EGON SCHIELE'S
PORTRAITS

EGON SCHIELE'S PORTRAITS

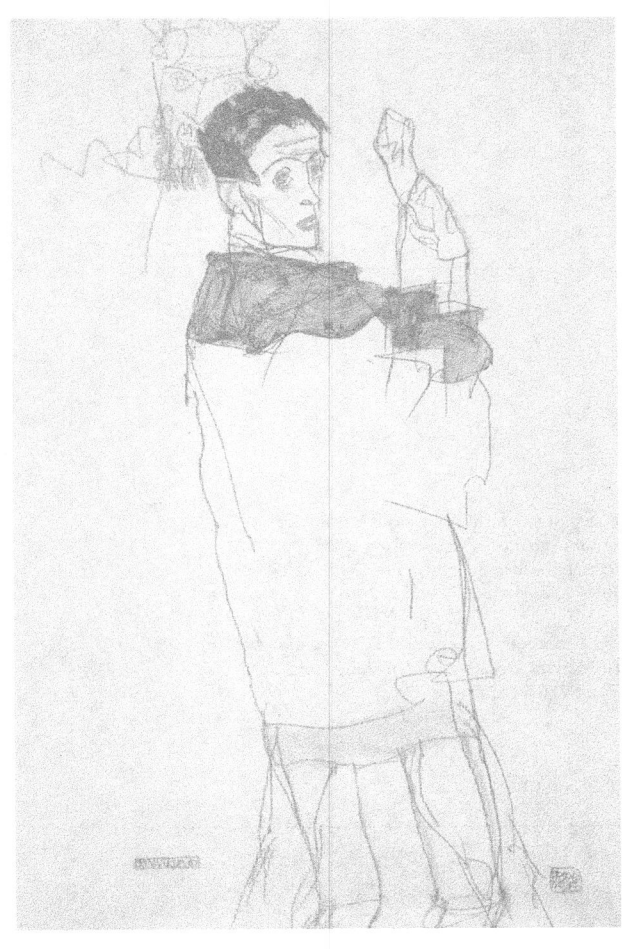

NEW
EDITION

Alessandra Comini

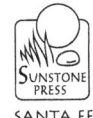

SUNSTONE
PRESS
SANTA FE

Sunstone books may be purchased for educational, business, or sales promotional use.
For information please write: Special Markets Department, Sunstone Press,
P.O. Box 2321, Santa Fe, New Mexico 87504-2321.

Printed on acid-free paper
∞
eBook 978-1-61139-309-5

Library of Congress Cataloging-in-Publication Data

Comini, Alessandra.
  Egon Schiele's portraits / by Alessandra Comini. -- New Edition.
     pages cm
  Includes bibliographical references and index.
  ISBN 978-1-63293-012-5 (softcover : alk. paper)
  1. Schiele, Egon, 1890-1918. I. Title.
  ND1329.S34C65 2014
  759.36--dc23
                                                2014021190

WWW.SUNSTONEPRESS.COM
SUNSTONE PRESS / POST OFFICE BOX 2321 / SANTA FE, NM 87504-2321 /USA
(505) 988-4418 / ORDERS ONLY (800) 243-5644 / FAX (505) 988-1025

Introduction to the New Edition

Certainly when I wrote *Egon Schiele's Portraits* decades ago I did not expect that it would be nominated for a National Book Award nor that Schiele's angular aesthetic would one day provoke an approving response from the New York world of high fashion.

And yet, with startling color-washed photographs by Eric Nehr of raw-boned male models intimately shot from directly overhead or frontally that matched the contortions of the artist's self-portraits, Egon Schiele was trumpeted as the artist who "may be the spring's most unexpected icon." So proclaimed the Sunday, March 8 issue of *The New York Times* Men's Fashion spring issue of 2009.

Not only has the Schiele phenomenon—his provocative art and tragically short life—penetrated fashion, but over the decades it has also inspired other artists, novels, plays, ballets, films, YouTube videos and forgeries. At the time of this writing there are well over two million and eighty thousand Internet entries for him.

When I first met them in Vienna during the late summer of 1963, Schiele's older sister Melanie (she pronounced her name: Me-la-*neee*) and younger sister Gertrude (Gerti) found it strange indeed that a young American art historian from the "Wild West" (actually, Texas) with an Italian surname and no Germanic background would have decided to research and write about their long dead brother. I described to them the epiphany I had undergone upon first seeing Schiele's riveting work in a small exhibition of Viennese Expressionism at the University of California in Berkeley. I was working on a master's degree in art history there and had just selected an esoteric medieval topic for my thesis. But then I saw—experienced, rather—Egon Schiele. Why such tension, why such pathos, why such urgency? I realized immediately that my scholarly future lay with him and that I must get myself to Vienna, where both his sisters still lived.

Because of that chance encounter with Schiele at the life-changing Berkeley exhibition, and with the financial support of my encouraging parents, the summer of 1963 found me in Vienna and happily ensconced in the dimly lit Studiensaal (study room) of the Graphische Sammlung Albertina. The Albertina Museum was the depository of the world's largest collection of Schiele drawings and watercolors as well as a rich archive of Schiele sketchbooks, letters, and photographs. The guards and staff, who referred to me as "das Schiele Fräulein," took an avuncular interest in my work but uniformly advised me not to bother interviewing the artist's sisters, as they were both confirmed recluses, did not even speak to each other, and were really quite crazy—"verrückt." Such negative advice redoubled my resolve to meet and interview them. After six weeks of working in the Albertina, taking notes and drawing small replicas of each Schiele artwork, I mailed off two carefully composed if grammatically shaky letters of self-introduction to Melanie and Gertrude, whom I felt I had already met through Schiele portraits and family photographs.

By the time surprisingly positive answers came to me from each sister, I had something unique to share with them concerning their brother. The Albertina owned eleven of the thirteen known watercolors Schiele had created while imprisoned during April of 1912 in the Austrian village of Neulengbach on charges of kidnapping, statutory rape and public immorality. His habit of inviting the local children to come and pose for him in the presence of what were deemed lewd images had aroused parental alarm. A little thirteen-year-old girl, who had run away from home and spent the night at Schiele's rented garden house, was the immediate cause of his arrest. The twenty some days Schiele spent in the basement cell of a crude country jail while awaiting trial resulted in his depictions of the cell, chairs and other objects, the corridor outside, its door to an exit, and four agonized self-portraits as prisoner. Schiele also kept a makeshift diary, and after he died it was published (and most probably heavily edited if not even embellished) by his collector friend, and supporter, the critic Arthur Roessler.

While waiting to hear back from the artist's sisters, I came across in the Albertina Schiele Archive an unanswered letter of inquiry from a German scholar asking exactly where in Neulengbach the artist had been incarcerated. It became clear to me that no one since the artist's death, neither relative nor scholar, had ever actually visited Neulengbach to see where the town jail was.

This realization was all I needed. Early on the morning of 27 August, as my diary for that day records, and armed with an effusive letter of introduction from the Albertina director, I rented a Volkswagen and drove to the little village of Neulengbach, some twenty miles southwest of Vienna. The tiny town possessed only one building—the district courthouse—that could possibly have housed any basement cells.

But my letter of introduction from the big city turned out to be a liability when I presented it to the uniformed official on duty at the courthouse. He read it aloud, slowly, with increasing pompousness, then waved me away, declaring that it was impossible for me to enter the building because there were "wichtige Regierungspapiere" ("important government papers") stored inside. Not even the fact that I had come all the way from California had any effect. Sadly, I walked away.

But not too far away. I circled back, then photographed the building's forbidding façade from behind a tree. The noon hour struck and several persons, including the unhelpful official, abruptly left the building. Propelled by some unknown force I entered the empty courthouse and immediately came upon a flight of stairs leading downward into the dark. Quickly descending I found myself in a damp cellar where, with a pounding heart, I recognized the long basement hall Schiele had drawn and described in his diary, "with the rubbish that lies in the corners and the equipment used by prisoners to clean their cells."

Somehow I managed to hold my Rolleiflex 2.8F camera steady enough to take a time exposure, capturing exactly the same view recorded by Schiele in his watercolor of 20 April 1912, entitled *I Feel Not Punished But Purified* . There was the same dismal band of gray paint running along the bottom of the limy whitewashed walls on both sides of the narrow corridor; there were the rough, heavy cell doors of thick wood; there was the same type of long-handled mop propped up on end to dry; and there, wedged above my head, was the wooden support beam Schiele had drawn, only now, fifty-one years later, it was sagging dangerously at the center. I was also able to ascertain which of the six cells had been Schiele's. The faithful depiction he drew of his cell interior included the initials "M H" carved on the inside of the door by a previous prisoner. The first cell door had no markings, but when I opened the door to the second cell, there were the "M H" initials! Not only did I photograph the telltale door, I also turned around and photographed the contents of Schiele's cell: no "wichtige Regierungspapiere" in sight; instead, only neatly stacked piles of firewood.

A few days later, when I elatedly showed my developed photographs to the Albertina staff, I was no longer "das Schiele Fräulein." Instead I was referred to from then on as "die Schiele Frau" (although this new rank carried no influence as far as getting the electric lights turned on during overcast days in the Studiensaal).

It was this—my photographs of Schiele's prison cell—that I had to offer Melanie and Gerti, although it was necessary to visit them separately since they were indeed not on speaking terms (it seems Melanie had appropriated a tomato from Gerti's garden during World War II). The photographs I had taken at Neulengbach accompanied my first book on Schiele, which included a translation of the artist's diary into English (*Schiele in Prison*, 1973). I presented both sisters with copies of this volume, and my friendship with them grew over the next eleven years. With the aid of a trusty, if heavy Tandberg tape recorder I was able to conduct interviews and preserve the cantilena of their pronounced Viennese accents. (These tapes were recently converted to CDs and are now in the Schiele archive of New York's Neue Galerie Museum for German and Austrian Art.)

Melanie Schiele especially became a true friend and was interested in my life and career at Columbia University. After completing a master's thesis on Schiele's self-portraits at Berkeley, I had begun teaching in New York during the years I wrote my dissertation on her brother's work. As early as our very first meeting (6 September 1963), she allowed me to photograph her next to the tall, black framed standing mirror that her brother had taken from the family home, and in front of which he executed his relentlessly intense and intimate self-portraits. When I brought Melanie the page proofs of my dissertation-turned-book, this *Egon Schiele's Portraits* (1974), she relived the events and people of her youth with relish as we slowly looked through the 335 illustrations together.

Over the years I also visited Schiele's younger sister who was sixty-nine when we first met. I could not help thinking how true to type these two sisters were: Melanie, tall, awkward, and totally without artifice, Gerti, petite, self-confident, and still the coquette of earlier days. Her bachelor son, Anton Jr.—Toni—had been painted by Schiele as a child and was touchingly solicitous toward his mother. During my visits he gently redirected Gerti's outbursts during our wide-ranging but frequently sidetracked Schiele discussions. She was game enough however to dress up for me in a typical Austrian dirndl, pose in a black chair Schiele had built, and playfully impersonate her brother's portrait of his wife Edith seated,

That night we conducted a spirited taped interview which lasted from eight in the evening until two in the morning. Visits to the impetuous Gerti were more exhausting and far less revelatory than were those to Melanie, whose single-track mind was set on elucidating for posterity all details she could recall about her gifted brother. Shortly before I was to return to America that first year of our acquaintanceship, Melanie afforded me the intimate form of address. My diary entry for 26 September 1963 records that moment: "showed Melanie all my new photographs, then we drank 'Brüderschaft' and pledged the 'Du.' Sad farewell at midnight." I visited Melanie every summer for eleven years until her death in October 1974. She died in her sleep at the age of eighty-eight.

One of the most helpful sitters, whom I interviewed several times over the years, was Schiele's sister-in-law, Adele Harms. She not only served as the artist's model after his wife Edith "got too fat," but also posed seductively for the artist's camera in front of the great standing mirror in Schiele's studio. Adele also garrulously submitted to my tape recording her reminiscences of her sister and her marriage to Egon. She was quite bitter that her brother-in-law had always portrayed Edith as looking so doll-like and "dumb" when in fact she was well educated and could converse in both English and French. Like Schiele, Adele seemed to have an obsession with the erotic—she frequently brought the conversation around to sex.

For example, when telling me about her father, whom Schiele portrayed in 1916, she mentioned casually: "My father, like all Germans, was bisexual"—a sweeping assertion noted down verbatim in my diary entry for that day ("Mein Vater, wie alle Deutschen, war bisexual").

One Sunday morning Adele telephoned me at six and with rolling rs and long, drawn-out tones shouted excitedly into the phone, "Fräu-lein Co-mi-ni! Hö--ren Sie gut zu! Ich hab' Ihnen was Wich-ti-ges zu er-zäh-len." (Miss Co-mi-ni! Listen care-fully! I have something im-por-tant to tell you.) "Ja?" I said sleepily. Adele pronounced solemnly: "E-dith warrr frrrüh rrreif!" "Was?" I lamely answered, not comprehending a term that translated literally as "early ripe." Adele repeated this information at a louder volume. When I still did not catch on, she screamed into my ear, "Die E-dith hat, mit zwölf Jah-rrren an-ge-fang-en zu *men-stru-IE-ren!*" Although I at last understood that Edith had begun to menstruate at the age of twelve, this gripping fact did not, somehow, appear in any of my books on Schiele. A few years later, Adele was forced to move into Vienna's Steinhof sanatorium ("Pavilion 25, for ever," she wrote me), where the ephemeral fame she had acquired as Schiele's sister-in-law hardly helped to allay her loneliness.

Another exceedingly informative sitter was Friedericke (Fritzi) Beer-Monti who lived in New York but who happened to be visiting in Vienna where I first met her in that productive summer of 1963. Her life-size portrait had been painted first by Schiele in 1914 (showing her plummeting with flailing fingers through a void), and then by Gustav Klimt in 1916 (in which she stands passive and immobile before a screen crowded with aggressively active oriental warriors). In this book I have quoted Fritzi's detailed reminiscences for me of her sittings with each master—Klimt, who portrayed her façade; Schiele who invested her with an angst-filled psyche. To my question as to what Schiele was like, she answered readily: "He was tall, thin, shy, and quiet. He spoke with Viennese intonation but not in heavy dialect. He dressed normally but even so he stood out in a crowd. One could tell there was something unusual about him. That fantastic head of hair! Those outspread ears!"

Fritzi explained to me that although Schiele liked and admired Klimt greatly he did not socialize with him. "When I think back on it now I can see that the artists of the time clearly fell into two different camps. You might call them the intellectuals versus the hedonists. Klimt and [Josef] Hoffmann were the hedonists—living the high life, always going out with lots of girls at night to Grinzing, holding what we thought of as bacchanals—while the other faction, which included the 'wild' painter Oskar Kokoschka as well, was considered the intellectual group, not so pleasure-loving, not so pleasure-seeking."

The division about which Fritzi spoke paralleled, I soon realized, the difference in attitude that characterized Vienna's artists and styles at the beginning of the twentieth century. The older Art Nouveau or Jugendstil generation—Klimt and Hoffmann included—was involved in a last nostalgic preoccupation with beauty and the façade. The younger Expressionist generation—represented by Schiele and Kokoschka—was gripped by the anxiety and self-concern that a compulsive confrontation with ugly "truth," such as the state of society or of an individual psyche, had forced into the open.

Seeking out Schiele's still living sitters took me to Switzerland. In Geneva I interviewed the not-so-helpful Erich Lederer, who had been portrayed in oil as a precocious fifteen-year-old by the artist at the end of 1912. The artist referred to his subject, who had a penchant for drawing, as a young "Beardsley." Erich's mother had been a close friend of Klimt's, and the family owned the largest private collection of Klimt oils and drawings. In fact it was Klimt who helpfully recommended Schiele to the Lederer family.

Now, in the summer of 1966, a reputation for being difficult had preceded Erich. And sure enough, his prurient similarity to Aubrey Beardsley revealed itself almost immediately. As soon as we had sat down in a restaurant to order dinner, Erich, in front of his long-suffering wife Lisl, turned to me and asked in an imperious voice: "Tell me, young lady, do you shave under your arms?" Only later that evening, when Erich settled down to examine the visual material assembled for my dissertation, did he abandon his impudent personal questioning and concentrate on Schiele.

A pattern was established over the next few days. We would meet after breakfast and slowly walk, by way of newspaper kiosks where the latest in porno magazines were kept under the counter for him, to the bank where Erich's vast collection of Schiele and Klimt drawings was kept in a vault. We spent the day looking at them. There was not much Erich could tell me about what it was like to sit for Schiele, but certainly this opportunity to study, sketch, and take notes on so many Schiele drawings was well worth the Swiss side trip.

As important as it was to interview Schiele's sitters and to photograph sites painted by the artist, it was equally imperative to see and examine as many Schiele works as possible. The largest and most important private collection of Schiele oils and graphic works in Vienna had been assembled by an ophthalmologist who kept the art in his large house at Coblenzgasse 16 in Grinzing. Dr. Rudolf Leopold was famed for being hard to meet, and so, becoming more complicitously Viennese by the day, I contrived to accompany two different scholars on pilgrimages to his collection. The first was with Herschel Chipp, the Berkeley professor who had organized the Schiele exhibition that so changed my life. Then four days later I returned with a former teacher at the University of Vienna, Gerhard Schmidt, who was writing a book on modern Austrian art. The fact that I had engineered *two* visits to see his collection greatly amused the formidable Dr. Leopold. He invited me back for dinner for more conversation about Schiele and the far-flung Schiele sites we both wanted to visit and photograph.

Still in pursuit of Austrian private collections of Schiele that first summer of research, 1963, I contacted Viktor Fogarassy in Graz, who, my Vienna mentors assured me, had a treasure house of superb Schiele and Klimt paintings and water-colors, as well as works by many other Austrian artists. The train trip southward to Graz via the high Semmering Alpine Pass took three hours and I had been invited to stay overnight. I stayed a week however at the family's urgent request. There were so many artworks to see in the long, three-story yellow manor house, and the four vivacious Fogarassy daughters were excited to have a guitar-playing American in their midst. I was shown to a yellow guesthouse that first evening where framed paintings and drawings were stacked by the dozens against the walls of the hall and one of the bedrooms. In my bedroom a Klimt landscape hung on one wall and a 1909 Schiele self-portrait with rigidly outspread fingers contemplated me from another wall at the foot of my bed. (It would become the cover for the hardback edition of *Egon Schiele's Portraits*.)

As with Schiele's sisters, an enduring friendship developed and I paid many return visits to Viktor Fogarassy and his wonderful, droll wife Dollie. The next summer I returned for an extended visit with the genial family who had "adopted" me—their word. I was taken by them to see other private collections in Graz and my sketches and note-taking became voluminous. On the afternoon of my departure, while I was busy packing in the yellow guesthouse, Dollie and Viktor knocked at the door, then entered carrying a mysterious piece of white cardboard about three feet high and two feet wide. Speaking in concert they said, "Don't forget to pack *this*." The "this" was a mat framing one of the gems of the Fogarassy collection—Schiele's 1913 black chalk and watercolor likeness of himself at work before an image he had drawn of Klimt. It was entitled by him *Erinnerung* (*Remembrance*). After much protest I packed up the precious gift—a gift twice precious, as it was a double-sided drawing with, on the verso, a black chalk study of a rowboat, seen from above, done around 1912. (*Remembrance* adorns the cover of this paperback edition of *Egon Schiele's Portraits*.) I have since given Schiele's *Remembrance* to the Dallas Museum of Art where over the years many classes of my students have been given the assignment to sketch it as best they could. Even in this computer age, I had discovered, one is better able to understand and remember a work of art if one tries to sketch it—connoisseur Bernard Berenson's tried and true technique.

On one visit to the Fogarassys in the fall of 1972, Viktor helped me carry Schiele's 1909 oil portrait of his sister Gerti out onto the guesthouse balcony for better light, then obligingly took my photograph with the elegantly silhouetted image. When I showed Gerti Schiele the photograph of her handsome portrait, which she had not seen for decades, her delight was heartening to behold. Proudly, she told me the story once again of how she and Egon, when she was just twelve and he sixteen, took an impromptu train ride that duplicated the itinerary of their parents' wedding trip. They rode all the way to Trieste where they stayed overnight in a hotel. Gerti admitted that she was easily persuaded to pose in the nude for her brother, and this led to other "secrets" which they kept from their parents. Of those years Schiele later wrote: "Have adults forgotten how they themselves as children were incited and aroused by the impulse of sex?.... I have not forgotten, for I suffered terribly from it."

These anguished words were written in Schiele's 1912 prison diary and it might have pleased him enormously to know that the basement corridor and cell in which he languished for some twenty days have recently been turned into a Schiele Museum, complete with Internet website. The architect Günter Wagensommerer was responsible for its tasteful conversion from neglected cell to didactic museum, with reproductions of the drawings Schiele made in prison. In October of 2006, Herr Wagensommerer was kind enough to drive me from Vienna to Neulengbach for a tour of the results, and it was indeed moving to enter once again the prison cell with "M H" carved on the door—some forty-three years after I first saw it. And in June of 2012 an international symposium was held at the Neulengbach museum in my honor—one hundred years after Schiele had been incarcerated and forty-nine years after my discovery of his prison cell.

Neulengbach's Egon Schiele Platz now hosts a yearly Schiele Workshop Festival featuring theater and dance as well as statements by visiting artists, after being "incarcerated" overnight in the prison cells (billed in English on line as "48 Hours Art Non-Stop in the Schiele Prison Cells"). In October of 2006 the town grade school of Neulengbach was host to a performance of *Der Maler Schiele aus Tulln* (*The Painter Schiele from Tulln*) by the Austrian playwright Gerald Szyszkowitz, who has also written dramas about Schubert and Schnitzler.

Neulengbach is not the only small Austrian town to host and boast a Schiele Museum. The artist's birthplace, Tulln on the Danube, where his father Adolf was stationmaster of the local railroad station (above which the family lived in four rooms), opened an ambitious Egon Schiele Museum in 1990 on the centenary of the artist's birth. The two-story building is on the site of Tulln's former district prison (suggesting preternatural association with Neulengbach). The museum has exhibits on both floors, including over one hundred photographs, original drawings and paintings from Schiele's early years. There is even a replica of Schiele's Neulengbach cell with reproductions of some of the prison drawings on the wall above the cell's humble cot.

And there is more. Lucky visitors to this museum are greeted by a life-size bronze effigy of Schiele. (Not even the more famous, longer-lived Klimt has yet rated a public statue, although resin statuettes of figures from his paintings are available on line.) The effigy has the same "fantastic head of hair" and "outspread ears" described by Fritzi Beer-Monti. Schiele stands on a raised pedestal with folded up easel and canvas under his right arm while his left hand clasps his breast as though welcoming the visitor, or perhaps, with this persistent plumber of the psyche and unembarrassed voyeur of the self, simply proclaiming his existence—"Ich!"

Behind the statue is a magnificent entry gate with metal letters EGON SCHIELE writ large upon it. More recently (1995) the museum extended its reach and furnished two rooms—one of them the room in which Schiele was born—at the original Tulln railroad station. Along with period furniture stands the original ceramic room stove into which Schiele's father once angrily threw some of his son's drawings.

The year 2013 saw publication of the Tulln Museum's handsomely illustrated monograph *Egon Schiele Der Anfang, The Beginning*, scrupulously edited by Schiele expert Christian Bauer.

When Melanie saw the shots I had taken of Tulln's railroad station—her childhood home—she pulled out a cache of old photographs, one of which showed a dress parade in front of the station honoring her father's twenty-fifth year of service. She told me that the first objects of Egon's incessant craving to draw were the passing trains, and that before he was five he began, to their mother's horror, crawling out of the dining room window and onto the slanting porch roof facing the tracks to get a better view for his amazingly detailed images. If his pencil and paper were confiscated by his parents he would then make trains on the floor out of bed sheets, a sheet for each rail car. One of the rare photographs to capture Schiele smiling shows the future artist proudly posing with his favorite toy locomotive.

There is a third small town museum devoted to Schiele because of terrestrial connections with the artist during his lifetime. From May to the beginning of August in 1911, Schiele rented an inexpensive garden house studio in his mother's German-speaking hometown of Krumau on the Moldau in Southern Bohemia—then part of the Austrian Empire (now Český Krumlov, belonging to the Czech Republic). With its imposing thirteenth-century castle and tower, fortresslike city hall, and boxy old houses with steeply pitched roofs facing a great bend in the river, Krumau was wonderfully picturesque. Craving isolation from Vienna's big city intrigues and complications, Schiele reveled in the simplicity of country life (the total town population was just below 9,000). As would occur the following year in Neulengbach however the artist's unconventional way of life—living openly with his model Wally Neuzil, and inviting pubescent girls to pose for him in the garden—turned the townsfolk against him. He was compelled to leave Krumau. But the artist would return a number of times to paint the desolate "dead city," as he tenderly called it.

When I first visited Krumau in 1967 it was a forgotten town, despite its lush Bohemian forest setting and famed blue river (then badly polluted with a white scum). The strictures of the Iron Curtain had indeed turned it into a dead city. But after the fall of Communism, a group of Schiele lovers from Austria and America, as well as local enthusiasts, cofounded and opened in 1993 the Egon Schiele Art Centrum in the grottolike basement of a sixteenth-century building complex that had once contained the town brewery. The Centrum houses a small permanent collection of Schiele's work as well as a documentary room devoted to the artist's life and art. It also features small changing exhibitions of painters, past and present (Klimt, Picasso, Giacometti, Dalí and contemporary artists). In addition to a shop and café, the Egon Schiele Art Centrum offers ten studios for working artists to rent. This would have appealed to Schiele, who was on friendly terms with his colleagues (one of whom married his sister Gerti), and who, in the last year of his life, organized a group show for the Vienna Secession's forty-ninth exhibition, even designing the show's lithographic poster *Tafelrunde* (*Round Table*).

Recently I found a crackling long distance call from Krumau on my answering machine: it was the jubilant message of a former student who, inspired by Schiele's haunting depictions of the old town, had driven with his parents up from Vienna to see it for himself. Little could the artist have known that the views of his mother's hometown he had so lovingly portrayed would one day help put Krumau on the map for foreign visitors. But he might not have been surprised, since he, like Gustav Mahler, believed that only later generations would truly comprehend and take to heart his art. "I shall go so far that people will be seized with terror at the sight of each of my works of 'living' art,'" Schiele wrote his uncle in 1911.

A recently opened (fall of 2001) four-story, white limestone-sheathed cube in the heart of Vienna's Museum Quarter could justifiably be characterized as a fourth Egon Schiele Museum. This is the Austrian government-financed Leopold Museum, named after the ophthalmologist with the passionate collector's eye who had been amassing art works for over five decades. Although the museum holdings span two centuries of Austrian art and run to some 5,000 items, the nucleus of the Leopold collection, turned Leopold Foundation, contains the largest Schiele collection in the world: some 224 works. They range from oil paintings on cardboard, wood, and canvas, to gouaches and watercolors, to black chalk, and pencil drawings on paper, and they encompass the whole of the artist's meteoric career. Three rooms are devoted to Schiele (and another entire room to Klimt) along with photographs, letters in the artist's distinctive hand, and sketchbooks. Among the gems of the Leopold Schiele holdings are several haunted self-portraits (*The Poet* and *The Self-Seer II*, both of 1911), important town- and landscapes (an entire exhibition was devoted to them by the museum in 2004-05), as well as two major allegories of 1912 *Cardinal and Nun* and *The Hermits*.

A few years before the opening of the Leopold Museum in Vienna, the Museum of Modern Art (MoMA) in New York was host to a well-received travelling exhibition: *Egon Schiele: The Leopold Collection*. Beginning in October of 1997, some 150 works by the artist were on display to the public. On New Year's Eve of 1997, four days before the show was to be taken down and flown to its next venue in Barcelona, representatives of two New York families delivered letters to MoMA claiming rights to two of the Schiele oil paintings in the exhibition: *Dead City (City on the Blue River) III* of 1911 and a 1912 *Portrait of Wally*—the latter a companion piece to Schiele's 1912 *Self-Portrait with Chinese Lantern Plant*, also in the Leopold Collection. Both claims alleged that the works had been stolen from the families' Jewish relatives in Vienna after the annexation of Austria by Hitler and never returned to their rightful owners. *Dead City*, which in fact had been sold by the original owner's sister-in-law, was returned to Vienna in 1999, but the high-stakes battle for *Portrait of Wally* lasted more than a decade. The suspense-filled finale was written only in July of 2010, just twenty-one days after the death of Rudolf Leopold. The main character of this precedent-setting drama did not live to see a settlement in which the Leopold Museum agreed to pay nineteen million dollars to the legal heirs for return of the painting to its collection.

The appearance in 2002 of a thick handbook of 148 confiscated Jewish collections in Vienna during World War II—Sophie Lillie, *Was einmal war: Handbuch der enteigneten Kunstsammlungen Wiens* (*What Once Was: Handbook of Vienna's Plundered Art Collections*)—energized various entities in both Europe and America. On 9 November 2008 a demonstration organized by the "Jewish Community of Vienna" and its sympathizers spread a zigzagging maze of yellow construction tape across the exterior walls and wide entrance staircase to the Leopold Museum. The yellow "police" tapes declared in two languages: "Raubkunst Tatort" and "Art Robbery Crime Scene." A video was made of the demonstrators in action and subsequent arrival of police. The dramatic result—a two-minute, fifteen-second video—was immediately released for worldwide YouTube audiences and is still in circulation.

I did not know when I visited Rudolf Leopold in 1963 that he was working on a new oeuvre catalogue of Schiele's works, one which he later maintained would definitively replace the bible of Schiele research—the 1930 oeuvre catalogue published by Otto Nirenstein-Kallir, and revised by him in a second edition in 1966. Dr. Kallir had relocated from Vienna to New York on the eve of Hitler's rise to power and founded the Galerie St. Etienne, which in 1941 presented the first Schiele exhibition in America. Now located on West Fifty-Seventh Street, it was and remains today one of the city's most respected art galleries, noted for high quality exhibitions, informative brochures, and dazzling website reproductions. Leopold's somewhat argumentative, and self-defensive oeuvre catalogue of 1972 (measuring almost three inches thick by twelve inches high and weighing in at ten pounds) would be outdistanced in unbiased scholarship and scope by that of Dr. Kallir's granddaughter, Jane Kallir. In 1990, after years of meticulous and inspired research, she published *Egon Schiele: The Complete Works*. In addition to the paintings, this copiously illustrated catalogue raisonné, brought out by both Harry N. Abrams of New York and Thames and Hudson of London, addressed the artist's graphic art—gouaches, watercolors, drawings, prints, and (rare) sculptures. There were co-editions in Holland, Spain, Germany, and France. A second, expanded edition of this definitive work appeared in 1998, and in 2003 Jane Kallir published a year-by-year study of Schiele's graphic work with over 300 color illustrations in a single, manageable (in size) volume, *Egon Schiele: Drawings and Watercolors*.

One of my first priorities upon beginning graduate study at Columbia University in the fall of 1964 had been to make contact with Dr. Kallir. Although I encountered official foot dragging in Vienna when it came time to assemble photographic materials for my first article on Schiele, Dr. Kallir's permission to reproduce a work in his collection arrived with lightning speed. I never forgot such cooperation. Recently I received a letter from Jane Kallir mentioning that she had been going through a thick file of letters between her grandfather and me. She commented: "It is clear that you looked to him as a mentor and guide to that confusing Austrian world, and he was thrilled to have found a young scholar as perceptive and enthusiastic as you." (In my 2004 book, *In Passionate Pursuit: A Memoir*, I was able to give further details of the help offered me by both Otto Kallir and his longtime associate at the Galerie St. Etienne, the knowledgeable and discerning Hildegard Bachert, to whom, in fact, the book is dedicated.)

My early work on Schiele also brought me into contact with the new director of the Solomon R. Guggenheim Museum, Thomas Messer. He was planning a truly ambitious Gustav Klimt/Egon Schiele exhibition for the Guggenheim, to open in February 1965. After a four-hour lunch and conference at the museum, Messer asked me, in a rich Czech accent, to contribute a catalogue chronology and essay on Schiele's drawings, which I was happy to do. He also proposed that I consider myself a "temporary staff member of the museum" (according to my flabbergasted diary entry of 12 August 1964) and fly immediately—at Guggenheim expense—to Europe to visit and cajole a few of the private Schiele and Klimt collectors from whom he hoped to borrow works. Three days later I was in Vienna, then Graz, then Munich, then Geneva, then Zurich, and finally Berne. All the loan requests were successful and I returned to New York just in time to register for classes on the 21st of September.

At the Guggenheim opening the following February I ran into a very excited Fritzi Beer-Monti and it was a delight to accompany her slowly down the museum's great spiral with so many major Klimt and Schiele works on the walls. Fritzi was simply elated that two of Vienna's greatest artists were being represented at so important a venue in America.

Three years later, in 1968, on the fiftieth anniversary of the artist's death, homage to Schiele was paid on both sides of the Atlantic. A selection of the artist's graphic work was presented by both the Galerie St. Etienne in New York and the Albertina in Vienna. Two other Viennese museums organized Schiele exhibitions as well: the Historisches Museum der Stadt Wien (now the Wien Museum) and the Österreichische Galerie Belvedere. The latter venerable institution put together an exhibition of major Schiele paintings and provided the public a richly illustrated catalogue.

From 1969 onward, the Serge Sabarsky Gallery on Madison Avenue began featuring works by Schiele. (During the 1980s Sabarsky published two volumes on Schiele and in the 1990s he organized the first three Schiele shows for Krumau's Egon Schiele Art Centrum.) In 1971 a travelling exhibition *Egon Schiele and the Human Form* made the circuit from Des Moines to Columbus to Chicago. Munich's famed Haus der Kunst museum held an important Schiele exhibition of 275 works along with an illustrated catalogue—mostly black-and-white plates—in 1975. The Seibu Museum of Art in Tokyo featured Schiele in 1979 and from then on almost yearly exhibitions of the artist's drawings and watercolors could be found at prestigious private galleries and museums in this country and abroad.

During these early years of increasing group or solo shows and publications on Schiele, I was substantially aided by two generous mentors in Vienna: Walter Koschatzky, the director of the Albertina who wrote that flowery letter of introduction so sneeringly dismissed by Neulengbach's provincial official, and Christian Nebehay, art and rare-book dealer whose gallery on the Annagasse often featured Klimt and Schiele drawings. After publishing a copiously illustrated *Klimt Dokumentation* in 1969, Christian turned his attention to Schiele, often travelling with me to some of the Schiele sites I wanted to photograph. With scrupulous documentation he published a number of books during the next thirty years on Schiele's life, his work, his letters and poetry, his sketchbooks, the Lederer family relationships with both Klimt and Schiele, and even a fascinating book about the role of the railroad in the artist's life (*Egon Schiele und die Eisenbahn*, 1995).

In 1986 New York's MoMA included Schiele works in a sumptuous, many faceted overview of Viennese art entitled *Vienna 1900—Art, Architecture and Design*. Also in 1986 Vienna's memorable *Traum und Wirklichkeit* (*Dream and Reality*) presentation at the Künstlerhaus included Schiele, as did a third major exhibition of that same year, *Vienne 1880-1938: L'Apocalypse Joyeuse*, in Paris's Centre Pompidou. Schiele seems to have clicked with the French public. A few years after the Paris exhibition one of my students, who had spent spring break in France, triumphantly brought me the latest issue of the popular French magazine *Match*, exclaiming "Look at this!" A full-page color photograph showed fifty-one-year-old film star Mireille Darc sitting on a wooden floor with a hardback copy of this Egon Schiele book in front of her on the floor as, with a contorted Schiele-like pose, she indulged in her literary "solitude."

To invoke another example of enthusiastic Schiele reception in France: the March 1995 issue of *Beaux Arts*—with an in-your-face Schiele female nude color detail on its cover—presented a lavishly illustrated (fifteen color plates), nine-page article on the artist titled "La Beauté Convulsive" (including a convulsively *reversed* reproduction of Schiele's 1910 drawing of *Gerti Nude*).

In 1994 an important solo showing of the artist's work, curated by Jane Kallir, travelled from Washington's National Gallery of Art to the Indianapolis Museum of Art and lastly to the San Diego Museum of Art. Authored by Jane Kallir, a generously illustrated catalogue accompanied the exhibition and included an essay by me concerning the sitters and sites of the artist—"In Search of Schiele." This was my first opportunity since 1976 to build upon some of the colorful interviews mentioned in this Introduction. In 2000-01 the Fondazione Antonio Mazzotta of Milan, in collaboration with the Albertina, showed some eighty of the Vienna museum's most important Schiele drawings

A second opportunity to share some of my early research arose in 2005 when Renée Price, director of New York's Neue Galerie Museum for German and Austrian Art, asked me to contribute an essay, "Pilgrimage to Schiele's Past," amplifying on my discovery of the artist's prison cell and quoting from interviews with sitters and early collectors. As has become the custom with the Neue Galerie, a lavishly illustrated catalogue with scholarly contributions was published, rivaling in size and heft the two Schiele oeuvre catalogues by Leopold and Kallir.

Also in 2005 some twenty paintings and eighty watercolors by Schiele were shown at Amsterdam's large Van Gogh Museum—a nicely apt connection, since the Austrian artist was born the same year Van Gogh died. This was a fact which Schiele treasured and more than obliquely acknowledged in some of his motifs. For this particular retrospective, because of a shared interest in the human body, the Dutch museum commissioned veteran performance artist Marina Abramovic and the dance group Krisztina de Châtel to perform in various spaces of the building's exhibition wing. The show's catalogue, written by Jane Kallir, devotes a chapter to this co-production.

Such linking of Schiele—master portrayer of the human figure and especially his own—with dance is not new. After a short version in 1982, the multimedia performance piece entitled *Pass the Blutwurst, Bitte (The Egon Schiele Story)* directed, choreographed and danced by lanky, tousle-haired dancer John Kelly, was staged at the New York Dance Theater Workshop in 1986. Both versions are preserved in two YouTube videos, the longer of which embeds the dancer and "Wally" within a life-size color reproduction of Schiele's 1915 allegory *Death and the Maiden.*

A live dance performance accompanied the 1993 opening of Krumau's Egon Schiele Art Centrum. And in May of 1995, at the University of Illinois in Chicago, Schiele's life was represented by the Itinerant Theater Guild in a theatrical dance production by the videographer Stephan Mazurek. Dancers performed twelve episodes from Schiele's life to a specially composed soundtrack by Rachel's, a post-rock American instrumental group which released a recording of the music in 1996. The album cover reproduces Schiele's *Autumn Trees* of 1911. For Rachel's, the three trees in the painting stood for the three instrumental players—piano, viola, and cello. In 2002 a contemporary all male British dance group, The Featherstonehaughs, performed for television cameras routines "inspired by intense images and characters portrayed in Egon Schiele's drawings and paintings." As early as 1977 the pop music world had paid homage to the artist in the form of mop-haired David Bowie's gesticulating pose for the cover of his album *Heroes*—a posture candidly inspired by Schiele's self-portraits.

Thanks in part to the books, exhibitions, catalogues, and events mentioned above, interest in Schiele has burgeoned over the past four decades since publication of this book. Attention to Schiele's poignant land- and townscapes has been paid in recent scholarship and in 2004 they became the subject of an intriguing monograph by Kimberly A. Smith, *Between Ruin and Renewal: Egon Schiele's Landscapes.* The author places emphasis on a conflict of resignation and regeneration in which Schiele's sober images echo not so much the psyche of the artist, but rather address and embody the decline of old world Austria in the face of the new modernism not only of art but also of society and politics. The marketplace had already confirmed the importance and appeal of this category of Schiele's work: in June 2003 the artist's 1916 view of Krumau on the Moldau sold at a Sotheby's auction in London for $20.93 million. (This was yet another looted painting from original Viennese owners during Nazi times—collectors who had bought it directly from Schiele. Its restitution to the heirs was this time nobly agreed to by the Neue Galerie der Stadt Linz, Wolfgang-Gurlitt-Museum.)

On a happier and more recent Schiele note, Vienna's august Belvedere presented a stunning exhibition in 2011, *Egon Schiele Self-Portraits and Portraits,* co-curated by Agnes Husslein-Arco and Jane Kallir. The year 1911 also saw the birth of an *Egon Schiele Jahrbuch,* founded by the Hungarian art historian Johann Thomas Ambrózy. During 2011-2012 the Leopold Museum presented its own superb one-man show, *Egon Schiele Melancholy and Provocation.* And in 2012 Jane Kallir published the lavishly illustrated book, *Egon Schiele's Women,* which will be the underpinnings for yet another Belvedere exhibition.

Schiele's ever growing popularity has inspired several popularizing biographies (fueled by a blend of research and literary imagination) and novels. Some of the better candidates are Joanna Scott, author of the 1990 novel *Arrogance*, Jean-Louis Gaillemin's *Egon Schiele: Narcisse échorché*, translated from the French in 2006 as *Egon Schiele: The Egoist*, and *The Pornographer of Vienna* published in 2008 by Lewis Crofts. One time removed but still fascinatingly connected to Schiele by using him as impetus, is the Peruvian writer Mario Vargas Llosa. In his novel of 1997, *Los cuadermos de don Rigoberto*, the sight of Schiele's erotic work by the protagonist Don Rigoberto when he was twelve years old propels him into ever expanding sexual adventures of his own.

From forging modern reincarnations of Schiele to actually forging his artworks is to be expected. In the 1980s the German forger Wolfgang Lammie produced a large number of homespun Schieles, passing them off for roughly $45,000 each to galleries and auction houses after "experts" had authenticated them. When Lammie was later convicted of forgery, in 1992, an unusually sympathetic court in Stuttgart found him to be a "passionate painter," motivated mostly by a desire to revenge himself on a market more interested in big names than unknown striving artists. He received a suspended prison sentence and was fined $25,000 as well as the means to pay the fine: permission to auction off his own genuine forgeries.

Another self-confessed, unabashed German forger of Schiele (etchings in particular) is Edgar Mrugalla, who has his own commercial web site with the usual links to Shop, Biography, Exhibitions, Press, Gallery, and Literature. He bills himself as "virtuoso," "genius," and "King of the Art Forgers." In 1987 the then forty--eight-year-old painter was sentenced to two years of "conditional" imprisonment for fraud. Ironically, he was released after having cooperated with the police to help expose forgeries, those of other artists as well as his own.

It makes perfect sense that a Museum of Art Fakes would come into being and that it would come into being in Vienna. This new museum, opened in 2005, is just across the street from the famous Hundertwasser House on Löwengasse and contains an extensive collection of forgeries—some "in the manner of" (as with its Bellini and Kollwitz examples); others, identical copies of existing works passed off as works by the original artist. In this latter category the museum has a collection of Edgar Mrugalla's "Rembrandt" etchings, and a convincing likeness of Schiele's 1909-10 watercolor and charcoal study of his sister Gerti in a plaid garment. In the museum shop an excellent copy of Schiele's single *Sunflower* of 1909 can be ordered. Under yet another category of "acknowledged copies" there is a magnificent, but ever so slightly off rendition of Klimt's first *Judith* of 1901 (the original is in the Belvedere), including a glittering copy of its identifying gold frame. The museum visitor is left pondering what the difference is between a falsified original and an original forgery.

Bidding for "original" Schiele artworks on eBay is not only unwise, but perilous. Warnings are routinely listed on the Internet, often in the form of reproducing an original Schiele alongside a forged one with earnest admonitions such as "Anybody can see, that the picture on the right is NOT painted by Egon Schiele."

The worldwide web encourages many hundreds of Schiele links, posters, quotes of the day, artist of the month, self-portraits a la Schiele, blogs, and videos. Some are amusing, others just plain awful. A music video of 2008 shows a tattoo artist industriously applying a needle to transfer Schiele's *Gerti in a Plaid Garment* on some willing customer's back. Would Gerti Peschka Schiele have been outraged or flattered?

Before there were distracting, ephemeral YouTube videos there were documentaries and movies about Schiele—some good, some average. The year 1980 proved to be a fertile year for Schiele film productions. In February Austrian and German television broadcast an eighty-nine-minute dramatized account of the painter's life. The movie was written by London director John Goldschmidt with the Schiele expert and gallery owner Wolfgang Georg Fischer, who would later (1994 and 2007) publish two useful and beautifully illustrated volumes on Schiele. In 1983 a dubbed version of the film was shown on British television, garnering an Austrian People's Education TV Award. The artist's early days are reviewed during location shots and his oeuvre is commented upon by a bevy of art historians.

Also released in 1980 was *Egon Schiele: Exzess und Bestrafung* (*Excess and Punishment*), filmed in sepia tones and directed by the Austrian Herbert Vesely with a European cast. The movie begins with incidents leading to the Neulengbach imprisonment disaster, with a mostly mute, very wide-eyed Schiele almost going insane. Unbridled emotions, alcohol, and sexuality occupy the narcissistic artist who lives only for his art. The end shows Schiele making love to his pregnant wife as she lies dying in his arms (he did in fact draw her on her deathbed) and contracting the influenza that killed them both. The movie can be characterized as purposefully provocative, featuring obsession over biography.

In May of 1979 I was contacted by the London filmmaker and director, Mick Gold, about making a movie for the Arts Council of Great Britain eponymously centering upon *Schiele in Prison*. The film would use my translation of Schiele's prison diary in its attempt to epitomize the situation of the modern artist in Emperor Franz Josef's decaying empire. By November of that boon year 1980, Gold's forty-eight-minute film was released and enthusiastically reviewed. We met recently in London and I learned with pleasure that he was involved in yet another Schiele production.

One of the more unusual and gratifying venues for a Schiele exhibition cum documentary on his life was the handsome museum devoted to Edvard Munch in Oslo. From April to June of 2007, Schiele paintings and works on paper were on view while at the same time influential or corresponding works by Munch were on display. The most striking example of course was the Norwegian artist's haunting *The Scream* of 1893. Its swirling vibrations of paint seemed actually to leap across the museum to Schiele's own agonized *Self-Portrait Screaming* of 1910.

"An isolation cell in which one is allowed to scream," so Karl Kraus characterized Vienna at the turn of the last century. Certainly Schiele's radical art reflected his time and place, but equally certain is that his unrelenting existential intensity links him to the anxiety and hopes of the present.

In 2014 the Neue Galerie Museum New York opened an exhibition of Schiele's portraits, curated by the author, thus crowning a half-century love affair with Egon Schiele.

As I follow the twenty-first century's continuing dialogue with Egon Schiele, it is with the joy of an early convert who watches her cause—once considered peripheral and esoteric—enter the mainstream of human concern.

—Alessandra Comini
Dallas, 2014

EGON SCHIELE'S PORTRAITS

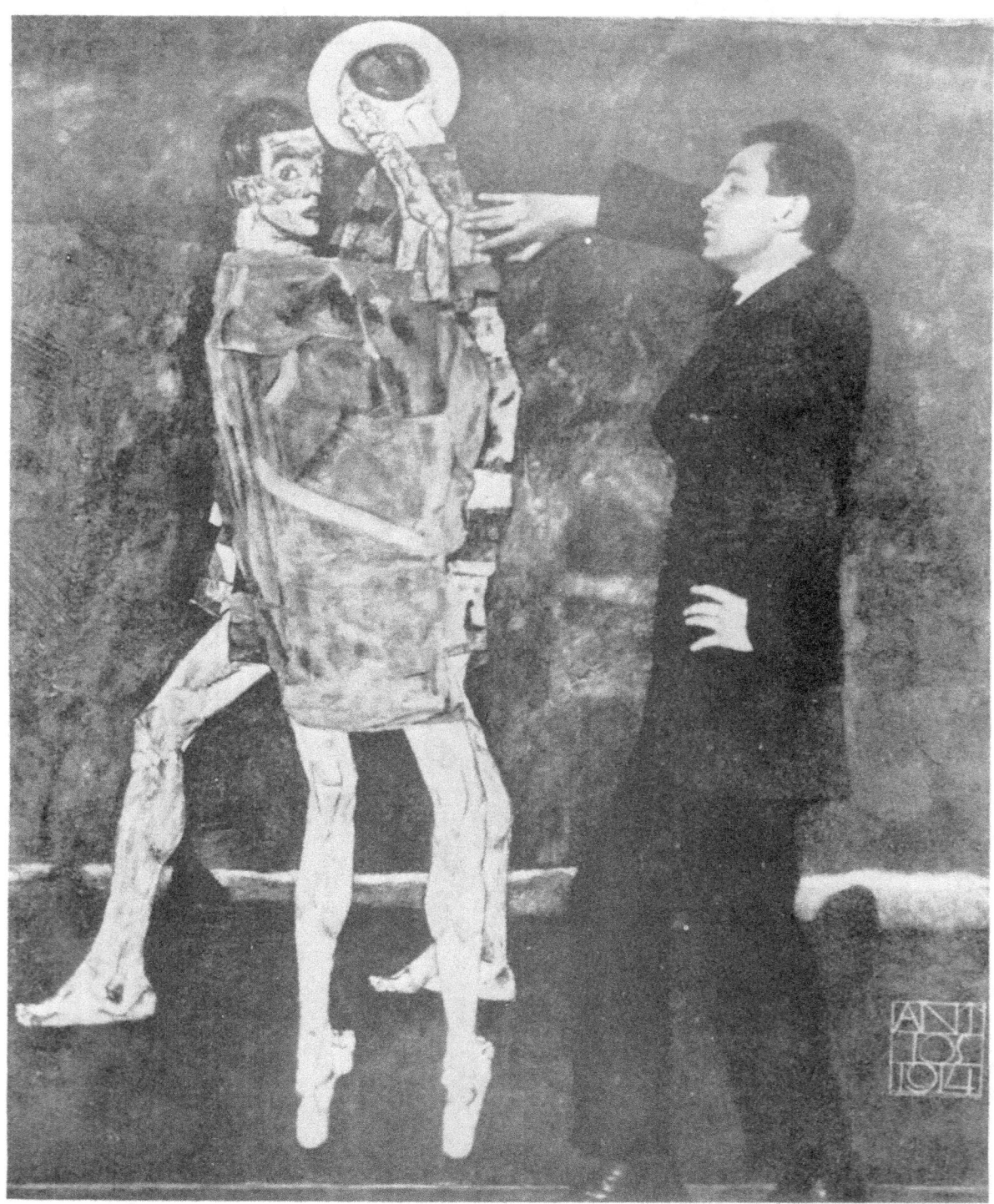

FRONTISPIECE: Egon Schiele standing before his painting,
Self-Portrait with Saint.

EGON SCHIELE'S PORTRAITS

Alessandra Comini

To my American mother and Italian father,

Megan and Tino

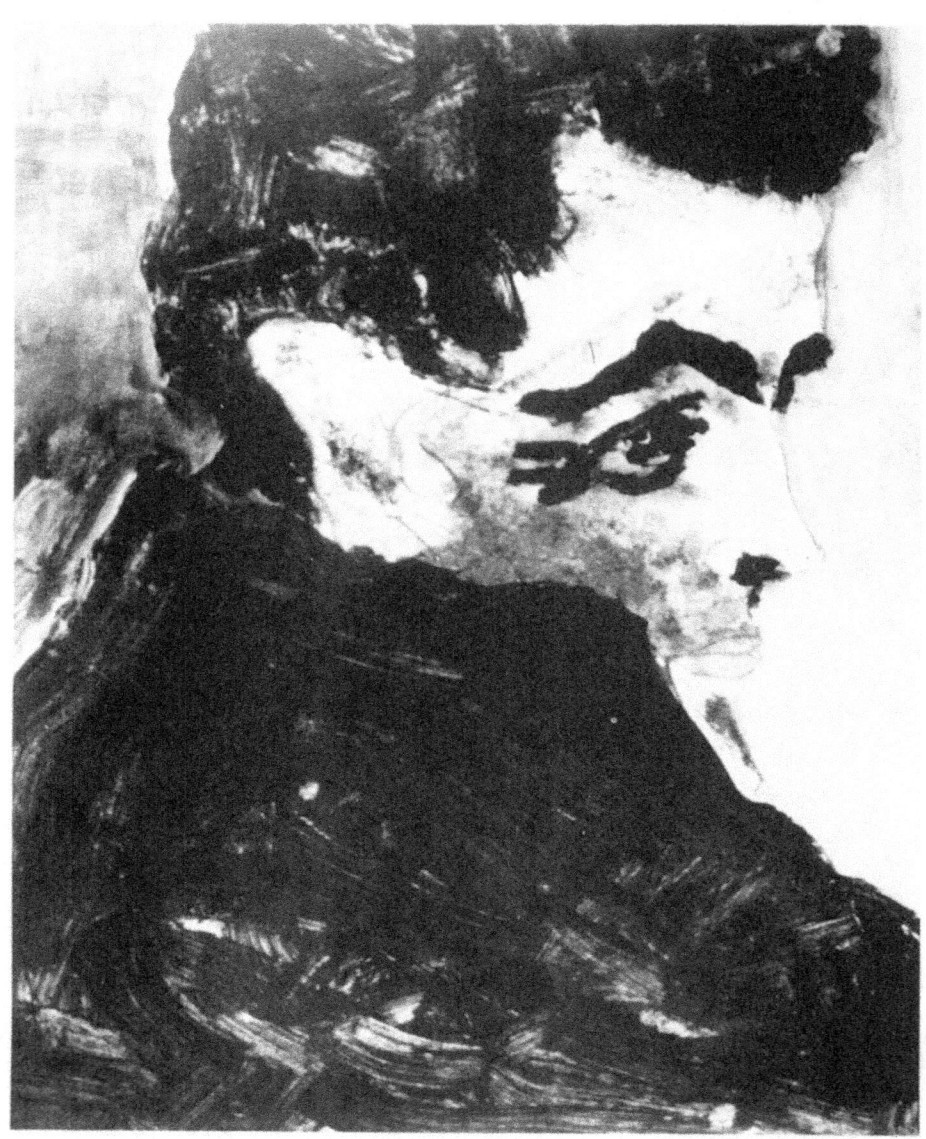

Erich Lederer, *Portrait of Egon Schiele*, ca. 1915.

Acknowledgments

THIS book—a decade in the making—is the result of a chance and decisive encounter with the work of Egon Schiele when I was a graduate student at the University of California at Berkeley in 1963. I attended an exhibition on Viennese Expressionism prepared by Professor Herschel B. Chipp and shown at the University Art Gallery. My "field" was medieval art, but the extraordinary draftsmanship and explorations of psyche revealed in Schiele's work held me spellbound. I became an instant convert to modern art, and simultaneously a vicarious Viennese—greedily absorbing the unique artistic and cultural atmosphere of fin-de-siècle Vienna. This has proved to be a vocation which I have never regretted, and I should like here gratefully to acknowledge all those who have helped, guided, and inspired me in my pursuit of Egon Schiele and his Vienna.

More than fifty years have elapsed since Schiele painted his portraits, yet some of his most important sitters are still living, and my research has benefited immeasurably from the recollections and reminiscences generously provided me. I owe the greatest thanks to Schiele's two surviving sisters, Frau Melanie Schuster and Frau Gertrud Peschka, who good-naturedly submitted over the years to numerous taped interviews and who gave me invaluable information about their brother's personality and life. Both sisters allowed me to study sketchbooks, read letter exchanges, and photograph drawings and watercolors in their collections. The devotion of Frau Melanie, now in her eighties, to the memory of her brother was an inspiration, and I shall always remember affectionately the sessions, frequently lasting nine or ten hours at a time, we spent together, as I arranged and transcribed her voluminous collection of letters to and from Schiele. Frau Gertrud also showed the greatest patience during my long visits and willingly made albums of photographs and other important documents available. I am indebted to her son, Herr Anton Peschka, Jr., for several informative conversations about Schiele and Austrian painting in general. Herr Peschka was also marvelously intuitive in his rephrasing of many of my questions to his mother when, in the wee hours, my German tended to falter, although Frau Gertrud's interest never flagged. I owe much to Schiele's sister-in-law, the late Frau Adele Harms, for her perceptive comments and vivid recollections. The late Dr. Otto Benesch kindly recounted his memories of sitting, when still in his teens, for a portrait by Schiele, and his widow, Frau Eva Benesch, has been of continuing generous assistance. Erich Lederer of Geneva, Switzerland, who was frequently portrayed by Schiele, went over all the photographic material of this book with me, and magnanimously allowed me first-hand study of his important collection of Schiele and Klimt works. In New York Mrs. Federica (Friederike) Beer-Monti (now of Honolulu), whose full-length portrait was painted by both Schiele and Klimt, assisted my study with detailed reminiscences based on diary entries. To all of these "Schiele sitters" I am especially grateful for the constant encouragement extended to me over a period of some ten years.

Despite the goodwill of those persons actually portrayed by Schiele, this book could have made little headway had it not been for the unusual generosity and aid of museums, galleries, and private collectors involved with Schiele. Hildegard Bachert of the Galerie St. Etienne in New York, the first gallery to promote Schiele in America, continually made available to me valuable primary and secondary material. Dr. Otto Kallir, the gallery's director, who published the pioneer work on Schiele in his oeuvre catalogue of 1930 (extensively revised and republished in 1966), gave his generous permission to reproduce certain works from his oeuvre catalogue, so that some of the lost Schiele canvases could be illustrated for discussion here. But Dr. Kallir's aid has gone far beyond provision of factual and visual material: since 1963 he has followed and encouraged my work on Schiele, carefully reading and criticizing this book in its ever-growing manuscript form. Another pioneering supporter of Schiele in America, Thomas M. Messer, director of The Solomon R. Guggenheim Museum, enriched and facilitated my work by inviting me to take part in the preparation and presentation of the museum's large Klimt-Schiele retrospective in 1965. His continued interest in my research has been a constant support. To Serge and Vally Sabarsky of the Serge Sabarsky Gallery, Inc. of New York I am particularly indebted for encouragement and "Viennese" information over the years, and for permission to reproduce works from their important private collection of Schiele. In London both Harry and Dr. Wolfgang Fischer of Fischer Fine Art Ltd. have proved to be allies of extreme amiability and efficiency, and Philip Wright of Marlborough Fine Art Ltd. has been of invaluable assistance in obtaining hard-to-find photographs. In Vienna Dr. Walter Koschatzky, director of the Albertina Museum, has given me unlimited time and ideal opportunities in which to study the immense Albertina Egon Schiele Archive, and I am particularly grateful to him for brushing aside red tape and also for personally photographing some of the vital material reproduced here. Other members of the Albertina staff who have aided me with photographs, translation help and advice are Dr. Alice Strobl, Dr. Hans Suesserott, and Dr. Erwin Mitsch. Dr. Rupert Feuchtmüller of the Niederösterreichisches Landes-Museum gave me an immediate welcome and liberally provided me with photographs and information. For similar assistance at the Historisches Museum der Stadt Wien, I am most grateful to the recently retired director, Dr. Franz Glück, to the present director, Dr. Alfred May, and to Dr. Hans Bisanz. For continually easing my path at the Osterreichische Galerie, I am indebted to the former director, Prof. Dr. Fritz Novotny, to the present director, Dr. Hans Aurenhammer, and to Dr. Gerbert Frodl. At the Museum des 20. Jahrhunderts I was cheerfully helped by the former director, Dr. Werner Hofmann, and the present director, Dr. Alfred Schmeller. Both immediate and long-range aid were offered by Dr. Margarethe Poch-Kalous, director, and Dr. Heribert Hutter of the Gemäldegalerie der Akademie der bildenden Künste, and the same is true of Prof. Walter Kasten, director of the Neue Galerie der Stadt Linz, Wolfgang Gurlitt Museum in Linz, and Prof. Dr. Wilfried Skreiner of the Neue Galerie am Landesmuseum Joanneum in Graz. The Galerie Würthle in Vienna and its director, Frau Luise Kremlaczeck, have also cooperated most helpfully.

Among the private collectors to whom I extend a general statement of thanks, I am materially and morally indebted to Viktor and Dollie Fogarassy of Graz, Erich and Lisl Lederer of Geneva, and Christian and Renée Nebehay of Vienna for food, lodging and cheer during long and repeated visits to study their splendid collections. Herr Nebehay, a Klimt scholar, rendered vital assistance in making his unique material available to me both before and after publication of his rich documentation on that artist. I am also very much indebted to members of the Nebehay Antiquariat and Art Gallery staff: Dr. Friedrich Heller and Dr. Hansjörg Krug and Frau Leopoldine Nemecek. Other private collectors whose cooperation has been germane to the realization of this book are Dr. Rudolf Leopold of Vienna, the family of Dr. Fritz Böck in Graz, Frau Daisy Kastner of Graz, and, in New York, Mrs. Helen Serger, Mrs. Alice M. Kaplan, and Ronald Lauder. I have further benefited from stimulating exchanges concerning things Viennese with the following: Professor Marianne Bonwit, Professor Jean Bony, Professor Patricia Carpenter, Robert Clark, Professor George Collins, James Demetrion, Dr. Johannes Dobai, Professor Wayne Dynes, Scott Elliott, Dr. Hans Fronius, Professor Julius Held, Professor Walter Horn, Lili Jensen, Professor William Jordan, Dr. Sidney Kahr, Dr. Robert Kantor, Eberhard Kornfeld, Felix Landau, the late Dr. Max Mell, the late Professor Alfred Neumeyer, Ingo Nebehay, Professor Linda Nochlin-Pommer, Professor Eugene Santomasso, Professor Gerhard Schmidt, Professor Carl Schorske, Professor Klaus Schrötter, Professor Peter Selz, Dr. Melvin Sigman, Professor Fritz Stern, Professor Josef Stern, Professor Eleanor Tufts, Horst Uhr, and Dr. Fritz Wotruba.

Special thanks go to Prof. Herschel B. Chipp, University of California, Berkeley, who sponsored my master's thesis on Schiele's self-portraits and who has continued actively to encourage my work. I am also grateful to Professors Joseph Bauke, Arthur Danto, Howard Hibbard, Theodore Reff, and Heinrich Schwarz, who formed the committee at the defense of my

Columbia University Ph.D. dissertation on the portraits of Egon Schiele. Among my colleagues at Columbia who through their practical example and encouragement proved to me that one can indeed teach and write at the same time, I would like to single out Professors James Beck, Robert Branner, George Collins, Howard Davis, Marion Lawrence, Barbara Novak, Dorothea Nyberg, Edith Porada, and the late Rudolf Wittkower. To my friend Isabelle Emerson, sensitive musicologist, courageous typist and resolute proofreader in spite of two lively children, I owe the realization of my heavily emendated manuscript, and to my ever-encouraging, consoling, and solution-devising editor Lorna Price of the University of California Press at Berkeley, I owe the niceties and consistencies of this book's final form.

Several generous and fortunately-timed grants provided the financial aid and release from teaching duties which were mandatory to the research for this book. I shall acknowledge these in chronological order. While I was still a graduate student two summer travel grants issued by the Department of Art History and Archaeology of Columbia University in 1965 and 1966 took me to Vienna, and a travel grant from the American Association of University Women for the year 1966–67 enabled me to conduct extended research in Vienna. As an assistant professor at Columbia, I received from the Columbia University Council for Research in the Humanities a welcome travel grant for the summer of 1971 to pursue research in Austria and Czechoslovakia. One of the greatest boons to the completion of this book occurred when I was named by the Council on the Humanities at Princeton University as the Alfred Hodder Fellow for 1972–73. Here, as "resident humanist," I have been given untrammeled free time and absolute privacy in an ideal intellectual environment, a regenerative experience that I wish might come the way of all active academics who find themselves sincerely torn between responsibility to their students and their research. I can not conclude without an acknowledgment of the idea-sparking influence extended by my undergraduate and graduate students—at Columbia, Berkeley, Southern Methodist University, and Yale. As Arnold Schönberg wrote in his manual on harmony: "This book I have learned from my students."

However the greatest debt of gratitude I owe is to my parents who creatively participated far beyond the demand of any family ties in the materialization of this book. My photographer father, Raiberto Comini, with his expert assistant Ray King, re-photographed, printed, and standardized unique photographic material which was indispensable but highly uneven in quality. My mother, Professor Megan Laird Comini of the Foreign Language Department of Southern Methodist University, devoted weeks upon weeks of her time to an exacting and merciless editing. Her combination of tactful and tenacious criticism is responsible for the final readability of this book. I sincerely appreciate the wonderful readiness of both my parents to make the far-off, long-dead Egon Schiele as much a part of their lives as he has been of mine.

ALESSANDRA COMINI

Contents

List of Illustrations

THE Albertina Egon Schiele Archive of the Graphische Sammlung Albertina, Vienna, is referred to as A.E.S.A. Oeuvre catalogue numbers are given for works by Klimt (Dobai) and Kokoschka (Wingler). For works by Schiele both the Kallir (K. for oils, Kallir for graphics) and Leopold (L.) oeuvre numbers are cited (see Concordance).

Illustrations within each chapter are designated "figures" here and in the text; those grouped after the text are designated "plates."

FIGURES

1. Photograph of the Schiele Family, *ca.* 1892. Left to right: Egon, Melanie, Marie, Adolf, Elvira. Courtesy Melanie Schuster, Vienna.
2. Egon Schiele, *Through Europe by Night, ca.* 1900, colored ink, Niederösterreichisches Landes-Museum, Vienna.
3. Egon Schiele, *Professor Strauch at His Easel*, 1906, red chalk, Niederösterreichisches Landes-Museum, Vienna.
4. Egon Schiele, *Profile Drawing of Gerti*, 15 March 1903, pencil on cardboard, Collection Gertrud Peschka, Vienna.
5. Photograph of Gerti, Melanie, and Egon Schiele, *ca.* 1903. Courtesy Melanie Schuster, Vienna.
6. Egon Schiele, *Sketch of Gerti*, 1907, pencil, Collection Gertrud Peschka, Vienna.
7. Egon Schiele, *Profile Drawing of Schiele's Mother*, 25 September 1906, red chalk and charcoal, Collection Melanie Schuster, Vienna.
8. Photograph of Melanie Schiele, *ca.* 1906. Courtesy Melanie Schuster, Vienna.
9. Egon Schiele, *Portrait of Melanie*, 29 September 1906, charcoal, Collection Melanie Schuster, Vienna.
10. Photograph of Egon Schiele, fall 1906. Courtesy A.E.S.A., Vienna.

11. Egon Schiele, *Mirror-Picture of Self*, 1905, colored pencils, Albertina, Vienna.

12. Egon Schiele, *Self-Portrait*, 6 September 1906, charcoal, Albertina, Vienna.

13. Barent Fabritius, *Young Man in Shepherd's Attire (Self-Portrait)*, *ca.* 1660, oil, Gemälde Galerie der Akademie der Bildenden Künste, Vienna.

14. Egon Schiele, *Self-Portrait with Hat 1907* (K.3; L.40), 1907, oil, formerly Collection Paul Vogel, Vienna. From *Egon Schiele: Oeuvre Catalogue of the Paintings* by Otto Kallir © 1930 and 1966 by Otto Kallir and Paul Zsolnay Verlag Gesellschaft m.b.H. used by permission of Crown Publishers, Inc.

15. Egon Schiele, *Self-Portrait 1907* (K.8; L.41), 1907, oil, Galerie St. Etienne, New York. From *Egon Schiele: Oeuvre Catalogue of the Paintings* by Otto Kallir © 1930 and 1966 by Otto Kallir and Paul Zsolnay Verlag Gesellschaft m.b.H. used by permission of Crown Publishers, Inc.

16. Anthony van Dyck, *Self-Portrait*, *ca.* 1618, oil, Gemälde Galerie der Akademie der Bildenden Künste, Vienna.

17. Photograph of the Life-Drawing Class at the Vienna Academy with Schiele in Left Background, *ca.* 1907. Courtesy A.E.S.A., Vienna.

18. Photograph of Gustav Klimt, *ca.* 1908. From Christian M. Nebehay, *Gustav Klimt Dokumentation*, Vienna, 1969.

19. Photograph of the Vienna Secession with the Academy in Back to the Right. Photograph by the author.

20. Photograph of the Wiener Werkstätte Showroom in 1907, Showing Works by Gustav Klimt and Georges Minne. From *Deutsche Kunst und Dekoration*, 1907.

21. Gustav Klimt, *Judith I* (Dobai 113), 1901, oil, Österreichische Galerie, Vienna.

22. Gustav Klimt, *Water Serpents* (Dobai 140), 1904, oil, private collection, Vienna.

23a. Egon Schiele, *Sheet of Seven Framed Compositions After Klimt Paintings*, 1908, pencil, private collection, New York.

23b. Egon Schiele, *Fairytale World* (K.65; L. 120), 1908, oil, private collection, Vienna. From *Egon Schiele: Oeuvre Catalogue of the Paintings* by Otto Kallir © 1930 and 1966 by Otto Kallir and Paul Zsolnay Verlag Gesellschaft m.b.H. used by permission of Crown Publishers, Inc.

24. Egon Schiele, *Two Men in Decorative Robes*, *ca.* 1909, pencil on cardboard, private collection, Dallas.

25. Egon Schiele, *Two Men*, *ca.* 1909, pen and wash drawing, Albertina, Vienna.

26. Photograph of Gustav Klimt, *ca.* 1912–14. From Christian M. Nebehay, *Gustav Klimt Dokumentation*, Vienna, 1969.

27. Egon Schiele, *Blue Pencil Sketch of Leopold Czihaczek*, 1907, blue pencil, private collection, Dallas.

28. Photograph of Leopold Czihaczek, *ca.* 1913. Courtesy Melanie Schuster, Vienna.

PLATES

The Expressionist Shift from Facade to Psyche

THE most persistent motif in the art of Egon Schiele (1890–1918), the Austrian painter and exponent of Viennese Expressionism, is the human figure. A contemporary of Arnold Schönberg and Sigmund Freud, he shared in that preoccupation with the psyche that found its first spokesmen in Vienna during the opening years of the twentieth century. Schiele's career was typically Expressionist—he worked with apocalyptic intensity, was actually imprisoned because of the "offensive" aspect of his art, and died quite unexpectedly at the age of twenty-eight, a victim of the influenza epidemic of 1918. He left a vast oeuvre of some three hundred oils and several thousand watercolors, sketches, and drawings. Portraiture, especially self-portraiture, was a tenacious constant in this artistic production, which ranged from lyrical but mysteriously uninhabited town- and landscapes to dark, brooding, ambiguous allegories. The portraits appear in every one of Schiele's creative years, and record major stylistic changes. The self-portraits reflect emotional states related to the artist's extraordinary private life—states which are intimately linked with the evolution of his radical idiom. The row of changing identities which Schiele provided himself and which he projected on canvas with obsessive regularity makes mandatory a chronological study of the relationship between his life and portraiture. Seen within the larger context of fin-de-siècle Austria, an analysis of the cultural influences which shaped Schiele's art can help explain the emergence of a distinctly Viennese, as opposed to German, Expressionism.

The singling-out of Schiele's portraits for a comprehensive study reflects my belief that the elusive element which this Expressionist artist sought in his portraiture accurately mirrors the collective cultural quest of his time: the inner self—psychological man, rather than the political, religious or economic man of times past. Internalization is a key word for the art forms at the beginning of our century. A general desire to probe, identify and express inner essences characterizes not only the type of painting which is now broadly labeled German Expressionism, but is also manifest in the dance, music and literature of the same period. Schiele was born in 1890, into that decade which nourished the short-lived but international movement Art Nouveau—called *Jugendstil* in Germany and *Secessionstil* in Austria. The ten years before the close of the nineteenth century might also be called the decade of the great and beautiful façade: art for art's sake, as communicated, for example, through the ethereal dance gestures of Loïe Fuller, Isadora Duncan, and the Wiesenthal Sisters. So competitively entrancing were the flares of cultural pyrotechnics that a sensitive representative of the "façade," Isadora Duncan, could recall of that period: "My soul was like a battlefield where Apollo, Dionysus, Christ, Nietzsche and Richard Wagner disputed the ground."[1] Redemption through art—that German aspiration first formulated by Schopenhauer—had been promised anew by Wagner and Nietzsche. The 1890s witnessed Theodor Herzl's successful attempt to spark a political goal for the Jewish people by appealing to the mystique and symbolism of a promised land, Zion. The decade also saw the obscure and eccentric writer Julius Langbehn propose to an enthralled German public the idea of a chiaroscuro-souled Rembrandt as the embodiment not only of the "Northern" culture of the past, but as spiritual model for a degenerate present.[2] In an industrialized society of increasing dehumanization and regimentation a few single voices condemning modern life and calling for greater individuality began to sound, and their heady demands for self expression awakened society to its own unarticulated rancors and desires, ultimately stirring the sleeping energies of a whole folk. Reason seemed shelved in an impassioned, national pursuit of the irrational. A need to unleash the subliminal self began to assail science and the arts alike, and the year 1900 introduced a decade that was restless rather than nostalgic, a decade in which a whole culture's attention shifted from the façade to the psyche.

One path to the psyche was art, and the new century saw an extraordinary change in the function of art from that of ornament to essence, as Expressionist artists and writers began to employ visionary means to probe the inner man. In the German-speaking world the processes of the mind and emotions which the young science of psychology had begun to explore were claimed for the artist by Kandinsky in his *On the Spiritual in Art* (published in Munich in 1912)—an essay (inspired by contacts with theosophy and recent theories of empathy) in which repeated key phrases evoked an alluring realm of *inner* "resonance," "necessity," "urge" and "soul vibrations."

As if in anticipation of the existential phenomenon that would concern the new century, Nietzsche had already asked:

"But how do we recognize ourselves? How can man know himself? He is a dark and hidden thing; whereas the hare is said to have seven skins, man can take off seven times seventy skins and still not be able to say: 'That is you as you really are,

1. Notes for the entire text appear in the Notes section below, pp. 189ff.

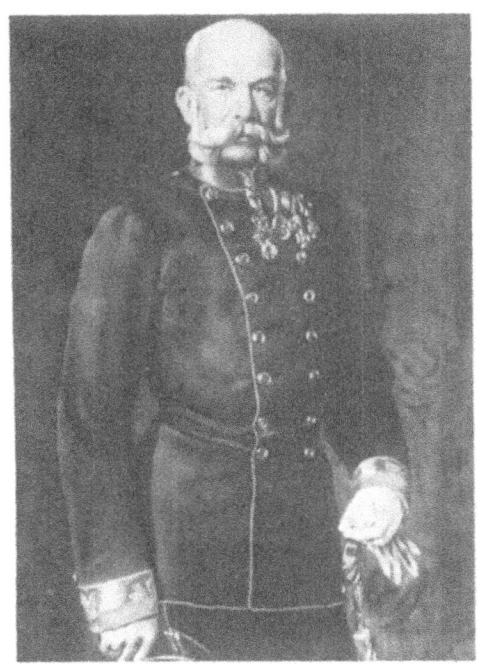

Emperor Franz Josef in an official portrait.

Photograph of Emperor Franz Josef posing
for an equestrian portrait.

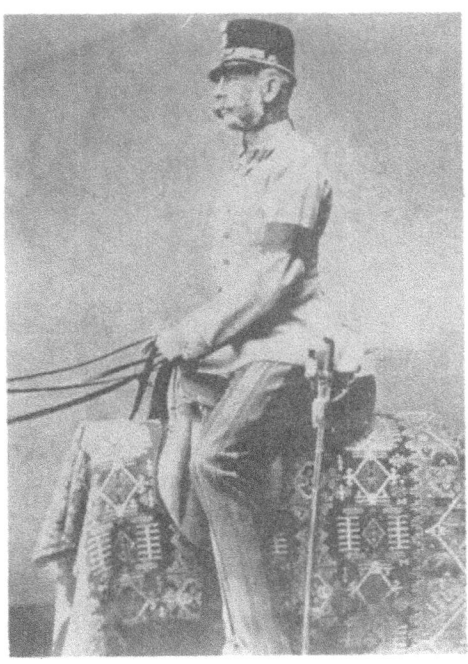

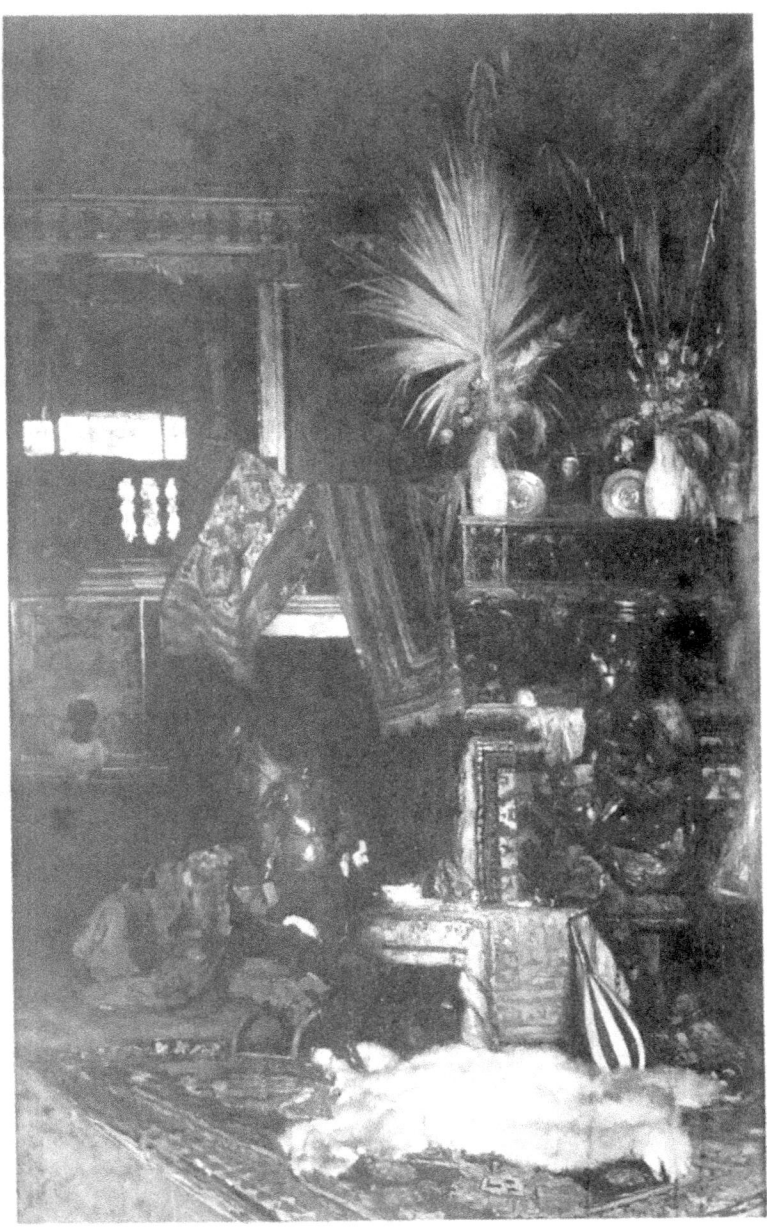

Eduard Charlemont, *Hans Makart in His Studio*, 1880, oil, Historisches Museum der Stadt Wien, Vienna.

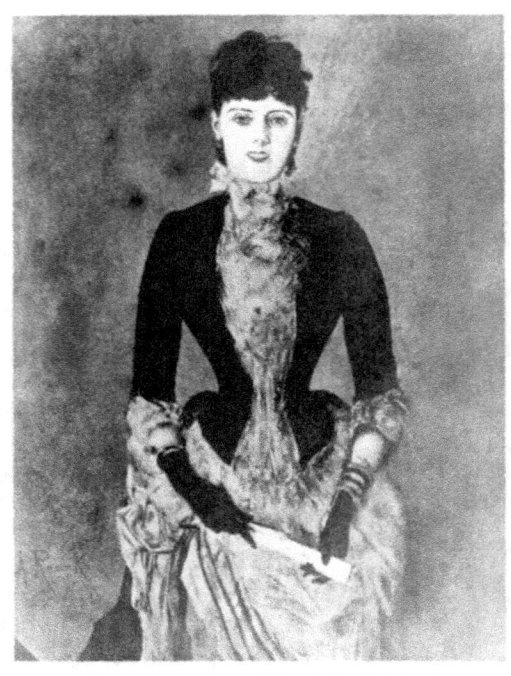

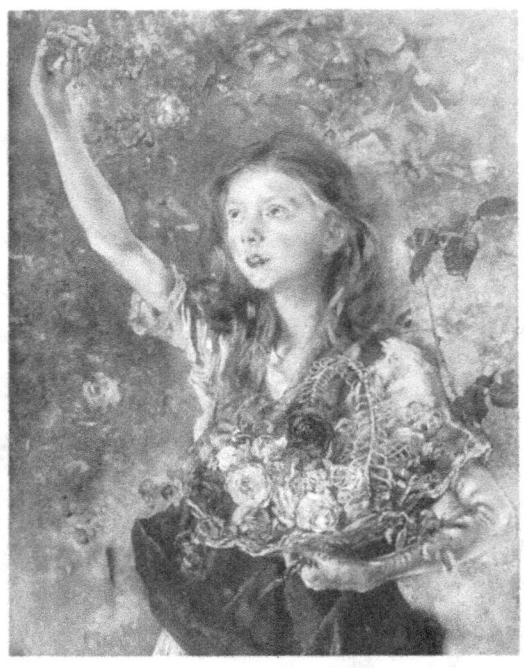

Anton Romako, *Portrait of Isabella Reisser*, 1885, oil, private collection, Vienna. From Fritz Novotny, *Der Maler Anton Romako*, Vienna, 1954.

Anton Romako, *Young Girl Picking Roses*, ca. 1883, oil, Österreichische Galerie, Vienna.

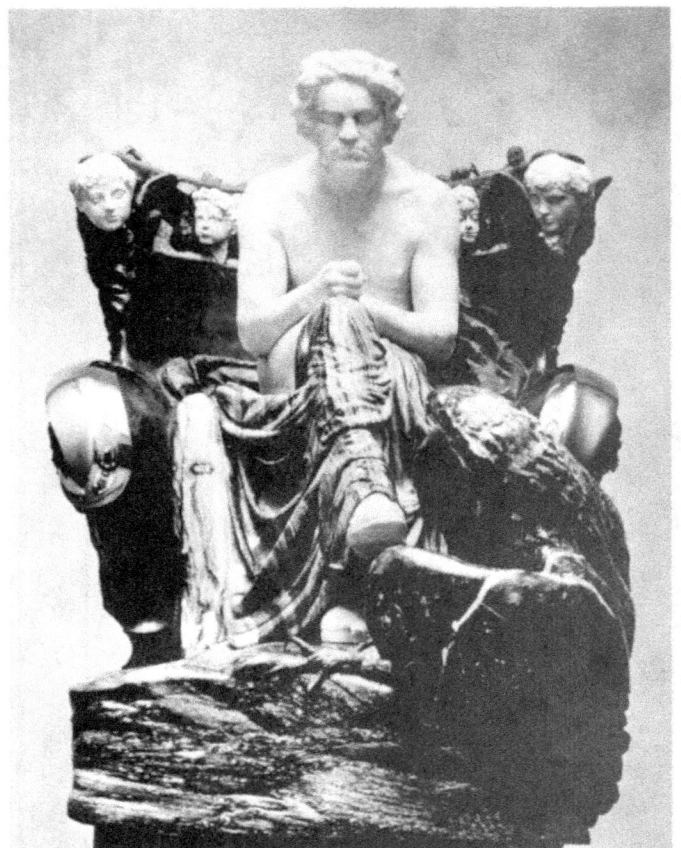

Max Klinger, *Beethoven Monument*, 1902, bronze, gold, colored marble, and semi-precious stones, Museum der bildenden Künste, Leipzig.

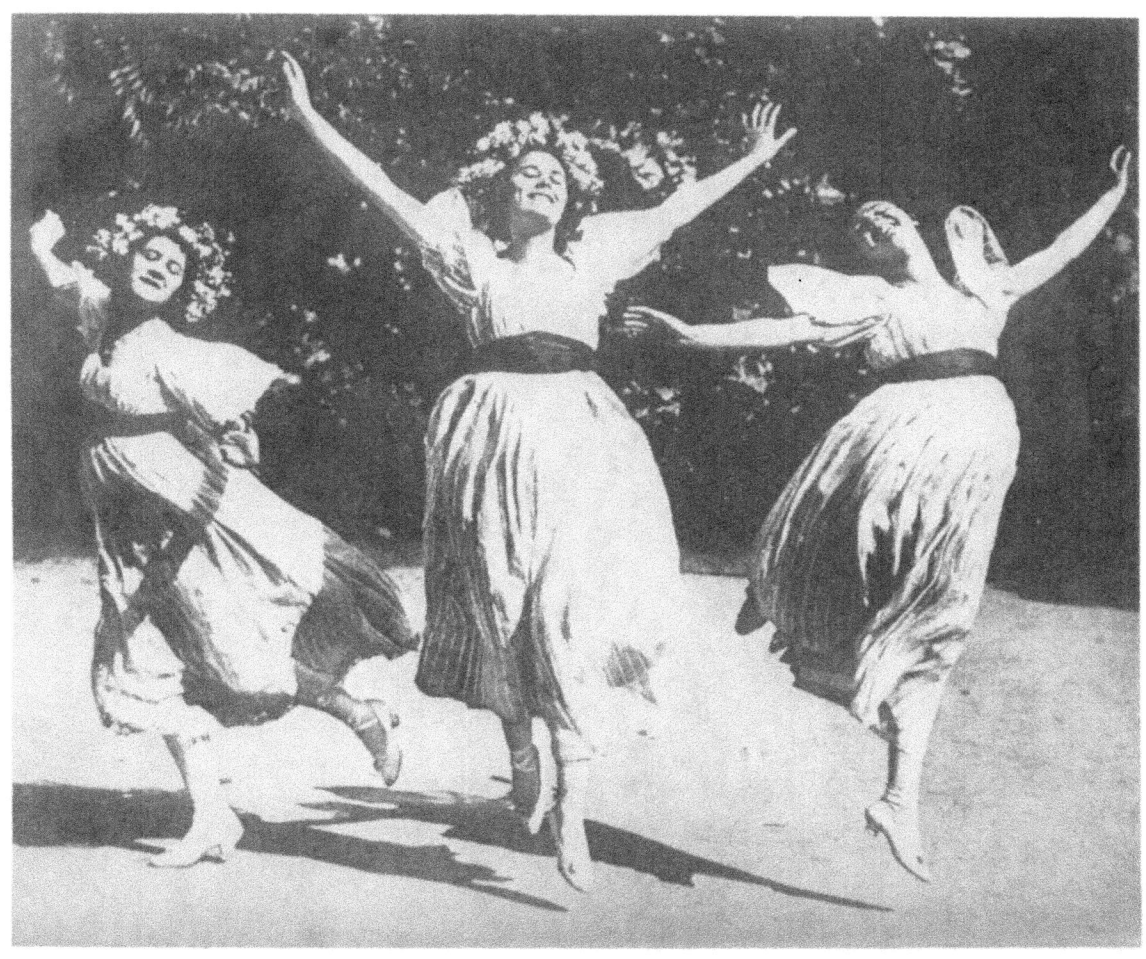

Photograph of the Wiesenthal Sisters, *ca.* 1908. *From* Rudolf Huber-Wiesenthal,
Die Schwestern Wiesenthal, Vienna, 1934.

Maximilian Lenz, *Marionettes, ca.* 1910, oil, present whereabouts unknown.
From 1. Internationale Jagd-Austellung Wien 1910 exhibition catalogue, Vienna, 1910.

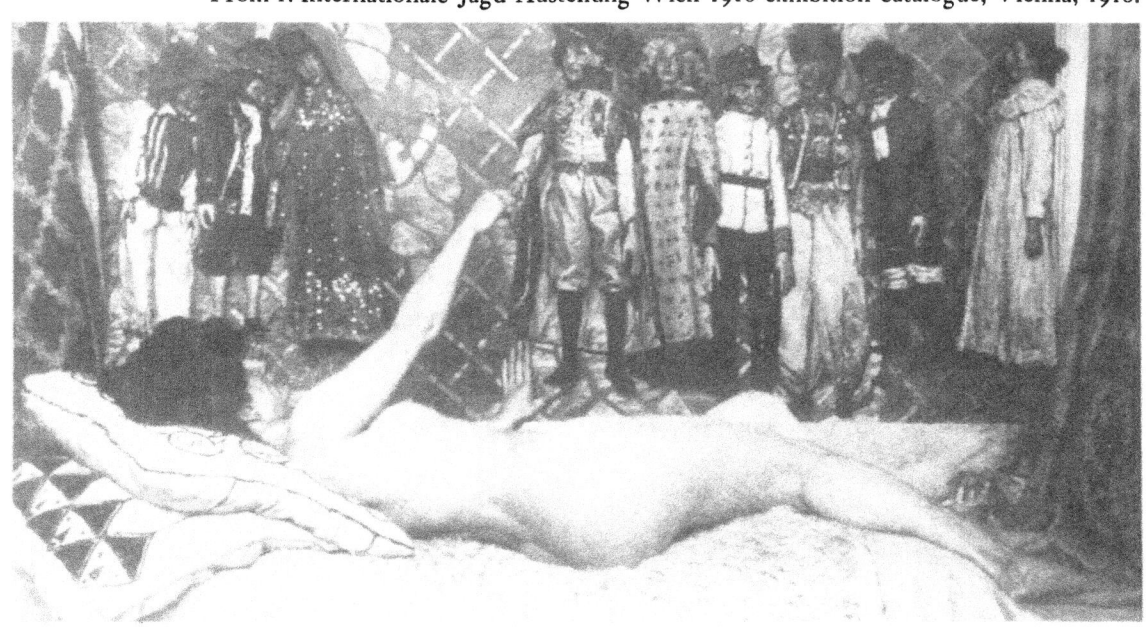

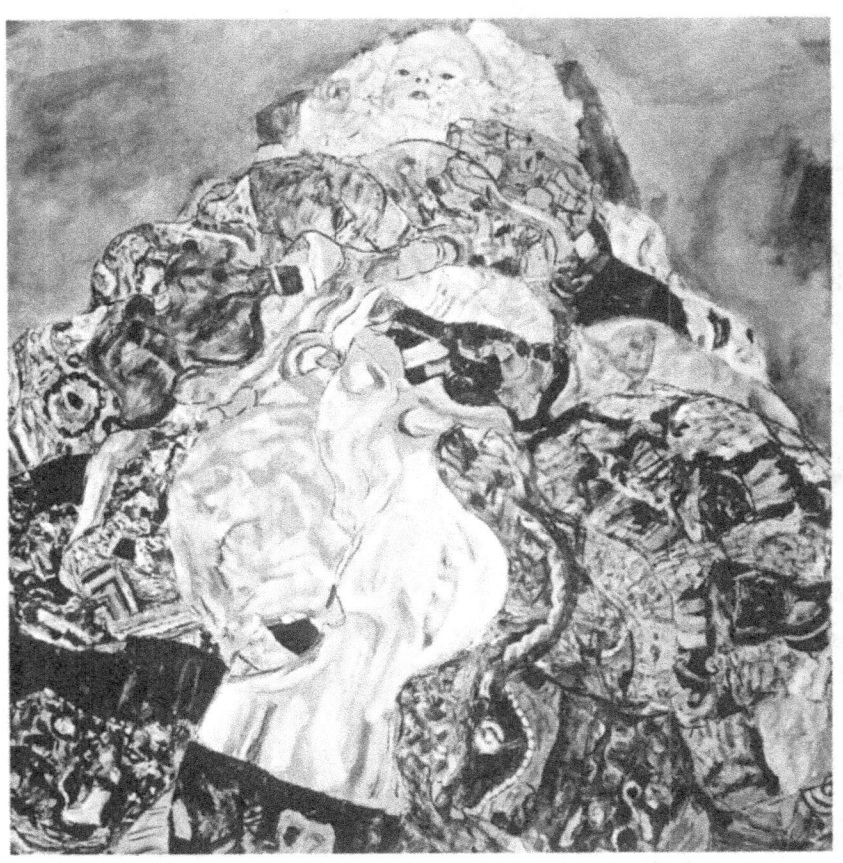

Gustav Klimt, *Baby* (unfinished; Dobai 222),
1917–18, oil, private collection, New York. Photograph Galerie St. Etienne, New York.

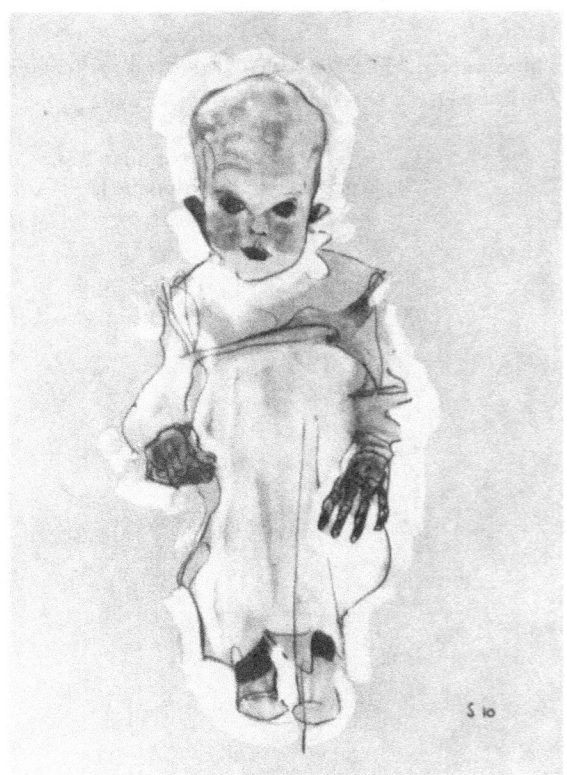

Egon Schiele, *Baby*, 1910, black chalk and
watercolor, private collection, Vienna.

that is no longer mere external appearance.' Besides, it is a painful and dangerous undertaking to dig down into oneself in this way and to descend violently and directly into the shaft of one's being"[3]

The shaft of one's being passed through subterranean strata of feeling. By the beginning of our century emotion, for artists, was to be trusted and exploited. Mary Wigman, pioneer of the new Expressionist dance, later described the creative process which first "freed" her dance from the façade of music:

"My purpose is not to 'interpret' the emotions. . . . My dances flow rather from certain states of being, different stages of vitality which release in me a varying play of the emotions, and in themselves dictate the distinguishing atmospheres of the dances. . . . Thus on the rock of basic feeling I slowly build each structure."[4]

It was this "rock" of basic feeling and states of being that the Austrian portrait painter Egon Schiele attempted, by virtue of natural inclination as well as cultural disposition, to uncover. For it was especially in recalcitrant Vienna that the rich motherlode of repressed emotions ran deepest.

To appreciate the Expressionist preoccupation with the psyche, it is instructive to look briefly back at the particular forces at work in that extraordinary city which nourished the sudden phenomenon of Expressionism in its art, music and literature. The distinctive love-hate relationship of Vienna's cultural spokesmen to their city plays a formative role. "An isolation cell in which one is allowed to scream!"[5] So Karl Kraus, satirist and controversial editor of *Die Fackel*, a privately published magazine which relentlessly exposed the intellectual and social foibles of the city for thirty-six years, once described turn-of-the-century Vienna. The dimensions of this cell were by no means meager. By the year 1900 the imperial city on the Danube had attracted over one and a half million inhabitants, drawn from all corners of the Dual Monarchy, and including a large number of Magyar and Slav peoples, whose growing demands for independence accelerated that conflict of nationalism which was ultimately to topple the Hapsburg monarchy. In the years between 1900 and 1914 however the political death signs of a situation which Kraus mocked as being "desperate but not serious," were ignored in a frenetic dedication to ritual and spectacle. The changing of the imperial guard, which the benign Kaiser Franz Josef personally supervised, provided a daily pageant and confirmation of the apparent stability of the Court—a stability whose Potemkinesque façade was about as durable as that support used by the Kaiser when posing for equestrian portraits. The educated upper middle class created its own symbol of enduring culture—the Ringstrasse—a protective ring of magnificent public buildings which effectively blocked off the factories and slum areas of the outlying districts. Built on the former site of Vienna's ancient military fortifications, this great avenue provided an impressive façade—an elegant yet superficial portrait of the inner city drawn and financed by its newly prosperous bourgeoisie. Such exploitation of pomp and luxury, which was the outward aspect of Kraus's isolation cell, had succeeded in mesmerizing its inhabitants during the closing decades of the nineteenth century.

If Vienna as a city was given to architectural self-portraiture to project a euphoric and still vital image, the musicians, writers and artists of the city were equally given to an unending depiction of their environment. The affectionate side of this portraiture was expressed in the operettas of Johann Strauss and Franz Lehár which depicted a carefree world wherein the aristocracy mingled with the people on easy, intimate terms. The narrowness and erotic license of this world of dashing army officers and coquettish working-class girls was reported with maudlin provincialism by the local press and dissected with melancholy irony in the stories and plays of Arthur Schnitzler. In the visual arts the most successful delineator of the glory that had been Vienna was Hans Makart (1840–1884). Through grandiose historical scenes and flattering official portraits he had become the unchallenged dictator of public taste at the time construction of the Ringstrasse was begun. When this portrayer of the Vienna façade was himself portrayed, it was within the context of the sumptuous, carpet-strewn atelier that contained the exotic paraphernalia of his inspiration.[6]

The same bourgeois society that lionized Makart found little to praise in the portraits of his great contemporary Anton Romako (1834–1889). Whereas Romako's glowing historical scenes continued the drama and élan of the Austrian Baroque heritage, the intensity of his portraiture emphasized the fragility of the individual's façade and pointed to the future course of Viennese portrait painting. In his genre or informal portraits and in his formal, commissioned works of the 1880s two trends were anticipated by Romako: the Jugendstil elaboration of environment into symbol and surface pattern, and the Expressionist concentration on the sitter surrounded by an abstract background or void. The girl picking roses in Romako's genre portrait is not shown against the panorama of a garden scene; she is set against a rich vegetation seen in as close a focus as is the sitter herself. This intensified juxtaposition of man and nature was developed by Vienna's foremost exponent of Jugendstil, Gustav Klimt (1862–1918), into a formula of ornate surfaces and isolated human elements. Romako's formal portraits, which often employed an empty background and an uncompromising frontality as direct bridges to the sitter's personality, shorn of any environmental definitions, forecast the existential single-mindedness of the Expressionist generation of Viennese painters: Richard Gerstl (1883–1908), Max Oppenheimer (1885–1954), Oskar Kokoschka (b. 1886), Paris von Gütersloh (b. 1887) and Egon Schiele. These artists penetrated the face to expose the psyche, and in their hands Romako's spatial void became an effective formal tool for a ruthless unmasking of the sitter.[7]

The persistence of portraiture as a major artistic expression of early twentieth-century Vienna was a phenomenon not seen elsewhere in Europe. It was directly related to the sense of Angst which accompanied the impending social and political bankruptcy of the nation and which was plunging the doomed capital into a last aesthetic utopianism.[8] A particular kind of hysteria was in the air, and it was the city's intelligentsia that was most aware of the contradictions presented by the public façade. It was an age of pronounced antisemitism. Austria had produced two charismatic political figures—Karl Lueger, leader of the Christian Social party, who as outspoken Mayor of Vienna (1897–1910), played a cat-and-mouse game with the Jewish community, declaring "*I decide who is Jewish*," and the more extreme antisemite, Georg von Schönerer, leader of the racialist Pan-German party. The natural isolation of the creative artist from society took on a trenchant sense of alienation for the Jewish intellectuals—an alienation summed up by Gustav Mahler, who referred to himself as three times homeless—"as a native of Bohemia in Austria, as an Austrian among Germans, and as a Jew throughout all the world."[9] The ambiguous attitude of the cultural avant-garde towards Vienna quickened withdrawal into a cult of the self. Such internalization was represented on the highest and most productive level by the brilliant young poet Hugo von Hofmannsthal, and on the lowest level by a whole society's plunge into apathy as even the petit bourgeois turned his attention to the behaviorist world of stimuli and sensations recently charted by Vienna's philosopher-scientist Ernst Mach. The cultural elite, which included Klimt and the other founding fathers of the Vienna Secession, substituted art for action and discarded the political for the cultural hero—the opera singer, theater actor, ballet dancer, literary critic, poet, architect, artist and musician. Confirmation of the spiritual superiority of these heroes and their patrons was achieved through a prodigality of portraiture. The entire artistic elite of Vienna joined forces in 1902 to create an appropriate setting for Max Klinger's famous and technically extravagant monument to Beethoven. His Zeus-like image of the city's adopted hero was given the place of honor in the Secession showrooms and Klimt decorated the walls with sumptuous friezes based on Schiller's "Ode to Joy." Mahler re-orchestrated for wind instruments the fourth movement of Beethoven's Ninth Symphony and conducted the Vienna Opera chorus on the opening day of the exhibition. The enthralled public was caught up in a multiple spectacle that inundated the senses and swayed the emotions through its seductive suggestion of a national mystique.

Such myth-making however still belonged to the age of the great façade, and the apotheosis of a cultural hero did not hold the same meaning or interest for the younger Expressionists as it had held for the older group of Jugendstil artists of the Secession. With the scandalous performance in 1908 of Kokoschka's play, *Murderer, Hope of Women*, (*Mörder, Hoffnung der Frauen*) (a boisterous public reaction required police intervention) the new hero of the Expressionist generation made his debut: Man. Man in his age-old conflict with sensuality, and cloaked in the anonymity of Everyman, but also Man-the-Self, transparent and painfully autobiographical. Kokoschka's short, tortured play can certainly be considered the first Expressionist drama, and in the same year the painter-author pursued the theme of self—an adolescent self racked by awakening sexual drives—in a "fairy story" of exquisite and shuddering imagery, *The Dreaming Boys*. This sort of open, frank acknowledgement of one of the fundamental aspects of the human experience was new for Vienna and began to mushroom during the opening decade of the century as self-concern was legitimized by art and science. Robert Musil called attention to sexual, sadistic aspects of the adolescent psyche in his first novel, *Die Verwirrungen des Zöglings Törless* (1906), and the unpopular assertions of Sigmund Freud and other psychoanalysists concerning bisexuality and the existence of unconscious sexual drives presented an inescapable "frontal" attack which blatantly differed from the refined sensualism with which sex had previously been viewed. The apparent abandonment epitomized in the flowing dance attitudes of the Viennese Wiesenthal Sisters and suggested in many of Klimt's allegorical works (figures 21 and 22; plates 15 and 17) was but one side of the hedonistic coin upon which the emotional commerce of Vienna depended. The other side revealed basic sexual inhibitions which received expression only through accepted forms and disguises. The "playful" nude woman who shares her charms with startlingly lifelike puppets in Secessionist artist Maximilian Lenz's painting *Marionettes* is typical of the hypocrisy and repression that characterized Viennese mores at the turn of the century. The same Klimt who pinioned neurotic society ladies in vises of multiple ornamental motifs was, in his private drawings, a sophisticated voyeur of auto-eroticism and lesbian love demonstrated by the models who posed for him. With the younger Expressionist generation the role of the artist as secret spectator of erotica changed to that of surcharged conduit. By 1910 the artist screamed his sexual frustrations aloud, not in an isolation cell but in public. The traditional self-portrait acquired a new exhibitionist function as the artist laid bare his hidden desires.

This wish to penetrate to essences as though by X-ray was shared by creative artists in other fields. The poet Georg Trakl produced an extraordinary self-portrait shortly before his suicide in 1914, and Arnold Schönberg painted a remarkable row of self-portraits and hallucinatory "color visions." The close-focus, heated emotionalism and existential anxiety of these intensified images betray the atmosphere of permanent tension in which the Expressionist artist existed—a tension from which the contemporary scientists of the psyche were no less free. The brilliant twenty-three year old Otto Weininger, accused in the Viennese press of having purloined his theories on bisexuality from Freud, committed suicide a few months after the 1903 publication of his immensely successful, if morbid, book *Geschlect und Charakter*. Although Freud played an unwilling role in Weininger's tragic drama, the awesome professor's treatment of the members of his own inner circle was at times methodically devastating. Freud's refusal to take into final analysis his gifted but fiercely independent disciple Viktor Tausk was a rejection, a psychic death, too great for the younger scientist to bear. The suicide note Tausk wrote to Freud on the morning he killed himself in 1919 has only recently been brought to light. The "façade" of Tausk's relationship with Freud was so discreet that half a century later Tausk's family was surprised to learn of the direct connection between Freud and Tausk's death.[10]

A lie—that is what the façade had become. Truth lay underneath and could only be exposed by probing, or even attacking, the psyche. The new aim of art, Kraus had written in the first issue of *Die Fackel*, was not what we bring (*"wir bringen"*) but what we destroy (*"wir umbringen"*).[11] A savage analysis of environment occurred in all fields. What Kraus criticized in language ("Every elaboration of information falsifies it"[12]) and Schönberg purged in music, Adolf Loos attacked in architecture. At the very time when the artisans of the Wiener Werkstätte were producing luxury items for the wealthy bourgeoisie, Loos aimed his purist theories directly at the Viennese love of sumptuousness, delivering the devastating invective:

"Man, as gregarious animal, used to have to employ different colors to distinguish himself; modern man uses his clothing as a mask. So monstrously powerful is his individuality that it can no longer allow itself to be expressed through clothing. Lack of ornamentation is a sign of spiritual strength."[13]

It was exactly this "monstrously powerful individuality" that the Viennese Expressionist artists strove to reveal. The pursuit of essence, the phenomenon of the self and of the other—these became the raison d'être of portraiture, enriching the genre with a new definition that included a violently subjective interpretation of reality—an interpretation so rigorous that an entirely new stylistic vocabulary had to be fashioned. It is thus not only the content—passage from the façade to the psyche—but also the new approach to form—from the environmental to the existential—which radically distinguishes even the portrait of a baby painted by the Jugendstil master Klimt from one by the Expressionist artist Schiele. How and why a whole generation of younger painters broke out of the isolation cell that was the Vienna of 1900 must now be examined in detail through the portraiture of an ideally representative artist of intrinsic quality, Egon Schiele.

CHAPTER I

1890-1909: Childhood and Student Years

THE SCHIELE FAMILY

EGON Schiele should logically have become a locomotive engineer, or a brakeman, or a petty official in the railroad office of some little Austrian town. For two generations before his birth, railroads had provided the occupations of the Schiele family. It was a source of pride that the paternal grandfather, Ludwig Schiele, had directed the construction and been the first general inspector of the impressively named Imperial Royal Privileged West Railway of Bohemia (present-day Czechoslovakia). Egon's father, Adolf Schiele, did not rise to such prominence, but he too was a railroad man and stationmaster of the small town of Tulln, about forty miles west of Vienna. Egon Schiele was born in Tulln and, as the only son in the family (figure 1), was expected to continue the tradition and aspire to be at least an engine driver. He was thus born into a family that was quite unprepared, by background or by custom, to understand the precocious manifestations of his artistic gifts.[1]

Egon, the sixth child born to Adolf and Marie Schiele, was the only son to survive. The first three children, all boys, were stillborn. The first living children were two girls, Elvira, born in 1883, and Melanie, born in 1886. Egon arrived 12 June 1890, and four years later a third girl, Gertrud ("Gerti"), completed the family.[2]

The boy's physical heritage was unpromising. His father had contracted syphilis just prior to his marriage.[3] However, he refused to admit that he had the disease, would not have it treated, and soon infected his young wife. A taciturn, serious man, but capable of fiery outbursts of temper, he died insane at the age of fifty-four, when Egon was fourteen years old.

Egon's mother, Marie Soukup, was from German-speaking Bohemia and eleven years younger than her husband. She was a strong-willed romantic, and had married against her family's wishes at the age of sixteen. The syphilitic infection from Adolf was an infelicitous wedding gift from which she suffered horribly for many years, bequeathing it in turn to her stillborn boys and to Elvira, who died from this bitter legacy at the age of ten.

From early childhood Egon was quiet and introspective, self-sufficient and intense, already distinguished by great dark eyes staring somberly out of a white face. He spent every possible moment with a pencil in hand covering paper, table tops, and walls with sketches. His two still-surviving sisters, Melanie and Gerti,[4] have described the young Egon as drawing uninterruptedly from morning to night, while his mother has written that he first began to draw at the age of eighteen months. His first drawings were—not surprisingly —of railroad trains. The Schiele family occupied four large rooms on the second story of the Tulln railroad station and before Egon was five he had adopted the disconcerting habit of crawling out of the dining room window onto the slanting porch roof facing the tracks—some fifteen feet below—in order better to see and draw the trains. The minute details he absorbed and the realistic images he was able to convey at such an early age are observable in a colored ink drawing done at about the age of ten and romantically entitled *Through Europe by Night* (figure 2). A many hued glow of sunset lights the sky and is reflected in the pool of water underneath the bridge. The child's delight in his own skill is evident in the beams of light from engine and caboose which penetrate the darkness, and in the wavering shape of the locomotive's smoke sensitively repeated in the scraggly silhouette of low hills in the background. The individual railroad cars, windows, wheel drivers, and the bridge show a remarkable perception and sureness of line. Later, Egon's first portrait sketches held the same insistence on veracity of detail.

He was never punished for misbehaving in the ordinary sense, but instead only for drawing pictures to the neglect of his studies. The family's attempts, now subtle, now rash, to encourage a more equal division of labor usually boomeranged. Once when Egon was about eight his father thought to win the reluctant student's cooperation by presenting him with a thick new sketchbook in which he would be allowed to draw one picture every day *after* completing his Latin. The sketchbook was given to Egon in the morning; when his father returned from work for the noonday meal the whole book had been filled. The boy had torn the pages out and arranged them throughout the house, like a little exhibition. Many of the sheets were of carefully drawn railroad cars, one to a page, and so formed "trains" going from room to room. Adolf Schiele was so angry that he took all the drawings, stuffed them into the stove, and set fire to them. Egon was horrified and wept futilely. Although his family more often rejected than accepted the precocity of its only son, Egon himself sensed that he was a *Wunderkind*, and as he grew older he learned to defend his drawing with a sharp and ready tongue.

He had few friends or playmates in Tulln, where he attended the elementary school, but spent his leisure time sketching the station grounds and garden. He kept an almost scientific watch over the family hens, making an exact written record of their breeding times. From his earliest days he was fascinated by the timetables and schedules of trains and streetcars. He had a passion for punctuality, constantly checking the family's routine by a clock. Another predilection, which he retained throughout his life, was that of studying his reflection in a mirror. He never entered a room that contained a mirror without going up to it at once and seriously examining his image.

EARLY SCHOOLING

Tulln had no *Gymnasium* (high school) so when Egon was eleven he was sent to the nearby town of Krems for further schooling. During the school week he lived with a relative but came home for weekends. Due to his father's employment Egon had the advantage of a railroad pass until he was fourteen, and this early commuting instilled in him a lasting pleasure in train trips. Even as an adult he would often hop aboard a train on the spur of the moment, without bothering to learn its destination, and would ride for hours looking out of the window and making sketches in his pocket notebook. When the train reached the end of the line he would just as enthusiastically catch the next train back.

In 1902 the family moved to Klosterneuburg, a picturesque old abbey town just a few miles northwest of Vienna. Egon was now twelve and Melanie and Gerti sixteen and eight respectively. Adolf Schiele was already suffering from the fits of insanity which now began to overshadow the last three years of his life. The spectacle of his father's slow mental deterioration made an unforgettable impression upon the son. The family had to adapt to the unpredictable presence of imaginary visitors—railroad inspectors and other dignitaries whom the father often produced, introduced and invited to stay for dinner. Out of compassionate complicity the family entertained these invisible guests and ceased to show surprise. Melanie took on the responsibilities of the eldest child, obtaining a position as clerk at the Klosterneuburg railroad station. The change of residence was the first of many. In four years at Klosterneuburg the Schiele family lived at four different addresses, due to their declining financial status and to the father's increasingly embarassing behavior. Egon tried to cheer his mother by telling her that she was "like Beethoven, always changing houses."

The year at Krems was not accredited by the abbey school at Klosterneuburg, which Egon now attended, and consequently he was a year older than the other boys in his class. His school work was so unsatisfactory that he had to repeat the First Class. This made him two years older than his classmates, from whom he haughtily remained aloof. He aroused the antagonism of his teachers by his willful indolence and was graded "unsatisfactory" in all subjects except freehand drawing, calligraphy, and gymnastics, in which he was regularly marked "praiseworthy," and often "excellent." His attention was only truly awakened in the drawing classroom where he applied himself industriously. At twenty, he looked back on his life in Tulln and Klosterneuburg:

"I received the clearly remembered impressions of my childhood from flat countrysides with tree-shaded springtime roads and raging storms. In those early days it seemed to me as though I already heard and smelled the miraculous flowers, the speechless gardens, the birds in whose shiny eyes I saw my rosy mirror image. Often when it was autumn I wept with half-closed eyes. When it was spring I dreamed of the universal music of life, then I rejoiced in the magnificent summer and laughed as during its splendor I painted for myself the white winter. Until that time I lived in joy, in joy that was alternately cheerful and melancholy; then began the times of obligations and the lifeless schools. Elementary school in Tulln, high school in Klosterneuburg. I went to cities that seemed almost endless and dead, and I mourned for myself. During this time I suffered the death of my father. My loutish teachers were my perpetual enemies. They—and others—did not understand me."[5]

One teacher did not belong in this category. This was Professor Ludwig Karl Strauch (1875–1955), a painter of local fame who had studied at the Academy of Fine Arts in Vienna (Akademie der Bildenden Künste) and who came to Klosterneuburg in 1905 to teach freehand drawing at the abbey high school. Under his tutelage Egon completed many assignments, ranging from still life studies of fruits and vegetables to detailed renditions of the view of Klosterneuburg from the drawing class window.[6] Strauch not only encouraged the boy at school but gave him private lessons at his own home as well, letting him paint beside him at a smaller easel. The enthusiastic pupil did several drawings of Strauch at work, of which the red chalk, *Professor Strauch at His Easel* (figure 3), done in the early months of 1906, is characteristic.[7] The admiration and respect which Egon felt for an established "painter" are reflected in the distinguished bearing, easy pose, and aristocratic silhouette with which he portrays his subject. The boy's early fascination by double images of the same subject, which later found important expression in the double self-portrait series of 1910–11 and again in 1915, is first evinced here. The left-hand portion of the drawing records Strauch's own subject matter—a self-portrait in profile with palette and brushes—and this lightly sketched image duplicates the figure of Strauch himself, standing at the right of his canvas in the same palette-holding, cigar-puffing pose.[8]

Under Strauch's tutelage Egon tried his hand at traditional subjects, and a red chalk drawing, *Madonna and Child* (plate 1), of around 1906 provides a dramatic contrast to Strauch's own watered-down Italianate style (plate 2).[9] Sentimentality is notably absent from Egon's rendition, in which the usual protective gesture of the mother's hands becomes the revelation of a compelling subject. The focal brilliance of Egon's drawing is concentrated in the pin-points of the mother's eyes. These eyes glow with hypnotic intensity as she touches the white form of her outsized child, who raises one large angular hand in benediction—a gesture which rejects naturalism and suggests the small adult Christ of Byzantine art. It is clear that Strauch's contribution to the young artist's education was in matters of technique and not style.

The flat two-dimensionality of Egon's *Madonna and Child* provides an important key to his future stylistic development. The composition of big, unmodeled areas, including the enlarged flattened halo, is impressive. These areas have however been interrupted by dramatic "apparitions" such as the hands and faces. Egon shows here a predilection for surface design which would before long lead him to overt emulation of Jugendstil features. Strauch's plasticity has been rejected for an expressive arrangement of form and an emphasis on mood (here almost sinister in effect), created by the remarkable long fingers, the audacious blocking-off of the mother's face by the child's head, and the compelling double stare. Such manipulation of surface design and intensification of mood became Schiele's stylistic formula underlying the radical portraits of 1910. However, years of high school and academic training would delay its application to portraiture.[10]

Egon spent almost all his time drawing, whether in school or out, but he did make a few friends, the closest of whom was an aspiring musician, Arthur Löwenstein (later portrayed by the artist as a member of the 1909 Neukunstgruppe, see plate 9). Löwenstein taught Egon how to imbed a row of steel pen points in the wooden desks at school until a "scale" was achieved, and the two boys would twang away at their improvised keyboards, happily disrupting the class. Or they would sit quietly during the lesson, one surreptitiously drawing and the other secretly composing, so that often the exasperated teacher would angrily snatch away their papers. A composite description of Egon by Strauch and other Klosterneuburg teachers gives a portrait of the young artist at this time:

"... [he was] always outside in the meadows, on the slopes, by the brooks, and drew sheet after sheet, mostly in pastel, of nature sketches. He drew quietly and with perseverance as if nothing existed except nature, pencil and drawing paper. His thin, earnest face with its dark eyes was immobile, and his black shock of hair, which was combed back, fell to his coat collar. An unusually quiet boy, not shy, but by no means gregarious, he was somewhat mannered in the way he intertwined his long hands. In his family circle he was considered a *Wunderkind*."[11]

Egon discovered a few other kindred spirits at Klosterneuburg. One of these was the art historian, Dr. Wolfgang Pauker (1867–1950). As custodian of the abbey museum, which included among its treasures the celebrated twelfth-century altar of Nicholas of Verdun, it may have been he who first inspired Egon's lifelong admiration for medieval art. Another friend was the landscape painter, Max Kahrer (1878–1937). Kahrer was twelve years older than Egon and had a family to support, but nevertheless found time and interest for the boy's work. Through his posters, which were more progressive than his Danube landscapes, he was the first to transmit the current Vienna Secession style to Egon. Together they talked of forming a "Union of Art, Drawing and Painting Institute," referred to by Egon in a letter to Kahrer headed Klosterneuburg, 1903. This letter is interesting not just for the boyish exaggeration of formal style, but also as one of the earliest firsthand revelations of ambitious projects and self-esteem:

"Through the obliging delivery of your brother Hans, I am able to announce to you in a few lines how industriously I have been laboring on the various items for our future 'Union of Art Exhibition.' Had I had more time for these drawings and paintings I would have gladly produced triple the amount. Since our mutual discussion of the 28th of this month I have undertaken to produce five works per day. I kindly urge you to remain true to our agreement so that our plan for the future may result in praise for us and fame for the . . . city of Klosterneuburg. May I further entreat you to go, if possible, to a book or art dealer in order to acquire perhaps a price list or some books in which better pictures can be found. The Alliance of Three shall remain united, it must and will come to pass. Hail! Your faithful companion Egon Schiele."[12]

Despite a certain degree of school comradeship, and his friendships with the older painters Strauch and Kahrer, Egon tended to remain by choice an outsider. He much preferred the company of his younger and favorite sister, Gerti. His earliest known portrait sketch of her is the *Profile Drawing of Gerti* (figure 4), done when he was only twelve years old. Neither timid nor overwrought, the sketch is remarkable for its sureness of line, self-taught hatchings, and organic relation of parts to the whole. Comparison with a photograph (figure 5) shows much similarity, from the turned-up nose to the sheen of the long hair. Egon himself must have been pleased with this drawing for he signed and dated it in large flourishing script. During their adolescent years Egon and Gerti had an intense relationship not without erotic overtones. He occasionally took her with him on his impromptu train rides and once, when she was twelve and he sixteen, he actually duplicated the itinerary of their parents's wedding trip and took her all the way to Trieste where they stayed overnight in a hotel.[13] Gerti was easily persuaded to pose in the nude for her brother, and this led to other secrets which they kept from their mother.[14] Their father was apprehensive and suspicious however and he once broke down a door to see what the two were doing in a locked room in the dark— on this occasion innocently developing negatives. Of these years Egon later wrote:

"Have adults forgotten how they themselves as children were incited and aroused by the impulse of sex? Have they forgotten how terrible passion burned in them and tormented them while they were still children? I have not forgotten, for I suffered terribly from it."[15]

It is obvious that Egon's early sexual curiosity was much greater and more strongly motivated than that of the average young boy. Awareness of the venereal origin of his father's deterioration is undoubtedly partly responsible for the unnatural preoccupation with sexual exploration which was to become the subject matter of his many erotic drawings. Furious sexual activity appeared to be Egon's way of exorcising any threat of insanity which he believed might hang over him. But on the other hand he never lost a basic respect for his father and continued to nourish in himself a nostalgia for his dead parent, which at times prompted him to seek out the places where his father had been,[16] and once even brought on the vision of a "visit" from his father.[17]

With Adolf Schiele's death on the first day of the year 1905, the family became a preponderantly feminine one. Elvira, the oldest sister, had died when Egon was three years old, but his mother and his two sisters, Melanie and Gerti, would all outlive him.

The family was left with only the pension of a railroad employee's widow and Melanie's small salary on which to exist. Adolf Schiele had actually died during the night of 31 December 1904, but the family lawyer counseled Frau Schiele to report the death as having occurred on the first day of the new year, so that she might be eligible for a slightly larger pension.[18] Leopold Czihaczek, the husband of Adolf Schiele's sister, was appointed Egon's legal guardian. An inspector at one of Vienna's railroad stations, and a typical petit bourgeois, Uncle Czihaczek had no doubts about the futility of painting as a career and felt that Egon should follow the family tradition. Against vehement opposition Egon tried to persuade his mother to let him leave the detested Klosterneuburg school.[19] She finally relented and allowed Egon to present himself with a portfolio of drawings at the Kunstgewerbeschule (School of Applied Arts) in Vienna—where both Klimt and Kokoschka had studied. The results were instant and sensational. The professors at first refused to believe the boy had made the drawings himself, but once convinced, they urged his mother to enter him immediately at the Vienna Academy of Fine Arts, where he could receive a more specialized training in painting. Czihaczek, infuriated, showed up at the Academy the next day and tried physically to block their entrance. But Schiele's mother, encouraged by the enthusiasm her son had aroused in the professors, made a courageous stand. Drawing herself up proudly she said to Czihaczek, "You may be the guardian of my children, but you are not my guardian, and I will do with Egon what I think best!"

The examining professors at the Academy also expressed amazement at the boy's drawings, and he was allowed to take the entrance examinations which included the submission of three finished portrait drawings. One of these was of the family charwoman, the others were a profile view of Egon's mother and a frontal portrait of Melanie. Comparison of the 1906 profile sketch of Marie Schiele (figure 7) with the early 1903 drawing of her daughter Gerti (figure 4) reveals substantial technical progress. The sketch of Gerti is essentially an outline drawing, but the portrait of Marie is a tonal conception, executed in charcoal, as required by the Academy. Cross hatchings and rubbings are effectively employed in the modeling of the face as well as in the hair, and a light smudge running along the length of the exterior of the profile-defining contour serves to set the head in relief as well as to absorb any faulty strokes. A white chalk heightening applied to the prominent surfaces of the face, chin, cheek, nose, and forehead, suggests a side illumination. Technical considerations have not precluded attention to facial individualization, and the family trait of a receding lower lip, so emphatically stressed in the portrait of Gerti, also appears here.

Melanie's squarish jawbone and large clear eyes, noticeable in a contemporary photograph (figure 8), are prominent in Egon's charcoal study, signed and dated 29 September 1906 (figure 9). The symmetrical features and close spacing between the lips and nose are emphasized by a side light which throws the right part of the face into a shadow broken only by the natural reflection of light on almost the whole of the protruding chin. These faithful observations are rendered tonally and complement the precisely drawn

contours of the face. The background here contrasts with the head by a movement from light to dark across the page in a direction opposite to the fall
of shadow on the face. The talent manifested in these test drawings obtained
for Schiele the entry "satisfactory" in the same book of Academy entrance
examination records in which, a few pages before, the notation "unsatisfactory"
is entered against the name of another youthful applicant—Adolf Hitler.

1906–1909: THE ACADEMY YEARS

At the beginning of the fall semester, 1906, at the age of sixteen, Egon
Schiele began study at the Vienna Academy. He faced not one, but two new
situations. His mother and sisters had taken a small apartment in Vienna, where
he slept until he was able to rent his first one-room studio the following year;
and, due to the strained finances of the family, it was arranged for him to
take his noon and evening meals in the home of his aunt and uncle Czihaczek.
Egon found their world a stodgy one, just as he found the rigidly controlled
life and teaching at the Academy stodgy. Eventually he and a circle of his
friends left the Academy in a huff, having acquired the reputation of rebels,
but in the meantime the three years of training in the basic disciplines of painting were valuable ones. They increased his technical facility, gave him a
sound knowledge of anatomy,[20] and later proved of practical value in improv-
ing his military status.[21]

The Vienna Academy had the distinction of being the oldest school of
art in Central Europe. It had long enjoyed royal patronage and since 1877
had occupied its own building in the Schillerplatz, just off the Opera Ring
in the center of Vienna, and only three blocks from the great Kunsthistorisches
Museum. The vast building not only contained classrooms, but housed a museum with 1,650 plaster casts of classical sculpture, the choicest of which were
exhibited in eight special rooms and the main assembly hall. In these rooms the
students worked on their daily assignments of copying from the antique.[22] The
ceiling of the great assembly hall had been painted by Anselm Feuerbach and
portrayed The Fall of the Titans. Feuerbach (1829–1880) was a prominent exponent of the lofty stage realism practiced by the "German Roman" painters
of the second half of the nineteenth century and had taught at the Vienna
Academy from 1873 to 1876, his late Classicist views leaving a firm imprint on
the curriculum. Continuing and championing Feuerbach's ideals at the time
of Schiele's acceptance into the Academy was Professor Christian Griepenkerl
(1839–1916), director of the School of General Painting. A conservative Classicist whose mind was fixed on Rome, Griepenkerl was famous for his stubborn
resistance against anything smacking of "modernism." A more progressive
faction among the professors at the Academy was represented by Heinrich
Lefler who, with Joseph Urban, founded in 1900 the Hagenbund, where later
both Kokoschka and Schiele exhibited their works. Because Strauch, his
teacher at Klosterneuburg, had studied with Griepenkerl, Schiele became
Griepenkerl's student during his third year at the Academy; had he worked
under Lefler the story of his years at the school might have been different.

The Academy possessed an important library of books, drawings, and watercolors, including a Dürer portrait drawing of 1503. Most important, the Academy had its own art gallery, based upon the former private collection of Baron Anton Lamberg-Sprinzenstein and gifts from the Emperor Ferdinand I. At the time Schiele was there, this gallery possessed 1,146 paintings, including 300 German and Netherlandish examples, 200 Italian paintings, and 180 modern works. The lectures on art history at the Academy were supplemented by mandatory visits to the school's own collection. Representative of the old masters on display during Schiele's years at the Academy were the following paintings: Dieric Bouts, *Crowning of Mary*;[23] Bosch (workshop), *Last Judgment Triptych*; Hans Baldung Grien, *Rest on the Flight into Egypt*; Lucas Cranach the Elder, *Lucretia*; Titian, *Tarquinius and Lucretia*, acquired by the Academy in 1907; Rubens, *Boreas Carrying Off Orithyia*; Rembrandt, *Portrait of a Young Woman in a Chair*; and Murillo, *Boys Playing Dice*. Two portraits by Christian Griepenkerl were also on view: *Josef Ritter von Führich* and *Hofrat Rudolf Eitelberger*. Considering the numerous self-portraits Schiele painted while at the Academy, it is interesting to note which self-portraits were on exhibition in the gallery at that time. They included canvases by Friedrich von Amerling, Ferdinand Georg Waldmüller, and Josef Abel. An early Van Dyck, not recognized until 1899 as a youthful self-portrait (figure 16), and a magnificent Barent Fabritius self-portrait, known then simply as *Young Man in Shepherd's Attire* (figure 13), were also on display. The precious quality of the Van Dyck and the arresting boldness of the Fabritius may well have attracted Schiele's attention and confirmed the assurance of his own self-portraits done at the Academy.

If the physical resources of the Academy were impressive, so was the curriculum. The brochure given to incoming students stipulated the following three-year program: classes in anatomy and perspective during the first year, theory of style in the second year, and color theory and color chemistry in the third. Lectures in art history and general history were to be attended for the entire three years. The student had to complete the School of General Painting before enrolling in any of the specialized schools of history painting, advanced sculpture, landscape painting, animal painting, copper engraving, and medal making.[24] A sheaf of class attendance certificates[25] indicates that Schiele followed the prescribed order of courses exactly.

First self-portraits

Schiele's attitude as a student changed considerably during his three years at the Academy. At first he applied himself with tremendous energy, determined to demonstrate his artistic worth to his disapproving uncle. The rapidity with which he assimilated new techniques is already apparent in a charcoal *Self-Portrait* (figure 12) dated 6 September 1906. A wide range of tonal gradations and a heightening or shadowing of neutral areas is achieved by rubbing and blotching. Comparison with another self-portrait, *Mirror-Picture of Self* (figure 11), done the year before, shows that Schiele had already sought to achieve this effect with more primitive means and technique—colored pencils and simple hatching. There is now also an advance in compositional sophistication; the naïve frontality, centrality, and careful balancing of flat, patternizing forms in the earlier picture are replaced by three-dimensional devices. The shoulders are set on a diagonal axis with the chin juxtaposed against the raised left shoulder, and the face is presented in three-quarter view, its cast shadow indicated by cross hatching.[26]

The charcoal *Self-Portrait* of 1906 indicates Schiele's attitude towards himself at this time. He was proud of wearing the broad white collar and flowing black cravat that distinguished the art students in Vienna. Being an "artist" had at last become an exciting reality. Gravely self-conscious, he posed for a photograph (figure 10) with the tools of his profession—tube of paint, brushes and palette—none of which, as a first-year student, he was as yet supposed to be using. He took pleasure in all objects that identified him as an artist, and proudly inscribed his drawing triangle with his name, class year, and school.[27] The stylized lettering he now employed shows familiarity with the posters, exhibition catalogues, and magazines of the current Jugendstil movement as represented in Vienna by the Secession.

The respect which Schiele felt for his new status did not long extend to his professors. He continued to draw assiduously, and brought home rolls of sketches daily, but he was by no means a docile or model student. At home he would mock and insult his teachers, calling them "asses." At school he openly criticized courses and soon became the leader of a group of young men who were impatient with the inflexible teaching methods of the Academy. He found ways to rebel at assignments he thought absurd. One week's project was to cover a large roll of paper with a single, continuous drawing, adding to it each day. While the other students worked, Schiele simply sat at his desk staring in front of him and not drawing a line. The next day in class this conduct was repeated, and the next, until the time arrived when the assignment was due. On this day Schiele suddenly began to draw and filled the roll with an exact ground plan of the Franz Josef Railway Station, where he had often wandered about, and which he knew by heart.[28]

Such erratic behavior naturally irritated his teachers and influenced their evaluation of his talent. Schiele's hostile conduct remained subterranean during the first two years at the Academy, but the final year brought an open conflict with Griepenkerl, who could support no insubordination or criticism from his students. The aging professor was still indignant over the sensation caused by the recent suicide of a former Academy pupil, the talented painter Richard Gerstl, who had been a rebellious student under him for two semesters in 1904 until the liberal Heinrich Lefler invited him into his special class. Griepenkerl had interpreted Gerstl's suicide as a defamation of the Academy and was in no mood to brook further signs of "anarchy" from his students. Schiele's arrogance had incensed him even before they met, for he had seen a self-portrait by Schiele which struck him as "the last word in conceit."[29] An oil *Self-Portrait with Hat 1907* (figure 14), possibly the painting which had of-

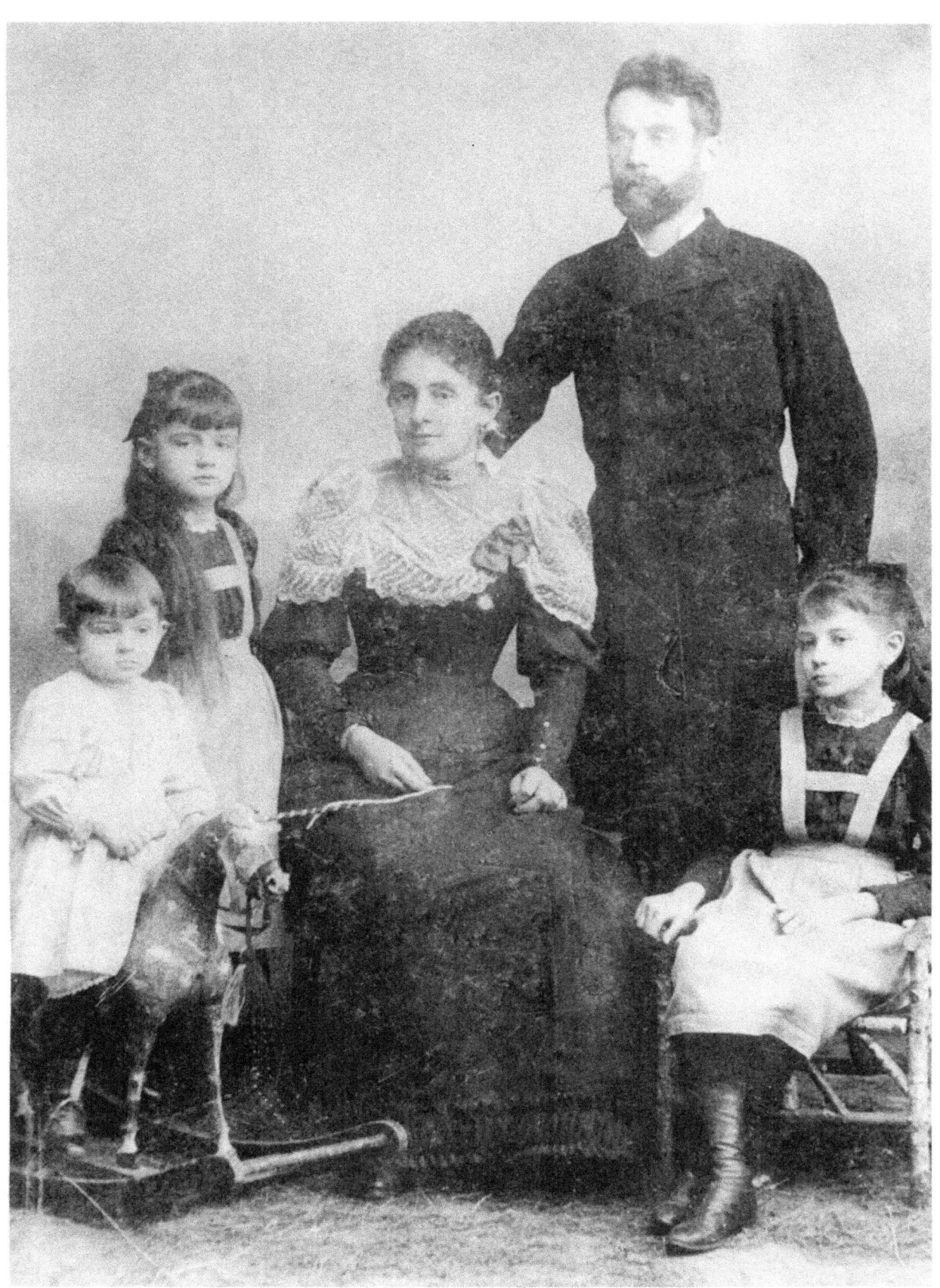

FIG. 1. The Schiele family, *ca.* 1892 l. to r: Egon, Melaine, Marie, Adolf, Elvira.

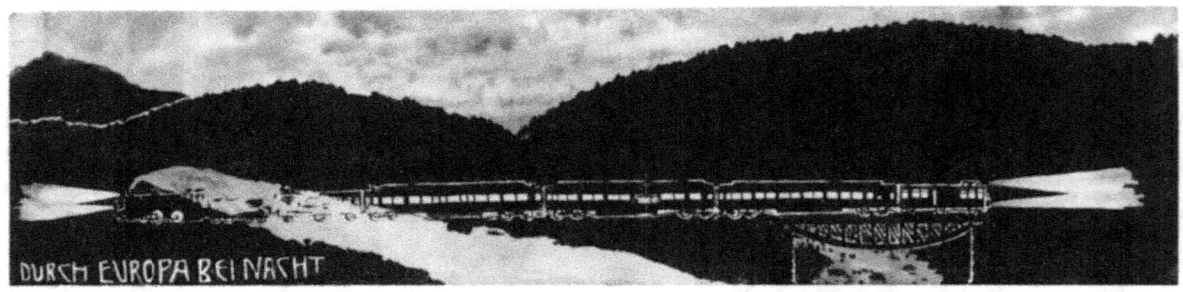

FIG. 2. Schiele, *Through Europe by Night, ca.* 1900, colored ink.

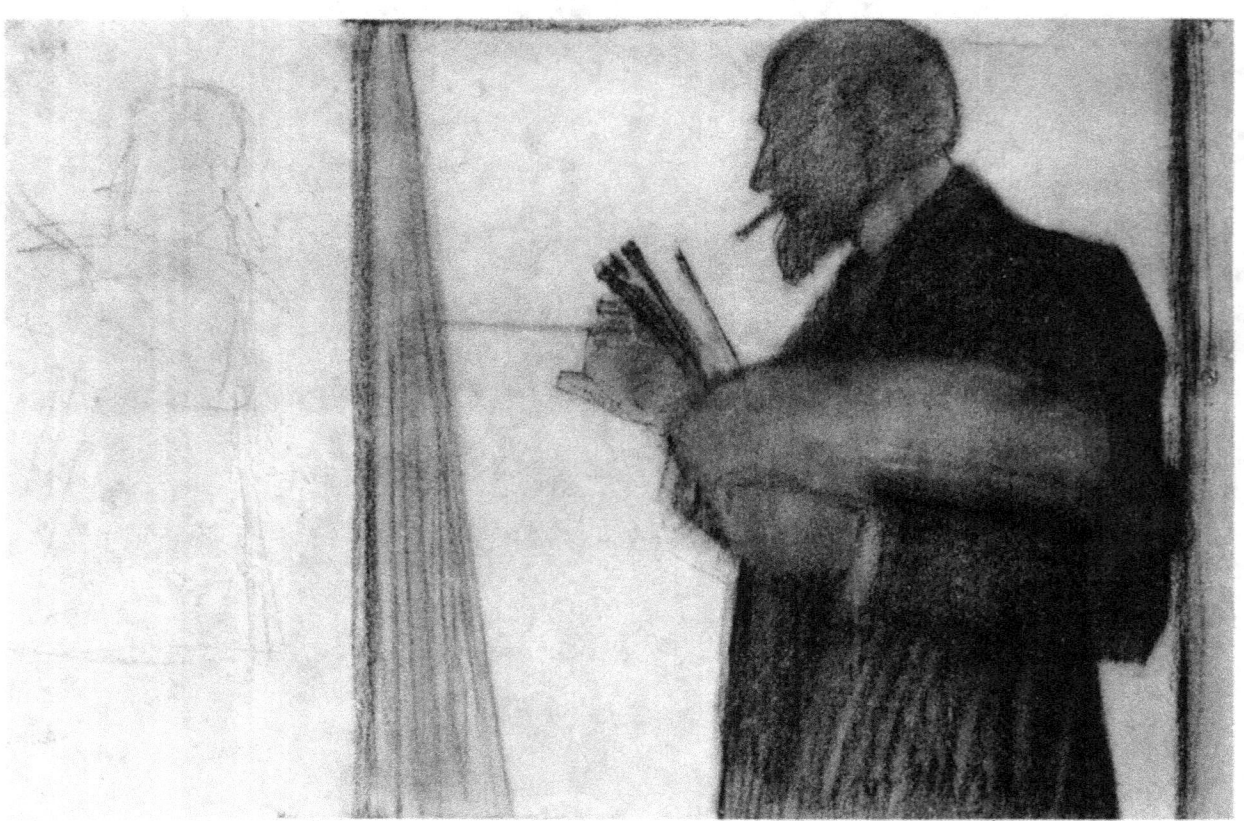

FIG. 3. Schiele, *Professor Strauch at His Easel,* 1906, red chalk.

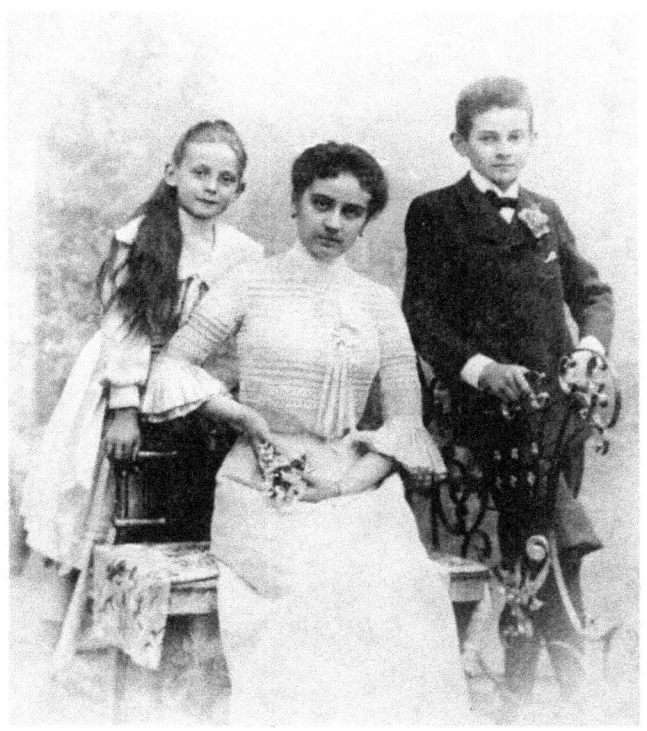

FIG. 5. Gerti, Melanie, and Egon Schiele, *ca.* 1903.

FIG. 4. Schiele, *Profile Drawing of Gerti*, 15 March 1903, pencil on cardboard.

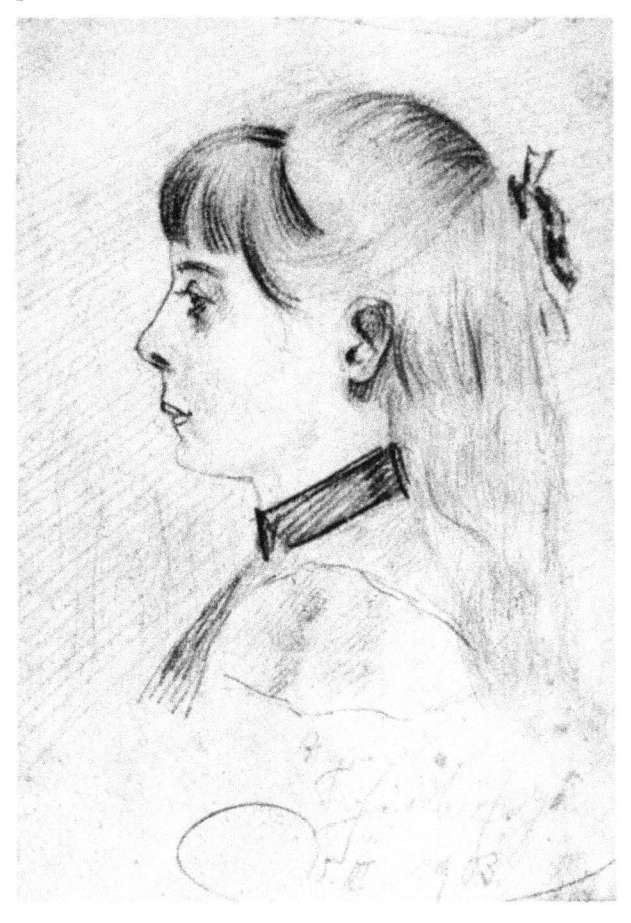

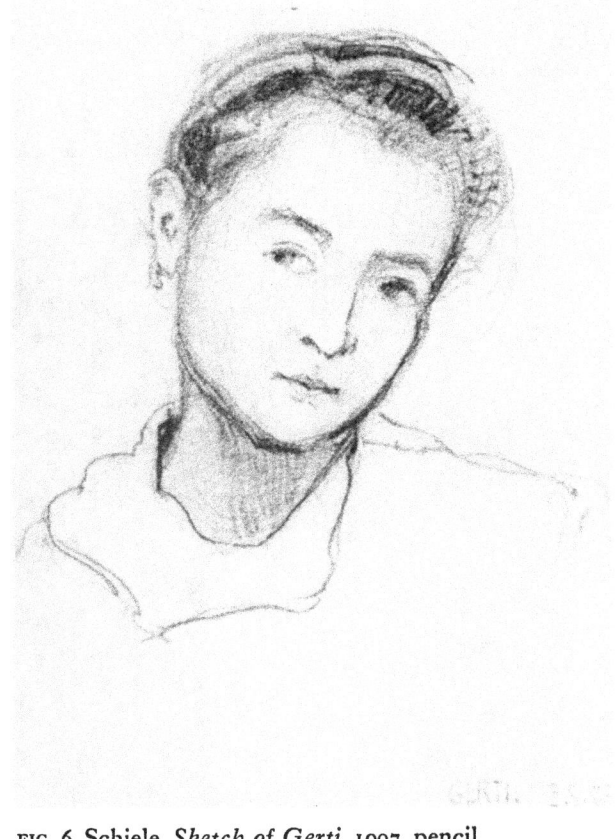

FIG. 6. Schiele, *Sketch of Gerti*, 1907, pencil.

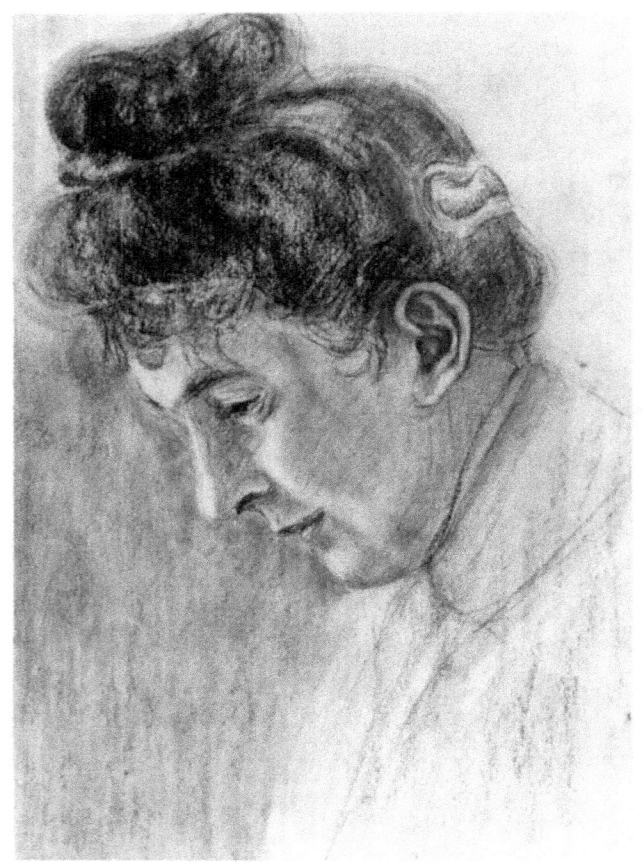

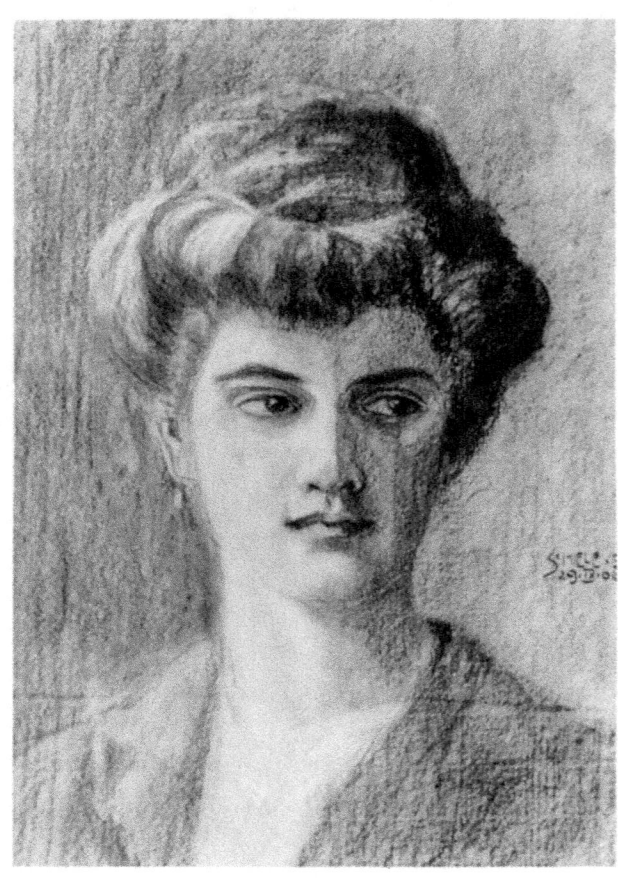

FIG. 7. Schiele, *Profile Drawing of Schiele's Mother*, 25 Sept. 1906, red chalk and charcoal.

FIG. 9. Schiele, *Portrait of Melanie*, 29 Sept. 1906, charcoal.

FIG. 8. Melanie Schiele, *ca.* 1906.

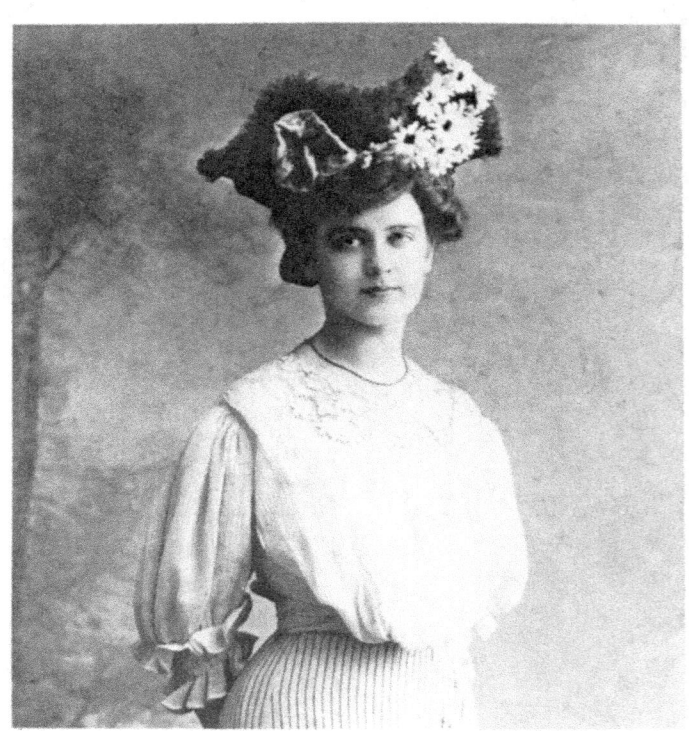

FIG. 10. Egon Schiele, Fall 1906.

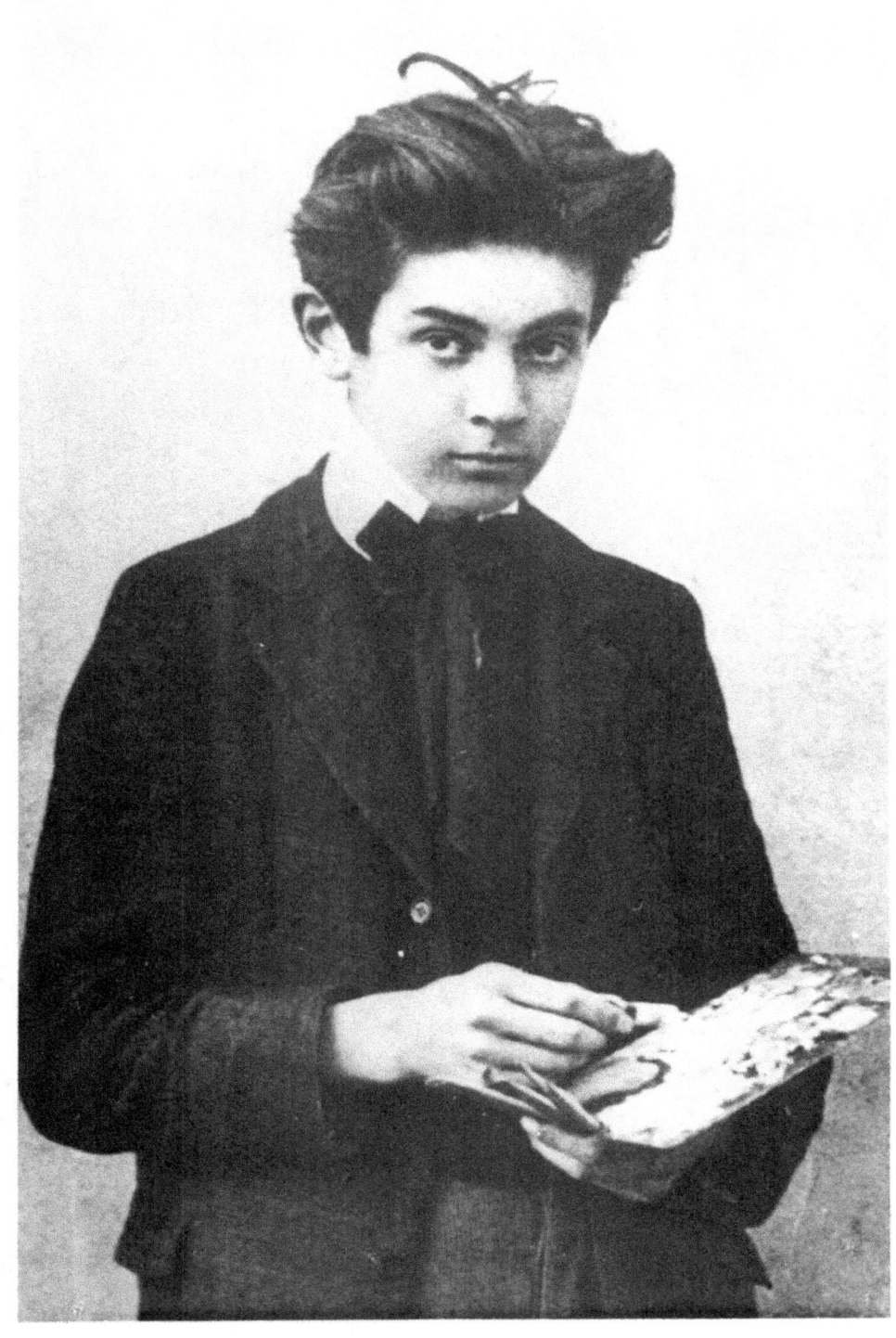

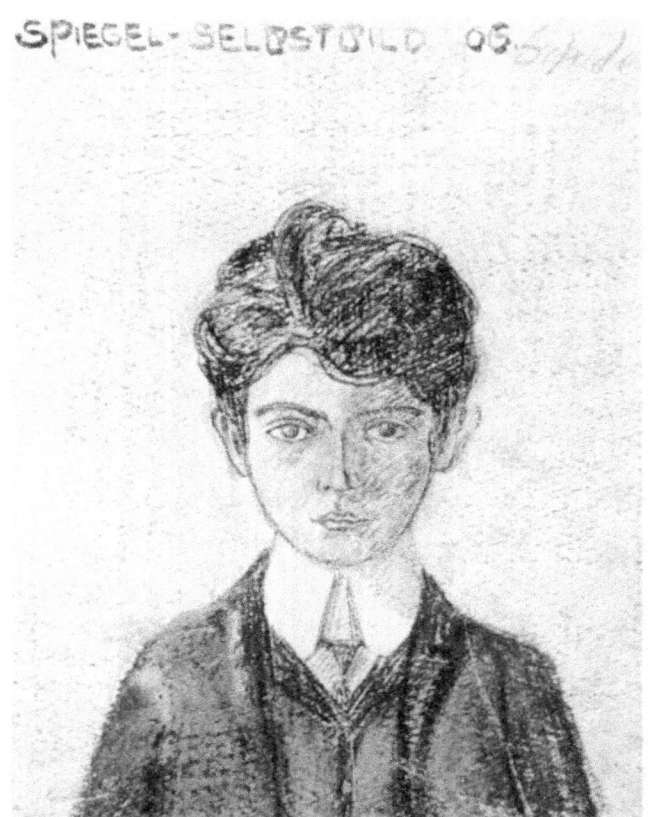

SPIEGEL-SELDSTBILD 05

FIG. 11. Schiele, *Mirror-Picture of Self*, 1905, colored pencils.

FIG. 12. Schiele, *Self-Portrait*, 6 Sept. 1906, charcoal.

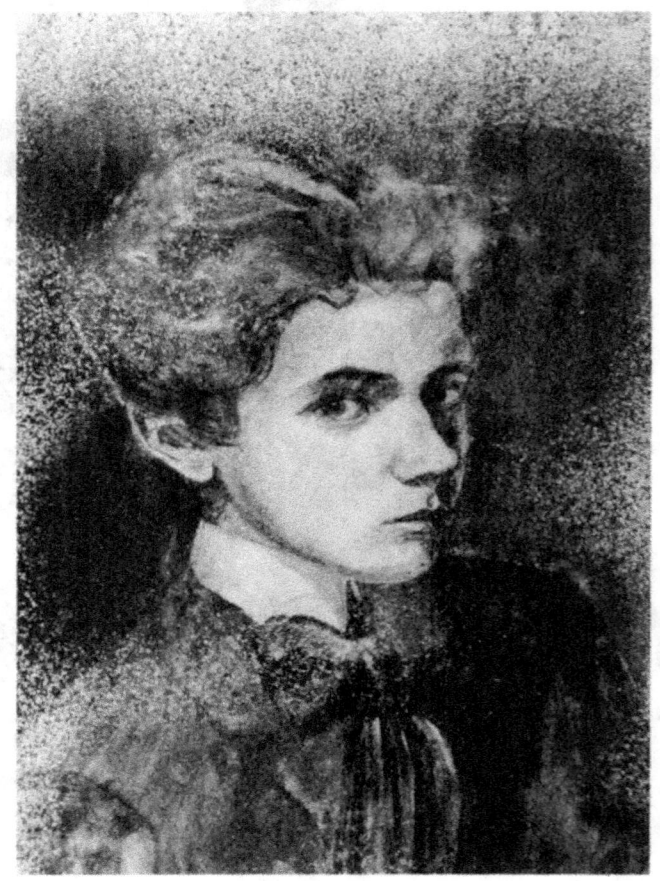

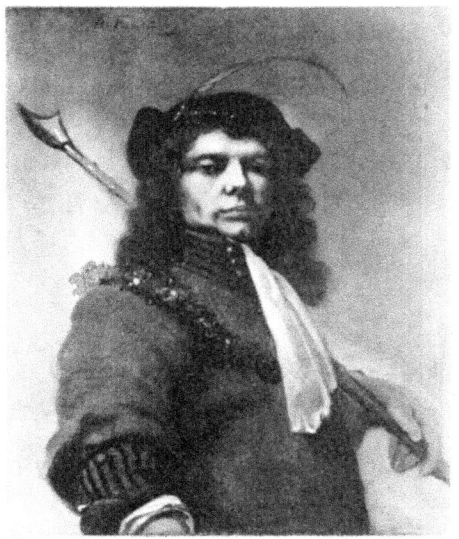

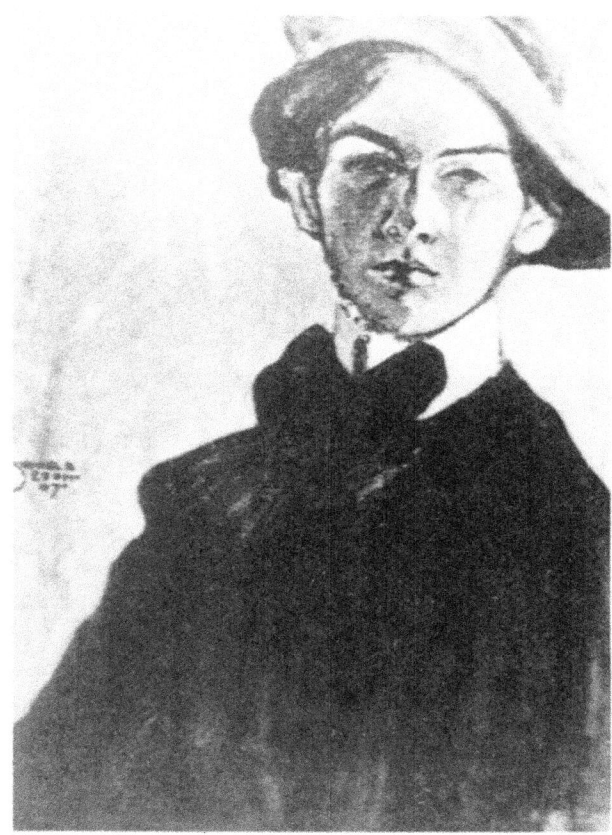

FIG. 14. Schiele, *Self-Portrait with Hat 1907*, 1907, oil.

FIG. 15. Schiele, *Self-Portrait 1907*, 1907, oil.

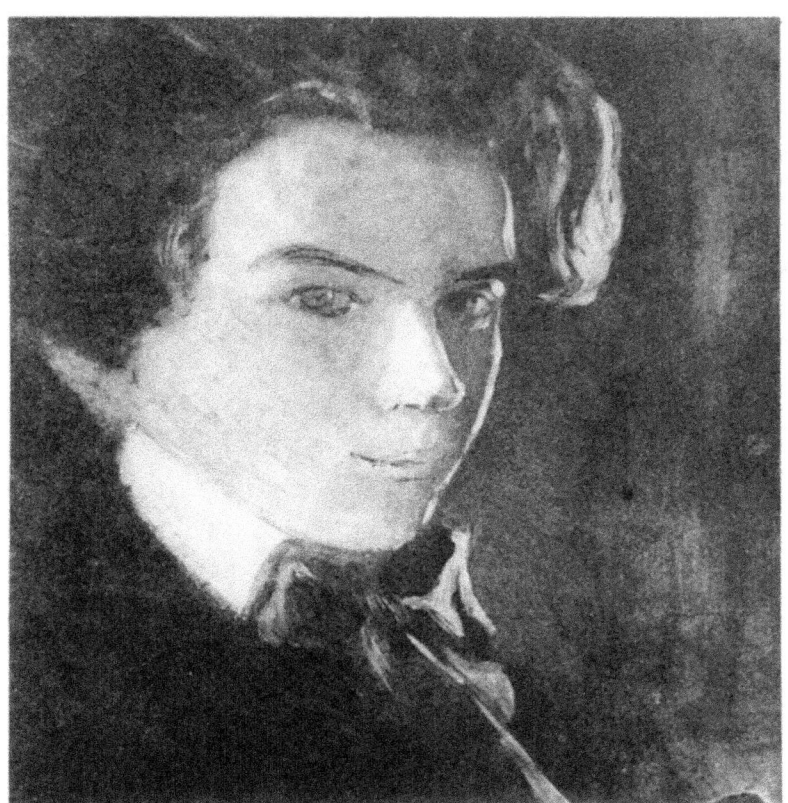

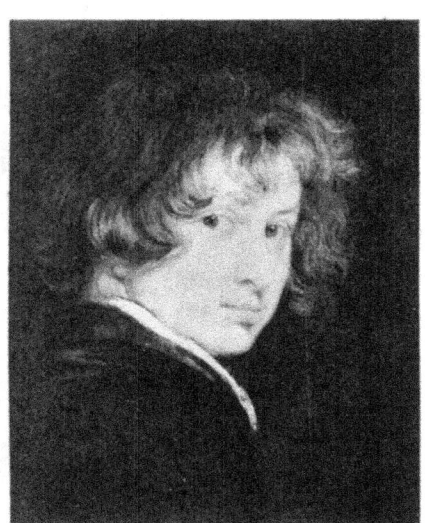

FIG. 16. Anthony van Dyck, *Self-Portrait*, ca. 1618, oil.

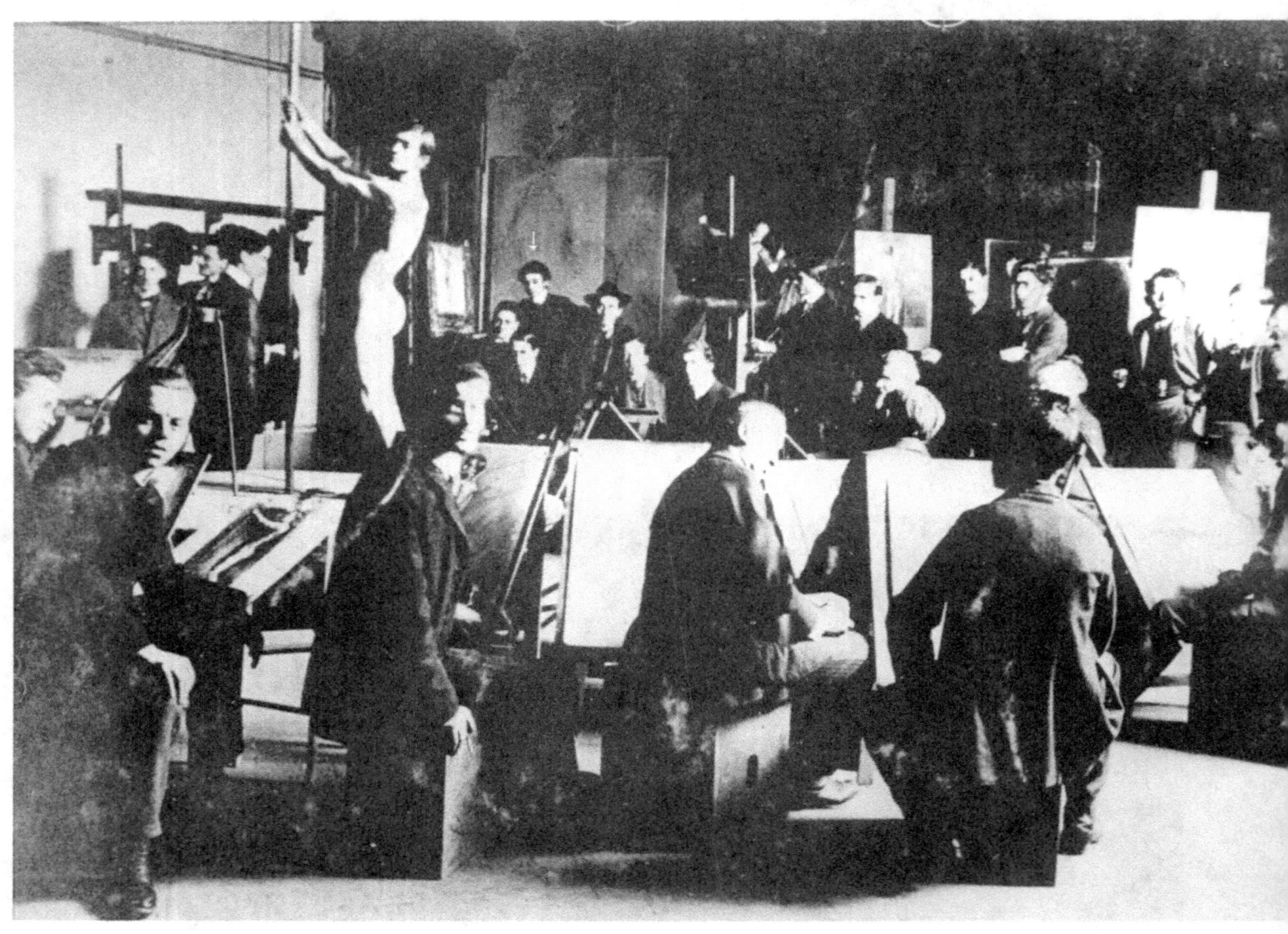

FIG. 17. The life-drawing class, Vienna Academy; Schiele in left background, ca. 1907.

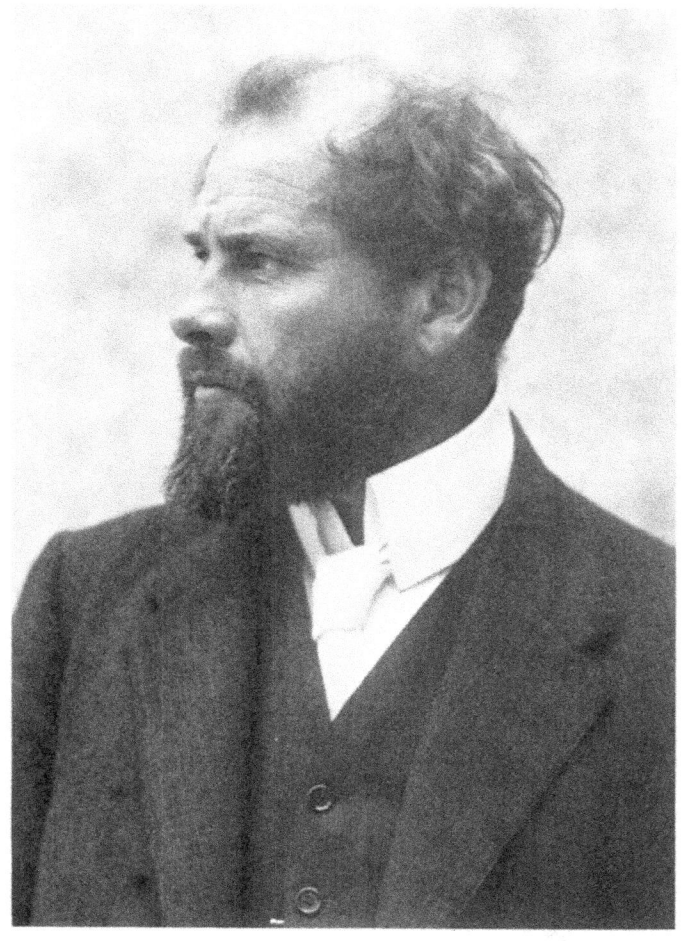

FIG. 18. Gustav Klimt, *ca.* 1908.

FIG. 20. The Wiener Werkstätte show-room, 1907, with works by Klimt and Georges Minne.

FIG. 19. The Vienna Secession with the Academy in back to the right.

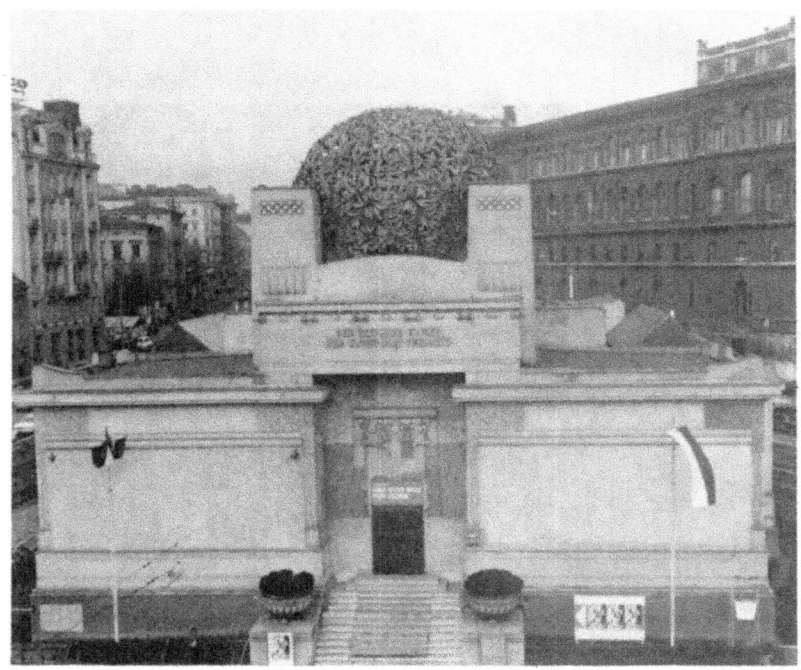

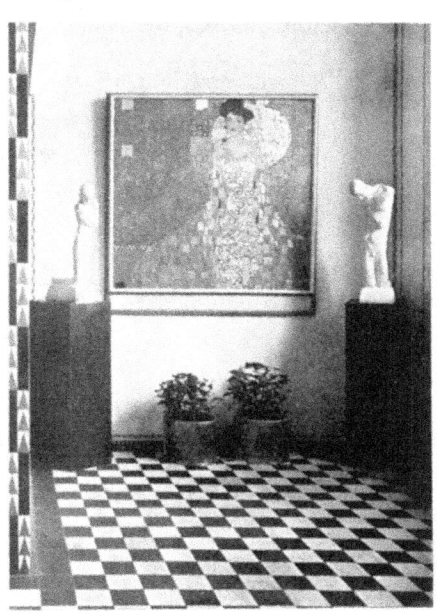

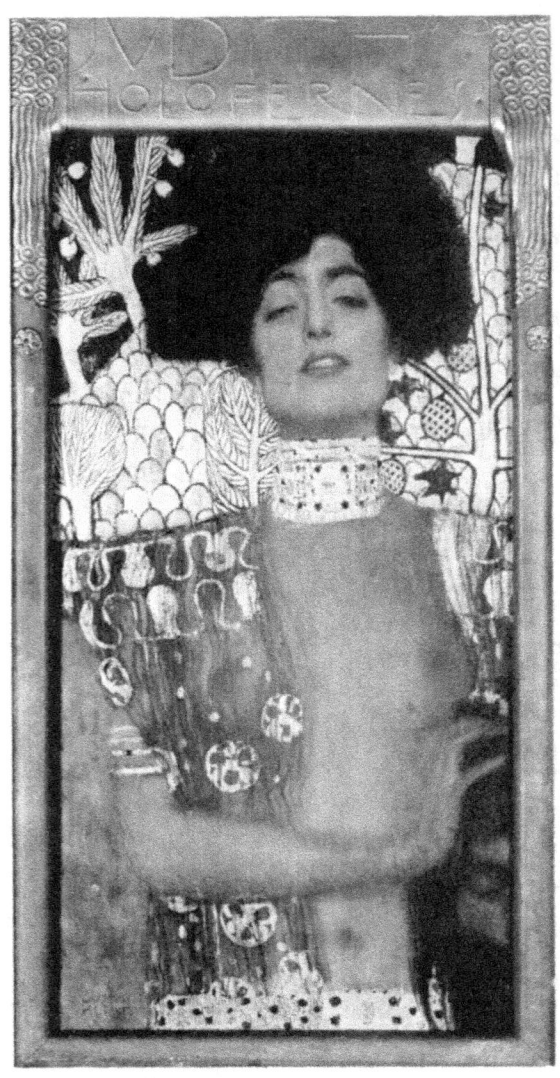

FIG. 21. Klimt, *Judith I*, 1901, oil.

FIG. 22. Klimt, *Water Serpents*, 1904, oil.

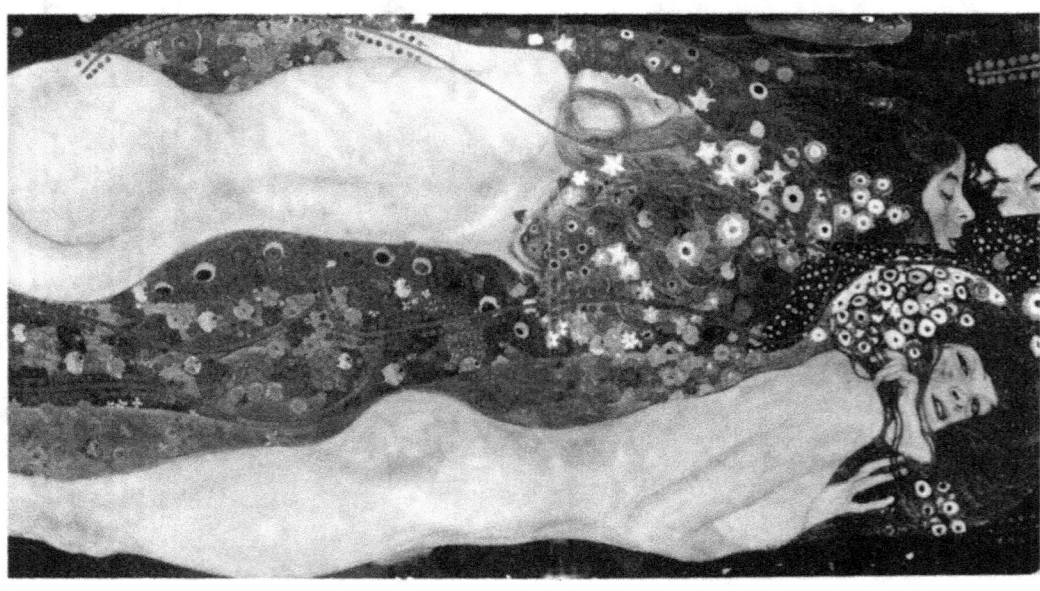

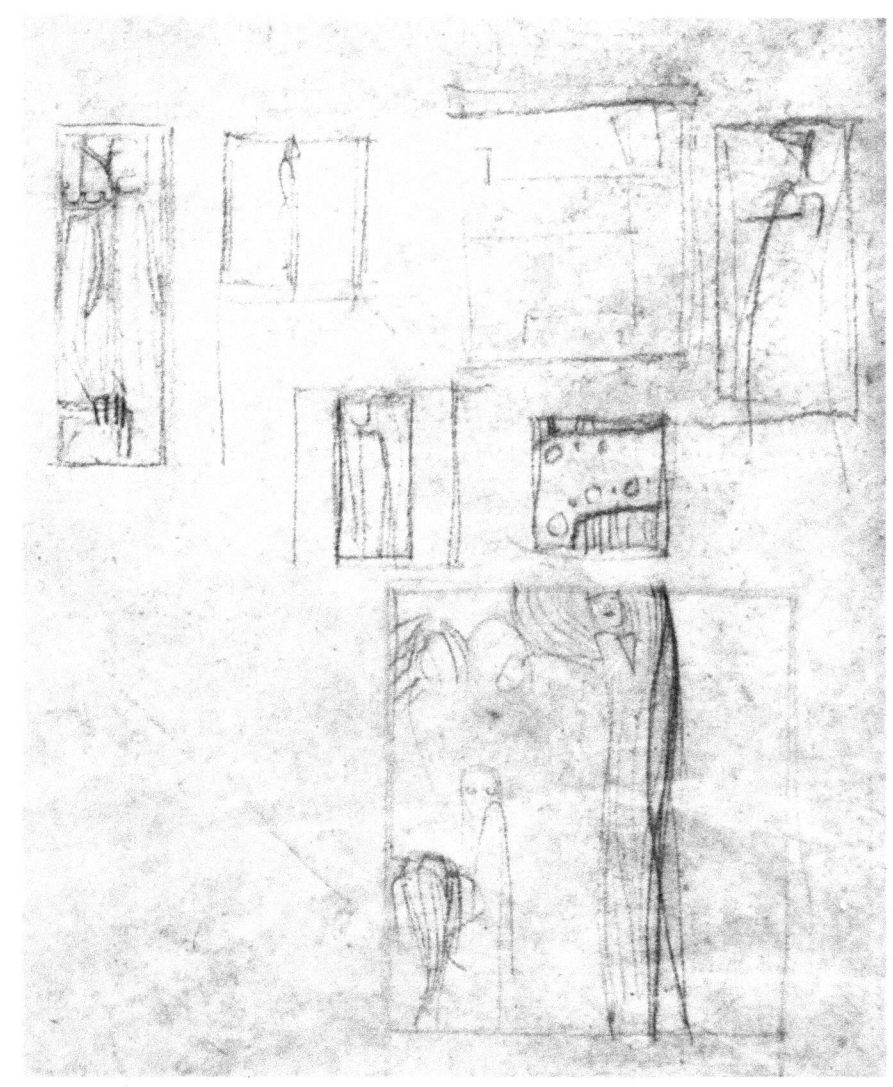

FIG. 23a. Schiele, *Sheet of Seven Framed Compositions after Klimt Paintings*, 1908, pencil.

FIG. 23b. Schiele, *Fairytale World*, 1908, oil.

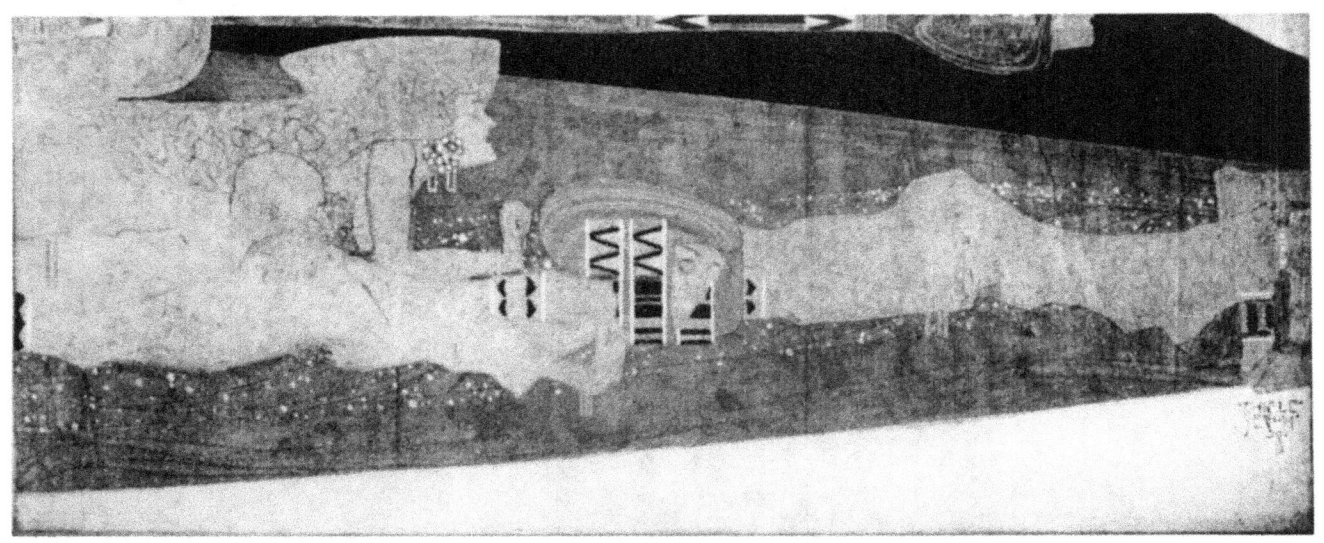

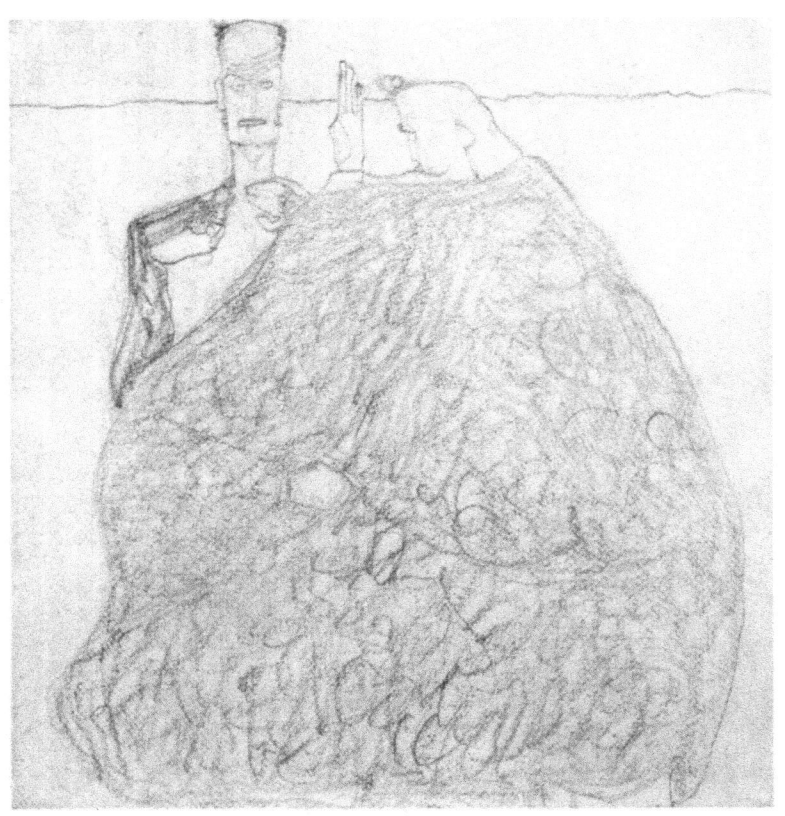

FIG. 24. Schiele, *Two Men in Decorative Robes, ca.* 1909, pencil on cardboard.

FIG. 25. Schiele, *Two Men, ca.* 1909, pen and wash drawing.

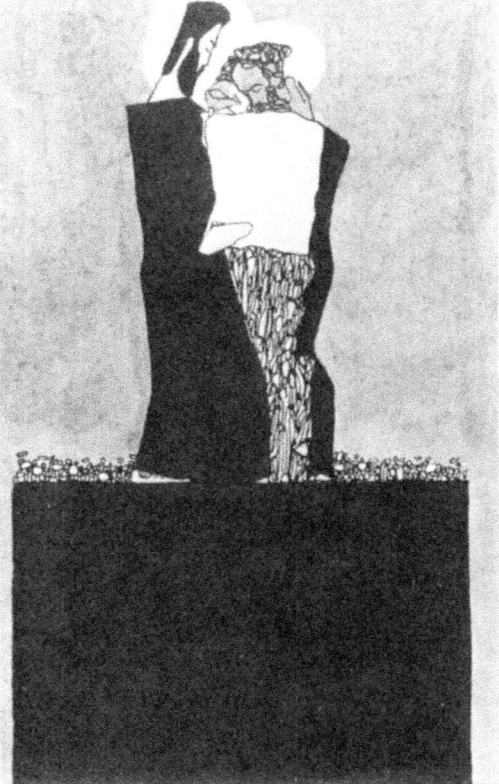

FIG. 26. Gustav Klimt, *ca.* 1912–1914.

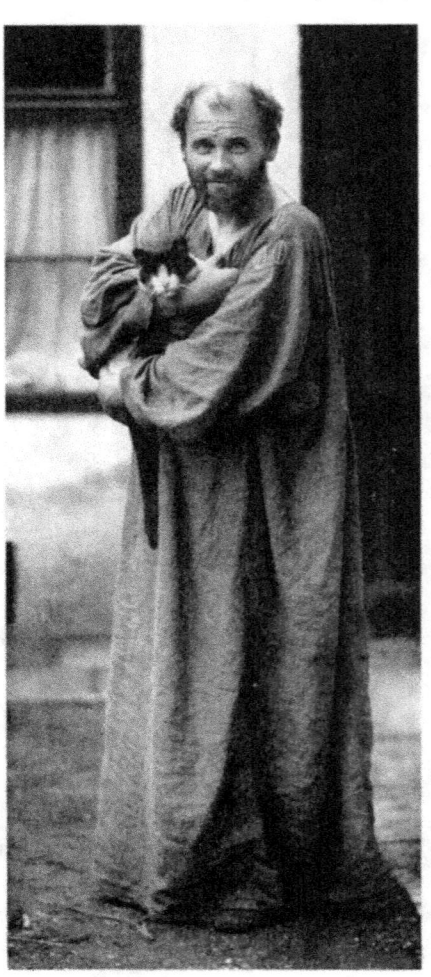

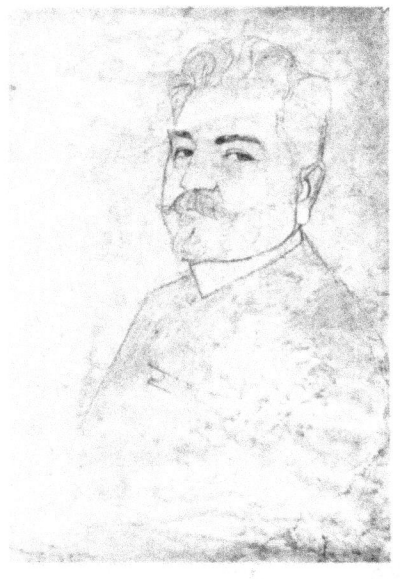

FIG. 27. Schiele, *Blue Pencil Sketch of Leopold Czihaczek*, 1907, blue pencil.

FIG. 28. Leopold Czihaczek, *ca.* 1913.

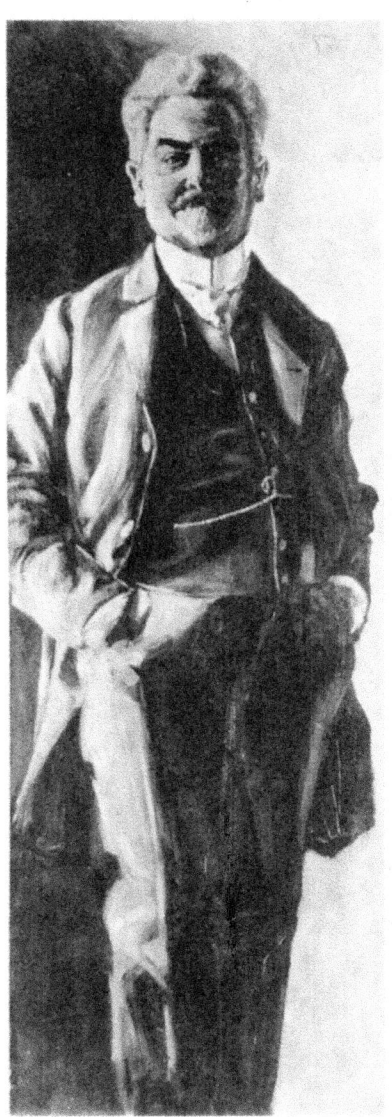

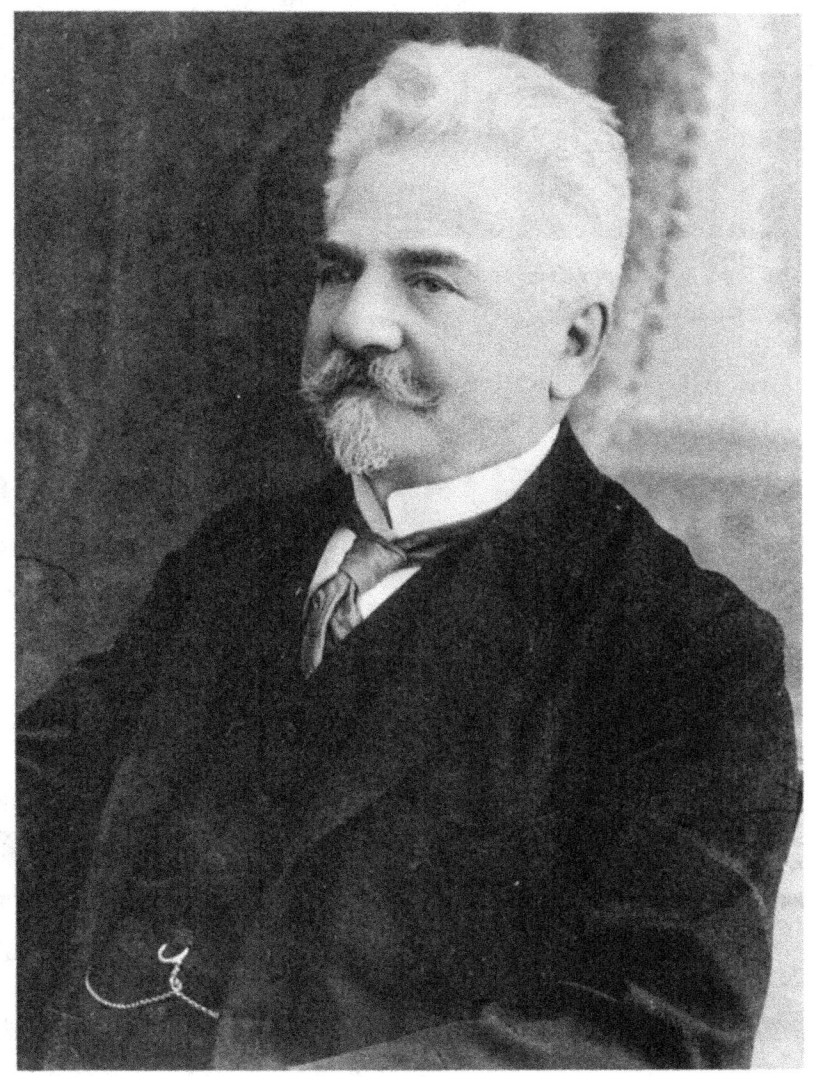

FIG. 29. Schiele, *Leopold Czihaczek I*, 1907, oil.

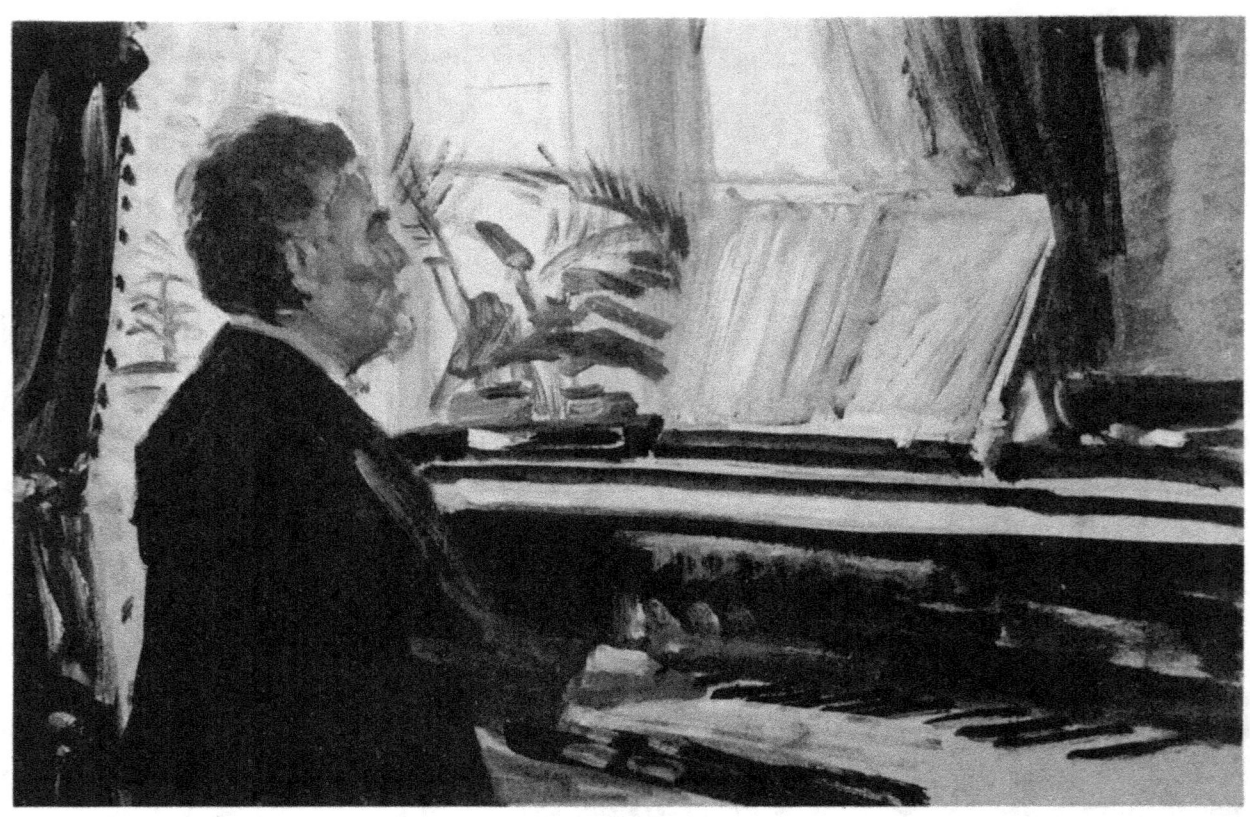

FIG. 30. Schiele, *Leopold Czihaczek at the Piano*, 1907, oil study.

FIG. 31. Leopold Czihaczek at the piano, *ca.* 1913.

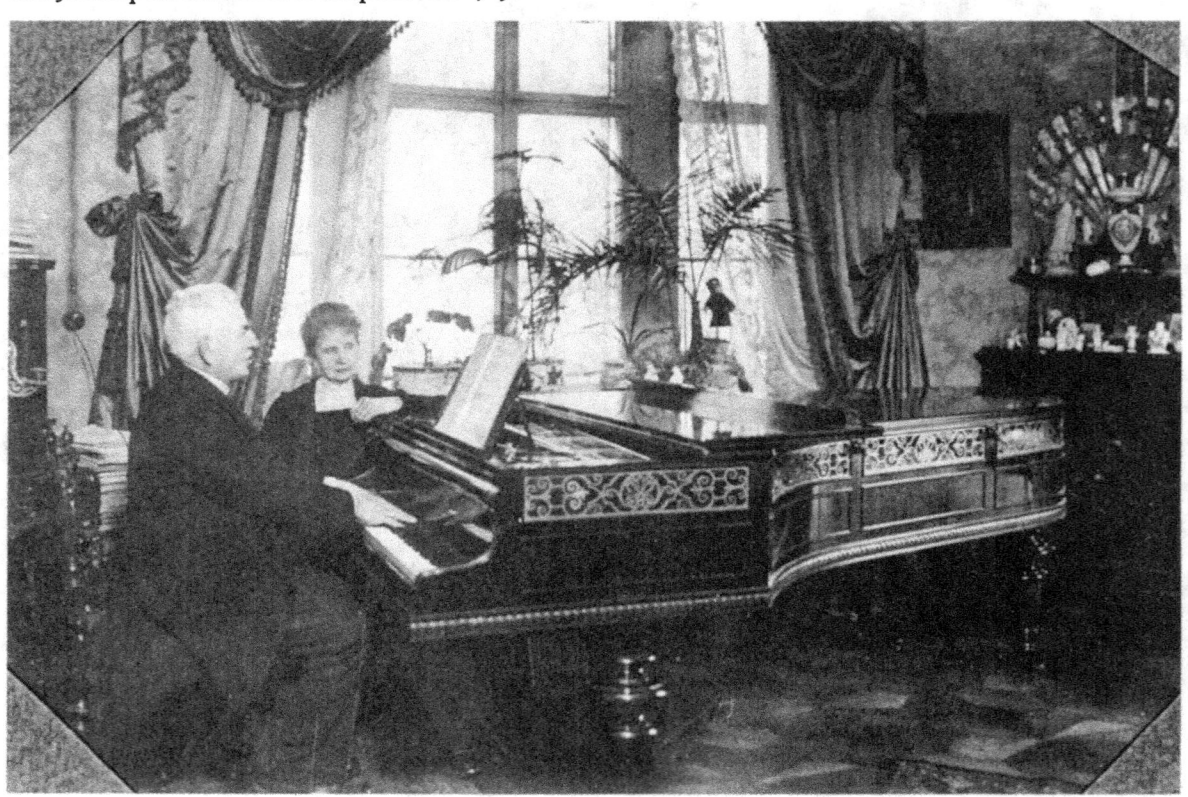

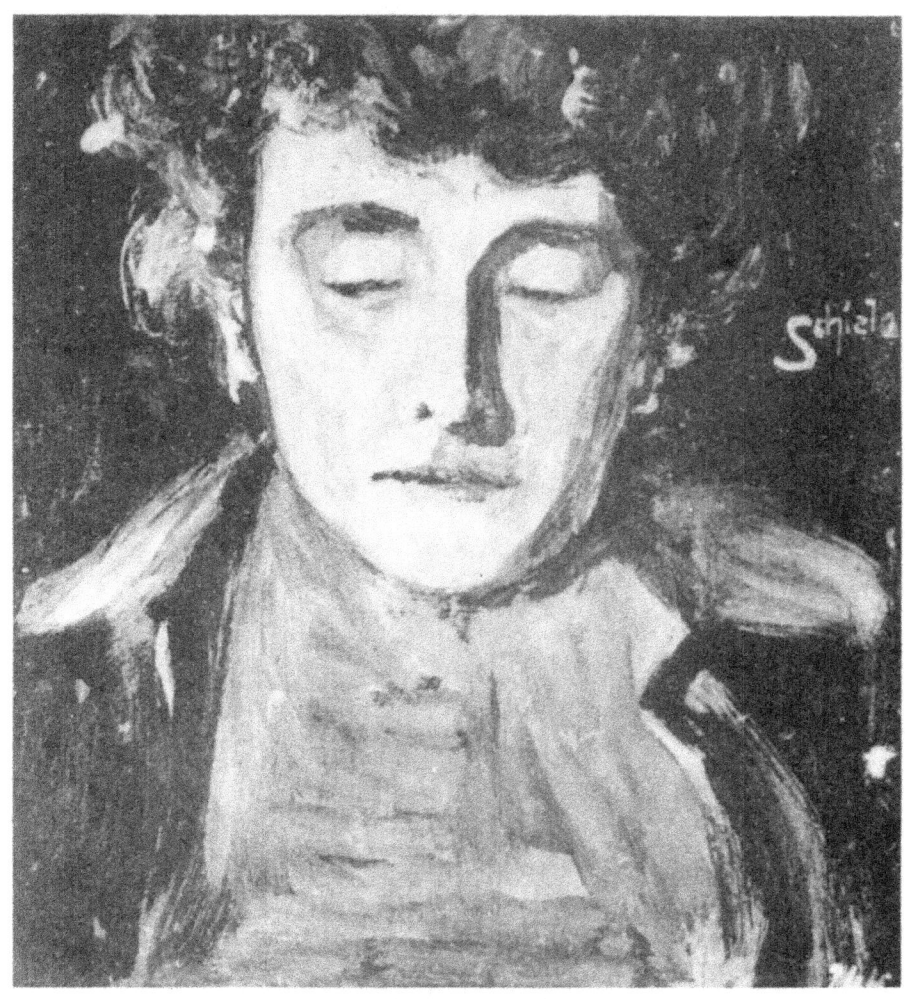

FIG. 32. Schiele, *Portrait of Schiele's Mother I*, 1907, oil on cardboard.

FIG. 33. Marie Schiele, *ca.* 1907.

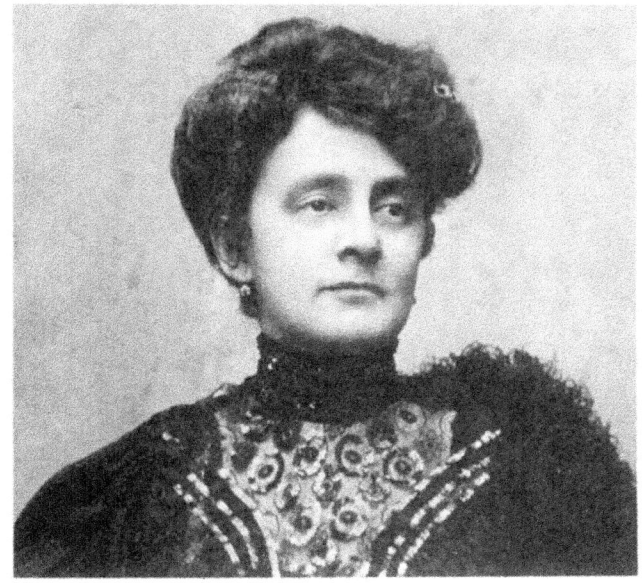

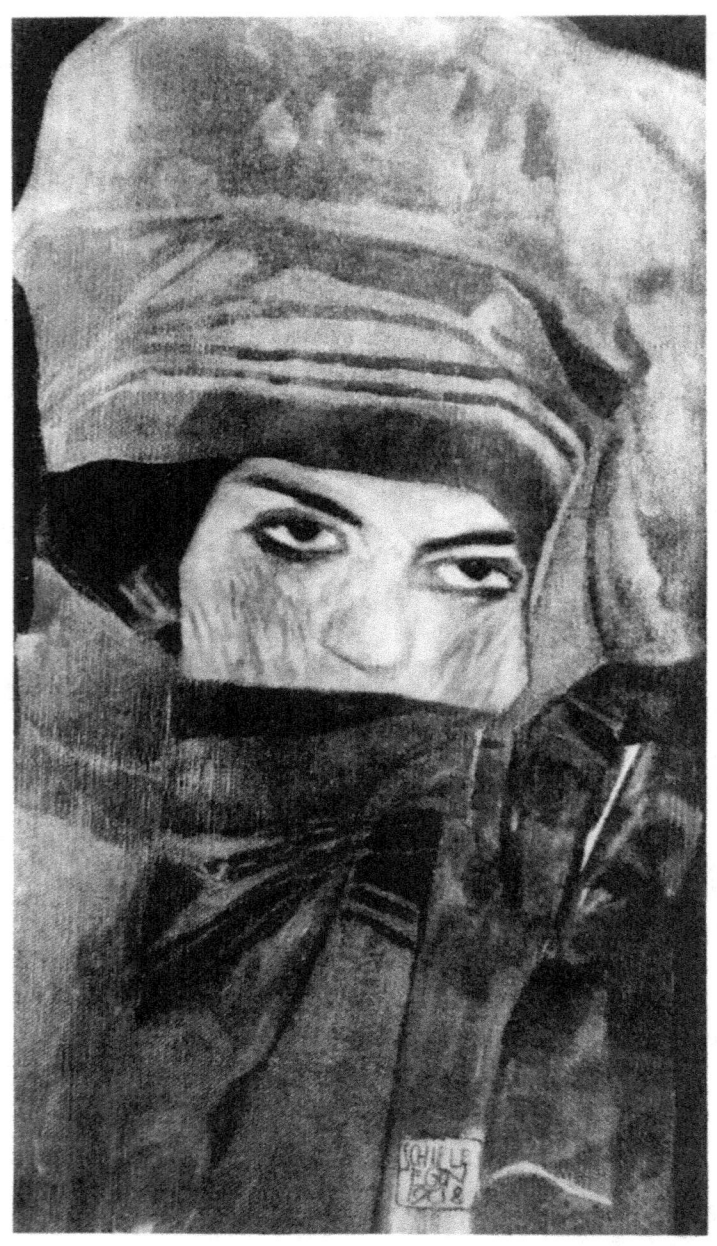

FIG. 34. Schiele, *Portrait of Melanie*, 1908, oil.

FIG. 35. Schiele, *Sketch of Melanie, ca.* 1908, pencil.

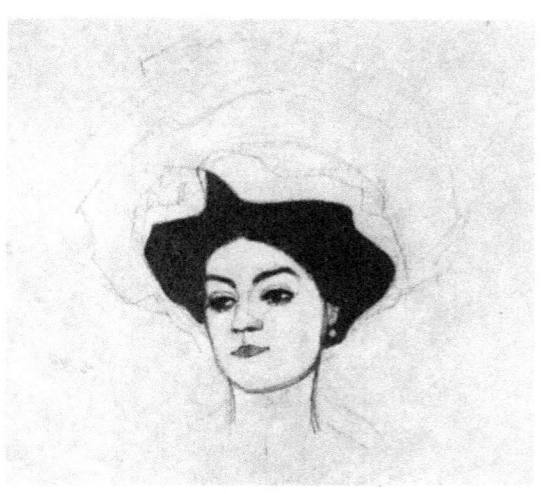

fended Griepenkerl, gives an excellent idea of the qualities which provoked him. Dressed in a painter's black smock and flowing necktie and in a serious, self-conscious pose, the seventeen-year-old painter does not deign to fix his glance upon the observer but stares out beyond him. His cherubic face is effectively framed by long black hair and an oversize painter's hat, artfully tilted over his left ear. No scenery or setting intervenes to support this self-reliant portrayal. Schiele no longer poses as artist at work as in the earlier photograph with palette, but as an entity, complete in himself. The "mannered" bearing referred to in the composite description of the young artist by his Klosterneuburg teachers is much in evidence here. Another oil, *Self-Portrait 1907* (figure 15), is similar in conception, with a closer focusing upon the face, where dramatic shadows flicker advantageously.[30] The general air of bravado combined with dandyism in these two self-portraits is noticeably akin to that of the Fabritius and Van Dyck self-portraits in the Academy art gallery (figures 13 and 16). It was perhaps the hint of self-sufficiency expressed in Schiele's self-portraits and personal bearing that his teachers interpreted as insolent smugness. Schiele made no secret of his critical attitude towards Griepenkerl's teaching methods, and the hostility between them grew. After months of ignoring the boy's impertinences, Griepenkerl finally shouted at him in a moment of exasperation, "You! Schiele! The devil has brought you into my classroom!" A photograph shows the young "hellion" in the Academy's life-drawing class (Figure 17). He looks not too different from his classmates, except that his extreme youth is most apparent. Schiele's last report card,[31] signed and graded by Griepenkerl, shows the intransigent old man's opinion of his pupil's talent: for painting of the human figure, practice in composition, industry, and progress, he marked him "satisfactory," the lowest classification one could receive and still pass.

1907: Meeting with Klimt

A short block from the Academy, on the Linke Wienzeile near the Karlskirche and not far from the Opera House, stood Joseph Olbrich's famous Secession building, designed and built in 1898 to provide a modern exhibition hall and headquarters for the avant-garde group around Klimt (figures 18 and 19). The two buildings stood back-to-back, impressive guardians of conflicting principles—conservatism and tradition on one hand, and freedom and modernism on the other. Although Klimt and his circle had withdrawn from the Secession in 1905 because of a policy disagreement, the work of modern foreign artists continued to be shown, and the activities of the Secession presented a progressive and stimulating contrast to the provincial exhibitions of the conservative Künstlerhaus. Some of the Academy professors, including Griepenkerl, as might have been expected, actually forbade their classes to attend the Secession shows, but this kind of forbidden fruit was all the more attractive to dissatisfied young pupils like Schiele. Across the street from the Secession building was the Café Museum, designed by Adolf Loos in 1899 as his answer to the decorative "excesses" of Viennese art. Its stripped, bare appearance had earned it the nickname "Café Nihilismus" (just as Olbrich's domed Secession building had previously been dubbed the "cabbage" by the public) and it was in this modern coffee house that Klimt, Josef Hoffmann and other members of the city's artistic intelligentsia could be seen. It was also here that the latest numbers of such avant-garde periodicals as *The Studio* and *Jugend*[32] were pored over by the art students who frequented the café hoping for a glimpse of the famous. Another place where an unknown art student might immerse himself unchallenged in the world of the "Klimtgruppe" was the elegant showroom of the Wiener Werkstätte (figure 20). Here during 1907 Klimt's allegory *The Three Ages of Life* (1905) was on permanent display, along with two of his major society portraits, *Frau Fritza von Riedler* (1906) (figure 20) and *Frau Adele Bloch-Bauer* (1907).[33] Here too Schiele first saw works by the Belgian sculptor Georges Minne (figure 20), who exerted an important influence upon his figure studies of 1910. But in 1907 it was not the gaunt expressiveness of Minne that claimed Schiele's attention, but rather the rich, ornamental, exquisite design and allegorical subject matter of Klimt.

Soon the boy began composing allegories of his own, with such titles as *"Guardian of Paradise"* and *"The Source."*[34] These rather lofty subjects were free variations on Klimt's famous University panels and at times incorporated specific Klimtian motifs, such as the old man from *Jurisprudence* (1903–1907) and the large suspended mask in *Philosophy* (1899–1907).[35] An additional source for the Klimt motifs now appearing in the sketches Schiele executed at home, away from the Academy, was the Secession-sponsored magazine *Ver Sacrum*. Although publication had ceased in 1903 after six years, and the lavish volumes were already becoming collector's items, Schiele had apparently been able to acquire a few issues through his Klosterneuburg friend, Max Kahrer, who in his Secession-style posters had already brought the elegant Jugendstil vocabulary to Schiele's attention.[36] One of the motifs Schiele took from *Ver Sacrum* was the figural supraporta showing a woman playing a lute, painted by Klimt for the private Dumba music room (1895–1898), and published during 1898 in two versions.[37]

To copy and improvise on Klimt's themes was one thing; to meet the man in person was quite another. However, Klimt was known for his generosity towards other artists, and this, coupled with Schiele's daily irritation over the methods of the Academy, gave the young painter courage. There were two places in which the famous artist could almost surely be found. One was the old Café Tivoli where he regularly ate an early morning breakfast consisting mainly of whipped cream; the other was his Josefstadt atelier—a spacious studio with furniture designed by Josef Hoffmann and set in an overgrown garden whose "wildness" was carefully cultivated by Klimt, who loved to roam about it dressed in the sandals and exotic blue smock which he always wore when working. Schiele decided to present himself at the atelier, and it was this fabled "wild" aspect of Klimt that he first came upon when he was shown into the garden. Somewhat taken aback in the presence of Klimt, who was twenty-eight years his senior, Schiele silently handed him a portfolio stuffed with drawings and asked simply, "Do I have talent?" As the master obligingly leafed through the seventeen-year old boy's work, his interest turned into astonishment. After a long silence he answered sternly, "Talent? Yes! Much too much!" A friendship based on mutual respect was immediately established and, although the two saw each other only infrequently, Klimt took pains to send Schiele models and to bring him to the attention of wealthy patrons. Occasionally he bought a drawing from Schiele to help him out financially, but more often he exchanged drawings, an event which always thrilled the younger artist.[38] It was Klimt who, toward the end of 1909, arranged a job for Schiele with the Wiener Werkstätte, as he had previously done for another unknown young painter, Oskar Kokoschka. Schiele's work for the famous arts and crafts association included fashion designs for men's clothing and for women's shoes, and post cards.[39]

Schiele's propensity for filial relationships (continued in his later friendships with Heinrich Benesch and Arthur Roessler, both older men) was fulfilled in part by Klimt. The resulting temporary influence upon Schiele's style was not the only significant outcome of their meeting. Acknowledgment of his talents by Vienna's leading artist was an important factor in increasing Schiele's already considerable self-esteem. His great artistic gifts had finally been conceded by his family, were recognized (if grudgingly) by the Academy, and now were praised by a famous painter. Schiele's vision of himself as an *artist* now elaborated upon his childhood dreams of greatness, as the reality of success seemed more and more within his grasp. For him, being an artist meant being one of a privileged group whose members' special talents carried them beyond the pale and domain of common man. His overestimation of this status was to cause him much bewildered grief vis-à-vis a society whose legal wheels continued to grind, making no distinctions between the financial debts owed by "geniuses" and those owed by the ordinary citizen.

In 1908 the architects, sculptors, and painters who had sided with Klimt in the 1905 Secession dispute realized an ambitious project. This was the organization of an extraordinary exhibition, the Kunstschau Wien 1908, organized in the spirit of a *Gesamtkunstwerk* in which the Wiener Werkstätte and other arts and crafts associations joined the artists in creating a magnificent, though temporary, exhibition hall. Almost every detail of this hall was exquisitely hand finished in accordance with a master plan dedicated to the celebration of the city's most progressive art movement, Jugendstil. The building, a complex of over fifty rooms, courts, and corridors, was designed by Josef Hoffmann, one of the original founders of the Wiener Werkstätte. The distinguished stage designer Alfred Roller directed the construction of a large garden with an open-air theater where the performance of young Kokoschka's play *Murderer, Hope of Women* caused a public scandal. The main feature of the 1908 Kunstschau was the exhibition of sixteen recent paintings by Klimt, on view during the duration of the show from May to October. It was here that Schiele had the opportunity of studying the master in depth.

Almost half of the sixteen works were landscapes; the others included three society portraits (*Frau Fritza von Riedler, Frau Adele Bloch-Bauer,* and *Frau Margaret Stonborough-Wittgenstein* [1905]) and the allegorical canvases, *The Three Ages of Life* (1905), *Danaë* (ca. 1907–1908), and *Water Serpents* (1907).[40]

To what extent Schiele absorbed the Klimt productions may be judged by several paintings and drawings created during the latter half of 1908. Of singular interest is a sheet of seven small framed sketches (figure 23a) of which at least two are recognizable redrawings of the Klimt compositions *Water Serpents* (figure 22; lower right on Schiele's sheet) and a famous earlier canvas not in the Kunstschau, the 1901 *Judith I* (figure 21; upper left on Schiele's sheet). Four of the remaining sketches deal with figures, possibly notations recalling Klimt portraits. These sketches appear on the verso of a blue-pencil drawing of Schiele's uncle, Leopold Czihaczek (figure 27), and suggest that the artist hurriedly selected an old drawing with a free side on which to jot down his impressions for himself or perhaps for a relative or friend to whom he was describing the Klimts he had seen. The several deviations from the originals in gesture and placement of the figures indicate that he was drawing from memory, and that it was the serpentine line and arbitrary cutting-off of the figure by its frame which most impressed him in Klimt's work. He soon painted a "Water Serpents" of his own, the *Fairytale World*[41] (figure 23b) of 1908, depicting several exotically coiffured nude females and one bald male floating in a vague and vaporous ambient. Their jewelry is heightened with gold and their forms are hardened into jagged stylizations more reminiscent of the repetitive figures in Klimt's 1902 *Beethoven Frieze* (which Schiele said he admired above any other Klimt) than of the flowing shapes of the *Water Serpents*. This tendency to harden and stratify Klimt's sinuous forms thus occurs quite early in Schiele. The trend is observable even in the sheet of seven sketches after Klimt discussed above, where a certain brittle emphasis squares shoulders and chins. Another sketch, copying Klimt's famous *Pallas Athena* of 1898, has the same angularization of forms.[42] Finally, one of Schiele's first major female nudes, a *Danaë* of 1909, was inspired by Klimt's *Danaë* on exhibition at the Kunstschau. There exist several detailed sketches for the typically Oriental background objects—birds, Japanese dwarf trees, and reeds.[43] The rhythmic figure contours of these sketches change to a bony whiplash of line in the completed oil, and the prominent gnarled hand of Schiele's *Danaë* heralds the expressive rawboned hands of his later portraits.

An interest in Oriental art expressed by the inclusion of Japanese background motifs in the *Danaë* is further evident in Schiele's *Portrait of a Lady* (plate 4) completed at the end of 1908. The pale, slant-eyed face and coiled black hair of the sitter are projected against a checkered gold background, and the harsh silhouette of her voluminous green- and blue-flecked red robe emphasizes the flatness of the picture plane. If the portrait is judged only as a work in the style of Klimt, it would appear that Schiele had deliberately resisted the hypnotic fluidity, delicacy, and refinement of those Klimt paintings in which similar checkered backgrounds (see figure 20) function like precious mosaics, defining, manipulating, and enhancing the foreground figure. Less talented painters than Schiele, the elegant if unassertive Max Kurzweil (1867–1916) for instance, were better imitators of Klimt. But the very qualities which make Schiele's picture only a second-rate Klimt are portents of the expressive style which he later developed. Klimt's nebulous ambients and constricting ornamentations were basically alien to Schiele's art, which strove to intensify and separate individual elements. The spaces that Klimt was compelled in his *horror vacuii* to fill would become for Schiele areas of luminous power, electrifying the contours of the figures set against them.

In evaluating Schiele's *Portrait of a Lady*, the pseudo-Oriental quality noted above is important. It is possible that Schiele was here not copying a Klimt portrait but rather was working from the same type of Orientally-clad (or really Oriental) model that Klimt himself enjoyed drawing (plate 3). Like all visitors to Klimt's atelier, Schiele must have been impressed by the painter's magnificent collection of antique Chinese screens, Japanese woodcuts, and Oriental vases, masks, robes, and textiles of all sorts.[44] Japanese art, in particular the works of Hokusai, was the object of general admiration in the Secession group around Klimt. *Ver Sacrum* had published articles on it, and one of the features of the 1908 Kunstschau was a collection of Japanese masks.[45] Schiele soon began to collect Japanese prints and, like Kokoschka before him, he admired their expressive outlines and vivid colors. The precise projections and daring foreshortenings of his later figure drawings trace part of their effectiveness to his early appreciation of Oriental art.[46]

It is generally conceded that Klimt exerted considerable influence on Schiele's increasingly sophisticated portrait style of 1909, of which the 1908 *Portrait of a Lady* is the immediate precursor. However, other works such as the *Fairytale World* of 1908 and the ambitious *Danäe* of early 1909, as well as various allegorical and thematic notations made during the Academy years, indicate that Klimt's initial impact on Schiele was also one of subject matter. The Klimt-engendered allegorical works discussed above are the first modest essays in a use of allegory that all his life served Schiele as an emotional release. Many of these later allegories are autobiographical: the artist himself appears, but in disguise.

The influence of Klimt upon Schiele's subject matter and style is confined to the Academy years, but the spiritual relationship of Klimt to Schiele emerged thematically, with unusual connotations, in two major canvases of 1912, *The Hermits* and *Agony*, two full years after Schiele had arrived at his own independent artistic idiom. The black pen and wash drawing *Two Men* (figure 25), done about 1909 as a design for a Wiener Werkstätte postcard, is an early expression of this theme. It also is indicative of the gravity with which Schiele evaluated his own stature as an artist. Two bearded monk-like figures of different age and physique, both dressed in black robes, stand facing each other on top of a flower-covered pedestal—an area which was probably meant to be inscribed with a seasonal message in the Wiener Werkstätte manner. The men's attention is centered upon a white tablet which rests on a tree stump and which the young man on the left (who may be interpreted as Schiele)[47] supports at the top with his left hand. A crayon is in his lowered right hand and he seems to be in the act of drawing. The older man on the right (Klimt) peers down over the top of the drawing and is raising both hands above it in a gesture of approval, or even benediction. Schiele has endowed both figures with halos, an attribute which he feels no shyness about sharing with the established master. One can imagine what Professor Griepenkerl's reaction to this "self-portrait" would have been. Further isolation from the ordinary world is achieved by strong black-white contrasts and stark silhouettes. A larger version of this composition done in pencil on cardboard, *Two Men in Decorative Robes* (figure 24), shows a portly Klimt (figure 26) wrapped in bulky robes and turning to gaze intently at the gaunt, exotically earringed younger man. Again a hand is raised in benediction. Schiele repeatedly characterized himself with furrowed brow, arched eyebrow, and drooped eyelid in numerous self-portraits of subsequent years. The single high horizon line is a characteristic Jugendstil device which functions effectively to link the two figures. The decorative space-filling nodules and the almost precious function of line and surface in both drawings are particularly reminiscent of Klimt's style as developed by the Wiener Werkstätte.[48] By such symbols as halos, pedestal and ascetic dress, Schiele's earlier image of himself as an artist now expands into a declaration of very special status.

Family portraits

The meeting with Klimt in 1907 and the subsequent visits to the Wiener Werkstätte showroom and the 1908 Kunstschau were exciting events that relieved the monotonous routine at the Academy. In the Czihaczek home, where Schiele was obliged to spend much of his free time, he was subjected to the strict and gloomy discipline of an elderly couple who had no children of their own and who overwhelmed the boy with lectures on morality, joyless home music appreciation sessions, and evenings in their box at the Vienna Burgtheater.[49] Schiele chafed particularly at this last "honor" and once when his aunt asked what he wanted for Christmas he replied passionately, "Never to have to go to the Burgtheater again!" On the other hand, Schiele's talent for mimicry and his outrageous imitations of the Academy professors, as well as his ability to reproduce the different nuances and variations of the Viennese dialect, both exasperated and captivated the pompous Leopold Czihaczek, who sometimes even invited him to perform at the dinner table. This encouragement often ricocheted however, as the boy began to use his growing knowledge of art to contradict and baffle the old man, challenging for instance a chance remark on the whiteness of the snow by insisting that it was blue. Defiantly, he could pursue such arguments with his uncle for hours.

Perhaps mercifully for Czihaczek, other hours were dedicated to posing for his nephew, who, when he was drawing, maintained complete silence.

During 1907 Schiele produced a half-dozen oil portraits of his uncle[50] as well as numerous studies. The *Blue Pencil Sketch of Leopold Czihaczek* (figure 27) is a typical example.[51] Comparison of this sketch with a photograph (figure 28) reveals, in the firm confident strokes, a meticulous observation of physical details. The likeness is succinctly attained by a few basic contours without calligraphic or tonal heightenings. The emphasis on Czihaczek's prominent black eyebrows introduces a romantic note in the otherwise neutrally photographic portrayal. This tendency to dramatize the aspects of force and authority in his uncle is a consistent feature of the oils, as for example in the imposing portrait *Leopold Czihaczek I* (figure 29). The deft halving of this almost life-size panel into areas of light and shadow reflects Schiele's technical lessons at the Academy, while the sensitive contour of the left arm and jacket reveals his basic feeling for linear design.

A second portrait, the oil sketch *Leopold Czihaczek at the Piano* (figure 30), has a unique place in Schiele's work because of the detailed background and surroundings. This is rare in Schiele who, from his earliest works onward, narrows his attention to only the sitter. (A fully particularized environment appears only twice again in Schiele's entire oil portrait production, both times in the last year of his life, 1918). The choice of a "moment musical" in Schiele's portrait of his uncle is not, as has sometimes been suggested, an attempt to emulate the well-known Klimt painting of 1899, in the Dumba music salon, of Schubert at the piano. The explanation is more mundane: Czihaczek was an accomplished pianist and extremely proud of the ornate *Flügelklavier* that took up a good half of his living room, as a photograph of Czihacek with Schiele's aunt, Marie, sitting by as faithful page-turner, shows (figure 31). A comparison of the picture and the photograph testifies to Schiele's almost photographic precision, as his brush moves to record (perhaps in grim humor) the cluttered background, from individual curtain ball fringes to the varying textures of the leafy potted plants. Schiele outdoes the photographer in effective design by showing his uncle's head against the bright windows, thus throwing the face into a shadow which mitigates the severe profile and creates a more dramatic effect.

The portrayals of Czihaczek suggest no affection on Schiele's part, and the portraits of his more immediate family convey, through their probing, simplifying technique, a distinct emotional distance. A small oil portrait of his mother (figure 32) done in 1907, and somewhat more sympathetic in feeling than similar frontal treatments of Czihaczek, makes use of the broad modeling and chiaroscuro learned at the Academy, while the arbitrary cropping-off of the top of the head is a result of Schiele's increasing preoccupation with close focus.[52] A photograph of his mother taken at about the same time (figure 33) shows how the abstract approach in the painting was able to present individual characteristics (the heavy-lidded eyes, firm mouth, wide nostrils) effectively. Contemporary sketches of his sisters range in style from the heavily cross-hatched technique of the Academy[53] to studies employing in both mood and technique a more delicate and exploratory approach (figure 6).

The influence of Klimt upon Schiele's portrayal of the members of his own family was not observable until the 1908 Kunstschau. Turning to his sisters as models, he produced a Secession-style portrait of each during 1908. The *Portrait of Gerti* (plate 5) contrasts in its easy sociability and fashionable elegance with the contrived mysteriousness of the partially veiled *Portrait of Melanie* (figure 34). The angular, asymmetrical design of Gerti's arms and shoulders stands out smartly against a light background, but a novel feature decisively differentiates this portrait from the compositionally similar one of Czihaczek standing (figure 29). It is the introduction in the background of an abstract shape which swells and spirals from left to right across the surface in rhythmic response to the figure of the girl and her jaunty hat. This is a first experiment with a decorative Jugendstil device which Schiele later transformed into the expressive "body halos" of the radical portraits of 1910.

A much closer focus is given to the *Portrait of Melanie*, whose eyes, as photographs show (figure 8), were her dominant feature. In the painting her right hand is just visible as she draws the concealing silver scarf across her mouth. The fanciful head-covering may have been provided by the girl herself, for she took enormous pride in designing and making her own hats.[54] A pencil *Sketch of Melanie* (figure 35), made before the oil portrait, shows the fascination which her spectacular hats and arresting eyes held for Schiele. The drawing is an excellent example of the Academy style he was trying to cast off, with its equal emphasis on all facial components, whereas the greater freedom employed in the brief indications of the headgear suggests Schiele's future graphic selectiveness. In another study for the portrait, Schiele concentrated exclusively on the eyes, drawing them twice—frontal, large, and very dark.[55] In the oil painting the gesture of drawing a veil across the lower face serves both to emphasize the eyes and to create a barrier (reflecting the emotional relationship existing between brother and sister). In the minds of Egon and Gerti, Melanie, who had been working to support the family since she was sixteen, had always been an adult (figure 5)—too old to join in their childhood games and temperamentally too practical to appeal to their imaginative natures. It is noteworthy that Schiele never painted a double portrait of his sisters, nor any group pictures of himself with them and his mother. The psychological aspects of human relationships did not concern him at this time. His interests were narrowed to the single figure, in consistency with his technical close searching of form.

Schiele's increasing assimilation of Klimt's portrait style is demonstrable in the earlier of the two 1909 paintings of Gerti, the *Portrait of a Woman with a Black Hat* (*Gerti*, plate 6).[56] The first of three portrait canvases painted for exhibition, at Klimt's personal invitation, in the Kuntschau of 1909, the picture is a larger, bolder, and more ornately executed statement of the 1908 oil (plate 5). Gerti wears the same double-breasted black coat and the billowing silhouette of the voluminous sleeves has been repeated and exaggerated. An ermine fur piece is around her neck, and she holds a decorative coverlet.[57] Although she looks directly at the beholder, a certain glazed fixedness in her eyes produces an impression of immobility, similar in effect to that of the static, mask-like faces of Klimt's contemporaneous female portraits.[58] The stark emergence of face and hands from a Klimtian setting of vividly colored and intricately patterned ornament is echoed by the handstitched pillow with its brown and creamy golden discs and orange dots against a bright green. Gerti holds the coverlet gingerly, as though it were some sort of unattractive reptilian thing. The white fur piece and Gerti's flaming orange-red hair isolate and intensify the face, and the black hat and coat are in strong relief against what Schiele had originally intended as a white background.[59] In spite of the profusion of Klimtian devices, Schiele's portrait of Gerti, with its angular contour and almost unrelieved isolation of the figure, has an elemental starkness comparable to that of Edvard Munch's 1892 portrait of his sister Inger. Both artists approached Expressionism through an intensified application of the Jugendstil decorative silhouette. Schiele would even more closely approximate Klimt's turn-of-the-century style in his next series of portraits, before discarding much of this older tradition and moving into a new artistic idiom.

CHAPTER II

1909-1910: Toward Artistic Independence

WITHDRAWAL FROM THE ACADEMY:
FORMATION OF THE NEUKUNSTGRUPPE

KLIMT'S invitation to contribute his canvases to the forthcoming 1909 International Kunstschau reinforced Schiele's self-esteem and quickened his dissatisfaction with the conservative teaching methods of his professors. The last known photograph taken during his student years (figure 36) shows a definite cockiness and combativeness added to the keen self-awareness that characterizes all photographs of the artist. When he jotted down the seven sketches of his fellow students at the Academy (figure 39)[1] on the back of a study for the 1909 painting Danaë, Schiele was in a particularly restless and critical mood. He seldom indulged in caricature, although the economy and speed of his drawing style eminently suited him for it, and the characterization of his comrades here, with their uniformly earnest yet bland features, hints at a new attitude towards the status and meaning of an "Academy" student. The dilapidated elegance of the stiff collars, oversized coats, and tight top hat is at odds with the dapperness of Schiele's early Academy self-portraits. The disenchantment suggested in these caricatures was given positive form by Schiele and some of his colleagues in a critique of the Academy's teaching methods presented to Professor Griepenkerl in 1909. Written as thirteen questions directed specifically at Griepenkerl, the censure was a remarkable plea for greater academic liberalism in "acceptable" subject matter, respect for the integrity of a student's individual development, and, finally, the creation of a contemporary "Austrian" art free of the slavish imitation of foreign traditions.[2] This bold document irreversibly terminated Schiele's career at the Academy. He withdrew at the end of the spring semester and stepped into a new world—the uncertain life of an independent but unknown young painter. Financially he was unequipped to take this step. No further help would be forthcoming from Leopold Czihaczek, who had previously at least been able to console himself with the "respectability" of the Academy, and his mother now expected and demanded support for herself and the fifteen-year-old Gerti. Schiele had moved out of his mother's house in 1907, and at the time of his withdrawal from the Academy was sharing a studio-sized room with another young man, an art restorer, in the Alserbachstrasse in Vienna's ninth district near the Danube canal. As with Picasso and Kokoschka and so many others, Schiele's first years of independence in a great metropolis were marked by real poverty and periods of semi-starvation. Nevertheless he was vain about his appearance and cut his own "starched" collars out of stiff white paper.

Nor did poverty interfere with Schiele's energetic and successful attempts to bring together the rebel elements of the Academy into an independent artists' organization. His Klosterneuburg friend, the musician Arthur Löwenstein, joined the group and during the summer of 1909 the name "Neukunstgruppe" ("New Art Group") was decided upon and Schiele elected president. A handwritten contract dated 17 June 1909 with the Pisko Salon, a small gallery with modernist sympathies attached to the great Pisko Auction Gallery, preserves the signatures of the original sixteen members of the Neukunstgruppe (figure 40).[3] Although some of these names have remained obscure, others, such as Tony (Anton) Faistauer and Franz Wiegele, became well-known artists. Also included in this list were the signatures of Anton Peschka, later Schiele's brother-in-law through his marriage to Gerti in 1912, and Erwin Osen, whose pretentious signing of himself as "Painter of Theater Art" presaged his future stormy relationship with Schiele. Two further artists who signed the Pisko contract merit remembrance if only because they were soon portrayed by Schiele in two major canvases: Hans Massmann and Karl Zakovsek. Each artist obligated himself to provide at least six paintings for the Pisko exhibition of their works, planned for December 1909, and Löwenstein agreed to perform several of his compositions. Two new members joined the Neukunstgruppe's first exhibition: Hans Böhler, a financially independent young artist who later became one of Schiele's most loyal patrons and collectors, and the talented Paris von Gütersloh, actor and poet as well as painter, and friend of Arnold Schönberg. These young artists who, out of disappointment with the outmoded teaching methods of the Vienna Academy, banded together to form the Neukunstgruppe during the summer of 1909 probably did not realize that they were repeating history. Exactly one hundred years earlier, on 10 July 1809, six earnest young students left the Vienna Academy to found their own group dedicated to the loftiest personal ideals in art, the Brotherhood of St. Luke. Of this group, so similar to Schiele's in revolutionary aspiration, the painters Friedrich Overbeck and Franz Pforr left Vienna to realize their German art in Rome, as founding members of the Nazarenes.

EARLY PORTRAITS OF THE NEUKUNSTGRUPPE

During the years 1909 and 1910 Schiele drew or painted portraits of six of the original members of the Neukunstgruppe. These constitute the first major portraits of persons outside his own family circle and may be divided stylistically as falling before and after the opening of the 1909 International Kunstschau, which was to exert decisive influence upon Schiele. A chronological examination of these portraits provides an illuminating answer to the question: where did Schiele derive his radical portrait style of 1910? The Neukunstgruppe portraits document Schiele's initial adoption of the Klimt format to portraiture and then an increasingly original application of Jugendstil techniques for psychological depth and new formal values.

Two basic compositions had been employed by Klimt in his portraiture. Although his standing figures were often centrally placed, the seated figures were customarily far to one side, so that a large surface area, usually elaborately ornamented, extended and aggrandized the area containing the visual ballast of chair, torso, hands, and face. This treatment is richly expounded in the 1907 *Portrait of Adele Bloch-Bauer*, which Schiele had seen in the 1908 Kunstschau. It was, among others, this work that Schiele must have had in mind when he began the portrait study of his Neukunstgruppe colleague, Anton Faistauer (1887–1930) (figure 38). Faistauer is seated in a chair with his hands folded. The head and torso are completely within the right-hand portion of the picture, while the legs and hands are to the left of a center axis, thus setting up an opposition of figure and "uninhabited" space in the best Klimtian manner.[4] The Klimtian ornamental overlay of surfaces is concentrated in the dense cluster of little rings which swarm along the entire side of the chair arm. Also Klimtian is a strong subjective emphasis on the hands and face, achieved here through color: fuzzy black hair, dark curling eyelashes, and open red lips accentuate the face which is otherwise uncolored and left in the light brown of the drawing paper, whereas the hands are yellow with prominent red knuckles.[5] A contemporaneous *Self-Portrait* by Faistauer, dedicated on the back to Schiele, and a photograph of Faistauer with Anton Peschka (figure 37) possess the same studied foppishness as in Schiele's portrait —where the precious Klimtian surface cultivation was subtly suitable.[6]

Schiele's study of Faistauer was not developed further, but the next two members of the Neukunstgruppe whom he sketched became the subjects of two large oils, both of which were exhibited in the 1909 Kunstschau. The *Portrait of Hans Massmann* (plate 8) and *Portrait of Anton Peschka* (plate 10), mirror each other compositionally. Both employ the Klimt-inspired disposition of the torso to one side of a center axis, but with the closer focus characteristic of Schiele. The elegant silhouettes of the young men extend across the canvases, continuing the curving shapes of their decorative armchairs. The solidity of the bodies contrasts with the busy patterns of the silver and pastel backgrounds. Neither head is in strict profile: Massmann's face turns a degree toward the beholder, whereas Peschka's is turned slightly away. The latter, more difficult "lost" profile, as well as the greater psychological tension conveyed through the outspread hands, suggests that the Peschka portrait was completed last. Like Klimt, Schiele has underscored the naturalism of his portrait heads by a contrasting abstract motif in the embellishment of the chairs and background. Unlike Klimt however he does not isolate the face and hands by intervening areas of shifting surface pattern, but retains the organic integrity of the body. The precise and continuous definition of body silhouette precludes the swallowing-up of the representational by the abstract.

A temperament fundamentally alien to the equivocal aspects of Klimt's portrait style is at work here. And yet, understandably, Schiele's use of the Klimt format and the decorative aspects in the Massmann and Peschka portraits caused viewers at the 1909 Kunstschau to dismiss him as a "weak imitator of Klimt."[7] Schiele himself considered these paintings as successful new statements of the older artist's style, and referred to himself jokingly at this time as "the silver Klimt." His imitation was not limited to painting; the provincal boy from Tulln now also began to parrot the colorful Viennese dialect so amusingly spoken by the laconic Klimt.

Consideration of a more three-dimensional work, the pencil *Study for the Portrait of Hans Massmann* (plate 7), demonstrates Schiele's basically organic approach to his subject.[8] The sparse indication of geometrical background areas (which in the painting itself received elaborate enrichment) suggests that, as observable also in the Faistauer portrait, for Schiele decoration (and also color) is a sequel to and not an inherent property of form. Through his graphic incisiveness form is revealed with poster-like clarity and immediacy, and not developed progressively in relation to an interacting environment. The secondary role that even interior modelling lines played at this time in Schiele's calligraphic grasp of his subject is apparent in a colored pencil sketch of a fourth Neukunstgruppe member, *Portrait Study of Arthur Löwenstein* (plate 9). The superficial, somewhat precious tone of the earlier Faistauer portrait (figure 38) has been replaced here by a more serious statement of character. The compositional motif of the self-enclosing folded arms reflects the mental isolation of the brooding or sleeping sitter and Schiele's irregular contour line begins to function on a subjective as well as a decorative level.

The Löwenstein portrait is also interesting for its disclosure, unconscious perhaps, of a new formal intention of the artist: to contravene the asymmetrical Klimt design by placing the figure directly on the centralized axis of the picture. This urge to energize the center of a portrait—so anti-Jugendstil in its unfluctuating and unrelieved intensity—was to receive significant external stimulus from a variety of sources now revealed to Schiele in the momentous Vienna Kunstschau of 1909.

THE INTERNATIONAL KUNSTSCHAU OF 1909

The emphatic success of the 1908 Kunstschau had prompted its directors to lay plans for an even more ambitious show the following year. This time it was not to be limited to Austrian and German artists, but to be international in scope, and in keeping with the special arts-and-crafts interest of the Klimt-Hoffmann group, impressive handicraft displays were secured from England and Germany. The works of foreign painters and sculptors were dispersed

among the Austrian entries according to nationality and medium. The artists
from abroad included the highly mannered Belgian master of Art Nouveau,
Jan Toorop (with twenty-two works including eight portraits), the Norwegian Edvard Munch (sketches for Ibsen's *Ghosts* only, no paintings) from
the north, and the Trieste-born, Rome-based Ernesto de Fiori (life-sized nude
figure murals, see figure 63) from the south of Europe. Switzerland was represented by Albert Trachsel, Giovanni Giacometti, and Cuno Amiet. (The
recent retrospective given by the Vienna Secession in 1904 explains the omission of Vienna's favorite foreign painter, the Swiss master Ferdinand Hodler.)
The French contribution reads impressively in the catalogue but requires
a quantitative clarification: Matisse (one painting identified as "The Lady
Gardener" and a figure study), Vlaminck (two landscapes), Bonnard (four
paintings), Vuillard (two works), and Gauguin (one painting, identified as
"Young Couple"). The following French artists exhibited a greater number
of works, averaging between three and five each: Henri Manguin, Jean Puy,
Charles Guérin, K. X. Roussel, and Louis Valtat. Felix Valloton was represented by five paintings (plate 28b) and Maurice Denis by two. The German
entries included sculptures by Ernst Barlach (seven small figures) and works
by Max Slevogt, Lovis Corinth (including two portraits, *The Priest Moser*,
1899, and *Tiny Senders*, 1904), Max Klinger, Thomas Theodor Heine, Bernhard Pankok (including an 1892 self-portrait), and Max Liebermann (including the *Portrait of Alfred Frieherr von Berger*). The Berlin-based artist, Emil
Orlik, sent numerous graphic portraits and Japanese sketches, and a handsome
memorial exhibition was mounted for the late Joseph Olbrich, architect of the
Secession. The English contribution included a large graphic section with
works by Charles Ricketts, Charles Shannon, Muirhead Bone, and Charles
Robert Ashbee. Several display cases contained handicraft by Charles and
Margaret Mackintosh, who had already impressed Vienna with their elegant
salon decoration for Fritz Waerndorfer, one of the original founders of the
Wiener Werkstätte.

In addition to the Belgian Toorop, whose large showing was a favorite
with the Klimt group, two other foreign artists dominated the 1909 Kunstschau by virtue of the number and importance given to their works. These
were the much admired Belgian sculptor, Georges Minne, with six large sculptures and drawings, including a kneeling figure from his famous *Fountain of
Five Boys*, and Vincent Van Gogh, whose works had first been shown to the
Viennese public by the Secession in 1903 and again in a large exhibition at the
Miethke Gallery in 1906.[9] Van Gogh was represented in the Kunstschau by
eleven paintings,[10] including four portraits and a version of *The Bedroom at
Arles*. Special rooms were set aside for the works of these artists. The two-to-
one ratio of what would now be termed Expressionistic art, as represented by
Van Gogh and Minne, to pure Jugendstil, as expounded by Toorop, presages
the course of modern art in Vienna and reflects favorably upon the liberal
tastes of the Kunstschau's directors. For it must be kept in mind that in Vienna
the younger Expressionist generation did not initially find themselves at odds

with their elders, the Klimt-Hoffmann group, but were actively supported and encouraged by them in an atmosphere of mutual admiration.[11] The young Kokoschka's title-page dedication to Gustav Klimt of his illustrated fairytale, *The Dreaming Boys*, published by the Wiener Werkstätte in 1908, and Schiele's proud designation of himself in 1909 as "the silver Klimt," are wholly in keeping with the sympathetic relations between the two generations. The most vehement criticism of the older group came not from the younger artists but from a distinguished colleague, the brilliant architect Adolf Loos, who fought a lonely battle against the decorative tendencies and aesthetic stylizations of Olbrich, Hoffmann, and Klimt. But in the first decade of Viennese Expressionism Schiele and Kokoschka could and did feel equal respect for Loos and Klimt. In restrospect it is clear that Loos's purist doctrines, as set forth in his 1908 essay, "Ornament und Verbrechen" ("Ornament and Crime"[12]), prepared the way and quickened a breakthrough to the direct, unadorned representation of "raw" form adopted by the Viennese Expressionist portrait painters.

This benevolent containment of the radical new form within what had previously been the avant-garde—paralleled in the city's musical world by the friendly relations and mutual respect between Mahler and the Schönberg circle—is nowhere better expressed than in the disparate character of the Austrian contributions to the 1909 International Kunstschau. Klimt had again been given a room of honor where eight drawings and seven major canvases adorned the walls (figure 42). Those works which were to hold particular meaning for Schiele were *Judith II* (see plate 15), both the 1903 and the 1907–1908 versions of *Hope*—a bold theme dealing with pregnancy (see figure 84)—and a portrait, titled simply *Old Woman*, (figure 41). The unusual austerity of this last work, with its dark, monolithic effect, is infrequent in Klimt's work: a simplified, non-fractured image contemplated in terms of plastic construction. Such isolation of the figure from its surroundings in order to intensify the image parallels the tendencies in the work of the younger artists.

The Kunstschau naturally featured many of the richly worked, highly ornate contributions of the Wiener Werkstätte. But direcly above the exuberant profusion of polychrome porcelain figures, inlaid furniture, colored glass mosaics, stage-set designs, and theater costume sketches hung the exploratory new works of Hans Böhler, Paris von Gütersloh, Max Oppenheimer, Egon Schiele, and Oskar Kokoschka. Schiele showed four paintings: the lost allegory *Current of Youth*,[13] and three portraits—those of Hans Massmann and Anton Peschka (see plates 8 and 10), and the 1909 portrait of Gerti (see plate 6). Kokoschka, as in the 1908 Kunstschau, contributed both sculpture and painting, including a small painted portrait sculpture of Lilith, the heroine of *The Dreaming Boys*, and a set of illustrations to a new fairy tale, *The White Animal Slayer*. These were both exhibited in the room dedicated to Toorop's works, but the Kunstschau directors were not able to find a setting of artistic kinship for Kokoschka's extraordinary painting later known as *The Trance Player* (figure 43). This was a portrait of Ernst Reinhold, the actor who had

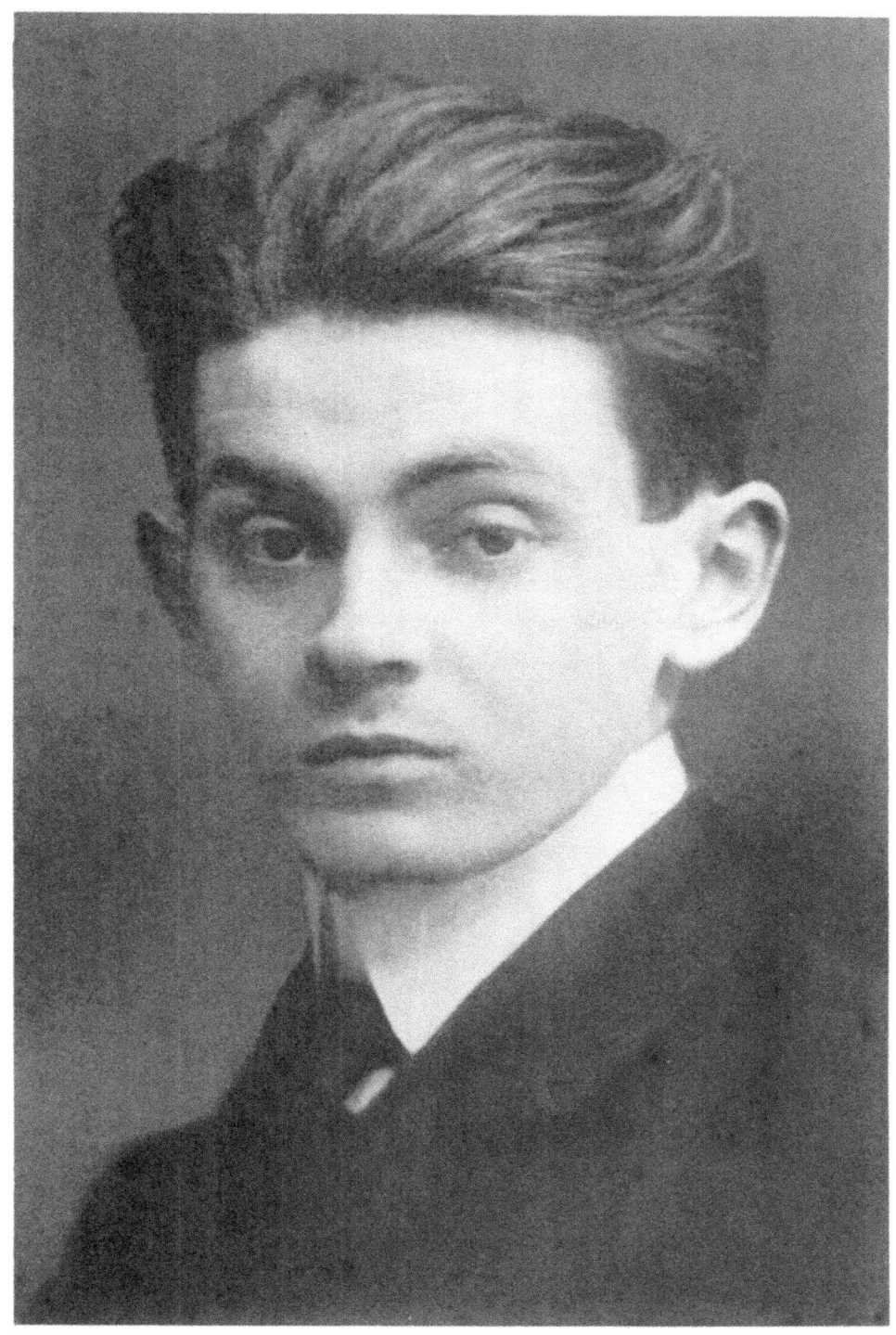

FIG. 36. Schiele at the age of nineteen.

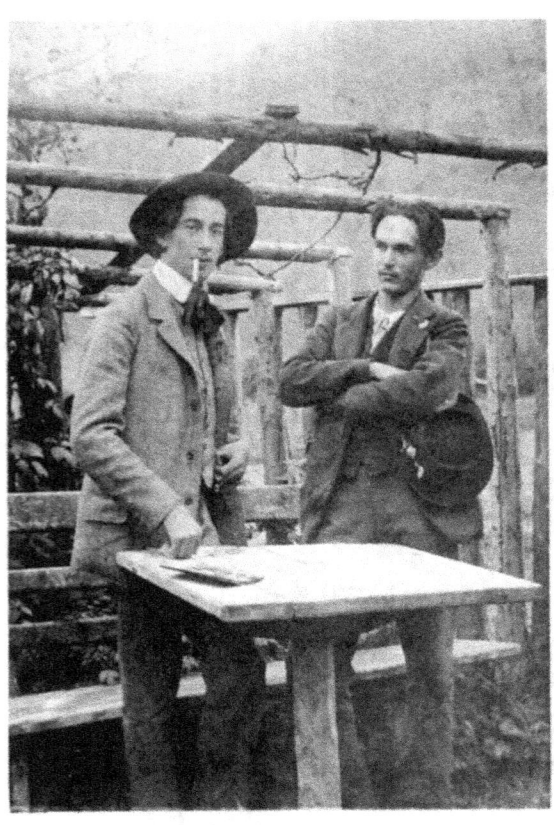

FIG. 37. Anton Faistauer and Anton Peschka, 1905.

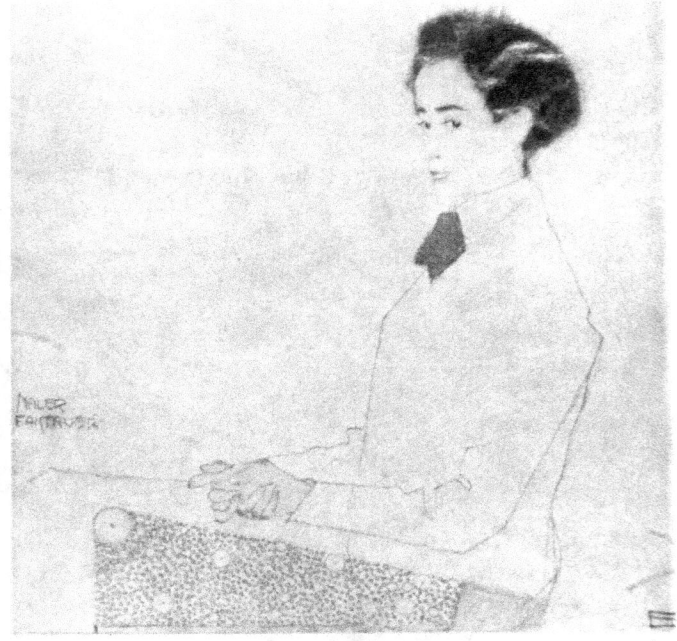

FIG. 38. Schiele, *Portrait Study of Anton Faistauer*, 1909, pencil with watercolor.

FIG. 40. The 17 June 1909 Neukunstgruppe contract with the Pisko Salon..

FIG. 39. Schiele, *Seven Caricatures of Fellow Students at the Academy, ca.* 1909, pencil.

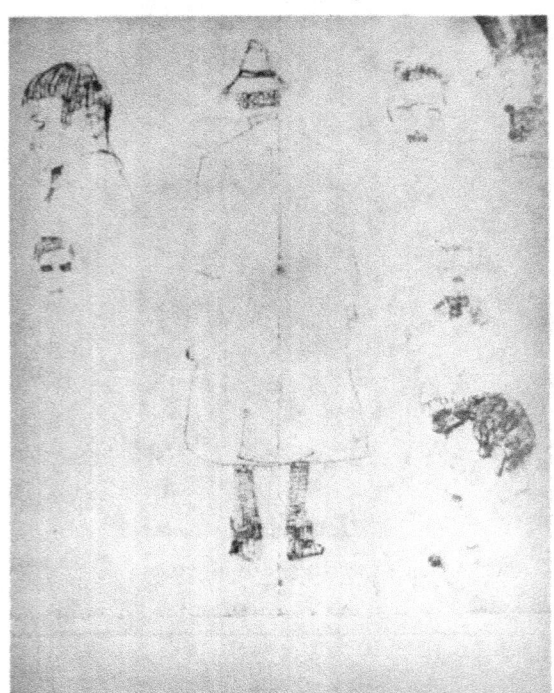

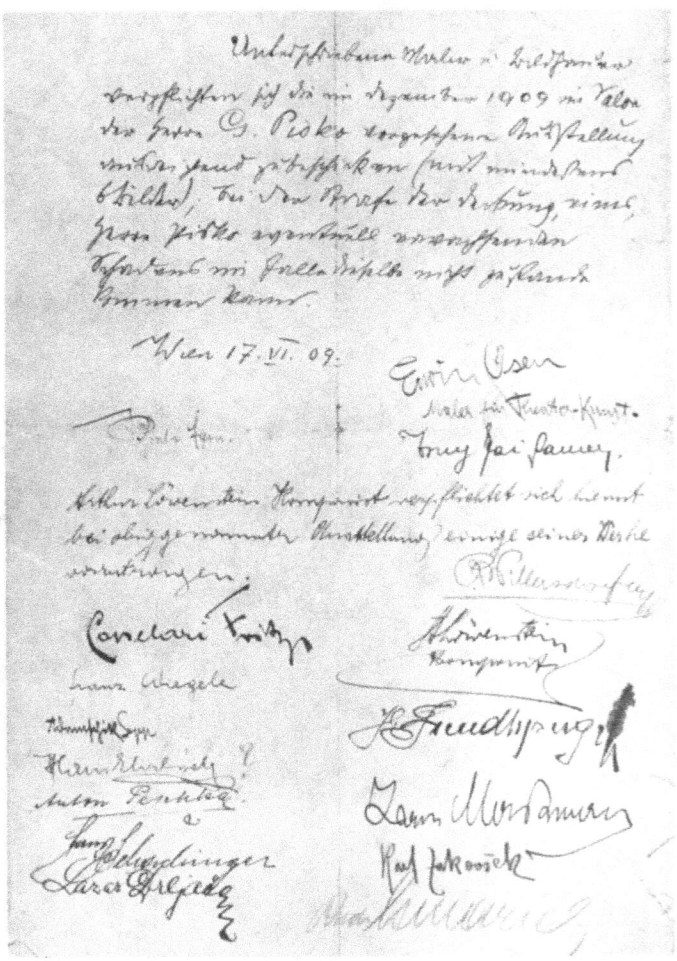

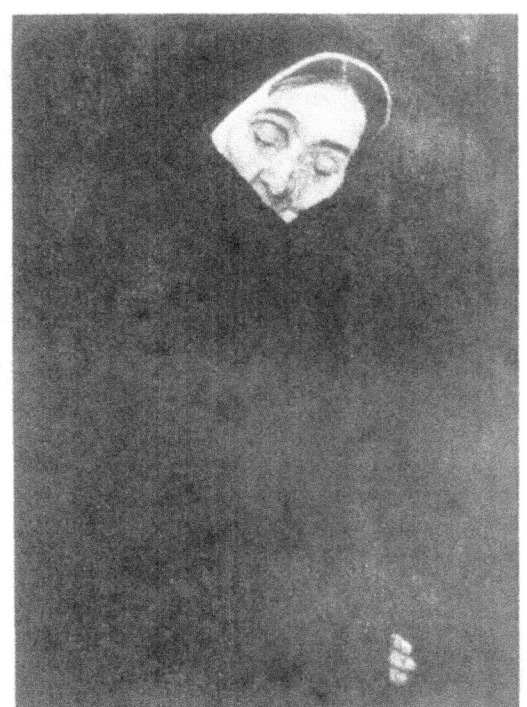

FIG. 41. Klimt, *Old Woman*, 1909, oil.

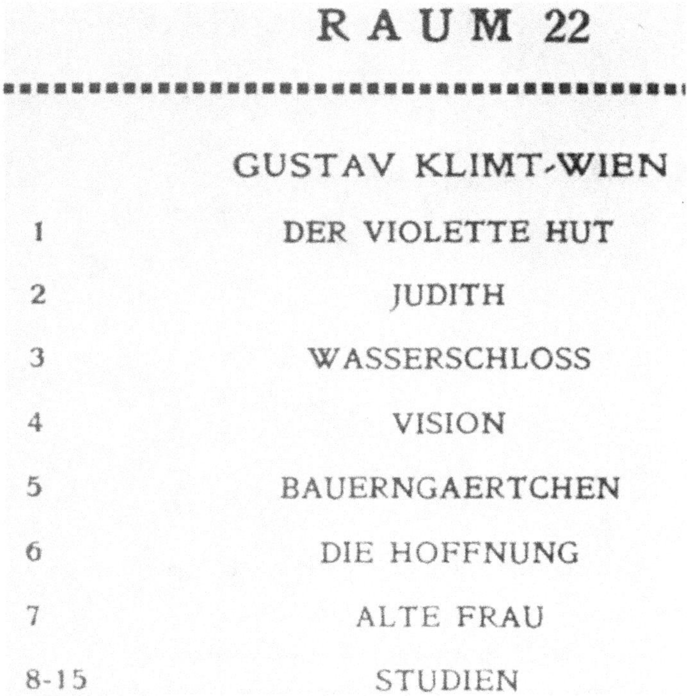

RAUM 22

GUSTAV KLIMT-WIEN

1	DER VIOLETTE HUT
2	JUDITH
3	WASSERSCHLOSS
4	VISION
5	BAUERNGAERTCHEN
6	DIE HOFFNUNG
7	ALTE FRAU
8-15	STUDIEN

FIG. 42. Klimt page from the 1909 Vienna International Kunst-schau exhibition catalogue.

FIG. 43. Kokoschka, *The Trance Player (Portrait of Ernst Reinhold)*, 1908, oil.

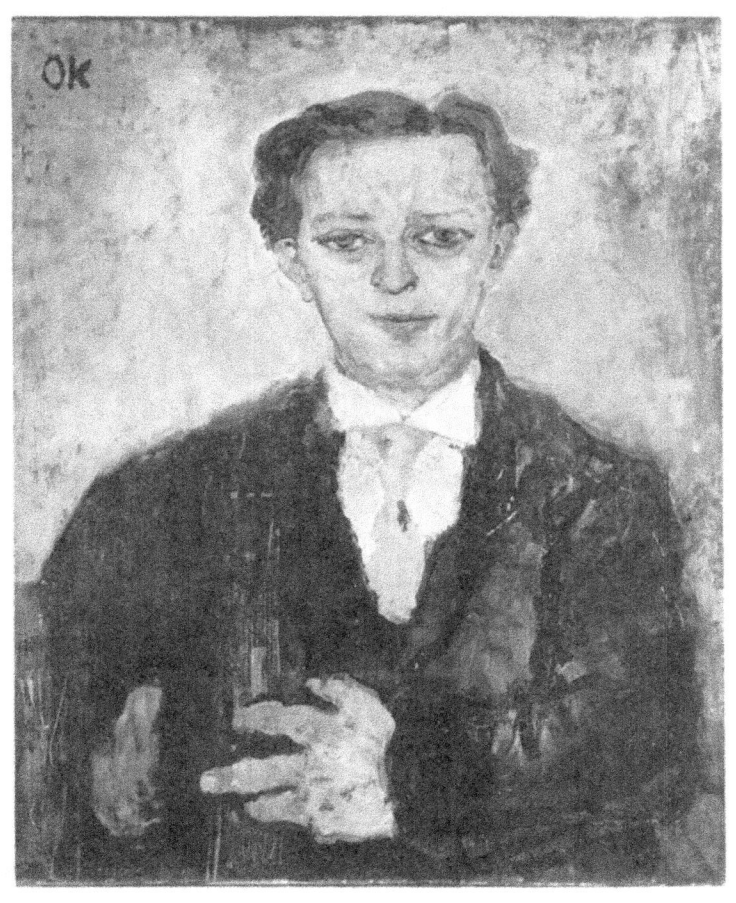

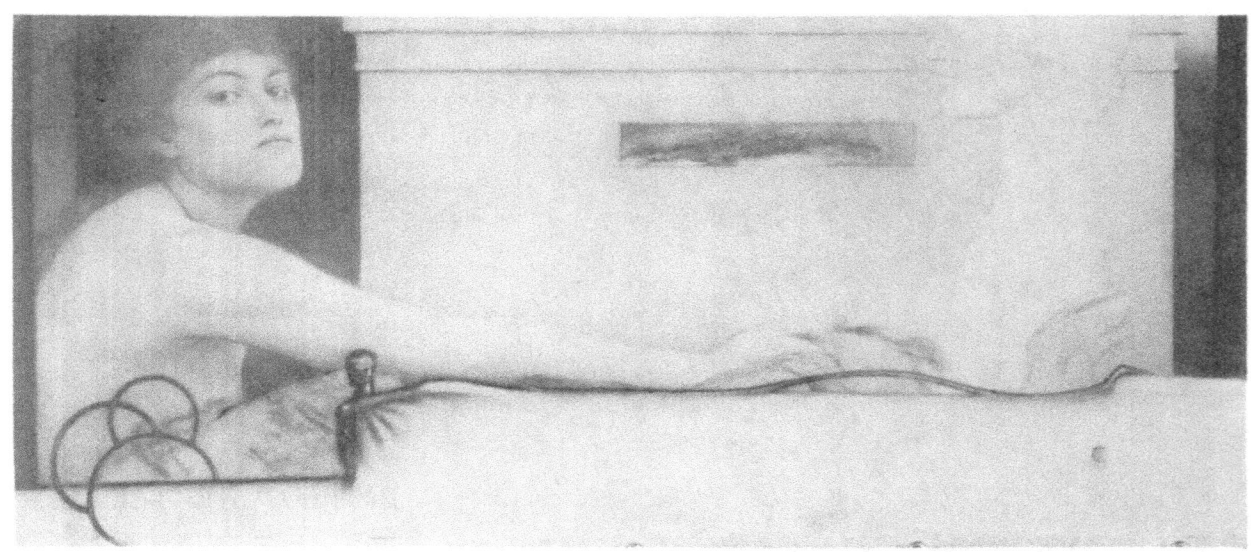

FIG. 44. Fernand Khopff, *The Offering*, 1891, pastel.

FIG. 45. Carl Moll, *Self-Portrait in Atelier*, 1906, oil.

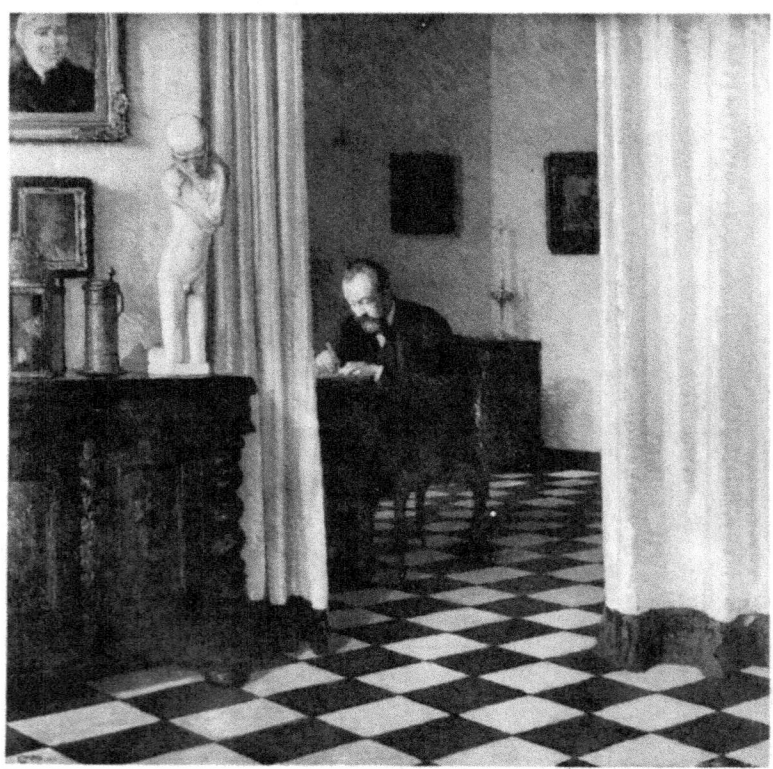

FIG. 46. Georges Minne, *Kneeling Boy*, 1898–1900, marble.

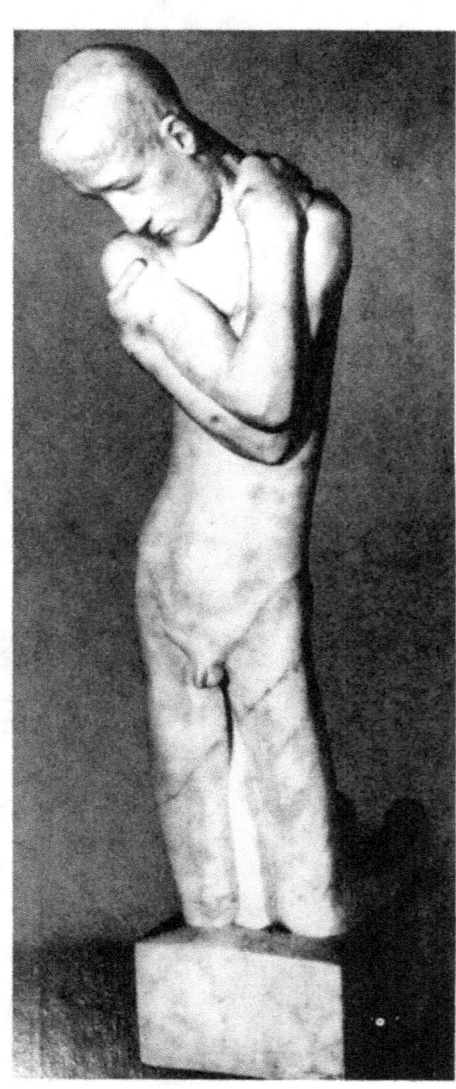

FIG. 47. Schiele, *Head Study of Anton Peschka*, 1909, charcoal.

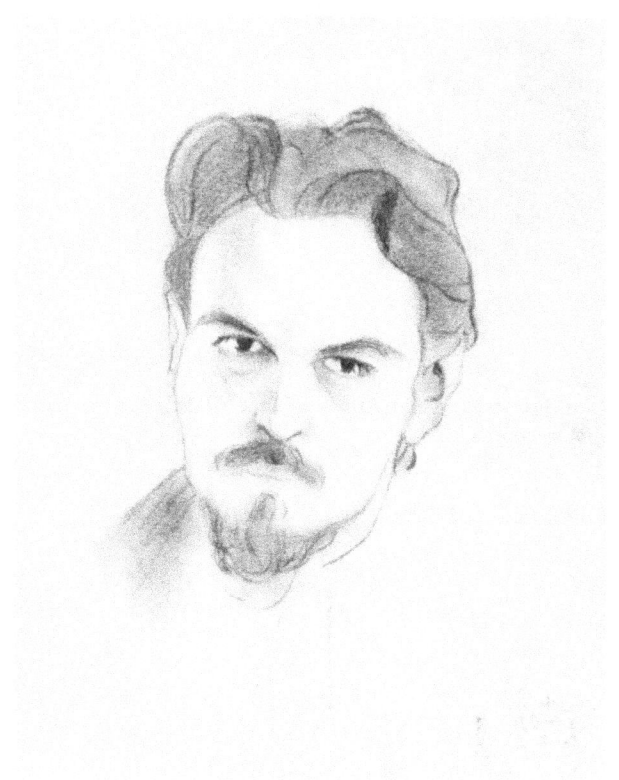

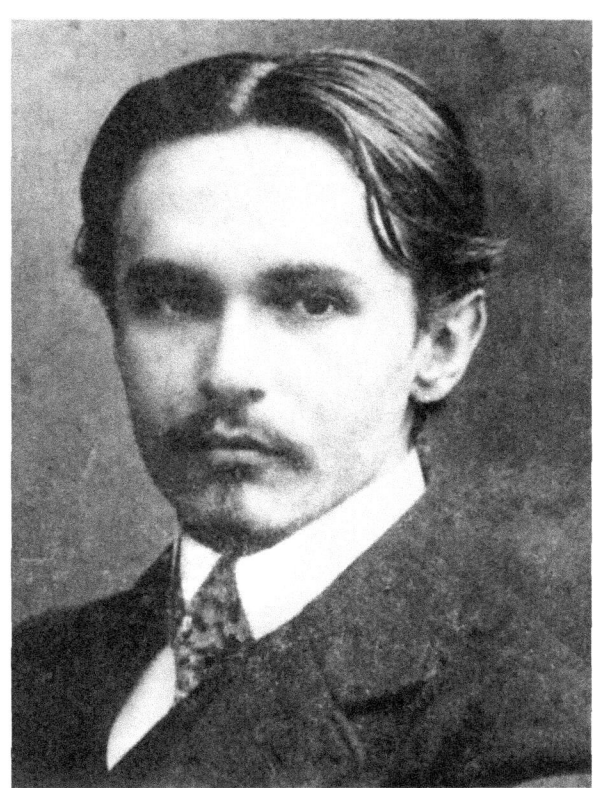

FIG. 48. Anton Peschka, *ca.* 1909.

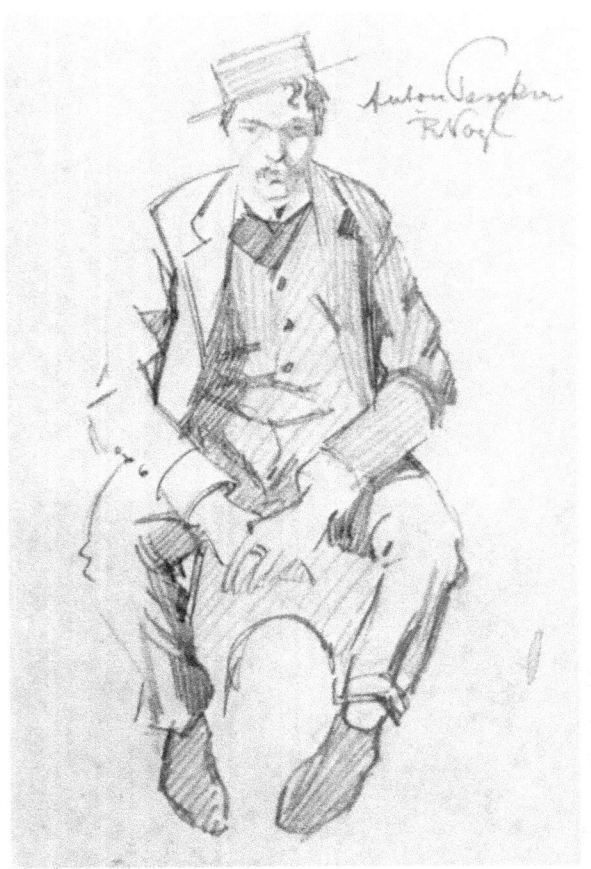

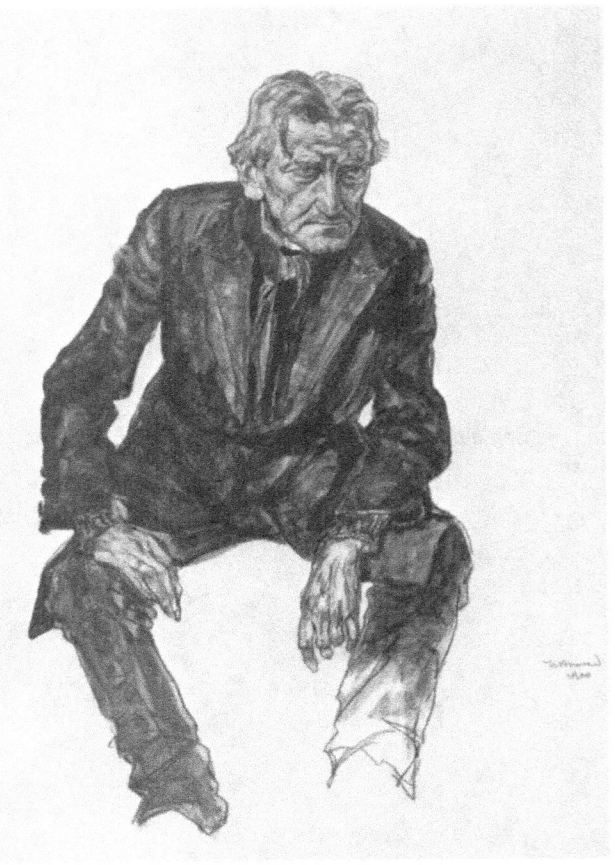

FIG. 49. R. Vogl, *Study of Anton Peschka Seated, ca.* 1910, pencil.

FIG. 50. Hugo Bouvard, *Study of an Old Man*, 1910, pencil and watercolor.

FIG. 51. Van Gogh, *The Zouave*, 1888. oil.

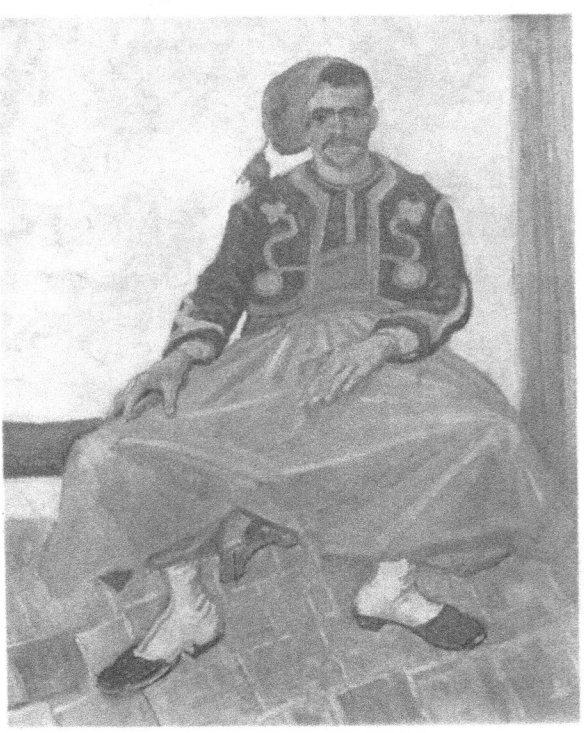

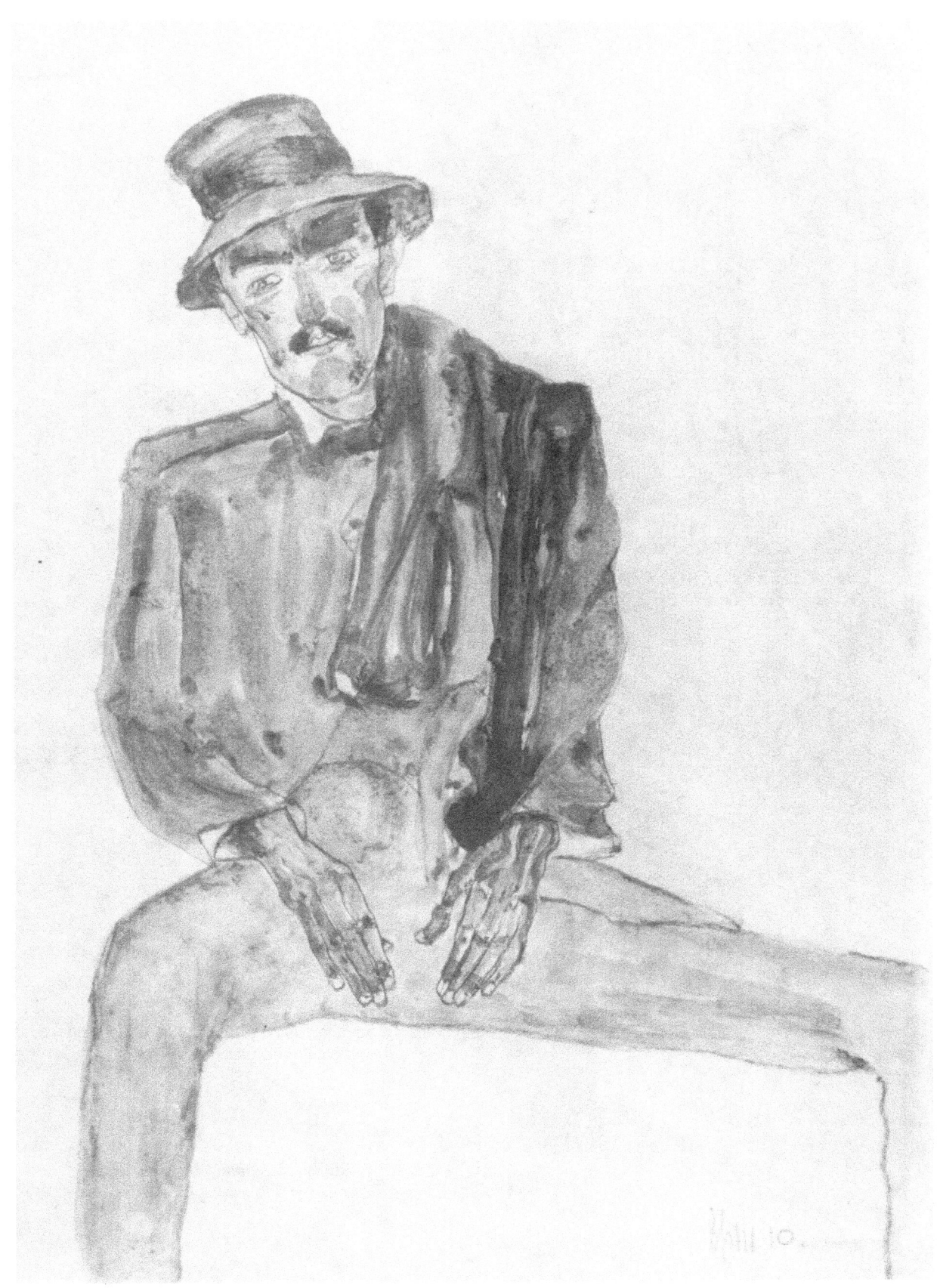

FIG. 52. Schiele, *Study of Anton Peschka Seated*, 1910, black chalk and watercolor.

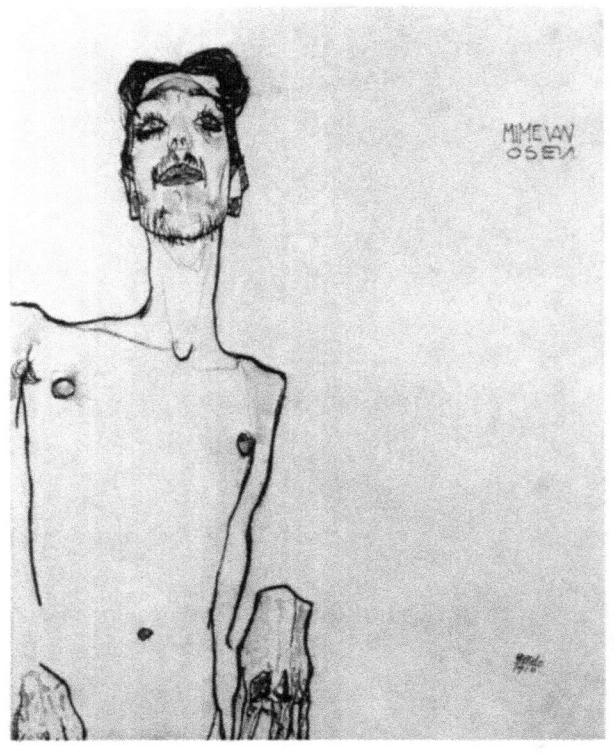

FIG. 53. Schiele, *Study of Mime van Osen Nude with Wrists Raised*, 1910, black chalk and watercolor.

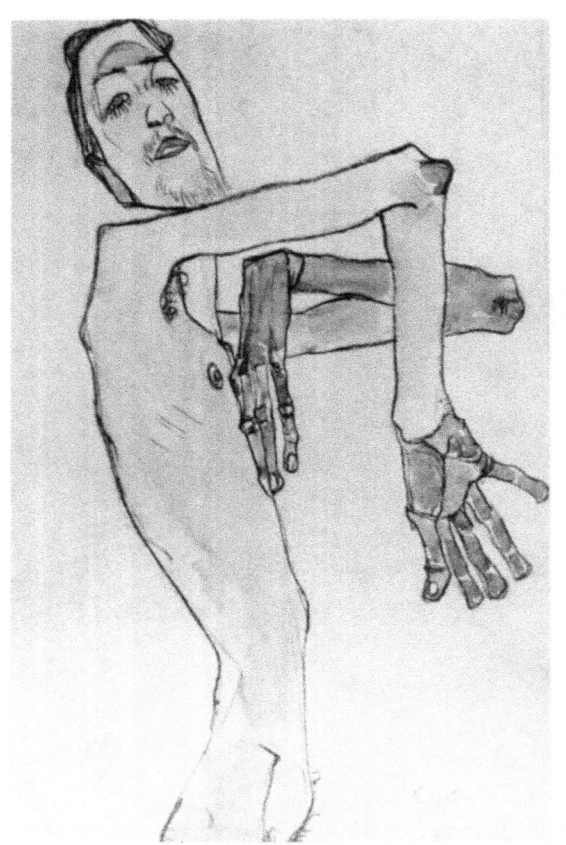

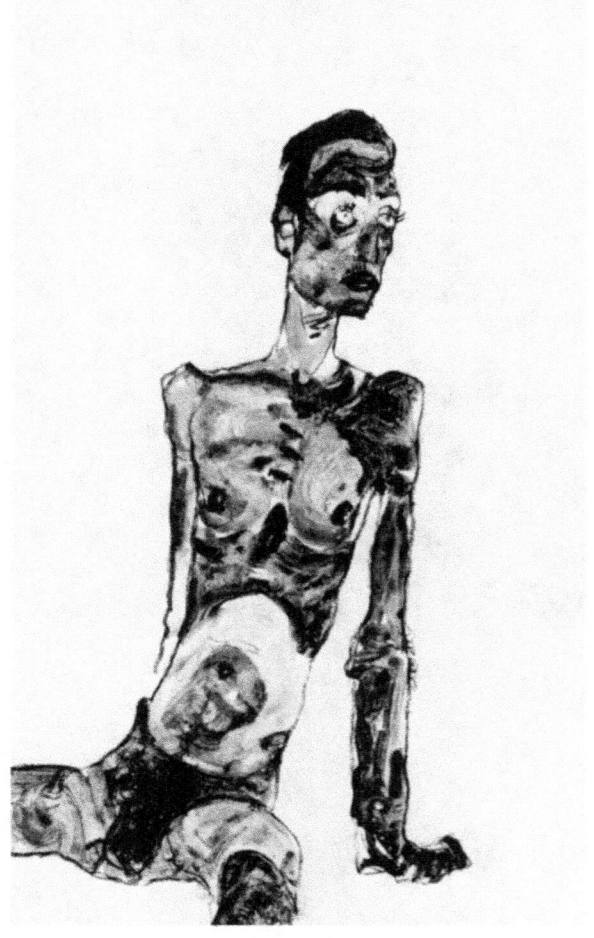

FIG. 55. Schiele, *Study of Mime van Osen Nude, Seated*, 1910, black chalk and watercolor.

FIG. 54. Schiele, *Study of Mime van Osen Nude with Elbows Raised*, 1910, black chalk and watercolor.

played the role of "Man" in the performance of Kokoschka's blood-curdling play *Murderer, Hope of Women* at the Kunstchau's Gartentheater in 1908. It hung next to a sentimental picture by Emil Orlik entitled *On Board, Second Class*, and Schiele's three portraits were flanked by etchings and woodcuts showing peasant scenes and village churches. The Kokoschka and Schiele portraits contrasted strongly with their neighbors and they also contrasted significantly with each other. The impetus of Kokoschka's "mad rush into painting" had swept him far beyond the Wiener Werkstätte vocabulary of his 1908 color lithographs for *The Dreaming Boys*. With startling unexpectedness, Kokoschka had created an Expressionist portrait. *The Trance Player*'s corporeal presentation is illuminated and transcended by an overwhelming subjectivism and psychic intensity. Schiele's Massmann and Peschka pictures, and the portrait of Gerti, are, on the other hand, still consciously within the Klimt format, with typical Jugendstil manipulation of line and surface.

The exposure to foreign artists in the 1909 International Kunstschau sparked significant consequences in the work of the Austrians. Not only the younger men but also mature painters, notably Klimt, were receptive to the powerful artistic stimuli from abroad. It would be an exaggeration to say that all Vienna began painting sunflowers after the impact of Van Gogh, but the appearance of this motif and its continued presence in the works of both Klimt and Schiele is directly traceable to influence of the Dutch painter. Other motifs associated with Van Gogh also inspired a sensitivity to similar subjects: both Klimt and Schiele painted single trees, angular and exquisitely fragile in the northern tradition; Schiele discovered a parallel to the boats at Saintes-Maries in the fat, bulgy fishing boats of Trieste, which he painted in cheerful colors, and he responded to the "Orientalism" of a gabled wooden bridge in Hungary[14] with the same enthusiasm as Van Gogh in his copy of Hiroshige. The early still-lifes of Kokoschka[15] which suddenly appeared along with his portrait oeuvre draw their stylistic and thematic treatment from Van Gogh. In 1911 Schiele paid homage to the Dutch artist by painting a paraphrase (*The Artist's Room in Neulengbach*, K.149) of *The Bedroom at Arles*,[16] which he had admired in the 1909 Kunstschau. Both Kokoschka and Schiele continued to draw inspiration in the use of arbitrary color and free contour from the works of Van Gogh, several of which were now permanently in Vienna. *The Bedroom at Arles* was in the collection of their mutual patron Carl Reininghaus, and other Van Goghs were owned by another mutual patron, Oskar Reichel. Throughout his life Schiele spoke of Van Gogh with admiration (although sometimes with wistful speculation on how nice it would be to have an understanding brother who could support him "as Theo did Vincent"), and in his prison diary of 1912 he contrasted the "stirring reality" of the Dutch painter's *Prisoners at Exercise* with the "theatrical" aspect of Alfred Roller's stage design for Mahler's important revival of *Fidelio*.[17] The impact of Van Gogh on the portraiture of both Schiele and Kokoschka was decisive and will presently be discussed in detail.

Several other foreign artists represented in the 1909 Kunstschau also influenced or served to fortify tendencies in contemporary Viennese painting. Toorop's maxim, paraphrased by the Viennese critic Ludwig Hevesi, that the rediscovery of the soul was the purpose of the new art, fired the imagination of his Austrian admirers, and contained a message for Klimt as well as for Schiele and Kokoschka. The features of Toorop's portraiture which particularly appealed to the Viennese artists were the frontality, the fixed, eerie quality of eyes that stared past the beholder, the enigmatic hand gestures, and the frequent asymmetrical relationship of the figure to its picture space. These qualities were also characteristic of Fernand Khnopff (figure 44), who was immensely popular with the Secession group.[18] Kokoschka and Schiele soon employed many of these elements for an intensified hallucinatory effect in portraiture. One of the major differences in the application of these elements in both Jugendstil and Expressionistic portraiture concerns the *particularity* of the individual portrait. The older tradition, obsessed with the idea of the *femme fatale*, used many of her attributes without discrimination so that Khnopff's relatives, Toorop's apostles, Hodler's fellow artists, and Klimt's society ladies all share certain qualities of sphinxlike mystery, apparent somnambulism, or rigid pensiveness which are not necessarily aspects of the sitters themselves. Although it might be argued, very reasonably, that all of Schiele's and Kokoschka's portraits resemble Schiele and Kokoschka themselves, it is also true that their work, unlike the portraiture of Jugendstil, achieves a distinct individuality in the sitters. Personal characteristics, through graphic or coloristic distortion, receive subjective emphases that often succeed in conveying the psyches of the subjects.

Other foreign artists left their imprint on Vienna more in the realm of subject matter than by stylistic innovation. Barlach's sympathetic portrayal of beggars and peasants touched a responsive chord in the new generation's awareness of and identification with the proletariat. Both Schiele and Kokoschka roamed Vienna in their early years searching for models in the working-class children of the streets. Some of the most compassionate works of both artists are their quick pencil sketches of the big city's gamins. Käthe Kollwitz's stark and tragic graphics were also influential.[19] The tendency of both Schiele and Kokoschka to heighten the realism of their child studies by an austere, selective line that bordered at times on caricature was reinforced by observation of the work of Toulouse-Lautrec, not represented in the 1909 Kunstschau but shown in good quantity that same year by the Miethke Gallery. Of the nineteenth-century masters, Schiele admired Lautrec next only to Van Gogh.[20]

Schiele felt a profound spiritual rapport with Munch. The older painter's sober view of humanity appealed to him, and he was impressed by the allegorical content of his work, especially in the prints, which had had circulation in Vienna since the Secession exhibition[21] of twenty Munch paintings at the end of 1903.[22] For older artists like Albin Egger-Lienz (1868–1926), the "Austrian Hodler," the example of Munch must have provided welcome corroboration in the development of a grave and monumental synthetic style.[23] For the younger generation Munch's themes had special significance. The dual interpretation of woman as something divine and something devouring expressed with such frequency and intensity in Munch's early works found a remarkable counterpart in the young Kokoschka's simultaneous concern with the reverent depiction of Lilith in *The Dreaming Boys* and the presentation of panic-ridden man as victim of woman's blood lust in *Murderer, Hope of Women*.[24] The prolific Austrian graphic artist, Alfred Kubin (1877–1959), working independently at this time in the remote village of Zwickledt, near Passau, also responded to the representation of woman as vampire.[25] For Schiele, four years younger than Kokoschka, this aspect of Munch's art had little appeal. His approach to the theme of woman, as expressed from 1910 on in his hundreds of drawings and watercolors of female nudes, was decidedly aggressive, devoted to the fullest possible exploration of the female as an accessible and erotic object, and alternated between orgiastic sexual participation and isolating masturbation. Death, loneliness, the sleepwalker's trance—these were the themes of Munch that found response in Schiele, still sensitive to the loss of his father. He also began to express these preoccupations in essays, poems, and aphorisms. An early landscape oil, *Girl by the Sea*,[26] recalls Munch's 1895 etching *Summer Night (The Voice)*, and Munch's 1899 lithograph of the painting *Three Stages of Woman* directly inspired a lost project by Schiele, *The Three Mothers*.[27] The far-reaching possibilities of direct expression through pictorial form, as revealed in Munch's prints, were realized in the same year, 1910, by such diverse artists as Schiele, in his row of male portraits, and Umberto Boccioni, the Italian Futurist, in his picture *Mourning*.

The attenuated figure sculptures of Georges Minne (figure 46) at the Kunstschau exerted a decisive influence on the Expressionists. Over fifty years later Kokoschka vividly recalled his first exposure to the Belgian artist:

". . . a small marble figure by George Minne, shown at the second Kunstchau, made a tremendous impression on me: 'Kneeling Boy.' Minne must have had models as skinny as my circus children. I can see his 'Kneeling Boy' before me today—after fifty years. . . . It was from Minne that I took over a preference for these fleshless young Gothic bodies. I was the first to show such models to students and have them draw from them. For the rest, the entire Vienna Kunstgewerbeschule was oriented towards ornament. Nothing but weeds and flowers and tendrils writhing about like worms."[28]

Minne's work had been introduced to Vienna by his friend and collector, Fritz Waerndorfer.[29] Waerndorfer owned drawings, sketchbooks, and sculptures by Minne, and his enthusiasm for the sculptor, who was still relatively unknown even in his native Belgium, was instrumental in the decision of the Secession directors to show fourteen of his sculptures in 1900. This was followed by a feature article and reproductions of his work in the second issue of the 1901 *Ver Sacrum*. Minne was hailed by critics as an "authentic Gothic artist"[30]—an epithet which would soon be applied by the same writers to Schiele. The sculptor's masterpiece, the 1898 *Fountain of Five Boys*, was exhibited at the 1900 Secession show. It was the quintessence of Minne's archaizing art in a Hodleresque repetition of his favorite motif—a gaunt kneeling

youth with arms crossed over his chest and attenuated fingers lightly touching
his shoulders. Soon afterwards the fountain group was acquired by the progressive Folkwang Museum in Hagen, the same museum which gave Schiele
a one-man show in 1913. A copy of one of the fountain's kneeling figures was
bought by the Secession painter, Carl Moll, who proudly included it and a
small Van Gogh portrait[31] in his 1906 painting *Self-Portrait in Atelier* (figure
45).[32] Two statues were bought by Waerndorfer, who exhibited them and
other Minne works in the newly opened (1903) display room of the Wiener
Werkstätte (see figure 20). Four Minne sculptures had been included in the
Secession Klinger-Beethoven exhibition of 1902, and his memorial for the poet
Rodenbach was displayed by the Secession late in the same year.

At the end of 1905 and beginning of 1906 the Miethke Gallery, responsible for so many "firsts" in Vienna at this time, gave a large Minne show, whose
enthusiastic reception by the critics[33] prepared wide public receptivity for the
important showing in the 1909 International Kunstschau. Kokoschka has acknowledged his early debt to Minne. Schiele was so powerfully affected by
the new angular forms and poignant motifs (wounded man, wrestling or
kneeling boys, nuns, mother mourning a dead child) in Minne's work that he
quickly adapted to his own purposes the taut, lean bodies with their evocation
of pathos, as will be observed in his radical self-portraits of 1910. He also directly borrowed motifs[34] and titles.[35] Not even Klimt, whose admiration for
Minne was no secret, proved exempt from influence: the main female form of
his painting *The Friends* (I, 1904–1907) strongly recalls a female figure exhibited by the Belgian sculptor at the 1900 Secession show.[36] Vienna's exposure to foreign artists during the first decade of the twentieth century, culmi-
nating in the ambitious 1909 International Kunstschau, quickened the way to
Expressionism for the younger artists, and also furnished a considerable and
beneficial stimulus for the older generation of Austrian artists.

A letter written by Schiele in 1910 sets forth his enthusiastic hope for a
new International Kunstschau and is an interesting indication of which painters
he considered desirable for inclusion:

> "Why couldn't there be a large International Kunstschau in the Künstlerhaus?
> I have told this to Klimt. For example: each artist has his own hall or his own room
> —Rodin, Van Gogh, Gauguin, Minne, the last ten years. . . . Klimt, Toorop, Stuck,
> Liebermann, Slevogt, Corinth, Mestrovič, etc. Only the *fine* arts. What an uproar
> for Vienna! Catastrophe!"[37]

The insistence on "only the *fine* arts," with its impatient dismissal of the previous Kunstschau inclusion of the arts-and-crafts element so dear to the hearts
of Klimt and Hoffmann, is an accurate reflection of the demise of an older
tradition and the coming of age of a new avant-garde.

1909: Family portraits and self-portraits

Under the impact of the renewed exposure to Klimt in the International
Kunstschau Schiele painted a second and much larger portrait of his sister
Gerti in 1909 (plate 14). This painting is one of Schiele's most elegant and

stylized essays in the Klimtian manner. The structural eloquence of the pose is based exclusively on a decorative contour which contains the ornament as well as the figure. Klimt had developed a similar organic figure "fill," and the silver and red orbs in Schiele's picture reproduce favored Klimtian shapes. These circlets dot the lining of a muff, turned inside out and held by Gerti on her lap. Slat-like bands of green, brown, gold, and red alternate with flowers to form a multi-faceted supporting pedestal for the figure. The major color areas are low-keyed: a black mantle falls from the shoulder, the dress is light brown with touches of pink, the flesh is also light brown and the hair is brown with dark olive-green strokes. The austerity of the colors is reinforced by the withdrawn aspect of the girl, whose face is turned partially away from the beholder and whose eyes are closed as if in daydream. Contemporary photographs of Gerti (plates 11 and 13) shows this same quality of reverie. Schiele has successfully transferred to canvas the features and mannerisms of the fragile young coquette. Several studies for the oil,[38] such as the *Sketch of Gerti Posing with Eyes Closed* (plate 12), trace the evolution of the picture's mood and document Schiele's elongation of the body contour and stylization of the drapery to create a vigorous, continuous silhouette. A preparatory notation shows, interestingly, that the figure was first composed within a narrow panel[39] and the oil itself has lateral additions to the canvas in order to create a large square area. The central placement of the figure within this square is similar to that in Schiele's earlier portrait of Gerti of the same year (plate 6), but the axial orientation is not the same. A slight diagonal determines the figure's position in the first portrait, whereas in the later portrait the rigid frontality of the seated figure, broken only by the turned head, is established by a vertical axis which runs down the center of the figure like a pole. This new placement, with its four elegant successive indentations from pedestal to waist to shoulder to head, effectively transposes Klimt's "spiral stream" to the center of the picture. The negation of Jugendstil asymmetry in favor of concentration on a "charged center" is a new discovery for Schiele. The stark isolation of the figure against a neutral background in both 1909 portraits of Gerti is still however a compositional rather than psychological element; e.g., hands do not yet assume importance. It is in the self-portraits of this period that Schiele first consciously begins to employ stylistic equivalents of emotional states of mind.

In 1909 Schiele painted two major self-portraits: *Self-Portrait Clothed* (plate 16) and *Self-Portrait Nude*[40] (plate 18). Both seem to be in response to the renewed exposure to Klimt, and are the last important works by Schiele which retain allegiance to him. The slim, oblong shape of the canvases[41] is a reflection of the architectonic shapes preferred by the Wiener Werkstätte and additional related mannerisms characterize the earlier *Self-Portrait Clothed*. Still within the Jugendstil formula of dramatic contrasts, large flat surface areas, and decorative silhouettes, it is further embellished by a slim vertical band of rectangles in subdued colors, running down the left side of the painting, like piano keys. Also reminiscent of the Wiener Werkstätte is the reversed T-square which both frames and cuts across Schiele's head and neck. The emphasis on the face and hands, with the blacking-out of all connective forms, recalls Klimt's stunning masterpiece of the same year, *Judith II* (plate 15), on exhibition at the International Kunstschau. In Klimt's work characteristic whiplash tendrils and swirls of clothing isolate the face and bare upper torso from the hands—remarkable for the tense articulation of the claw-like fingers. Tucked away on the lower right is the half-concealed head of Holofernes (considered by some to be a Klimt self-portrait): this may have inspired Schiele to do a sly paraphrase of the painting, with the reversed T-square actually decapitating him (perhaps as a sort of John the Baptist; Klimt's *Judith* was frequently referred to as a "Salome"). Most notably akin to the Klimt picture is Schiele's emphasis, both compositional and coloristic, upon the hands. The fingers are rigidly outspread, the lines in the palm are lightly but minutely indicated in grayish white over garishly rosy flesh, and the mounts are prominent. Such postured use of the hands to suggest inner tension (see also *The Trance Player*, figure 43), and other early portraits by Kokoschka)—soon to become a hallmark of Viennese Expressionism—attests the younger artists' receptivity to the "ugly" in Klimt—that poignant combination of elegance and repulsiveness which is so pronounced an aspect of his allegorical works.

The limpness of the hands in the second and larger self-portrait is as effective as their rigidity in the first. The *Self-Portrait Nude* is an intentionally "shocking" exposure and a provocative juxtaposition of opposites. Schiele stands with his body in profile and his face turned slightly toward the beholder. His long arms hang slackly at his sides and the fingers, flattened against a bit of cloth which covers the penis, bend inward at the first joint of the bright red knuckles. The artist's glance conveys the intense concentration with which he was studying his mirror image and is in contrast to the lethargic attitude of the body. The brow is furrowed and the right eye squints—two characteristics which Schiele repeated in the majority of his self-portraits during the next three years. The dark shock of hair frames his forehead and he sports, for the first time in an oil portrait, a trim moustache (symbol of his new independence?).[42] In effective, almost brutal contrast to the "prettiness" of the flowery support and Wiener Werkstätte style drapery falling down the sides of his body is the emphatic presentation of the jutting ribcage, swelling, relaxed stomach, and pubic hair. Schiele's "inelegant" depiction of himself in favor of a somewhat dramatized anatomical veracity presents undeniable similarities with the elderly male nude in Klimt's 1903–1907 mural *Jurisprudence* (plate 17).[43] This emaciated figure, with its swollen abdomen and pathetically bulging bones, had excited admiration and revulsion in disparate amounts—public indignation finally forced government rejection of *Jurisprudence* along with the other two panels (*Philosophy*, 1900, and *Medicine*, 1901) originally commissioned for the University of Vienna. The notoriety made the works almost a required study for aspiring young painters[44] and Klimt became an even more sought-after portrayer of Viennese society.

Several studies for the 1909 *Self-Portrait Nude* exist, indicating that Schiele moved slowly toward the nudity of the final oil through a process of decorative disrobings.[45] One of the earliest studies, a crayon sketch, *Self-Portrait with Hair Band* (plate 19), shows the artist with his hair bound by a Wiener Werkstätte ribbon. He slouches with one long hand hanging limply and the other raised to his cheek where the weight of his fingers pulls the skin down underneath one eye. This gesture becomes one of Schiele's favorite contrivances in self-portraiture and appears as late as 1915 in the great double self-portrait *Soaring* (figure 106). In contrast to pointing directly to the breast—a traditional *Ecce Homo* pose to draw attention to one's own suffering—Schiele's gesture implies a private, and perhaps unsolvable, symbolism. The frequent occurrence of drawing attention to the eye with a V-shaped gesture of the hand certainly functions on one level as a second and "secret" signature, contained in the pun implicit in the artist's name ("schielen" means "to squint" in German) and remarked upon by contemporary hostile critics:

"That just in our day and age an artist exists whose name is Schiele is probably no accident. He is still squinting at things which others already see. But squinting is exactly suitable to this particular artist."[46]

In later self-portraits and photographs this "signature" gesture is expanded to one in which the fingers are spread in a V-shape over the mouth to frame pursed lips, at the same time still pulling the flesh down underneath one eye (see plate 32, and figure 79). In view of Schiele's lifelong exploration of and fascination by all aspects of erotica, such gestures could have held multiple significance for him.[47] Perhaps the meaning to which he himself gave the most value is that which springs most readily to the eye of the modern beholder: the inescapable drawing of attention to the self—a bold and unusual exhibitionism. Certainly Schiele must be placed along with Van Gogh, Munch, and Picasso, among those creators whose psycho-sexual history is patently present, if never fully explainable, in their art and directly affects its content and form.

In summary, the most startling feature of Schiele's second self-portrait of 1909 is the nudity. There is no reference to his identity as an artist. The collar and cravat of the Academy self-portraits are absent; the association with Klimt indicated in the 1909 pen drawing *Two Men* is not evoked—Schiele is alone and naked. He had been praised by Klimt, he had broken with the Academy and founded his own art group, and he had exhibited as an independent artist in the great International Kunstschau of 1909. For the nineteen-year-old Schiele the establishment of his status as an artist appeared accomplished. Now his thoughts turned towards himself and the recognition of that self by his colleagues. He returned to the portrait row of fellow artists which he had begun before the 1909 Kunstschau.

1910: MORE PORTRAITS OF FELLOW ARTISTS

Two studies of Schiele's old Klosterneuburg friend Max Kahrer, a watercolor (plate 20) and a black chalk drawing (plate 21), already indicate what would soon be an active rejection of the Klimt format. The basic step was away from the asymmetrical, profile composition of the earlier Neukunstgruppe portraits (Faistauer, Massmann, Peschka, and Löwenstein), and toward the central or frontal (or both) disposition of subject which had already been partially essayed in the two portraits of Gerti. The black chalk portrait of Kahrer[48] incorporates many features which Schiele developed later that same year in a series of oil portraits. The subject is seated in the central part of the picture, without any background accessories or indication of support, and he faces the beholder, in unseeing meditation. The hands, not so much enlarged or deformed as compositionally and calligraphically emphasized, have an interpretive character of their own. Schiele had an affectionate regard for Kahrer, whom he once described with tender mockery as "that grumpy old Kahrer, who speaks as little as I do."[49] The thumb-concealing clasped hands reflect Kahrer's consistent modesty and passivity, even when his work was criticized unfavorably. Schiele found this quality lovable but irritating, and once exclaimed with grieved exasperation: "If he would at least defend himself! Occasionally let himself get thoroughly angry! But he does not do this . . . only defends himself through passive tolerance. . . . Poor, dear fellow!"[50]

The impression of pathos in the chalk portrait of Kahrer is also present in the watercolor study. The rumpled hair, disheveled beard, and baggy jacket, all in broad strokes of blue-purple, brown-red, and violet wash, contrast with the delicately penciled face and help emphasize the isolation suggested in the quiet self-containment of the folded arms. A sense of pathos is one of the distinctive features of Expressionist portraiture, and of Viennese Expressionism in particular. Although Chaïm Soutine's haunting works might be described as "distressing," it is unlikely that the various page boys and choirboys he portrayed would all have experienced psychic or physical traumas. The pictures by Kokoschka and Schiele however could be partly characterized as portraits of "distressed" or "disturbed" persons, almost as if these were the subjects specifically sought by the Viennese artists. Lovis Corinth's extraordinary *Portrait of Eduard Graf Keyserling* (1900), although not among his canvases exhibited in the 1909 International Kunstschau, may surely be considered a prototype of this sort of tragic portraiture. Within the Austrian tradition itself, Anton Romako's hypersensitive portraits had served as models for Klimt's own paintings of the high-strung, inbred, overrefined, aristocratic ladies of Viennese society. This element of temperamental hysteria, already fastidiously fixed by Klimt in a "preservative" of encasing ornament, became part of the elusive psychic "reality" sought by Vienna's Expressionist painters and scientists of the psyche.

The Poldi Lodzinsky commission

The new goal in portraiture became penetration rather than static display, exposure rather than embellishment. What is of extreme interest in Schiele's art is that he applied his "psychic drill" to responsive subjects from both sides of the tracks. His colleague Anton Faistauer rightly pointed out that if Klimt could be considered the portrayer of the moneyed society that dwelt within the magic circle of the Ringstrasse, Schiele could qualify as the painter of the city's proletariat—discovering his models on the streets of Vienna's outlying districts.[51] Often these models remain anonymous: small children, coaxed to pose for "just a few minutes,"—boys and girls with thin, undernourished, white bodies and the pinched, wizened faces of world-weary adults. But whether in a commissioned work such as the oil *Portrait of Poldi Lodzinsky* (plate 23), or in a single watercolor study—representative of a whole series of similar works—of an unidentified street child such as the *Girl in Black* (plate 22), both of 1910,[52] Schiele's aim was the same—to plumb and lay bare the psyche. The basic formula was: an "existential" or environmentless isolation of the figure, a composition stressing a central axis, frontality, a close focus that cuts off part of the lower body, and a predominance of the eyes and hands. Schiele's insistence upon introducing a "disquieting" element, such as oversized, gnarled fingers, is particularly trenchant in the Poldi portrait. It was commissioned by Josef Hoffmann's Wiener Werkstätte, which had been entrusted with the entire decoration of the Palais Stoclet in Brussels, and was intended for use in a stained glass window of that building. Klimt had worked on a decorative frieze for the Stoclet dining room for five years (*ca.* 1905–1909; first mounted in 1911), and Schiele's contribution was expected to be in the same elegant Werkstätte tradition. Schiele's work was never executed, very probably because, despite its Jugendstil trapping of the bright multi-colored shawl, the portrait was far too intense for the delicate and restrained spirit of the Palais Stoclet interior. The deliberate, adamantine elongation of the face and hands and the stiffness of the pose must have seemed inadmissably "ugly" in comparison with the rhythmic delicacy of Klimt's frieze. But these very traits add to the ambiguity (the lip-shaped opening formed by the two pressed-together thumbs functions discreetly but unmistakably as a vulval reference[53]) and epigrammatic qualities which place this picture among the "disturbing-disturbed" portraits of the Expressionist generation.

LATER PORTRAITS OF THE NEUKUNSTGRUPPE

The cheerful Wiener Werkstätte colors of the Poldi Lodzinsky portrait were exchanged for restrained, low-keyed ochres, browns, and reds on white in the austere *Portrait of the Painter Karl Zakovsek* (plate 25). A preparatory sketch (plate 24) exhibits a candid and intimate search for the eloquent form achieved in the painting and reflects Schiele's closer acquaintance and more relaxed relationship with the sitter, a fellow member of the Neukunstgruppe. The areas emphasized in the study are the emaciated face and bony hands. In the final oil these expressive areas, distributed on either side of the centrally placed body, produce a wavering diagonal countermovement operating as a handsome equivalent to the frail figure of the sitter, whose left hand droops pathetically like a broken wing and whose fleshless right hand appears ready to snap under the weight of the immense head which it supports. Unmistakable is the tribute to Van Gogh's *Portrait of Dr. Gachet* (plate 26). Although this was not among the paintings on display during the 1909 International Kunstschau, Schiele owned a copy of the Meier-Graefe monograph on Van Gogh (1910) in which the Gachet portrait appeared as a plate.[54]

The effect of pathos achieved in Schiele's picture by the manipulation of exaggerated natural forms is specifically enhanced, as in the preliminary study, by one commanding feature: the exaggerated elongation of one shoulder. This "extended shoulder" device may be observed in many Viennese Expressionist portraits and seems to have made its debut at the International Kunstschau where both Kokoschka (*The Trance Player*, figure 43) and Schiele (*Gerti Schiele*, plate 14) used it to great advantage. In the Zakovsek portrait this feature is not only eloquent in itself but adroitly relates two isolated elements—the head and the hand.

One of the younger Viennese artists who early adopted the extended shoulder device was the versatile and largely neglected painter Max Oppenheimer, known as Mopp (1885–1954). Five years older than Schiele, Mopp had finished his studies at the Vienna Academy in 1903 and had already exhibited a self-portrait in the 1908 Kunstschau as a member of the avant-garde group encouraged by Klimt. By 1909 Mopp was quick to follow Kokoschka's lead in the new extravagant "pathological" portrait, as can be seen by comparing their two separate paintings, both made that year, of Vienna's beloved bohemian poet, Peter Altenberg (plates 27a and 27b).[55] The influence of Van Gogh is attested to in both works through the existential concentration on the subject, the close focus, the surface importance of the brushwork as a tactile feature with emotional value, and the application of arbitrary colors to suggest a psychological intensity. Much of the boldness of Kokoschka's more radical portrayal is due to his disregard of traditional painterly values, but the more technically conservative Mopp portrait compares favorably from the point of view of the Expressionist syntax.

Both portraits employ a "body halo" or "astral glow" which runs its own expressive course around the contour of the figure. This feature, although much heightened by the Viennese artists, also finds an immediate precedent in the self-portraits of Van Gogh. Its adoption by Gerstl, Kokoschka, Mopp, Schiele, and other artists of the Viennese Expressionism circle (but not characteristic of German Expressionism portraits in general) may however also indicate a local response to a theory discussed by a man whose writings on occult color notions eventually influenced Kandinsky[56]—the Austrian philosopher and Goethe scholar, Rudolf Steiner (1861–1925). Steiner had spent eleven years in Vienna as a student, and, although he moved to Germany in 1890, his book *Theosophie*, published in 1904, was enormously popular in both Germany and Austria and was already in its third edition by 1910.[57] Building upon the theosophy of Madame Blavatsky and the specific color keys offered by the team of Annie Besant and C. W. Leadbeater, Steiner proposed a theory of psychic vibrations in which thoughts and feelings assumed definite colors and forms to create, around the body of each person, a "human aura"—a field of supersensitivity, an "astral glow." This astral glow was visible to the clairvoyant and to the developed "spiritual eye." In painting, of course, the insertion of such an aura or distinct area of paint between the figure and its background served to elucidate and project the subject and was not unknown as a technical effect in previous periods of art, acquiring in some instances a symbolical significance, as for example in the Christian aureole and mandorla. In other cases, as with the portraits of Rembrandt, the painterly light contributed both chiaroscuro relief and subjective mood. The function of the Expressionist body halo, as inherited from Munch and Van Gogh but already germinally present in Vienna in the luminous glow of Anton Romako's works, was to make an emotional extension of and comment upon the inner state of the sitter as "perceived" by the hypersensitive spiritual eye of the painter. The aura could also transmit its own emotional energy into the surrounding background space by means of swatches of paint and bundles of incised lines or scratches (see especially the portraits of Kokoschka). Schiele's use of Steiner's phrase, "my astral light,"[58] leaves no doubt as to its significance for him, and the aura soon became a hallmark of his portraits. As early as 1910 Schiele's friend, the artist Paris von Gütersloh, wrote about the "atmospheric impression" in Schiele's portraiture.[59] Schiele's calligraphic development of this basically painterly instrument is one characteristic that distinguishes his portraits from those of the more coloristically inclined Kokoschka and Mopp.

As an indication of which contemporaries he admired, it is interesting that Schiele, in 1910, sought out Mopp—another portrait painter, and one who had gained entry into the world of such differing representatives of Viennese cultural life as Peter Altenberg and Arnold Schönberg, whose portraits he had painted in 1909 (see plate 27a and figure 122) and Arthur Schnitzler, whom he painted in 1910. According to Mopp[60] Schiele suddenly appeared in his atelier one day—solemn-eyed, and with the close-cropped head of an ascetic—and announced that he would like to show him his paintings. Mopp obligingly followed Schiele back to his small fifth-story studio where mountains of drawings rose from the floor. He looked carefully at the paintings, which struck him as bizarre and ornamental, but containing an intensity that seemed somehow related to his own work. When he expressed this opinion, Schiele replied, "That is why I came to you." Their first meeting turned into a marathon of two days and three nights during which the two young men roamed the city and its surrounding hills and avidly exchanged ideas on art. Within a few weeks of their meeting each did a portrait of the other. Schiele's was in black chalk and watercolor (plate 27c) and Mopp's was an oil (plate 27d).[61] They are excellent examples of the two contrasting approaches to Expressionism in Vienna—the linear, as represented by Schiele and Gütersloh, and the painterly, as used by Mopp, Faistauer, Wiegele, Kolig, Felix Albrecht Harta, Johannes Fischer, and Kokoschka. Schiele's study of Mopp depends on the incisive power of a continuous, dramatic contour line. The compatibility of this Jugendstil trademark with Schiele's own graphic propensity accounts not only for its persistence in the artist's restless search for new form, but provides a key to understanding his unique brand of Expressionism. Color plays a substantial but accessory role, filling rather than creating the form. The garish yellow-greens of the face and hands intensify the black of the suit, but all the colors adhere strictly to the silhouette of the figure. The accentuation of the hand is also present in Mopp's portrait of Schiele, in which the elongated fingers of the left hand rest lightly on the rigid right, whose paired and spread fingers are locked in one of Schiele's gestures—not "secret" this time, but rather, according to Mopp, an expression of pure disgust upon hearing what low prices their drawings, which Mopp had been trying to peddle, had fetched. An animated shoulder silhouette distinguishes both portraits and Mopp's version augments the graphic activity by the use of a body glow of varying width and intensity that encircles the figure. Schiele's gaunt appearance in this portrait is a true reflection of his actual undernourishment at this time and not just the result of Mopp's usage of the pathetic. Schiele's drawing, of compositional and emotional intensity, manages to suggest Mopp's well-known obsession with personal elegance.[62]

The fact that an exaggerated sort of psychosomatic (or "psychological") portrait, as developed by Gerstl, Mopp, and especially Kokoschka, had already been in existence in Vienna for a good two years before Schiele's fully awakened interest in the subject, has not previously been emphasized with regard to Schiele's work. Schiele was by no means the "inventor" of Expressionist portraiture in Vienna; rather, he shared in that legacy of hypersensitivity to the neurotic which extended from Romako through Klimt, and which during his own lifetime and in his own city would see exploration of the psyche legitimized as a science.

The alacrity of Schiele's response to the unmasking approach to portraiture is evident in his further portraits of his future brother-in-law, Anton Peschka, one of the original members of the Neukunstgruppe. The large oil portrait of Peschka which Schiele had exhibited in the 1909 Kunstschau (plate 10) had been very much within the Klimt format. Comparison of a charcoal sketch of Peschka (figure 47) done towards the end of 1909 with a contemporary photograph (figure 48) points up Schiele's strong instinct for psychological dramatization. The designations "mild" for the photograph and "sinister" for the portrait sketch are perhaps too sweeping, but the conversion of the amiable, easy-going painter into a person whose physiognomy denotes strength and powers of concentration (by means of the heightened forehead, arched brows, firm jaw, powerful nose, and recessed eye) does represent a remarkable pictorial transformation which however still preserves an almost mirrorlike fidelity.

Schiele's final portrait of Peschka, a watercolor of early 1910 (figure 52), extends far beyond creative verisimilitude. In a frontal splay-legged posture reminiscent of Van Gogh's *The Zouave* (figure 51),[63] Peschka sits relaxed, his head tilted to one side and his hands hanging flaccidly across his legs.[64] He wears the tall, broad-brimmed painter's hat, and an overcoat is slung across his left shoulder. In contrast to the capable but unimaginatively literal portrait of Peschka in almost the same pose drawn by a mutual colleague, R. Vogl (figure 49), Schiele's picture shows no explanatory support but allows the pose to operate autonomously, concentrating attention upon form and silhouette. An inner modeling of the "soapy" application favored by Schiele at this time distributes black heightenings along the clothes and flesh, and the gnarled hands are shown in vivid, amplified detail. The selectivity of Schiele's exaggeration of natural forms to achieve an intense psychological presence is set into instructive relief by a further comparison with a watercolor study of an old man, also done in 1910, by an artist unknown to Schiele at this time—the Viennese military painter Hugo Bouvard (figure 50).[65] Bouvard's portrait is remarkable in many aspects and much of its initial impact of almost Expressionist starkness is due to elements present also in the Schiele portrait: the compelling frontality, lack of supporting environment, emphasis on the hands, legs truncated by the lower edge of the painting, and forceful statement of form through its vivacious silhouette. The areas between the arms are employed as positive elements as are the vigorous interior modeling strokes of the brush. Close scrutiny of Bouvard's portrait however reveals nothing more than a powerful realism—a realism concerned primarily with outward appearances. Bouvard's objective picture is fully within the tradition of Academic realism and continues the naturalistic tradition of Menzel, Trübner, and Leibl in Germany, and of Carl Schuch and Rudolf von Alt in Austria.

The final, logical step in Schiele's subjective realism occur in his studies of a sixth member of the Neukunstgruppe, the "theater" painter, Mime van Osen (figures 53, 54 and 55). The figure is now nude. Exposure of the sitter's psyche depends upon a corresponding exposure of his body—introducing an extraordinary quality of vulnerability into Schiele's austere format. Osen, one of the original signers of the 1909 Pisko contract, was an ingratiating rascal of the most colorful sort, and his aggressive, magnetic personality spellbound the young Schiele during their first years of acquaintance.[66] He had once worked for the Austrian Lloyd and thus been able to travel without cost to Constantinople, an experience that provided him with a springboard for countless stories of vagabond journeys through the Orient. Osen's hero was Rimbaud, whose poetry he could quote from memory and whose life, travels, and sexual predilections he attempted to emulate. It was from Osen that Schiele learned of the Rimbaud poem, *Le Bateau Ivre*, a German translation of which Schiele memorized and often recited for his friends.[67] Osen represented much that Schiele was himself too shy to do, and the naked strutting and extrovert mimicry recorded in most of his portraits of Osen are reflective of the model's own irrepressible exhibitionism and interest in pathological expression.[68] The achievement of new form and psychological effects in the portraits of Peschka and Osen encouraged Schiele to return to the probing of himself—the cheapest and most available model. The nude self-portrait would absorb much of Schiele's painterly attention during the years 1910 and 1911.

Along with the other members of the Neukunstgruppe, and following close upon the vanguard of Gerstl and Kokoschka, Schiele had by the end of 1909 completely shaken off or transformed two separate styles of portraiture. He had rejected the Academy tradition, within which he had been trained, for the avant-garde idiom of Klimt, the vocabulary of which he had at first merely repeated but then employed creatively in a new syntax. Small wonder that by the time of the December showing of the Neukunstgruppe at the Pisko Salon, Vienna's critics bemoaned the disappearance from Schiele's work of the "silver Klimt" and decried the "purposeful intonation of the ugly or morbid, the outrageous gesticulations, and completely unnatural use of color."[69] The imputation of scandal associated with this new "ugly" art of Schiele and his Neukunstgruppe circle is recalled by one of the visitors to the Pisko exhibition, the Austrian poet and playwright, Max Mell. Over fifty years later, he still remembered the excitement caused by this group:

"In those days there was a municipal jury of art, and I served on it with the architect Joseph Hoffmann. It awarded prizes in the various arts and encouraged artists. But there was an atmosphere of notoriety connected with the Neukunstgruppe of Schiele—it was not, unfortunately, the kind of group to which a civic prize could be awarded, not in the Emperor Franz Josef's Vienna!"[70]

CHAPTER III

1910: The Radical Portraits and Self-Portraits—Into the Void

THE GREAT NUDE PORTRAIT SERIES: SELF-PORTRAITS AND GERTI

WHEN he was twenty Egon Schiele painted three major self-portraits in rapid succession: *Self-Portrait Kneeling with Raised Hands* (figure 56), *Self-Portrait Standing with Hands on Hips* (figure 58), and *Self-Portrait Sitting with Raised Arms* (figure 59).[1] These portraits are remarkable for several reasons. First, for sheer size: they constitute the largest canvases yet attempted by the artist. Up to this time his largest work had been the second 1909 "flowery pedestal" portrait of Gerti (plate 14), which measured 55¼ x 55⅛ inches.[2] The *Self-Portrait Sitting with Raised Arms* is 59¾ x 59 inches and the other two, although now lost, may be presumed to have been of like size, since they are similar in format and since all three nude self-portraits, together with a companion nude portrait of Gerti, immediately went into the collection of the industrialist Carl Reininghaus, an avid collector of "sensational" pictures, who later wanted Schiele to paint a lifesize mural of erotic themes for his elegant Vienna flat in the Schmalzhofgasse.[3] A second noteworthy feature of these self-portraits is that the stylistic devices of Klimt, still traceable in Schiele's 1909 works, have been discarded and an independent artistic idiom initiated. The mellifluous Jugendstil contour line is now a surgical knife and the Art Nouveau dream wakes to oppressive reality, made inescapable by a sense of overbearing physical presence. Taut, gesticulating, and emotionally charged, the figures are in complete contrast to the slyly exposed, flaccid body of Schiele's 1909 *Self-Portrait Nude* (plate 18), with its accompaniment of Wiener Werkstätte drapery and flowery support. The new bodies look as fleshless as x-rays and seem barely able to contain their straining skeletons.

These skeletal ensembles present a further singular aspect of the series:

what now constitutes a self-portrait for Schiele has radically changed. It is no longer the face, or half torso, but the entire body that demands portrayal. To reveal the psyche now requires, for Schiele, literal revelation of the body. Is this nudity exhibitionism or exposure? Or both? Projected with poster-like clarity, the bodies are silhouetted as brittle solid objects against an empty area that functions less as a neutral background and more as the foil of a Void. The potentially corrosive *Angst* of this Nothingness (the "chasm" sensed by Rilke behind Van Gogh's figures and objects) is kept at bay by a powerful physical vibrancy. Bony bulges erupt along the flung-out shoulders of the standing figure; thorny nodes break the straight torso, thigh, and knee lines of the kneeling figure; and stretched flesh duplicates the jagged structure of its skeleton in the seated figure which is painted against an electrifying yellow ground, the chosen void against which Schiele has elected to examine the self, out of context, with abandoned egocentricity.

A watercolor study for the kneeling self-portrait (figure 57) first comprehends the expressive quality of this new angular silhouette and indicates to what extent it was later enhanced through the extreme figure stylization in the oils. In the seated self-portrait oil, the abdomen takes on a hard, circular shape, indented like some resistant metal between the sharp ridges of the pelvic bones. In all four versions the "electrified" hair stands away from the head, and the outspread limbs heighten a sense of physical presence and contribute to the powerful emotional intensity set up by the vibration between void and solid. These stylistic effects serve Schiele's new concept of self-portraiture. There is now no interest in indicating the artist's connection with his work, with another artist, or with society. The content is self; there is no frame of reference except self. And the achievement of a naturalistic physical likeness is not the objective. Instead, Schiele is concerned with *what happens* to his physical likeness as the impact of his inner feelings and sensations is registered upon it. In the scores of self-portrait studies that preceded these oils, Schiele allows and even encourages himself to become gripped by such powerful emotions that his very physiognomy is affected.

The association with the vagabond painter, Osen, to whom no secret of psyche or body was sacred, probably hastened Schiele's discovery of the rich motif of the naked self. Nevertheless it must be asked why Schiele's work assumed such imperious intensity at this time, and how he fashioned the new artistic vocabulary called for by this concentrated vision of himself. There are several external and internal explanations. One is the concern with self that prevailed in turn-of-the-century Vienna. When Schiele, at sixteen, left the small provincial villages which had comprised his world, he came to a city which was the intellectual stronghold and crossroads of Central Europe—a metropolis however whose spokesmen and citizens, in the face of social disaster, were plunged into a last, insistent commitment to the pleasure principle. Living in the same city, moving in the same environment, and receptive to the same stimuli as Otto Weininger and Sigmund Freud, Schiele partook in that general phenomenon of preoccupation with the psyche. Schiele's self-

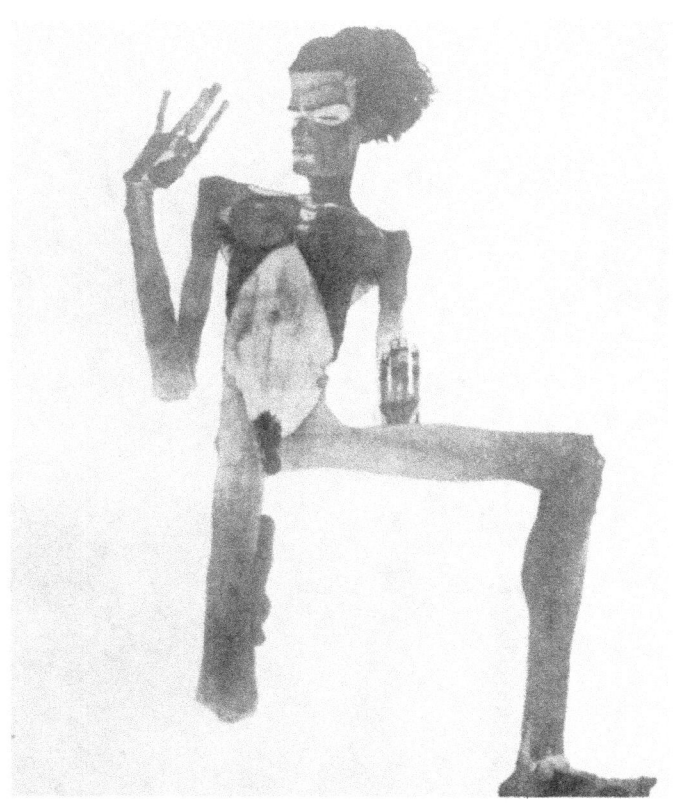

FIG. 56. Schiele, *Self-Portrait Kneeling with Raised Hands*, 1910, oil.

FIG. 57. Schiele, *Study for Self Portrait Kneeling with Raised Hands*, 1910, black chalk and watercolor.

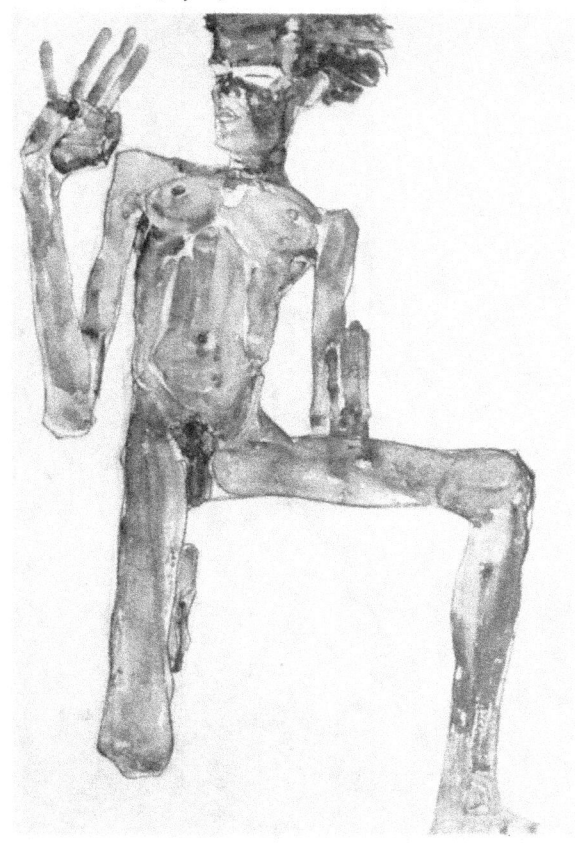

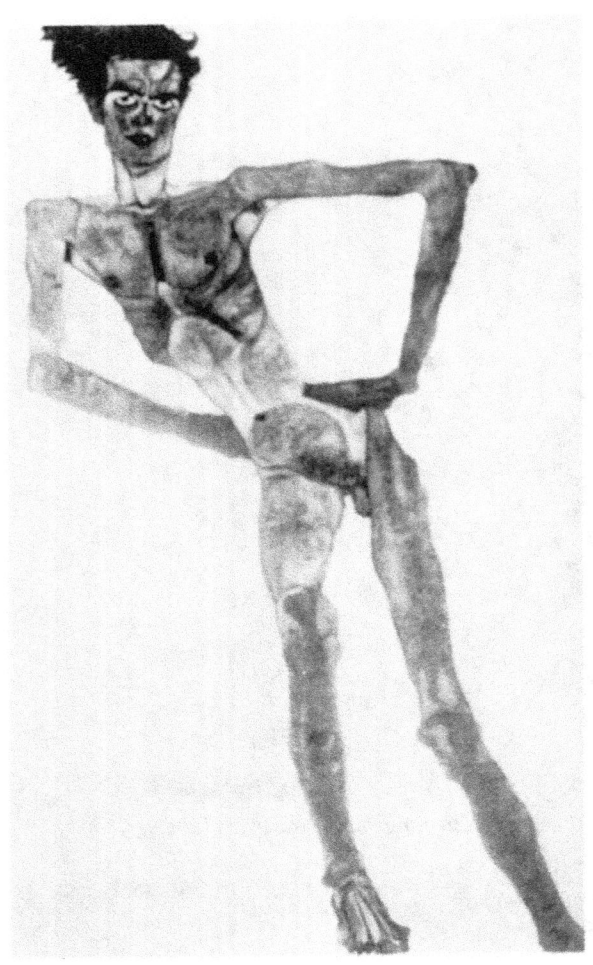

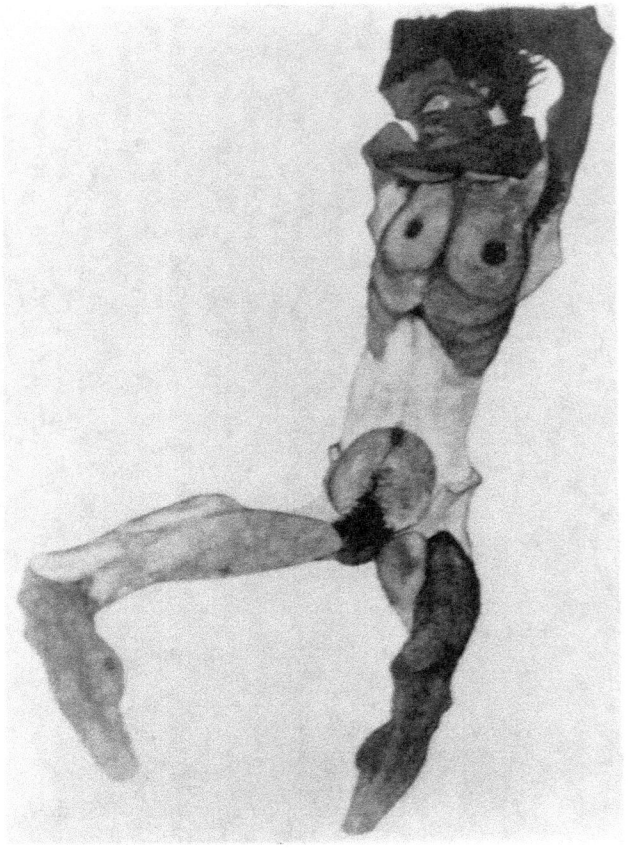

FIG. 59, Schiele, *Self-Portrait Sitting with Raised Arms*, 1910, oil.

FIG. 58. Schiele, *Self-Portrait Standing with Hands on Hips*, 1910, oil.

FIG. 60. Max Klinger, *Christ on Mount Olympus*, 1897, oil.

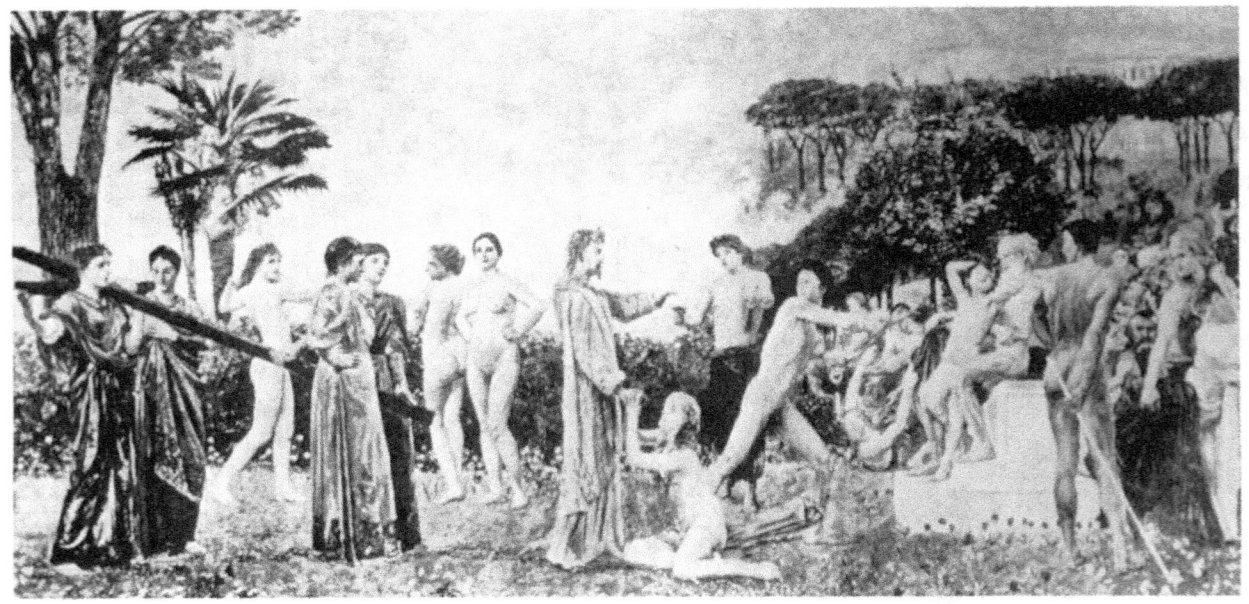

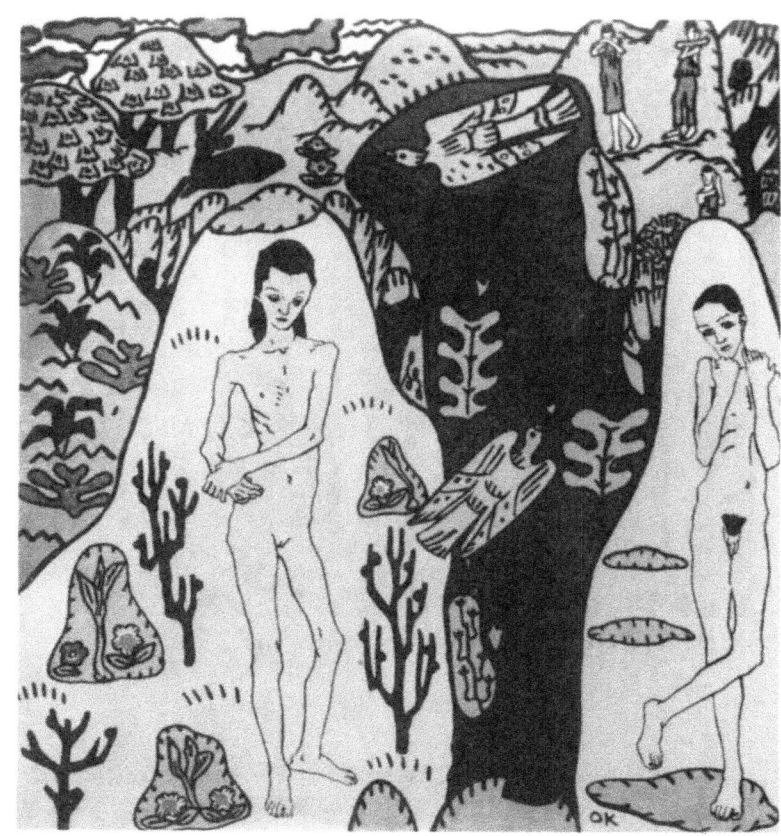

FIG. 61. Kokoschka, illustration from the book *The Dreaming Boys*, 1908, color lithograph.

FIG. 62. Ferdinand Hodler, *Spring*, 1901, oil.

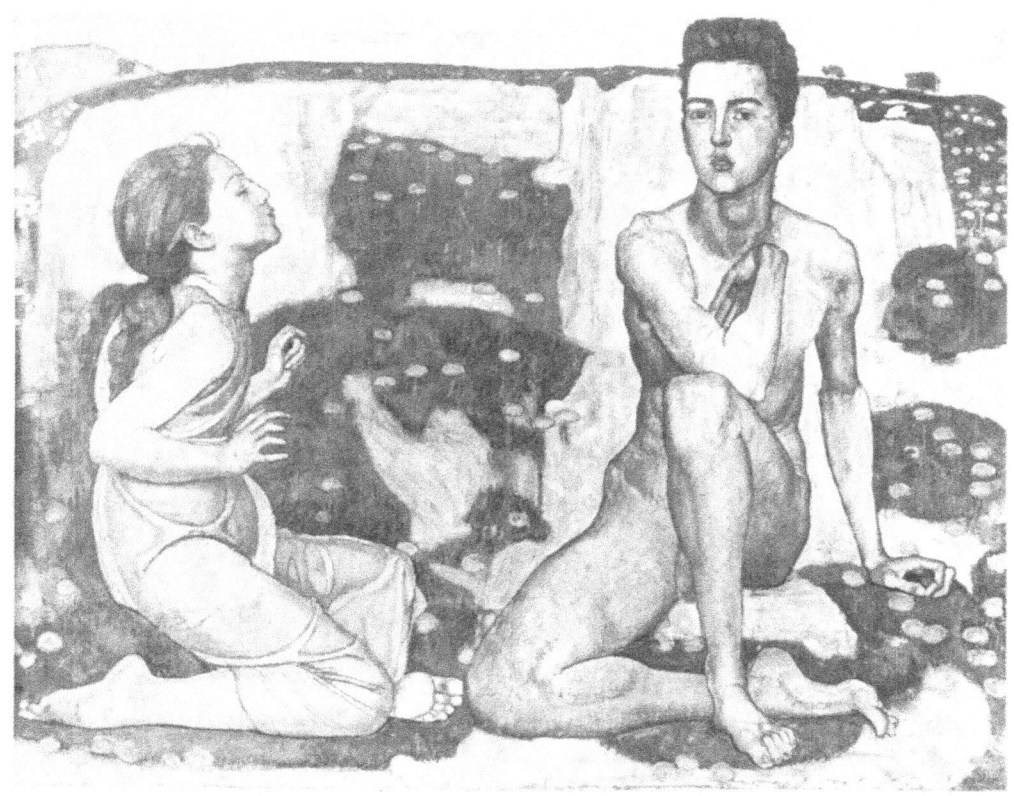

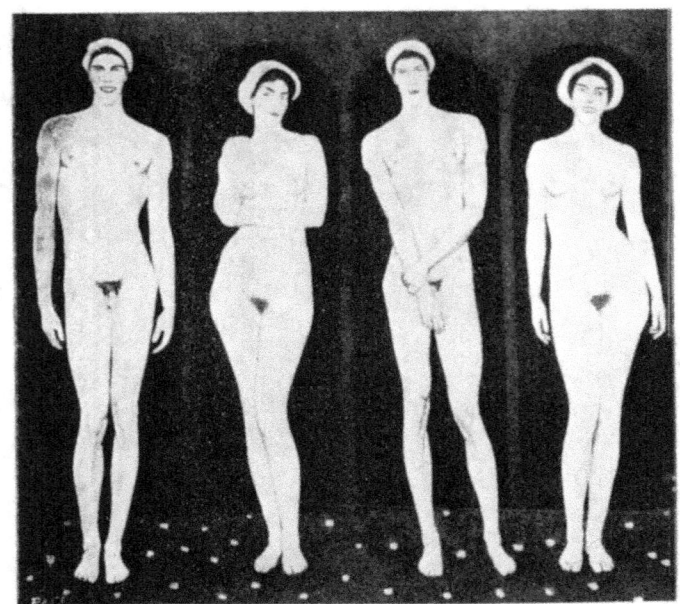

FIG. 63. Ernesto de Fiori, *Mural, ca.* 1908–1909, oil.

FIG. 64. Richard Gerstl, *Self-Portrait Nude*, 1908, oil.

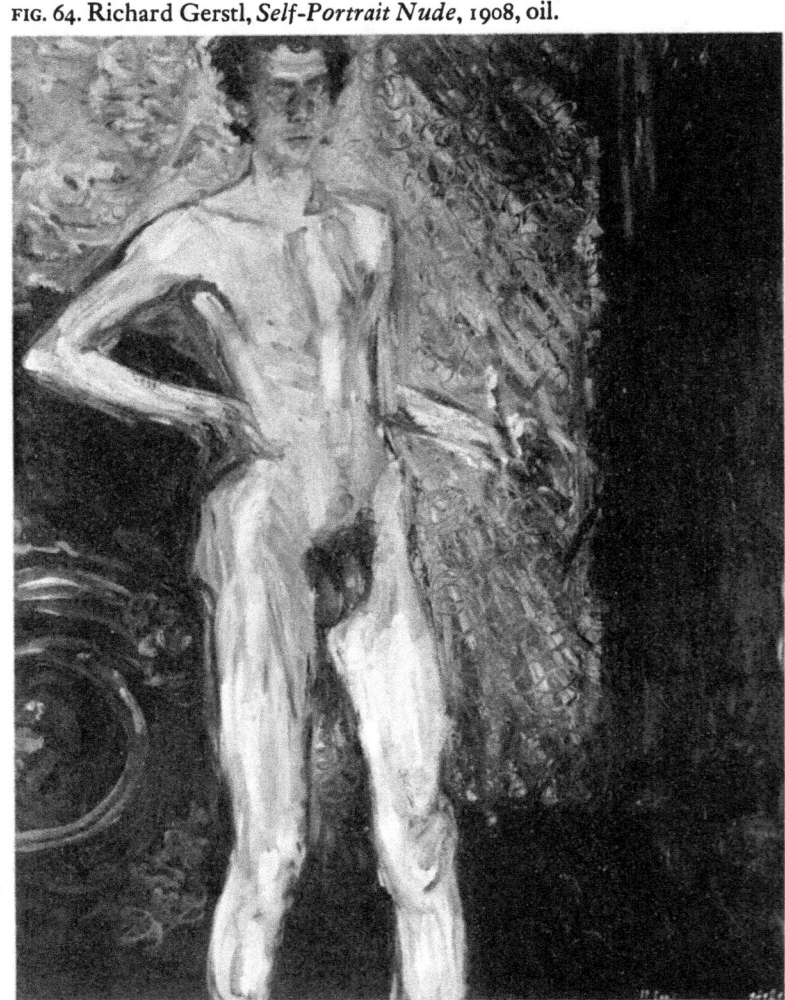

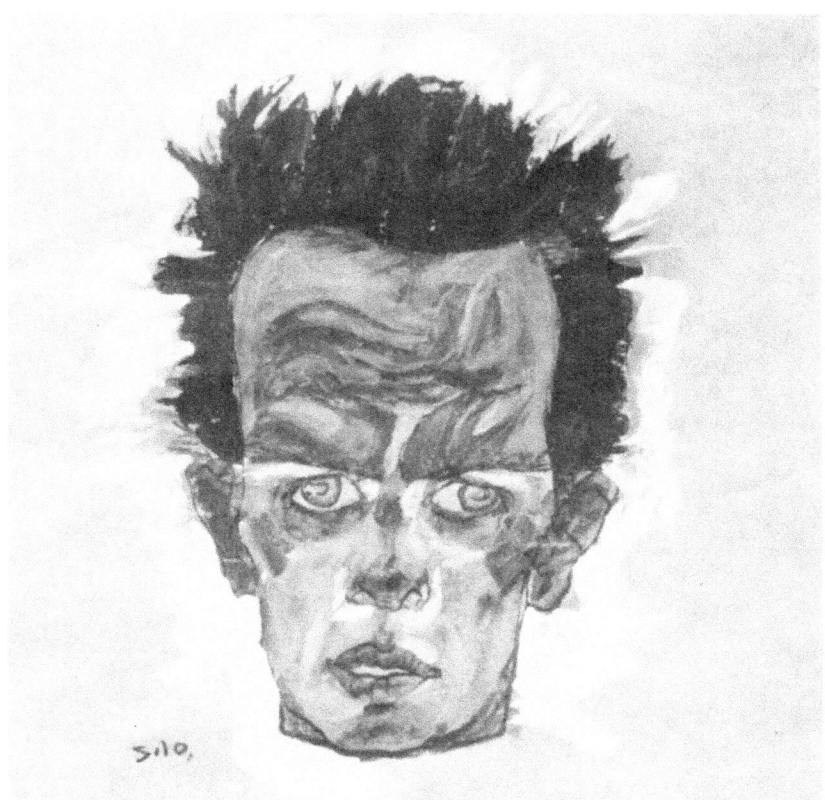

FIG. 65. Schiele, *Self Portrait with Wrinkled Forehead*, 1910, black chalk, watercolor, and gouache.

FIG. 66. Schiele with wrinkled forehead, 1914 (photograph by Anton Josef Trčka).

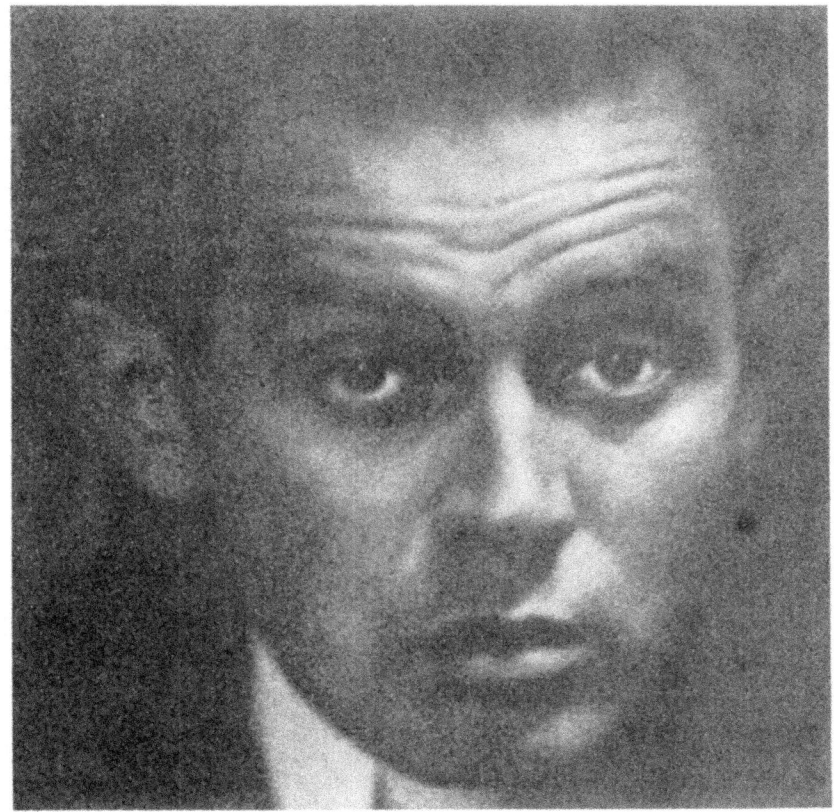

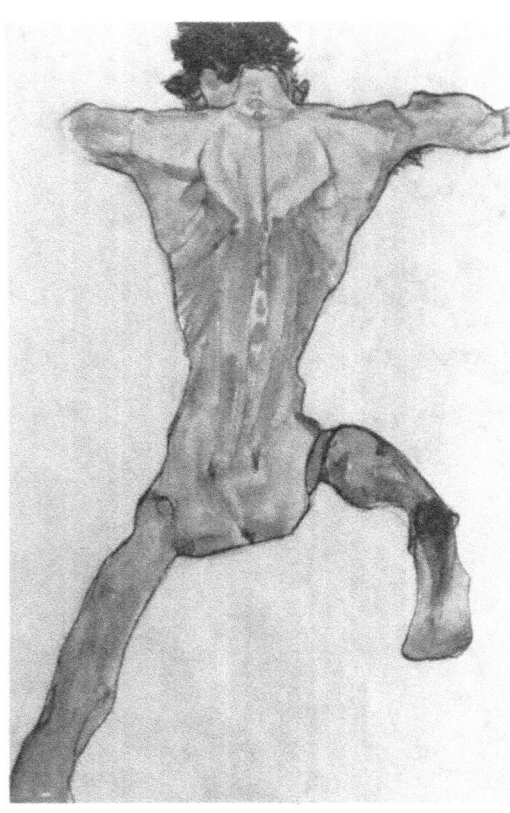

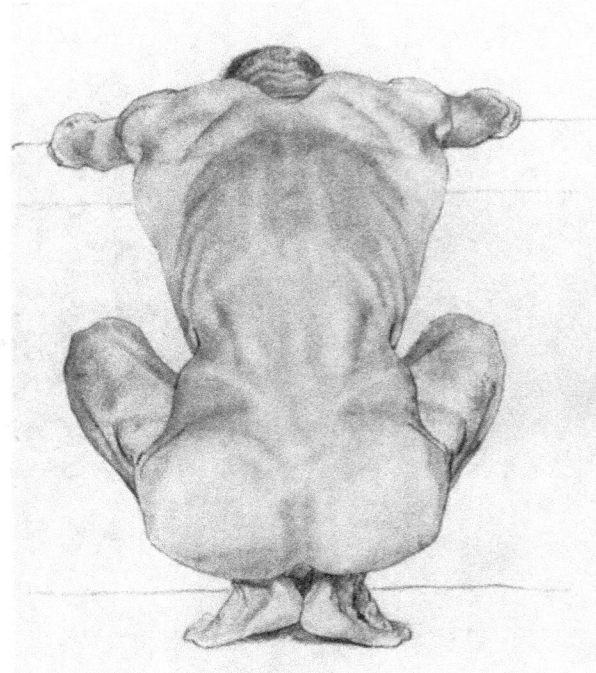

FIG. 68. Franz Wiegele, *Male Nude from the Back*, 1908, pencil.

FIG. 70. Schiele, *Self-Portrait Nude Leaning Forward*, 1910, black chalk and watercolor.

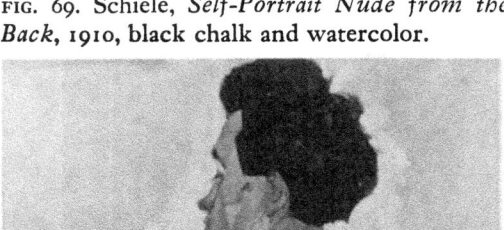

FIG. 67. Schiele, *Nude from the Back (self portrait?)*, 1910, black chalk and watercolor.

FIG. 69. Schiele, *Self-Portrait Nude from the Back*, 1910, black chalk and watercolor.

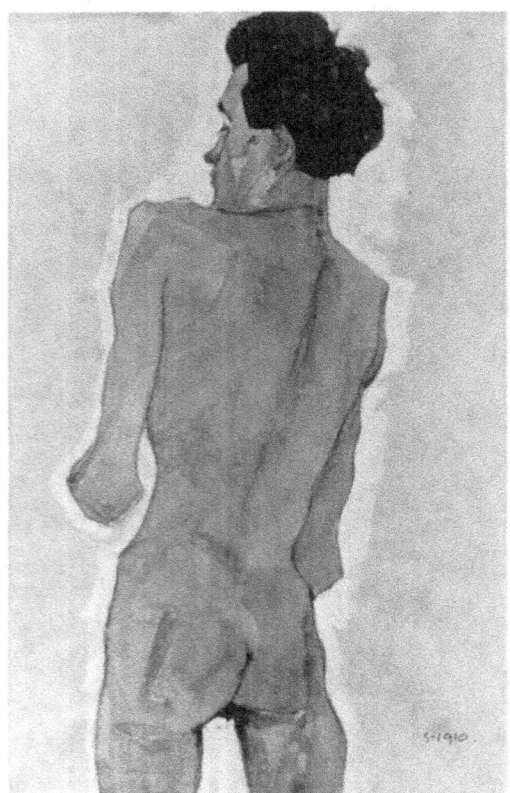

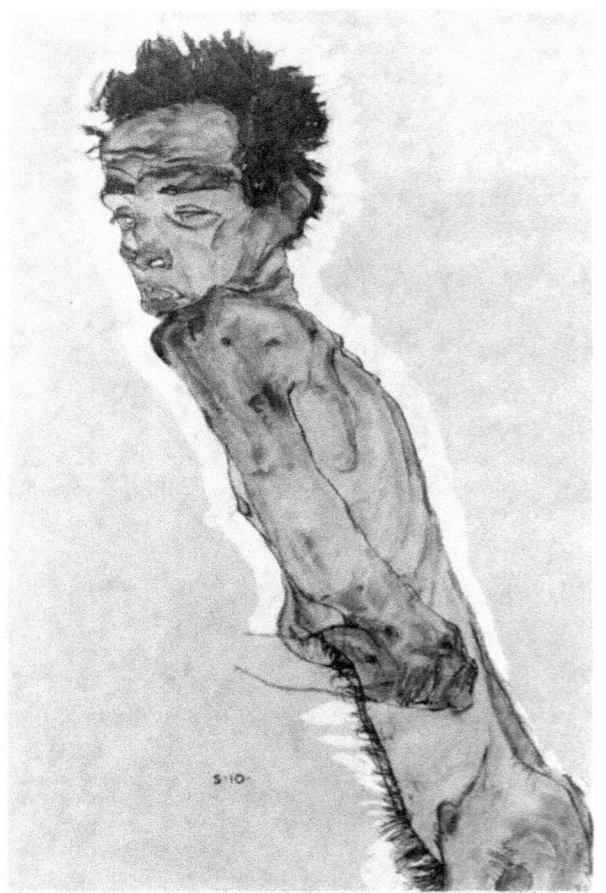

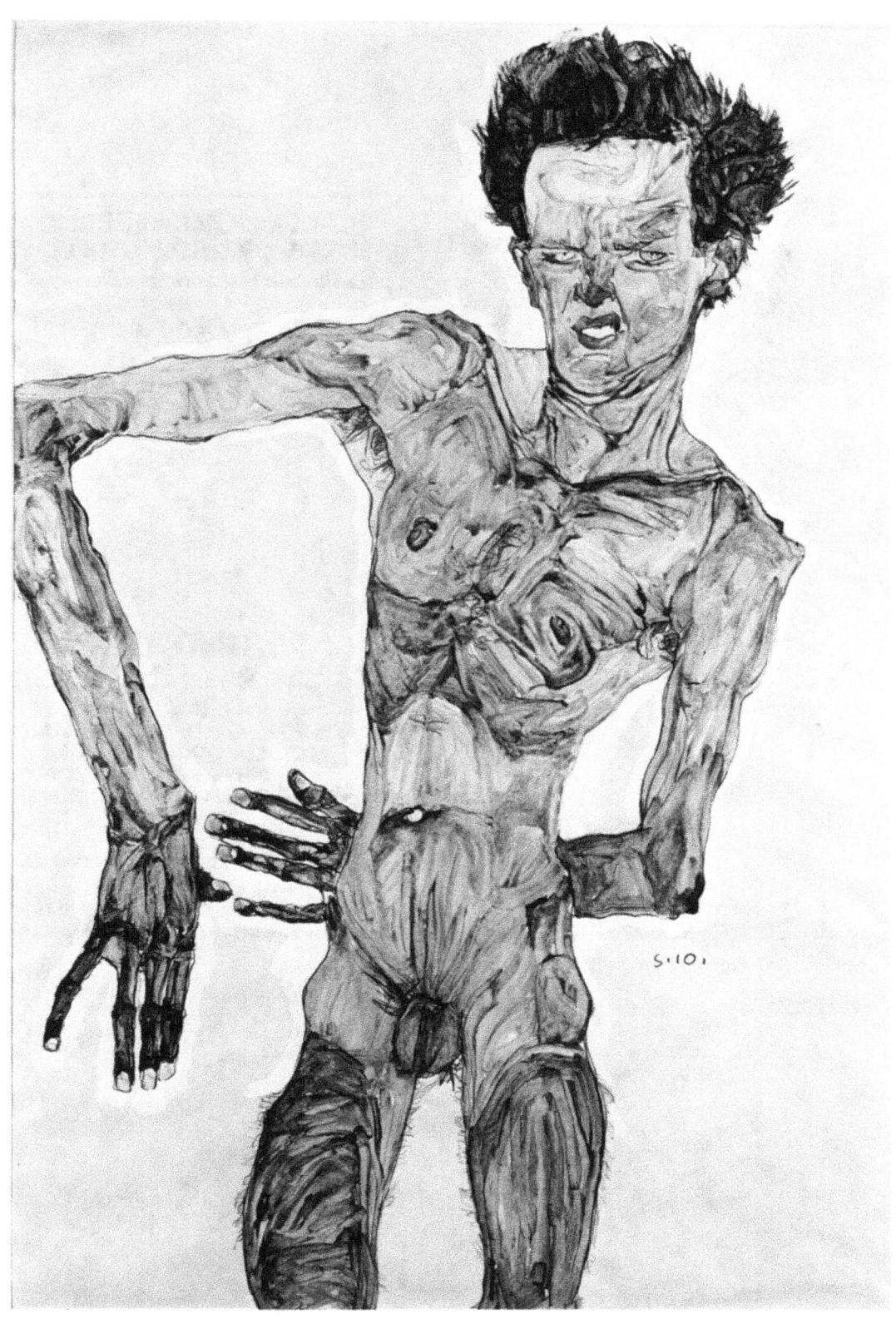

FIG. 71. Schiele, *Self-Portrait Nude Facing Front*, 1910, pencil and gouache.

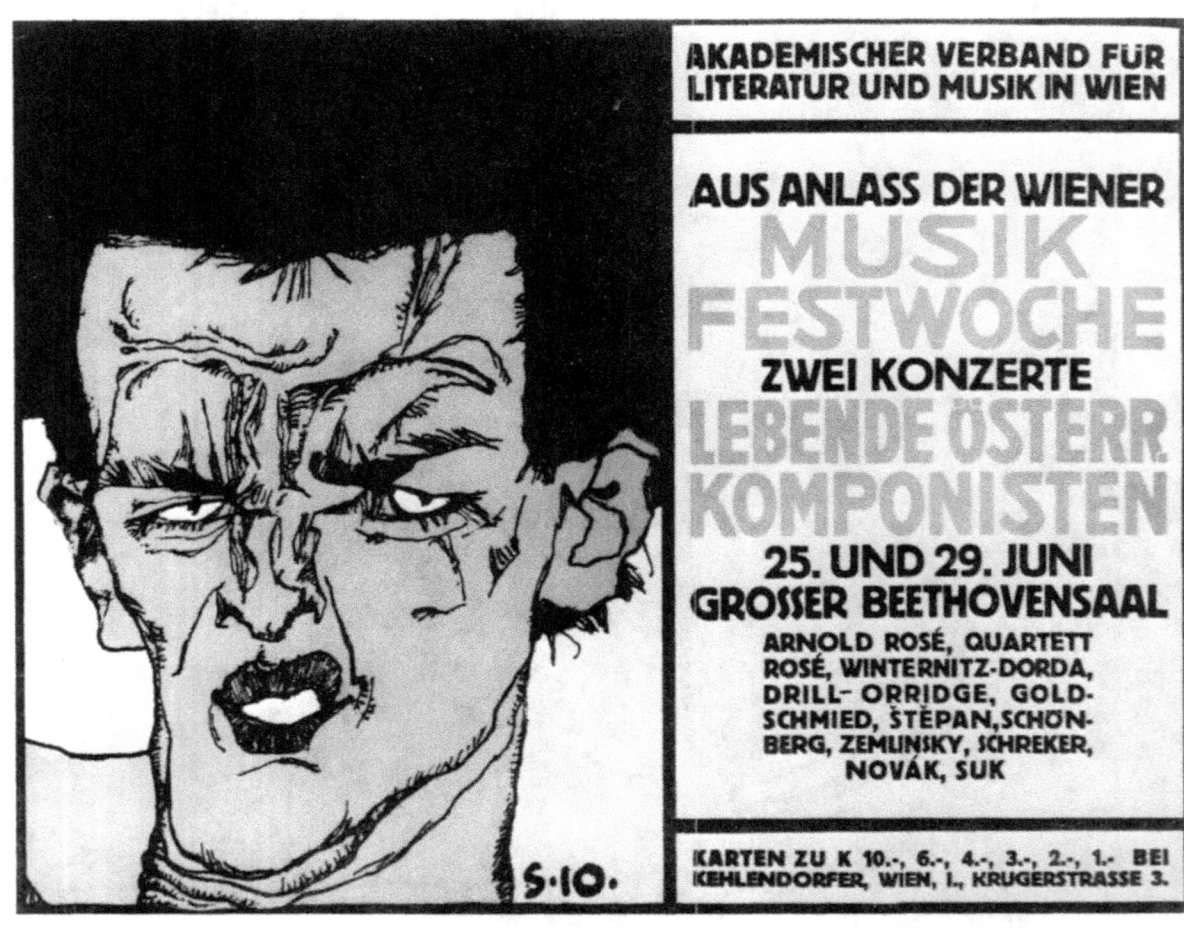

FIG. 72. Schiele, *Self-Portrait Poster for Vienna Music Festival*, 1910.

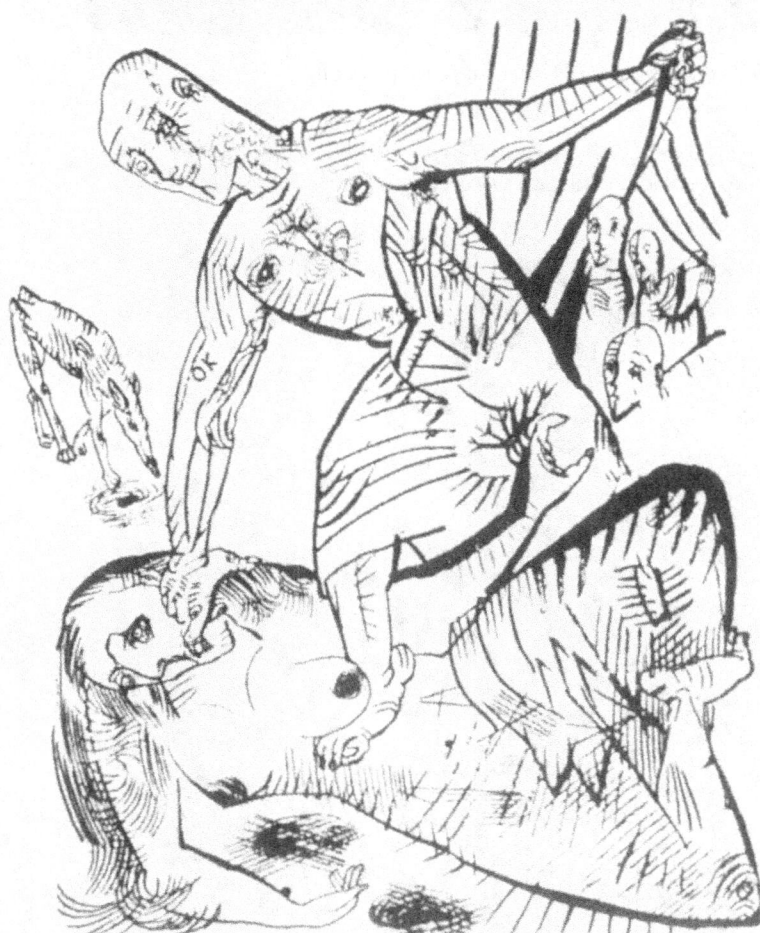

FIG. 73. Kokoschka, illustration in *Der Sturm* for *Murderer, Hope of Women*, 1910.

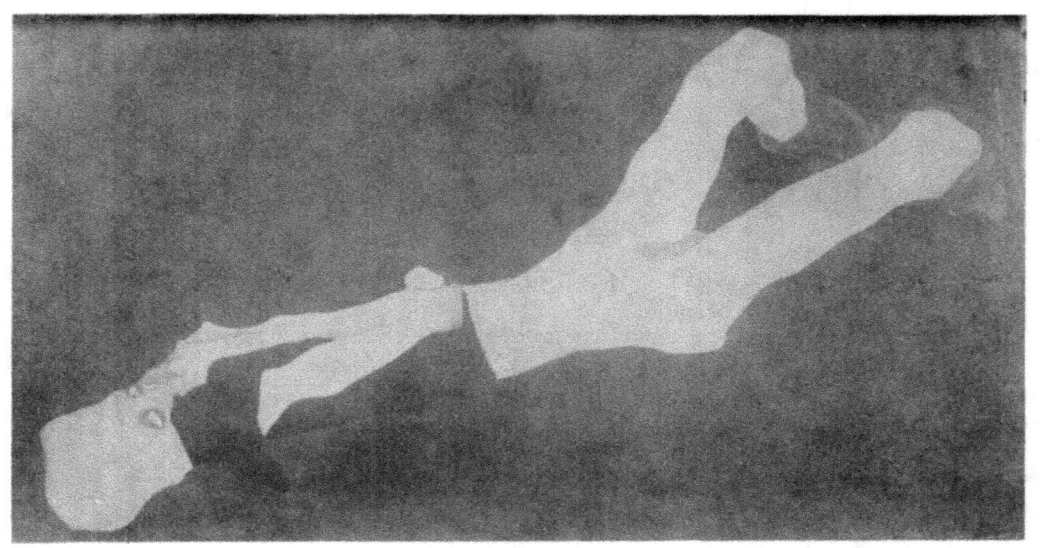

FIG. 74. Schiele, *Self-Portrait with Trousers Pulled Down*, ca. 1909–1910, oil.

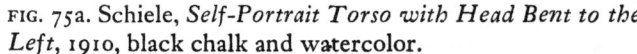

FIG. 75a. Schiele, *Self-Portrait Torso with Head Bent to the Left*, 1910, black chalk and watercolor.

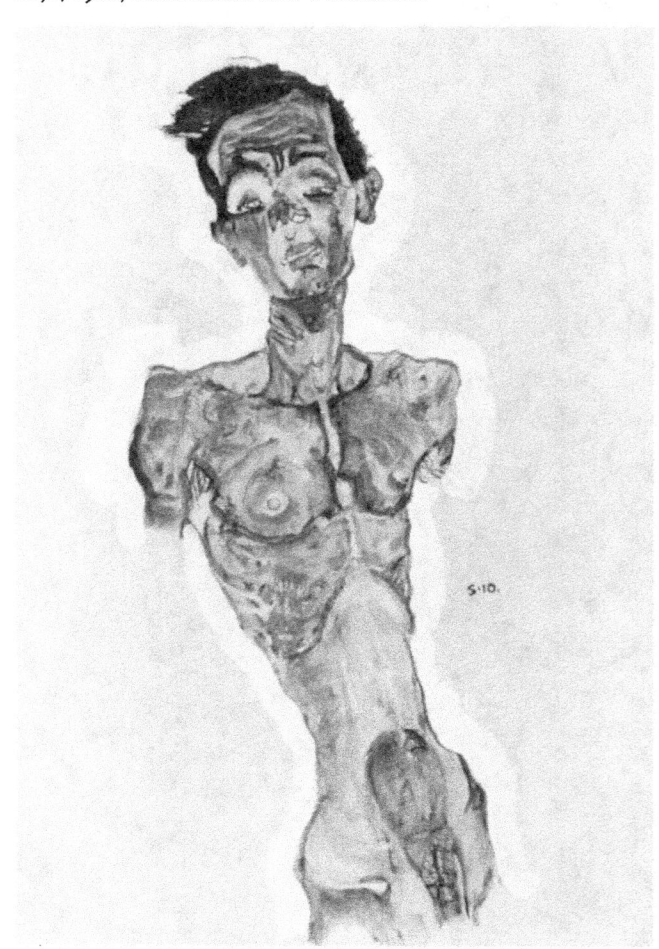

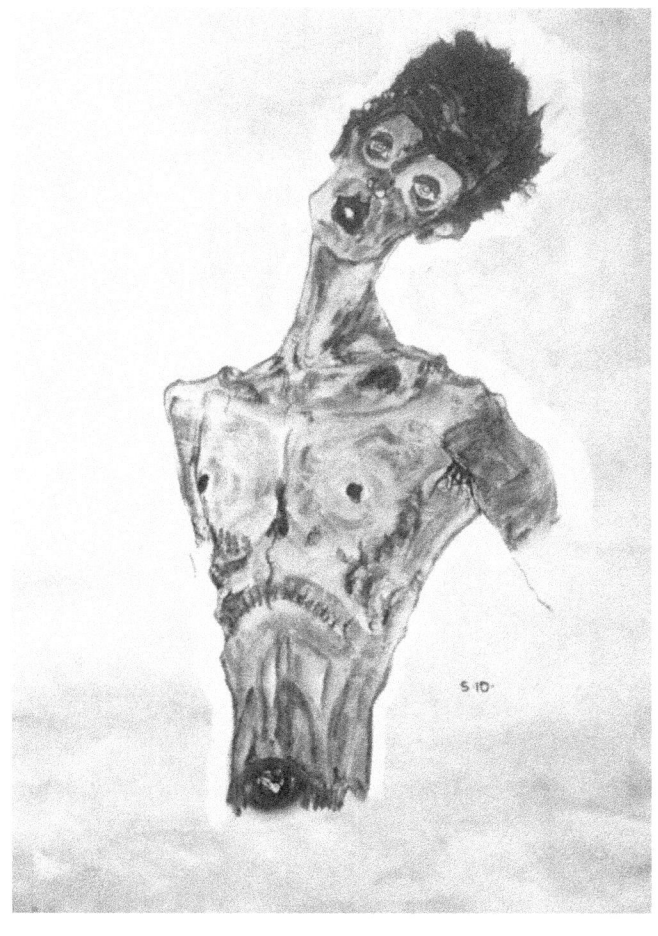

FIG. 75b. Schiele, *Self-Portrait Torso with Head Bent to the Right*, 1910, black chalk and watercolor.

FIG. 76. Schiele, *Delirium*, 1910, oil.

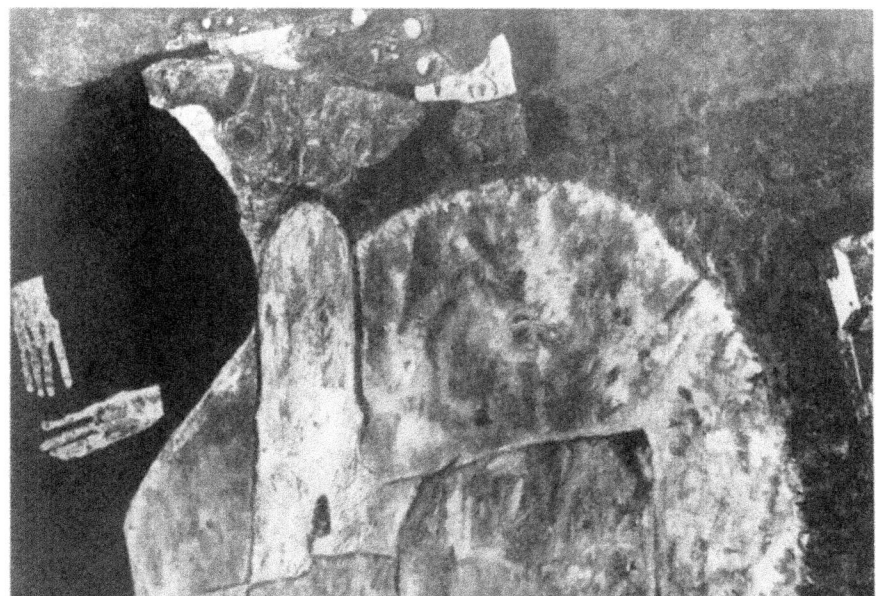

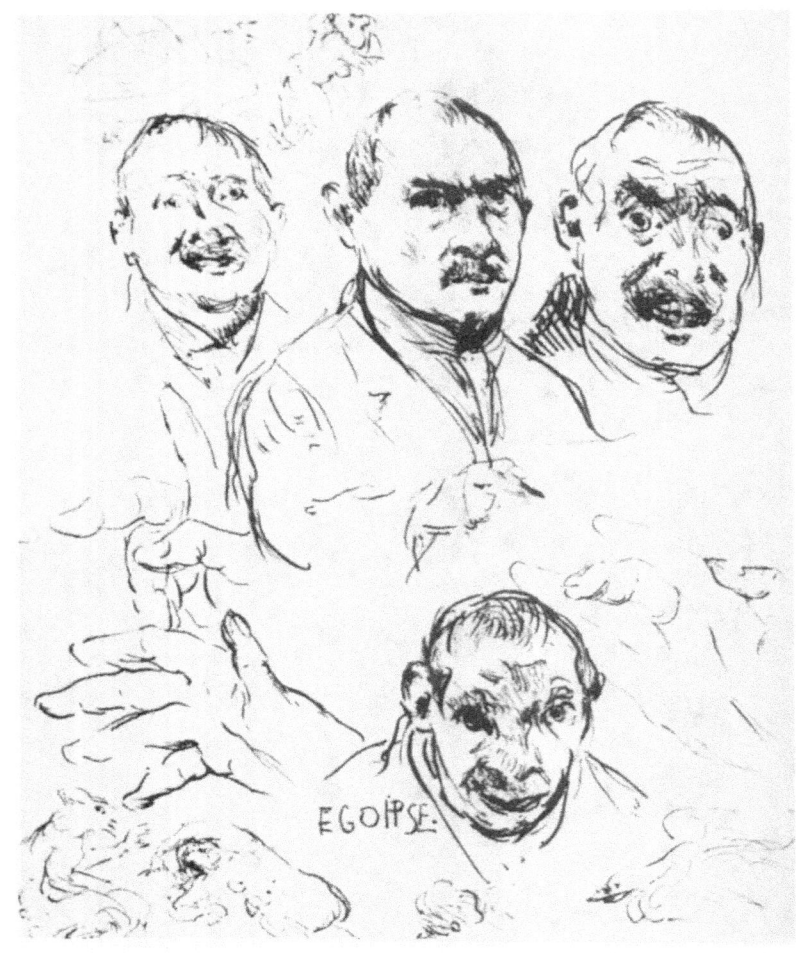

FIG. 77. Lovis Corinth, *Ego Ipse*, 1914, etching.

FIG. 78. Alfred Kubin, *Self-Contemplation*, *ca.* 1900, pen and sepia.

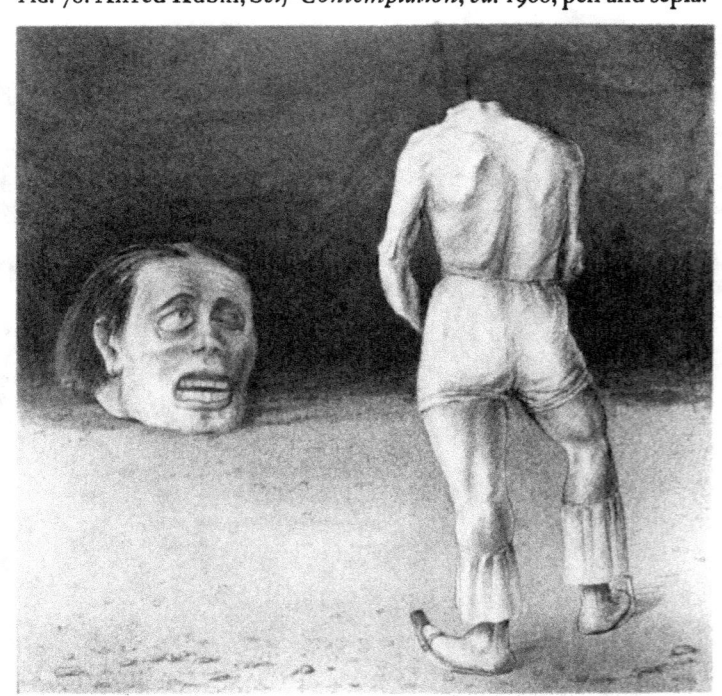

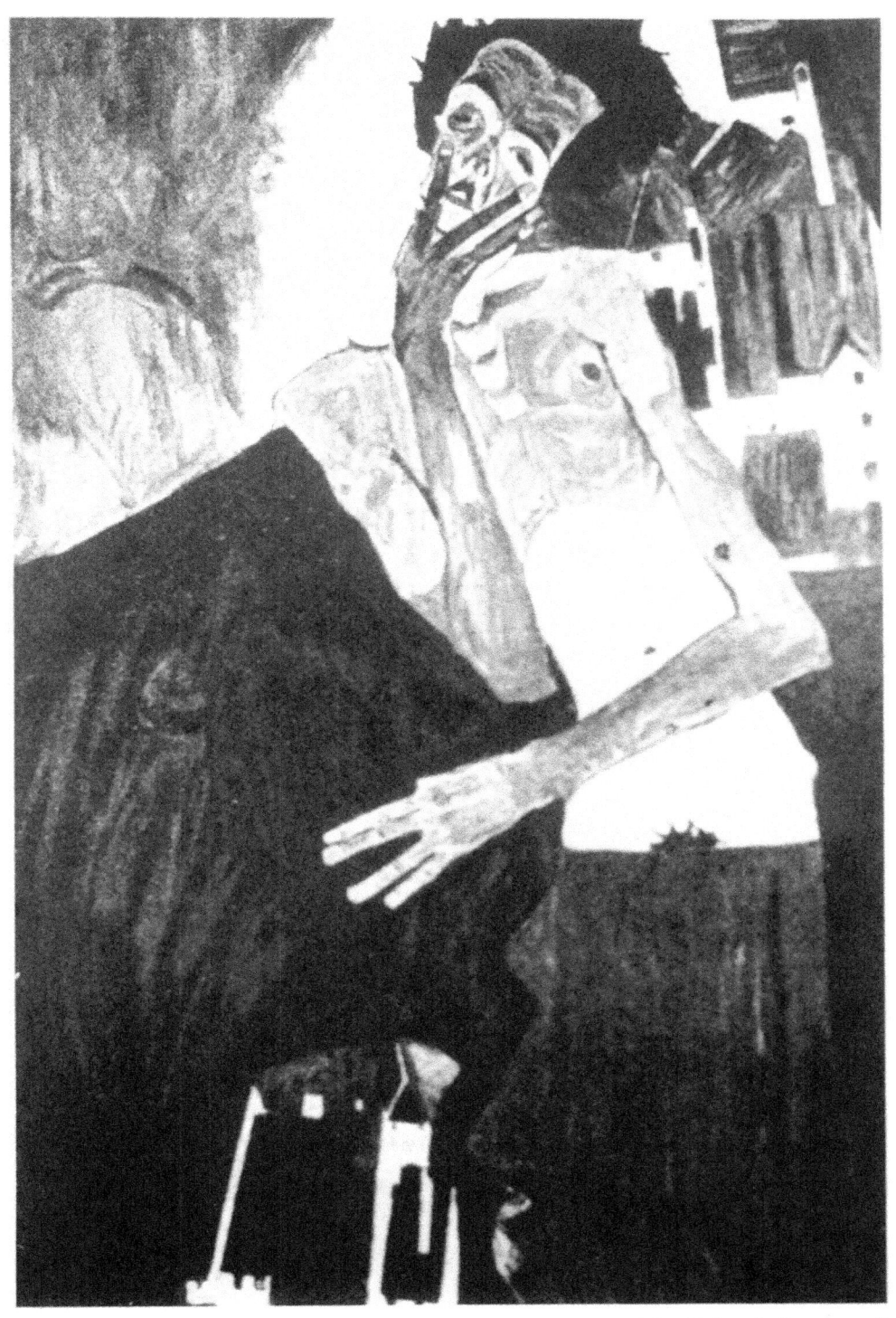

FIG. 79. Schiele, *Melancholia*, 1910, oil.

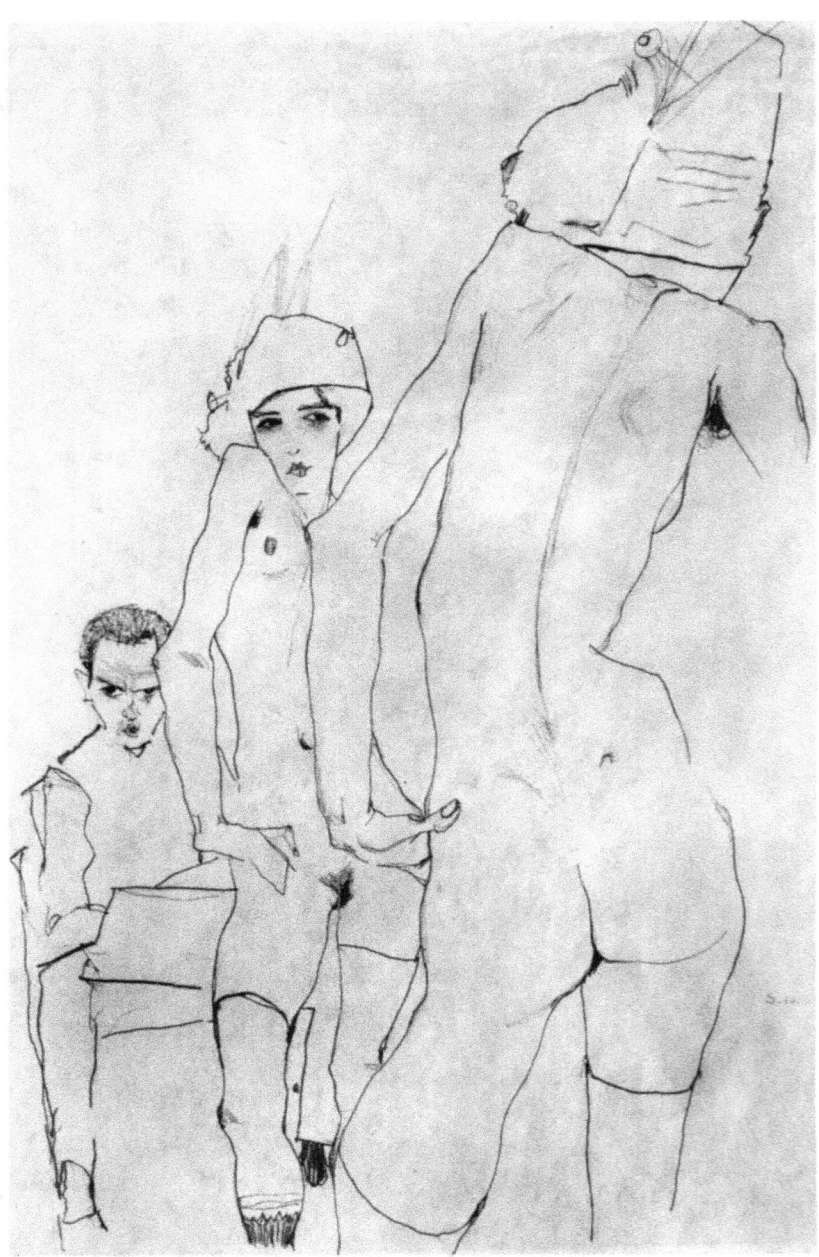

FIG. 80. Schiele, *The Artist and His Model*, 1910, black chalk.

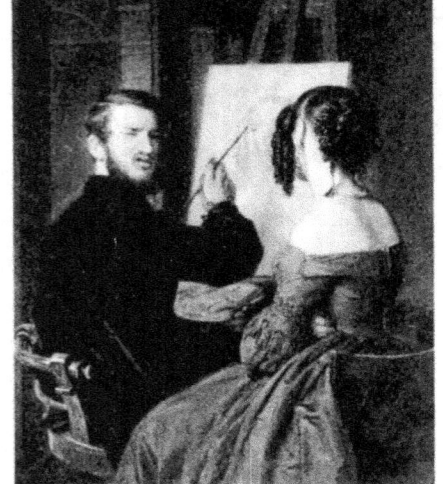

FIG. 81. Johann Baptist Reiter, *Self-Portrait with Model*, 1845, oil.

portraits, and those of Gerstl and Kokoschka as well, deal intuitively with those aspects of sex and personality given scientific identification and analysis by Freud and subjective interpretation by Weininger. With the same persistence that had characterized his boyhood study of the breeding times of the family hens, Schiele now embarked upon the empirical, although at times visionary, autoscopy which continued throughout his life. His findings were recorded in literally hundreds of sketchbook notations, drawings, watercolors, and oils—a total oeuvre of self-portraits numbering more than those of even Rembrandt, Corinth, or Max Beckmann.

The preoccupation with self was of course also traditional with Northern European artists from Dürer to Van Gogh, and the same sort of quizzical or brooding intensity with a double emphasis on face and hands is found in the affirmative early self-portraits of Dürer and those of the invincibly honest Van Gogh.[4] Schiele's self-concern was coupled, as was theirs, with the awareness of being different from most people. Whether as the object of tears or of praise, he had been treated since childhood as something special, openly referred to as a *Wunderkind*, and admired as a young genius. Isolation and poverty further contributed to his concentration on self. He had already rejected two socially established institutions—his family and the Academy. He lived a basically solitary life in his self-imposed withdrawal from society. Unfortified by the present-day semistatus of the self-declared, alienated beatnik or "hippie," without the social prestige of Klimt in a class-conscious Vienna, and destined to exist upon the whims and good will of a few patrons for almost the whole of his artistic career, Schiele was keenly aware of his apartness and dependence upon self. He could rarely afford to hire models, he had as yet no regular mistress, and his most available and frequent model was naturally himself. Living alone, introspective by temperament, and existing in an age characterized by self-infatuation, Schiele's self-scrutiny, in which he allowed exaggerated pantomime of face and body to externalize mental states, increasingly commanded his artistic attention.

The self-portrait drawings, watercolors, and oils produced in such great quantity beginning in 1910 and continuing for eight years, have one feature in common: they are all mirror images. Schiele always drew from nature, and when he made his own portrait he relied on the reflection of his image. At only one time in his life did he draw himself from memory—during the twenty-four days in 1912 when he was without a mirror, in a prison cell. The variety of complex standing poses, as well as the frequent employment of positions which could only be mirror images (figure 80), suggest that a full-length mirror was part of the basic equipment of his atelier. This supposition is verified by a photograph taken in 1916, showing Schiele gazing at his image in front of a large mirror (figure 117)[5], a huge pier glass which had been in the family home at Tulln until Schiele begged it from his mother in 1907 for his first studio.[6] As he did with most objects pertaining to his atelier, Schiele had painted it (the frame and base) black. Despite its size and weight he took the mirror with him whenever he changed residence. The intense communication with a silent mirror image during this difficult year (1910) of great social isolation had profound effects upon a further series of oil self-portraits begun at the end of the year, the row of "Self Seers," in which a ghostly double image or *Doppelgänger* appears.

Schiele's arrival at a new kind of self-portraiture entailing a monumental depiction of his whole body in the nude had historical and local sources, and also followed direct precedents, traceable to certain works exhibited in the Kunstschau of 1908 and the International Kunstschau of 1909. Imperial Vienna had long been surfeited with heroic renditions of nude male and female figures in the Baroque ceiling frescoes and fountains of its palaces and public squares, and, by 1900, the turbulent gymnastics of these custodians of an earlier tradition no longer appealed to public taste. Preferences moved to the "intellectual" ensembles of Anselm Feuerbach, the robustly pantheistic creations of Arnold Böcklin and Franz Stuck (based like those of Feuerbach on a forceful realism), the static figure compositions of the poetical Hans von Marées, and the sensuously intended, glittering, and curiously porcelain-like figures of Hans Makart. Their programmatic and symbolic approach and the stylistic importance of contour line and surface arrangement of color masses served as a springboard for the hyper-aesthetic Viennese Jugendstil. This brand of intellectual painting, encompassing both neo-classicist and Romanticist features, and its Secessionist offshoot were both ultimately rejected by Vienna's Expressionist painters. It would be misleading to speak of Baroque or Gothic roots for Gerstl's and Kokoschka's painterly Expressionism, or Schiele's linear Expressionism, without taking cognizance of this intervening tradition. As part of a revolt against neo-classicism, the embracing of two previous art styles, Gothic and Baroque, which had received full and congenial development in Middle Europe, also represents the new national consciousness characteristic of German and Austrian Expressionism. The further discovery of such sources as folk, Oriental, and primitive art by the Expressionists (Schiele was an enthusiastic collector of objects from all three modes) exemplifies the "instinctive" northern denial of the southern classical tradition and is a phenomenon of Expressionism which received contemporary recognition and interpretation in the writings of Wilhelm Worringer.

By 1910 the following masters were included in Vienna's collection of modern painting housed in the Lower Belvedere: Feuerbach was represented by several figure drawings; Böcklin by his *Portrait of Lenbach, Idyl of the Sea, Venus Genetrix*, and *Silence in the Woods*; Stuck by several nymph- and satyr-peopled woodland scenes; Marées by an idyllic landscape; and Makart by his five celebrated panels of nude female figures, *The Five Senses*. (These panels by Makart, along with his *Rheingold Maidens*, played an important role in Klimt's art.) But the most famous contemporary treatments of monumental nudes in the Belvedere at this time were Max Klinger's large, decorative canvases, *The Judgment of Paris* and *Christ on Mount Olympus* (figure 60). The latter was exhibited in Vienna in 1899 and was immediately acquired for the state as the result of its enthusiastic public reception, during which the work was endorsed as the apotheosis of modernity.[7] In Klinger's juxtaposition of Christian and pagan ideals several nude male figures are given prominent display: the aged Zeus is shown enthroned with the boy Ganymede arching upward between his knees; flanking the throne are two magnificent male nudes, one of whom is Eros who lunges away from the approaching figure of Christ. A partially draped Dionysus offers his goblet to Christ. The realism, firmness of outline, hard musculature, dry colors, and almost metallic modeling of these nude male figures recall two early Renaissance artists revered by both Klinger and Schiele: Mantegna and Signorelli. Schiele owned and carefully studied Richard Hamann's illustrated handbook, *Die Frührenaissance der Italienischen Malerei* (Jena, 1909), which devoted twenty-one plates to the works of Signorelli. With a rare flash of modesty, he once remarked to a friend, the future art historian Otto Benesch, that compared to Signorelli, he [Schiele] was but an "insignificant dwarf."[8]

The influence of Hodler, Kokoschka, de Fiori, and Minne

Although Renaissance and neo-classical treatments of the nude figure were among the older prototypes available to the historically conscious Schiele, there were other, more recent and widely discussed portrayals which presented direct formal antecedents. Of cardinal importance for him was the work of the great Swiss painter of eurythmic allegories, Ferdinand Hodler (1853–1918). Hodler was considered second only to Rodin by the Klimt generation in Vienna, and in the winter of 1903–1904 the Secession had staged a large Hodler retrospective[9] that assured his permanent influence on Austrian artists, from Klimt and Egger-Lienz to Kokoschka and Schiele. Carl Reininghaus, patron of both Kokoschka and Schiele, had bought seven paintings from the Hodler exhibition,[10] and it was thus that Schiele, in the home of the same art lover who had commissioned him to paint an erotic mural, acquired a first-hand knowledge and appreciation of Hodler's somber works. He frequently referred to him as the greatest living painter besides Klimt.[11] A lost self-portrait as a monk sitting on a mountaintop[12] was apparently directly inspired by Hodler's *View into Eternity*, in the Reininghaus collection. The Swiss painter's imposing mountain landscapes, with their high horizon line, anthropomorphic isolation of individual trees, and planar construction of nature into horizontal bands, made a permanent impact upon Schiele's (and Klimt's) own landscapes from 1911 on, notably, *Autumn Trees* (K.145, 1911), *Autumn Sun (Sunrise)* (K.165, 1912), *Setting Sun* (K.183, 1913), and *Four Trees* (K.225, 1917). Hodler's painting, *Eurhythmy*, showing a dragging procession of five elderly men in ascetic dress, was a model for Schiele's many hermit and monk figure compositions of 1912 to 1915, but in 1910, at the time of Schiele's first monumental nude self-portraits, it was another aspect of Hodler that attracted and excited him. This was the quality of mystery and tension with which Hodler endowed his nude boys in such paintings as *View into Eternity* (1903), *The Admired Youth* (1903), and the frequently exhibited and reproduced *Spring* (1901). The extent to which both Kokoschka, in *The Dreaming Boys* of 1908 (figure 61), and Schiele, in his three nude self-portrait oils of 1910, availed themselves of the formal elements in Hodler's figural work may be swiftly ascertained by comparison of these works with the portrayal of the nude boy in *Spring* (figure 62). The kinship is unequivocal. Hodler's youth is rendered against an almost abstract background (aureole-like here; schematized in *View into Eternity* and *The Admired Youth*).[13] The body is defined by a vivid and rhythmically drawn contour line, with a simplified interior modeling. The essentially realistic figure assumes a difficult, unnatural pose with the inward-bent right elbow resting on the raised left knee, forming an energetic vertical movement continued by the neck and head. To either side of this frontal shaft the tensed left arm and relaxed right leg extend in asymmetrical and disproportionate volume. Through postural distortion and an enhanced realism the figure becomes an expressive carrier—of mood in Hodler, and of emotion in Kokoschka and Schiele. Although Kokoschka soon abandoned Hodler's tightly structured figural syntheses in favor of an explosive and raw pigmental building of forms, he continued to employ the evocative gestures that distinguish Hodler's work. Schiele also incorporated these latter elements in his portraiture. He always remained close to Hodler in his linear comprehension of the subject, tectonic organization, and definitive, separatist color application. The predilection for allegory, expressed by Kokoschka and Schiele in the service of their differing life philosophies, is another mutual trait inherited in part from the Rosicrucian symbolism of Hodler, who stressed, through his parallelism, rhythms, and symmetry, the eurhythmical relation between man and nature.

It is possible that Schiele's eye was first quickened to the possibilities of Hodler's form through an analysis of its manifestations in Kokoschka's booklet *The Dreaming Boys*, a copy of which was one of his first acquisitions from the Wiener Werkstätte, in partial payment for the designs he contributed to the fashion department.[14] Schiele had also been able to observe Kokoschka's translation of Hodler's figure style in the 1908 Kunstschau, where a monumental design for a dance-hall wall tapestry called *The Dream Bearers* had been exhibited by Kokoschka. This canvas, now lost, presented a life-sized procession of nude figures executed in tempera. Kokoschka recalls that it was painted in several colors, without shading and with heavy outlines—similar stylistically to *The Dreaming Boys*.[15]

The 1909 International Kunstschau had also exhibited a mural of life-sized nude male and female figures. This was the painting entered by Ernesto de Fiori (1884–1945) (figure 63).[16] De Fiori had studied in Munich where he had been exposed to Hodler, and the latter's influence is much in evidence in this mural which shows two young men and two young women standing in various frontal attitudes upon a flowery meadow, at the back edge of which four arches rise to separate and frame their figures. Each figure is nude except for a turban—a singular feature which later turned up in a fragment for a large group composition by Schiele.[17] The pose of the male with arms crossed in front of his body and with the weight on the right leg was repeated by Schiele in his 1913 *Double Portrait of Otto and Heinrich Benesch* (plate 110). The Hodleresque qualities of de Fiori's work obviously appealed to the directors of the Kunstschau as well as to Schiele, for along with two paintings by Van Gogh, it was one of the few works selected for reproduction in the exhibition catalogue. Aside from the "remembered" features of de Fiori's mural which appeared in the later works by Schiele mentioned above, the immediate effect of this mural in 1909 must have been an affirmation of his own urge to monumentalize. Although almost repellent in their saccharine passivity, de Fiori's nudes are impressive as large poster-like forms defined by powerful, continuous silhouettes against a neutral background. Schiele's 1909 *Self-Portrait Nude* may have been partially inspired by his contact with de Fiori's work, and by 1910 he was ready to express his own muralistic statement of the completely nude male form. His interest in the Italian artist continued long after this initial encounter, and in 1913 and 1915 he unsuccessfully attempted to trade some of his works for a terra cotta figure by de Fiori.[18]

The monumental male nude as rendered by Hodler, Kokoschka, and Ernesto de Fiori had been studied at first hand by Schiele, either in Carl Reininghaus's private collection or in the two Kunstschau exhibitions. The treatment of this theme by yet another artist supplied a precedent second in importance only to Hodler as a stylistic source for Schiele's own work. This was the sculpture of Georges Minne, whose kneeling figures from the *Fountain of Five Boys* were well known to Schiele from the Wiener Werkstätte collection (figure 20) and from the International Kunstschau. With slight variations in the placement of hands or turn of the head, the *Fountain of Five Boys* figures all reproduced the same basic motif—a kneeling nude youth whose raised arms not only cross his chest but actually cradle his body in isolated self containment. Schiele himself had employed this protective self-hugging gesture in his portrait of the timid Max Kahrer; in Minne's work the great pathos inherent in this pose spurred Schiele to further experimentation, but not, as one might have expected, in literal application to himself. And herein lies a salient feature of Schiele's radical nude self-portraits of 1910. They are not expressions of withdrawal but compulsive revelatory statements. In communication with his mirror, Schiele played the role of voyeur to his own acts of exhibitionism, satisfying two urges at once. The self-encasing gesture, with the emotional overtones conveyed by Minne, was transferred intact by Schiele to two kinds of portrait subjects towards whom he felt a strong protective sympathy: the street urchin[19] and his sister Gerti. One of the "secrets" Schiele had apparently successfully kept from his mother, now that he lived alone in his own studio, was that he was working on a large portrait of his younger sister—a portrait for which she came to pose almost daily and one in which she would appear completely nude (plate 28a). This work,[20] now lost, was purchased by the ubiquitous Reininghaus as a companion piece for the three nude self-portrait oils. Two fine preparatory studies[21] exemplify the radical selectiveness with which Schiele moved from an initially decorative and, like the second 1909 "flowery pedestal" portrait of Gerti, prop-sustained conception (plate 29) to an increasingly austere formalization (plate 30). Although the second study's slicing-off of the top of the head by the picture frame is retained in the oil, the emphasis on the genitals is softened and the long legs, truncated at the ankles, repeat the mutilation of the lopped-off head—a none too subtle symbolism which might well have alarmed Frau Schiele! The exposure afforded by the modest, self-protective hug of the arms is at once raw and tender—a pictorial equivalent of Frank Wedekind's compassionate drama of the disastrous events in the lives of schoolchildren raised under a system of sexual hypocrisy, *Frühlings Erwachen* (*The Awakening of Spring*) of 1891. Schiele's extraordinary portrait of his young sister must be counted among those sympathetic yet chilling exposures of the adolescent psyche bequeathed to our century by Munch's *Puberty* (of which Schiele may well have been thinking), Kokoschka's *The Dreaming Boys*,[22] and E. L. Kirchner's *Fränzi*.

The existential concentration achieved by vigorous contours and vastly simplified interior modeling in Schiele's studies and portrait of Gerti owes part of its immediacy to the precedent set by yet another contributor to the 1909 International Kunstschau. The stark realism of Felix Valloton's *Naked Woman* (plate 28b) must have been staggering for a young painter nourished on the sumptuous, hothouse aesthetics of Klimt's ethereal nudes. Valloton's poster-like clarity probably contributed to the rapidity with which Schiele now cast off the Academic formula of naturalism in his search for a heightened reality. This progress is easily observed by comparison of the two 1910 watercolor studies for the nude Gerti portrait with Valloton's *Naked Woman*. Schiele's two studies share the sharp relief and distinctness of detail of the Valloton work, and the factual realism of both artists approaches an almost sadistic objectivity. The Swiss painter's statement (embroidering on that hint of "earthy" realism found in Manet) is analogous to the broad naturalism of his literary friend Octave Mirbeau, whereas Schiele's realism is emotional as well as literal, evoking through meticulous execution and subjective emphases a trance-like super-reality similar to that in Franz Kafka's writings. In the final version of the Gerti portrait, Schiele's transformation of the clenched right hand into a thrashing claw and his accentuation of the raised left shoulder add to the effect of a painful racking of body and emotions. Makart's panels of the five senses have been left far behind in this expression of adolescent yearning and half-fearful expectation.

It is both extraordinary and in keeping with the singular environment of Vienna's cult of self that, contemporaneous with and even slightly preceding the nude self-portraits by Kokoschka (allegorical in *The Dreaming Boys* and *Murderer, Hope of Women*) and Schiele, a third Viennese artist should have evolved the same approach to self-portraiture. This occurs in the remarkable *Self-Portrait Nude* of Richard Gerstl (figure 64), painted in the year of his suicide, 1908. In many ways Gerstl's portrait is more startling, by virtue of its seemingly incurious confrontation, than Schiele's posed gymnastics, and the agitated surface swirls and scratchings drawn into the pigment by both ends of Gerstl's brush attest the intense emotional discharge that accompanied this deceptively objective statement. Although it is doubtful whether either Schiele or Kokoschka saw this particular work of Gerstl's, the fact of its creation in Vienna during the first decade of the twentieth century is of keen phenomenological interest and is one more reflection of the multiple stirrings of Expressionism in that city.

Experiments in self-portraiture

The sources and prototypes for Schiele's own radical oil self-portraits of 1910 were substantial. But the artist's introspective temperament and the unique aesthetic atmosphere of the Viennese *mise en scène*, with its emphasis on self-engrossment, further propelled him towards a psychosomatic exploration of self. Nevertheless the formal solutions posed in the three self-portrait oils of 1910 were not arrived at overnight. An exhaustive experimentation was carried out. Dozens of drawings and watercolors were devoted to the observation of various aspects of the artist—in street dress, draped only in a sheet, nude half-figure studies, or "decapitated" head studies. Consideration of key examples from these voluminous studies will aid in establishing the mental processes leading to Schiele's choice of the entire nude body as his most effective vehicle for self-expression.

In the 1910 *Self-Portrait in Street Clothes Gesturing* (plate 31) Schiele draws himself up in a precious, theatrical pose. His bony fingers are spread self-consciously against his partially-bared chest—a variation, with definite narcissistic implications, on the Minne gesture of self-enclosure. An exaggerated neck emphasizes the physical separation of head from garment, and the body itself seems to resist the encumbrance of clothing as one naked shoulder extrudes from the jacket. The tautness of the spread fingers is repeated in the face with its pursed lips, narrowed eyes, and arched brows. Flesh, hair, and drapery are colored a uniform gray by energetic strokes of the brush, the pressure of which varies in subjective emphasis. The artist is his own appreciative audience, as the image in the mirror engages in deliberate dramatics.

In another series Schiele experiments with "secret" gestures, returning to the treatment of hand on cheek originated in the 1909 crayon drawing, *Self-Portrait with Hairband* (plate 19). A heavily-worked gouache dating stylistically from the first half of 1910, *Self-Portrait with Hand to Cheek* (plate 32), depicts the artist in a similar pose but with all expressive vehicles heightened as the worked swirls of red, blue, and purple in the drapery repeat and prolong the concentration upon self. Both hands are now shown in full with vigorously specified knuckles and fingernails. The exaggerated length of the fingers is echoed by the face with its great swelling forehead. Again the skin under the right eye is pulled down to reveal the white of the eyeball, and the left eye is narrowed and stares into space. This gouache self-portrait, with its "secret" gesture, was to serve as the basis for a major thematic statement toward the end of 1910 (*Melancholia*, figure 79).

Perhaps in reaction to the obvious theatrics of the gesticulating self portraits, Schiele also explored a quite contrary method of psyche-tapping. In a
series of images showing himself from the bust up, he posed the problem of
conveying maximum expressiveness in the face and upper torso without the
emotive benefit of hand gestures. (Possibly the example of Kokoschka's *Self-
Portrait Bust*, executed in clay and colored in "blood" reds, lay in the back of
Schiele's mind, for the work had caused much comment at the 1908 Kunstschau.) The extraordinary *Self-Portrait Screaming* (plate 34) records a paroxysmal outburst. It is the same sort of frustrated, prolonged shriek to which
Karl Kraus was referring in his description of Vienna as an isolation cell in
which one was allowed to scream. It is noteworthy that another Viennese
critic, Hermann Bahr, the author of *Expressionismus* (1916), was to characterize the shriek as the most prominent trait of Expressionism. Schiele's picture
might well be imagined as in answer to Munch's famous painting, *The Scream*.
But in Schiele's picture there are no outside forces pressing in. The scream is
the escaping energy of inner forces that have come to a furious boil. Sharply
contrasting colors of flesh and clothing are used exclusively to intensify emotion. The single tooth gleams a malicious white against the red tongue. Underneath the arched black eyebrows white has been slapped over the flesh tone,
creating a startling effect of movement.

One of a series[23] of such drawings, the *Self-Portrait Draped* (plate 33)
introduces yet another approach towards expressive portraiture. Except for
the face and hands and a glimpse of legs, the figure is hidden by a draped robe.
The flesh is brightly colored in yellows, oranges, and red-browns, and is in
stark contrast to the almost ghoulish expanse of drapery which has been reserved and left the white color of the paper. This unpainted robing is as eloquent as the worked-over garments of such a drawing as the *Self-Portrait
Screaming*. Its dramatic effect is secured by boldness of definition and un-
broken expanse of flat areas. Sometimes the drapery contour corresponds with
the frame beneath, and sometimes it billows out to create an expressive pattern
of its own. The emphasis on the isolated face created by an outline use of garments may possibly have suggested consideration of the "decapitated" head,
which absorbed Schiele's attention in another large group of self-studies.

Almost as though he were attempting to create a twentieth-century sequel to the eighteenth-century sculptor Franz Xaver Messerschmidt's celebrated series of "character heads," Schiele embarked on a row of violently
colored watercolor portrayals of heads showing himself in the grip of various
mordant emotions.[24] In one such study, *Self-Portrait with Wrinkled Forehead*
(figure 65), the portrait likeness is reduced to a stylization of physical features
in order to facilitate the spontaneous capture of mood. The forehead is dark-
ened and clouded by a deep purple, while dabs of black watercolor become
wild strands of hair. The glance of the disembodied head is not level, but has
the same outward-turned eye used before in Schiele's portraits, and the eyebrows are knitted to emphasize the furrows in the brow. This wrinkling of the
forehead by contracting or arching the eyebrows was a cultivated habit, and
a photograph taken four years later (figure 66) shows the artist with an almost

identical expression. Schiele's mother, upon seeing such a drawing on her occasional visits to the studio, would scold her handsome son for painting himself "so *ugly*." His answer was always the same, "It *has* to be this way."[25] The extent to which distortion of features was maintained within a still recognizable portrait likeness is observable in a close view of the face (figure 72) based on a full-figure self-portrait watercolor (*Self-Portrait Nude Facing Front*, figure 71). This electrifying image soon became associated with the avant-garde literary and musical circles in Vienna when it was reproduced as a poster advertising lectures by Egon Friedell on "Shaw oder die Ironie," and "Besser als Shakespeare"; again as a handbill announcing two concerts by the Rosé Quartet of compositions by living Austrian composers, including Arnold Schönberg;[26] and finally through reproduction as the cover for Robert Müller's short-lived militant magazine, *Der Ruf*, which published four volumes in 1912 and included essays, poems, and drawings by the country's leading writers and artists.[27]

From exploration of the expressive qualities inherent in gesture, drapery, and facial expression, Schiele turned to the depiction of his body in the nude.[28] A monumental and "brutalized" statement of form was sought, and the means employed were trenchant contour and eccentric coloring. The *Nude from the Back (Self-Portrait?)* (figure 67), one of a great number of such studies done throughout 1910 (some of himself, some of other models), exhibits the decisive transformation of the elegant Jugendstil silhouette into a vehicle for the surface operation of abstract lines and shapes. The "mutilation" suggested in all these works through a compositional amputation of extremities reinforces the element of raw exposure conveyed by the butcher-shop reds, crimsons or the gangrenous greens, yellows, and blues with which the flesh is ribboned. These formal aspects inspire a greater response to the pathos of the vulnerability of the flesh than does a similar effort by Schiele's Neukunstgruppe colleague, Franz Wiegele, whose Academic study, *Male Nude from the Back* (figure 68), strives towards an enhanced realism through a minute stippling of the lapidary form, but does not achieve the oppressive "presence" of Schiele's hallucinatory images.

Finally, three significant watercolor studies, all employing the astral body glow which occurs in most of the major oil portraits and self-portraits of 1910, form a commentary on how Schiele's concentration on his own nude body produced the kind of tortured image presented in the three monumental self-portrait oils purchased by Reininghaus. In the first work, *Self-Portrait Nude from the Back* (figure 69), the body alone conveys the man. As though setting himself a challenge, Schiele turns his back to the mirror, denying any contribution from gesture or facial expression. One continuous stroke of the black chalk maps the dips and bulges of the silhouette, while organizing the form into rhythmic interrelations. The angular left elbow juts into the concavity of the waist and finds an interlocked repetition of the same elements on the right. In a similar way the inward curve of the chin is taken up by the outward curve of the rising shoulder. Color is again employed expressively rather than in imitation of nature. The hair is dark matte purple and the flesh is a coruscant orange encrusted with glittering purple strokes. The edges of the dramatic contour line are brought into relief by the luminous body halo, a ragged and continuous frame of white that reiterates the form it encompasses.

In contrast, the second work, *Self-Portrait Nude Leaning Forward* (figure 70), has a double intention: to render expressively the body and to chronicle seismographically a shattering emotion. The scanning of the figure was in this instance so rapidly committed to paper that a first-sketched elbow remains abandoned and rejected in the final drawing, a fossilized witness to the evolution of concept during the act of creation. Schiele's body is now turned sideways to his mirror and the upward thrust of the humping silhouette rushes to meet the colossal head pivoted to a three-quarter profile. The rigid body and head are visually and symbolically interchangeable with a giant phallus. The eyes respond separately to the body's spasm. Deep lines slit the forehead, and all hair on the body and head stands on end, as though in reaction to an electrical current. The skin is tinged purple, and the great head of tangled hair is colored violet and blue. Crimson tints overlap and define both flesh and hair, and the vivid red of the lips is repeated in the lid of the open eye. Now the astral glow, usually a continuous stroke in these studies, circumscribes the head in agitated, individual stabs of the brush and gleams in luminous white against the brownish paper.

When Schiele stands before his mirror full-face, *Self-Portrait Nude Facing Front* (figure 71), a terrifying image appears. This is not a picture of symbolic castration nor is it a picture of actual masturbation (although these portrayals will follow). It is a fascinated look at the self—experiencing orgasm and held at bay while, with remorseless insistence, the crayon flashes to record the accompanying physical manifestations. The figure appears convulsed in a spasm: the torso is jerked into a skin-splitting stretch, the turgescent chest seems about to burst, and the hands, still in a position which could afford friction, are violently flung back and away. Every member of the body echoes the effect of the spasm: the limp penis and splayed fingers are incapacitated in its paralyzing grip but share the pulsating roseate tonality of the gasping mouth, dilated nostrils, and strained heart area. The face is twisted into an involuntary grimace and the wild hair stands on end. The whole figure is so charged with sensation that it gives off an incandescent glow. It is this type of emotion-racked image that Schiele elected to formalize in the three Reininghaus self-portraits.

What emotion is this that demands such violent and repeated public exposure? Schiele wrote a description of his inner state at the time of these self-portraits:

"An eternal dreaming full of the sweetest abundance of life—restless, with frightened pains inside the soul. It blazes, burns, waxes toward battle—spasm in the heart. Poised —and madly excited with aroused lust. Powerless is the torment of thinking, senseless to reach for thoughts. Speak the tongue of the creator and give. Demons! Break the power! Your language—your symbols—your might."[29]

But Schiele the poet is more euphemistic than Schiele the artist. The "aroused lust" is given specific depiction in the row of nude self-portrait watercolors and oils, all of which might be properly referred to as exercises in self-agitation. For these pictures do concern the artist's sexual drives and sensations, but they deal with the particular kind of release imposed on him by his isolated situation—masturbation. Schiele "exposes" an act usually performed in private. And, as though the mirror were a sudden intruder, hands and arms are flung out, frozen in rigid postures. Various possible connotations are introduced: compulsion, self-denial, interruption, release, and guilt—all this before the audience of a looking-glass. The apparently guilty nature of Schiele's feelings towards this activity, perhaps influenced by erroneous speculation on the causes of his father's insanity, is interpretable not only through the spasm and other painful attitudes in which he often presents himself, but also by the visual punishments meted out so prominently to the accessory agents—his hands—either through rigid petrification or compositional amputation.[30] The latter generates signal pathos in a series of nude torso studies represented by the *Self-Portrait Torso with Head Bent to the Left* (figure 75a) and the *Self-Portrait Torso with Head Bent to the Right* (figure 75b). An uncompleted oil, *Self-Portrait with Trousers Pulled Down*[31] (figure 74), painted at the end of 1909 or beginning of 1910, is probably the earliest statement of this theme of masturbation and guilt. Schiele thought enough of this work to photograph it before utilizing the canvas as the backing for another picture. Our photograph shows, on the wall behind the canvas, a watercolor[32] that is related to the two 1910 torso self-portrait studies reproduced here. Two years later, Schiele was still so fascinated by the theme of masturbation-compulsion-guilt, that he submitted several new self-portrait drawings (plates 74, 75a and 75b) dealing with this subject to the SEMA Association in Munich, which had invited him to contribute to a portfolio of lithographs by contemporary artists.

Nevertheless, in regard to Schiele and his row of self-portraits dealing with masturbation, the question must be asked: does the crime fit the punishment? Did Schiele *really* feel guilty about this activity, or was it not perhaps simply too spectacular a motif—with all its connotations of the suffering, feeling individual—to be passed up by an artist who wished both to be unusual and to shock an apathetic public? Did he want to become, like Klimt with his rejected University panels and Kokoschka with his shocking play, a notorious public figure, a *cause célèbre?* And what of the theme of auto-eroticism itself? Ever since Wedekind's bold treatment in *Frühlings Erwachen*, in which a young boy works himself to orgasm in the privacy of a toilet chamber while contemplating, cajoling, and finally flushing to watery death a reproduction of Palma Vecchio's *Venus*, masturbation had become legitimate fare for the arts, just as it recently had for psychology. It did not require the appearance of a Freud on the horizon for amateur psychologists to savour contemplating the "ills" of this activity (Wagner had once "analyzed" Nietzsche's problems as all due to "excessive masturbation" and advised him in a letter to either marry or write an opera). Also familiar was the phenomenon of the substitution of pain for pleasure, with its attendant punishments of hallucinations of mutilation—not necessarily expressed by castration or mangling of the offending organ, but through proxy dismemberment of other body extremities. Schiele, whether in sincerity or simulation, seems to have been clearly aware of this aspect, and it is interesting that he only applied such suggestions of punishment to himself. Voyeurism, rather than compulsion or guilt, is the context of Schiele's many studies of female nudes masturbating, either singly or in pairs. Consciously following in the tradition of Rodin and Klimt, whose drawings of lesbians and single female nudes masturbating were much sought, Schiele exploited only the erotic aspect of this type of scenario for which he found occasional female models to pose, omitting the psychological dimension. Possibly the reason for this lack of interest in his professional models' psyches was that these pictures were his main means of support: there was always a market for his handsome, titillating and daringly specific drawings and watercolors of erotica.

Several aspects of Schiele's nude self-portrait studies parallel formal features in Kokoschka's work. As has been pointed out, Schiele's use of the body halo recalls the shimmering painterly aureole given by Kokoschka and Mopp to their portrait subjects. The emotion-charting interior modeling is similar in application and in combinatons of hue to Kokoschka's own watercolor studies of nude figures at this time. But whereas the calligraphic grids drawn on the skin of Kokoschka's semi-nude (allegorical) self-portrait figures illustrating *Murderer, Hope of Women* (figure 73) [33] represent, in the artist's own words, a network of nerves, Schiele's brush-swirling treatment of the flesh was intended as a seismographic reading of physical sensations.

Neither are Schiele's tormented self-portrayals of 1910 the result of passionate alliances with women. In this respect he differs from Kokoschka, whose early self-portraits frequently occur (as do those of so many of the German Expressionists) in the narrative context of a blissful or agonized relationship with a woman. There is the aspect of awakened passions in *The Dreaming Boys*, a terrifying mutual blood lust in *Murderer, Hope of Women*, and an alternately consuming and enthralled battle of wills in his later self-portraits with Alma Mahler. Kokoschka, or his allegorical substitute, appears with a woman; in 1910 Schiele appears alone.

The compositional dismemberment employed by Schiele in many of the nude self-portrait studies of this year has a more literal parallel (figure 78) in *Self-Contemplation* by his compatriot, Alfred Kubin. Although never on the monumental scale of Schiele's compositions, Kubin's pen-scrawled visions of cadavers, sexual dramas, and demon-infested countrysides contained many hallucinatory combinations which impressed later artists (including de Chirico, who had met him in Munich in 1910). Kubin's treatment of the masturbation theme in *Self-Contemplation*, drawn about 1900, is characteristic of a particularly Germanic autobiographic obsession with the sexual fields of experience. The amputation here is actual decapitation, with the isolated head providing an enormous self-audience for the action suggested by the body's stance, fall of the arms, and stiff, upward-pointing shoes. The idea of a watching but disembodied head, symbol of consciousness and rationality (and in this case observing an act which is the result of the instinctual, "animal" side of man) was an important element of Jugendstil, especially as established by the Viennese circle. Redon's sinister eye of consciousness is a foreign equivalent. One thinks of Klimt's theater panels and allegories in which the huge faces are often compositionally enhanced by being the focal point of an undershot perspective. These heads function as concentrated forms of individual consciousness that contrast with the oblivion or unconsciousness of ecstasy, sleep, or death.

In Klimt the watching head is but one aspect of the Viennese Jugendstil urge to create a total environment of a female-dominated aesthetic—also exemplified in the exterior decoration of the Secession building as well as in much second-rate architecture of the period. To Kubin, Schiele, and other exponents of Expressionism (in Germany, Paul Klee) the watching head took on a more personal and terrifying aspect. In the difficult to read, but thematically important self-portrait oil of late 1910, *Delirium* (figure 76),[34] Schiele combines the watching head motif with body dismemberment and finger paralysis in an almost clinical study of masturbation and orgasm. As though indicating a time sequence, five overlapping self-portrait heads, inclined to the right and in varying stages of excitation, all top one nude body, whose dark schematic contours offer a double reading as the erect torso, rounded off and distinctly separated from the high rib cage, repeats in giant form the upward thrust of the penis below. The specific but arrested hand friction is displaced to the far left of the picture and is all the more prominent for the black void against which the fingers project. To the far right are a tower and roof tops, a favorite motif of Schiele's taken from his townscapes of the city of Krumau—his mother's home town in Bohemia. In view of the combination of confessional intimacy and scientific objectiveness presented in *Delirium*, the remarks by Paris von Gütersloh concerning the painting and published in his monograph on Schiele in 1911 seem actually to confirm what the writer so adamantly denies:

"In ... *Delirien* [*sic*] ... Schiele has suddenly entered the midnight soul of the artist. ... But one should once and all forbid that the senile eroticism of critical old men hears merely the 'also' behind the younger artist's sensual form, which can also be understood as unchaste. It is no longer suitable to accuse a painfully maturing artist also of the marks of puberty of his human being; it should be pointed out to them that the compassion of impotence resembles damned closely the insinuation of masturbation, and that any random artist does not provide the suitable object on which to demonstrate one's knowledge of pathological nomenclature."[35]

The remarkable cinematic[36] serialization of the heads in *Delirium* presages a similar "scientific" study pursued by Lovis Corinth in his etching *Ego Ipse* of 1914 (figure 77), in which four self-portrait heads reveal different degrees of sexual arousal and are accompanied by two Leda-and-the-swan scenarios with the addition in one of a fox, in the others, suggestive finger gestures.

The phallic significance of the Krumau tower motif is reinforced by a final painting dealing with autoeroticism, *Melancholia* (figure 79), painted towards the end of the year. This time both the study and the completed version of his painting *Dead City*, as Schiele called this townscape,[37] are quoted, to the lower left and upper right of the figure respectively. The figure pose, with raised hand pulling down the skin of the right eye and also enclosing the open mouth in a stretched V gesture repeated by the lowered left hand, derives from the gouache study *Self-Portrait with Hand to Cheek* (plate 32) and also from the earlier crayon sketch *Self-Portrait with Hair Band* of 1909 (plate 19). In *Melancholia* the genitals are veiled by a semi-transparent cloth that falls from below the hips, and the amputation occurs in the stressed concealment from view of both thumbs. This picture summarizes Schiele's symbolic repertoire of male sexual attributes: the townscape towers and overt hand gestures referring to masturbation. It is conceivable that the enclosing V gesture over the mouth alludes to what is desired by the artist: the vulva, and oral sex. *Melancholia* should however also be interpreted on another level, that of the artist whose work—the two versions of *Dead City*—yields insufficient consolation or companionship in the oppressive loneliness of a solitary existence.

Judging from such grim self-portrayals as *Delirium, Melancholia,* or any of the three Reininghaus nude self-portrait oils, what sort of person could one expect the artist to be? Perhaps only an attenuated echo of his own drawings? Heinrich Benesch, a man of modest means but with an appetite and appreciation for art that was to inspire his young son Otto to become an art historian, after chancing upon some of Schiele's works for the third time in three years,[38] was curious. In a reminiscence he wrote:

"I decided immediately to make the personal acquaintance of the artist and wrote him at his studio in the Grünbergstrasse. After a few days I received a post card with the stamped date 22.XI.1910 upon which was printed in the distinctive block lettering used by Schiele: "On Friday afternoon, if you like, at 2 o'clock. Cordially, Egon Schiele." That afternoon turned out to be my lucky day. I went and found a thin young man of more than average height and with an erect, unaffected posture. A pale but not sickly small face, great, dark eyes and luxuriant dark brown hair which stood up from his head in uncontrolled long strands. His manner was a little shy, a little timid, and a little self-conscious. He did not speak much, but when one spoke to him his face was illuminated by the glimmer of a quiet smile. He laid out his drawings before me, but left me alone, and busied himself somewhere in the studio. . . . The basic feature of his personality was seriousness, but not a gloomy, melancholy, head-hanging kind. It was rather the quiet seriousness of a man absorbed by a spiritual mission. . . . Schiele's nature was childlike (not childish)."[39]

As Benesch came to know Schiele better he frequently observed him at work:

"The sureness of his hand was almost infallible. When drawing he most often sat on a low footstool, the drawing-board with its paper on his knees, and the right hand with which he drew propped on a support. . . . An eraser was unknown to him. . . . Schiele created his drawings only directly from nature. . . . The coloring was always added from memory, without any model. . . ."[40]

A drawing dating from 1910, *The Artist and His Model* (figure 80), bears out Benesch's description of the artist at work. For once Schiele is not concerned with himself. His lips are pursed now from concentration, his forehead furrowed not by pain or cramp but by absorption, his eye narrowed only by the intensity of his gaze. As a feat of difficult draftsmanship this drawing is extraordinary. Schiele sits outside the picture to the left, his model stands with her back to him facing the great standing mirror. Her image is reflected so that it faces the beholder, and behind her is mirrored the figure of the artist himself. The facile handling of this intricate arrangement is pure virtuosity. The assemblage of matching points such as shoulder to shoulder, elbow to elbow, wrist to wrist, and knee to knee is perfect in its alignment and complicated perspective. Schiele's employment of the mirror stratagem, involving the reflected images of both artist and model, recalls Matisse's thematic fascination by the same situation, in particular his early painting *Carmelina*[41] of 1903. But whereas the Frenchman's careful structures are often touched by a note of sly humor in the fragmented inclusion of self, Schiele's picture does not diverge from the initial direct confrontation in which his eyes bore into the model and his right hand flashes to record his impression. An Austrian precedent for this kind of humorless intensity exists in Johann Baptist Reiter's *Self-Portrait with Model* (figure 81) of 1845, in which the artist squints and scowls at his young model. The excruciating meticulousness of approach in Reiter's earnest picture is replaced by a spontaneous grasp and reduction of form in Schiele's drawing, but the serious spirit of the preoccupied artist is common to both works. Moreover Schiele's picture is about drawing and construction of form, and not a commentary on the relation of the artist to his model, such as was for example to become a topic of Die Brücke artists. In this respect there is a correspondence to the objective manipulation of intervals, voids, and solids in Matisse. One of the aesthetic drawbacks of Schiele's numerous "gloomy" allegories—pictures of gaunt men and women, mothers and children—is a certain spiritual and technical heavy-handedness that informs the compositionally welded forms. This formal "brutalization," so characteristic of Expressionism in general in its reaction to the over-refinement of Jugendstil, was employed by Schiele to distinct advantage towards the end of 1910 in his first portrait commissions. The unflinching scrutiny with which he had literally laid himself bare in the self-portraits was now directed with an equal intensity towards others.

COMMISSIONED PORTRAITS: PATRONS AND FRIENDS

By the end of 1910 Schiele had completed six major oil portraits.[42] Of these one had been a labor of love, the portrait of his Neukunstgruppe colleague, Karl Zakovsek (plate 25); the rest were commissions. These portraits were all approximately the same size, 40 by 40 inches, and were thus only about two-thirds the size of the large nude portrait of Gerti and the three self-portrait oils that had gone into the Reininghaus collection. Schiele's stubborn reservation of the largest canvases in his possession for self-portraiture and for his grandiose allegories often provoked perplexed comment from his friends, who could not understand why the artist saved these canvases for personal, "non-commercial" paintings when at the same time poverty and a lack of raw materials forced him to execute some of his best figure, portrait, and land-scape studies on wrapping paper or cardboard. It was due to a small group of friends and patrons who began to gather about Schiele in the fall of 1910 that the means were provided for a series of relatively large oil portraits.

Portrait of Arthur Roessler

One of the first commissioned portraits by the artist was of Arthur Roessler (1877–1955), influential art critic for the socialist newspaper *Arbeiter Zeitung*. Roessler was a prolific writer, who not only contributed regularly to Austrian and German publications[43] but also produced several books varying in subject matter from a travelogue on Dalmatia to monographs on Waldmüller and Rudolf von Alt. He had first seen Schiele's work at the December 1909–January 1910 Pisko Salon exhibition of the Neukunstgruppe, which he reviewed favorably with particular emphasis on Schiele, to whom he referred as an "outsider," comparing his "great earnestness" to the spirit of Gothic art.[44] Roessler immediately befriended Schiele and continued to give him reviews and publicity in his paper. Their friendship, occasionally punctuated by dramatic arguments and jealous misunderstandings,[45] was mutually bene-ficial, and Roessler's activities on the artist's behalf did much to further his reputation, especially in Germany. In his reminiscences of Schiele, Roessler wrote down his first impression of the artist in a description that corroborates and augments the one given by Heinrich Benesch:

"The impression which I received of Schiele's personality at our first meeting was singular and powerful. . . . It was the impression of having before me a per-sonality extraordinary in its entire character, a personality of such markedly pro-nounced unusualness, that its mere presence might not always be pleasing to every-one, and often not even to itself. . . . Even within a group of well-known men with imposing countenances, Schiele's uncommon appearance stood out, as I was able to observe later on many occasions. He had a tall, slender, supple figure, with narrow shoulders, long arms, and long-fingered, bony hands. His face was beardless and sunburned, and framed by long strands of unruly dark hair. His broad, angular forehead was furrowed by horizontal lines. The mobile features of his face were usually fixed in an earnest, almost sad expression, as though suffering from inner, weeping grief. When spoken to he turned large, dark, astonished eyes—which had had first to chase away the dream that possessed them—upon his interlocutor. His relaxed behavior, never violent with rudeness or impetuous with passionate excite-ment, the undeniable peculiarity of even the smallest and least expressive of his slow gestures, and his laconic, aphoristic manner of speaking created, in harmonic ac-cordance with his outward appearance, the impression of an inner nobility that was felt even more convincingly since it was obviously natural and in no way intentional."[46]

For Schiele the home of Roessler and his wife Ida, proved to be not only a physical haven, but also a lending library and circulating museum. Roessler's study[47] was crammed with the latest art books and periodicals and filled with exotic folk objects, Gothic wooden statues, and contemporary paintings. Some of these items changed hands as Schiele traded pictures for objects that caught his eye, in particular two Javanese shadow puppets that hung on the wall. These became, in Roessler's words, Schiele's "favorite toys." Roessler filled Schiele's ears with anecdotes about great artists past and present, passing on to him Winckelmann's alleged remarks to Tischbein about perceiving animal types in human faces, and exhorting Schiele to study Gavarni's repertoire of human types. He stimulated Schiele's interest in primitive cultures and Oriental art; as a direct result, Schiele acquired two expensive publications, *Das Weib im Leben der Völker* (a pseudo-scientific geographical peep show of nude women from all parts of the world) and the more sedate Oskar Münsterberg's *Chinesische Kunstgeschichte*—two richly illustrated volumes on Chinese art.[48] Roessler also communicated his interest in Early Christian art and Gothic manuscripts to Schiele, and Ida Roessler sought to divert his literary tastes from Rimbaud. To the twenty-year-old painter she lent the work of another precocious artist, the verse playlet, *Der Tor und der Tod*, (1893), written by Hofmannsthal when he was only nineteen. But this choice of a piece of literature glorifying the blasé Epicurean, as well as Roessler's enthusiastic recommendation of Gavarni's caricatures, seems to indicate a certain lack of acumen on the part of the well-meaning but frequently overbearing Roesslers towards their young protégé. It was the earnest, mystical, humanitarian Rainer Maria Rilke, and not the aesthete Hofmannsthal, who eventually displaced Rimbaud in Schiele's admiration.

Schiele's response to Roessler and his stimulating world of letters and art appears to have undergone a rapid change from an initial filial deference to an emphatic projection of self into the person of the older, married, and professionally established man. Visual evidence as well as the tone of their lengthy correspondence bears this out. An early study, *Arthur Roessler Standing with Arms Akimbo* (plate 35), recalls Schiele's portrait of his uncle Czihaczek (figure 29) in its sensitivity towards the sitter's own poise and authority. That this open, self-assertive pose was actually a habitual stance of Roessler's may be observed in a 1913 photograph of Schiele and Roessler standing before the tiny island castle Schloß Orth, a popular Austrian tourist spot in the Salzkammergut (plate 36). Schiele's clenched fist and lowered eyes contrast significantly with Roessler's expansive, confident bearing. The artist's personal shyness however is more than outweighed by the exquisite surety of line in his study of Roessler. Taken solely as an exercise in the rendition of contemporary dress, the technical execution in this drawing is remarkable. Alternating light with heavy pressures, Schiele guides the black chalk in rapid, firm strokes that set up a lively dialogue between similar but unequal small areas within the total form. The organic approach to portraiture exhibited in this drawing and in Schiele's previous studies of Gerti, Max Kahrer, Zakovsek, and Mopp, with full articulation given to parts of the body, contrasts with the Jugendstil segmentation then current in Vienna. The emphasis in the older style on face and hands, with an attendant neglect or obscuring of organic relationship, not only had been practiced by Klimt in his "icon" portraits of Vienna's *grandes dames* but was also favored by many other artists of his generation. This approach predicated that drapery was either to be treated as a decorative area (Klimt's ornate color wedges; Koloman Moser's swirling folds) or suppressed. The latter method gave rise to an effective portraiture in the tradition of découpage silhouettes, always popular in Vienna.[49] It was within this tradition that Viktor Hammer, a leading contemporary exponent of a kind of Holbeinesque realism, worked when he sketched Arthur Roessler's portrait (plate 37) in 1917.[50] The garments are treated as a dead area quite without modeling and only faintly indicated, while the face and hands are faithfully reproduced in microscopic detail and shading. The greater vitality of Schiele's sketch is due in substantial part to his animation of the drapery area. This treatment, periodically rediscovered in art, is typical of Expressionism in general, whether staked out in strident color blocks as with members of Die Brücke, or used as arenas of nervous calligraphic or textural activity, as with Schiele and Kokoschka. Especially in Vienna the vitalization of clothing frequently takes on a corporeal aspect that closely mirrors and heightens the psychosomatic reverberations in the sitter. This development in painting is far in advance of most contemporary Viennese portrait photography,[51] which still employed the Art Nouveau asymmetrical figure disposition and decorative isolation of extremities, as typified in a contemporary photograph of Karl Kraus (after p. 2). The pictures that Schiele, in collaboration with the photographer Anton Josef Trčka, took of himself in 1914 continued this exploration of the poignant equation of gesticulating body with animated clothing (figures 100–102a).

Another reason for the vivid immediacy of Schiele's and Kokoschka's portrait sketches is the application of a stringent selectivity as opposed to the photographic literalism of an artist like Viktor Hammer. This may be fruitfully examined in two further studies of Roessler, one by Schiele, *Portrait Head of Arthur Roessler, Frontal* (plate 39),[52] and one by Kokoschka, *Portrait Head of Arthur Roessler in Three-Quarter View* (plate 38). In both sketches salient features such as the length of the head with its high forehead and square jaw are rendered minimally but forcefully through an economical use of contour, pencil pressure, and shading. The pronounced difference in psychological response, however, is informative. For Schiele, Roessler represented not only a figure of social importance but also something akin to a magician—a man of the world who could arrange exhibitions, influence other critics, produce patrons and even conjure money on occasion. The alert and forceful mien of Schiele's portrait reflects the awe he felt in the presence of qualities so foreign to his own nature and previous experience. Kokoschka and Roessler never hit it off, primarily because Kokoschka was by nature a headstrong and elusive protégé and Roessler, unlike the artist's close friend and protector Adolf Loos, tended to be a demanding, possessive patron. In addition, Roessler could never bring himself to accept what he termed Kokoschka's "color massacres."[53] Kokoschka's sketch of Roessler is manifestly objective and even disinterested (compare his portrait of Franz Hauer, plate 114). The receding hairline, which in Schiele's portrait bristles energetically, is a mark of age in Kokoschka's version, and it is the fleshiness rather than the straightness of the prominent nose which is emphasized. Kokoschka's resistance to Roessler, the critic, is symptomatic of his lifelong contempt for public opinion. Schiele was all too vulnerable to local intrigue, and his instinctive response to an authoritative father figure formed part of the close bond that held him to Roessler all his life.

The urgency of Schiele's need to identify with the image of success that Roessler represented to him is witnessed in the total revision of his portrait project. The preparatory sketches discussed above indicate that a frontal portrait was contemplated, but on 6 October 1910 Schiele wrote to Roessler: "I am changing the entire portrait, and must think over several things."[54] The changes were completed by the end of the month, at which time the artist announced that the "rosy-red Roessler" was ready to be framed, signed, and photographed.[55] The finished portrait (plate 42) presents a memorable figure —a figure that bears physical resemblance to the Roessler of the preparatory studies and photographs but that also in many ways recalls Roessler's own description of Schiele. Compositionally the painting bears an unmistakable similarity to the flowery-pedestal portrait of Gerti (plate 14). As in the Gerti portrait, the stiff frontality of the torso is broken by a profile turn of the head, with eyes closed as if in dream. Again austerity and intensity are the emotional qualities procured by the central placement of the figure against a neutral background and by the trance-like shudder suggested in the contraposition of the raised and lowered shoulders. In the Roessler portrait the extended shoulder treatment is even more exaggerated. The Schiele-Gerti resemblance of this portrait is strongest in the picture's most salient feature, the immense tensed hands which cross the body in a thumb-concealing gesture of self-containment that is diametrically opposed to Roessler's extroverted nature. This is a startling interpretation! Schiele has transformed this enterprising man of action into a passive receptacle for paroxysmal visions—himself. Kokoschka's 1909 *Portrait of Constantin Christomanos* (plate 40), author and court reader to the Empress Elisabeth, presents some remarkable formal parallels to Schiele's work, especially in the self-hugging gesture of the enormous, tremulous hands. The similarity between these two shivering visionaries, painted by two different but contemporaneous artists, answers the question that must be asked of the new Expressionist approach: *whose psyche was being exposed—the sitter's or the artist's?* Were the persons portrayed intrinsically pathetic individuals or was the pathos contributed by the artist? Viewed through the distorting lenses of existential *Angst*, the psychic frailties of Everyman spoke to the receptive artist whose eyes were fixed on human pathos. His subjects did indeed reflect the world viewed through the temperament of Expressionism.

Four years after the Roessler oil, Schiele again portrayed his friend, this time in an etching (plate 41) for which a close study exists (plate 43). Although reduced to the essentials of face and hands, with a single line indicating the shoulders, these organically "uncompleted" portraits are not reversions to the Jugendstil segmented portrait style. They are instead nondecorative essays in construction, and, as with the master constructionist Cézanne, to whom Schiele paid homage in his carefully structured landscapes, the selectivity depends upon a strongly implied interlocking of unstated but powerfully felt forms. Schiele's empathic interpretation of Roessler is scarcely altered in these later works of 1914. The head is again turned to the side against a raised shoulder, the open eyes narrow upon some inner specter, and the hands are raised away from the head, palms out, as if warding off interruption. The rapport of these portraits with Schiele's self-portraits as saint or monk at this time confirms the artist's continued sympathetic indentification with Roessler.

The Roessler 1910 oil portrait is a recognizable extension of Schiele's own concerns and sensitivities. It would be accurate, although incomplete, to say that in all the portrait commissions painted this year, the sitter was always essentially Egon Schiele. However not everyone painted by the artist appreciated such an Expressionist transmutation.

Portrait of Otto Wagner

Perhaps no client portrayed by Schiele had greater right to feel himself "betrayed" than Otto Wagner (1841–1918; plate 47), Vienna's most revered and influential architect at the turn of the century. The sixty-nine-year-old Wagner, holder of a professorial chair at the Vienna Academy since 1894, and the man to whom the building of the city's ambitious metropolitan railway network had been entrusted, had an awesome reputation. In spite of his multiple achievements in the past, he had been able to move with the times and looked with affability on modern movements and the work of talented younger men. His battle against historicism and his vigorous pleas for functionalism made him an Austrian equivalent of America's Louis Sullivan. His belief that creative activity must take account of the technical and social developments of contemporary life had been expressed in his important book of 1895, *Modern Architektur*, in which he declared that "all the rest is archaeology." Now wealthy enough to be no longer dependent on designing public projects to please the Emperor Franz Josef, the aging architect took a vicarious delight in forwarding the work of progressive young artists, and when his good friend and former Secession colleague Klimt, seconded by Roessler, strongly recommended Schiele, Wagner responded with magnanimity and imagination. Sympathetically disposed towards the young painter and his work, the architect agreed to meet the former Academy student and to take a look at his drawings.

Wagner received Schiele cordially, then and there buying a few of his drawings, and told the young man that this sort of piecemeal selling to individual clients was too slow and on too small a scale. He immediately suggested that Schiele paint a whole series of famous Viennese cultural personalities—painters, sculptors, architects, musicians, poets, critics, prominent collectors and teachers, perhaps even politicians—and that these portraits then be sent as a traveling exhibit around Europe and possibly also to America. He then proposed to the enthralled young artist that he, Wagner, would serve as the first sitter. Klimt, he said, should be the second, and Hoffmann, Bahr, Altenberg, Hofmannsthal, Kraus, Mahler, and others could follow, each supplying the necessary painting materials and canvas for his own portrait. Schiele enthusiastically reported the results of the Wagner meeting that same evening to Roessler,[56] and kept him advised through letters of the accommodating old man's weekly visits during October and November to his humble studio in the Alserbachstrasse—a visit which involved climbing stairs to what was the "first floor if you were coming from heaven." Nevertheless, as soon as preliminary hand and torso studies[57] had been made and the face sketched on the canvas, Wagner's visits became less frequent until finally he appeared no more. Roessler, who conveyed Schiele's urgent requests to complete the sittings, reported that Wagner excused himself on the basis that he was now too busy and that since Schiele had painted the face, he could certainly find some other model on which to base the figure. When further pressed, the venerable architect lost his temper, admitting that he no longer wanted to come.

In addition to the stair-climbing ordeal involved, another reason for Wagner's further lack of interest in sitting for Schiele is strongly indicated by an examination of one of the watercolor studies for the portrait (plate 44), and of the portrait fragment itself (plate 46). When one compares the well-groomed, dignified Otto Wagner as he appears in his photograph (plate 47) with the emaciated, squinting, wizened old man of Schiele's renditions, the question of personal vanity looms large. There can be little doubt that, generous as Wagner was in his championing of young artists, he did not care to see himself aged and debilitated as a contribution to the new visionary portraiture. It will be recalled that Kokoschka's portraits too were accused of adding years to their sitters' ages. That personal pride was the reason for Wagner's inability to accept Schiele's ravaging interpretation is confirmed by the fact that he soon selected the photograph reproduced here as the basis for a line-drawing "official" portrait of himself, published and distributed as a post card (plate 48) on the occasion of the city-wide celebration of his seventieth birthday in 1911.[58] A compositional notation for the Wagner portrait in one of Schiele's sketchbooks (plate 45)[59] indicates that the artist contemplated a close-focus, frontal portrait, cut just below the waist, and with the employment of the extended shoulder treatment to establish a slightly off-center pyramid. Contrary to the sketchiness of the hands in the watercolor study, the hands in the final oil would have been large, bony, and prominent, while the furrowed brow, pointed beard, and angular shape of the head would have continued to receive emphatic treatment. A possible influence on Schiele's gaunt and frontal conception may have been Rodin's bust of the bearded C. M. Dalou, reproduced in an 1898 issue of *Ver Sacrum*.[60] The influence of this work on the sculptor Gustinus Ambrosi's haggard bronze portrait bust of Otto Wagner (1917) is unmistakable. Ambrosi, friend and colleague of Schiele, completely assimilated the Frenchman's style and subject matter.[61]

Schiele's disappointment over the loss of Otto Wagner as a sitter destroyed his enthusiasm for the proposed portrait series of famous Viennese, and nothing more came of the project. He gave the Wagner portrait fragment to Roessler, who soon felt obliged to chide him concerning his petulant dismissal of Wagner's well-meant aid:

"You should be less eager to advertise your relationship with Klimt than to bear in mind sometimes also to consider the reaction of *Oberbaurat* Wagner, and not brusquely and in bad taste reject well-meaning friendship. Bluffing alone does not do it, believe me."[62]

Schiele apparently heeded this advice, for toward the end of 1911, he reported in a letter to Anton Peschka that he had been to see Wagner, "who was naturally very friendly and gave me 20 [K]ronen for nothing."[63]

Portrait of Erwin Graff

Although the Wagner portrait remained only a fragment, four others were brought to completion by the end of 1910. They rank in innovative interest with the Zakovsek and Roessler portrayals. One of these was the *Portrait of Dr. Erwin Graff* (plate 50), a gynecologist stationed at the Women's Clinic of the Vienna Medical School. Graff became acquainted with Schiele early in 1910 at a private showing of the artist's work at one of the weekly soirées held by Carl Reininghaus. One result of this meeting was the permission received by the artist to draw the women patients in the doctor's clinic—an opportunity somewhat paralleled by an event in Kokoschka's life when he was taken by Loos in 1909 to the Steinhof sanatorium in Vienna to paint the incurably ill Ludwig Ritter von Janikowsky. The depiction of the mentally or physically infirm, which had previously received treatment at the hands of such distinctly non-related individuals as Hogarth, Goya, and Géricault, had become in the late nineteenth century a focus of artistic and literary attention. Exploration of psychic functions had appeared in Munch and Strindberg long before Freud's scientific interpretations of psychotic symptoms had become matters of general knowledge and discussion. The pathographic investigations of Schiele and Kokoschka, Klee and Meidner, Kubin and Kafka were phenomenological counterparts of the new psychology, but they, like the young science itself, were heirs of a pre-existing cultural disposition that had begun with Kierkegaard and Nietzsche toward social and private vivisection of the psyche. In a pilgrimage much like that made later by Thomas Mann, Kokoschka traveled to a Swiss sanatorium where he painted the tubercular patients, including Adolf Loos's wife, Bessie. In Dr. Graff's clinic Schiele drew studies in the nude of pregnant women, newborn and stillborn babies, and sickly little girls. He refused to show these sketches to Graff's sister-in-law, remarking that such things were not for ladies to see.[64]

This fascination by illness and death, which because of the insanity and deaths in his own family held intimate connotations for Schiele, seems to have been transferred like a communicable disease to the figure of Dr. Graff in

Schiele's eerie, anemic portrait. The doctor appears as a shrunken-headed cadaver in a state of rigor mortis. A creamy, lackluster body halo surrounds the figure and in the resultant morbid atmosphere the prominently bandaged finger has the impact of a grim joke. The painter's subjectivity in this macabre interpretation is confirmed when the oil portrait is compared with a beautiful preliminary drawing, *Three Head Studies of Dr. Graff* (plate 49). The three progressively developed profiles indicate that the sitter was a healthy, well-groomed, and even handsome gentleman, apparently fully in possesion of his mental and physical faculties. Schiele's imposition of his own artistic diagnosis of the doctor abandons, in the oil portrait, the extended shoulder treatment developed in the Zakovsek and Roessler portraits in favor of a body symmetry that works to overwhelm and isolate the puny, undersized head, whose vulnerability is manifested in its uneven, serrated silhouette. The compositional approach in this painting is germane to the more painterly but equally visionary effect of other Viennese Expressionist works, such as, for example, in Mopp's shimmering interpretation of 1911, *Portrait of Heinrich Mann* (plate 51). In both the Schiele and Mopp examples, as well as in many portraits by Kokoschka, the form is stretched vertically, as though on a spit, along the center of the canvas, and the figure is enveloped by an astral body glow that activates or sets off the surrounding space. But the portraits of Mopp and Kokoschka grant their sitters some degree of individuality. In contrast especially to Kokoschka, who at this time aggressively painted his subjective response to each sitter, Schiele's attention was focused primarily on self-extension, whether through self-portraiture or portraits of others. This self-projection did not dismay Dr. Graff, who was apparently less demanding than Otto Wagner; he not only accepted the painting but remained a lifelong friend, and it was he who attended the artist on his deathbed.

Portrait of Oskar Reichel

Another medical man, Dr. Oskar Reichel, was portrayed by Schiele this year. Credited by many as the rediscoverer of Anton Romako, Dr. Reichel was a perceptive collector and active patron of the younger Viennese painters, including Kokoschka (as early as 1907), Mopp, Paris von Gütersloh, and Anton Faistauer. His interests extended to foreign as well as Austrian artists, and an exhibition of his collection held at the Miethke Gallery in February of 1913 included works by Manet, Gauguin, Toulouse-Lautrec, Van Gogh, Munch, and Khnopff, as well as five works by Schiele and paintings and drawings by all of the above-mentioned local artists.[65] It was Roessler who introduced Schiele to this important and extremely wealthy patron, and it was Roessler who persuaded Reichel to sit for his portrait. Just how receptive the doctor was to this suggestion is indicated in the same letter in which Roessler chided Schiele for bragging about his friendship with Klimt. He reminded the artist: "Due to my mediation you received further commissions from . . . Dr. Reichel (who permitted himself to be portrayed by you only after my urgent persuasion)."[66] Dr. Reichel's doubts may have been justified, from his point of view. Two preliminary watercolors, *Head and Torso Study for the Portrait of Dr. Reichel* (plate 56) and *Head Study for the Portrait of Dr. Reichel* (plate 55) are decidedly formidable. Again, it is almost as though the doctor has become the victim of one of the diseases he is accustomed to treat. The pale eyes stare out in glowering concentration from beneath the weight of an immense hydrocephalic forehead, while, especially in the face study, the viscid application of dark colors tinged with yellows and greens suggests the traditional black-bile complexion of the "melancholiac." The loss of vital secretion is hinted at by a single watercolor dribble that flows unchecked from the side of the head. At some point the frontality contemplated in these brooding studies was dismissed. The final oil, *Portrait of Dr. Oskar Reichel* (plate 54), is a profile view of arrested motion in which the body takes on a sculptural rigidity as though lignified. As in the Dr. Graff portrait, both physical and psychic disorders are suggested. The left hand raised to the head recalls a characteristic gesture of the hard-of-hearing; in the tensed right hand the concealment from view of the thumb parallels the "amputation" in Schiele's self-portraits. The frowning, sclerotic immobility conveys a hesitant indecisiveness that was actually displayed by Reichel in regard to his portrait. At first he did not wish to buy the painting and it was acquired by the collector Hermann Eissler. Reichel then purchased it from Eissler and later resold it to a member of the Eissler family.[67]

When Schiele visited Reichel's home to view the doctor's famed Romako collection, he must have seen two Kokoschka oils hanging on the wall. One was the *Still Life with Tortoise and Hyacinth* and the other a picture of Reichel's son, *Portrait of Hans Reichel* (plate 52), both painted before 1910. The pose of young Hans Reichel, with his left hand raised to his head and the right hand tensed in front of him,[68] is rather similar to the stance adopted in Schiele's portrait of the father; in fact, Schiele's painting might be considered a variant on the frontal Kokoschka pose, given a quarter turn to the right. Schiele's curious decision to change his portrait of Dr. Reichel from a frontal to a profile composition coincides, interestingly, with a strikingly similar treatment introduced the same year by Kokoschka in his *Portrait of Herwarth Walden* (plate 53), dynamic publisher of the Berlin-centered periodical *Der Sturm*. The half-torso depiction of a male figure standing in full profile is an innovation that appears in the work of each of these artists only once during 1910. Kokoschka's portrait was painted in Berlin where it was exhibited at Cassirer's in June of the same year. A reasonable possibility exists that Schiele knew of the Walden portrait (through reproduction or hearsay), since Dr. Reichel had entertained Kokoschka as a house guest during the winter of 1907–1908 and continued to collect the artist's works and keep informed of his whereabouts and activities.[69] It is even conceivable that Schiele changed his portrait to the Kokoschka Walden format at the express request of Dr. Reichel. Roessler liked to tell the following anecdote about why Dr. Reichel had never been successful in getting Kokoschka to paint his portrait: "Oskar Kokoschka, whom the Viennese collector Reichel had asked to paint his portrait, looked at the man attentively for a long time and then suggested: 'You know what, doctor? I'd much rather paint you a still life!' ' "[70]

If Dr. Reichel had hoped to find a new Kokoschka in Schiele, he was disappointed, as the double exchange in the portrait's ownership indicates. Nevertheless he remained, with Reininghaus, one of Schiele's most important patrons, and a man whom Schiele, in his artless "business correspondence," did not hesitate to half-threaten, half-cajole into buying more of his works. The following letter, written by Schiele to Reichel on 31 January 1911, is typical of the artist's high-handed relationships with his patrons:

"Without wishing to flatter you, I know in Vienna no one more knowledgeable about art than you. Therefore I have selected and sent to you this picture of mine from an entirely new series. In a short time you will be completely convinced by it, as soon as you begin not to look at it, but in to it. The picture is the one about which G. Klimt has said that he was glad to see such faces. It is SURELY, presently, the best that has been painted in Vienna. Whoever laughs at it must be observed as to how he laughs; he is hostile to my art, envious of my art, etc. Why should I always remain silent when this is the truth? E.S."[71]

Portrait of Herbert Rainer

Comparison of Kokoschka's *Portrait of Hans Reichel* with another major commission completed by Schiele this year, the *Portrait of Herbert Rainer* (plate 58), provides an opportunity to explore the two artists' separate interpretations of the same theme—an adolescent boy. Both portraits are characteristically Expressionist in their pathetic effect. In both pictures the summarization of the whole body by means of large surfaces continues the Hodler-Munch tradition.[72] Pallid hands and faces, strained, arrested gestures, bodies enveloped in formless or monolithic drapery, and isolation of the frail figures against a surface-charged void—these are the salient formal elements that produce the ensembles in both portraits. The unquestionable dramatic power conveyed by the hallucinatory portrait "presence" of these works may be compared to that of the eerie naturalism of the half-sung, half-spoken dialogue developed in Viennese music at this time. Schönberg's hybrid new *Sprechgesang*, introduced to the public for the first time in his *Pierrot Lunaire* of 1912, had the same heightened realism as did the exaggerated natural forms of Expressionist portraiture. One thinks of Schönberg's own earlier attempts in painting and of the similar emphasis he gave to the ghostly or uncanny—the frontally conceived, phosphorescent, apparitional heads that stared with huge eyes into their own visions (figure 119). Schönberg's essays in paint resulted in an autumn showing of his portraits, nature studies, and "color visions" in 1910. In the same year Schiele wrote in an essay entitled *Vision*: "I thought of my colored portrait visions and it seemed to me as if only once had I spoken to all those."[73] Similar terminology seems to have developed simultaneously in those creative fields for which the *intensification* of artistic expression was a mutual aim.

One of the preparatory studies for the Rainer portrait (plate 57) indicates the extent to which this intensification had become a working formula for

Schiele. A seemingly effortless portrait verisimilitude, destined to receive heightened enforcement in the oil, commands only part of the artist's attention. Equal concentration is given to the establishment of a powerful encasing contour, to gesture, and to the articulation of the oversized hands. On the canvas Schiele's continued search for a trenchant silhouette appears in the partially overpainted area of the boy's left elbow. In both the study and the oil the hands are insulated by enveloping swatches of thickly applied pigment. This organic isolation is distinctly related to the artist's many mother-and-child allegories (*The Dead Mother I*, plate 69; *Mother*, K.116; *Madonna*, K.134; *Mother and Death*, K.135; and *Dead Mother II* ["*Birth of Genius*"], plate 70) in which a similar womblike encasement is employed. The Rainer picture contains a self-projection of the artist's own childlike expectations of aid and recognition, as voiced so repeatedly in his letters. Whereas the dancelike pose of Kokoschka's Reichel boy recalls the entranced figure sequences and ballet postures of his *The Dreaming Boys* and continues his preferred outwardly oriented self-expression, the constrained, hemmed-in conception of Schiele's Rainer boy portrait communicates a sensitive and trusting exposure rather than a dream-like exhibitionism.[74] Schiele's portrait was found acceptable and another commission was given to the artist by Herr Rainer that year, the now lost portrait of Herbert Rainer's sister (K.IV).[75]

Portrait of Eduard Kosmack

While the isolating pictorial concentration displayed in Schiele's Rainer boy parallels in many respects the intense portraiture of Edvard Munch, a more specific evocation of the Norwegian master may be observed in Schiele's last major commission of 1910, completed in November, the *Portrait of Eduard Kosmack* (plate 61). The formal debt of this portrait to Munch's *Puberty* (plate 60) is unmistakable. The idea of conscious exposure, conveyed by the resolute frontality of body and unaverted glance, must have appealed to Schiele. Munch's simplified background, in which an expanding organic form rises as a visual symbol of the young girl's emotional state, has been carried one step further in Schiele's portrait where an actual void now functions as counterpart to the sitter it contains.

The draining of this space around the sitter differentiates Schiele's portrait of Kosmack not only from its Munch prototype, but also from its Kokoschka and Mopp counterparts. In Schiele the astral body glow intervenes between solid and void; in Kokoschka the ghostly efflorescence around the silhouette transmits a motor discharge that electrifies the entire remaining surface. This difference in reaction to the *horror vacui* previously expressed by Klimt is stated on a purely compositional level as well. Kokoschka's figures are usually larger than Schiele's in relation to the canvas and therefore take up more surface area.[76] And Kokoschka often extends the figure across the canvas, whereas Schiele insists on a concentrated portrait core that frequently appears to be compressed by or wedged within the surrounding void. In portraits dating from the middle years of Schiele's career, the austerity of empty space is tempered by a geometrical fracturing of the surface into an expressive carrier (see especially the *Double Portrait of Heinrich and Otto Benesch*, plate 110), and in the late works a new painterly activation of the surface is introduced (*Portrait of Paris von Gütersloh*, plate 190). In 1910 however the primary dependence upon a painstakingly defined expressive solid inserted into a void relates Schiele's portraits to the forceful graphic clarity of Hodler (as, for example, in that master's 1907 *Portrait of the Sculptor Vibert*), whereas Kokoschka's energized surfaces actually continue the space-filling tradition of Klimt. The "psychic" energy of individual artistic temperaments may express itself through multiple surface-filling forms, as with Klimt or Bresdin, or it may isolate elements into concentrated essays on synthetic construction, as with Schiele or Modigliani.

Kosmack's bibliographical data and his relationship to the artist provide explanations for two striking aspects of his portrait that might otherwise have to be interpreted on stylistic grounds alone. A feature in common to all the preparatory studies and to the painting itself is the commanding glance of the refulgent blue eyes. In the watercolor, *Study for the Portrait of Eduard Kosmack, Seated* (plate 62), the astral body glow and "melancholic" coloring of the face force into prominence the incandescent region of the eyes. The asymmetrical Klimtian figure disposition across the surface marks this study as one of the earliest Schiele made for the portrait. In a later watercolor, *Study for the Portrait of Eduard Kosmack, Frontal with Left Hand Raised to Forehead* (plate 63), the eyes receive added emphasis through the sitter's conspicuous gesture and through the new frontal treatment of face and torso. The sketch closest to the final oil, *Study for the Portrait of Eduard Kosmack, Frontal with Clasped Hands* (plate 64), provides a less overt but equally effective intensification of the sitter's forceful gaze by means of a rhythmically repeated symmetry that affects all paired parts of the body—knees, hands, elbows, shoulders, ears—in a regular, mesmeric progression to the luminous eyes. A photograph of Kosmack (plate 59a) confirms the wiry physique, but tells nothing of the radiance or compelling quality of the eyes. Should Schiele's arresting depiction be considered solely in the light of an Expressionist adaptation of the watching heads of consciousness in Jugendstil art and architecture, or as a continuation of the staring Medusa faces popularized by Franz Stuck and Khnopff? Even the affinity with Munch's *Puberty* ends here, for the gaze of Munch's young girl is fixed on her thoughts, whereas Kosmack's stare is one of determined will power directed outward and aimed at the beholder. There is a more personal explanation. Kosmack was an enthusiastic and successful amateur hypnotist.[77] It was this prepossessing faculty, a power capable of transforming its frail owner into an image of authority with access to the mind's innermost secrets, that Schiele wished to incarnate and project against a void of subsconsciousness. Both sitter and subject matter therefore were eminently suited to Expressionist interpretation.[78]

The second salient feature of the Kosmack portrait is the apparent reference to a natural environment suggested by the large decaying sunflower to one side of the sitter's knees. Whereas present-day psychology might interpret the sunflower as a sexual symbol,[79] the historian explains the presence of this wilting sunflower as a continuation of one of the nineteenth century's most favored motifs, employed by writers and painters from Oscar Wilde to Van Gogh, and as the new Expressionist style's heightening of the morbid side of Jugendstil.[80] In his letters, poems, and essays Schiele frequently dwelt upon the particular tenderness he felt like the poet Trakl for autumn, the season of glorious decay that reminded him that he was but a pilgrim in this world. His landscapes repeatedly treat the subject of autumn, often centering on the anthropomorphic motif of several slender trees whose fragility is emphasized by the wooden splints with which they are braced for winter; and sunflowers continue as a favorite subject of the artist all his life. But to return to the Kosmack sunflower—there is, as with the hypnotic gaze, a further explanation to be found in the personality of the sitter himself and his relationship to the artist. Eduard Kosmack was the publisher of two important Viennese art journals, *Der Architect* and *Das Interieur*, and a nephew of the painter Adolf Hoelzel. Kosmack published his uncle's theories on art and later became a director of the Wiener Werkstätte. At the instigation of Arthur Roessler, he agreed to reproduce one of the most spectacular of Schiele's early paintings, *Sunflower* (Plate 59b) in a 1911 volume of *Das Interieur*.[81] Schiele's inclusion of the sunflower in his portrait of Kosmack may thus also be understood as a souvenir of their collaboration and a silent "reminder" of the mutual project underway. That this was Schiele's way of paying a compliment or sealing a bargain is substantiated by his 1917 *Portrait of Dr. Franz Martin Haberditzl* (plate 150), the first museum director to acquire Schiele's works for a public institution in Austria. In this portrait the director of the Österreichische Staatsgalerie is shown holding and admiring a recent work by Schiele, a watercolor, curiously enough, of a sunflower.

The close-focus, gesticulating, dramatic portraits painted by Schiele at the end of 1910 were the result of an energetic search. Countless experiments and several major formal statements in self-portraiture had brought the artist to consider frontality as the preferred solution for the psychic exposure demanded by Expressionist portraiture. In his portraits of others he proceeded from the melodramatic and facilely communicated pathos of the Zakovsek, Graff, and Reichel portraits to the more stringent expressiveness of the Roessler, Rainer boy, and Kosmack portraits. These powerful statements depended upon certain formal features such as the extended shoulder, or emphasized symmetry, suggestions of "mutilation," an astral body glow, and the projection of the sitter against a void that at the most symbolized the realm of the psyche and at the least melancholic isolation.

It is strange yet germane to the artist's temperament that at the very time when he had developed a radical portrait style which was receiving acceptance from at least a part of Vienna's avant-garde, Schiele made himself unavailable for further portrait commissions. He left the city and began a troubled quest for seclusion and communication with nature that was to take him from village to village and terminate in his arrest and imprisonment.

CHAPTER IV

1910-1914: Isolation and Thematic Absorption in Self

SCHIELE'S apparent sabotage of his prospects as a leading portrait painter of the new Vienna avant-garde was partially caused by a powerful Wanderlust. Periodically the need to get away seized Schiele irresistably and was responsible for impromptu railway trips even to points distant as Trieste. This restlessness, compounded with a sense of social inadequacy in the educated, articulate world of his patrons and new friends, made Schiele particularly sensitive to the intrigues inherent in being the protégé of a local clique in which each member was in covert competition with the others. The frustrations of commissions that did not materialize, abandoned projects, and deferred payments are recorded in Schiele's correspondence with Roessler. Nevertheless, and until the weather permitted more extensive travel, Schiele was confined to Vienna for the winter and, in a typical response, began to retreat into himself. He moved to a more outlying district, Meidling, and found a studio in the Grünbergstrasse, where the vast bordering parks of Schönbrunn castle gave him some comfort.[1] This longing to retire to nature is a feature shared by so many German Expressionist artists that it has often been remarked upon as one of the movement's most salient aspects, continuing that nostalgic search begun by Gauguin for an "unspoiled" environment. One thinks of the "retreats" of Nolde, Pechstein, Kirchner, Campendonk, and Marc, and also of the slightly earlier group-attempts to create ideal artistic communities in rural atmospheres, such as Worpswede and Dachau—the German equivalents of Pont-Aven. In Austria, too, artists sought out nature as a necessity; the Bohemian Forests were "discovered," Klimt spent some twenty summers at the Attersee, and Kubin lived for fifty-three years in an isolated country house.

In his new-found isolation Schiele produced the erotic watercolors sought by his clients and brooded upon the inhumanity of his penniless existence in a soul-destroying metropolis. Judging from his autobiographical essays and letters these grim ruminations were in much the same character as those of Rilke, who would eventually replace Rimbaud as his favorite writer and whose autobiographical *The Notebooks of Malte Laurids Brigge* (published 1910) parallels some of Schiele's experiences and perceptions.[2] Surrounded by the dozens upon dozens of gesticulating self-portrait studies that had gone into the painting of his three nude oil self-portraits, Schiele must have brooded too over the scornful words his uncle Czihaczek had recently used to describe him: "Egon takes after his father in all his bad characteristics, especially in his vaulting ambition, haughtiness, and pretentiousness."[3] Unable yet to enjoy on any permanent basis the companionship and activities delineated in his drawings of erotica—although his good looks brought him several short-lived affairs at this time—Schiele continued to speculate on himself and to consult the image his mirror held. His output of portraits of others, even portrait sketches, dropped markedly towards the end of 1910, and during the following two years was at a minimum. On the other hand, his self-portraits proliferated in all media. Many are allegories, involving one or two other figures, male or female, all usually dressed in ascetic garments. The self-portraits produced during these years of isolation, first in Vienna, and then in the country, do however fall into distinctive groups that display specific and changing thematic interests. Examination of prominent individual works of this period will indicate these various motifs and note alterations in style. It will be seen that the development of both style and theme continues to be manifestly related to Schiele's personal history.

1910–1911: THE SELF-SEERS—DOUBLE SELF-PORTRAITS

Three oils constituting a series that Schiele called the "Self-Seers" illustrate a new and major concept. The paintings are: *Self-Seers I* (figure 82), painted in December of 1910, and *The Prophet* (figure 86) and *Self-Seers II ("Death and Man")* (figure 87), both painted in 1911. All are *double* self-portraits. Schiele's occasional reference to the final painting[4] of the series as "Death and Man" specifies at least one level of interpretation: the ancient *vanitas* or memento mori theme in which death stalks his victim, a popular subject in German art and literature since the days of the Housebook Master and Dürer. Schiele had been exposed to a local memento mori at the Academy art gallery, where there hung on permanent display a painting of the subject by the monogrammist H. F., presumably the Basel painter Hans Fries, who worked under Holbein's influence.[5] Just as the autumn tree appealed to the artist as a symbol of man's transient state, so did this traditional theme and several of Schiele's mother-and-child allegories (plates 69 and 70) deal with "Death" taking the mother, and the simultaneity of death and new life. If Hofmannsthal's *Der Tor und Der Tod* had held any interest for Schiele at all, it would probably have been found in the scene in which Death appears as a musician to the world-weary Claudio. The memento mori in painting had been re-popularized in

1872 by Arnold Böcklin in his much admired *Self-Portrait with Death Playing the Violin* (figure 83), a work that received frequent reproduction in art publications both on and after the occasion of Böcklin's death in 1901. Lovis Corinth had responded with a more robust version in his ponderously sardonic *Self-Portrait with Skeleton* of 1896, in which the artist and a studio skeleton share equal portrait space and stare out challengingly at the beholder who is coerced into making morose comparisons. Schiele's interpretation in the Self-Seers series and in the later allegorical self-portrait *Death and Maiden* (plate 129), returned to the intense earnestness of his Gothic predecessors.[6]

Certain formal devices in the Self-Seers group, such as the arrested hand gestures and the compositional suggestion of various limb amputations or dislocations, are familiar through their earlier use in the 1910 self-portraits dealing with masturbation, especially *Melancholia* and *Delirium*, and this solitary search for sexual release certainly figures as one of the initial thematic concerns of Schiele's new series. One of the conventional fears accompanying an indulgence in masturbation is that it may be detected in expressions of the face. In *Self-Seers I*, following an almost Dorian Gray-like use of the painted double, Schiele transfers the consequences of this act to the countenance of his grimacing image in the foreground, while his "own" features remain relatively unclouded.[7] However the increasing dehumanization and sexless aspect of the remaining two double self-portraits document not a specific physical habit but an impending and deeply rooted personality crisis. It is in this light that the whole series will be considered.

The most important aspect and the thematic innovation of these self-portraits is the appearance of a double. In one form or another the *Doppelgänger* had fascinated German Romantic writers from Goethe and Jean Paul Richter to Kleist and E.T.A. Hoffmann, and in the nineteenth century the motif had received greater psychological implications, particularly within the *Besserungsstück* genre of Vienna's Grillparzer and Raimund.[8] More recently Dostoevsky, in his novels *The Brothers Karamazov* and *The Double* (the latter illustrated by Kubin with sixty drawings in 1913), had revived and expanded the personality dissociation of Hoffmann's *Doppelgänger* into an interpretation of the double as a projection of the subconscious self. It is indeed extraordinary and in keeping with the general Expressionist anticipation of psychoanalytic concerns that, probably unaware of such literary parallels, Schiele intuitively explored the existence and implications of the "other self" in his Self-Seers series. A closer study of the three paintings will indicate that the primary theme, whether begun as an essay on autoeroticism or as "Death and Man," soon became an expression of the divided self. The presence of the subconscious had already been symbolized by the astral body glows and voids of the 1910 portraits. Now the division of self became in part a battle before the mirror, between the artist as creator of and as vessel for his own image.

The title of the first painting, *Self-Seers I*, announces this thematic concern. Prolific self-portraiture before a mirror had brought a new being into existence, and Schiele now sees a second self who must also be portrayed, and against whom possibly the accusation may be leveled: "It is not I who masturbate, but you—my other self." With a possessive attachment he forces this entity to undergo what he has experienced and exposes the raw new being to total self-confrontation. Schiele the conscious artist kneels behind his creation and with his left (thumbless) hand directs its attention upon itself. In ghostly mimicry of its master the apparition jerks up its left hand. Schiele's eyes look directly into the mirror that reflects his creation, his mouth is open as if urging the creature to look upon himself and see. The creature is a stylized image of Schiele: it combines the pursed lips, the narrowed eye, the raised eyebrow, the puckered forehead, and the electrified black mass of hair of the 1910 self-portrait drawings. In a hypnotic state, equivalent to the somnambulistic dissociations of personality described by Hoffmann and Dostoevsky, it obeys the exhortations of its creator. A black garment binds the two figures together. They kneel upon an abstract plane that combines with the dark background that envelops them. The darkness is broken only by the exposed white flesh of their bodies and a luminous triangle of light behind their heads. In this double act of self-seeing the created image seems to succumb to the powerful spectacle of itself. Rilke's description of a terrifying battle between image and reflection experienced by Malte Laurids Brigge (in which the hero is suddenly unable to remove a mask he has tried on) depicts a similar hallucinatory experience:

"Hot and angry, I rushed to the mirror and with difficulty watched through the mask the working of my hands. But for this the mirror had just been waiting. Its moment of retaliation had come. While I strove in boundlessly increasing anguish to squeeze somehow out of my disguise, it forced me, by what means I do not know, to lift my eyes and imposed on me an image, no, a reality, with which, against my will, I became permeated: for now the mirror was the stronger, and I was the mirror. I stared at this great, terrifying unknown before me, and it seemed to me appalling to be alone with him. But at the very moment I thought this, the worst befell: I lost all sense. I simply ceased to exist. For one second I had an indescribable, painful and futile longing for myself, then there was only he: there was nothing but he."[9]

The struggle before the mirror between "Sein" and "Schein," and the artist's power to mimic the looking-glass by creating a reflection of his own image continued to fascinate Schiele. One of the sheets from a sketchbook of 1911 (figure 85) contains a face in the lower center of the page which is unmistakably related to the 1910 double self-portrait. Although the virile growth of hair, the frown, and the pursed lips are repeated faithfully, the eyeballs are now enormous and seem no longer to be socketed in a living face but in a skull. In the head to the right this idea of a skull is carried a step further by depriving it of hair. A direct precedent for these skull-like faces is seen in the background of Klimt's much-discussed painting of a pregnant woman, *Hope* (figure 84), which Schiele had admired in the 1909 Kunstschau. Behind an actual skull shown in profile in Klimt's painting, three emaciated faces stare out frontally in varying stages of awareness, and the gaunt face on the far left displays the squinting eye so consistently employed in Schiele's work.

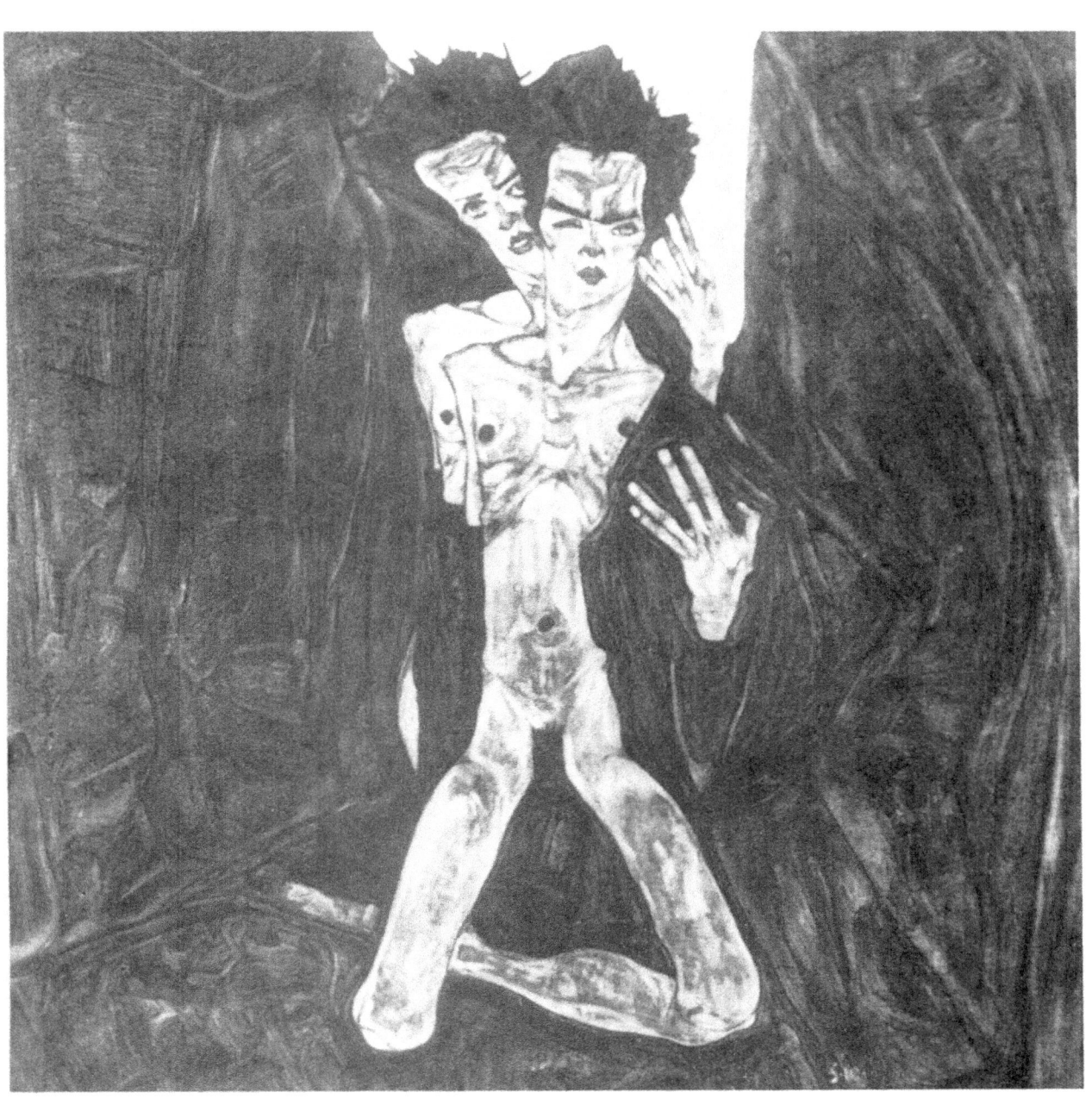

FIG. 82. Schiele, *Self-Seers I*, 1910, oil.

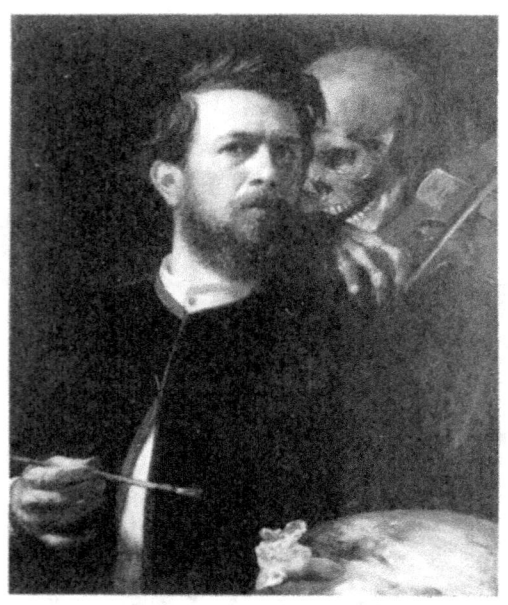

FIG. 83. Arnold Böcklin, *Self-Portrait with Death Playing the Violin*, 1872, oil.

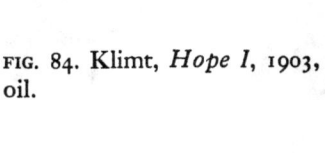

FIG. 84. Klimt, *Hope I*, 1903, oil.

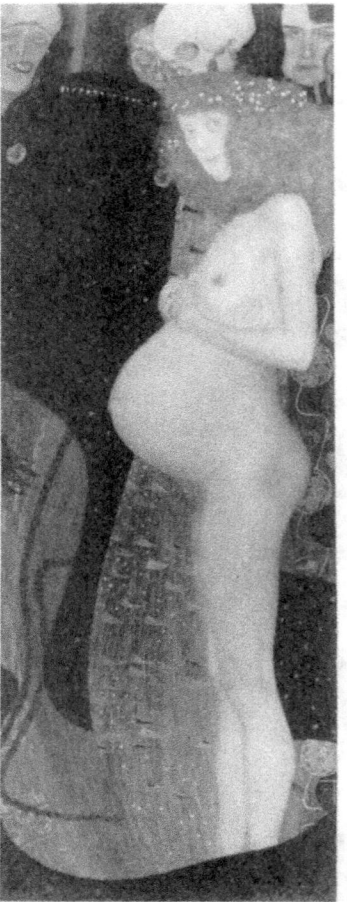

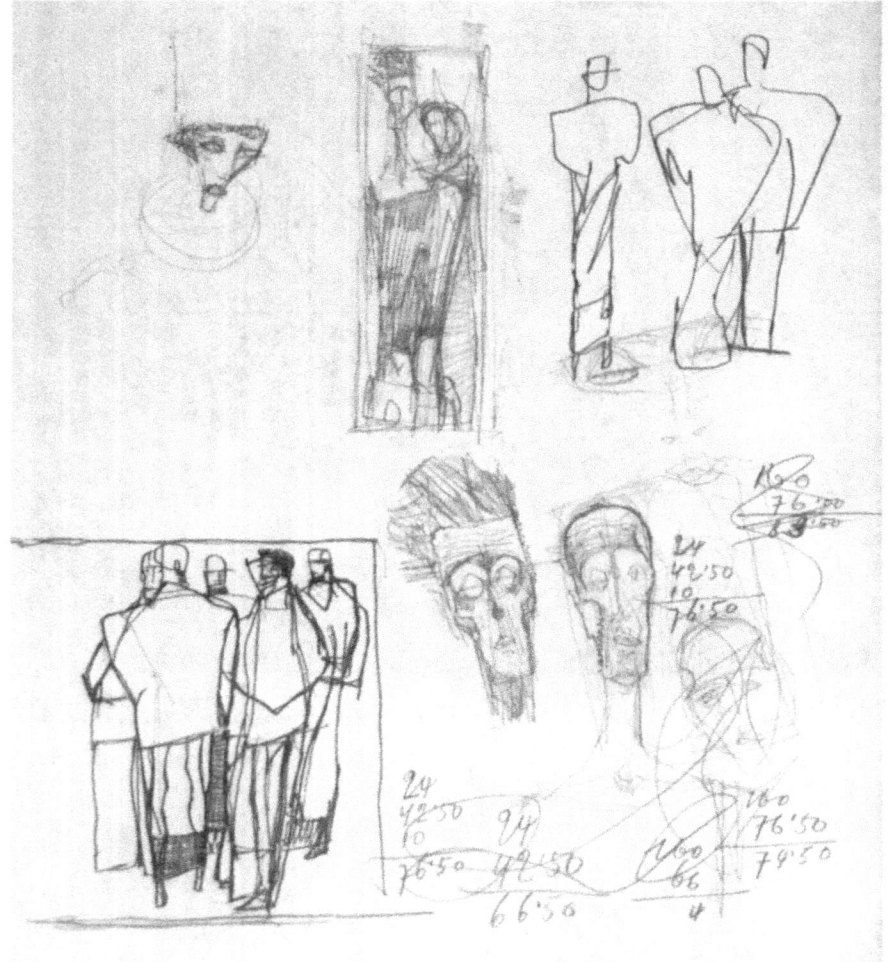

FIG. 85. Schiele, A.E.S.A. Sketchbook XII, 1911, pencil, p. 10 *recto*.

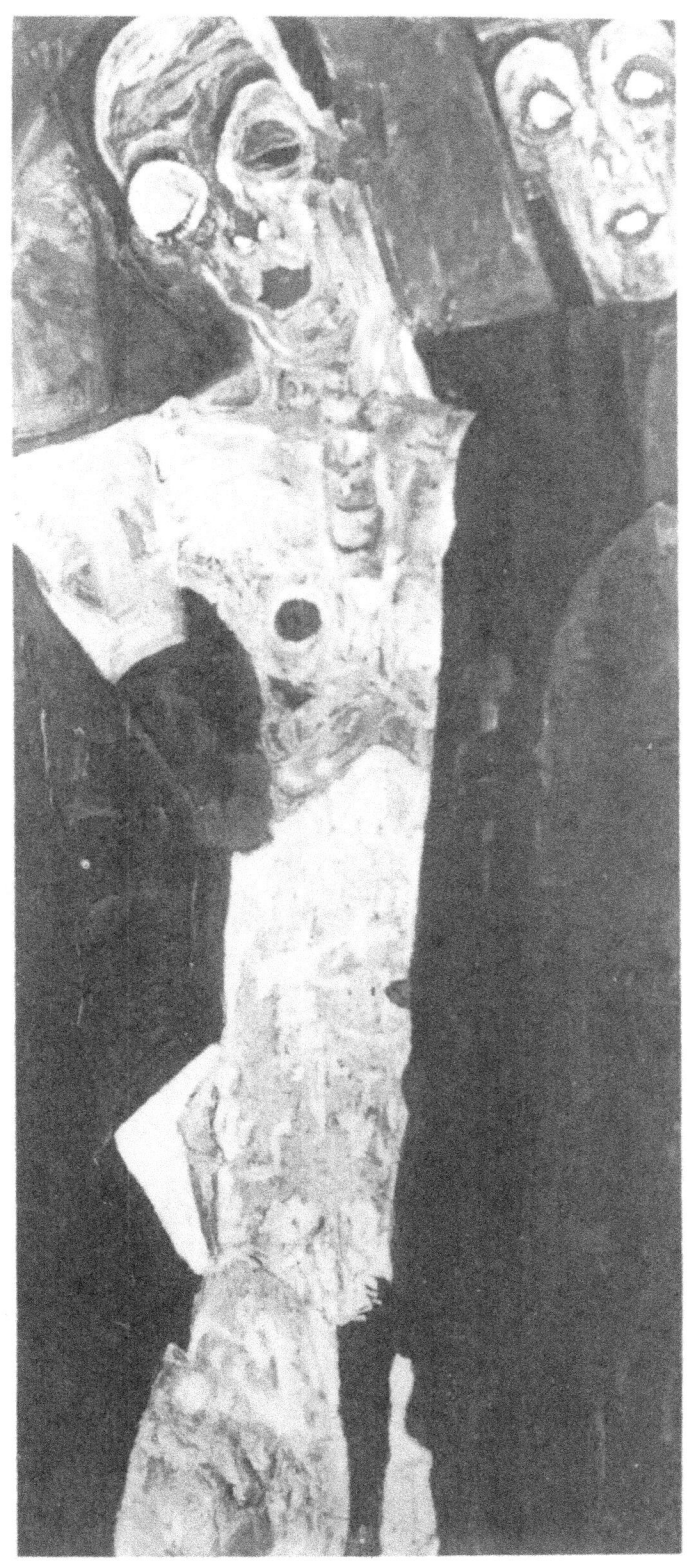

FIG. 86. Schiele, *The Prophet*, 1911, oil.

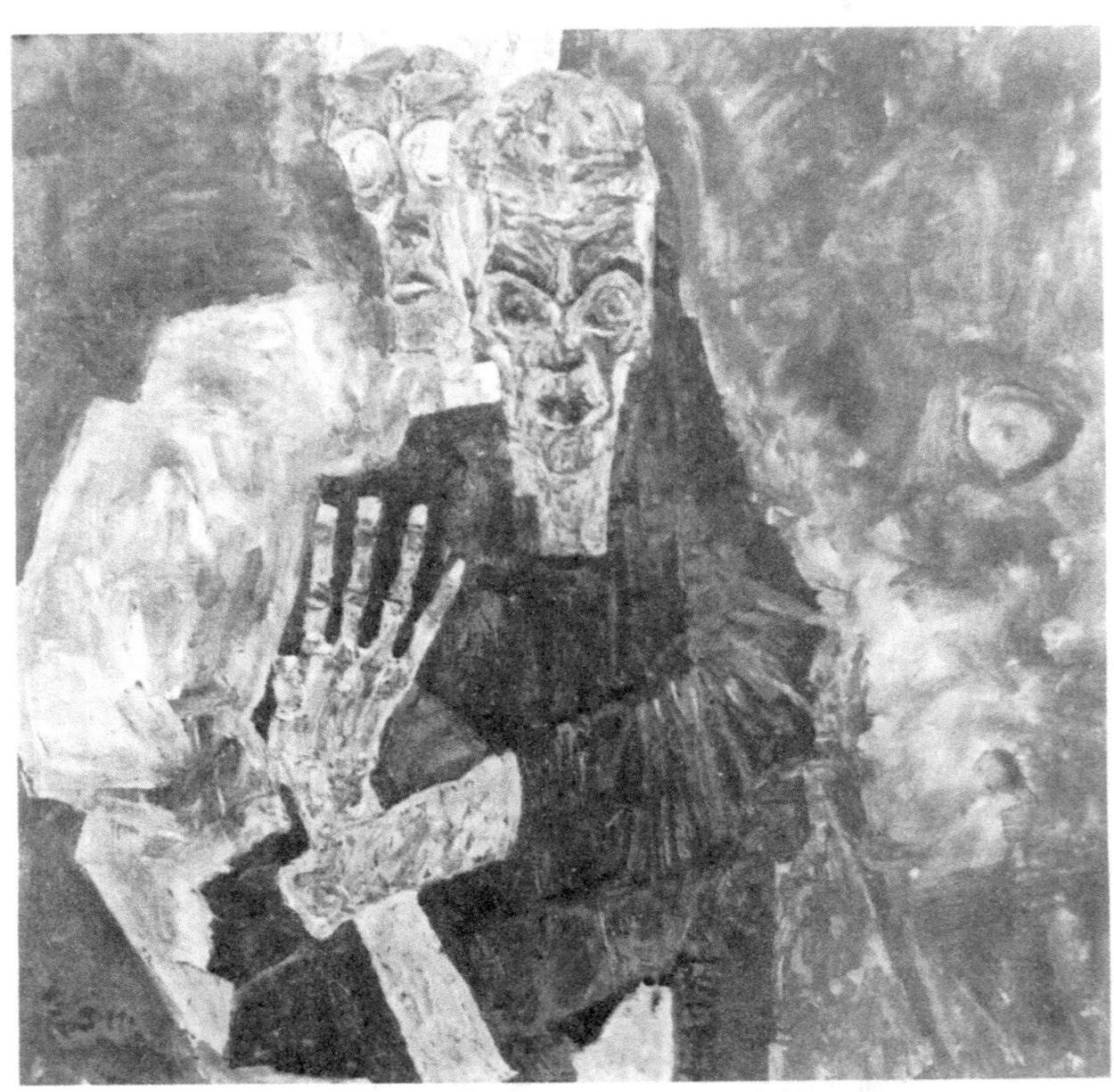

FIG. 87. Schiele, *Self-Seers II ("Death and Man")*, 1911, oil.

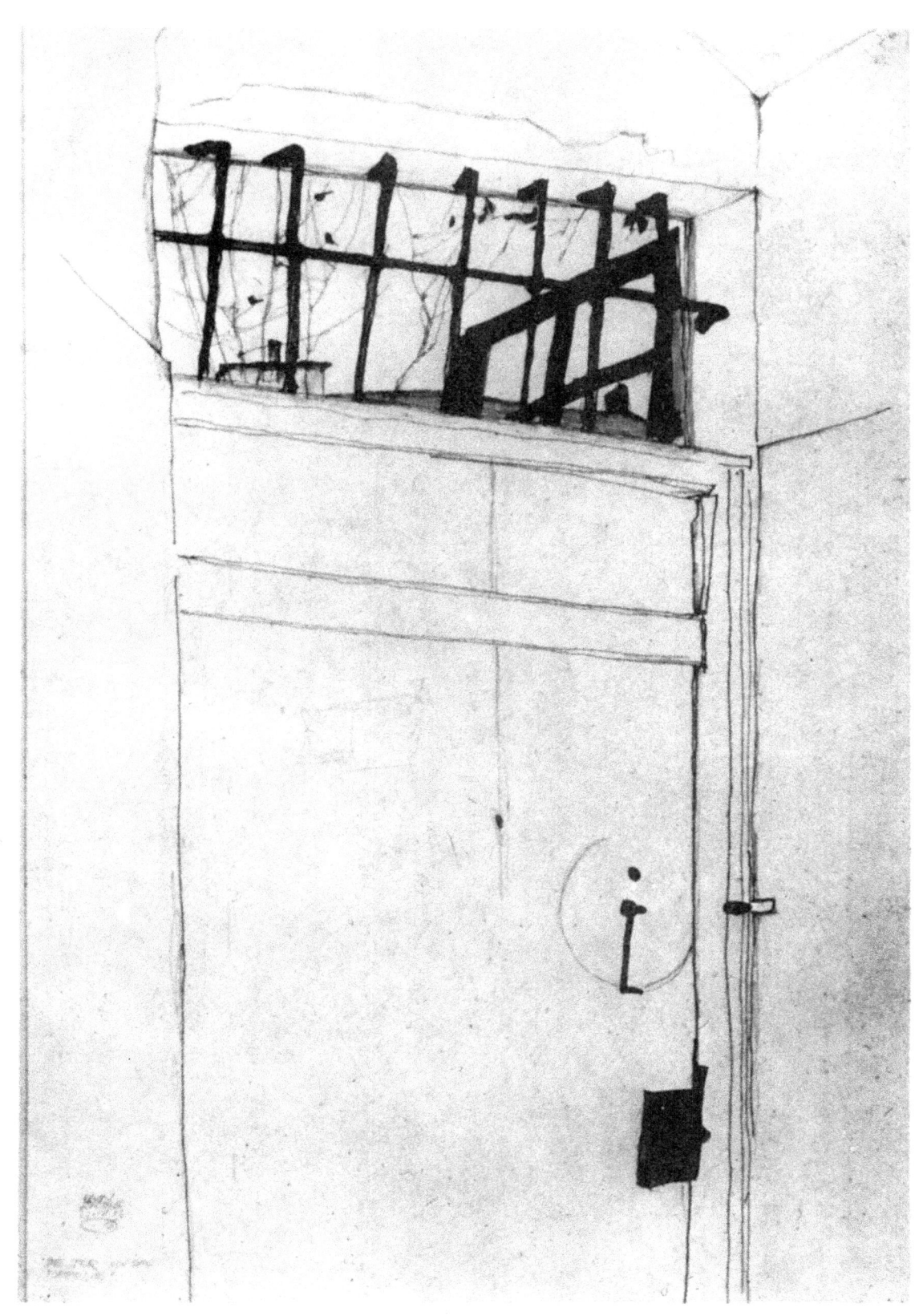

FIG. 88. Schiele, *The Door Into the Open!*, 21 April 1912, pencil and watercolor.

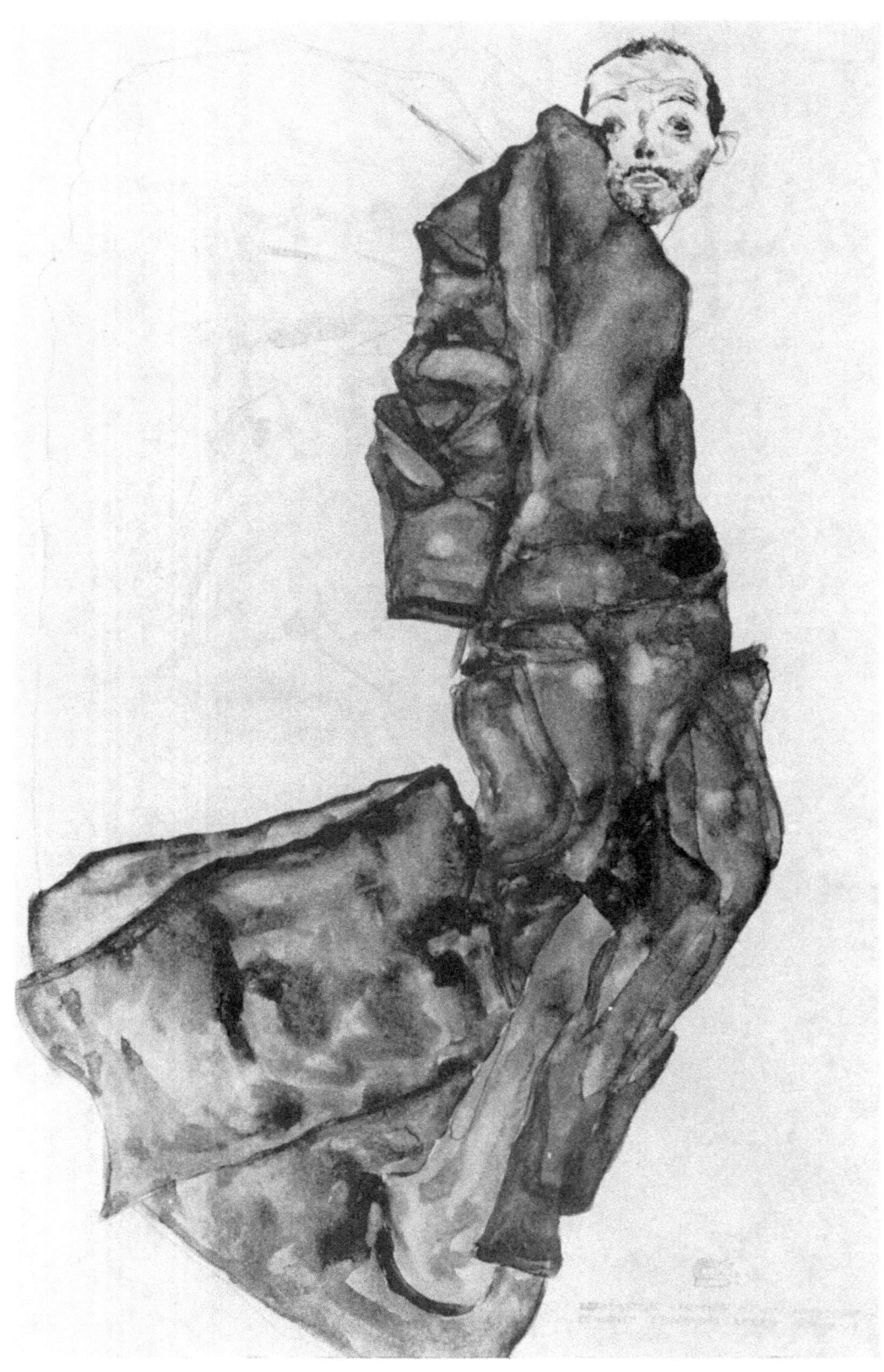

FIG. 89. Schiele, *Hindering the Artist is a Crime, It is Murdering Life in The Bud!*, 23 April 1912, pencil and watercolor.

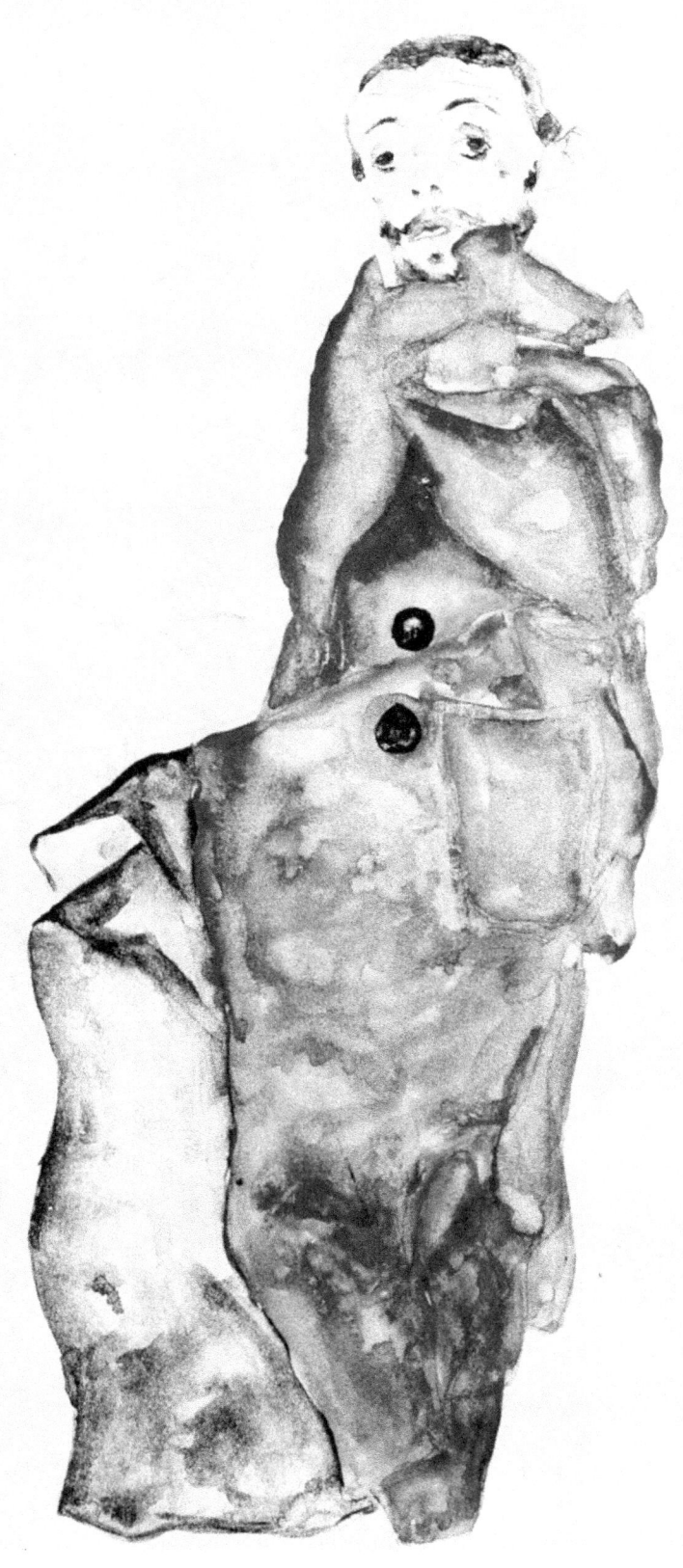

FIG. 90. Schiele, *I Love Antitheses*, 24 April 1912, pencil and watercolor.

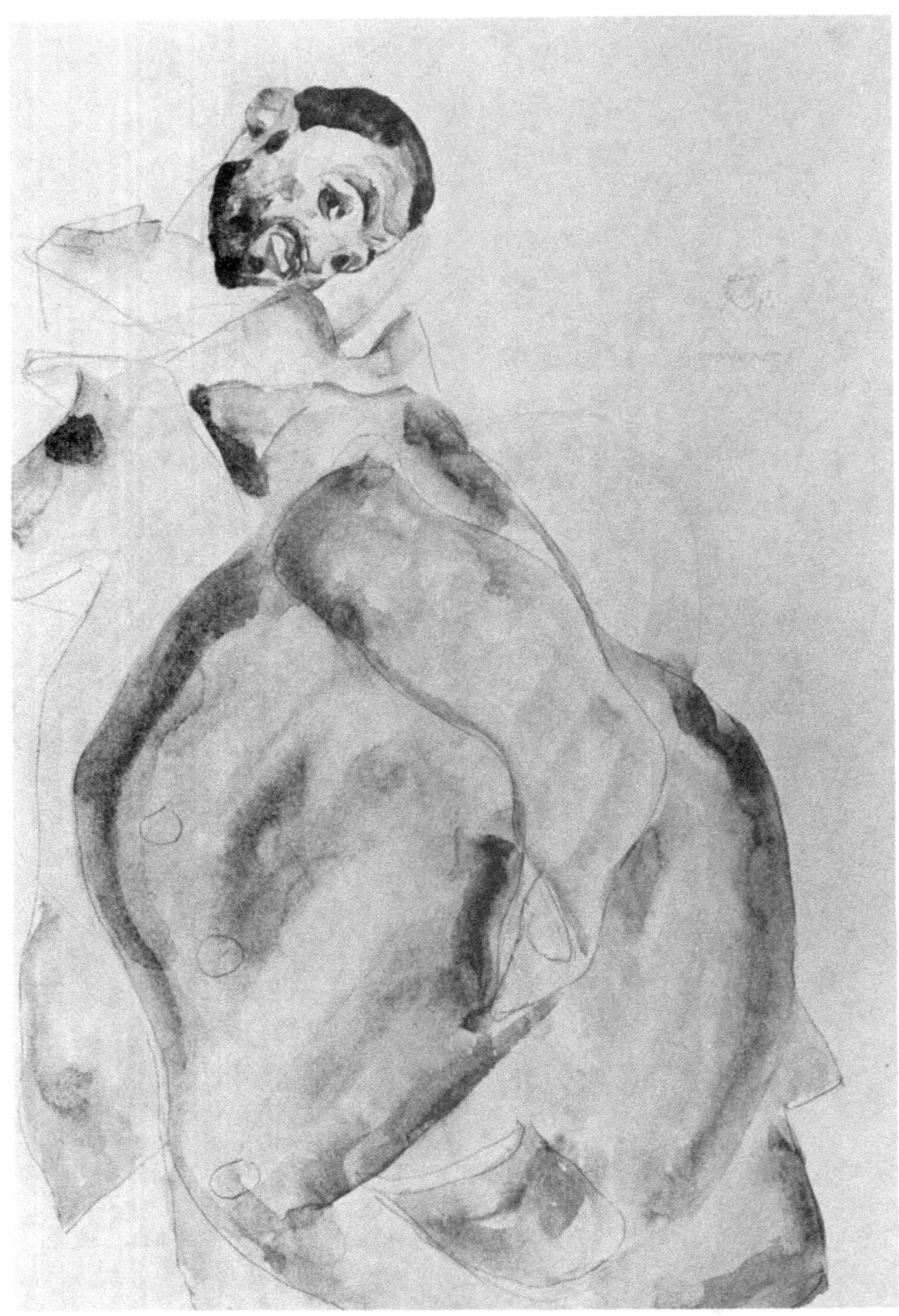

FIG. 91. Schiele, *Prisoner!*, 24 April 1912, pencil and watercolor.

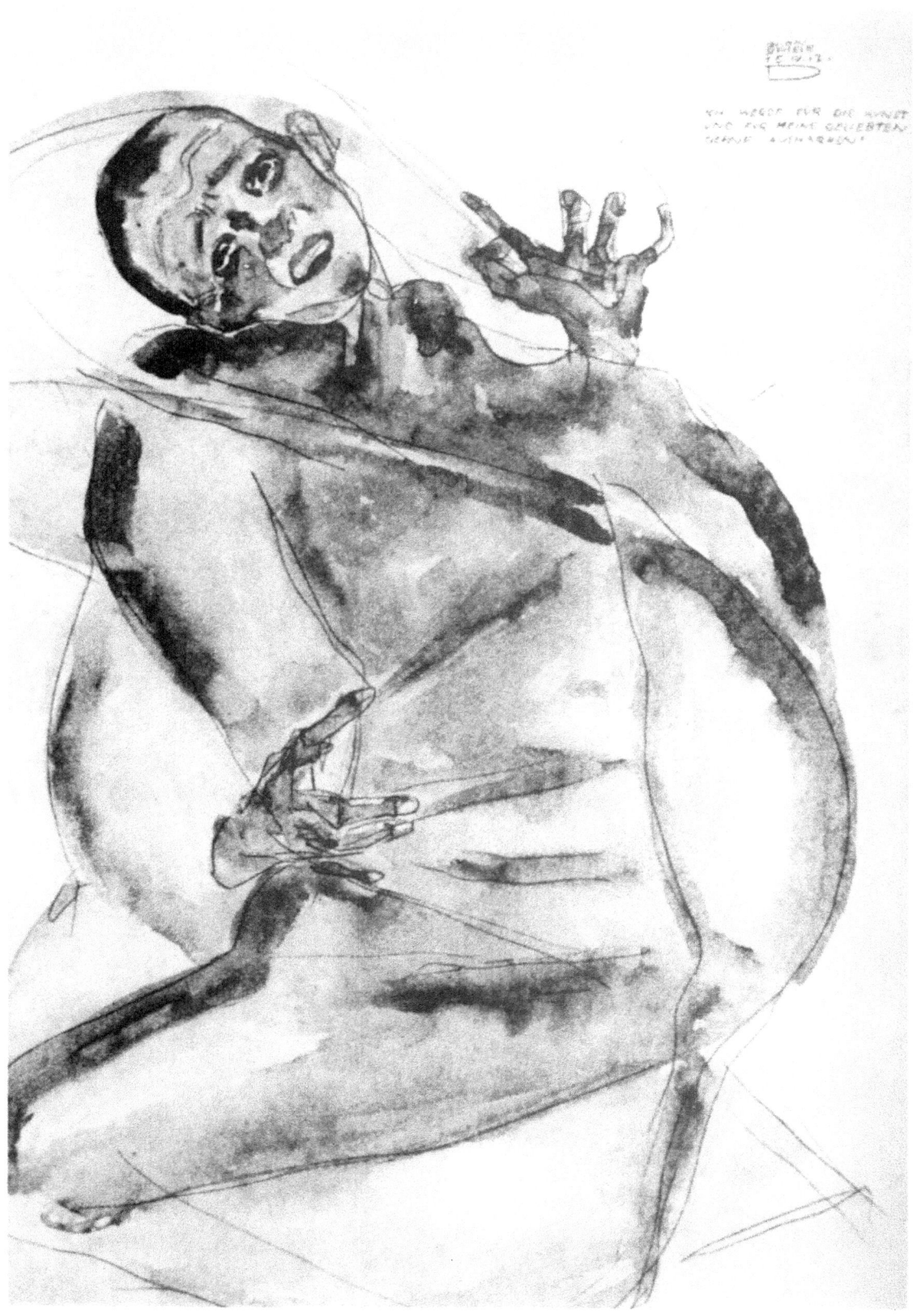

FIG. 92. Schiele, *For My Art and for My Loved Ones I Will Gladly Endure to the End*, 25 April 1912, pencil and watercolor.

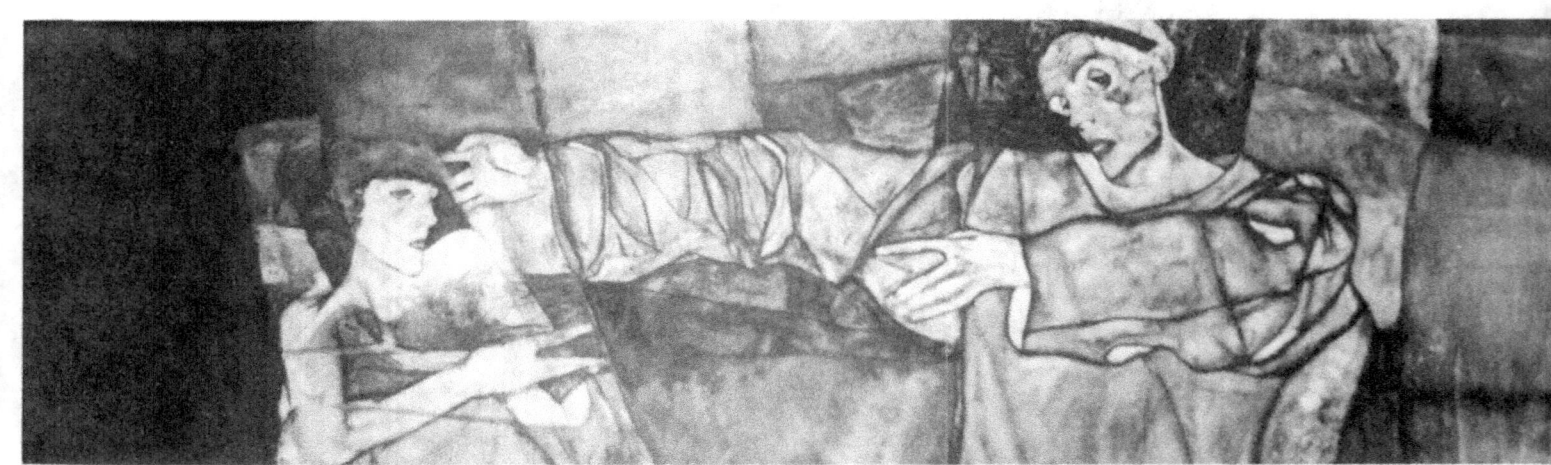

FIG. 93. Schiele, *Self-Portrait with Model ("The Sleepwalkers")* 1913, oil.

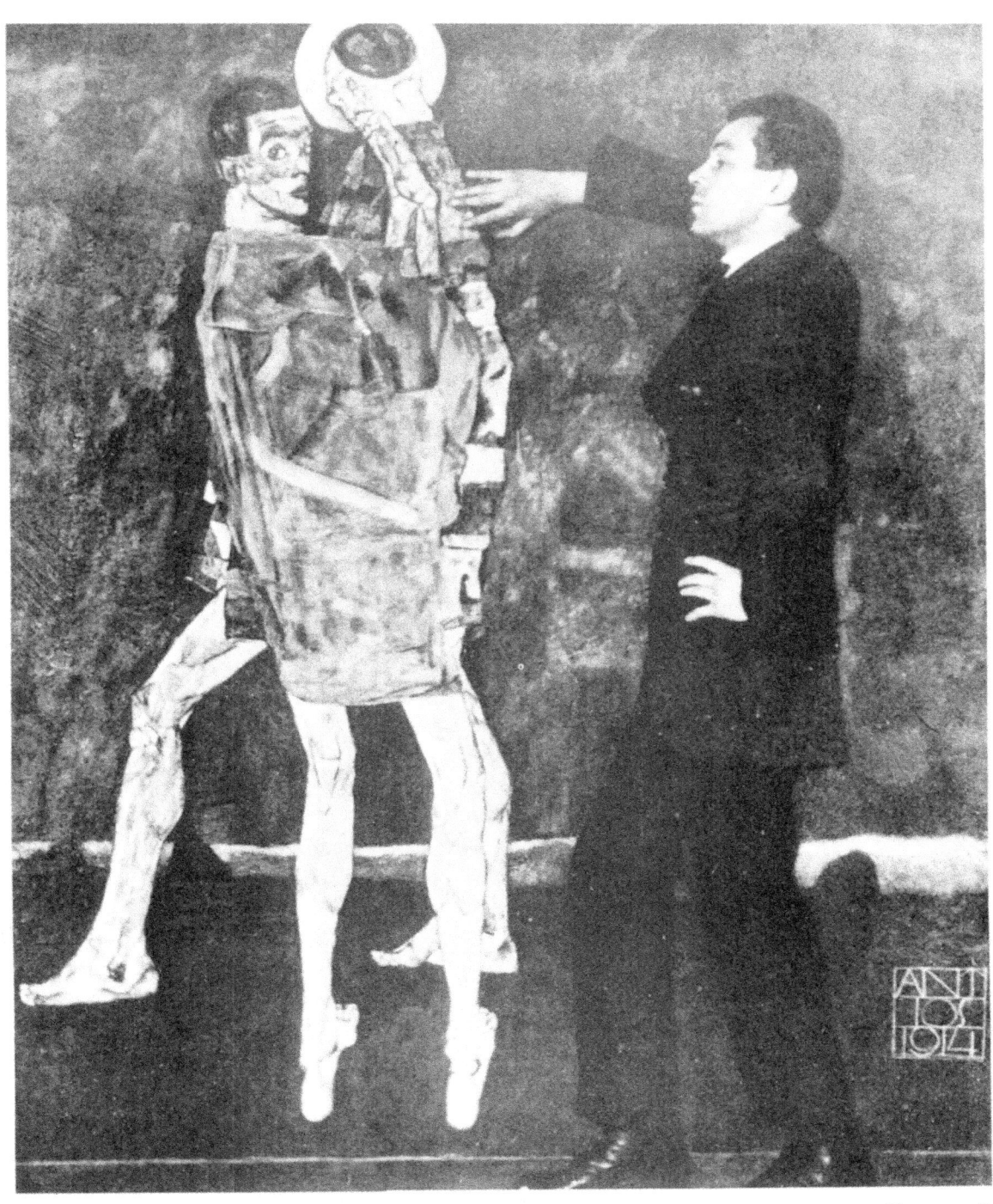

FIG. 94. Schiele, *Self-Portrait with Saint ("Encounter")*, 1913, oil.

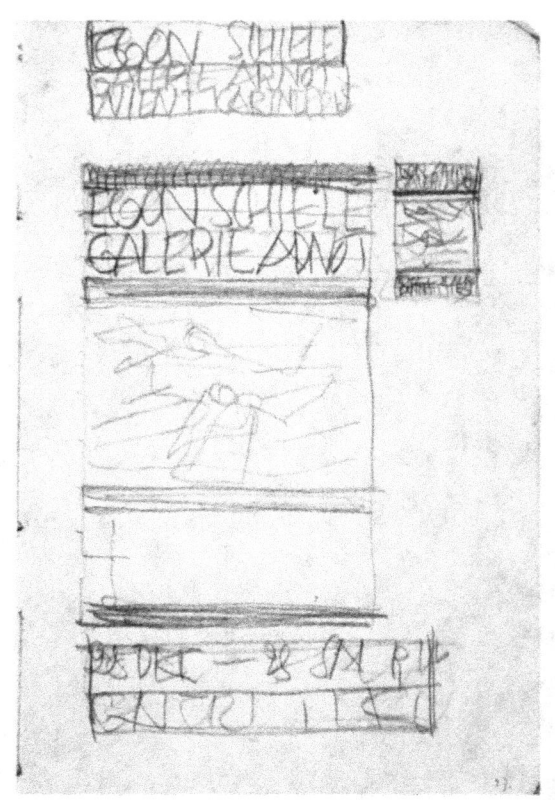

FIG. 95. Schiele, A.E.S.A. Sketchbook VI, 1914,
pencil, p. 27 *recto*.

FIG. 96. Schiele, *Self-Portrait as St. Sebastian*, 1914, pencil.

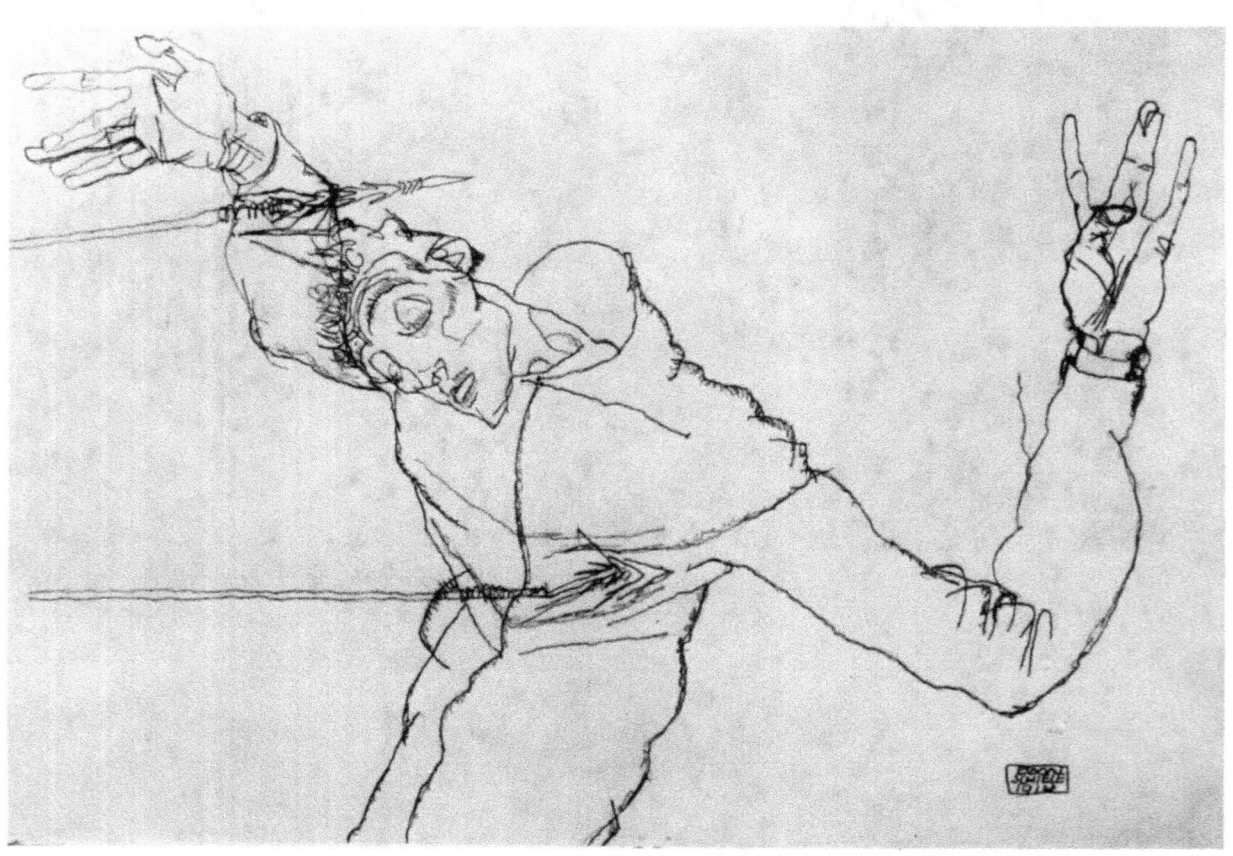

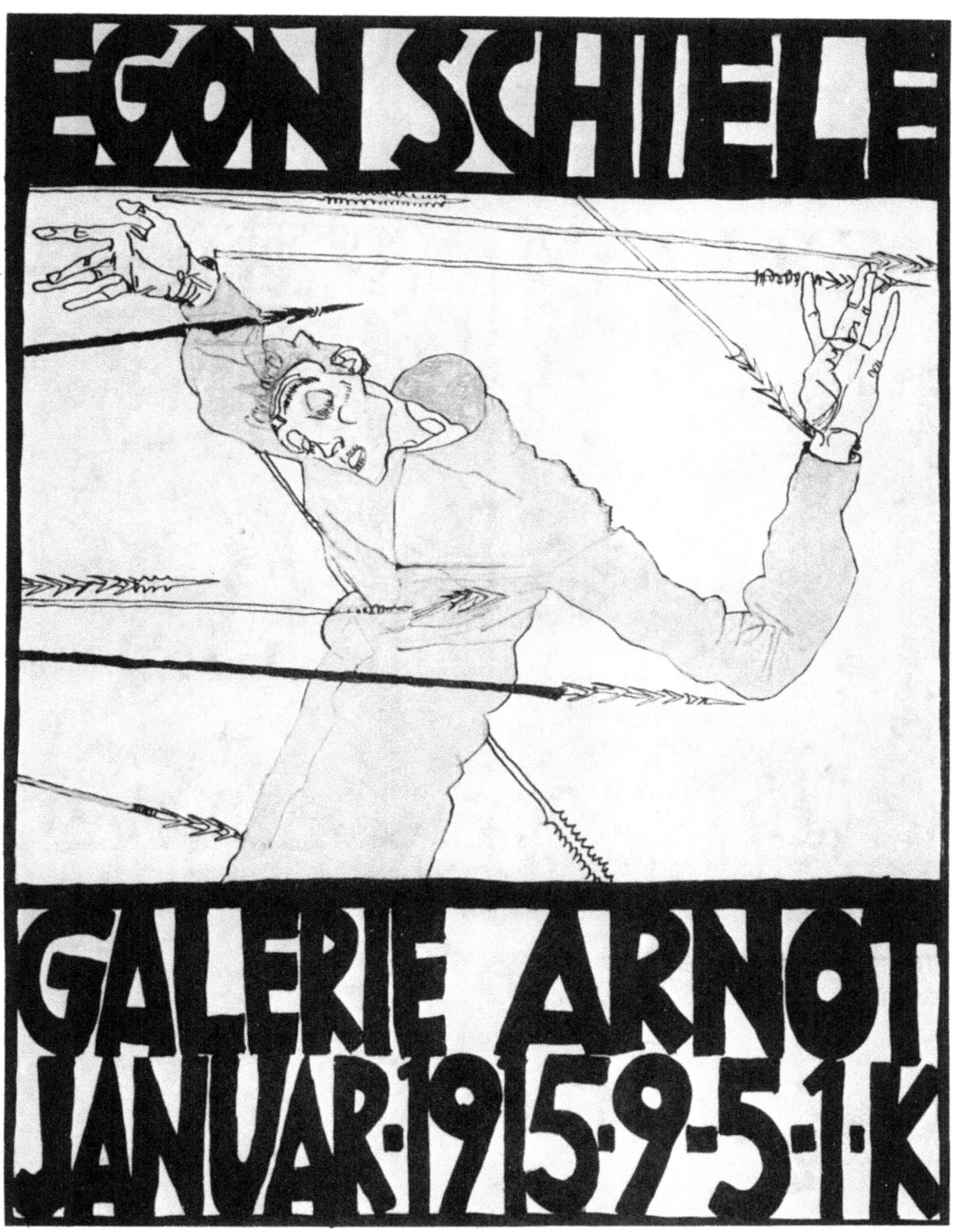

FIG. 97. Schiele, *Poster Design for the Arnot Gallery*, 1914, ink, black crayon, and watercolor.

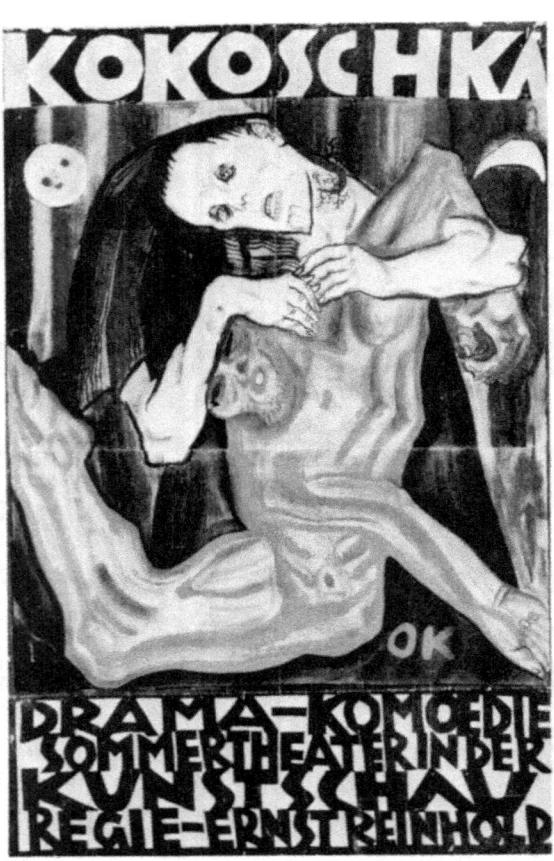

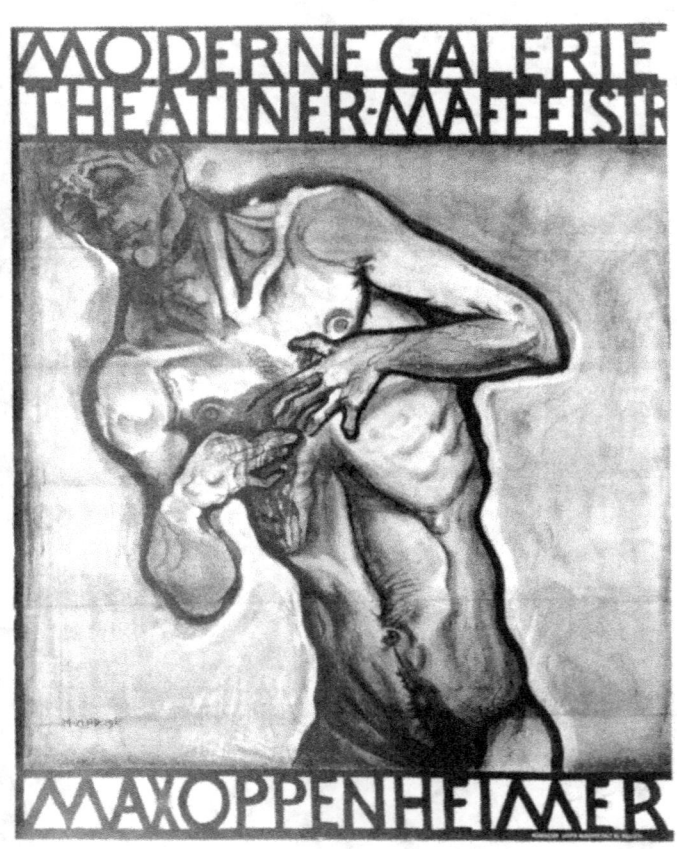

FIG. 98. Kokoschka, *Poster for the 1908 Vienna Kunstschau*, 1908, color lithograph.

FIG. 99. Max Oppenheimer (Mopp), *Poster*, 1911, color lithograph.

The large-socketed eyes of the two faces from Schiele's notebook, whether staring or veiled by lids, strongly suggest a somnambulistic state, and in the small framed two-figure arrangement sketched directly above them the idea of somnambulism takes form in a compositional study for the second painting in the double self-portrait series, *The Prophet*. Gone is the imperative self-confrontation of *Self-Seers I*; now the two images of Schiele appear to share a trancelike state of paralyzed wills and suspended action. The title, always important with the artist, may be meant to apply to one of the figures or both. Perhaps it is still Schiele, the creator, who stands in back and to the right, draped in dark garments, and with his right arm encircling and possibly divesting himself of the nude being whose head sags. As in the previous painting Schiele's eyes and mouth are open while the creature's squint has now completely closed one huge eye. And yet there is only one "real" eye in the picture—that of the droopy-lidded creature—for Schiele's eyes are really only sockets (especially noticeable in color).[10] Aside from the possibly intended ironic meaning of a sightless seer, there is, emphatically emphasized, the condition under which he operates as a seer or prophet—a somnambulistic state—that favored arena of Expressionist art and literature in which suppressed daytime fears emerge as hideous but somehow bearable nocturnal visualizations.

The return to the title "Self-Seers" in the third and final double self-portrait of this series re-emphasizes what is being perceived, the self or selves —the creator and the created. Heavily articulated areas spell out the greater corporeality of the double or "created," and contrast it noticeably with the vaporous, more spiritualized and less explicitly indicated "creator" figure behind. An ambiguous ruddy flesh-colored area, encompassing the entire right side of the canvas and built up by a variety of disjointed strokes circulating in various directions, suggests the presence of a third and nude torso, seen at much closer range and cut off at the neck and groin. Another vaguely defined area corresponds to the right shoulder of the back figure, where creamy whites repeat the pallor of its face and hair. The forward figure is again characterized by pursed lips, arched brows, and wrinkled forehead, but now both eyes are closed. The arm amputation practiced in *The Prophet* has been exchanged for a variation on the rigid hand gesture of the first Self-Seers portrait. This gesture, although dissociated organically, is made by the left hand of the foreground creature, and it seems to be caught and firmly pressed against by the encircling left arm of the back figure. The paired frontality of the faces in the two previous portraits is varied here by a quarter turn of the back head, whose socket-like eyes and open mouth still resemble the corresponding figure's appearance in *The Prophet*. The skeletal aspect of both heads has been greatly heightened in *Self-Seers II*. An important change in this final portrait is the draping of the previously nude front figure; nevertheless the bare flesh of the lower torso is revealed by the cloth that is bunched up under the arms. From the point of view of the erotic and revelatory connotations of nakedness, the series presents a self-portraiture that is increasingly sexless (the torso is progressively cut off above the knees in *The Prophet* and at the stomach in *Self-Seers*

II) and increasingly ambiguous (as to the spatial relation and physical presence of the two figures). Typical of all three works is the dominating, willful aspect of the back or creator figure. "Speak the language of the creator and give," Schiele had urged himself when writing about the "cramps" that seized him. The role of creator and created—in this case a materialization of the artist's own reflected image—surely is one of the multiple premises of the Self-Seers series and may well be related to the momentary creative incapacitation voiced in *Melancholia*, where the artist stands emotionally drained and divorced from two examples of his work.

Nevertheless the change from the expressive and powerfully vital single self-portraits of 1909 and 1910 to the successively dehumanized double images of these three paintings is too sudden and too profound to be explained fully by the above interpretations alone. The repeated presence of the double may be interpreted as having a significance that goes beyond the announced thematic intentions of the artist. For the paintings are not products of self-analysis but of *self-absorption*: a fixation which can three times beget a paired self-image. Schiele's "self-seeing" springs from a voyeuristic urge that now serves a fixed libido in which even the sexual object becomes the self. The "seeing" of an identical self or double not only displaces the "hated" masturbation but also provides a "safe" love object.[11] The quickened pace of depersonalization that overtakes this series, with its frozen, intellectualized images, designates a personality crisis which is endemic in the self-mirroring narcissistic confines of Expressionist morphology: schizophrenia. The dehumanization present in the Self-Seers is a gesture of withdrawal from the framework of the world and from the more familiar aspects of self. The growing dissociation, observable here, of the emotional from the intellectual life is essentially schizoid. The pictorial form has suffered correspondingly: line and color lose their individual impact as they are combined in raw and ambiguous definitions of mass. The discerning portrait characterization is replaced by a lifeless mask. The self-seer concept has become a thematic guise for an unhealthy withdrawal and self-infatuation. Reflected in the three double self-portraits is the threat of a narcissism capable of withering the artist's creative powers.[12] Schiele's next series of self-portraits becomes all-important in determining whether this crisis is overcome, and whether his painted descriptions of schizophrenia are of an artistic rather than pathological nature, cultivated rather than paranoid.

Family portraits: casual and allegorical

Schiele's self-preoccupation and the isolation of his Meidling studio left little place in his attention or oeuvre for the members of his family. Frau Schiele had an irksome (to Schiele) habit of reminding her son of his filial duties and occasionally, to underscore her point, she would mail him post card reproductions of Whistler's *Mother*! Her constant demands for an accounting of his time, money, activities, and friends left him little zest for visiting the family apartment.[13] Nevertheless Schiele did occasionally come by in search of free models, and comparison of a photograph of his sisters (plate 65) with two pencil sketches—a 1910 portrait of Melanie (plate 66) and a 1911 drawing of Gerti (plate 67)—demonstrates the discerning characterization of which he was capable when his attention was deflected from himself. Both sisters are dressed for the street, and their "public" attitudes are beautifully caught in the quick sketches by their brother. The solemn frontal portrait of Melanie reflects the impression of awkward reserve conveyed in the photograph, whereas the coquettish grace and self-assurance of Gerti in the same photograph are transferred with equal perception to her portrait. In a family that did not hesitate to discuss with friends the charge of "lesbian" hurled at the older sister when she gave a few night's shelter to the family maidservant after sudden dismissal from service by Frau Schiele,[14] a personality distinction of at least the depth indicated in the photograph is to be expected in Schiele's portraits.

Schiele liked to draw his mother when she was asleep—a short respite from her vigorous reproaches—and a watercolor portrait of 1911 (plate 68) shows Frau Schiele napping on the couch, her hands crossed on her lap and her hair spread about her head. The couch and her clothing are blocked off into unequal rhomboids containing patches of watercolor pigments that have been allowed to combine on the paper while still wet, producing gently luminous values.[15] The thin black lead pencil used here and in the portrait of Gerti was adopted by Schiele in 1911 in preference to the black chalk ("schwarze Kreide") with which his previous drawings, including the sketch of Melanie, had usually been made. The use of the more recalcitrant graphite corresponds with a new delicacy developed in 1911 in which the artist experimented with the gradual delineation of focal points by repeated strokes (see especially the area around the eyes in both the mother and Gerti portraits). When he returned to the black chalk in 1913 it was to combine a forceful new geometrical definition with the posterlike immediacy distinctive of the works of 1910. Abstraction and omission play a tremendous role in Schiele's 1911 watercolor portrait of his mother. Only the head is treated naturalistically, while the undefined body lies beneath glowing color wedges which contain and fix it as if in the constriction of a tomb. The mummified impression is accentuated by the vertical reading enforced by the placement of the signature and date. This is a stratagem frequently employed by the artist in his drawings of recumbent figures; it results in an enhancement of the somnambulistic qualities with which he often endows his pictures.[16]

That the sleep depicted by Schiele in the 1911 watercolor portrait of his mother held profound symbolic implications for him is confirmed in several allegorical canvases painted at this time concerning sleep and death. All of these, though ostensibly dealing with the universal theme of mother and child, may be regarded as biographical wish-projections on Schiele's part, and thus hidden but not too "secret" portraits of himself and his mother. One example typifies—in its subject-matter, its title, and the circumstances behind its creation—these allegories. *The Dead Mother I* (plate 69) was painted within the space

of a few hours on 24 December 1910. It was done as the result of a conversation
with Roessler in which Schiele had complained of his mother's total lack of
understanding or sympathy for him. Roessler suggested that the artist sublimate his distress about his relationship with his mother by painting a series
of statements on the different kinds of motherhood. All the paintings were to
be of the same size and executed on wooden panels. Schiele appeared to like
the idea but left the art critic's house without further comment. As Roessler
learned the next day,[17] Schiele had gone straight to the railway station and
impulsively climbed aboard the Paris Express. He traveled as far as Feldkirch
where he waited two hours for the return train, arrived home in the early
morning of the twenty-fourth, and without eating or sleeping began immediately to paint *The Dead Mother*. He brought the completed still-wet painting
to Roessler that same evening and for years considered it one of his best works.[18]
Since Roessler had suggested themes like "Blind Mother" (actually painted
by Schiele in two versions of larger format in 1914, K.194 and K.195), "Un-
wed Mother," and "Stepmother," it is particularly interesting that the first
motif Schiele selected to soothe his troubled feelings was that of the "dead"
mother. This substitute expression of a death wish, or at least the contemplation
of death as it applied to the mother (the baby in the picture is alive and stirs
actively within its blanket; the pink, orange, and red flesh tones of the child
contrast overtly with the ashen colors of the mother's face and hand), may
not be as sinister as it first appears however. Schiele's letters at this time suggest that he had thoroughly absorbed and agreed with Rilke, who in his *Kleine
Novellen* and through the voice of Malte Laurids Brigge proposed that dream
and death are more real and important than life, and that death is part of a
greater whole, functioning as the supreme consummation of existence.

Artistic prototypes for Schiele's painting may of course be found; Roessler
himself in a 1914 review[19] made a comparison with Klinger's 1889 etching
cycle *On Death*, in which one of the illustrations, "Mother and Child,"[20] shows
a baby crouching on the body of its mother, who has been laid out and prepared for burial. Other contemporary precedents of equal visionary effect
and thematic severity come to mind, such as Segantini's *The Wicked Mothers*
of 1894. This eerie picture of a mother impaled on a spiny tree as punishment
for having abandoned her baby was greatly admired in Vienna; it had been
reproduced in *Ver Sacrum*[21] and acquired by the State at the turn of the century. Another forerunner of Schiele's painting was Munch's *Death and the
Child (The Dead Mother)* of 1899–1900, which had been exhibited in the 1904
Secession show and reproduced in the catalogue.[22] Otto Benesch has recorded
that another Munch work, the 1899 lithograph *Three Stages of Woman*, inspired a large work by Schiele (since destroyed) entitled *The Three Mothers*,
in which the middle figure, a pregnant woman being consumed with "inner"
fire, was naked, as was the center figure in Munch's work.[23] Fritz Waerndorfer
of the Wiener Werkstätte owned Minne's marble statue *Mother with Dying
Child*, and similar themes were treated by Käthe Kollwitz in her etchings
Woman with Dead Child and *Pregnant Woman*, on display in the Secession

at the time Schiele painted his *The Dead Mother*.[24] Finally, several of Klimt's paintings dealing with the mother-and-child theme may have impressed Schiele. Klimt's *Three Ages of Life* (1905; on exhibition at the Wiener Werkstätte, 1907, and at the 1908 Kunstschau) presented an old woman and a young (healthy) mother and child. His *The Family* of 1910 showed a mother and two sleeping children, in a new "darker" style, and this same theme had been used by Schiele in 1910 in a small tempera (K.116) titled simply *Mother*. Schiele later received thematic and compositional inspiration from the older painter in an allegory entitled *Mother and Death* (K.135, 1911) that shows Death, with features similar to Schiele's, confronting a large, pregnant woman.

When the artist's own early *Madonna and Child* (plate 1), is recalled however the basic originality of his *The Dead Mother*, as well as the unique set of circumstances giving rise to it, may also be appreciated. (The vicarious return-to-the-womb experience expressed as a secondary motif is perhaps a predictable response from a son whose feelings toward his over-protective, demanding mother are ambivalent.) A second version, painted in 1911 and modestly subtitled by Schiele "Birth of Genius" (plate 70), shows the mother with her eyes shut in death while her baby, its eyes wide with wonderment, pushes energetically out of a womb-like encasement. These two "Dead Mother" allegorical portraits in which the death of a mother is caused by the birth of a remarkable child (a genius) prefigure an extraordinary letter written by Schiele to his mother three years later. It leaves no doubt as to the autobiographical significance of the paintings and the deadly serious self-esteem of the author. He writes:

"You are at the age when, I believe, one has the driving desire to want to see the world with a pure soul, unrestrained and unhindered, and to want to rejoice in the fulfilled and revealed fruits—whose wilfullness is innate and grows independent roots. This is the great separation. Without doubt I shall be the greatest, the most beautiful, the most valuable, the purest, and the most precious fruit. Through my independent will all beautiful and noble effects are united in me—this also, no doubt, because of the man. *I shall be the fruit which after its decay will still leave behind eternal life; therefore how great must be your joy—to have borne me?*" [Italics mine].[25]

SOLITARY SELF-PORTRAITS OF 1911

With the exception of a portrait painted to pay a dentist's bill[26] Schiele produced no identifiable portrait oils[27] in 1911, the year following his successful formulation of an original Expressionistic portraiture. Instead he busied himself with troubled self-portraits and morose allegories that expressed his concerns with sex, life, and death. His other important works in the oil medium this year were townscapes of what he tenderly referred to as the "dead city" Krumau, where he lived in seclusion from May to the beginning of August, and anthropomorphic interpretations of those motifs in nature from which he always derived the most solace—huge decaying sunflowers, which filled the surfaces of his canvases like the faces of intimate friends seen at close range, and pictures of isolated, fragile trees. But this aspect of his oeuvre was outweighed by a continued fascination with the self. The many self-portraits of 1911, whether mere pencil jottings in a notebook, watercolor- or gouache-heightened drawings, or formalized oils, express principally three aspects of the artist's personal life: sexual longing, a studied public dandyism, and hermaphroditic visions of the projected self. How the problem of a potentially extreme narcissism raised by the creation of a double in the Self-Seers series was ultimately resolved can be observed by turning now to several further examples of self-portraiture created during the year 1911.

Perhaps with no artist other than Schiele could it be considered a healthy sign to have shown, in a self-portrait dealing with masturbation, the actual physical activity rather than the arrested or "punished" act. And yet, judging by a stylistic chronology that led towards a more geometricized rendition of the face and a new vigorous watercolor flecking of the flesh, this was the concluding note of those portraits dealing with the subject. This final aspect paralleled other portrayals of sexual desire expressly directed toward the opposite sex. The evolution may be observed in three representative pictures. The watercolor *Self-Portrait with Bare Stomach* (plate 71) is a striking example of mutilation by symbolic amputation inflicted by the artist while confronting his passion-racked image in the mirror. As in *Delirium* a phallic connotation is suggested by the extended shaft of bare stomach.[28] Next, the emotions of guilt and compulsion are formalized in a forceful new variation on the 1910 nude self-portrait oils in a painting which Schiele entitled *The Lyric Poet* (plate 72), and it is noteworthy that the self-assertion portrayed here replaces the immobility and generalization of the Self-Seers. Neither the technique nor the motif is ambiguous now as the artist returns to the single-figure self-portrait and to a more personal, immediate image. The very title implies artistic expression of the poet's own feeling rather than that of outward event or imposed theme. The skeletal image has been abandoned; the fringe of a beard grows along the jaws of a living face. A pulsating application of red, orange, yellows, and green in the face, hands, and legs indicates that this figure is no ghostly emanation but a body of real flesh and blood, writhing in the "agitated longing" of the 1910 literary self-portrait. The shooting, upward thrust of the right hand, clasped tightly by the left (both with the concealed or "amputated" thumb and V-shaped gesture of previous works relating to sexual desire), is a compositional and physical repetition of the erect penis which is painted a flaming red. The straight lines of the dark shirt falling open across the torso frame a rectangle of pale white flesh which further reiterates the upward jolts of movement. The head falls back limply on the shoulder, the lips are pressed together, and the eyes are partially closed. The forehead breaks into contorting ripples and the long hair stands stiffly on end. A second slim rectangle of flesh is formed by the drapery at the shoulder, and it points toward a halo of light that surrounds the head. The somnambulistic mood of the Self-Seers is shattered by the need to express the demanding physical state and human needs. In *The Lyric Poet* Schiele's vision of himself is *rehumanized*: it deals with an emotion rather than a concept. The third picture in this series, the watercolor *Self-Portrait Masturbating* (plate 73), is "healthy" in the sense previously suggested, because overpowering physical dictates and not castrating guilt are emphasized in this almost scientific depiction of self-gratification.

When, at the end of the year, Schiele was requested by the Delphin Verlag of Munich to submit an original lithograph for publication with fourteen others in a portfolio of SEMA artists (a venture to which Klee, Kubin, and Mopp also contributed), he once again chose the subject of autoeroticism. The two versions (plates 75a and 75b) which Schiele submitted in January of 1912 to the publishing house, and a related study (plate 74), constitute his last major statement on the theme, as though the proclamation of his "problem" to the world had automatically achieved a resolution. The drawing chosen for reproduction by the Delphin Verlag in April of 1912 (plate 75b)—the more "sinister" of the two images—creatively sums up the expressive devices developed in 1910 and 1911: the "punishment" through compositional amputation, the extended shoulder, and the astral body glow. The merciless self-exposure of this lithographic self-portrait must be understood as a final link in the chain of those public portrayals of solitary sexual desire.[29]

With the realization that his desires could be expressed and even partly consummated by pictorial representation, Schiele now confessed more ambitious longings to canvas. Perhaps inspired by the encounters at his country studio with Valerie Neuzil, a model who was soon to become his steady and extremely devoted mistress, Schiele contemplated a heterosexual relationship in his painting *Vision* (plate 76). The painting is a frank revelation of the loneliness of his sexual life. Looking down upon an ample bed upon which his figure takes up pitifully little room, the artist portrays himself—his eyes almost closed and his right arm flung across the width of the bed, fingers relatively relaxed. In his wakeful half-sleep, or dream, the figure of a nude woman joins him, and his left hand, reaching out to touch her, grows in size and desire. The large fingers knuckle and claw at the "vision" and come to rest not upon a human companion but upon a pillow (or perhaps a sheet of drawing paper—the inanimate conveyor of this apparition). Brightly colored bits of material to either side of the bed serve as abstract reminders of the tower motif from Krumau which Schiele had previously incorporated on a symbolic level into paintings of sexual longing. The concrete phantom in *Vision*, although summoned forth by the artist, has a tradition in painting and continues the Middle European fascination with the folk belief in nocturnal visitations of demonic incubi and succubi.

Fuseli's nightmare visions furnish eighteenth-century examples of the visit of various forms of incubi to sleeping women. The less frequent materialization of a succubus (as separate from the "temptation" visions besetting dozing or awakened saints in traditional art) presented in Schiele's picture has a probable recent precedent in Hodler's eerie and controversial work of 1890,

The Night (plate 77), which, although dealing with Death, had struck an indignant public as thinly veiled obscenity. Hodler's picture presents a trio, a couple and two single figures, representing different aspects of peaceful and disturbed sleep and of fulfilled and unrequited longing. These figures surround in pinwheel fashion the center figure, a male nude (Hodler himself) who starts back in horror at the hooded visitation that squats most corporeally between his spread legs. The psychological and philosophical implications of Hodler's many-figured work are more daring than the concerns of Schiele's autocentric painting, but the thematic directness of both bespeaks a willingness to grapple with sexual reality that is of an utterly different character from that of the "disguised" eroticism of Vienna's fin-de-siècle art, as represented for example by Maximilian Lenz's *Marionettes* (after p. 2). Schiele soon materialized his vision of the opposite sex in the devastatingly bold oil "portrait" of his mistress "Wally" (Valerie Neuzil), *Reclining Woman with Upturned Skirt* (plate 90).[30] A raw exposure of the genitals is effected by the apparent butcher-shop hacking-off of the legs at the hip (they are actually pulled back against the shoulders). Schiele's upturned, straight-on view continues Klimt's equally revealing studies of female nudes, and contrasts with the method of another German Expressionist usually considered brutally explicit, Max Beckmann, whose repeated motif of the spread-eagled figure seems almost subtle by comparison. The intimacy of Schiele's picture is matched by the intimacy of its size: 12⅝ x 9½ inches on wood, rather like a private icon or peep show. Taken as a series, the three masturbation portraits, *Vision*, and the *Reclining Woman with Upturned Skirt* document a psychological refutation of the threatening schizoid narcissism apparent in the Self-Seers. As Schiele projects his physical needs upon canvas he passes from sterile, ingrown self-absorption to vital, outwardly-oriented expression of self.

Two other aspects of the artist's personality were concurrently given definition in self-portraiture. In a letter written to Roessler at the beginning of the year, Schiele complained of his continued poverty in the following indignant terms:

"Will things go any further? I can't, I haven't been able to work for days. I don't even have any wrapping paper. . . . I have headaches, I am chained. Will no one help me? If only I could have an exhibition, then I would be out of it. But no, I can't even draw, so I must write in order to borrow money, now, in the very best years and days in which I want to work. . . . What times! Shall I become a merchant? Or a salesman? . . . Who will help me? I can't buy a single canvas; I want to paint but have no colors. . . . I am sick. . . . The artist should at least not have to worry every month about getting the money owed to him! Whoever can deal with the artist, writes at least. Why should I be silent about all this? . . . I am extremely sensitive, and all these people have absolutely no idea how they should behave towards an artist."[31]

This concern over his position as an "artist" is reminiscent of that in the early Academy self-portraits and was also reflected in Schiele's growing idiosyncratic dress and manner in public. Despite his lack of funds he was a foppish dresser and, drawing on his Wiener Werkstätte experience, designed all his own clothes down to the last detail. One spectacular suit which he ordered made at this time was of dark linen with a double row of buttons down the front, the sleeves and trouser legs very narrow at the top and belling out at the cuffs. When in this splendid attire, he refused to be seen carrying a package or even a roll of his drawings in the street because he considered it beneath his dignity. A photograph (plate 78), a sketchbook page (plate 79), and an oil, *Self-Portrait Standing* (plate 80), all convey the image of a dandy. Those same features which in the watercolor *Self-Portrait with Bare Stomach* had displayed torrential emotion—the pursed lips, the arched brows, and the wrinkled forehead—can also convey studied insouciance. This apparent contradiction in the artist's personality was explained by Schiele himself as being "either from embarassment or in defense." At twenty-one he was simultaneously a recluse and a public sensation. He was genuinely reserved but also arrogant; he was both modest and egotistical. In one breath he could and did say, "I am the shyest of the shy" and "I am divine!" He liked to speculate that should he have children they would have to be "either cretins or geniuses," a comment reflecting preoccupation with his family history and an unshakable belief in his artistic gifts. He also spoke of an overpowering urge to play the fool in public:

"Sometimes it tempted me downright irresistibly to appear as a 'horror of the bourgeois' ['Spießerschreck'—the same epithet hurled by the public at Kokoschka], to express in word or action something which I know must have a strange, even repulsive effect on others . . . my outward bearing does not agree with my inner needs."[32]

These words and actions express a genuine dualism which Schiele's nature not only contained but thrived upon; a dualism which extended to the subjects of his paintings throughout his life: on the one hand sensitive, lyrical town scenes and landscapes, trees and flowers—all motifs which exerted a calming influence on him—and on the other tortured, obsessive explorations of all forms of erotica. The dualism that denies a purely idyllic interpretation of his "dead" townscapes and spindly trees also occurs in his erotic scenes and self-portraits. In the difficult-to-read formal allegories set down on dark-colored canvases, Schiele's presentation of embracing couples or single sexually involved figures is often marked by ambiguity and clouded by deliberate obscurity. Contours mingle impossibly or vanish at crucial junctures, color functions symbolically rather than definitively, and the very sex of his figures is often indeterminable. But in the intimate realm of his drawings and watercolors this ambiguous duality can become unmistakably explicit. A series of self-portraits done in 1911 dwells upon hermaphroditic qualities and changes in Schiele's own body. At times, in this row of watercolors, suggestions of feminine attributes supplement the natural felinity of Schiele's lithe body. The fragility of a hairless frame is accentuated and, as in the 1910 self-portraits, the breasts and turgid nipples are emphasized and modeled by color. The pelvic structure is widened, the hip becomes voluptuous, and the penis disappears altogether, not in a symbolic amputation but in an identification with and vicarious experience of the opposite sex. Or, as in the crimson-red watercolor *Self-Portrait with Raised Leg* (plate 81), the angular characteristics of his lean body are depicted with an accompanying wiry insistence on the hairs of the chest, armpit, and pubic area, while topping the body is a female face whose features are relaxed in a swoon. In other self-portraits of this character the same female head (possibly Wally, but also similar to another model depicted by Schiele during the latter half of 1910 and 1911) tops the artist's body while he/she caresses an erect penis; in another work the same face performs fellatio on "its" own body.[33] In these most intimate of his drawings we see Schiele actually transformed into the object of his own desire. This duality or "plurality" is powerful because it has not remained at subconscious level but has been recognized and subjected to conscious examination from the vantage point of living simultaneously inside and outside the body. Just as he had previously explained to his mother, "It *has* to be this way," Schiele again spoke of the compulsion he felt to make such works:

"Certainly: I have made pictures which are 'horrible'; I do not deny that. But do they believe that I liked to do it or did it in order to act like a 'horror of the bourgeois.' No! This was never the case. But yearning too has its ghosts. I painted such ghosts. By no means for my pleasure. It was an obligation."[34]

The obligation to which Schiele refers includes his recognition and portrayal of the "horrible" side of himself. By such visual depiction of all aspects of his sexual character he arrived independently and as though instinctively at concepts just beginning to be verbalized by Vienna's psychologists. Schiele's self-findings were, to him, revelatory and phenomenological, rather than personally shattering; in this sense he, like Krafft-Ebing before him, was more a "collector" of psycho-sexual data than an actual *medium* of it—in contrast to his contemporary Otto Weininger, whose tormented contemplation of bisexuality, which clumped women and Jews together as personifications of contemptible weakness, contributed to a suicidal self-hatred. The contrasting visions of himself that Schiele presents are all reconcilable qualities of a single personality in the light of modern psychoanalytic interpretations.

The works discussed above were made for the most part in Krumau, where Schiele had rented an inexpensive studio in May of 1911. But by the beginning of August he wrote Roessler that the townspeople were harrassing him and that he was being forced to leave town.[35] Still determined not to have to settle in the capital, he immediately found a new retreat in the small village of Neulengbach, about twenty miles from Vienna. The first months there were among the happiest and most creative in his life. By the middle of August he was installed with an adequate supply of paints and canvases in a rustic garden house that rented for $150 a year.[36] His spirits rose and he wrote his uncle Czihaczek that he would stay in Neulengbach forever. The letter, dated 1 September 1911, is a good example of his chronic desire for approval from those in authority: it partly demands, partly begs for understanding and recognition, and concludes with a list of aggressive aphorisms on art.[37] In an out-burst of affection for his new environment he painted, in conscious and close imitation of the Van Gogh *Bedroom at Arles* (in the collection of his patron Reininghaus), a small and gay-colored view of his own bedroom (K.149).[38] This new delight in color brightens Schiele's last oil self-portrait of 1911, *Self-Portrait with Fingers Spread Apart* (plate 82). Although the thumbtip concealing V-shaped finger gesture of the previous self-portraits prominently persists, this work is a real self-portrait rather than a thematic personification or an embodied expression of an inner state. Schiele no longer shows himself in an enigmatic background that hovers to envelop his figure, but instead shar-ing a setting that contains several recognizable objects. Applying the unusual perspective observed in his recent paraphrase of Van Gogh, he has tilted up the white table top behind him. On the table a multifaced black ceramic "Janus" pitcher[39] projects one of its profiles beyond the artists's head to the right—a second-image introduction that he can not resist, but of infinitely more serene connotations than those of the Self-Seers series. A brightly colored Wiener Werkstätte cloth lies on the table to the right, and to the upper left may be seen what is probably the lower part of one of the artist's townscapes, or perhaps a piece of the decorative cloth he liked to keep in his studio. From the eye of the Janus vase protrudes a branch of winter cherry, one of the artist's favorite plants. As he had done once before for a short time in 1909, Schiele has grown a debonair moustache, somewhat transforming his delicate appearance with a suggestion of self-assertion and virility. The long fingers and furrowed forehead seem to convey sensitivity instead of an eruption of emotion. The contours delineating Schiele's body are delicate and serene, in contrast to those in *The Prophet*, *Self-Seers II*, and *The Lyric Poet*; the con-tinuation of the line of the neck by the sloping left shoulder is not an expres-sion of violent truncation but of exquisite fragility.[40]

The confidence which Schiele felt in his own artistic destiny fairly glows in a letter written in September 1911 to the patron he had portrayed in 1910, Dr. Oskar Reichel. Although full of unfinished thoughts and grammatical errors, the entire letter is worth quoting, for it gives a remarkable view of the artist's philosophy, his polar conception of himself, and his attitude towards others.

"I have become aware: earth breathes, smells, listens, feels in all its little parts; it adds to itself, couples itself, falls to pieces, and finds itself, enjoys what life is, and seeks the logical philosophy of all, all in all; days and years of all transitoriness, as far as one wishes and is able to think, as far as the spirit of beings is with great con-tents; through our air, our light, it [the earth] has become something or many things, even to creators who are necessary, and has partially perished, consumed in itself, back into itself again, and begins the smaller or greater cycle, everything that I want to call divine germinates anew and brings [forth] and creates, out of the power which few see, a creature.

"The transitoriness of the material is determined in the sense of an existence; a sure becoming and passing away, a coming; life, in which concept one should understand the endless disintegration which, however, can be kept in life through organic means, yes, it [life] can become retroactive, far back, so that it, by these means, can give no complete death.

"There was, is and will be the old or the new primal spirit, which wants, which out of something, out of unions, out of interminglings, must bring forth, must create; the real great Mother of all, of everything similar but still separate, who wills, and so was, is and will be the wish always out of these our eternal means, to be able to create the most manifold human beings, animals, plants, living creatures in general, as soon as this physics is present, just so soon does the common will of the world exist.

"I possess the immediate means within myself that can draw [portray by drawing], in order to record, to wish to fathom, to invent, to discover, with means within myself, which already have the great power to kindle themselves, to burn themselves up and to shine like a thought out of the eternal light, and to glow into the darkest eternities of our little world, which consists of only so few elements.

"All disguises for us are, anyway, for naught; since they conceal us, instead of having the urge to interweave with other organs.

"When I see myself completely, I shall have to see myself, and will have to know what I want, not only what goes on within myself, but also how far I have the ability to see what means are mine, out of what puzzling substances I am made, out of how much of the more, what I recognize, what I have so far recognized within myself.

"I see myself evaporate and breathe forth stronger and stronger; the oscillations of my astral light become swifter, sharper, simpler, and like a great recognition of the world.

"So I bring forth out of myself always more, always something further, an endlessly brighter shining, as far as love, which is everything, enriches me in this way and leads me to this to which I am instinctively drawn; which I want to tear into myself, so that I may create again a new thing which I, in spite of myself, have perceived.

"My existence, my decay, transposed to enduring values, must bring, sooner or later, my strength to other strongly or more strongly developed beings, like a believing revelation of religion.

"The farthest away will notice me, the more distant ones will look at me, and my negative ones [unbelievers in him] will live by my hypnosis!

"I am so rich that I must give myself away."[41]

This extraordinary letter by the twenty-one-year-old Schiele reveals an unequivocal yearning for identification outside and beyond the self. The conflicting desires to assert and to efface that ego which has been the motivation and often the subject matter of his creativity seek resolution in unity with a greater whole, the universe. Schiele's language echoes several partially digested philosophic sources. The *Zusammenhang* aesthetic surrounding Klimt's allegories, and voiced in Ricarda Huch's *Ver Sacrum* article "Symbolistik vor Hundert Jahren,"[42] emphasizes the same awareness of the grandiose and minute forms of nature as in the opening phrases of Schiele's letter.[43] Throughout the self-evaluation which rings like a manifesto, there is a good deal of Nietzsche adopted *en bloc*. The conclusion smacks of Zarathustra's words:

"For these men of today I do not wish to be *light*, or to be called light. *These* I wish to blind. Lightning of my wisdom! put out their eyes!"[44] Also like Nietzsche's is the desire expressed for a self-annihilation through conscious participation in a (Bergsonian) flow of continuous creation in which the joy of becoming contains intrinsically the joy of destruction. Schiele emphasizes again and again the transitoriness of sensed time and experience, repeating Nietzsche's recognition of eternal recurrence, but desiring to "interweave" with it, sensing that through "endless disintegration" life can become "retroactive." Like Hofmannsthal, with whom he shared a constant preoccupation with death, Schiele feels the "old" as well as the "new primal spirit" and he yearns for a union with the preexistent contents of the "puzzling substances" from which he is formed. The pantheistic appreciation of nature parallels that of Rilke; Schiele's "light" which will shine "as far as love" recalls that poet's words, "To love is to give light with inexhaustible oil."[45] The theosophic language of Steiner is recognizable in the phrase, "oscillations of my astral light."[46] Much of the latter half of Schiele's letter is about artistic creation. But how does Schiele write about art? He writes about *himself* and art. Compared to Cézanne's cautious reservations concerning the fulfillment of his painterly aims, or the rapturous discoveries which Van Gogh recorded in an almost grateful spirit, Schiele's literary outbursts are colossal declarations of a self-centeredness that pleads for, while zealously proclaiming, the assurance of regeneration in the eternal existence of art. This emotional confidence in his special status as an artist and in what might be called the aesthetic imperative was to be drastically tested at Neulengbach the following year.

1912: ALLEGORICAL DOUBLE PORTRAITS WITH KLIMT

The loneliness that speaks out to the beholder in the solitary self-portraits of 1911 was of a spiritual as well as physical nature. The "philosophic" letters to patrons like Dr. Reichel were bids for an intellectual exchange and sympathy that had been lacking in Schiele's life ever since his self-imposed exile from Vienna. His occasional visits to the city had been disappointing, involving him either in family squabbles (Gerti, according to their mother, was seeing too much of her brother's former classmate, the painter Anton Peschka) or in the manual labor and paper work that went along with shipping paintings to and from different exhibitions.[47] Back in the seclusion of his village retreat Schiele stretched a very large canvas (71¼ x 71⅛ inches) and set about creating for himself a worthy companion. The result was a double portrait, but not of the sort fashioned during the orgy of self-infatuation that had produced the row of Self-Seers. Schiele titled this new painting of the opening months of 1912 *The Hermits* (plate 84).[48] In the center of the canvas stands Schiele with his left hand on his waist while his right hand, fingers spread in the familiar V gesture with "missing" thumb joint, rests against his upper thigh. The companion standing to his left is not any second image of himself but the spiritual master of his late teens, Gustav Klimt. Both figures are shown in monk-like clothing. Schiele had once before been attracted to the idea of showing himself and Klimt together as a pair of monks or ascetics. This was the pen and wash drawing of 1909, *Two Men*, and its pencil variation, *Two Men in Decorative Robes* (figures 25 and 24). The costume inspiration for these early drawings had probably come from Klimt himself. Although not in the least tempted to reject the carnal pleasures of life, it was Klimt's delight to dress in the ample robes (designed by himself) and open sandals of a monk, an idiosyncrasy which his full beard carried to perfection. Schiele's imitation of the older artist in regard to dress had caused the children of the village of Krumau to call him the "Lord God painter,"[49] and this mode of attire appealed to his ascetic side. In the monk's habit with its significance of withdrawal from the world, Schiele saw not only a symbol of his retreat from Viennese society, but also the suggestion of an identity—hermit or monk—that corresponded to a period which he greatly admired, the Middle Ages. Schiele's somber allegories and gothicized figure style had won him the appellation "Gothiker" from his critics, and it was an epithet that he was pleased to incorporate into his own description of himself. The ascetic guise of Schiele and Klimt as monks in 1909 and as hermits in 1912 may surely be read in both cases as a symbol of separateness, if not actual withdrawal, from an alien and uncomprehending world (the public scandal and official rejection of Klimt's university murals must have seemed to the younger artist a parallel to the misunderstanding encountered by his own work). The prominent crown of thorns worn by Schiele in *The Hermits* reinforces this concept of the martyred artist who is the object of public mockery.

The question must be asked however whether this new double portrait is simply a thematic retroversion or whether a new statement concerning the artist's attitude towards himself and Klimt is contained in this large—lifesize—and impressive work. In the early drawing *Two Men* the artists are shown oblivious to the world and engrossed in an act of creation—the monk Schiele drawing while the monk Klimt makes a gesture of approval. In *The Hermits* of 1912 Schiele is not represented as artist at work, nor is there any suggestion of an exaltation of his art. His stance is notably defiant: the elbows are flung out akimbo, completely covering Klimt's body on the right, and one bare, crossed foot seems almost impatiently to tap the ground in belligerent expectation. With tight-clamped lips, Schiele cocks his head to one side and his great eyeballs roll up deliberately to meet and rivet the beholder's gaze. The two figures are no longer elevated on a pedestal, but stand on ground level. They confront the world, but as monks—huddling together in ascetic isolation. This painting was considered by contemporaries as Schiele's great homage to Klimt. But is it? Examination of one of the first compositional sketches (plate 85) indicates otherwise: the monkish robes are clearly indicated and the two figures are recognizable, showing that Klimt, with his beard and stocky build, was originally conceived as being in front, while Schiele, with a younger, narrower face, is half-hidden behind him—just the reverse of the final painting. Klimt is in profile and appears to be taking a step forward. His left arm reaches around to clasp Schiele's. A heavy dot indicates Schiele's eye and his mouth is open, as if saying something to the older man. Klimt's face is taut with concentration upon what would appear to be the simple act of walking. Under his raised eyebrows there is a faint, ragged indication of a great eyeball—a large, staring eyeball—with a tiny shrunken pupil. When one looks again at *The Hermits* there now appears a feature so blatant that the first impulse is to correct one's interpretation or dismiss it altogether. Klimt is shown as a blind man or as a sleepwalker. His large protruding eyeballs are veiled by tightly closed lids. He is arrested in mid-step, as the figure of Schiele stops and turns to face and *look* at the beholder. Klimt's head is bent in sightlessness or sleep, his mouth is open as though in the effort of listening attention, and he presses against Schiele to sense what has happened to interrupt their progression. A carefully worked-out pen and wash drawing (plate 83), in which the figure placement of the final painting is proposed, confirms this reading: to the right the sagging face of Klimt is drawn a second time, enlarged, and in each case the eyes are shown "blind" or closed. In both the painting and its studies therefore Klimt is directed by, and dependent upon, Schiele. As an expression of a spiritual father-son relationship *The Hermits* is hardly one of simple esteem. It is instead a morbid prediction, and a prolonged speculation on that dictum inherent in each successive generation, that he who was strong shall diminish, and he who was weak shall grow strong. The older man, blind or in a trance, is unaware, as though existing in a dream state. He is led by his "son," or successor, whose steadfast gaze—first conceived in an arresting self-portrait study (plate 88)[50]—consciously places him in the real world, the world of the present. Every detail supports the contrast projected by Schiele. Klimt's shoulder slopes in a straight line from his long bare neck, emphasizing his fragility, while Schiele's broad shoulders are accentuated by colorful epaulets of Wiener Werkstätte material. To the lower left are two red winter cherries, one clinging tenaciously to its upright branch, the other fallen to the ground. This hardly subtle symbolism pointedly refers to the two men, one full of promise and defiant, the other tired and in a state of senility. Directly below and to the left of the cherry plant is a remarkable triple assertion of Schiele as artist and creator of this picture—his signature and the year printed in white three times on the dark ground.[51]

The great disparity between the professional status of Schiele and Klimt at this time must be considered as having direct bearing upon the meaning of *The Hermits*. The young Schiele of 1912 was still almost penniless, continually having to beg or bully friends and patrons for funds. He moved in very different circles from Klimt, the wealthy and favored painter of Vienna's society ladies. It was Klimt who had arranged Schiele's participation in the International Kunstschau and his employment at the Wiener Werkstätte, Klimt who sent him models and brought his work to the attention of rich patrons. He represented the fabulously successful and internationally acclaimed artist, and yet he was actually a rough man of humble background who, with the animal magnetism of a Rasputin, had climbed from poverty and anonymity to fame and social acceptance. Schiele always carried his milieu with him. If he brooded over the inequality in their social status, his use of monk's clothing in *The Hermits* may have been unconsciously influenced by a motive other than symbolic asceticism. By robing Klimt and himself alike, he brought the older man to his level. The father-son aspect of this painting assumes a predictable course as Schiele lashes out in retaliation. In a wild fantasy the young artist plays God and strikes Klimt blind, or at least reduces him to the trance-like, helpless state of a sleepwalker. He assaults Klimt as a fellow artist by depriving him not only of his sight but of his hands, whereas his own are emphasized by the double V gesture and long, vital fingers. It is Schiele's statement concerning himself and Klimt *as artists* that assigns this allegorical double portrait of two "hermits" such a prominent place in his oeuvre. For, much as he admired him, Schiele truly believed that the *epoch* which Klimt represented was dead, and he saw himself as the bearer of a vigorous new art. Klimt too must have been made aware that his art was considered by many as facile and old-fashioned—very possibly through the cantankerous reviews of his University panels written by Karl Kraus—for after about 1910 a deep-going change may be observed in Klimt's work as he shed much of the statically ornamental, and even repainted older works from his "gold" period.

One painting was not enough for such a complex theme. More modest in size (27½ x 31½ inches), *Agony* (plate 87) is nevertheless a major statement presented again in terms of a personal allegory of Schiele's relationship to Klimt.[52] The two protagonists are still ascetic figures and their physical characteristics still indicate reference to Schiele and Klimt, but the positions are now reversed. Klimt is a powerful figure with his arms raised and bent in a circle in front of him. He advances upon Schiele with the compelling gaze of a hypnotist, his hands in the gesture of a sorcerer casting a spell. Schiele, his face white and skull-like, his red-rimmed eyes rolling upward, falls backward in a swoon.[53] Several compositional tryouts for *Agony* appear in Schiele's sketchbooks. One page shows a vigorous figure recoiling from a second figure whose back is turned towards the beholder;[54] on other pages the response of the "Schiele" figure changes to limp surrender (plate 86).[55]

The sense of claustrophobic domination in *Agony* is enhanced by the piling-up of abstract, rocklike areas of color—the closest Schiele comes to employing features of Cubism and Futurism. This geometrical fracturing of the background is a formal equivalent to the "charged" surfaces of Kokoschka's portraits, and will be used by Schiele again in other major works of 1912 and 1913, interestingly all also two-figure compositions.[56] In *Agony* the churning background adds emotional comment to the pantomime of the two figures. Succumbing to his "agony," Schiele's hands are pressed to his heart and on the exposed right palm is a round mark, possibly suggesting stigmata. Lighter blocks of color spread a ray, or "astral light,"[57] across him, further intimating the divine quality of his suffering. One gesture of Schiele's potency remains. In yellow letters against dark brown he has signed the painting not at the usual lower left or right but in close proximity to Klimt, at a level with his face. By allowing physical domination to the figure of Klimt, Schiele has focused compositional attention upon himself. The interesting reversal of roles in *Agony* tends to support the powerful ambivalence of Schiele's attitude towards his spiritual master, as first exposed in *The Hermits*. Perhaps Schiele himself was unaware of his feelings until he attempted these testimonials of his personal and historical relationship to a famous living artist. The allegorical subterfuge of hermits and monks generalizes but does not ameliorate the conflict between the "old" style of painting, as personified by Klimt, and the new, "modern" art, as represented by Schiele.

1911–1913: Interlude—portraits of Wally

Schiele's great faith in the primacy of his status and destiny as an artist, asserted in *The Hermits* and in the previously cited philosophical manifesto addressed to Dr. Reichel, received moral support in the modest person of Valerie Neuzil. A red-headed young Viennese model with haunting blue-green eyes, Wally had been sent to Schiele by Klimt, and she followed the artist from Krumau to Neulengbach, settling down with him in the small garden house there. She became his devoted companion and mistress, posing for love and managing the more mundane aspects of the household, even taking batches of Schiele's erotic drawings around to various sure clients in Vienna —an activity that subjected her to occasional lewd interrogation by some of the more curious customers and sent her back to Schiele in tears. During the years 1911 to 1914 Wally posed for scores of erotic works, none of them however again as devastatingly overt as the small oil previously discussed, *Reclining Woman with Upturned Skirt* (plate 90). The upturned skirt that revealed the lace-trimmed bloomers then in vogue remained a favorite contrivance with Schiele, and a watercolor such as the 1913 *Wally in Red Blouse* (plate 91) is, aside from its artistic quality, noteworthy for two reasons: the fetish-like importance of shoes, stockings, and garters for Schiele's brand of eroticism, and, for once, the lack of a signature-enforced vertical reading for this type of earthy, non-allegorical recumbent figure motif.

That Wally represented more than just a sexual object for her lover is certainly indicated in the tender oil portrait of 1912, *Wally* (plate 92). The focus is very close, marking a break with the portraits of 1910, and the frame cuts the top of the head and crosses the torso just below the upper arms. No arms or gestures are needed to convey the gentle nature that looks out from the great, expressive eyes. The inclined head suggests wistfulness and docility, and the wide lips speak perhaps more of generosity and receptivity than of the sensualism perceived in Schiele's erotic drawings by his customers. Schiele found her long nose, straight brows, and frivolous bangs fascinating, and these were the features which, along with the lucent eyes and generous mouth, he emphasized in his portrait drawings of her. Wally's gentle spirit began to pervade his works: a third version of the mother-and-child motif painted at this time (1912, K.155) shows a live mother in place of the previous "dead" mother, and the features approximate Wally's. The sprig of winter cherry that Schiele had used to decorate his last oil self-portrait of 1911 (plate 82) also adorns the portrait of Wally, and when he painted a companion piece, the *Self-Portrait with Winter Cherry* (plate 94),[58] the presence of this plant not only linked the two portraits but continued the lyrical mood. The close focus, geometrical head halo, frame cutting, placement of the winter cherry branch, and inclination of the head all match the Wally portrait to which it is spiritually so akin. Both pictures are painted on wood and are distinguished by a technique of thin, diluted oil glaze in which the individual strokes of the brush are permanently fixed, creating a rich surface texture that complements the intimate glow of the jewel-like hues. Schiele appears armless, and therefore non-gesticulating. In a desire to represent a state of being—"I am so rich that I must give myself away"—rather than transitory emotions, the artist has returned to the face as a primary object of expressiveness. A beautiful watercolor study (plate 89) for this portrait presents an illuminating contrast to the similarly posed but bristling self-portrait study (plate 88) executed in preparation for *The Hermits*. Brimming over with fulfillment in his creative life and companionship in his private life, Schiele shows himself as he is: a thin—not emaciated, delicate—not rent apart, sensitive—not suffering, young man. The buoyant impression of his body, much more rounded than in the angular portraits of 1910 and 1911, is reiterated by the jaunty sprig of winter cherry. The harmony suggested in these two companion portraits is the subject of a drawing in one of the artist's sketchbooks (plate 95). Lying side by side, the partners raise their arms in a double gesture of communication and concord. The few lines with which Schiele has captured likeness and pose are characteristic of the many little figures and scenes which fill his notebooks. Schiele took Wally everywhere with him, even to the Roessler summer house in Altmünster, where he posed for a photograph with her, dressed in her "English" suit (plate 93).[59] A sedate-enough looking couple in public, the intimacies of their private life were recorded by the artist in drawings and watercolors, and the possessiveness he began to feel towards her is best epitomized in a "testimony" he once compelled her to write and sign in one of his sketchbooks: "I say today, 8 June 1913, that I am not in love with anyone in the world. Wally."[60] Schiele's later unwillingness to give up Wally in spite of his marriage to another woman caused tempestuous scenes between mistress and wife and had predictable thematic repercussions in the artist's work.

APRIL 1912: THE PRISON SELF-PORTRAITS AND THEIR AFTERMATH

By the final months of 1911 the thematic function of Egon Schiele's Self-Seers series had been completely abandoned and the artist's vision of himself rehumanized as he found external solutions to his personal problems and experienced a heightened self-esteem. The strong duality of his nature seemed momentarily resolved in his art. The opening months of 1912 found him isolated, but no longer alone, serene in the peaceful seclusion of Neulengbach, and with enough materials for his work. In this soothing country atmosphere he created the lyrical portraits of himself and Wally and painted some of his most beautiful town- and landscapes.

On 13 April 1912 this period of rich productivity was brought to a sudden and brutal end. Schiele's reputation for "pornographic" drawings, the comings and goings of his mistress, and his invitations to the village children to come and pose for him in the isolated little garden house on the outskirts of town, had aroused first the indignation and then the hostility of the provincial country folk, until at last legal steps were taken to rid Neulengbach of its undesirable inhabitant. Two constables confiscated his drawings and Schiele was arrested and locked up without bond in a basement cell of the Neulengbach district court. The charges against him were "immorality" and "seduction," but apparently the prisoner was not informed of them for over a week. The first charge alleged that Schiele, while entertaining and drawing child models in his studio, had through the careless or willful display of erotic drawings contributed to their corruption. This was an accusation that did not come as a surprise to his friends in Vienna. Heinrich Benesch had often warned Schiele to be more judicious as to what sort of drawings he left lying around when children came to pose.[61] Concerning the second charge, which alleged that he had seduced a young girl of the village, Schiele insisted in letters and other writings that he was innocent.[62] Whatever the validity of the accusations against Schiele (and he had reason to believe that his own uncle Czihaczek had been instrumental in bringing them to bear), the charges were sufficient to hold him in prison for twenty-four days, first at Neulengbach during the month of April, and then, sometime after 1 May, at the larger town of St. Pölten.[63] He was released, after a court trial, on 7 May. At the trial he was fined, and one of his drawings was burned by the judge in symbolic condemnation of his work. The humiliation of his arrest, imprisonment, and trial left an indelible imprint upon Schiele's personal and artistic development.

Schiele kept a diary, sketched, and made at least thirteen watercolors and one finished drawing during his imprisonment at Neulengbach. With one exception these watercolors were signed, dated exactly, and given special titles by the artist. Studied in connection with the diary,[64] which makes reference to most of them, they present a dramatic story, in which the act of drawing, mainstay of Schiele's art, becomes his moral support as he struggles to comprehend his arrest. The watercolors are divisible into three distinct groups that indicate the artist's thoughts concerning first his imprisonment, then himself, and finally his art. The first seven[65] deal with the prisoner's immediate surroundings—the cell, the corridor, the "door into the open"—and with objects near him—the chair, the water pitcher, and his own clothes. All seven pictures are based directly on factual objects, with meticulous veracity of detail. Before Schiele was permitted to receive drawing materials he tried to paint landscapes and heads on the cell walls with his own spittle. This type of imaginary drawing was displaced by the artist's habitual method of working directly from nature, as soon as he obtained pencil, paints, and paper.

Seven drawings later, and despite an attempt to infuse his humble subject matter with symbolic value (the last watercolor of this group, showing two chairs, a bucket, and a water pipe, is entitled "Art Can Not Be Modern: Art Is Primordially Eternal"), Schiele could no longer bear to record the oppressive reality of his surroundings (figure 88). His thoughts turned inward, upon a vision of himself as an unjustly suffering prisoner, and in three consecutive days he drew four self-portraits. For perhaps the first time in his life he portrayed himself without reference to a mirror image. The contemplation of himself, undistracted by a physical reflection, reached new depths of introspection. On the day that he executed the first self-portrait, Schiele addressed in his diary the God of his childhood days, for whom until now he had had little use. He wrote:

"Look down here, universal Father, . . . and consider whether you wish to tolerate that this shameful, debasing torture is being prepared for me. . . . When I stumble it is with your will that I stumble on your paths. But to suffer through your will? To be imprisoned through your will? . . . This is why I call to you: hear me, lend me your unlocked ear!"[66]

In the self-portrait of that same day, 23 April, Schiele further tried to attract the attention of the Being upon whom he had called. In an almost atavistic gesture he presented himself as a votive offering (figure 89). It is a pitiable creature that he portrays, one incapable even of resistance to suffering. Lying motionless upon his narrow cot, a coat thrown over his long frame, he turns his head feebly to one side, revealing an unshaven, hollow-eyed countenance. The hands, so important to Schiele's art when he wishes to convey emotion, are lacking—a symbol of his impotence in this situation. The great overcoat is painted a stifling orange with two large blue buttons down the front. Yellow cloth is under his legs and at his feet is the gray prison blanket. Schiele has signed and titled the picture at the bottom right, requiring a vertical reading that produces a distinct shock on the beholder, since the figure now appears not recumbent but uneasily erect, as though pinned to some rack of torture. The title is an appeal to both divine and profane authority: "Hindering the Artist Is a Crime, It Is Murdering Life in the Bud!" Corresponding to the change in subject matter from surroundings to self, the decorative capital letter that appears underneath the date in the whole prison series changes from the "G" for *where* (*Gefängnis*=prison) to a "D" for *when* (*Dienstag*=Tuesday). This concern for the exact day of the week continues for the rest of the series except for the final picture which is undated.

The next day Schiele turned his thoughts towards a very real being, the authority[67] who had placed him in jail. In his diary he wrote:

"Not very far from me, so near that he would have to hear my voice if I were to shout, there sits in his magistrate's office a judge, or whatever he is. A man, that is, who believes that he is something special, who has visited churches, museums, theaters, concerts, yes, probably even art exhibitions. A man who consequently is numbered among the educated class which has read or at least heard of the life of the artist. And this man can permit me to be locked up in a cage!"[68]

In the first watercolor for that day, 24 April, (figure 90) Schiele again portrays himself. Recumbent on the planks that form his cot, he now lies on his side with his legs drawn up underneath the blanket and coat, seeking warmth against the chilly April weather outside and the perpetual dampness of his basement cell. His coat is colored an oppressive orange-red and the two large buttons are almost offensive in their cheerful commonplaceness and great size. Together with the effect of the formless drapery they suggest the incongruous aspect of a clown. The hands are still pressed out of sight. Once again the picture is signed to secure a vertical reading. The decorative letter is now an "M" (*Mittwoch*=Wednesday) and the title reads bitterly: "I Love Antitheses."

But the suffering reflected in the first self-portrait and the dismayed sarcasm presented in the second drawing of himself still did not bring a response from the fellow human beings who controlled Schiele's fate. There was no answer to his call, and we know that he did call aloud:

"Yesterday: cries—soft, timid, wailing; screams—loud, urgent, imploring; groaning sobs—desperate, fearfully desperate. Finally apathetic stretching out with cold limbs, deathly afraid, bathed in shivering sweat."[69]

Only one picture, one word, can describe Schiele's condition on that day, 24 April: "Prisoner!" (figure 91). The prisoner lies stretched out at full length, his body seized by paroxysms and the red lips drawn back over his chattering teeth in a hideous grin of seeming insanity. His head snaps forward as though broken at the neck.Hair and beard are uncared-for. The great overcoat writhes in response to his convulsions, the empty sleeve flaps aimlessly. Suffering appears to have dulled his brain; it is a mindless body that churns in anguish. Here is a being who has cried out, a man who has shrieked in agony and then fallen into apathy.

"And yet," wrote Schiele, continuing his diary entry of 25 April, "for my art and for my loved ones I will gladly endure to the end." This statement becomes the title for a self-portrait painted on 25 April and marked "D" (*Donnerstag*=Thursday) (figure 92). The title announces a change in Schiele's vision of himself. It is the decision to endure, the determination to last out and survive this horrible imprisonment. Now he can suffer, now he can unashamedly voice his agonies. For the first and only time in this row of four self-portraits Schiele shows his hands. They are claws, flailing empty space, clutching at his blanket—so tensely that the fingers send creases shooting across the material. The reappearance of the hands as expressions of suffering is a gesture of return to the living. Schiele has cut his hair and beard. He shows himself full face, with his head thrown back. His distress is great, but he will experience it as a conscious human being, not as the benumbed creature of the previous self-portrayals. He has sworn to endure for the sake of art and for his loved ones. With this decision, the need to depict himself as a suffering prisoner is appeased, for this is the last self-portrait of the Neulengbach series. The final group of prison pictures exhibits fresh dimensions of Schiele's artistic resources. In a drawing and a watercolor of three oranges on his blanket ("All

Things Balance out Physically Most Surely" and "My Wandering Path Leads Over the Abysses") he first transforms reality, and then, in a shimmering watercolor of Trieste fishing boats, he escapes the dismal reality of his present surroundings by turning to the world of memory and fantasy. This capacity to adjust and the robust, objective quality of these later works supply proof of the intactness of Schiele's artistic powers during the Neulengbach confinement, despite the threat to sanity which this experience contained. As before, in periods of personal crisis, Schiele was able to sublimate suffering through art.[70]

In his prison diary Schiele had gloomily speculated on what the charges against him might be:

"If only I knew why they have stuck me in here. It could not have happened because of the drawing. Or could it? In Austria anything is possible. Here, where Waldmüller had to write the tax office a begger's letter, where Romako was driven to suicide by the lack of understanding and the jealous envy of incompetents, where university professors sneered at Klimt in the most shameful, self-tainting way."[71]

This calling to mind of previous artists who had suffered at the hands of society seems to have comforted Schiele (the allusion to Romako's suicide is especially interesting), and a walk in the prison courtyard at St. Pölten with the other inmates prompted him to recall another artist:

"A walk in the prison courtyard. Roller is surely a great artist, but his prison yard in *Fidelio* is still only theater, whereas the painting of the prison courtyard by Van Gogh is the most stirring truth, great art."[72]

When Schiele finally learned that one of the charges for which he was to be brought to trial would be based on his confiscated erotic drawings, he again recalled other artists, exploding indignantly to his diary:

"It is a scandal! An almost unbelievable crudity! Vulgarity! And a great, great stupidity! It is a cultural blasphemy, a shame for Austria that such a thing can happen to an artist in his own country. I do not deny it: I have made drawings and watercolors that are erotic. But they are still always works of art—that I can attest, and people who understand something of this will gladly affirm it. Have other artists made no erotic pictures? Rops, for example, made only such kinds. But one has never imprisoned an artist for this. . . . I could mention the names of many, many famous artists, even that of Klimt, but I do not want to excuse myself by this at all— that would not be worthy of me. Therefore I do not deny it. I do declare as untrue, however, that I showed such drawings intentionally to children, that I corrupted children."[73]

It was with this kind of reasoning, based on an established tradition of the freedom of great artists to produce erotic art, that Schiele attempted to console himself. His confidence in his status as an artist, his belief in artistic privilege, revolted at the thought of legal prosecution on such grounds.

The charges against Schiele were "immorality" and "seduction," and yet at the trial it was *as an artist* that the judge condemned and publicly disgraced him. The remembered spectacle of watching one of his own works deliberately set aflame in open court seared his senses. Shattered and humiliated, he shied away from discussing the incident with his friends. The loss of security in his status as "artist" and the fact of his imprisonment and trial weighed long upon Schiele's mind, strongly affecting both his personality and the thematic material of his painting. The day after his release he concluded his diary:

"Vienna, 8 May 1912

"For 24 days I was under arrest! Twenty-four days or five hundred and seventy-six hours! An eternity!

"The investigation ran its wretched course. But I have miserably borne unspeakable things. I am terribly punished without punishment.

"At the hearing one of the confiscated drawings, the one that had hung in my bedroom, was solemnly burned over a candle flame by the judge in his robes! Autodafé! Savonarola! Inquisition! Middle Ages! Castration, hypocrisy! Go then to the museums and cut up the greatest works of art into little pieces. He who denies sex is a filthy person who smears in the lowest way his own parents who have begotten him.

"*How anyone who has not suffered as I, will have to feel ashamed before me from now on!*" [74]

1912–1913: Allegorical double-portraits with Wally

"How anyone who has not suffered as I, will have to feel ashamed before me from now on!" These closing words of the prison diary now molded the character of Schiele's vision of himself and of the world. The symbolic guise of monk and hermit in the double portraits with Klimt made before the Neulengbach arrest now became a protective identity. Schiele's belief in the infallibility of the artist had been based on an aesthetic individualism. In a course that in many ways parallels that of another firm and tragic believer in the aesthetic imperative, Stefan George, Schiele chose in the face of shattering reality to dissociate himself by retreating into a proud isolationism from which, through his work, he hurled daring symbolic darts at the world. The delusion of persecution already hinted at in the concluding remarks of his letter to Dr. Reichel ("The farthest away will notice me, . . . and my negative ones will live by my hypnosis!") now began to assume dramatic proportions as Schiele eagerly embraced the role of social outcast. He needed sympathy and he craved revenge on the society which had condemned him. Both longings were realized in a new kind of painting that once again forces us to broaden the definition of Schiele's portraiture. On another of the wooden panels previously used to paint the idyllic portraits of himself and Wally at the beginning of the year, he now set down for himself a permanent lamentation, *Woman in Mourning* (plate 96). Although both the title ("Die Trauerende") and general appearance of the woman's face recall works of Minne, there can be no doubt that Schiele's painting is a very personal work in response to a particular situation. The woman is Wally, her features stamped with grief. [75] Comparison with a study (plate 97) for the earlier oil portrait of Wally (plate 92) demonstrates by what simple means Schiele is able to preserve and yet imprint his suffering upon the familiar features of his sorrowing companion, who had attempted in a small way to alleviate the gloom of his prison cell by throwing oranges through the bars of his window (the first prison watercolor had even been entitled "The Single Orange Was the Only Light"). The usually straight bangs curl in unheeded disarray, a skeletal emaciation is suggested by the fall of the head scarf about the face, and the dark pupils of the great eyes are moist with compassion. As though in incarnation of Wally's distressed thoughts there projects behind and beyond her head to the left a pale profile whose features are unmistakably those of Schiele. He presents himself as a delirious counterpart to her melancholy. To the extreme left a single sunflower from which all but a few petals have been plucked stands as a reminder of the artist's own recent spiritual mutilation. Schiele later wrote in praise of Wally's loyalty at this time.

From the recognition of his suffering achieved in this and another portrait of the grieving Wally,[76] Schiele turned his attention to retaliation. Feeling himself wronged by society, he now attempted to outrage it by attacking one of its institutions, the church. He painted his notorious *Cardinal and Nun* (plate 98). The posterlike crudeness of this work actually enhances the dramatic quality of its sacrilegious theme—an especially audacious subject to have been painted by a subject of the Emperor Franz Josef—a subject who had recently been imprisoned and brought to trial for "immorality." Although this was a familiar theme in art dating back to Bosch, Schiele's version was imbued with such intimate expressions of lust and guilt that a double scandal was involved, on the personal as well as the ecclesiastical level. The inclusion of his and Wally's own portrait features was a tormented bid for attention from the society that had attacked him as an artist. Schiele intended not ony the sacrilege implicit in the identification of the two protagonists as "cardinal" and "nun," but also a literal portrayal of sexual intercourse. The shocking orange-scarlet of the cardinal's robe tellingly enacts the drama as it pierces and then pushes into the black garments of the nun. But Schiele was not only defying the world at large in *Cardinal and Nun*: he was also challenging Klimt. If *The Hermits* contained a prediction of his primacy over Klimt as an artist, *Cardinal and Nun* documents Schiele's competition with him on his own ground, for the picture is unquestionably a deliberate parody of one of the older painter's most celebrated works, *The Kiss* (plate 99). Painted in 1908 and exhibited in the Kunstschau of the same year, it had been a sensation, although Klimt's mesmeric handling of the abstract and the representational side by side, aided by a glorious ornamental overlay, somewhat softened the narrative fact that here too a monk-like figure indulges in pleasures of the flesh. Schiele's treatment of the representational in a drastically simplified, abstract manner produced exactly the opposite effect, magnifying the "affront" presented by *Cardinal and Nun*. The fact that Klimt's figures, who also kneel to embrace, seem literally to merge and melt into one another, in the tradition of Rodin, emphasizes by contrast the aggressive, unilateral aspect of Schiele's painted statements of heterosexuality that is continued in the later portraits with his wife.

Schiele seemed to thrive on the thematic casting of himself and Wally as a sort of present-day Abelard and Héloïse, and he painted or drew projects for several more versions of the monk-nun motif in which his and Wally's features are recognizable.[77] This series was continued into 1913; a representative example is the ambitiously large *Self-Portrait with Model* [*"The Sleepwalkers"*] (figure 93).[78] Schiele's robes and tonsured head establish his monk's identity and, in an interesting variation on *Agony*, it is now he who is the aggressor, advancing with long arms stretched out towards the object of his desire, Wally—who responds with a gesture familiar in Schiele iconography, the V-shaped finger spread. Set against a background of tumbling blocks of color, this painting recalls *Cardinal and Nun*, but differs from it in the somnambulistic appearance of its protagonists. The earlier work delineated an act of passion and simultaneous reaction; this painting is more restrained and generalized, assigning to the heterosexual urge the same trance-like compulsion that Schiele had previously associated with his autoerotic portraits. The religious self-portraits with Wally had originally served Schiele only as a castigation of society, but as the months passed they seemed to suggest an increasingly appealing "identity." They also reflected his first meaningful and longlasting relationship with a woman, an alliance which because of the painful experience of Neulengbach he chose to depict under the protective veiling of asceticism.

1913–1914: THE ASCETIC SELF-PORTRAITS:—FROM MONK TO SAINT

Schiele had traveled in August of 1912 to Munich, where his works were being assembled for inclusion in the Secession exhibition at the end of the year. A notebook kept during this visit contains several lists of contemporary artists and their dealers, all checked off as Schiele made the rounds of the Munich galleries.[79] Included were the names of Rops and Pascin, and of the German Expressionists Kirchner, Schmidt-Rottluff, Nolde, Pechstein, Meid, Beckmann, Marc, Klee and Jawlensky. Schiele also bought a copy of the just published almanac edited by Kandinsky and Marc, *Der Blaue Reiter*, which he kept on display in a glass showcase in his studio (figure 114). Although Schiele shared the prevalent interest of his German colleagues in Oriental, Gothic, primitive, and folk art, his first-hand exposure to the techniques and themes of the German Expressionists had surprisingly little effect upon his own work. Only in 1916, when he tried his hand at a few woodcuts, is there any apparent result from his acquaintance with the Brücke and Blaue Reiter groups.[80] The geometrical fracturing of his portrait backgrounds during 1912 and 1913 may be considered however as a superficial incorporation of the methods of Cubism as practiced in Germany in the works of Feininger, Marc, and Macke. The Cubist analysis of structure, as practiced by Braque and Picasso, held no appeal for the artist, but the Cubist planes suggested an interesting alternate method for refraction of the astral body glow. On the whole Schiele was, as he had been since 1911, much too absorbed in himself and his thematic statements through self-portraiture to respond radically to other specific artistic stimuli.

This is demonstrated in the self-portraits of 1913 and 1914, which continue the antisocial portrayal of hermit or monk. The greater part of Schiele's painted oeuvre was devoted to land- and townscapes during these two years, and even allegories played a less important role than formerly, as the artist sought the mental diversion and health-restoring consolation which a return to nature always provided him. Other than the *Self-Portrait with Model* [*"The Sleepwalkers"*] of 1913 only one oil self-portrait was painted during these years and it was left uncompleted. This was the intriguing 1913 *Self-Portrait with Saint ("Encounter")* (figure 94), now lost, and known only through the photograph reproduced here, taken in 1914 and showing the artist himself standing to the right and "completing" the picture. The difference between the apparently sophisticated and self-possessed Schiele in the flesh and the timid, uncertain ascetic in the painting is impressive. The painted Schiele of 1913 stands with his back to the beholder, his face turned back over his shoulder almost reluctantly. A blue cloth covers the upper torso, emphasizing the bareness of the legs. The delicate watercolor study for this painting entitled by the artist *Remembrance* (plate 100a) reveals two interesting features not carried over into the painting itself: Schiele stands with a piece of drawing chalk in his hand, and the second figure, who does not share his world but is only an image which the artist has begun to draw, has the monk's beard equated with Klimt in *The Hermits* and *Agony*. Schiele was right-handed, but he has shown himself here holding the chalk in his left hand. If this seems partially to contradict his role as artist, the painting confirms the ambiguity, for the chalk is no longer shown and the artist seems about to step into his own picture behind the striding figure of the saint who has replaced the Klimt-monk of the preparatory study.

Although Schiele never completed this painting, he nonetheless entered it in a contest sponsored by Reininghaus the following year, with the explanation that it was a study for a mural, planned to extend some eighteen feet or more to the right. The public was to "imagine" a row of blind figures, each leading another. (The judges were apparently not willing to work *their* imaginations overtime however, for Schiele did not win the contest.) The ambitious size projected for this work is an example of Schiele's life-long urge to do great frescoes—his sketchbooks and letters are full of such projects—and reflects the general Expressionist predilection for large works and triptychs, an inheritance of the mural tradition of Munch, Hodler, and locally Klimt and Egger-Lienz. Many studies exist for the "blind" figures who were to be appended to this Bruegelesque work, and they are all Schiele. One example, *Self-Portrait from the Back with Hand to Cheek* (plate 100b), is particularly illustrative of the tortured character of the series.[81] It repeats a gesture first emphasized as early as 1909 and 1910. In still another way Schiele has reverted to the spirit of his early self-portraits. The delicate stroke of the graphite adopted in 1911 and 1912 has been abandoned in favor of the thick chalk or black crayon characteristic of 1910. There is however one important difference between the 1913 portrayals of self and those of the previous years: *Schiele no longer shows himself totally in the nude.* The implication is significant. The self-portraits of the 1913 series are in a sense rehabilitative, whether attempting to elicit society's commiseration for "blindness" or appealing for the ascetic dignity automatically ascribed to a hermit or monk. They are all integral parts of a new emotional self-respect. In this fragile convalescence Schiele seems carefully to avoid that nude confrontation before the mirror which had in the past called forth such total psychic exposure. It was several years before the artist again essayed nude self-portraiture in any media, and even longer before he employed it for major formal statements in oil.

In the bid for sympathy represented by the 1913 self-portraits it was but one short step from monk to saint. In keeping with Schiele's particular bent of personality—the real or fancied persecution, mistrust, and intrigue that he felt on all sides (his optimistic entering of the uncompleted *Self-Portrait with Saint* in the Reininghaus competition and his subsequent bitter disappointment at not having placed is typical of the "failures" towards which he as though instinctively steered)—this new portrait identity could not be just any saint, it had to be a *martyred* saint. And, significantly, Schiele chose a public event to make his saintly debut. A one-man show of his work was scheduled to open in December of 1914 at the Arnot Gallery in Vienna. A page of sketchbook designs for the exhibition poster (figure 95) marks Schiele's inspiration to present himself as St. Sebastian. The motif was then worked out in one of the artist's most eloquent drawings, the *Self-Portrait as St. Sebastian* (figure 96). We behold a limp figure, successor to the swooning monk of *Agony*, with arms outstretched as though affixed to an invisible crucifix. The head, with its open mouth and bulging eyes, hangs forward within the great diagonal formed by the extended left shoulder. Two arrows penetrate the body and the fingers are spread in rigid expression of pain. The continuous contour of the figure is itself pierced by quivering linear darts in a sensitive stylistic counterpart of agony. A gaping collar emphasizes the fragile neck, and the drapery humps along the shoulder in empathy. At some point during the sketching of the right hand Schiele decided upon a duplicate gesture to match the double V gesture of the left hand (an unerased sixth finger attests to the effective compositional change). This device is crystallized in the final design for the poster (figure 97) which was heightened with watercolor touches and placed within a bold hand-printed text. As if in compensation for the simplification of contour line projected for lithographic reproduction, Schiele has streaked the surface of his picture with eight more arrows, several of which pierce his body. There had been quite a few reproductions of the St. Sebastian motif in Schiele's copy of the Hamann book on Early Italian painting, and he no doubt knew the Mantegna version at the Kunsthistorisches Museum, but a more recent and far more notorious image of martyrdom suggests itself as a source for this public display of the artist as a tortured human being. Kokoschka's poster of 1908 advertising the performance of *Murderer, Hope of Women* at the Kunstschau (figure 98) had pictured a gruesome scene in which the raw, apparently flayed skin of a man is held in the grasp of a raging woman. Mopp had followed with a morose nude self-portrait poster in 1911 (figure 99) that shows the artist dipping his hands in the blood of his own wound.[82] Schiele's thematic choice in his *Self-Portrait as St. Sebastian* poster was undoubtedly chiefly influenced by his own personal history of persecution and torment attendant on the Neulengbach arrest. The theme however was quite within the context of current Viennese Expressionism, whose frequent portrayals of the paranoid were now a part of that unique cultural stockpile so frequently raided by Freud.

A further observation can be made concerning Schiele's depiction of himself now as a saint. If we were not familiar with the development of the artist's vision of himself from nude vessel of sexual cravings to ascetic monk and were to see only the St. Sebastian self-portrait, our conclusions about the artist's feelings of persecution and isolation from society would be correct but incomplete. From the vantage point of chronology and from comparison with earlier works, e.g., the 1909 drawing *Two Men*, such features as the absence of a halo and the covering of the traditionally bare torso of St. Sebastian assume special meaning. Schiele is not sanctified by his suffering as he was once sanctified by his art; it is as a human being that he suffers the tortures of the saint. The clothing heightens this personal identification and at the same time shows that the artist is not yet ready to reveal his nude body to artistic penetration. There have been no major nude self-portrait statements since the Neulengbach arrest. After the "sin" of *Cardinal and Nun* (who are clothed), Schiele appears to have been engaged in a long and arduous "penance" through ascetic self-portraiture. He must first suffer the martyrdom of a saint before the "redemption" through sainthood is his.

Two opinions of Schiele and his art at this time, one written by his Munich dealer, Hans Goltz, and the other by the artist himself, are instructive in summing up the difficult course of his life and work so far. On stationery boasting the names of Schiele, de Fiori, and Kandinsky in its letterhead, Goltz wrote the following exasperated and revealing message:

"I confirm having received 2 new pictures and 20 drawings. But, Herr Schiele, no matter how pleased I always am with your drawings, and how gladly I make allowances for the most bizarre whims, who will buy the pictures? I have there very, very little hope. You must not blame me if I, who have readily followed all artists of the new direction and who have facilitated for some their being understood, express my misgivings to you. What appeared to us only a year ago, yes, even half a year ago, as extraordinarily vigorous and therefore, but only therefore, promising for the future, must not become congealed into that form. It was one *way* out of the goal that has become diminished, that has already been reached. The 'isms' that were extraordinarily necessary as ways and as destruction must gradually clarify themselves into a calm, vigorous art. Otherwise, regardless of all personal understanding the art dealer can no longer achieve anything and must now with a heavy heart revert to less strong but, at least by comparison, comprehensible artists. I do not wish, with these words, to play the role of the admonishing father, I merely want to prepare you for a total financial failure which your pictures—on their present level, as well as those of others—must suffer. Even the well-meaning and perceptive part of the public is beginning to become impatient and hungers for calm and clarity."[83]

The "unsellable" aspect of the difficult works of which Goltz complained mattered not a whit to Schiele. His point of view is expressed in the following letter to a patron in which he sums up his life in a petition for the kind of spiritual understanding that would automatically provide financial help:

"I expect you to visit me on Tuesday or Wednesday between 2–4 o'clock in order to purchase one of the two *Cities*. Do not come if you feel in any way suspicious toward me or my proposition. To tell the truth, I am asking you because since the summer of 1913 I have been accumulating debts amounting to 2,500 K[ronen]—quite explicably, since during the entire long period from August until now I have sold one picture for 350 K. How then and by what means shall I get along?

"I became independent when I was 19 years old, I had to pass innumerable obstacles, perhaps like no one else, and this weakens one. These restrictions found expression in pictures. All colleagues were enemies: I began to hate Vienna, wanted to remain in isolation in Krumau, but could not since I had no money at my disposal. I needed Vienna and moved to Neulengbach to be by myself and still have Vienna in close proximity. I became respectable, and fate willed that a girl took a liking to me and managed things so that of her own will she [came] to me. I sent her away. They convinced themselves that she was untouched, but nevertheless the case came before the court. At that time I was cruelly humiliated because of my kindness—I lost all faith in otherwise trustworthy people—I lived through difficult, difficult hours, learned to know the whole morass of people and many misunderstood, true human beings.

"Of those who knew me best nobody made a move except Wally, whom I had known only a short time and who acted so nobly that she captivated [me], and Herr Benesch. I began to think deeply. I became aware of people with open souls and their saintly hearts, and I thought about liars and evil people. Thus I came to the conclusion that the pure, true human being must live eternally. I felt disgust for my melancholy countryside at Neulengbach, previously so tenderly beloved, and as a contrast, was lured to the border. In 1912 I stayed in Bregenz and saw nothing but the lake's various kinds of storms and distant white sunny mountains in Switzerland. I wanted to begin a new life, but I haven't yet been able to do so; so far I have not succeeded in anything in my life. I long for free people; no matter how much I love Austria, I mourn for her. I understand more and more the essays by Egger-Lienz, except that he boxes the ears—this I shall not do.

"Goltz in Munich wrote to me that a well-to-do gentleman would like to enable me to spend a rather long period of time in Paris. If not, I shall do everything I can to get to Paris, Berlin, or Munich, the sooner the better.

"This can not go on forever. I believe in important human beings who will recognize me, who will give me, not as a painter but as an artist, the tools to create.

"Herr Hauer, I wish to retain the exalted impression I have of you; therefore, prove yourself."[84]

The genuineness of Schiele's belief in his lifelong persecution at the hands of an unfeeling fate, as described above, is not to be doubted. At the time of the writing of this letter Schiele had become a bitter recluse. He preferred isolation to the company of friends. The festering resentment and self-pity absorbing his thoughts since his release from prison had infected his mind and had received thematic treatment in his canvases. His oil self-portraits no longer showed him alone but required the foil of a second figure serving either as object of attack or as director of attention upon Schiele himself. Publicly disgraced as an artist, he had adopted the antisocial personation of monk or hermit, advancing himself by the end of 1914 to the status of martyred saint. These ascetic self-portraits were the beginning of a painful search for personal and social identity. The hope of residing in a more enlightened city, such as Paris or Berlin or Munich, was never realized. Schiele was to remain dependent upon the Vienna he professed to hate, in an attachment that witnessed the gradual emergence of the artist from isolation as the social realities of a world war and marriage were borne in upon him. The firm conviction expressed in this letter of 1914 that his artistic talents would be "recognized" did not find gratifying realization until 1918, the last year of his life.

CHAPTER V

1912-1914: *Major Portrait Commissions*

T HE dejection which overtook Schiele after the Neulengbach arrest considerably worried his friends in Vienna. It was Klimt who thought of forcing the young artist out of his withdrawal by arranging for his introduction to an important patron of the arts, the industrialist August Lederer. Herr Lederer was the wealthy owner of a distillery in Györ (Raab), Hungary, and maintained a residence in Vienna. His wife, Serena, was talented artistically and had long been a close friend of Klimt, with whom she had studied painting for many years. The Lederer home contained the largest private collection of Klimt's works, including some twenty paintings. Klimt had portrayed several members of the family, including Serena, of whom he had made an oil portrait in 1899, and he knew that besides introducing Schiele to a family that was sympathetic to the arts and influential, he would also be exposing him to the youthful atmosphere of the Lederer household, dominated by the spirited presence of two sons, Fritz and Erich, aged twenty-three and fifteen, and the beautiful eighteen-year-old daughter Elisabeth. The introductions took place, and Schiele made a favorable impression. Almost immediately he was invited to spend Christmas at the Hungarian estate of this affable Jewish family, with a commission to paint the younger son's portrait. One of Schiele's sketchbooks contains in August Lederer's handwriting the factory address and train schedule to Györ, followed by Schiele's exclamation: "Saturday!"[1] On Saturday, 21 December 1912, he took the train to Hungary and was given such a spectacular welcome by the family that he sat down the very next day and wrote a spirited account of his adventures to his mother and a more lengthy chronicle to Arthur Roessler. Schiele's elation at his surroundings and reception bubbles over in the letter to his mother, in cheerful contrast to his former morose mood:

"I feel simply wonderful. I arrived here yesterday at quarter to twelve and was picked up immediately by private car. The Györ distillery is a very large one including three freight tracks and their own railroad cars and locomotives—in short, very large. The house is conformable and is furnished entirely by the Wiener Werkstätte. The people are extremely elegant and highly amiable towards me, perhaps I shall paint all of them in time. We went to the theater and other places. The city is almost as large as Linz. The car is always waiting. Servants, grey with silver buttons."[2]

To Roessler Schiele wrote in greater detail, mentioning that he had already made five drawings, "each of which pleases the Lederers, and they are amazed at how adroitly I work while they watch."[3] The letter concludes with an amusing and characteristic plea for practical advice via return mail as to how much he should tip the Lederer servants. In a second letter to Roessler, written on 24 December, Schiele describes roaming through Györ and discovering an old gabled wooden bridge which impressed him as "completely Asiatic, as though Chinese."[4] This bridge soon became the subject of one of Schiele's most unusual landscapes (*The Bridge*, K.181), and the attraction it held for him illustrates how, as in other critical periods of his life, he was compellingly drawn to landscapes and town scenes.

1912–1913: PORTRAIT OF ERICH LEDERER

But the immediate concern was the portrait of young Erich, and in the same letter to Roessler Schiele tells of the enthusiastic industry with which he had set about this task: "the picture will be 140 x 55 cm. I've made about 20 colored sketches for the portrait."[5] Erich was not a difficult subject to observe because, like his mother, he was of an artistic bent and often kept Schiele company by bringing his own crayons, squatting over a drawing board on the floor, and working as tirelessly as the artist who had come to portray him. A watercolor sketch by Schiele *Erich Lederer Drawing on the Floor* (plate 101) shows the young boy in his fashionable Eton jacket with its wide, starched collar, crouched on the floor, his heels against the wall, and leaning on his elbows—totally absorbed in the act of drawing. Only two lines in Schiele's sketch are extraneous to the subject: a line above the boy's drawing hand to signify a piece of paper and a line by the foot to indicate the wall of the room. This bare suggestion of a setting is noteworthy, for it tells even more succinctly than the early date, still 1912, that this is one of Schiele's first sketches, and that he is just beginning to close in for a more austerely Expressionistic study of his subject. The candid and almost anecdotal manner of this early sketch reflects both Schiele's visual astuteness and his social shyness. A markedly sympathetic attitude towards his subject is evident in Schiele's first letter to Roessler from Györ, as he describes Erich: ". . . the boy I am painting is 15 years old, with a long, aristocratic face. He is a born painter, and draws also, like Beardsley; only he has never observed nature, and that is his misfortune."[6]

One of the results of Erich's labors was a *Portrait of Schiele* (plate 102) which, in spite of a certain awkwardness and hesitancy of line, spontaneously conveys the great somber eyes peering out of a gaunt face with the head so character- istically cocked to one side. Dating from the Győr visit is a "composite" draw- ing—a portrait of the bearded Klimt, begun as a jest by Schiele one evening and then added to with increasing verisimilitude by all the members of the Lederer family.[7] In citing Beardsley with reference to young Erich, Schiele was probably referring to the subject matter as well as to the natural ease of the boy's drawings; later letters from Erich to Schiele are almost exclusively concerned with accounts of the boy's philandering and high-flown talk of sexual adventures.[8] That their conversations were not the shared intimacies of two equals, but rather the boastful outbursts of a high-spirited adolescent just beginning to sow his wild oats to a reticent but apparently interested young man with a reputed penchant for things erotic, is indicated by the tone of Erich's letters to Schiele in 1915, in which the polite "Sie" form of address is maintained despite the spicy personal reportage.[9]

The verso of *Erich Lederer Drawing on the Floor* contains a quickly exe- cuted pencil drawing of Erich in profile with one hand raised to his head, a sketch which was rejected by Schiele as unsatisfactory and not heightened with any watercolor touches as were most of the other portrait studies. One of these, done in the first days of 1913, demonstrates Schiele's characteristic "propless" approach to his sitter. In *Erich Lederer with Hands Folded* (plate 103) emphasis is given to the sitter's face, which Schiele had found so "long and aristocratic." The large head, unruly mop of hair, arched brows, great eyes with their luxuriant dark lashes, full rosy lips, and elfin ears and chin are set off by vibrant watercolor touches in the clothing: an orange-red collar, a purple tie, and a black jacket. Creases in the paper indicate that Schiele had folded back the sides of the sheet to approximate the narrow oblong of the canvas selected for the portrait. The sitter is presented without any of the props—chair or stool—which would ordinarily explain his posture, heightening the intensity of rendition, almost as though in this town of distilleries Schiele were extracting the pure essence of his sitter from the atmosphere in which he lived and breathed. The efficacy of the presentation appears upon comparison of this drawing with a slightly earlier study, dated 1912, *Erich Lederer Stand- ing with His Hands in His Pockets* (plate 104) which was completely worked out in watercolor. More introspective than the later studies, it shows the head turned away from the beholder and the eyes downcast. The boy, of delicate, exotic appearance, is shown against a fully articulated background—a patch- work of gaily colored rhomboids, parallelograms, and triangles which recalls the Wiener Werkstätte drapery seen in previous canvases and watercolors. The presence of a decorative background may have functioned as a psycho- logical filler, compensating for a lack of familiarity with the subject. The 1912 date and the evident self-consciousness (manifested in this study by pensive- ness) suggest that this is another of the earliest sketches.[10]

As the acquaintance between artist and model deepened, the studies of

Erich progressively reveal more outgoing characteristics, and in the later studies the boy's head is almost always turned directly towards his new friend and confidant. Indeed it is the bold precocity of Erich Lederer—half boy, half man—which Schiele strove to capture in the final oil. What he intended can be ascertained in the 1913 preparatory drawing *Erich Lederer Standing with Hand on Hip* (plate 105). The study,[11] heightened by black, blue, and red watercolor touches, has been lightly sized by Schiele with a square grid for transfer to canvas. The frontality of the previous studies has been exchanged for a side view of the torso, suggesting an arrested movement, as though the boy had paused in mid-step to thrust his hand on his hip and turn his head inquiringly towards the beholder. The unusual physiognomy is rendered with the same emphasis on size as in the other studies, but with somewhat less exaggeration. The chin is more rounded and the hair has become manageable. With his exquisite feeling for the pairing of similar forms, Schiele has accented the double pattern of arm at right angles to the body and the emphatic protrusion of the boy's ear from his head. On the left the continuous silhouette of the figure creates a narrow, wavering spatial void which runs the length of the sheet and accentuates the verticality of the enclosing oblong. Whereas the figure is placed to the left of the center axis, the outthrust arm, bent at the elbow and forming a triangle, introduces diagonal thrusts into the right half of the picture which extend to where the elbow touches the edge of the frame. Thus the half-length figure takes compositional and psychological possession of its space, at once simulating and opposing the enclosing oblong. Although the scrawny look of some of the earlier studies has been toned down here, the excited tumbling of the drapery has lost none of its autonomy. The sleeve, jacket-front, and trousers are rendered in mobile, bumpy contours while abstract pockets of vigorous lines collect as interior modeling at the shoulder and inner trouser-leg. A second set of lines in the lower torso indicates that Schiele wished to contrast the bony protuberance of the out-thrust hip and its awkward bell shape with the narrow chest and slender shoulders; an observation of the undeveloped adolescent body comparable in sensitivity to that of Donatello's *David*. Of the paired members of the body Schiele has shown only one ear and one hand in this final study. As can be expected of the artist by now, the hand functions as a character index and compositional tour de force, and great delight has been taken in emphasizing with black dabs of watercolor the isolating or coupling play of space around the fingers.

It was the stance determined in the study just examined which was adopted for the oil *Portrait of Erich Lederer* (plate 106),[12] but with the figure extended to almost full length. The hand on hip, which in the preparatory study had been recorded in its natural fall, now receives a vicarious Schiele tension, with the long, pale fingers stretched in a double V gesture—but as a decorative rather than "secret" device. To the lower right of the canvas a colorful passage of horizontal stripes and triangles recalls the decorative background motifs introduced in the watercolor study *Erich Lederer Standing with His Hands in His Pockets*. This hint of environment (a similar building-up of background forms and chair cushions may be observed in the watercolor study of Elisabeth Lederer, plate 107b) and the impression of interrupted action conveyed in the half-turn of the body indicate a new and less "tragic" attitude towards portraiture on Schiele's part. No longer does the prospect of an adolescent sitter provoke that somber, Munch-like response formulated in the 1910 *Portrait of Herbert Rainer* (plate 58). The portrait of the Rainer boy furnished an occasion for a general statement on the universal themes of loneliness and vulnerability. The child himself exhibits no distinctive character traits; he is literally an object surrounded by a void, a generalized, static icon. The Lederer portrait, on the other hand, does not function as a symbol. It deals with a specific personality presented within a narrative and even candid context. Schiele's new receptiveness towards other persons as individuals now begins to characterize most of his portraits during these middle years.

The diminishing of Schiele's subjective comprehension of other people's psyches is interestingly demonstrated in two studies[13] of Elisabeth Lederer (plates 107a and 107b), made during the same period as the painting of Erich. The artist responds to the magnetism of the great dark eyes, so similar to Erich's in their exotic effect, but he does not cloud them over with intimations of Angst or somnambulistic reverie. Character differences between the brother and sister also receive comment. Schiele had shown the more aggressive Erich with arms and legs and even an ear projecting, angular and all askew, while the older, more reserved, and perhaps shyer Elisabeth is presented with her arms close to her body and with the hands clasped in a gesture of self containment. The projected oil portrait of Elisabeth by Schiele was never begun; it was Klimt who was to remain the portrayer of the Lederer women, completing oil portraits of both the daughter (*Portrait of the Baroness Elisabeth Bachofen-Echt*) and the maternal grandmother (*Portrait of Charlotte Pulitzer*) by 1915.

The sojourn in Györ began an enduring friendship with the Lederer family and Schiele visited them often at their Vienna residence during the next years, sometimes to give drawing lessons and sometimes just to chat or, later, to discuss war news.[14] Schiele drew Erich many more times (plates 108a and 108b) although he never painted another portrait of him.[15] The patronage of this sympathetic and influential family was an important factor in Schiele's eventual personal rehabilitation and one which deepened his appreciation of and interest in others.

1913: DOUBLE PORTRAIT OF HEINRICH AND OTTO BENESCH

Shortly after his St. Pölten trial Schiele had written Roessler that the pictures he had been permitted to make in prison would be given only to his closest friends.[16] Heinrich Benesch was one of these friends. The description of Schiele which Herr Benesch wrote upon the occasion of their first meeting in November of 1910 has already been cited in connection with the 1910 self-portraits. Since that time the older man, a civil servant with only a modest income, had become an enthusiastic customer and loyal personal friend. Notwithstanding the fact that he had a wife and teen-age son to support, Herr Benesch had purchased and assembled a sizeable collection of Austrian artists. The walls and even the doors of his house were hung from top to bottom with paintings. The first time Schiele visited the Benesch home he was shown the collection, which at that time consisted mostly of works of the Romantic school. When Benesch later asked what he thought of it, Schiele with his customary candor answered: "Well, some of them aren't *too* bad."[17] Later Benesch came to agree with Schiele and changed his tastes in favor of more contemporary Austrian artists. His favorite foreign artist was Cézanne, whom he often discussed with Schiele. Frau Benesch was a little appalled at the bohemian appearance of her husband's protégé and, although he was a frequent visitor, it was never for dinner. Nevertheless Benesch saw Schiele either at home or in his studio once a week for many years, and a lively friendship developed between the artist and Benesch's young son Otto, the future Rembrandt expert, whom Schiele referred to affectionately as "Benotto." Otto followed Schiele's work with admiration and deep thought. As early as March 1912 he had written and timidly presented to the artist an imaginative essay on *The Hermits*, then on exhibition at the Hagenbund. The filial relationship which Schiele both observed and shared in the Benesch family during these early years of independence not only bore fruit pictorially but also proved of emotional benefit to him. Although, typically, he took offense at both Heinrich and Otto on different occasions, his relationship with them was of a more stable and less demanding nature than the stormy friendship with another father-figure, Arthur Roessler. The older Benesch's help was often of a material nature. More than once he had sent money to Schiele upon receipt of one of the artist's not-too-rare pleas, mailed from some Austrian outpost, for return fare to Vienna. "Herr B will fix things," was one of Schiele's frequent statements in times of trouble, and indeed "Herr B" smoothed over many matters for him, from reconciling acquaintances or clients Schiele had unintentionally estranged to settling such mundane matters as exhibition transport costs. It was Heinrich Benesch who visited Schiele three times during his Neulengbach imprisonment and who escorted him back to Vienna from St. Pölten after his release, arranging for the transfer of his personal effects from Neulengbach. It is not surprising that Schiele gave him three of the most impressive prison watercolors—two self-portraits (figures 89 and 91) and the interior scene entitled *The Door into the Open!* (figure 88).[17a]

The idea of a life-size double portrait of father and son (plate 110) was probably arrived at mutually. Following close upon the completion of the Lederer portrait, this new project served as a continued stimulus to Schiele and prevented him from turning his thoughts inward once more. Having observed with satisfaction the therapeutic benefits that involvement with a commissioned work had produced upon Schiele, it was probably the older Benesch, then fifty-one, who gently urged realization of this challenging task.[18]

Although in the final oil both figures are standing, Schiele's first solution to the difficult problem of placement, offered by any double portrait, was to draw the older Benesch seated to the right with his son standing behind him on the left, as in the drawing *Benesch Double Portrait Study, Heinrich Seated and Otto Standing* (plate 111a). A profile or three-quarter view of Heinrich as opposed to a full frontal view of Otto appears to have been Schiele's intention from the beginning. The stance of young Otto, who at seventeen already towered above his father, was also first determined in this early study. The boy stands with his weight on the right foot, the narrow right shoulder sloping correspondingly, and the arms hanging close to the body with the hands lightly clasped in front. Otto's long, bony face, of the kind so favored by Schiele, wears a reflective expression. The outward-turning left eye (denoting the cerebral concentration which is prominently stressed in the completed painting) was also established in this drawing. As in the final oil, Otto's stance with clasped hands is curiously reminiscent of one of the standing male nudes in the Ernesto de Fiori mural that had impressed Schiele at the 1909 Kunstschau (figure 63). The rhythmic motif of a double projection of ear and elbow which Schiele had recently used to great advantage in the portrait of Erich Lederer is again essayed here and developed throughout the studies of Otto. Only the hands are treated differently in the oil.[19]

In regard to a triple study of his hands done on one piece of paper by Schiele and entitled *The Folded Hands* (plate 109), Otto wrote a description years later of the hurried concentration with which the artist worked:

"The number of drawings which he made in preparation for a portrait was legion. I was frequently able to observe him at work, particularly when he was doing the life-size double portrait of my father and me. . . . Schiele drew rapidly, the pencil slid across the white surface of the paper as if guided by the hand of a ghost, as if in a game, and the position of the hand was at times that of the brush handling of East Asiatic painters. The eraser was not used—if the model changed position, the new lines were placed next to the old with the same unerring sureness. Incessantly one sheet of paper after the other was placed on the board, so swiftly sped the production. It was unavoidable that now and then a drawing was lost—in the studio there were always plenty of discards underfoot. But how Schiele penetrated the model with his dark eyes! How nerve and muscle were captured! (*The Folded Hands*) Schiele *never* added colors to his drawings *in front of the model*, but always afterwards from a completely retained memory of the natural object."[20]

The important change in favor of a composition in which both figures stand appears in the drawing, *Benesch Double Portrait Study, Heinrich Standing Right and Otto Standing Left* (plate 111b). Heinrich is now seen at his full height, his body and face turned at almost a right angle to the viewer. The conception of Otto is essentially unchanged: his face wears the same meditative expression, now intensified by the addition of lines in the forehead, cheek, and chin. (In the final oil the boy's greater height is emphasized by allowing the top of the canvas to cut off the top of the head.) Schiele contrasts the substantial width of Heinrich's head with the attenuated shaft of Otto's face and emphasizes the boy's high forehead by raising and leveling the hairline. The narrowness of the head is further stressed by the long cheek line, now continuous with the lapel line of the jacket. The modeling of the jacket is in much greater detail here, with a re-drawing of the left sleeve, suggesting, as does the relationship of the figure to the paper, that this drawing was begun as a study of Otto alone. The overlay of lines on this sleeve establishes the actual moment of the new compositional inspiration. As can be observed also in the previous double portrait study, where a triple entry of lines indicates how the artist determined the height of the seated Heinrich's head in relation to the arm of his son, so in this study a hairline drawn at approximately the same point reveals that Schiele again intended to show Heinrich seated when he decided to include him in this drawing. Suddenly he changed his mind and quickly drew in Heinrich's head as if he were standing—perhaps even asking him at this point to stand up. The sketchiness and overlap of the few lines denoting Heinrich's collar and jacket complete the visual evolution of this change of plan. As is brought out in Otto's description of how Schiele drew, a change in the position of the sitter did not bother him at all: he erased nothing, but simply applied new lines next to the old ones.

Careful planning of the space between the figures was now needed, and in later studies Schiele began to back the figure of Heinrich farther from Otto, while a three-quarter view of Heinrich leaning slightly away from his son with his head in profile and his back towards the beholder was developed.[21]

This pose apparently satisfied Schiele until he had actually transferred the composition to canvas and completed most of the painting. A careful look at the oil discloses the remnants of this "old" posture, still sufficiently visible to produce a double image. The old pose shows Heinrich with both hands thrust in his pockets, and the portrait must be imagined in this earlier state in order to fathom what Schiele was attempting and why he was dissatisfied. The austere shapes that were beginning to receive color upon the canvas—gray-green clothes and creamy faces against a gray background—presented very simply two figures, one frontal with hands clasped and leaning slightly to the right of his axis, the second facing inwards but leaning back with hands in pockets and face turned to look over his shoulder at the observer. The result was two figures disturbingly unrelated to each other. What Schiele had desired to express concerning and differentiating father and son now functioned too blatantly on a physical, compositional plane, and distracted from the more subtle characterizations also present. For Schiele had contrasted father and son not only in terms of size, age, and physiognomy, but also in terms of personality: Heinrich appears as an active, self-confident man who responds readily to the world about him, and who expects to engage the attention and respect of persons in his company; Otto is shown as a young man absorbed in thought, deferential to the authority of his father, passive in response, but alert to his own world—an intense dreamer very much in tune with Schiele's own nature. But now the physical emphasis on the spatial void separating father and son overshadowed these qualities. The figures had to be related to each other, as they were in real life. The distinctions expressed by the individual gazes, and so unswervingly advanced in the preparatory drawings, were left unaltered, but a radical change in gesture was introduced directly on the canvas. The older Benesch was given a "new" left arm which was raised to shoulder height and extended towards Otto, thus bridging the canvas and the gap between the two figures. The fingers of this raised left hand are not fully extended but bend inwards at the tips, repeating the tenser gesture of Otto's tautly clasped fingers, and giving both figures a feature in common. The raised arm gesture is compositionally a dramatic success; its significance however is open to multiple interpretation. The extended arm suggests authority, possession, affection, possibly domination. It was this last quality that the Benesch family ascribed to the painting. Fifty years after its completion Otto Benesch's wife, Eva, wrote:

"The painting was frequently discussed in the circle of our family and acquaintances —there were always new interpretations and new riddles to be solved. Later its true meaning was recognized. Had Schiele captured here—consciously or unconsciously —a profound psychological situation? Heinrich Benesch liked to dominate. At times his son's flight of thought began to appear eerie to him. *The glance into the spiritual world*, beyond all outer barriers, was already recognized by Schiele in the then seventeen-year-old [boy] and expressed in the portrait—a spiritual world in which Otto Benesch of course dominated."[22]

The insight into a spiritual-intellectual world to which Eva Benesch refers is substantiated by Schiele's geometric fracturing of the background into kinetic emblems denoting directions, energies, and intensities—the most notable area being the extended triangle which begins with its apex at Otto's left outward-turning eye and then extends to the opposite edge of the canvas, encompassing his head and continuing beyond in an ever-widening expansion. The passage of time has given this double portrait more significance than the mere determination of who dominates whom: Schiele's carefully conceived portrait holds general interest as a sensitive statement about the inbuilt tensions and ties of a father-son relationship.

The systematic "Cubist" background fracturing in the Benesch double portrait had been employed by Schiele, it will be remembered, in four previous major paintings of this period—interestingly all also two-figure compositions: the two self-portraits with "Klimt" (plates 84 and 87) and two self-portraits with Wally (plate 98 and figure 93). After these works Schiele developed a less geometric and more organic division of the background, especially in his landscapes, in a personalized reflection of Hodler's eurythmic principles. The appearance of a "charged" background in the Benesch portrait and the fact that it is a double portrait invite comparison with Kokoschka's 1908–1909 double portrait of the Viennese art historians Hans and Erika Tietze (plate 113). There are certain formal similarities, such as the placing of the figures at right angles to each other, obtaining a profile as contrasted to a frontal portrayal of the sitters. The emphasis on gesture is even greater in the Kokoschka portrait, and the silent dialogue of the hands suggests a confrontation of active and passive forces comparable to the depiction of forceful extrovert and reflective states established in Schiele's portrait. Equally effective is the emotion-conveying role of the charged background in both paintings. Schiele, the born draftsman, fractures the background into hard-edged wedges, whereas Kokoschka, the instinctive colorist, loads his canvas with amorphic swatches of color reminiscent, in their bold harmonies, of the Fauves. A reverse process is then observable: Schiele fills his geometric areas with a fabric of short, stubby brushstrokes, while Kokoschka scratches into the paint a wiry network of line bundles. This sensitizing of the surface is always carried to a greater extreme in Kokoschka, who allows the implanted color swatches an almost sinister aggressiveness as they nibble away at the human contours. Schiele never permits the forms of his figures to be dissolved or even penetrated by their charged atmosphere; on the contrary it is the sheer force of their corporeal presence which often indents or stamps an after-image or "body halo" in the background about his figures, as in the area around Heinrich Benesch's hand, or the mimetic wedge just under his raised left arm. Contemporary reaction to both these portraits was one of horror, and little attention was paid to the difference in means employed to obtain the spell-binding intensity—Kokoschka's active, often calculatedly morbid atmosphere with its intimation of the subject's physical decay, and Schiele's brittle integrity of the whole, the fragile *Dasein* existentially engaging the void which is its setting. Schiele's figures are isolated; Kokoschka's figures are surrounded. Both suggest the pathos in life deeply sensed by the two artists. It is doubtful whether Schiele knew the Tietze portrait at the time he painted the Benesch double portrait since he did not come into contact with Dr. Tietze until much later, in 1918,[23] but the common intention voiced by different techniques in these two double portraits is another testimony to the general phenomenon of Expressionism in the younger generation of painters in Vienna at this time.

Although today the universality of the Expressionist *Drang* among these avant-garde artists is apparent, there is evidence that Schiele would greatly have resented a comparison of his Benesch double portrait with the Tietze portrait by Kokoschka. For the one-man exhibition of Schiele's works at the Arnot Gallery in January of 1915, Otto Benesch wrote a long foreword to the catalogue which was published before Schiele had a chance to read it.[24] In this essay Otto traced Schiele's primary inspirations to the Gothic past (Grünewald appealing to the painter in him and Dürer attracting the draftsman) and to the more recent Wiener Werkstätte. He wrote of Schiele's having passed from the stage of being "a capable Klimt-disciple" in his early works, to the painting *Agony*, in which "Schiele goes beyond anything which those around Klimt have accomplished." Otto concluded:

"In *Resurrection* [K.176] he manifests greater congeniality with the old masters than with the cultivated Vienna that was his childhood before *Sturm und Drang*. If the present time, which counts a Kokoschka among its own, equals old art in power of expression, may it permissibly be accused of affectation because it surpassed the Klimt period?"[25]

This enthusiastic essay, placing Schiele between Klimt and Kokoschka, with Gothic roots, apparently roused the immediate indignation of Schiele, for a remarkable defense of the essay exists in the form of a nine-page handwritten letter to Schiele from Otto, dated 10 January 1915. In this letter Otto expresses his surprise at hearing that his introduction had "stirred up some dust." He reminds Schiele that he had tried to show him the manuscript before publication, had made an appointment to meet him at the Arnot Gallery and had arrived there punctually with the manuscript, but that Schiele had not made an appearance. He condemns the circle of painters *around* Klimt as dangerous imitators, and then bravely writes: "You too, Herr Schiele, were once one of 'those around Klimt.' The change that led you into different directions can only have been a descent or an ascent. It surely was an ascent."[26] The vehemence of Schiele's objection to being mentioned in the same breath with Kokoschka can be judged by the sarcasm of one of Otto's concluding remarks: ". . . and Kokoschka is not so bad that it would be a sin to mention his name or to mention it next to yours." The fact that Kokoschka had begun to paint Expressionist portraits from the beginning of his career, whereas Schiele had arrived at this kind of portraiture only after shedding the Klimt-Wiener Werkstätte style—a development which Otto had pointed out in his essay— was evidently a sore point with Schiele. It is an interesting reflection on Schiele's opinion of the uniqueness of his art that as late as 1915, with several one-man exhibitions at home and abroad behind him, he should have been so incensed by Otto's well-meant catalogue introduction. It may be deduced from this incident that the "priority" in Expressionistic portraiture which Kokoschka claims to this day,[27] was already a disputed point in artistic circles at that time.

1914: ETCHED PORTRAIT OF FRANZ HAUER

Although Schiele and Kokoschka may both have resented being compared with one another, they continued to share and even portray mutual patrons as late as 1914. Franz Hauer was the well-to-do owner of a Vienna beer hall, the Reichenberger Beisel in the Griechengassel, from which it derived its more popular name, the "Griechenbeisl."[28] Hauer was a self-educated connoisseur and discriminating collector of contemporary Austrian art. He had turned the garden of his Döblinger home into a gallery where several hundred of the best works by prominent Austrians were displayed, among them paintings by L'Allemand, Fahringer, Sterrer, Egger-Lienz (with a whole room devoted to him), Faistauer, and Kokoschka. Hauer was as renowned for his generosity in helping young unknown painters as he was for his collection, and it was Arthur Roessler who in 1912 gave Schiele the idea of inviting Hauer to see his work, then on display at the Hagenbund. Schiele wrote him the following to-the-point letter: "Dear Herr Hauer: I have heard that you are one of the few who acquire pictures from the youngest. Would you not like to visit me or look at the exhibition of the Hagenbund where some of my works can be seen?"[29]

The response was immediate and substantial. Within two days Hauer had seen the show, visited Schiele in his studio, and bought three of his most recent paintings, even though they were not yet completed.[30] From the time of this first meeting Hauer evinced a lively interest in Schiele's works and well-being and was, on Schiele's part, admitted to that circle of father-figure friends upon whom was bestowed the dubious honor of frequent "emergency" requests for return train fare to Vienna. Although most of Schiele's correspondence with Hauer deals with money problems, advances, and payments, some important personal insights can be gained. Hauer, who had already acquired two of the artist's "unpopular" allegories (*Conversion I*, K.158, and *Agony*), was also eager to obtain the large 1913 allegory *Resurrection* (K.176).[31] The exchange of letters concerning this work, which both men called "Graves," deals mainly with reports on its progress and the increased price which the artist felt entitled to charge. However, Schiele wrote that if Hauer still wanted to pay only the original 700 Kronen for the painting, it would be acceptable, but:

"Consider, dear Herr Hauer, that otherwise I have sold small pictures (landscapes) to people for 600 Kronen, therefore, I know how kindred-souled to me the man is who owns the Graves."[32]

Schiele respected Hauer sufficiently to confide to him some of his painterly aspirations and methods:

"For the present I am primarily thinking about pictures which I would like to paint. I am also making studies, but I find and know that copying after nature is meaningless for me, since I paint better pictures from memory, envisioning the landscape. I am now observing primarily the physical movement of mountains, water, trees, and flowers. Everywhere one is reminded of similar stirrings of joy and sorrow in plants. Painting alone does not suffice me, I know that qualities can be created WITH colors. An autumnal tree can be experienced in summer more profoundly, and with one's being and heart. It is this melancholy that I would like to paint."[33]

Schiele's interesting statement about observing the physical movement of mountains, water, trees, and flowers, and being reminded on all sides of similar stirrings of joy and sorrow in plants, corroborates the extremely personal attitude exhibited in his landscapes and his tendency to read human emotions into nature. This emotional personification differs from the more scientific detachment of Klee, who, for instance, made the replanting of a bergamot cut in his garden an occasion to discuss and draw in his diary the capillary action involved,[34] or who, in his Bauhaus years, used the examples of mountains, watermills, and plants to illustrate principles of energy projection inherent in a line. The longing to express through color the "melancholy" of an autumnal tree experienced in summer is the key to Schiele's approach to form: a double interpretation which depends upon his unique graphic ability to recapture the perceived object and his response to the "shape" of its emotional content.

It may again be asked whether the "melancholy" which both Schiele and Kokoschka expressed in their separate portraits of Franz Hauer (Schiele, plates 112 and 115; Kokoschka, plate 114) was not as much a product of the attitude towards portraiture exhibited by Viennese Expressionism in general as of the portrait subject himself. Or, as might perhaps also be justifiably inquired of Freud, would a study of citizens of any other European city have resulted in the same pathological findings of anxiety and repression? Franz Hauer was an interesting example of the new bourgeois patron of the arts who, by dint of actual capital as well as genuine appreciation, was taking over the role of collector and connoisseur in imperial Vienna. It was this new, moneyed middle class to which the young rebel artists like Kokoschka and Schiele gave their allegiance. Hauer's beginnings had been humble. Apprenticed to a butcher in his youth, he became proprietor of the Griechenbeisl through marriage with the previous owner's sister-in-law. Physically ravaged, as both portraits indicate, he suffered from tuberculosis contracted during long years of hard work. But he was inwardly sustained by a passion for art, and his later financial stability, coupled with the fear of a shortened life-span, gave him an almost frenetic hunger for the acquisition of painting. To the neglect of his five children, left motherless since 1907, he concerned himself exclusively with covering the walls of his home and gallery with works of art, leaving the operation of the Griechenbeisl to a manager. A lonely man, isolated by his tastes from his business associates, he became the friend of other solitary men and was one of the first to champion Adolf Loos. The unspoiled sincerity and directness of Hauer must have touched responsive cords in Schiele and Kokoschka, who both had suffered from the vague promises, financial tightness, and jealous intriguing of the typical Viennese collector of art. The ability of both artists to sense and portray the melancholy in Hauer was at once a compliment to the man whom they found sympathetic and an extension of themselves through a receptive agent.[35] The somber Hauer was an ideal subject for Viennese Expressionism, a movement whose adherents were predisposed towards pathos. The intriguing "El Greco" quality of spirituality that flickers in both artists' portrayals may be read as an appreciative response to that master, whose long-neglected work had become one of the major art "discoveries" of the new century, and whose quivering distortions appealed to both the brutalizing and abstractive approaches within Expressionism.

The Hauer portraits were realized in different media: Schiele's studies[36] resulted in the 1914 etched portrait (plate 115), and Kokoschka completed his oil portrait of Hauer in the same year. The final products, although in different media, again exhibit the significant difference in approach by which in each instance a "pathetic" portrait was achieved. Kokoschka's "crude" figure appears in the richness and complexity of a whole, or at least broader, personality, with accompanying associations (the room with its multipaned window and window box, the chair, and the open book in Hauer's lap). Schiele's portraits up to this time, including the Lederer and Benesch pictures, have remained more existential in approach, centering upon one or a very few characteristics which are then intensified. His initial response to the small size of the copper plate had been to focus on Hauer's face, and at first even an imaginary face, as in the interesting first attempt at etching, *Head of a Man* (Kallir[37] No. 3a, 1914), engraved on the right-hand portion of the same plate upon which

Schiele's friend, the graphic artist Robert Philippi, had demonstrated the etching method by incising the full figure of a standing Oriental. The exclusive "precise" attention given Hauer's face in the etched portrait had been cultivated in the pencil studies where the only other feature is a hand or, as in the example reproduced here (plate 112), an unspecified husk of drapery which extends to the waist and is expressed by a single dark irregular contour pierced at right angles along its length by a lighter angular scribble. The lively calligraphy establishing the beard and face in this study contrasts with the sparse treatment of the clothing, which by its very economy channels attention to the apex of graphic activity, the head. Was it perhaps the bristly strands of Hauer's beard which attracted this extraordinary linear concentration? A comparison with the recently executed studies of the bearded Heinrich Benesch (plates 111a and 111b) discourages such speculation; the brittle, multiple handling of linear elements in the Hauer study suggest instead that Schiele was simply anticipating the "feel" and look of a copper plate.[38]

Although Schiele's etching of Hauer deals only with the face, and Kokoschka's portrait with the whole man, the same heavy-lidded introspection is described by both artists in their final portraits. Kokoschka punctuates the characterization by means of the forgotten half-turned page of the book held in the fingers of the huge left hand, Schiele by means of the glazed, recessed left eye—already essayed in the study, and similar in effect to the outward-turned eye of Otto in the Benesch double portrait. The physical frailty apparent in the worn, lined face is further communicated by the heavy fall of the ill-fitting clothes in the Kokoschka version and through the dwarfing awkwardness of the formless jacket in Schiele's portrait. Schiele's aggrandizement of all graphic elements functions with the intensity of barbed wire in certain areas (notably the cheek and forehead wrinkles), sometimes fraying, as in the beard and hair areas, sometimes fracturing in a crystalline explosion about the eyes. Kokoschka employs similar stresses through the application of color tensions in a passage of tonalities from red and blue to greens.

The untimely death of Franz Hauer in June 1914 from peritonitis deprived not only Schiele and Kokoschka, but many lesser-known Viennese artists, of a sensitive and generous patron.

Two portrait "obligations"

Before the portrait commission by Fräulein Friederike Beer, Schiele's oil portraits of women had been limited to the members of his own family and to his mistress, with two exceptions—both portraits done in settlement of debts. The first, the 1911 *Portrait of Trude Engel* (plate 116) was the exasperated solution to the problem of staggering dental bills. Trude Engel was the daughter of Dr. Hermann Engel, recommended by Roessler to Schiele as a dentist willing to accept paintings in payment for his work.[39] One of the first paintings thus destined was the now lost *Revelation* ("Die Offenbarung," K.X, 1911), and a letter of "explanation" written by Schiele (obviously at Engel's request) makes clear that the dentist was not a man to appreciate the artist's recondite allegories.[40] A portrait of his daughter was another matter however and the awkwardly rigid figure of the homely young girl set against a cinnabar-red, layered triangle and crowned by her best feature—the loosened black hair which displaces a comb by its falling weight—was the quickly painted offering which apparently met with satisfaction.[41] The second female portrait prior to Friederike Beer's commission had also been done to fulfill an obligation. This was the very small 1912 portrait of Arthur Roessler's wife Ida (plate 118), who had unsuccessfully tried to divert Schiele's literary tastes from Rimbaud to Hofmannsthal. In mood, size, and medium, it is a continuation of the five oils on wood which Roessler described as having been painted within a period of four days.[42] As in the preceding portraits in this series (plates 92 and 94), the focus is much closer than that of the 1910 works, and only the head is shown. Judging from a photograph of Frau Roessler (plate 117), we must conclude that Schiele's portrayal endowed his subject with a flattering elegance. The handsome format derives from the artist's Wiener Werkstätte fashion-design days.[43] An organic gray shape on the white background accentuates the blue-black forms of the hat and fur piece which frame the blond hair and light silhouette of the face. This highly complimentary[44] and rather superficial picture is atypical of Schiele's oeuvre, but the very fact that he could so effortlessly produce this kind of portrait heightens the stylistic interest of the strange and at first glance repulsive, life-size portrait which he now painted of Friederike Beer (plate 123).

1914: PORTRAIT OF FRIEDERIKE BEER

Friederike Beer was the first total stranger whom Schiele had ever painted. She represented a completely different type and class of woman from any that he had ever painted before. Fräulein Beer was twenty-three years old, just a few months younger than the artist himself, when Schiele painted her. Daughter of the owner of two Viennese night clubs, the Gelber Saal and the Kaiserbar, schooled in Belgium and England, and recently returned from a trip around the world, she belonged to Vienna's young Jewish intelligentsia. Her most attentive suitor was a Neukunstgruppe colleague of Schiele's—Hans Böhler, who, with his older cousin Heinrich, encouraged and supported Schiele, often taking him along on painting expeditions to Krumau. Friederike was an enthusiastic collector of Wiener Werkstätte products and dressed by preference only in the hand-printed fabrics designed by its fashion department. A photograph (plate 119) confirms the description she gives of herself at this period:

"I was good-looking, young, and interested in music and art. What was I doing at twenty-three? Nothing! Just living—going to the theater, to art exhibitions, to the opera. In those days I was so wild about the Wiener Werkstätte that every single stitch of clothing I owned was designed by them. When I got an apartment of my own all the furniture, even the rugs, was made by them. I was really a walking advertisement for the Wiener Werkstätte."[45]

Concerning the portrait commission, she recalls:

"I had often seen Schiele at art exhibitions in the company of my friend the painter Hans Böhler. Schiele was tall, thin, shy, and quiet, but he stood out in a crowd. One could tell there was something unusual about him. He really appeared rather spectacular. That fantastic head of hair! I decided that I wanted Schiele to paint my portrait, but I didn't know him and I was too shy to ask him, so Böhler asked him for me. The sittings began in May and I went out to his atelier at Hietzinger Hauptstrasse 101 every morning during the summer months. Both Schiele and I were rather embarrassed and quiet. I didn't want him to think that I was 'eine Dame' after all! I wore a Wiener Werkstätte dress that was black, green, and white, which I later left there as a present for Wally, whom I never met, because Schiele told me she liked it so much from the painting. During the sittings I never dared to go up and see what Schiele was doing, and saw only the finished product. Schiele was very polite and always accompanied me back to the streetcar stop."[46]

Two studies for the portrait show the zig-zag patterned silk Wiener Werkstätte dress just described and document the initial search for a pose. In one of the studies[47] Friederike is shown standing in profile, and in a second (plate 120) she is seated on the floor with her legs drawn to one side and her left arm raised, elbow out, across her chest. At this time Schiele's attention was concentrated on the zig-zag divisions and folds of the dress in relation to its outer contour and only a few cursory lines reproduce the heavy oval of the face. But chance intervened to suggest the posture of the final oil. Friederike recalls the event:

"The previous summer my family and the Böhlers had been in South America and I had bought some of the little hand-woven dolls made by the natives in La Paz. One day I brought some of these little dolls with me to Schiele because I thought they would please him. He was delighted with them, asked me to lie down on a low mattress which was on the floor, with my arms about a pillow, and then he began to strew the dolls over me, like confetti, one at the crook of my arm, one on my back, another on my shoulder, two on my legs, and then he included them in the painting."[48]

A page from Schiele's sketchbook (plate 121) fairly vibrates with excitement at the compositional possibilities of this new recumbent pose.

In the oil (plate 123) Schiele's penchant for omitting supporting objects, such as the pillow seen in the sketchbook notations, is slyly exercised, leaving a posture that is inexplicable and disquieting. The lack of any background articulation calls to mind the work of 1910 and interrupts the suggestion of "environment" which had begun to characterize the allegorical self-portraits and portrait commissions of Schiele's middle years—whether on a still life basis, as with the introduction of objects in the recent portraits of himself, Wally, and Erich Lederer, or in the form of commentary, as with the geometric areas signifying emotional tension in *The Hermits*, *Agony*, and the Benesch double portrait. Still another feature in the Friederike Beer portrait recalls earlier devices. As in the prison self-portraits, which also presented a recumbent figure, Schiele now accentuated and further compounded the ambiguity of the unsupported pose by enforcing a vertical reading through the placement of his signature.

Further evidence of compositional traction and psychological strain distinguish the portrait. The perfect oval of Friederike's face contends, in its almost bland symmetry, with a riotous progression of orange, yellow, gold, cream, and red color wedges that erupt from the original green, black, and white slattings of the dress and which cascade like tumbling dominoes across the cloth. The jewel-like quality of these small areas of glowing color recalls similar areas in the windowpanes, shutters, and tiled roofs of Schiele's townscapes of 1913 and 1914. A dark brown body halo plays about the entire contour, giving an afterglow to the tarnished yellow background. Angular abstractions and a ghostly white color in the prominent bare feet (Schiele had asked Friederike to remove her shoes) seem to vie with the face for attention. Perhaps those shoeless feet unconsciously express the only erotic access Schiele had to this girl so near his own age and yet of such a different world; certainly the looming nakedness of the feet is a reverse statement of the eroticism expressed by the detailed depiction of shoes and stockings in so many of Schiele's female nudes. This fetishistic emphasis distinguishes for example the contemporaneous watercolor *Female Model with Legs Spread Apart* (plate 122), an extraordinary manipulation of form in which the same blandness of facial expression is contrasted with the ragged, rocky cascade of angular extremities. This watercolor and the portrait of Friederike Beer both announce an increasing geometrization of the human figure which became a hallmark of Schiele's work in 1914, and which attempted a new abstraction of plastic concentration in space by substituting the typical for the individual. It was this generalized treatment of Friederike's face and an ignorance of the key to the apparently strained, upright pose which caused some of Schiele's contemporaries to criticize the portrait. Anton Faistauer complained about the "barbarian brightness" and "raw membrification," and deplored the "empty mask" of a face.[49] Friederike tells the following anecdote about the painting's reception at home: "Schiele suggested when the portrait was finished that I hang it from the ceiling, and indeed I did for a while. Our maid went to the market a few days later and told everybody: 'My mistress has been painted and she looks as though she lies in the tomb!'[50]

Perhaps after a time even the staunch-hearted, agreeable Friederike tired of Schiele's "tomblike" conception, for in the late fall of 1915 she commissioned a second life-size portrait of herself, this time from Klimt. With the completion of this work in 1916 (plate 124) Friederike Beer became the only person to have had portraits painted by Klimt, the Viennese master of Jugendstil, and Schiele, the Viennese master of Expressionism.[51] Her own reminiscences again set the scene and provide fascinating details for a comparison:

"After the Schiele painting was completed, I decided that I also wanted to be painted by Klimt. But although I could afford Schiele's price-range, Klimt was quite out of the question until my friend Hans Böhler said that he would like to make me a very special present, perhaps a pearl choker. I answered that I would rather have a portrait by Klimt, and that is how it came about. When I went out to Klimt's garden house in Hietzing I was really prepared for anything, because I knew how eccentric he was with that beard and always going about in a sort of monk's robe and sandals. But when he opened the door for me I wasn't prepared for one thing! He wore a big monocle in one eye and looked me sedately up and down without saying anything! That was rather unsettling. Finally he said to me: 'What do you want to come to me for? You have just had your portrait done by a very good painter.' I was afraid he was going to turn me down and so I answered quickly that yes, this was certainly true, but that through Klimt I wanted to be made immortal, and he accepted that. During the following painting sessions (November to April), I never had the courage to step up and look at what Klimt was doing, and, as with the Schiele portrait, I only saw the finished product. Klimt's atelier was of course something quite superb. His whole home was filled with Wiener Werkstätte designs and objects, and he had wall-to-wall Wiener Werkstätte rugs all about. He always had three or four models in another room and after working with me for a few hours he would give me a book to read from his vast library and leave me for an hour, disappearing into the room with the models. He would take my hand and just stand there, holding it, studying it, turning it over without speaking—so long that it made me feel eerie. The most striking quality about him was perhaps his animalism. He was actually 'animalisch'; he even *smelled* like an animal! One could really be afraid of him, and I felt that he did not study me at all with the shy aloofness that Schiele had."[52]

Many individual studies of the hands and face are preserved,[53] their intense isolation echoing the concentrated scrutiny which had made Friederike feel ill at ease. Other preparatory drawings are devoted solely to drapery studies, with hands and face only lightly blocked in. Klimt's piecemeal approach also omits any reference to what dominates the background in the painting—a large Oriental screen with figures of fighting warriors on horseback. This background was not taken from a real screen, but rather transformed into one by Klimt who magnified the crowded design on an ancient Korean vase in his studio. Klimt's studies were never projected as existing in a vacuum or against a void, and the delicate, wavering, multiple-contour treatment of form that was the cachet of his drawing style compensated in the portrait studies for his *horror vacuii* that was always at work even when isolating certain features. In Schiele's studies for his portrait of Friederike, where the long silk dress almost totally conceals her body, he conveys a feeling of taut limbs stretching and projecting with hard-edged intensity against the cloth, whereas Klimt's sketches extend the mellifluous quality of the garment to the figure, equating pleats with hands and feet by the same soft meandering stroke, a stroke which takes active sensual delight in the caress of multiple textures. As it had occurred with Schiele, a chance event, occasioned by the sitter herself, determined the final pose of the Klimt portrait. Friederike recalls this moment:

"Klimt made me try on Chinese and Japanese robes of which he had a large collection. When I told him that I had had a dress made out of hand-blocked Wiener Werkstätte silk that I called my 'Klimt dress,' he asked me to bring it and was enthusiastic and decided to paint me in it. Once as I started to slip my fur coat over the dress when leaving his atelier, I asked permission to put the coat on as I would like to wear it in public had I more courage, and then I put it on with its beautiful Wiener Werkstätte lining out and the fur inside. Klimt was enchanted and said it was just the thing, and so he painted me that way—standing with my fur coat turned inside out." [54]

Friederike's moment of courage was caught forever as Klimt recorded her cocked head in the final painting, and bore down with tenacious delight upon the new decorative motif presented by the patterned silk lining. A strange similarity to Schiele's portrait appears as Friederike's pearly, immobile face emerges, iconlike, from a sheath of busily painted background and overlay. But unlike Schiele's burnished colors and metallic atmosphere, Klimt's pastel shades of yellow, pink, and green, his use of white to break up orange and violet, and his gray-soaked blues and red madders (a combination found in his landscapes of this period) all work to reduce the contrast of figure and background, to achieve an opulent, atmosphere of exquisite delicacy.

No greater contrast in statement of formal artistic purpose could have been asked of Klimt and Schiele than that presented in these two portraits. The same subject, rendered in both cases with almost no interest in psychological penetration, became the figurative foil for a statement of abstract content: in Klimt's case the overwhelming activity of the ferocious but painted warriors was checked by the impressive passivity of the ornamental presence of the sitter and her garments, as force and object are forever fixed in a complementary coexistence serving the single function of decoration. Schiele's portrait wilfully suppressed all traces of supporting environment and foreswore the subjective, interpretive potential of portraiture.

With Friederike Beer he did not rely on the cocky adolescent appeal of the Erich Lederer portrait, nor present the dramatic confrontation of two personalities as in the Benesch double portrait, nor contemplate the tragedy of a prematurely aged and sickly Franz Hauer. As though recoiling from the obvious decorativeness of the Werkstätte dress (which, after all, represented his artistic roots), Schiele introduced an unsupported upright posture, endowing the figure of Friederike Beer with flailing fingers, plummeting feet, and wrenched head, all quickening the crescendo of the tumbling color slats, pinning it like a butterfly to a setting which is a compositional and allegorical void. Why did he place the figure of this secure young woman in a void? Certainly she had not experienced enough at the age of twenty-three to suggest the pathos which Schiele's similar employment of space—with its connotations of the subconscious—conveyed in the radical portraits of 1910. Her face shows no evidence of suffering; in fact it has little to distinguish its round, placid shape. Schiele has not only denied character to Friederike Beer, he has also stripped her of her own personal environment. The sophistication of her precious Wiener Werkstätte silk dress has been altered, almost attacked, by the dart-like intrusion of rag dolls from a primitive culture. There is nothing else—no clue to the sitter's personality or status. Schiele's apparent return to the

1910 "existential" void may be interpreted perhaps as an unconscious striking-out at the carefree Friederike Beer and the social order she represented. The disquiet and unrest which Schiele produces here would seem to be his own uncomfortable reactions to the world of wealth and culture. This was the same world which Klimt found congenial and nourishing, and which elicited in his portrait of Friederike Beer the self-confident introduction, in the form of the oriental screen, of his own aesthetic tastes. One aspect of his sitter did, curiously enough, impress Klimt: upon completion of the portrait he remarked to her with satisfaction: "Now people can no longer say that I paint only hysterical women!"[55] And yet it was the very healthiness of this girl, so at ease in her environment, which caused Schiele to react defensively. Just as decoration is the true motif in Klimt's portrait, so the expression of a personal anxiety, bordering almost on hostility, becomes the actual subject of Schiele's work. In both paintings the portrayal of the subject functions on a secondary level—a fate inherent in any commissioned portrait, and an invitation to artistic commitment that has immortalized many a modest personality.

CHAPTER VI

1914-1916: Emergence from Isolation and New Directions in Style

THE PHOTOGRAPH AS SELF-PORTRAIT

SCHIELE'S personal anxiety, as it was communicated in his portrait of Friederike Beer and in the transformation from hermit to martyred saint in his self-portraits since 1912, found further expression in 1914. The flesh-and-blood Schiele of 1914 who posed for a photograph in front of his uncompleted 1913 *Self-Portrait with Saint* (figure 94) presents an undeniable inconsistency in the artist's image of himself—the timid painted ascetic versus the sophisticated real-life dandy—hinting, perhaps, at an impatience with the severity of the thematic vision of self as monk. The wish to present a new image, more worldly and more sophisticated, is evident here and in a whole series of photographs of himself which Schiele had taken by the portrait photographer Anton Josef Trčka in March of 1914. Trčka, who photographed Klimt the same year, was also a sculptor, a painter, and a poet, and the professional rapport between the photographer and his model invests the pictures with an elegant sensitivity. In some of the photographs, such as the photograph of Schiele with eyes closed (figure 100), former self-portrait canvases of the artist were imitated, in this case the 1911 double pose employed in *The Prophet* and *The Self-Seers II*. In other pictures, such as the above-mentioned photograph of Schiele standing before his *Self-Portrait with Saint*, the artist actually "completes" his painting, whereas in other examples, such as the photograph of Schiele with wrinkled forehead (figure 66), the portrait aspect of the sitter is emphasized with pale face and hands inked about by a dark ground. The singling out of the face and hands for a close-focus treatment approximates Schiele's own methods and also recalls such contemporary avant-garde photography as that of Edward Steichen,[1] but a more specific model for Schiele's and Trčka's joint effort may have been the melodramatic hand-to-face photograph of Aubrey Beardsley reproduced in Schiele's personal copy[2] of Hermann Esswein's 1912 monograph on the English illustrator. In other photographs Schiele appears in front of completed works, and in one photograph of Schiele with his carved wooden horse (figure 101), he self-consciously poses in front of one of his cityscapes with a favorite object, the little carved horse that he had once obtained by trade with a child on the street. This toy appears in two of Schiele's oils,[3] and in 1915 a similar horse, with boy rider, figures in an exhibition poster designed by Schiele for a showing of his works at the Kunsthaus in Zurich—displacing the previous St. Sebastian poster motif.

The majority of Trčka's photographs show the artist in rigidly posed pantomime, and an example such as the photograph of Schiele with arms raised above his head (figure 102a) indicates the unusual extent of Schiele's own participation in the creation of this series. The photographic print has been substantially painted over by Schiele: an astral glow encompasses the agitated figure, broad vertical and horizontal strokes establish a confining frame—Karl Kraus's isolation cell—and a double signature and date affirm the identity and workmanship of the artist. Schiele painted over and signed a number of Trčka's prints and even some of the negatives. Clearly he considered these photographs as a new kind of self-portraiture. The existence of such photographs is of cardinal importance. Here is an artist, not yet twenty-four, who has already drawn and painted more self-portraits than possibly any other artist in history. He is now compelled to supplement these with photodramas (figure 103)—with their possibilities of unlimited reproduction. Once again Schiele's own body is the primary motif of his art. In a perpetual interplay the subject becomes the object and the object becomes the subject. As is the case with Stefan George, who also posed for numerous photographs throughout his long life (emphasizing what he believed were the "Dantesque" features of his massive profile), one may search in vain for a smile in the photographs of Schiele.[4] This public gravity is directly related to the earnest self-awareness with which both artists considered their creative missions.

The self-portrait photographs raise an interesting question: what was the source of the unusual poses assumed by Schiele in the three-quarter and full-figure shots? Could there be a connection with contemporary dance gesticulation of such local performers as the three Wiesenthal sisters, who first intrigued Vienna with their conception of ballet? (Kokoschka for example had responded with a portrait sculpture of Grete Wiesenthal.) Schiele knew of the Wiesenthal sisters; in fact a postcard sent him in 1910, with a photograph of Else Wiesenthal on the front, was found among his private papers at the time of his death.[5] But a close look at the poses of the three Wiesenthal sisters (after p. 2) and those struck by Schiele reveals a difference so profound as to suggest the quintessence of Jugendstil versus Expressionism: the ethereal, floating figures of the dancers could almost have been painted by Klimt for one of his University panels, whereas the studied, contorted attitudes of Schiele coincide essentially with those in his painted self-portraits. Two worlds are reflected: the new "modern" dance of the Wiesenthal sisters was really a last nostalgic expression of the nineteenth-century preoccupation with beauty and the façade; "modern" painting, such as Schiele's, was a first symptom of the anxiety and self-concern of the twentieth century. If this criterion is accepted, the ecstatic transports of Isadora Duncan must also be classified as a fin-de-siècle phenomenon. Her appearance at the Secession, clothed only in red roses from the bouquets brought by her admirers, had enthralled Viennese society at the beginning of the century,[6] but her stripping-to-the-skin performances, dedicated to the revelation of beauty, were still in the spirit of art for art's sake, whereas the nude self-portraiture of Gerstl, Kokoschka, and Schiele had a very different aim: exposure of sexual torment and psychic trauma.[7] The name of one contemporary dancer does emerge however not as an influence, but as the creator of a remarkable psychosomatic Expressionism in the dance. This is Mary Wigman. A pupil of the great Rudolf von Laban, Wigman worked from the principle that dance movement evolves from emotion (see Introduction). During 1914, when the Laban school moved from Munich to Zurich, she choreographed and appeared in her first solo dance, the immediately famous *Witch Dance I*. Her angular style and concern with "ugly" silhouette (figure 102b) versus changing body space presents a striking parallel to Schiele's body manipulations.[8]

Like Wagner however whose life just as frequently followed the story line of his operas as vice versa, Schiele not only lived but *became* his pantomimes. The exaggeration of posture in the 1910 and 1911 mirror images was always based on a real source, the psychosomatic repercussions of the artist's own emotions. The four self-portraits wrung out of Schiele in prison represent four agonizing stages through which he had lived. The ascetic mien of the monks and hermits who had subsequently represented Schiele's vision of himself was well suited to his own temperament and truthfully reflected his inner feelings. And now, as portrait commissions and increased participation in European exhibitions began to lure him out of isolation, he again lived his pantomime and began to imitate in real life the confident image projected in the series of self-portrait photographs.

THE HARMS SISTERS AND A NEW REASON FOR SELF-PORTRAITURE

In November of 1913 Schiele had rented a top-floor studio at Hietzinger Hauptstrasse 101 in Vienna's outlying thirteenth district, Hietzing. This studio, near the forests of the imperial animal preserve, the great Lainzer Tiergarten, served as the artist's permanent home and atelier until a few months before his death. From his studio windows Schiele had a good view of a house almost opposite his own, Hietzinger Hauptstrasse 114. This building proved of particular interest because of two of its residents, the young and attractive sisters Adele and Edith Harms. The girls used to stand at the window watching and discussing the painter at work. When Schiele discovered their attention, he responded with outlandish pantomimes and began drawing large pic-

tures of himself wearing nothing but his short, sleeveless painting jerkin (plate
125a). He would hold these brightly colored drawings out of his window to
tease and shock the girls. Scribblings in his sketchbook reflect the course of
his thoughts (plate 125b). Through the next months Schiele learned what he
could about the Harms family from gossip at the local stores. Herr and Frau
Harms had come to Vienna from Hanover, bringing with them a step-son, Fritz,
and the two girls. The dark-haired sister, Adele, was Schiele's own age, and
the blonde sister, Edith, was two and a half years younger. They had attended
cooking and sewing schools and were proficient in English and French. The
spectacle of this petit bourgeois family fascinated Schiele, who only a few
years before had criticized the middle-class tastes of his aunt and uncle
Czihaczek. He bombarded the sisters with flamboyantly written invitations
to come and visit him in his atelier or to go on an outing with him. For almost a year his letters were ignored (but carefully kept) by the sisters. When
he once chanced upon them in a park his elation was so great that he made
a complete fool of himself, genuinely frightening the girls with an outburst
of obscenities hissed in the coarsest Viennese dialect. A note of 10 December
1914, written in several colors, invites the sisters to attend a movie with him
in the company of a chaperone, Wally, and also attempts to excuse his scandalous conduct in the park:

"Dear Fräulein Ed. and Ad. or Ad. and Ed. I believe that your Frau Mama will permit
you to go with Walli [sic] and me to the movies, or to the Apollo, or wherever
you want. You may rest assured that in reality I am entirely different from an
'Apache.' That is nothing but a momentary pose out of bravado. If you would
like, therefore, to entrust yourselves to me and Walli, I would be delighted, and I
await your reply as to which day would be convenient for you."[9]

This time an answer rewarded Schiele's efforts:

"The movies are agreeable to us, and the one on Monday the 14th, at the Park-Kino,
Ewers' 'Launen einer Weltdame.' ['Whims of a Woman of the World.'] With
Walli [sic], naturally. Who will take care of getting the tickets? My mother must
know nothing about this. Sincerely, Adele and Edith."[10]

Schiele's unusual method of courting the Harms sisters—by flapping drawings of himself out the window—gave him a new reason for self-portraiture,
and he set about producing such pictures with zest. The *Self-Portrait in Jerkin
from the Back* (plate 126c) typifies this new row of self-portraits which
served as a kind of personal advertisement. Schiele's pose, looking back over
his shoulder, and with his left arm raised, clearly indicates that he is working
from his mirror. He has not portrayed himself as a monk but simply as Schiele
—a stylized Schiele whose pose is exaggerated and whose face and figure are
recognizable even from an across-the-street distance. The picture indeed acts
as an effective poster. It is also an excellent example of the further abstraction
of Schiele's figure style. Although still drawing from nature, his delight in
tense linear patterns grasps all geometric suggestions, and countless small areas
are marshalled into independent abstractions. The bones of the face, with its

indented and raised planes, are like pounded copper. A hollow carves into the left thigh; the contour of the raised arm follows a craggy course of its own which is abruptly checked by the paper's edge. A repetition of minute rhythmic forms appears in the inverted V between the eyebrows and the V line intersecting the bent wrist which is rendered in a bold and seemingly effortless foreshortening. The silhouette of the opaque, thickly painted gold jerkin leads a separate existence as it clings to the neck and falls away from the torso in front. In the garment paint is still applied as a contour-defining area across which linear horizontal ripples move. But the skin is given a new plasticity by means of a flecking technique of dry smudges of color—red, green, and yellow. By facial stylization Schiele has moved to a generalized concept which gives him new freedom to organize surface and emphasize three-dimensional plasticity. The underlying anatomical structure upon which the exaggeration of physical characteristics is based registers with a new "hardness" compared to that in similar self-portrait studies of even only a year before, such as the *Self-Portrait in Jerkin with Raised Arms* of 1913 (plate 126a)—a study for one of Schiele's ascetic allegories. In both drawings the familiar hallmarks appear—the arched brows, wrinkled forehead, and rumpled hair, but in the later work these features are incorporated for their surface values as well as their emotional qualities. The rapid geometrization of Schiele's style now is singularly characteristic, in its most exaggerated form, of the year 1914 and, as comparison with the similar 1913 self-portrait demonstrates, the changes within Schiele's cohesively graphic approach are clearly datable year by year—unlike the difficult-to-establish chronology of Klimt's drawings.

Although in this year of greatest abstract flamboyancy Schiele's line is angular and brittle, wiry and tense, and hypersensitive to anatomical dictates to the point of grotesque exaggeration, it is still based on organic structure, and so differs importantly from the distortion practiced by members of Die Brücke.[11] For these German Expressionists—Kirchner, Heckel, Schmidt-Rottluff, and Pechstein—line and color are often one, and the visual impact is based on deformation of the figure and on shock qualities of vivid color relieved of naturalistic definition. The muscular, emotional slashes of Kirchner's strokes (plate 126b) are often independent of the physical structure of their subject, whereas Schiele's chalk always attests an organic source, even in the abstract variations of patterned response to form. Compared to Kirchner, both Schiele and Kokoschka seem much more within the boundaries of traditional art, evoking Gothic and Baroque forms respectively. The Fauve-inspired autonomy of Kirchner's simple vibrating colors and ragged, flat shapes has little interference from the organic and formal elements governing the portraits of Schiele and Kokoschka. This insistence upon the creation of a corporeal reality, will remain one of the distinguishing features of Viennese Expressionist portraiture.

Once Schiele had established personal contact with the Harms sisters, the role of his self-portrait "posters" diminished and he continued his double courtship along more conventional lines. In the meantime he was hard at work on a new—and final—self-portrait with Wally.

ALLEGORY AS CONFESSION: A LAST SELF-PORTRAIT WITH WALLY

Schiele and Kokoschka seem more tradition-bound than their German colleagues also in their predilection for allegorical portraiture. With the notable exception of Beckmann, the portraits and self-portraits of the German Expressionists might be said to be either situation pictures—real or hypothetical (one thinks of Kirchner's *Self-Portrait with Model*, 1907; the triptych *To the Sick Woman*, 1912–13; or the *Self-Portrait as Soldier*, 1915) or psychological pictures (the single large self-portraits of Meidner, Kirchner, and Schmidt-Rottluff). Although the psychological portrait figures prominently in Viennese Expressionism, the situation portrait often tends to be handled in an allegorical fashion. We have already seen this in Kokoschka's *The Dreaming Boys* and *Murderer, Hope of Women* and in Schiele's Self-Seers series, *The Hermits*, and *Woman in Mourning*. Thus when the practical question arises: what did Schiele think and do about Wally during his courtship of the Harms sisters, the answer is to be found in allegory. Schiele's large canvas *Death and Maiden ("Man and Girl")* (plate 129) completed in the spring of 1915, is, in spite of the titular reference to the ancient motif of Death and the Maiden, a grim and thinly concealed confession of a love that has grown stale. Schiele, his face in a now familiar stylization, is still dressed in the ascetic or monk's habit of the earlier allegorical double portraits, and Wally, identifiable by her red hair, high cheekbones, and long nose,[12] is stripped to the lace-trimmed undergarments in which Schiele had previously portrayed her. The two figures embrace in a mindless clutch, grasping at one another automatically and staring off past each other into space.

The theme of this embrace had been in Schiele's mind for quite some time and several drawings for the project appear in sketchbooks of 1914 and 1915.[13] Although essayed in many variations, the essential character of this embrace is one of noncommunication. The rocky landscape considered in one of the compositional sketches is epitomized in the painting by lumpy areas of green, gold, and tan, but a large cloth intervenes between the figures and the background, staging the action on sheets that writhe in response. A sense of frustration is conveyed by the poses of the tumbling figures, the emphasis of space between their facing upper legs, and the symbolic multiple hindrance of the multi-point underskirt. The tenacity of Wally's embrace is repeated in the intertwining of her hands, the separate gestures of which are overt references to intercourse.[14] The fingers of both of Schiele's hands are spread in V gestures (Adele and Edith?[15]) and the thumbs are again "missing" (a guilt-feeling towards Wally?) Neither his thoughts nor his body are really with Wally, and in an action displacement illustrative of his thwarted lust, he fastens his great red lips upon her hair. This gobbling action may be traced to a specific source known to have been admired by the artist. A detail of *The Damned* from Signorelli's great fresco cycle at Orvieto, reproduced in the Hamann book (in Schiele's possession) on early Italian painting (plate 128), shows a winged demon snatching and sucking at a woman's hair. This scene may have remained unconsciously in Schiele's memory until his own chilling use of it in *Death and Maiden*.[16] The fin-de-siècle interpretation of female hair as an encompassing agent, menacing the male, is never utilized by Schiele, and the confessional aspect of his work distinguishes it from another recent, "personal" treatment of the traditional theme, Munch's etching *Death and Maiden* of 1894. Munch's depiction is an expression of resentment at woman's sensuality and her readiness to great even death with a lover's embrace; Schiele's version is an acknowledgment of new sexual longing unappeased by the present love object.

Obvious parallels to another Viennese pictorial statement on love between the sexes and, again, between two specific and identifiable persons, are suggested by this work of Schiele's. Kokoschka's well-known painting of himself with Alma Mahler (plate 127), completed a year before Schiele's canvas and entitled *The Tempest* ("Die Windsbraut"), was brought before the public in 1914 through unusual circumstances. Following one of his many "breaks" with Alma Mahler, and stimulated by the excitement of the outbreak of war, Kokoschka impetuously decided to sell this intimate portrait of himself and Vienna's famous widow in order to raise money to buy a horse and a dragoon's uniform. It was shown at the same 1914 Munich Secession exhibition in which Schiele's works were to be seen, and reproduced that year in *Deutsche Kunst und Dekoration*.[17] Kokoschka's work is also presented in allegorical terms—the "bride" is the "tempest" and the two lovers lie in a boat buffeted about by the waves of their stormy love. Like Schiele's picture it is a statement of farewell to the present love who in Kokoschka's portrait sleeps contentedly at the side of her wakeful and brooding lover. It seems reasonable to postulate a definite relationship between the two works. Knowledge of Kokoschka's much discussed canvas must have encouraged Schiele to air his own personal dilemma in allegorical terms. Both "allegories" are of the twentieth century in that they relate to and depict a specific biographical event, rather than presenting a vague, general alienation of the sexes as symbolized by the Salome, vampire, or femme fatale of Jugendstil association.

THE DOUBLE SELF-PORTRAIT SERIES OF 1915

Schiele's simultaneous courtship of the Harms sisters and his continued deception of Wally, including inducing her to act as chaperone to the two girls so that he could take them to the movies, might well have given him good reason to feel as though he were two different persons. Without this knowledge of the turn of events in the artist's personal life, the entry of a double into the self-portraiture of 1915 would appear to be a grave retroversion to the second self produced during the narcissistic crisis of the 1910–1911 Self-Seers series. However, to whatever extent the double role Schiele was now playing in real life entered into his self-portraits, the element of a continued personal narcissism can not be lightly dismissed. A trick photograph which Schiele now had taken of himself (figure 104) indicates the abiding fascination of this self-love. At the end of 1914 his favorite sister, Gerti, had married his best friend and the model for many of the nude male studies of 1910, Anton Peschka.[18] With a curious blind spot engendered by loyalty and affection for the less gifted Peschka, Schiele was to encourage and champion his works for the rest of his life, often going out of his way to have his brother-in-law's paintings included in exhibitions. Contemplation of the new, official relationship between two persons dear to him, as well as comparisons of Wally (who represented his bohemian past) with the Harms sisters (whose anticipated seduction promised something "new," and who symbolized the petit bourgeois world with which he was slowly coming to terms) must have led Schiele to consider the idea of marriage. Oscillating between social and antisocial tendencies, he once again turned inward, seeking assurance from his two selves. The extraordinary double self-portrait trick photograph[19] presents a tender and nostalgic mood. Although posed, there is an intimacy which reflects a new, less violent awareness of self. Schiele's features are not drawn into the disfiguring contortions characteristic of the 1914 Trčka photodramas, but are quiet and pensive. The right-hand figure seems to look with affectionate interest at the introspective image by its side. There is no statement of "apartness" from social conventions—Schiele is dressed with taste but inconspicuously. The hand has no expressive function and serves only to hold a cigarette which in itself introduces a note of sociability lacking in previous photographs.

Awareness of a dual nature with opposing drives is intensified in the unusual *Double Self-Portrait* (figure 105) watercolor of 1915. Neither head dominates the composition, but the anchorlike position of the lower head provides physical stability for the inclined upper head. This reinforcement is repeated at an emotional level as the pensive, determined countenance of the lower head suggests an answering support for the questioning, anxious expression of the upper head. The calm confrontation of the double self-portrait photograph becomes more demanding as Schiele turns from the passive role of photographed object to the active role of recording artist. Confronted with his mirror image, Schiele's response is, as always, a perceptive indication of inner emotion. Here the phenomenon of a schizoid state is given a self-conscious and literal description. Anxieties are transmitted through line, as contours become marked by angular eruptions. Other lines fleck the flesh, forming isolated areas of graphic energy. The hair of both heads is drawn in bristly individual strokes reminiscent of the 1910 self-portraits. Two quick swirls emphasize the pivoting neck of the lower head, and equally brief lines indicate the drapery of both figures. In this picture of disparate aspects of personality the hands are not shown.

The outcome of such double self-portrait photography and drawings[20] was the large and eerie canvas of 1915 entitled *Soaring*[21] (figure 106). Just as one aspect of *Death and Maiden* implied a farewell to Wally, *Soaring* may be interpreted on one level as a leave-taking of the guise of hermit and saint in which Schiele had consistently appeared in his formal oil self-portraits since the Neulengbach arrest of 1912. The debonair Trčka photographs of 1914 had already indicated an impatience with this gloomy role. *Soaring* is the largest ($77\frac{1}{2}$ x $65\frac{1}{4}$ inches) and last work in which the artist presents himself in ascetic dress. It is also one of the last major self-portraits of Schiele's career. This allegory, which by its title ("Entschwebung") has to do with a soaring up or away, presents two male figures, both Schiele, clothed in short tunics and apparently floating, one above the other, against or above a rocky background similar to that in *Death and Maiden*. The background appears tilted on end and quite close to the protagonists. Although the two figures are clothed in a somber brown, the background is shot with color: vivid green clumps of grass alternate with light-blue, white, black, red, and yellow flowers resembling daisies. The legs of both figures are bent at the knee and held together, and their hands are raised in distinctive but motionless gestures. The upper figure touches his fingers together as though in prayer and the lower figure raises both hands, fingers spread in the double V gesture already observed in *Death and Maiden*. The right hand of this lower figure touches the cheek in a pose reminiscent of earlier hand-to-cheek self-portraits, while the whereabouts of the "missing" thumb is explained in the matching gesture of the left hand which is palm front to the beholder. Schiele's secret sign language is at work again here, indicating furthermore a possible "E" for Edith in the raised left hand and an uncrossed "A" for Adele in the raised right hand (see also figure 107).[22]

If one aspect of this work concerns the choice between two new love objects (and even the partially plucked petals of the daisies seem to suggest the old ritual "She loves me, she loves me not"), an equally significant meaning may be assigned to the severance or separation of personalities explicitly treated in *Soaring*. For a further choice is also being made, a choice between the celibate of narcissistic self-sufficiency (represented by the ashen-fleshed upper "religious" figure) and that of the more socially oriented flesh-and-blood member of the human community (symbolized by the more rosy-hued lower "lay" figure whose feet at least seem still anchored to the ground). This shedding of the solitary personality, the monklike reification of which is shown floating out of sight, may thus also perhaps be correctly read as a conscious dismissal of Schiele's double of the Self-Seers series. This conjecture appears to be borne out in all further double portraiture, in which the artist consistently presents himself in heterosexual context.[23]

For Schiele and Kokoschka the phenomenon of floating took on escapist connotations different from the time-space fantasies and sexual abandonment in the work of, for example, Chagall and, later, Picasso. But Kokoschka's *The Tempest* is still within the realm of normal daydreams, whereas Schiele's depiction of split personality enters that of hallucination. The intellectualization of Schiele's technique contrasts with the emotional language of Kokoschka's vigorous brushwork. The attitudes struck by the two protagonists in *Soaring* no longer receive psychological furtherance through an empathic rendition of drapery (so fully exploited, for example, in the four prison self-portraits and in *Self-Portrait as St. Sebastian*). It is the dissociation of symbol from emotion which contributes to the other-worldly effect of this Expressionist allegory of self.

In conjunction with the effect of personal and world events on Schiele's life, *Soaring* seems to have been a kind of catharsis; it is the artist's last "pathological" self-portrait to be formalized in oil.

Soaring may also be considered as dealing with the concept of personal resurrection about which Schiele had written so earnestly to Dr. Reichel in 1911. It is related thematically to a large allegory painted by Schiele in 1913 and entitled *Resurrection* ("Auferstehung," K.176). The earlier work is a caustic reflection on the literal meaning of the word sarcophagus—"flesh-eating"—and the resultant impossibility of a "ressurection." The figures struggle to raise their decomposing bodies from coffins. Their hands and faces feebly express the hopelessness of their efforts. The generality of theme and of the protagonists in *Resurrection* (the male figure in the lower coffin possibly symbolizes Schiele, but the absence of portrait features indicates a more general interpretation) is in contrast to the distinctly personal aspect of *Soaring*. *Soaring* does not share the bitterness of its earlier counterpart. No longer formally connected with a religious concept (Schiele avoided the connotation of the German "Auferstehung"—Resurrection—and used the neutral "Entschwebung"—soaring up or away—in his title), the 1915 *Soaring* indulges in a determined, if somewhat gruesome, declaration of a personal resurrection. The lower figure whose feet appear rooted to the ground, calls attention to himself by pulling down the skin under his eye with his right hand, and gesturing upward towards the second figure, or "apparition," with his left. This double bid for attention seems to accompany a plea. It is possible to imagine Schiele saying, "What I have seen with my eyes and suffered in my soul has sanctified me and I shall rise from the dead." (One recalls the constant reference to "suffering" in the prison diary and the words to Dr. Reichel: "a sure becoming and passing away, a coming . . . no complete death . . . I see myself evaporate and breathe forth stronger and stronger . . .") If anyone is worth resurrecting, *Soaring* seems to say, is it not the former prisoner, hermit, monk, and martyred saint, Schiele? As though in answer, a second figure—a spiritualized image of himself which has at last earned the saintly right to levitate—floats effortlessly in an attitude of kneeling prayer above the earthbound Schiele. Perhaps the second image does not co-exist with Schiele, but is intended as a visual projection of the future. Just as the artist did not hesitate to call upon God in his despair at Neulengbach, so he has no qualms about borrowing and transforming a religious concept for his personal interpretation. The theme of this painting however is not the existence of God but that of Schiele.

A year later Schiele's ambivalent attitude towards religion revealed itself in this jingle jotted down in his 1916 sketchbook:

That there is a God in heaven I believe / not unjust are his acts.[24]

Punctuation to the contrary, the juxtaposition of words effectively introduces, especially when spoken, a second reading, the meaning of which is quite the reverse of the first. Schiele was obviously perfectly aware of the possible comical shift in meaning; his penchant for ambiguity would have responded to the jingle's dual possibilities.[25]

I have suggested that *Soaring* worked as a catharsis for the artist. Schiele now consciously moved toward the society whose attention he had previously wished to attract by assuming first the guise of fornicating cardinal and then of martyred saint. In 1915 this same society influenced him significantly. Two important events affected Schiele's life this year and contributed to his emergence from isolation. He was drafted into the army and he married. These two events placed him in a relationship to society that needed no intermediary guise. The status of soldier and married man provided an identity within the framework of the human community. The effect on his style, especially in portraiture, reflects the course of the Expressionist movement in general once social integration of the artist-outsider had occurred: a distinct lessening of subjective orientation as, in the reality of war, art made peace with society. The Expressionistic psyche, full of *Angst*, naked and revealed to the world, now became in a sense man's new façade.

1915: MARRIAGE—PORTRAITS OF EDITH HARMS AND HER FAMILY

On 28 June 1914 the heir to the Austrian throne, the Archduke Franz Ferdinand, was assassinated at Sarajevo. In Vienna Karl Kraus was stunned into silence; the *Fackel* did not appear. In the following succession of political maneuvers that saw the four Central Powers lining up for a death struggle against the Western Allies, the younger generation of artists in Vienna reacted according to their individual temperaments. To the restless Kokoschka the war offered a romantic chance for adventure and escape from a torturous love affair; for Schiele, still absorbed in his ascetic role, the meaning of the war dawned only slowly. In his note to Gerti on the eve of her wedding in November 1914, he had written: "We are living in the mightiest period the world has ever seen.... Whatever happened before 1914 belongs to a different world."[62] The practical meaning of these lofty words was impressed upon him in February of 1915 when he received a military summons and wrote Roessler: "Went to the recruiting office today and was sent home definitely. I am contemplating getting married—most advantageous, perhaps not W[ally]."[27] In spite of his rather frail physique, he realized that he might not escape the draft a second time. Moreover the practical aspects of marriage were becoming increasingly attractive to him. His selection of a mate however was not Wally— hardly a surprise when we remember her ghoulish role in *Death and Maiden*— but one of the Harms sisters. The older, Adele, had placed herself out of the running by declaring she was "really a nun"[28] (see plates 138 and 139 to the contrary). The pace of Schiele's courtship of Edith (plate 130) was speeded by a second military summons in May. He wrote to his brother-in-law, Anton Peschka, who was already in the army:

"Shall exhibit in the Munich Sezession, summer to October, and in August at the Kunsthaus, Zurich. We have founded a new group which I'll write you about when

I get the opportunity. I would have had everything now—Monday I will be inducted! Maybe I'll come through this too?"[29]

Until this time Schiele had still considered the war as an irritating spectacle. A few days prior to this second summons, on a post card to Peschka, he had made the following accusing connection between the Italian Futurists and Italy's role in the war:

"We are sitting right now in the Café Wunderer and waiting for the decision of Italy. . . . A major blame falls on Marinetti and the rest of the Futurists!"[30]

Schiele was not deferred again. On the last day of May he sent a post card to Peschka announcing simply:

" 'Physically fit!' Must report for service in Prague, 21 June!"[31]

As a married man Schiele would have the right to be joined by his wife in Prague and eventually to live outside the barracks. This was on his mind in a letter to Peschka written 9 June:

"Also write me: When I get to Prague, will I live by myself? Will this be allowed? How much free time or duty does one have, and does one have to sleep in the barracks at the beginning?"[32]

The practical considerations that figured in Schiele's somewhat hasty marriage to Edith must be emphasized in order fully to appreciate the extraordinary range of his ensuing portraits of her. On 17 June 1915, the anniversary of his own parents' wedding, Egon Schiele, a Catholic by birth, and Edith Harms, a professed Protestant, were married in an evangelical service. The only witness was Edith's father, Johann Harms. The delay in obtaining the dispensation which would have been required by the Catholic Church for mixed marriages was thus avoided. Two silent and rather grisly companions stood guard over the couple during their wedding night in Schiele's atelier: *Death and Maiden* and *Soaring*. Three days later Schiele reported for duty, and by 25 June he had installed his new bride in the Hotel Paris at Prague.

Schiele responded to the state of matrimony with characteristic individuality. Edith had of course been aware of his relationship with Wally and had insisted that the association be ended so that their marriage might be begun in an atmosphere of "mutual trust and purity."[33] She agreed to their seeing each other for "one last time," and a meeting was arranged at the Café Eichberger in Hietzing where Schiele was accustomed to go bowling in the evenings. When Wally arrived Schiele greeted her in silence, handed her a letter, and said, "Here. Everything is in here." The letter was not a sentimental farewell but a remarkable formal document couched in legal terms, in which he "obligated" himself "from this date on to undertake a yearly summer vacation trip of several weeks" with Wally.[34] She failed to appreciate the offer and rejected the suggestion with indignation. She never saw Schiele again; a short time later she died at an army field hospital where she had volunteered as a nurse. Schiele's unusual proposition is consistent with the unrestrained self-pampering of an egocentricity which was ready to accept the social benefits of marriage but did not believe the conventional obligations applied to him. This early wish to conduct simultaneous relationships with both a wife and a mistress becomes a thematic obsession in his allegorical self-portraiture of 1917.

After completing a few weeks of basic training Schiele was transferred back to Vienna where he was permitted to go home when off duty. His army duties included guarding factories and Russian prisoners of war. During August he was able to complete a lifesize oil portrait of Edith. An early study (plate 131) reveals that a sitting pose was initially contemplated. As he had done with Friederike Beer, Schiele sat high above his model, looking down on her from above and obtaining a combination of rounded form and inclusive silhouette. A photograph taken that year (plate 136) shows Edith wearing the same black and white striped dress seen in the studies. She had made the dress from Schiele's atelier curtains, and Schiele always declared it was his favorite. The portrait studies show what it was about the dress that appealed to him: the long stripes, with their constantly shifting indication of the form beneath, presented a tantalizing challenge. Schiele's multiplication of the rippling stripes and his light-handed enlivenment of their wavering course record his enthusiastic response, just as once in prison he had enjoyed testing his technical prowess by reproducing the intricate folds of his creased handkerchiefs. A second compositional idea is documented in a further study (plate 132). Edith now stands and faces the observer, her arms hanging at her sides. Although the dress stripes continue to receive full and animated treatment in this and other studies, the features of the face are in relatively abbreviated terms. The hem of the overblouse, as it curls out from its belt, the cuffs, the buttons and their buttonholes, the flaps of the collar, even Edith's bangs, all receive greater description than does the face. One can surmise a great deal about the character of the clothes, but very little about the personality of the model; at the most, perhaps, she is "sweet." The final oil *Portrait of Edith Schiele Standing* (plate 133) shows the same approach. Compared with Schiele's trenchant psychological pictures of Zakovsek, Kosmack, Reichel, and Roessler, and even with the more recent Benesch double portrait, there is little in this large, formal portrait of the artist's wife to indicate the dimension or cast of her character. Reviewing for a moment Schiele's major oil portraits of women—Gerti, Wally, Trude Engel, Ida Roessler, Friederike Beer, and now Edith—it becomes apparent that only two of these women can strike the beholder as possessing any real personality or indications of inner life. These were the two with whom he had had "illicit" relations—his sister and his mistress. All the rest are presented with mask-like faces, and often with stiff, wooden bodies.

What is the reason for Schiele's puppet-like portrayal of his wife of two months? Why does she stand so rigidly, with huge wooden clogs for shoes (so unlike the minutely depicted high heels that belong to the paraphernalia of her husband's foot and stocking fetish), with hands tensed in duplicate gestures, and with the glazed stare and apple-red checks of a china doll? Why all the compensatory graphic energy extended to the drapery in this characterless portrait? *Where is the psyche?* Is this an example—so common to the Expressionist movement whether due to suicide or sudden sapping of creativity—of Expressionism burning itself out? The answer lies partly with this general phenomenon and partly with the sitter herself. Schiele did not marry a psyche; he very circumspectly wed a façade: not Wally the bohemian, but Edith the petite bourgeoise incarnate. The blandness of the portrait is a character reading after all, referring to Edith's own personality and virginal inexperience. This young coquette, trained in the respectable art of teasing but not yielding, had, after all, given herself in marriage to a sophisticated connoisseur who had engaged for years in the observation, acting out, participation in and recording of erotica. It was predictable that the limited background and prim mentality of Edith and her inherited middle-class code of values and aspirations could not long fascinate or satisfy Schiele.

A series of double portraits stemming from this first year of their marriage reveals more than any psychological analysis the initial course of their conjugal relationship. In most of these drawings Schiele wears a nightshirt and a nightcap that matches the black nightcap worn by Edith in their photograph (plate 136), and Edith wears the familiar striped dress. The tone of this series changes from a lyrical incipient embrace modestly resisted and gently insisted upon, *Embrace* [*I*] (plate 134), to a floor-thrashing clutch of lust in which Schiele's features are correspondingly distorted, *Embrace* [*II*] (plate 135), to the exhaustion and numbed acceptance of a timid after-embrace, *Embrace* [*III*] (plate 137). Perhaps it is a reflection of Edith's prudery that causes Schiele to clothe the figures in these three intimate portraits. In the first two drawings Edith's face remains calm, modestly turned aside; in the third picture her expression is clouded and dazed. As though vaguely sensing inadequacy, she clings more tightly to her partner. It is Schiele's face however that most fully expresses the frustration of their embraces: from the tender expression of the first drawing in which his eyes dream, one half closed and the other staring, to the face contorted by desire in the second drawing, to the mindless mask in the third.

What explanation may be offered for the extraordinary spectacle presented in *Embrace* [*III*]? The "embrace" of husband and wife is reflected for them in the artist's mirror. Is Schiele now masturbating in front of and for an audience? Is this a statement of differing levels of sexuality—a virile young man's comprehension of his partner's apparently limited physical desire and libidinal participation, and his attempts to arouse both her and himself? Or does the "catatonic stupor"[35] suggested by the fixed stare and awkward position of Schiele's body refer to a (real or feared) impotence? Whatever the full message of this remarkable picture, it, like *Soaring*, seems to have been a catharsis, for later intimate portrayals of Schiele with Edith document mutual action and sexual accord.

In regard to Edith's "inadequacy," was it likely that a young girl of her restricted upbringing could immediately supply Schiele with the sexual variety

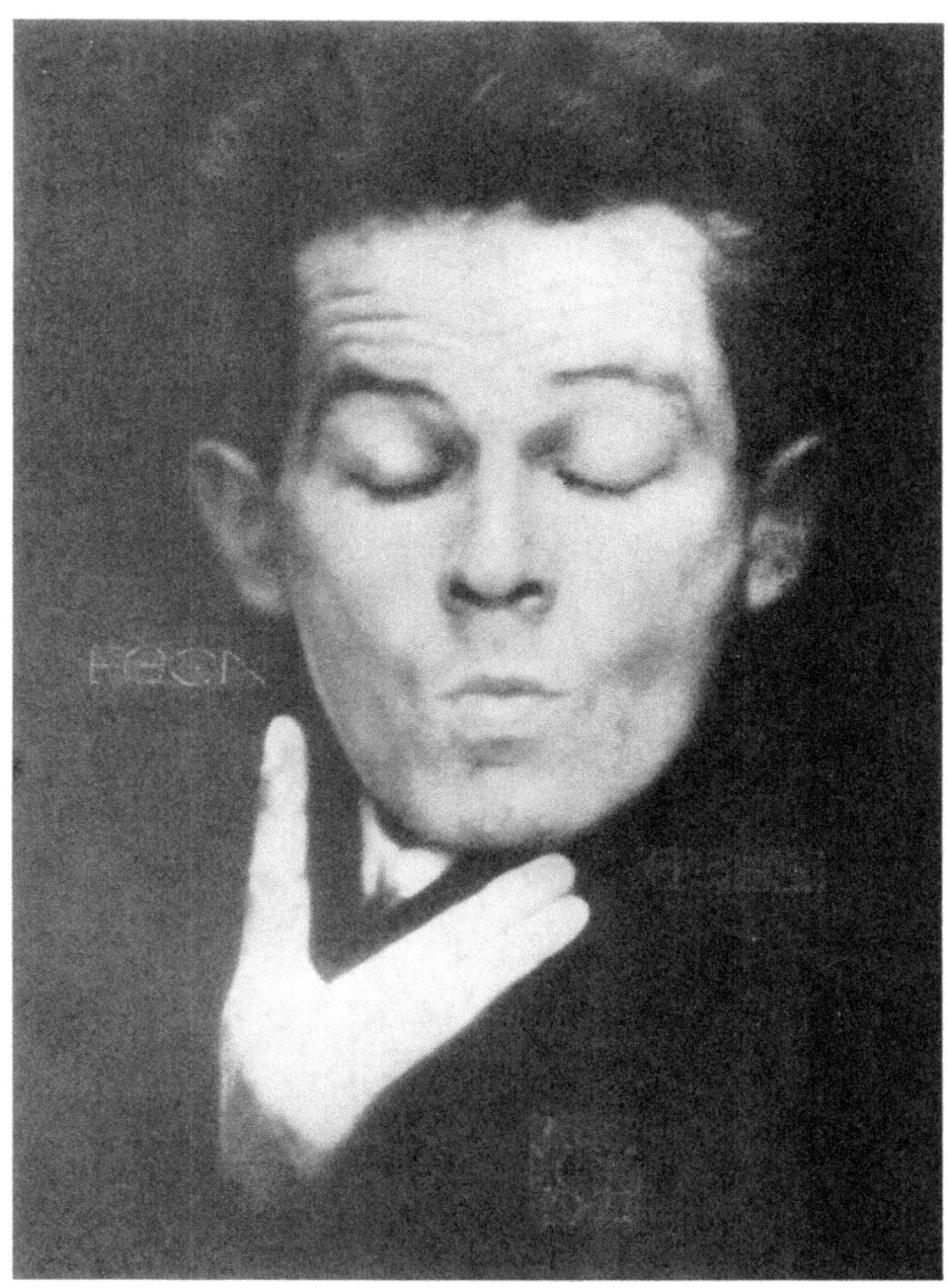

FIG. 100. Schiele with his eyes closed, March 1914 (photograph by Anton Josef Trčka).

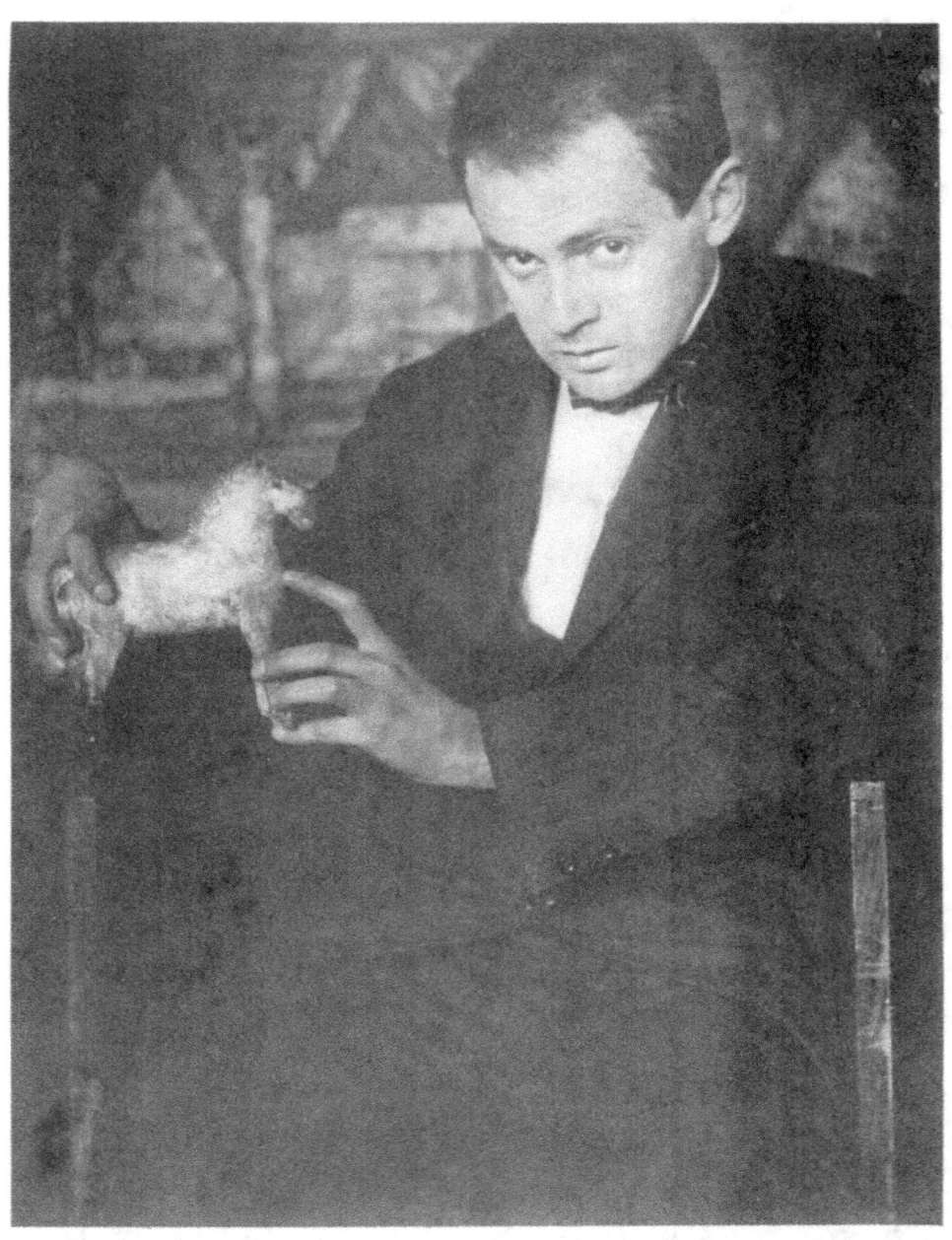

FIG. 101. Schiele with his carved wooden horse, March 1914 (photograph by Anton Josef Trčka).

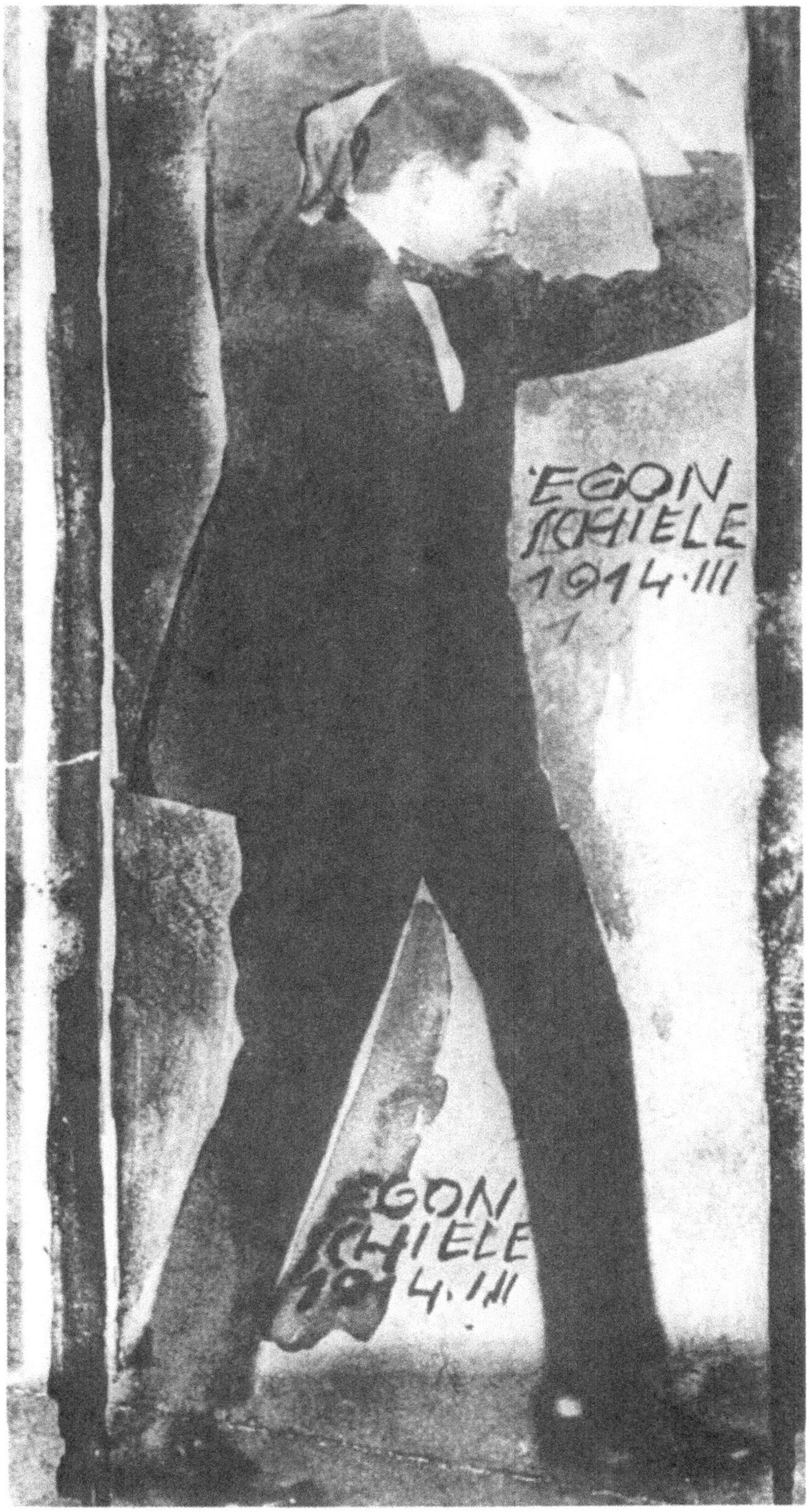

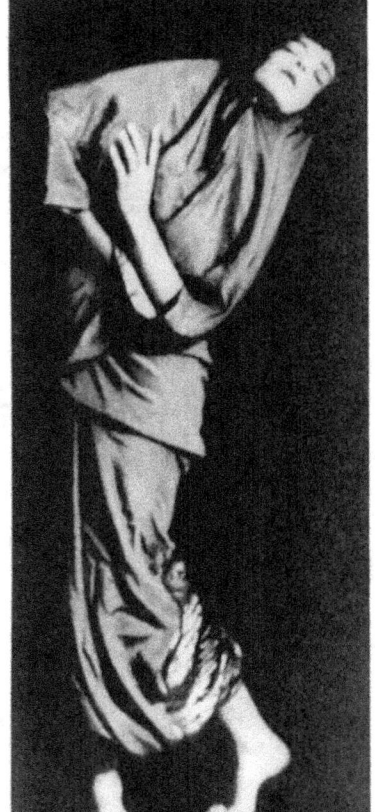

FIG. 102a. Schiele with arms raised above his head, March 1914 (photo by Anton Josef Trčka).

FIG. 102b. Mary Wigman in *Dream Vision 5, ca.* 1917.

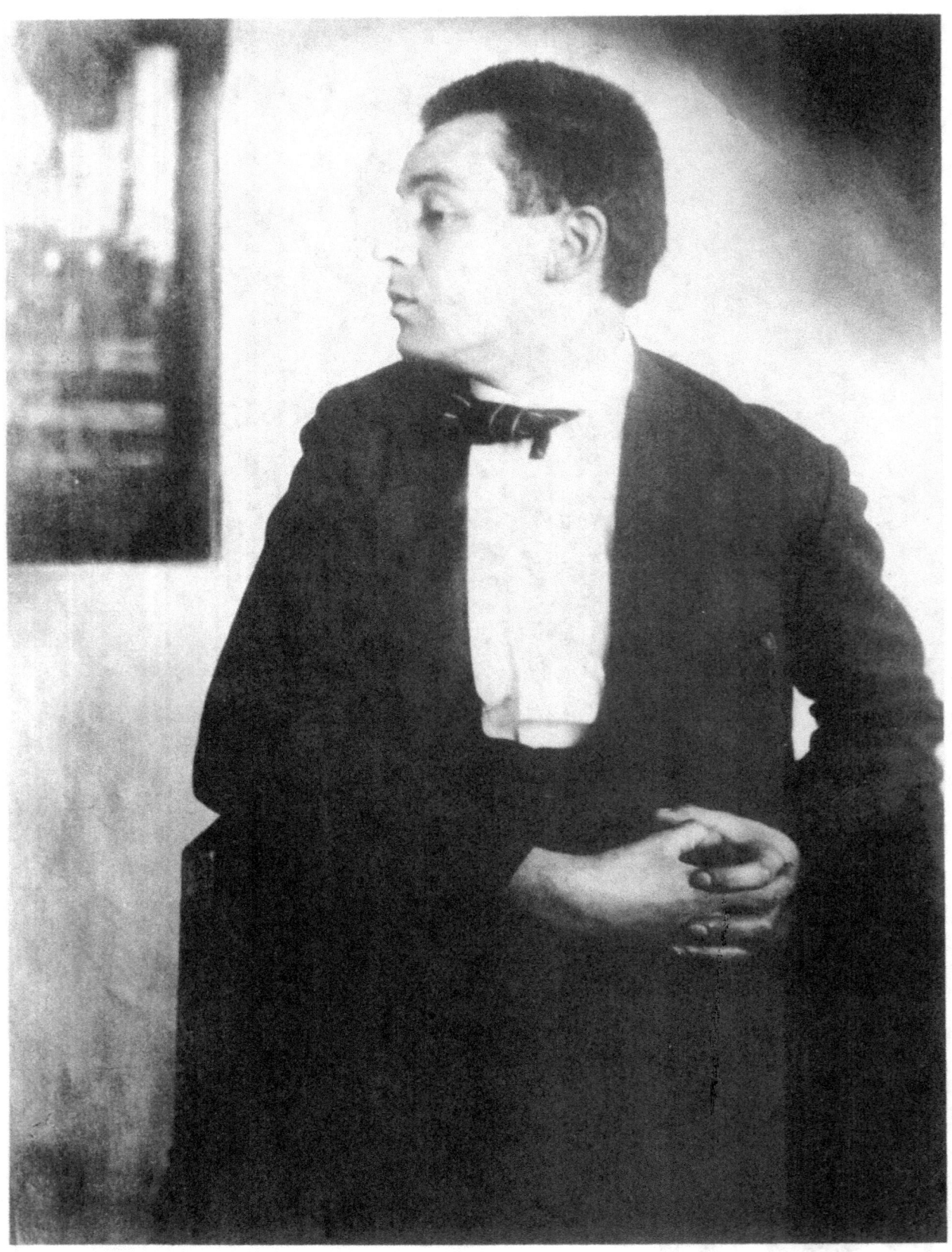

FIG. 103. Schiele looking to the left, *ca.* 1914.

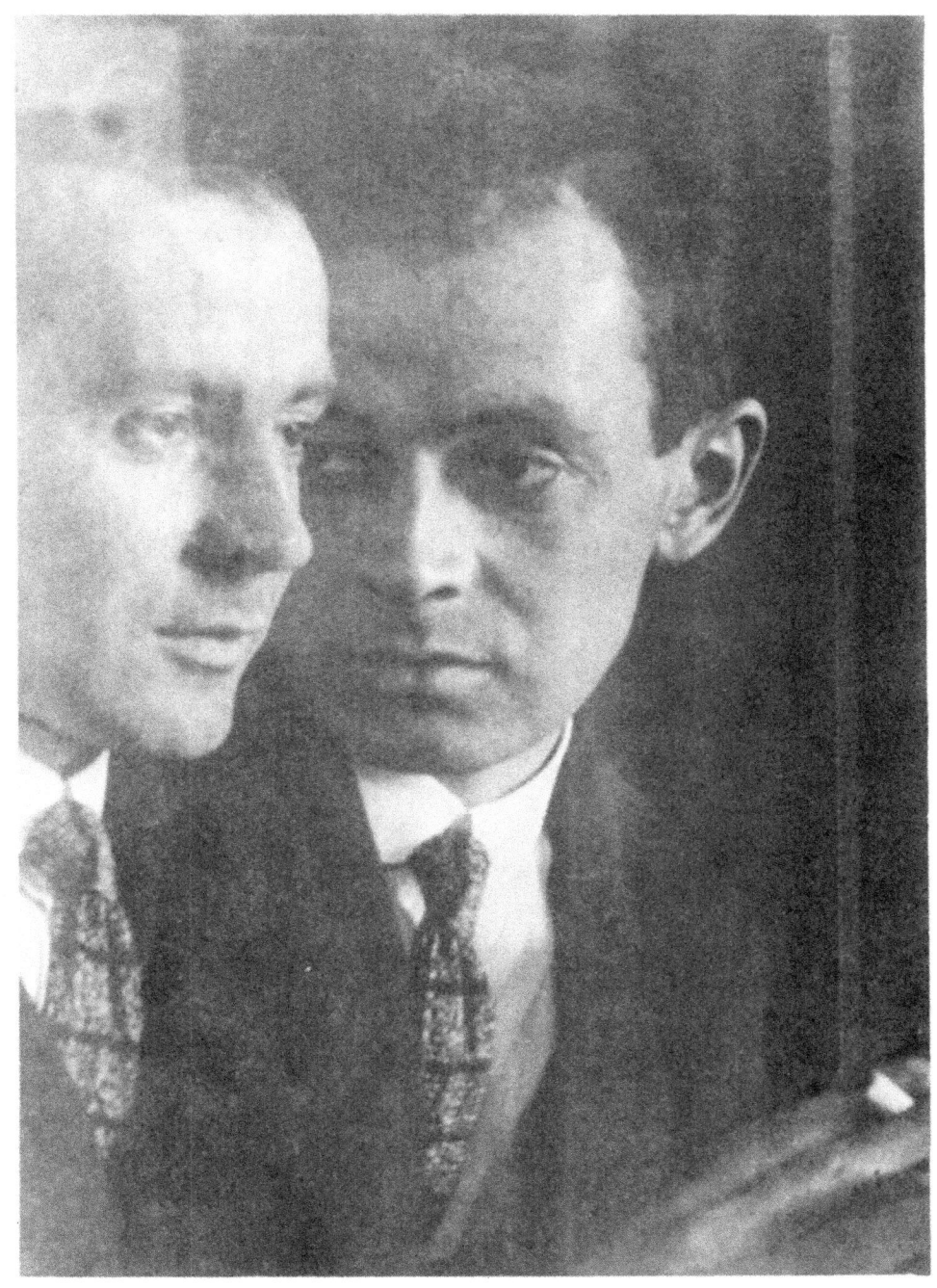

FIG. 104. Trick photograph of Schiele shown twice, *ca.* 1915.

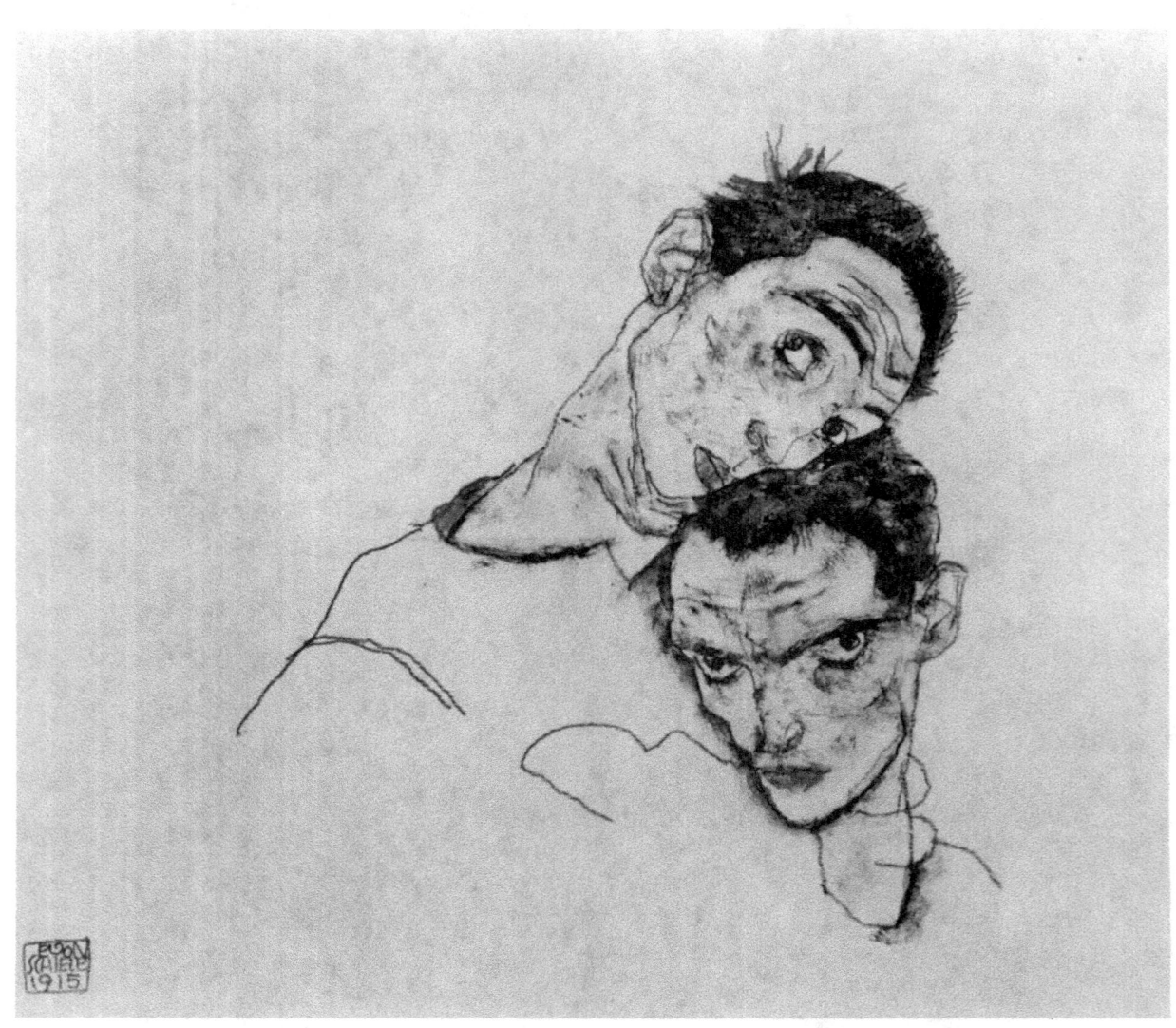

FIG. 105. Schiele, *Double Self-Portrait*, 1915, black chalk and watercolor.

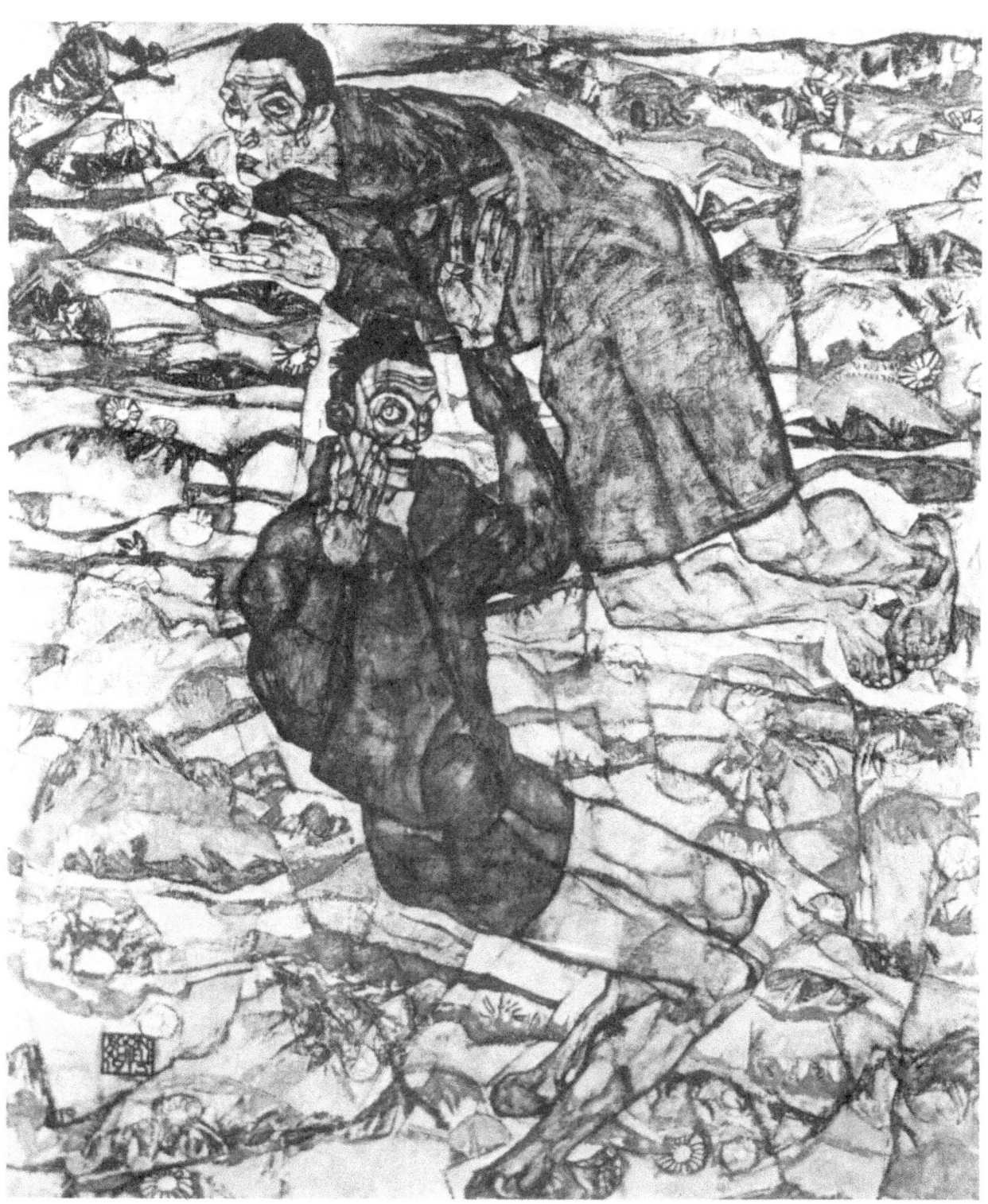

FIG. 106. Schiele, *Soaring*, 1915, oil.

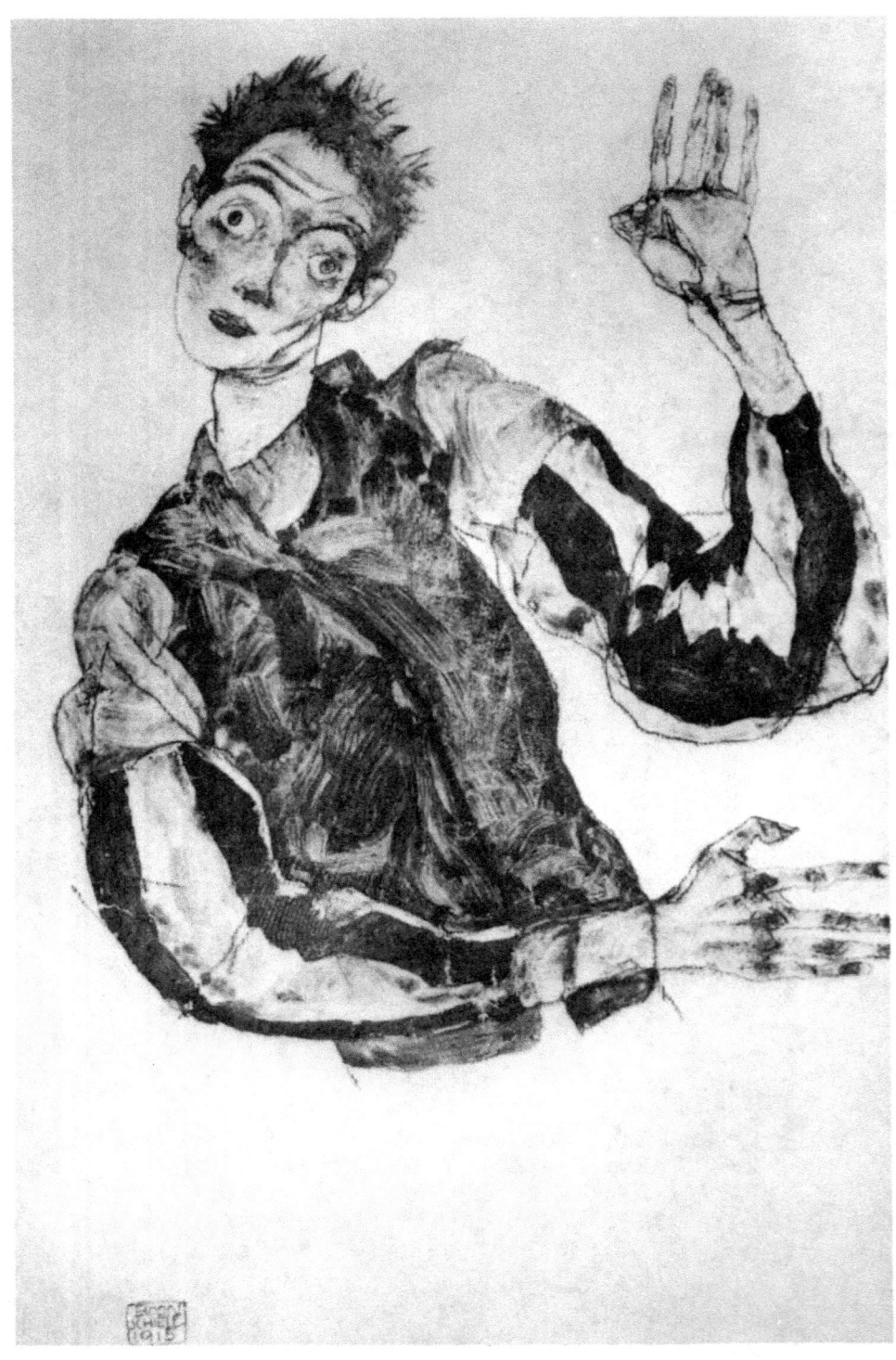

FIG. 107. Schiele, *Self-Portrait with Raised Left Hand*, 1915, black chalk and watercolor (printed as a post card in Schiele's lifetime).

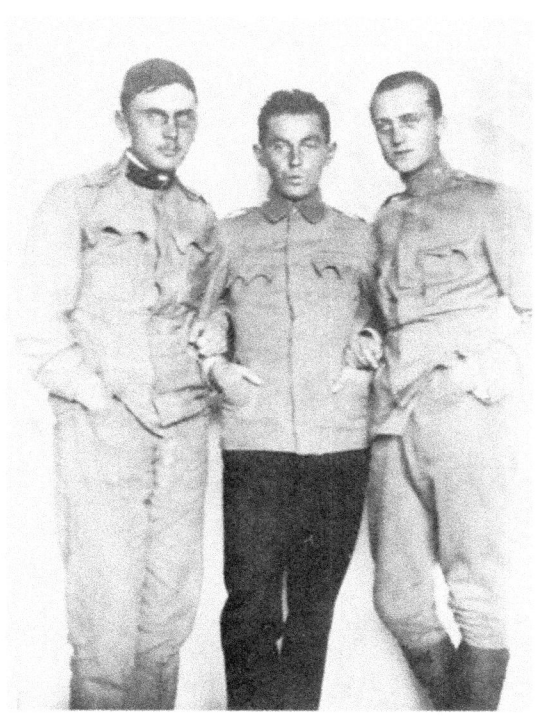

FIG. 108. Schiele (center) with two army comrades, *ca.* 1916.

FIG. 109. Schiele, *Portrait of a Russian Prisoner of War,* 1915, pencil and watercolor.

FIG. 110. Schiele, *Portrait of a Soldier,* 1916, pencil and watercolor (printed as a post card in Schiele's lifetime).

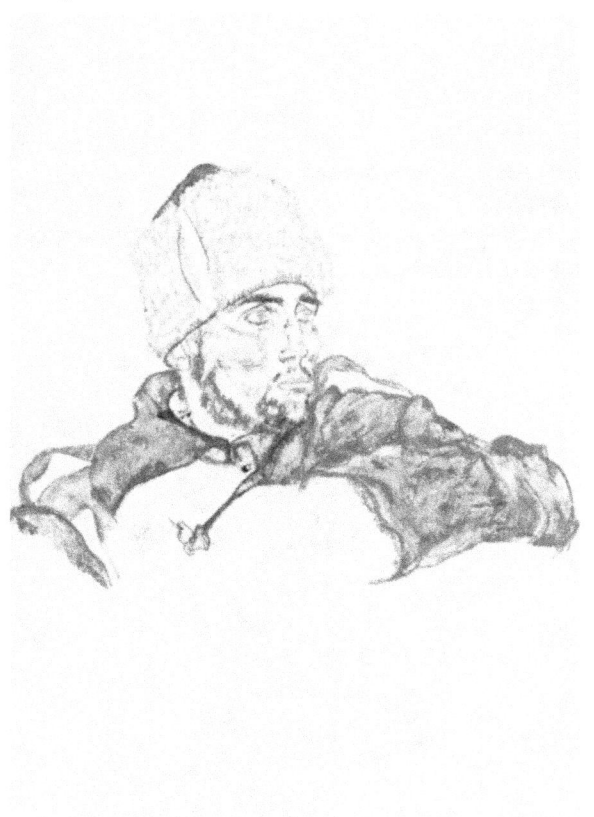

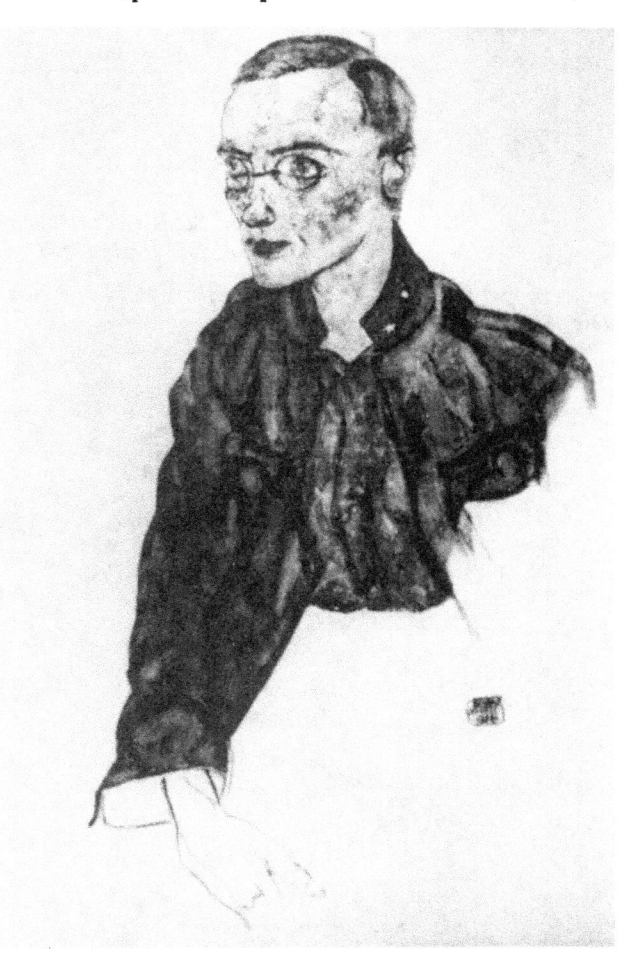

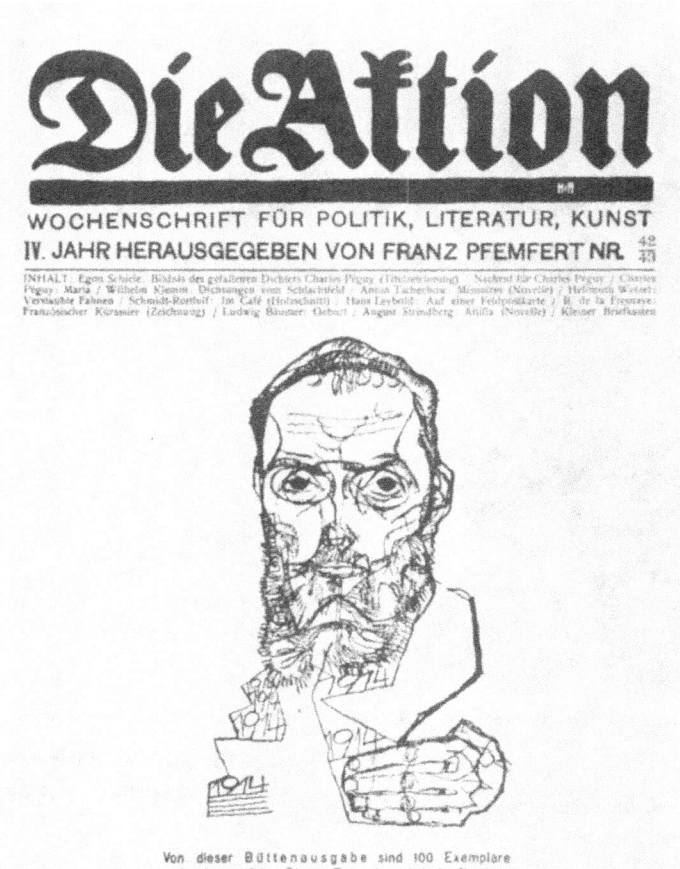

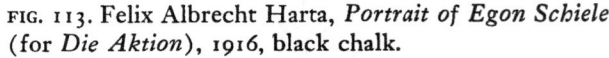

FIG. 111. Schiele, *Portrait of Charles Péguy* (reproduced on the cover of *Die Aktion*, No. 42/43, 1914).

FIG. 112. Schiele, *Portrait of Felix Albrecht Harta* (for *Die Aktion*), 1916, black chalk.

FIG. 113. Felix Albrecht Harta, *Portrait of Egon Schiele* (for *Die Aktion*), 1916, black chalk.

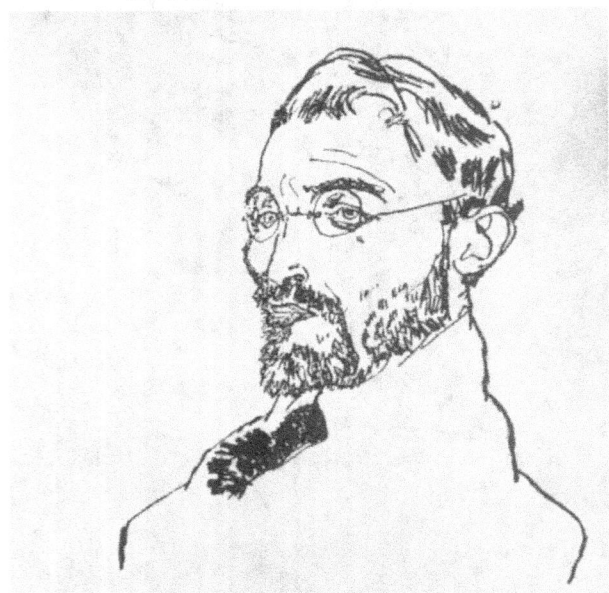

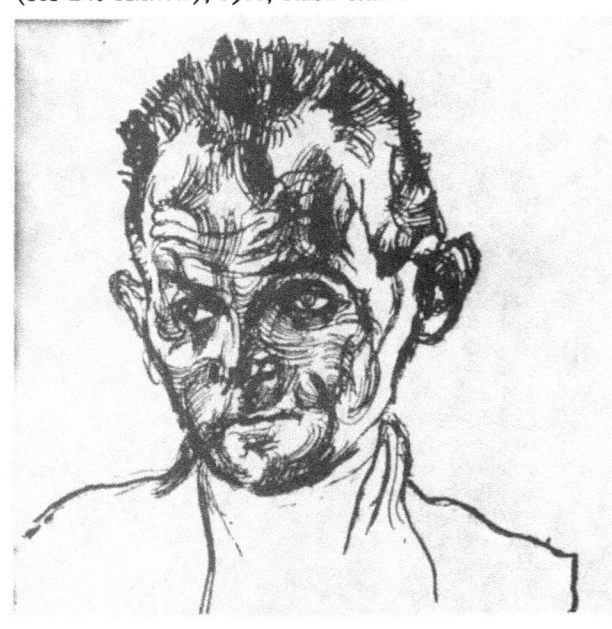

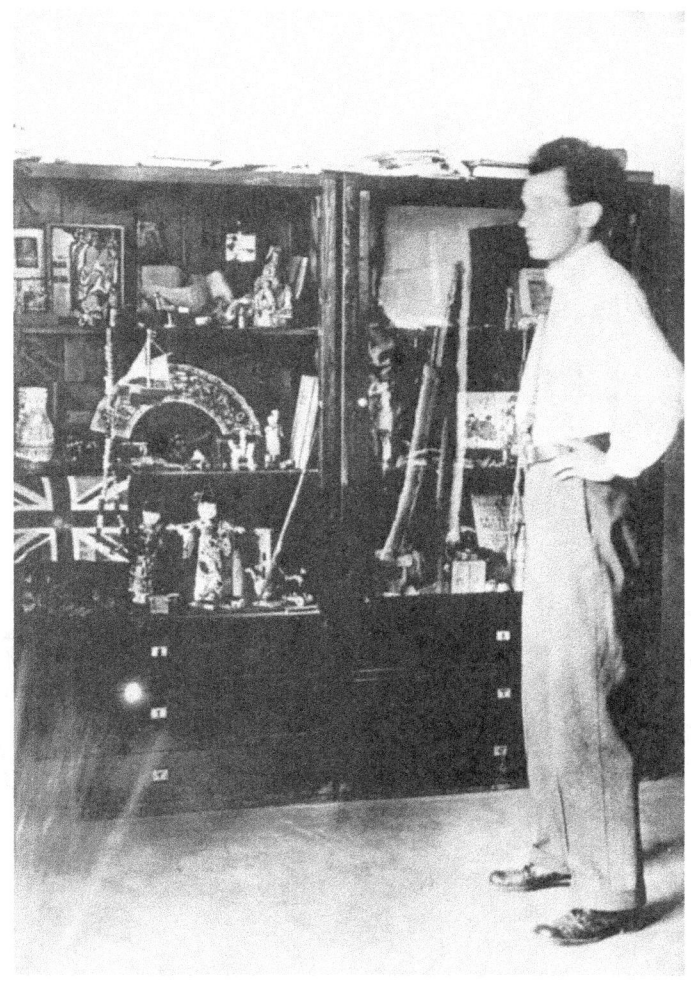

FIG. 114. Schiele before his display cabinets, 1916 (photograph by Johannes Fischer).

FIG. 115. Schiele seated, 1916 (photograph by Johannes Fischer).

FIG. 116. Anton Peschka, *Portrait of Egon Schiele*, *ca*. 1916, oil.

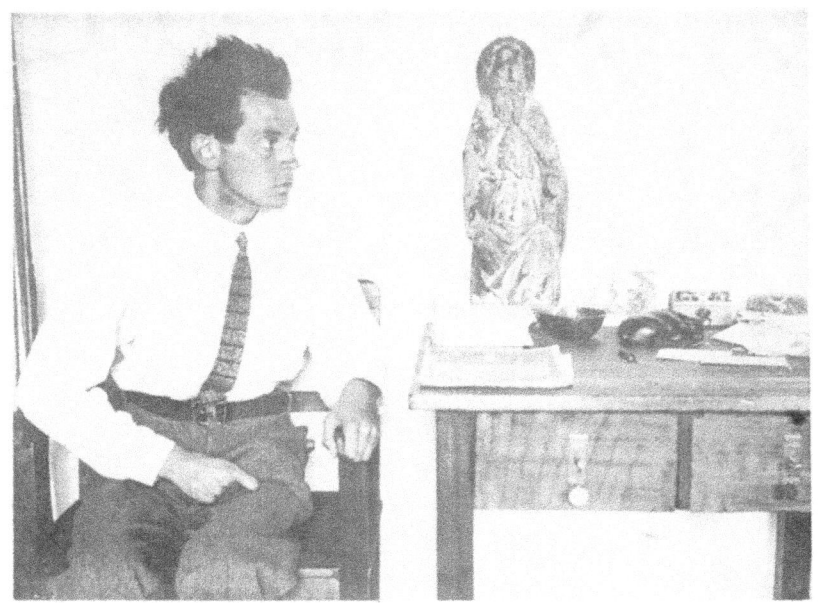

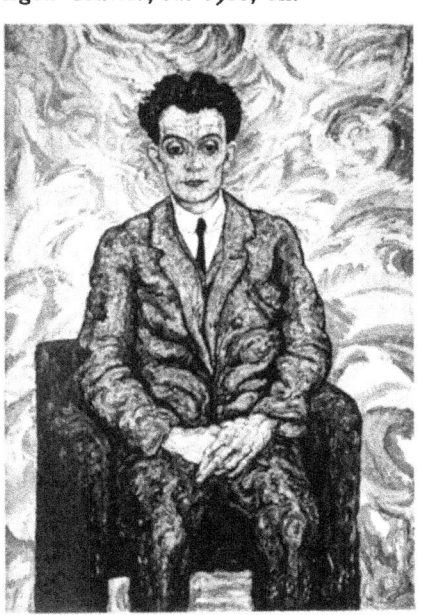

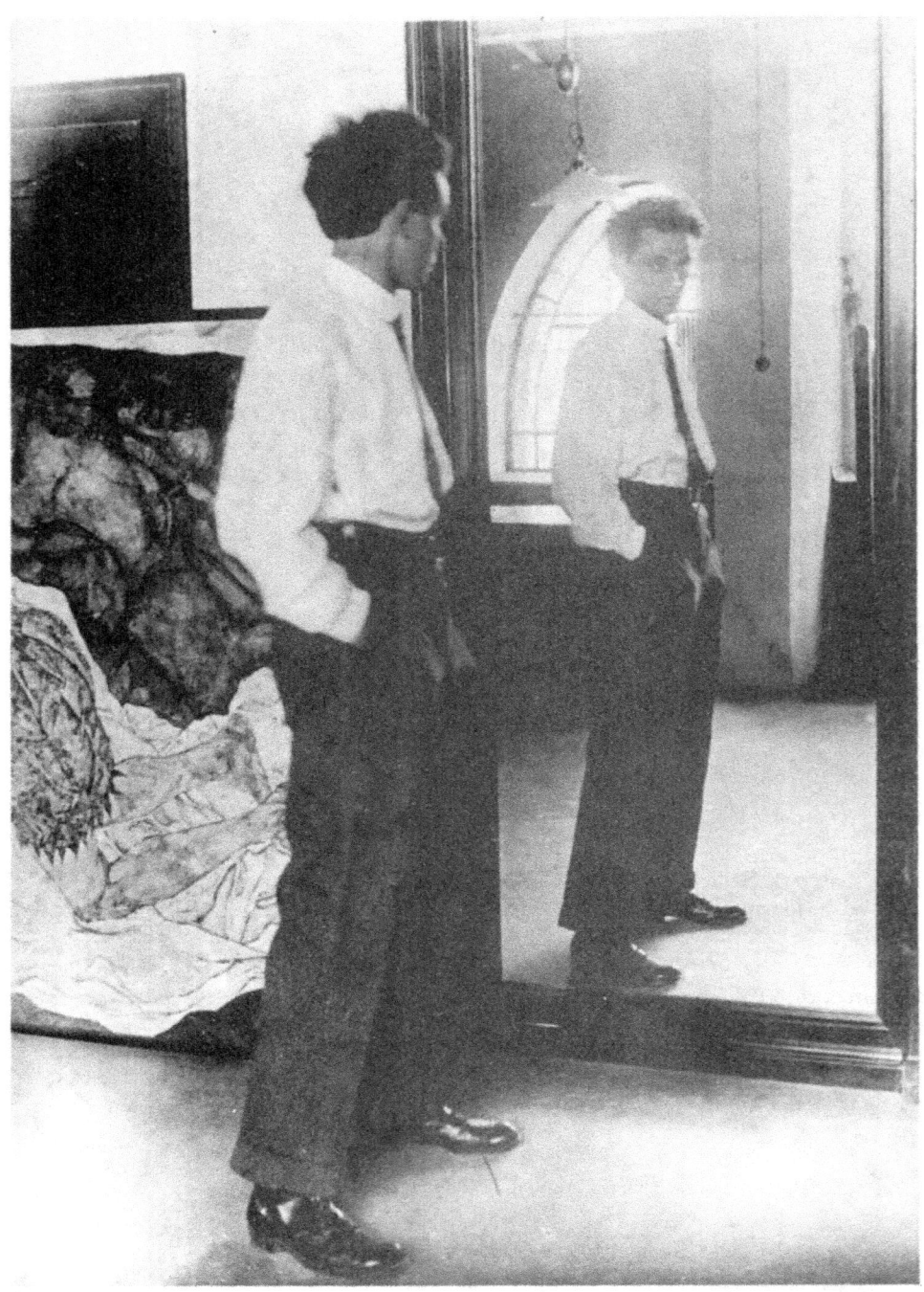

FIG. 117. Schiele standing before his mirror, 1916 (photograph by Johannes Fischer).

and excitement of his former life? Schiele may have asked himself this question as he worked on the formal portrait of his wife, reflecting on the barriers that he must one by one break down. Indeed the first barrier, the physical, is conspicuously symbolized in his painting: Edith's identical hand gestures— the fingers curved to meet the thumb, creating in each instance a hollow area —refer to defloration and its prior state (the left hand holds a round object, effectively "blocking" its cavity). The notched flaps of Edith's white collar may also be considered as referring, in Schiele's overt sign language, to a ruptured hymen. Two years later the artist transferred exactly the pose of this "virginal" portrait of Edith to a painting of almost equal size, showing a nude woman with a masklike face. He entitled this painting *The Virgin* (K.221).

A 1915 watercolor study for *Soaring, Self-Portrait with Raised Left Hand* (figure 107), exemplifies the extreme geometric treatment of the face notable in both *Soaring and Embrace* [III]. The Don Juanian course of Schiele's fantasies, possibly expressed here again through the spelling-out of the letters "E" for Edith and "A" for Adele by the fingers of the left and right hands respectively, continued after the artist's marriage. The "unconquered" Adele became increasingly desirable in his eyes and in 1917, as part of his efforts to entice her, he persuaded the self-identified "nun" to pose for his camera in her underclothes (plate 138) as well as in the nude.[36] Schiele's photograph is of interest other than as the documentation of a seduction. It incorporates all of his fetishes—the high heels, black stockings, garters, dentillated underslip, and fragile band containing a potential torrent of hair—and catches the model in a provocative, intimate pose that bears all the hallmarks of a Schiele drawing, as comparison with a watercolor portrait of Adele done the same year makes clear (plate 139). It frequently occurs in Schiele's portraits of women that the more physically intimate or "illicit" the portrayal the greater the character delineation, as in this portrait of Adele which captures so well the pleased complicity of the photograph.

Schiele had begun to keep a "war" diary in March of 1916 and on 17, 22, and 24 April[37] he made references to being at work on a portrait of his seventy-two-year-old father-in-law, Johann Harms (plate 140). Although the artistic tastes of Herr Harms, a retired factory foreman, ran more towards the old masters (a copy of a Franz Hals portrait hangs on the wall behind his head in the photograph reproduced here), he got along quite well with his son-in-law, and a sympathetic bond was established that is noticeable in the portrait and its studies. There was reason for a certain rapport between the two men. Herr Harms was, like Schiele, shy and reticent. He nevertheless had strong ideas on certain subjects: for example, his daughters must master English because, he believed, it would soon be the world's leading language. He was proud of being a Protestant in Catholic Austria and was fiercely interested in German politics, subscribing to Maximilian Harden's daring weekly journal, *Die Zukunft*, which specialized in criticisms and scandalous exposés of the court camarilla around Emperor Wilhelm II. Supported now by a Viennese relative, and remote from the concerns of daily life, Herr Harms lived quietly in a world of speculation and reminiscence. Schiele's sympathetic portrait (plate 142) dwells on this aspect of the pensive old man[38] and incorporates one of the sitter's idiosyncrasies as well: his insistence on always wearing a frock coat, winter or summer. The slumping figure is spread across the canvas in a compositional diagonal reminiscent of Schiele's 1910 Van Gogh-inspired picture of Zakovsek and a similar impression of fragility is obtained. In accordance with their disposition along the diagonal, the right hand and the legs loom large and close to the beholder, while the shoulders and the hand supporting the head appear small and delicate, thus emphasizing the man's isolation in his own thoughts.

Two new features appear in the portrait of Harms. The sitter now shares the scene with a simple wooden chair (one of two made by Schiele for his studio), thus defining the background as an environment. Although this background would be austere in many artists' work, for Schiele the introduction of a sustaining prop borders on scenical profusion. This new tendency to fill his canvas is fortified by a second new feature—Schiele's brushwork, which visits each of the three major areas of the picture—man, chair, and background —with an extended thoroughness. The thick overlay of pigments imparts a warmth and cohesion previously absent from Schiele's portraits. The same approach is observable in preparatory pictures such as the *Study for the Portrait of Johann Harms* (plate 141) where a generous profusion of oil pigments—ochre and mossy dark greens—knit loosely together to produce a vibrant three-dimensionality. This is the technical direction Schiele's portraits will take from now on: a swing towards the painterly—a swing that seems antipodal to the artist's natural calligraphic grasp of his subject, and even to his own mode of thinking in relation to painting. In referring to the progress of his work on the Harms portrait, for example, he noted in his diary: "I drew my father-in-law small and large on canvas," and then, "I painted the dark background in the portrait of my father-in-law."[39] The Harms canvas is the first in a series of what may be referred to as Schiele's "painterly" portraits. The wider scope of technical interests and the change from an existential to an environmental exposition of subject seem an accurate reflection of the events—marriage and the war—which have drawn the artist out of isolation and into society.

Changes were also rapidly taking place in Schiele's relationship with Edith. The unpredictable military relocations, fortunately still within commuting distance of Vienna, and the constant apprehension of being shipped to a more remote outpost worked to bring the new husband and wife closer together. In a diary written in the hospital while recovering from an appendicitis attack, Schiele mused over their first days in Prague: "She [Edith] entertained herself perhaps at times during the period when I couldn't get away, but at that time we were not yet as close as we are today (for otherwise she would not have accepted invitations)".[40] The loneliness and boredom of military life which had earlier caused Schiele to write his mother in the understandable outburst: "My comrades constantly receive cakes and tarts and mail from home, I have not yet received anything from anywhere,"[41] made the days and nights spent away from Edith and the Hietzinger Hauptstrasse atelier long and painful. The reunions were all the more memorable, and Edith became not only more lovable in his eyes but more sexually desirable. Entries in the 1916 war diary show that she assumed a new importance in his thoughts, and he often dreamed of her. His pencil elaborated his dreams and the only drawing ever to appear in the intimacy of Schiele's sketchbooks that could really be termed "pornographic" was made during this period of enforced continence (plate 143). Even here, after the satisfaction of giving visual form to his fantasies, Schele has marked over the exaggerated penis with heavy canceling lines. The few scribbles with which he had unmistakably indicated his own face are an excellent example of the expressive shorthand technique he employed to jot down figure or compositional ideas.

When Schiele was able to be with Edith again he recorded their activities in several different ways. In his own diary he meticulously drew circles and other symbols to indicate the number of times per night they had intercourse, and he had Edith keep a similar journal in which she too was to keep track of their unions, distinguishing between times spent in bed ("nude") and on the couch ("clothed").[42] Like Goethe and Strindberg, Schiele could make love with one hand while recording it with the other, capturing on paper certain moments as in the 1916 sketch of himself and Edith before the ever-present mirror, *Lovers* (plate 144). The frenzied quality of the 1915 embrace series is here replaced by a mood of mutual desire (even the high-heeled shoe is present). Edith's passivity is now tender permissiveness and Schiele's face has lost the masklike quality of the earlier drawings. A new compatibility is evident. Such graphic recording of intimate moments represents a not unnatural desire to hold and make permanent such events.

Schiele also moved to create a more formal monument to his marriage, a double oil portrait of himself and Edith. In the war diary of 1916 he twice refers to the double portrait (K.XLIX), mentioning work on Edith's head and on her "checkered" skirt.[43] The portrait is lost, but we have an idea of it from a detailed compositional sketch (plate 145).[44] The environment acknowledged in the Harms portrait has been greatly expanded. Schiele and Edith sit side by side on separate chairs facing the beholder. Schiele's arms are crossed against his chest and he wears a checkered shirt (familiar from other self-portraits of the time; figure 128b). Two studies of Edith alone, drawn just above this sketch, indicate the two separate gestures considered for her: in the right-hand sketch she sits with her hands in her lap; in the left her hands are raised to her shoulders. This latter pose is the one given her in the double sketch, where indications of a checkered skirt indicate that her initially nude figure would have been clothed in the final portrait. This painting, with its formal rigidity and the separation of the two protagonists, would have differed significantly from the intimate embraces of the previous watercolor and chalk double portraits. Perhaps the reason for this is the showpiece intention of the work, for behind the two figures the background is completely filled with little framed drawings, one on top of the other, like a wall hung with paintings. The artist had already had himself photographed in front of several of his works. The projected double portrait with Edith would have been a continuation of this idea and would have presented the world not only with a memorial of Schiele's marriage but apparently also with an inventory of his works. The increasing "sociability" of Schiele's portraiture is reasserted in this sketch. The artist's painterly attention is next expanded to include his fellow artists and army comrades.

THE ARMY: PORTRAITS OF SOLDIERS AND FELLOW ARTISTS

If Schiele's marriage to Edith Harms and his "contract" offer to Wally had disclosed him as an unconventional husband, his term of service in the Austrian army revealed him as a very ordinary soldier, sharing in the usual apathy and typical viewpoints of the enlisted man.

His slight physical frame and mild manner had soon convinced his superiors that he was no combat soldier and he was assigned to guard duty in factories and prison camps. At first this had brought him to the environs of Vienna, but in May of 1916 he was assigned to the obscure village of Mühling near Wieselburg in Lower Austria. Edith joined him at this new post, which was within a hundred miles of Vienna, and Schiele was able to make occasional visits to the capital.

Army life greatly curtailed Schiele's artistic production in oil. The number of canvases completed during his years of military service averages around ten each year, in contrast to the average thirty paintings a year produced formerly. Schiele compensated for this by sketching and drawing as much as possible, even when on guard duty. He seldom portrayed himself as a soldier. He disliked the uniform intensely and always changed to civilian clothes whenever possible. A rare exception is a 1917 watercolor self-portrait in uniform with raised right hand which was used as the title page of a portfolio of Schiele's drawings published by Richard Lányi in the same year. In general however the self-pity and resentment which had earlier, during his jail term in Neulengbach, caused him to portray himself four times as a prisoner apparently did not provoke a similar reaction to army life. The protest associated with previous guises—hermit, monk, and saint—was not expressed in regard to his new state. He chose to draw his surroundings (the beautiful canvas *The Mill*, K.217, was executed during his stay at Mühling from on-the-spot drawings) and his army companions. The portraits, often heightened by watercolor, display a relaxed side of the artist and frequently provide sympathetic as well as apt characterization. A 1916 watercolor *Portrait of a Soldier* (figure 110) and a photograph of the same man shown linking arms with Schiele (figure 108)[45] both convey a similar impression of the nameless man's serious and reserved nature. A moving passage in the war diary records Schiele's conversation with some German-speaking Russian prisoners concerning peace and the idea of a United States of Europe; at another time the whole question of war was debated, and Schiele ended his entry with the dangerous and "unpatriotic" conclusion:

". . . it is quite odd how listless all soldiers whom I have met so far are. Each one desires the end of the war, regardless of in what way. To me especially it makes no difference where I live, i.e., [for] which nation I live. In any case I am leaning far more toward the other side, that is toward our enemies; their countries are much more interesting than ours. There is real freedom, and there are more thinking individuals than with us. However, what shall one say today about the war? It is a pity for every hour that it lasts."[46]

The watercolor *Portrait of a Russian Prisoner of War* (figure 109) is an example of the compassionate portrayals drawn by Schiele of these men with whom he had spoken of a universal desire for peace and freedom. The above works were considered as single works by the artist and not as preparations for oil portraits, but compositional notations in his war diary indicate that he was considering at least one formal portrait at this time.[47] The same chair used in the portrait of his father-in-law and in the double portrait of himself and Edith appears here. While the individual sketches of his army companions were still drawn without a supporting background, Schiele's conception of formal oil portraiture from now on includes reference to an environment.

There is at least one documentable instance in which Schiele did not sketch a portrait from life, as was his custom. An urgent message dated 4 October 1914 from Franz Pfemfert, the editor of the Berlin periodical *Die Aktion*, and written on the back of a *Die Aktion* post card reproduction of Schiele's sketch of the young Viennese Expressionist poet Hans Flesch von Brunningen, contained this request: "Can you draw a portrait of the great poet Charles Péguy from the enclosed photograph? He has just been killed in action. I would be very grateful to you if you could send me the drawing really quickly."[48] Schiele's response was published on the front page of a 1914 issue of *Die Aktion* (figure 111). In addition to the evidence of humanist sympathies which recognized no nationalist division among artists, Schiele's drawing of Péguy presents an interesting contrast to the life sketches just discussed. The basic features are in a skull-like enclosure characterized by metallic "dents" and abstract linear areas that recall the "poster" self-portraits in a jerkin of the same year. Flurries of graphic decoration assert the artist's own energetic emendation of the probably static mien of the photograph model, and the date 1914 has been lettered six times in emphasis on the year of the poet's death. Only the original photograph could confirm a suspicion that the "missing thumb joint" gesture is also an element furnished by Schiele.

In his postcard request Pfemfert had also expressed the desire to publish a special Schiele edition of *Die Aktion*, if the artist would create some woodcuts. By 1916 Schiele's idea was to contribute a series of portraits of the Vienna-based contributors to *Die Aktion*, including Harta, Gütersloh, Mopp, and himself, with each artist doing his own interpretation of all the others. This project could also serve as basis for a formal portrait series of his colleagues. With this in mind Schiele wrote to Harta proposing that he and Gütersloh meet at Schiele's studio in Vienna on a forthcoming Sunday, "to draw, respective to painting, each other."[49] The meeting took place a little later than planned (apparently only Harta came). Gütersloh and Schiele did not portray each other until 1918, but the outcome of the Harta-Schiele encounter was included in Pfemfert's promised "Schiele edition" of *Die Aktion*, published in 1916. This special number carried a Schiele self-portrait from 1915 on the cover, a study of a nude model, an original woodcut, *The Bathers* (Kallir 13), a poem by the artist entitled "Abendland," and two short critiques on Schiele's art, as well as the Harta-Schiele portrait exchange. Schiele's sketch of Harta (figure 112), although done only in black chalk, has much in common with the soldier and prisoner watercolor portraits of the same year (1916) in its new emphasis on plastic qualities achieved through repeated tonal strokes within the main contours. The portrait is less brittle than the Péguy drawing of two years before and attests to a growing interest in the coloristic rather than the decorative or abstract aspects of the graphic process.

In 1908 Kokoschka had painted a somewhat sinister portrait of the artist Harta, with his hands raised in an enigmatic gesture and his face distorted by a myopic squint;[50] Schiele's portrait is by contrast an objective rendition concerned primarily with outer appearances. Harta's portrait of Schiele (figure 113), which seems to dwell obsessively on the subject's receding hairline, is hardly more involved with a psychological interpretation than Schiele's, and the passivity of the model seems subservient to the energy of the coloristic graphic modeling.[51]

At least one close friend and colleague did not care for the new composure and objectivity of Schiele's portrait of Harta as it appeared in *Die Aktion*. Schiele had recently suggested to Peschka that he subscribe to *Die Aktion* and that he buy the series of portrait post cards done by Harta, Mopp, and himself.[52] In a good-natured letter of 13 January 1917 Schiele wrote Peschka the following:

"During the same days I heard that you considered my drawings in the *Aktion* as 'Griepenkerl's' ideas—I admit that particularly these drawings are tame—but not all of those from that period."[53]

In referring to his *Die Aktion* paintings as "tame," Schiele used a word which, in a larger and not negative sense, might be used to distinguish all the later portraits from the violent, psyche-searing portraits of 1910. Innovative color usages and plastic interests are partly responsible for this softening of style. A parallel is also found in the artist's private life, in which the new domesticity with Edith and the routine of army duty exerted their own "taming" influences upon the former Academy rebel and free-living bohemian.

Examination of an oil portrait by Peschka of Schiele at this time (figure 116) is eloquent evidence as to why Schiele had recommended the *Die Aktion* portrait series to his brother-in-law. Peschka approached this portrait with an enthusiastic eclectism. It is the painterly and tactile Expressionism of Mopp, Faistauer, and Kokoschka that Peschka has drawn upon liberally to fill and surround the heavy contours that painstakingly spell out his image of Schiele. The colors are harsh: undiluted lead-whites, sulphurous yellows and oranges, and gaseous blues and violets. The portrait is decidedly not "tame." One feature does echo the model as we have come to know him through his own self-portraits and photographs: the element of tension suggested in the pose of the hands, in which one hand clasps and covers the other. This concealment of part of the hand is familiar and may be observed in a candid shot of Schiele taken at the time of the Peschka portrait (figure 115) (compare also the photograph of Schiele with Roessler, plate 36).

Another photograph, one in a series taken by the artist Johannes Fischer in 1916, shows Schiele standing in front of two black cabinets in his Hietzinger Hauptstrasse atelier (figure 114). Study of the contents of these cabinets, in which Schiele kept his beloved collection of treasures, is rewarding. Several books are displayed, including *Der Blaue Reiter*, brought from Munich in 1912. There are also two Japanese dolls, a statuette of a seated Buddha, an Oriental fan, a hair belt, a Union Jack, a small carved Gothic madonna and child, a toy sailboat, miscellaneous cups, saucers, and vases, and numerous wooden folk carvings, Western and Oriental, of little dolls, birds, and animals, including the wooden horse that appears in two of the artist's paintings. Schiele's collection is thoroughly typical of the "exotic" and folk interests of Expressionism.

The candid, unposed quality that characterizes Schiele in the last two photographs examined is in significant contrast to the contorted self-portrait photodramas of early 1915. Being a soldier and a married man was not a disguise for Schiele, it was an identity. He seemed prepared now to confirm the words written to Dr. Reichel in 1911 before the Neulengbach crisis: "All disguises for us are, anyway, for naught; since they conceal us. . . ." The acceptance, through sometimes devious channels, of this social identity provided the artist with a new capacity for objectivity in his attitude towards others and in his art. The gloomy company of monks, hermits, and saints which had dominated the self-portrait canvases of the last four years was banished. Schiele's emergence from isolation would henceforth be reflected in the new thematic concerns of his allegorical self-portraiture. It was with a more stable and extroverted attitude and with a new set of technical interests—plasticity and color—that Schiele turned towards his last great series, the "painterly" and "environmental" portraits of his later style.

1917-1918: *Schiele's Later Portraits— Return from the Void*

SCHIELE'S "old master" procedure in portraiture—involving dozens of preparatory studies of the subject—had always been germane to his art. The all-too-general term "Expressionism" frequently implies frenetic speed of execution, "destruction" of form, and surrender to emotion. Schiele's early radical portraits were not capitulations to passion but rather conscious exploitations of it, involving an internal iconography, experimentation, and creative revision. The intense subjective orientation of these works had produced a corresponding agitation of graphically defined form. In the late portraits, as Schiele's objectivity increased, the amount of invested emotional content diminished. His portrait canvases began to explore the construction of form through color as well as line, and surroundings provided a positive element in the arrangement of shapes in conjunction with other shapes. Are Schiele's final portraits still Expressionist in the sense of being an extension of the self or the communication of an emotion?[1] An answer would have to be formulated with an acknowledgment of the fact that form rather than content gradually became the more expressive force in Schiele's new objective portraiture. This development may be studied in Schiele's last group of portraits.

COMMISSIONS: FROM EXISTENTIAL TO ENVIRONMENTAL PORTRAITURE

At the beginning of 1917, through the influence of Roessler, Benesch, and other friends, Schiele was transferred to Vienna where, after several months' duty at a state warehouse, he was assigned to the Heeresmuseum which had been converted into a supply house for the Vienna Arsenal. His hours were from seven in the morning to five in the afternoon. He was allowed to live at home and received special permission to wear civilian clothes when off duty. With such a regular schedule Schiele was able to spend much more time painting and at least thirteen major oils were completed in this year, over half of them landscapes. Despite the war he was invited to contribute to exhibitions in Vienna, Munich, Amsterdam, Copenhagen, and Stockholm. Schiele's artistic prospects were good and his mood optimistic.[2]

One of the officers Schiele met at his new Vienna post was Karl Grünwald, an art enthusiast who in civilian life had been a successful cloth merchant. Grünwald proved to be the catalyst for a number of painters, poets, and musicians whose lives had been disrupted by the war. Numerous meetings were held at Grünwald's home and the outcome was the formation of an ambitious new art group, "Kunsthalle." The Kunsthalle planned to rent a hall for exhibitions and lectures and to publish a yearbook, an art portfolio, and possibly a monthly journal. In the tradition of the Secession which had built its own exhibition hall, the Kunsthalle planned to erect a special house after the war. At the beginning of March Schiele wrote an enthusiastic description of the group to Peschka:

"Now listen:
We have founded a new group. 'Kunsthalle.' Everything, in the largest dimensions, moves along with giant steps. It was in the air. Fine arts, literature and music. The whole world of Austrian artists is roused. The founders are artists and friends of art. Among others are Arnold Schönberg, Gustav Klimt, Jos[ef] Hoffmann, A[nton] Hanak, Peter Altenberg, along with many others—the best art historians, etc., it is not a society, there are only work groups."[3]

Schiele's reference to "the best art historians" points up the intimate relationship that existed in Vienna between practicing artists, their critics, and scholars. Although they subsequently became authorities on other periods of art, the young Hans Tietze and Otto Benesch were both champions of the new Expressionist generation. Ludwig Hevesi, Leopold Liegler, and Max Eisler were also among the group of Viennese critics and historians receptive and sympathetic to contemporary events in the world of art.

Among the original Kunsthalle founders were listed the names of both Schiele and Grünwald. By May of 1917 Schiele had completed an oil portrait[4] of his friend and superior officer in what was to be the first of a series of newly commissioned portraits, all of approximately the same large rectangular format (*ca.* 55 x 43 inches). A black chalk study (plate 146) employs two elements henceforth to distinguish Schiele's portraits and portrait studies: the point of view from which the sitter is observed—from above—and an interior modeling of the face and clothes. This effect is achieved by laying the chalk on edge and varying the pressure of the strokes. The view from above, with its challenging perspective, had been in vogue since Post-Impressionism and held special appeal for Schiele. His practice of sitting on a high stool in front of his subject has been mentioned, and may be inferred here. The backward cant and diagonal axis of Grünwald's figure suggest a certain restlessness. It is this quality of unrest that marks a more fully worked watercolor study (plate 147). Now the sitter squirms in his (unshown) chair, in a zigzag pose that encompasses the swing of his lower torso out towards the left, the pull of his interlocked fingers towards the right, and the bend of his elbow and head on the left. Again the view is from above, and the face and hands are lightly modeled with the brush while more vigorous strokes give a partial coloring to the jacket. The small detail of a mole or birthmark on the sitter's forehead is indicated in this and the previous sketch. Schiele's pleasure in recording Grünwald's distinctive features is apparent in the emphasis on the leanness of the face with its high receding forehead and long nose. A suggestion of physical alertness complements the élan of this organizer for the Kunsthalle.

The final *Portrait of Karl Grünwald* (plate 148) combines the mood of restless energy and the high viewpoint with a single exemplar from the world of environment—that same chair built by Schiele himself and introduced in the portrait of his father-in-law. And indeed, the Grünwald picture invites comparison with the *Portrait of Johann Harms* (plate 142). As a pair they present handsome embodiments of the ancient contrast between the active and the contemplative life. A spiritual kinship to Michelangelo's Giuliano and Lorenzo effigies suggests itself all the more strongly because of a similar focus and dependence upon contrapposto to impart mood and character. Schiele's concentration upon the specific personality of his sitter, free from stylized gestures and psychic duress, is new. That forceful enhancement which in 1910 could turn Roessler, a man of action, into a spastic visionary is withheld now in favor of a new objectivity. With significant exceptions the above observations also apply to the other works in Schiele's last portrait series.

The motif of Grünwald's interlocked fingers—hands joined rather than flung apart—introduces a new and important psychological factor into this last series of portraits. Whereas the radical pictures of 1910 as well as the works of the middle years had almost uniformly shown the sitters with their hands emphatically apart, not touching each other (exceptions are the *Girl*, K.100 and *Portrait of Eduard Kosmack*, plate 61 of 1910, and the figure of Otto in the 1913 *Double Portrait of Heinrich and Otto Benesch*, plate 110), the new series of 1917–18, beginning with the Grünwald portrait and with only one notable exception (*Portrait of Paris von Gütersloh*, plate 190), would focus upon the concept of somatic fusion rather than psychic fission. This was to be expressed in compositional and symbolic form through a new psychosomatic integrity—conveyed in a linking of the hands, whether by direct contact or by means of a mutually held and connective object, such as a book or chair arm. Almost as though the unpredictable electrical storms which had previously wrenched the hands apart in emotional or psychic overcharge had now been harnessed and their currents conducted through a regulated personality circuit. The vastly more peaceful aspect of the last portraits reflects a matured, comprehensive interest in the psyche itself rather than an over-weighted preoccupation with its individual behavior and manifestations.

In his letter to Peschka describing the Kunsthalle Schiele had mentioned the composer Arnold Schönberg as one of the group's co-founders. He soon set about making preparatory studies for a portrait (not realized[5]) of the famous man, himself a former "Expressionist" painter. The controversial leader of Vienna's avant-garde music was forty-three years old at the time of Schiele's portrait sketches, and a contemporary photograph (figure 118) shows that he had already attained the portly appearance often acquired by men of short, stocky build as they approach middle age. It was this physique among other features, that Gerstl had emphasized in his 1906 *Portrait of Arnold Schönberg* (figure 121). For Schiele's colleague, Mopp, the composer's bulk had provided an opportunity for dramatic compositional emphasis in his 1909 *Portrait of Arnold Schönberg* (figure 122). Fifteen years later Kokoschka in his *Portrait of Arnold Schönberg* (figure 120) of 1924 would also stress that pudgy powerhouse of a body which had for years supplied its owner with the energy to teach during the day and compose through the small hours of the night. Turning from these testimonials concerning Schönberg's physical build to Schiele's studies of the man, the beholder is in for a surprise. The gaunt figure in Schiele's *Portrait Sketch of Arnold Schönberg* (figure 125) is not the result of any wartime malnutrition but the product of empathy. Schiele had already lent his own tortured self-portrait features to a poster advertising a concert of the composer's music;[6] now he projected upon his real-life model the attenuation which the intensity of the man's bearing and work declared. Whether or not Schiele knew the quality of pathos and searching intricacy of his sitter's creations from first-hand experience or from hearsay, he responded to those very qualities in the man before him. In the portrait sketch the crinkled folds in Schönberg's vest and sleeve seem to echo the convolutions of keen mental activity and it is upon the head that Schiele concentrates his greatest attention. Capitalizing upon suggestions of facial assymetry, he intensifies the sitter's analytical expression. A luminous pearly white area streaks like a flash down the top of the head in subjective indication of a topography of thought, while in the hand a vivid red speaks of the taut physical grasp maintained upon the chair arm,[7] a gesture which Schiele intended to endow with his new hand-object-hand linking motif, as worked out in a separate black chalk study of Schönberg's hands (figure 124). A second watercolor study, *Portrait Sketch of Arnold Schönberg with Left Arm Raised* (figure 123) presents minute but effective variations in the face where a semicircular slash calls attention to the left eye and a vertical line in the jawbone frames the twisted lips. Schönberg's arm is raised, as though in explanation or emphasis, a gesture that anticipates Kokoschka's Schönberg portrait of seven years later.

Comparison with the Kokoschka, Mopp, and Gerstl portraits is in order, for four different Schönbergs are presented in this fascinating line-up covering a period of eighteen years. Richard Gerstl's portrait of 1906 is less concerned with Schönberg the composer than it is with Schönberg the man. The young painter's unconquerable infatuation with Mathilde Schönberg and the resulting traumatic break with the Schönberg circle in 1908 contributed directly to Gerstl's suicide. The alert, responsive glance recorded in his portrait of Schönberg lights up the trusting and affectionate expression of the man who was to accept him into his own family and who within two years was to confront him as a rival for his own wife.[8] Mopp's portrait shows the public Schönberg of 1909—a man who faced vicious public disturbances at each concert-hall performance of his music, who was constantly frustrated in his attempts to complete the mammoth orchestration of his "Gurrelieder," and who, in a further surcharge of energy, had recently seriously taken up painting. Primarily through the application of the expressive shoulder device, already noted as the common property of the Viennese Expressionist portrait painters at this time, Mopp has attempted to convey the pressures that surrounded the overburdened but tireless musician. Schönberg seems to glance apprehensively to his left. A repainting of the right arm documents Mopp's none-too-subtle inspiration to make his sitter appear more helpless, with his hands drawn up behind his back. Had Schiele painted Schönberg in 1909 or 1910 a similar terse personification of Expressionist *Angst* would probably have been the result. Indeed Schönberg himself has left a document of the kind of frightening hallucinatory self-awareness with which he was visited at this time in a *Self-Portrait* (figure 119) done around 1909. At the opposite pole stands Kokoschka's picture. The postwar Schönberg of 1924 was a man exactly half a century old, who had outlived his wife by one year, who had recently abandoned the Jewish faith, and who for the past six years taught in the retirement of the small city of Mödling, just outside Vienna, where he lived in a house whose walls were covered with his own paintings: "Faces and eyes, eyes everywhere."[9] As a profound characterization of the father of Expressionism in music, Kokoschka's portrait appears much more distant and objective in approach than his searingly revelatory pictures of the 1910s. The view from above does not discharge a claustrophobic sense of pressing space, but instead draws attention to the short stature of the composer. The question here is not one of personal disparagement[10] (as can for instance be observed in the first of Kokoschka's two portraits of the sharp-tongued Karl Kraus) but of a change in the technical interests and content of Kokoschka's own tempered Expressionism after the war. Cool blues and greens set down in fluid patches in the clothing and background give the prevailing tone and act to subdue the burst of orange that accompanies the gesture of the hand raised to the forehead as indication of the *locus* or moment of inspiration. A gesture emphasizing the intellect rather than emotion, it contrasts with the jerky pantomimes of Kokoschka's "black" portraits of the 1910s, in which his sympathetic views of Vienna's intelligentsia invariably presented them as suffering heroes (visual counterparts to his writings and public lectures affirming the supremacy of culture). Kokoschka's postwar portrait of Schönberg deals with a new orchestration of man with his mood-environment that is substantially independent of discordant mannerisms.

Schiele's portrait sketches of Schönberg also abandon the forced pathos of earlier Viennese Expressionism. The Schönberg of 1917 was a man who, despite his active military status (from July to October he was on garrison duty in Vienna), had redoubled his participation in the cultural life of the city, directing a "seminary" for composition that was frequently disrupted by the transfer of its students to the front. Schiele's recognition of the energy, endurance, and creativity of his model was objective; his response however was subjective: he endowed Schönberg with a gaunt body closely approaching his own (figure 115). In this regard the Schönberg sketches are still "Expressionistic" and differ significantly from the objective, non-transforming approach displayed in the other commissioned portraits of 1917–18. It was probably one of the "emaciated" Schönberg sketches exhibited the following year in the one-man showing of Schiele's works given by the Secession which provoked the comment from an otherwise friendly critic that Schiele's portraits of other people always contained something of his own features.[11] Perhaps the most remarkable aspect of Schiele's sketches of Schönberg is the truly visionary presentation of the composer—an impressive image which, although hardly corresponding to the hearty physical impression of Schönberg at the time of the studies (figure 126), chillingly forecast the shrunken frame and wizened features of the aged Schönberg (figure 127).

One of the persons responsible for Schiele's transfer to less strenuous duty in the Heeresmuseum was the distinguished Rubens expert, Franz Martin Haberditzl. As the recently appointed director of the Österreichische Staatsgalerie, Dr. Haberditzl's influence was considerable, and when he took an interest in a contemporary artist's work it was with the full authority of his position as buying agent for the great museum he represented. During 1917 he acquired several drawings and a new oil portrait of Edith (plate 171) by Schiele for the museum and towards the end of the year he gave a private commission to the young artist to paint his portrait.[12] At their first meeting Schiele had not been prepared for the keen and lively understanding of modern art displayed by his client, and he enthusiastically described the interview to Roessler.[13] Neither had he been prepared for the physical appearance of the man, for Haberditzl, despite his active direction of museum activities, suffered from a chronic ailment which would eventually confine him to a wheelchair. As in the earlier etched portrait of the sickly Franz Hauer, Schiele responded with a particular sympathy to the physical frailty of his sitter. In dozens of preparatory sketches he explored the means by which the museum director's lean and delicate physiognomy might be expressed to give an idea of his vitality of spirit. Preliminary frontal views[14] were discarded for the greater contrast between silhouette and interior modeling involved in the three-quarter view. Several sketches were devoted to establishing the gesture and character of the hands. In such drawings the stroke of the chalk varies greatly, lightly touching the paper when conveying internal structure, and pressing down heavily when establishing the containing contour or difficult foreshortening of a thumb seen straight on. In the three-quarter view *Study of Dr. Haberditzl Looking to the Right* (plate 149) the scholar glances up as though interrupted in his task of sorting through the drawings he holds, and in a second sketch dealing with this theme, the physical energy suggested by this same small narrative incident is converted into mental force, as the emphasis shifts from action to contemplation. This was the interpretation towards which Schiele had been working, and after the three-quarter profile and the fall of the loose-fitting suit had been established in other drawings,[15] this pose was transferred to canvas in the final oil, *Portrait of Dr. Franz Martin Haberditzl* (plate 150). Haberditzl sits stiffly erect in one of the artist's home-made chairs, with a portfolio leaning against a leg of the chair. He has been looking at one of Schiele's watercolors, a sheet of sunflowers, and now contemplates the images and thoughts called up in his own mind. As in the *Portrait of Eduard Kosmack* seven years earlier (plate 61), the image of a sunflower acts as a token of the relationship between the artist and his model. But now the sunflower is a picture within a picture, and other objects such as the chair and portfolio share the scene, all gently insisting that the lightly indicated background surrounding the figure is just that, a localized setting and not a void. Though austere in effect the Haberditzl portrait represents a further step in Schiele's move away from purely existential portraiture.[16]

A great number of studies had gone into the hard-won final concept of the portrait. It is small wonder that Schiele complained about being asked to sell his preparatory drawings before completion of a particular project. The importance of these sketches for the evolution of his paintings is discussed in forceful terms by Schiele at this time in a letter to the art dealer Richard Lányi:

". . . my drawings have simply no other purpose than as preparations for pictures to be painted—they are intended only for myself, and they have immense value for me because I have the 'closest' conception of a work before me. Unfortunately, many of my, to me, most valuable drawings have too often been taken away from me, and so it came about that many large pictures have already had to remain incomplete in their first bud, and people are finally deluded and think that my drawings are already pictures."[17]

It was exactly because so many clients did consider Schiele's drawings "already pictures" that he was subjected to the predicaments described above. Edith also exerted pressure on him. Ambitious and with a sound head for business, she soon realized how much more easily drawings could sell than canvases. She urged Schiele to abandon or interrupt work on his paintings and use his extraordinary gift of speed to turn out drawings. He frequently gave in to her practical arguments and applied himself to the production of hundreds of drawings during 1917 and 1918. Many of these (mostly nude female figure studies) have a forced quality. At their best they display a rhythmical sustainment and masterful abridgement of form of the sort for which Matisse was later also to strive. On the whole these later drawings maintain Schiele's virtuosity of line but have little inner content. He realized the dangers[18] inherent in such artistic peddling and often had misgivings, but in the face of the poverty and debts which persisted despite his growing reputation, he continued this mass production. However, the great number of preparatory drawings executed for each commissioned portrait during these last years afforded Schiele the important compensation of approaching his subject in depth.

By the end of 1917 Schiele had completed the portraits of two supporters of the Kunsthalle, Grünwald and Haberditzl, and had drawn the preliminary sketches for the portrait of a third distinguished member, Schönberg. Clearly the former rebel and voluntary social outcast was now moving in an august circle. The war had a great deal to do with Schiele's new social contacts and with his equally new interest in his colleagues in the fields of music and literature. That quickened sense of brotherhood which had led the members of the proposed Kunsthalle to rally around the cause of preserving art was symptomatic of many intellectual centers in Europe just before and during the First World War.

An entry under the date 2 January in Schiele's pocket calendar for 1918[19] shows an appointment for a portrait sitting with the writer Robert Müller. Only three years older than Schiele, Müller was a prolific and sharp-tongued essayist who had already fathered several of Vienna's revolutionary (and short-lived) cultural magazines. In 1912, as the leader of a group of Nietzsche-oriented poets around the Burgtheater, he had brought out four issues of the bellicose avant-garde periodical, *Der Ruf*. For the cover of the third issue of this publication, subtitled *Krieg*,[20] a Schiele self-portrait of 1910 had been used. An idea of Müller's emphatic convictions may be obtained from the essay on Theodore Roosevelt included in the *Krieg* issue. After praising Roosevelt's cult of physical health, he complains:

"... our painters and writers believe they have to ruin themselves in order to become creative, because Heinrich Mann maintains somewhere that excesses make one productive . . ."[21]

An interesting contraversion of the Romantic celebration of physical frailty, Müller's views parallel those expressed a few years later by Karl Jaspers when he warned the Expressionist artists against a consciously cultivated neuroticism in their imitation of the childlike and the exotic.[22] In his several portrait sketches of Robert Müller, Schiele attempted to reproduce his sitter's almost intimidating intensity. His forthright manner seemed to dictate only one possible pose—frontal—and this is the view from which Müller is presented in two black chalk drawings (plates 151 and 152). In Hodleresque fashion the looming figure takes possession of the surrounding space, and the resolute stare polarizes the beholder's attention. A photograph of Müller in military uniform (plate 154) shows the same earnestness. The long crooked nose and tightly pressed thin lips are recorded in Schiele's sketches, but the emphasis is on the contracted brow and fixed gaze. In both studies the hands are clasped at a level with the waist. This gesture, although firm, is, in the context of Viennese Expressionism, relatively subdued. It is in the earlier, prewar works of both Schiele and Kokoschka that a specifically emotive implication is given to the (often enlarged) hands. Although the sitter is a bona fide "Expressionist," no gesticula-

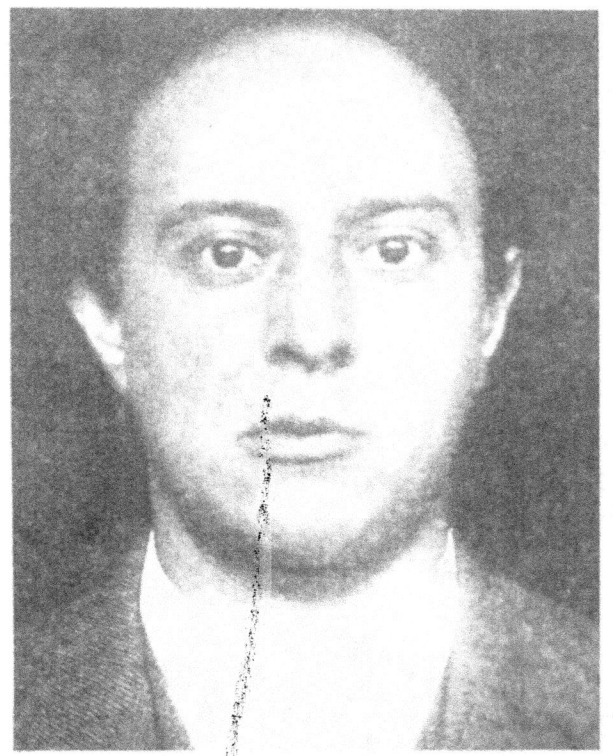 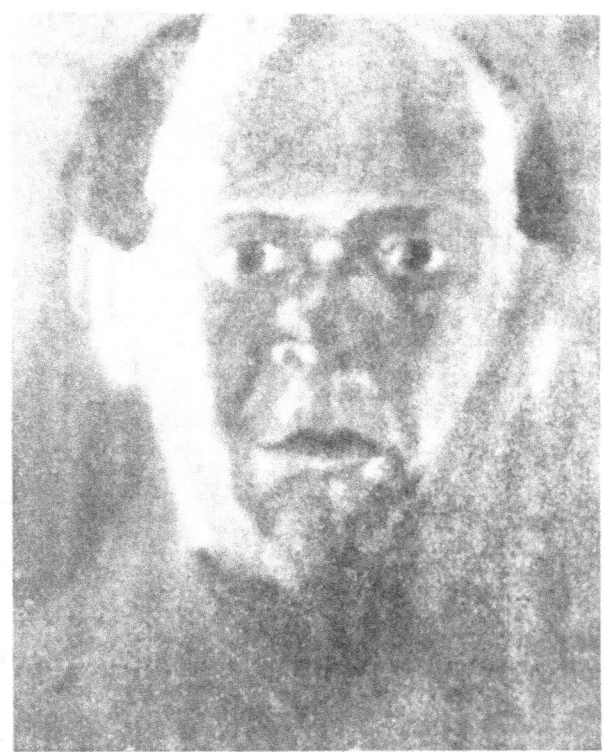

FIG. 118. Arnold Schönberg *ca.* 1914.   FIG. 119. Arnold Schönberg, *Self-Portrait, ca.* 1909, oil.

FIG. 120. Kokoschka, *Portrait of Arnold Schönberg*, 1924, oil.

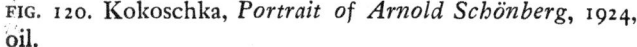

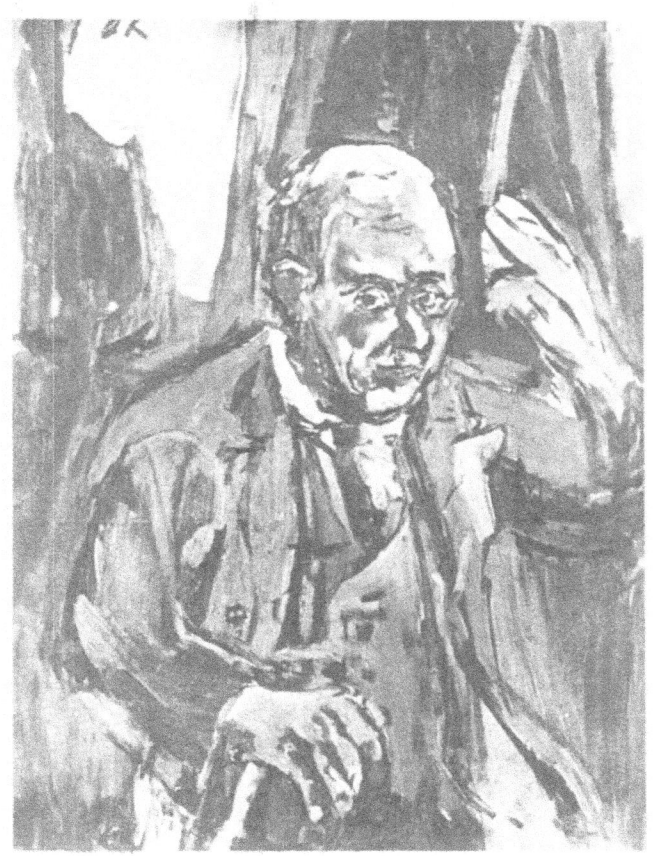

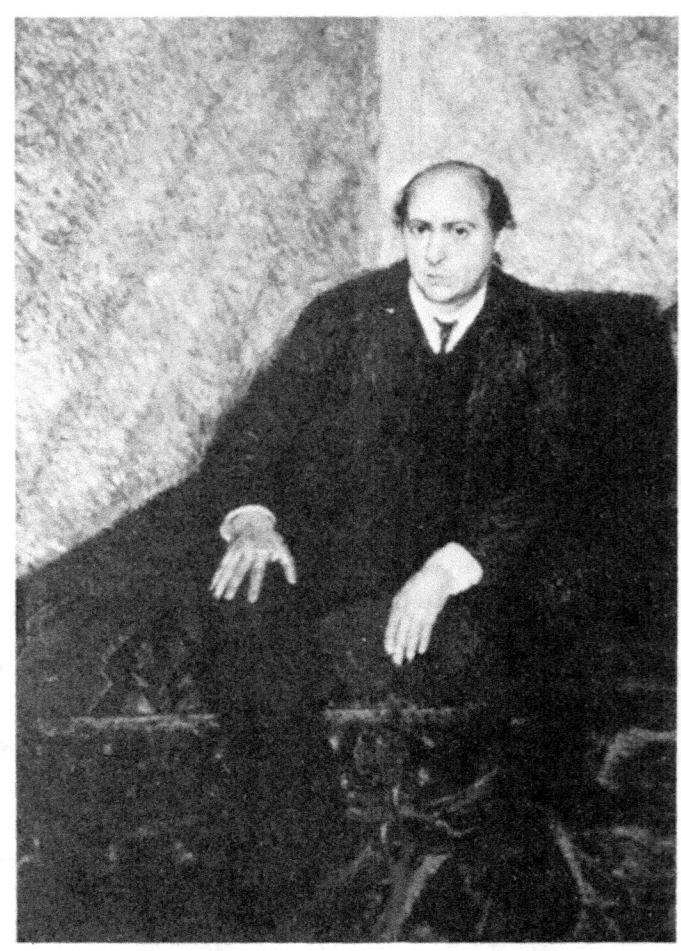

FIG. 121. Richard Gerstl, *Portrait of Arnold Schönberg*, 1906, oil.

FIG. 122. Max Oppenheimer (Mopp), *Portrait of Arnold Schönberg*, 1909, oil.

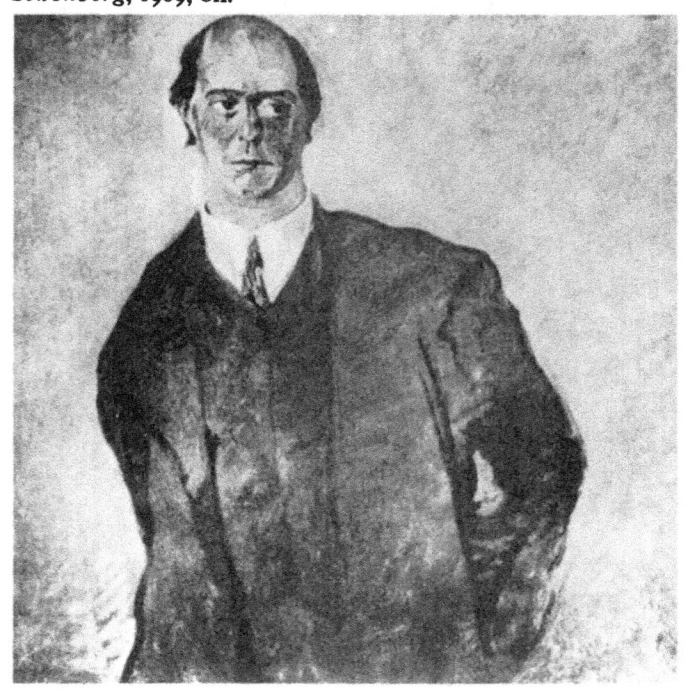

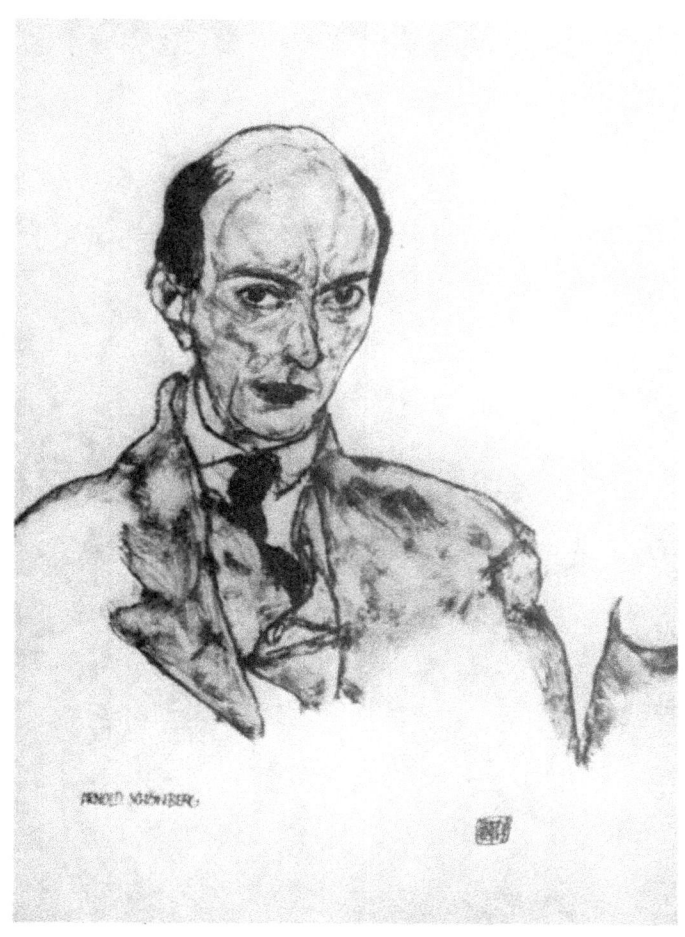

FIG. 123. Schiele, *Portrait Sketch of Arnold Schönberg with Left Arm Raised*, 1917, black chalk and watercolor.

FIG. 124. Schiele, *Study of Arnold Schönberg's Hands*, 1917, black chalk.

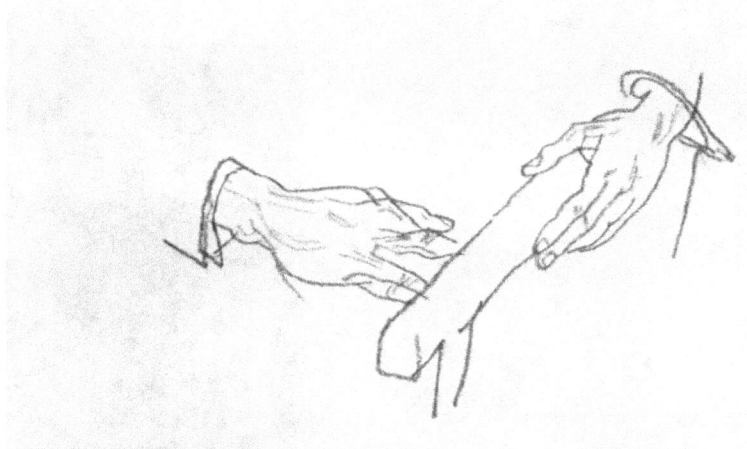

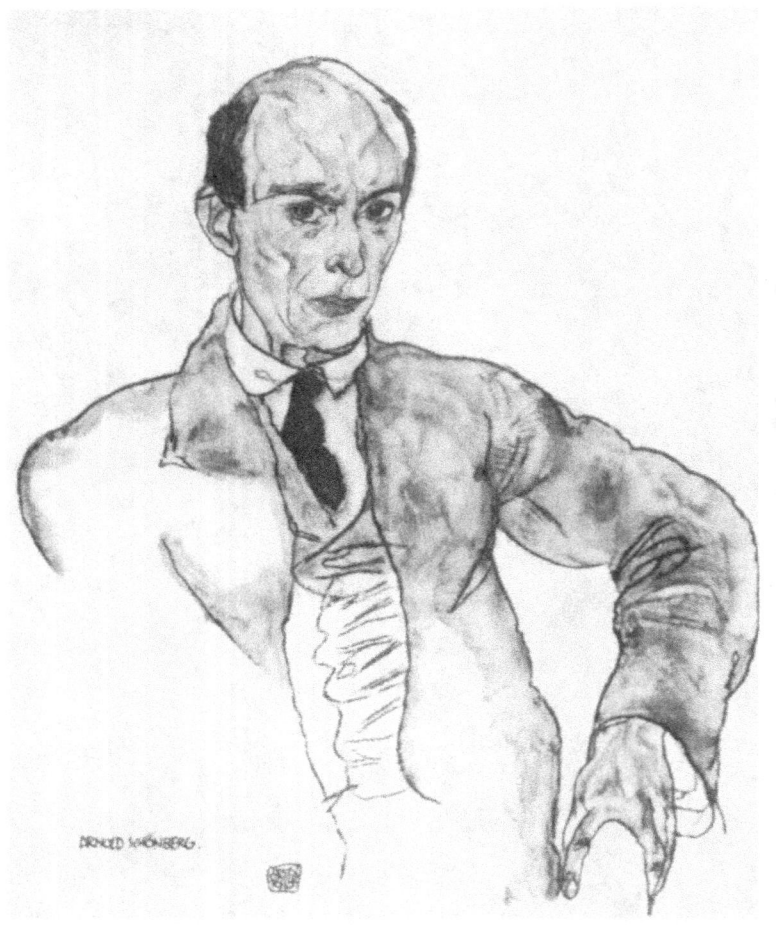

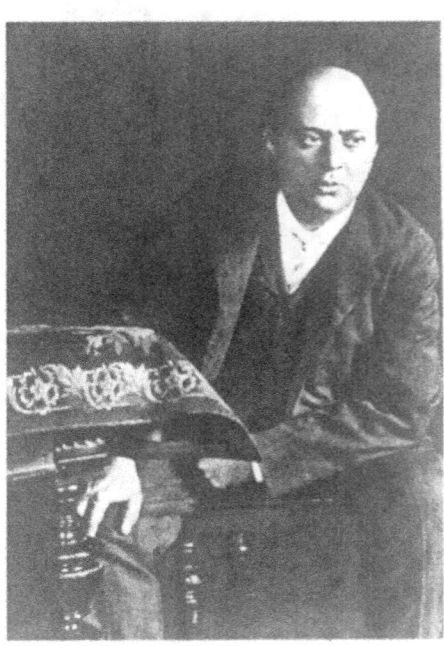

FIG. 125. Schiele, *Portrait Sketch of Arnold Schönberg*, 1917, black chalk and watercolor.

FIG. 126. Arnold Schönberg *ca.* 1917.

FIG. 127. Arnold Schönberg *ca.* 1950.

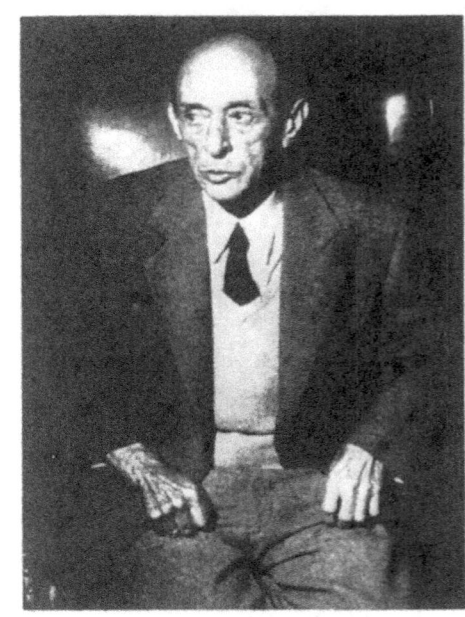

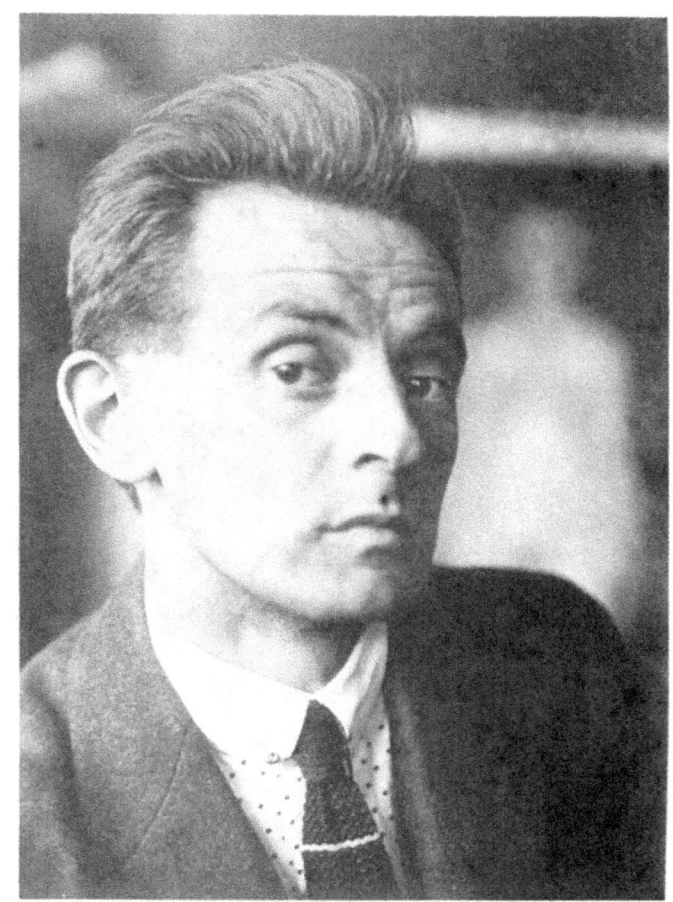

FIG. 128a. Egon Schiele, 1918.

FIG. 128b. Schiele, *Self-Portrait in Checkered Shirt*, 1917, black chalk and watercolor.

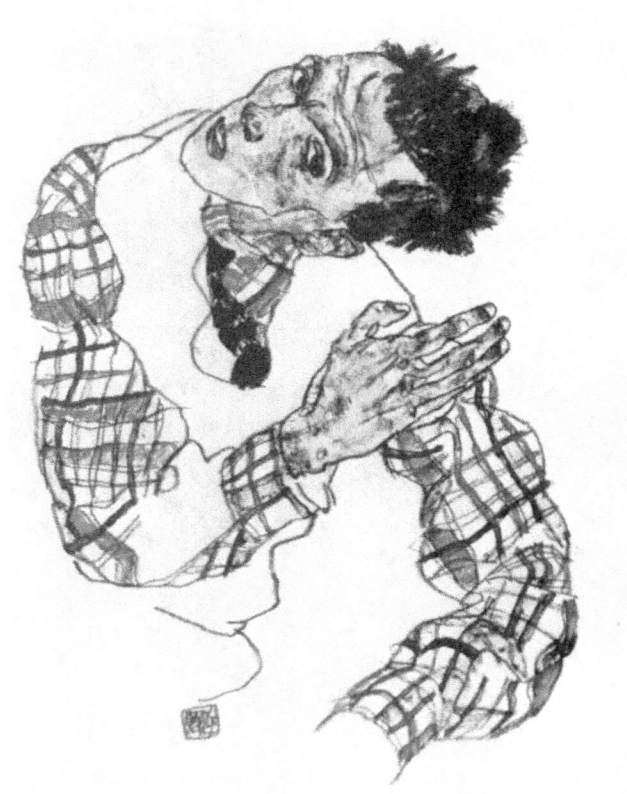

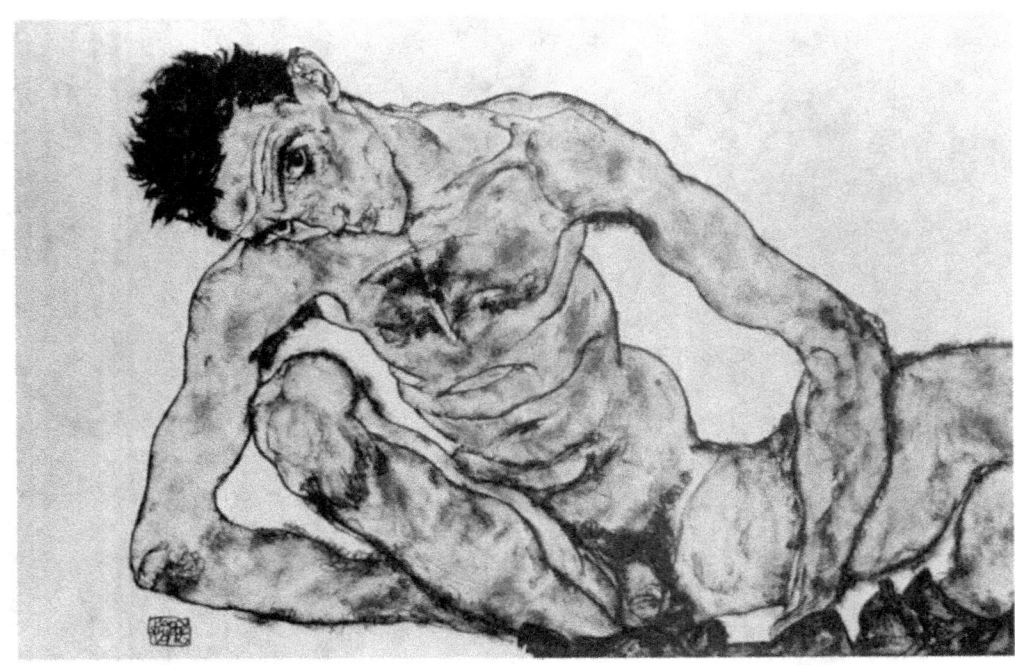

FIG. 129. Schiele, *Self-Portrait Squatting I*, 1916, black chalk and watercolor.

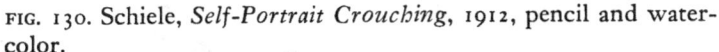

FIG. 130. Schiele, *Self-Portrait Crouching*, 1912, pencil and water-color.

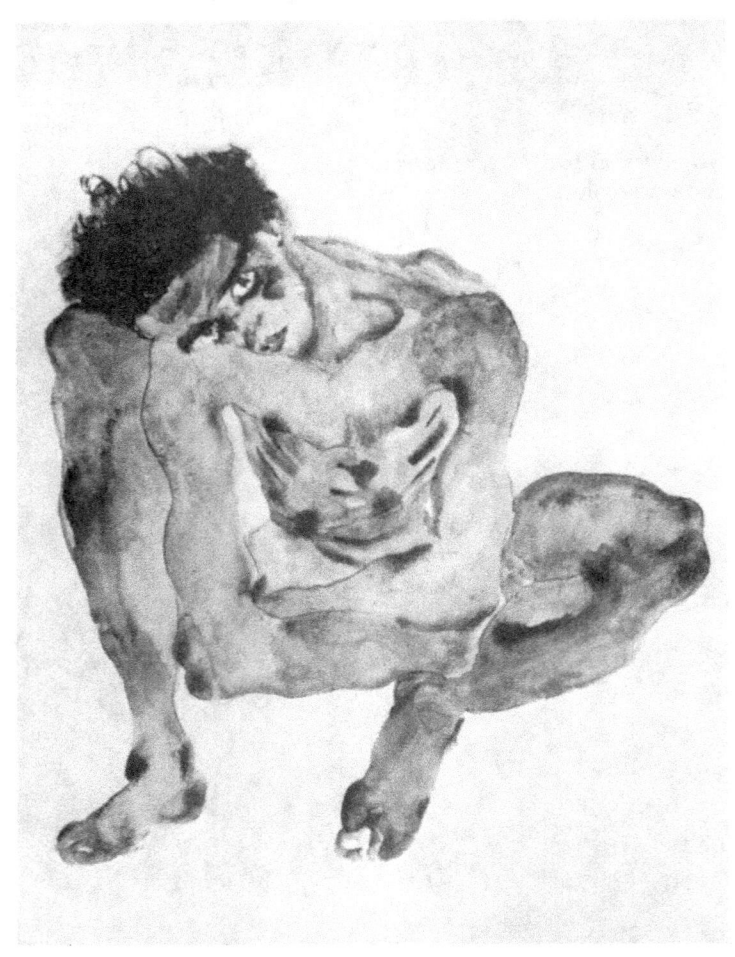

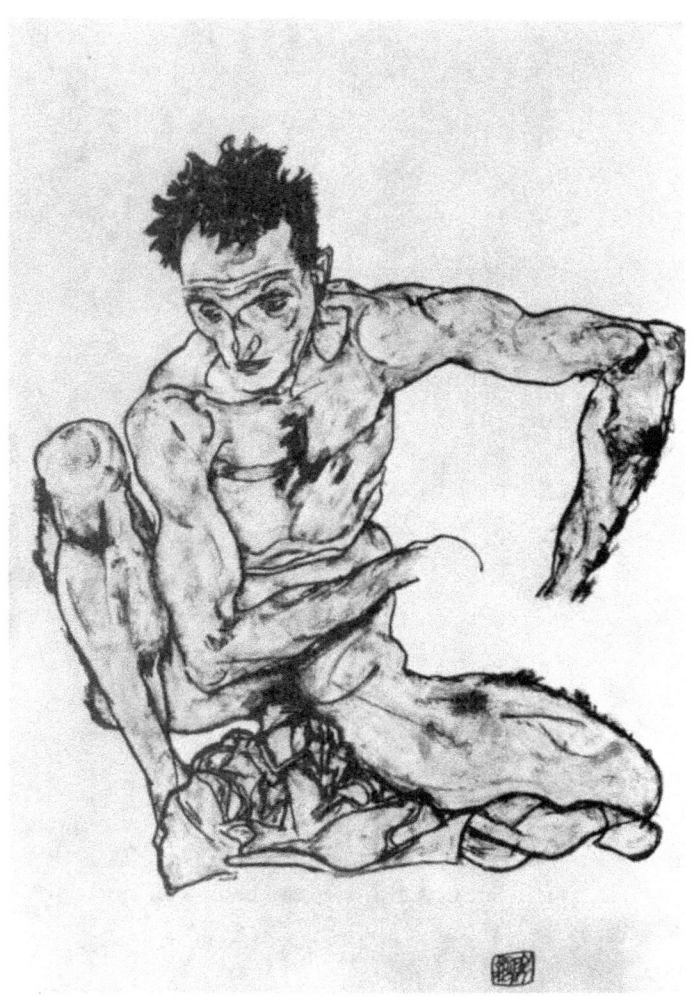

FIG. 131. Schiele, *Self-Portrait Squatting II*, 1917, black chalk and watercolor.

FIG. 132. Schiele, *Self-Portrait Squatting III*, 1918, black chalk.

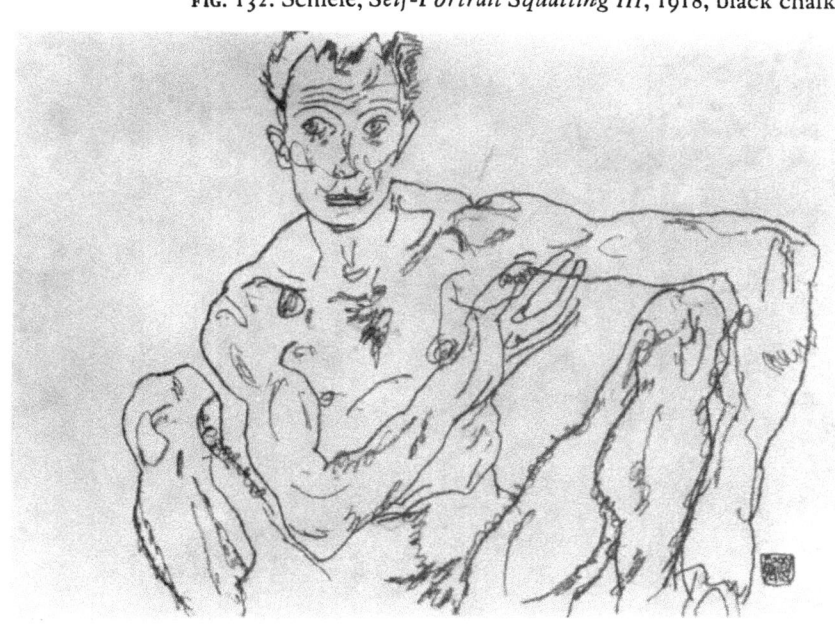

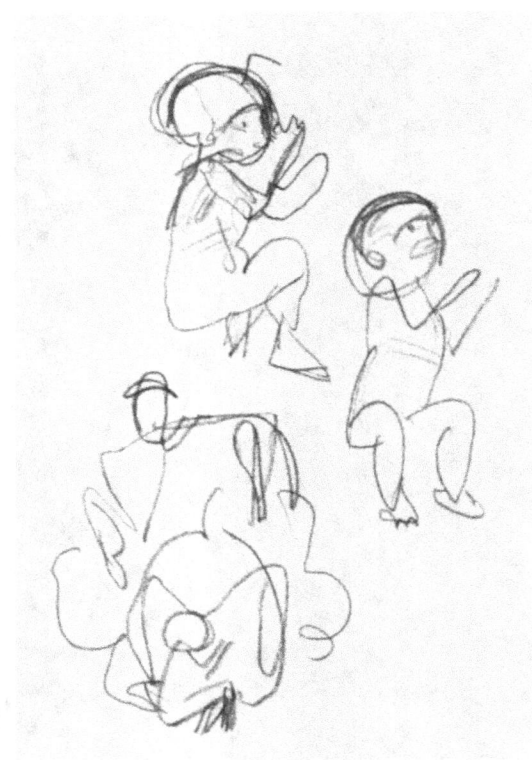

FIG. 133. Schiele, A.E.S.A. Sketchbook VII, 1917–1918, pencil, p. 5 *recto*.

FIG. 134. Schiele, A.E.S.A. Sketchbook VII, 1917–1918, pencil, p. 2 *recto*.

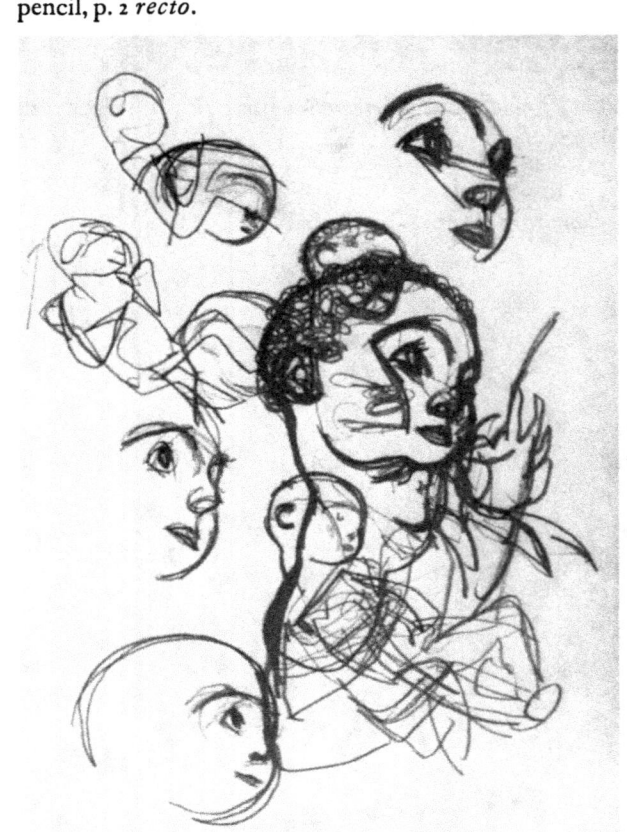

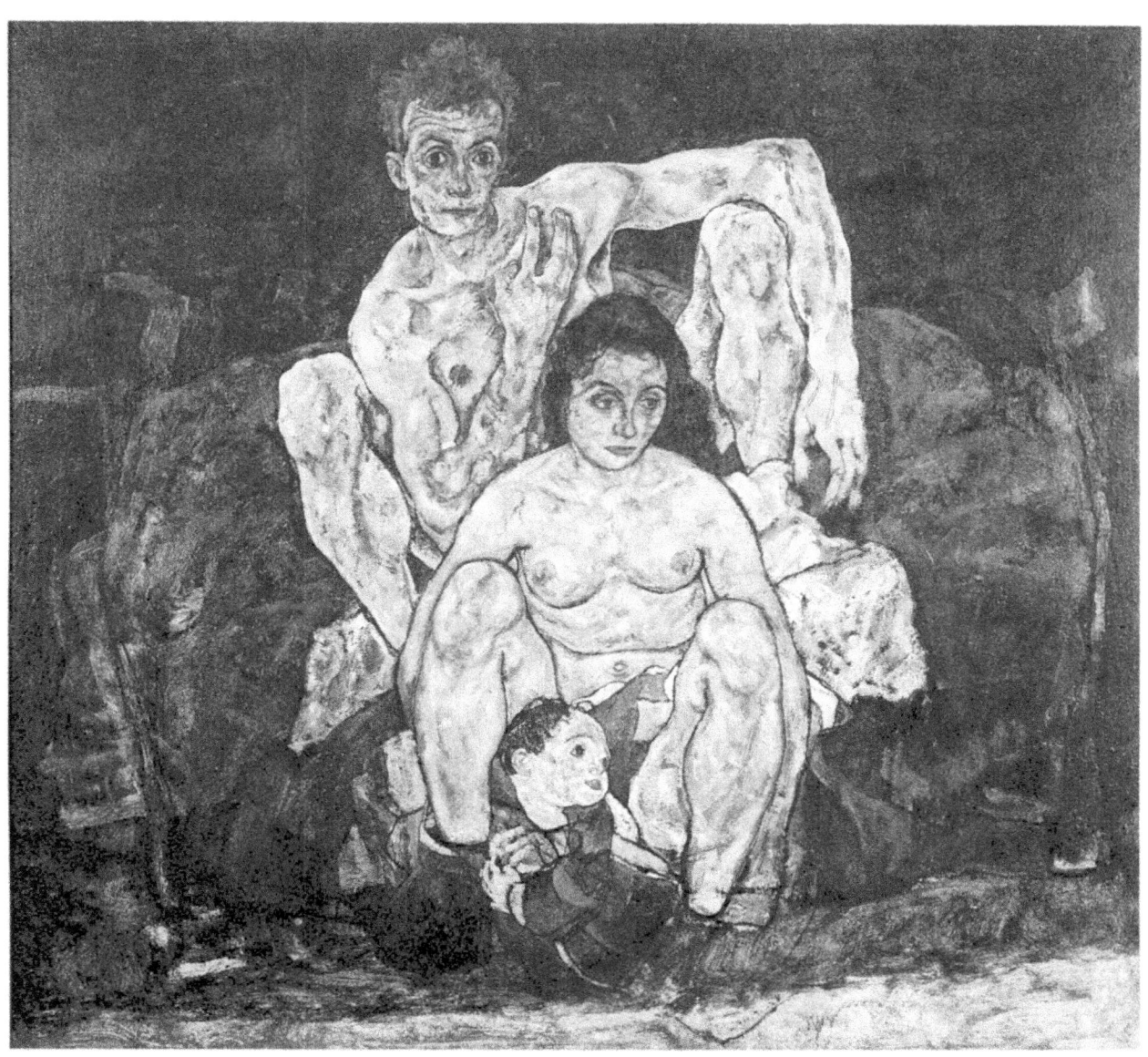

FIG. 135. Schiele, *The Family*, 1917–1918, oil.

tory pantomime determines Schiele's presentation of Robert Müller. The hands neither avoid nor clutch each other; they are joined in repose. Psychologically their union suggests a unification of the ego; compositionally they complete an oval disposition of form. This connective gesture of the hands, whether holding an object, as in the Haberditzl portrait, or directly joined, as in the portrayals of Grünwald and Müller, continues the new "fusing" formula which we can observe emerging as a pattern in Schiele's later commissions.

Although uncompleted and only a fragment, the oil *Portrait of Robert Müller* (plate 153) illustrates the new technical means by which Schiele now intended to dramatize his sitter. An impasto application of the brush responds in density to the model's concentrated expression. Müller's dark form emerges from a fiery yellow and orange background and flickering dabs of white, pink, orange, and light blue on the brownish-white skin and clothes animate the forms while emphasizing the viscosity of the oil pigment on the surface. Would Schiele's humble black chair ultimately have been provided as "environment" for the sitter? The other completed portraits at this time would so indicate, but this conclusion remains in the realm of speculation. So also must the possible course of Müller's own life, ended prematurely by suicide in 1924 when he was thirty-seven.

The use of color to generate mood and underscore personality was the concrete result of an approach Schiele had visualized as early as 1913, when, in a previously cited letter, he wrote Franz Hauer: "Painting alone does not suffice me, I know that qualities can be created WITH colors"[23] (A convenient reversal, for an artist, of theosophical theories of colors created by mental states, levels and emotions.) Concurrent with the new manipulation of oil pigments was the increasingly coloristic effect of the preparatory black-and-white drawings. The tendency, as early as 1915, towards calligraphic interior modeling within the form-defining outlines had appeared in Schiele's sketches of fellow soldiers and prisoners of war. This technique coincided with a return to the black chalk previously favored in 1910. By 1917 and 1918 Schiele worked exclusively with black chalk or charcoal in his portrait studies, whose coloristic quality differentiates them from the stark poster-like works of 1910. Another distinguishing feature is the implied plasticity of the subject. This is conveyed through a selective principle in which discontinued contours force the white areas of the paper to function as volume. Schiele's portrait sketch of another Expressionist writer, Franz Blei, (plate 156), exemplifies this later drawing style. A single line indicates the shoulder; otherwise only the paper surface intervenes between the face and hands. The white area operates as a constructive element. That powerful sense of organic cohesion basic to Schiele's figure and portrait studies is therefore still present, even if supplied by the beholder's imagination. Schiele's emphasis on the face and hands again agrees with practices in contemporaneous photography, as observable in a photograph of Blei (plate 155) taken in 1918, the year of Schiele's drawing. Nevertheless, as the relaxed attitude of the crossed arms suggests, this portrait-sketch concentration on face and hands is only a means to an end and not the end itself, as might have been the case in 1910. Another drawing, *Portrait Sketch of Franz Blei, Frontal* (plate 157), while still abbreviating detail, indicates the equal importance that figure disposition (and a calm one at that) played in the artist's conception. Schiele's interior modeling is now notably more objective. Comparison with the dramatically posed portrait sketch of yet another Expressionist writer, Carl Otten (plate 158), done four years earlier, clearly illustrates this. In 1914 the graphic detail was not structurally informative, but abstractly decorative. This non-organic commentary was imposed on basic contours, whereas in the late drawings of 1917 and 1918 a form-defining modeling is often inserted between the outlines of the face and hands. The frequently interrupted contours of the Otten drawing give way to more continuous, sweeping strokes in the Blei sketches. The three-dimensional, pictorial quality sought now by Schiele in his oil portraits is already evident in the new tonality of his preparatory sketches.[24]

An idea of the proposed Blei portrait had it been realized in oil may be had from a work completed by Schiele shortly before March of 1918, the *Portrait of Viktor Ritter von Bauer* (plate 159).[25] The subject was an Austrian foreign officer who had served as Ambassador in Rome before the war. Karl Grünwald obtained the commission for Schiele. A certain distance, or perhaps shyness, is reflected in Schiele's attitude towards his sitter. There is no psychological contact between the artist and his model, who stares into space and sits with loosely flung-out arms and legs. The arms form an oval with the hands connected visually through their position on or under the right chair arm. There are few clues to personality. The totally bald head lends a startling note to an otherwise unremarkable appearance. As though in compensation, Schiele has introduced an artificial note of warmth: his black studio chair has been given a cheery yellow color in the portrait and a brightly striped cushion contrasts gaily with the chalk-white suit of the model. For the first time in Schiele's portraiture the background is clearly divisible into floor and wall, and these are both painted yellow. Certainly this environmental note marks a return from the void—that void which had so consistently characterized the radical portraits of 1910. What makes this relatively impersonal portrait an Expressionist picture and heir to the Van Gogh portraits it so clearly recalls is the stark and unrelieved concentration on the human figure. Although there is no communication between the artist and his model, there is also nothing to intervene. The presentation is almost overbearingly direct, and the artist attempts to "create qualities with colors" in the hot chrome and citron yellows that completely surround the enigmatic figure. Permeating the contiguous hues of the color scale is a distinct melancholy, a melancholy paradoxically in a major key, the primary color yellow. The picture's intensity depends not on gesture or facial expression but on an unresolved tug of war between the formal elements that compose it—line and color. Neither merging nor receding, these two elements vie in topical insistence upon the man and his sparse environment.

As though in recognition of the formal stalemate inherent in this type of separatist assignment of color to background and contour to figure definition,

Schiele took a new step in the next (and last) two portrait commissions he completed. In his *Portrait of Guido Arnot* (plate 162), he included several of the books, canvases, and folk art objects from his own studio. Finding this a compatible substitute for the painterly co-existence of model and background, he literally surrounded his sitter with books in his final commission, the *Portrait of Dr. Hugo Koller* (plate 163).[26]

Schiele's *Portrait of Guido Arnot* contains more references to himself than to the art dealer whom he was portraying. Arnot, whose gallery was located on the Kärntnerring in the center of town, had given the artist a one-man show in December of 1914 and had bought works from him ever since. The tone of his correspondence reveals that he was a shrewd businessman. In arranging an exhibition of Schiele's works for November of 1916, he extracted the promise of a 25 per cent commission on any work the artist might sell directly to a client during the three months after the show.[27] A glimmering of Arnot's wary ways may be had in the alert and tensed position in which Schiele shows him. This particular characterization of Arnot through posture was suggested in a quick notation in the artist's sketchbook and immediately worked out in a second sketchbook drawing in which the varying strokes and overlaid contours document the febrile excitement of Schiele's creative vision, and contrast with the more definite lines of later preparatory studies of Arnot's face and hands.[28] In the final oil the pose speaks of Arnot; all the rest belongs to the artist. As twice before, in the portraits of Kosmack and Haber-ditzl, Schiele includes a special object from the outside world to testify to his relationship with the model and, in effect, to seal a promise of patronage. The object this time is not a sunflower but Schiele's carved wooden horse, the same little horse with which he had been photographed in 1914 (figure 101) and which he had painted in his *Still Life with Books* (K.218) of 1916. Other recognizable items from the artist's collection surround the horse in the upper right background: a rag doll with bonnet and baby, and a little puppet. In front of Arnot and cutting diagonally across the bottom of the picture is a table. Ten books of various size and binding are propped up in a row along this table and to the right stands a small Egyptian statue. All of these items, as well as the cushioned chair (used by Edith) were Schiele's.

As a further step back from the void and towards a localized portraiture, the Arnot picture is an advance over the Ritter von Bauer portrait. But far more important features distinguish this work than the mere presence of additional paraphernalia. The new wealth of setting gives Schiele a chance to juggle perspectives, flatten planes, and tilt objects in the best manner of Cézanne. As Schiele's approach to portraiture expands to include environment, his spiritual model in the mainstream of modern art changes from Van Gogh to Cézanne. Even earlier than his portraiture Schiele's landscapes had exhibited a trend away from emotional immediacy (e.g., the 1912 *City Hall, Krumau*, K.142) to analytical construction (e.g., the 1916 *Mödling*, K.215). One of the factors resulting from the Van Gogh-like directness characteristic of the Ritter von Bauer portrait is the lack of any barrier between the artist or beholder and the model. In the Arnot portrait Schiele introduced an ef-

fective intervention in the form of the book-laden table. The radical disposition of objects within ambiguous and flattened planes strongly indicates
a conscious emulation of Cézanne.[29] Further assimilation of Cézanne's techniques is noticeable in arbitrary color accents with which Schiele helps equate
on the surface different planes in depth: the deep rose-red of the rug is repeated
in the page tops of several books; the orange-yellows of the chair cushion appear in the long vertical band (floor, wall—or table?) to the right and in some
of the background objects; and the gray-white of the carved horse occurs
again in Arnot's suit, the floor molding to the left, and the table top. This
surface interlocking of back- and foreground objects speaks of ambitious
structural interests. Nevertheless, Schiele's primarily graphic approach, which
was based on the outline of the drawing chalk and not on the stroke of the
brush, was to rule out that final creation of space through color achieved by
the French master. Furthermore the hard edges of Schiele's forms would continue to be composed on the surface rather than in space, as a perpetual heritage
from his Jugendstil beginnings.

The *Portrait of Dr. Hugo Koller* (plate 163) confirms the new constructionist tendencies in Schiele's portraiture. The amiable-looking bibliophile,
husband of the landscape-artist Broncia Koller, sits in a comfortable armchair
and gazes thoughtfully past the pages of a book held open on his knee. Schiele's
viewpoint is even higher than in the previous Grünwald or Arnot portraits
and it allows him to display the large number of books and volumes that tum-
ble companionably about the sitter.[30] The books were not part of the original
conception as jotted down in a sketchbook (plate 161a). In the sketch Koller's
position leaning against one corner of the chair is much the same as in the
final portrait, but in place of books only one other object is indicated, a small
four-legged stool or low table in the upper left corner. It may be assumed that
Schiele noted down this compositional idea at the Koller home[31] rather than
in his studio, for another drawing, *Armchair Study for the Portrait of Dr.
Hugo Koller* (plate 160), is devoted exclusively to the observation of these
two pieces of furniture—the side table and upholstered chair. This drawing,
which responds to the outlined form rather than to the textural feel of the
objects under study, is typical of the painstaking methodology underlying
Schiele's later portraits. Still another drawing, *Study of Dr. Koller with Left
Arm Raised* (plate 161b), meticulously reproduces one of the tiny circles
(upholstery button?) indicated in the armchair study, while essaying a new
figure disposition. The variation in pose absorbs the artist's interest here and
the lower part of the face is left undefined.[32] In other sketches the facial characteristics and structure of the head receive the greatest attention.[33] Such
multiple probing of every aspect of his sitter had been basic to Schiele's approach to portraiture from his earliest years, but these later preparatory drawings exhibit an untroubled, dispassionate approach that not only allows the
pose to develop from observation of the subject's own personal habits (as in
the Lederer and Benesch portraits of the middle years), but also permits recognition and inclusion of those inanimate personal objects to which the sitter
has lent the stamp of his own individuality. Thus Dr. Koller's favorite read-

ing chair and his collection of old books receive prominent space in the final oil.

The building-block arrangement of books in the Koller portrait both enhances and duplicates the position of the model. A wavy row along the bottom of the canvas produces a barrier between spectator and sitter similar to the one in the Arnot portrait, but now the diagonal movement is far less pronounced, and the row of books relates as a compositional repetition to the sagging horizontal lines of the armchair and the books above. To the left a tower of old volumes climbs precipitously up to meet this topmost row of books, forming an apex directly behind Koller's head. The extended shoulder device (drawn with exaggerated exuberance in the initial compositional sketch) receives low-keyed treatment in the final version and, unlike the same feature in the earlier Ritter von Bauer portrait, it no longer projects against a void but is backed by the chair. The softening of this Expressionist hallmark through environmental containment allows attention to focus on the much larger gesture of which the asymmetrical shoulder line is only a part. This is the continuous circle or oval formed by the arms, that "linking" motif which we have seen receive increasingly definitive formulation ever since its first appearance in the Grünwald portrait. The out-thrust, angular, off-balance posturing of the commissioned portraits of 1910 has been definitely abandoned. There are no overt implications of anxiety or self-protection in this new gesture, which suggests repose as well as harmonious self-containment.[34] Schiele's ability to relate objectively to others is also reflected in the greater portion of the body shown. Usually only the feet are cut off now, whereas formerly the torso was frequently shown in only three-quarter length.[35] As the *Lebensraum* of Schiele's models increases and fills with specific, intimate objects, so does the somatic extension into a no longer hostile space. Space is no longer regarded as void but as environment.

It has often been said of the Expressionist movement that its artists burned themselves out. The new trends noted in Schiele's last series of portrait commissions support this oversimplified but appropriate statement. The ordeal of a general world war ended the luxury of purely self-centered and private emotion for many artists and left them different men. Kokoschka's portraits just before and during the war evince a similar aspect of "burning out," or of passing from the existential to the environmental. His 1914 portrait of Franz Hauer (plate 114), it will be remembered, presented the subject in a room, sitting with an open book on his lap before a pane-glass window. Other (though not all) portraits done during these years also include background fragments, usually in the form of a partially shown armchair.[36] It is significant, in this regard, that Kokoschka was known for his insistence on doing his portrait commissions in the room where his sitter lived, so as better to penetrate the subject's personality.[37] The objectivity promised (if not always delivered) in this attitude was shared by Schiele in his portrait of Koller. The Koller commission occasioned the first thorough study by the artist of a person, other than himself, in his own surroundings. The result incorporated a new formal interest in construction—the environment, and a sympathetic, rather than formidable, interpretation of personality. The Arnot and Koller portraits are strong indications of what the future course of Schiele's commissioned portraiture[38] might have been—descriptive, objective, and essentially non-Expressionistic in content—in short, a return from the void.

FAMILY PORTRAITS

The change in attitude that distinguishes Schiele's later portraits from those of 1910 is cogently illustrated in the 1918 *Portrait of Anton Peschka, Jr.* (plate 167).[39] Schiele's four-year-old nephew, Toni, sits quietly on the edge of a large chair, holding a violet and looking out at the beholder with solemn eyes. His serious demeanor is much the same as that displayed in a photograph taken at this time (plate 166). In the portrait his head is on a level with the chair arms and the chubby little legs hang down without reaching the floor. The child's small size in relation to his surroundings is further emphasized by the multi-colored horizontal stripes of the chair's upholstery which climb out of the picture to an unspecified height. The obvious sentimentality elicited by this contrast of child and chair compares with the maudlin stratagems of Biedermeier art, as pursued well into the closing decades of the nineteenth century. Ernst Klimt's *Portrait of a Boy* (plate 165) of 1885 is an elegant example of this kind of sententious child portraiture, and one with which Schiele may have been personally acquainted. It was not young Toni Peschka's blood relationship to the artist that exempted him from the intense emotions conveyed by the void-surrounded children of Schiele's early portraits, but rather the fact that his portrait was made late in Schiele's career. Earlier watercolor portraits dating from 1915 showing Toni nursing at his mother's breast are striking in their merciless, almost sadistic rendition of the child as a vapid, voracious human organism.[40] A preparatory watercolor of 1917, *Study of Anton Peschka, Jr., Frontal* (plate 164), traces the decision to conceal at least one hand or arm in the final portrait, a feature which abandons the "linking" hands formula used concurrently in Schiele's portraits of adults, and which thus effectively contributes to an impression of fragility similar to that in Ernst Klimt's portrait. In the final oil the tonal exuberance of the cheerfully striped chair back and cushion is accompanied by warm red-browns in the floor and background and thick creamy whites in the clothing. Schiele's delight in jewel-like colors, dating from his Wiener Werkstätte days and frequently expressed in the multi-colored roofs of his townscapes, prevents this portrait from assuming the austere quality of his work of 1910. Nevertheless a basically graphic approach persists despite the striving towards a more painterly use of color. Schiele's child still retains the existential or metaphysical force of its watercolor studies, in which the figure is convincingly projected against the white surface of the paper. For Schiele, the introduction of color remains very much a property of the environment with which he now surrounds, rather than defines, his figures; the state of being of his figure conveys less emotional tension but as much immediacy of presence as the radical portraits of 1910.

In 1915 Schiele had employed the figure of the infant Toni twice[41] in the same painting, a work which he partly repainted and signed in 1917. This picture, *Mother with Two Children* (plate 168), is a general thematic statement in the tradition of Schiele's earlier mother-and-child allegories. The ashen head that looms like a skull from its shawl does not invite comparison with Gerti, the child-model's mother, but rather stands as a symbol for a life on the wane, a life that has served its purpose—procreation. Conversely, the rosy-cheeked, brightly clad babies do not exist for the sake of providing two different views of Toni but rather as symbols of contrasting life attitudes—introvert and extrovert, religious and worldly, dependent and self-sufficient, passive and active, perhaps even a predication of death and life.[42] Schiele made numerous compositional notations for this work[43] and when the young Toni was not available, he occasionally substituted the figure of a small Japanese doll that he kept in his studio.[44] Indeed the intended aspect of folk art on a monumental scale suggested by the gay colors and wooden poses in this picture is confirmed in a 1915 pencil and tempera drawing of folk art objects from Schiele's collection in which the painting is shown reduced to a miniature statue or panel.[45] The double appearance of Toni in *Mother with Two Children* is the first of several late allegories in which Schiele posed a figure from real life (in the other cases himself) with invented or symbolically generalized figures.

If Schiele's treatment of the theme of motherhood could now abstain from specific comment on his own mother, so also could the portrait sketches of his mother evince a new emotional confidence, free of any symbolic overtones.[46] The black chalk *Portrait of Marie Schiele* (plate 169) presents a sympathetic view of a woman worn by the privations and uncertainties of war. The spontaneity of pose conveyed by the turn of the head, relaxed hands which lightly link with each other, and changing contrapposto affords an off-balance construction that is harmoniously stabilized through a fluid system of massed lines and white intervals. The coloristic use of the chalk is expanded by smudging and blending contours. It is perhaps an ironic demonstration of Schiele's excellence as a draftsman that his most painterly effects are achieved in drawings such as this rather than in the formal oil medium.

The major family portrait executed in Schiele's later style was the almost life-size *Portrait of Edith Schiele Seated* (plate 171). Although signed and dated 1918, it was painted during the opening months of 1917 and may be placed chronologically as just preceding the row of commissioned portraits that began with that of Karl Grünwald. The faint indication of floor and walls meeting at an angle behind the chair is the only sign of environment. Just such a room corner had been suggested in the 1916 portrait of Edith's father (plate 142), and a pensive mood similar to that of the Harms painting further relates the two portraits, which are of the same size[47] and which if hung side by side would show the protagonists facing each other. Schiele evidently decided rather late on the direction of his wife's gaze to the right, for most of the preparatory sketches show Edith with her face turned to the left. In a letter to Lányi, dated 16 March 1917, the artist invited him to come by his atelier on the following Sunday, and asked:

"If possible bring me, from the drawings to be reproduced, the two which are listed in the collection of the Staatsgalerie. (The Russian and my wife seated.) You can have the drawings back by Monday already, and I need them most urgently."[48]

The importance of preparatory studies for Schiele has been noted in regard to the Haberditzl portrait, but in this case the "urgent" need to refer to such a drawing may have been occasioned by a contemplated major change in the portrait of Edith. A photograph of the work in its original state shows that Edith was initially painted wearing a brightly checkered skirt. Known as the Scottish style, this pattern was considered the latest fashion in Vienna at that time, and it may be presumed that Schiele had faithfully reproduced the dress of which his wife was so proud, just as he had previously shown her in the striped dress made from his studio curtains. The letter to Lányi quoted above refers to a drawing of Edith in the possession of the Staatsgalerie, and in fact that museum's director, Dr. Haberditzl, was highly interested in the progress of Schiele's new portrait of Edith since he intended to acquire it for the Staatsgalerie. After viewing the completed work however he asked Schiele to change the "proletarian" pattern of the skirt. Schiele complied with this request.[49] The drawing that he asked Lányi to bring by his studio may have been similar to the watercolor *Study of Edith Schiele Seated with Hand to Cuff* (plate 176) in which the checkered pattern of the skirt had not been indicated, in order to study the effect of a neutral skirt. The change was apparently not carried out until the following year, when Schiele signed and dated the portrait. At this time he reworked the picture, laying an opaque white over the checks in the skirt, changing the round contours of the collar into a dentillated outline, tucking the left thumb out of sight, permitting the shoes to show, and adding a black string tie with red tassel to the neck of the white blouse.

It is noteworthy that Schiele's new oil portrait of Edith did not contain any of the overt symbolism in the hand gestures such as had appeared in the 1915 portrait of Edith standing (plate 133). Instead, as indicated in the study reproduced here and in the original and final versions, Schiele was experimenting with the linked-hand gesture—and continuous oval motif—of the commissioned portraits of 1917–18. This compositional effect, with its suggestion of serenity and repose, was thus first definitively formulated by Schiele in this portrait of Edith.[50] There is one salient resemblance to the 1915 portrait of Edith. We once again behold a face which is wooden and characterless. This is especially remarkable considering the sympathetic treatment given the face in the preparatory studies. Other watercolors in this series were devoted exclusively to the face and its expressive sensibility, such as the study *Edith in Three-Quarter View* (plate 172). The explanation does not lie with Schiele's capabilities as a draftsman but rather with the occurrence of a certain state of mind that seemed frequently to overtake him when working in the oil medium. He became overly self-conscious and his whole style stiffened. The spontaneity of his graphic rendition became weighty and formalized. The blank expression on Edith's face[51] is perhaps also related to an indecision or conflict in Schiele's own mind about the nature of his wife. Photographs of her capture two different Ediths, the one worldly and seductive (plate 175), the other unassuming and modest (plate 170). This dual conception of Edith helped influence Schiele's decision to paint a new allegorical self-portrait with wife and mistress.

The disparity between Schiele's photographs and portraits of Edith contrasts interestingly with the harmonious agreement displayed in the oil portrait and photographs made by Klimt of his mistress Emilie. Klimt's 1902 *Portrait of Emilie Flöge* (plate 174) presents the same easy elegance and poise as does his fashion photograph of her (plate 173).[52] For Klimt, who lived openly with Emilie for some twenty years, there were no repressed or conflicting images such as preoccupied Schiele in his first stages of social respectability.

LAST SELF-PORTRAITS: AS LOVER, AS HUSBAND, AS LOVER-HUSBAND

Schiele's self-assignment, as manifested in his last major self-portraits, into two separate roles—that of lover and that of husband—evinces a growing restlessness in his personal life. The desired simultaneous relationship with Edith and Wally had not materialized, but several years of marriage and extramarital affairs had provided his imagination with two ideal and distinct self-images—lover and husband. These two concepts now provided the thematic inspiration for three large oil self-portraits.

Two canvases of life-size female nudes painted in 1917 shed light on the genesis of the first self-portrait. One work was entitled *The Virgin* (plate 177); the other received no specific title, but might well be called "Desire" (*Reclining Woman*, K.222). Both figures are set down with broad, dark contours against a vivid background of yellow—a color which according to his own testimony held erotic significance for the artist.[53] The virgin stands stiffly erect, facing front, and with her hands clenched at her sides. Her face (strangely reminiscent of those blank Austrian Baroque faces of Peter Strudel, Daniel Gran, and J. M. Rottmayr) has the round, perfect, anonymous features of a painted doll, and there is no indication of personality or emotion save in the hands which curl into loose fists, forming the same apertures as those which figured symbolically in the 1915 *Portrait of Edith Schiele Standing* (plate 178a). The similarity with that portrait is striking: not only are the canvases of almost identical height,[54] but the poses are so alike that the later work might almost have been drawn from a tracing of the first. Another equation of Edith with *The Virgin* was made by Schiele in still a different but no less obvious form. One of the photographs he took of Edith in 1917 (plate 178b) shows her posing, fully dressed, next to the still-stretched canvas (seen in its first version, showing the figure with long wavy hair down to the waist). She turns her back to it, places her hand defiantly on her hip, and looks out at her husband with a pleased, self-conscious smirk. By contrast, the protagonist in the second painting "Desire" is shown in the throes of emotion. Her legs are thrust wide apart and bent in at the knees and her arms are crossed behind her head. She lies on a blue-edged white sheet, its wrinkles and folds seeming to echo the writhings of the body upon them. Her nipples and cheeks are a deep crimson and the fingers of her left hand are tensed in a gesture reminiscent of Schiele's self-portraits of masturbation.[55]

Neither of the above works can be considered specific portraits, but they offer palpable materializations of their creator's fantasy. It is almost predictable that Schiele should now (thematically) come to the aid of one of these ladies. He chooses the reclining nude—not to be identified as Wally[56]—in preference to the virgin-Edith, and paints his nude body alongside hers in another life-size work of 1917, *The Embrace ("Lovers")* (plate 179). The bedsheet with blue piping again crumples into expressive folds under the tossing weight of two bodies, and the yellow background is shot with greens and whites. Schiele's embrace is passionate and the hard musculature of his body contrasts with the softer, supple form of the woman whose dark brown hair fans out luxuriantly on the pillow. She presses Schiele's mouth closer to her ear and the fingers of her left hand spread to form a wide V on her lover's back while the organic form of the sheet between her thighs symbolizes the approaching physical union of their bodies.

The marked emphasis on the different hues and textures of the bodies recalls Klimt's uncompleted *Adam and Eve* begun the same year as Schiele's *The Embrace*. Klimt's use of a darker tonality for the male body in earlier works such as *The Kiss* and *Death and Life* (before 1911, worked over in 1916) may have been adopted from his observation of Egyptian art.[57] There can be little doubt that Schiele had noted and appreciated this painterly distinction between the sexes by Klimt. Nevertheless, the harmony that typifies Klimt's canvas finds no duplication in Schiele's work. *Adam and Eve*, with its dreamy melancholic pace and its rhythmic figure parallelisms, and *The Embrace*, with its violent tempo and thrashing bodies, are characteristic not only of the different personalities of their creators, but also of the contrasting viewpoints of their art affiliations—elevation versus pursuit of beauty.

Schiele's portrayal of himself as the lover in *The Embrace* brings attention to an important fact. He has *shown himself nude in a major canvas for the first time since 1911*—following a thematic withdrawal of over five years. I have previously identified one of the causes for this cessation of nude self-portraiture with the deep trauma inflicted at Neulengbach. The young man who, to clothe his spiritual vulnerability, had borrowed the guises of hermit, monk, and saint, had also taken care to cover his physical nudity. The thematic self-portrait statements of the next five years all had as their protagonist a clothed Schiele. In the two double portraits with Klimt of 1912, *The Hermits* and *Agony*, Schiele was dressed in a monk's habit; in the 1912 *Cardinal and Nun* he was robed in scarlet. He wore a tunic in the 1913 *Self-Portrait with Saint*. In the two great self-portrait canvases of 1915, *Death and Maiden* and *Soaring*, he was clothed, and he was clothed in the lost 1916 *Double Portrait with Edith*. One of the last paintings in which Schiele had emphasized his nudity was *The Lyric Poet* of 1911 (plate 72), which presents a surprising analogy with *The Embrace* of 1917. It was the depiction of himself in *The Lyric Poet* as a flesh-and-blood being, suffering from the longings of sexual desire, that had broken the succession of increasingly dehumanized double self-portraits begun with *Self-Seers I* of 1910 and continued by *The Prophet* and *Self-Seers II* in 1911. Now, almost six years later, it is again expression of his sexual drive that enables Schiele to throw off the last vestiges of allegorical masquerading and return to the theme of his nude body. There are nonetheless still a few reservations. In the role of lover Schiele has a practical justification for his nudity. Furthermore, he has turned his back to the beholder—his mirror. Even his face is only partially seen. And yet there can be no doubt as to the artist's identification or wish-identification with the male figure in *The Embrace*. The image of self as lover has been given full expression in this important and bold painting.

In the more intimate realm of his drawings and watercolors, Schiele had already made a first cautious return to what had always been his most powerful means of self-expression—nudity. A watercolor dating from the latter half of 1916, *Self-Portrait Squatting I* (figure 129), shows him sitting on the floor with his legs spread wide apart. Confronting his mirror, Schiele has deliberately presented an image shorn of any thematic guise. At first glance it would appear that he has returned to the solitary statements of his earlier years, and indeed the low, squat, extended left shoulder and downward turn of the head recall a watercolor of early 1912, *Self-Portrait Crouching* (figure 130). These two studies provide an excellent measure of the progress of Schiele's emotional objectivity towards himself. Although both pictures are Expressionist in the sense that they exploit and relentlessly display the self, the works are, in the precisely documentable span of Schiele's iconography, poles apart. The earlier image, thinly penciled and fluidly colored with ice-blue hues that convey the shudder which seems to take hold of the crouching frame, is distinguished by an animal-like intensity. The enormous, insomnia-ringed eyes glow with the intensity of a wild creature's and the sense of something dumb and bestial is enhanced by the squatting haunches and the folded arms which swing like short, inarticulate forepaws and cover the source of the figure's sexual drive. The later self-portrait contains the same penetrating observation but the concentration is now diffused: this is not the study of a body wracked by emotion, but rather simply of a body. There is no outer reverberation of inner violence, no involuntary contortion. The expression of Schiele's face is more a gaze of critical scrutiny than an animalesque reaction to physical longings. A thoroughgoing technique introduces other factors in this study of self which go beyond that of narcissistic exhibitionism (the concealed hands and non-erect penis negating, for once, the theme of masturbation). A vigorous contour now permeates the entire body with equal emphasis. All parts share the expressiveness of line, from the knobby knee to the humping neck as it merges into the extended left shoulder. But the line is no longer limited to silhouette: horizontals, arcs, and delicate grids spread across all surface areas of the body in anatomical reflection and modeling. The plastic impression achieved by line is strengthened by a dry, flecking application of color to the structural highlights, suggesting the play of light and shadow.

The *Self-Portrait Squatting I* of 1916 represents the first in a series of nude studies in which the artist was searching not for an emotion, but for a unique "signature" pose which could be associated with himself in a major work. During 1917 and 1918 the invention of this pose was often on his mind and experimentation was not limited to those times when he was actually posturing in the nude before his mirror. A spontaneous combination of three essential features of the pose as finally conceived—the extended left shoulder line, the "broken" or "open" position of the arms, and the raised right hand with bent thumb and V gesture—may be seen in the 1917 *Self-Portrait in Checkered Shirt* (figure 128b). This is not a drawing of psychological depth; the pose with its sudden swivel suggests an impulsive look in the mirror. Schiele's head is bent to one side and his expression is quizzical. Obvious delight has been taken in coloring the "civilian" shirt and a sculptural dimension is attained by dabbling the skin surface with flecks of color.[58]

The picture for which Schiele was conducting his investigations in posture and three-dimensionality was to be a monumentalization of a vision of self as husband and founder of a family. The ineluctability of the life-cycle in nature and the eternal renewal (through death and regeneration)—these thoughts had been central to the philosophic speculations and artistic concerns which had molded Schiele's formative years. Klimt's obsession with this dual theme had given rise to the great spirals of floating humanity in his University panels, and had been more specifically treated in *Hope, Three Ages of Life*, and *Death and Life*. Klimt was to treat it again in the unfinished *Bride* of 1917–18. All of these works were presented as allegories. It is characteristic of Expressionism, and of Schiele in particular, that a theme so universal in significance should be viewed in expressly personal terms. Schiele entitled his ambitious new work "Squatting Couple,"[59] but within a few years after his death it was already known by its present title, *The Family*.

The Family (figure 135) was begun in 1917 and remained partly unfinished, although Schiele exhibited it in Vienna and Zurich during 1918. One of the first pages of a 1917–18 sketchbook (figure 133) contains what is probably the first full compositional notation for this painting. Each of the three figures received further attention in other studies, but the final version of the work is quite similar to the sketchbook idea. In the oil the squatting couple is presented frontally with the baby—a boy—twisting sideways at its mother's feet. The trio is stacked in three non-receding levels which share the visual prominence of the foreground. The symbolic and compositional relation of the figures to one another overrides placement in depth. The baby (whose lower torso and legs are uncompleted[60]) is enclosed within the legs of its moher and the V-shape disposition of its body completes the large oval formed by the mother's figure. Both mother and child look off to the right, the baby alertly, the mother with with an introspective expression. Several pages in

Schiele's 1917–18 sketchbook are devoted to developing the pose of the child and the articulation of its head and face (figure 134). These studies of a vigorous and attractive baby agree in their sympathetic approach with Schiele's last-mentioned portrayal of his nephew, and are in marked contrast to the earlier depictions made at Dr. Graff's clinic of gruesomely wasted or dead babies. The man who once used to assert that he should not have children, because they would be born either idiots or geniuses, demonstrates in these tender studies a mellowed attitude.

As the baby's clothed form is contained within the legs of its mother, so the figure of the mother is framed within that of the father and husband. His angular, extended body is painted the same yellowish-brown hues as in the 1916 *Self-Portrait Squatting I*, while the mother's skin is tinted with rose and white, and the baby's face and hands are pink and gray. A certain separateness of identity, a melancholic non-communication, is present in these three interlocked figures. In contrast to the averted gazes of the mother and child, the father stares towards the beholder, although Schiele's use of the recessive eye indicates meditation as well as confrontation. The child's form receives and returns the downward thrust of the mother's oval shape, while the diagonal disposition of the father's figure creates an independent rectangle. The knee levels of the two upper figures trace a gentle rising zigzag which culminates in the father's extended left shoulder. The father's arms are in the broken or open position noted in the preparatory studies, and this compositional element contrasts with the linked continuity of forms in the mother and child. The dominance of the father's figure is secured by the gesture of his right hand which, held with bent thumb and V-shaped gesture against his chest, emphasizes himself. Schiele's psychological and compositional separation of the man (himself) from the unit which forms mother and child may perhaps be interpreted as paralleling actual family relationship during the first months following the arrival of a baby, rather than as an Expressionist comment on the conflict between the sexes.[61] Schiele's position behind the rest of the family also recalls an earlier theme in which his appearance behind a second figure conveyed the suggestion of creativity. It will be remembered that one of the interpretations offered for the row of Self-Seers in 1910–11 included this idea of the creator standing behind his created work, a second image of himself, just as the baby son is now an image of self.

Despite the universal theme represented by this "family," the picture is not devoid of details. In keeping with Schiele's new environmental portraiture two objects are introduced into the background: to the upper left is a chair and extending across the center of the picture is what appears to be a bed, but which is in fact the low sailcloth couch ("Lotterbett"), of Schiele's atelier.[62] Sitting on this the artist could work directly from his mirror.

It is interesting that Schiele did not endow the woman in *The Family* with the features of his wife.[63] Although the fact that Edith had grown too plump for Schiele's taste in nude portraiture accounts for the use of a model, it does not explain the absence of Edith's likeness in a painting whose the-

matic content deals with the concept of a family and in which the artist includes a self-portrait. The explanation surely lies in the fact that Schiele was
interpreting a "grandiose" and traditional theme rather than recording an
actual domestic situation. Edith did not become pregnant until the spring of
1918.[64] Schiele's selection of this particular model however still links her with
Edith once the "code" is understood. He had employed her before as the
actual physical model—with references to Edith—in *The Virgin* (plate 177).[65]
It should be observed that he did not use the more voluptuous model who had
been the subject of "Desire," and who had appeared with him in *The Embrace.*
The introduction into *The Family* of a model whom Schiele had previously
associated with virginity and purity follows a certain logic. The thematic
(and actual) transformation of virgin into mother agrees with the stereotyped
concept of woman as either mistress or wife—a concept related to the centuries-
old "prostitute-madonna" opposition. This assignation of two contrasting
roles to the female was to provide the basic motif for Schiele's final major
self-portrait.

There is no doubt that from its first inception Schiele intended to portray himself in *The Family*. It is in complete conformity with his egocentric
polar vision of himself to include self-portrayal as the generative force of a
universal theme. Nevertheless the artist's generalized physical appearance in
The Family no longer conveys the specified, violent emotions of the earlier
radical self-portraits. The preparatory studies, and there are many, of himself
for *The Family* indicate a new employment of the "typical" for the sake of an
advancement in technique. Two further drawings in the "squatting" series
may be examined briefly as illustrative of Schiele's late drawing style, which
abandoned the 1910 exploration and exploitation of the individual and instead
strove for the creation of types. The 1917 watercolor *Self-Portrait Squatting
II* (figure 131) exhibits early stages of this new tendency. While still conveying the individualized aspects of such features as the shoulders and knee,
the body silhouette is dominated by a sweeping contour which imparts equal
emphasis to all areas. The continuous, firm, and evenly applied line is used for
formal definition rather than expressive content. This single-minded purpose
is not obscured by a geometrized abstraction of individual areas such as had
characterized the 1914 "poster" self-portraits. The face is rendered in a stylized
formula with no particular expression given the features. The eyes do not
glance at the beholder-artist but gaze downward, reflecting attention. Such
individual features as the hands and feet are covered by the drapery or simply
cut off. There is no affirmative need to include the penis. This is not a drawing
of how an individual looks or feels but of how a figure appears in a certain
pose. The painterly approach begun in the 1916 *Self-Portrait Squatting I* is
intensified, with the plastic volumes of the body modeled by colored daubs
of green, red, and yellow. Hair on the legs and arms is not indicated by the
individual decorative lines of 1914 but by thick strokes of the chalk backed
by a blur of color. Even the hair of the head, formerly depicted by vigorous
strokes of the brush, partakes of the new modeling treatment: colors are put

to work against each other rather than simply applied at the same time, thus brown and blue-black indicate dips and risings of the hair rather than merely texture as formerly.

A second study for *The Family*, the 1918 *Self-Portrait Squatting III* (figure 132), shows the extent to which Schiele's generalizing figure contour has led, and at the same time determines the facial expression, as the artist prepares to transfer this particular pose to canvas. Without the benefit of subsequent watercoloring of highlights, the dry chalk operates as a coloring agent. After expressing the body silhouette in far more simplified terms than the 1916 or 1917 studies (note especially the wavering line of the raised left shoulder), the chalk is applied to numerous small areas in tonal strokes. The earlier line of 1910, which expressed "anatomical truth" to the extent of over-statement, is now used far more delicately and with a sense for pictorial "art-truth." The need to express has shifted from the act of expression to the means by which expression is achieved.

As finally executed in *The Family*, the figure of Schiele, by means of its quieter conception, lends a new importance to the face. A photograph of Schiele taken at this time (figure 128a) shows the artist as he appears in *The Family*: suddenly aged by overwork, solemn and alert, his eyes vital and aware. The self-portrait in *The Family* truthfully reflects this moving image: a mellowed Schiele who can contemplate his identity not only as one link in the eternal chain of life, but more specifically as husband and founder of a family.

The artist's separate images of self as lover and as husband had been formal-ized and formulated in two sizable paintings, *The Embrace* and *The Family* respectively. Schiele was irresistibly drawn to the idea of merging these two concepts, which so exactly mirrored his life, into a single work.

The large, unfinished painting, *Man and Woman* (plate 180), begun in 1917, was still incomplete (and untitled) at the time of Schiele's death in October, 1918. The lower half of the canvas is empty and has been thinly overpainted. In the upper part of the picture are the nude figures of a man and a woman. The man, bearing Schiele's features, lies on a level above the woman, with his right arm crossed over that of his partner. The unsatisfactory placement of the figures in relation to the picture surface, and the fact that it is an unfinished work, have caused the painting to be generally neglected by critics.

Schiele's sketchbooks provide the key to this mysterious work and its seemingly elusive theme. There is no doubt that the inevitable combination of the artist's two visions of himself as lover and husband was intended to be expressed in this painting. On a page from the 1917–18 sketchbook (plate 181) Schiele set off in a four-line "frame" a compositional drawing for *Man and Woman*. The man and woman in the painting are immediately recog-nizable and it is clear from this little sketch that a third figure, that of another woman, was also planned. Smaller than the others, she occupies the lower part of the picture but extends only half the length of the other figures. Is she supposed to be a child? The developed breasts contradict this. If not a child, such as in *The Family*, who does she represent? Schiele often drew female figures in imaginative compositions that were never realized on canvas. As early as 1915 he had mused over the idea of an Amazonian woman (plate 182) encompassing the slight frame of a male. In a sketchbook from the year 1918, on one of several pages devoted to little framed drawings of paleolithic and folk art motifs (plate 184), is the amusingly recognizable fat figure of the Venus of Willendorf. The presence of this figure suggests that at least some of the objects in these little sketches had been seen by Schiele at the Vienna Naturhistorisches Museum. A few pages later in the same sketchbook (plate 183), the obese Willendorf physique is found dominating a three-figure composition that intersects with another framed drawing for *Man and Woman*. This is the only appearance of a woman of such dimensions during the compositional formulation of the painting. Nevertheless the idea of several females of different body types is related to similar drawing in the 1917–18 sketchbook (plate 185). Here the male figure (or Schiele) seems to play the part of Paris, exposed to the attractions of three goddesses.[66] The delightful torture of this situation is intensified by the bonds that bind his arms to his chest—in Schiele's case perhaps the restricting fetters of matrimony. Two of these women are transferred to a compositional sketch for *Man and Woman* drawn in the upper left-hand corner of the same page. Here it can be observed that the figure of the second woman was first drawn only half-size and then redrawn in heavy strokes. Apparently Schiele altered this sketch only after several further considerations of the size and disposition of the second female figure. One of the first pages devoted to this painting in the 1918 sketchbook[67] reverses the direction in which the three figures lie. The second female figure is smaller but has the developed body of an adult. On the verso of this page (plate 186) Schiele repeated the new direction in which the figures lie and centered the body of the second female in relation to the embracing couple. It is interesting that sketches on the right-hand page of this notebook have first limited the number of "performing" or "temptress" females to two, and then to one. An entranced Schiele squats and claps his hand in private appreciation.

In this last examined compositional sketch for *Man and Woman*, the second female figure, who may be designated as the mistress image, has her arms raised behind her head and her legs spread open. This is a pose strongly reminiscent of that of the model with whom Schiele appeared as lover in *The Embrace*. The reappearance of her figure type (including the long dark curly hair) and pose in the sketches for *Man and Woman* supports an interpretation of the two female figures as representing two separate objects of love: mistress and wife.

To reinforce this theory the first female figure must also be identified. On further examination of the painting it is apparent that the model in Schiele's arms is the same model used for *The Virgin* and for *The Family*. In these two works the round face and apple breasts, resilient body and small pubic area of the woman are identical with those of the figure in *Man and Woman*, and in direct contrast to the full-breasted, complaisant mistress-figure in the sketches for the painting. The prototypes for the first female figure in *Man and Woman* are drawn from the model who represents a substitute for Edith, and whom Schiele has previously employed as personifying such irreproachable concepts as virginity and motherhood. Thus, the two female personae of *Man and Woman* derive their physical type and conceptual identity from two models who symbolized to Schiele opposing concepts of mistress and wife.

The combination of the artist's image of himself as lover and as husband in a single picture is verified by the figure of Schiele himself. Present not only in the painting but in all the compositional sketches, he has portrayed himself with a consistency of pose unmistakable in its implications. The physical relation of his lower torso, genital area, and upper thighs to the figure of his wife is one of emphatic non-contact. In progressive studies (plates 181, 185, and 186) Schiele's body is placed higher and higher, formally stressing the physical void between the two figures. In weird counterbalance his arms press tighter and tighter around the neck and shoulders of the woman sharing this sterile embrace. In further sketches in the 1918 sketchbook, as the mistress image becomes more precise, he essays departure from the wife figure,[68] then focuses on the compensation of a neck and shoulder embrace,[69] and develops this compositional solution in a final double-portrait study (plate 187). Here, as the relationship to the wife-figure assumes final articulation, the mistress-figure grows not only in size and spatial commitment but in gesticulative power as well. Four framed stick figure indications of the mistress (similar to the redrawn figure in plate 185) show her recumbent and full length with knees and head lifted as before, but with her elbows now supporting her raised back. The lower composition on the left-hand page reveals that Schiele at one time considered clothing the wife-figure.

Looking again at the painting *Man and Woman* for some physical indication of the entire theme as disclosed in the sketchbooks, a careful study of the lower half of the canvas reveals that a full-length female figure has been painted out. The figure—still visible under the paint—is as large as the other two and lies on its back in the same horizontal placement with its head to the far right. It is nude, the legs are separated, and the arms are stretched and bent behind the head. The mistress-figure did thus exist once on canvas. Why has it been painted over? Aside from the possibility that Edith, a real-life wife with real-life complaints, may have had something to do with the slow progress of this work, certain internal features suggest that the mistress-figure was never worked out in detail on canvas during Schiele's lifetime. The blotted-out figure is difficult to read, but enough details are discernible to reveal that it is clumsy and poorly proportioned. The legs are much too short for the long torso and appear almost deformed. The torso itself is painted in two ill-matching extended halves, whereas the arms are elephantine, with a coarse heavy contour foreign to Schiele's work. Furthermore, the steadily evolving conception of the figure lifting itself on its elbow, developed in the sketchbooks, is completely absent. The simplest pose has been adopted: that of a figure lying flat on its back. The separated legs are an unsuccessful substitution for the difficult-to-render raised knees of Schiele's conception, and are not even convincing on a two-dimensional plane when compared with the subtle modeling of the other woman's legs. It is not possible to ascribe the clumsily realized figure of the mistress to Schiele.[70] The fact that *Man and Woman* was abandoned by Schiele (probably after his March 1918 Secession success) indicates that the theme, compositionally solved and partially blocked out on canvas, simply held no more interest for him.[71] It is also conceivable that Schiele was affected by the prospect of his and Edith's expected first child and that a symbolical affirmation of his masculinity—as husband and lover—was no longer necessary.

PORTRAIT OF A FELLOW ARTIST: PARIS VON GÜTERSLOH

The last major oil portrait painted by Schiele may in a very real sense be considered a self-portrait statement and an assertion of Schiele's own identity as artist. Although depicting Schiele's good friend and neighbor in Hietzing, the painter Paris von Gütersloh (plate 188), the portrait is also, on a symbolic level, an homage to the Artist—the Artist who, as physical vessel of the creative flow, is set apart from other people.

The two painters had been friends ever since their mutual debut in the 1909 International Kunstschau. It was Gütersloh who had written the first study of Schiele, jumping into the psychoanalytic arena in defense of Schiele's painting *Delirium*.[72] Gütersloh had published his first book, an Expressionist novel titled *Die tanzende Törin*, in 1910, and his further literary activities included collaboration with Pfemfert in Berlin, an essay for the 1912 Piper collection of articles on Arnold Schönberg in which he discussed Schönberg as a painter, a second book, *Die Vision vom Alten und vom Neuen* in 1912, and the founding with Franz Blei of a socialist periodical *Die Rettung*, in 1918. His activities were not limited to art and literature however. He was also an actor and producer, and during 1911 and 1912 he had worked as scenic designer for Max Reinhardt. Schiele very much admired Gütersloh's multiple gifts.

Sketchbook notations (plate 189) for the portrait show that Schiele wished from the beginning to establish a pose that would signify the actual moment of artistic inspiration. The seated frontal figure with palms raised, drawn three times in the sketchbook pages, suggests the grave, erect figure of a Christ of the Last Judgment and there is something of this solemnity in the final oil *Portrait of Paris von Gütersloh* (plate 190). The artist sits in a tensed position, staring straight ahead and with his hands raised slightly above shoulder level. The right hand is shown palm out and the left hand, held slightly lower, is turned with palm inward. Like an electrical conduit, Gütersloh's gesture draws the beholder's attention into its own orbit. As though riveted upon some inner vision the eyes are widened with intensity. The puckered, tight mouth and furrowed brow reinforce this impression. In a lithograph (Kallir 16) and in numerous preparatory drawings,[73] one of which is reproduced here (plate 191), Schiele worked within this narrow formula to produce a facial expression of the greatest mental concentration, an appearance which Gütersloh had given himself in more than one self-portrait.[74]

To his own canvas Schiele communicated not only the highly pitched intellectual sensibilities of his gifted friend, but also a prominent physical feature, Gütersloh's crooked nose. A *Mirror Self-Portrait* (plate 192) by Gütersloh shows that he in no way minimized this Michelangelesque distinction; in fact he bestowed it upon others as a mark of spiritual rapport. Gütersloh's *Portrait of Egon Schiele* (plate 193), done as part of Schiele's project for mutual portraiture,[75] is an earnest and amusing case in point. Although Schiele's magnificent crop of hair is definitely his own, the twisted axis of his nose is a gift from the author of the portrait. The compliment is returned in Schiele's sketches of Gütersloh and receives a two-fold emphasis in the portrait oil through a continuation of the distorted axis in the wavering line of the flapping blue necktie (the movement of which also imparts a sense of creative energy).

The Gütersloh portrait is unfinished, but there is enough brushwork in the areas surrounding the figure to demonstrate that this would have been the most painterly of Schiele's portraits. The specific function of Schiele's coloration becomes clear when the Gütersloh portrait is compared with a kindred work, Kokoschka's *Self-Portrait* of 1917 (plate 194). Both portraits have rejected the excessive pantomime and contorted figure distribution of prewar times to concentrate upon a comparatively subdued but eloquent gesture. The thick meanderings of Kokoschka's loaded brush act architecturally to re-enact an inner turbulence on the body surface. Schiele's brushwork is commentary, not construction; his pigments do not become contours. He works instead to amplify the mood of the sitter. With a new freedom and signal verve Schiele's brush lays down incandescent areas of vivid yellow, gold ochre, carmine and vermilion reds which ignite the background into a glow that is reflected on the briefly sketched chair. The environment iterated with the greatest emphasis here is not one of physical objects but rather the flaming forge of the artist's own sparked imagination. The light brown shirt and trousers are shot through with luminous patches of white, and Gütersloh's figure shines out against a black, or "negative," body glow. This reference to the astral glow of 1910 (described in Gütersloh's monograph on Schiele as the "atmospheric pressure of human beings") points up the reappearance of Expressionistic qualities which link this, the most personal and subjective of Schiele's late single portraits, with the radical works of 1910.

Gütersloh's raised hands communicate that sense of tension, of duality and of non-resolution so frequently observed in Schiele's self-portraits. From an iconographical point of view, the gesture—which both attracts and repels, displays and conceals—breaks the sequence of portraits, dating from 1917, in which the hands were linked within the framework of a compositional oval.

It is significant that this single deviation from the ovoid pattern should appear in a portrait with which Schiele could so fully identify himself—that of an admired fellow artist. The double-V gesture is Schiele's, the luxuriant growth of hair is his, the lined, inquisitive forehead, and the slight, wiry frame are all attributes of the second image that forces its way into this sympathetic and (like the Schönberg sketches) deeply felt portrait. The Gütersloh portrait occupies a pivotal position in Schiele's oeuvre. The creation of a visionary atmosphere through the employment of dramatic posturing points back to the radical portraits of 1910, but the full somatic presentation of the sitter characterizes the later portraits, although the conversion of the surrounding void into a spiritual rather than material environment is a new feature. The undeniably Expressionistic rendition of Gütersloh suggests, I believe, that Schiele's future portraiture might have followed two separate and simultaneous courses: in the commissioned works a continuance of the "accepted" veristic presentation of the patron-sitter as defined by his setting; in the portraits of close friends and of self an intensified approach based on painterly form. This deliberate move from expressive content to expressive form characterizes all of the artist's later portrait work and may also be observed in his last land-scapes (e.g., *The Waterfall*, K.243).

Work on the Gütersloh portrait began as early as January of 1918 and was still in progress at the end of May, according to Schiele's calendar entries.[76] The painting was one of three portraits exhibited shortly after Schiele's death in the December 1918-January 1919 Secession show of contemporary portraiture—a show which Schiele had worked to organize.[77] As one of the very last works by the artist the Gütersloh portrait may be fruitfully examined within the context of this show. The painterly enforcement of Schiele's graphic approach to portraiture has been discussed and demonstrated. Just as the Gütersloh portrait sums up the past achievements of Schiele's art and points to its future course, so Schiele's place in Austrian Expressionism may be judged by a comparison of this portrait with other major entries in the Secession show. The jump in the exhibition's line-up from a shared German-Austrian Jugendstil to the local brand of Expressionism, with the prominent absence of any of the Brücke or Blaue Reiter representatives, accurately reflects the isolation of Viennese Expressionism from the mainstream of German Expressionism. For example, one of the two major German artists to be substantially represented in the show was the grand old dictator of Munich's flamboyant and vigorous Jugendstil, Franz von Stuck. The spirited subject of his *Portrait of a Lady*[78] sparkles darkly from the mysterious depths of her canvas with an elegance that must have vied with the two Klimt female portraits in the same show.[79] The other German master on exhibition was the Berlin-based Lovis Corinth, who can not be correctly labeled either as a Jugendstil or as an Expressionist artist. His *Portrait of Dr. Karl Schwartz*,[80] with its subtle commentary on the stability of the sitter's personality, marks Corinth as an important creator of that kind of psychological portrait more readily associated with Kokoschka. Except for these distinguished outsiders, the majority of artists listed in the Secession catalogue were local Viennese. The impressive silhouette and empty characterization produced within the Jugendstil format by artists such as the now forgotten Hermann Grom-Rottmayer (1877–1953) in his *Portrait of a Lady*[81] provided instructive contrasts to the more talented but equally facile portraits of Emil Orlik, as in the latter's *Portrait of Eugen D'Albert*.[82] The realist Viktor Hammer, whose portrayal of Arthur Roessler I have contrasted with Schiele's, exhibited fifteen portraits in various media, and Egger-Lienz was represented by two Hodleresque portraits. Hugo von Bouvard, who had once painted the sister of Schiele's subject Friederike Beer, also exhibited. Several of Schiele's Academy colleagues, such as Josef Dobrowsky, Harta, and Faistauer, were well represented. The entries of Harta and Faistauer revealed solid painterly talents that on the whole rejected Expressionist tendencies. Kokoschka's policy of boycotting Viennese exhibitions[83] explains the absence of his paintings in this one, although several works by a promising but obscure artist, Edmund Pick-Morinó (b.1877) were reminiscent not only of Kokoschka but also, in use of powerful, half-defined forms, of Gerstl, whose works had been hidden away in storage and were generally unfamiliar in 1918.

The profound characterization, impassioned execution, and arresting spiritual quality of the *Portrait of Paris von Gütersloh*, as judged alongside the other Secession show entries, revealed Schiele not only as an artist of sustained force and originality but also as a fairly entrenched "old master" of Expressionist portraiture in Vienna.

FINAL IMAGES

The Vienna Secession exhibition of March 1918 was given over to a one-man show of Schiele's paintings. The event was a definite success. Five works, including three portraits, were sold for prices ranging from 3,000 to 5,000 Kronen.[84] Schiele wrote the following enthusiastic report to Peschka:

"On opening day, and especially on Sundays, our exhibition was so well attended that it was hard to walk around. One saw only enthusiastic or shocked people who blocked the paintings."[85]

Newspaper critics who had previously delighted in calling Schiele the "Freud-student" and in analyzing his portraits as examples of "dementia praecox" now almost all found nothing but compliments for the genius in their midst.[86]

Commissions poured in: decoration of the Burgtheater, portraits (fourteen commissions by October, including one from the wife of the Saxonian ambassador), illustrations for a newly founded art periodical, *Der Anbruch*, and the request and funds from a local graphic arts society for two lithographs.[87] Schiele was recognized by his colleagues as the first artist of the city (Klimt had died in February) and was entrusted with the organization of group shows for Austria and abroad. In May the Arnot Gallery gave Schiele a large graphic show,[88] and prices for his drawings trebled. With enough money for the first time in his life to do as he wished, Schiele moved into a garden house with a two-story studio at Wattmanngasse 6, near the Schönbrunn zoological garden,[89] and even hired a personal secretary to handle his growing business correspondence. He envisioned projects for making stained-glass windows and monumental frescoes, and spoke of opening a school for artists. Edith was expecting their first child. The perpetual rumors that the war would soon be over seemed at last to have foundation. Never had Schiele had so much for which to live. Never had his prospects been better or his spirits more buoyant.

The enthusiastic reception of Schiele's work at the March 1918 Secession could not have been foreseen. There was no assurance of success when Schiele designed a publicity poster for the exhibition showing himself with a group of his friends seated around a table. This final self-image is, therefore, of extraordinary interest and assumes special significance within the artst's long row of self-portraits.[90]

The idea for the poster had long been in Schiele's thoughts. In January of 1917 he had written Peschka:

"I intend to do a large figure painting, with all my closest friends, life size, seated at a table."[91]

The theme was evidently abandoned until later that year or at least the beginning of 1918 when the artist took it up again in the form of a large painting (K.244) and a small painted design on cardboard (K.239). A sketchbook page (plate 195)[92] shows the idea worked out in some detail. The chairs pushed out at different levels, the L-shaped table with a single figure at its head, and the earthenware vases are carried over into the lithographed Secession placard, *Round the Table (The Friends)* (plate 197). Nine figures of monkish bearing and dress are seated in high-backed wooden chairs, each absorbed in the books or papers in front of him. The youngest is the slim young man at the head of the table. In contrast to the cropped, bald, or tonsured heads of most of the others, he has a full head of hair. He is, of course, Schiele.

The eleven chairs in the poster have personal significance for the artist. They are duplicates of the two high-backed wooden chairs with arms that he had designed and built for his studio, and in which most of his later portrait sitters were shown.

The four water pitchers or jugs on the table represent a class of objects which had always held a certain mystique for Schiele. They are recurring objects in his work, beginning with the days at Neulengbach, where they appear with both happy and painful connotations (*The Artist's Room in Neulengbach*, K.149, and the prison drawing, "Organic Movement of the Chair and Pitcher").

Two of the chairs in *Round the Table* are, significantly, empty, and one of them occupies a place of honor directly opposite the figure of Schiele. The death of Klimt had greatly shocked Schiele. On the morning of 11 January, while dressing, the older artist had suddenly been felled by a stroke which left his right side paralyzed. Hospitalized, (two days later his unguarded studio was broken into and robbed) he lingered on for a few weeks, but died on 6 February 1918 at the age of fifty-six. The following day Schiele went to the hospital morgue and made three portrait sketches of the emaciated corpse (plates 198a, 198b, and 198c). The newly shaven face revealed the previously bearded Klimt in a way he had never shown himself in life.[93] Schiele's calendar entry for 9 February shows an appointment notation for Viktor Ritter von Bauer struck through and the name Klimt written in large letters with the time of his funeral.[94] For the issue of *Der Anbruch* dated 15 February 1918 Schiele contributed a terse epitaph:

Gustav Klimt
An artist of unbelievable perfection
A man of rare depth
His work a shrine[95]

The empty chair opposite Schiele's own in *Round the Table* may, I believe, be understood as symbolizing the missing friend and artist.[96] Close study of the lithographic poster copies reveals in fact the scrawl of Klimt's distinctive signature faintly indicated on the right-hand page of the book in front of the empty chair. The partly shown book or manuscript in front of the second empty chair (to the right) has no "signature" and the identity of the person it might represent can only be conjectured.[97]

The symbolic reference to Klimt leaves no uncertainty concerning the professional identity of the nine figures around the table. They are artists, and their monkish garments set them apart from society—a theme dear to the heart of Schiele. Schiele not only sits among them but at their head. In *Round the Table* Schiele has turned aside from images of himself as lover and husband and has returned to the self-confident conception of himself as an artist in the 1909 *Two Men* (figure 25)—this *before* his success at the March Secession exhibition. The self-affirmation is thus not the antiphonal product of society's capricious recognition.

What is the character of Schiele's identity assertion in *Round the Table?* Is the ascetic garb and the inclusion of his colleagues, physically and symbolically, a protective gesture? Does he require the presence of other artists to reinforce his own social identity? The poster's close relation to another projected work suggests the answer. The (wine?) jugs which appear with such prominence in *Round the Table* are also seen in a strikingly related composition from the 1918 sketchbook (plate 196). This sketch appears above yet another compositional formulation of *Man and Woman* and shows several men kneeling and facing each other across a long table. This is not another version of the Secession poster, but a study for one of Schiele's rare religious projects, a Last Supper. Heinrich Benesch records that Schiele was planning a monumental rendition of this theme and that when he visited the artist at the new Wattmanngasse studio, which had a ceiling some twenty feet higher than the Hietzinger Hauptstrasse atelier, Schiele had already stretched and set up the canvas for this painting.⁹⁸ The crude single-plane rendition and ascetic appearances of the figures in the sketch are very similar in spirit to the Secession poster. The jugs are common to both. It is interesting to note that Schiele had introduced such earthenware vases once before in connection with another religious project, a Deposition.⁹⁹ The salient inclusion of these jugs in *Round the Table* strengthens the placard's kinship with the projected Last Supper painting. Schiele has allowed all the implications associated with a Last Supper prominent manifestation in *Round the Table*. He does not take refuge in the company of his colleagues, but sits, in Christ's place, at their head. He is their leader, their chief. He shows himself not only as an artist, a public figure, and social leader, but also as the spiritual master of an elite group. Schiele's self-portraiture has run the full gamut from hermit to monk to martyred saint to Christ. In his own words: "I am the most perfect of the perfect; I am divine!"¹⁰⁰ The psychic injury inflicted by the Neulengbach crisis had altered but never diminished Schiele's egocentric self-esteem. This ultimate step in what might appear to be paranoid grandiosity follows the classical development of that "dementia praecox" or schizophrenia which Schiele's critics had so facilely professed to read in the "Freud-student's" paintings. However, as with Gauguin's earlier self-portrait equations of himself with Christ, such "paranoia" is perhaps more securely attributable to knowledgeable, artistic license. The 1918 *Round the Table* poster, with its Christ-identification implications, is not only the logical outcome of the proud self-esteem manifest in the 1909 *Two Men*, but actually a welcome indication of the artist's basic mental health. If the Expressionist psyche had become the new façade of World War I, so Schiele's identity as "artist" was at last publicly exposable as *both* façade *and* psyche for this lavishly gifted, totally self-centered, frustrating, and, in spite of himself, sympathetic young man of twenty-eight years.

*   *   *

The new Wattmanngasse garden atelier was large and difficult to heat. October of the year 1918 brought an unusually severe winter and the great influenza epidemic that ravaged Europe during the last months of the war spread to Vienna. Coal and oil were almost impossible to obtain. Schiele wrote his company commander begging for an allotment of coal. The townspeople scoured the Vienna woods for branches and twigs to burn. Schiele cancelled business appointments in the city and forbade Edith, now in her sixth month of pregnancy, to leave the protective isolation of their home. The number of influenza deaths multiplied and in some cases streetcars were converted into public hearses. On 26 October Edith came down with the dreaded infection and developed pneumonia also. On the evening of the 27th Schiele took his moribund wife in his arms and held her through the night, kissing her repeatedly. In a desperate gesture to arrest her ebbing spirit, he sketched her portrait as she lay on the pillow (plate 199a). He then placed a pencil and paper in Edith's hands and in her last moments of consciousness she wrote a tragically disjointed message (plate 199c) of her love for him:

"27 October 1918.
I love, I love you unendingly and always *more* boundlessly and . . . lessly your Edith"[101]

At eight o'clock in the morning Edith died. Schiele had already contracted the influenza from her and the next day was unable to remain on his feet. He was put to bed in the Harms house, where Adele also lay ill with the same virus. Four days later, as Edith's funeral cortege passed his window, Schiele was in his death agony. He died during the night of 31 October-1 November at one o'clock in the morning. His last words were: "The war is over . . . and I have to go. Mama!"

During the next three days Schiele's friends came to see his body on the deathbed. He had suffered severely in the last days, but Dr. Graff gave him sedation during the final hours, and his death was easy. The hand of his raised left arm pillowed his head, and the right arm lay naturally across his breast. The anguish of his self-portraits was erased; his face was calm. Schiele's last portrait (plate 200) was drawn with tenderness by death.

        *   *   *

If Schiele could have left a last portrait of himself it might well have been these words of his, written before the Neulengbach imprisonment in 1911:

"Sooner or later there will arise a belief in my pictures, writings, and words which I speak rarely but most concentratedly. My pictures up to now are perhaps but prologues—I don't know. . . . Those who believe that painting is something in itself are mistaken. Painting is an ability. I am thinking of the warmest colors next to each other, colors which blend, melt away, break, appear in relief. A bumpily laid-on sienna with green and gray and beside it a blue-cold star, white, white-blue. . . . The painter also can look. To see however is something more."[102]

Notes

DR. OTTO KALLIR's two Schiele oeuvre catalogues form the groundwork upon which any study of Egon Schiele must build. These two works are: Otto Nirenstein (-Kallir), *Egon Schiele; Persönlichkeit und Werk* (Vienna, 1930), and Otto Kallir (-Nirenstein), *Oeuvre Katalog der Gemälde*, 2nd ed., revised (Vienna, 1966), and henceforth referred to in notes and text of this book as "Kallir, *Oeuvre Catalogue.*" The 1930 edition documents paintings of Schiele's lost in two world wars, and the carefully revised edition of 1966 includes those Schiele's which have come to light in recent years that are accepted as genuine by Kallir.

Rudolph Leopold, a Viennese opthalmologist and important collector of Schiele, has published a catalogue raisonné of Schiele's work (*Egon Schiele: Gemälde, Aquarelle, Zeichnungen*, Salzburg, 1972). Regetably, it was issued too late for consideration in the text of this work, but is referred to in these notes as: Leopold, *Catalogue Raisonné*. Leopold accepts a greater number of works than does Kallir, especially among the early landscapes, and a concordance of the two oeuvre numberings for Schiele paintings referred to here follows the plate section of this book.

All references to paintings in these notes are to the second edition of Kallir's oeuvre catalogue unless otherwise specified, and the notation "K." followed by a number indicates the Kallir oeuvre numbering in the second edition of his catalogue.

INTRODUCTION: *The Expressionist Shift from Facade to Psyche* (pp. 1–7).

1. Isadora Duncan, *My Life* (New York, 1927), p. 151.
2. See Fritz Stern, *The Politics of Cultural Despair* (New York, 1965), for an illuminating discussion of the phenomenal success in Germany and abroad of Langbehn's book *Rembrandt als Erzieher*, first published anonymously in 1890, and consequently sold in over forty printings by the end of 1891.
3. Friedrich Nietzsche, *Schopenhauer as Educator*, trans. by James W. Hillesheim and Malcolm R. Simpson (Chicago, 1965), pp. 4–5.
4. Mary Wigman, "Composition in Pure Movement," (1946) in *The Creative Process*, ed. Brewster Ghiselin (New York, 1952), pp. 78–80.
5. Karl Kraus, *Die Fackel*, Nos. 251–52 (Vienna, April 1905), p. 34. Kraus has finally received a sympathetic and long overdue introduction to the English-

speaking world in Frank Field's informative study, *The Last Days of Mankind: Karl Kraus and His Vienna* (New York, 1967).

6. Shortly after Makart's death in 1884 Rudolf von Alt set himself the task of recording the artist's extraordinary studio for posterity. His painting of Makart's studio (1885) is in the Historisches Museum der Stadt Wien, Vienna.

7. Romako's importance for later Viennese portrait painting is treated by Hans Bisanz in "Edvard Munch og Portrettkunsten I Wien etter 1900," *Arbok for Oslo Kommunes Kunstsamlinger 1963*, pp. 1–43.

8. This concept is formulated and analyzed at length by Carl E. Schorske, "Politics and the Psyche in Fin de Siècle Vienna: Schnitzler and Hofmannsthal," *American Historical Review*, LXVI:4 (1961), 940–44.

9. Alma Mahler, *Gustav Mahler: Memories and Letters*, trans. by Basil Creighton (Seattle, 1968), p. 98.

10. The fascinating and long-suppressed story of Freud and Tausk is given full account by Paul Roazen in his book *Brother Animal* (New York, 1969).

11. Kraus, *Die Fackel*, No. 1 (April 1899), p. 1.

12. "Jede Ausschmückung der Information verfälscht sie." Quoted by Paul Schick, *Karl Kraus* (Hamburg, 1965), p. 54.

13. "Die herdenmenschen mußten sich durch verschiedene farben unterscheiden, der moderne mensch braucht sein kleid als maske. So ungeheuer stark ist seine individualität, daß sie sich nicht mehr in kleidungsstücken ausdrücken läßt. Ornamentlosigkeit ist ein zeichen geistiger kraft." [*sic*] Adolf Loos, *Sämtliche Schriften*, ed. Franz Glück (Vienna, 1962), I, p. 288.

CHAPTER I: *1890–1909: Childhood and Student Years* (pp. 9–27)

1. Schiele's grandfather possessed a substantial talent for drawing. An impressive portfolio of his student drawings of architectural and engineering projects is in possession of Gertrud Peschka, Vienna. In this collection are studies of the Erechtheum, the Pantheon, contemporary house façades, groundplans, and waterworks, all rendered with minute detail.

2. Egon Schiele's paternal grandfather was Ludwig Schiele (1817–1862). His son Adolf (1850–1905) married Marie Soukup (1862–1935) and his daughter Marie (1853–1937) married Leopold Czihaczek (1842–1929), who became Egon's legal guardian in 1905. The first daughter of Adolf and Marie Schiele, Elvira, lived only ten years (1883–1893), Egon lived twenty-eight years (1890–1918), and the two other daughters, Melanie (b. 1886) and Gertrud (b. 1894), are still alive at the time of this writing (1973).

3. This information comes from Melanie Schuster, personal interview, Vienna, 12 January 1967.

4. The two Schiele sisters Frau Melanie Schuster and Frau Gertrud Peschka, both live in Vienna. For simplification they will be referred to in the text simply as Melanie and Gerti.

5. "Die bildhaft nackwirkenden Eindrückle der Kindheitszeit empfing ich von ebenen Ländern mit Frühlingsalleen und tobenden Stürmen. Es war mir in jenen ersten Tagen, als hörte und roch ich schon die Wunderblumen, die sprachlosen Gärten, die Vögel, in deren blanken Augen ich mich rosa gespiegelt sah. Oft weinte ich mit halben Augen als es Herbst war. Wenn es Lenz war, träumte ich von der allgemeinen Musik des Lebens, alsdann freute ich mich über den herrlichen Sommer und lachte, als ich in seinem Prangen mir selbst den weißen Winter malte. Bis dahin lebte ich in Freude, in wechselnd heiterer und wehmütiger Freude, dann begannen die Mußzeiten und die leblosen Schulen.

Volksschule in Tulln, Realgymnasium in Klosterneuburg. Ich kam in schier endlos und tot scheinende Städte und betrauerte mich. In dieser Zeit erlebte ich das Sterben meines Vaters. Meine rohen Lehrer waren mir stets Feinde. Sie—und andere—verstanden mich nicht." Arthur Roessler, ed., *Briefe und Prosa von Egon Schiele* (Vienna, 1921), pp. 18–19. (Henceforth referred to as *Briefe and Prosa*.) The following year Roessler published *Erinnerungen an Egon Schiele* (Vienna, 1922). (Henceforth referred to as *Erinnerungen*; citations in the notes refer to the 2d ed., 1948.)

6. The Klosterneuburg studies are preserved in the Niederösterreichisches Landes-Museum in Vienna. A present-day view from the same window shows an almost identical scene, except for the growth of trees, and is testimony to the extraordinary exactitude with which Schiele worked.

7. This and a second pencil sketch of Strauch at work were among the drawings left to the Niederösterreichisches Landes-Museum from the Strauch estate in 1955. This museum is an important deposit for the early works of Schiele and also contains works by Klimt and Kokoschka.

8. Compare Ludwig K. Strauch's painting, *My Family*, reproduced in the catalogue of the *3. Kunstausstellung des Vereines heimischer Künstler Klosterneuburgs*, 1914, item 40. This catalogue also contains reproductions of works by another of Schiele's Klosterneuburg friends, Max Kahrer.

9. I am indebted to Dr. Rupert Feuchtmüller, director of the Niederösterreichisches Landes-Mueum, for first bringing my attention to the existence of these two works. Although the Strauch *Madonna and Child* reproduced here is dated 1946, and could not therefore have been the actual prototype for Egon's work, it is wholly typical of the older painter's sugary naturalism which was so adamantly rejected by Schiele.

10. These expressive devices appear first in Schiele's town and landscapes of 1907–1909, especially in the paintings of individual autumn trees and sunflowers, both of which functioned for him almost in the capacity of self-portraiture, so great was his lifelong attachment to these two motifs.

   A second interesting comparison of similar subject matter treated by Schiele and Strauch can be seen in their separate paintings of a holiday crowd in the town square: Schiele's *Before the Feast of St. Leopold in Klosterneuburg* (K.16, 1907) and Strauch's version of the same event, *ca.* 1907 (Niederösterreichisches Landes-Museum, Inv. No. 72). The composition is basically the same, with a single viewer, placed in the lower left foreground, observing a crowd gathering on the other side of the street. Strauch's rendition is that of a heavy-handed Impressionism, whereas Schiele's focuses much closer and emphasizes the separation which the street creates between the viewer (a young boy) and the crowd. Again mood (loneliness) and surface composition characterize Schiele's work.

11. "... [er war] immer draußen auf den Wiesen, an den Hängen, an den Bächen und zeichnete Blatt auf Blatt, meist Pastell—Natureindrücke. Er zeichnete still und unentwegt, als gäbe es nichts als Natur, Bleistift und Zeichenpapier, sein schmales, ernstes Gesicht mit den dunklen Augen unbeweglich, die schwarze, nach rückwärts gekämmte Haarmähne bis auf den Rockkragen fallend. Ein seltsam stiller Bursche, nicht scheu, aber durchaus nicht gesellig, etwas maniriert in der Art, wie er seine langen Hände ineinanderlegte, ... Im Kreise der Verwandtschaft reichte man ihn als Wunderkind herum." This description was printed in a newspaper article preserved in the Albertina Egon Schiele Archive (abbreviated henceforth as A.E.S.A.). The article is from the *Neue Freie Presse*, 1927 (publication date not preserved with the clipping).

12. "Durch die gefällige Überlieferung Ihres Herrn Bruders Hans teile ich Ihnen

in einigen Zeilen mit, wie fleißig ich an den einzelnen Werker für unsere zukünftige 'Union-Kunstausstellung' arbeite. Wenn ich längere Zeit zu diesen Zeichnungen und Malereien hätte, würde ich sehr gerne das Dreifache leisten. Ich nahm mir seit unserer gemeinschaftlichen Besprechung vom 28. d. M. vor, pro Tag je 5 Werke herzustellen. Ich bitte Sie freundlichst, an unserem Vorschlag festzuhalten, damit unser Zukunftsplan zum Lobe für uns und zum Ruhme . . . Stadt Klosterneuburg ausfalle. Ferner ersuche ich Sie, wenn es Ihnen möglich ist, in eine Buch- oder Kunsthandlung zu gehen, um Preiskurante oder solche Bücher, wo bessere Bilder sich befinden, vielleicht zu bekommen. Vereint soll bleiben der Dreibund, es muß und wird geschehen. Heil Ihr tr. Compagnon Egon Schiele." Roessler, *Briefe und Prosa*, p. 151.

13. Gertrud Peschka, personal interviews, Vienna, 3 March 1967 and 21 September 1971, and Melanie Schuster, personal interview, Vienna, 6 September 1963.

14. One of these sketches, done about 1908, is in the possession of Melanie Schuster, Vienna, and shows Gerti from the back, nude, standing with legs spread, and pubic hair emphasized. Melanie stresses her brother's unnatural affection for their younger sister during their adolescent years, casting herself as the responsible, sober breadwinner of the family. However, she admits that she also posed in the nude for her brother. Personal interview, Vienna, 19 September 1963. Gerti freely acknowledges her own nude posing, and has verified the 1910 *Female Nude Standing* (K.110) as a portrait of herself. Personal interview, Vienna, 18 February 1967.

15. "Haben die Erwachsenen es vergessen, wie verdorben, d.h. sexuell-triebhaft an- und aufgeregt sie selbst als Kinder waren?—haben sie vergessen, wie die fürchterliche Leidenschaft in ihnen brannte und quälte, als sie noch Kinder waren?—Ich habe das nicht vergessen, denn ich habe entsetzlich darunter gelitten." Roessler, ed., *Egon Schiele im Gefängnis* (Vienna, 1922), p. 33.

16. See Schiele letter to his brother-in-law, Anton Peschka, 12 July 1913, Roessler, *Briefe und Prosa*, p. 102.

17. Schiele wrote a description of this vision on a post card from Krumau, dated 25 August 1910, collection Gertrud Peschka, Vienna. No portrait sketch of his father has been preserved.

18. According to Melanie Schuster, personal interview, Vienna, 27 August 1966. Thus Schiele was fourteen when his father died, not fifteen as sometimes recorded.

19. The Klosterneuburg school records show that an announcement of intention to withdraw was made on 29 May 1906, and that Egon left at the end of the term, 9 July 1906. Thus he completed only three grades, having had to repeat the First Class.

20. One of Schiele's anatomy exercise tablets from this period is in the A.E.S.A. It is entitled "Fragen und Antworten aus der Anatomie" and has an Ex Libris design drawn by Schiele.

21. A draft law of 5 July 1912 permitted those who could submit proof of higher education to enter the Army with the status of "Einjährigfreiwilliger" (one-year volunteer). On 23 October 1913 Schiele asked for a Certificate of Attendance and received a Triennium diploma on 1 May 1914. (Both documents are in the A.E.S.A.)

22. Many of Schiele's charcoal copies after the antique are preserved in the collections of his sisters. They are almost without exception head or limb studies only, and thus preclude positive identification of the specific plaster casts which served as models.

23. With the exception of the Titian *Tarquinius and Lucretia* (acquired in 1907), all the paintings listed in the text still bear the old inventory numbers (of

1891–1910) in the latest catalogue of the Academy (*Katalog der Gemälde Galerie*, Vienna, Akademie der Bildenden Künste in Wien, 1961).

24. Schiele's personal copy of this brochure is preserved in the A.E.S.A. The category "Guest" is underlined in pencil throughout, and indeed he was so classified during his first two years at the Academy. He changed to "regular student" in his final year, 1908–1909. "Guests" were defined as those who partook of instruction in one of the Schools on a temporary basis. They had the same rights as regular students except that they were not eligible for school stipends or prizes.

25. In the A.E.S.A.

26. Further progress along these lines may be observed in a second charcoal self-portrait signed and dated later the same month: 22 September 1906 (Collection Harry Fischer, London; reproduced in the Fischer Fine Art Limited catalogue *Egon Schiele* [London, November–December 1972], p. 9).

27. Collection Melanie Schuster, Vienna.

28. There is an interesting parallel to this precocious conduct in the life of Arthur Rimbaud, who was shortly to become Schiele's favorite poet. During the first three hours of an interschool competition for the Latin poetry prize the fourteen-and-a-half-year-old Rimbaud sat sulkily at his desk without writing a word. Suddenly he penned eighty lines of prize-winning Latin. See Rimbaud, *Collected Poems*, trans. by Oliver Bernard (Baltimore, 1962), p. xxxii.

29. Reported by Ludwig K. Strauch in "Egon Schiele Erinnerungsbuch," 23 September 1950, A.E.S.A.

30. A second oil self-portrait of this type is in the Collection Melanie Schuster, Vienna. It is not accepted in either the original or revised Kallir *Oeuvre Catalogue*.

31. Dated 31 July 1909. In the A.E.S.A.

32. As early as 1907 Schiele was trying his hand at designing title pages for *Jugend*. One of these sketches shows a half figure of Gerti in profile and is inscribed "Jugend 1907 Nr." Formerly Collection Wolfgang Hainisch, Vienna.

33. One of the many laudatory articles on the Wiener Werkstätte published in Alexander Koch's Darmstadt-based *Deutsche Kunst und Dekoration* reproduced photographs of the showroom as it appeared in 1907. See *Deutsche Kunst und Dekoration*, XX:2 (1906–1907), 328–33, *passim*.

34. The *Guardian of Paradise*, hand-titled by Schiele in Secession-style characters and dated 6 May 1907, is in the Collection Gertrud Peschka, Vienna. On the left is a large-winged angel and at the right an old man begging entrance (to Paradise). Various shades of purple have been splattered on the paper. *The Source*, also hand-titled and dating from the same year, shows a female nude beside a waterfall in a forest setting, and is also in the Collection Gertrud Peschka, Vienna.

35. The old man from Klimt's *Jurisprudence* (Dobai 128) is in Schiele's *Guardian of Paradise* (note 34), and a variation on the huge *Philosophy* (Dobai 105) "mask," with a similar relationship to the much smaller human forms, occurs in an untitled watercolor in the Collection Melanie Schuster, Vienna. This somewhat awkwardly executed picture is of two nude young people, a boy and a girl, each with long wind-blown hair. The boy, seated at the right, gazes at the girl, on the left. Long wavy snake-like lines extend across the picture and wrap themselves around the body of the girl. Behind the two figures an enigmatic female mask of large proportions stares straight ahead.

36. For an example of Max Kahrer's poster art see the catalogue, *Wien um 1900*, Kulturamt der Stadt Wien, 5 June to 30 August 1964, plate 61. Schiele's copies

of individual issues of *Ver Sacrum* were formerly in the possession of Melanie Schuster, Vienna.

37. Schiele's little picture, done on canvas, represents, at the far left, a woman with a lute, and, at the right, a large, very decorative tree. Collection Gertrud Peschka, Vienna. The Klimt supraporta designs (Dobai 69 and 89) were reproduced in *Ver Sacrum*, I: 3 (1898), 19, and Nos. 5–6, p. 25. Land- and townscapes dating from *ca.* 1907 in the collections of both sisters reveal that Schiele was also studying the pseudo-pointillistic surface treatment and stacked horizontal planes of Klimt's landscapes.

38. See Schiele's letter of 27 November 1910 to Arthur Roessler, Roessler, *Briefe und Prosa*, p. 47, and two transcriptions of letters to Roessler in the A.E.S.A., the first not dated (probably 1910) and the second written 4 January 1911.

39. A pair of gay multi-striped women's high heeled shoes designed and painted by Schiele for the Wiener Werkstätte is in the A.E.S.A. Three color post cards were published in 1910 (Nos. 288–90), one a portrait of Gerti. For other post card designs, see below, note 48. In 1913 Schiele obtained a modeling position for Gerti in the Wiener Werkstätte's fashion department.

40. The complete list of Klimt entries in the 1908 Kunstschau, as given in the exhibition catalogue, p. 47, is: (1) "Drei Alter," (2) "Liebespaar," (3) "Porträt der Frau Geheimrat R.," (4) "Porträt der Frau A.B.," (5) "Porträt der Frau St.," (6) "Pergament," (7) "Freundinnen," (8) "Rot und Schwarz," (9) "Buchenwald," (10) "Bauerngarten," (11) "Rosen," (12) "Sonnenblume," (13) "Blühender Mohn," (14) "Apfelbaum," (15) "Danaë," (16) "Wasserschlangen." Drawings by Klimt were also on exhibition. For the most complete treatment of the 1908 Kunstschau see Christian M. Nebehay, *Klimt Dokumentation* (Vienna, 1969), Chapt. XXX, especially pp. 393–415. Joseph A. Lux wrote an extensive review of the Kunstschau in *Deutsche Kunst und Dekoration*, XXIII: 1 (1908–09), 33ff. (see especially pp. 48–49 for Klimt). In Schiele's effects at the time of his death was a reproduction of Klimt's *Portrait of Frau Margaret Stonborough-Wittgenstein* (Dobai 142) identified in his handwriting as "Frau Wittgenstein." It shows an earlier state of the portrait in which the background and dress are not as ornate as in the final version (reproduced in Nebehay, *Klimt Dokumentation*, p. 412).

41. This canvas (K.65) is one of the most interesting early Schieles to come to light since publication of the 1930 edition of the *Oeuvre Catalogue*. Its discovery confirms the earlier dating for Klimt's influence on Schiele proposed here and corroborated by the many 1907 and 1908 sketches after Klimt themes or paintings found in the collections of Schiele's sisters.

42. This study is a pencil drawing in the Collection Melanie Schuster, Vienna. It is a full-figure frontal presentation of Pallas Athena, with upper torso and raised spear arm in the same pose as that of Klimt's *Pallas Athena* (Dobai 93). The head is drawn a second time with emphasis on the helmet. Two specific features from the Klimt original are included: the small female statue and the grimacing archaic Greek face-disc worn as a breast medallion. The drawing is signed and is dated 1908. Schiele may have copied from the original or from a reproduction of it published in the 1898 special edition of *Ver Sacrum*, p. 2.

43. A colored pencil sketch for some of the background elements in *Danaë* (K.92) exists in a private collection, U.S.A. A second, very detailed drawing of the background motifs with color notations and two framed figure compositions, one of them sized for transfer to canvas, exists on the verso of a 1910 nude female watercolor (Inv. No. 30996) in the Albertina. I am grateful to the director, Dr. Walter Koschatzky, for allowing me to examine and photograph the versos of Schiele drawings in the Albertina (some of them previously pasted to their mats).

44. Concerning the books on Japanese art in Klimt's library see Alice Strobl, "Bemerkungen zur Ausstellung Gustav Klimt," in the Albertina Catalogue *Gustav Klimt und Egon Schiele zum Gedächtnis ihres Todes vor 50 Jahren* (Vienna, 5 April–16 June 1968), pp. 16–17. (Henceforth referred to as *Albertina Catalogue Klimt-Schiele.*) For Schiele's library on Oriental art, see below, Chapter III, note 48.

45. A photograph of these masks as displayed at the Kunstschau appears in *Deutsche Kunst und Dekoration*, XXIII:1 (1908–09), 68.

46. The ornate cover for a collection once owned by Schiele of twelve woodcuts by Japanese masters still exists; possession Melanie Schuster, Vienna.

47. Otto Benesch was the first to identify these figures as Klimt and Schiele. This identification (expressed in conversation only) was published by Erwin Mitsch, *Egon Schiele, Zeichnungen und Aquarelle* (Salzburg, 1961), p. 5. Mitsch however misinterprets the drawing tablet and support as part of Klimt's garment.

48. Three other pen and wash drawings in this same series of Wiener Werkstätte designs are preserved in the Albertina. One depicts a Christ child giving a blessing and standing on a flowery pedestal whose decorative nodules are repeated in the clothes and hair of the figure; the second is of two wrestling lads; and the third shows two monks (not Klimt and Schiele) below a rigid figure resembling a crucified Christ.

49. The prominence of the theater in the life of the cultured middle class in the Vienna of the early 1900s is described by Stefan Zweig in his autobiography, *Die Welt von Gestern* (Stockholm, 1944).

50. K. 5, 6, 7, 52, 53, and I (lost).

51. The verso of a 1910 portrait study of Arthur Roessler in the Albertina (Inv. No. 31170) contains a particularly fine watercolor sketch of Czihaczek seated with legs apart, hands on his knees, holding a cigar and wearing a hat. It is signed and dated 1908. During the years 1910 and 1911 Schiele's extreme poverty and lack of drawing material often drove him to use the verso of a completed drawing or watercolor for a new work.

52. The same device is applied in two similar female portraits of the same year, K.10 and K.11 (sitters not identifiable).

53. A characteristic example is the colored-pencil profile sketch of Melanie reproduced in the Felix Landau Gallery Catalogue *Egon Schiele* (Los Angeles, 1967), figure 10. (Henceforth referred to as *Landau Catalogue Egon Schiele.*) The drawing is not identified in the catalogue and bears the initials and date "ES '10" in a strange hand. Stylistically the drawing dates from around 1907.

54. By her own account Melanie was a fanatic when it came to hats. Whenever she had completed a new creation she went at once to a photographer to have it recorded. When the family was living in Klosterneuburg, the photographer did the work gratis, using the finished pictures as fashion advertisements in his show window (personal interview, Vienna, 6 September 1963). The Schiele interest in documentation of self was not therefore limited to Egon.

55. This pencil and black chalk study is in the Collection Gertrud Peschka, Vienna.

56. Aside from the visual evidence, both sisters have confirmed in personal interviews the identification proposed here.

57. Melanie says she lent Gerti her own fur piece for the painting and that she made both the hat and coverlet (personal interview, Vienna, 27 October 1966).

58. Compare especially with two standing female portraits by Klimt: the 1902 *Portrait of Emilie Flöge* (Dobai 126), and the 1905 *Portrait of Frau Margaret Stonborough-Wittgenstein.*

59. The painting is reproduced here in its original state, as it is in Kallir, who points out the change in background since 1930. Now the background is silver, shot

with pinks, blues, and whites, with pinwheel-like ornamentations. In the 1930 edition of the *Oeuvre Catalogue* Dr. Kallir interprets the coat as being open, revealing a colored, patterned dress beneath, but close examination of the photograph of the painting in its original state, and of the same unchanged areas in the painting today, reveals that the coat is buttoned up (the top button of the right-hand row of double buttons is clearly visible, and that it is Melanie's ornamental coverlet and not a dress which shows the colored patterning.

CHAPTER II: *1909-1910: Toward Artistic Independence* (pp. 29-48)

1. One of the two persons identified in this drawing is the painter Anton Kolig (1886-1950). He did not leave the Academy with Schiele and his friends, but continued his studies until 1912. He married the sister of another artist and friend of Schiele, Franz Wiegele (1887-1944), who also did not withdraw from the Academy, but was one of the original members of the Neukunstgruppe founded by Schiele.

2. Quoted in full by Arthur Roessler, *Der Maler Anton Faistauer* (Vienna, 1947), pp. 15-16. The objections voiced in this critique had long been in the air. A dissatisfaction with the tradition-locked methods of the Academy had been expressed in a long editorial entitled "Die Reformierte Akademie," published in *Ver Sacrum*, II:8 (1899), 26-30. In his 1903 history of Austrian art, the perceptive critic, Ludwig Hevesi, predicted a new Austrian art which would shake off foreign influences, old and new, and find its own idiom. "Sie will sich nicht mehr italienisch ausdrücken, aber auch das Englische wird nicht ihre Muttersprache werden." ("It will no longer express itself in Italian, but neither will English become its mother tongue.") (*Österreichische Kunst im 19. Jahrhundert*, Vol. 2, Leipzig, 1903, p. 282).

3. The contract reads:

   "Unterschriebene Maler u. Bildhauer verpflichten sich die im Dezember 1909 im Salon der Herrn G. Pisko vorgesehene Ausstellung ausreichend zu beschicken (mit mindestens 6 Bilder[n]); bei der Strafe der Deckung, eines, Herrn Pisko eventuell erwachsenden Schadens im Falle dieselbe nicht zustande kommen kann." ("The undersigned painters and sculptors pledge to send a sufficient number of works to the exhibition planned for December 1909 in the Salon of Mr. G. Pisko [a minimum of 6 pictures] to cover any possible loss occurring to Mr. Pisko in case the exhibition can not materialize.")

   The signatures, so far as they are legible, read: "Schiele Egon, Arthur Löwenstein [with a note obligating himself to present some of his musical works at the exhibition], Canelari[?] Fritz, Franz Wiegele, Adamschik Sepp, Hans Ehrlich, Anton Peschka, Hans Schachinger, Lazar Dreacik[?], Erwin Osen Maler für Theater-Kunst, Tony [Anton] Faistauer, R. Pillersdorfer, H. Freudsberger[?], Hans Massmann, Karl Zakovsek, Rud[olf] Csmarich[?]."

   In a sketchbook of 1910 Schiele referred to the "current exhibition at Pisko's" in an essay on the meaning of the terms "Neukunst" and "Neukünstler"; see Roessler, *Briefe und Prosa*, pp. 17-18.

4. In my judgment this is the earliest instance of Schiele's complete application of Klimt's seated portrait formula with the figure disposed to one side of the main axis. Schiele also made sketches in this format for an unrealized portrait of Czihaczek (see my commentary published in Christian M. Nebehay, *Katalog Egon Schiele, Frühe Werke und Dokumentation*, XIV [Vienna, April 1968], item 2, reproduced figure 2, and item 3, p. 4). These Czihaczek drawings are compositionally related to the Peschka and Massmann portraits and may be dated slightly later than the Faistauer portrait sketch.

5. Schiele had also considered a standing pose for the portrait of Faistauer. A pencil and pastel sketch with a square grid for transfer to canvas shows Faistauer standing in profile with hands clasped in front and one leg indicated, Marlborough New London Gallery, London, reproduced in the catalogue *II. Internationale der Zeichnung* (Darmstadt, 1967), p. 339; not identified as Faistauer.

6. The Faistauer *Self-Portrait*, a charcoal drawing of *ca.* 1909, is in the collection of the Gemälde Galerie der Akademie der Bildenden Künste, Vienna. For another portrayal of Faistauer at this time, see the portrait (present location unknown) by Paris von Gütersloh reproduced in Arthur Roessler, *Kritische Fragmente* (Vienna, 1918), p. 59.

   Schiele's early friendship with Faistauer later cooled, although they remained in professional contact. Faistauer was jealous of Schiele's presidency in the Neukunstgruppe and tried to undermine his authority. Schiele himself was quite devoid of jealousy of his colleagues. The collector Heinrich Benesch recorded Schiele's earnest answer when Benesch mentioned that he would like to buy a painting by Faistauer to supplement the many Schiele works he had already acquired. Schiele responded, "Yes, one should certainly own a Faistauer." (Heinrich Benesch, handwritten essay entitled "Mein Weg mit Egon Schiele," dated November 1943, in the album compiled by Max Wagner, "Egon Schiele Erinnerungsbuch" [pp. not numbered], A.E.S.A. Hereafter referred to as "Mein Weg mit Egon Schiele." This essay was eventually published as a book by Dr. Otto Kallir under the same title [New York, 1965], slightly expurgated; see Chapter V, note 22.) Later, speculating on which of his friends would come to help him if they knew he was in trouble, Schiele wrote disapprovingly in his prison diary (Roessler, *Egon Schiele im Gefängnis*, p. 8) about Faistauer's "Jesuit" manner. After Schiele's death Faistauer wrote a book, *Neue Malerei in Osterreich; Betrachtungen eines Malers* (Vienna, 1923), in which he devoted chapters to both Klimt and Schiele. A gifted colorist of conservative tastes, Faistauer did not remain with the avant-garde group around Schiele but devoted himself to a more traditional style of painting. His book contains remarkable comments on the Expressionist movement: "Die sogenannte expressionistische Bewegung, von Kandinski begründet, ist eine östliche Angelegenheit. . . . Die Juden, insbesondere die Ostjuden—an der Sozialrevolution am stärksten beteiligt—erscheinen als die Hauptträger des Expressionismus." ("The so-called Expressionist movement, founded by Kandinsky, is an Eastern affair. . . . The Jews, particularly the eastern Jews—most deeply involved in the social revolution—appear as the main carriers of Expressionism.") *Ibid.*, p. 26.

7. Heinrich Benesch, "Mein Weg mit Egon Schiele."

8. A second study for the Massmann portrait is in the Collection Rudolf Leopold, Vienna (reproduced *Albertina Catalogue Klimt-Schiele*, figure 132). This drawing is the closest to the portrait and has a square grid for transfer to canvas. The face and hands are heightened by watercolor.

9. Donald Gordon gives a partial listing of the forty-five Van Gogh works shown in the January 1906 exhibition of the Miethke Gallery ["Kirchner in Dresden," *Art Bulletin*, XLVIII (1966), 339, n. 26]. Because of the possible value for future study of "Van Gogh and Vienna" I cite the entire list as described in the Miethke catalogue below, along with the gallery's indication of which paintings were for sale (signified here with an asterisk): (1) "Knabenkopf,"* (2) "Platz in Auvers,"* (3) "Erdgräber,"* (4) "Orangen mit Blumen" [added by hand, "Blühende Mandelbäume"], (5) "Feld mit kleinem Haus,"* (6) "Viadukt in Arles,"* (7) "Mohnfeld,"* (8) "Hutten in Auvers,"* (9) "Botte," (10) "Getreidefeld,"* (11) "Hospital,"* (12) "Schlucht,"* (13) "Garten,"*

(14) "Grünes Korn,"* (15) "Garten in Asnières,"* (16) "Strohhütte in St. Maries," (17) "Kleine Häuser in Auvers,"* (18) "Mann mit der Pfeiffe,"* (19) "Arlesierin,"* (20) "Blühender Baum," (21) "Sonnenblumen," (22) "Landschaft," (23) "Boulevard in Arles," (24) "Eisenbahnbrücke," (25) "Landschaft," (26) "Gehölz,"* (27) "Landschaft b. Auvers,"* (28) "Ein Park,"* (29) "Blick auf Montmartre,"* (30) "Porträt eines Zouaven,"* (31) "Porträt,"* (32) "Porträt," (33) "Trauben,"* (34) "Frau,"* (35) "Absynth,"* (36) "Seine-Ufer,"* (37) "Sonnenuntergang üb. d. Rhone,"* (38) "Boulevard Extérieur,"* (39) "Ernte in der Provence,"* (40) "Knabenporträt,"* (41) "Das Paar am Waldesrand,"* (42) "Porträt,"* (43) "Mohnblumen,"* (44) "Olivenhain,"* (45) "Hof des Irrenhauses in Arles."*

I am most grateful to Dr. Alice Strobl of the Albertina, Vienna, for her kindness in relaying to me the contents of the Miethke catalogue.

10. Listed in the 1909 International Kunstschau catalogue as "Das Schlafzimmer," "Olivenhain," "Die Amme" (reproduced in the catalogue), "Hospital in Arles" (reproduced in the catalogue), "Sonnenuntergang über der Rhone," "Ruderboote," "Frauenkopf," "Blumenstück," "Die Trinker," "Porträt," "Sonne."

11. Richard Gerstl, who refused to have his paintings exhibited alongside any works by Klimt, is an exception.

12. Adolf Loos, "Ornament und Verbrechen" in *Sämtliche Schriften*, I, pp. 276–88.

13. The composition and subject matter of this lost painting are not known. Schiele's sisters cannot recall it, nor could I find any of the other still-living visitors to the 1909 exhibition who retain any memory of this work beyond the fact that it was an allegory. It may be presumed that the painting was similar in style to the Klimtian *Fairytale World* (K.65), painted the year before (see Chapter I, note 41).

14. See Chapter V, below, visit to the Lederer family.

15. The only extant example is *Still Life with Pineapple* (Wingler 3), *ca.* 1907, Dahlem Museum, Berlin.

16. De La Faille 484. One of three versions.

17. Roessler, *Egon Schiele im Gefängnis*, p. 21. See further Chapter IV, my article, "Egon Schiele in Prison," *Albertina Studien*, No. 4, (1964), 123–37, and my book, *Schiele in Prison*, Greenwich, 1973. Schiele knew Van Gogh's copy (de La Faille 669) of the Doré engraving from his personal copy (formerly in the possession of Melanie Schuster, [Vienna] of Julius Meier-Graefe's monograph, *Vincent van Gogh* (Munich, 1910), where it is reproduced full page on p. 35. Schiele greatly admired Alfred Roller, and Beethoven was his favorite composer.

18. Fernand Khnopff, whose paintings and sculptures were shown by the Secession in its first (1898), second (1898), seventh (1900), and eighth (1900) exhibitions, was featured in the December 1898 issue of *Ver Sacrum*. His powerful thematic as well as formal influence upon Klimt would make a rewarding study.

19. The 1910 November–December Secession exhibition, "Die Kunst der Frau," included two Kollwitz etchings identified as "Frau mit totem Kind" (item 270) and "Schwangere Frau" (item 271). Klimt had already treated the theme of the pregnant woman in his two daring versions of *Hope*, exhibited in the 1909 Kunstschau, and Schiele made several powerful nude studies of pregnant women in 1910.

20. Many of Schiele's 1910 female nude watercolor studies exhibit Lautrec's arbitrary color, selective line, and unusual angle of view. A notable example of this influence on Schiele is a 1910 watercolor portrait of Gerti (clothed),

entitled *The Spiteful Girl (Die Hämische)*, Collection Gertrud Peschka, Vienna.

21. December 1903–February 1904, nineteenth Secession exhibition. This was a group show and included works by Cuno Amiet, Axel Gallén, Hodler, Hans von Marées, and Jan Thorn-Prikker as well as the twenty canvases by Munch. This was not the first time that the Vienna Secession had shown Munch; in November–December of 1901 two paintings were included in a review of Scandinavian art, and in the November–December exhibition of 1902 three etchings were shown. Again in January of 1904 Munch graphics were featured. In the opening months of 1912 just before Schiele's own one-man show at the same gallery, the Hagenbund presented eleven paintings and thirty-one graphics by Munch (including the *Alpha and Omega* series) in a group show of Norwegian artists. In the International Schwarz-Weiß exhibition held in Vienna in 1913, Schiele had the satisfaction of seeing some of his own drawings next to five graphic works by Munch.

22. Among Vienna's budding Expressionists only Richard Gerstl would have been old enough to have received a direct impression from this important exhibition. Gerstl was twenty in 1904 and a student at the Academy, Kokoschka was seventeen and majoring in chemistry at high school, and Schiele was only thirteen and still in Klosterneuburg.

   The nineteenth Secession catalogue reproduced two of Munch's figure paintings: *Portrait of the Four Linde Boys*, 1903 (item 33), and *Death and the Child (The Dead Mother)*, 1899–1900 (item 51). Schiele may have seen this catalogue by the time he painted his *Portrait of Herbert Rainer* (K.106) and his *The Dead Mother I* (K.115), both at the end of 1910 (see plates 58 and 69).

   Ludwig Hevesi, informative and usually astute historian of the Vienna Secession gives a curiously unenthusiastic report on the Munch works in the 1903–1904 exhibition (*Acht Jahre Sezession* [Vienna, 1906], p. 459).

23. Especially striking is the similarity in formal pictorial aims between Munch's canvas *Fertility, ca.* 1898 (item 50 at the 1904 Secession show), and many of Egger-Lienz's peasant-in-nature pictures. Of the four Munch paintings in the Vienna Kunsthistorisches Museum (*Park in Kösen*, 1906; *Bathing Men at the Sea*, 1907; *Summer Night at the Shore*, ca. 1902; and *Double Portrait of the Painter Paul Hermann and Dr. Paul Contard*, 1897), none was acquired before 1916. Thus Munch was not on public display in Vienna except for the Secession-sponsored exhibitions. *The Summer Night at the Shore* was formerly in the collection of Alma Mahler, where Kokoschka may have had occasion to study it.

24. An interesting local precedent also existed for Kokoschka's treatment of the man-woman conflict. The 1899 December edition of *Ver Sacrum* featured poems and drawings by Ernst Stöhr (1860–1917) concerning this same theme. One of Stöhr's drawings shows a wild-eyed woman vampire crouching over the prone, weakly protesting figure of a man. The accompanying text (pp. 8–9) runs:

   "Was lockst Du mich zur süssen Lust / Mit rothem, dunklem Mund? / Ich sink' an Deine heisse Brust— / Ach! Küsse mich gesund! / Wie brennt Dein Mund so fieberheiss / und loht in wilder Glut! / Mein armes Leben ist der Preis / Du trinkst mein Herzensblut."

   ("Why do you entice me to sweet lust / With your red, dark mouth? / I sink onto your hot breast— / Ah! Kiss me that I may get well! / How your mouth burns as in hot fever / And blazes in wild fire! / My poor life is the price / You drink my heart's blood.")

Hofmannsthal's play *Elektra* (1903) is another possible influence on Kokoschka's play.

25. Kubin was also influenced in this respect by the works of Beardsley, Ensor, Rops, and Klinger. The 1905 Paris meeting with his hero Redon further strengthened his lifelong fascination by the sinister and mysterious. His remarkable autobiography, *Die andere Seite*, published in 1909, provides, along with Kokoschka's early plays, yet another instance of the contribution to Expressionist literature by the Austrian Expressionist artists.

26. This small oil, *ca.* 1907, formerly in the Collection Melanie Schuster, Vienna, (not listed in Kallir) shows a young girl in profile, leaning against a tree and staring out to sea at the sunset.

27. Known to us only by description. See Otto Benesch's essay, "Memories of Paintings by Egon Schiele which are No Longer Existent" (hereafter referred to as "Memories"), in Kallir, *Oeuvre Catalogue*, pp. 63–64; and Otto Benesch, *Edvard Munch* (London, 1960), p. 26–27.

28. Ludwig Goldschneider, *Kokoschka* (Greenwich, 1963), p. 10.

29. An interesting written description by Waerndorfer of Minne's appearance, character, and impecunious working conditions is quoted in Friedrich Haack, *Die Kunst der Neuesten Zeit* (Stuttgart, 1925), p. 398. See also *Deutsche Kunst und Dekoration*, XXV:1 (1909–10), 244.

30. See the feature article on Minne by the art critic Arthur Roessler, soon to be Schiele's most articulate champion, in *Deutsche Kunst und Dekoration*, XXV:1 (1909–10), 241ff. See Haack, *Die Kunst der Neuesten Zeit*, p. 398.

31. De La Faille 477.

32. Moll's painting was exhibited in the 1908 Kunstschau.

33. Most favorably reviewed in the short-lived and little-known but important art periodical, *Hohe Warte* (*The Watch Tower*), II:3 (1905–1906), 48. This exceptionally spirited magazine was issued twice monthly by the distinguished writer Joseph August Lux, with active collaboration by Josef Hoffmann, Peter Altenberg, Alfred Roller, Koloman Moser, and Arthur Roessler, from 1904 to 1908. It was intended as the Austrian response to the English arts-and-crafts movement, and featured articles by Frank Brangwyn and Charles Mackintosh. Further important contributions were by or about Otto Wagner, Joseph Olbrich, Henry van de Velde, Peter Behrens, Hermann Obrist, and August Endell.

34. See Chapter I, note 48. Schiele's Wiener Werkstätte post card design of two wrestling boys was possibly inspired by Minne's figure group of the same subject.

35. See Chapter IV, plate 96, *Woman in Mourning*. "Die Trauernde" was the German title of Minne's 1886 statue of a mother mourning her dead child (Puyvelde 2) and an 1888 statue of a mother mourning two children (Puyvelde 5). It must be noted that the Leo van Puyvelde oeuvre catalogue (Brussels, 1930) is incomplete.

36. Klimt also borrowed heavily and sometimes literally from another sculptor, Auguste Rodin, one of the heroes of the Viennese Secession circle. The full extent of Klimt's debt to Rodin (especially as regards quotations from *The Gates of Hell*) has yet to be determined.

37. "Warum könnte nicht eine große internationale Kunstschau im Künstlerhaus sein?—Ich habe dies dem Klimt erzählt. Zum Beispiel: jeder Künstler hat seinen eigenen Saal oder sein eigenes Zimmer.—Rodin, Van Gogh, Gauguin, Minne, die letzten zehnjähr . . . Klimt, Toorop, Stuck, Liebermann, Slevogt, Corinth, Mestrovič usw. Nur *bildende* Kunst. Welch ein Schrei für Wien!—Katastrophe!" Letter of 1910 (not dated, probably November) to Arthur Roessler, Roessler, *Briefe und Prosa*, p. 47.

38. Some informative sketches for the oil exist. The earliest appear to be two pencil drawings (signed and dated 1909) formerly in the collection of the Oddone Tomasi family of Trento. Tomasi (1884–1929) was a colleague of Schiele's at the Vienna Academy. The first drawing, quite faint, is the most "naturalistic" of the series and is a simple profile study of the seated Gerti, placed according to the Klimt formula to one side of the central axis of the paper while the hands stretch across to the other side. Her thin dress is not pulled down over her shoulders in this drawing. The second Tomasi sketch again places the figure to one side but the body is now frontal. (For reproduction of the first Tomasi sketch, see Nebehay, *Katalog Egon Schiele, Frühe Werke und Dokumentation*, figure 5.) A more worked-out version of the frontal pose with head in profile, used in the final painting, is owned by Gertrud Peschka, Vienna. In this black and red pencil drawing, also signed and dated 1909, Gerti is shown with black high-laced shoes, and her body appears almost squat in comparison with its elongation in the painting.

39. This first compositional notation appears on the verso of a 1910 female nude watercolor in the Collection Otto Manley, Scarsdale, New York.

40. These portraits are listed in reverse order in Kallir and are identified as *Self-Portrait* (1909) I (K.90) and *Self-Portrait* (1909) II (K.91). Stylistic and conceptual advances prompt the chronology I have suggested in the text. The larger, more ambitious scale of the *Self-Portrait Nude* (K.90) would also indicate a later dating.

41. But see Kallir, *Oeuvre Catalogue*, p. 188, for notes on the original dimensions of the *Self-Portrait Nude* (K.90), which was initially some four inches wider.

42. With two exceptions Schiele was always clean-shaven. He grew a moustache for a few months at the end of 1909, apparently after his participation in the International Kunstschau, and again for a period during 1911–1912.

43. Other Klimt prototypes of this sort are the large allegory, *Three Ages of Life* (Dobai 141), exhibited in the 1908 Kunstschau (in which the spent, sagging figure of an elderly female nude appears, also in profile), and the 1903 version of *Hope*, showing a nude, red-haired, pregnant female, shown in the International Kunstschau (see above note 19). The "ugly" in Klimt, and its influence on other painters besides Schiele, have yet to be studied and should prove fruitful.

44. Richard Gerstl's impressive *Self-Portrait as Partially Nude Model* of about 1908 must also be considered in the light of this Klimt heritage. In its central, frontal wedging of the figure with its astral body glow into an unornamented but worked surface-void, Gerstl's portrait anticipates many of the salient features of the Expressionist portraiture of Kokoschka and Schiele.

45. One of these is a quick sketch set down on a sheet of polka music, Collection Gertrud Peschka, Vienna. Another is a watercolor study in the possession of the Kornfeld and Klipstein Gallery, Berne. This watercolor shows Schiele standing with a purple drape falling in tectonic folds down the front of his body. His left arm is raised and the hand twines back around the neck.

46. "Daß in unseren Tagen just ein Zeichner Schiele heißt, ist wohl kein Zufall. Er schielt noch nach Dingen, nach denen andere schon schauen. Zum Schielen aber ward eben just dieser Schiele eingesetzt." Unsigned review of Schiele's work in the *Österreichische Volkszeitung*, 2 November 1917 (A.E.S.A.).

47. A specifically sexual interpretation has been offered by Dr. Robert Kantor of Atherton, California, who, in conversations with me during the summer of 1967, interpreted the V-shaped spread of Schiele's fingers as a representation of the vulva and the enlarged eye as a reference to a testis. Some chapters in Paul Schilder's book *The Image and Appearance of the Human Body* (New York, 1951) offer corroboration for such an interpretation. Providing a Freud-

ian explanation of Schiele's imagery of 1909–18 is, it seems to me, not only presuming upon a not yet (at that time) fully formulated Freudian orientation, but is also unfairly yoking a nineteenth-century moralist with a twentieth-century hedonist.

48. The "soapy" application of pigment and the thin pencil contour, both characteristic of Schiele's 1911 style, suggest that the watercolor study of Kahrer is the later, chronologically. A third 1910 study of Kahrer exists in a private collection in Vienna and is entitled "Vision Max Kahrer." I have not had an opportunity to examine this work.

49. See the chapter "Ein wahrhaft guter Kollege" in Roessler's *Erinnerungen*, p. 27 and pp. 50–51.

50. "Wenn er sich doch wenigstens wehren wollte! Sich gelegentlich gründlich austoben wollte! Aber er tut das nicht . . . wehrt sich nur durch passive Duldsamkeit. . . . Armer, lieber Kerl!" *Ibid.*, p. 51. Roessler's paraphrase of this outburst includes the phrase: "Dazu ist er, der überzeugte Sozialdemokrat, persönlich zu vornehm, zu duldsam." ("He, the convinced social democrat, is personally too genteel, too tolerant for that.") Schiele's political interests and comprehension were slight and of a naïvely idealistic nature [personal interviews with his sisters, sister-in-law, and his friends Otto Benesch, Erich Lederer, and Mrs. Federica Beer-Monti; and see his ingenuous speculations on a world community in his *War Diary*, transcribed in my article, "Egon Schieles Kriegstagebuch 1916," *Albertina Studien*, IV:2 (1966), 86–102]. The epithet "überzeugte Sozialdemokrat" smacks more of Roessler, who was a critic for the *Arbeiter Zeitung*, than of Schiele. It should be strongly pointed out that either through elaboration or omission Roessler frequently edited the reminiscences and quotations from Schiele which he presented to the public.

51. Faistauer, *Neue Malerei in Österreich*, pp. 11–19.

52. The *Portrait of Poldi Lodzinsky* is dated 1908 by Kallir in the second edition of the *Oeuvre Catalogue* (p. 156). In the first edition the painting was placed in the year 1910 (N.61) with the notation that it was signed later. For stylistic reasons I can not agree with Dr. Kallir's 1908 dating. A preparatory study of this painting, *Girl with a Scottish Shawl*, was formerly in the Collection Erwin Neubauer, Vienna. It too displays the graphic style characteristic of Schiele's 1910 work.

53. Werner Hofmann gives a similar interpretation of the Poldi Lodzinsky portrait in *Egon Schiele—Die Familie* (Stuttgart, 1968), p. 20.

54. The Van Gogh portrait is reproduced on p. 73 of the Meier-Graefe monograph. See also note 17 above.

55. For an interesting confirmation of the impression made by Peter Altenberg, with his double aspects of bungling helplessness and sly humor, compare the portrait (almost a caricature) of him done in bold Secession style by Gustav Jagerspacher and formerly hung in Adolf Loos's Kärntner Bar of 1907.

56. For the fullest discussion of the influence of theosophy on Kandinsky (and on Mondrian) see Sixten Ringbom, "Art in 'The Epoch of the Great Spiritual'— Occult Elements in the Early Theory of Abstract Painting," *Journal of the Warburg and Courtould Institutes*, XXIX (1966) 386–418.

57. In Vienna Steiner's local circle of devotees met at the home of the theosophist Marie Lang. As an indication of the widespread interest in theosophy and its theorists in Vienna at this time, it is interesting to note that Alma Mahler wrote Annie Besant in 1914 asking her to accept her as a student in Sanskrit; see Alma Mahler-Werfel, *And the Bridge is Love* (New York, 1958), p. 78.

58. Schiele could discourse at length on this feature of theosophy, picked up probably indirectly through his well-read colleague, Paris von Gütersloh, who

may have been exposed to Steiner's work through his contact with Kandinsky and the Munich circle. Schiele's most important written statement concerning the astral body light is contained in a lengthy manifesto-style letter of September 1911 to his patron Dr. Oskar Reichel (see Chapter IV, "Solitary Self-Portraits of 1911"). Cf., Chapter V, note 40.

59. Gütersloh's 1910 essay on Schiele's painting, "Versuch einer Vorrede," was used as the text for a little monograph, *Egon Schiele*, published in 1911 (Vienna). This essay was republished in the book edited by Arthur Roessler, *In Memoriam Egon Schiele* (Vienna, 1921), pp. 24–29.

60. Mopp's description of their first meeting and the resulting portraits also mentions that Schiele's pictures were painted with backgrounds of applied tinfoil, see his book *Menschen Finden Ihren Maler* (Zurich, 1938), pp. 34–35.

61. Mopp also included a portrait of Schiele in an allegorical painting of the same year, 1910, entitled *Descent from the Cross*. This painting (present location unknown) contained portraits of Heinrich Mann, Peter Altenberg, Karl Kraus, Tilla Durieux, and a self-portrait as well. A photograph of the painting is in the A.E.S.A.

62. Schiele's hint of Mopp's fastidiousness, and the peculiarly effeminate quality of Mopp's portraiture, observable in his oil of Schiele and also present in his early portraits of Peter Altenberg (plate 27a), Heinrich Mann (plate 56), Adolf Loos, Oskar Reichel, Arthur Schnitzler, Ferruccio Busoni, and Arnold Schönberg (figure 122), perhaps reflect Mopp's own sexual preferences. It is doubtful however whether Mopp was ever one of the models for Schiele's watercolor studies of paired male homosexuals.

63. *The Zouave* had been exhibited in the 1906 Miethke Gallery show (item 30; see note 9 above.

64. A second version of this portrait exists. It shows Peschka asleep, wearing the same hat, with his head tilted to one side, arms folded across his chest, and legs spread apart; pencil and watercolor, in the possession of the Kornfeld and Klipstein Gallery, Berne (misidentified as a self-portrait).

65. For further comparison of Bouvard and Schiele see Chapter V. note 51.

66. Schiele took over Osen's studio for a while in June of 1912 because it was the cheapest one available. By July of the same year he was already writing Roessler about the great disappointment he had suffered at the hands of Osen (who, apparently, cheerfully signed his name to Schiele's drawings and sold them as his own), see Roessler, *Briefe und Prosa*, pp. 69–70. Roessler's account of Osen, identified rather transparently as "Mr. Naso," in an essay entitled "Begegnung mit dem Abenteurer," was contributed to a book edited by Fritz Karpfen, *Das Egon Schiele Buch* (Vienna, 1921), pp. 73–80. This brought on a successful lawsuit by Osen and thus the revised edition (1948) of Roessler's 1922 book, *Erinnerungen*, while listing this chapter in its table of contents, deletes it in the text. This incident is characteristic of the intricacies attendant on all aspects of Schiele research and publications. See also Chapter V, note 22 concerning suppression of material on Osen.

The best characterization of the controversial Osen is given by himself in the following spirited letter to Schiele (original in the A.E.S.A.):
"Lieber Egon Schiele!
Leider ist es schon am 1 Sept. zu kommen mir unmöglich, da ich in Wien furchtbar viel zu erledigen habe. . . . Willst DU denn Besuch riskieren? Dann muß ich in Wien noch ein Porträt fertig machen und einige Zeichnungen auf dem Steinhof für den Naturforscher Tag, wo Dr. Kronfeld spricht, über den pathologieschen Ausdruck im Porträt. . . . Ich simmuliere schon alle Krankheiten damit ich früher los komme. . . . Also jetzt kommt der Alte Pump auf **DEINE WELTBEKANNTE** Menschenfreundlichkeit: Ich kann mir

in Wien kein Atelier soffort [*sic*] nehmen weil ich dann nach Prag und Berlin in kurzer Zeit muß und auch das Subjekt das ich noch malen muß, nur bis 14. Sept. in Wien bleibt. Da bitte ich Dich, möchtest Du mir erlauben, das ich im Vorzimmer, am Clos oder wo in Deiner Gotterburg, das Ungeheuer porträtiere. . . . Herzlichst, Dein Osen 1913"

("Dear Egon Schiele!

"Unfortunately it will be impossible for me to come as soon as Sept. 1, since I have terribly much to do in Vienna. . . . Do YOU then want to risk a visit? Besides I still have to finish a portrait in Vienna and a few drawings at Steinhof for the "Science Day" where Dr. Kronfeld will be speaking on the pathological expression in portraiture. . . . I am already simulating all diseases so that I may get away sooner. . . . So now the old sponger comes to the subject of YOUR WORLD-FAMOUS philanthropy: I can not immediately rent a studio in Vienna, since I will have to go to Prague and Berlin shortly, and also because the subject whom I still have to paint will be in Vienna only until Sept. 14. I beg you, therefore, to permit me to paint the monster in the entrance hall, the toilet, or anywhere else in your sacred castle. . . . Most cordially, Your Osen 1913")

67. Stimulated by Osen's admiration of the poet, Schiele bought the Insel publication, *A. Rimbaud, Leben und Dichtung* (Leipzig, 1907). This book is still in the possession of Gertrud Peschka and contains Schiele's enthusiastic underlinings of the "color" phrases, such as "Sah silberne Sonnen" in the poem, "Das Trunkene Schiff" (*Le Bateau Ivre*), pp. 174–77.

It is interesting that the name of Rimbaud was cited in connection with Kokoschka to explain the "disturbing" quality of the latter's precocious entries in the 1908 Kunstschau; see Edith Hoffman, *Kokoschka, Life and Work* (London, 1947) p. 38.

In an anecdote about how Kokoschka used to earn his meals as a student by reciting fantastic stories to restaurant customers, Arthur Roessler refers to the influence of Rimbaud's *Le Bateau Ivre* on Kokoschka's narrative style; see *Der Malkasten: Künstler-Anekdoten* (Vienna, 1924), p. 91 and hereafter referred to as *Der Malkasten*.

68. Osen sometimes earned a living by mime performances in cabarets. See also the reference to a lecture on the pathological expression in portraiture in his letter cited above, note 66.

A black gouache portrait of Osen, nude, and seen from the back, dated 1910 has recently been acquired by the Niederösterreiches Landes-Museum in Vienna, and a second watercolor study of Osen, nude, with elbows raised, also dated 1910, was formerly in the Collection Melanie Schuster, Vienna.

69. Undated and unidentified Viennese newspaper clipping (*ca.* January 1910) in the A.E.S.A. A favorable review published in *Die Graphischen Künste*, XXXIII:2–3 (1910), 55, discussed Schiele's "suffering bodies of the modern city dweller."

70. Max Mell, personal interviews, Vienna, 23 July 1963 and 26 February 1967. A poster design for the Neukunstgruppe Pisko exhibition, drawn by Faistauer on a narrow cardboard panel and showing a mysterious, gothicized frontal half-figure is in the possession of Gertrud Peschka, Vienna.

CHAPTER III: *The Radical Portraits and Self-Portraits* (pp. 49–78)

1. The order in which they were painted is not known. I believe a fragment of a fourth painting related to this row of large nude self-portraits of 1910 may

be seen on the verso of the 1915 portrait, *Edith Schiele Standing* (K.205), which I examined during the Guggenheim Museum Klimt-Schiele exhibition of 1965 in New York. This verso is reproduced in a short article by Wolfgang Fischer, "Zur Rückseite von Egon Schieles 'Porträt Edith Schiele' und die Berichtigung einer Datierung," *Albertina Studien*, III:2 (1965), 103. Kallir also refers to the verso of this painting (*Oeuvre Catalogue*, p. 406) and discusses its 1910 origin. A second, female, figure blocked in over the male nude seems to me to be of a later date, conforming to stylistic and compositional concerns of 1915, and not, as both Fischer and Kallir indicate, concurrent with the male figure.

2. The 1909 portraits of Massmann (47¼ × 43¼ inches), Peschka (43¼ × 39¼ inches), and Gerti (39⅜ × 39¼ inches), all exhibited in the 1909 Kunstschau, were Schiele's largest previous works.

3. This project was never realized. For an account of Reininghaus's proposal see Roessler, *Erinnerungen*, pp. 45–46. Also reminiscences of Max Mell and Gertrud Peschka concerning the "notorious" bacchanalian parties given by Reininghaus; personal interviews, Vienna, 26 February 1967 (Mell), and Vienna, 18 February 1967 (Gertrud Peschka).

4. Nevertheless I can not agree with Dr. Heinrich Schwarz's citing a Dürer self-portrait as a source for Schiele's self-portraiture; cf. below, Chapter IV, note 29. Our varying opinions have been fortified by friendly discussions on this and other aspects of Schiele during the past several years, and I am most indebted to Dr. Schwarz and his vast knowledge of the Austrian tradition for many helpful suggestions.

5. The photograph was taken in Schiele's Hietzinger Hauptstrasse 101 atelier. To the left may be seen part of the large 1915 painting, *Death and Maiden* ("Man and Girl"; K.207). The mirror still exists and is in the possession of Melanie Schuster, Vienna. Its base was left behind in Neulengbach after Schiele's arrest there in 1912.

6. Melanie Schuster, personal interview, Vienna, 19 September 1963.

7. See Hevesi, *Acht Jahre Sezession*, pp. 433–34, and David C. Preyer, *The Art of the Vienna Galleries* (Boston, 1911), pp. 314–16.

8. Otto Benesch, "Memories," p. 64. Also, Otto Benesch, personal interview, Vienna, 16 August 1963, and a handwritten letter of 10 January 1915 from Benesch to Schiele (private collection) in which he writes about: ". . . the work of a Mantegna, Signorelli (which has produced such a great impression upon you." [". . . den Werken eines Mantegna, Signorelli (der auf Sie einen so großen Eindruck wirkt]."] Cf. Chapter V, note 26. Schiele liked to tell an anecdote about Signorelli that he had learned from Arthur Roessler (recorded in Roessler, *Der Malkasten*, pp. 9–10) in which Signorelli is supposed to have painted such a realistic picture of his dead son that he called it "Victory of Art over Death," Adele Harms, personal interview, Vienna, 24 January 1967. Other artists of Schiele's circle were also impressed by these two Italian masters. Mopp's painting *Anatomy* in the Historisches Museum der Stadt Wien is based on Mantegna's *Dead Christ* in the Brera, Milan.

9. The Vienna Secession had first exhibited works by Hodler in 1900 (the two side panels to *The Retreat from Marignano*) and again in 1901 (*The Chosen One* and *Spring*). The large 1903–1904 Secession exhibition, arranged by the Viennese artists Carl Moll and Koloman Moser, included thirty-one paintings by Hodler. These are listed in the nineteenth exhibition catalogue of the Vienna Secession as follows: "Abendruhe," "Die Poesie," "Bildnis des Grafen von Romaun," "Waldlied," "Berner Landschaft—Abend," "Bewunderung," "Sommerlandschaft," "Blümlisalp," "Ergriffenheit," "Berner Landschaft—

Mittag," "Rückzug von Marignano—Mittelbild," "Eurythmie," "Rückzug von Marignano—Seitenbild," "Die Wahrheit," "Die Empfindung," "Die Enttäuschten," "Wilhelm Tell," "Die Nacht," "Jüngling, vom Weibe bewundert," "Der Tag," "Rückzug von Marignano—Seitenbild," "Die Lebensmüden," "Die Jungfrau," "Heilige Stunde," "Blumenweise," "Der Frühling," "Apfelbaum," "Blick ins Unendliche," "Im Walde," "Der Traum," "Weib am Bache." For Ludwig Hevesi the Hodler entries were the high point of the exhibition and he wrote about them at length (*Acht Jahre Sezession*, pp. 452–57). The exhibition was covered in *Deutsche Kunst und Dekoration*, XIV:2 (1904), 605, and included a reproduction of *Spring*. An article on Hodler in a later issue [XVII:1 (1906), 281ff] reproduced *Night, Day, Truth, The Admired Youth*, and, again, *Spring*.

Although the two Hodler rooms became the immediate popular focus of the Secession exhibition, the other participating artists are noteworthy. Hodler's friend and fellow countryman, Cuno Amiet, was represented by thirty works, and Edvard Munch had twenty (see Chapter II, notes 21 and 22). Axel Gallén, Hans von Marées, and Jan Thorn-Prikker were also represented. For further information, and reminiscences by Cuno Amiet and Koloman Moser concerning this important Hodler retrospective see Cuno Amiet, Hans Ankwicz-Kleehoven, and Koloman Moser, *Hodler und Wien* (Zurich, 1950).

10. The seven Hodler paintings acquired by Carl Reininghaus from the Secession exhibition of 1903–1904 are identified in the nineteenth exhibition catalogue as "Blümlisalp," "Die Lebensmüden," "Die Wahrheit," "Ergriffenheit," "Sommerlandschaft," "Weib am Bache," and "Blick ins Unendliche." An eighth painting, "Kastanienbaum," was also acquired by Reininghaus at this time (see Amiet, Ankwicz-Kleehoven, and Moser, *Hodler und Wien*, p. 16).

11. Personal interviews: Otto Benesch, Vienna, 16 August 1963; Melanie Schuster, Vienna, 25 November 1966; Gertrud Peschka, Vienna, 18 February 1967. Roessler records that once while leafing through some gothic manuscripts, Schiele remarked to him that the illuminations were so monumental that not even Hodler measured up to them (see Roessler, *Erinnerungen*, p. 35).

12. Otto Benesch, "Memories," p. 63. Benesch indicates Hodler's mountain scenes as a source.

13. The "electrified hair of the Schiele 1910 self-portraits is also present in the three Hodler examples discussed in the text.

14. Schiele's copy, with the cover lithograph printed in red instead of the usual black, was from the first edition, of which only a handful of copies were sold before 1910; Collection Melanie Schuster, Vienna. The second handcrafted Wiener Werkstätte item to be acquired by Schiele was a silver pocketwatch and chain, Collection Melanie Schuster, Vienna.

15. Goldschneider, *Kokoschka*, p. 10.

16. Ernesto de Fiori's career as a painter was short. In 1901 he studied painting at the Munich Academy, but ten years later, on a trip to Paris, he was so impressed by the "unsurpassable" accomplishments of Cézanne and Renoir that he took up sculpture instead. His first attempts in this medium brought him immediate fame. He is remembered today as a sculptor of portrait busts of famous personalities. His 1925 bust of Jack Dempsey is an example. In the 1909 International Kunstschau, de Fiori was represented by three murals (room 7, items 10, 22, and 33).

17. See the painting *Female Nude Seen from the Back* (K.179), 1913, Collection B. F. Dolbin, New York.

18. Schiele's attempts to acquire a figure by de Fiori are recorded in the letters to the artist from his Munich dealer Hans Goltz, preserved in the A.E.S.A.

(*ca.* forty letters). References are made to a plaster cast of a girl and to a terra-cotta figure in letters dated 13 October and 2 September 1913, and 16 November 1915. Two photographs of one of de Fiori's attenuated male figures (very close in style and intensity of gesture to Minne's work) are reproduced in *Zeitschrift für Bildenden Kunst*, XXIII:10 (July 1912), 234.

19. *The Standing Boy with Arms Raised to Head*, a watercolor of 1910 (Albertina, Vienna), is one of several similar studies by Schiele in a close variation of the Minne pose. One is reminded of Kokoschka's statement concerning the strong impression made upon him by Minne's kneeling boy statute at the International Kunstschau and his subsequent application of the Belgian's "skinny" style to his own drawings of Vienna street children (see Chapter II, p. 37).

I wish to acknowledge informative conversations with Albert Alhadeff concerning his research on the work of Georges Minne. Professor Alhadeff has uncovered important drawings which trace Minne's discovery and development of the "self-hugging" motif. It is my opinion that the source for this gesture in Minne may have been Masaccio's *Baptism of the Neophytes*.

20. Gerti herself readily testifies that she was the model for this painting (personal taped interview, Vienna, 18 February 1967), and this is borne out by the preparatory studies.

21. A third study, in the possession of the Felix Landau Gallery, Los Angeles, indicates an earlier stage in which Gerti is dressed and seated, with arms crossed about her body, and with her hair, tied with a ribbon, hanging down her back (see *Landau Catalogue Egon Schiele*, figure 5; not identified as Gerti and misdated as *ca.* 1908).

22. The Minne self-embracing gesture also characterizes the nude male hero of the eighth and last color lithograph in Kokoschka's *The Dreaming Boys*, and is repeated in the three small figures in the landscape of the same illustration. Another motif used by Kokoschka in the third color lithograph of the series is the figure of the nun, which recalls Minne's bust *The Nun*, then in the possession of Fritz Waerndorfer and on display at the Wiener Werkstätte.

23. A fine example of this series, showing Schiele pulling a garment over his head, is in the Collection Alice M. Kaplan, New York.

24. A contemporary of Schiele, the Viennese sculptor Franz Metzner (1870–1919), seems also to have had in mind a continuation of the Messerschmidt idea. He created a series of grimacing heads.

25. Melanie Schuster, personal interview, Vienna, 6 September 1963.

26. The two posters both date from 1910 and were reproduced photomechanically, see Otto Kallir, *Egon Schiele: The Graphic Works* (New York, 1970), plate 12.

27. Notices of forthcoming cultural events in *Der Ruf* refer to further public appearances by Egon Friedell and the Rosé Quartet in 1912.

28. In late 1908 or 1909 Schiele had painted a very small ($9\frac{3}{4} \times 7$ inches) oil of himself in the nude standing over a mirror. (This painting is not accepted by Kallir; first reproduced in *Art International*, VIII:9 (1964), 45, but against the wishes of the author of the accompanying essay on Schiele, Otto Benesch.) The signature appears to be of a later date, and the history of the work is not clear. Reminiscent of Klimt in its decorative silhouette, this tiny self-portrait perhaps represents a private homage to that artist's celebrated allegory *Medicine*, in which a nude female figure is seen from below, floating and detached from a spiraling mass of humanity. (Schiele's transferal of a figure motif from the female to the male sex has already been observed in his 1909 *Self-Portrait Clothed*, with its several references to Klimt's *Judith*.) Johannes Dobai, compiler of the excellent oeuvre catalogue on Klimt (Johannes Dobai and Fritz

Novotny, *Gustav Klimt*, Salzburg, 1967), was the first to suggest a connection between this small nude self-portrait of Schiele and the floating female figure in Klimt's *Medicine* (see Dobai, "Gustav Klimt—Art Nouveau Painter," in the Guggenheim Museum Catalogue, *Gustav Klimt and Egon Schiele*, New York, 1965, p. 25; hereafter referred to as *Guggenheim Catalogue Klimt-Schiele*). I am grateful to Dr. Dobai for the time he took in going over the Schiele material assembled here and for his helpful observations.

29. "Ein ewiges Träumen voll süßesten Lebensüberschuß—rastlos, mit bangen Schmerzen innen, in der Seele.—Lodert, brennt, wachst nach Kampf,—Herzenskrampf. Wägen—und wahnwitzig rege mit aufgeregter Lust.—Machtlos ist die Qual des Denkens, sinnlos, um Gedanken zu reichen.—Spreche die Sprache des Schöpfers und gebe.—Dämone! Brecht die Gewalt!—Eure Sprache,—Eure Zeichen,—Eure Macht." Roessler, *Briefe und Prosa*, p. 20.

30. Schiele's overt sign language in the "allegorical" self-portraits and his actual depictions of masturbation dictate the above interpretation. For similar conclusions dealing with far more recondite subject matter, see Theodore Reff, "Cézanne's Bather with Outstretched Arms," *Gazette des Beaux-Arts*, CIV:1 (1962), 173–90.

31. Identifying title is mine. Not known to Kallir; Leopold 149, and dated by him as 1910. This work is now partially marked over and is attached as backing to the verso of a later work, *Still Life with Books* (K.218, dated by Kallir according to the signed date as 1916; Leopold 253, placed by him as 1914). The studio photograph reproduced here comes from a collection of glass negatives found among Schiele's effects at the time of his death. The negatives are now in the A.E.S.A.

32. Now in the Collection Gertrud Peschka, Vienna, signed and dated 1910.

33. Four illustrations were published in *Der Sturm*, Berlin, II, Nos. 20, 21, 24, and 26 (June–August 1910). Kokoschka also recalls painting a network of nerves on the actors' skins in the performance of his play at the 1908 Kunstschau (see Goldschneider, *Kokoschka*, pp. 14–15).

34. Kallir has always dated this (lost) painting 1911, but evidence points to completion before the end of 1910. Included in the picture on the extreme right is part of a Krumau townscape for which Schiele painted a tempera study in 1910 (K.117). This townscape was also included by Schiele in a reliably dated and related self-portrait of 1910, *Melancholia* (K.114; see note 37 below). Both *Delirium* and *Melancholia* were reproduced in the monograph on Schiele written by Paris von Gütersloh in 1910 and published in 1911 (see Chapter II, note 59). *Delirium* is referred to by title in the text.

35. "In . . . *Delirien* [*sic*] . . . hat Schiele . . . die Mitternachtseele des Künstlers plötzlich betreten. . . . Aber der senilen Erotik kritischer Greise sollte man es endlich verbieten hinter der sinnlichen Form eines Jungen, die auch unkeusch verstanden werden kann, nur das 'Auch' zu hören; es geht nicht mehr an, einem qualvoll erwachsenden Künstler auch noch die Pubertätsnoten seines Menschen nachzusagen; es sollte ihnen bedeutet werden, daß das Mitleid der Impotenz dem Insinuieren einer Masturbation verdammt ähnlich sieht, und daß irgend ein Künstler nicht das geeignete Objekt ist, seine Kenntnis der pathologischen Nomenklatur daran zu demonstrieren." Gütersloh, *Egon Schiele*, pp. 27–28.

36. Schiele was in fact a great movie fan. During his almost two-year residence (1909–October 1910) in the Alserbachstrasse he frequently visited a movie house that occupied the ground floor of his own apartment building. He had struck up a friendship with the owner, who allowed him to spend many hours in the theater which, unlike Schiele's cold studio, was comfortably heated.

37. Kallir has changed the title of this work (a tempera on paper study for the oil dated by Schiele as 1911, K.140) from the previous *City on the Blue River* (*The Dead City*) to simply *City on the Blue River*. I am however retaining Schiele's own title (several handwritten references in notebooks and letters, A.E.S.A.) for this painting in my text. Schiele was especially impressed by the Gothic aspect of his mother's hometown Krumau, and its autumnal austerity continued to fascinate him. He returned to the village regularly, and as late as 1917, painted a series of townscapes. The inclusion of both the study and the oil versions of *The Dead City* (K.140) in *Melancholia* indicates that the townscape was near completion by the end of 1910.

38. Benesch had first seen works by Schiele in a group exhibition of local artists held at Klosterneuburg in 1908. The following year he came across the Schiele entries in the International Kunstschau, canvases which he considered "weak imitations of Klimt." In the autumn of 1910 a second group exhibition of Klosterneuburg artists again included works by Schiele, and Benesch was especially impressed by his painting, *Sunflower* (K.97).

39. "Ich beschloß sofort, den Künstler persönlich kennenzulernen und schrieb ihm in sein Atelier in der Grünbergstraße. Nach wenigen Tagen erhielt ich eine Postkarte mit dem Datumstempel 22. XI. 1910, auf der in eigenartiger, von Schiele angewandten Bloschrift stand: 'Am Freitag Nachmittags wenn lieb. ab 2h Bestens, Egon Schiele.' Deiser Freitag wurde für mich zum Glückstage. Ich kam und fand einen schlanken, jungen Mann von mehr als mittlerer Größe und aufrechter, ungezierter Haltung. Blasses, aber nicht krankhaftes, schmales Gesicht, große dunkle Augen und üppiges, halblanges, dunkelbraunes, zwanglos emporstehendes Haar. Sein Verhalten war ein wenig scheu, ein wenig zaghaft und ein wenig selbstbewußt. Er sprach nicht viel, aber wenn man ihn ansprach, war sein Gesicht immer von dem Schimmer eines leisen Lächelns erhellt. Er legte mir Zeichnungen vor, ließ mich aber allein und kramte irgendwo im Atelier herum. . . . Der Grundsatz seines Wesens war der Ernst, aber nicht ein düsterer, melancholischer, kopfhängerischer, sondern der ruhige Ernst des von seiner geistigen Aufgabe erfüllten Menschen. . . . Schieles Natur war kindlich (nicht kindisch)." Heinrich Benesch, "Mein Weg mit Egon Schiele."

40. "Die Sicherheit seiner Hand war fast unfehlbar. Beim Zeichnen saß er wohl öfter auf einem niedrigen Schemel, das Reißbrett mit dem Zeichenblatte auf den Knien, die zeichnende rechte Hand auf die Unterlage gestütz. . . . Er kannte keinen Radiergummi. . . . Schiele schuf seine Zeichnungen nur vor der Natur. . . . Die Kolorierung erfolgte immer ohne Modell aus dem Gedächtnisse. . . ." *Ibid*.

41. Museum of Fine Arts, Boston.

42. Two further, smaller oil portraits had also been completed: the unidentified *Girl* (K.100), a profile portrait still in the Klimt format; and the Wiener Werkstätte-commissioned *Portrait of Poldi Lodzinsky* (K.63), now dated as 1908 by Kallir and accepted as 1910 by myself (see Chapter II, note 52).

43. Roessler contributed to the Viennese *Hohe Warte* and the *Almanach der Wiener Werkstätte*, and from 1909 was a feature writer for *Deutsche Kunst und Dekoration*, producing articles on Minne, Mestrovič, and Schiele. He supplied the catalogue foreword for the 1906 Miethke Gallery show of Van Gogh. In 1911 he founded his own art periodical, *Bildende Künstler*, which survived for only one year. The third volume was devoted to Schiele and included nine reproductions of his works. After Schiele's death Roessler published several books on the artist, editing his letters and prison diary and writing detailed reminiscences of their friendship and conversations (see Bibliogra-

phy). His editing frequently involved re-wording or omission (see Chapter II, note 50), and his reminiscences, directed to the general public, tended to play down Schiele's erotic interests and erratic conduct. He presented the artist as a shy, often inarticulate, kindly dreamer, who was the first to be shocked by offers to buy his "innocent" drawings of erotica. See especially the somewhat fabricated chapters in *Erinnerungen*, "Kakophonisches Intermezzo" and "Der Reiche Mann." Quite a few of Roessler's own prejudices (notably antisemitism) go into his condemnation of the inevitable "capitalists" who appeared on the scene to buy Schiele's erotic work. The true reason for Schiele's resentment of these patrons was their lecherous curiosity concerning his relations with the models he drew.

44. This review, dated 1909, is reprinted in full from the *Arbeiter Zeitung* in Roessler, *Kritische Fragmente*, p. 128. Two copies of this book were in Schiele's possession at the time of his death.

45. These arguments are documented in a series of unpublished letters between Schiele and Roessler which are now in the Historisches Museum der Stadt Wien, to which the Roessler estate was willed. The quarrels usually concerned financial matters, pictures exchanged or recalled, and accusations of intrigue. Roessler and his wife often sought to tempt Schiele's collector's instinct by offering to trade objects in their home that had caught the artist's eye—a Chinese tablecloth, a guitar—for watercolors and paintings.

46. "Der Eindruck, den ich bei unserer ersten Begegnung von Schieles Persönlichkeit empfing, war eigenartig und stark. . . . Es war der Eindruck, eine dem gesamten Wesen nach ungewöhnliche Persönlichkeit vor sich zu haben, eine Persönlichkeit von so markant ausgeprägter Sonderart, daß sie, schon in ihrer bloßen Gegenwart, vermutlich nicht immer für jedermann angenehm sein mochte, oft genug nicht einmal für sich selber. . . . Sogar im Kreise berühmter Männer von bedeutendem Aussehen fiel Schiele als ungewöhnliche Erscheinung auf, wie ich später mehrmals beobachten konnte. Von hoher, schlanker, geschmeidiger Gestalt, mit schmalen Schultern, langen Armen und langgefingerten, knöchernen Händen, einem von langsträhnigem, wildzausigem, dunklem Haar umrahmten bartlosen und sonnverbrannten Antlitz mit breiter, querfaltig gefurchter, kantiger Stirn, einem Antlitz, dessen plastische Gesichtszüge meistens einen ernsten, fast traurigen Ausdruck trugen, wie von Schmerzen, die nach innen weinen, mit großen und dunklen Augen, aus welchen er, angeredet, gleichsam immer erst einen Traum scheuchen mußte, trat er einem frappierend entgegen. Sein gelassenes, nie aus Unerzogenheit heftiges oder in leidenschaftlicher Aufwallung unbeherrschtes Benehmen, die unleugbare Eigenart in der kleinsten, an Ausdrucksbedeutung geringsten seiner langsamen Gesten, seine wortkarge, aphoristische Sprechweise bewirkten, in harmonischer Zusammenstimmung mit seinem Äußeren, den Eindruck von innerlicher Vornehmheit, die um so eindringlicher empfunden wurde, als sie offenbar ganz Natur und keineswegs Absicht war." Roessler, *Erinnerungen*, pp. 5–6.

47. The Roessler estate collection in the Historisches Museum der Stadt Wien contains two photographs of Roessler's study, taken around 1914. In one of these two Schiele canvases can be seen on the back wall: *Portrait of Ida Roessler* (K.150) of 1912 and *Setting Sun* (K.183) of 1913. On the right wall is Anton Faistauer's portrait of Ida Roessler. The two Javanese shadow puppets later acquired by the artist from Roessler can also be seen in the photograph. The popularity of such puppet figures in Vienna at this time may be traced to the artist Richard Teschner (1879–1948), whose marionettes (exhibited at the 1908 Kunstschau) and risqué puppet shows attracted many fellow artists, including Klimt.

48. Albert Friedenthal, *Das Weib im Leben der Völker*, 2 vols. (Berlin, 1910), and Oskar Münsterberg, *Chinesische Kunstgeschichte*, 2 vols. (Esslingen a N., 1910). The works are now in the collections of Schiele's sisters.

49. An example is Emil Orlik's popular etching of Gustav Mahler (1902), in which the profile head is given full tonal articulation while only a few sparse lines indicate the clothing.

50. A companion sketch of Ida Roessler by Viktor Hammer also exists, Historisches Museum der Stadt Wien, Vienna.

51. A good idea of the state of Austrian and German portrait photography at this time may be had from a special number of *The Studio*, "Art in Photography," published in 1905 and containing introductory essays with representative examples arranged according to countries.

52. Drawn in 1910, but signed (by Schiele) later and misdated "1908."

53. Roessler's review of Kokoschka's one-man exhibition at the Hagenbund in 1911 is illuminating in this respect. Here are some excerpts: "I must hear all too often that Kokoschka works with and attempts to be effective through 'mystical means'—I wish he would do this by painterly means, it would be more artistic. Until now I have considered Kokoschka artistically impotent; I no longer do so, since I have seen evidence of his talent as a painter. He brews his colors from poisonous putrescence, from fermenting juices of disease. . . . Artistically evaluated they are a color massacre." ("Ich muß allzu oft hören, daß Kokoschka mit 'mystischen' Mitteln arbeite und zu wirken trachte—ich wollte, er täte das mit malerischen Mitteln, es wäre künstlerischer. Ich hielt Kokoschka bisher für künsterisch impotent, tue das nun nicht mehr, weil ich Beweise dafür sah, daß er als Maler Begabung hat. . . . Seine Farben braut er sich zusammen aus giftiger, Fäulnis, gärenden Krankheitssäften. . . . Künstlerisch gewertet sind sie Farbengemetzel.") Roessler, *Kritische Fragmente*, pp. 94–97.

54. "Ich ändere das ganze Porträt, und muß Verschiedenes überdenken." Roessler, *Briefe und Prosa*, p. 43.

55. *Ibid.*, pp. 43–44.

56. See the chapter entitled "Ein Missglücktes Projekt," in Roessler, *Erinnerungen*, pp. 19–22.

57. A pencil study by Schiele signed and titled *Otto Wagnerhände* exists, private collection, Vienna.

58. This post card portrait of Wagner was later sent to Schiele by Roessler in 1912 and was found among the artist's effects at the time of his death. It is now in the A.E.S.A.

59. The sketch reproduced here is from the A.E.S.A. Sketchbook XII, p. 8 verso. A second compositional sketch for the Wagner portrait appears on p. 19 recto of the same sketchbook.

60. *Ver Sacrum*, I:5–6 (May–June 1898), 33.

61. When Schiele's wife, Edith, died the artist sent Ambrosi a letter asking him to come out to the house and make a cast for a marble copy of her hands. Ambrosi arrived to find Schiele also dead, and it was thus that he was in the position to take the artist's death mask, copies of which are now in the Albertina, the Historisches Museum der Stadt Wien and the two sisters' collections.

62. "Sie sollten weniger beflissen sein Ihren Verkehr mit Klimt zu kolportieren, als darauf bedacht, zeitweilig auch Oberbaurat Wagners Verhalten zu erwägen und wohlmeinende Freundschaft nicht geschmacklos zu brüskieren. Der Bluff allein tuts nicht, das dürfen Sie mir glauben." Roessler to Schiele, letter of 4 January 1911, Historisches Museum der Stadt Wien, Vienna; transcription kindly supplied me by Dr. Franz Glück. Neither did anything come of Klimt's agreement to pose for Schiele as the second sitter in the series. That Wagner

had proposed the idea to Klimt is confirmed in a letter from Schiele to Roessler dated 27 November 1910 in which he jubilantly reported; "Klimt was here, he wants to exchange drawings with me, and next week he will pose for me, because—because he saw O. Wagner." ("Klimt war bei mir, er will mit mir Zeichnungen tauschen, und wird nächste Woche mir sitzen, weil—weil er den O. Wagner sah.") Roessler, *Briefe und Prosa*, p. 47.

63. ". . . der natürlich sehr freundlich war und mir 20 K[ronen] für nichts gab." Letter of 29 August 1911, A.E.S.A.

64. This and other information concerning Schiele's relationship with Dr. Graff and the sketches made at the clinic was given to me by Adele Harms, personal interview, Vienna, 24 January 1967, and by Graff's friend Max Mell, personal interview, 26 February 1967. I would speculate that several of the watercolor studies of unidentifiable female models, both clothed and nude, which have always been considered to have been of obliging prostitute models, also belong to the series of drawings produced at Graff's clinic. It must be recalled that in 1910 Schiele did not have the money to hire prostitutes, in any capacity. The poignant, sympathetic drawings of pregnant women and listless, ailing children are primarily the result of the opportunity to observe these subjects at firsthand, and not, as has been suggested, in thematic response to Munch's work (see Erwin Mitsch, *Albertina Catalogue Klimt-Schiele*, p. 79. Figures 142, 144, and 145 in this same catalogue are examples of the kind of drawings made by Schiele in Graff's clinic).

65. A catalogue to the exhibition, "Privatsammlung Dr. Oskar Reichel, Wien" with an introduction by Reichel, was published by the Miethke Gallery and dated 21 February 1913. Five works by Schiele are listed: *Madonna* (K.134), *The Ascetics* (K.XIX), and three drawings. A copy of this catalogue is in the Historisches Museum der Stadt Wien.

66. "Weitere Beträge erhielten Sie auf meine Fürsprache hin von . . . Dr. Reichel (der sich nur auf mein dringendes Zureden von Ihnen porträtieren ließ)." Roessler to Schiele, letter of 4 January 1911, Historisches Museum der Stadt Wien, Vienna.

67. Another watercolor study for the Reichel portrait exists in a private collection in New York (reproduced, Leopold, *Catalogue Raisonné*, p. 685) and is closest to the "hard-of-hearing" stance in the final painting.

   Schiele's efforts to collect payment on the Reichel portrait met initially with small success. In a letter of 1 May 1911 he wrote Roessler: "E[issler] does not want to give me any more for the Dr. R[eichel] portrait. Herr A. R—r, you could be truly so kind as to go to Dr. E. so that he gives at least 800 Kronen for it, which is the rate for the other pictures, . . ." ("E[issler] will nichts mehr hergeben für das Dr. R[eichel]-Porträt. Herr A. R—r Sie könnten wirklich so lieb sein und zum Dr. E. gehen, damit er doch wenigstens 800 Kronen dafür gibt, womit die übrigen Bilder angeschrieben sind, . . .") Roessler, *Briefe und Prosa*, p. 54.

68. In 1953 Hans Reichel gave Peter Selz an account of Kokoschka's procedure in painting this portrait: the preparations included asking the boy to hold an orange in his right hand. This orange was subsequently painted out, producing the claw-like effect in the painting. See Selz, *German Expressionist Painting* (Berkeley, 1957), pp. 165–66 and notes 22–24.

69. As late as 1916 Schiele mentioned seeing two new Kokoschkas at Reichel's house; see my article, "Egon Schieles Kriegstagebuch 1916," p. 101, entry of 9 July.

70. "Oskar Kokoschka, den der Wiener Sammler Reichel aufgefordert hatte, sein Porträt zu malen, sah den Mann lang und aufmerksam an und schlug dann vor:

'Wissen S' was, Herr Doktor? Da mal i Ihna do liaber a Stilleben [*sic*]!' "
Roessler, *Der Malkasten*, pp. 90–91.

71. "Ich weiß, ohne Ihnen schmeicheln zu wollen, keinen Kunstwissendern in
Wien als Sie. Darum, ausgesucht, hab' ich Ihnen dies mein Bild aus der ganz
neuen Reihe geschickt. In gewisser Zeit werden Sie so vollständig überzeugt
sein davon, sobald Sie beginnen, nicht daraufzusehn, sondern hineinzuschaun.
Das Bild ist jenes, worüber G. Klimt geäußert hat, er wäre froh, solche Ge-
sichter zu sehen. Es ist SICHER, gegenwärtig, das Höchste, was in Wien
gemalt wurde. Wer darüber lacht, derjenige ist zu beachten, wie er lacht,
derjenige ist feindlich zu meiner Kunst, neidisch zu meiner Kunst usw. Warum
soll ich immer still sein, wenn es die Wahrheit ist. E.S." Roessler, *Briefe und
Prosa*, pp. 143–44. Schiele also had his arguments with Reichel. The following
year in a letter to Roessler dated 3 March 1912, he complained: "I shall never
be able to forget that someone who owns a Van Gogh can speak so coarsely;
I must deny that he has any understanding, especially of Van Gogh; every
botanist is a collector." ("Ich werde niemals vergessen können, daß ein Mensch,
der einen Van Gogh hat, so roh sprechen kann; ich muß ihm das ganze Verständnis, besonders für Van Gogh, verneinen; Sammler ist jeder Botaniker.")
Roessler, *Ibid.*, p. 65.

72. Munch's *Portrait of the Four Linde Boys* had been exhibited in the 1904
Secession show and was reproduced in the exhibition catalogue (see Chapter
II, note 22.) As has been mentioned, Hodler's allegories of youth, such as
Spring (figure 62) and *Adoration*, were well-known in Vienna.

73. "Ich dachte an meine farbigen Porträtsvisionen und es kam mir vor, als ob ich
einmal nur mit jenen allen gesprochen hatte." Roessler, *Briefe und Prosa*. p. 23.

74. An instructive comparison may be made between the fully developed Expressionism of Schiele's Rainer boy portrait and the Jugendstil conception of his
earlier unidentified *Girl* (K.100) of 1910 (see note 42).

75. Mentioned in the artist's notes. Nothing is known of its dimensions or format.
See Kallir, *Oeuvre Catalogue*, p. 488.

76. Important exceptions are Kokoschka's *ca.* 1908 *Portrait of Karl Kraus* (Wingler 12) and the 1913/14 *Self-Portrait with Raised Brush* (Wingler 87). In these
canvases Kokoschka's placement of the figure in the lower half of the picture
and the "felt" weight of the oppressive upper half of the painting seem to
anticipate the portraits of Giacometti and Francis Bacon.

77. I am indebted to Christian M. Nebehay of Vienna, a friend of Kosmack's,
for this important information and for kindly providing the photograph used
here. It will be noted that Schiele misspelled Kosmack's name on the three
studies reproduced here; he did so occasionally in the letters he wrote to
Kosmack as well. A fourth study for the painting exists in the collection of
the Neue Pinakothek, Munich. A black chalk drawing, clearly of 1910 origin,
but dated later by Schiele in pencil "1911," it shows the figure frontal with
both arms lowered and hands tensed.

78. It is interesting to note that one of the rare male portraits executed by Klimt
(Dobai 70) adopts features which are considered hallmarks of Expressionist
portraiture. This portrait is a reverse statement of the power of vision, for it
depicts a blind man, presented with great realism, in strict and rigid frontality,
against a non-decorated void (cf., Chapter II, note 43).

79. Dr. Kantor has suggested that the sunflower in this portrait represents the
female aspect of himself that Schiele was not permitted to know; that the
artist could not admit feminine tendencies personally, but could do so artistically. Personal interview, Atherton, 6 August 1967 (cf., Chapter II, note 47).

80. The immediate impression suggested by the presence of this sunflower in the

Kosmack portrait is that it is a relic of the earlier Klimt-influenced paintings in which similar floral fragments appear, as in the second 1909 "flowery pedestal" portrait of Gerti and the 1909 oil portrait of Anton Peschka. The first of the three compositional studies reproduced here (plate 62) shows that the painting was indeed begun in the Klimt format. Nevertheless Schiele's correspondence (letter to Roessler of 18 October 1910, Roessler, *Briefe und Prosa*, p. 44) indicates that the portrait was not finished until the end of the year, a fact to which the internal stylistic development would have strongly pointed even without documentation. It is characteristic of Schiele's chronic difficulties with his clients that the portrait had still not been paid for by the end of 1914 (letter to Roessler of 11 December 1914, Roessler, *Ibid.*, pp. 83–84).

81. *Das Interieur*, XII (1911), p. 8.

CHAPTER IV: *1910–1914: Isolation and Thematic Absorption in Self* (pp. 79–112)

1. Schiele moved to the Grünbergstrasse studio in November of 1910. He had previously lived in the Alserbachstrasse, near the Emperor Franz Josef Railway Station, a location much closer to the Ringstrasse and the center of town.

2. Adele Harms has repeatedly emphasized that this was one of her brother-in-law's favorite books (personal interview, Vienna, 24 January 1967). As must often occur in the case of persons who survive a famous relative by many decades, some of the "recollections" are based upon, or at least acutely sharpened by, the information exchanged in the course of interviews or statements contained in early publications on the personage involved. Conversely, certain family stories are so treasured by all relatives concerned that their over-repetition seems at times a block towards further analytic and more objective reminiscences. I have endeavored to admit only those details about Schiele which the three surviving relatives have corroborated either through unanimity or through an unshakable consistency over the eight-year period in which I have been privileged to interview them.

3. "Der Egon gerät in allen übeln Eigenschaften, vor allem im Hochhinauswollen, dem Nobeltun und Anspruchsvollsein, dem Vater nach." Quoted by Schiele to Roessler, Roessler, *Erinnerungen*, p. 72.

4. Although the first edition of Kallir's *Oeuvre Catalogue* lists *The Prophet* (N.76) before *The Self-Seers II* (N.77), the second edition places them in reversed order. Because of the internal development presented in this series and discussed in the text, I have retained the original chronology. Dr. Kallir has informed me that the arrangement in the second edition does not necessarily reflect a chronology within the subject groups (personal interview, New York, 9 November 1967). *The Self-Seers II* and *The Prophet* went into the collection of Dr. Oskar Reichel, who had recently been portrayed by the artist, while *The Self-Seers I* was bought by the distinguished art critic and historian, Max Hevesi.

5. Akademie der Bildenden Künste Gemälde Galerie, Inv. No. 573. The skeleton Death appears with an hourglass behind a man of middle age.

6. This aspect of the memento mori was taken up by Kokoschka in an illustration to Albert Ehrenstein's *Tubutsch* (1911) in which a poet is shown with Death looking over his shoulder. Alfred Kubin explored the theme with increasing insistency throughout his long life, titling his pictures "Death Takes the Artist."

7. It is interesting that Schiele thought enough of this revelatory personal statement to write Roessler: "I want to know WHO gets my picture the 'Self-Seers'. Perhaps I will not even give it to him. Not everyone ought to have something

by me.' ("Ich will wissen wer mein Bild die 'Selbstseher' bekommt, vielleicht gib ich's demjenigen gar nicht. —Nicht jeder soll von mir was haben.") Letter of December 1910, Roessler, *Briefe und Prosa*, p. 48.

8. For a full if rambling discussion of the role of the *Doppelgänger* in German Romantic and post-Romantic literature, see Ralph Tymms, *Doubles in Literary Psychology* (Cambridge, 1949). Mr. Tymms's book has led me to many literary parallels for the *Doppelgänger* as it appears in painting, and I am grateful to Professor Marianne Bonwit of the German Department of the University of California at Berkeley for first calling my attention to literary doubles and to the Tymms book.

9. Rainer Maria Rilke, *The Notebooks of Malte Laurids Brigge*, trans. by M. D. Herter Norton (New York, 1964), pp. 94–95.

10. A similar device is used most effectively in yet another well-known German variation on the memento mori theme, Hans von Marées's haunting double portrait of himself with the painter Franz von Lenbach (Neue Pinakothek, Munich) of 1863. In the Marées portrait such features are employed as the single "real" eye (an effect attained by the veiling aspect of the spectacles and the position of Lenbach's head, which partly covers Marées's left eye), the distinction between a partially concealed, dark figure and an exposed, light figure, and finally the compositional placement of Marées behind Lenbach in the traditional disposition of the memento mori or of the inspiring muse theme. Both Schiele's *The Prophet* and Marées's double portrait with Lenbach utilize basically similar means to produce the eerie *Doppelgänger* effect, but the titular and hallucinatory aspects of Schiele's picture go beyond the physical confrontation of the Marées portrait.

11. I formerly believed that the anal entry suggested by the back figure in *Self-Seers I* might refer to a latent homosexuality in Schiele (see my Ph.D. dissertation, "Egon Schiele's Portraits," Columbia University, 1969). I no longer hold this view; in fact Schiele's creative, if exhibitionist, release in self-portraiture seems to me now not only "therapeutic" but substantially heterosexual, healthy, and unrepressed.

12. For an intriguing discussion of a parallel situation in the life and work of Hugo von Hofmannsthal—resulting in a long creative hiatus—see Gotthart Wunberg, *Der frühe Hofmannsthal: Schizophrenie als dichterische Struktur* (Stuttgart, 1965). I am grateful to Professor Joseph Bauke of the German Department of Columbia University for first calling this book to my attention.

13. Roessler quotes Schiele as complaining to him that his mother had absolutely no understanding for him and very little love (Roessler, *Erinnerungen*, p. 26). Melanie Schuster has a collection of some fifteen letters and post cards written by Schiele's mother to him. These letters paint an exaggerated picture of a "martyred" mother enduring financial and psychological suffering at the hands of her undependable, elusive, and hopelessly wayward son.

14. This charge against Melanie is typical of the whole Schiele family's morbid fascination with sex. Schiele's mother allowed Arthur Roessler to publish a letter written to her by Schiele on 13 March 1913 in which he discussed Melanie's "downfall" at length (see Roessler, *Briefe und Prosa*, p. 31). It is curious that in Vienna, a city whose citizens' enthusiasm for lawsuits is proverbial, this damaging letter could have been published while Melanie was still alive. The Schiele family continued to follow this pattern of libelous incrimination, and even while Schiele was living the mother united with Melanie to charge Gerti's husband, Anton Peschka, with forging and selling "Schiele" works.

15. A similar watercolor of Gerti sleeping, also done in 1911, exists in the Albertina (Inv. No. 31252).

16. To "correct" these pictures of recumbent figures by reproducing them horizontally is to ignore the symbolic intention of the artist. This watercolor portrait of Schiele's mother was unfortunately recently reproduced horizontally on the same page where three other 1911 drawings showing sleeping female figures, all signed to enforce a vertical reading, were reproduced vertically (see *Albertina Catalogue Klimt-Schiele*, figures 172–75; see also a prison self-portrait in the same catalogue, figure 190).

17. The conversation and incidents leading to the painting of *The Dead Mother* are described by Roessler in *Erinnerungen*, pp. 62–63; see also p. 28.

18. Letter to Roessler, 24 May 1911, Roessler, *Briefe und Prosa*, p. 56.

19. Roessler, *Kritische Fragmente*, p. 147.

20. Max Klinger, *Vom Tode II*, Op. XIII, 4.

21. *Ver Sacrum*, II:5 (1899), 17, and IV (1901), 77. The influence of Segantini's haunting canvas of 1894 on Paul Klee's etching *Virgin in a Tree* (1903), with its analagous sinister fin-de-siècle mood, can be satisfactorily demonstrated, I think, although the genesis of Segantini's picture through three earlier heavy-handed phases (*Fruit of Love*, *Angel of Life*, and *The Unvirtuous*) which progress from the saccharine to the decorative, reveals artistic preoccupations quite different from those of Klee or Schiele.

22. Item No. 51 in the 1904 Secession exhibition (cf., Chapter II, note 22).

23. Otto Benesch, *Edvard Munch*, pp. 26–27, and Otto Benesch, "Memories," pp. 63–64. Benesch says that Schiele abandoned this work even though it was nearly completed.

24. 1910 November–December Secession exhibit entitled "Die Kunst der Frau." The Kollwitz items were Nos. 270 ("Frau mit totem Kind") and 271 ("Schwangere Frau").

25. "Du bist in dem Alter, wo, ich glaube, der Mensch die Sucht hat, die Welt mit reiner Seele, ungehalten und ungehindert sehen will und Freude über die vollbrachten, dargelegten Früchte sehen will, ihren Eigenwillen, der angeboren ist und selbständige Wurzeln trägt. —Das ist die große Absonderung. Ohne Zweifel werde ich die größte, schönste, kostspieligste, reinste und wertvollste Frucht sein—in mir haben sich durch meinen selbständigen Willen alle schönen und edlen Wirkungen vereinigt;—schon auch des Mannes wegen. *—Ich werde die Frucht sein, die nach ihrer Verwesung noch ewige Lebewesen zurücklassen wird; also, wie groß muß Deine Freude darob sein—mich gebracht zu haben?—*" (Italics mine.) Letter of 31 March 1913, Roessler, *Briefe und Prosa*, p. 29.

26. *Portrait of Trude Engel* (K.126); see Chapter V and plate 116.

27. One painting, *Black Girl* (K.125), in which the hair, arms, and dress are not clearly distinguishable, seems to be an allegory rather than a portrait. The sitter is a model seen in other group figure allegories of the same year (K.133, K.134) and may possibly be Valerie Neuzil, the model who became Schiele's mistress towards the very end of the year and of whom he painted more traditional and recognizable portraits the following year.

28. Self-portraits of this type should be interpreted within the context of the 1910–11 works dealing with masturbation and its symbolic punishment by amputation of secondary offending members, and not, as has recently been suggested, as a reference by the artist to himself as St. Sebastian (see Erwin Mitsch, *Albertina Catalogue Klimt-Schiele*, p. 80). Schiele's presentation of himself in this role did take place but his thoughts did not turn towards the theme of self as martyred saint until after his imprisonment at Neulengbach in 1912.

29. Without the knowledge that both lithographic self-portraits deal with the theme of masturbation and guilt, continuing the artist's autoerotic self-portraits of 1910 and 1911, a quite different interpretation of the two pictures is possible: see Heinrich Schwarz, "Schiele, Dürer, and the Mirror," *The Art Quarterly*, XXX:3–4 (1967), 210–23. Dr. Schwarz proposes that the Schiele self-portrait lithograph published in the SEMA portfolio had as its model the Dürer pen-and-brush drawing at Weimar of a male nude in three-quarter length (recognized by Franz Roh in 1916 as a Dürer self-portrait).

    I do believe that Schiele made intentional paraphrases on the following works by other artists: Klimt's *Judith* (cf. Chapter II, figure 21), Van Gogh's *Bedroom at Arles* (cf. below, note 38), and Klimt's *The Kiss* (cf. p. 106 and plate 99).

30. Comparison with her photograph and with other Schiele portraits of Wally (see plates 91, 92, 93, 95, 96, 97, and 98; and figure 93) confirms that this too is a portrait. It was acquired by Roessler.

    The intensity of Schiele's picture presents an interesting contrast with the almost playful eroticism of Chagall's similarly posed oil of 1913, *Nude in Movement* (Meyer 153).

31. "Wird es denn fort so weiter gehen? Ich habe, ich kann seit Tagen nichts arbeiten. Nicht einmal Packpapier hab' ich. . . . Ich habe Kopfschmerzen, bin gefesselt, will mir niemand helfen? Wenn ich nur eine Ausstellung machen könnte, wäre ich draußen; aber nein, ich kann nicht einmal zeichnen, also muß ich schreiben, mir Geld ausleihen, jetzt in den allerbesten Jahren und Tagen, wo ich arbeiten will. . . . Welche Zeiten! Soll ich Kaufmann sein? oder Verkäufer? . . . Wer wird mir helfen. Ich kann keine Leinwand kaufen, will malen, habe keine Farbe. . . . I am sick [*sic*]. . . . Der Künstler soll sich doch wenigstens nicht darum kümmern müssen, ob er monatlich das schuldige Geld kreigt! Wer mit dem Künstler umgehen kann, der schreibt doch wenigstens. Warum soll ich zu alledem still sein? . . . Ich bin äußerst empfindlich und alle diese Leute wissen absolut nicht, wie sie sich benehmen sollen dem Künstler gegenüber." Letter of 10 January 1911, Roessler, *Briefe und Prosa*, pp. 49–51.

32. "Manchmal lockte es mich geradezu unwiderstehlich, als 'Spießerschreck' aufzutreten, in Wort oder Tat etwas zu äußern, von dem ich weiß, daß es auf andere befremdend, ja sogar abstoßend wirken muß . . . meine äußeren Verhältnisse sich mit meinen inneren Bedürfnissen nicht in Übereinstimmungen befinden." Roessler, *Erinnerungen*, pp. 39–40. Paraphrases of Schiele's remarks in the text above have been drawn from the reminiscences of his sisters, personal interviews, Vienna, 1963–1972. The present-day Viennese artist, Fritz Hundertwasser (b. 1928), presents an interesting parallel to Schiele's occasional opprobrious conduct in public. Hundertwasser is a reserved and quiet-spoken man, completely devoted to the exercise of his talents, who despite substantial European success based on solid artistic merit, periodically succumbs to various exhibitionist urges, such as stripping to the flesh during public lectures. The well-known provincialism of the Viennese middle class may have something to do with the desire of a man such as Schiele, Kokoschka, or Hundertwasser to shatter public complacency by appearing as a "Spießerschreck."

33. Watercolor examples of this type are in the collection of Rudolf Leopold, Vienna, and in several private collections in California and New York.

    It is possible that Klimt may have introduced Schiele to the content of Sar Peladan's work (*L'Androgyne*), with which he had become familiar in 1901 (see Dobai, *Gustav Klimt*, oeuvre catalogue, p. 386). Certainly an ambiguous character marks much of the figural art at the turn of the century. Perhaps the most intriguing example is Peter Behrens' famous color woodcut *The Kiss*

(1896–97) in which the gender of the two lovers—at first glance apparently of different sexes—is actually indeterminate.

Mario Praz refers to the hermaphroditism characteristic of the fin-de-siècle in his book *The Romantic Agony*, trans. Angus Davidson (2d ed., New York, 1956); see especially his discussion of Renée Vivien, p. 376.

34. "Gewiß: ich habe Bilder gemacht, die 'schrecklich' sind; ich leugne das nicht. Aber glaubt man, ich tat das gern und nur, um als 'Spießerschreck' zu wirken? Nein! Nie war das der Fall. Aber auch die Sehnsucht hat ihre Gespenster. Solche Gespenster malte ich. Durchaus nicht zu meinem Vergnügen. Es war ein Muß." Roessler, *Erinnerungen*, p. 40. Such hermaphroditic transformations could also be the subject of a joke in Schiele's circle. Roessler liked to recount the following Saxonian anecdote: 'What are you working on now?' a professor in a Dresden academy asked a colleague. 'Now I am painting a female nude.' 'So? And what does your wife say to that?' 'Nothing. This is how I'm doing it: I paint myself in the mirror, and afterwards I transpose myself into a female.' (" 'Was arbeiden Se denn jezd?' fragte ein Dresdener Akademie professor einen [*sic*] Kollegen. 'Ich male jezd weiblichen Agd.' 'So? —Un was sachd denn die Frau Gemahlin dazu?' 'Gar nichds. Ich mache sie das nämlich so: ich male mich selbsd im Schbiechel und hernach dransbonier ich mich ins Weibliche.' ") Roessler, *Der Malkasten*, p. 33.

35. Schiele reported to Roessler that his association with undesirable political elements had turned the town against him, because he was "red" (letter of 31 July 1911, Roessler, *Briefe und Prosa*, p. 58) but, as was soon to happen in Neulengbach, his eccentric conduct and appearance as well as his reputation for "pornographic" drawings must have been sufficient to ostracize the artist and his visiting model.

36. Roessler, *Briefe und Prosa*, p. 61. To increase his feeling of security, and probably under the influence of his more military-minded friend Anton Peschka, Schiele acquired a pistol at this time.

37. Original, possession Gertrud Peschka, Vienna, transcription kindly provided me by Anton Peschka, Jr., Vienna.

38. *The Artist's Room in Neulengbach* ("*My Living Room*") (K.149), 1911. To the best of my knowledge Peter Selz was the first to point out the resemblance of this painting to Van Gogh's work (*German Expressionist Painting*, p. 158), and he draws attention to the fact that whereas the Dutch painter's bedroom had three openings (one window and two doors), Schiele's room is completely closed and isolated. This is one of the several paintings that Schiele signed with a triple signature (cf. note 51 below).

39. A speculation on my part that this black form in the shape of a face must have been some kind of ceramic vase was gratifyingly confirmed in the winter of 1966 by my discovery in Gertrud Peschka's home of a five-faced black variation of a Janus vase which Frau Peschka identified as having belonged to her brother.

40. A related watercolor in the Albertina, *Self-Portrait Lunging* (Inv. No. 31156), also showing Schiele clothed and with a moustache, differs from the previous troubled self-portraits in a similar way by its rendering of the artist's image in vigorous action rather than paralyzed by emotion.

41. "Ich bin wissend geworden; Erde atmet, riecht, hört, fühlt in allen den kleinen Teilen; erwirbt, paart sich, zersetzt sich und findet sich, genießt, was ein Leben ist und sucht die logische Philosophie aller, alles in allem; Tage und Jahre, aller Vergänglichkeiten so weit man denken will und kann, so weit der Spiritus der Wesen mit großem Gehalt ist; sie ist durch unsere Luft, unser Licht zu Etwas oder Vielem geworden, selbst zu Schöpfern, die notwendig sind, und

ist zum Teil gestorben, verbrannt in sich, wieder—in sich zurück, und beginnt den kleineren oder größeren Kreislauf, alles, was ich göttlich nennen will, keimt von neuem und bringt und erschafft aus der Gewalt, die wenige sehen, ein Geschöpf. —Die Unvergänglichkeit des Materiellen im Sinne eines Daseins ist bestimmt; ein sicheres Werden und Vergehen, Kommen; Leben, worunter man das unaufhörliche Verwittern vestehen soll, das aber durch organische Mittel zum Leben aufgehalten, ja, bis weithin rückgängig werden kann, so daß es mit diesen Mitteln keinen vollständigen Tod geben kann. —Es war, ist und wird der alte oder neue ungewachsene Geist da sein,—der will, der aus etwas, aus Zusammenkünften, aus Mischungen bringen muß, gebären muß; die eigentliche große Mutter von allen, allen ähnlich, doch vereinzelt, die will und so war, ist und wird der Wille immer aus diesen, unseren unendlichen Mitteln, die mannigfaltigsten Menschen, Tiere, Pflanzen, Lebewesen im allgemeinen erschaffen können, sobald diese Physik da ist, sobald der allgemeine Wille der Welt besteht. Ich habe das unmittelbare Mittel bei mir, das, um niederzuschreiben, einzeichnen kann, um erforschen zu wollen, um zu erfinden, um zu entdecken, mit Mitteln aus mir, die schon die starke Kraft haben, selbst zu zünden, selbst zu verbrennen und zu leuchten wie ein Gedanke, vom ewigen Licht, und zu leuchten in die dunkelsten Ewigkeiten unserer kleinen Welt, die nur aus so wenigen Elementen besteht. —Alle Deckmäntel für uns sind sowieso für nichts, weil sie uns verbergen, anstatt die Sucht haben, zu verweben mit anderen Organen. —Wenn ich mich ganz sehe, werde ich mich selbst sehen müssen, selbst auch wissen, was ich will, was nicht nur vorgeht in mir, sondern wie weit ich die Fähigkeit habe, zu schauen, welche Mittel mein sind, aus welchen rätselhaften Substanzen ich zusammengesetzt bin, aus wie viel von dem mehr, was ich erkenne, was ich an mir selbst erkannt habe bis jetzt. —Ich sehe mich verdunsten und immer stärker ausatmen, die Schwingungen meines astralischen Lichtes werden schneller, unvermittelter, einfacher und ähnlich einem großen Erkennen der Welt. So erbringe ich stets mehr, stets Weiteres, endlos Scheinenderes aus mir, so weit mich die Liebe, die alles ist, auf diese Art bemittelt und mich zu dem führt, wohin ich instinktiv gezogen werde, was ich in mich zerren will, um von neuem ein Neues zu bringen, was ich trotz mir erschaut habe. —Mein Wesen, mein— Verwesen, auf bleibende Werte umgesetzt, muß auf andere stark oder stärker ausgebildete Wesen meine Kraft über sie erbringen, früher oder später, wie eine gläubig scheinende Religion. —Die Weitesten werden mich beachten, Entferntere werden mich anschauen und meine Negativen werden leben von meiner Hypnose! —Ich bin so reich, daß ich mich fortschenken muß." I am grateful to my mother, Professor Megan Laird Comini of the German and Italian Departments of Southern Methodist University, for her help in the translation of this difficult letter.

42. *Ver Sacrum*, I:2 (1898), 7–18. This article, presented in the form of excerpts from "a yet uncompleted work on Romanticism" by Ricarda Huch, was chosen to accompany the illustrations of Klimt's works, to which this second issue of *Ver Sacrum* was dedicated. Huch discusses the *Zusammenhang* aesthetic as already visible in Runge's work—a combination of "mathematics, music, and colors" (p. 18).

43. The common heritage of the *Zusammenhang* aesthetic and its thematic concerns seem also to have influenced Kokoschka's imagery and thought. In a public speech, "Von der Natur der Gesichte," given at Vienna's Musikvereinssaal in February of 1912, Kokoschka, speaking of different kinds of awareness, alluded to two motifs (frequently found in Schiele's work): the unborn child and the tree. Kokoschka also spoke of an absence of death

through a re-formation ["There is no longer a place of death because visions dissolve and disperse—however only in order to gather together again in a different manner." ("Es gibt keinen Platz des Todes mehr, weil sich die Gesichte wohl auflösen und zerstreuen, doch nur, um sich in anderer Weise wider zu sammeln")], of a reverberation of the world through one's own soul: ". . . as an uncontrolled human being quiveringly reflects in his own soul the vibrations of the entire world. . . ." (". . . als ein regelloser Mensch von der ganzen Welt mit der eigenen Seele widerbebt. . . ."), and, using the simile of a burning lamp, of the existence of all former things within the self: "Consciousness is the grave for things where they cease, the Beyond into which they enter. So that at their end they appear no longer to exist in anything more concrete than in the vision within me. They breathe out their spirit as a lamp burns and draws the oil from the wick. In this measure each thing has released itself into the Beyond, as it looks at me." ("Bewußtsein ist das Grab für die Dinge, wo sie aufhören, das Jenseits, in dem sie eingehen. So daß sie alsdann bei ihrem Ende in nichts Wesentlichem mehr zu bestehen scheinen, als meinem Gesicht in mir. Sie hauchen ihren Geist aus, wie die Lampe leuchtet und läßt vom Docht das Öl ziehen. In diesem Maß hat jedes Ding sich seiner selbst entledigt in das Jenseits, wie es mich anschaut."). See Otto Breicha and Gerhard Fritsch, *Finale und Auftakt Wien 1898–1914* (Salzburg, 1964), pp. 238–42.

44. Friedrich Nietzsche, *Thus Spoke Zarathustra*, in *The Portable Nietzsche*, trans. and ed. by Walter Kaufmann (New York, 1954), p. 401.

45. Rilke, *The Notebooks of Malte Laurids Brigge*, p. 209.

46. Another reference to Steiner's theory appears in an aphorism Schiele wrote his uncle Czihaczek at this time (see note 37): "I paint the light which comes from all bodies." ("Ich male das Licht welches aus allen Körpern kommt.")

47. On 24 April 1911 the Miethke Gallery gave Schiele a one-man exhibition. Heinrich Benesch reports meeting the artist in the street on his way to the show to collect, as he jubilantly told Benesch, "the first thousand." (H. Benesch, "Mein Weg mit Egon Schiele.") Benesch gives the date as 1910, and this is the date given by Kallir for the Miethke Gallery exhibition (*Oeuvre Catalogue*, p. 512). Nevertheless printed invitation cards exist in the sisters' collections and in the A.E.S.A. with the date 18 April 1911 hand-corrected to read 24 April 1911, and Schiele refers to the Miethke show in letters written to Roessler during 1911 dated 3 and 6 February, 17 March, and 1 May (see Roessler, *Briefe und Prosa*, pp. 51–54). There was no money for Schiele to collect however and by the end of the week only one drawing had been sold. He reported this to Roessler, asking pathetically if he didn't know anybody who might come and buy (letter of 1 May 1911, *Ibid.*, pp. 53–54).

There is no mention in Schiele's correspondence of the important Hagenbund exhibition of twenty-five paintings by Kokoschka in February of the same year. The year 1912 was a much busier year for Schiele. He sent works to Budapest and Cologne and to three different exhibitions in Munich, while at home some of his paintings were shown by the Hagenbund in March and, at the end of the year, by the Vienna Secession.

48. *The Hermits* was exhibited in the Hagenbund show of March 1912 (No. 226) and received favorable reviews. Friedrich Stern, writing in the 11 April 1912 issue of *Feuilleton* discussed Schiele's creative use of Cubistic elements, and the Munich periodical, *Die Kunst für Alle*, wrote to Schiele asking permission to reproduce *The Hermits* in their review of the Hagenbund show (letter of 28 March 1912, A.E.S.A.). This evidence for the dating of *The Hermits* before Schiele's arrest at Neulengbach was only recently made available to

me and changes the interpretation given in my master's thesis ("Egon Schiele: The Artist's Vision of Himself," pp. 77–84) in which the work is discussed as part of Schiele's reaction to his imprisonment.

A glass negative of *The Hermits* was made by Schiele in his studio, and is now in the A.E.S.A. It best shows the traces of a previous figure composition not entirely painted out by Schiele. It also shows *The Hermits* placed upside-down on the artist's easel (in order that it might be seen right side up in the camera). To the right in this negative may be seen a portion of Schiele's canvas of 1917, *House with Drying Laundry* (K.229), in its first version.

49. Letter to Roessler, 25 May 1911, Roessler, *Briefe und Prosa*, p. 56.

50. As with my earlier interpretation of *The Hermits* (see note 48 above), I formerly believed this closely related study originated *after* Schiele's incarceration, and so discussed it in my article, "Egon Schiele in Prison," *Albertina Studien*, II:4 (1964), 123–137.

51. Schiele employed this triple signature and date several other times, always in pictures that were particularly meaningful to him. They are: *Procession* (K.133), 1911; *Mother and Death* (K.135), 1911 (in which the artist appears as a monk—Death—to confront a pregnant woman); and the previously discussed *The Artist's Room in Neulengbach* (K.149), 1911 (see note 38 above).

It is curious that, considering the importance of the plant symbolism in this painting, major disagreement exists as to what type of plant is shown. The present owner of the work sees a single rose growing (". . . wächst eine einzige Rose," Leopold, *Catalogue Raisonné*, p. 212), whereas in the painting two red husks are clearly visible, their shapes identical to the winter cherry plant included by Schiele in other works of this period (plates 82, 92, and 94). See note 58 below.

52. In the first edition of Kallir's *Oeuvre Catalogue The Hermits* and *Agony* were listed in the order presented here (N.106 and N.108 respectively). As mentioned before (see note 4 above), the grouping within subject categories in the second edition of the *Oeuvre Catalogue* is not necessarily chronological. The order indicated in the first edition would, in my opinion, be the correct one.

During the whole of 1912 a singular development takes place in Schiele's self-portraiture. As if in reaction to the solitary portraits or double visions of himself of 1910 and 1911, he is now almost hesitant to show himself alone. An exception is the oil self-portrait bust painted on a small wood panel, *Self-Portrait with Head Lowered* (no Kallir numbering; Leopold 202), which was conceived as a study for *The Hermits*. Another self-portrait bust painted on wood, *Self-Portrait with Raised Naked Shoulder* (K.173; Leopold 209) matches in size, medium and mood a similarly agitated portrait of *Wally* (K.153; Leopold 208). The lyrical *Self-Portrait with Winter Cherry* was conceived as a companion piece to the "winter cherry" portrait of *Wally* plate 92) and in the five "allegorical" portrayals of self painted this year, the artist always appears with a companion: *The Hermits* (plate 84), *Agony* (plate 87), *Woman in Mourning* (plate 96), *Cardinal and Nun* (plate 98), and *Conversion I* (K.158; not reproduced). The lost painting *The Ascetics* (K.XIX), also of this year, may be presumed to have been related to *The Hermits* and *Agony*.

53. An interesting "precedent" for *Agony* showing a young boy fainting into the arms of an older, bearded monk-like figure may be seen in the second color lithograph ("rot-fischlein") illustration of Kokoschka's *The Dreaming Boys*.

54. A.E.S.A. Sketchbook II, 1912–13, pencil, p. 22 recto, Albertina, Vienna.

55. An indication of canvas measurements and the notation in Schiele's hand "Speisezimmer Györ" (dining room Györ) suggests that this painting was destined for a specific location—the dining room of the August Lederer family in Györ, Hungary (see Chapter V). The drawing on the left-hand page of the sketchbook shown in this plate contemplates the canvas in place over a small ornate fireplace. It is possible that the Lederers, friends of both Schiele and Klimt, had seen and admired *The Hermits* and asked Schiele to paint a second version for them. The measurements indicated by Schiele in the sketchbook—193 × 186 centimeters—are close to the measurements of *The Hermits* (181 × 180.5 centimeters). Schiele must have dropped the Györ project, for the final version of this theme, *Agony*, was much smaller and went into the collection of another patron, Franz Hauer (see Chapter V).

56. The earliest instance of this kind of geometrical background fracturing in Schiele's figurative work is in a difficult-to-read allegory of 1911, showing three (?) figures—a woman and two skull-headed males?—entitled *Procession* (K.133).

   At the time of Schiele's allegorical double portraits of 1912 the Austrian artist Adolf Hoelzel (1853–1934), founder of the German school of "absolute art" and teacher of Emil Nolde, Johannes Itten, and Oskar Schlemmer, was making interesting semi-abstract compositions in Stuttgart. These works included peasant-like figures in landscapes which had been broken down into geometrical and organic statements of structure. Hoelzel had exhibited in the 1908 Kunstschau, and his theories concerning the "spirited use of media" were known to Viennese artists through an article on the artistic means of expression published in *Ver Sacrum* in 1901. Schiele may have become acquainted with Hoelzel's work when he painted the portrait of Eduard Kosmack, the nephew of Hoelzel, in 1910 (cf. Chapter III).

57. See Chapter V, note 40.

58. The plants in both these portraits, as well as in the *Self-Portrait with Fingers Spread Apart* (plate 82) closely resemble the winter cherry that grows in abundance in both Krumau and Neulengbach. This "balloon vine" or "Jerusalem cherry" with its bladderlike husks seems to have had a special appeal for Schiele (perhaps he knew of the French term for it, "*amour en cage*"), for he often kept sprigs of it in his studio.

59. A better photograph of Wally, wearing the same "English" suit, is reproduced in the Historisches Museum der Stadt Wien Catalogue *Egon Schiele: Leben und Werk* (Vienna, 1968), figure 11. Identification of the photographs of Wally has been confirmed for me by three persons who knew her: Melanie Schuster, Gertrud Peschka, and Erich Lederer.

60. "Sage heute am 8. Juni 1913 daß ich in niemandem auf der Welt verliebt bin. Wally." A.E.S.A. Sketchbook "I" (1913), p. 20 recto. Further portrait sketches of Wally are in the collections of Melanie Schuster, Rudolf Leopold, the Griechenbeisl Gallery, Vienna, and Viktor Fogarassy, Graz.

61. Heinrich Benesch, "Mein Weg mit Egon Schiele."

62. *Ibid.* See also Schiele's diary entry under "Wieder ein Tag, Maitag!", Roessler, *Egon Schiele im Gefängnis*, pp. 21–30.

63. There is no longer any record of Schiele's trial at the St. Pölten courthouse. In the summer of 1963 I discovered and photographed the primitive basement cell at Neulengbach in which Schiele was imprisoned. For a fuller account of Schiele's prison drawings and how they faithfully reproduced physical details of the cell and corridor as they may still be seen today, see Comini, *Schiele in Prison*.

64. Roessler published this diary four years after Schiele's death. A vigorous

effort on my part to examine the original has proved fruitless. The circumstances surrounding its removal from the rest of the Roessler estate apparently do not permit admission of the manuscript into the public domain. Judging from Roessler's "editing" of Schiele's war diary of 1916, the original of which is in the Albertina, I feel obligated to suggest that Roessler may have tampered with the diary to some extent. I can not however jump to the drastic conclusion proposed by Rudolf Leopold in his recent claim that the entire prison diary was fabricated by Roessler (Leopold, *Catalogue Raisonné*, p. 666 and p. 682). This assertion is untrue.

65. Since publication of my article on Schiele in prison one more watercolor from the prison series has come to my attention. It shows a pair of green hose flung over a stool and is dated 21 April 1912 (with a decorative "G" for "Gefängnis" —prison) and entitled "Souvenir of the Green Stockings." This watercolor is in the Collection Gertrud Peschka, Vienna and is reproduced in Comini *Schiele in Prison*, p. 89, plate 30.

66. "Schaue herzu, Allvater, . . . und denke, ob du dulden willst, daß mir diese schamvoll niederdrückende Qual bereitet wird. . . . wenn ich strauchele, tu ich's auf deinen Wegen mit deinem Willen—aber leiden mit deinem Willen? —gefangen mit deinem Willen? . . . ich rufe darum zu dir: höre mich, leih mir dein unverschlossenes Ohr!" Roessler, *Egon Schiele im Gefängnis*, p. 15.

67. The late Dr. Otto Benesch kindly shared with me the fascinating information he had uncovered concerning the personality of the judge who passed sentence upon Schiele and who shocked the courtroom by setting fire to one of the artist's drawings. This judge, a Dr. Stövel, was, as Schiele had supposed in his diary, a man of culture and interest in the arts. He was in fact an avid collector of the paintings of the Austrian Jesuit artist, Franz Stecher (1814–53), who had decorated Jesuit churches in the United States as well as Austria. This artist was mentally unbalanced, and his paintings reveal a morbid scatological mingling of religious and sexual elements, done in a weird neo-Blake style (see Martha Reinhardt, *Franz Stecher*, Vienna, 1957). Thus the judge who condemned Schiele for his undisguised erotic art was himself a collector of it, in a more "acceptable" form. In this respect Dr. Stövel represents the neurotic obsession with the erotic through "permissible" disguises characteristic of the overrefined sensualism of the pre-World-War I culture of Vienna.

68. "Gar nicht weit von mir, so nahe, daß er meine Stimme hören müßte, wenn ich schreien würde, sitzt in seiner Amtsstube ein Richter oder was er sonst ist, ein Mann also, der was Besseres zu sein meint, der studiert hat, der in der Stadt gelebt hat, der Kirchen und Museen, Theater und Konzerte, ja wohl auch Kunstausstellungen besucht hat, der also zu den Gebildeten zählt, der vom Leben der Künstler gelesen oder wenigstens gehört hat,—und dieser Mann kann es leiden, daß ich in einem Käfig eingesperrt bin!" Roessler, *Egon Schiele im Gefängnis*, pp. 15–16.

69. "Gestern: Rufe—leise, zage, klagend; Schreie—laut, drängend, flehend; stöhnende Schluchzlaute—verzweifelt, angstend verzweifelt;—schließlich dumpfes Hingestrecktsein, kaltgliedrig, todesbang, schauerschweißbenäßt." *Ibid.*, p. 16.

70. After his transfer to the jail at St. Pölten, Schiele also modeled out of bread the face of a fellow prisoner. Two photographs of this little sculpture are reproduced in the published version of Heinrich Benesch's memoirs, *Mein Weg mit Egon Schiele*, figure 6 (see Chapter II, note 6).

71. "Wenn ich nur wüßte, warum man mich da hereingesteckt hat. Wegen der Zeichnung kann es doch nicht gut geschehen sein. Oder doch? —In Österreich ist alles möglich, hier, wo Waldmüller dem Steueramt einen Bettelbrief

schreiben mußte, wo Romako vom Unverstand und eifersüchtigem Neid der Nichtskönner zum Selbstmord getrieben wurde, wo Universitätsprofessoren in schändlichster Selbstbefleckung Klimt höhnten." Roessler, *Egon Schiele im Gefängnis*, p. 17.

72. "Spaziergang im Gefängnishof. Roller ist gewiß ein großer Künstler, aber sein Gefängnishof in "Fidelio" ist doch nur Theater, während das Gemälde Gefängnishof von Van Gogh packendste Wahrheit ist, große Kunst." *Ibid.*, p. 21. For Schiele's knowledge of Van Gogh's picture *Prisoners at Exercise* (de la Faille 669) see Chapter II, note 17. Alfred Roller's new decorations for the recent Mahler production of *Fidelio* had caused a general stir in Vienna and had received praise from Hermann Bahr, who referred to Roller's prison backdrops as "heroic reality" (see the 1911 *Almanach* printed by Brüder Rosenbaum, Vienna, pages not numbered).

73. "Es ist ein Skandal! Eine fast nicht zu glaubende Roheit! Gemeinheit! Und große, große Dummheit! Es ist eine Kulturschande, eine Schande für Österreich, daß einem Künstler in seinem Vaterland so etwas passieren kann. Ich leugne es nicht: ich habe Zeichnungen und Aquarelle gamacht, die erotisch sind. Aber es sind doch immer Kunstwerke—das kann ich sagen, und Leute, die davon was verstehen, werden es gern bestätigen. —Haben andere Künstler keine erotischen Bilder gemacht? —Rops z.B. hat nur solche gemacht. Aber eingesperrt hat man deshalb nicht einen Künstler. . . . Viele, viele berühmte Künstlernamen könnte ich nennen, auch den von Klimt; aber ich will mich damit gar nicht entschuldigen, das wäre meiner nicht würdig. Ich leugne also auch nicht. Als unwahr erkläre ich aber, daß ich Kindern solche Zeichnungen absichtlich gezeigt habe, daß ich Kinder verdorben habe." Roessler, *Egon Schiele im Gefängnis*, pp. 30–33.

74. "Wien, 8. Mai 1921.

"24 Tage war ich in Haft! —Vierundzwanzig Tage oder Fünfhundertsechsundsiebzig Stunden! —Eine Ewigkeit!

"Die Untersuchung ist kläglich verlaufen, —ich aber habe elendiglich Unsagbares gelitten. Bin furchtbar bestraft ohne Bestrafung.

"Bei der Verhandlung wurde ein Blatt von den beschlangnahmten, das, welches in meinem Schlafzimmer aufgehängt war, vom Richter im Talar feierlich an der Kerzenflamme verbrannt! —Autodafé! Savonarola! Inquisition! Mittelalter! Kastratentum, heuchlerisches! —Geht doch in Museen und zerstückelt, die besten Kunstwerke. Wer das Geschlecht verleugnet ist ein Unflat und beschmutzt niedrigst die eignen Eltern, die ihn zeugten.

"*Wie wird sich fortan jeder, der nicht litt wie ich, vor mir schämen müssen!*" *Ibid.*, p. 38.

75. Not identified by either Kallir or Leopold as Wally.

76. K.153, a companion piece to Schiele's *Self-Portrait with Raised Naked Shoulder* (K.173); see discussion in note 52 above.

77. *Conversion I* (K.158) of 1912 is a hard-to-read composition in which two female figures (one of them Wally) seem to kneel underneath the figure of the monk-Schiele, whose robes surround the trio. The series takes on a domestic aspect in 1913 in a gouache on parchment work entitled *The Birth* (private collection), in which Schiele stands behind Wally who holds a small, gesticulating baby contained in the same type of embryonic encasement seen in the previous mother-and-child paintings. Since the artist has now substituted his mistress for his mother in this type of "allegorical" portraiture this may be judged as a positive change in his approach to the mother-and-child theme.

78. A fragment of a lost painting, it measures 27½ × 95½ inches. Collection B. J. Dolbin, New York.

79. This notebook is in the possession of Melanie Schuster, Vienna.
80. One of the postcards Schiele sent his mother from Munich was a reproduction of Franz Marc's *The Yellow Cow* (post card in the possession of Melanie Schuster, Vienna). Marc's rhythmical treatment of nature must have appealed to him as a variant on the Hodler parallelisms in his own landscapes. Because of Schiele's direct exposure to the works of Die Brücke and Der Blaue Reiter in Munich as early as 1912, I can not agree with Dr. Schwarz's statement that the German Expressionist qualities of Schiele's 1916 woodcuts are indebted primarily to his colleague, the graphic artist Robert Philippi (1877–1959); see Heinrich Schwarz, "Die graphischen Werke von Egon Schiele," *Philobiblon*, V:1 (Hamburg, 1961), 50–69. Schiele was also well acquainted with German Expressionist woodcuts from Franz Pfemfert's Berlin periodical *Die Aktion*, to which his colleagues Mopp, Gütersloh, and Harta regularly contributed, and in which his own 1916 woodcuts were published. The "crude" style of Schiele's woodcuts seems to me more likely to be a direct and perhaps even impatient response to his medium. Schiele's exasperation with the slower techniques involved in any kind of printmaking once caused him to complain that in the time it took him to engrave one plate, he could have drawn a hundred pictures (Roessler, *Erinnerungen*, p. 67).
81. Other studies (private collection, Europe) include two fully worked gouaches on parchment for the principals as seen in the oil, and further studies exist in private collections in Germany, Austria, and the United States. Otto Benesch describes another large mural project of 1913, now lost, which included Schiele, Klimt, the Benesch father and son, and other close friends, all robed as monks (see Benesch, "Memories," p. 64). Another 1913 project for an allegorical portrait of himself as a blind man being wept over by Wally was executed in gouache on parchment (private collection).
82. Another artist with a penchant for showing himself as "persecuted" was of course James Ensor. (See his lithograph poster for the 1898 show of his works at the Salon des Cents.) Ensor's torments were of another sort than Schiele's however and dealt with demons and sexual apparitions more in the tradition of the Temptation of St. Anthony.
83. "Ich bestätige Ihnen 2 neue Bilder und 20 Zeichnungen erhalten zu haben. Aber Herr Schiele, so sehr ich mich stets über Ihre Zeichnungen freue und auch bei den bizarrsten Launen gerne mitgehe, wer soll die Bilder kaufen? Ich habe da sehr sehr wenig Hoffnung. Sie dürfen mir nicht verübeln, wenn ich, der ich doch gerne allen Künstlern der neuen Richtung gefolgt bin, und dessen Verstehen wohl manchem ein wenig erleichert habe, Ihnen gegenüber mein Bedenken ausspreche. Was noch vor einem Jahr, ja noch vor einem halben Jahr uns ausserordentlich stark und deshalb, aber auch nur deshalb zukunftsreich erschien, das darf nicht in der Form erstarren. Es war ein *Weg* um aus dem wässerig gewordenen Ziel, das schon erreicht ist. Die "Ismen," die als Wege und als Zerstörung ausserordentlich notwendig waren, müssen sich nun allmählig abklären zu ruhiger kraftvoller Kunst. Sonst kann der Kunsthändler bei allem persönlichen Verständnis nichts mehr ausrichten und muss nun mit schwerem Herzen auf weniger starke, aber dafür wenigstens lesbare Künstler zurückgreifen. Ich will mit diesen Worten keinen ermahnenden Papa spielen, ich will Sie nur vorbereiten auf einen gänzlich finanziellen Misserfolg, den Ihre Bilder auf Ihrer jetzigen Stufe sowohl als auch die der anderen erleiden müssen. Auch der wohlwollende und verständnisvolle Teil des Publikums beginnt ungeduldig zu werden und hungert nach Ruhe und Klarheit." Letter of 1 April 1913, A.E.S.A.
84. "Ich erwarte von Ihnen, daß Sie mich am Dienstag oder Mittwoch 2–4h

besuchen werden um eines der beiden Städte zu kaufen. Kommen Sie nicht, wenn Sie sich irgendwie mistrauisch zu mir oder meinem Vorschlag verhalten. Ich wünsche dies darum von Ihnen, weil ich um die Wahrheit zu gestehen, seit Sommer 1913 2500 K[ronen] Schulden habe,—ganz erklärlich, weil ich in der ganzen langen Zeit vom August bis jetzt, ein Bild für 350 K verkauft habe. Woher und auf welche Art soll ich mich also fortbringen?

"Mit dem 19. Jahre wurde ich selbständig, ich hatte unzählige Hindernisse zu passieren, wie keiner vielleicht und das schwächt. Diese Hemmungen kamen in Bildern zum Ausdruck. Von den Kollegen waren alle Feinde; ich begann Wien zu hassen, wollte in Krumau einsam bleiben, konnte aber nicht weil ich kein Geld zur Verfügung hatte. Ich brauchte Wien und zog nach Neulengbach um einsam zu sein und doch dabei Wien in nächster Nähe zu haben. Ich wurde keusch und das Schicksal wollte es, daß ein Mädchen mich gerne sah und es so weit brachte, daß es selbständig zu mir. Ich schickte es fort. . . . Man überzeugte sich, daß es unberührt war, trotzdem kam es vors Gericht. Damals wurde ich gemein erniedrigt für meine Güte,—ich verlor jeglichen Glauben an sonst glaubhafte Menschen, —ich erlebte schwere, schwere Stunden, lernte allen Morast von Menschen kennen und viele unverstandene wahre Menschen.

"Von meinen nächstbekannten rührte sich niemand ausser Wally, die ich damals kurz kannte und die sich so edel benahm, daß diese fesselte und Herr Benesch. Ich begann schwer zu denken—ich empfand Menschen mit offener Seele und ihr heiliges Herz, und ich dachte über Lügner und böse Menschen nach. So kam ich auf den Gedanken, daß der reine, wahre Mensch ewig leben muss. Mir ekelte vor meiner früher so innig geliebten melancholischen Landschaft in Neulengbach—es trieb mich also Gegensatz an die Grenze, ich blieb 1912 in Bregenz und sah nichts als den verschieden stürmenden See und ferne weisse sonnige Berge in der Schweiz. Ich wollte ein neues Leben beginnen, aber bis jetzt konnte ich nicht, nichts gelang mir noch in meinem Leben. Ich sehne mich nach freien Menschen, so lieb mir Österreich ist, ich beklage es. Ich verstehe immer mehr die Aufsätze von Egger-Lienz, nur daß er ohrfeigt —das werde ich nicht tun.

"Goltz in München schrieb mir, daß ein wohlhabender Herr mir einen längeren Aufenthalt in Paris ermöglichen möchte, wenn nicht, so werde ich alles tun um nach Paris, Berlin oder München zu kommen, je früher desto besser.

"Auf die Dauer geht dies nicht so. Ich glaube an bedeutende Menschen die mich erkennen werde, die mir abgesehen von dem Maler,—dem Künstler das Werkzeug geben werden damit er bilden kann.

"Ich wünsche Herr Hauer von Ihnen den erhabenen Eindruck zu behalten, darum erweisen Sie sich." Letter to Franz Hauer, 25 January 1914, Historisches Museum der Stadt Wien, Vienna; transcription kindly provided me by Dr. Franz Glück.

CHAPTER V: *1912–1914: Major Portrait Commissions* (pp. 113–153)

1. "Samstag!" Sketchbook A (July–December 1912), p. 20 verso, Collection Melanie Schuster, Vienna.

2. "Mir geht es einfach ausgezeichnet, ich kam gestern um viertel 12 Uhr hier an und wurde gleich mit dem Herrschaftswagen abgeholt. Die Spiritusfabrik Györ ist eine ganz große samt drei Schleppbahnen und eigenen Waggons und Lokomotiven, kurz sehr groß. —Das Wohnhaus dementsprechend und völlig von der Wiener Werkstätte eingerichtet. Die Leute sind äußerst elegant, und höchst liebenswürdig zu mir, vielleicht male ich alle mit der Zeit. Wir

waren im Theater und verschiedenes. Die Stadt ist fast so groß wie Linz. —Immer wartet die Equipage. Diener, grau mit Silberknöpfen." Roessler, *Briefe und Prosa*, p. 28.

3. ". . . wovon jedes Lederers gefällt und diese erstaunt sind, wie sicher ich arbeite, wenn sie zusehen." *Ibid.*, p. 74.

4. ". . . ganz asiatisch, wie chinesisch." *Ibid.*, p. 75.

5. ". . . das Bild wird 140 × 55 cm groß. Habe zirka 20 farbige Blätter zum Porträt gemacht." *Ibid.*

6. ". . . der Knabe, den ich male, ist 15 Jahre alt, langes vornehmes Gesicht, und malt natürlich und zeichnet auch wie Beardsley; nur hat er noch nie die Natur beobachtet und das ist sein Schaden." *Ibid.*, p. 74.

7. Erich Lederer, personal interview, Geneva, 28 Nov. 1966. I wish to express my gratitude to Herr Lederer and his wife Lisl for their generous hospitality on the occasion of my visits to them and for their continued substantial encouragement and aid. Herr Lederer's personal memories of Schiele are vivid and informative.

8. Erich Lederer, personal interviews, Geneva, 28 November 1966, 10 February 1967, and 8 December 1972, and Venice, 28 September 1971.

9. Several of these letters are in the possession of Melanie Schuster, Vienna. The young Erich seems to have had even less luck with Klimt in this respect. In one of his 1915 letters to Schiele he mentions a visit by Klimt to Györ and complains about his lack of interest in the local dancing girls during a night out at the theater (Letter of 4 August 1915, possession of Melanie Schuster, Vienna).

10. A variation on this pose is the watercolor study of 1912 in the Staatliche Graphische Sammlung, Munich. In this study the boy is shown with his hands raised against his body in two contrasting gestures: the left hand is pressed against the hip in a loosely clenched fist, palm up, while the fingers of the right hand point upward in a snapping motion towards the left shoulder. The head is tilted as in the example reproduced here, but the eyes turn back towards the beholder. The general impression conveyed is somewhat precious as opposed to the dreaming attitude of *Erich Lederer Standing with Hands in His Pockets.*

11. Another 1913 pencil and watercolor study, *Erich Lederer with Arm over Chair*, is in the Collection Erika Sieber, Vienna. The seated pose was rejected in favor of the standing one established in the study *Erich Lederer Standing with Hand on Hip.*

12. Due to copyright restrictions Dr. Kallir did not reproduce or fully identify the *Portrait of Erich Lederer* in either the original or revised edition of the *Oeuvre Catalogue*. I am indebted to Herr Lederer for allowing me to reproduce the portrait here for the first time in color. Although the work is signed and dated 1912 by Schiele, the later 1913 studies indicate that the composition was actually conceived in its final form and the painting completed in the first days of 1913.

13. A third study in pencil exists in a private collection, Europe.

14. The Lederers were among those friends of Schiele who worked to get him transferred to the War Archives in Vienna during the war. Schiele makes frequent reference to the Lederers in his War Diary (see Comini, "Schieles Kriegstagebuch 1916," 86–102). Erich Lederer recalls that the day after Schiele's death he came out to the Hietzinger house to see the body, but, because of the high degree of contagion in the influenza epidemic, Schiele's mother would not allow him to enter the room in which the body lay; instead she set up a mirror by the door, so that the young man could look at his friend

one last time (Erich Lederer, personal interview, Geneva, 28 November 1966).

15. Two of these drawings, one from 1914 and the other from 1917, were reproduced by Roessler in one of the first articles to appear on Schiele after his death (see Arthur Roessler, "In Memoriam Egon Schiele," *Deutsche Kunst und Dekoration*, XLIV:1 (1919), 227–43.

16. Letter to Roessler, 18 May 1912, Roessler, *Briefe und Prosa*, pp. 66–67.

17. I owe this and other information about the Benesch's friendship with Schiele to the late Dr. Otto Benesch who kindly reminisced at length for me, and who supplied helpful information concerning Schiele's Neulengbach prison period. Personal interview, 16 August 1963. Frau Eva Benesch has offered continuing generous assistance.

17a. Schiele also gave Heinrich a small "sculpture"—the head of a fellow prisoner modeled out of bread, cf. Chapter IV, note 70.

18. In a letter to Schiele dated 18 March 1913 (A.E.S.A.) Heinrich Benesch asked the artist to do his portrait. This double portrait of father and son must have resulted from this request.

19. When Schiele sketched Otto alone, he seated the boy in order to study intensively the movements of his hands, and it was at this time that he observed the knuckle-rubbing gesture of young Otto which accompanied his cogitation and which became an enduring habit with him. In the watercolor entitled by Schiele *The Folded Hands* (plate 109) three detailed portrayals of this absent-minded massaging of the knuckles of one hand by the fingers of the other were drawn, one above the other. An even more exaggerated version was used in the painting with the knuckles showing white as they press through the resistant fingers and the veins standing out rigidly along the back of the hand.

20. "Die Zahl der Blätter, die er zur Vorbereitung eines Bildnisses schuf, war Legion. Ich konnte ihn oft bei der Arbeit beobachten, besonders als er das lebensgroße Doppelporträt von meinem Vater und mir schuf. . . . Schiele zeichnete rasch, der Stift glitt, wie von Geisterhand geführt, wie im Spiel, über die weiße Papierfläche, mit einer Handhaltung, die zuweilen die der Pinselführung ostasiatischer Maler war. Radiergummi wurde nicht verwendet—änderte das Modell die Haltung, so wurden die neuen Linien neben die alten mit gleicher unfehlbarer Sicherheit gesetzt. Unablässig wurde ein Papierblatt nach dem anderen aufgezogen, so eilte die Produktion dahin. Daß hie und da ein Blatt leer lief, war unvermeidlich—im Atelier gab es stets eine Menge Abfall, der mit Füßen getreten wurde. Doch wie bohrte sich Schiele mit seinen dunklen Augen in das Modell! Wie wurde Nerv und Muskel erfaßt! (*Die Gefalteten Hände*) Die Farben gab Schiele seinen Blättern *nie vor dem Modell*, sondern immer nachträglich aus der mit Naturanschauung vollgezogenen Erinnerung." Quoted from the Otto Benesch original manuscript in the A.E.S.A. of an article later published in *Art International*, 9/10 (1958), 59.

21. See the 1913 pencil drawing *Benesch Double Portrait Study, Heinrich Standing with Right Arm Raised* in the Albertina, Vienna. Here Otto's shoulder and arm are twice lightly sketched in to the left while Heinrich's right hand is shown holding two match-shaped objects and is raised, as if to attract Otto's attention.

22. "Oftmals wurde das Gemälde in unserem Familien- und Bekanntenkreise diskutiert—immer von neuem gab es ein Deuten und Rätselraten. Später erkannte man seinen wahren Sinn. Hatte Schiele—bewußt oder unbewußt—hier eine tiefgehende psychologische Situation erfaßt? Heinrich Benesch dominierte gerne. Der Gedankenflug des Sohnes begann ihm zuweilen unheim-

lich zu werden. *Der Blick in die Geisteswelt* über alle äußeren Schranken hinweg wurde von Schiele bereits an dem damals Siebzehnjährigen erkannt und in dem Porträt zum Ausdruck gebracht—eine Geisteswelt, in der Otto Benesch ganz selbstverständlich dominierte." Eva Benesch, foreword to Heinrich Benesch, *Mein Weg mit Egon Schiele*, pp. 6–7. Reiterated in a personal interview, Vienna, 30 January 1967. Whereas I have quoted from Frau Benesch's foreword to the published version of the Heinrich Benesch original manuscript in the A.E.S.A. (see Chaper II, note 6), I have chosen to quote the Benesch text directly from the manuscript. The published version omits some of Heinrich Benesch's personal opinions on Schiele's art, strikes out a reference to the painter Anton Faistauer, and elides an unfavorable characterization of the painter Mime van Osen.

The physical history of the Benesch double portrait has an ironic twist, for it never became the property of the family. Immediately upon completion the painting was whisked away for exhibition in the one-man showing of Schiele's works at the Hans Goltz Gallery in Munich (26 June–15 July 1913). Heinrich Benesch was unable to pay the fee he himself believed this major work deserved, and when Carl Reininghaus offered to buy it from Schiele for 600 Kronen, Schiele accepted (see Schiele's letter to Roessler of 15 June 1913, Roessler, *Briefe und Prosa*, p. 78). This apparently caused no hard feelings, for Schiele's correspondence with Benesch remains on a friendly level until July 1917 (see note 26 below). From Reininghaus the ownership of this painting passed to Wolfgang Gurlitt, and finally to the Wolfgang Gurlitt Museum in Linz.

Otto Benesch records that at the time Schiele was working on the double portrait he was sketching a life-size group of about twelve figures on an enormous canvas, now lost. The figures were wearing long habits like those of monks, and represented close friends of the artist, among them the two Benesches and Klimt (see Otto Benesch, "Memories," p. 63–64). Two fragments of nude female figures from this painting have been preserved and were identified by Benesch (K.178 and K.179), and I believe a further portion showing the clothed, striding lower torso of one of the men is to be identified on the verso of the 1915 landscape *Single Houses* (K.208). The present owner, Herr Viktor Fogarassy, Graz, has kindly allowed me to examine and photograph this fragment, which is painted in black, red, brown, and gray tones.

23. On April 1918 Schiele wrote Roessler that Dr. Tietze had approached him in regard to doing an article on his paintings (Roessler, *Briefe und Prosa*, p. 91). This article was published in *Die bildenden Künste*, II (1919), 99–110. The Kokoschka portrait was owned by the Tietzes and not publicly exhibited until 1941.

24. This foreword was reprinted in Roessler, *In Memoriam Egon Schiele*, pp. 30–37.

25. "Größere Kongenialität mit Altmeistertum, denn mit dem kultivierten Wien, das vor Sturm und Drang seine Kindheit gewesen, bekundet er in der *Auferstehung* [Resurrection, K.176]. Wenn die Gegenwart, die einen Kokoschka zu den ihren zählt, an Wucht des Ausdrucks alter Kunst gleichkommt, darf man ihr erlaubterweise Affektation vorwerfen, weil sie die Klimtperiode überholte?" *Ibid.*, pp. 36–37.

26. "Sie, Herr Schiele, waren auch einmal einer von 'denen um Klimt.' Die Wandlung die Sie in andere Bahnen lenkte, kann nur ein Abstieg oder Aufstieg gewesen sein. Wohl war es ein Aufstieg" (private collection). Frau Eva Benesch kindly read through this letter with me and has acquiesced to my

quoting from it here. This partially documented argument between Otto Benesch and Schiele appears to have resolved itself with time. However another tiff with the Beneschs is recorded in a testy letter written by Schiele to Heinrich on 31 July 1917:

"Lieber Herr B!

"Ich habe Ihnen den Vorschlag gemacht 2 Jahre lang nichts von mir zu erwerben, bis sich die Zweifel gelegt haben. Ich habe auch gar nicht die Absicht an Zweifelnde zu verkaufen. Das erwähnte Blatt werde ich für Sie bei mir hinterlegen lassen, auch wenn Ihnen fernerhin das eine oder andere zusagt, und nach 2 Jahren können Sie's haben. Ich will damit nicht unsere Freundschaft zerstören, sondern festigen. Freundliche Grüße, Egon Schiele 1917."

("Dear Herr B!

"I have suggested to you not to buy anything from me for 2 years until the doubts have abated. I do not have any intention of selling to those who doubt. The drawing referred to I shall have put aside for you at my place, also if henceforth you like one thing or the other, and after 2 years you may have it. I do not want to destroy our friendship through this, but strengthen it. Friendly greetings, Egon Schiele 1917"). From the A.E.S.A., Folder of transcripts of letters, the originals of which are not in the A.E.S.A.; location of original undetermined.

27. "... I have had to drag [Schiele] about with me ever since he exhibited his drawings side by side with mine at the second Kunstschau. The point was always made that his linear style compared with mine, as though there were even the slightest resemblance." Statement by Kokoschka to Goldscheider, see Goldscheider, *Kokoschka*, p. 9. More recent derogatory comments on Schiele by Kokoschka were reported in the 24 October 1966 issue of *Der Spiegel*, p. 172.

28. In a letter to Heinrich Schwarz, Kokoschka describes Franz Hauer as "... einer der letzten großen und echten Wiener mit Kultur zu einer Zeit, wenn Adel und Bürgertum bereits diese österreichische Kultur zu verschachern begonnen hatten. ..." ("... one of the last great and genuine Viennese with culture at a time when nobility and bourgeoisie had already begun to barter away this Austrian culture ...") See Schwarz, "Die graphischen Werke von Egon Schiele," 50–69. Schwarz discusses the Schiele and Kokoschka portraits and studies of Hauer, gives a chronological oeuvre numbering for the Schiele graphic works, and points out that a "Self-Portrait" etching which Schiele showed Roessler is not the head engraved on the same plate as a figure by Philippi, as had previously been assumed, but the head which appears on the verso of the Hauer portrait plate. I am grateful to Dr. Schwarz for bringing to my attention a book by Hauer's son which contains information about the Hauer gallery (see Leopold Hauer, *Der Maler Leopold Hauer, Selbstbiographie*, Vienna, 1962).

29. "Geehrter Herr Hauer,

"Ich habe gehört, daß Sie einer von den Wenigen sind, die Bilder von den Jüngsten erwerben. Möchten Sie mich nicht besuchen, oder die Ausstellung des Hagenbundes ansehen, wo von mir einige Arbeiten zu sehen sind?" Letter dated 12 July 1912; this and other transcriptions of the Schiele–Hauer correspondence kindly provided by Dr. Franz Glück, former director of the Historisches Museum der Stadt Wien, Vienna.

30. Hauer paid Schiele 900 Kronen for *Autumn Land* (K.XXVII) (1912), *Conversion I* (K.158) (1912), and *Agony* (plate 87).

31. Schiele later bought this painting back from Hauer in order to exhibit it in the 1916 Kriegsausstellung held in Vienna, for which occasion he gave it the grandiose title: *Heroes' Graves—Resurrection—Fragment for a Mausoleum.*

This new title was simply a matter of expediency and did not reflect on the original meaning of the painting, for, as Schiele complained, neither he nor any of the other artists he was responsible for including in the Kriegsausstellung were really "painters of war," but the paintings had to have some connection, even the most far-fetched with war. See Schiele letter to Peschka, 30 May 1917, in Roessler, *"Briefe und Prosa,* pp. 123–24.

32. "Bedenken Sie lieber Herr Hauer, daß ich aber sonst anderen Leuten kleine Bilder (Landschaften) um 600 Kronen verkauft habe, also ich weiß wie sympatisch mir der Mensch ist, der die Gräber besitzt." Letter of 11 August 1913 to Hauer, transcription provided by Dr. Franz Glück.

33. "Vorderhand denke ich hauptsächlich über Bilder nach die ich malen möchte. Studien mache ich auch, aber ich finde und weiß, daß das Abzeichnen nach der Natur für mich bedeutungslos ist, weil ich besser Bilder nach Erinnerungen male, als Vision von der Landschaft. —Hauptsächlich beobachte ich jetzt die körperliche Bewegung von Bergen, Wasser, Bäumen und Blumen, überall erinnert man sich an ähnliche Regungen von Freuden und Leiden in den Pflanzen. Die Malerei allein genügt mir nicht, ich weiß, daß man MIT Farben Qualitäten schaffen kann. Inniger und mit dem Wesen und Herz empfindet man einen herbstlichen Baum im Sommer, diese Wehmut möchte ich malen." Letter of 25 August 1913 to Hauer, transcription provided by Dr. Franz Glück.

34. See entry No. 770 (May 1906) in Paul Klee, *Tagebücher* (Cologne, 1957), pp. 214–25.

35. Compare Kokoschka's drawing of Arthur Roessler (plate 38) for a "non-pathetic" portrayal of a man who was not particularly sympathetic to the artist.

36. At least two other pencil studies by Schiele for the Hauer portrait exist. One, showing Hauer's face turned to the right, as in the final etching, is in the Collection Leopold Hauer, Vienna. A second study depicts Hauer in left profile with his hands raised to his face, and is in the Collection S. and G. Poppe, Hamburg. There is interesting evidence that Schiele did at one time intend to paint an oil portrait of Hauer. The verso of the 1917 painting *Edge of Town* (K.231) has a portrait sketch of a bearded man (noted but not identified by Kallir; not noted by Leopold) whose features bear an unmistakable resemblance to Franz Hauer. I am grateful to Dr. Wilfried Skreiner of the Neue Galerie, Landesmuseum, Joanneum in Graz for allowing me to examine the painting and its verso and for generously providing me with photographs.

37. In his article "Die graphischen Werke von Egon Schiele," (see note 28 above) Heinrich Schwarz attempted a chronology of Schiele's graphic works. The recent oeuvre catalogue by Dr. Otto Kallir, *Egon Schiele: The Graphic Works*, (Vienna, 1970) now provides a complete and expanded list of the artist's work in the media of etching, lithography and woodcut. The Kallir oeuvre catalogue numbering is used here. (In the text "Kallir" followed by a number refers to the oeuvre numbering of a graphic work.)

   The demonstration plate with Schiele's *Head of a Man* was later cut into two parts. Dr. Schwarz was the first to draw attention to the existence and meaning of this formerly double plate.

38. Early in 1914 Schiele had suggested making a few etchings if Roessler would supply the money and tools (see the chapter, "Wie Schiele zur Radierung kam," Roessler, *Erinnerungen*, pp. 67–69). The preparatory study for the 1914 etched portrait of Roessler (plate 43) also displays a needle-like treatment in which outer contours set intersecting or parallel lines of hatching into motion, and inner areas generate grids and moons of graphic response.

39. See Schiele's letter to Roessler of 17 March and 10 August 1911, Roessler,

Briefe und Prosa, p. 53 and pp. 59–60. Several unpublished letters between Schiele and Dr. Engel are in the A.E.S.A. and in the possession of Melanie Schuster, Vienna.

40. Roessler, *Briefe und Prosa*, p. 161. This letter constitutes one of Schiele's rare statements on the meaning of a work, and because certain passages shed light also on the Self-Seers series and *Agony*, I give it here. Of special interest are Schiele's references to the "astral light" and the union of positive and negative electricity:

"September 1912

"Dear Dr. Engel:

'The Revelation'! The revelation of a particular human being. It can be a poet, an artist, a man of learning, a spiritualist. Have you noticed what an impression a great personality exerts on his contemporaries? That would be one. The picture must emanate light. Bodies have their own light which they use up while living; they burn up, they are unilluminated. The figure in the back? One half is supposed to portray the vision of so great a human being that the one who has just been influenced kneels down in intoxication, bows before the greatness that looks without opening its eyes, that decays, from which the astral light pours forth in orange or other colors to such excess that, hypnotized, the bowing figure flows into the large one. On the right everything is red-orange, red-brown. On the left is thus the being which resembles him, which in a different way equals the large one on the right. (Positive and negative electricity unite.) This is to indicate that the little one kneeling melts into the radiating large one. These would be a few comments about my picture, 'The Revelation'. Egon Schiele."

("September 1912

"Lieber Dr. Engel

" 'Die Offenbarung'!—Die Offenbarung eines betreffenden Lebewesens. Ein Dichter, ein Künstler, ein Wissender, ein Spiritist kann es sein. —Haben Sie schon gespürt, welchen Eindruck eine große Persönlichkeit auf die Mitwelt ausübt? —Das wäre eine. —Das Bild muß von sich Licht geben, die Körper haben ihr eigenes Licht, das sie beim Leben verbrauchen; sie verbrennen, sie sind unbeleuchtet. —Rückwärts die Figur? —Die eine Hälfte soll also die Vision eines so großen Menschen porträtiert zeigen, daß der, der eben beeinflußt, hingerissen sich niederkniet, sich beugt vor der Große, die schaut, ohne die Augen zu öffnen, die verwest, der das astralische Licht orange oder andersfarbig ausströmt, in dem Übermaß, daß der Gebeugte hypnotisiert in den Großen fließt. —Rechts ist alles rot-orange, rot-braun. —Links ist also das ihm ähnliche Wesen, das andersartig, dem rechten großen gleichsteht. —(Positive und negative Elektrizität vereinigen sich.) So soll bedeutet sein, daß der kniende Kleine in den strahlenden Großen hineinschmilzt. —Das wäre Einiges über mein Bild, 'Die Offenbarung'. Egon Schiele.")

41. Dr. Engel's voracious "claims" to further paintings as Schiele's reputation grew finally exasperated Schiele so much that he attempted to retrieve some of his works, see letters to Roessler, *Briefe und Prosa*, pp. 90–91.

    This motif of a frontal female figure enclosed by the falling triangle of her own loosened hair appears in two allegories and their studies executed in the same year, *Procession* (K.133) and *Madonna* (K.134). In my opinion these figures are not to be associated with Trude Engel. Dr. Kallir informs me that Dr. Engel cut out and repainted a portion of the portrait which he considered too intimate (personal interview, 26 September 1972, New York).

42. See the chapter, "Hoffnungsfunke," Roessler, *Erinnerungen*, pp. 22–24. The five oils on wood mentioned by Roessler are Schiele's *Self-Portrait with Win-*

ter Cherry and the matching *Wally* (plates 92 and 94), another portrait "pair" of the same personae (K.153 and K.173; see discussion in Chapter IV, note 52), and the intimate portrait of Wally, *Reclining Woman with Upturned Skirt* (plate 90). A letter from Schiele to Roessler, saying that he would expect Frau Roessler at his studio "to paint," indicates that the project had been under consideration since November of 1910 (Roessler, *Briefe und Prosa*, p. 46).

43. A 1912 pencil study for the Ida Roessler portrait is in the Historisches Museum der Stadt Wien (Inv. No. 115164). In contrast to the oil it shows the sitter in three-quarter length.

44. A 1917 pencil sketch of Ida Roessler by the realist Viktor Hammer, done as a companion piece to his sketch of Arthur Roessler (plate 37) and now in the possession of the Historisches Museum der Stadt Wien, gives an interesting mirrorlike exactness against which to measure Schiele's idealized portrait. Anton Faistauer also painted a portrait of Ida Roessler in 1914.

45. Personal interview, Vienna, 23 August 1963. Mrs. Federica (formerly Friederike) Beer-Monti, who, since 1934, has resided in the United States, has generously and repeatedly described her encounters with Schiele and Klimt for me, and I am most indebted to her for perceptive analyses of the artistic situation in Vienna before World War I.

   Apparently further sittings for the completion of this portrait, begun in October, were made in December of the same year, for one of Schiele's sketchbooks contains entries for Fräulein Beer against the dates 1–5, and 14, 15 December, from 10 to 12 noon (see A.E.S.A. Sketchbook VI, pp. 4 verso and 5 recto).

   As a regular client of the Wiener Werkstätte Friederike had already unknowingly come into contact with Schiele's sister Gerti, who modeled women's fashions during the years 1912 and 1913. When I showed her several photographs of Gerti in various Wiener Werkstätte dresses, Mrs. Beer-Monti recognized one of the gowns as "a green dress I bought right off the model!" (personal interview, New York, 16 February 1968).

46. Personal interview, Vienna, 23 August 1963, and letter to me, 21 November 1966.

47. Not reproduced here; Collection Federica Beer-Monti, Honolulu.

48. Personal interview, Vienna, 23 August 1963.

49. Anton Faistauer, *Neue Malerei in Österreich*, p. 19. Faistauer was comparing Schiele's and Klimt's portraits of Friederike Beer and decided that the Klimt version was superior because of its "gentleness." He drew no conclusions about the Expressionistic elements in Schiele's work, but only condemned them as poor work.

50. Personal interview, New York, 9 March 1967.

51. The historically fortuitous event of a third portrait of Friederike Beer by Kokoschka *almost* occurred. Here is Mrs. Beer-Monti's reminiscence:

   "Kokoschka asked if he could paint me and I was of course delighted. But at that time he was still recovering from his war wounds, and he was recuperating at the Field Hospital set up temporarily in the Palais Palffy on the Augustinerstrasse in the center of Vienna. So I had to go to him. I went—just once! You see, I was dressed in my Wiener Werkstätte dress which was really an eye-stopper and quite elegant, and when I walked into that courtyard of wounded men lying about, so weak and listless, I felt—well, I felt unhappy and wrong. Kokoschka sensed this and I left, promising to come back another time. But I never did, and that's why I haven't had a portrait done by Kokoschka" (personal interviews, Vienna, 23 August 1963, New York, 16 February 1968, and Honolulu, 3 August 1970).

   An interesting comparison with Schiele's portrayal of Friederike Beer does exist however in the full-length portrait of her sister Charlotte, painted at about the same time by Hugo Bouvard, the artist who in 1910 had created watercolor portraits of a remarkable intensity (figure 50). By 1914 Bouvard had become, in Mrs. Beer-Monti's phrase, "the Raphael Soyer of his time," and devoted himself to society portraits and the depiction of military events. His portrait of Charlotte Beer (now in the Collection Aris Demertzis, New York) is in subdued colors, showing her reclining on a couch and gazing out frontally. Her dress and a supporting pillow are of Wiener Werkstätte design, but these are the most advanced features in a painting which has otherwise returned to the tradition of Hans Makart's portrait of *Charlotte Wolter as Messalina* (1875, Historisches Museum der Stadt Wien).

52. Personal interviews, Vienna, 23 August 1963, and New York, 16 February 1968. Klimt received the equivalent of $7,000 for this portrait, an enormously high sum at that time.

53. Four studies are in the Collection Federica Beer-Monti, Honolulu, and five others were recently offered for sale by Christian M. Nebehay, *Katalog Gustav Klimt, 56 Zeichnungen*, XI (Vienna, 1967), figures 48–52.

54. Personal interviews, Vienna, 23 August 1963, New York, 16 February 1968, and Honolulu, 3 August, 1970.

55. Klimt's remark quoted to me by Mrs. Federica Beer-Monti, personal interview, Vienna, 23 August 1963.

CHAPTER VI: *1914–1916: Emergence from Isolation* (pp. 133–153)

1. See for example Steichen's portrait photograph of Clarence H. White (plate XXIV) in the 1905 special number of *The Studio*; cf. Chapter III, note 51.

2. Among Schiele's effects at the time of his death; possession Melanie Schuster, Vienna.

3. See the 1916 *Still-Life with Books* (K.218) and the 1918 *Portrait of Guido Arnot* (plate 162).

4. A mistaken identification was made in the Marlborough Gallery Catalogue *Egon Schiele* (London, 1964), p. 23 insert, where, along with four photographs of Schiele, a fifth, showing a young man whose face is distorted by a face-splitting grin, was reproduced and identified as Schiele. This is not a photograph of Schiele but of his colleague, the painter Hans Böhler, as Böhler's mistress of some fifty years promptly and indignantly informed me and the Marlborough Gallery.

5. This post card, dated 17 March 1910 (signature illegible), is in the A.E.S.A.

6. For reviews of Isadora Duncan's appearances in Vienna see Hevesi, *Acht Jahre Sezession*; at the Secession, 6 February 1902, pp. 368–70; at the Carl-Theater, 8 and 10 January 1904, pp. 516–23. Few dates occur in Isadora's own writings, but she describes her rose-bedecked appearance at the Secession building (incorrectly referred to by her as the Künstler Haus) in connection with her first visit (1902) to Vienna with Loïe Fuller's troupe (*My Life*, p. 98).

7. If any one dancer exerted a direct influence on the form of Schiele's photographic pantomimes it would have been Ruth St. Denis, whom he had seen and admired at the Ronacher theater. Roessler reports that once while admiring the dancing movements of his Javanese shadow puppets, Schiele remarked that, compared with the puppets, Ruth St. Denis was a heavy cannon. (See Roessler, *Erinnerungen*, p. 36.) An undated (*ca.* 1930?) article in the A.E.S.A. by Fritz Karpfen published in the *Weltpresse*, No. 219, p. 4, describes an alleged short but passionate friendship between Ruth St. Denis and Schiele.

Schiele did make several drawings and watercolors of dancers, male and female, during the years 1911–14, and it is interesting to note that he occasionally gave such drawings "action" titles such as "Dancer" and "Fighter," motifs eminently suitable to his cult of the expressive, speaking body and his love of clear outline.

8. See Mary Wigman, *The Language of Dance*, trans. by Walter Sorell (Middletown, Conn., 1966), p. 113, and Hans Brandenburg, *Der Moderne Tanz* (Munich, 1921), pp. 199–203. Although the Viennese Expressionist portraits precede Wigman's work by several years, an exploration of a possible cross-fertilization between Laban's theories, Hodler's eurythmic canvases, and Steiner's anthroposophic writings might throw further light on the sources of Expressionism in Vienna and Munich.

I am grateful to Dr. Walter Sorell of the Theater Arts Department of Columbia University for discussing Mary Wigman in relation to Expressionist painting with me (personal interviews, New York, 8 and 10 November 1968).

9. "Liebes Fräulein Ed. und Ad. oder Ad. und Ed. ich glaube, daß Ihre Frau Mama Ihnen erlauben wird, mit Walli [*sic*] und mir in's Kino oder in's Apollo oder wohin Sie wollen, zu gehen. Sie können beruhigt sein daß ich in Wirklichkeit ein ganz anderer bin,—als 'Apache,' das ist eine bloß momentane Pose aus Übermut. —Wenn Sie also Lust haben, sich mir und Walli anzuvertrauen, so würde ich mich freuen und erwarte Ihrerseits die Antwort an welchen Tag es Ihnen conveniert."

In the A.E.S.A. "Walli" is Schiele's spelling of Wally. Adele Harms testifies that it was Wally, Schiele's mistress, who first served as chaperone for their meetings (personal interview, Vienna, 24 January 1967).

10. "Mit Kino sind wir einverstanden und zwar Montag den 14. im Park-Kino zu Ewers 'Launen einer Weltdame.' Natürlich mit Walli [*sic*]. Wer besorgt die Karten? Meine Mama darf davon nichts wissen. Herzlichst Adele und Edith." Undated, in the A.E.S.A. The movie referred to was a silent film starring Tilla Durieux.

11. The gallery lists in Schiele's Munich diary (see above, Chapter IV, note 79) indicate his familiarity with the German Expressionists. It is possible to determine his knowledge of other contemporary artists at this time from a letter written to him by the Dresden art dealer Emil Richter. This letter, dated 30 June 1914, boasts the names of some 250 contemporary artists in its letterhead, including Schiele's, and Schiele went through the list with his pencil, underlining his own name, and the names of the other artists whose works he knew. Some names, such as those of Hodler, Lautrec, Munch, Picasso, Rodin, Rops, Signac, Valloton, and Whistler, are underlined as might be expected; others, also underlined, are interesting as further indications of Schiele's knowledge. These include: Besnard, Brangwyn, Carrière, Daumier, Derain, Forain, Israels, Khnopff, Klinger, Meid, Menzel, Slevogt, Steinlen, Stuck, Toorop, Zorn, and Zuloaga. Names apparently not familiar to Schiele include: Daubigny, Ensor, Fantin-Latour, Rysselberghe, Vogeler, and Wright (letter in the A.E.S.A.).

12. Comparison with photographs and drawings of Wally and the testimony of Adele Harms indicate the female figure is Schiele's mistress and not his future wife.

13. See A.E.S.A. Sketchbook V (1914), p. 15 recto, p. 15 verso, p. 16 recto, and Sketchbook VI (1915), p. 9 verso, p. 10 recto, and p. 29 recto.

14. Cf., *Portrait of Edith Schiele Standing* (plate 133) and discussion in the text below.

15. The double V gestures here seem a definite allusion to the two new women in a Don Juanian roving of seductive fancy. For a transformation of the gesture

into a more specific reference cf. *Soaring* (figure 106), discussion in the text, and note 22 below.

16. Another source for *Death and Maiden* may have been a Kollwitz etching "Tod und Frau," No. 367 in a Secession exhibition of November 1911–January 1912 and reproduced in the catalogue. In Kollwitz's work the skeleton Death bites into the back of a kneeling female nude with a small child.

17. XXXIV:2 (1914), 342. After Schiele was befriended by Alexander Koch, the enlightened publisher of *Deutsche Kunst und Dekoration*, an agreement was made to exchange some drawings for a subscription to this important art periodical; see letter of 19 October 1916 to Schiele, A.E.S.A.

   Later Schiele was able to examine another portrait by Kokoschka of himself and Alma Mahler when their mutual patron, Dr. Oskar Reichel, acquired the 1913 painting *Dancing Pair* (Wingler 77). Schiele could also have seen Kokoschka's earliest (1912) double portrait of himself and Alma Mahler (Wingler 71) in reproduction in *Die Kunst*, XXVII (1913), 464.

18. Schiele wrote separate letters to Gerti and Anton Peschka on the eve of their wedding. The letter to Peschka is of particular interest in shedding light on their relationship:

"23 November 1914
"Dear Anton Peschka!
"We have known each other for a long time. Life has been sad for you. You were educated by experiencing a great deal. The times must change. You have a great fault without which you should grow. You must be master and you must direct. Whoever lives with deliberation will advance faster. We must not be peasants or people rooted in the soil—that already must separate us. We must never again wish for the past—that would be a going back. Therefore, I do not want to stay here with you, but to go to Berlin after the war and have the courage to begin life again. For this I wish for you and for myself perception, clarity, and luck. Most cordial greetings, Egon Schiele."

("23 November 1914
"Lieber Anton Peschka!
"Wir kennen uns lange—das Leben war für Dich traurig—Du wurdest dadurch erzogen, weil Du viel erlebtest—die Zeit muß anders werden. Du hast einen großen Fehler an Dir, ohne den Du wachsen müßtest.—Du sollst Herr sein und dirigieren. Wer mit Überlegung lebt, wird schneller fortkommen. Wir dürfen nicht Bauern sein oder bodenständige Leute, schon das soll uns unterscheiden,—die Vergangenheit dürfen wir nie wieder wünschen,—das wäre Rückkehr. Darum möchte ich mit Euch nicht hierbleiben,—sondern nach dem Krieg nach Berlin und den Mut haben, von Neuem zu leben beginnen,—dazu wünsche ich Euch und mir Erkenntnis, Klarheit und Glück. Herzlichste Grüße, Egon Schiele.") Roessler, *Briefe und Prosa*, pp. 104–05.

19. An interesting precedent exists for Schiele's trick photograph. Around 1890 Maurice Guibert took a double portrait photograph of Toulouse-Lautrec showing the artist seated on a stool before his canvas (on which a self-caricature has been drawn) and facing his model, Lautrec again, seated on a stool vis-à-vis. While it is not possible to ascertain whether Schiele or his photographer (presumably Schiele's neighbor, the painter Johannes Fischer) knew of this picture, a local precedent may be found in a photograph by Nicola Perscheid of a young girl in a mirror, reproduced in *Deutsche Kunst und Dekoration*, XXI:1 (1907–08), 113.

20. A 1915 self-portrait drawing entitled "The Seers" shows Schiele three times, floating with hands raised (reproduced on an invitation card to a tenth anni-

versary exhibition of Schiele's death given by the Würthle Gallery in Vienna in October, 1928; invitation card in the A.E.S.A.).

21. Translated as "Transfiguration" by Dr. Kallir. Due to the thematic importance implied in Schiele's word choice ("*Entschwebung*," "soaring up" or "away"), I am retaining this meaning in the title given in the text.

   An unpublished Schiele sketchbook in the possession of Dr. Kallir (hereafter referred to as Kallir unpublished Schiele Sketchbook) contains a multifigure, framed sketch in which the two central figures repeat exactly the poses in *Soaring*. On pp. 15 and 16 of the same sketchbook (pages reproduced in Kallir, *Oeuvre Catalogue*, p. 85) notes made by Schiele for a Mausoleum project (not realized) refer twice to a painting titled "Resurrection of Eternal Life." Schiele was apparently playing with the idea of expanding *Soaring* into a triptych. An interesting compositional study for *Soaring* is in the A.E.S.A. Sketchbook V, 1915, p. 12 recto, Albertina.

22. This is the interpretation insisted upon by Adele Harms (personal interview, Vienna, 24 January 1967).

23. For parallels in this "floating away from the problem" in cases of paranoid schizophrenia see Dr. Alan A. Stone's discussion of schizophrenia and disturbances in the body image, *The Abnormal Personality Through Literature* (Englewood Cliffs, 1966), pp. 68–69 and p. 136.

24. "Daß ein Gott im Himmel ist glaube ich/nicht ungerecht sind seine Taten." A.E.S.A. Sketchbook IX (1916), p. 8 verso. The same sketchbook page also contains a clumsily set down musical theme, further indicating that this page was Schiele's eclectic page for noting things which appealed to him and which he wished to remember.

25. I am indebted to Professor Emeritus Julius S. Held, formerly of the Art History Department of Columbia University, who went over all the Schiele sketchbooks in the Albertina with me in the summer of 1963, and who taught me how to read Schiele's Gothic script. Professor Held has substantiated my interpretation of this jingle.

26. "Wir leben in der gewaltigsten Zeit, die die Welt je gesehen hat. . . . Was vor 1914 war, gehört zu einer andern Welt." Roessler, *Briefe und Prosa*, p. 39.

27. "War bei der Musterung und wurde endgültig heimgeschickt. —Habe vor, zu heiraten,—günstigst, nicht vielleicht W[ally]." *Ibid*, p. 85.

28. An assertion to which the late Adele Harms still maintained allegiance in my last interview with her (Vienna, 24 January 1967).

29. "Werde in München, Sezession, Sommer bis Oktober ausstellen und im August im Kunsthaus, Zürich. Wir haben einen neuen Bund gegründet, darüber schreib' ich gelegentlich. Alles hätte ich jetzt—Montag werde ich gemustert! Vielleicht komme ich auch dorthin?" Roessler, *Briefe und Prosa*, p. 106.

30. "Wir sitzen gerade im Café Wunderer und warten auf die Entscheidung von Italien. . . . Eine Hauptschuld fällt auf Marinetti und die übrigen Futuristen!" *Ibid.*

31. " 'Geeignet!' am 21. Juni nach Prag einrücken!" *Ibid.*, p. 107.

32. "Schreibe mir auch: wenn ich nach Prag komme, will ich für mich wohnen, wird dies gestattet? Wie lange hat man frei oder Dienst, und muß man anfangs in der Kaserne schlafen?" *Ibid.*, p. 108. Due to the Triennium he had earned at the Academy, Schiele was entitled to the military status of "Einjährigfreiwilliger"; see Chapter I, note 21. He was later promoted to the rank of corporal.

33. These sentiments are expressed in a still-existing long and emotional "manifesto" from Edith to Egon (in the A.E.S.A.).

34. Roessler gives a detailed account of this in a reminiscence not intended for the general public in the A.E.S.A., "Egon Schiele Erinnerungsbuch." The story is substantiated by Adele Harms and both Schiele sisters.

35. It is interesting that contemporary criticism of Schiele's portraiture actually introduced, in a derogatory sense, the concept of "stupor catatonicus" (see citations by Herbert Waniek, "Egon Schiele und Ich," *Ver.* [15 November 1917], 106–107).

36. These glass plate negatives were found among Schiele's effects at the time of his death and went into the possession of Melanie Schuster. Adele has stated to me that her "nunish" avocation was successfully impinged upon by Schiele in 1917 (personal interview, Vienna, 24 January 1967). Apparently Edith was aware of the situation but tolerated it, accustomed by this time to her husband's ways.

37. This diary runs from 8 March to 30 September 1916 and is today in the A.E.S.A. For the entries cited here see Comini, "Egon Schieles Kriegstagebuch 1916," pp. 86–102.

38. Writing to Peschka on 13 January 1917 Schiele reported: "On January 5 my father-in-law died of old age. I liked him a lot, he was tall and thin, 76 years old. In the spring of 1915 [1916], when I was in Liesing, I drew and painted him. The portrait is 140 × 110 cm. He is seated. And when I was in Vienna for the funeral, I made a death mask of him. It turned out very well and interesting." ("Am 5. Jänner starb mein Schwiegervater an Altersschwäche, ich hatte ihn sehr gerne, er war groß und mager, 76 Jahre alt. Im Frühjahr 1915 [1916], als in Liesing war, zeichnete und malte ich ihn. –Das Porträt ist 140 × 110 cm groß–er sitzt.–Und als ich zu der Leichenfeier in Wien war, nahm ich ihm die Totenmaske ab, sie wurde sehr gut und interessant.") Roessler, *Briefe und Prosa*, p. 116. This death mask is still extant and was formerly in the possession of Adele Harms, Vienna.

39. "Ich zeichnete klein und groß auf Leinwand meinen Schwiegervater. . . . Ich malte an dem Porträt meines Schwiegervaters den dunklen Grund." Comini, "Egon Schieles Kriegstagebuch 1916," p. 98 (17 and 22 April).

40. "Sie [Edith] unterhielt sich vielleicht in der Zeit wo ich nicht fortkonnte zeitweise, doch damals waren wir noch nicht so nahe wie es heute ist (denn sonst hätte sie nicht Einladungen angenommen)." Diary scrap dated 26 August 1915, possession Walter Neurath, London; published by Wolfgang Fischer, "Unbekannte Tagebuchblätter und Briefe von Egon Schiele und Erinnerungen einer Wiener Emigrantin in London," *Albertina Studien*, II:4 (1964), 172–73. In the commentary to these diary entries Dr. Fischer misinterprets a mention by Schiele of his 1915 portrait of Edith (K.205, plate 133) as referring to the 1917–18 portrait of her (K. 232, plate 171) and redates the painting as 1918. In a later correction of this mistake ("Zur Rückseite von Egon Schieles 'Porträt Edith Schiele' und Die Berichtigung einer Datierung," *Albertina Studien*, III: 2, p. 102), Dr. Fischer misread an identification painted by a foreign hand on the back of the canvas as "Edith Schiele Wien 1915"; the correct reading is "Edith Schiele Wien 1925."

41. "Meine Kameraden bekommen fortwährend Kuchen und Torten und Post von zu Hause, ich bekam noch von nirgend wo was." Roessler, *Briefe und Prosa*, p. 35. This and two other letters to his mother on pp. 34–35 are incorrectly dated 1915 in an obvious publishing error; they should read "1916."

42. Edith's diary was formerly in the possession of Adele Harms, Vienna, who says Schiele "forced" her sister to write it (personal interview, Vienna, 24 January 1967). It is now owned by Dr. Kallir, New York. Klimt showed a similar compulsion to note down virile moments with models, and a Klimt diary of 1918 (possession Christian M. Nebehay, Vienna) is filled with X's.

43. Comini, "Egon Schieles Kriegstagebuch 1916," p. 98 (9 and 23 April).

44. This sketch is found on p. 107 of a sketchbook owned by Dr. Kallir and recently published by him in facsimile, *A Sketchbook by Egon Schiele* (New York, 1967). A loose page is seen reproduced to the right in the illustration given here, showing a quick sketch of Schiele's 1915 *Portrait of Edith Standing*, done probably from memory since the painting had apparently already gone into the collection of the art dealer Guido Arnot, whom Schiele was shortly to paint.

45. Of the several photographs showing Schiele with army companions of the most disparate types an interesting feature is observable in all. Invariably the other men link arms with Schiele, or hold on to him as though commonly inspired by some protective instinct for their shy and fragile comrade-at-arms. Schiele's fellow artists also portrayed him with a mild, dreamy countenance that is much at odds with the artist's own self-portraits prior to 1917 and 1918 (see portraits by Mopp, plate 27d; Harta, figure 113; Peschka, figure 116; and Gütersloh, plate 193).

46. ". . . wie unlustig alle Soldaten sind mit denen ich bisher zusammen kam ist ganz eigentümlich—ein jeder wünscht das Ende des Krieges, gleichgültig auf welche Art.—speziell mir ist es egal wo ich lebe, d.h. welcher Nation ich lebe —jedenfalls aber neige ich weit mehr auf die drübere Seite, also unsere Feinde— ihre Länder sind viel interessanter als unsere—dort gibt es wirklich Freiheit— und Denkende mehr als bei uns. Was soll man aber heute über den Krieg sagen,—schade um jede Stunde der Fortdauer." Comini, "Egon Schieles Kriegs- tagebuch 1916," pp. 94 and 97 (12 March and 4 April).

47. *Ibid.*, reproduced p. 95, plate 9. I have not been able conclusively to identify the sitter. He looks like a prematurely aged Max Oppenheimer, who however spent most of the war years in Switzerland.

48. "Können Sie nach der beiliegenden Photographie ein Bild des grossen Dichters Charles Péguy zeichnen? Er ist soeben gefallen. Wenn Sie mir die Zeichnung recht schnell senden könnten, wäre ich Ihnen sehr dankbar." Post card in the A.E.S.A. An interesting parallel occurs with Klimt, who also usually only drew from life. Christian M. Nebehay, in his richly detailed *Gustav Klimt Dokumentation* (Vienna, 1969), has demonstrated that Klimt's famous profile sketch of the actor Carl Blasel (1897) was based on a photograph (p. 117).

49. "uns gegenseitig zeichnen resp. malen." Post card dated 25 July 1916, A.E.S.A.

50. Wingler 13.

51. A watercolor portrait done by Harta of Schiele (Collection Melanie Schuster, Vienna) again exemplifies the painterly approach of this artist who had once complained of England that there was no Baroque to be seen in that country (remark quoted by Federica Beer-Monti, personal interview, New York, 9 March 1967). Schiele's new interest in developing a more coloristic technique is supported by the fact that he now began to collect drawings and watercolors by Harta, Kolig, Faistauer, and Johannes Fischer—all artists distinguished by a painterly approach. Schiele's collection of works by his colleagues is now in the possession of Melanie Schuster, Vienna.

52. Letter to Peschka of 31 October 1916 (Roessler, *Briefe und Prosa*, pp. 115–16). Schiele described *Die Aktion* thus: "there are the wildest fellows in it" ("es sind die wildesten Kerle drin" p. 116).

53. "In denselben Tagen hörte ich, daß meine Zeichnungen aus der 'Aktion' Du für 'Griepenkerls'-ideas hieltst—ich gebe zu, daß gerade diese Blätter zahm sind—nicht aber alle aus dieser Zeit." *Ibid.*, p. 116. This letter is of further interest for the information it gives concerning the whereabouts of Schiele's colleagues at this time:
"Faistauer is with the pass control at the Salzburg railroad station. Gütersloh

is still with the Red Cross in Vienna; Harta is in training in Mostar; Jungnickel, inducted in Bavaria, is almost always on furlough and is in Vienna; Kolig is with the War Press Department, Wiegele a prisoner in Algiers, Lang in Moscow, only Fischer is still a civilian. Thus we are all scattered. Kokoschka was discharged from Berlin through Prince Lichnowsky. His nerves are entirely ruined. In Germany a number of the youngest and most promising artists were killed in action. Oppenheimer [Mopp] is in Zurich (civilian). Böhler in Vienna, he is Swiss."
("Faistauer ist bei der Paßrevision in Salzburg am Bahnhof.—Gütersloh ist noch beim Roten Kreuz in Wien, Harta ist beim Train in Mostar, Jungnickel in Bayern eingerückt und hat fast immer Urlaub und ist in Wien, Kolig ist im Kriegspressequartier, Wiegele in Algier in Gefangenschaft, Lang in Moskau, nur Fischer ist noch Zivil.—So sind wir alle zerstreut.—Koskoschka wurde durch Fürst Lichnowsky von Berlin aus enthoben.—Er ist mit seinen Nerven ganz kaput.—In Deutschland fiel eine Reihe der jüngsten und zukunftsreichsten Künstler. Oppenheimer [Mopp] ist in Zürich (Zivil). Böhler in Wien, er ist Schweizer.") (p. 118.)

CHAPTER VII: *1917–1918: Schiele's Later Portraits* (pp. 155–87)

1. An important discussion of the distinction between contemporary (French and German) interpretation of the term "Expressionism" is given by Donald E. Gordon, "On the Origin of the Word 'Expressionism,' " *Warburg Journal*, XXIX (1966), 368–85.

2. His penchant for travel was also satisfied, for his new work in Vienna brought him into contact with Hans Rosé, a first lieutenant in charge of the Austrian post exchanges. Rosé planned to publish a monograph on these supply centers and "ordered" Schiele to travel around Austria to make on-the-spot drawings of each of the twenty-eight posts. (See Wolfgang Fischer, "Egon Schiele als 'Militaerzeichner," *Albertina Studien*, IV:2 [1966], 70–82.) This assignment took him to many towns in the Tyrol during June and July of 1917.

3. "Nun höre:
"Wir sind von neuem zusammengetreten.—'Kunsthalle'—in den größten Dimensionen läuft alles mit Riesenschritten. —Es lag in der Luft. —Bildende Kunst, —Literatur und Musik. Die ganze österreichische Künstlerwelt ist auf. —Die gründer sind Künstler und Kunstfreunde. Unter anderen sind Arnold Schönberg, Gustav Klimt, Jos[ef] Hoffmann, A[nton] Hanak, Peter Altenberg und viele andere mit,—die besten Kunsthistoriker usw., es ist kein Verein, es gibt nur Arbeitsgruppen." Roessler, *Briefe und Prosa*, pp. 118–22. Schiele goes on to copy the text of the Kunsthalle's "Declaration" for Peschka. This singular text declares that art is more than "a matter of bourgeois luxury," and that the artists of the present have a spiritual obligation to unite in order to preserve and regenerate Austrian art in the face of and beyond war. The ambitious plans of the Kunsthalle were not realized; by the end of the war several of the founders, including Klimt and Schiele, were dead.

4. The Grünwald portrait is listed in a bill of lading for the Munich Glaspalast dated 21 May 1917 and written in Schiele's hand (possession Melanie Schuster, Vienna).

5. A small framed sketch by Schiele in the Kallir unpublished Schiele Sketchbook, p. 18, is in my opinion a compositional study for the projected oil portrait of Schönberg. The figure is shown frontally, seated with legs spread apart. The hands are balled into fists and rest on the upper legs. The bald

dome and dark patches of hair at the sides of Schönberg's head are clearly recognizable in this and a second sketch on the same page.

6. See Chapter III, note 26.

7. In the portraits and photographs of Schönberg assembled here and extending over a period of eighteen years an idiosyncracy in dress is evident: he apparently almost never buttoned his jacket.

8. Gerstl left a series of extraordinary self-portrait drawings which attest the severe emotional crisis that resulted in his suicide. These drawings, ranging from pointillistic jigsaw puzzles to fauve fragmentation and coloring, are discussed on a purely stylistic basis by Otto Breicha, "Gerstl, Der Zeichner," *Albertina Studien*, III:2 (1965), 92–101.

9. Darius Milhaud, as quoted by Ralph W. Wood in *The Music Masters*, ed. A. L. Bacharach, vol IV (Baltimore, 1957), p. 300.

10. Schönberg himself was quite satisfied with the portrait, and a few year later he contributed a catalogue essay for a retrospective of Kokoschka's work (Mannheim, 1931).

11. Josef Bernhard, "Wiener Expressionismus," *Österreichs Illustrierte Zeitung*, XXVII:26 (31 March 1918), 461–62. The Schönberg portrait sketch exhibited in the March Secession show is listed as item 294 in the catalogue.

12. Haberditzl's correspondence with Schiele (1917–18) is preserved in the A.E.S.A. and in the Collection Melanie Schuster.

13. Roessler, *Erinnerungen*, pp. 51–53 (Roessler takes credit for introducing Schiele to Haberditzl). A letter to Schiele from Carl Reininghaus dated 16 July 1915 (possession Melanie Schuster, Vienna) suggests that Haberditzl might be of influence in obtaining a better military assignment.

14. A superior example of this row of frontal studies is in the Collection Ingo Nebehay, Vienna. The face is modeled with great delicacy and the arms hang down in front of the body in a relaxed position.

15. Several of these studies exist in private collections in Vienna, Geneva, and the United States.

16. The portrait was probably completed in late November or December of 1917. A letter from Haberditzl to Schiele dated 24 December 1917 thanks him for the pleasant and interesting hours spent in his company, mentions that the portrait is being framed, and that part payment is enclosed (possession Melanie Schuster, Vienna).

   A 1923 portrait of Haberditzl by Herbert Boeckl (1894–1965) provides a later glimpse of the scholar who was by that time confined to a wheelchair existence. The difficulty involved in not showing Haberditzl's wasted body was overcome by Boeckl (one of the more "painterly" of the younger Viennese Expressionists) by the simple device of placing the sitter in the extreme lower right of the canvas where he is cut off just below the shoulders by the picture frame (private collection, Austria).

17. ". . . meine Zeichnungen lediglich keinen anderen Zweck haben, als Vorbereitungen für zu malende Bilder zu sein,—daß sie nur für mich bestimmt sind und für mich von ungeheurem Wert sind,—weil ich die 'nächste' Vorstellung für ein Werk vor mir habe.—Leider wurden mir nur zu oft meine für mich wertvollsten Blätter weggenommen und so kam es, daß schon viele große Bilder in ihrem ersten Keim stekken blieben und man schließlich getäuscht wird und glaubt,—daß meine Blätter schon Bilder sind." Roessler, *Briefe und Prosa*, letter of 16 March 1917, p. 172.

18. Such plethora gave rise to the production of Schiele forgeries even during his lifetime.

19. A.E.S.A., p. 31 verso.

20. An advertisement in the back of this issue of *Der Ruf* announces plans for another magazine to be edited by Müller: *Das Zeitalter*—"the semi-monthly voice of our radical youth, will appear from January 1913 on" (apparently not realized).

21. "... unsere Maler und Literaten glauben, sie müßten sich ruinieren, um schöpferisch zu werden, weil Heinrich Mann irgendwo behauptet, daß Ausschweifungen produktiv machten ..." *Der Ruf*, I:3 (Vienna, 1912), p. 18. According to Hans Heinz Hahnl in an article titled "Der Politiker des Geistes" (*Neue Zürcher Zeitung*, No. 427, p. 53 [12 September 1971] Müller was editor or co-editor of at least thirteen different Expressionist periodicals.

22. Written in response to his visit to the great Cologne Sonderbund Exhibition of 1912 (where Schiele was represented by three canvases, including the *Self-Seers I*); Karl Jaspers, *Strindberg und Van Gogh, Versuch einer Pathographischen Analyse unter vergleichender Heranziehung von Swedenborg und Hölderlin* (Berne, 1922), pp. 130ff.

23. Letter of 25 August 1913, transcription provided by Dr. Franz Glück; see Chapter V, text, and note 33.

24. Neither the Carl Otten nor the Franz Blei sketches resulted in oil portraits. Both sitters were active critics and writers whose literary activities were centered more in Munich and Berlin than in Vienna. They contributed to Pfemfert's *Die Aktion* and shared strong communist sympathies. Carl Otten (1889–1963) was the co-editor of the Munich magazine *Die neue Kunst* (1913–14) and the author of several Expressionist books: *Reise nach Albanien* (1913), *Die Thronerhebung des Herzens* (1918), and *Der Sprung aus dem Fenster* (1918). Franz Blei (1871–1942) had been connected with the literary publications of the Wiener Werkstätte and helped found the cabaret "Fledermaus" in 1907. As early as 1899 he had contributed an article on Beardsley to *Pan* (V:4, 256ff.), and it was he who coined the phrase "cerebral erotic" for Klimt, fifteen of whose drawings were used to illustrate Blei's German translation of Lucian: *Die Hetären Gespräche des Lukian* (Leipzig, 1907). Blei may have been introduced to Schiele by their mutual friend Paris von Gütersloh, with whom he published the periodical *Die Rettung* in 1918–19.

25. An appointment in Schiele's pocket calendar for 1918 (A.E.S.A.) records a portrait sitting for Viktor Ritter von Bauer for 13 January. The portrait was item 16 in the 1918 March exhibition of Schiele's works, so it must have been completed by the end of February. Entries noting appointments with Blei continue into May.

26. Entries in Schiele's pocket calendar for 1918 (A.E.S.A.) show a sitting appointment for Guido Arnot on 21 April and for Dr. Koller on 6, 27, and 28 May. In a letter to Roessler dated 24 May 1918, Schiele wrote that he had to complete the Koller portrait which he had begun because Dr. Koller was leaving for the country at the beginning of June. (Roessler, *Briefe und Prosa*, p. 91).

27. This exhibition is not listed in Kallir and I have not been able to determine whether it was held. In a letter to Arnot dated 17 November 1916 Schiele asks him not to open the exhibition until the 26th of that month (Roessler, *Briefe und Prosa*, p. 179). Thirteen letters to Schiele from Arnot are preserved in the A.E.S.A. and cover the period from 25 February 1915 to 19 September 1917.

28. Schiele's initial compositional idea for the Arnot portrait is recorded in A.E.S.A. Sketchbook VII, 1917–18, p. 12 recto and p. 13 recto. A black chalk study of Arnot, dated 1918, is in the Collection Viktor Fogarassy, Graz. The stratagem of a "barrier" between artist and model had been utilized in similar fashion by Cézanne in his 1895 *Portrait of Gustave Geffroy* (Collection René Lecomte, Paris).

29. Schiele had tried in vain to acquire a copy of Fritz Burger's famous study of stye in modern art, *Cézanne und Hodler* (Munich, 1913). A letter to Schiele from the Munich dealer Hans Goltz dated 14 December 1915 advises him that the book is entirely out of print and that he therefore can not send him a copy (letter in the A.E.S.A.).

30. The high viewpoint taken in this last portrait series recalls certain portraits by Degas, in particular those of Carlo Pellegrini (*ca.* 1876–77) and Diego Martelli (1879). Schiele's book-filled portrait of Koller has a predecessor in Degas's portrait of Edmond Duranty (1879). I have been unable to determine how specific Schiele's knowledge of the French artist was. It is likely that their mutual interest in Japanese prints partly accounted for the bird's-eye perspective present in the works of both, but Schiele may well have benefited from a study of the other's portraits.

31. The daughter of Hugo and Broncia Koller, Silvia, was also an artist. Schiele did a watercolor portrait of her dated 31 August 1918. It is a strange portrait: the young girl is seen in profile with her arms appearing like stumps cut off just above the elbows (private collection, Vienna).

32. Another portrait sketch of this type—unusual for Schiele—with all the details of the figure and chair worked out, but with the face left blank, is in the Collection Serge Sabarsky, New York.

33. Several such sketches exist in private collections, Vienna, and one in the National Gallery of Arts, Washington, D.C. A detailed face study of Dr. Koller is in the Collection Viktor Fogarassy, Graz, and an interesting profile study of Koller's head and upper torso is in the Collection Serge Sabarsky, New York. (This latter reproduced as plate 59 in the catalogue *Egon Schiele and the Human Form*, Des Moines Art Center, (20 September–31 October, 1971; essay by James T. Demetrion).

34. For a sober discussion of the psychological expression conveyed by the hands when in an attitude of apparent "repose," see Walter Sorell, *The Story of the Human Hand* (London, 1968), pp. 155–56.

35. In Freudian psychology this appreciation of the somatic integrity of other individuals is considered a sign of the adult stage of psycho-sexual development. See Paul Schilder, *The Image and Appearance of the Human Body*, p. 173.

36. See also the following portraits by Kokoschka: *Carl Moll* (Wingler 88, 1913–14); *Albert Ehrenstein* (Wingler 90, 1914); *Lady with Stuart Collar* (Wingler 97, 1914); *Brother and Sister* (Wingler 98, 1914); *Anton von Webern* (Wingler 99, 1914); *E. Ludwig* (Wingler 100, 1914); *Ludwig von Ficker* (Wingler 104, 1915); *Heinrich von Neumann* (Wingler 106, 1916); *Hermann Schwarzwald II* (Wingler 107, 1916); *Nell Walden* (Wingler 112, 1916); *The Exiles* (Wingler 113, 1916–17); *The Friends* (Wingler 119, 1917–18); and *The Artist's Mother* (Wingler 121, begun 1917). All of these portraits contrast with the earlier "void" portraits of 1908–12.

37. Roessler relates the following anecdote in this regard: "Kokoschka was on a visit to Vienna and spoke of Berlin which he did not like. Asked about his immediate plans he said: 'Well, first I must go again to Berlin to finish the picture of Tilla Durieux. Cassirer does not give me any peace. Why don't I finish the picture here? No, no, I can not do that; I can do a portrait of someone only in the room in which this person lives. He does not have to be there. I don't look at him anyway when I paint. Well, if he is there, that's better, but he can walk around as he pleases. It is best if he stands behind me while I paint. You know—I must smell him!'"
("Kokoschka war zu Besuch in Wien und erzählte von Berlin, wo es ihm nicht gefalle. Auf die Frage nach seinen nächsten Plänen sagte er: 'Jo, z'erst

muaß i wieder nach Berlin, dös Bild von der Tilla Durieux fertig maln. Der Cassirer, der gibt ma ka Ruah. —Warum i dös Bild net da fertig mach? —Na, na, dös kann i do net; i kann das Porträt von an Menschen nur in dem Zimmer machen, in dem der Mensch lebt. Dabei sein braucht er net, i schau ihn eh net an beim Maln. —No, wann er da is, is scho besser, aba er kann umananda gehn, wia er wüll. Am besten is, er steht hinter meiner, wann i 'n mal. Wissen S',—riachn muaß i ihn!' ") Roessler, *Der Malkasten*, p. 22.

38. During May and July of 1918, Schiele made composition notations and preparatory sketches for what would have been a group portrait. The commission came from a Viennese painter Lilly Steiner, instrumental in her role of patroness in the career of Adolf Loos as well. (His 1910 house for the Steiner family marks a turning point in modern architecture and was one of the first private houses to be built of reinforced concrete.) The family consisted of Herr and Frau Steiner and two daughters, Maria and Eva (Eva later married Otto Benesch). Schiele drew several stick-figure composition ideas for the four-figure portrait (A.E.S.A. Sketchbook VIII, pp. 34 verso–35 recto) and made a good dozen individual studies (the majority of these studies are in the collection of Eva Steiner-Benesch, Vienna). Work on this project during the months of May and June is documented in letters from Lilly Steiner to Schiele (possession Melanie Schuster, Vienna) and in a letter from Carl Reininghaus dated 28 June 1918 (A.E.S.A.) in which he asks Schiele to delay completion of the Steiner portraits that have begun until his return from Paris.

39. The portrait was left unfinished at the time of Schiele's death and shows signs of having been worked over by a different hand. Gertrud Peschka concedes that her husband completed the feet (personal interview, Vienna, 3 March 1967). See also Kallir, *Oeuvre Catalogue*, p. 474.

40. One of these is in the Collection Gertrud Peschka, Vienna.

41. In a letter to Anton Peschka dated 16 December 1915 concerning this painting, Schiele referred to "the little Toni used twice" ("der kleine Toni zweimal verwertet"). Roessler, *Briefe und Prosa*, p. 111.

42. A watercolor in the possession of the Galerie St. Etienne, New York, is a close study for the right-hand "active" figure in *Mother with Two Children*.

43. Kallir, *A Sketchbook by Egon Schiele*, pp. 21, 53, 56, 59–60, 62, 66, 69, 74, 77, 82, 92, 105, and 108. Some of these compositional sketches show a mother with only one child; others show an emaciated second child lying in a cradle. A second oil painting, begun in 1915 and left unfinished, *Mother with Two Children* (K.211) presents a similar contrast between an active child with open eyes (on the right) and a passive, or "dead," child with eyes shut (on the left). The sorrowing face of the mother in this version also suggests the idea of death.

The decision to show a mother with two children may have been prompted by Schiele's memory of the gloomy Klimt canvas of 1909–10, *The Family* (Dobai 163), in which a mother is shown holding a baby in each arm.

44. *Ibid.*, pp. 73, 75–76. For a view of the doll probably used by Schiele, see the photograph of Schiele before his cabinets, figure 114.

45. Neue Galerie der Stadt Linz, Wolfgang Gurlitt Museum, Linz, reproduced in *Albertina Catalogue Klimt–Schiele*, figure 257, and in Des Moines catalogue *Egon Schiele and the Human Form*, plate 50. Other recognizable objects from Schiele's collection of folk art in this 1915 pencil and tempera work are a small wooden duck and the horse and rider that appeared in his 1916 *Still Life with Books* (K.218).

46. It will be recalled that in 1910 and 1911 Schiele had been concerned with the dead-mother theme, often in conjunction with himself (as the "birth of

genius"). As late as 1914 Schiele had done three allegories showing a mother with children: one, *Blind Mother I* (K.193), shows a mother suckling two babies; a second, *Blind Mother II* ("*Young Mother*") (K.194), shows one child nursing at its mother's breast, while a third, *Mother with Two Children* (K.195), shows two babies enclosed in their mother's arms. The latter picture is closest in mood and composition to the Klimt prototype of 1909–10 (cf., note 43 above).

47. The *Portrait of Johann Harms* measures 55⅛ × 43½ inches; the *Portrait of Edith Schiele Seated* is 55 × 43 inches.

48. "Wenn möglich bringen Sie mir von den zu reproduzierenden Blättern die beiden, die im Besitz der Staatsgalerie angegeben sind. (Russe und meine Frau sitzend.) Sie können die Blätter schon Montag wieder haben und ich brauchte sie sehr notwendig." Roessler, *Briefe und Prosa*, pp. 172–73.

49. Otto Benesch has emphasized that Dr. Haberditzl requested the change not because such a "proletarian" costume would be out of place in a state gallery, but simply because it was too decorative for his own tastes (personal interview, Vienna, 16 August 1963).

50. After establishing the direction of Edith's gaze as it appears in the final portrait, Schiele worked for a time with the idea of showing his wife holding a piece of paper (one of his drawings?). A detailed sketch with watercolor touches of blue and green in the background appears on p. 2 of the Kallir unpublished Schiele Sketchbook. Edith is shown seated with both arms extended away from the body to the left, while her body and gaze swivel to the right. Three further drawings, one augmented with red ink, on pp. 8 verso and 9 recto of the same sketchbook, continue this idea of Edith holding a piece of paper out away from her lap. One of the drawings studies the grasp of her fingers on the paper. Apparently this idea was then transferred to the Haberditzl portrait.

  Schiele also used the linked hand pose for his sister-in-law in a handsome watercolor study of 1917, *Portrait of Adele Harms* (Albertina, Vienna), in which the hands are studied as they have fallen together naturally, instead of being artificially posed.

51. Discussing with me Schiele's portraits of her sister, Adele once burst out with great emotion, "But why did he always have to paint her looking so *dumb*!" (personal taped interview, Vienna, 24 January 1967).

52. Klimt posed and photographed eight pictures of Emilie Flöge dressed in various fashions of his own design. These photographs were reproduced in *Deutsche Kunst und Dekoration*, XIX:1 (1906–07), 65ff.

53. Schiele remarked frequently that yellow was "the color of passion, of eroticism" (personal interviews, Melanie Schuster, Vienna, 20 February 1967; Gertrud Peschka, Vienna, 18 February 1967; Adele Harms, Vienna, 29 January 1967; and Erich Lederer, Geneva, 11 February 1967).

54. The *Portrait of Edith Schiele Standing* measures 70¾ × 43¼ inches; *The Virgin* is 71 × 25½ inches.

55. According to Dr. Rudolf Leopold of Vienna, the present owner of this work, the genitals were originally also exposed (personal interview, Vienna, 30 August 1963). A fold of the bedsheet now covers them.

56. The dark-haired model who appears alone in "Desire" and with Schiele in *The Embrace* had begun to pose for Schiele after Edith became, in the artist's own words, "too fat" (personal interviews, Melanie Schuster, Vienna, 20 February 1967 and 24 September 1971, and Adele Harms, Vienna, 29 January 1967). There may be a certain irony intended in Schiele's selection of this particular model as the "mistress" figure in his canvases. According to Erich Lederer, who knew her, this model adamantly preferred her own sex, and

occasionally brought along a female friend to Schiele's studio so that he might sketch them together; Schiele was only too pleased to comply (personal interview, Venice, 27 September 1971).

57. As suggested by Dr. Johannes Dobai, letter to me of 6 July 1967. Franz von Stuck however, painting in Munich at the turn of the century, had employed a similar distinction between the body tones of the sexes.

58. Two compositional drawings on p. 34 of the Kallir unpublished Schiele Sketchbook are unmistakably related to the watercolor *Self-Portrait in Checkered Shirt*. They show Schiele seated with his head bent to the right and his right arm raised across his chest, while his left arm hangs down across his lap. This "open" pose—with hands held apart—contrasts with the linked gestures in the commissioned portraits at this time (cf. discussion of the two paintings *The Family and Portrait of Paris von Gütersloh* in the following text).

59. Exhibited under this title in the March Secession exhibition of Schiele's works in 1918.

60. Werner Hofmann, in *Egon Schiele—Die Familie*, introduces a traditional Freudian speculation concerning this seeming amputation of the child's lower limbs. He mentions a possible reversed Oedipus complex which compels the father to free himself of his son-rival in this manner. Hofmann then dismisses this theory as unnecessary (p. 15). I would agree. There is also some evidence to support the theory that Schiele did not originally plan to include a baby in his "Squatting Couple." Melanie testifies that the first time she saw the canvas there was a large bunch of flowers at the woman's feet, and that the child was painted in only later (Melanie Schuster, personal interview, Vienna, 6 September 1963). Schiele's own title "Squatting Couple" would further confirm this.

61. Klimt also made a statement on a new mother's divided loyalties between her husband and her child in a beautiful drawing of *ca.* 1913 (private collection, Vienna; reproduced *Albertina Catalogue Klimt-Schiele*, figure 108). The drawing shows the nude figure of a woman kneeling to embrace her baby on a bed. Behind her kneels the nude figure of her husband, encompassing her figure in his embrace, but turning his head away from the scene as he concentrates on obtaining his own satisfaction.

62. Melanie recalls that by 1916 Schiele had built a low couch, actually a platform and mattress covered with sailcloth, large enough for two persons. It was placed vis-à-vis his standing mirror. A second looking-glass on the ceiling provided further views of the models whom he posed on this couch (Melanie Schuster, personal interview, Vienna, 6 September 1963). This description largely agrees with one given by Mrs. Jella Pollak who visited Schiele's studio as a young art student in the summer of 1917 (reported in Wolfgang Fischer, "Unbekannte Tagebuchblätter und Briefe von Egon Schiele und Erinnerungen einer Wiener Emigrantin in London," pp. 175–89).

The fact that Schiele included two pieces of his own furniture in *The Family* is consistent with his new environmental approach to portraiture and succeeds in further personalizing this "allegorical" self-portrait. Because of the steady chronological advance in Schiele's work in this direction (—his return from the void—), I can not agree with Werner Hofmann's contention that the principal interpretation of *The Family* is one of "Werdens und Vergehens" (becoming and passing) set in an interior which, by its "few spatial indications" and through its "earthy coloring" is actually transformed into a "nature metaphor"—a "transformation of the interior into a scene of apparent landscape character." (Hofmann, *Egon Schiele—Die Familie*, pp. 3–4, 25–26.)

63. Identification of the female figure in *The Family* as the artist's wife is a com-

mon error. It was, for example, so identified at Canada's "Expo '67," where the painting was on exhibition, and in the Österreichische Galerie Catalogue, *Egon Schiele–Gemälde* (Vienna, April–September 1968), item 69.

64. In a diary formerly in the possession of Adele Harms, Edith mentions her pregnancy in an entry dated 18 April. Adele was of the opinion that her brother-in-law painted *The Family* only because it was a good general theme and not because of any particular excitement at having a baby. According to Adele, Edith considered Schiele's liaisons a threat to their marriage and became pregnant in order to bind her wandering husband more closely to her (personal taped interview, Vienna, 24 January 1967).

65. Schiele employed this model for another work of 1917, the uncompleted *Squatting Women* (K.241). In this painting the model is shown twice–both times nude and sitting in a pose similar to that in *The Family*. The artist began a companion piece to this work which was also left unfinished at the time of his death. Not accepted by Kallir (Leopold 297), it might be entitled *Squatting Men* (formerly in the possession of the Felix Landau Gallery, Los Angeles). It is a frontal view of two male nudes sitting with bent legs and clasped hands (there are evidences of overpainting by a foreign hand). Although the faces are generalized they resemble Schiele's face in *The Family*, and a preparatory self-portrait drawing (formerly in the possession of the Gallery Kornfeld and Klipstein, Berne) leaves no doubt that the model for *Squatting Men* was Schiele. Both *Squatting Women* and *Squatting Men* were conceived as part of a monumental wall fresco for Schiele's mausoleum project (cf. Chapter VI, note 21). Because of the somewhat anonymous quality of both the female and male figures in these two works, I would not interpret Schiele's use of himself for the male model as a meaningful return to the double self-portrait series of 1910–11 or that of 1915.

66. The poses and figure relationships of the three female figures in this compositional sketch were transferred almost exactly to a large uncompleted canvas begun probably in 1917, *Three Female Nudes Standing* (K.245). In this fragment the center figure is the same model seen in *The Virgin*, *The Family*, and the uncompleted *Squatting Women* (see above, note 65), while the more active figures to either side both resemble the model with long curly hair used by Schiele for his "mistress" paintings of 1917, *Reclining Woman*, and *Embrace*. The figure to the left holds both hands up in an ostentatious double-V gesture, and the picture seems to present a lesbian implication. This particular sort of voyeurism on Schiele's part had been the subject of drawings and watercolors since 1910 and was re-inforced now by acquaintance with a model who was willing to pose with her female friends for such scenes (see note 56 above).

67. A.E.S.A. Sketchbook VIII, 1918, p. 15 recto.

68. *Ibid.*, p. 21 recto.

69. *Ibid.*, p. 22 recto.

70. Apparently another person attempted to finish the painting after Schiele's death, made a start, and then simply painted the figure out.

71. In addition to the general example provided by the Brücke scenes of nudes-in-forest, there is a local figural precedent for Schiele's picture of one male nude in the company of two nude or partially nude females. In 1911 Schiele's Academy colleague Franz Wiegele began work on a large oil, *Figures in the Forest*—a painting which occupied his attention for over a decade. A male nude stands between two women, with his right arm around the shoulder of the completely nude woman who has entered the forest from the left. The man's glance is directed towards this woman and they both ignore their

companion, a partly clothed woman on the right side of the canvas who kneels and appears to be picking flowers (Österreichische Galerie, Vienna).

72. See Chapter II text, and note 59.

73. A particularly fine study is in the Albertina and a second, of equal quality, is in the Collection of Mr. and Mrs. D. Thomas Bergen, London. The Akademie der Bildenden Künste in Vienna owns a complete figure study, minus the head, for the portrait.

74. Notably in the *Self-Portrait Before Easel* of 1913 (Historisches Museum der Stadt, Wien, Vienna). This painting gives a good indication of Gütersloh's miniaturist's delight in spatial ambiguities (a picture within the picture to the upper left mirrors the real image as projected presumably on a third surface, the artist's canvas).

75. See Chapter VI text, and note 49.

76. Two appointments for Gütersloh's sittings are shown in Schiele's calendar diary for 1918 (A.E.S.A.). They are dated 7 January and 29 May. Karl Grünwald was the first owner of the Gütersloh portrait.

77. Schiele mentions this fact in a draft of a letter to an army superior dated 2 October 1918 (Roessler, *Briefe und Prosa*, pp. 181–83). Two conflicting dates given in the catalogue for the show reflect the delay arising from Schiele's untimely death on the last day of October. (The catalogue cover carries the dates November–December 1918, while the inside flyleaf bears the dates, December 1918–January 1919, and the text entries show a cross by Schiele's name.) The three works by Schiele exhibited in this Secession show were: *Portrait of Dr. Hugo Koller*, number 158 (reproduced in the catalogue); *Portrait of Paris von Gütersloh*, number 159; and *Portrait of Guido Arnot*, number 160.

78. Reproduced in the catalogue to the show, *LII. Ausstellung der Vereinigung Bildender Künstler—Secession* (December 1918–January 1919), (henceforth referred to as *Secession LII. Ausstellung*); present whereabouts unknown.

79. Klimt's two entries are identified simply as a portrait of a lady and a portrait of a young girl. The latter must have been the *Portrait of Mäda Primavesi* (Dobai 179).

80. Reproduced in *Secession LII Ausstellung*. Corinth's portraits of the painter Fritz Proels and Tini Senders are also listed in the Secession catalogue. As I have mentioned, certain works by Corinth, such as the *Portrait of Eduard Graf Keyserling* (1900) at the Munich Staatsgalerie, strongly prefigure portraits by Kokoschka in the next decade. Certainly a rewarding study could be made of the sources and styles of Corinth and of his specific role in German Expressionism, not only in portraiture but in landscape and allegory as well.

81. Reproduced in *Secession LII Ausstellung*; present whereabouts unknown.

82. Reproduced in *Secession LII Ausstellung*; present whereabouts unknown. Among Orlik's etchings and lithographs were included the portraits of Ferdinand Hodler, Max Slevogt, Wilhelm von Bode, Richard Strauss, Gustav Mahler, and Wanda Landowska.

83. In his capacity as one of the organizers for the Kunsthalle and Secession shows in 1917 and 1918, Schiele had written Kokoschka asking if he would be willing to exhibit. In a letter to Schiele dated 6 January 1918 Kokoschka politely but bitterly answered: ". . . although I wish all success to the efforts of the society as you have established it, I shall not participate in any exhibition in Vienna, a position which I have maintained for many years. Since I have no indication that the opinions of the circles which concern themselves there with art have improved towards my art, I should never again be inclined to feel at home there, not even with the least important of my works." (". . . obwohl ich

den Bestrebungen der Vereinigung, wie Sie sie zusammengesetzt haben allen Erfolg wünsche, mich doch an keiner Ausstellung in Wien betheiligen werde, wie ich es schon seit vielen Jahren gehalten habe. Da ich kein Anzeichen besitze, dass sich die Gesinnung der Kreise, die sich dort mit Kunst beschäftigen, meiner Arbeit gegenüber so gebessert hätte, dass ich Lust hatte, auch nur mit der Geringsten meiner Arbeit mich dort jemals wieder heimisch zu fühlen.") Letter in the Josef Hoffmann–Egon Schiele Archive in the Vienna Rathaus, Inv. No. 109.837. These words from Kokoschka indicate that his virulent dislike of Schiele occurred only later, as he saw the spotlight of Viennese Expressionism diverted from himself.

84. A Secession sales record in the A.E.S.A. dated 10 April 1918 lists the paintings and prices charged. The three portraits sold were: *Edith Schiele Seated*, 3,000 Kronen, to the Staatsgalerie; *Viktor Ritter von Bauer*, 3,000 Kronen to Karl Grünwald; and *The Family* (listed as "Squatting Couple") 5,000 Kronen, to Hans Böhler.

85. "Unsere Ausstellung war am Eröffnungstag, und besonders an Sonntagen, so besucht, daß man nicht mehr gut gehen konnte. Man sah nur mehr begeisterte oder entsetzte Menschen, welche die Bilder verstellten." Letter of 14 March 1918, Roessler, *Briefe und Prosa*, p. 126.

86. For the pejorative comments see Herbert Waniek, "Egon Schiele und Ich," pp. 106–07. For the praise see the contribution by Max Eisler to *In Memoriam Egon Schiele*, entitled "Egon Schiele in der Sezession [*sic*] 1918," pp. 38–40.

87. Schiele discusses his new obligation in the art world in the draft of a letter to a superior in the army (Roessler, *Briefe und Prosa*, pp. 181–83). A letter to Schiele from one of the editors of *Der Anbruch*, Otto Schneider, dated 25 April 1918 (possession Melanie Schuster, Vienna) gives the information that the wife of the Saxonian ambassador was anxious to make his acquaintance in regard to commissioning a portrait. I am grateful to Dr. Franz Glück for supplying me with photographs of those pages from *Der Anbruch* (1917–19) which reproduced drawings by Schiele. Later issues of *Der Anbruch* published works by the German Expressionists Ludwig Meidner, Kirchner, and Schmidt-Rottluff. A measure of Schiele's "acceptability" after his March Secession success is given by the fact that a local magazine of women's fashions, *Die Damenwelt*, to which Klimt had previously contributed, now asked to publish drawings by Schiele (see letter from Roessler to Schiele dated 10 July 1918, A.E.S.A.). Concerning Schiele's commissions for lithographs, see, Roessler, *Erinnerungen*, pp. 68–69 and Kallir, *Egon Schiele: The Graphic Works*, pp. 41–43. Even before the end of the Secession show, Schiele was invited by a group of artists in Prague to make the poster and arrange a show of some two hundred works under the title "Junges Österreich" (recorded in a group of six letters from the Prague Kunstverein preserved in the A.E.S.A. and covering the dates 27 March to 8 June 1918).

88. Schiele's show at the Arnot Gallery received favorable criticism even from the conservative art critic A. F. Seligmann (*Neue Freie Presse*, 28 May 1918).

89. The Hietzinger Hauptstrasse studio exists today and is still rented by artists. The garden house atelier in the Wattmanngasse was left intact until a few years ago, when it was remodeled. The main divisions stand however and the present owner was able to provide me with an exact plan of the large two-story studio used by Schiele.

90. A "portrait" by Schiele in still another medium exists. This is the so-called *Self-Portrait in Bronze*. I now agree with Dr. Kallir that the bronze head (modeled in clay by Schiele; cast in bronze only after his death) is not a self-portrait but rather just a "head." It is slightly under life size and dates from

1918. Conceived in realistic terms, the head is mild in mood (mouth closed, eyes non-protruding) and rendered in modeled, rounded forms. At present there are from twenty to twenty-five copies of the head in bronze and in 1964 ten stone copies were made. A sculptured article more directly from Schiele's hand exists in the Collection Gertrud Peschka, Vienna. This is a squatting female nude (headless) in stone, in a pose probably inspired by Rodin. (The contorted poses in many of Schiele's female nude drawings also suggest familiarity with the French sculptor's *Crouching Woman* of 1882.)

91. "Ich habe vor, ein großes Figurenbild zu malen, mit allen meinen Nächstbekannten, lebensgroß, bei einer Tafel sitzend." Roessler, *Briefe und Prosa*, p. 116.

92. The compositional sketch reproduced here is from Kallir, *A Sketchbook by Egon Schiele*, p. 111. An earlier pencil sketch is reproduced in the La Boetie Gallery catalogue, *Egon Schiele and his Circle* (New York, May–June 1971), item 2. Another detailed study appears in the A.E.S.A. Sketchbook VIII, loose page number 3. Even after the poster was printed, the composition was on Schiele's mind: he sketched it on a letter written to him on Secession-letterhead paper by the president of the Secession, Richard Harlfinger, dated 21 May 1918 (A.E.S.A.).

93. One of the sketches was included in the March Secession show (No. 295); it was Schiele's wish never to sell them.

94. Pocket calendar for 1918, A.E.S.A.

95. The epitaph appears in *Der Anbruch*, I:3 (15 February 1918, Vienna), p. 1.

Gustav Klimt
Ein Künstler von unglaublicher Vollendung
Ein Mensch von seltener Tiefe
Sein Werk ein Heiligtum

Schiele felt, as did many, that the Klimt house and studio should be bought by the government and preserved as a museum of the "Klimt-Glaube." When nothing was done about the house (even after it was broken into by thieves; see letter from Schiele to Peschka dated 30 January 1918, Roessler, *Briefe und Prosa*, p. 126) Schiele began negotiations with his colleague Harta, whose mother-in-law owned the house, to rent it himself (Harta, letter of 21 September 1918 to Schiele, possession Melanie Schuster, Vienna; and Harta, letter of 1 October 1918 to Schiele, A.E.S.A).

96. The theory that the empty chair opposite Schiele's in *Round the Table* symbolized the recently deceased Klimt was advanced by me in my 1964 master's thesis, "Egon Schiele: The Artist's Vision of Himself," p. 157. Although Dr. Kallir questioned this hypothesis when he read the thesis in 1964, he now concurs with this suggestion and has discussed it at length in his introduction to *A Sketchbook by Egon Schiele*, pp. 9–11. (See also his discussion in Kallir, *Egon Schiele: The Graphic Works*, p. 40.) Figure II in the sketchbook introduction reproduces a color sketch for *Round the Table* in which plates, instead of books, are shown in front of the figures. Dr. Kallir also identifies a drawing on p. 92 of the sketchbook (reproduced in Kallir, *Egon Schiele: The Graphic Works*, plate 13a) as the first draft for *Round the Table*. Here we disagree. I read the same drawing as a compositional sketch, redrawn four times, for *Mother with Two Children*.

97. Several important figures in the Viennese art world died in 1918, but all after the March printing of Schiele's poster (Otto Wagner, 11 April, and Koloman Moser, 18 October.) Schiele's idol, Hodler, would be an obvious suggestion,

but his death date, 19 May, discounts the idea. The figures who do appear in the poster represent colleagues such as Harta and Gütersloh, but a definitive and complete identification is not possible; for a good attempt however see Kallir, *Egon Schiele: The Graphic Works*, p. 40, and p. 52, notes 12 and 13. Hildegard Bachert of New York has suggested to me the intriguing idea that the nine persons in Schiele's poster might portray the actual exhibitors in the March show—nine figures for the nine major artists represented (personal conversation, 27 July 1972, New York).

98. Heinrich Benesch, "Mein Weg mit Egon Schiele." Benesch also writes that on his last visit to Schiele, in mid–October 1918, the artist showed him a row of just completed watercolor studies of earthenware jugs. (One of these studies is in the Albertina and a second is in the Collection Melanie Schuster, Vienna.)

99. These appear in a sketch for that project in the A.E.S.A. Sketchbook IX, 1916, p. 6 recto. In this drawing three jugs are clearly indicated, and the two on the left have been gone over again with thick strokes.

100. Melanie states that when Schiele entered a room he liked to announce himself by booming in a solemn voice: "Make way for the Godhead! Here comes the Divinity!" (personal interview, Vienna, 11 February 1967).

101. "27. Oktober 1918.

"Ich habe ich Dich unendlich liebe und liebe Dich immer *mehr* grenzenlos und . . . los deine Edith" In the A.E.S.A. Schiele also made a second deathbed drawing of Edith, her head weakly supported by one hand (collection Rudolf Leopold, Vienna; reproduced, Leopold, *Catalogue Raisonné*, p. 493).

102. "Früher oder später wird ein Glaube zu meinen Bildern, Schriften, Worten, die ich selten, aber am konzentriertesten spreche, entstehen. Meine bisherigen Bilder sollen vielleicht Vorreden sein,—ich weiß nicht. . . . Die haben unrecht, die glauben, daß Malen schon etwas ist. Malen ist ein Können. Ich denke an die wärmsten Farben zu einander, die verfließen, die zerrinnen, brechen, erhaben sind, hügelig aufgetragen Siena mit grünen und grauen und daneben einen blaukalten Stern, weiß, weißblau. . . .Schauen kann auch der Maler. Sehen ist aber doch mehr." Roessler, *Briefe und Prosa*, p. 144.

Concordance

COMPARISON table of the oeuvre catalogue numbers listed by Otto Kallir (1966; second edition of the original 1930 oeuvre catalogue) and Rudolf Leopold (1972) for the paintings by Egon Schiele reproduced in this book.

Kallir	Leopold	Kallir	Leopold	Kallir	Leopold
3	40	109	144	159	203
5	30	110	141	174	223
7	31	111	140	175	234
8	41	112	145	177	243
9	32	—	149	180	228
62	116	113	161	192	256
63	143	114	165	205	267
64	129	115	167	206	265
65	120	123	169	207	266
66	128	124	194	213	270
86	131	126	188	219	279
87	132	127	181	220	282
88	133	128	172	221	277
89	136	129	173	223	273
90	135	130	171	224	276
91	134	131	175	232	285
97	139	136	176	233	286
101	147	138	170	234	294
102	148	150	200	235	292
103	152	151	211	236	293
104	154	152	212	237	295
105	153	154	201	238	290
106	160	156	210	240	289
107	151	157	218	242	299

Selected Bibliography

THE following bibliography lists the primary and secondary sources that were found to be of use in the preparation of this book. These sources have been divided into the following categories:

1. Material Pertaining Directly to Schiele
2. Material Relating to Schiele's Colleagues and Contemporaries
3. General Background Material
4. Contemporary Periodicals
5. Exhibition Catalogues (arranged chronologically)
6. Unpublished Material

Other sources not here mentioned are specifically referred to in the notes. Not listed are the portfolios of original graphics and reproduced works by Schiele. These and a comprehensive listing of exhibition catalogues and articles (through 1966) may be found in Otto Kallir, *Egon Schiele, Oeuvre Katalog der Gemälde* (Vienna, 1966).

1. MATERIAL PERTAINING DIRECTLY TO SCHIELE

Benesch, Heinrich. *Mein Weg mit Egon Schiele*. New York, 1965. (Foreword by Eva Benesch.)

Benesch, Otto. *Egon Schiele als Zeichner*. Vienna, 1950. (Portfolio with twenty-four reproductions of drawings and watercolors.)

Chipp, Herschel B. "A Neglected Expressionist Movement—Viennese 1910–1924," *Artforum*, I:9 (1963), 21–27.

———. "An Early Sketchbook of Egon Schiele," *Artforum*, II:7 (1964), 32–33.

Comini, Alessandra. "Egon Schiele in Prison," *Albertina Studien*, II:4 (1964), 123–37.

———. "Egon Schieles Kriegstagebuch 1916," *Albertina Studien*, IV:2 (1966), 86–102.

———. "From Façade to Psyche: The Persistence and Transformation of Portraiture in Fin-de-Siècle Vienna," *Acts of the 22nd International Congress of Art Historians 1969*, Budapest (1972), 411–14; 467–70.

———. "Vampires, Virgins, and Voyeurs in Imperial Vienna," in Thomas B. Hess and Linda Nochlin (eds.), *Woman as Sex Object* (Art News Annual XXXVIII), New York (1972), 207–21.

———. *Schiele in Prison*. Greenwich, 1973.

Faistauer, Anton. *Neue Malerei in Österreich; Betrachtungen eines Malers*, Vienna, 1923.

Fischer, Wolfgang. "Egon Schiele als 'Militaerzeichner,'" *Albertina Studien*, IV:2 (1966), 70–82.

———. "Unbekannte Tagebuchblätter und Briefe von Egon Schiele und Erinnerungen einer Wiener Emigrantin in London," *Albertina Studien*, II:4 (1964), 172–73.

———. "Zur Rückseite von Egon Schieles 'Porträt Edith Schiele' und die Berichtigung einer Datierung," *Albertina Studien*, III:2 (1965), 102–103.

Freiberg, Siegfried. *Ihr werdet sehen. . . . Ein Egon Schiele-Roman*. Vienna, 1967.

Gütersloh, Paris von. *Egon Schiele*. Vienna, 1911.

Hofmann, Werner. *Egon Schiele—Die Familie*. Stuttgart, 1968.

Kallir (–Nirenstein), Otto. *Egon Schiele, Oeuvre Katalog der Gemälde*. Vienna, 1966. (With essays by Otto Benesch, "Memories of Paintings by Egon Schiele which are No Longer Existent," and Thomas M. Messer, "The Reaction to Schiele's Work in America.")

———. *A Sketchbook by Egon Schiele.* 2 vols. Facsimile and commentary. New York, 1967.

———. *Egon Schiele: The Graphic Work.* Oeuvre catalogue. New York, 1970.

Karpfen, Fritz, ed. *Das Egon Schiele Buch.* Vienna, 1921.

Koschatzky, Walter, ed. *Egon Schiele, Aquarelle und Zeichnungen.* (Essay and selection by Erwin Mitsch.) Salzburg, 1968.

Künstler, Gustav. *Egon Schiele als Graphiker.* Vienna, 1946.

Leopold, Rudolf. *Egon Schiele: Gemälde, Aquarelle, Zeichnungen.* Catalogue raisonné. Salzburg, 1972. (1973)

Liegler, Leopold. "Egon Schiele," *Die Graphischen Künste,* 3(1916), 70–80.

Mitsch, Erwin. *Egon Schiele, Zeichnungen und Aquarelle.* Salzburg, 1961.

Nirenstein(–Kallir), Otto. *Egon Schiele: Persönlichkeit und Werk.* Catalogue raisonné. Vienna, 1930.

Roessler, Arthur. *Erinnerungen an Egon Schiele.* 2d ed. Vienna, 1948. (1st ed., 1922.)

———. "In Memoriam Egon Schiele," *Deutsche Kunst und Dekoration,* XLIV:1, (1919), 227–43.

———. *Kritische Fragmente.* Vienna, 1918.

———, ed. *Briefe und Prosa von Egon Schiele.* Vienna, 1921.

———, ed. *Egon Schiele im Gefängnis.* Vienna, 1922.

———, ed. *In Memoriam Egon Schiele.* Vienna, 1921.

Schwarz, Heinrich. "Die graphischen Werke von Egon Schiele." *Philobiblon* (Hamburg), V:1 (1961), 50–69; VI:2 (1962), 154.

———. "Schiele, Dürer, and the Mirror." *The Art Quarterly,* XXX:3–4 (1967), 210–23.

Tietze, Hans. "Egon Schiele." *Die bildenden Künste,* II (1919), 99–110.

Waniek, Herbert. "Egon Schiele und Ich," *Ver* (15 November 1917), 106–07.

2. MATERIAL RELATING TO SCHIELE'S COLLEAGUES AND CONTEMPORARIES

Amiet, Cuno; Ankwicz-Kleehoven, Hans; and Kolo Moser, *Hodler und Wien.* Zurich, 1950.

Bahr, Hermann. *Gegen Klimt.* Vienna, 1903.

———. *Rede über Klimt.* Vienna, 1901.

———. *Secession,* Vienna, 1900.

Bardi, P. M. *Ernesto de Fiori.* Milan, 1950.

Bender, E., and W. Y. Müller. *Die Kunst Ferdinand Hodlers.* 2 vols. Catalogue raisonné. Zurich, 1941.

Benesch, Otto. *Edvard Munch.* London, 1960.

———. "Hodler, Klimt und Munch als Monumentalmaler," *Wallraf-Richartz Jahrbuch,* XXIV (1962), 333–58.

———; Paris von Gütersloh; Otto Mauer; and Herbert Tasquill. *Herbert Boeckl.* Vienna, 1947.

Berend-Corinth, Charlotte. *Die Gemälde von Lovis Corinth.* Catalogue raisonné. Munich, 1958.

Breicha, Otto. "Gerstl, Der Zeichner," *Albertina Studien,* III:2 (1965), 92–101.

De La Faille, J. B. *L'Oeuvre de Vincent van Gogh.* Catalogue raisonné. 4 vols. Paris–Brussels, 1928.

Dobai, Johannes, and Fritz Novotny. *Gustav Klimt.* Catalogue raisonné. Salzburg, 1967.

Doderer, H. *Der Fall Gütersloh.* Vienna, 1930.

Eisler, Max. *Anton Hanak.* Vienna, 1921.

———. *Gustav Klimt,* Vienna, 1921.

Geretsegger, Heinz and Max Peintner. *Otto Wagner.* London, 1970.

Goldschneider, Ludwig. *Kokoschka.* Greenwich, 1963.

Hammer, Heinrich, and Franz Kollreider. *Albin Egger-Lienz.* Innsbruck, 1963.

Hauer, Leopold. *Der Maler Leopold Hauer, Selbstbiographie.* Vienna, 1962.

Hodin, J. P. *Oskar Kokoschka.* The Artist and His Time. London, 1966.

Hoffmann, Edith. *Kokoschka, Life and Work.* London, 1947.

Hofmann, Werner. *Gustav Klimt.* Greenwich, 1972.

Kandinsky, Wassily, and Franz Marc. *Der Blaue Reiter.* Munich, 1912.

Karpfen, Fritz. *Der Bildhauer Gustinus Ambrosi.* Vienna, n.d.

Klee, Paul. *Tagebücher.* Cologne, 1957.

Kokoschka, Oskar. *A Sea Ringed with Visions.* Translated by Eithne Wilkins and Ernst Kaiser. London, 1962.

———. *Die Träumenden Knaben.* Vienna, 1908.

Kubin, Alfred. *Die andere Seite.* Munich, 1909.

Loos, Adolf. *Sämtliche Schriften.* Edited by Franz Glück. 2 vols. Vienna, 1962.

Lux, Joseph August. *Otto Wagner.* Munich, 1914.

Meier-Graefe, Julius. *Felix Vallotton.* Berlin 1898.

———. *Vincent van Gogh.* Munich, 1910.

Milesi, Richard. *Franz Wiegele.* Catalogue raisonné. Klagenfurt, 1957.

Muther, Richard. *Die Belgische Malerei im Neunzehnten Jahrhundert.* Berlin, 1909.

Nebehay, Christian M. *Gustav Klimt Dokumentation.* Vienna, 1969.

Novotny, Fritz. *Der Maler Anton Romako.* Catalogue raisonné. Vienna, 1954.

Oppenheimer, Max [Mopp]. *Menschen Finden Ihren Maler.* Zurich, 1938.

Osborn, Max. *Emil Orlik*. Berlin, 1920.

Pirchan, Emil. *Gustav Klimt*. 2d ed. Vienna, 1956. (1st ed., 1942).

———. *Hans Makart*, Vienna, 1942.

Puyvelde, Leo van. *George Minne*. Catalogue raisonné. Brussels, 1930.

Stefan, Paul. *Oskar Kokoschka*. Dramen und Bilder. Leipzig, 1913.

Roessler, Arthur. *Der Maler Anton Faistauer*. Vienna, 1947.

———. *Der Maler Hans Böhler*. Vienna, 1929.

———. "George Minne," *Deutsche Kunst und Dekoration*, XXV:1 (1909–10), 241ff.

———. *Rudolf von Alt*. Vienna, [1910?].

Schneditz, Wolfgang. *Alfred Kubin*. Vienna, 1956.

Strobl, Alice. *Gustav Klimt*. Salzburg, 1962.

Waissenberger, Robert. *Die Wiener Secession*. Vienna, 1971.

———. "Hagenbund 1900–1938. Geschichte der Wiener Künstlervereinigung," *Mitteilungen der Österreichischen Galerie*, XVI:60 (1972), 54–130.

Wingler, Hans Maria. *Oskar Kokoschka*. Catalogue raisonné. Salzburg, 1958.

3. GENERAL BACKGROUND MATERIAL

Andreas-Salomé, Lou. *In der Schule bei Freud: Tagebuch eines Jahres 1912/13*. Munich, 1965.

Basil, Otto. *Georg Trakl*. Hamburg, 1965.

Benesch, Otto. *Kleine Geschichte der Kunst in Österreich*. Vienna, 1950.

Berghahn, Wilfried. *Robert Musil*. Hamburg, 1963.

Brandenburg, Hans. *Der Moderne Tanz*. Munich, 1921.

Breicha, Otto, and Gerhard Fritsch. *Finale und Auftakt Wien 1898–1914*. Salzburg, 1964.

Buchheim, Lothar–Günther. *The Graphic Art of German Expressionism*. New York, 1960.

Burger, Fritz. *Einführung in die Moderne Kunst*. (Die Kunst des 19. und 20. Jahrhunderts.) Berlin, 1917.

Cremona, Italo. *Die Zeit des Jugendstils*. Translated by Marlis Ingenmey. Munich, 1966.

Du. Kulturelle Monatsschrift, April 1963. Conzett und Huber, Zurich. (Entire number devoted to Vienna 1900–18.)

Duncan, Isadora. *My Life*. New York, 1927.

Edschmid, Kasimir, ed. *Briefe der Expressionisten*. Frankfurt, 1964.

Engelhard, Josef. *Ein Wiener Maler Erzählt*. Vienna, 1943.

Feuerstein, G.; H. Hutter; E. Köller; and W. Mrazek. *Moderne Kunst in Österreich*. Vienna, 1965.

Field, Frank. *The Last Days of Mankind: Karl Kraus and His Vienna*. New York, 1967.

Freud, Ernst L., ed. *The Letters of Sigmund Freud*. Translated by Tania and James Stern. New York, 1964.

Gordon, Donald E. "Kirchner in Dresden," *Art Bulletin*, XLVIII:3–4 (1966), 335–66.

———. "On the Origin of the Word 'Expressionism,'" *Warburg Journal*, XXIX (1966), 368–85.

Grimschitz, Bruno. *Österreichische Malerei vom Biedermeier zur Moderne*. Vienna, 1963.

Groner, Richard. *Wien wie es war*. Vienna, 1965.

Haack, Friedrich. *Die Kunst der Neuesten Zeit*. Stuttgart, 1925.

Hemleben, Johannes. *Rudolf Steiner*. Hamburg, 1963.

Hevesi, Ludwig. *Acht Jahre Sezession*. Vienna, 1906.

———. *Altkunst–Neukunst: Wien 1894–1908*. Vienna, 1909.

———. "Modern Painting in Austria," *The Studio*, (Special Summer Number: The Art-Revival in Austria), London (1906), i–xvi.

———. *Österreichische Kunst im 19. Jahrhundert*. 2 vols. Leipzig, 1903.

Hofmann, Werner. *Das Irdische Paradies*. Munich, 1960.

———. *Moderne Kunst in Österreich*. Vienna, 1965.

Hofstätter, Hans H. *Geschichte der europäischen Judgendstilmalerei*. Cologne, 1963.

———. *Symbolismus und die Kunst der Jahrhundertwende*. Cologne, 1965.

Holthusen, Hans Egon. *Rainer Maria Rilke*. Hamburg, 1958.

Jaspers, Karl. *Strindberg und Van Gogh, Versuch einer Pathographischen Analyse unter vergleichender Heranziehung von Swedenborg und Hölderlin*. Berne, 1922.

Johnston, William M. *The Austrian Mind*. Berkeley, 1972.

Jones, Ernest. *The Life and Work of Sigmund Freud*. Edited and abridged by Lionel Trilling and Steven Marcus. New York, 1961.

Kantor, Robert. "Art, Ambiguity and Schizophrenia," *Art Journal*, XXIV:3 (1965), 234–39.

Karpfen, Fritz. *Österreichische Kunst*. Vienna, 1923.

Keyserling, Arnold. *Der Wiener Denkstil: Mach, Carnap, Wittgenstein*. Graz, 1965.

Kuhn, Charles L. *German Expressionism and Abstract Art*. The Harvard Collections. Cambridge, 1957. (Introductory essay by Jakob Rosenberg.)

Lux, Joseph A. "Kunstschau-Wien 1908," *Deutsche Kunst und Dekoration*, XXIII:1 (1908–09), 33–61.

Mach, Ernst. *The Analysis of Sensations and the Rela-*

tion of the Physical to the Psychical. Translated from the 1st German edition (1897) by C. M. Williams. Chicago, 1914.

Madsen, Stephan Tschudi. *Sources of Art Nouveau.* Translated by R. I. Christopherson. New York, 1956.

Mahler, Alma. *Gustav Mahler, Memories and Letters.* Translated by Basil Creighton. Seattle, 1968.

Mascha, Ottokar. *Österreichische Plakatkunst.* Vienna, 1916.

Masur, Gerhard. *Prophets of Yesterday.* Studies in European Culture, 1890–1914. New York, 1961.

Meyers, Bernard S. *The German Expressionists. A Generation in Revolt.* New York, [1957?].

Nietzsche, Friedrich. *Thus Spoke Zarathustra. The Portable Nietzsche.* Translated and edited by Walter Kaufmann. New York, 1954.

Nostitz, Helene von. *Aus dem Alten Europa.* Hamburg, 1964.

Novotny, Fritz. *Painting and Sculpture in Europe 1780–1880.* Baltimore, 1960.

Pfemfert, Franz. *Das Aktionsbuch.* Berlin, 1917.

Praz, Mario. *The Romantic Agony.* Translated by Angus Davidson, 2d ed. New York, 1956.

Preyer, David C. *The Art of the Vienna Galleries.* Boston, 1911.

Raabe, Paul. *Ich schneide die Zeit aus. Expressionismus und Politik in Franz Pfemferts 'Aktion.'* Munich, 1964.

Rathke, Ewald, *Jugendstil.* Mannheim, 1958.

Reininghaus, Hugo von. *Demarkationslinien der Modernen Kunst.* Munich, 1910.

Rheims, Maurice. *The Flowering of Art Nouveau.* Translated by Patrick Evans. New York, n.d.

Rieder, Heinz. *Geburt der Moderne: Wiener Kunst um 1900.* Graz, 1964.

Rilke, Rainer Maria. *The Notebooks of Malte Laurids Brigge.* Translated by M. D. Herter Norton. New York, 1964.

Rimbaud, Arthur. *Collected Poems.* Translated by Oliver Bernard, Baltimore, 1962.

Roazen, Paul. *Brother Animal.* New York, 1969.

Roessler, Arthur, ed. *Der Malkasten: Künstler-Anekdoten.* Vienna, 1924.

Schick, Paul. *Karl Kraus.* Hamburg, 1965.

Schilder, Paul. *The Image and Appearance of the Human Body.* New York, 1951.

Schmidt, Gerhard. *Neue Malerei in Österreich.* Vienna, 1956.

Schmutzler, Robert. *Art Nouveau.* Translated by Edouard Roditi. New York, 1962.

Schnitzler, Arthur. *Jugend in Wien.* Vienna, 1968.

Schonauer, Franz. *Stefan George.* Hamburg, 1960.

Schorske, Carl E. "Politics and the Psyche in Fin De Siècle Vienna: Schnitzler and Hofmannsthal," *American Historical Review,* LXVI:4 (July, 1961), 1–32.

———. "The Transformation of the Garden: Ideal and Society in Austrian Literature." Speech delivered at the XIIe Congrès International des Sciences Historiques, Vienna, 29 August–5 September 1965. Berkeley, 1965.

Selz, Peter. *German Expressionist Painting.* Berkeley, 1957.

———, and Mildred Constantine, eds. *Art Nouveau.* Art and Design at the Turn of the Century. (The Museum of Modern Art, New York.) New York, 1959.

Sharp, Dennis. *Modern Architecture and Expressionism.* New York, 1966.

Sokel, Walter H., ed. *An Anthology of German Expressionist Drama.* New York, 1963.

———. *The Writer in Extremis.* Stanford, 1959.

Sotriffer, Kristian. *Malerei und Plastik in Österreich.* Von Makart bis Wotruba. Vienna, 1963.

Stern, Fritz. *The Politics of Cultural Despair.* Berkeley, 1961.

Stone, Alan A., and Sue Smart Stone, eds. *The Abnormal Personality Through Literature.* Englewood Cliffs, 1966.

Taylor, A. J. P. *The Habsburg Monarchy 1809–1918.* London, 1948.

Tymms, Ralph. *Doubles in Literary Psychology.* Cambridge, 1949.

Wagenbach, Klaus. *Franz Kafka.* Hamburg, 1964.

Weininger, Otto. *Geschlecht und Charakter.* Vienna, 1903.

Werfel, Alma Mahler. *And the Bridge is Love.* New York, 1958.

Wigman, Mary. *The Language of Dance.* Translated by Walter Sorell. Middletown (Conn.), 1966.

Worringer, Wilhelm. *Abstraktion und Einfühlung.* Munich, 1908.

Zweig, Stefan. *Die Welt von Gestern.* Stockholm, 1944.

4. CONTEMPORARY PERIODICALS

Die Aktion. Nos. 11, 15, 20 (1914). Edited by Franz Pfemfert, Berlin.

———. Nos. 3–4, 31–32 (1915).

———. Nos. 35–36 [(1916). Egon Schiele Heft].

Der Anbruch. I:1 (15 December 1917), 1. (1917–19 only). Edited by Otto Schneider and Ludwig Ullmann, Vienna.

————. I:2 (15 January 1918), 1, 3.

————. I:3 (15 February 1918), 1.

Bildende Künstler. I:3 (1911). (12 issues only.) Edited by Arthur Roessler, Vienna.

Deutsche Kunst und Dekoration. (Edited by Alexander Koch, Darmstadt.) XIV:2 (1904), 605.

————. XIX:1 (1906–07), 65ff.

————. XX:2 (1906–07), 328–33, *passim.*

————. XXI:1 (1907–08), 113.

————. XXIII:1 (1908–09), 68.

————. XXV:1 (1909–10), 244.

————. XXXIV:2 (1914), 342.

Die Fackel. I:1 (April 1899), 1. Edited by Karl Kraus, Vienna.

————. VII:251–52 (April 1905), 34.

Die Graphischen Künste. XXXIII: 2–3 (1910), 55. Vienna.

Hohe Warte. II:3 (1905–06), 48. Edited by Joseph August Lux, Vienna.

Das Interieur. XII (1911), 8. Vienna.

Der Ruf. I:3 (1912), 18. Edited by Robert Müller, Vienna. (4 issues only.)

The Studio. Special Number (1905), "Art in Photography." London.

Der Sturm. II:20, 21, 24, 26 (June–August 1910). Edited by Herwarth Waden, Berlin.

Ver Sacrum. Organ of the Vienna Secession: Vienna, 1898; Leipzig, 1899; Vienna, 1900–03.

5. EXHIBITION CATALOGUES

1902: *Klinger: Beethoven.* Vienna: XIV. Ausstellung der Vereinigung Bildender Künstler Österreichs Secession, April–June 1902.

1904: *XIX. Ausstellung.* Vienna: Secession, December 1903–February 1904.

1906: *Vincent van Gogh: Kollektiv Ausstellung.* Vienna: Galerie H. O. Miethke, January 1906.

1908: *Kunstschau Wien 1908.* Vienna, 1908.

1909: *Katalog der Internationalen Kunstschau Wien 1909.* Vienna, 1909.

1910: *1. Internationale Jagd-Ausstellung Wien 1910.* Vienna, 1910.

1910: *Die Kunst der Frau.* Vienna: Secession, November–December 1910.

1912: *Ausstellung der Secession.* Vienna, November 1911–January 1912.

1913: *Internationale Schwarz-Weiss-Ausstellung.* Vienna, 1913. (Forewords by Peter Altenberg, Paris von Gütersoh, Emil Rheinhardt, and Paul Stefan.)

1913: *Privatsammlung Dr. Oskar Reichel, Wien.* Vienna: Galerie H. O. Miethke, 21 February 1913.

1914: *3. Kunstausstellung des Vereines heimischer Künstler Klosterneuburgs.* Klosterneuburg, 1914.

1918: *Kollektivausstellung in der 49. Jahresausstellung.* Vienna: Secession, March 1918. (One-man show of Schiele's works.)

1919: *Secession Bildnisse.* Vienna: Secession, December 1918–January 1919.

1940: *Les Hodler du Musée d'Art et d'Histoire.* Geneva: Musée d'Art et d'Histoire, 1940. (Preface by Waldemar Deonna and essay by Daniel Baud-Bovy.)

1956: *Egon Schiele. Bilder, Aquarelle, Zeichnungen, Graphik.* Berne: Gutekunst und Klipstein, 1956. (Introductions by Otto Benesch and Arthur Roessler.)

1957: *German Art of the Twentieth Century.* New York: Museum of Modern Art, 1957. (With essays by Werner Haftmann, Alfred Hentzen, and William S. Lieberman.)

1958: *Katalog der Schausammlung.* Linz: Neue Galerie der Stadt Linz Wolfgang Gurlitt Museum, 1958.

1960: *Egon Schiele.* Boston: Institute of Contemporary Art, 1960.

1960: *Expressionismus: Literatur und Kunst 1910–1923.* Marbach: Schiller-Nationalmuseum, 8 May–31 October 1960.

1960: *Les Sources du XXᵉ siècle.* Paris: Musée National d'Art Moderne, 1960.

1961: *Katalog der Gemälde Galerie.* Vienna: Akademie der Bildenden Künste in Wien, 1961.

1962: *Kunst von 1900 bis Heute.* Vienna: Museum des 20. Jahrhunderts, 21 September–4 November 1962. (Opening exhibition.)

1963: *Viennese Expressionism 1910–1924.* Berkeley: University Art Gallery of the University of California, 5 February–10 March 1963. (Introduction by Herschel B. Chipp.)

1963: *Zeugnisse der Angst in der Moderne Kunst.* Darmstadt: Mathildenhöhe Darmstadt, 1963.

1964: *Austrian Expressionists.* New York: Galerie St. Etienne, 1964.

1964: *Egon Schiele.* London: Marlborough (New London) Gallery, 1964.

1964: *Secession. Europäische Kunst um die Jahrhundertwende.* Munich: Haus der Kunst, 14 March–10 May 1964.

1964: *Wien um 1900.* Vienna: Kulturamt der Stadt Wien, 5 June–30 August 1964.

1965: *Egon Schiele. Watercolors and Drawings from American Collections.* New York: Galerie St. Etienne, March–April 1965. (Introduction by Thomas M. Messer.)

1965: *Gustav Klimt and Egon Schiele*. New York: The Solomon R. Guggenheim Museum, 1965. (With essays by Johannes Dobai, James Demetrion, and Alessandra Comini.)

1965: *Jugendstil and Expressionism in German Posters*. Berkeley: Berkeley Art Gallery, 16 November–9 December, 1965.

1966: *Richard Gerstl*. Vienna: Wiener Secession, June–July 1966. (Essay by Otto Breicha.)

1967: *Egon Schiele*. Los Angeles: Felix Landau Gallery, 1967.

1967: *Katalog Gustav Klimt, 56 Zeichnungen*. Vienna: Christian M. Nebehay Gallery, 1967. (Catalogue XI.)

1967: *II. Internationale der Zeichnung*. Darmstadt: Mathildenhöhe Darmstadt, 1967. (Introduction by Werner Hofmann.)

1968: *L'Art en europe autour de 1918*. Strasbourg, 8 May–15 September 1968.

1968: *Egon Schiele*. New York: Galerie St. Etienne, 31 October–14 December, 1968.

1968: *Egon Schiele—Gemälde*. Vienna: Österreichische Galerie, April–September 1968.

1968: *Egon Schiele: Gemälde, Aquarelle, Zeichnungen*. Salzburg: Museum Carolino Augusteum, July–August, 1968.

1968: *Egon Schiele: Leben und Werk*. Vienna: Historisches Museum der Stadt Wien, 1968.

1968: *Katalog Egon Schiele, Frühe Werke und Dokumentation*. Vienna: Christian M. Nebehay Gallery, April 1968. (Catalogue XIV.)

1968: *Katalog Gustav Klimt und Egon Schiele zum Gedächtnis ihres Todes vor 50 Jahren*. Vienna: Graphische Sammlung Albertina, 5 April–16 June 1968. (Forewords by Walter Koschatzky, Paris von Gütersloh, and Otto Benesch; introductions by Alice Strobl and Erwin Mitsch.)

1969: *Egon Schiele Drawings and Watercolors, 1909–1918*. London: Marlborough Fine Art Ltd., February–March, 1969.

1971: *Egon Schiele and His Circle*. New York: La Boetie Gallery, May–June, 1971.

1971: *Egon Schiele and the Human Form*. Des Moines: Des Moines Art Center, 20 September–31 October, 1971. (Essay by James T. Demetrion.)

1972: *Egon Schiele: Oils, Watercolors, Drawings, and Graphic Works*. London: Fischer Fine Art Ltd., November–December 1972.

1972–73: *Expressionists*. New York: Serge Sabarsky Gallery, Inc., October 1972–February, 1973.

6. UNPUBLISHED MATERIAL

Comini, Alessandra. "Egon Schiele: The Artist's Vision of Himself." M.A. thesis, University of California at Berkeley, 1964.

Harms, Adele. Taped personal interview, Vienna, 24 January 1967.

Harms–Schiele, Edith. Diary, 1915–18. Collection Otto Kallir, New York; formerly Collection Adele Harms, Vienna.

Jaffe, Anne B. "The Nature of the Tragic in the Portraits of Soutine and Kokoschka." M.A. thesis, Columbia University, 1955.

Klimt, Gustav. Diary, 1918. Collection Christian M. Nebehay, Vienna.

Peschka, Gertrud. Taped personal interviews, Vienna, 18 February and 3 March 1967.

Schiele, Egon. Diary pages from a trip to Munich, 1912. Collection Melanie Schuster, Vienna.

———. Sketchbook A (July–December 1912), pencil, Collection Melanie Schuster, Vienna.

———. Sketchbook B (1915–16), pencil, Collection Melanie Schuster, Vienna.

———. Sketchbook (1918), pencil, colored inks, and watercolor, Collection Otto Kallir, New York.

Schuster, Melanie. Taped personal interviews, Vienna, 23 January and 18 February 1967.

Wagner, Max, compiler. "Egon Schiele Erinnerungsbuch." November 1943–September 1950. With reminiscences by, among others, Heinrich Benesch, Arthur Roessler, and Ludwig K. Strauch. Manuscript in the A.E.S.A., Vienna (handwritten).

Index

NOTE: Egon Schiele's portrait subjects are identified in this index by capital and small-capital letters. They appear separately in the main index, and in more condensed form under Schiele, work, portraits, where the listing is limited to portraits that are the subject of major text discussions. Sketches and studies attached to such portraits and illustrated in this book are not indexed separately, but are comprehended in entries under Schiele, work, portraits, q.v. Works by Schiele mentioned but not illustrated in this book are not indexed separately.

Artists other than Schiele, mentioned only in connection with exhibitions and museums, are not indexed separately. In general, persons mentioned in the text only one time are not indexed. Exceptions are some artists, and all periodical publications pertaining to Viennese culture.

168; use of line, 10, 22, 32, 39, 45–46, 50, 52, 54, 59, 75, 109, 137, 140, 163, 164, 166, 168, 173–174, 176, 177; head halos, 12, 24, 88, 100, 110; composition, 12–13, 18, 26, 32, 39, 42, 43, 54, 73, 74, 77, 116, 134, 165–168 *passim*; expressiveness of hands, 13, 22, 40, 42, 43, 47, 56, 57, 75, 76, 81, 82, 83, 88, 89, 103, 109, 116, 142, 147, 162, 171, 172, 180, 181; *see also* V-shaped gesture; facial characterization, 13, 40, 41, 43, 57, 58, 60, 76, 77, 82, 83, 97, 98, 100, 109, 116, 129, 137, 138, 145, 146, 147, 162, 163, 164, 170, 171, 173, 176, 177, 180, 181, 182; psychological dramatization, 13, 46, 47, 50, 56, 57, 59, 60, 75, 78, 145; extended shoulder device, 18, 44, 56, 57, 69, 71, 73, 78, 89, 109, 159, 167, 173, 174, 175, 177; use of ascetic garments, 24, 80, 96, 98, 106–107, 108, 110, 138, 140, 141, 184, 185, 186, 225n81; detailed background, 25; close focus, 25, 26, 31, 43, 58, 71, 78, 83, 99, 100, 133; compositional dismemberment, 25, 47, 56–63 *passim*, 78, 81, 83, 88, 89, 90, 100, 102, 140, 167, 174; *see also* close focus, "missing" thumb; astral glow, 26, 44–45, 59, 60, 73, 76, 77, 78, 81, 88, 89, 98, 107, 122, 129, 134, 181, 232n40; use of color, 32, 46, 48, 54, 57–60 *passim*, 73–77 *passim*, 82–93 *passim*, 98, 102, 103, 106, 115, 120, 124, 129, 131, 137, 141, 148, 152, 158, 163–168 *passim*, 171–177 *passim*, 181, 232n40; self-protective hug of arms, 32, 42, 55, 56, 57, 69; organic approach to subject, 32, 67, 137; use of drapery, 39, 58, 68, 75, 83, 88, 103, 109, 115, 116, 126, 130, 141, 145, 146; sexual symbolism, 41, 43, 56, 60–64 *passim*, 78, 81, 83, 84, 87–92 *passim*, 106, 129, 138, 146, 171–172; use of nudity, 41, 50, 55, 59, 83, 108–109, 110, 135, 172–173, 174; V-shaped gesture, 41, 57, 64, 88, 93, 95, 98, 107, 109, 116, 138, 141, 172, 174, 175, 182, 247n66; "signature" pose, 41, 57, 174; pose, 42, 43, 47, 54, 57, 60, 61, 69, 71, 74–78 *passim*, 83, 116, 128, 145, 160, 165, 171, 174, 180, 182; existential approach to subject, 43, 125; application of pigment, 47, 76, 137, 148, 163, 202n48; skeletal bodies, 49, 50; wild, "electrified" hair, 50, 58, 60, 82, 88, 137, 140, 206n13; use of mirror, 51–52, 57, 60, 65, 80, 81, 82, 88, 135, 136, 140, 146, 149, 173, 174; double image in self-portraits, 52, 80–84 *passim*, 88, 133, 139–142 *passim*; outward-turned eye, 57, 58, 119, 121; geometrization, 76–77, 88, 98, 100, 107, 115, 116, 121, 122, 127, 128, 129, 136–137, 147, 165, 176, 222n56; "painterly" portraits, 77, 148, 153, 168, 176, 181, 182; plant symbolism, 77–78, 87–88, 97, 100, 106, 161, 165, 213–214n80, 221n51, 222n58; use of object in portrait to seal patronage relationship, 78, 165; somnambulism, 82, 83, 85, 88, 97, 107; skull-like head, 82, 83, 98, 151, 169; vertical reading of recumbent figures, 85, 102, 103, 129, 216n16; use of graphite pencil, 85, 108; use of black chalk, 85, 108, 163, 169, 177; "missing" thumb, 88, 93, 95, 138, 141, 151; delicate ambiguity 91–92, 108, 128–129; types of background environment, 93, 122–123, 128, 138, 141, 148–153 *passim*, 157, 161, 164–169 *passim*, 175, 181, 182; triple signature, 97, 218n38, 221n51; painting on wood with diluted oil glaze, 100; "propless" sitter, 115, 128, 131;

method of working, 119, 120; emotional content in landscapes, 124; graphics, 125–126, 225n80; view from above, 128, 156, 157, 166; creation of types, 129, 176; use of carved wooden horse, 134, 165; plasticity, 137, 152, 156, 157, 160, 163, 164, 174, 176–177; sign language, 141, 147; use of preparatory studies, 155, 161–162, 165, 166, 169, 170; linked-hand gesture, 157, 158, 162–163, 164, 167, 169, 170, 181; objective approach to subject, 157, 160, 164–168 *passim*, 173, 174, 182; contrapposto, 157, 169; probing of sitter's personality, 165–169 *passim*; painting in oil on wood, 232–233n42; backgrounds of applied tinfoil, 203n60

Schiele, Egon, work

allegorical works: 23, 91, 138, 169, 216n27, 222n56; mother and child, 12–13, 76, 85–87, 99–100, 224n77, 245n46; self-portraits, 80–84, 91–92, 109–110, 137, 141–142, 145, 153, 171–180; double portraits, 95–99, 105–107, 108, 138–139, 225n81; *Fairytale World* (fig. 23b), 22, 23; *The Dead Mother I* (pl. 69), 76, 80, 85–86, 87; *Dead Mother II* ("Birth of Genius") (pl. 70), 76, 80, 87; lost *Self-portrait with Saint* ("Encounter") (pl. 94), 108; *Mother with Two Children* (pl. 168), 168–169; *Round the Table* (*The Friends*) (pl. 197), 184–186. *See also* Self-portraits with others

army portraits: *Portrait of a Soldier* (fig. 110), 150; *Portrait of a Russian Prisoner of War* (fig. 109), 151; portrait of Charles Péguy for *Die Aktion* (fig. 111), 151, 152

portraits: *Portrait of a Lady* (pl. 4), 22–23
  Marie SCHIELE I (fig. 32), 25
  Leopold CZIHACZEK I (fig. 29): 25, 26; sketches and studies, 22, 25, 195n51, 196n4
  Melanie SCHIELE (fig. 34), 26; sketches, 15–16, 26
  Anton PESCHKA (pl. 10): 31–32, 34, 35, 42, 46, 205n2; studies 46–47
  Hans MASSMANN (pl. 8): 31–32, 34, 35, 42, 205n2; studies, 32, 197n8
  Gerti SCHIELE: 42, 145; portrait (pl. 5), 26; *Woman with a Black Hat* (pl. 6), 26–27, 34, 35, 39, 205n2; 'flowery pedestal' portrait (pl. 14), 38–39, 44, 49, 55–56; nude portrait (pl. 28a), 55–56; sketches and studies, 39, 55–56, 67, 85, 201n38, 207n21
  Poldi LODZINSKY (pl. 23), 43, 209n42
  Karl ZAKOVSEK (pl. 25): 43–44, 65, 78, 145, 148; studies, 43, 67
  Heinrich and Otto BENESCH (pl. 110): 55, 77, 118, 120–122, 131, 145, 157, 166; studies, 119–120, 126, 228n21
  Arthur ROESSLER (pl. 42): 69, 70, 78, 145; etching (pl. 41), 69–70; studies, 67, 68, 69–70, 195n51
  Otto WAGNER (pl. 46): 70–72
  Dr. Erwin GRAFF (pl. 50): 72–73, 78; studies, 73
  Dr. Oskar REICHEL (pl. 53): 74, 78, 145
  Herbert RAINER (pl. 58): 75–76, 78, 199n22, 117
  Eduard KOSMACK (pl. 61): 76–78, 145, 157, 161, 165
  Paris von GÜTERSLOH (pl. 190): 77, 157, 180–182, 183

PLATES

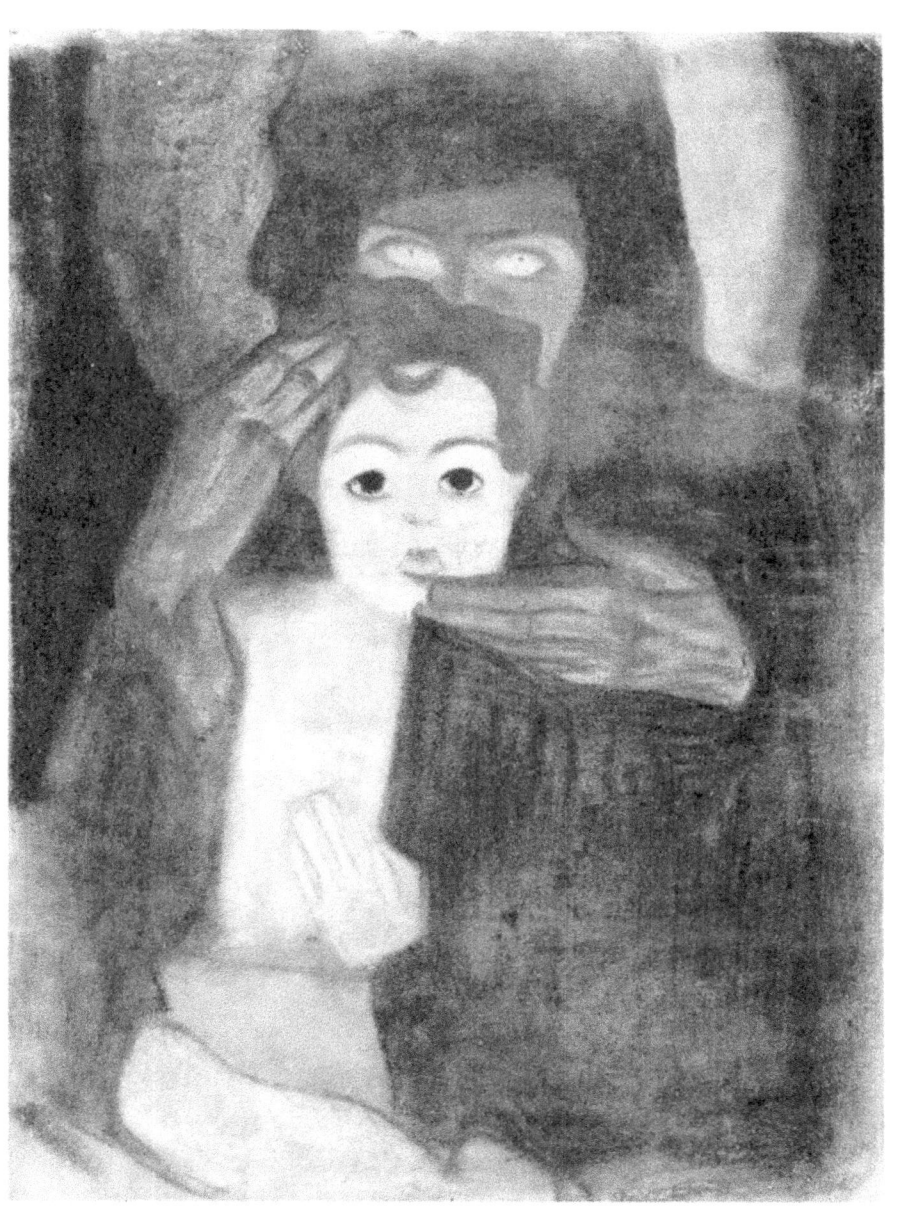

PL. 1. Schiele, *Madonna and Child*, *ca.* 1906, red chalk with white chalk and charcoal heightening.

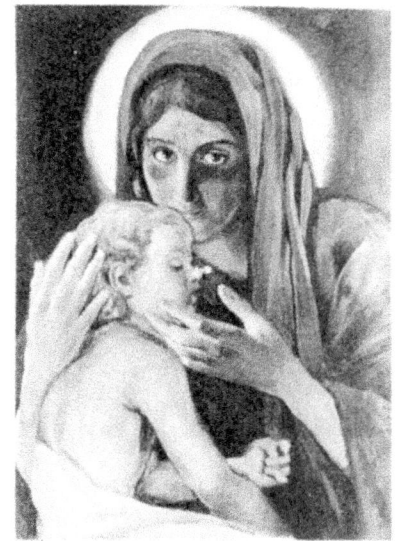

PL. 2. Ludwig K. Strauch, *Madonna and Child*, 1946, oil.

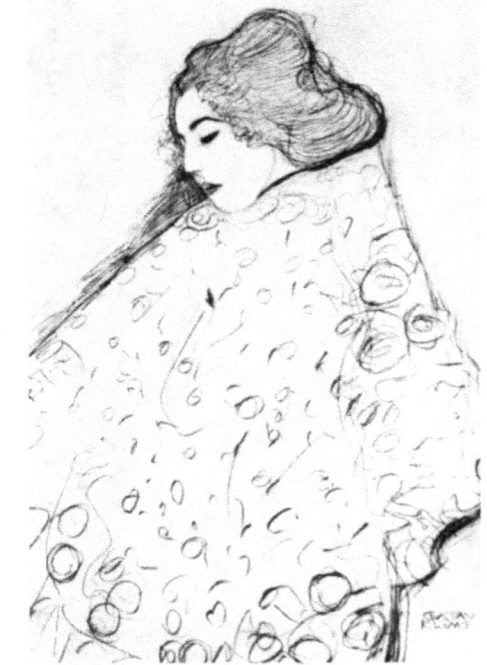

PL. 3. Klimt, *Portrait Sketch of an "Oriental" Model*, *ca.* 1906–1919, red and blue pencil and white chalk.

PL. 4. Schiele, *Portrait of a Lady*, 1908, oil.

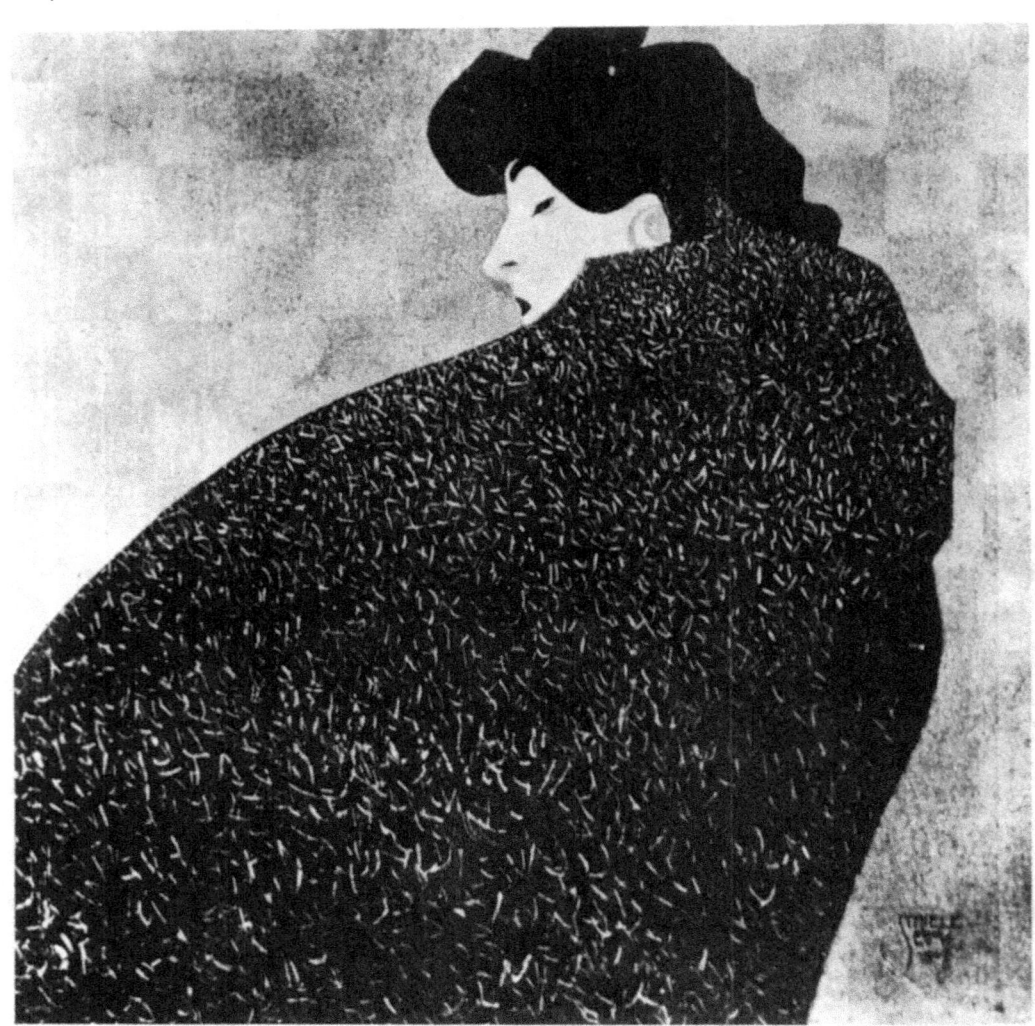

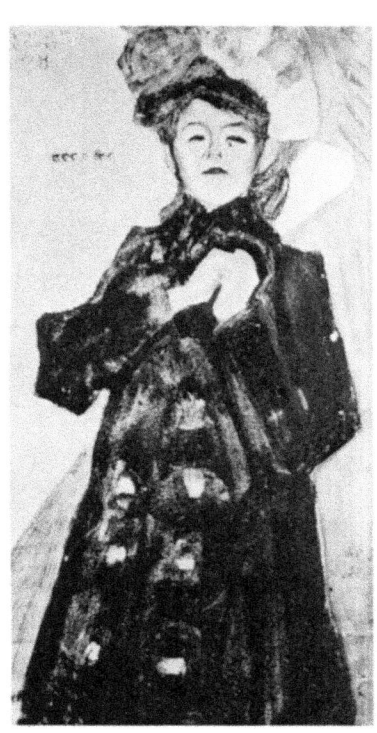

PL. 5. Schiele, *Portrait of Gerti*, 1908, oil.

PL. 6. Schiele, *Portrait of a Woman with a Black Hat (Gerti)*, 1909, oil.

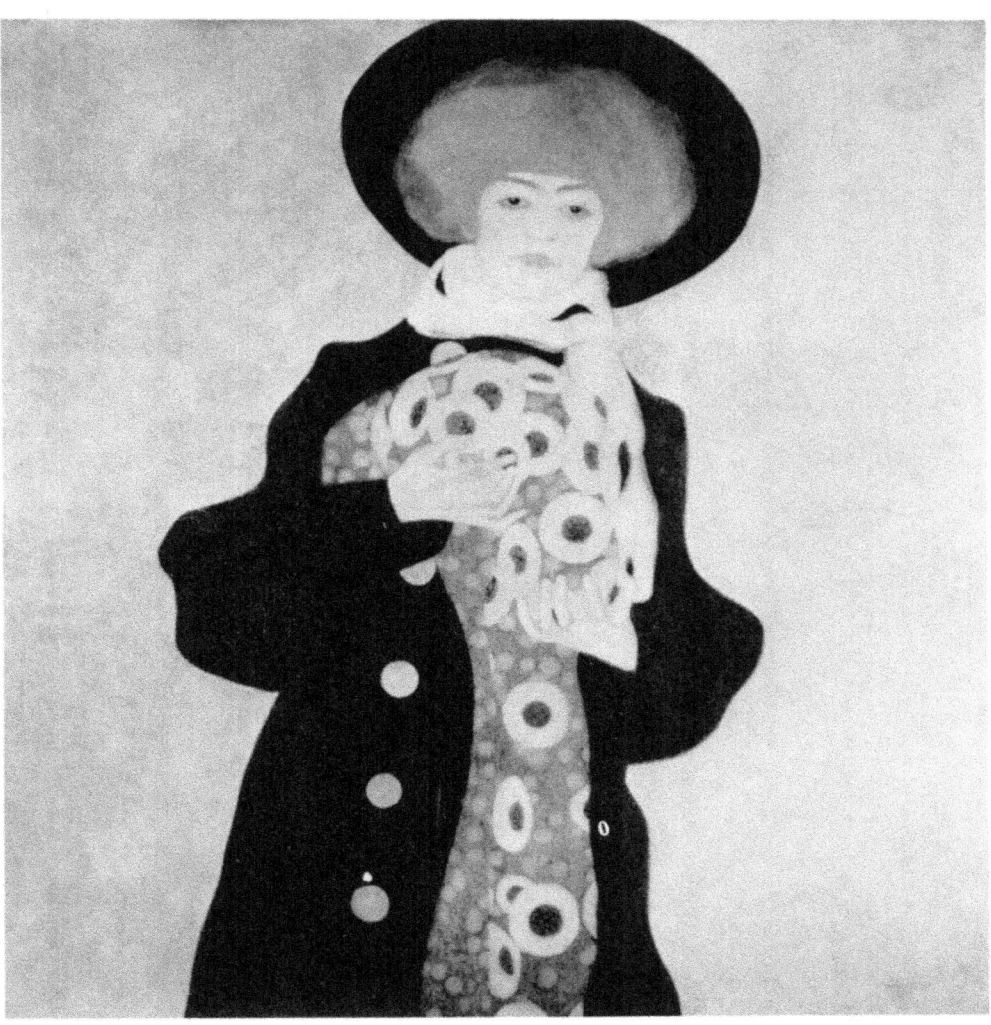

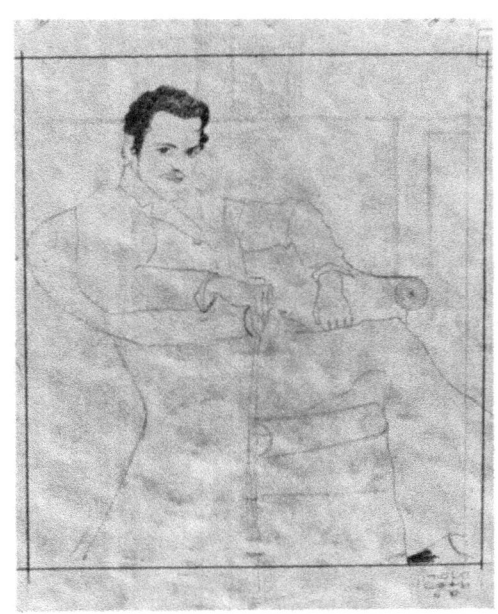

PL. 7. Schiele, *Study for the Portrait of Hans Massmann*, 1909, pencil.

PL. 8. Schiele, *Portrait of Hans Massmann*, 1909, oil.

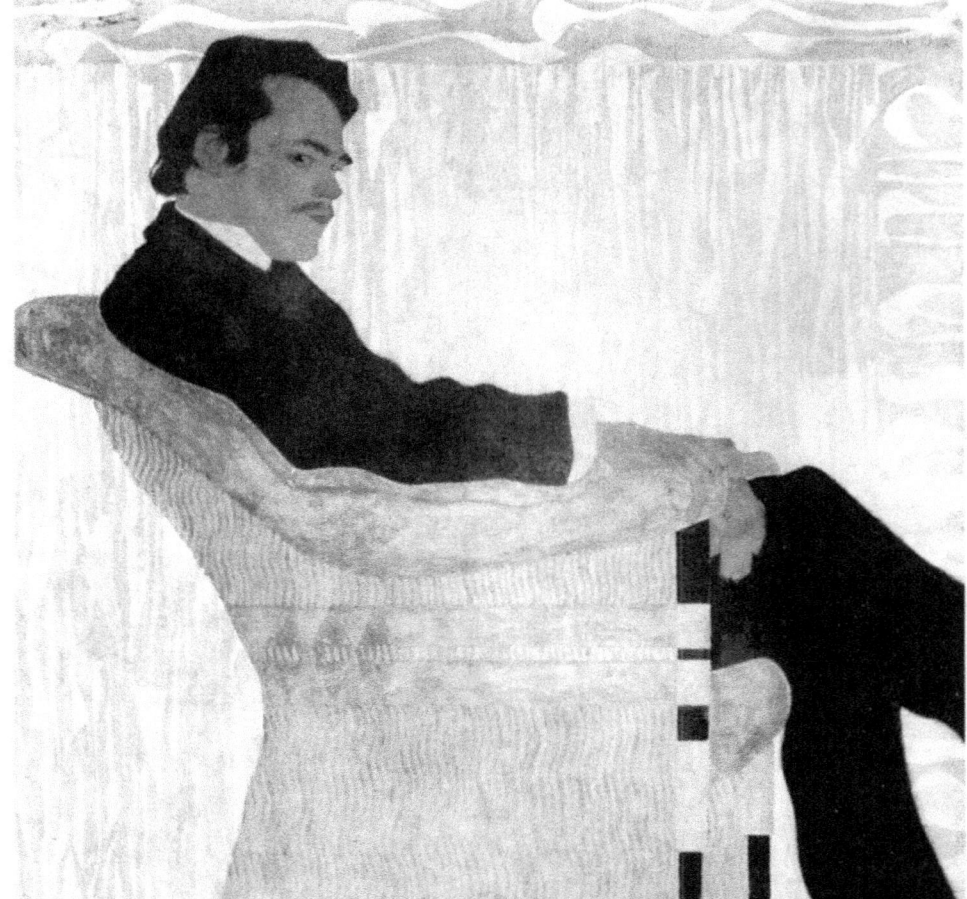

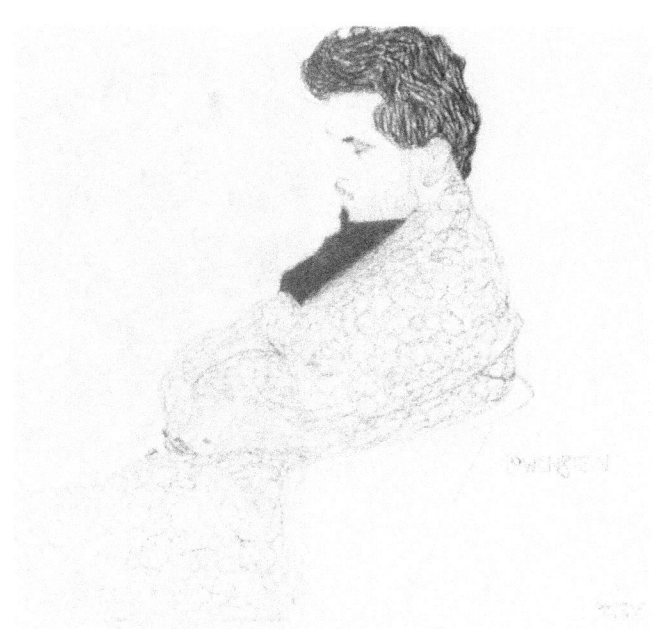

PL. 9. Schiele, *Portrait Study of Arthur Löwenstein*, 1909, colored pencil.

PL. 10. Schiele, *Portrait of Anton Peschka*, 1909, oil.

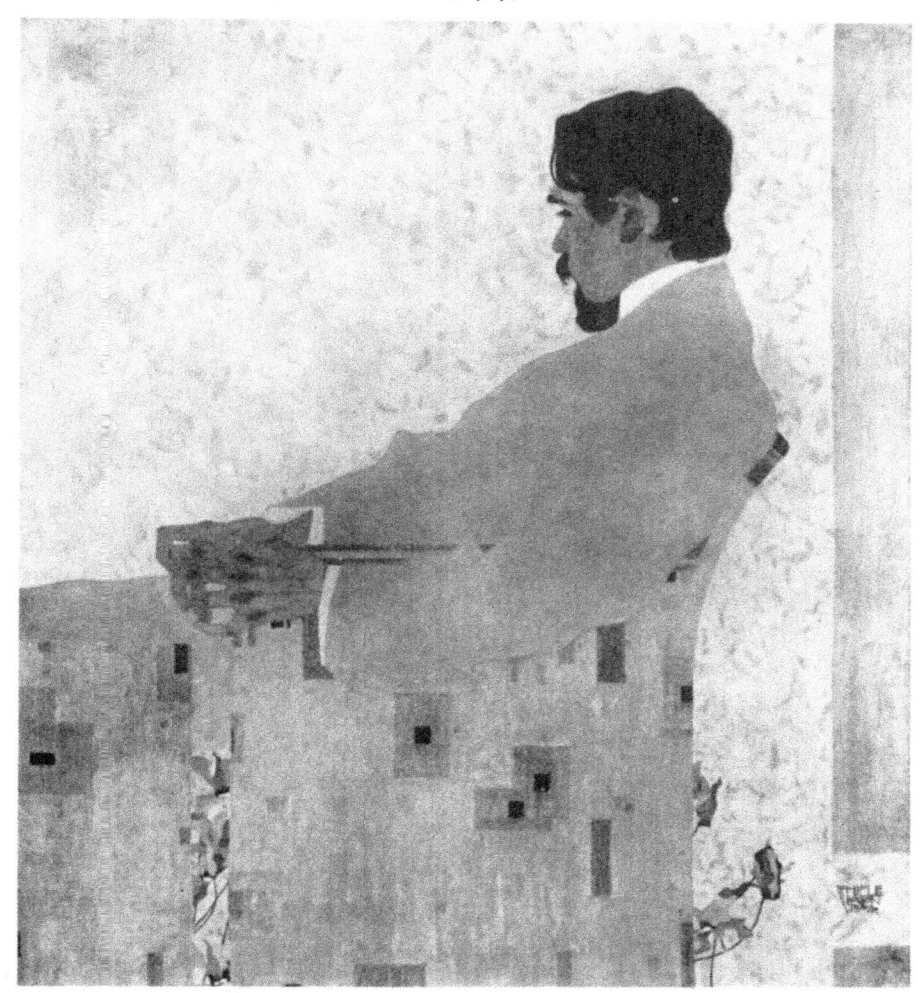

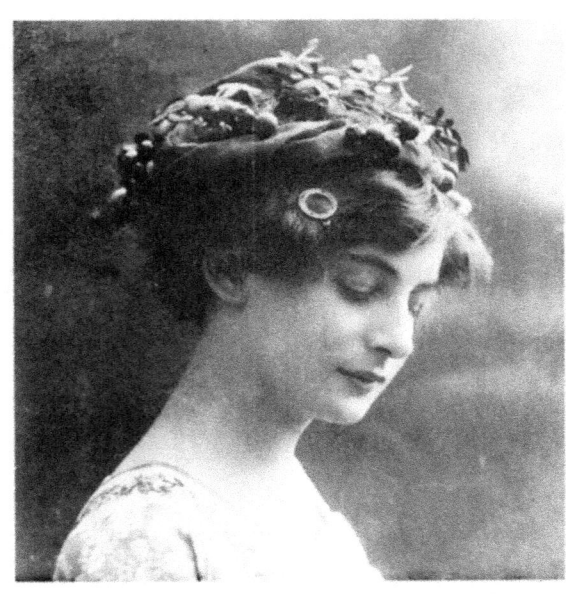

PL. 11. Gerti Schiele, *ca.* 1909.

PL. 12. Schiele, *Sketch of Gerti Posing with Eyes Closed*, 1909, pencil.

PL. 13. Gerti Schiele as a Wiener Werkstätte clothes model, *ca.* 1911.

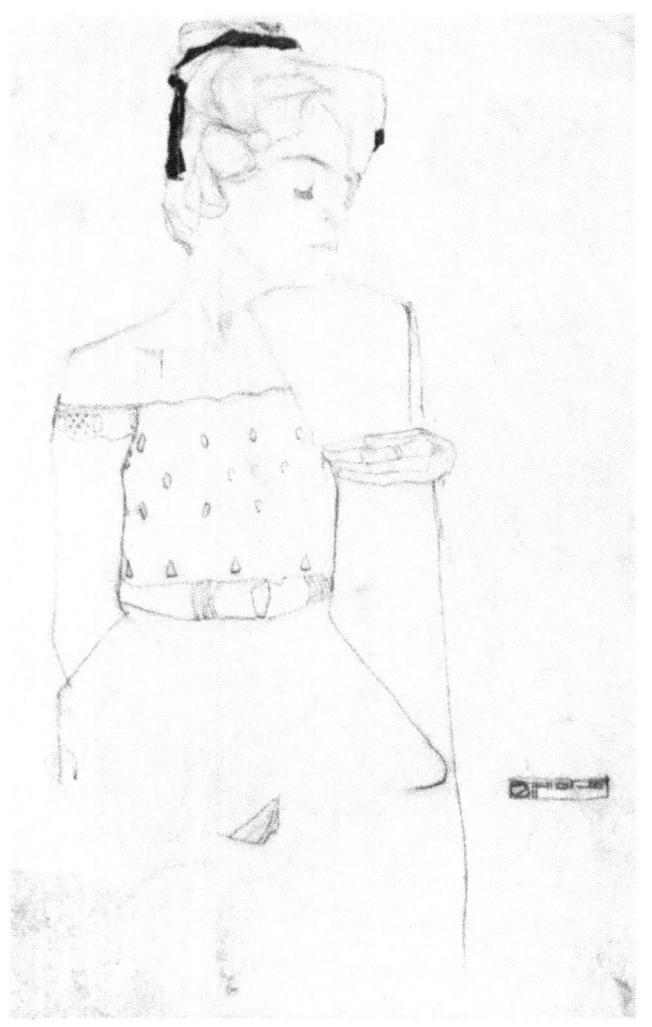

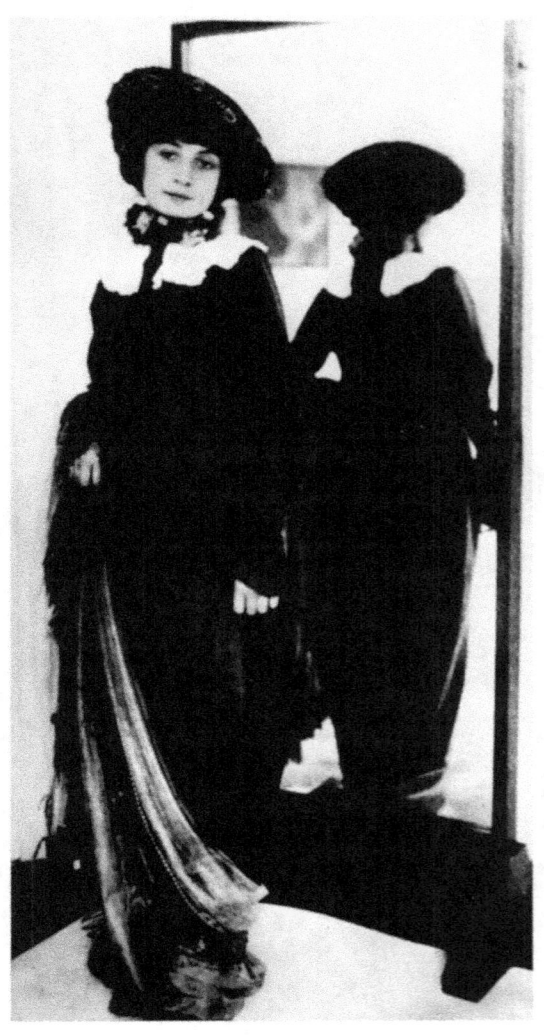

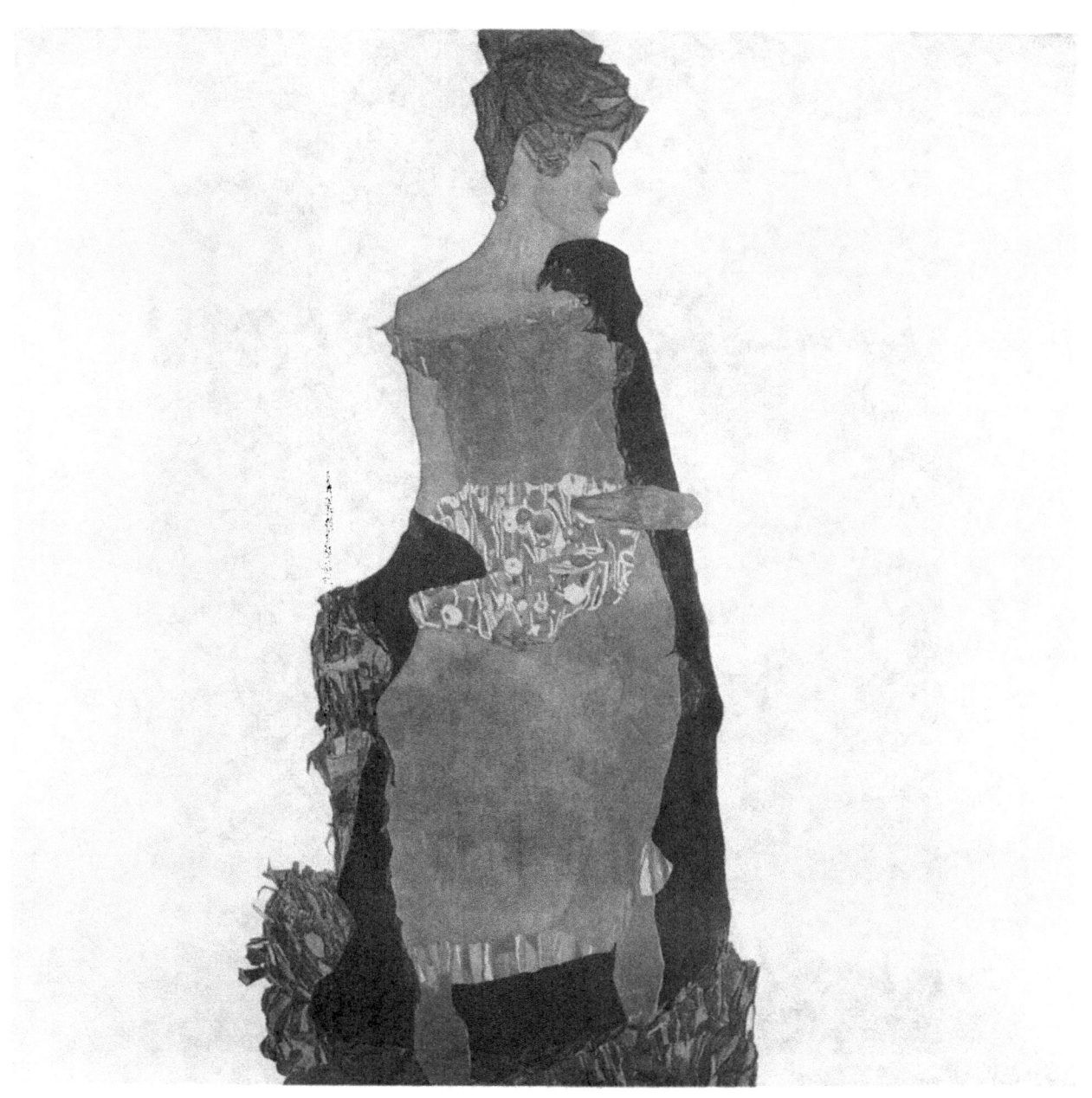

PL. 14. Schiele, *Portrait of Gerti Schiele*, 1909, oil.

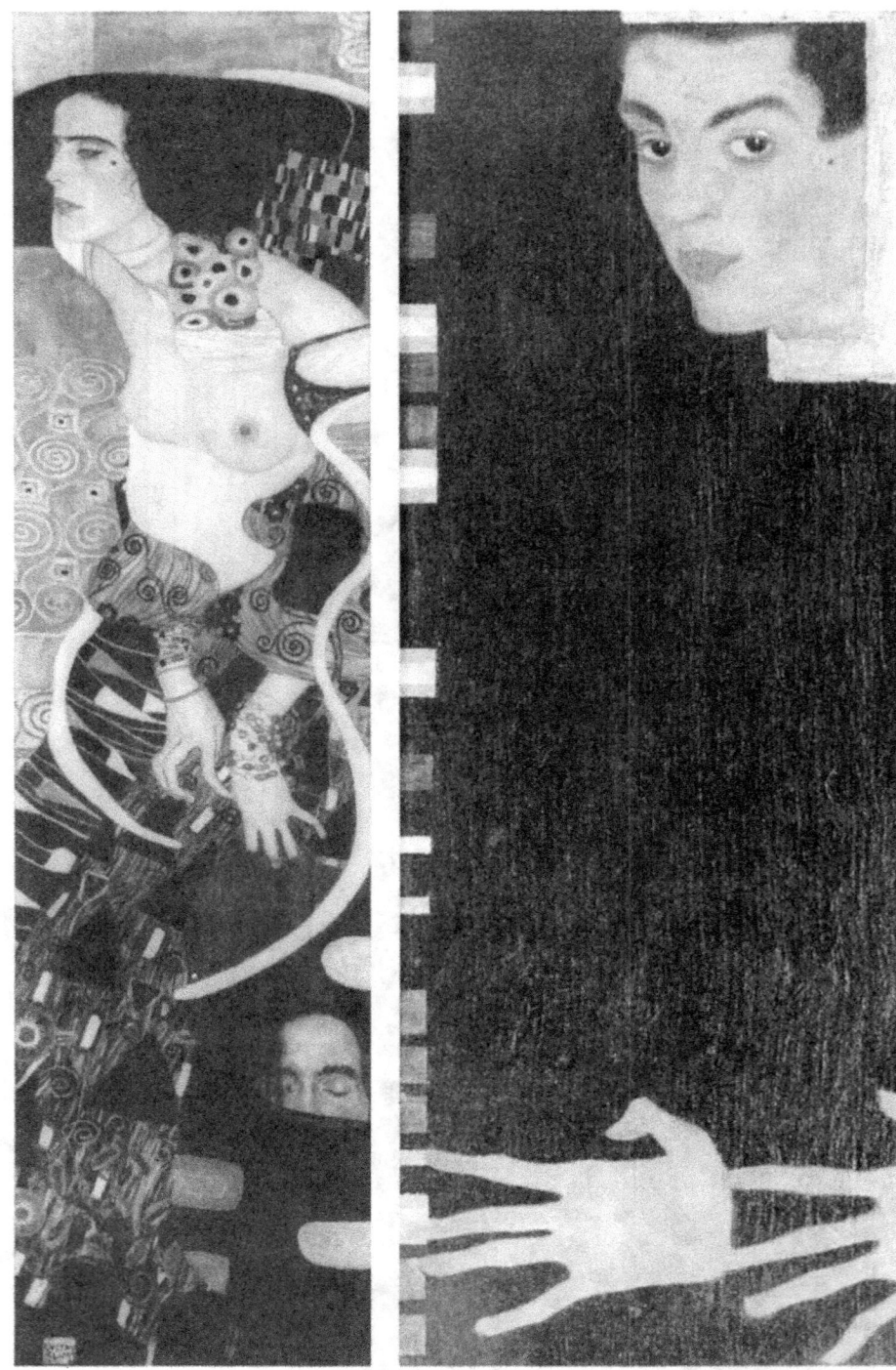

PL. 15. Klimt, *Judith II*, 1909, oil.   PL. 16. Schiele, *Self-Portrait Clothed*, 1909, oil.

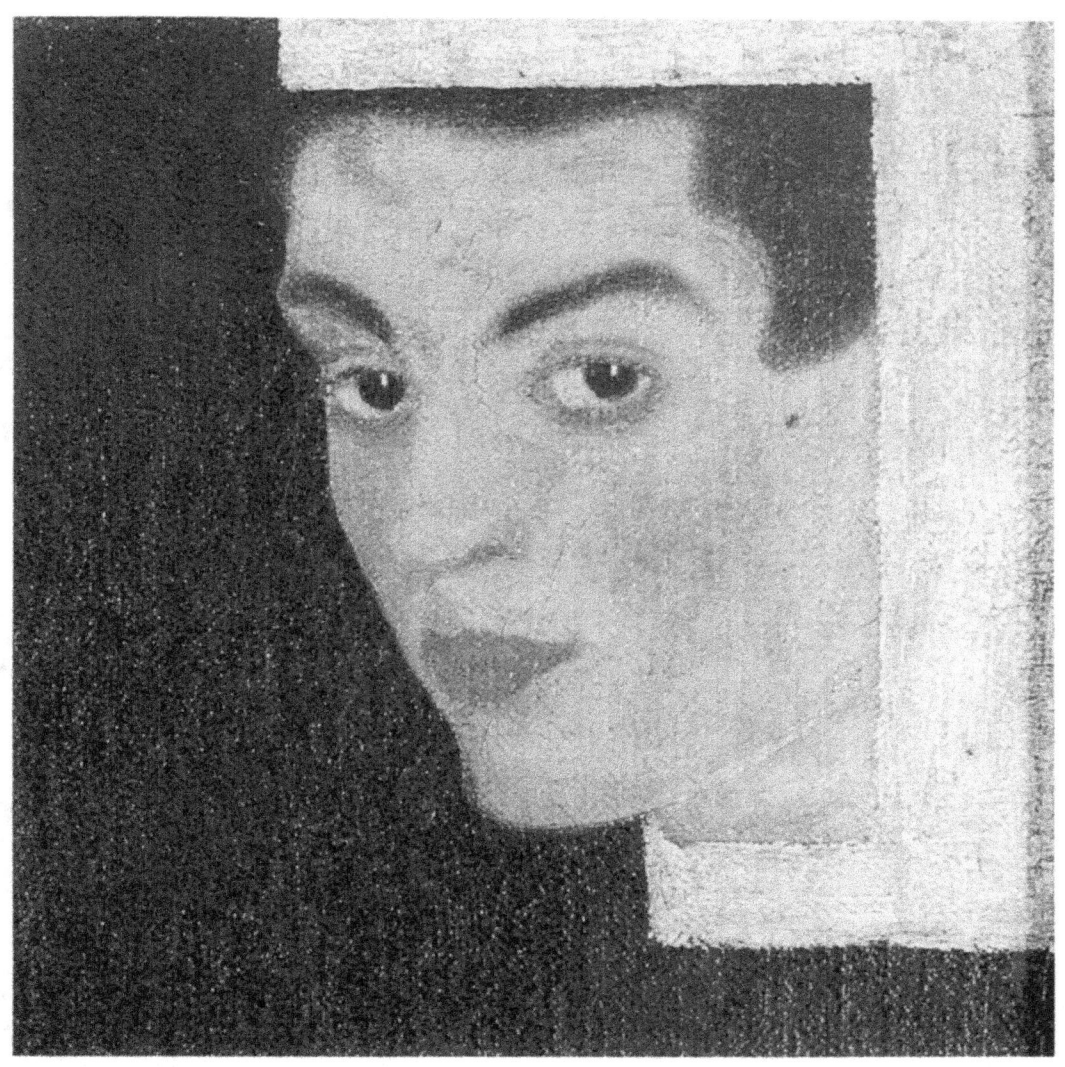

Schiele, *Self-Portrait Clothed*, 1909, oil, detail.

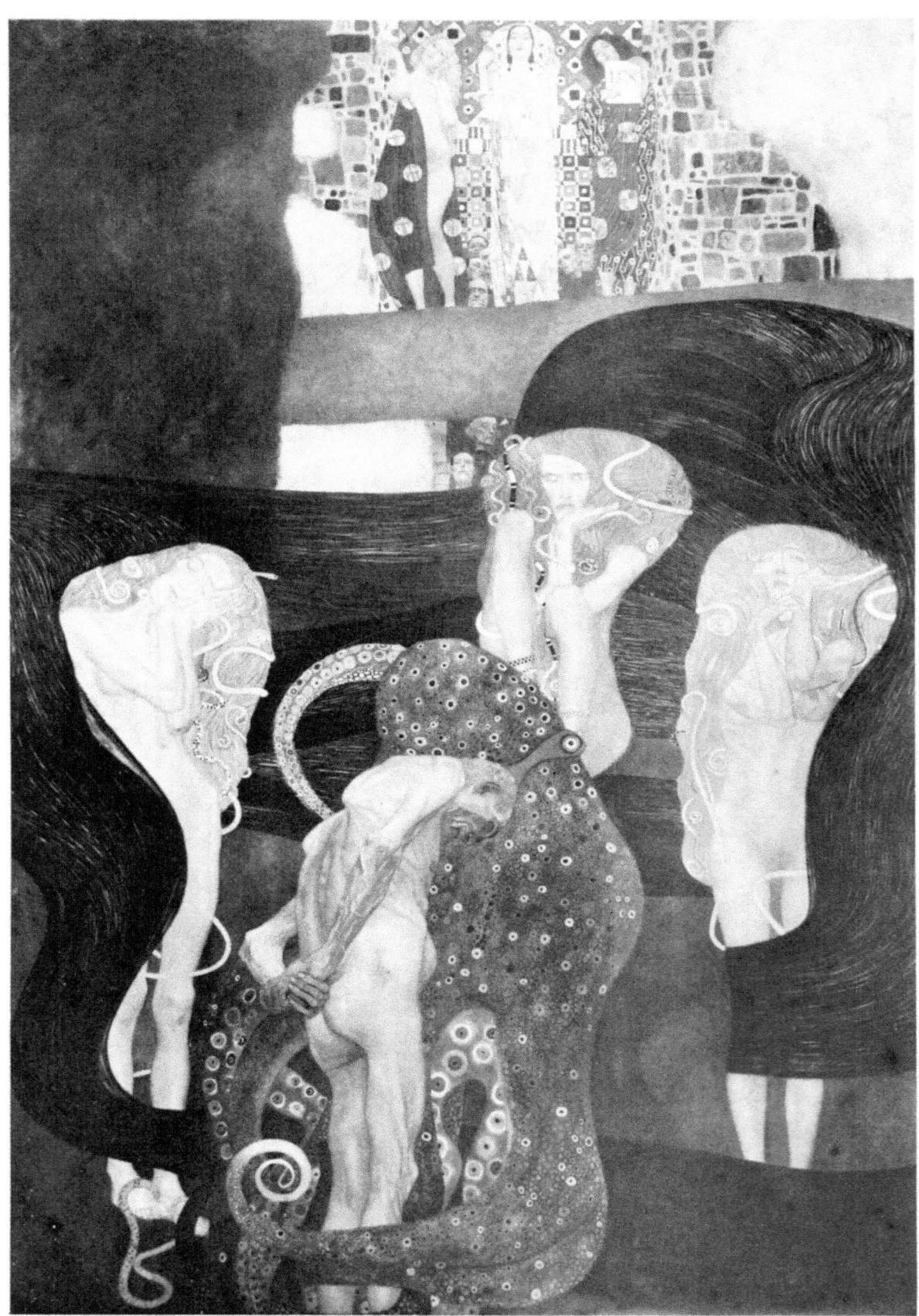

PL. 17. Klimt, *Jurisprudence*, 1903/1907, oil.

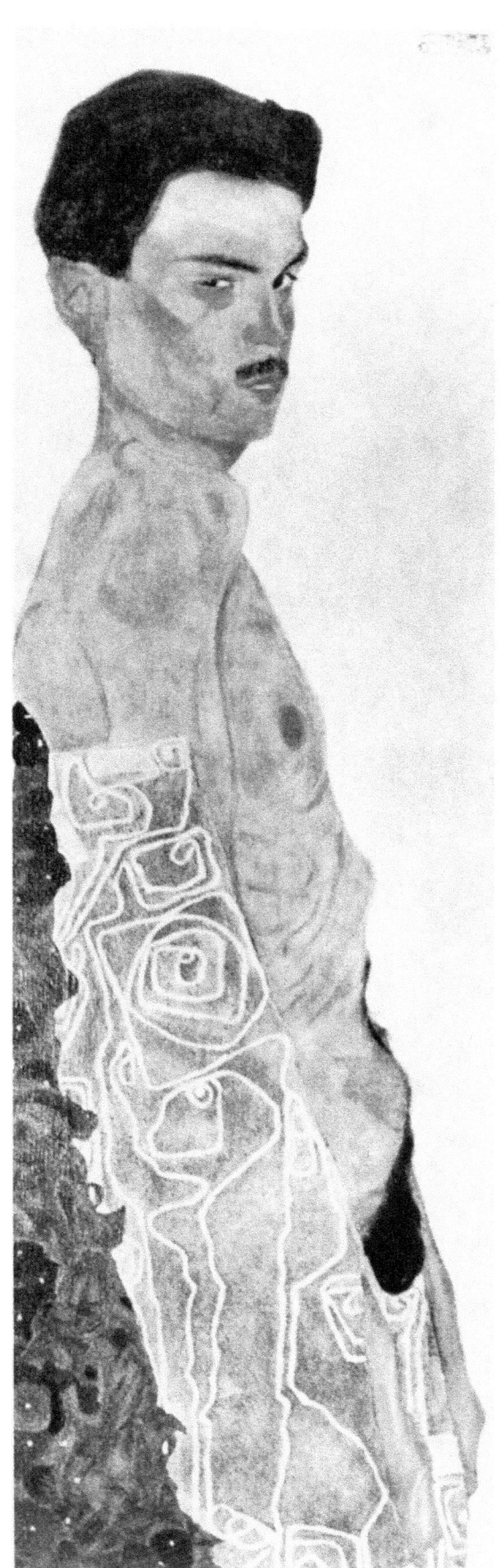

PL. 18. Schiele, *Self-Portrait Nude*, 1909, oil.

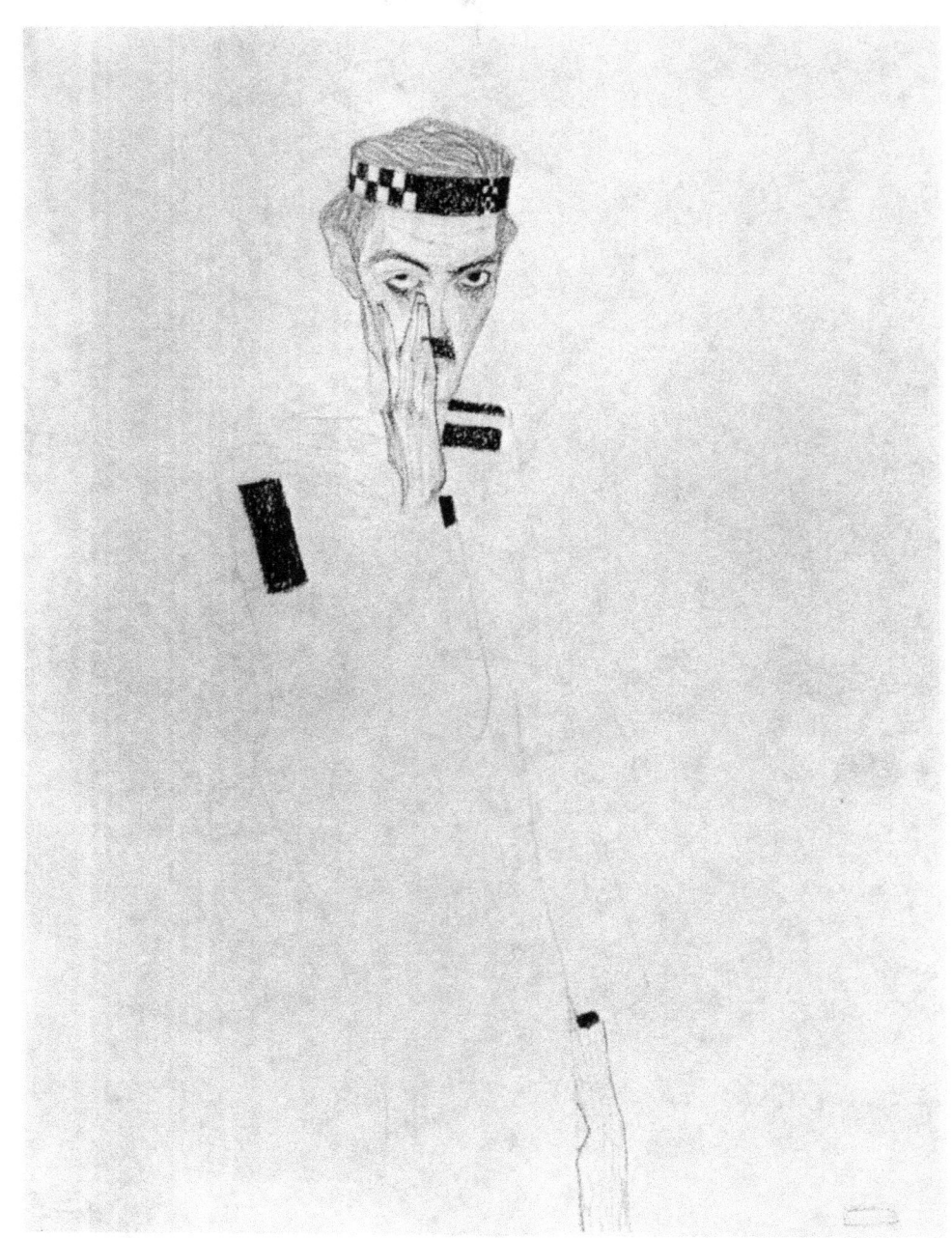

PL. 19. Schiele, *Self-Portrait with Hair Band*, 1909, colored crayon.

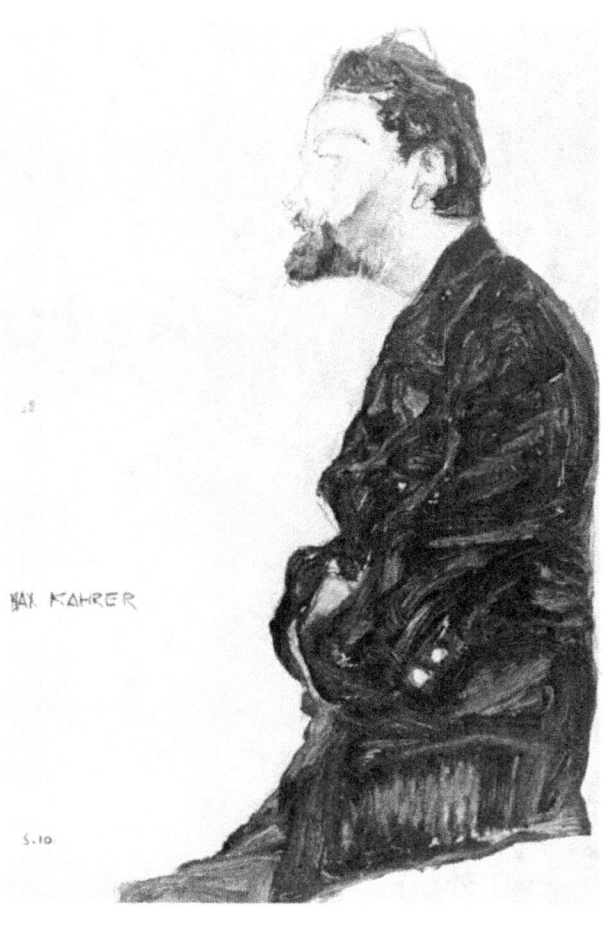

PL. 20. Schiele, *Portrait of Max Kahrer*, 1910, black chalk and watercolor.

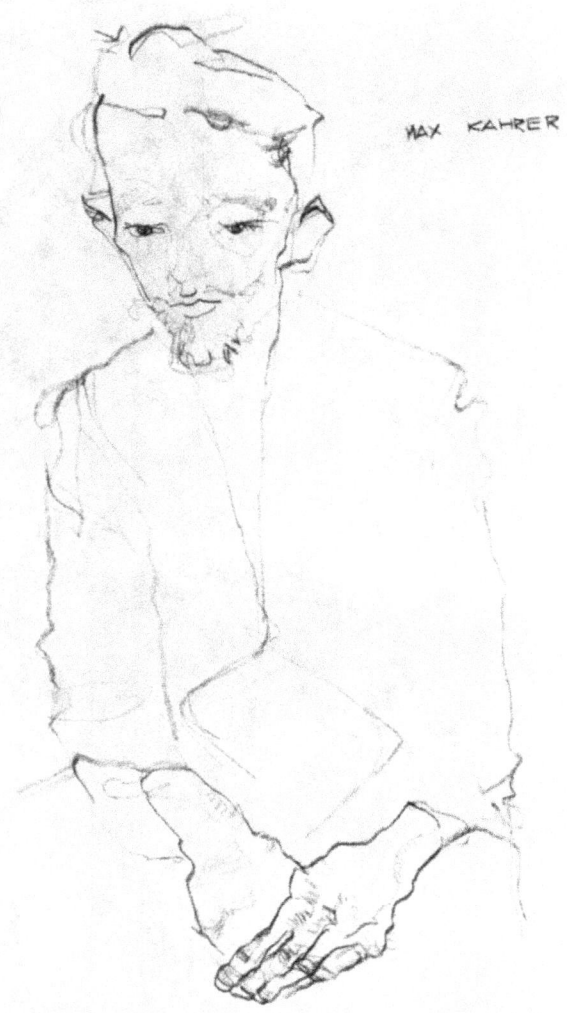

PL. 21. Schiele, *Portrait of Max Kahrer with Hands Crossed*, 1910, black chalk.

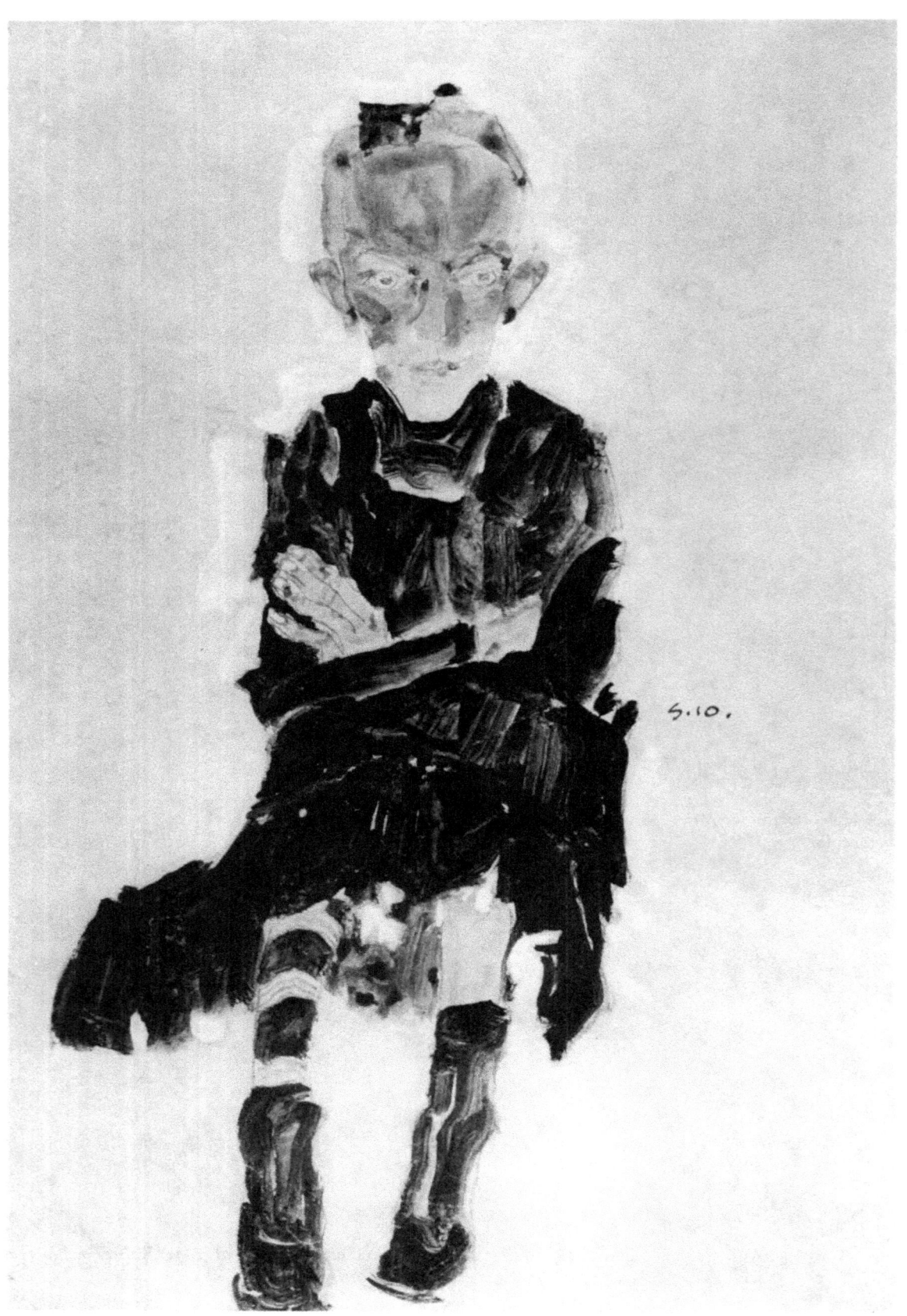

PL. 22. Schiele, *Girl in Black*, 1910, black chalk and watercolor.

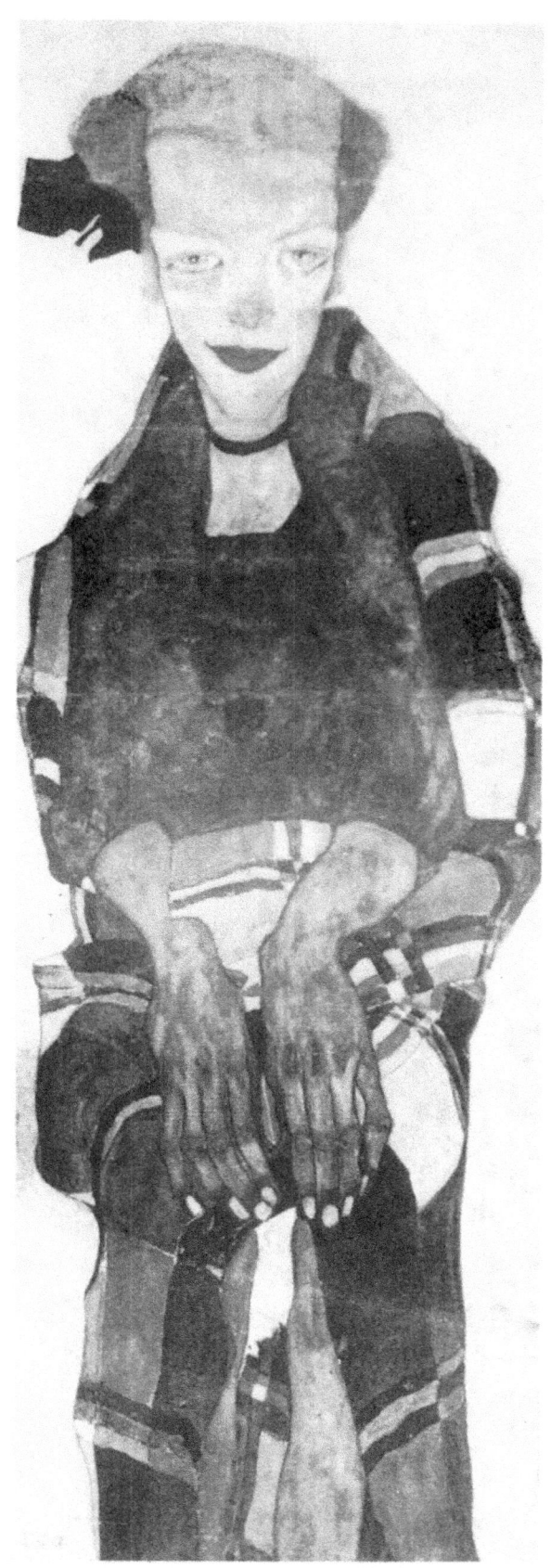

PL. 23. Schiele, *Portrait of Poldi Lodzinsky*, 1910, oil.

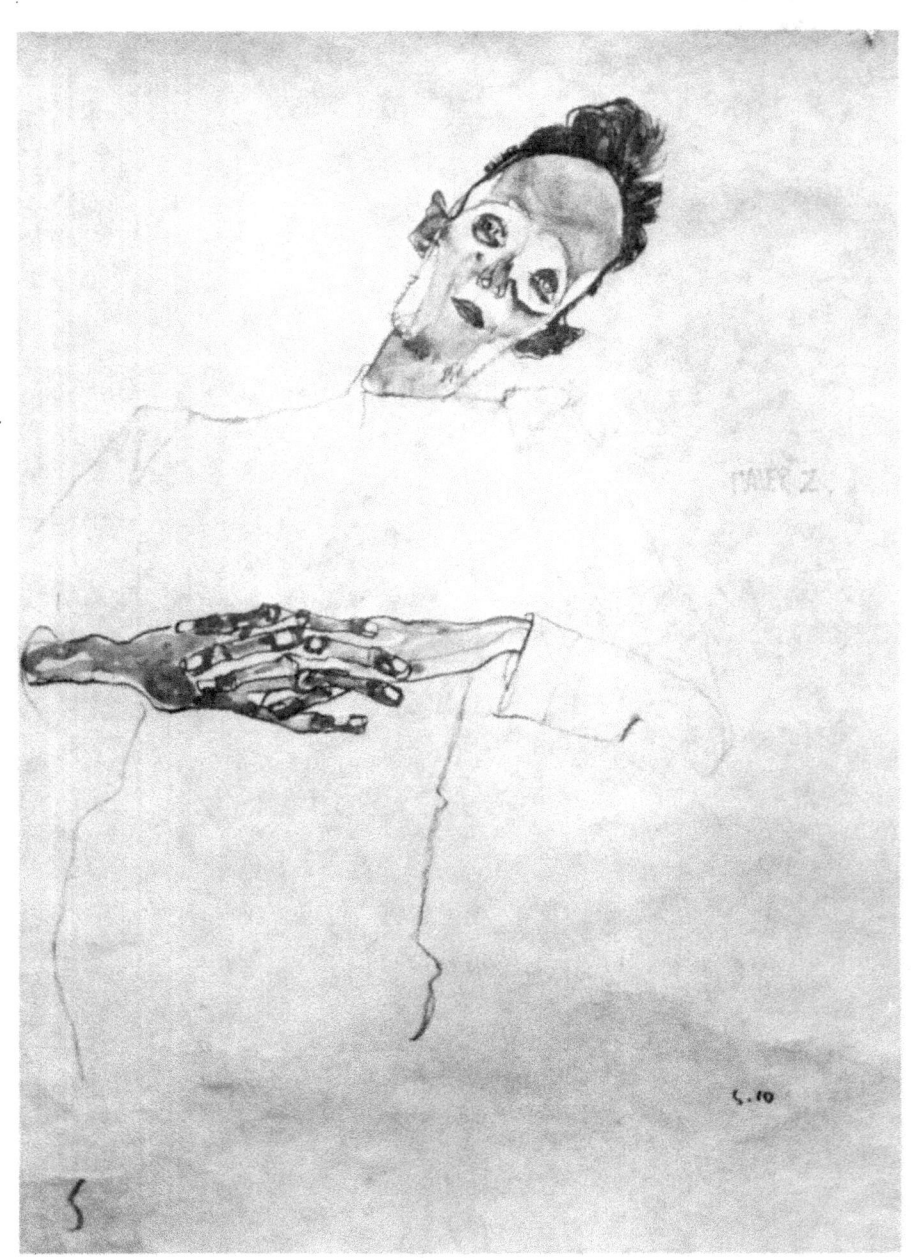

PL. 24. Schiele, *Study for the Portrait of Karl Zakovsek*, 1010, black chalk
and watercolor.

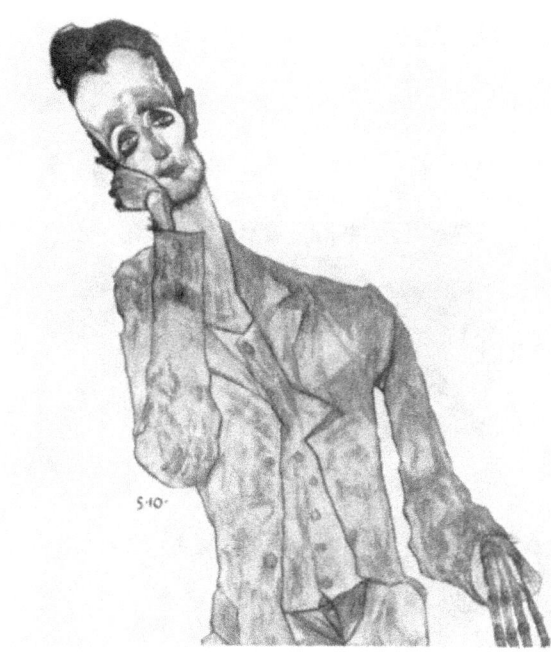

PL. 25. Schiele, *Portrait of the Painter Karl Zakovsek*, 1910, oil.

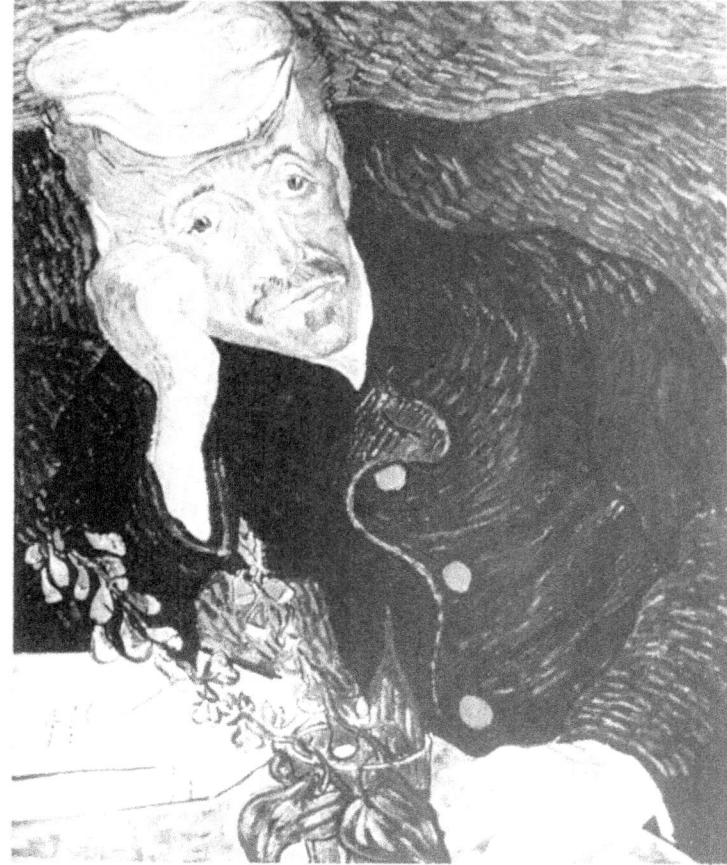

PL. 26. Van Gogh, *Portrait of Dr. Gachet*, 1890, oil.

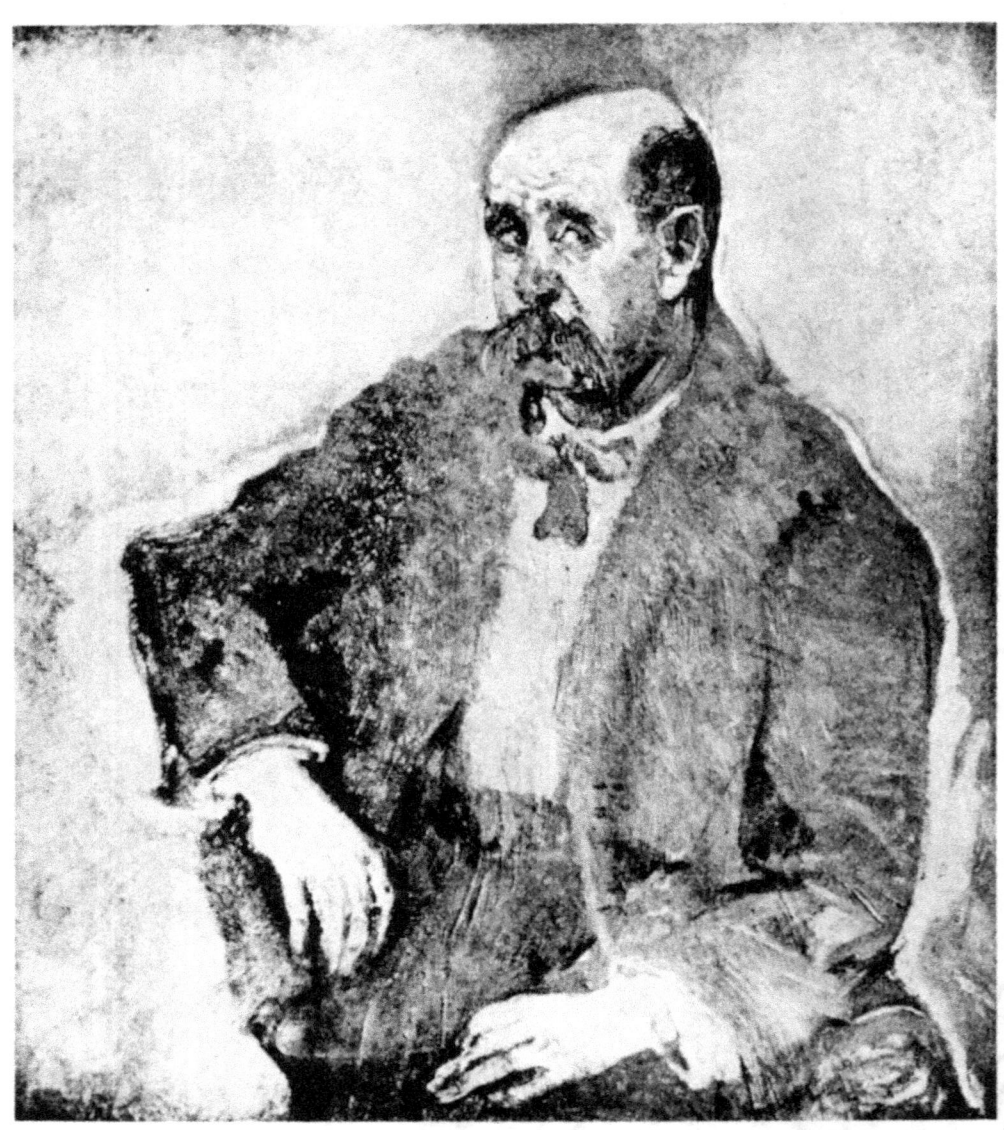

PL. 27a. Max Oppenheimer (Mopp), *Portrait of Peter Altenberg*, 1909, oil.

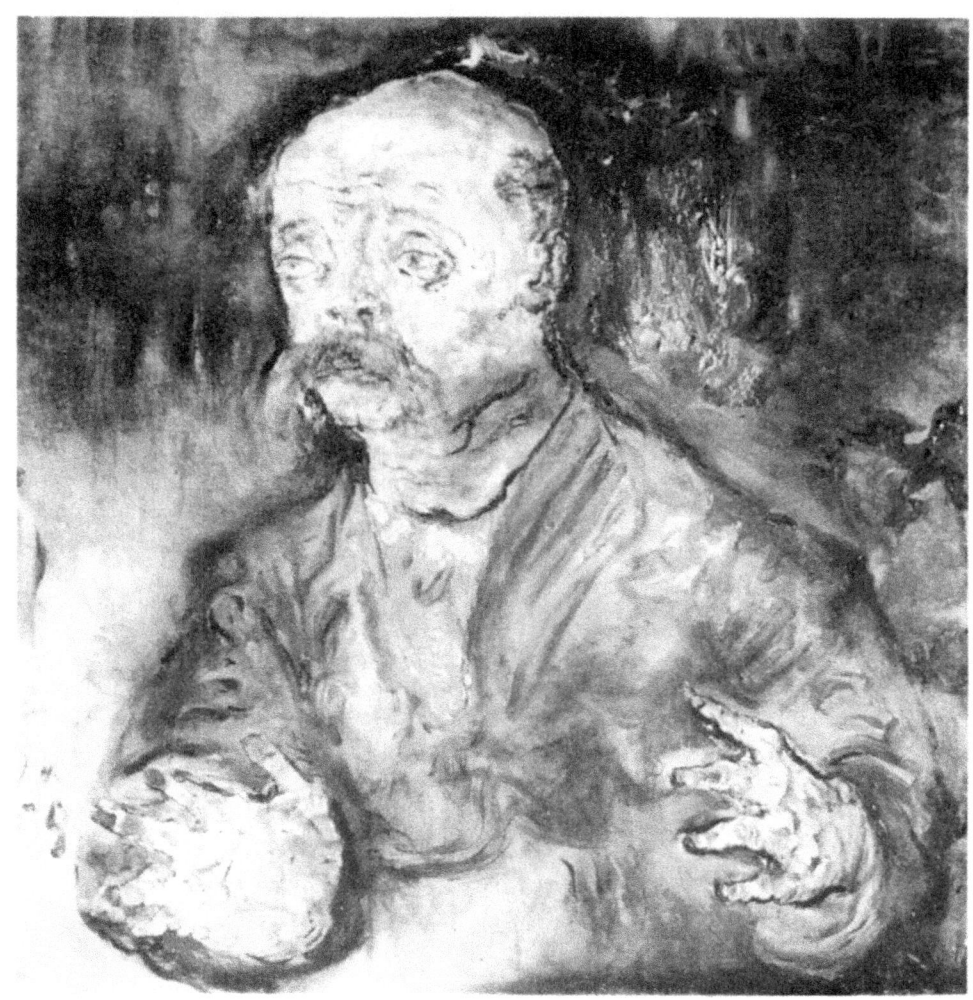

PL. 27b. Kokoschka, *Portrait of Peter Altenberg*, 1909, oil.

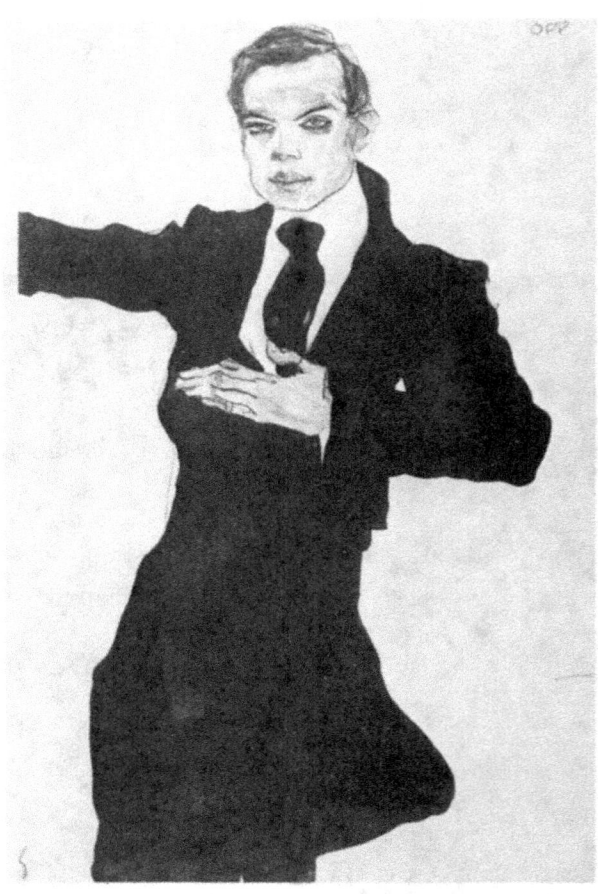

PL. 27c. Schiele, *Portrait Sketch of the Painter Max Oppenheimer (Mopp)*, 1910, black chalk and watercolor.

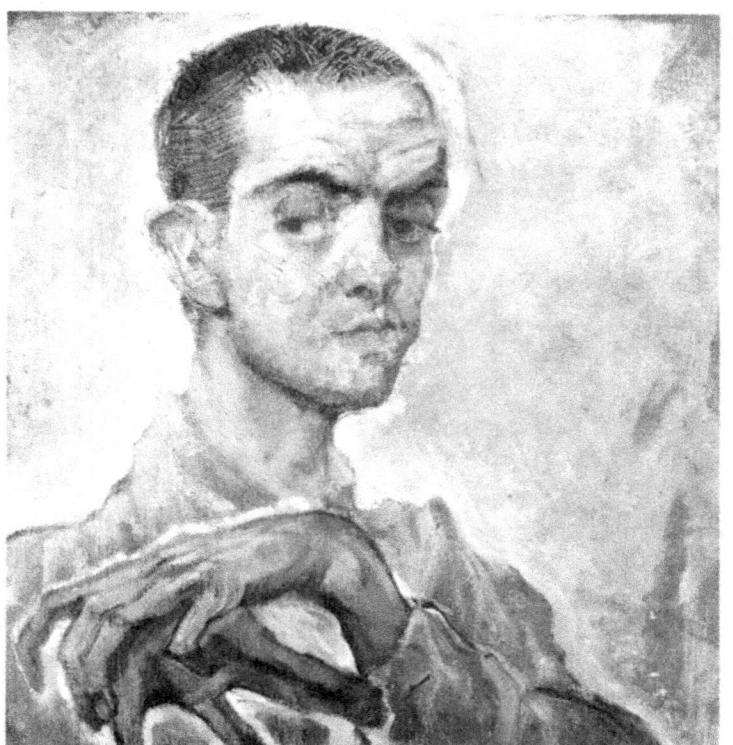

PL. 27d. Max Oppenheimer (Mopp), *Portrait of Egon Schiele*, 1910, oil.

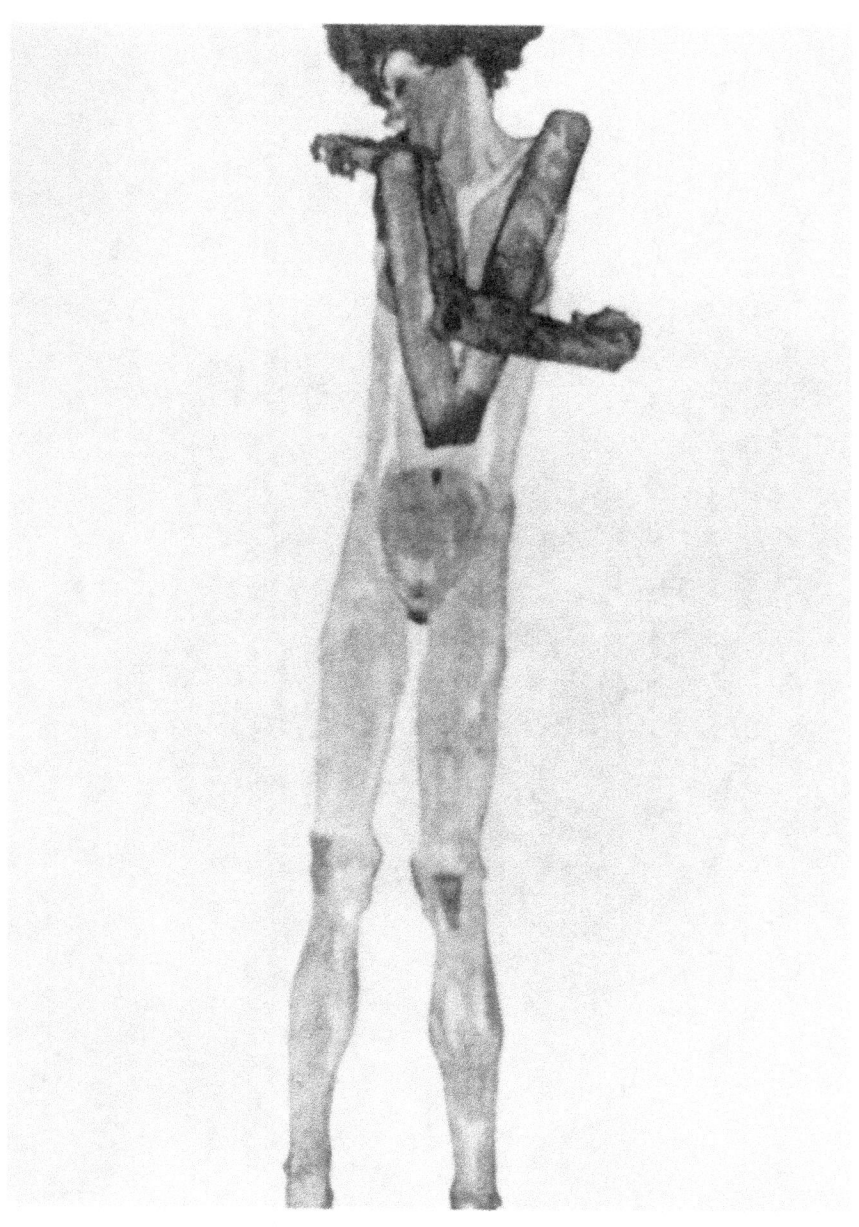

PL. 28a. Schiele, *Portrait of Gerti Nude*, 1910, oil.

PL. 28b. Felix Valloton, *Naked Woman*, 1904, oil.

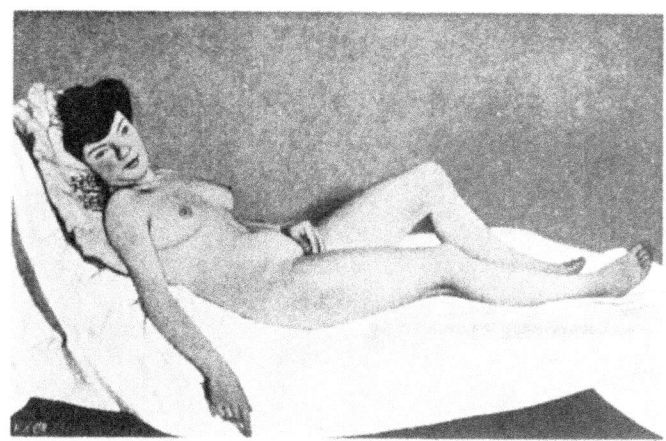

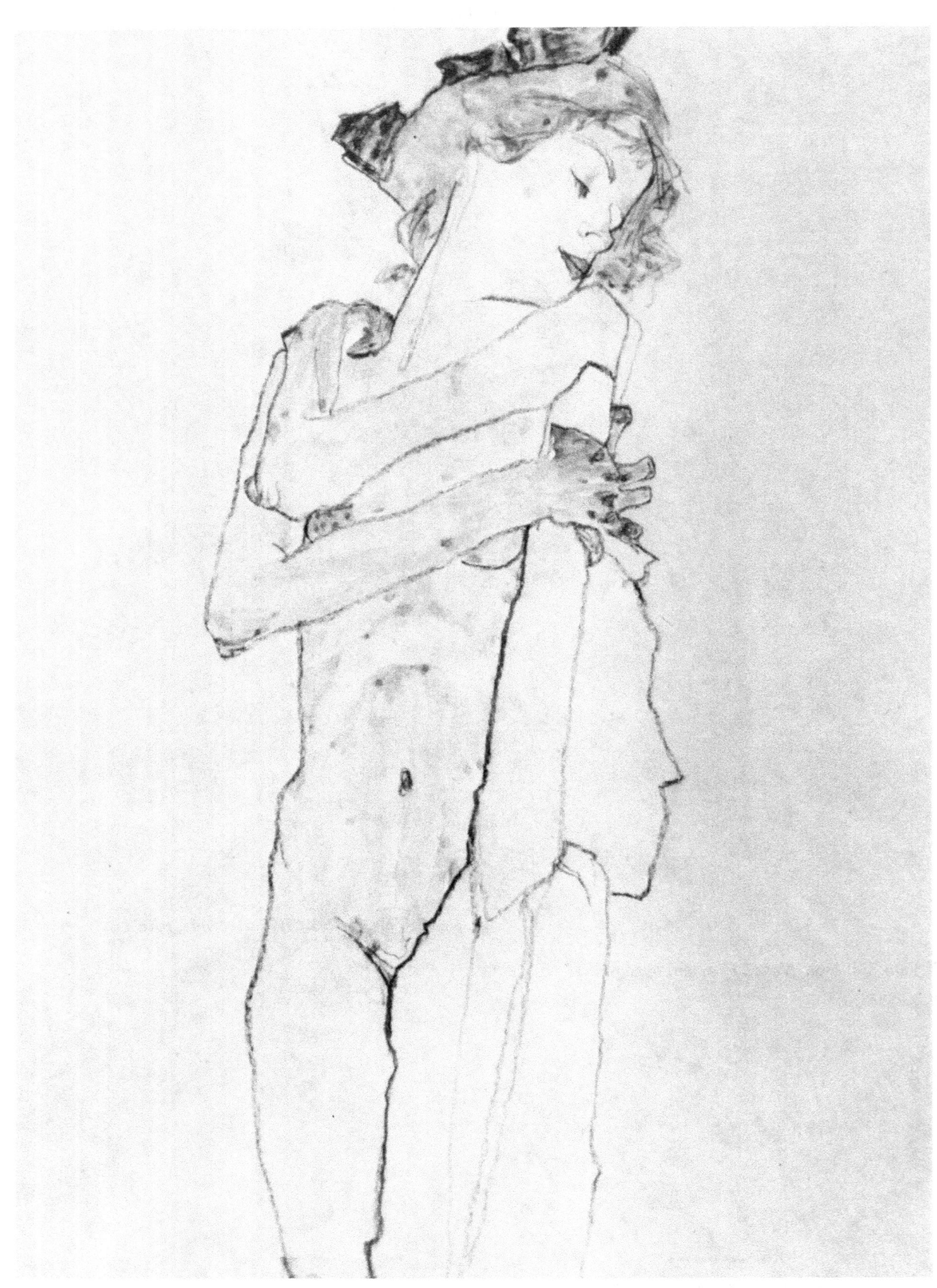

PL. 29. Schiele, *Study for the Portrait of Gerti Nude with Head Turned Right*, 1910, black chalk and watercolor.

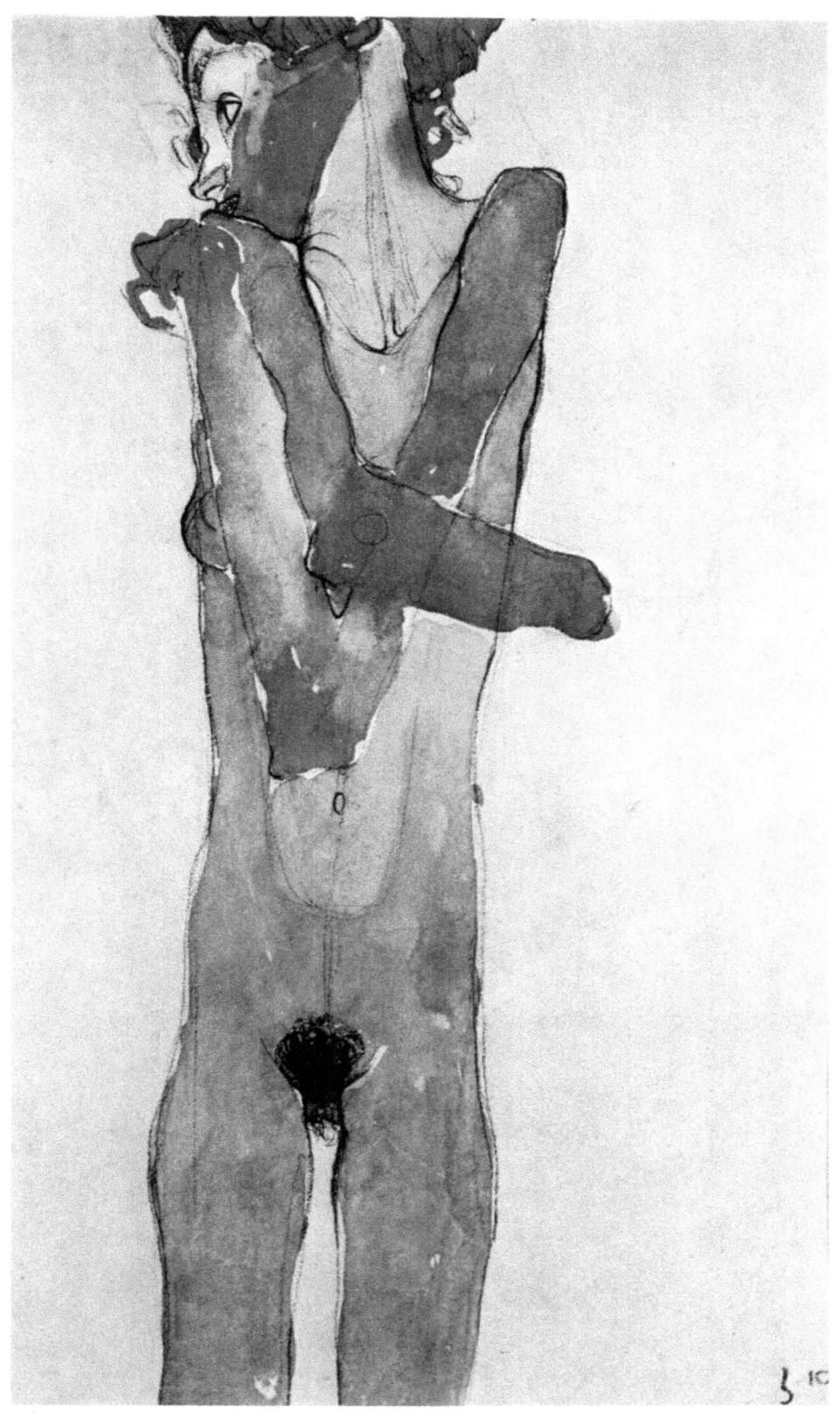

PL. 30. Schiele, *Study for the Portrait of Gerti Nude with Head Turned Left*, 1910, black chalk and watercolor.

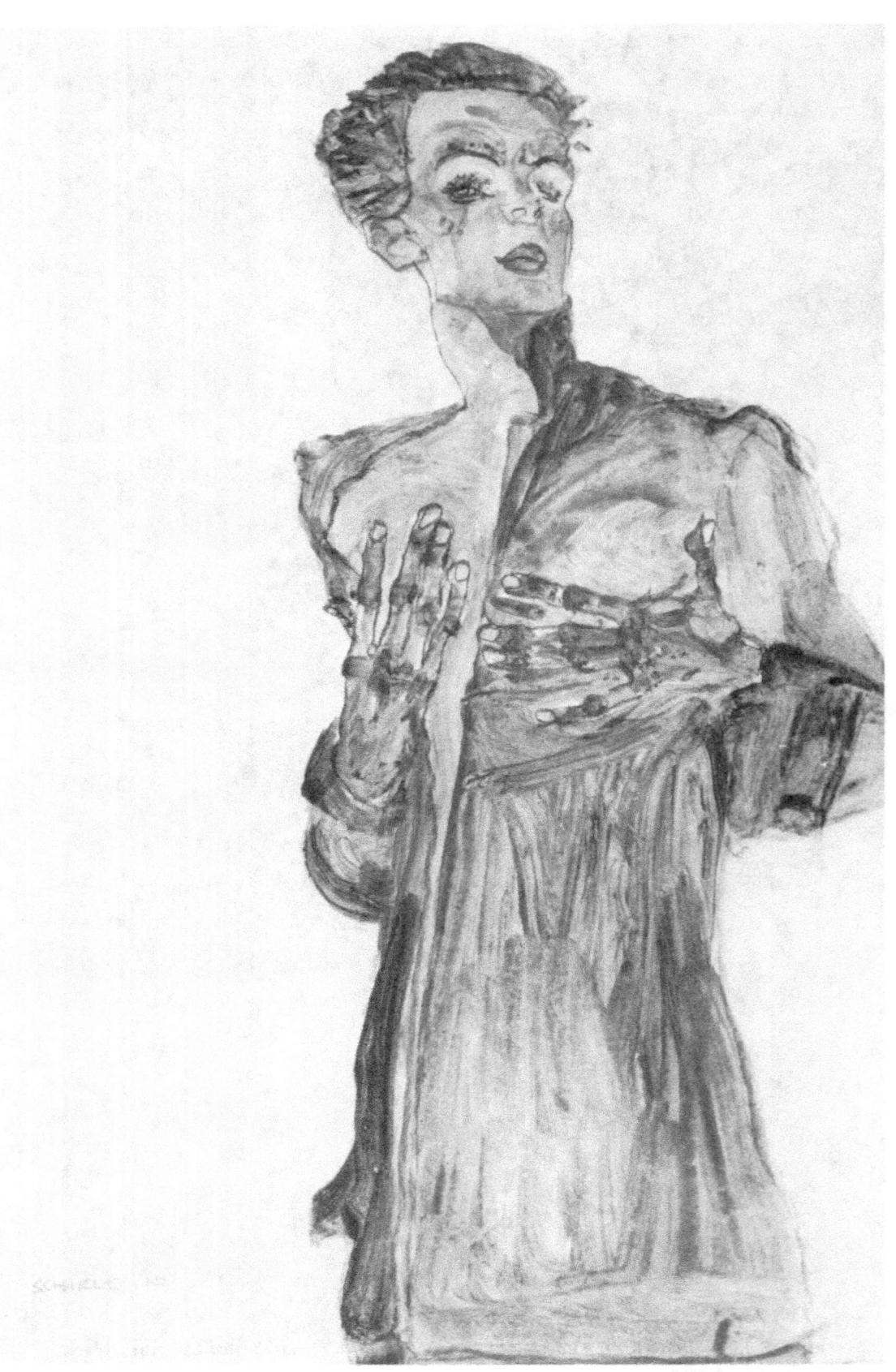

PL. 31. Schiele, *Self-Portrait in Street Clothes Gesturing*, 1910, black chalk and gouache.

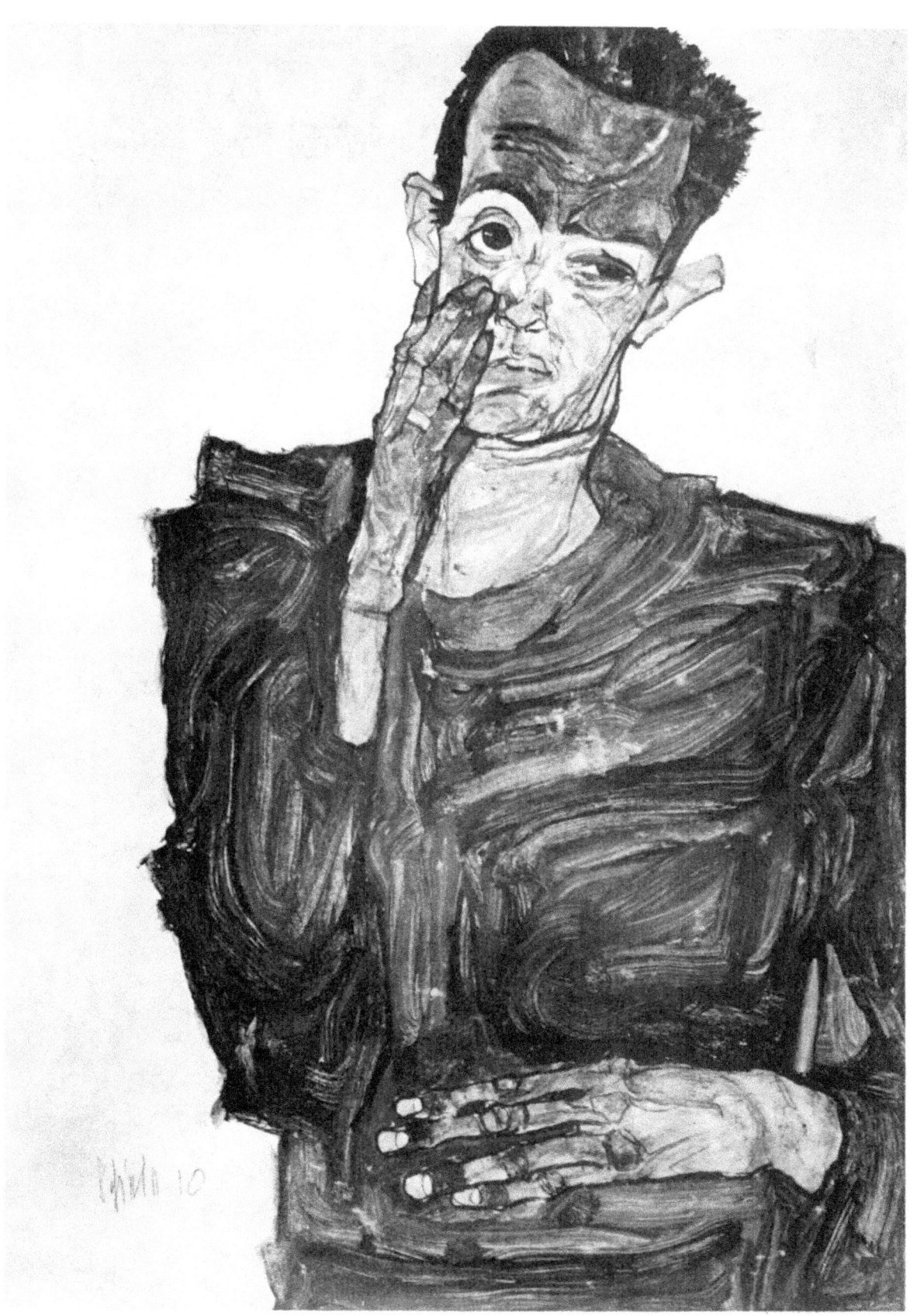

PL. 32. Schiele, *Self-Portrait with Hand to Cheek*, 1910, black chalk and gouache.

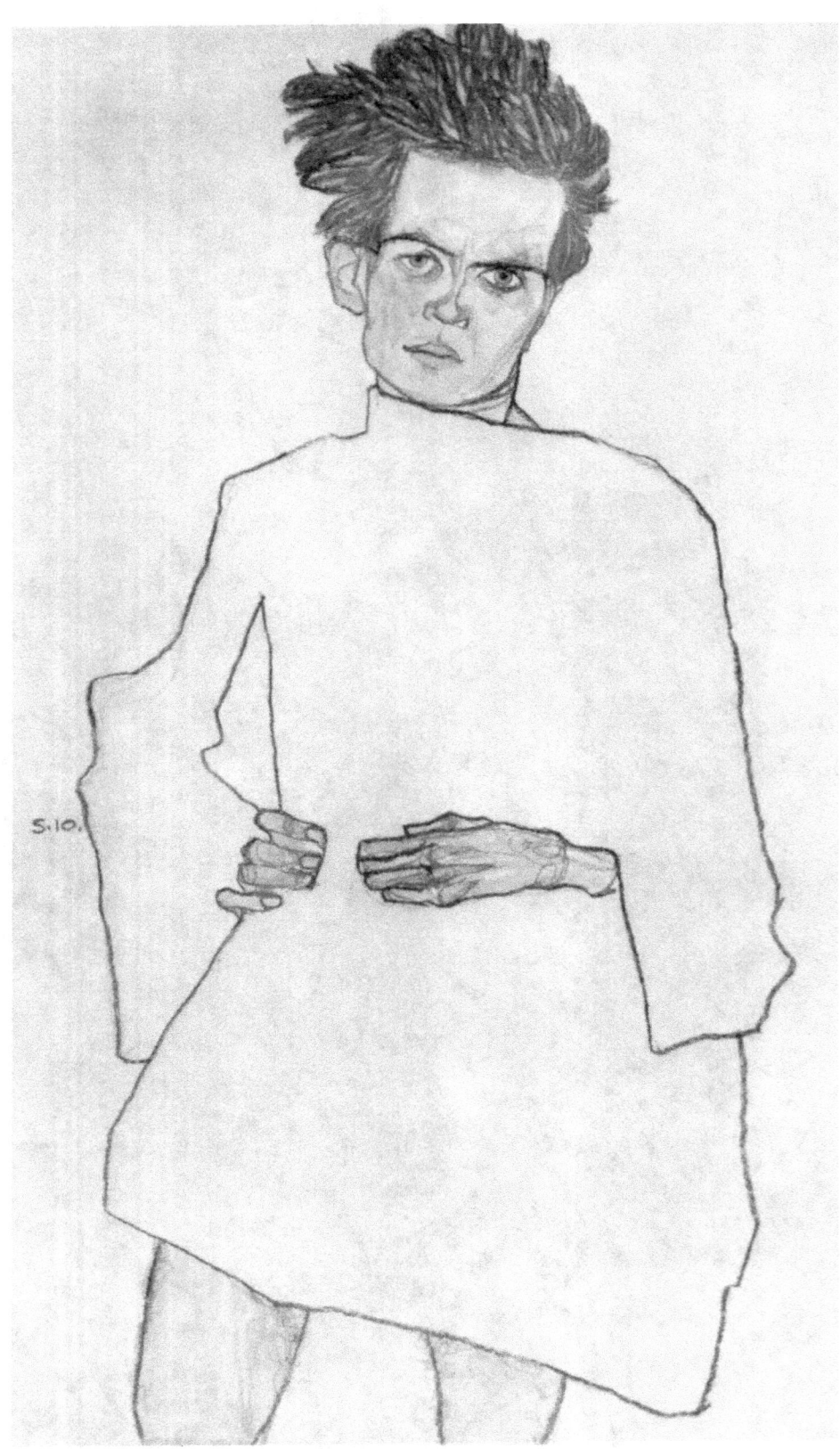

PL. 33. Schiele, *Self-Portrait Draped*, 1910, black chalk and watercolor.

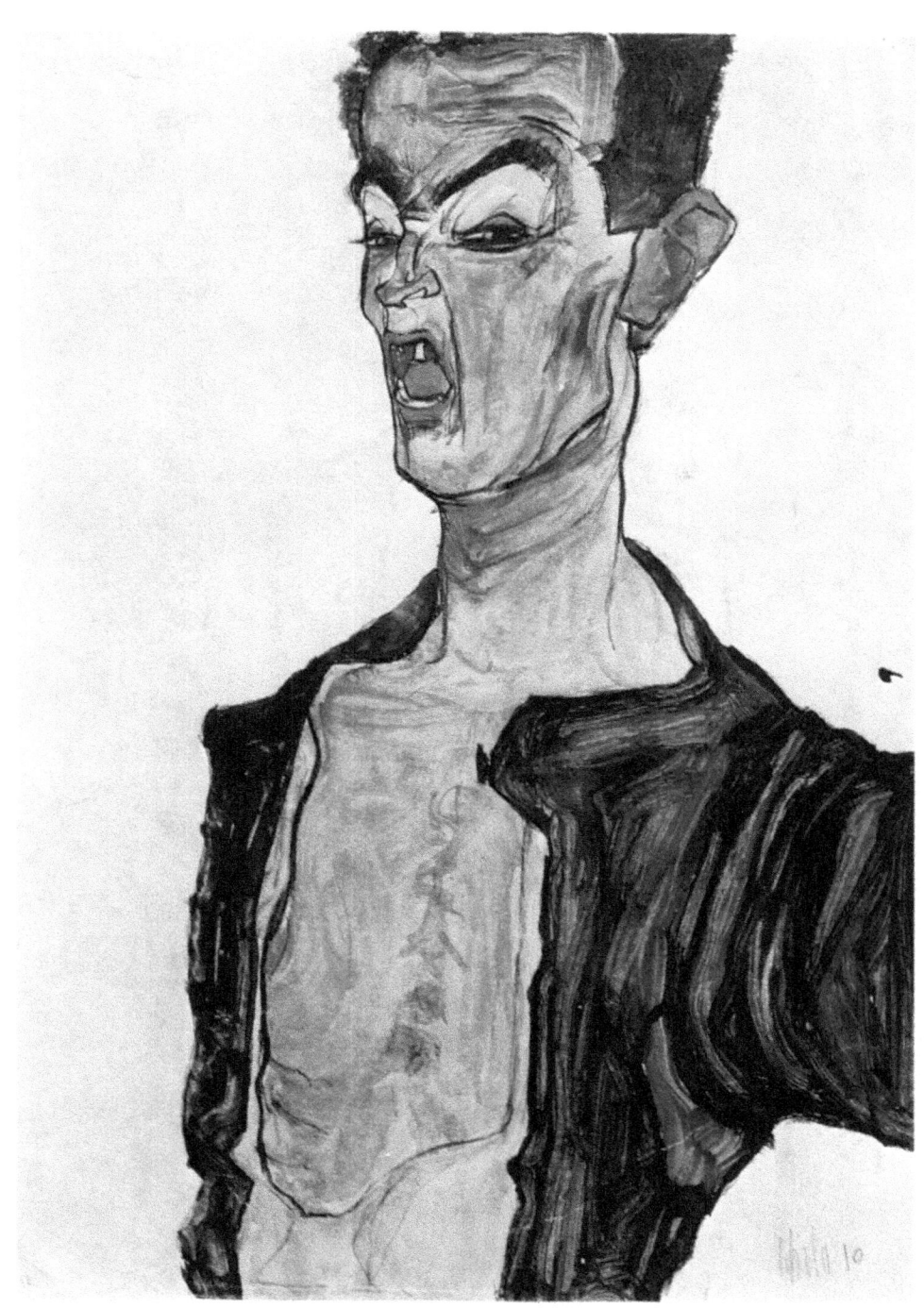

PL. 34. Schiele, *Self-Portrait Screaming*, 1910, black chalk and watercolor.

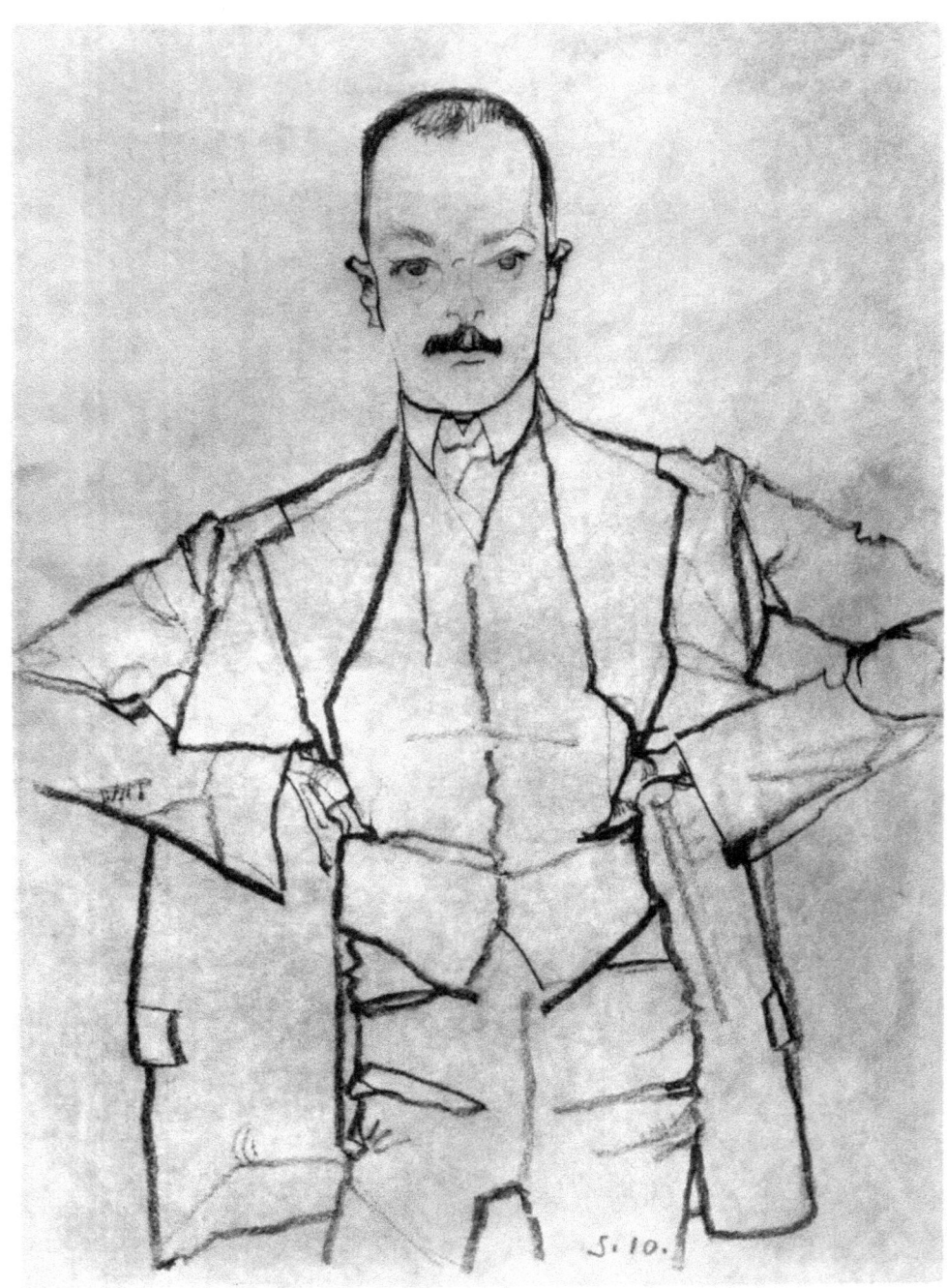

PL. 35. Schiele, *Arthur Roessler Standing with Arms Akimbo*, 1910, black chalk.

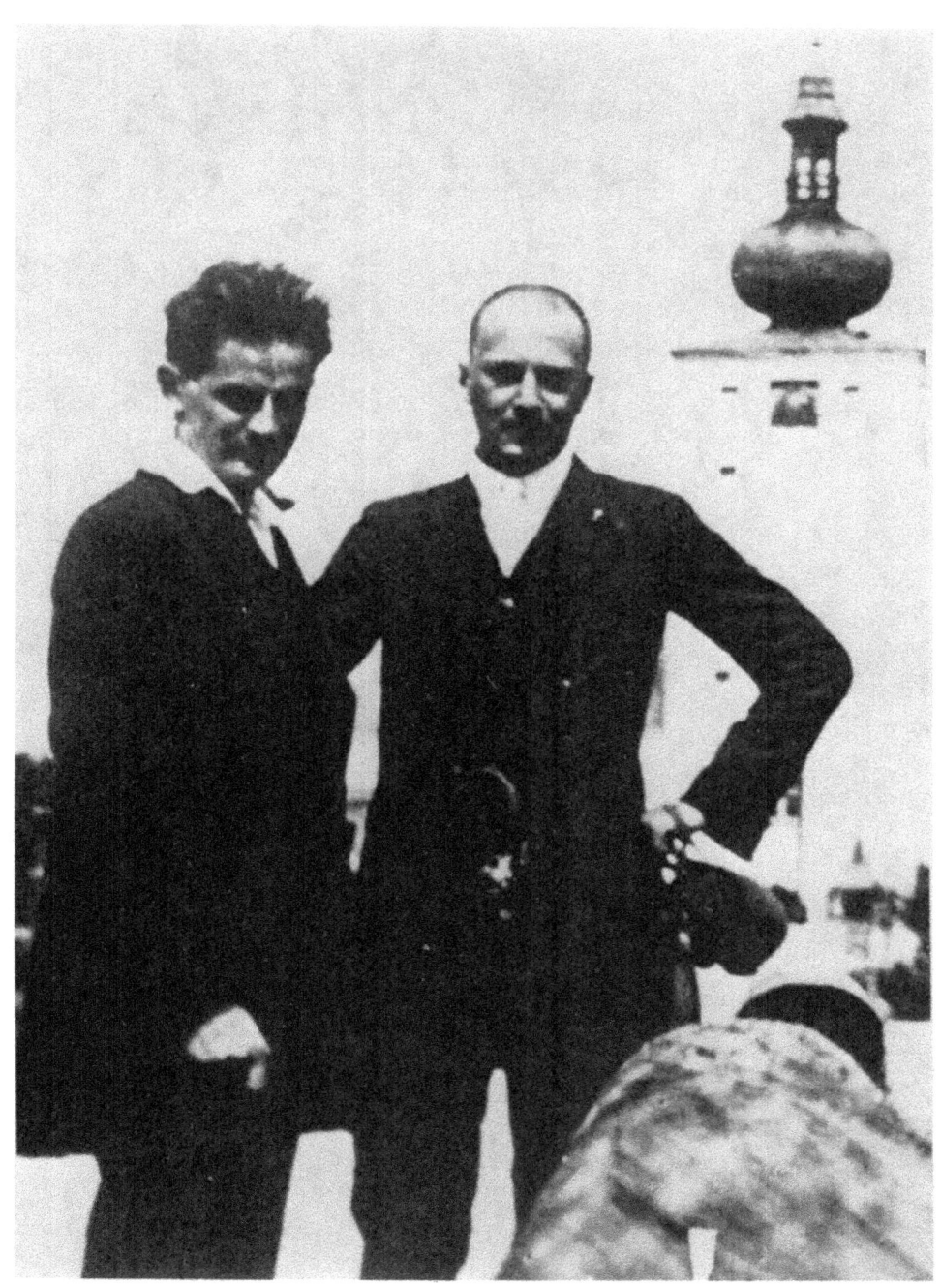

PL. 36. Egon Schiele and Arthur Roessler at Schoß Orth, 1913.

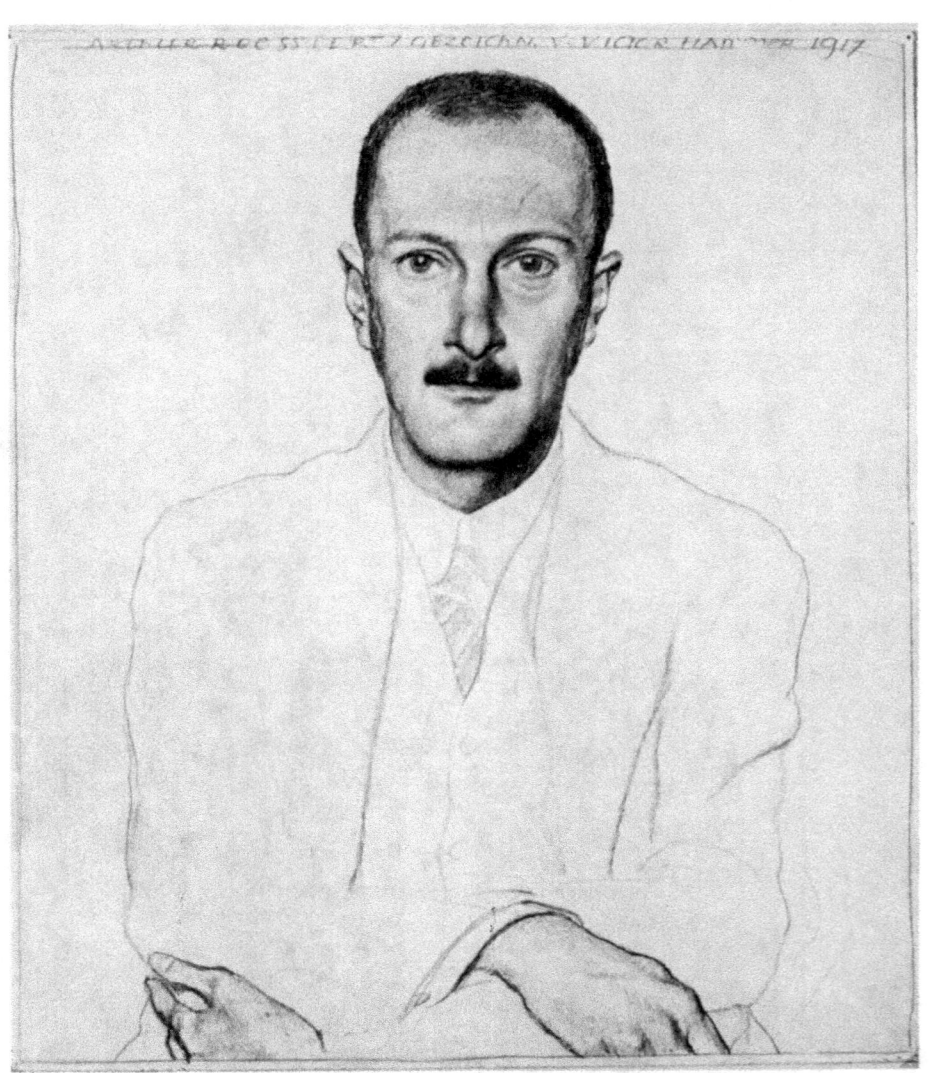

PL. 37. Viktor Hammer, *Portrait Sketch of Arthur Roessler*, 1917, pencil.

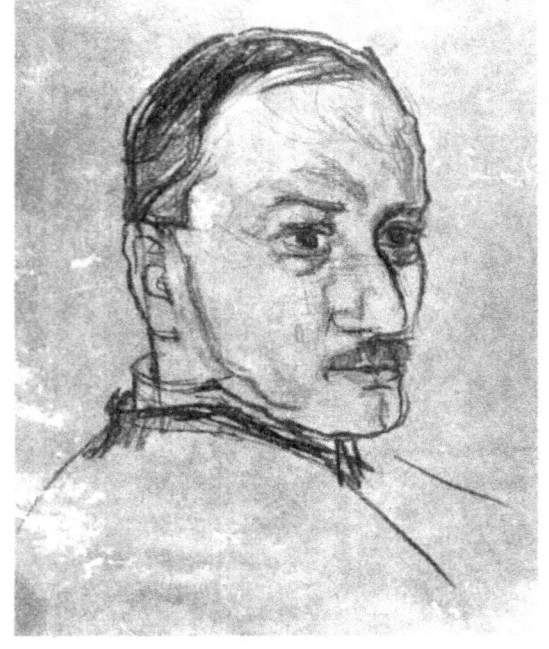

PL. 38. Kokoschka, *Portrait Head of Arthur Roessler in Three-Quarter View, ca.* 1912, pencil.

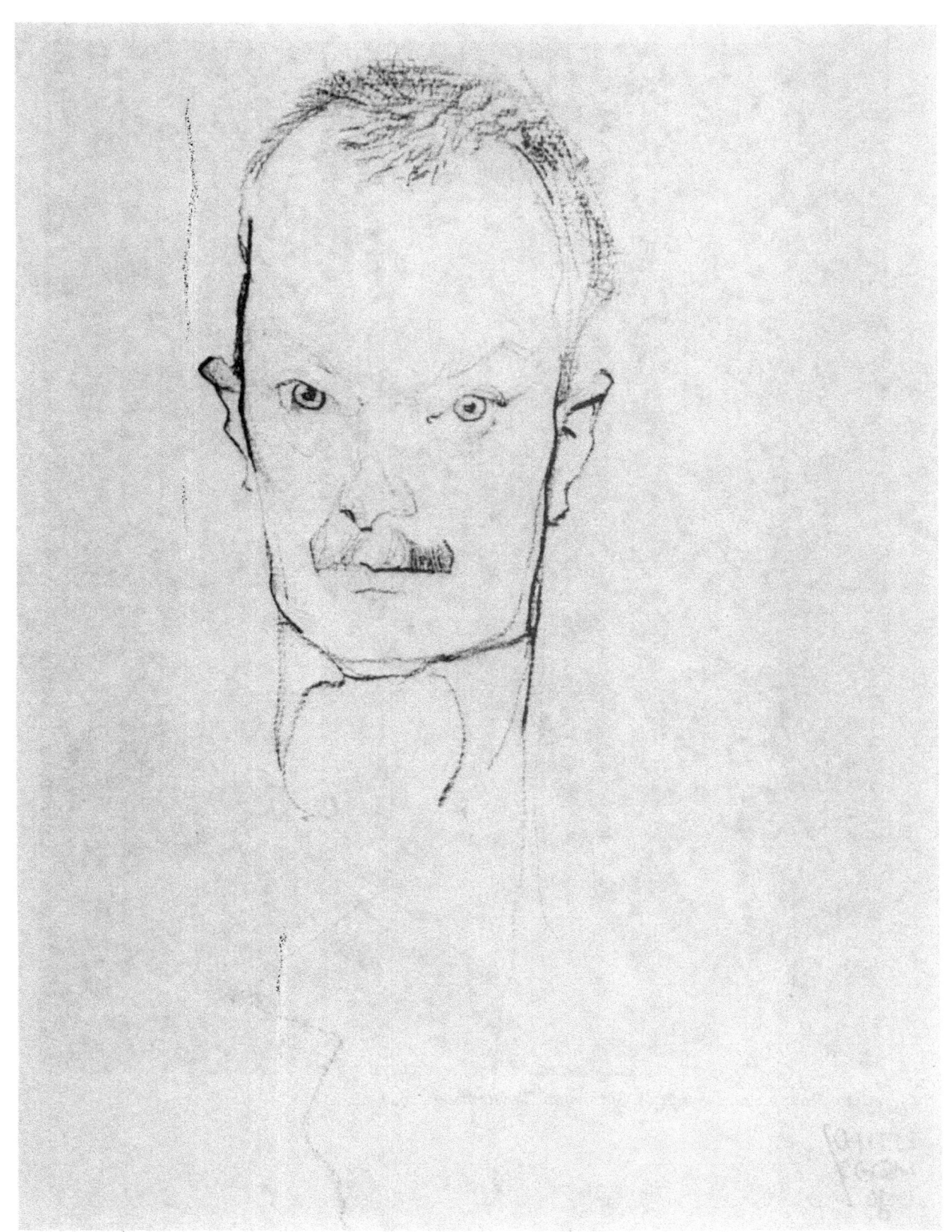

PL. 39. Schiele, *Portrait Head of Arthur Roessler, Frontal,* 1910 (misdated 1908), black crayon.

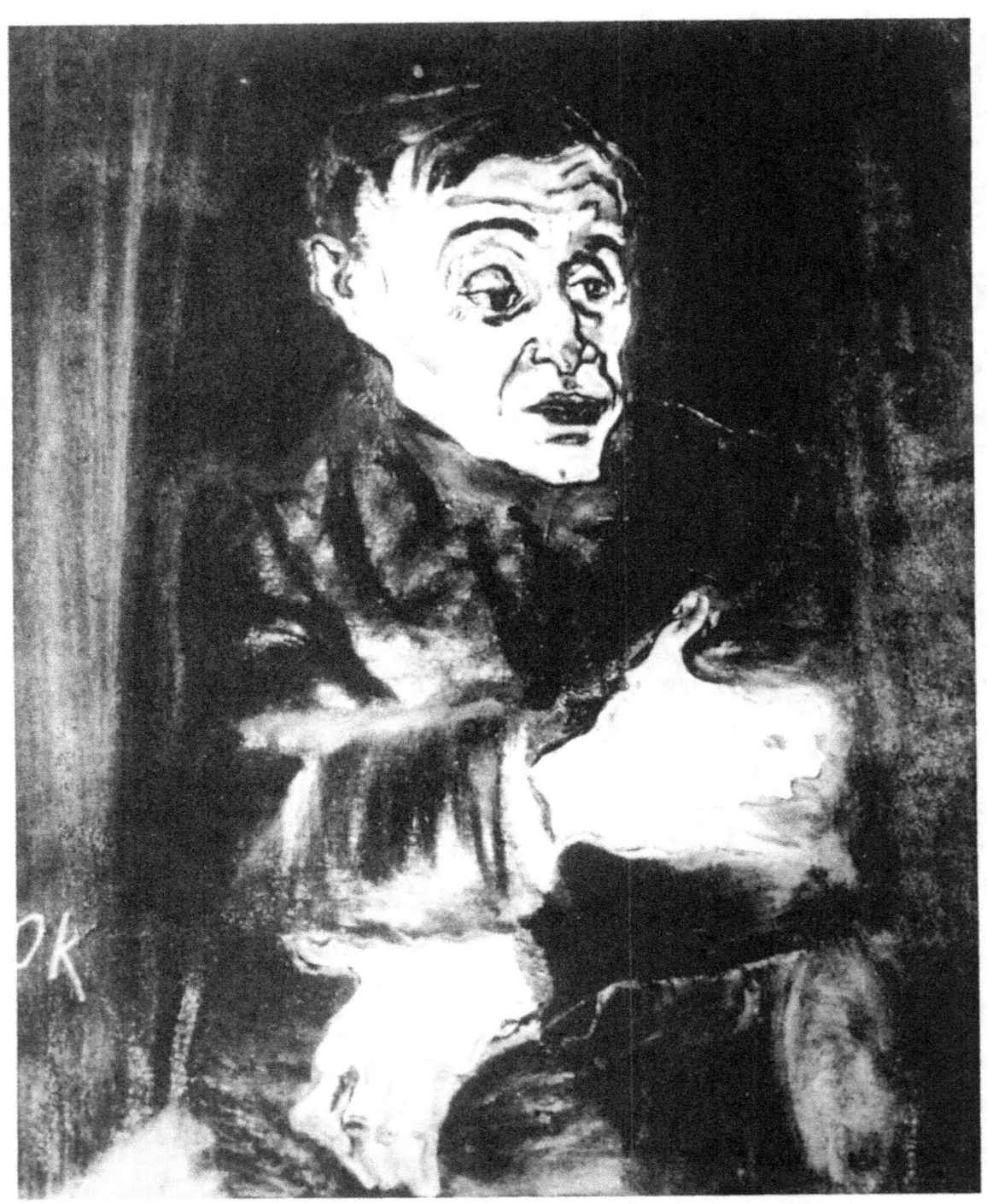

PL. 40. Kokoschka, *Portrait of Constantin Christomanos*, 1909, oil.

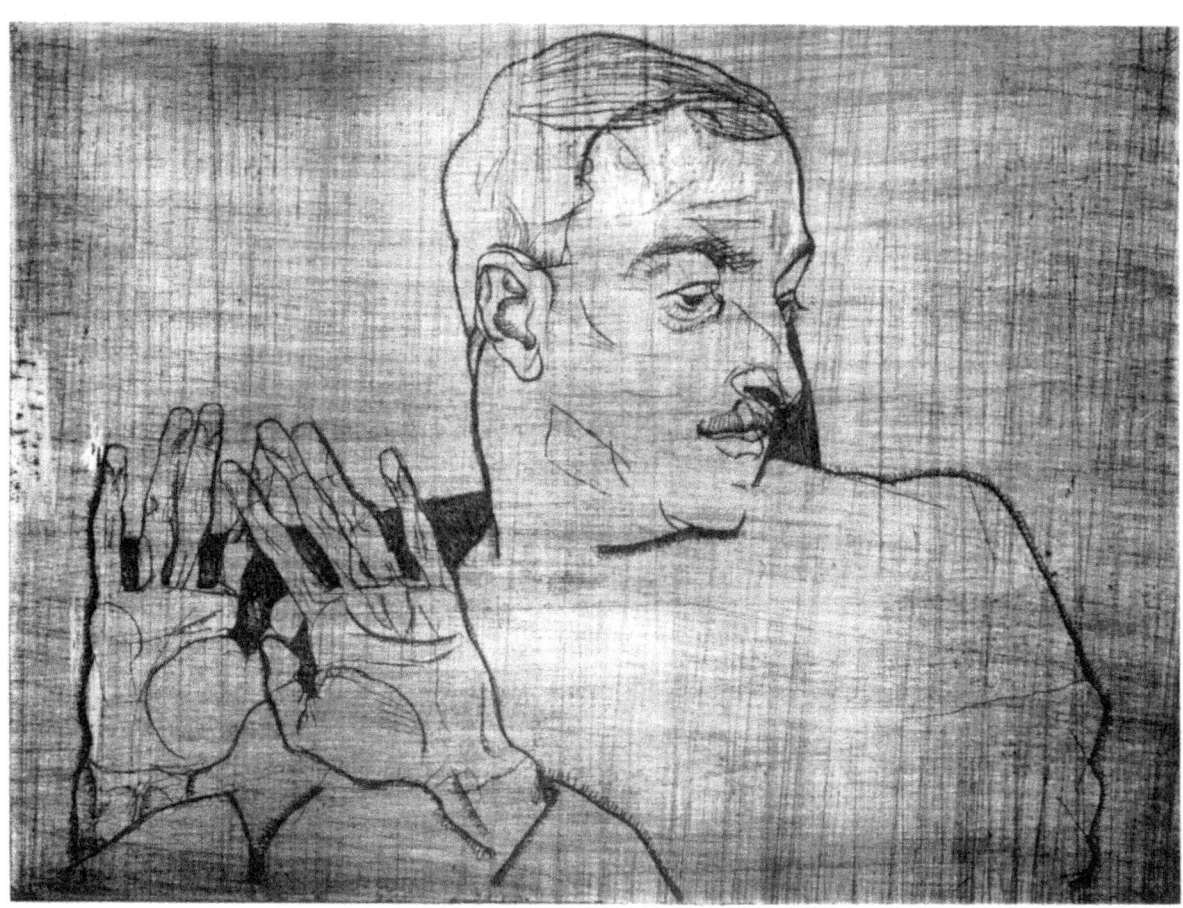

PL. 41. Schiele, *Etched Portrait of Arthur Roessler*, 1914, etching.

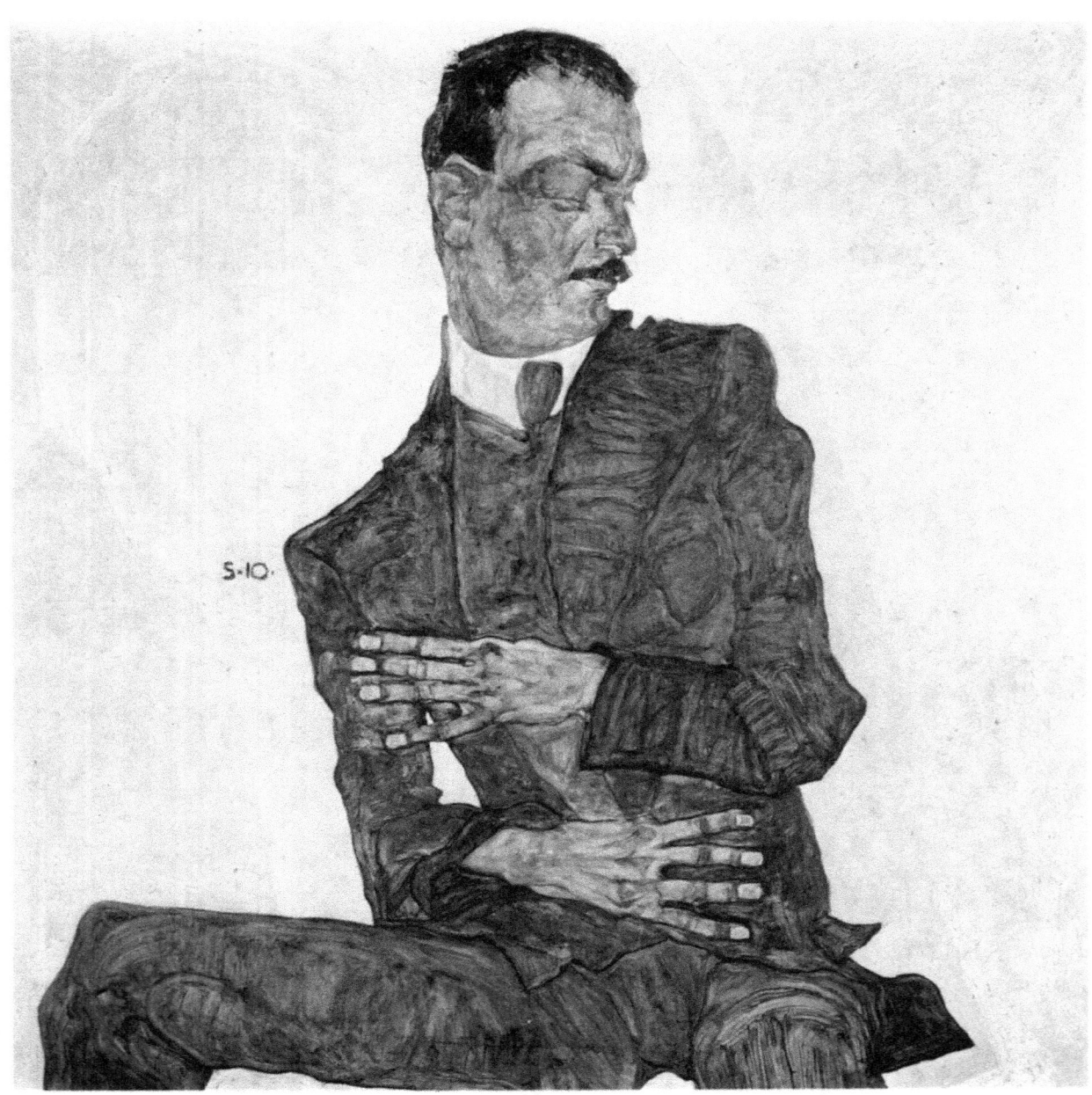

PL. 42. Schiele, *Portrait of Arthur Roessler*, 1910, oil.

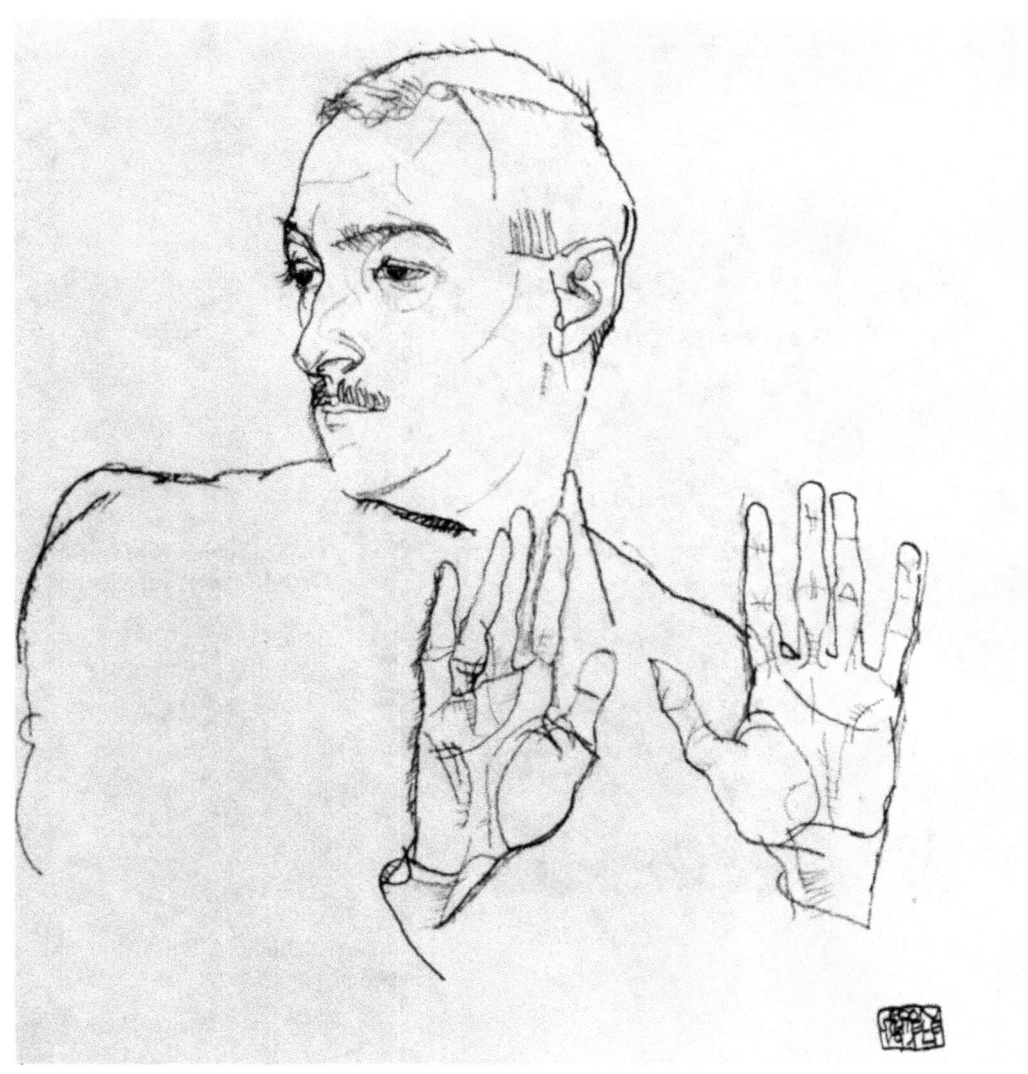

PL. 43. Schiele, *Study for the Etched Portrait of Arthur Roessler*, 1914, black chalk.

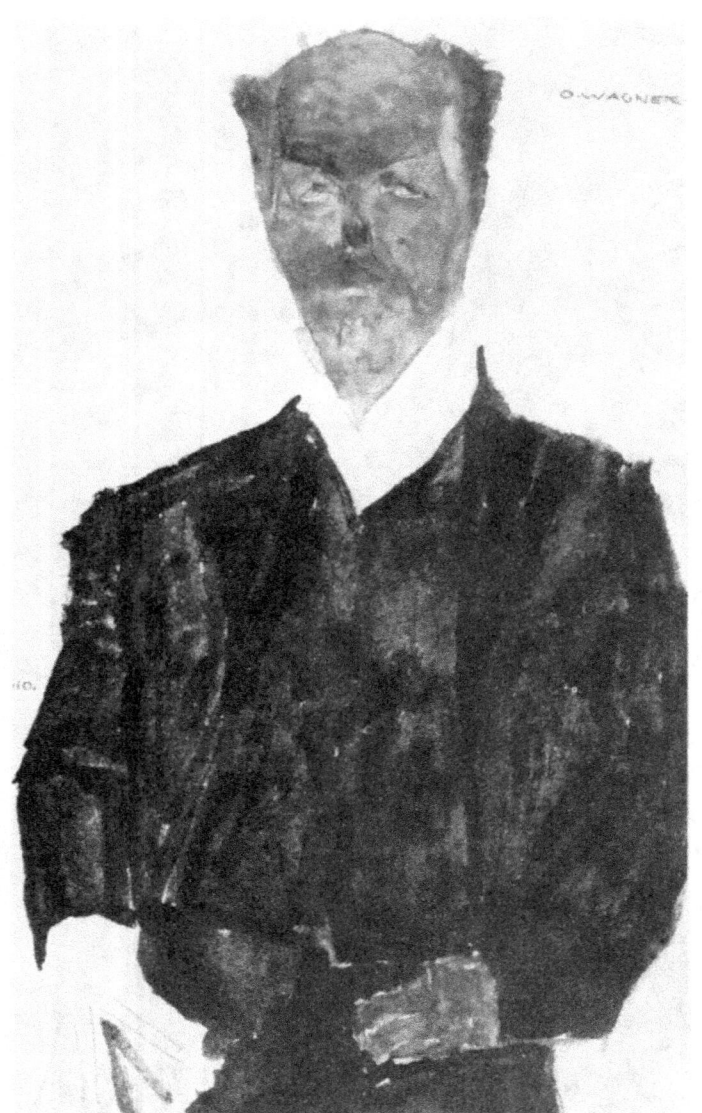

PL. 44. Schiele, *Study for the Portrait of Otto Wagner*, 1910, pencil and watercolor.

PL. 45. Schiele, A.E.S.A. Sketchbook XII, 1910, pencil, page 8 *verso*.

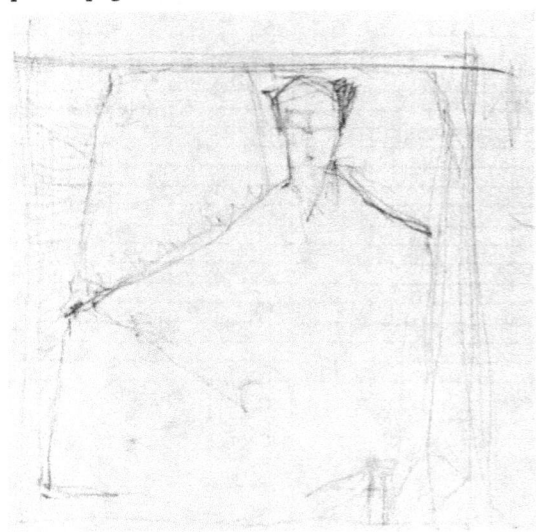

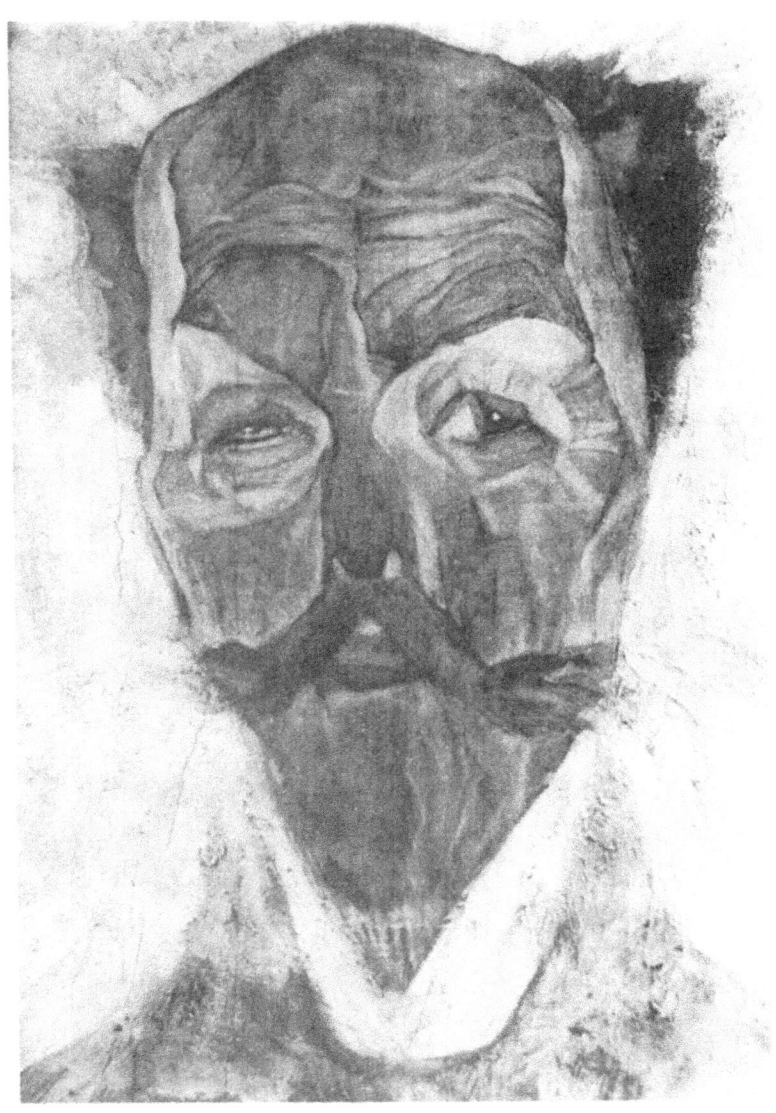

PL. 46. Schiele, *Portrait of Otto Wagner* (fragment), 1910, oil.

PL. 48. *Portrait of Otto Wagner*, 1911 (post card).

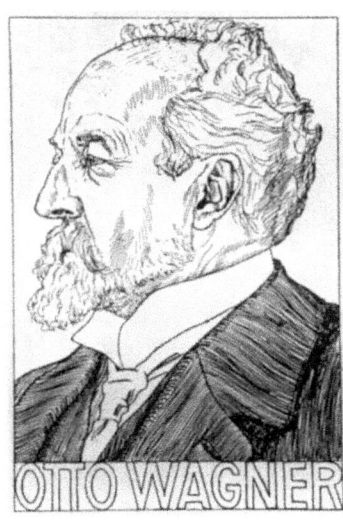

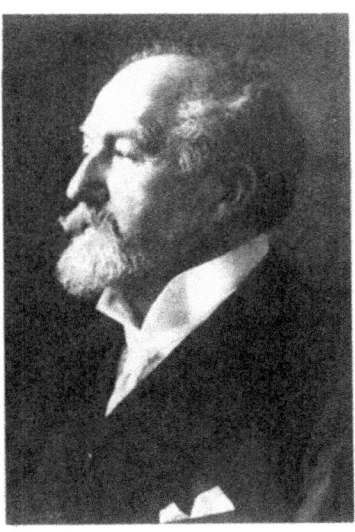

PL. 47. Otto Wagner, *ca.* 1910 (helio-gravure).

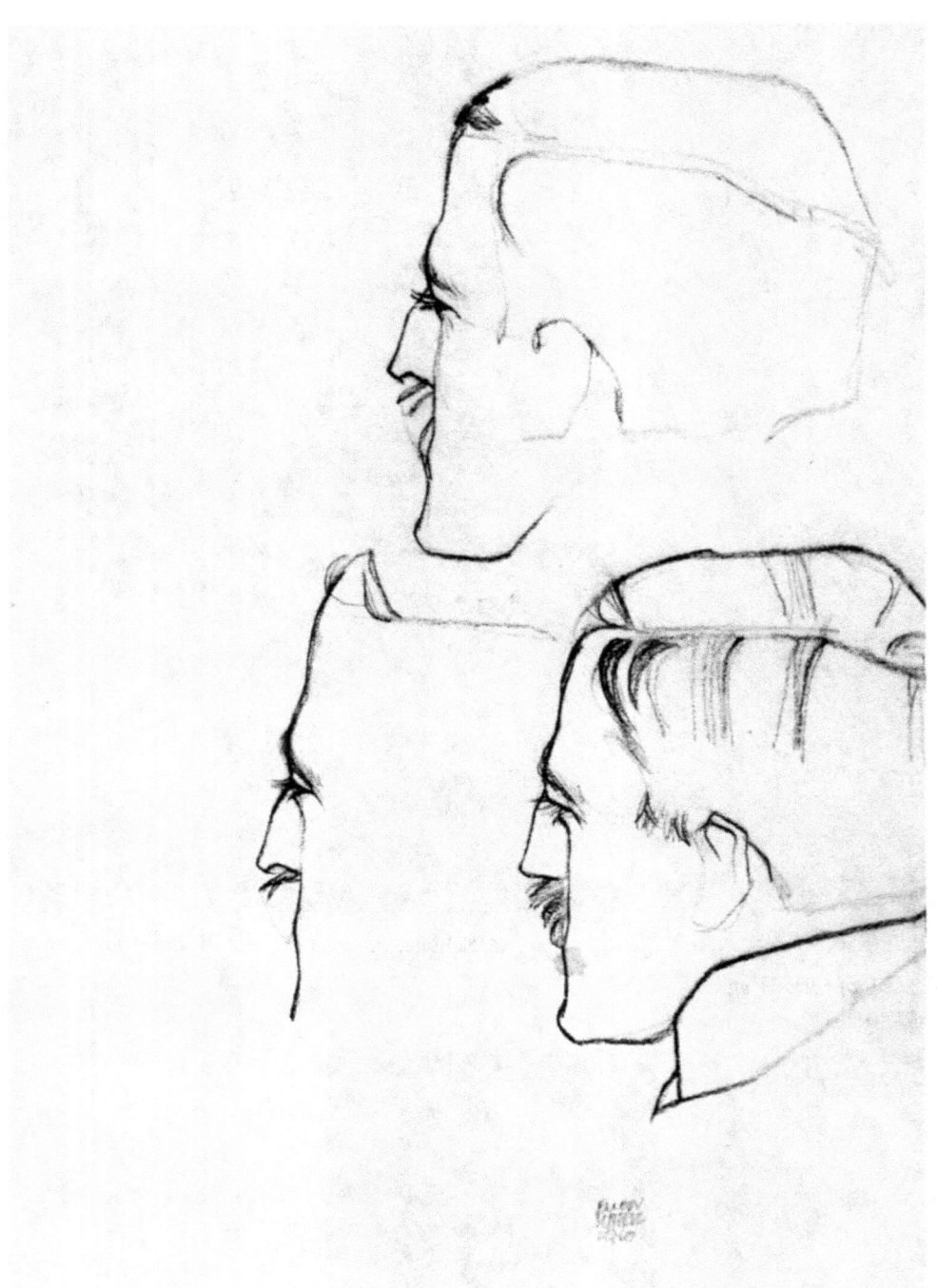

PL. 49. Schiele, *Three Head Studies of Dr. Graff*, 1910, black chalk.

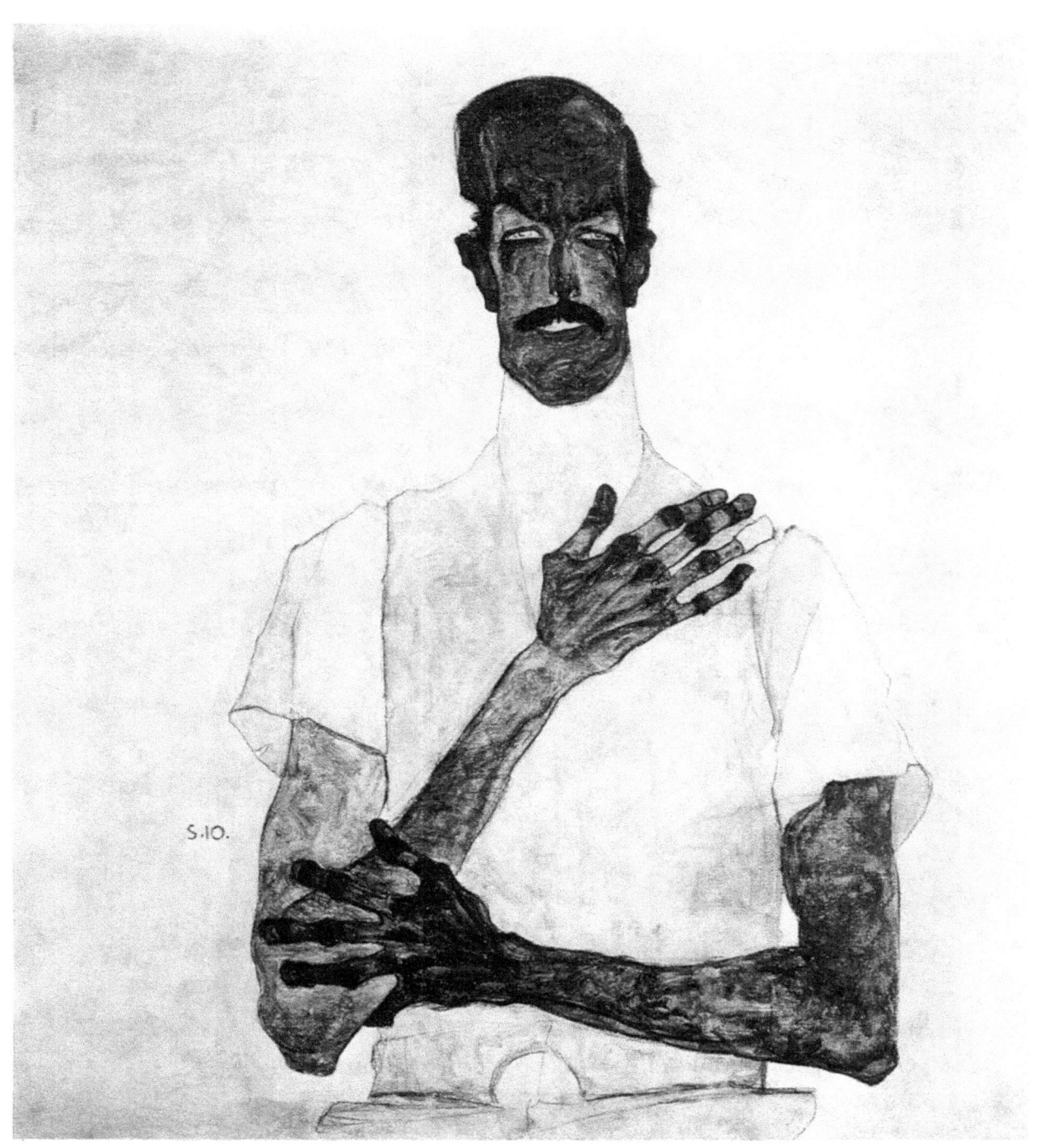

PL. 50. Schiele, *Portrait of Dr. Erwin Graff*, 1910, oil.

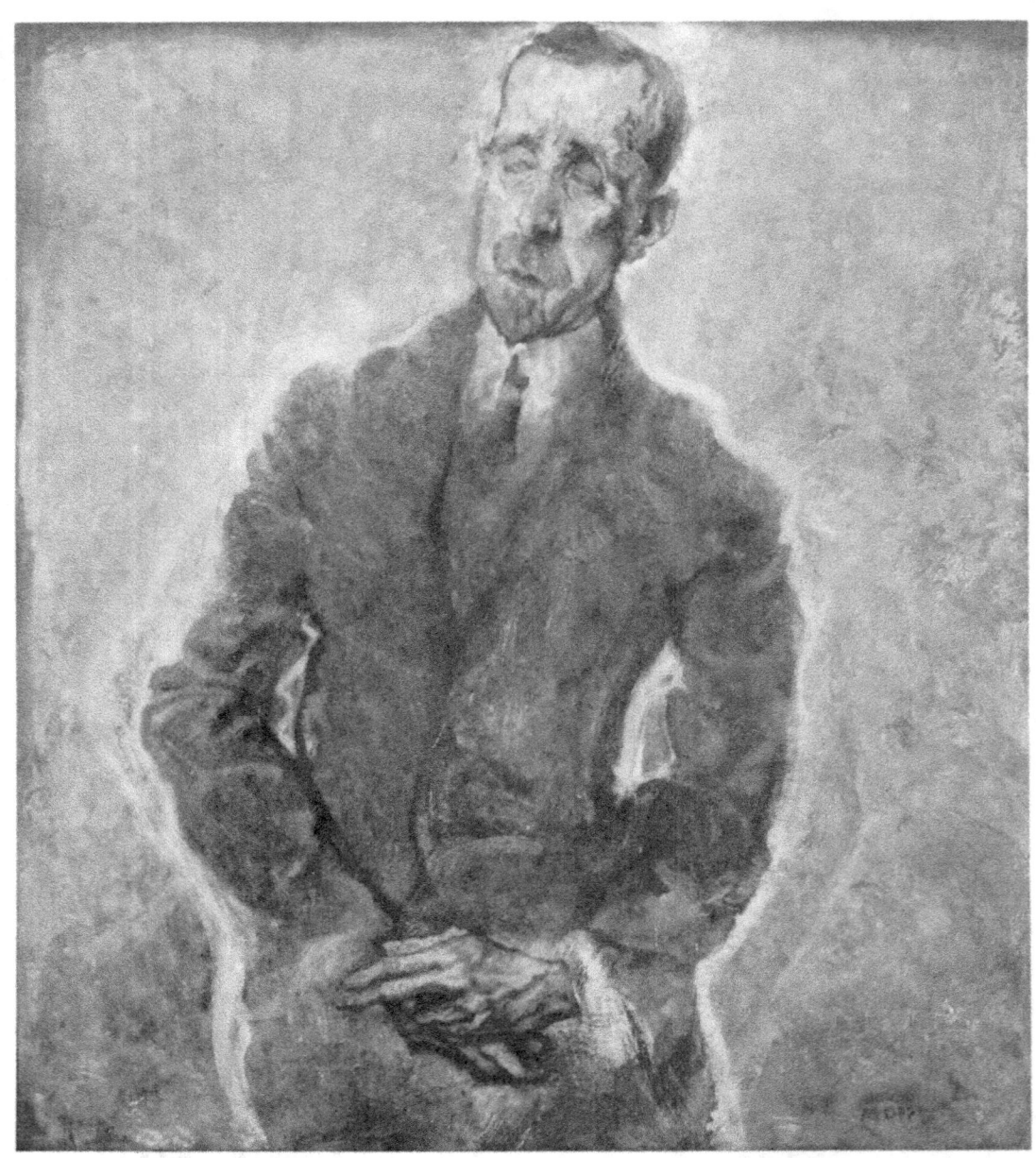

PL. 51. Max Oppenheimer (Mopp), *Portrait of Heinrich Mann*, 1911, oil.

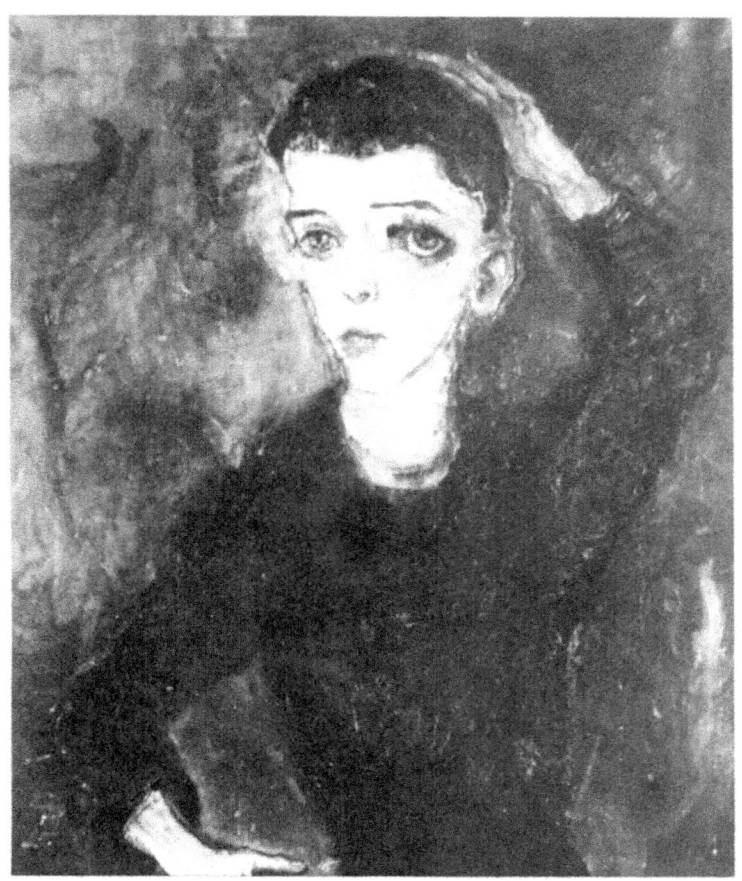

PL. 52. Kokoschka, *Portrait of Hans Reichel*, 1909, oil.

PL. 53. Kokoschka, *Portrait of Herwarth Walden*, 1910, oil.

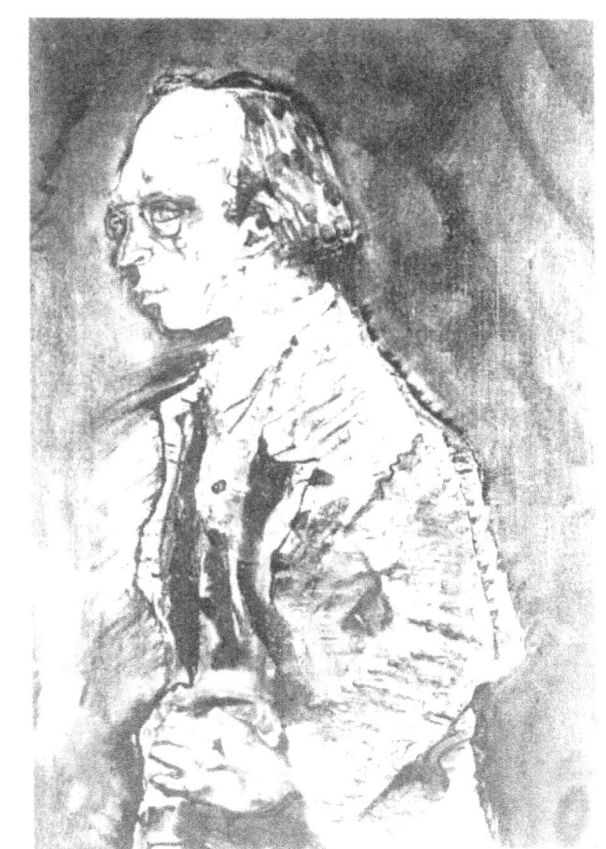

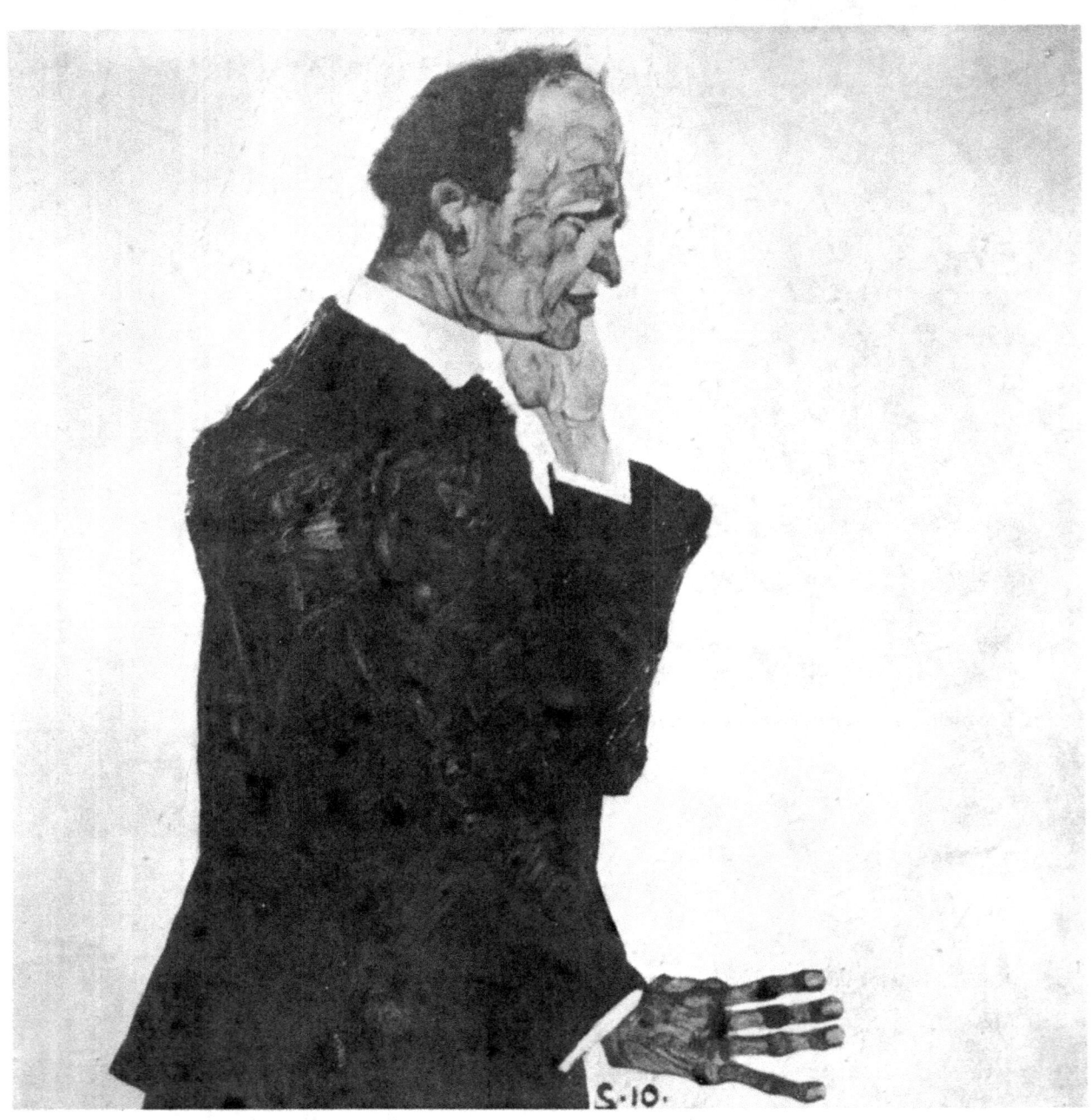

PL. 54. Schiele, *Portrait of Dr. Oskar Reichel*, 1910, oil.

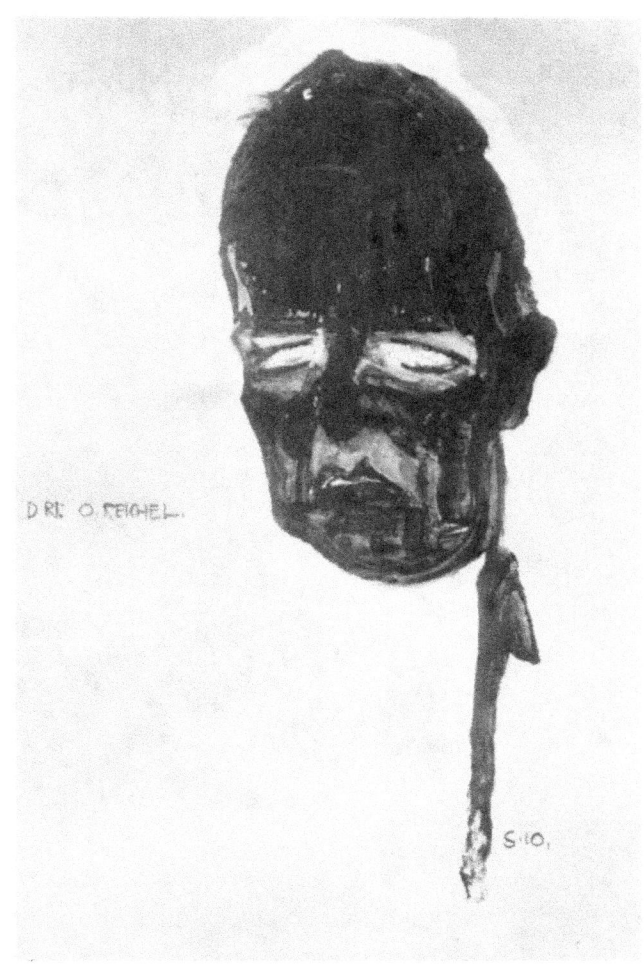

PL. 55. Schiele, *Head Study for the Portrait of Dr. Reichel*, 1910, pencil and watercolor.

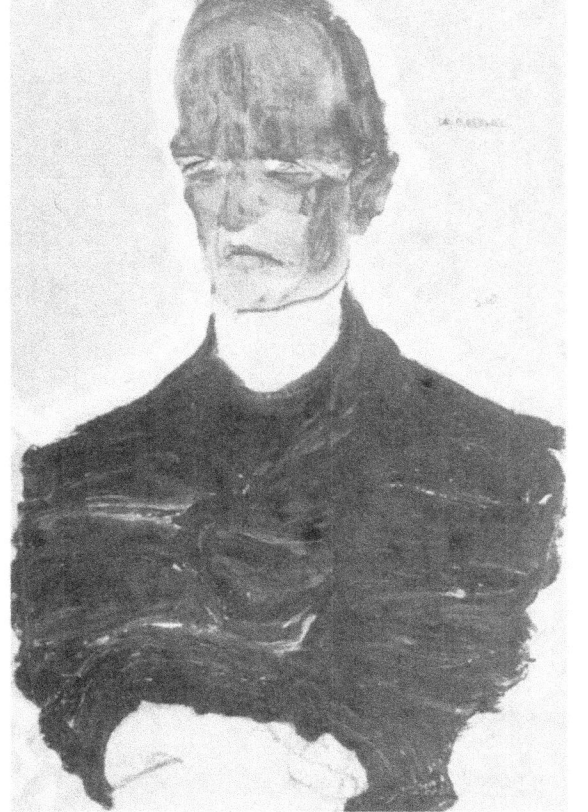

PL. 56. Schiele, *Head and Torso Study for the Portrait of Dr. Reichel*, 1910, pencil and watercolor.

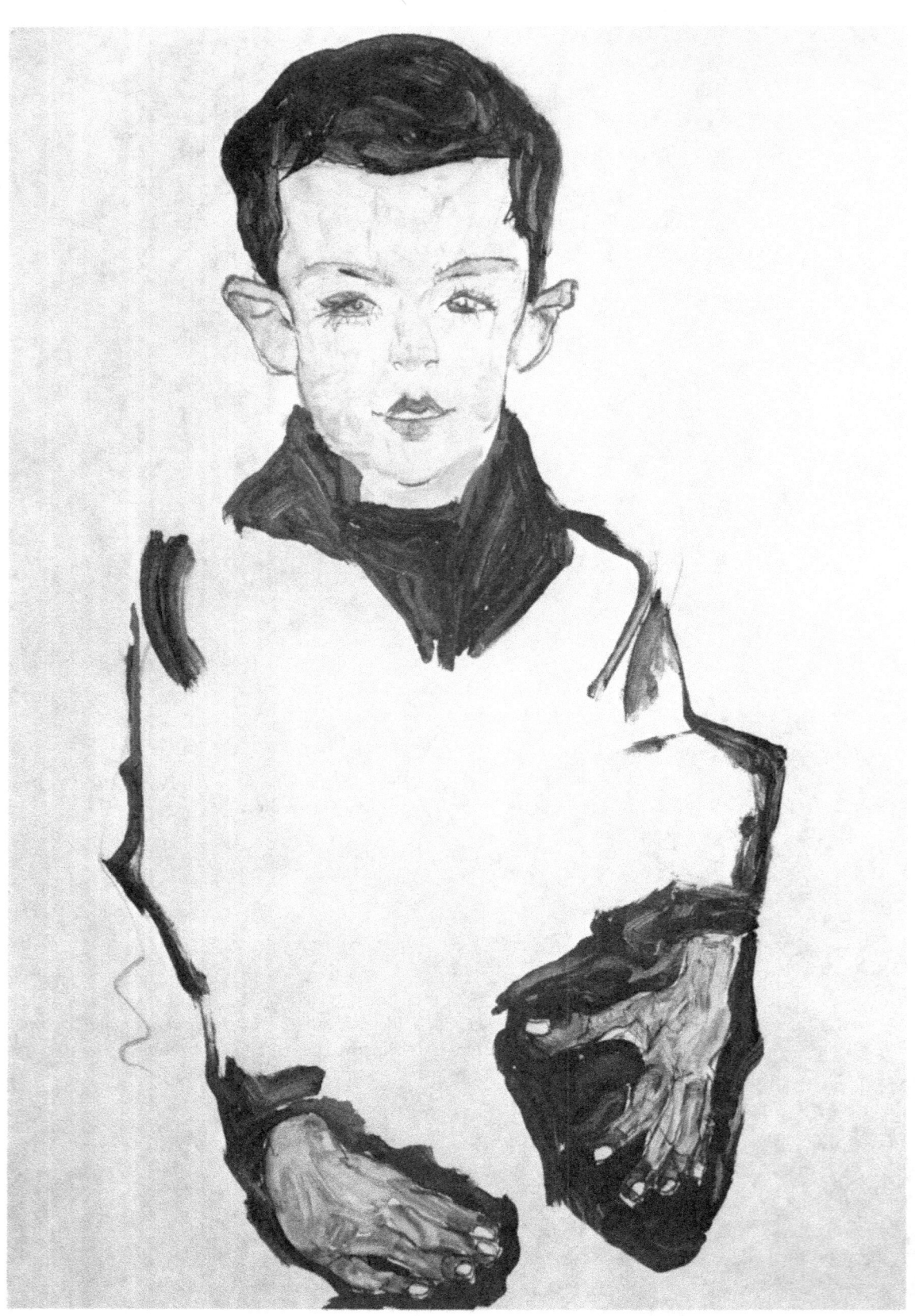

PL. 57. Schiele, *Study for the Portrait of Herbert Rainer*, 1910, pencil and watercolor.

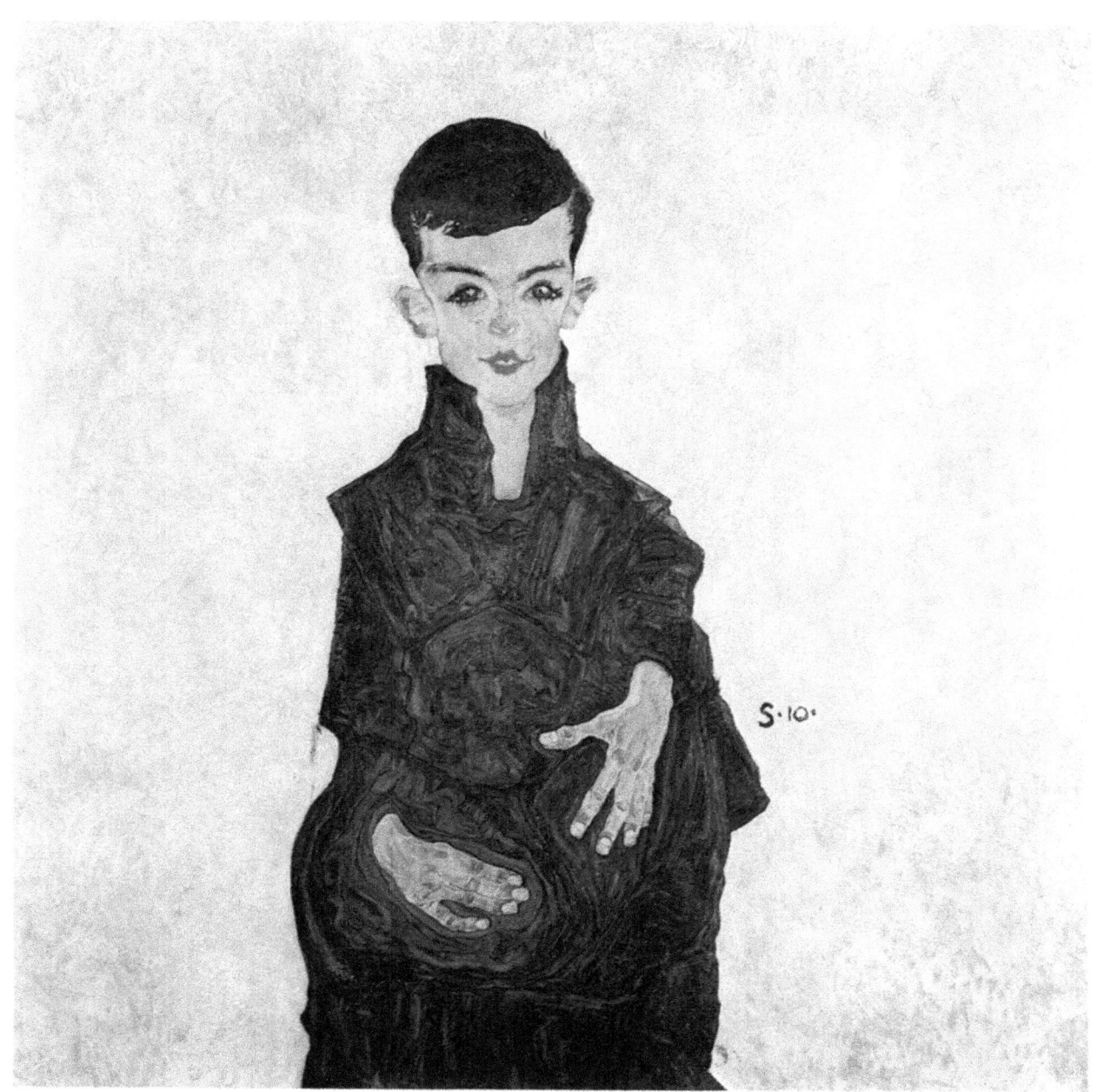

PL. 58. Schiele, *Portrait of Herbert Rainer*, 1910, oil.

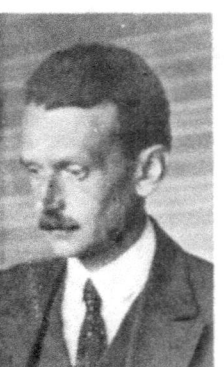

PL. 59a. Eduard Kosmack, *ca.* 1918.

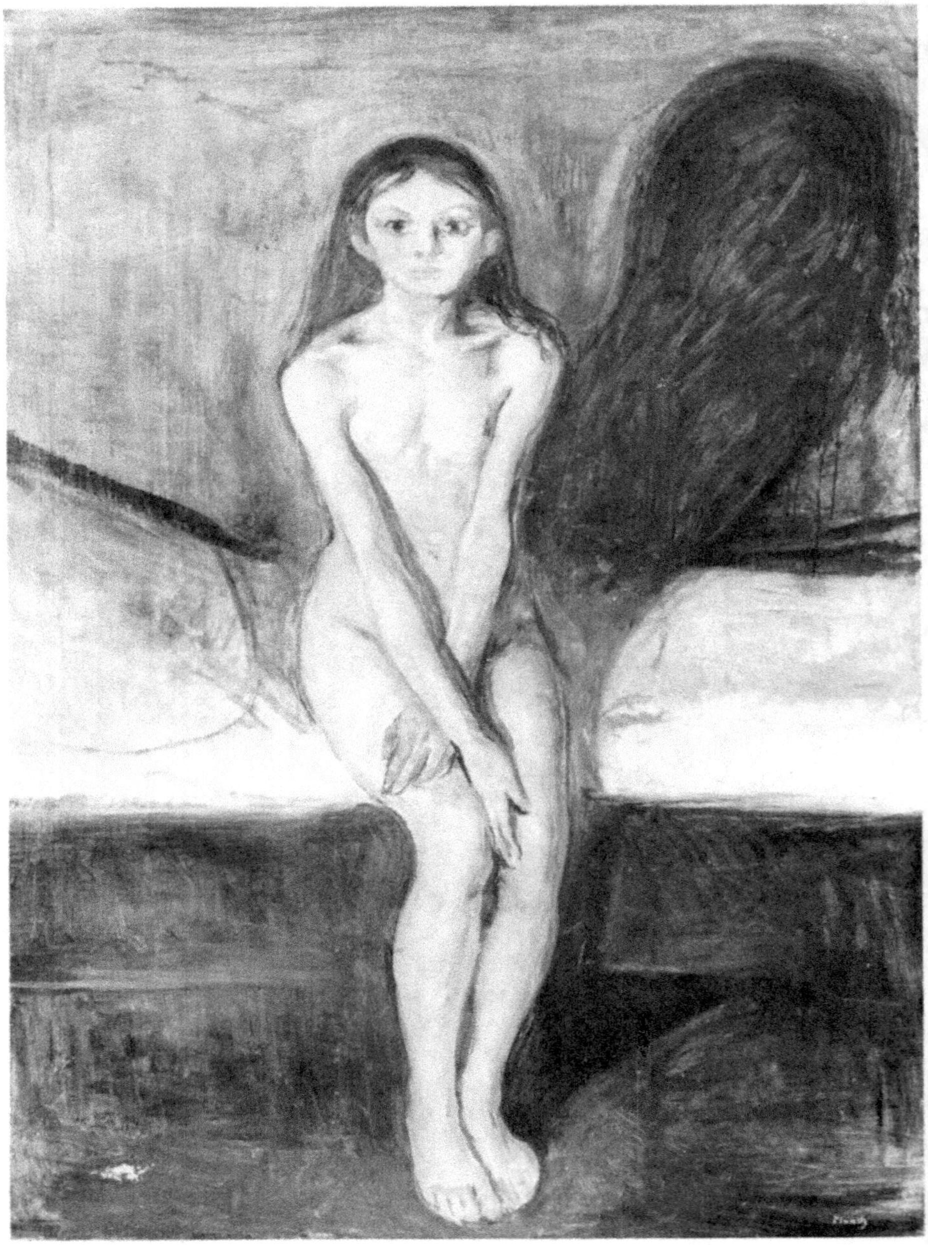

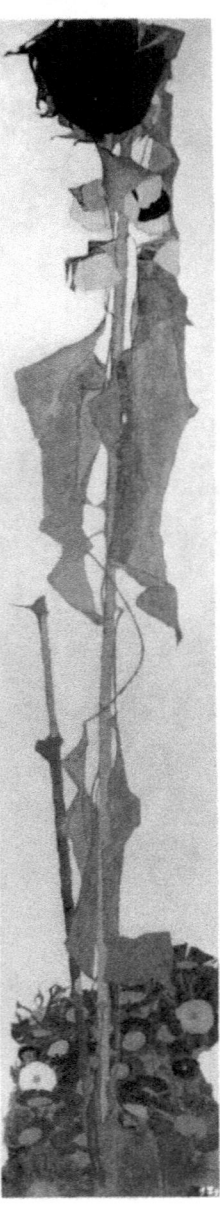

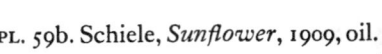

PL. 60. Edvard Munch, *Puberty*, 1894, oil.

PL. 59b. Schiele, *Sunflower*, 1909, oil.

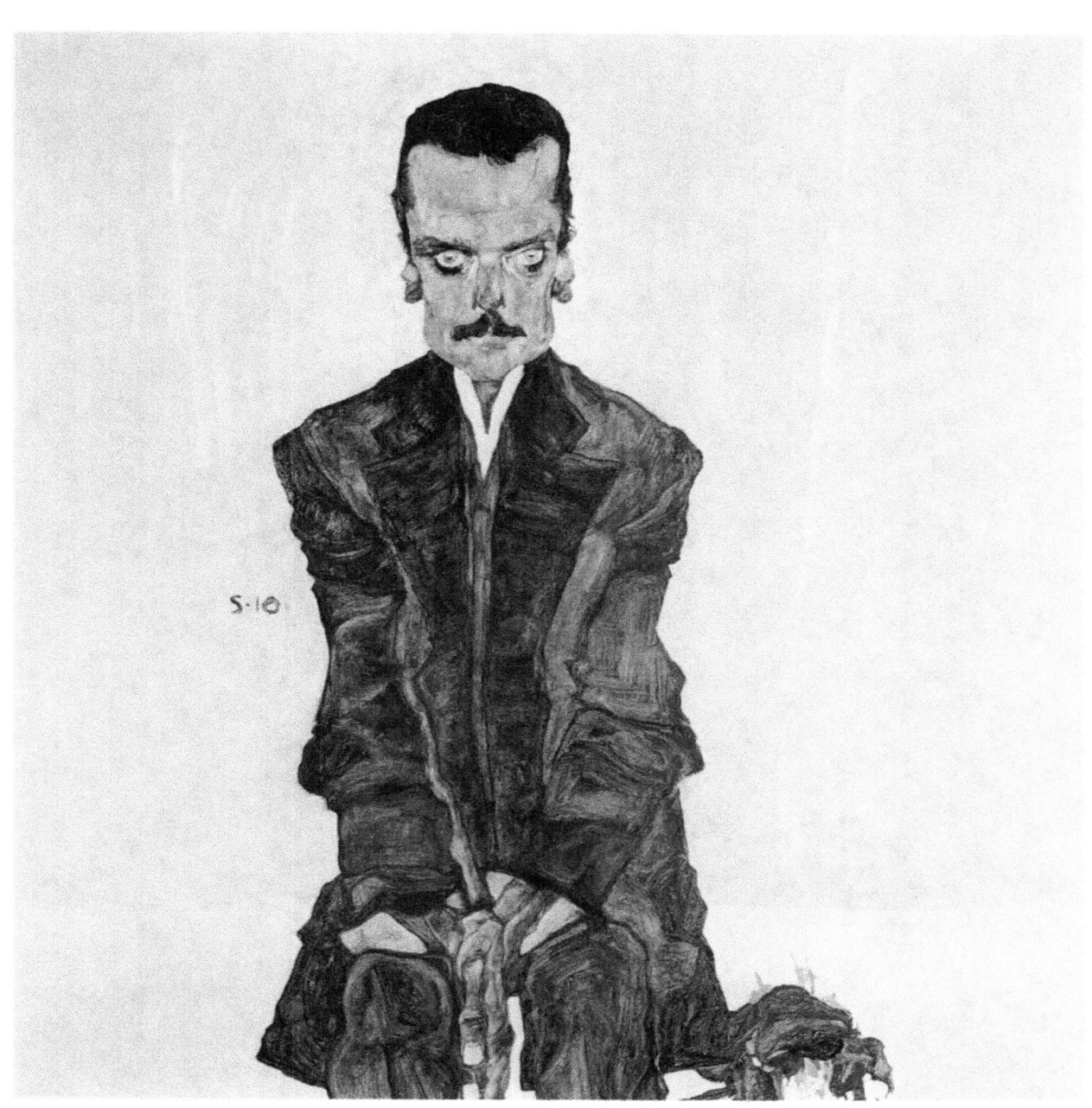

PL. 61. Schiele, *Portrait of Eduard Kosmack*, 1910, oil.

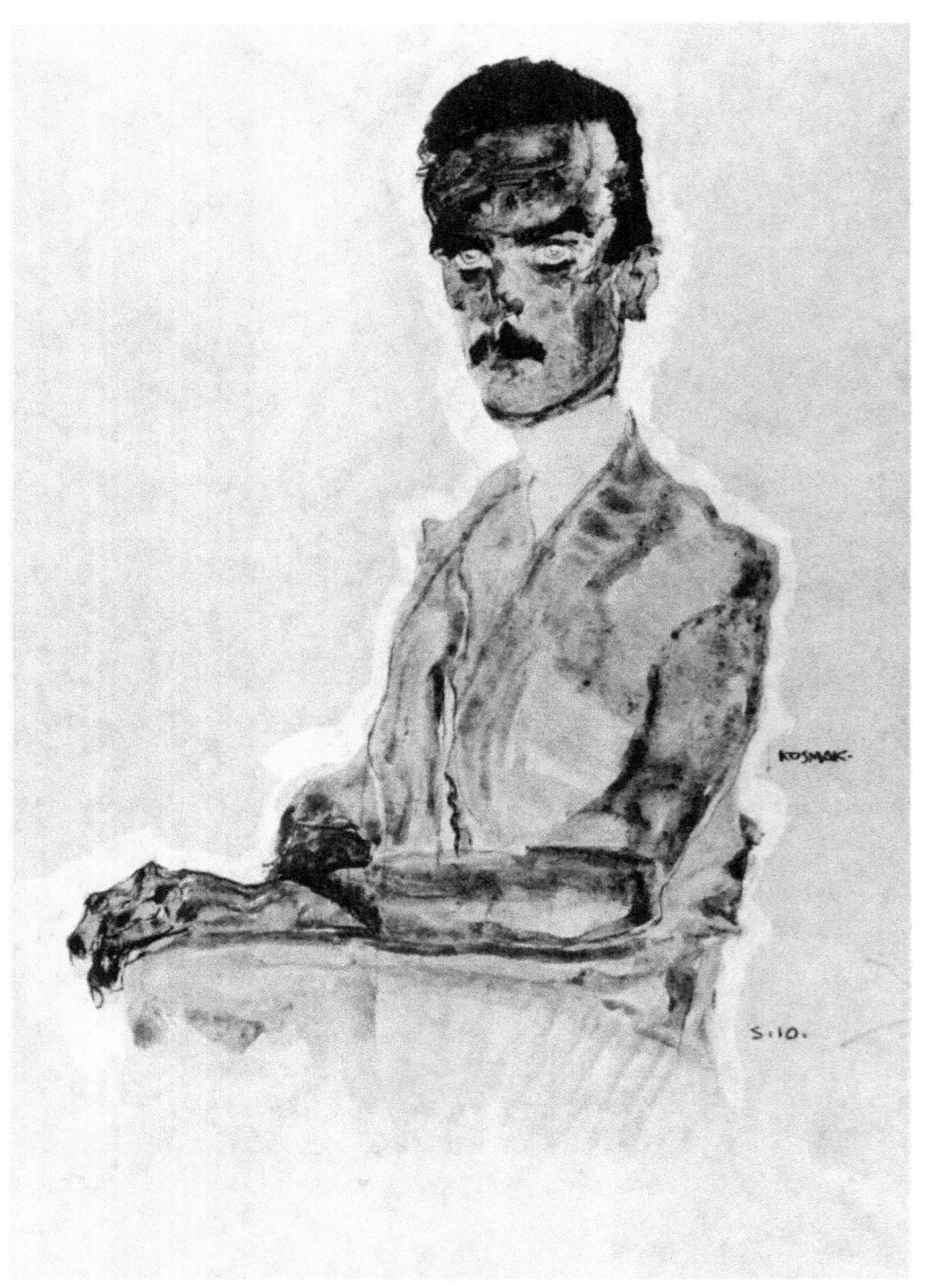

PL. 62. Schiele, *Study for the Portrait of Eduard Kosmack, Seated*, 1910, black chalk and water-color.

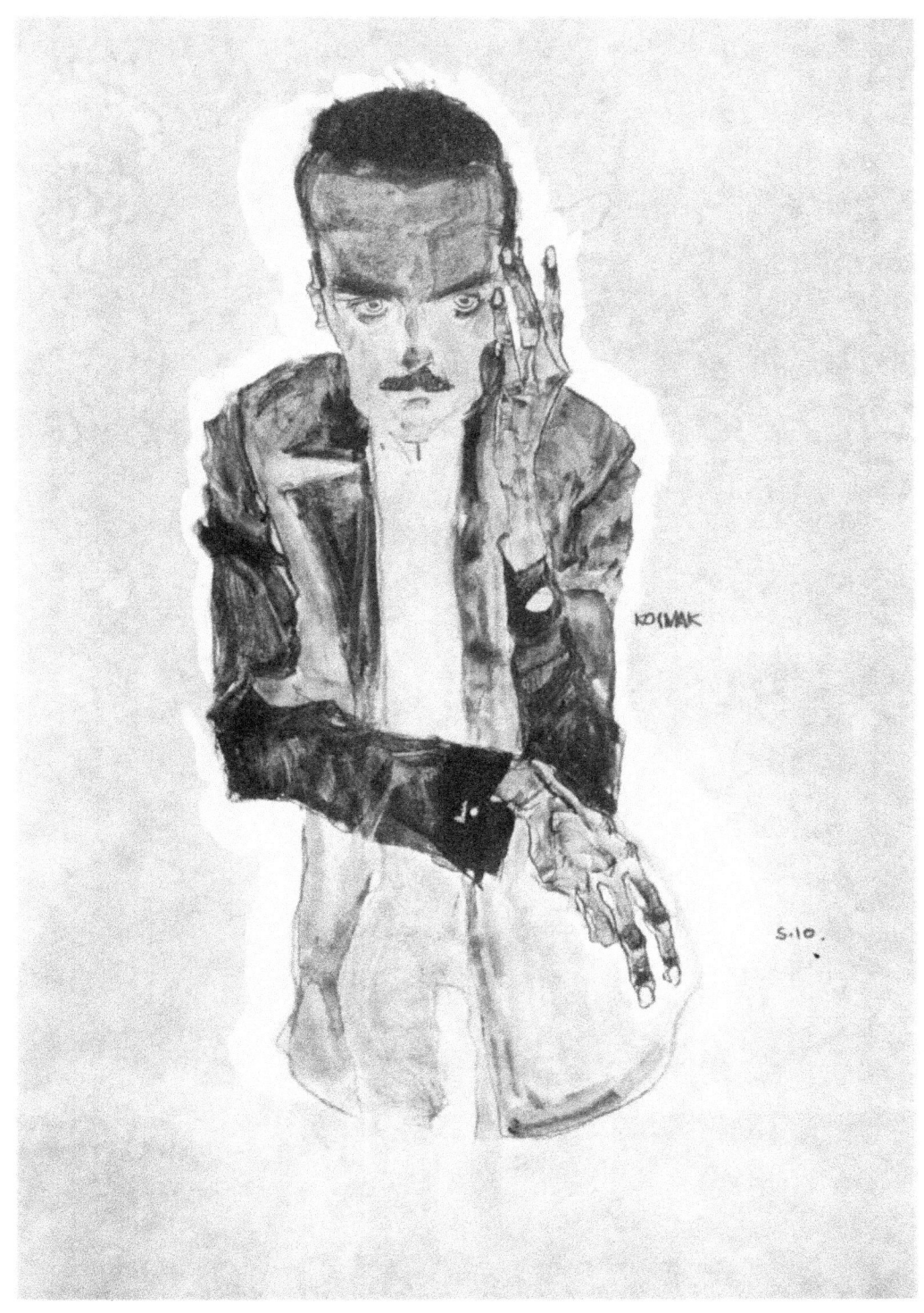

PL. 63. Schiele, *Study for the Portrait of Eduard Kosmack, Frontal with Left Hand Raised to Forehead*, 1910, black chalk and watercolor.

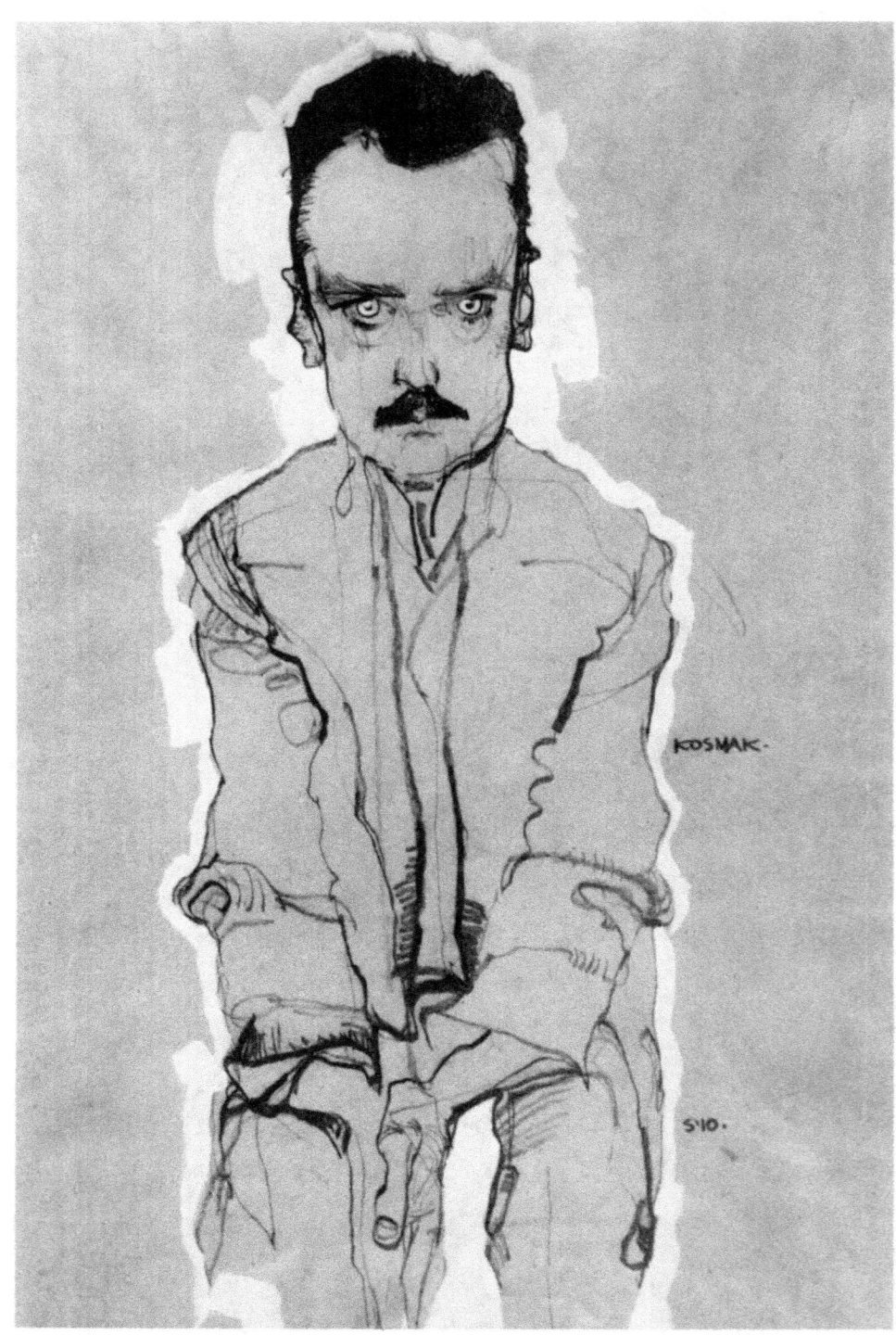

PL. 64. Schiele, *Study for the Portrait of Eduard Kosmack, Frontal with Clasped Hands,* 1910, black chalk and watercolor.

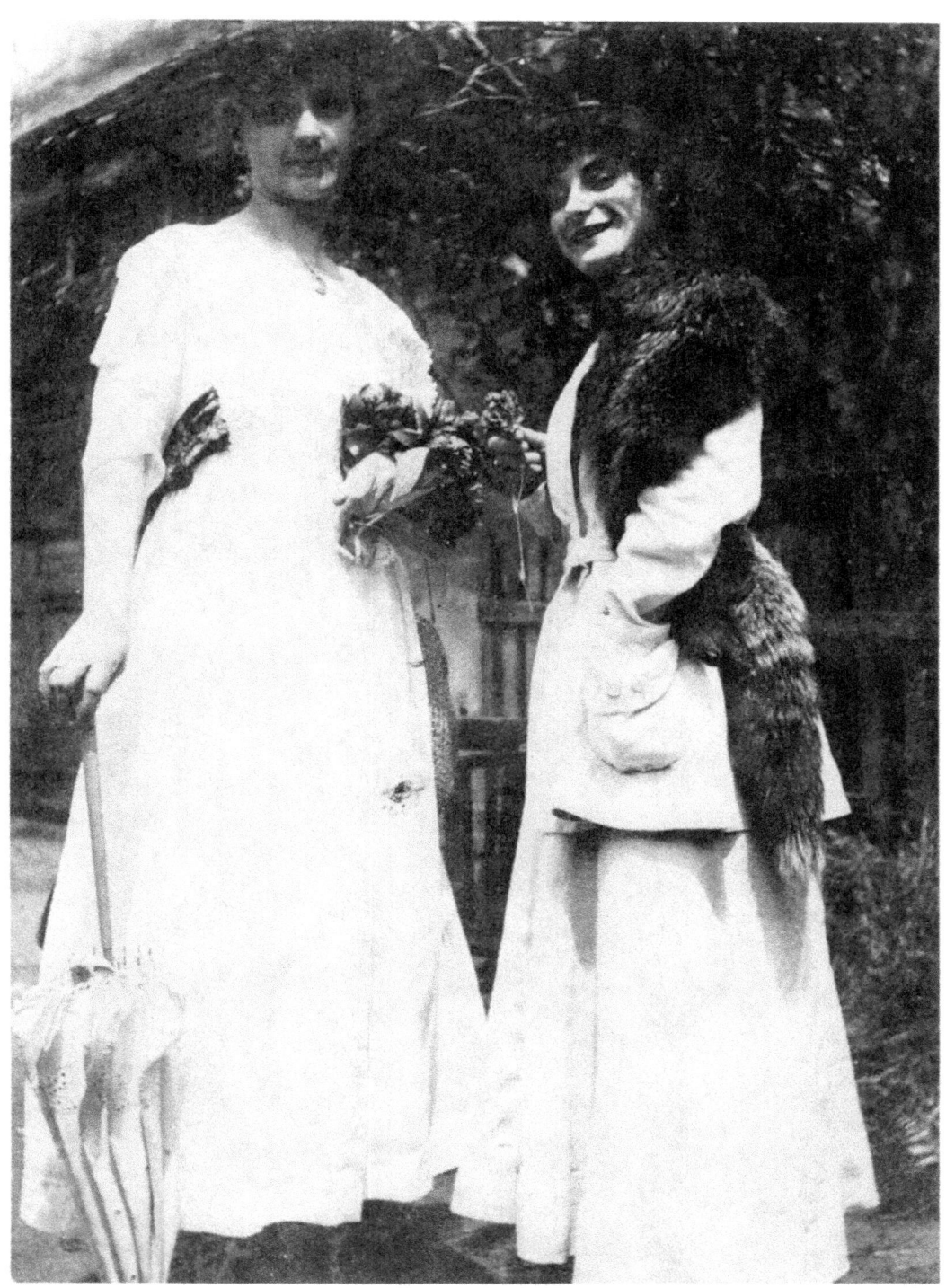

PL. 65. Melanie and Gerti Schiele, 1919.

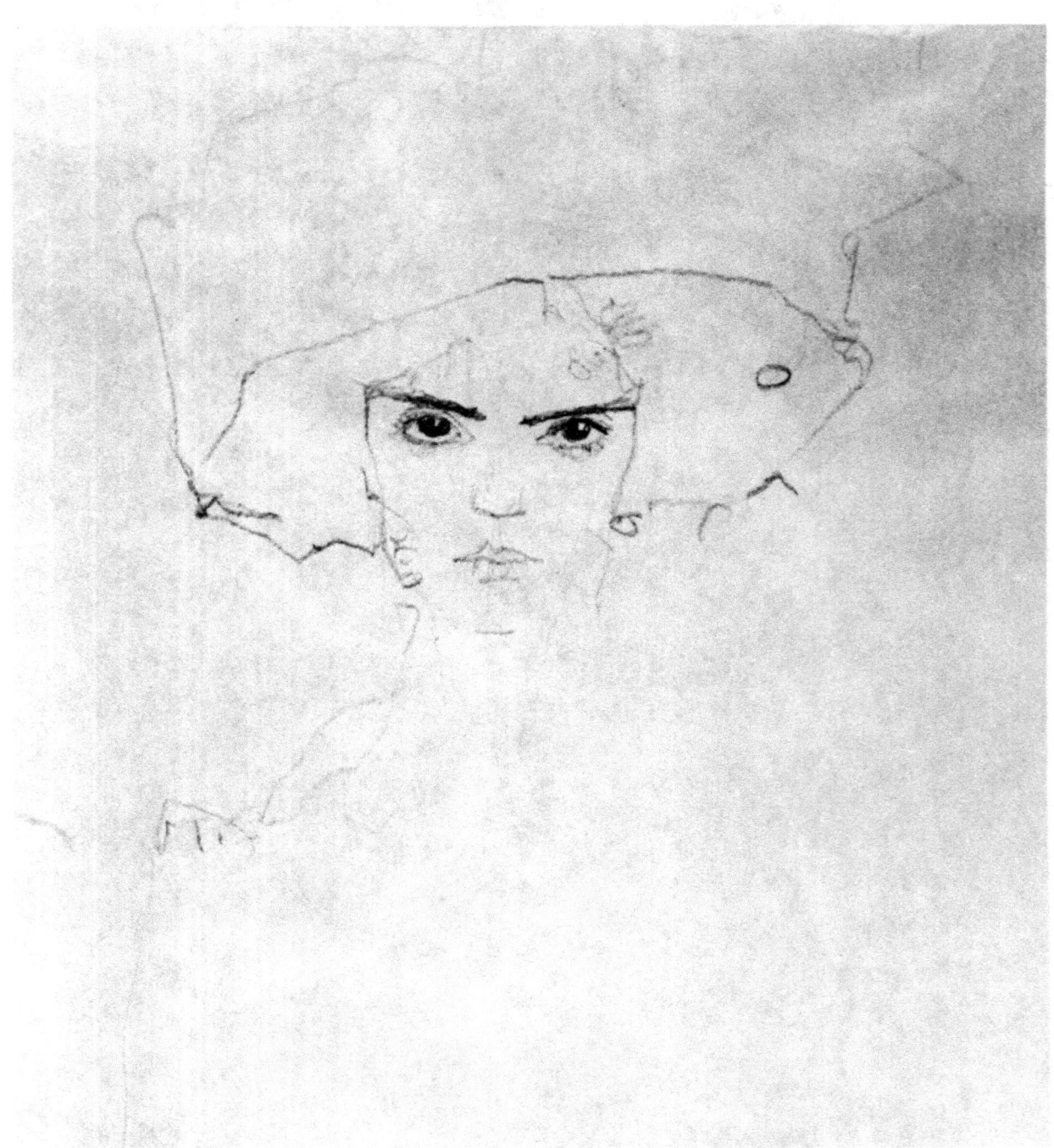

PL. 66. Schiele, *Portrait Sketch of Melanie*, 1910, black chalk.

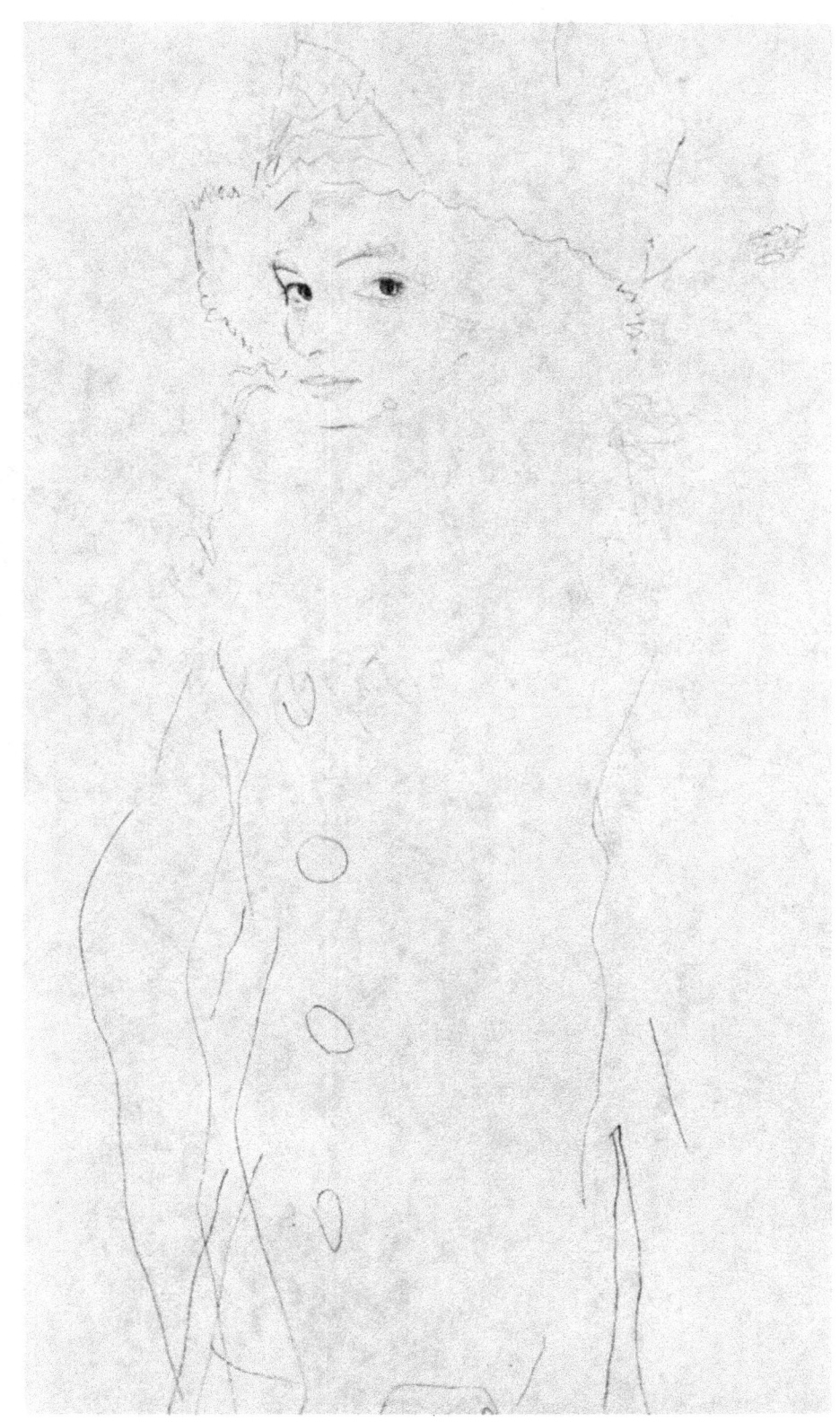

PL. 67. Schiele, *Portrait Sketch of Gerti*, 1911, pencil.

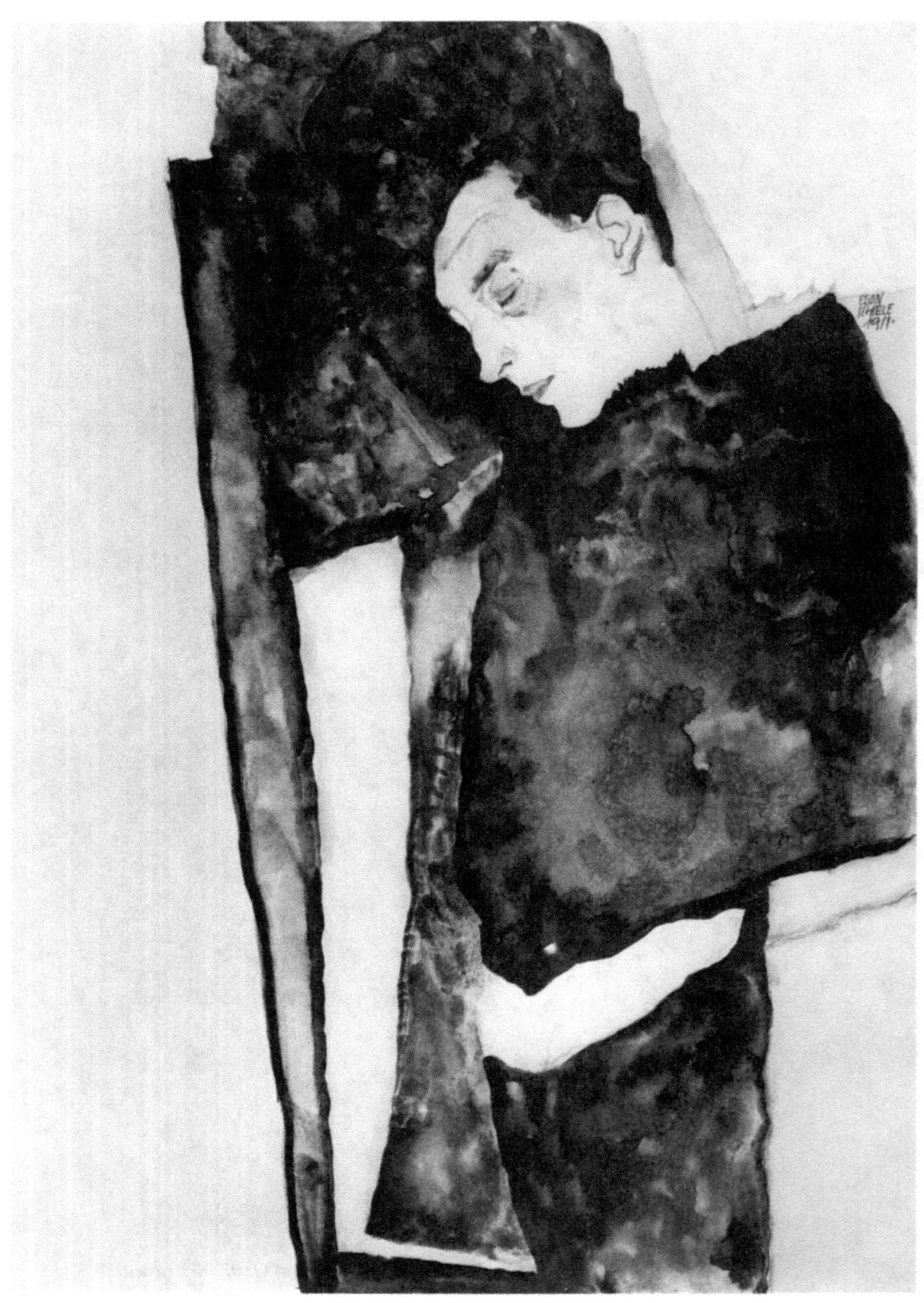

PL. 68. Schiele, *The Artist's Mother Asleep*, 1911, pencil and watercolor.

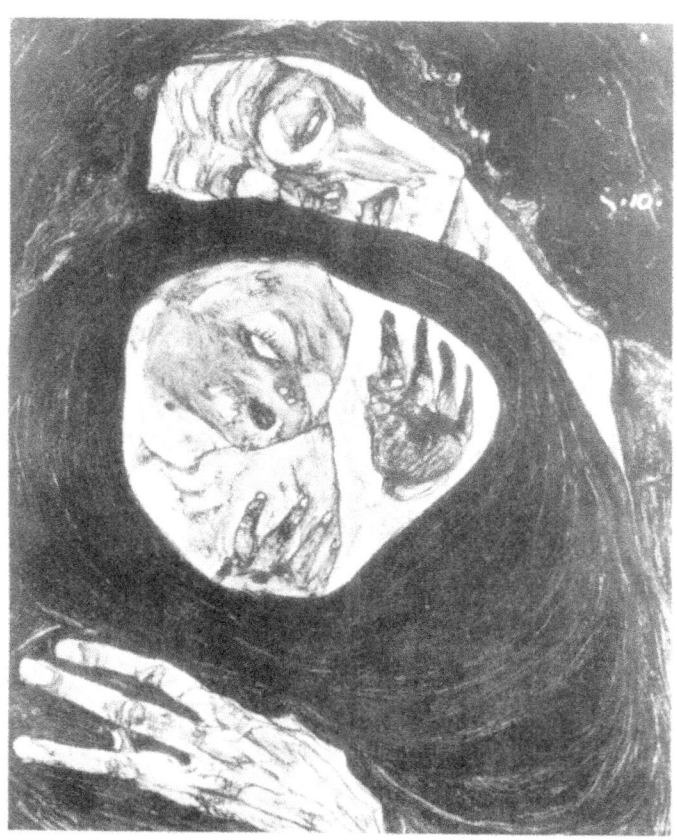

PL. 69. Schiele, *The Dead Mother I*, 1910, oil.

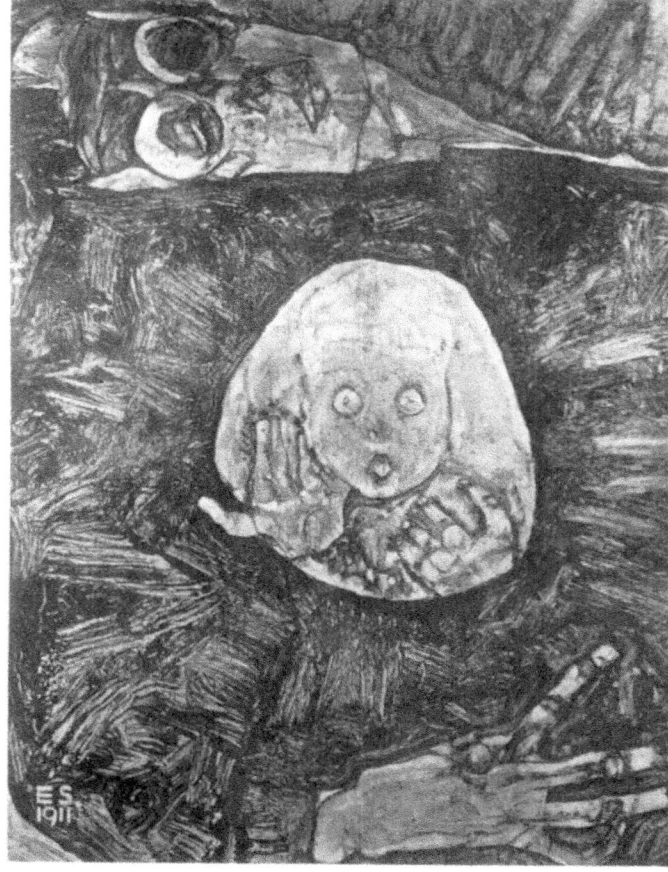

PL. 70. Schiele, *The Dead Mother II ("Birth of Genius")*, 1911, oil.

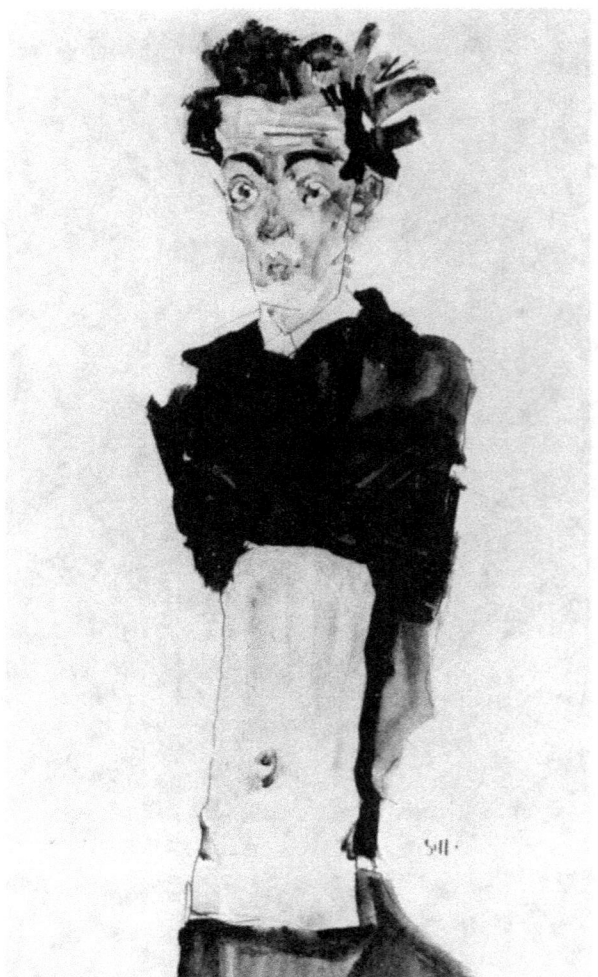

PL. 71. Schiele, *Self-Portrait with Bare Stomach*, 1911, pencil and watercolor.

PL. 72. Schiele, *The Lyric Poet*, 1911, oil.

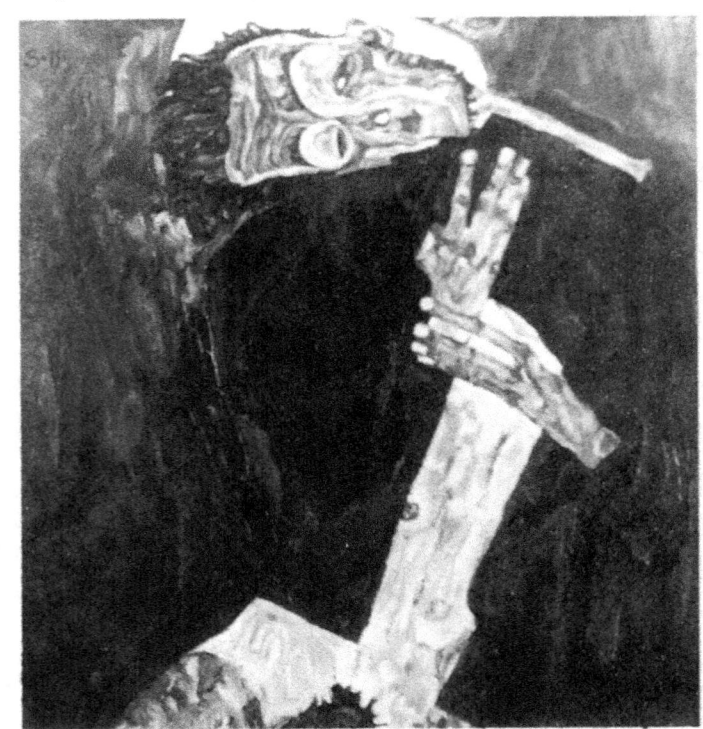

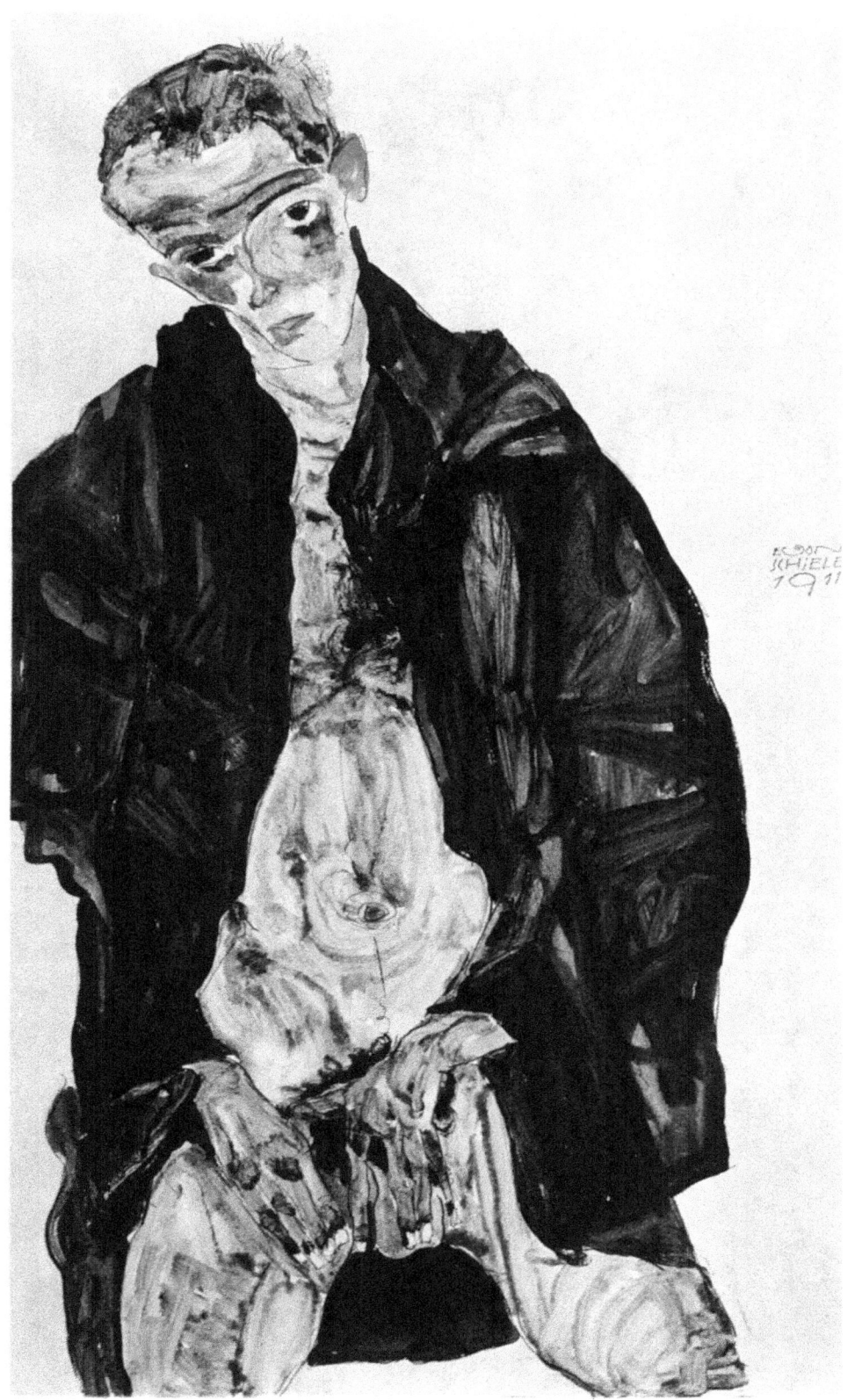

PL. 73. Schiele, *Self-Portrait Masturbating*, 1911, pencil and watercolor.

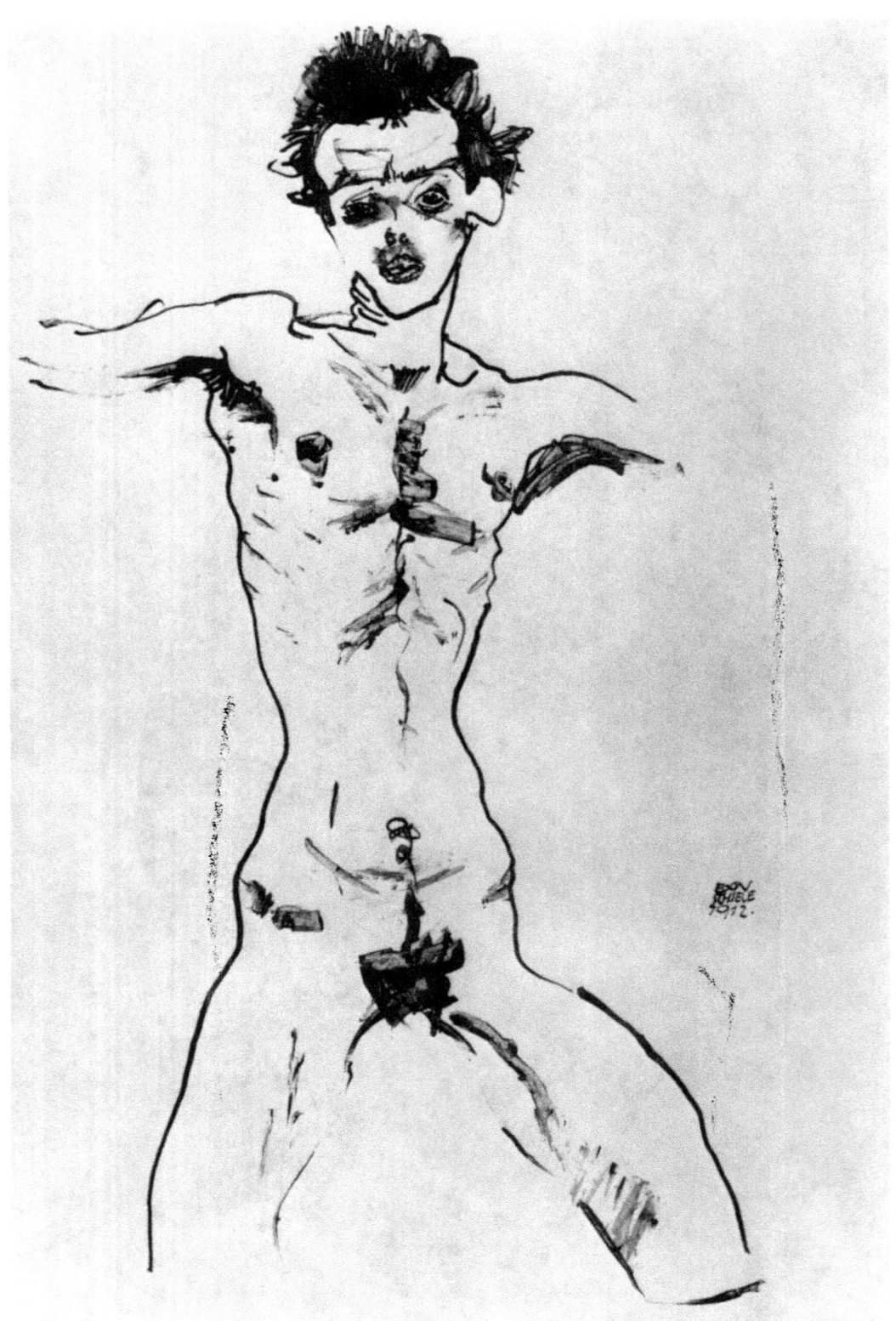

PL. 74. Schiele, *Self-Portrait Nude Study*, 1912, black chalk and watercolor.

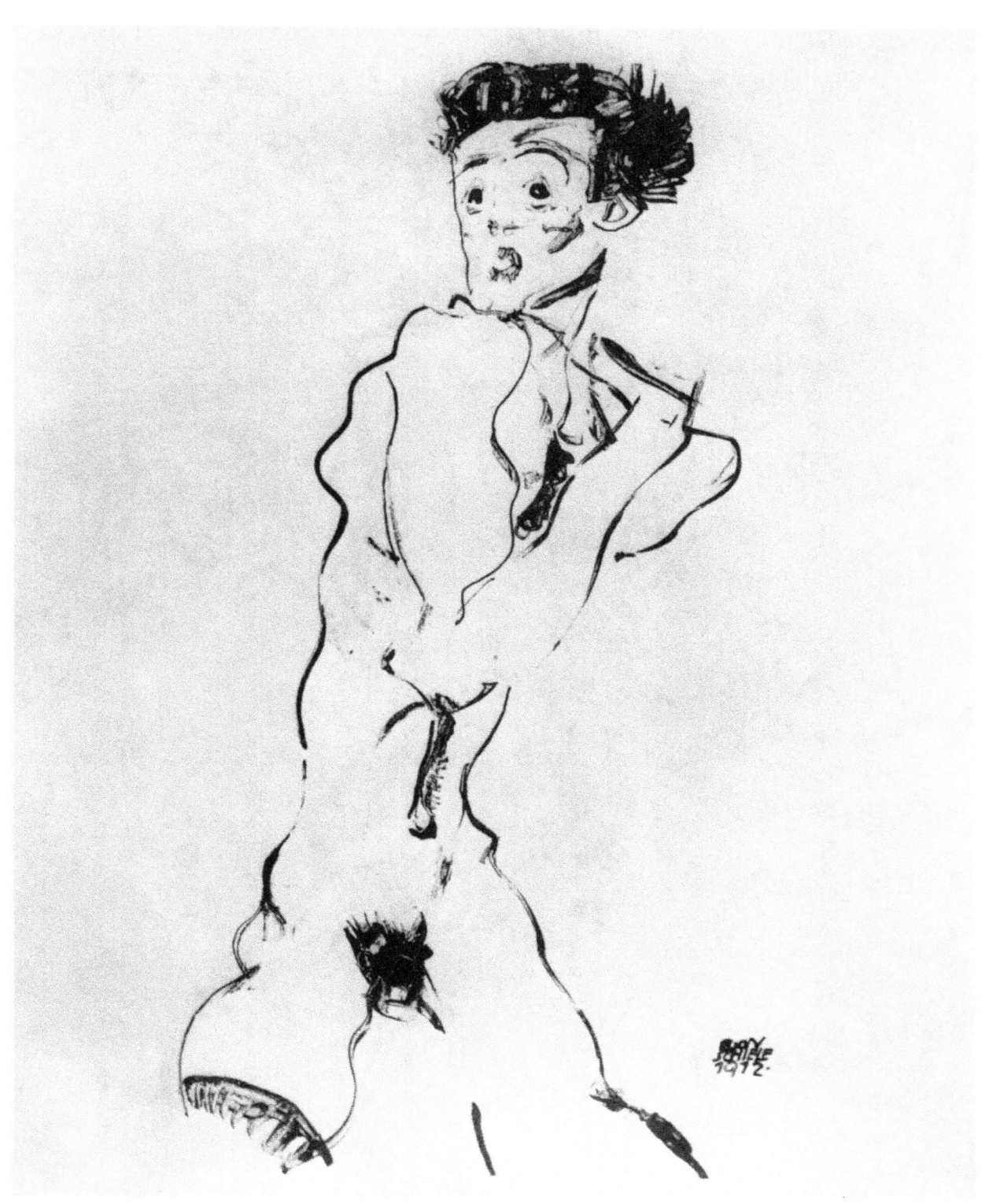

PL. 75a. Schiele, *Self-Portrait Nude II* (*"Male Nude [Self Portrait] II"*), 1912, lithograph.

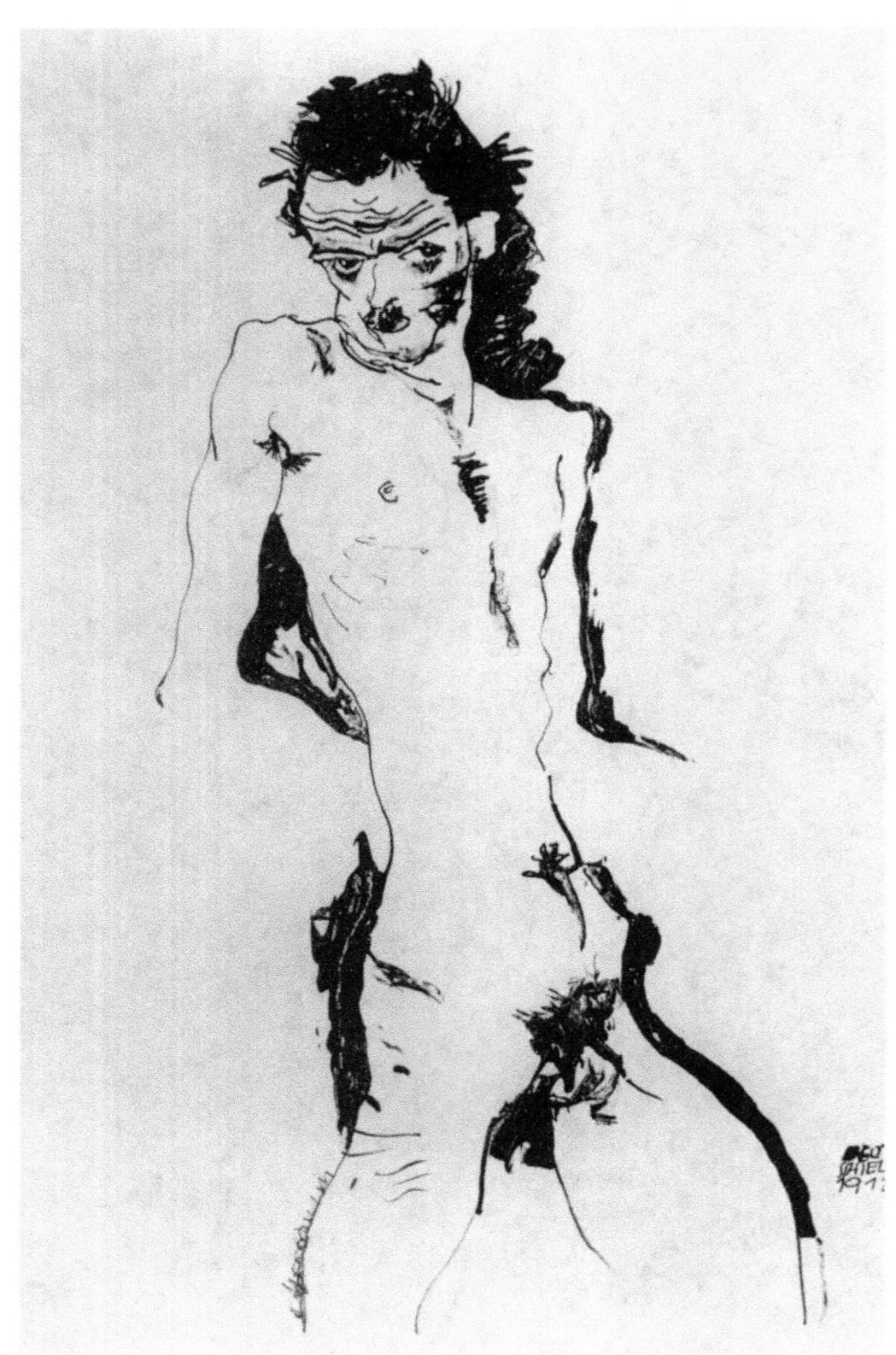

PL. 75b. Schiele, *Self-Portrait Nude I* (*"Male Nude [Self Portrait] I"*), 1912, lithograph.

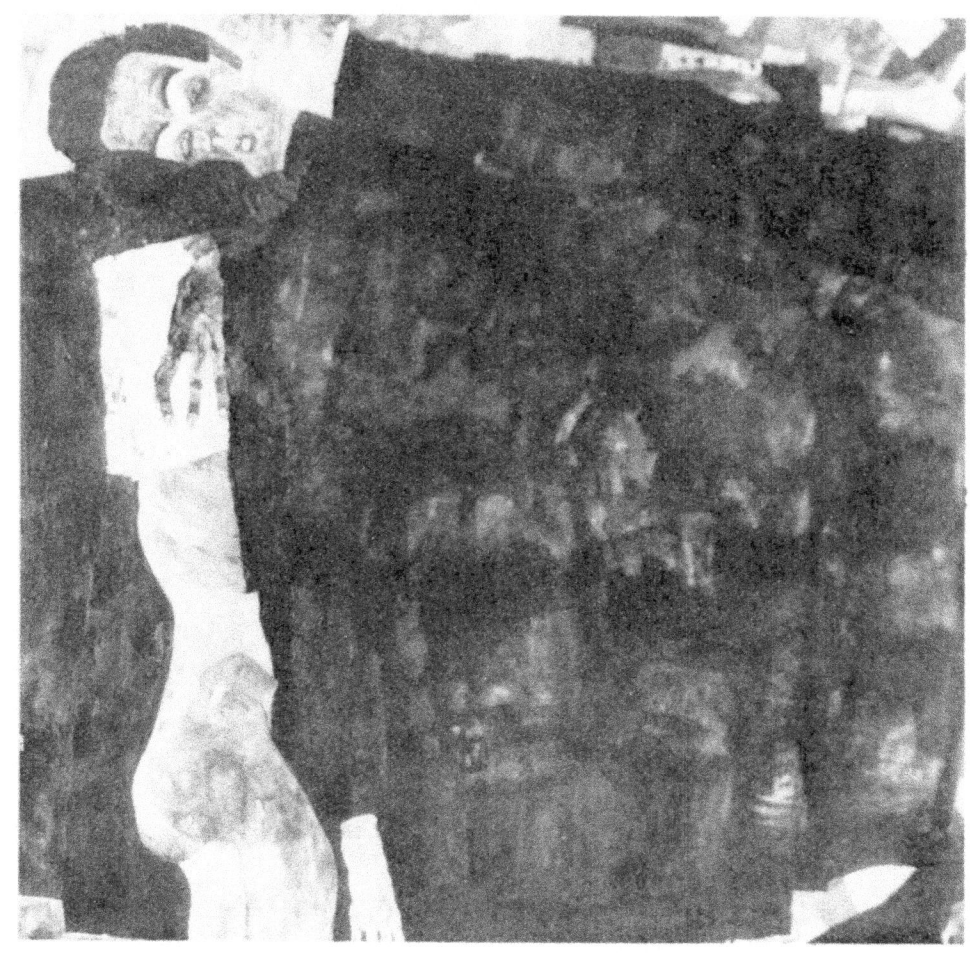

PL. 76. Schiele, *Vision*, 1911, oil.

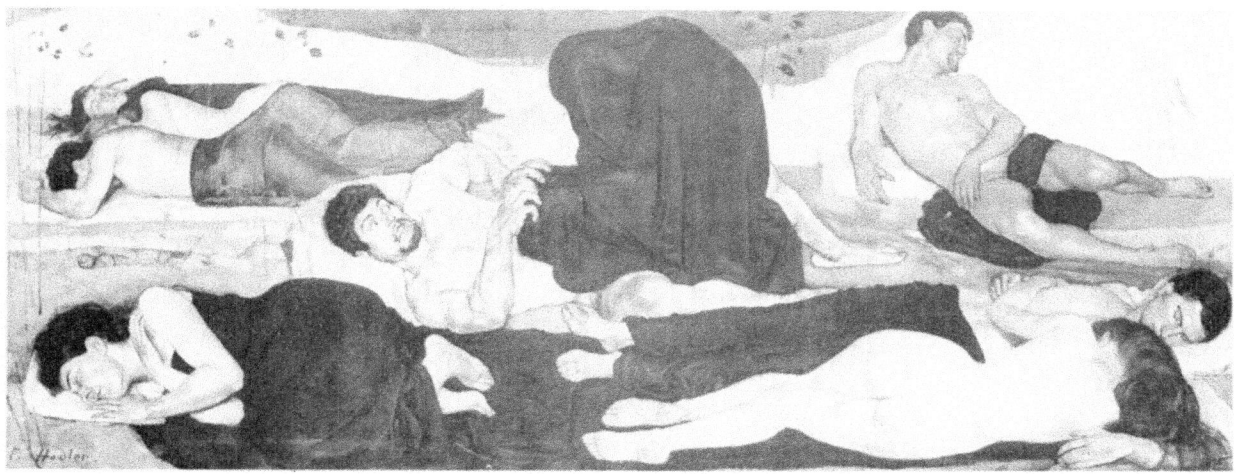

PL. 77. Ferdinand Hodler, *The Night*, 1890, oil.

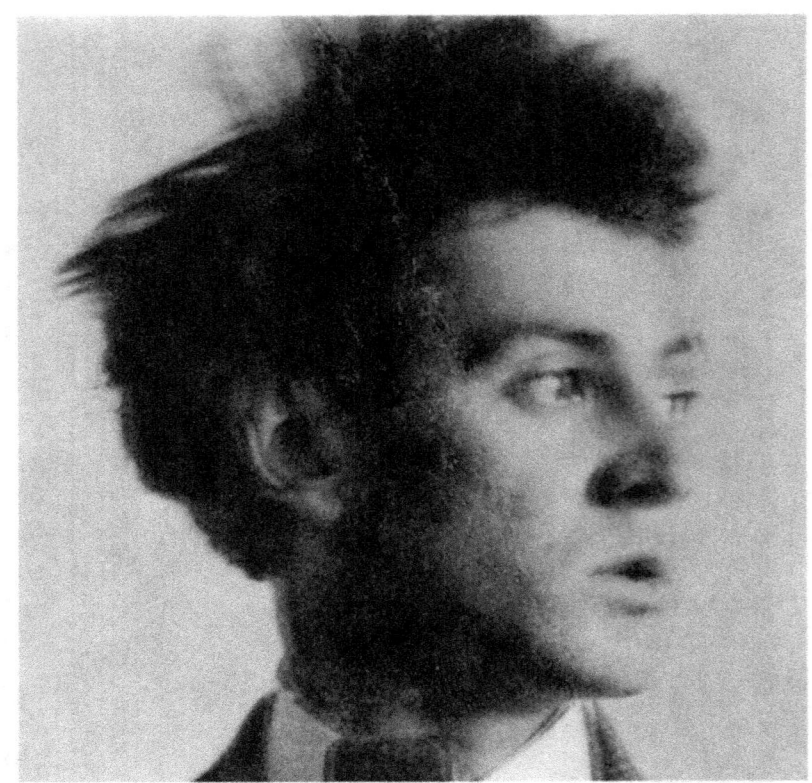

PL. 78. Egon Schiele *ca.* 1911.

PL. 79. Schiele, *Self-Portrait Sketch*, *ca.* 1911, pencil.

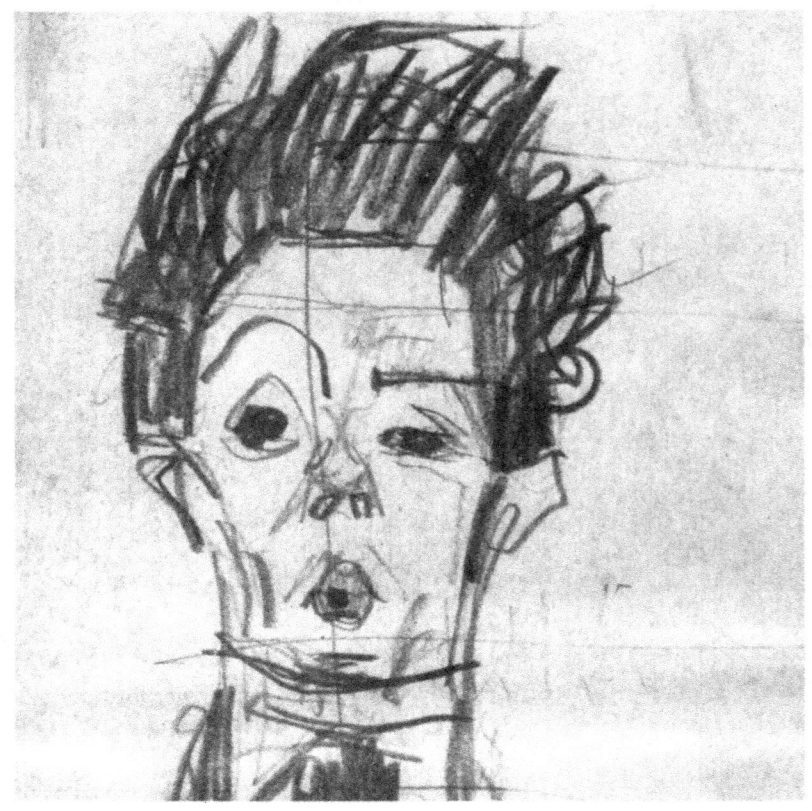

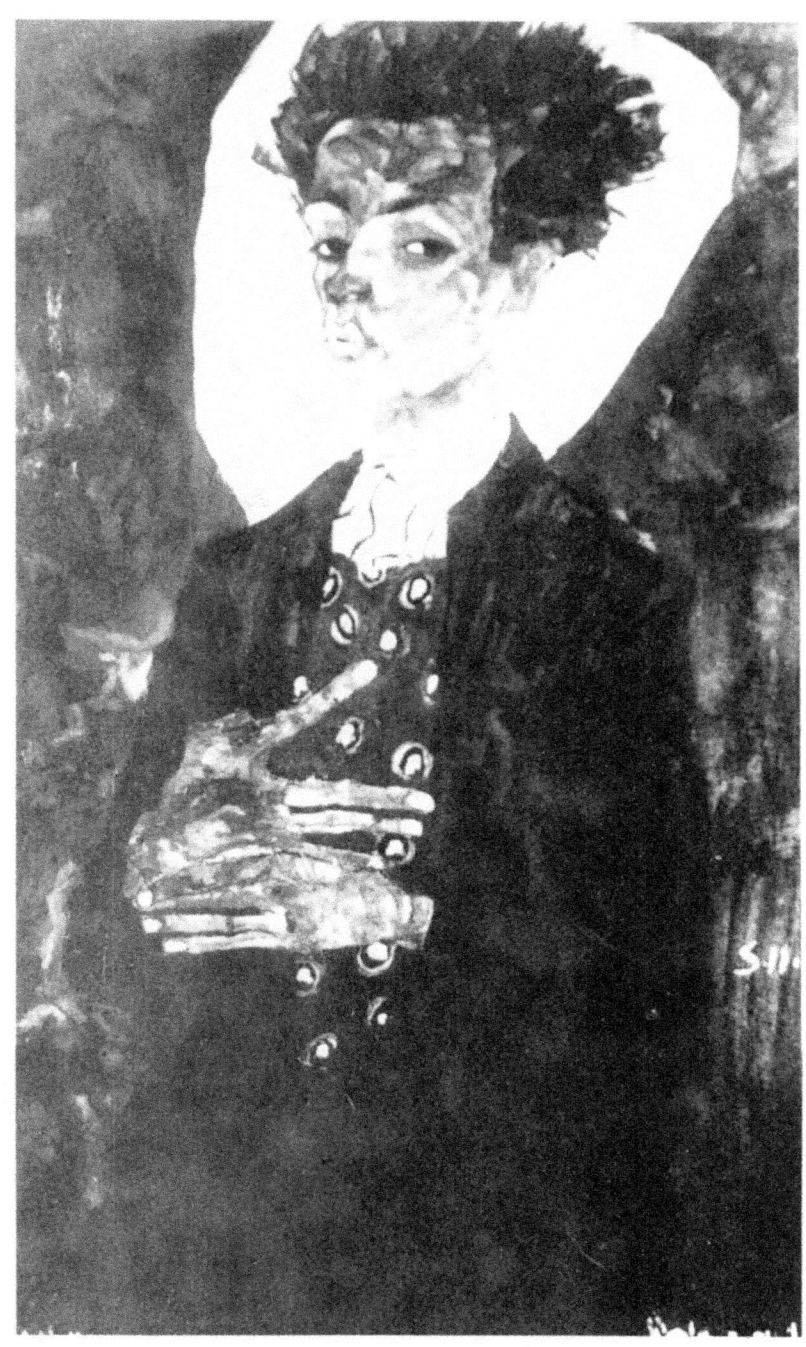

PL. 80. Schiele, *Self-Portrait Standing*, 1911, oil.

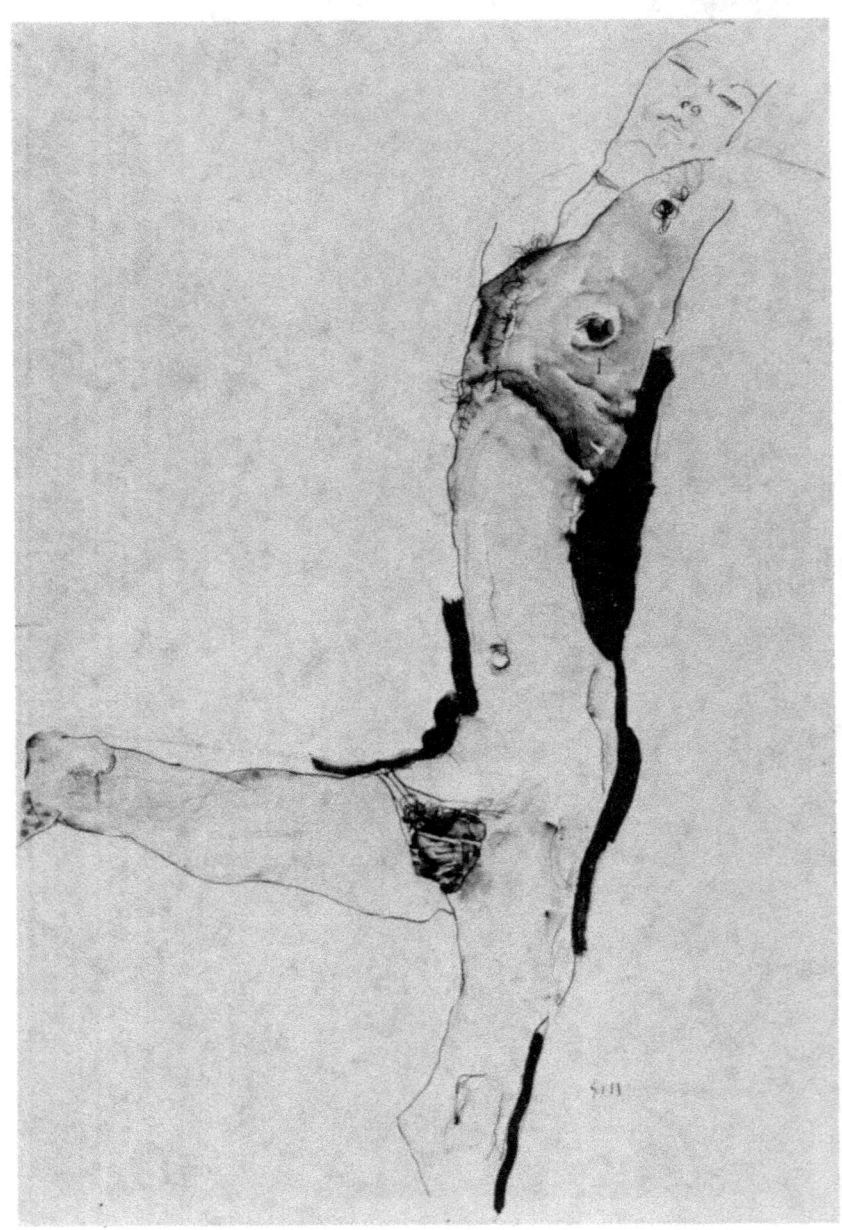

PL. 81. Schiele, *Self-Portrait with Raised Leg*, 1911, pencil and watercolor.

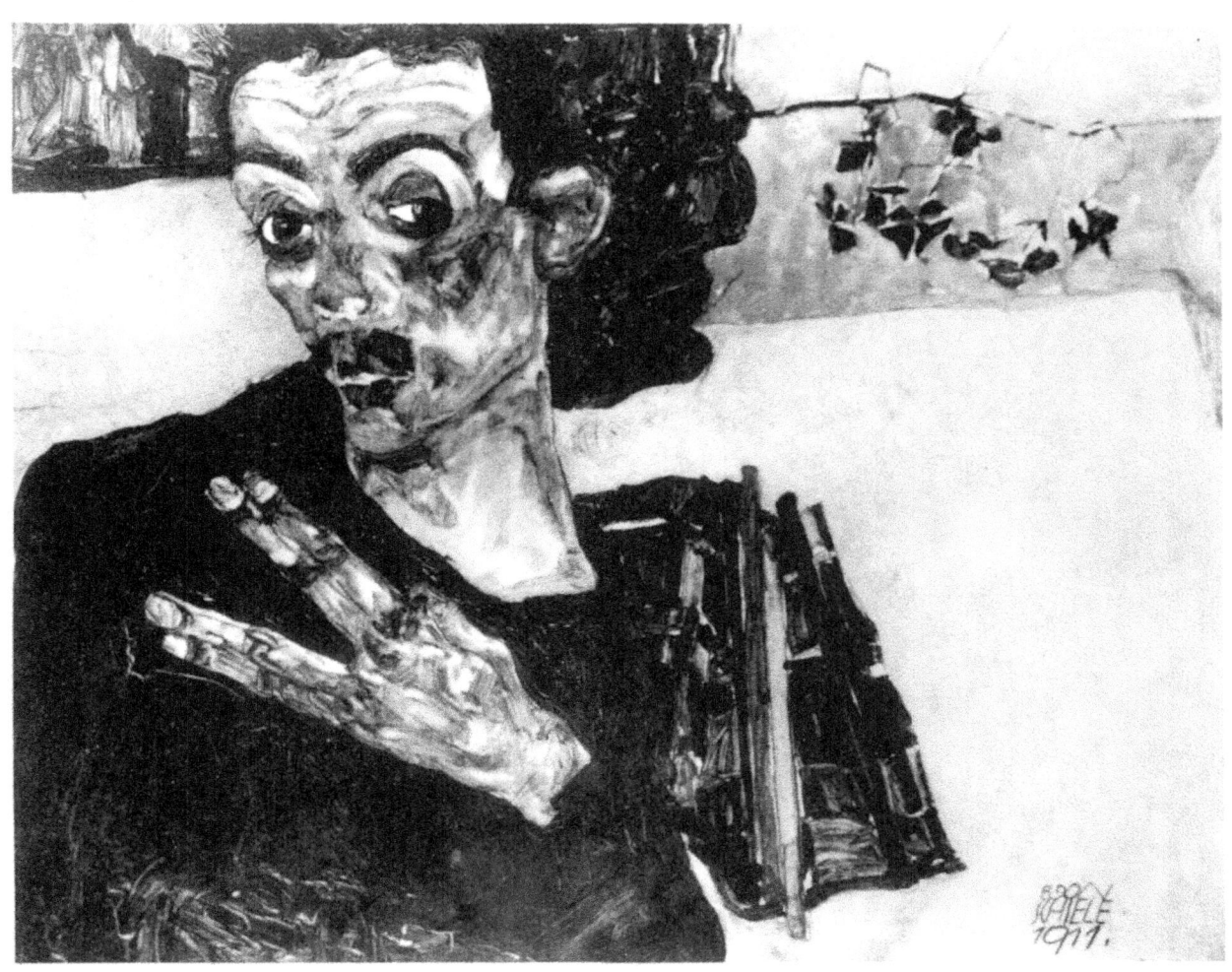

PL. 82. Schiele, *Self-Portrait with Fingers Spread Apart*, 1911, oil.

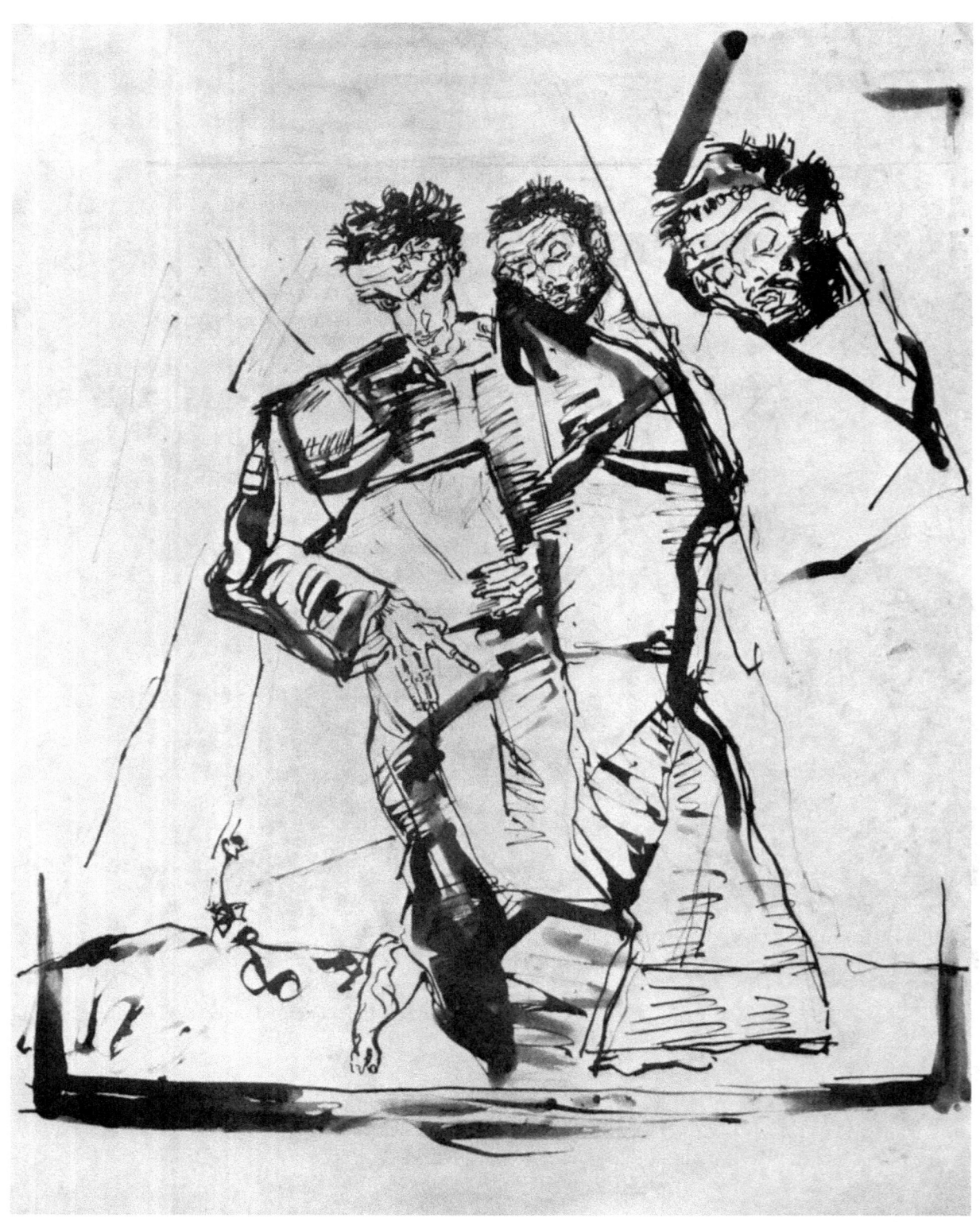

PL. 83. Schiele, *Study for The Hermits*, 1912, pen and wash drawing.

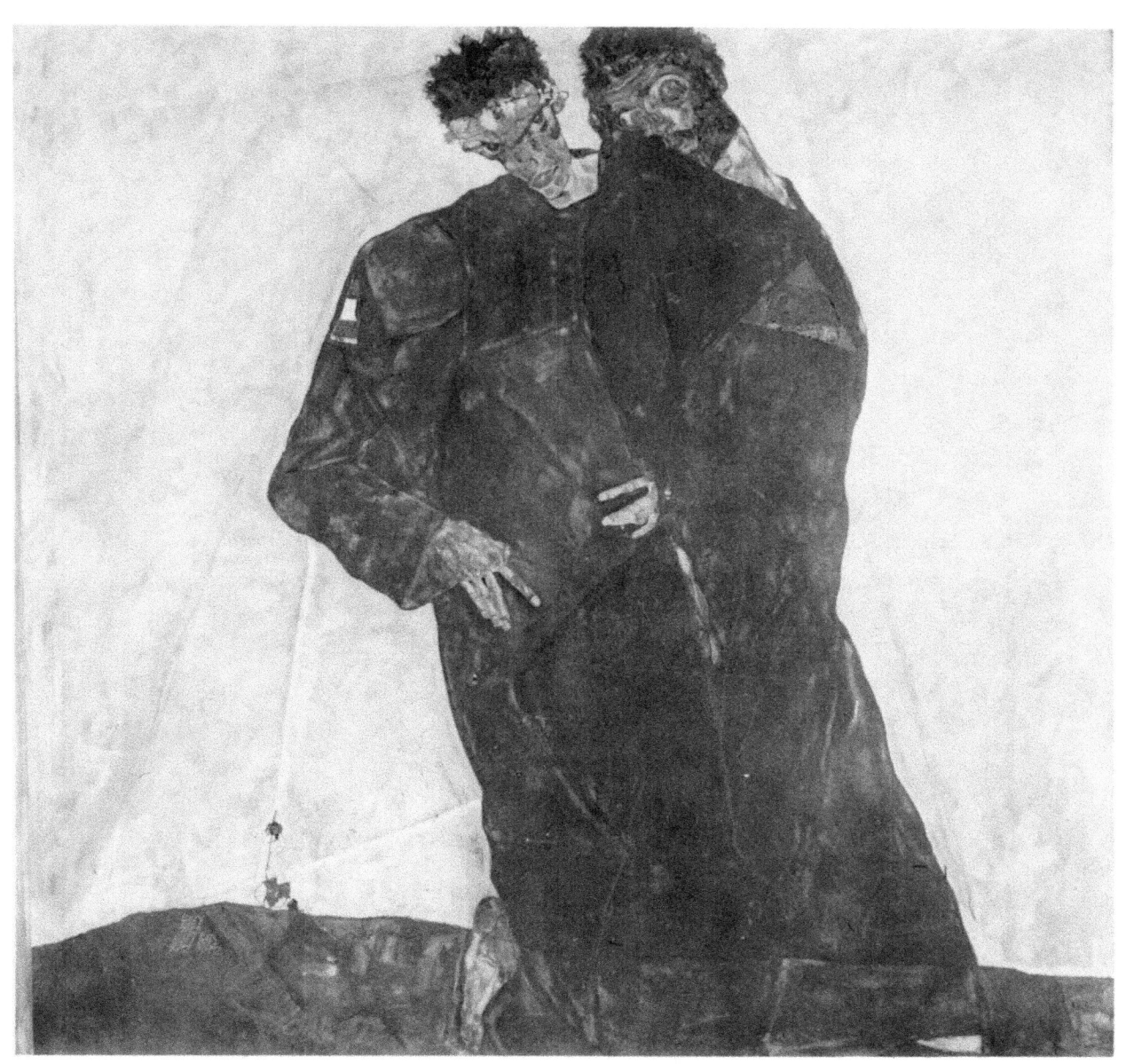

PL. 84. Schiele, *The Hermits*, 1912, oil.

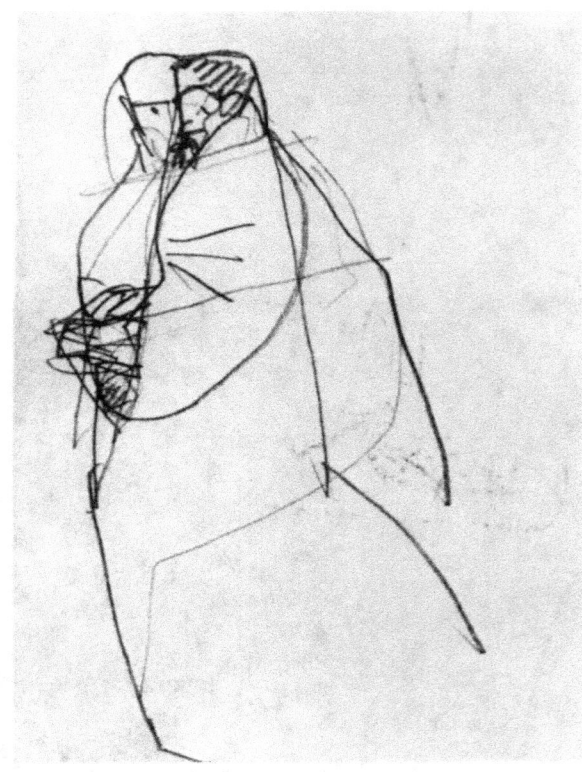

PL. 85. Schiele, A.E.S.A. Sketchbook I, 1912, pencil, p. 26 *verso*.

PL. 86. Schiele, A.E.S.A. Sketchbook II, 1912–1913, pencil, pp. 17 *verso* and 18 *recto*.

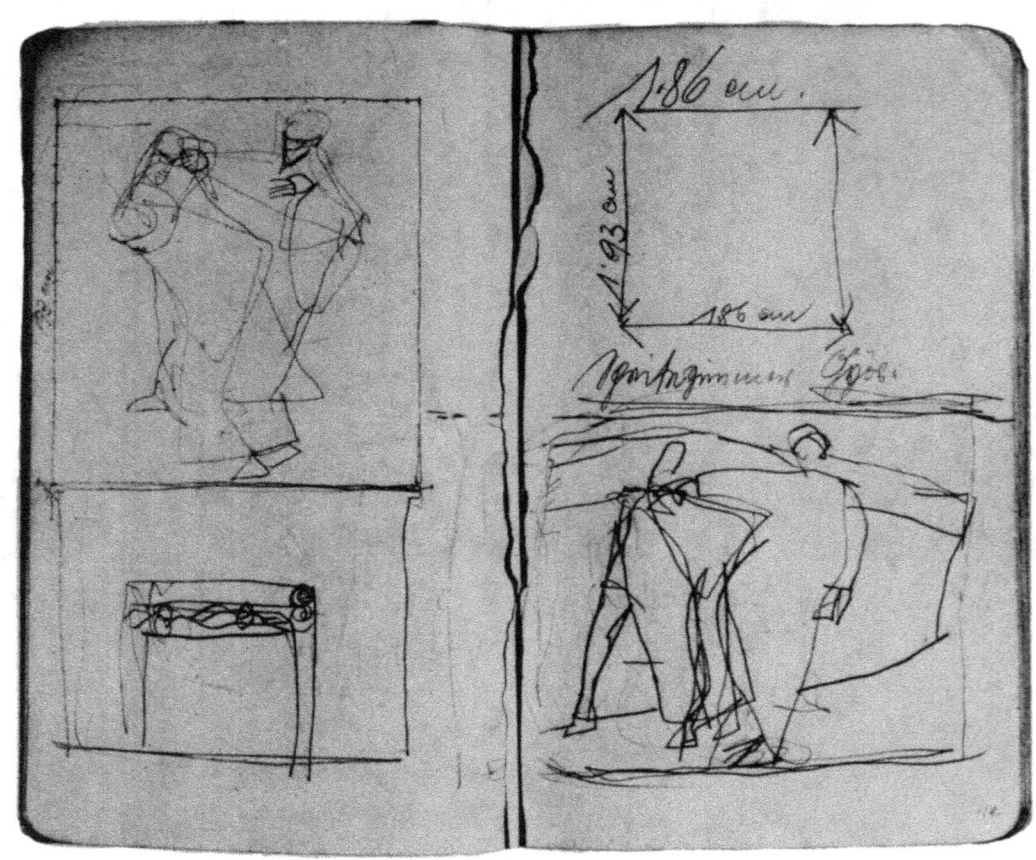

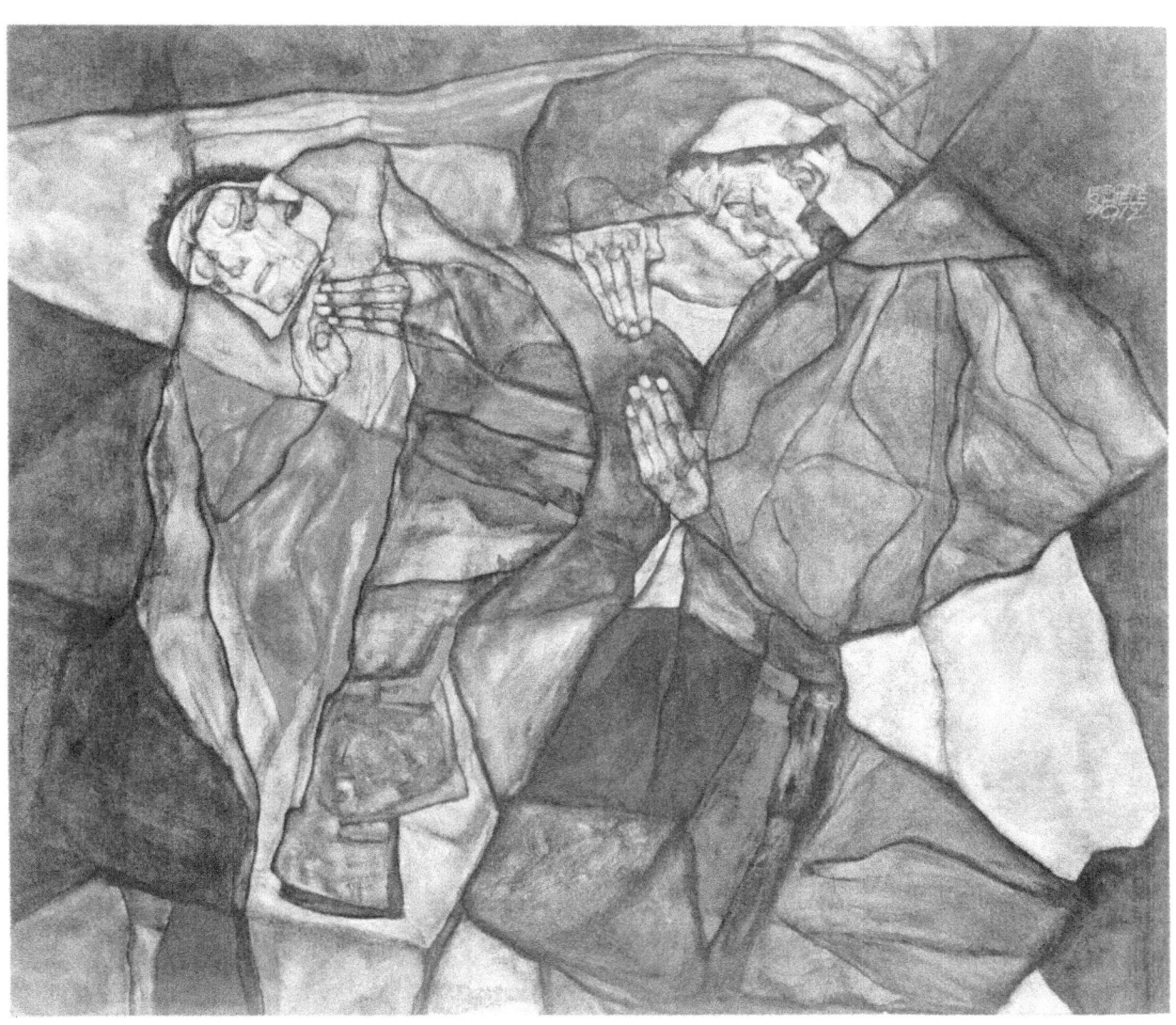

PL. 87. Schiele, *Agony*, 1912, oil.

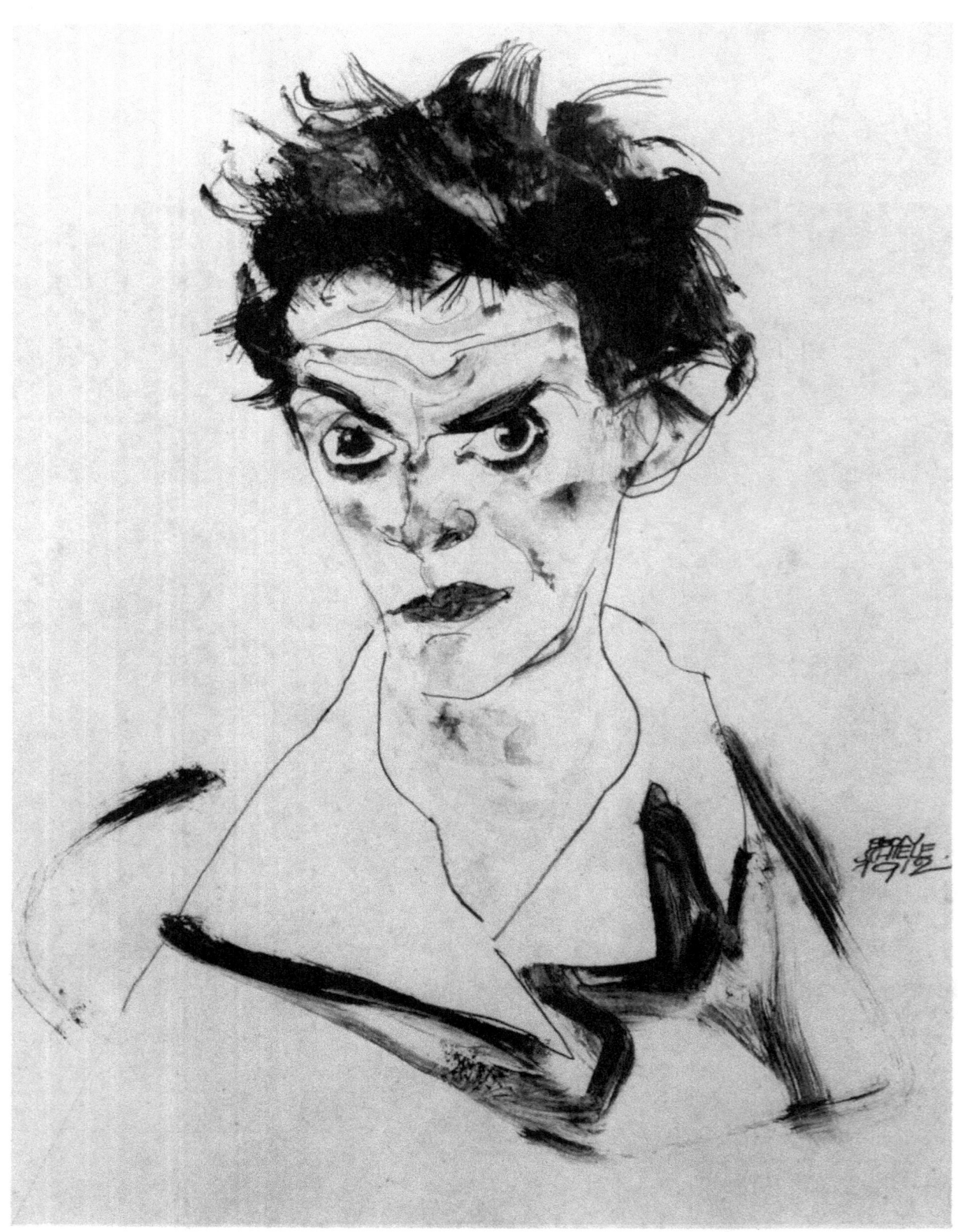

PL. 88. Schiele, *Self-Portrait Study for The Hermits*, 1912, pencil and watercolor.

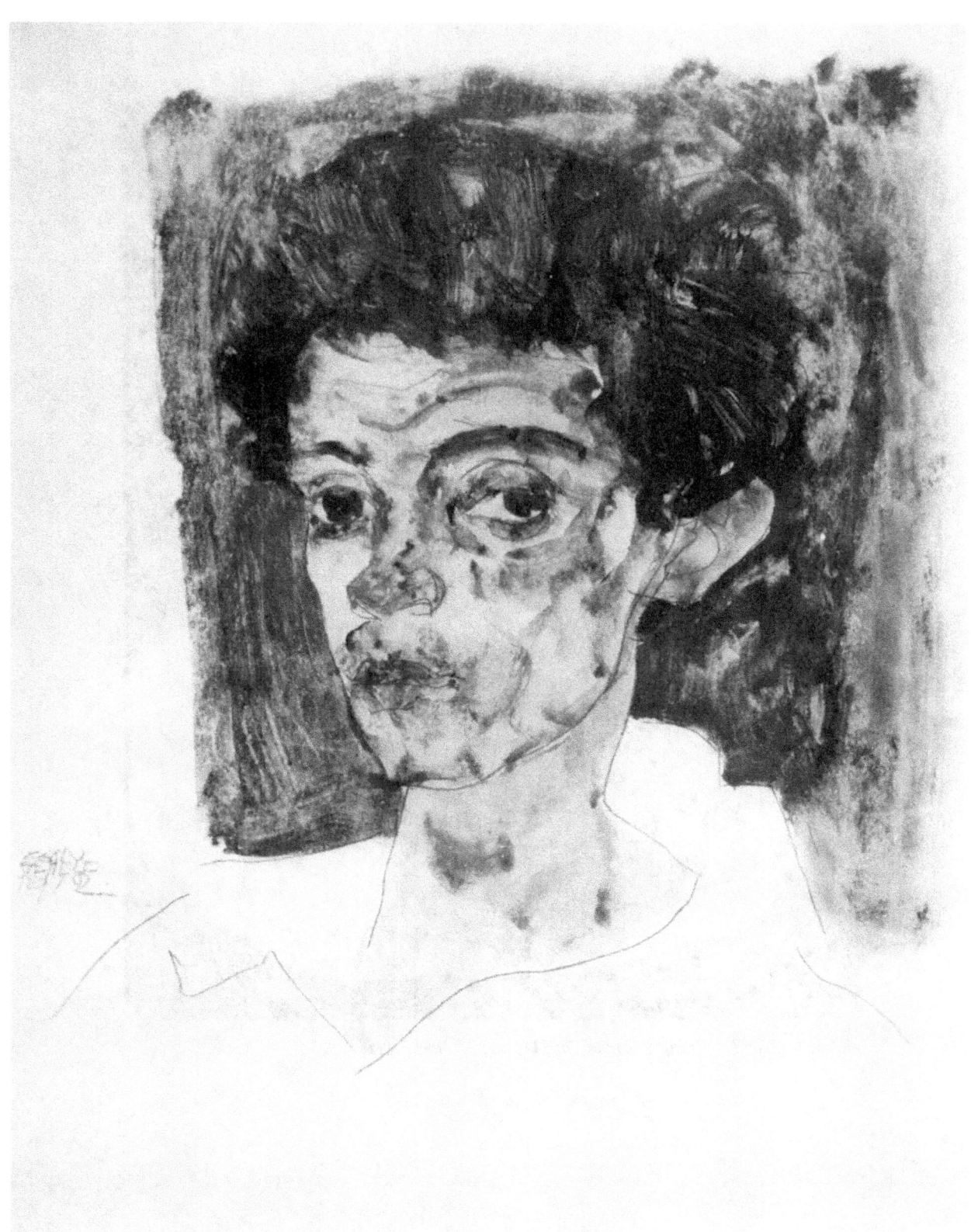

PL. 89. Schiele, *Study for Self-Portrait with Winter Cherry*, 1912, pencil and watercolor.

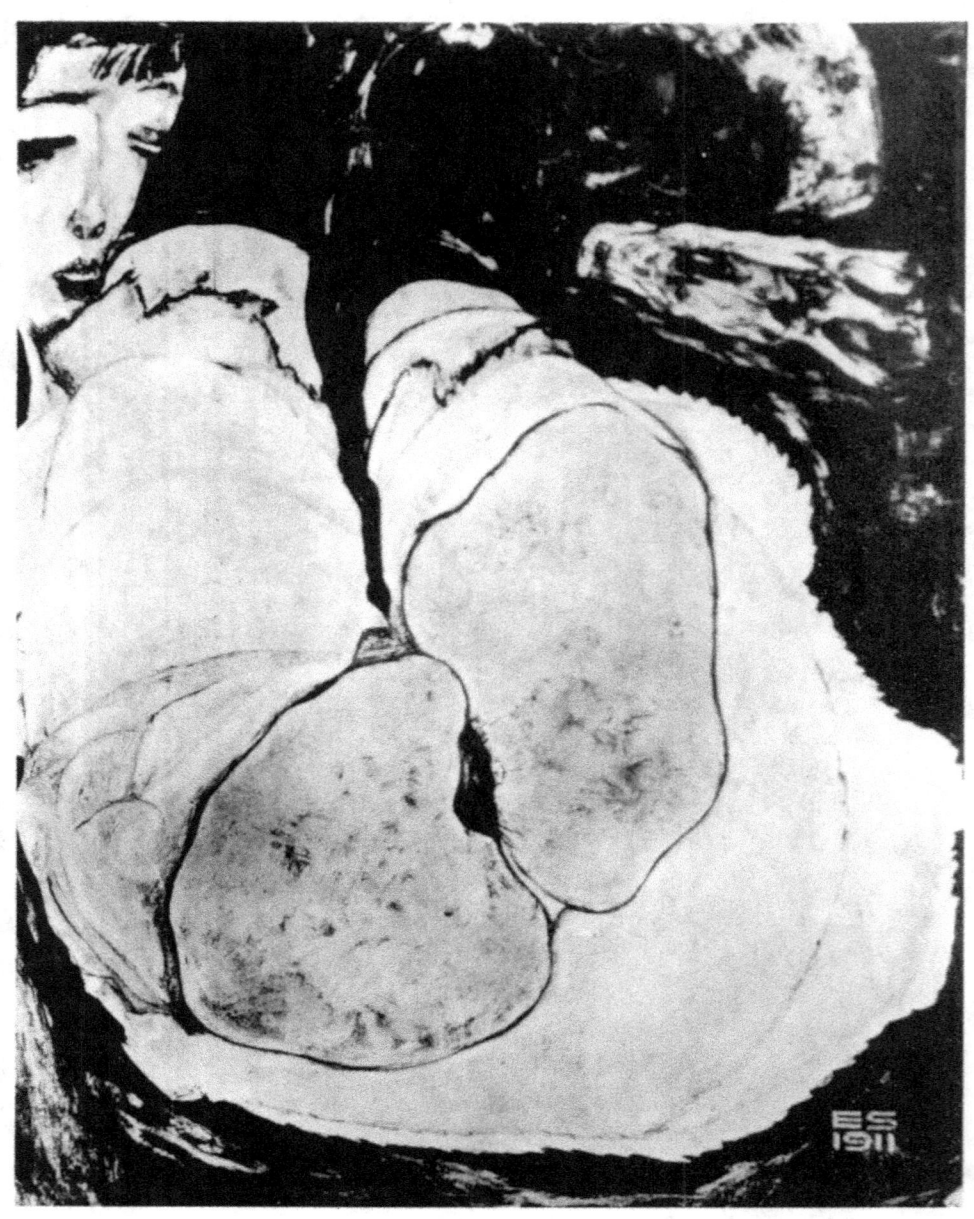

PL. 90. Schiele, *Reclining Woman with Upturned Skirt*, 1911, oil.

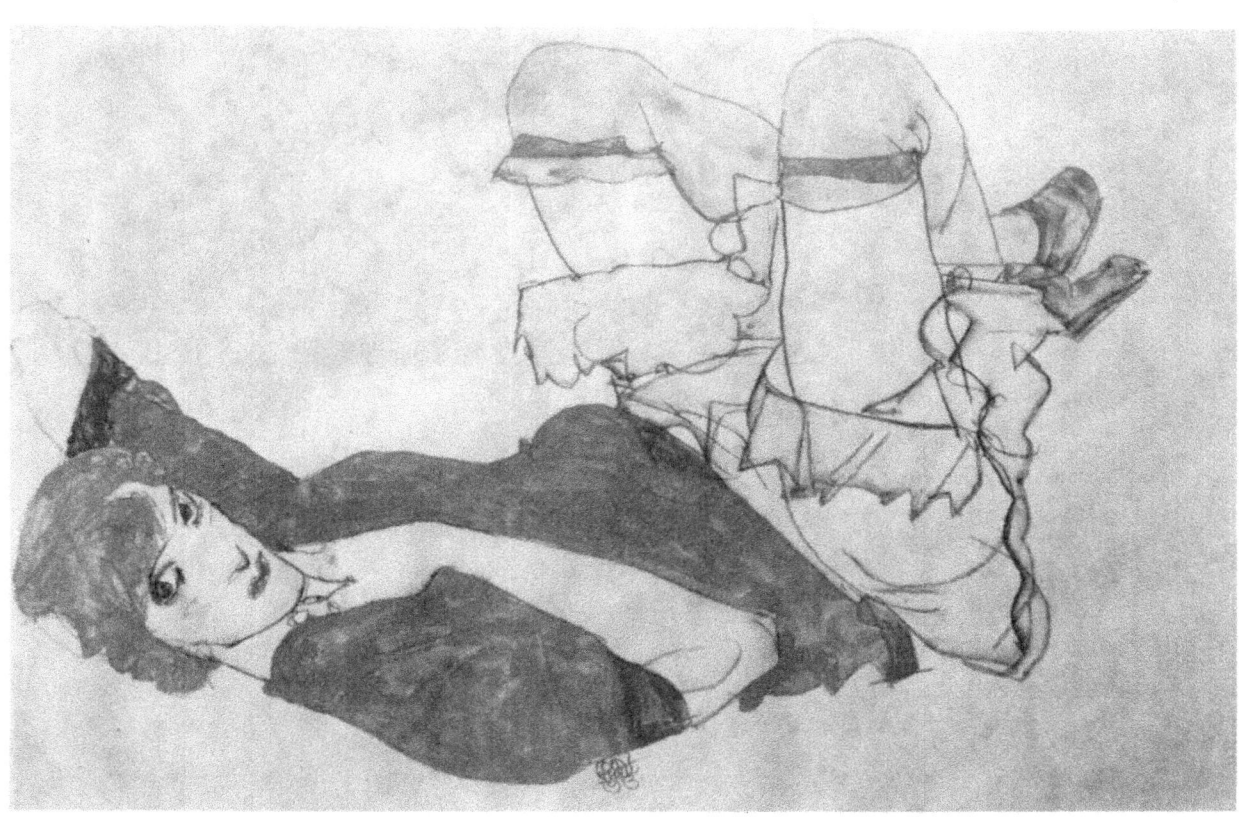

PL. 91. Schiele, *Wally in Red Blouse*, 1913, pencil, watercolor, and tempera.

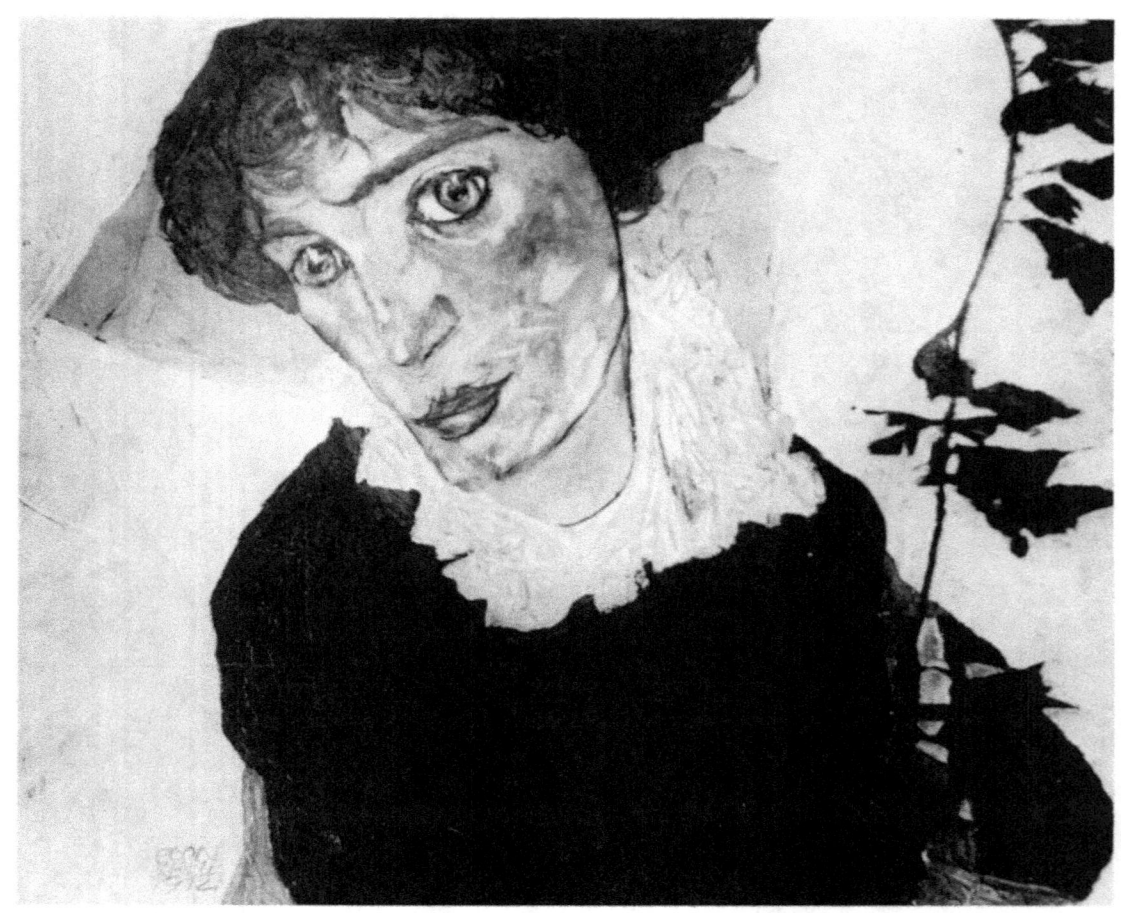

PL. 92. Schiele, *Wally*, 1912, oil.

PL. 93. Egon Schiele and Wally, 1913.

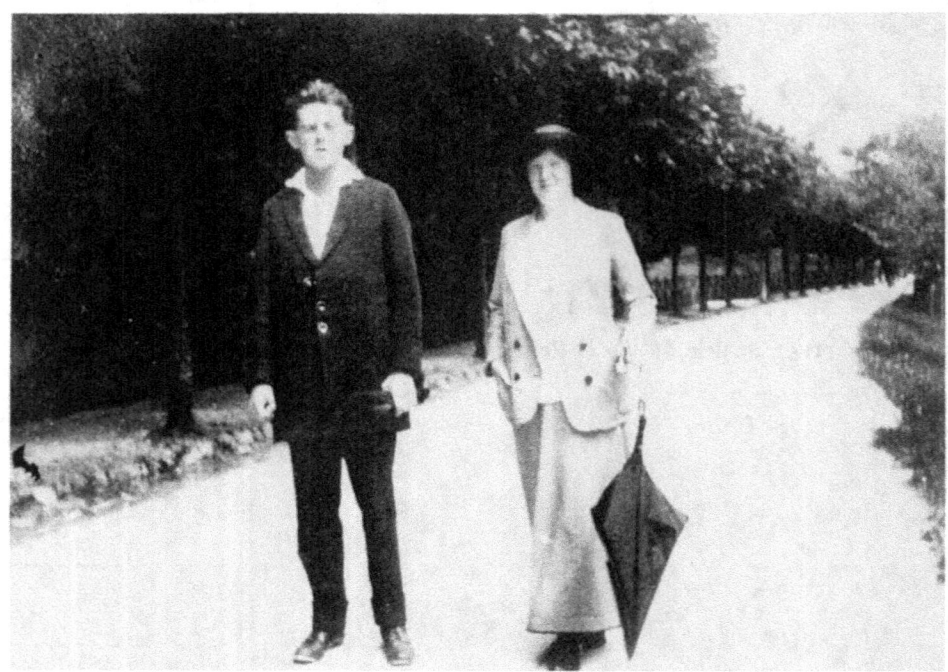

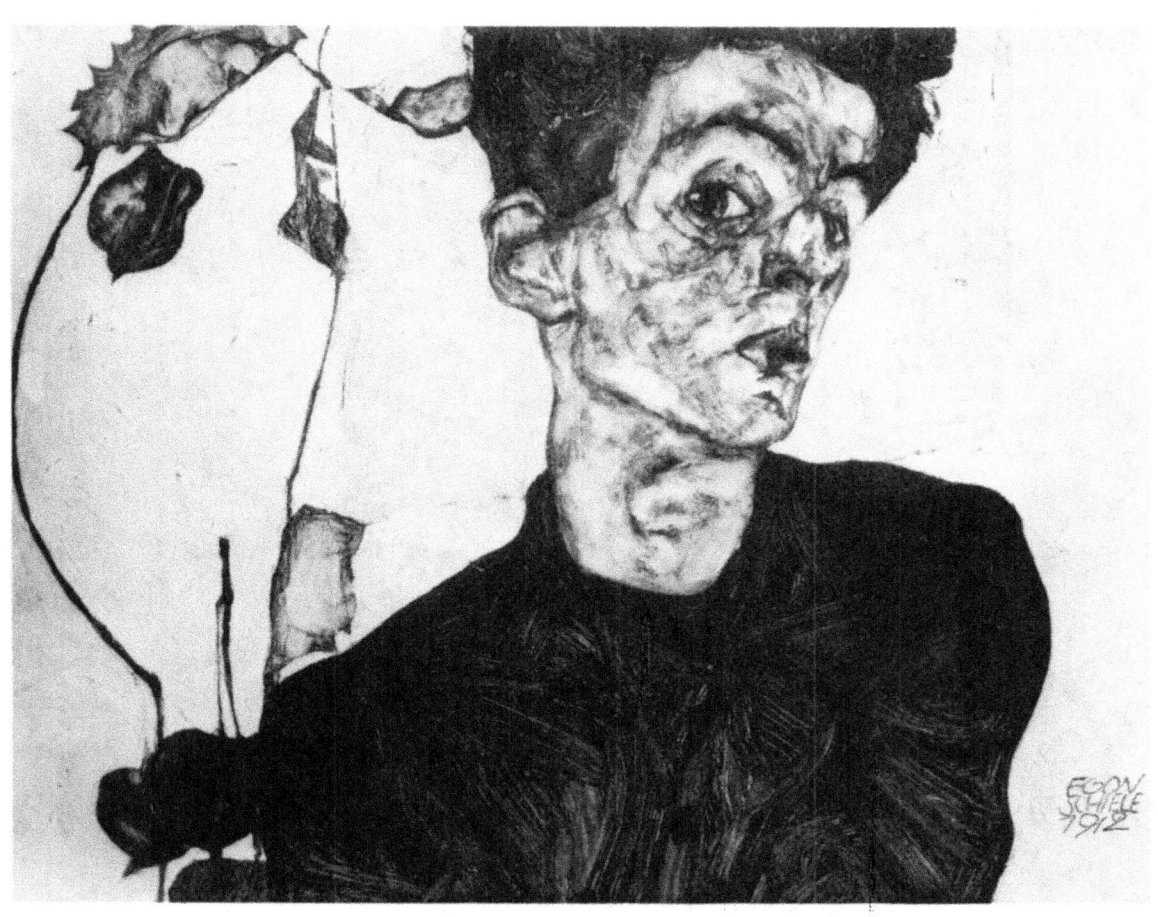

PL. 94. Schiele, *Self-Portrait with Winter Cherry*, 1912, oil.

PL. 95. Schiele, A.E.S.A. Sketchbook II, 1912, pencil, p. 11 *verso*.

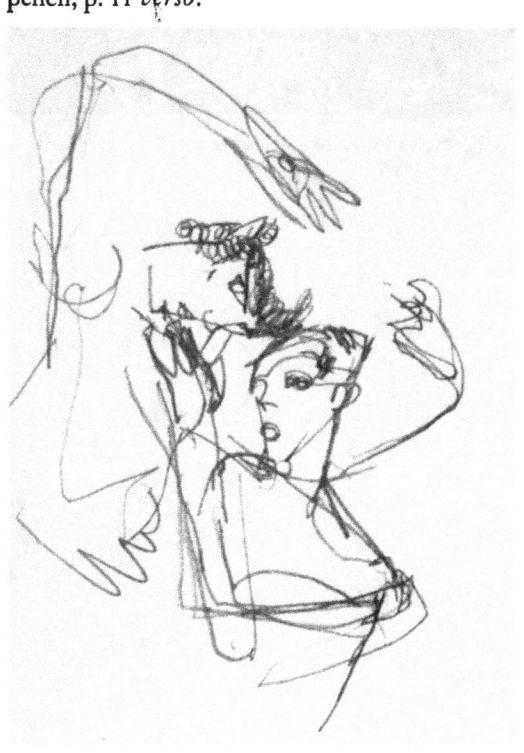

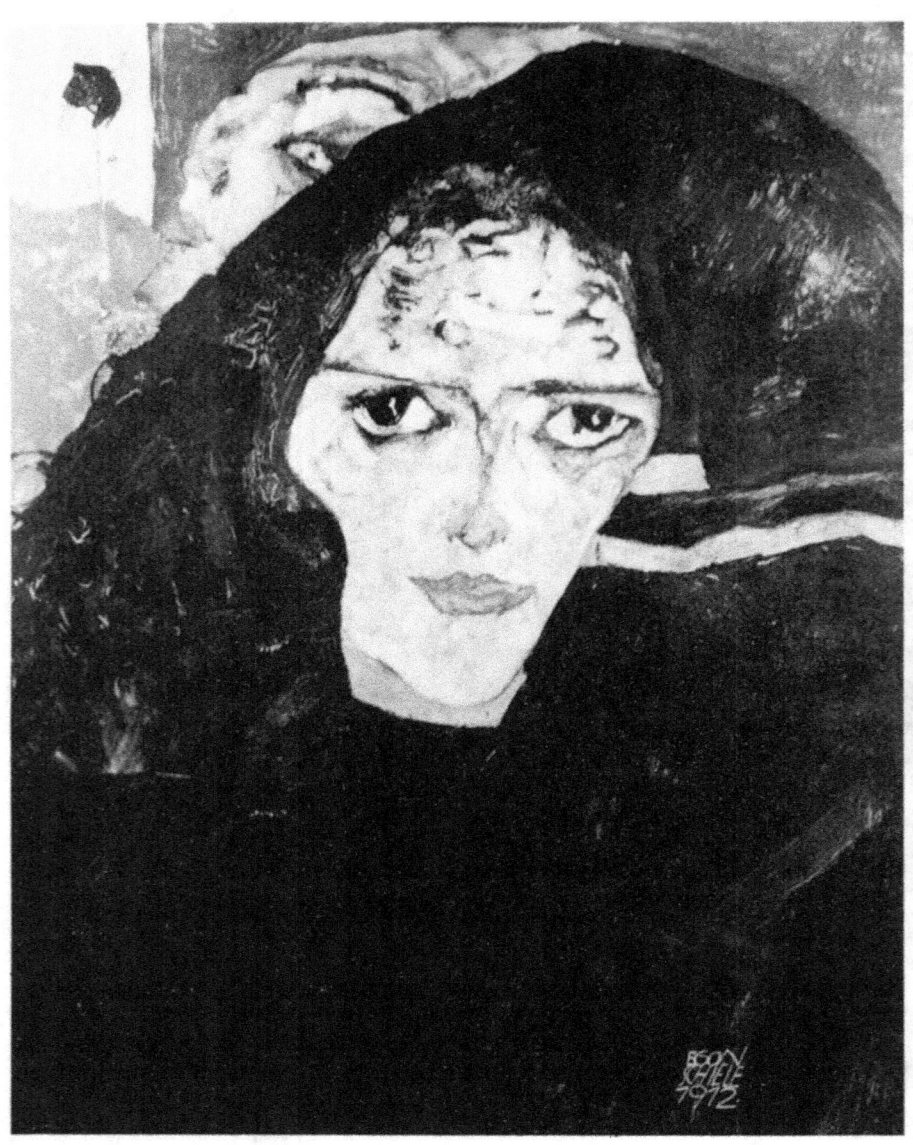

PL. 96. Schiele, *Woman in Mourning*, 1912, oil.

PL. 97. Schiele, *Study for the Portrait of Wally*, 1912, pencil.

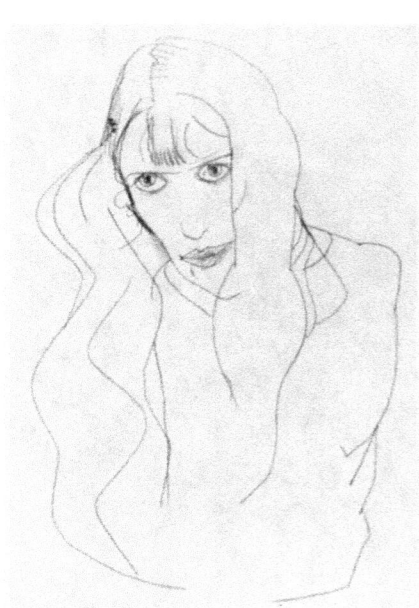

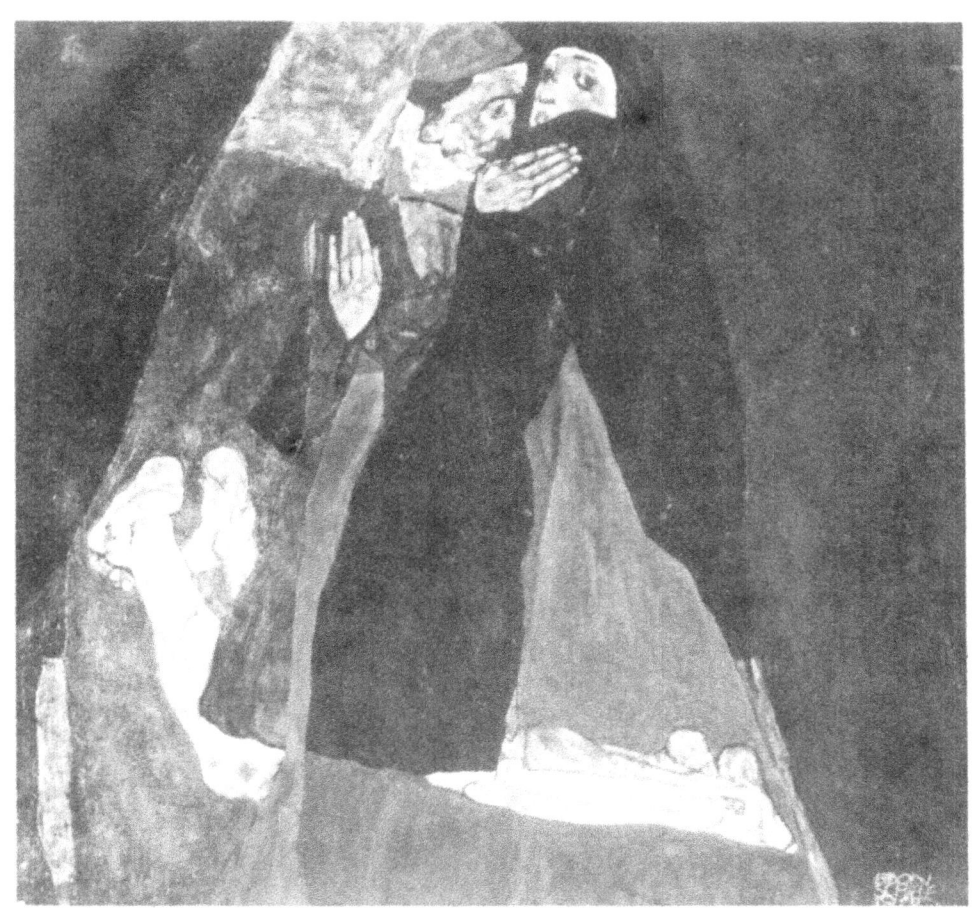

PL. 98. Schiele, *Cardinal and Nun*, 1912, oil.

PL. 99. Klimt, *The Kiss*, 1908, oil.

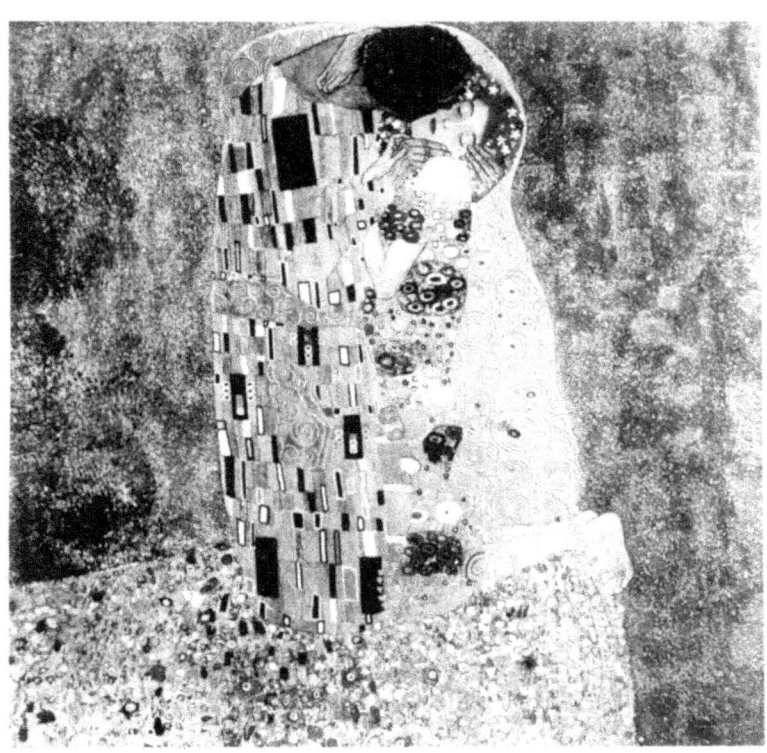

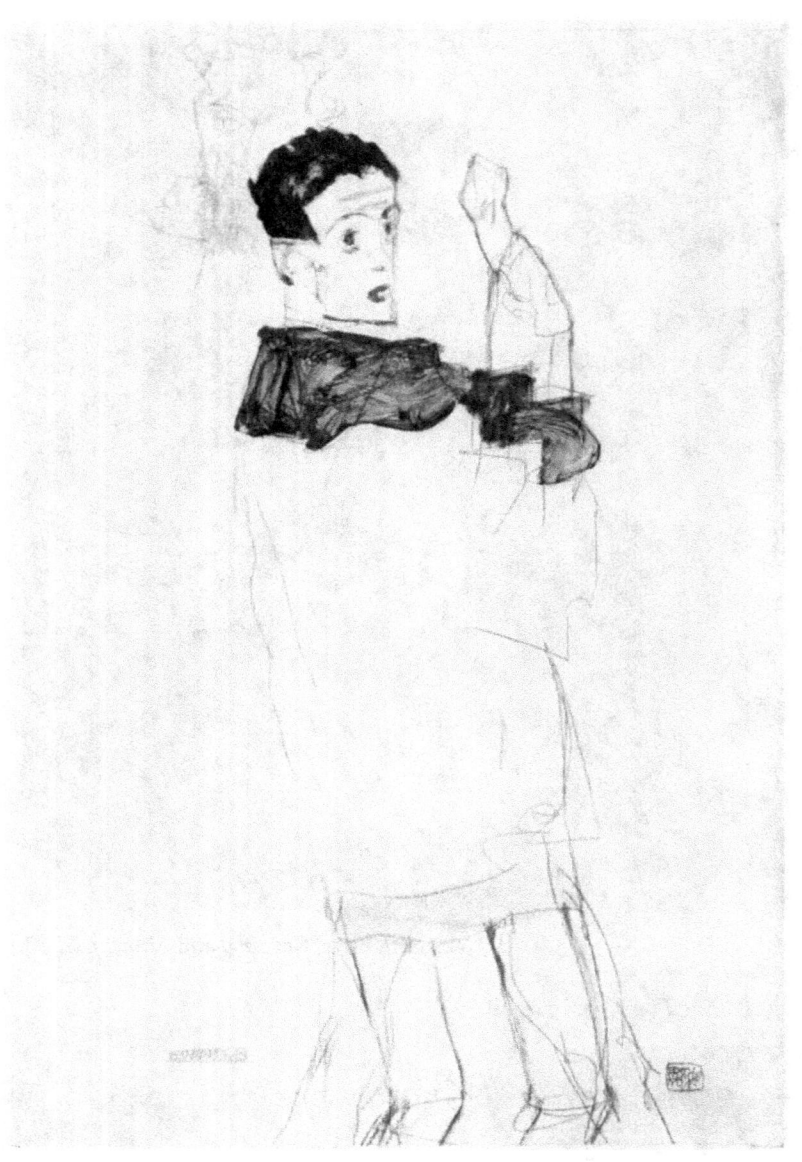

PL. 100a. Schiele, *Remembrance*, 1913, black crayon and watercolor.

PL. 100b. Schiele, *Self-Portrait from the Back with Hand to Cheek*, 1913, black crayon.

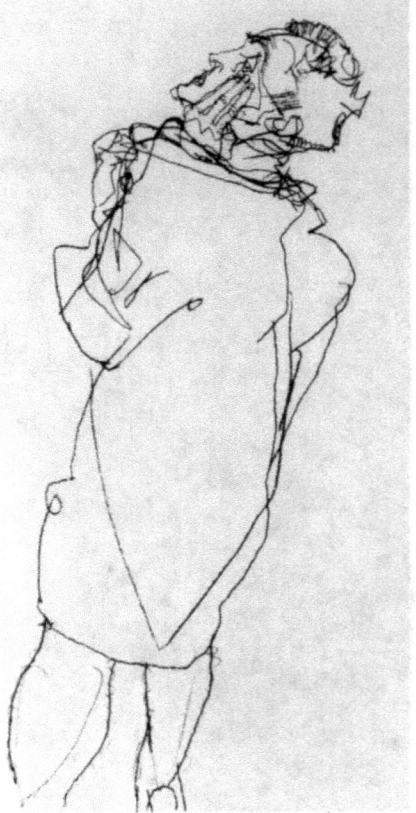

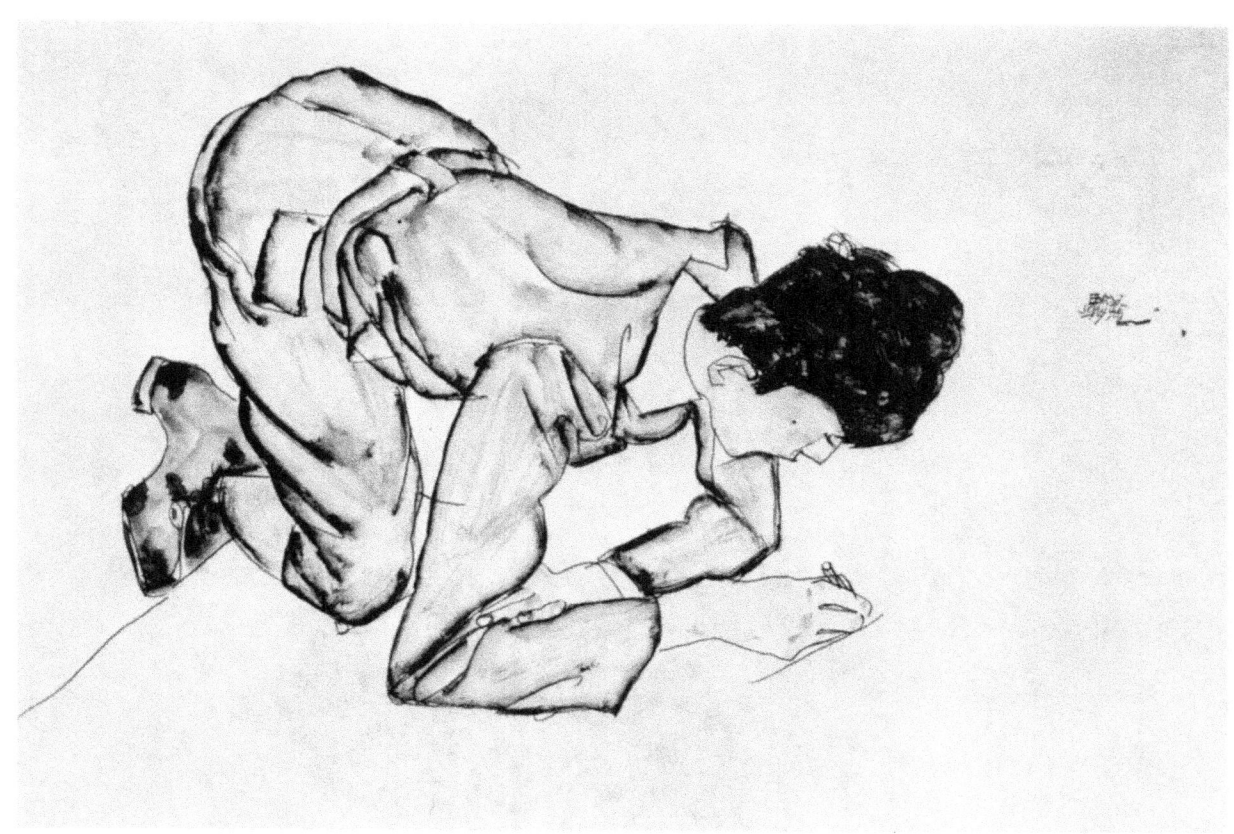

PL. 101. Schiele, *Eric Lederer Drawing on the Floor*, 1912, pencil and watercolor.

PL. 102. Erich Lederer, *Portrait of Egon Schiele*, 1913, charcoal and colored crayon.

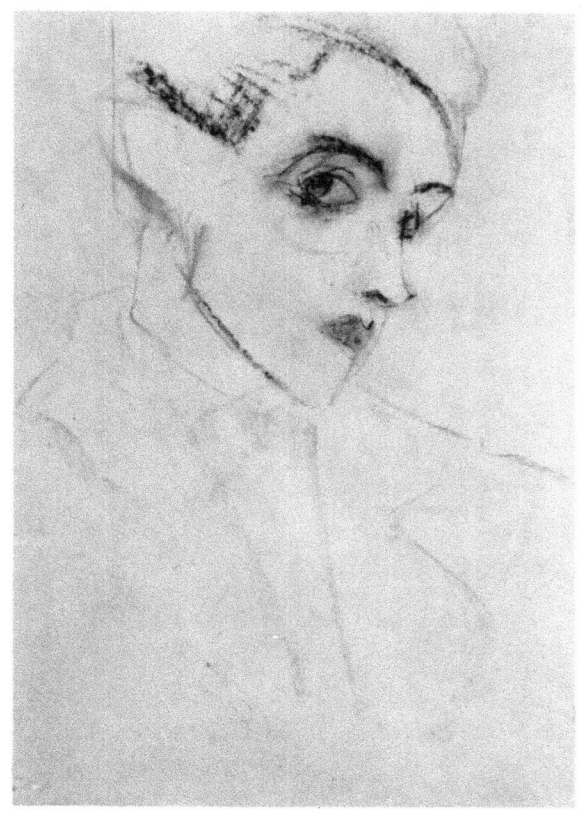

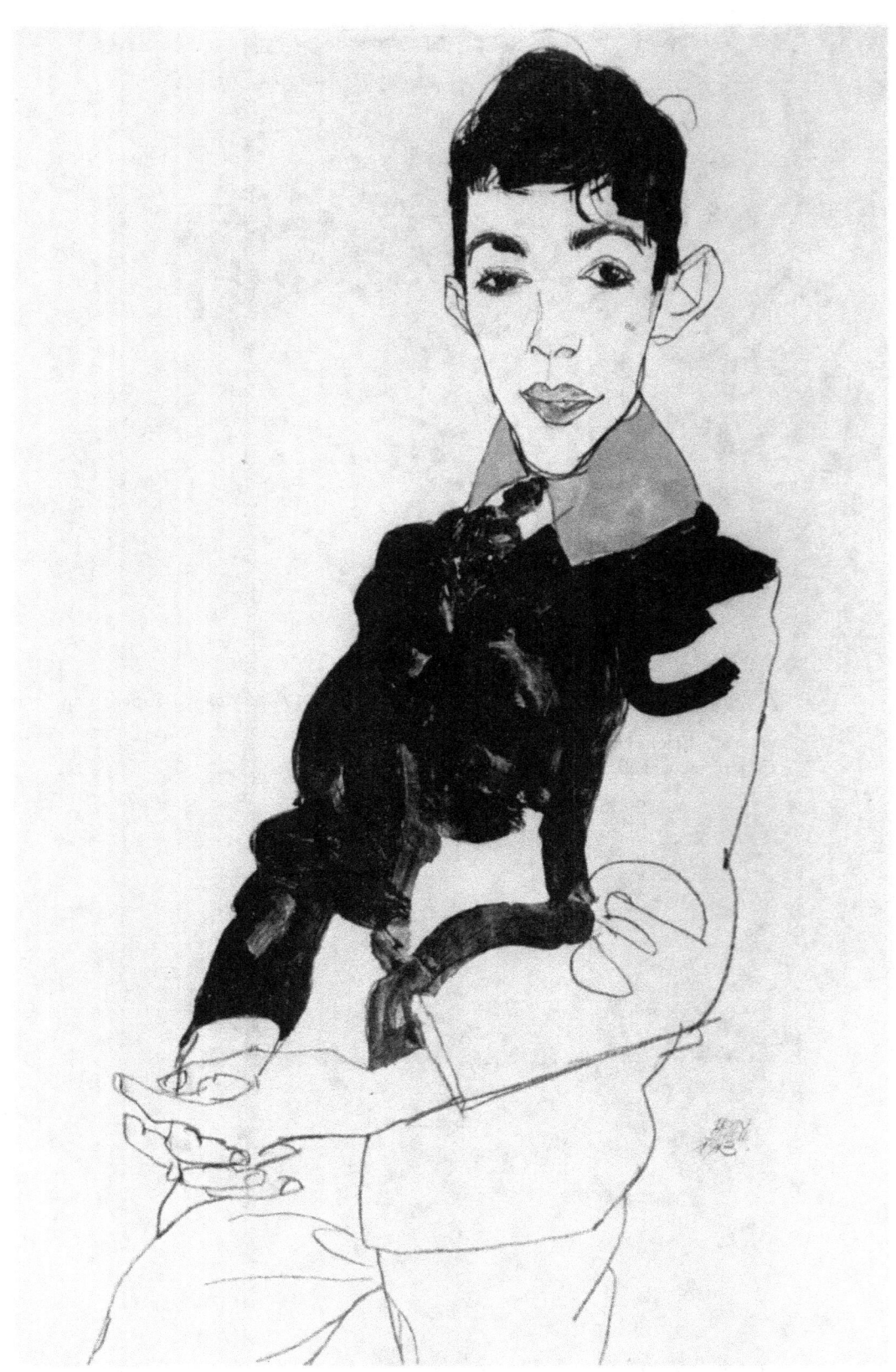

PL. 103. Schiele, *Erich Lederer with Hands Folded*, 1913, pencil and watercolor.

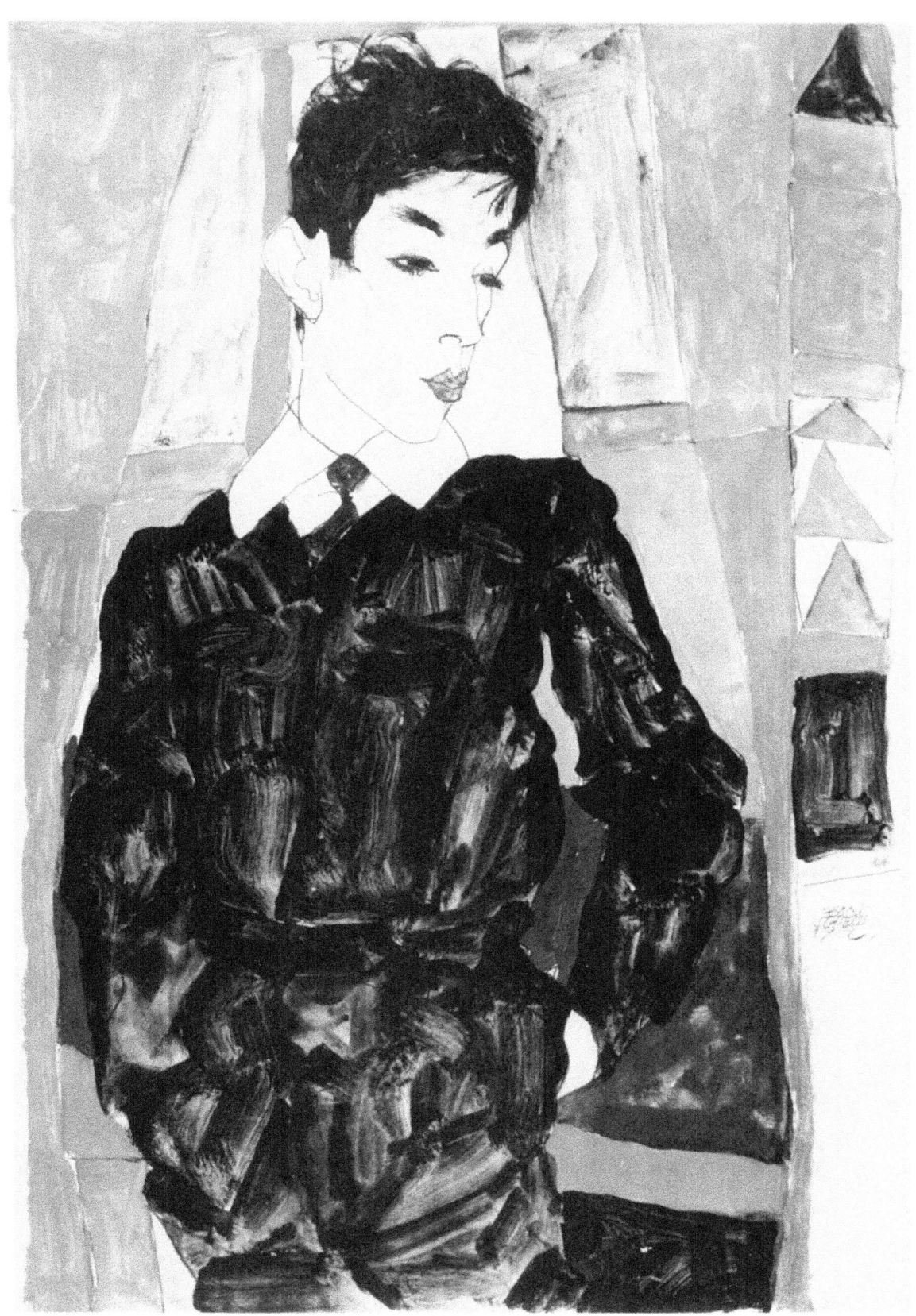

PL. 104. Schiele, *Erich Lederer Standing with His Hands in His Pockets*, 1912, pencil and watercolor.

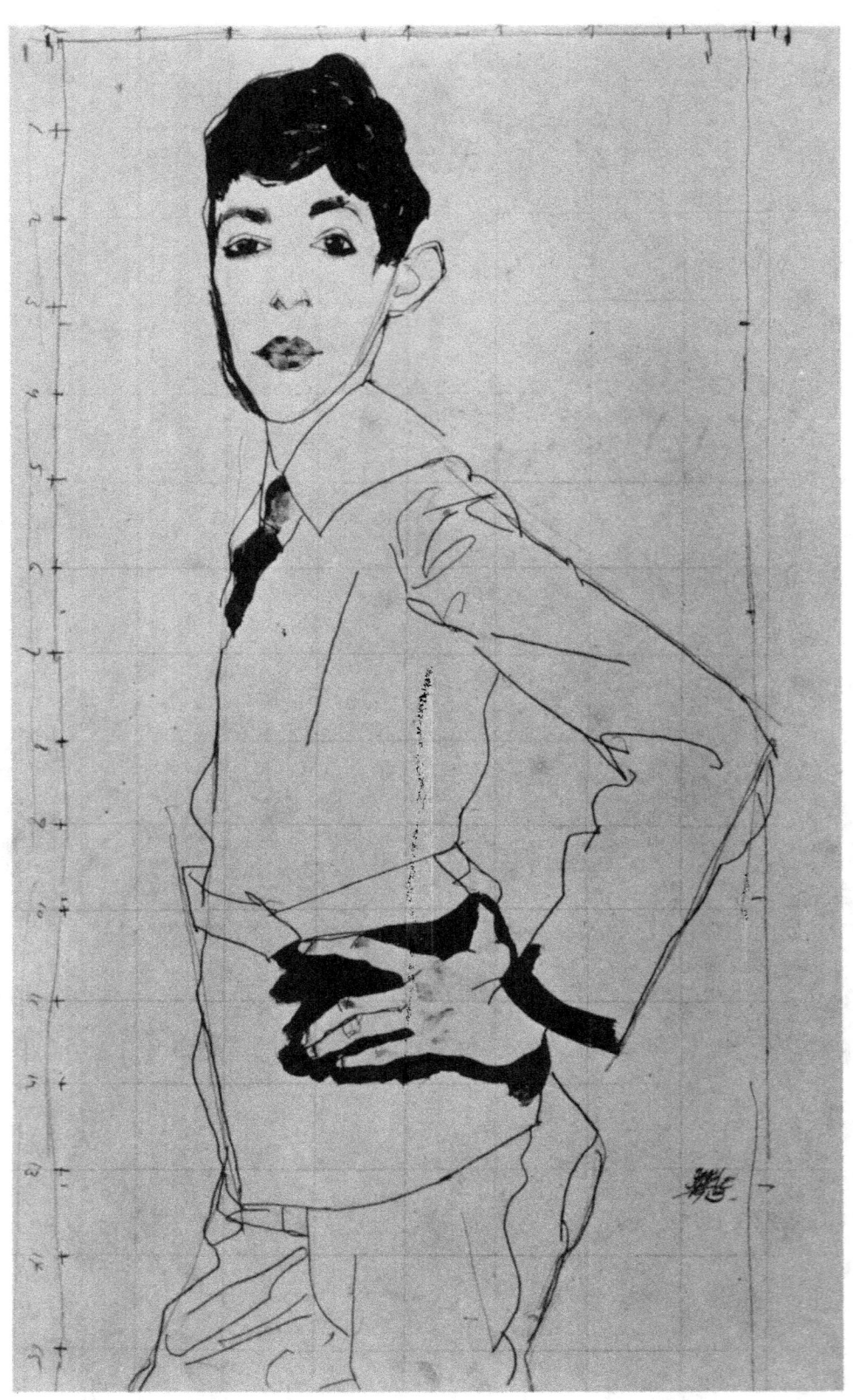

PL. 105. Schiele, *Erich Lederer Standing with Hand on Hip*, 1913, pencil and watercolor.

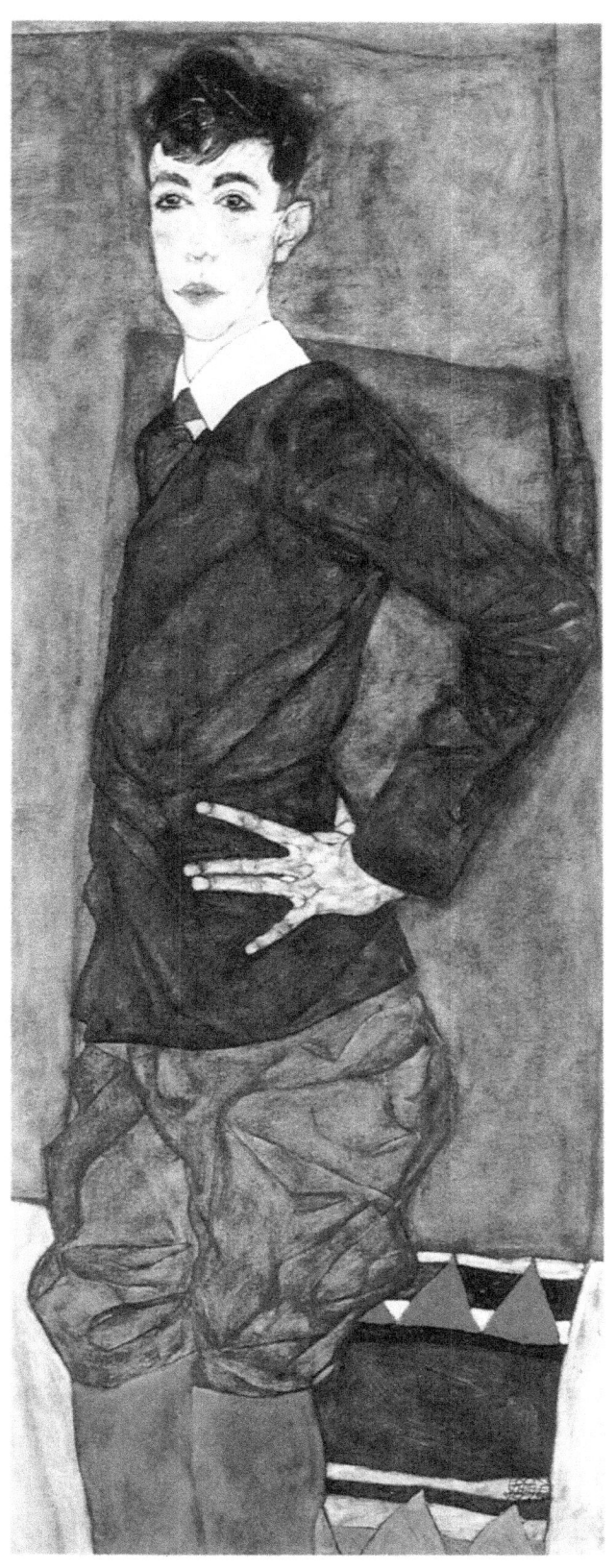

PL. 106. Schiele, *Portrait of Erich Lederer*, 1912–1913, oil.

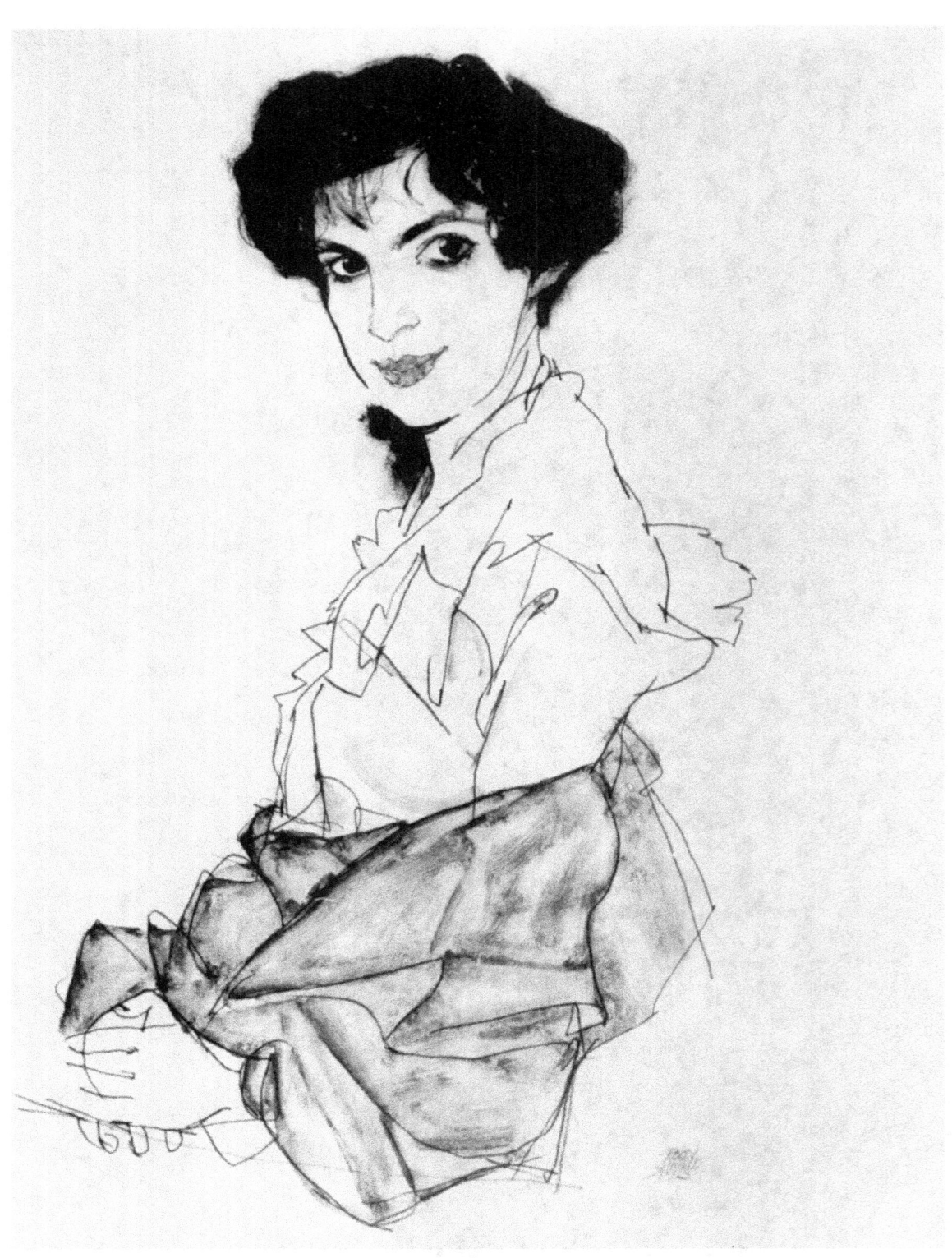

PL. 107a. Schiele, *Elisabeth Lederer Seated with Hands Folded*, 1913, pencil and watercolor.

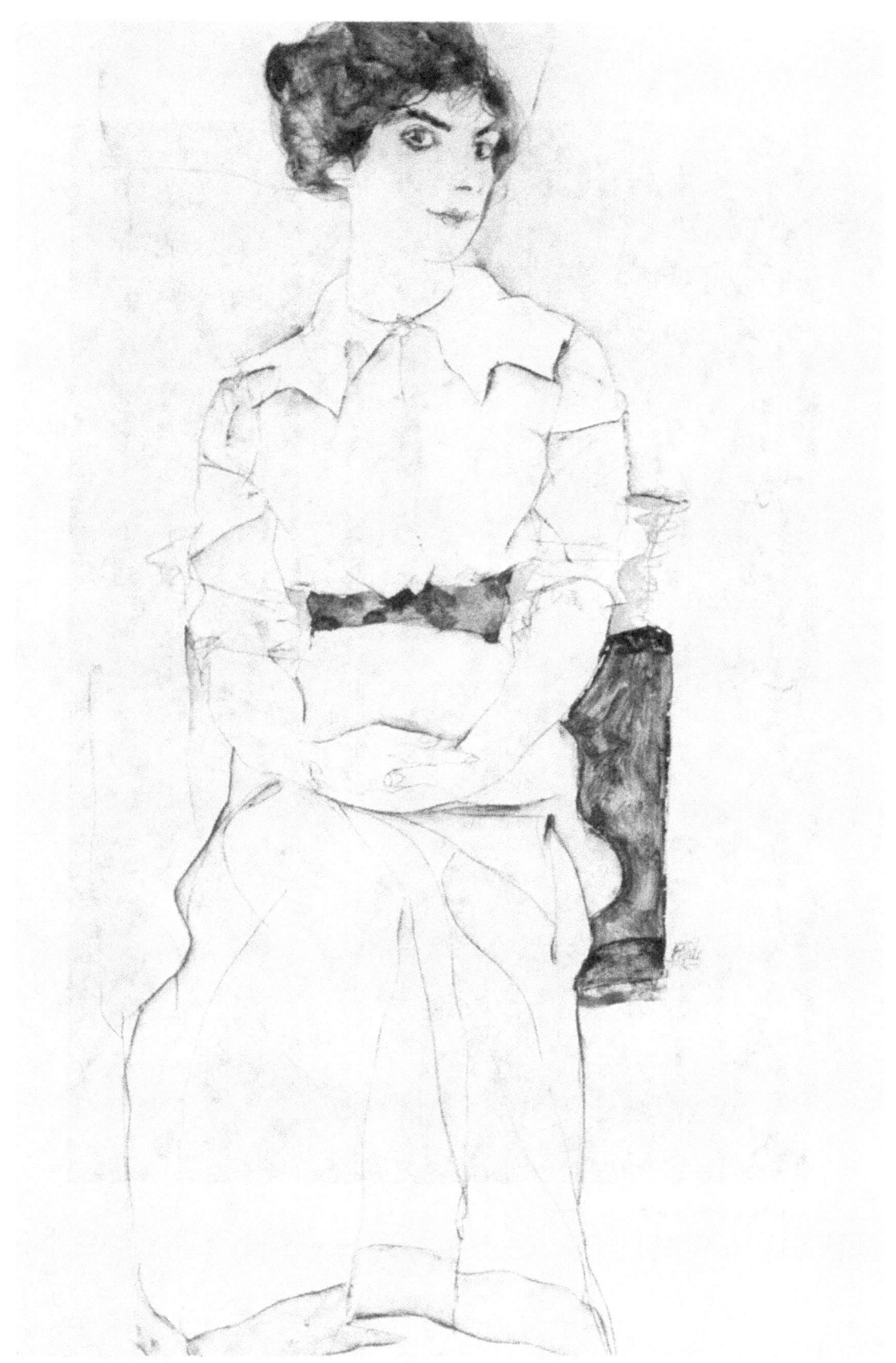

PL. 107b. Schiele, *Elisabeth Lederer Seated, Full-Figure*, 1913, watercolor.

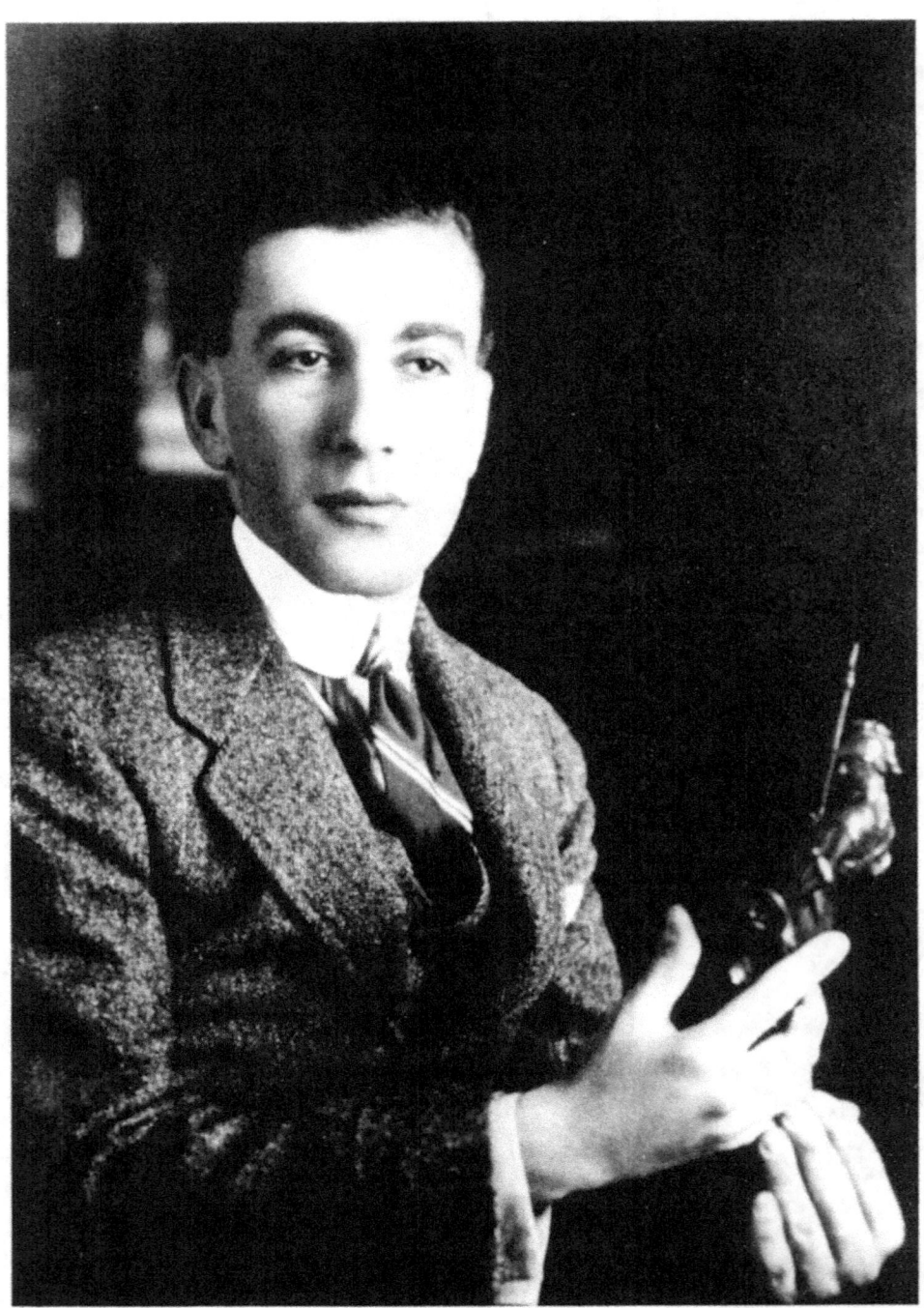

PL. 108a. Erich Lederer, ca. 1915.

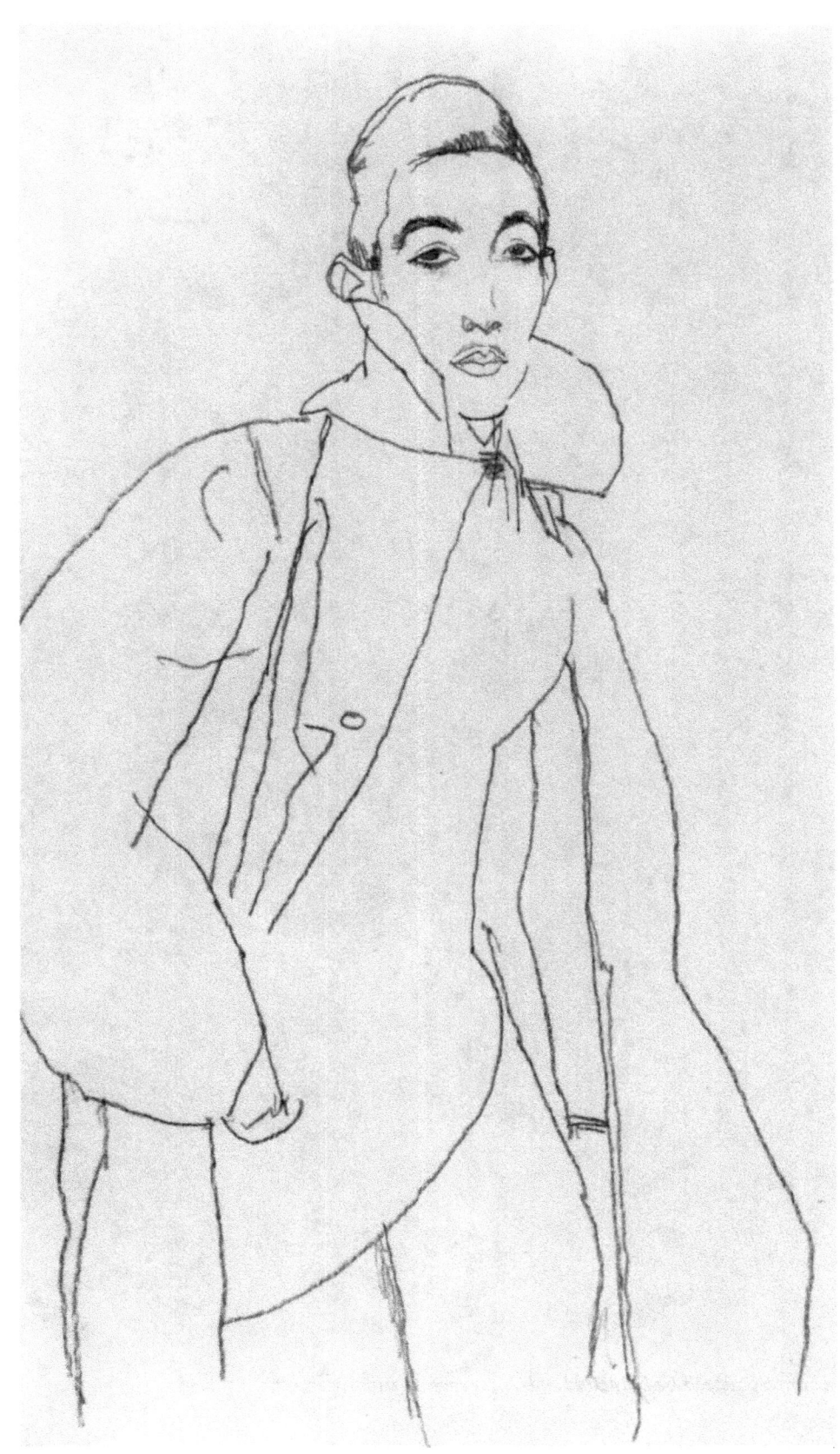

PL. 108b. Schiele, *Study of Erich Lederer in a Coat, ca.* 1915, black chalk.

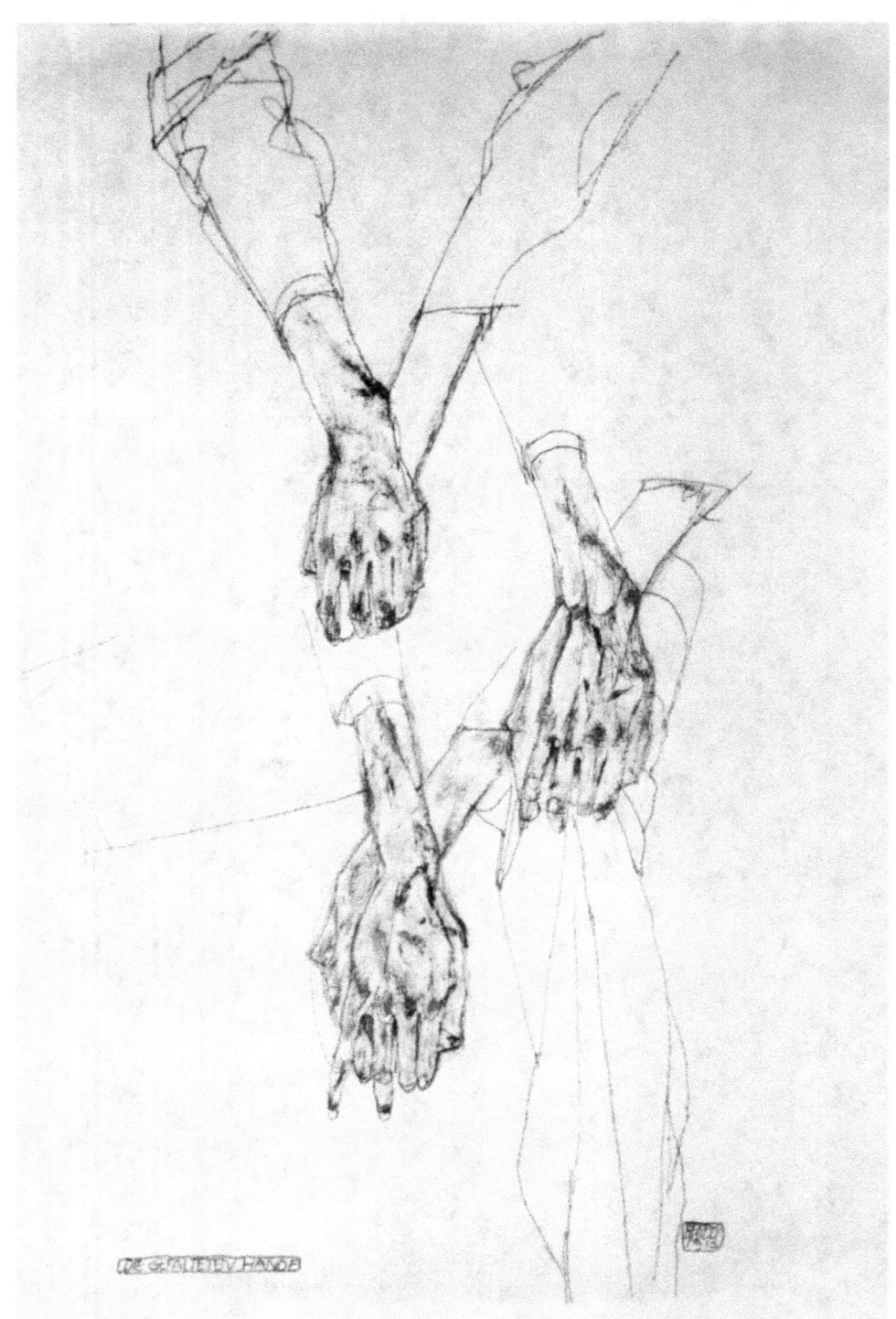

PL. 109. Schiele, *The Folded Hands*, 1913, pencil and watercolor.

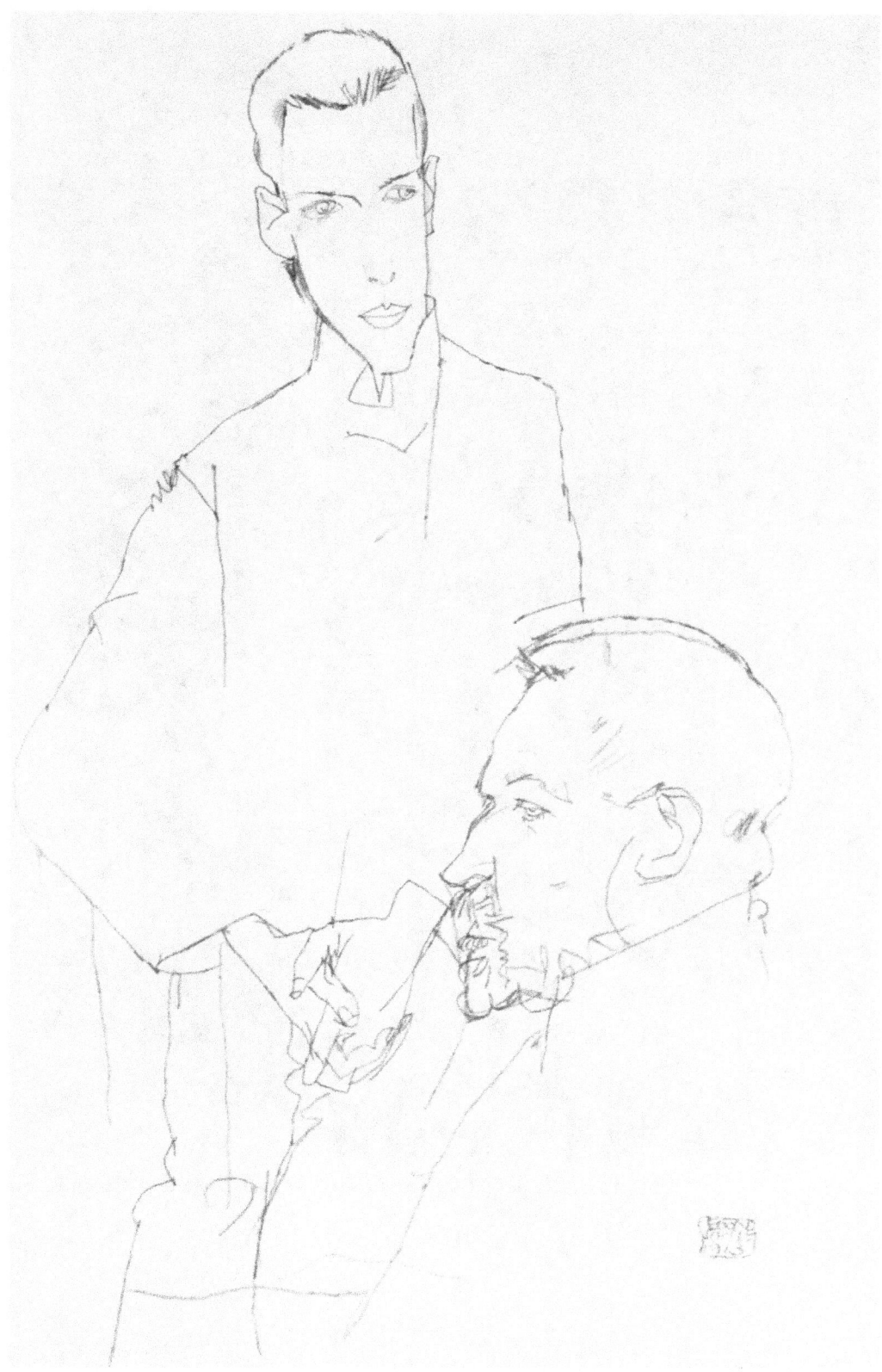

PL. 111a. Schiele, *Benesch Double Portrait Study, Heinrich Seated and Otto Standing*, 1913, pencil.

PL. 110. →

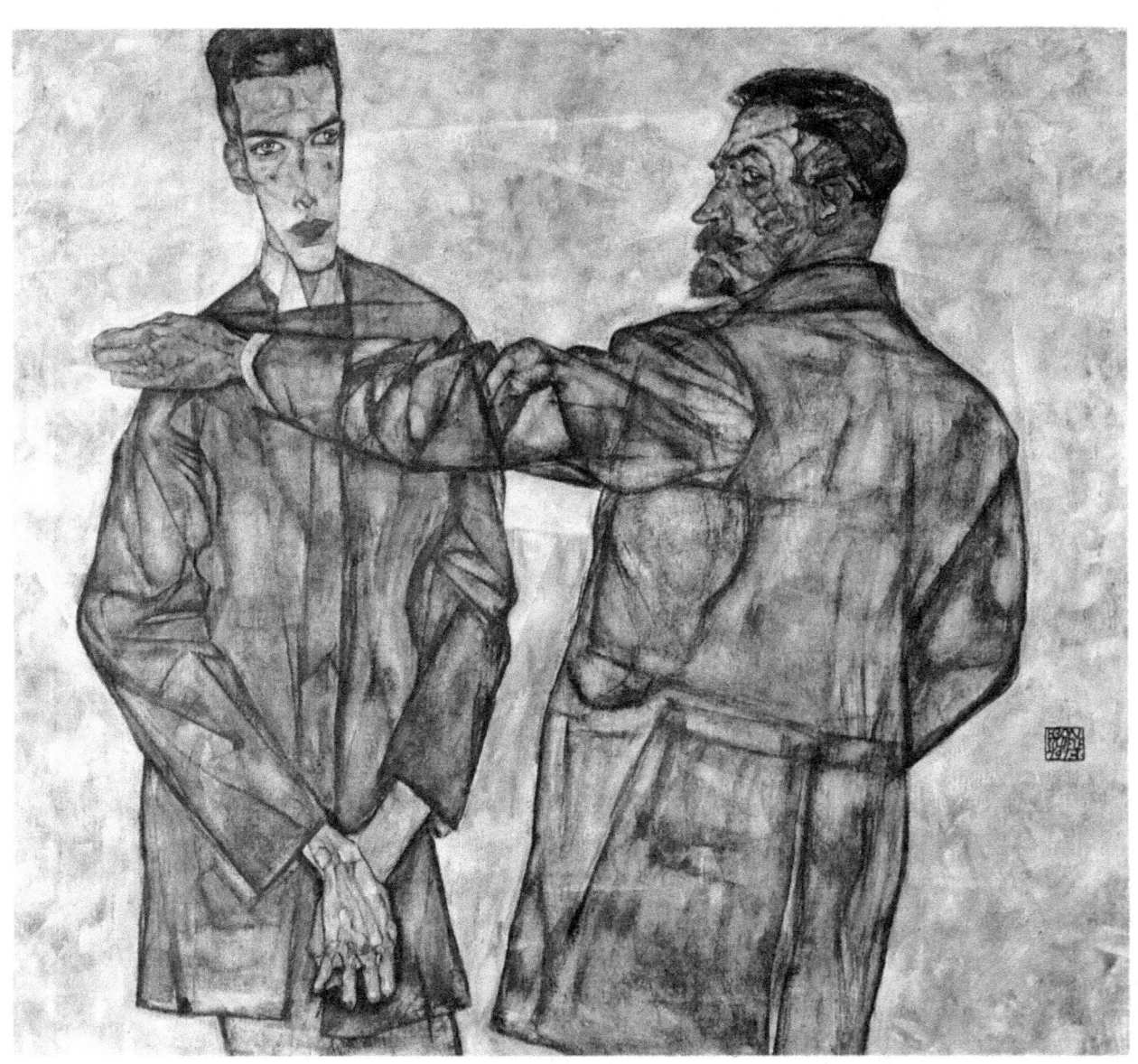

PL. 110. Schiele, *Double Portrait of Heinrich and Otto Benesch*, 1913, oil.

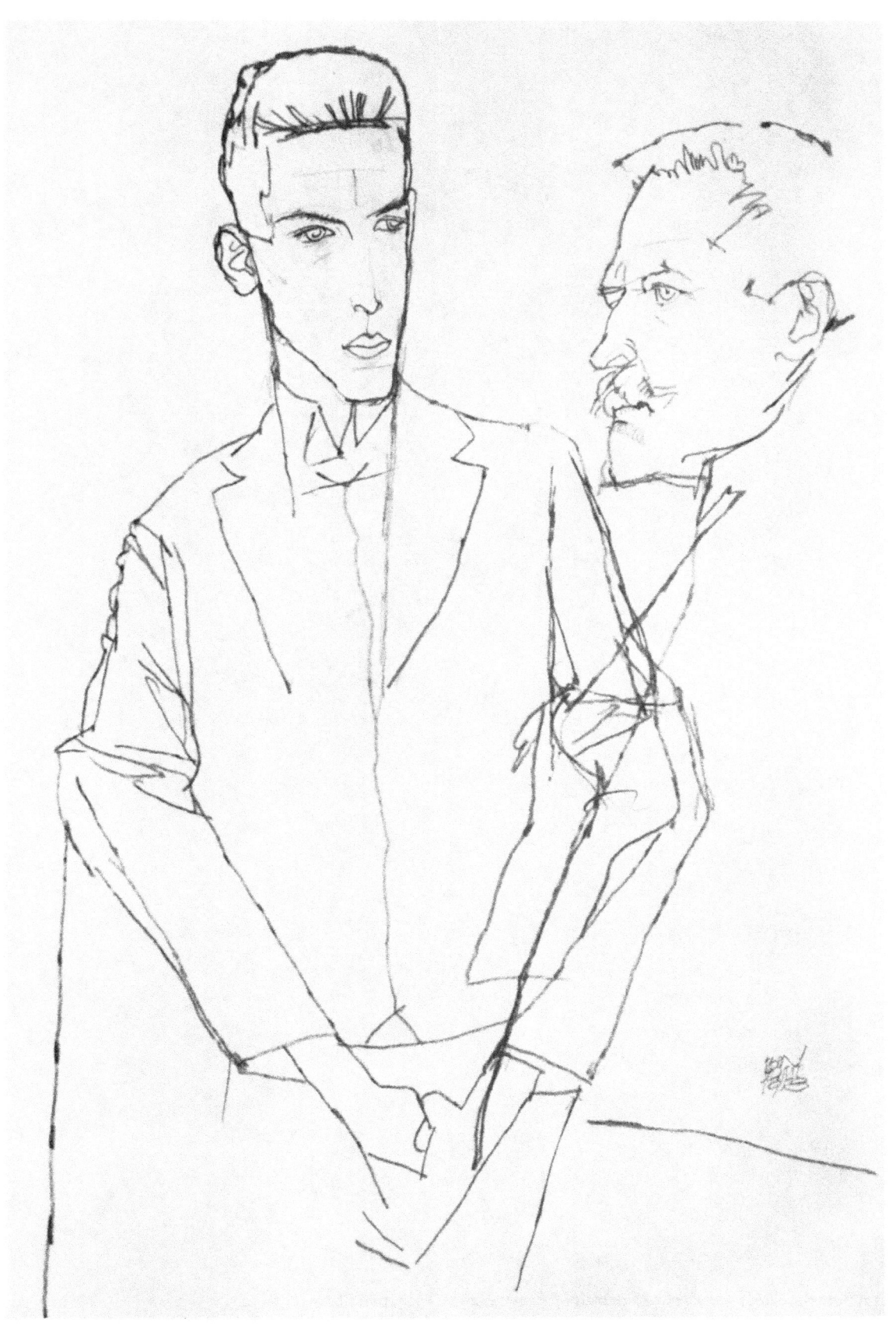

PL. 111b. Schiele, *Benesch Double Portrait Study, Heinrich Standing Right and Otto Standing Left*, 1913, pencil.

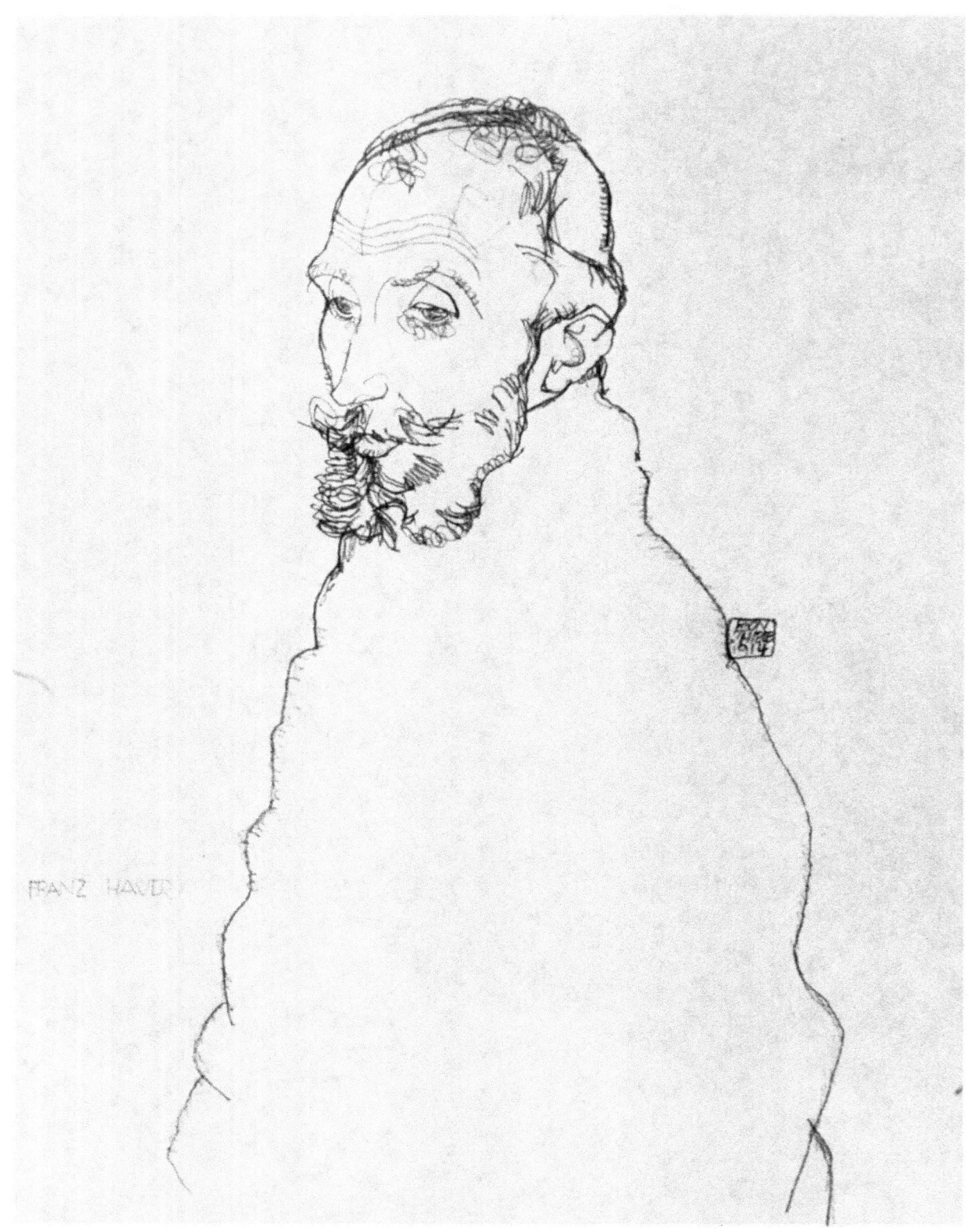

PL. 112. Schiele, *Study for Etched Portrait of Franz Hauer*, 1914, pencil.

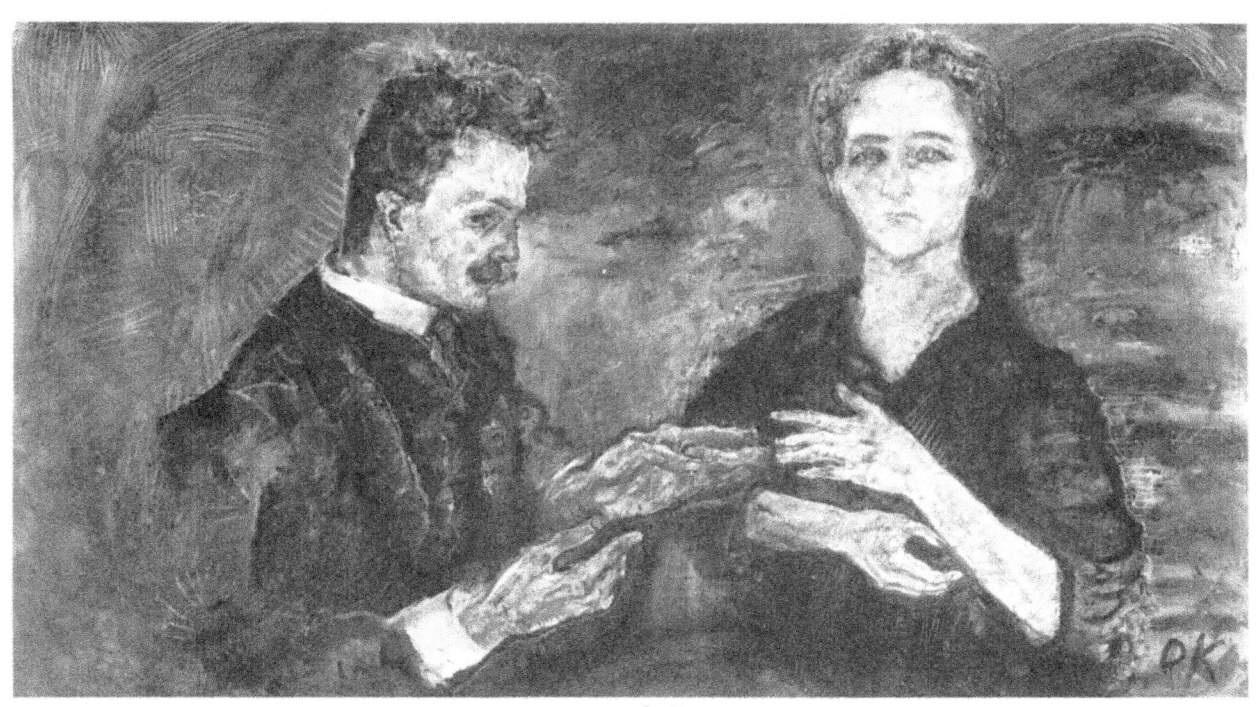

PL. 113. Kokoschka, *Double Portrait of Hans and Erika Tietze*, 1909, oil.

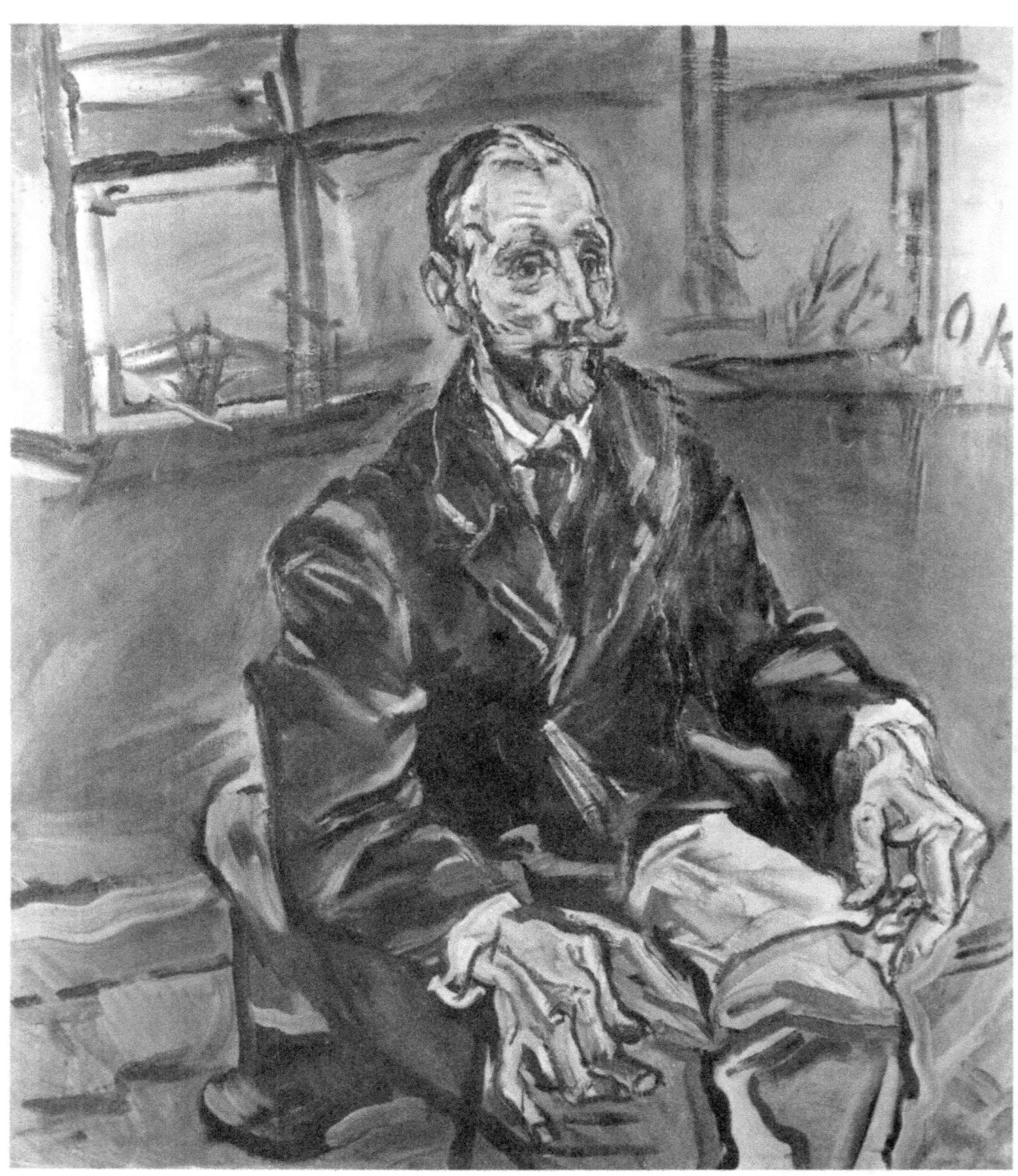

PL. 114. Kokoschka, *Portrait of Franz Hauer*, 1914, oil.

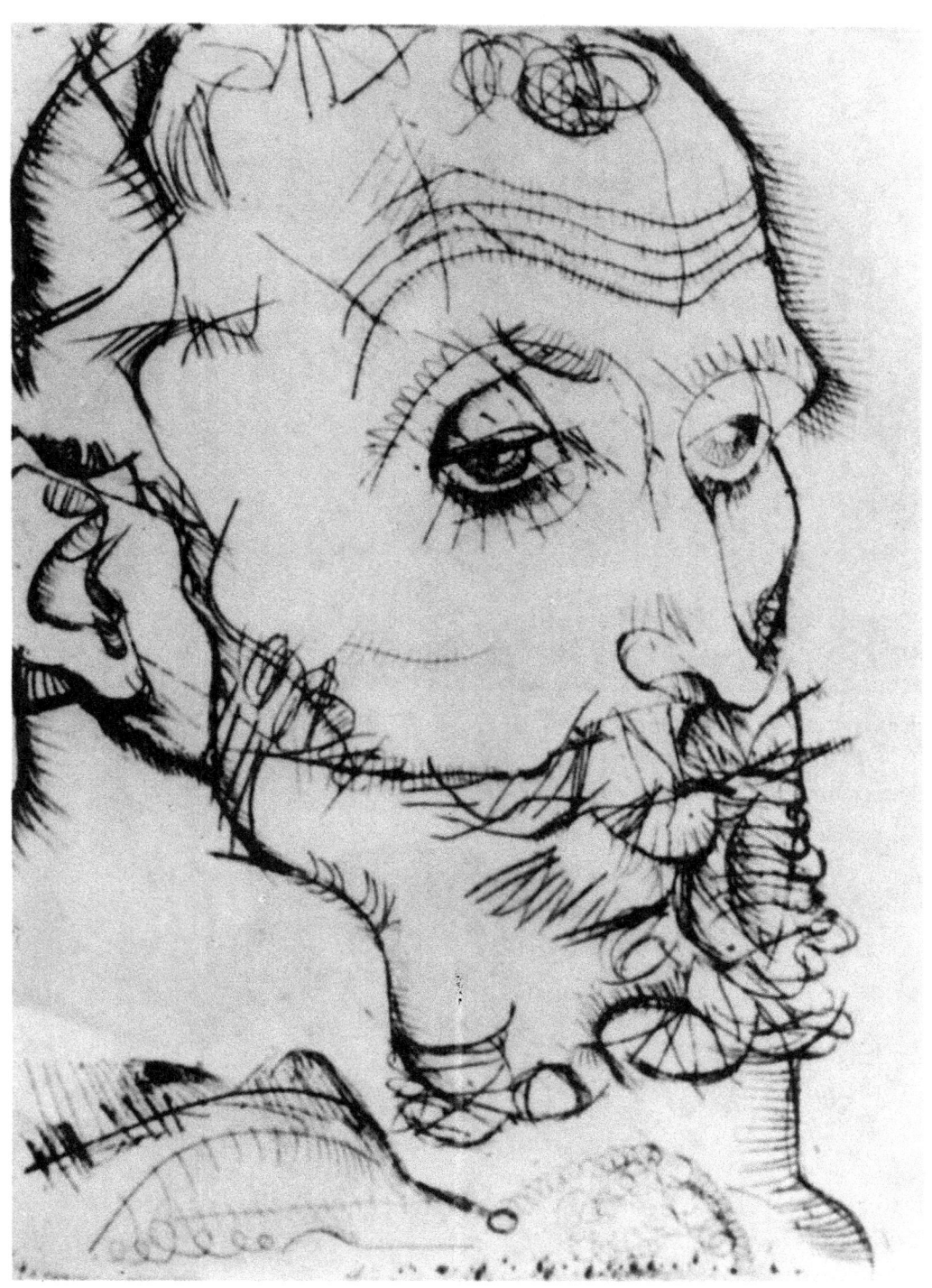

PL. 115. Schiele, *Portrait of Franz Hauer*, 1914, etching.

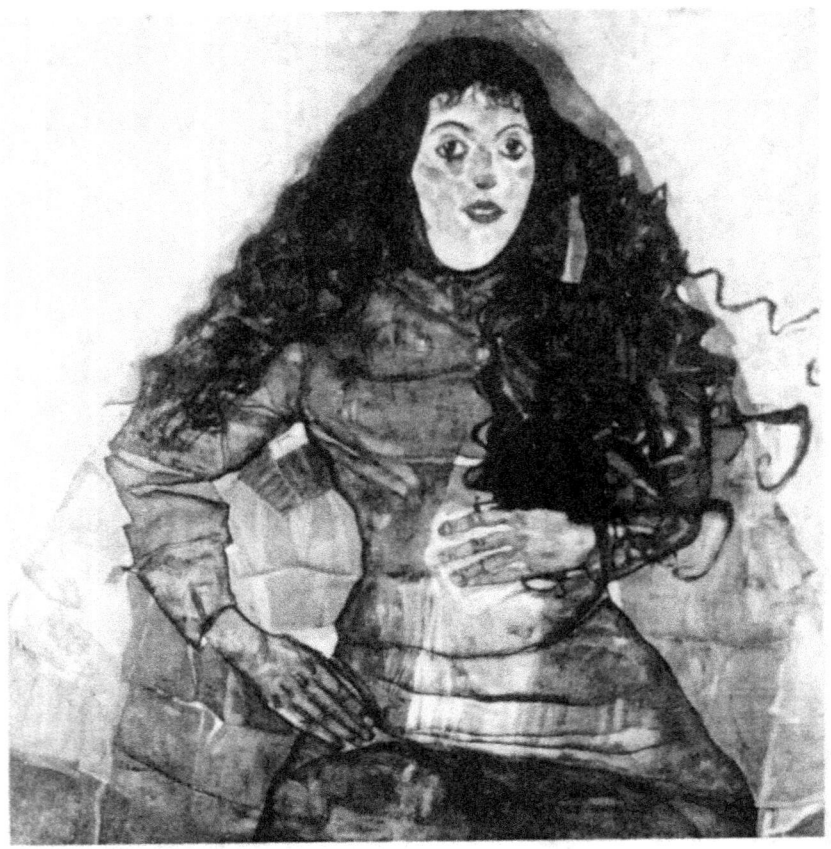

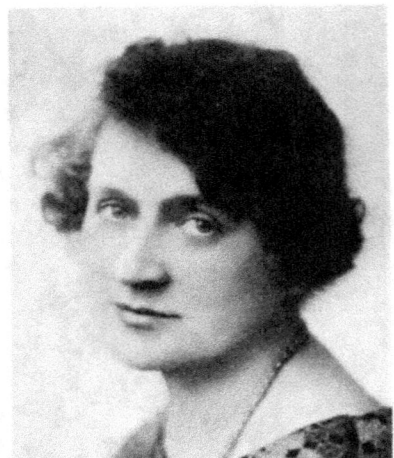

PL. 116. Schiele, *Portrait of Trude Engel*, 1911, oil.

PL. 117. Ida Roessler, *ca.* 112.

PL. 118. Schiele, *Portrait of Ida Roessler*, 1912, oil.

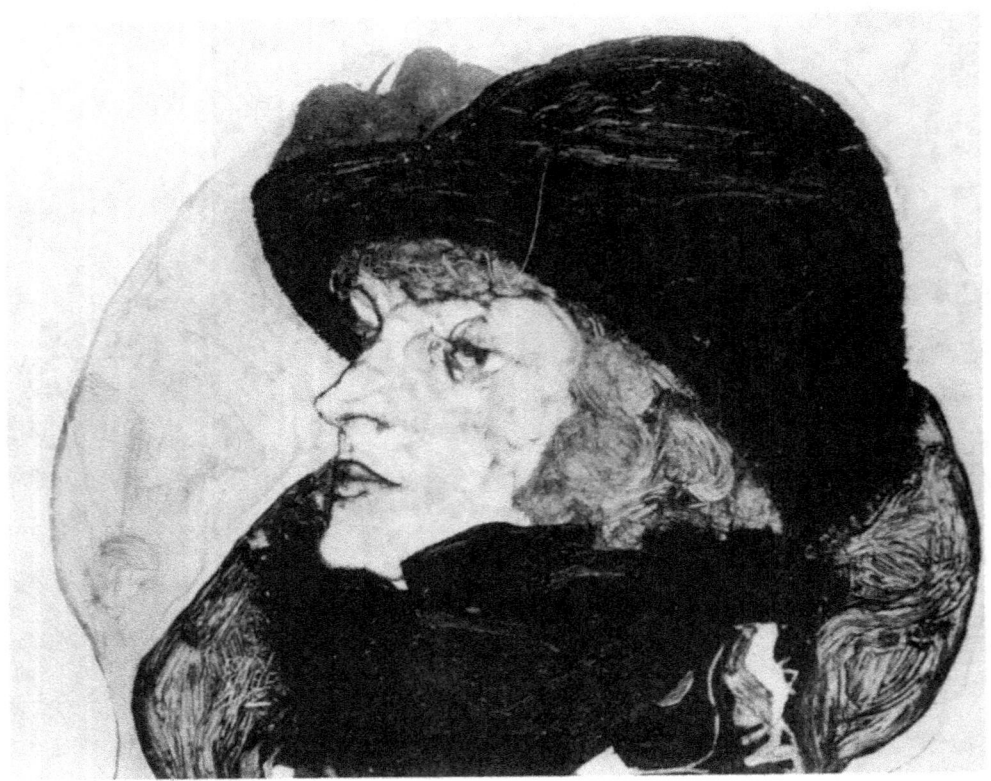

PL. 119. Friederike Beer, 1916.

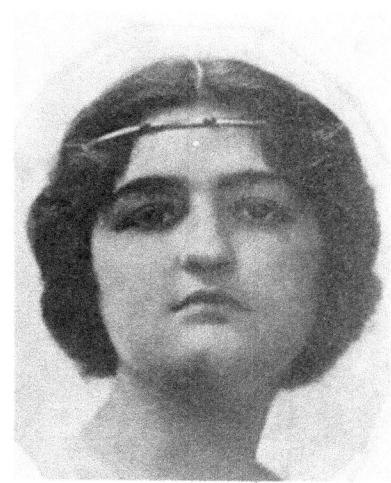

PL. 120. Schiele, *Study for the Portrait of Friederike Beer*, 1914, pencil.

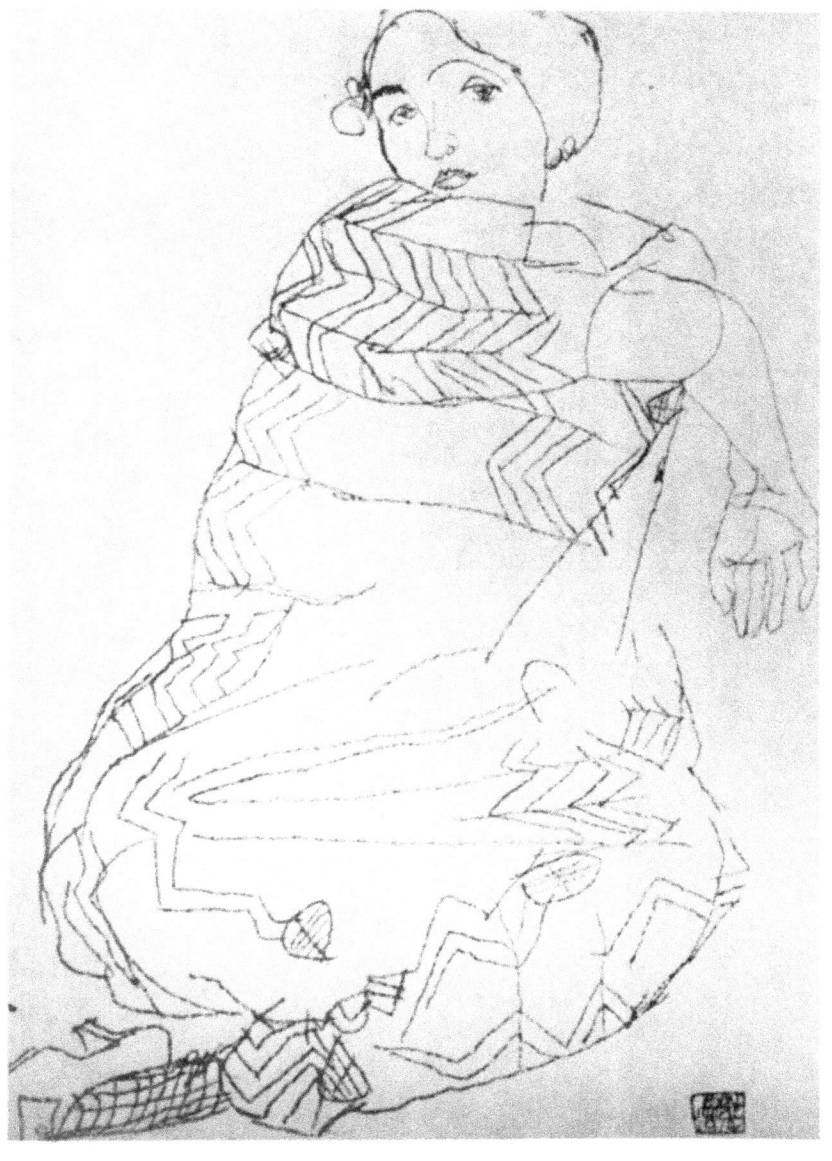

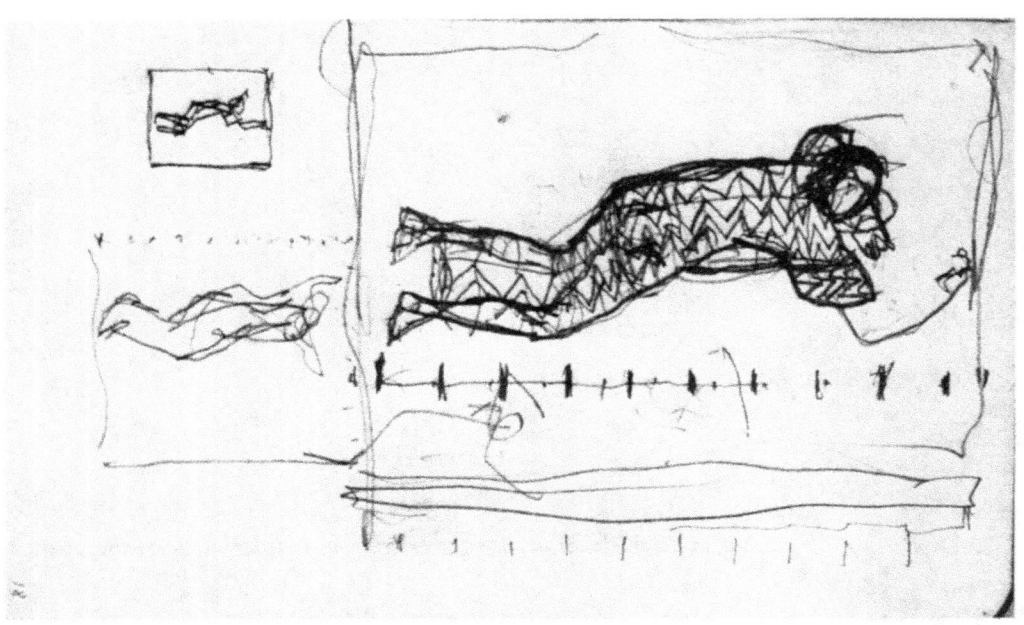

PL. 121. Schiele, A.E.S.A. Sketchbook V, 1914, pencil, p. 18 *recto*.

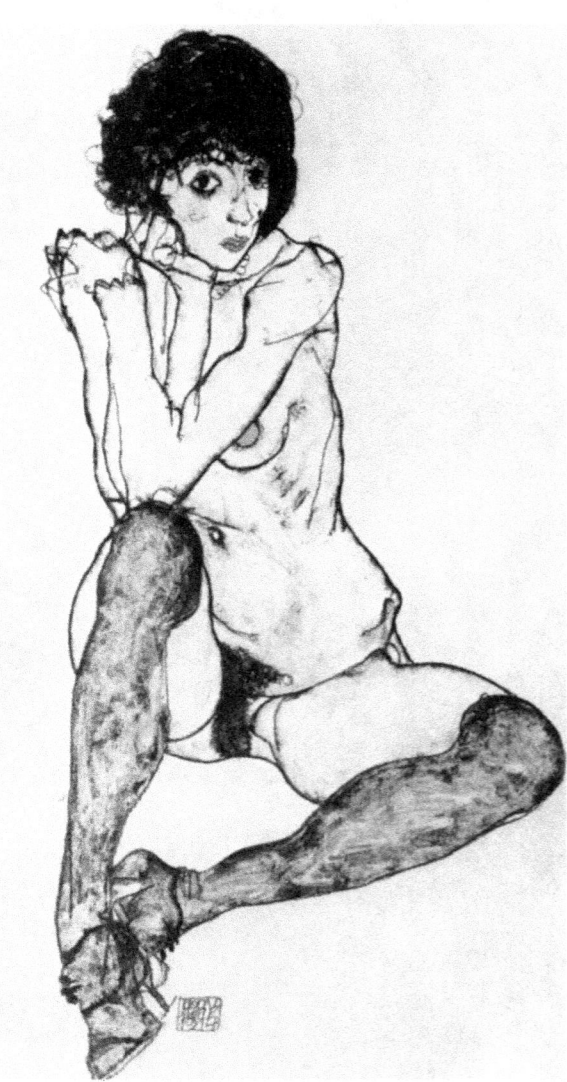

PL. 122. Schiele, *Female Model with Legs Spread Apart*, 1914, black chalk and watercolor.

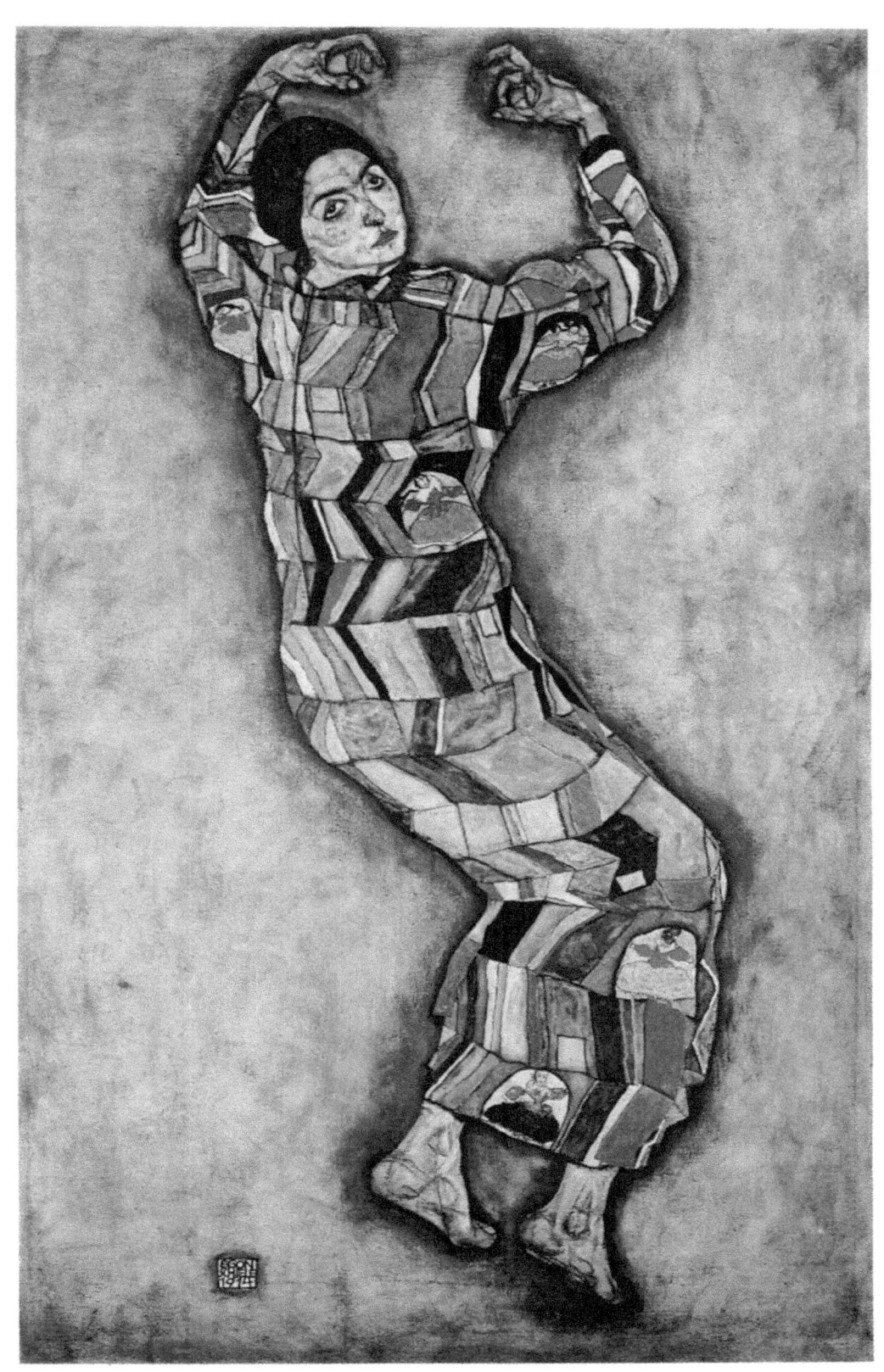

PL. 123. Schiele, *Portrait of Friederike Beer*, 1914, oil.

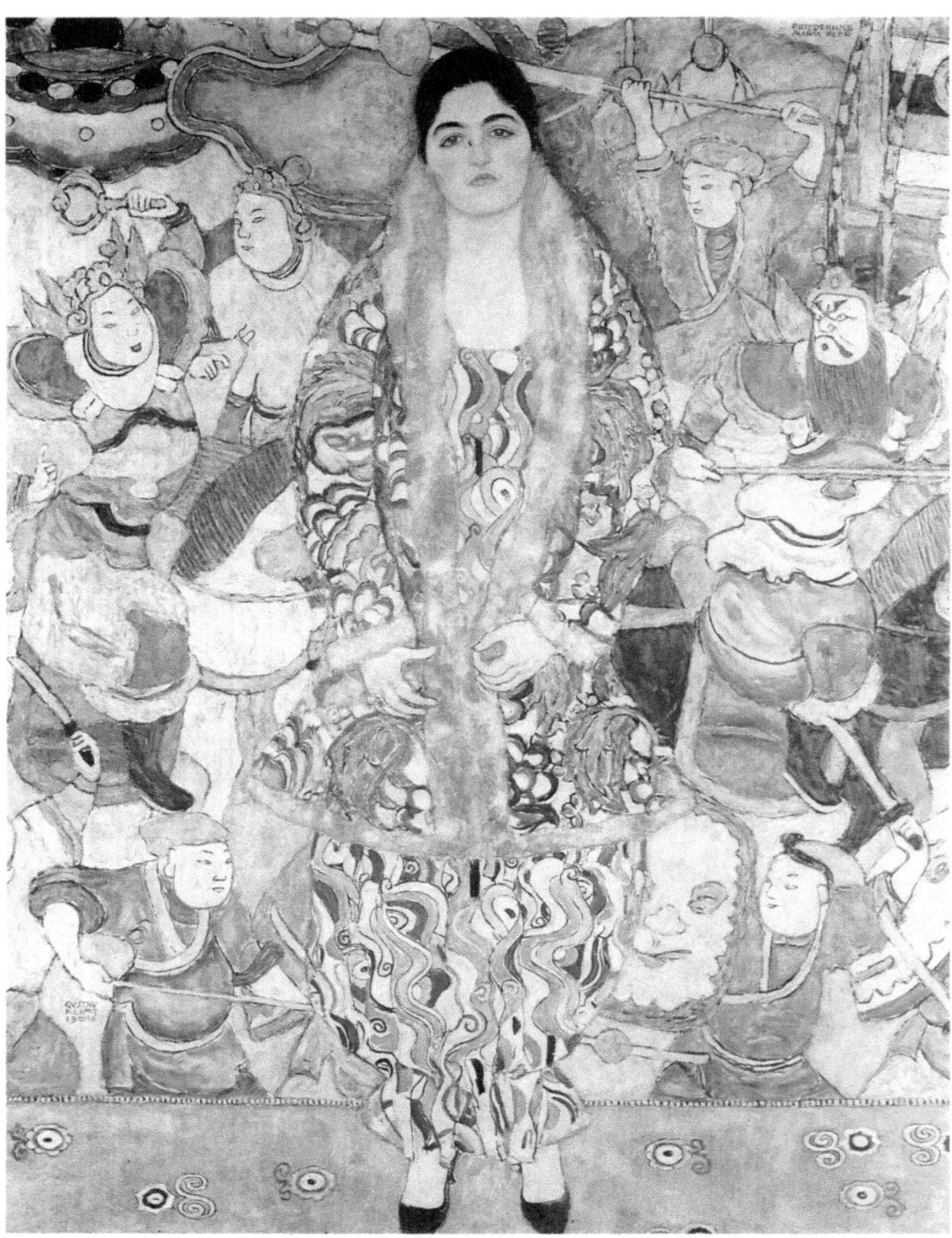

PL. 124. Klimt, *Portrait of Friederike Beer*, 1916, oil.

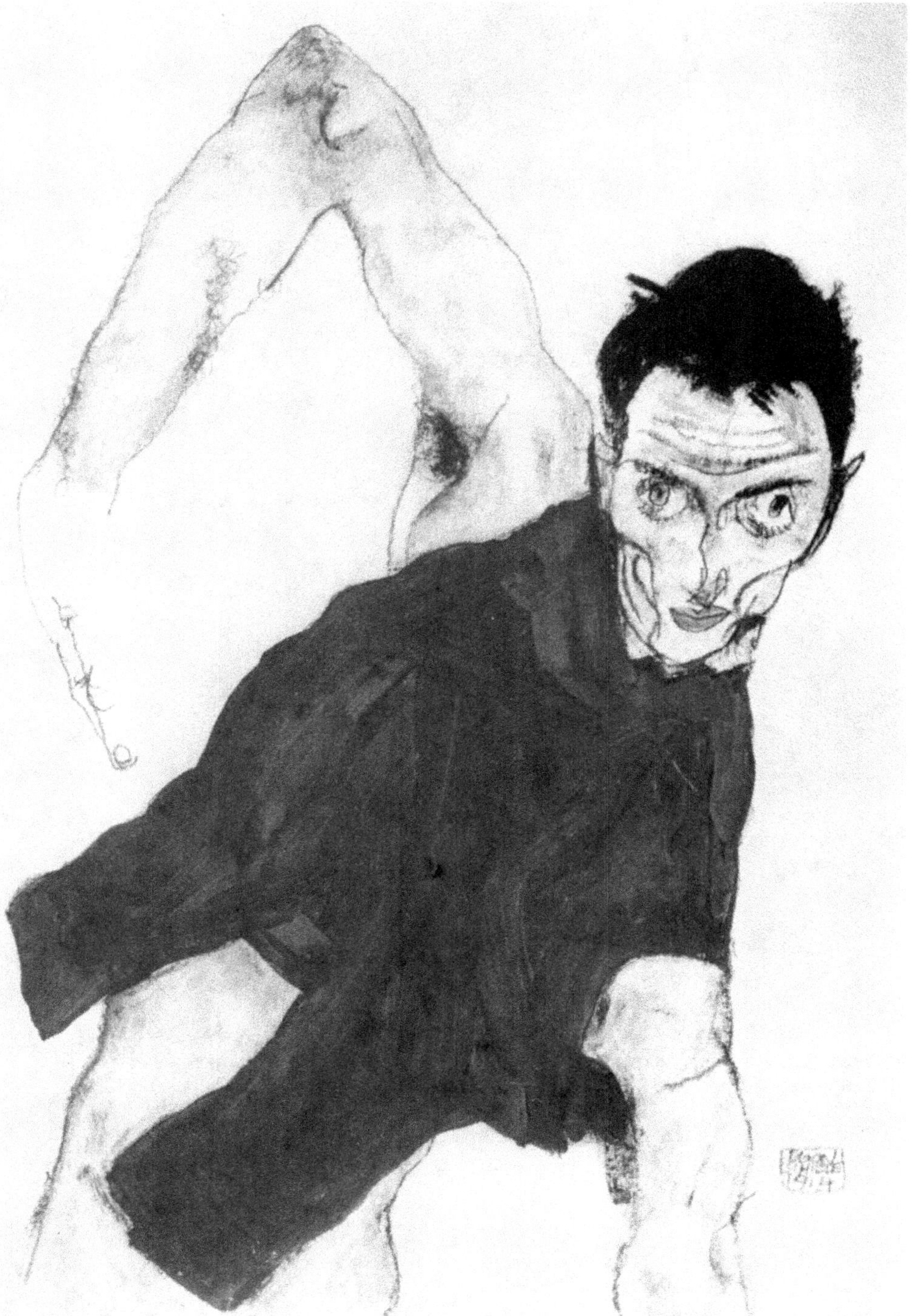

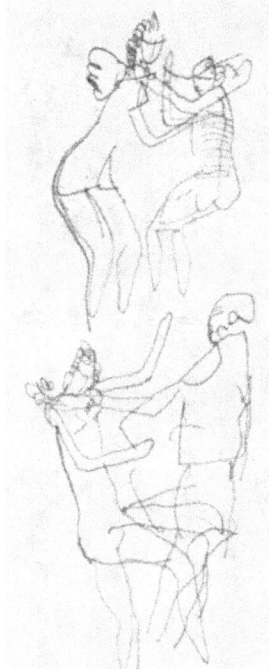

PL. 125a. Schiele, *Self-Portrait in Jerkin with Right Elbow Raised*, 1914, black chalk and watercolor.

PL. 125b. Schiele, A.E.S.A. Sketchbook V, 1914, pencil, p. 6 *recto*.

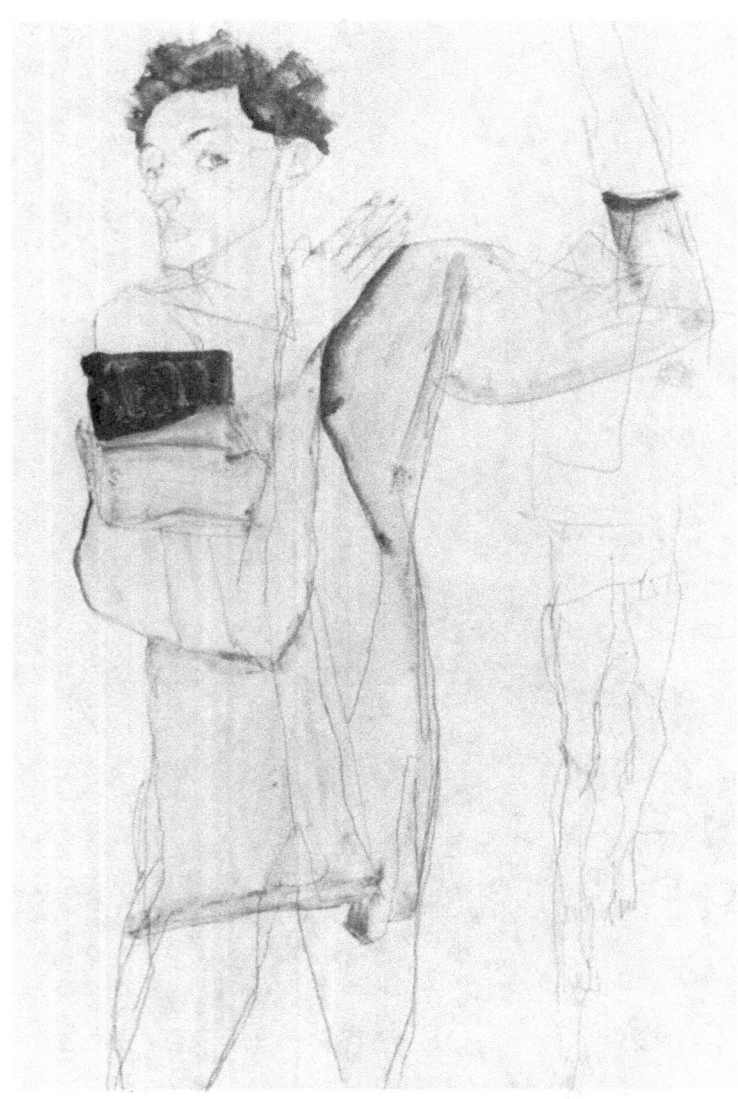

PL. 126a. Schiele, *Self-Portrait in Jerkin with Raised Arms*, 1913, pencil and watercolor.

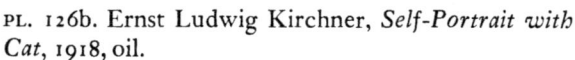

PL. 126b. Ernst Ludwig Kirchner, *Self-Portrait with Cat*, 1918, oil.

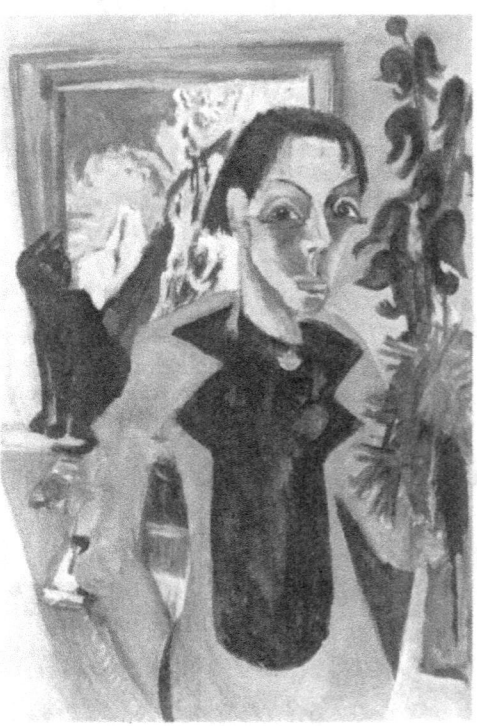

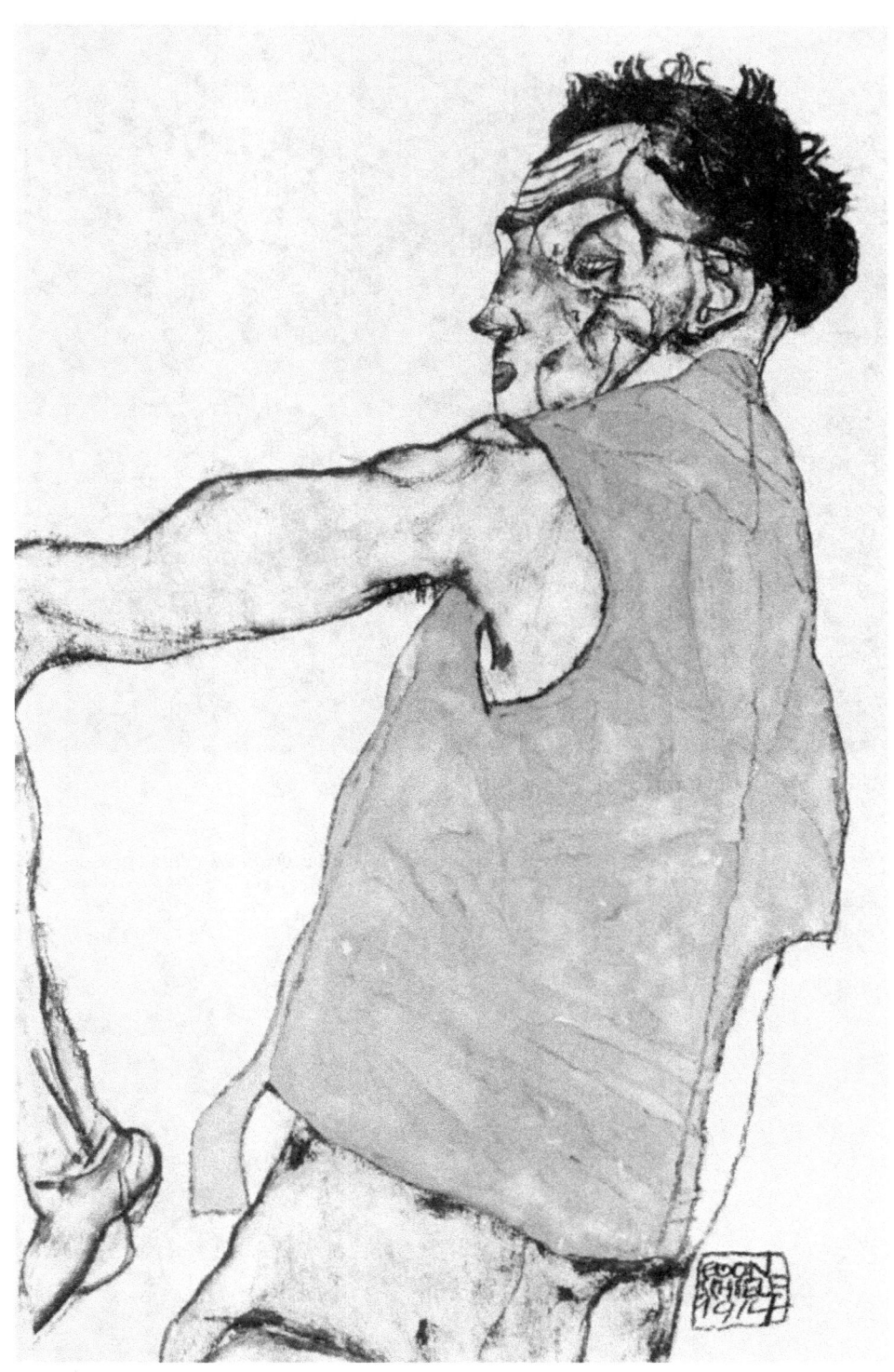

PL. 126c. Schiele, *Self-Portrait in Jerkin from the Back*, 1914, black chalk and watercolor.

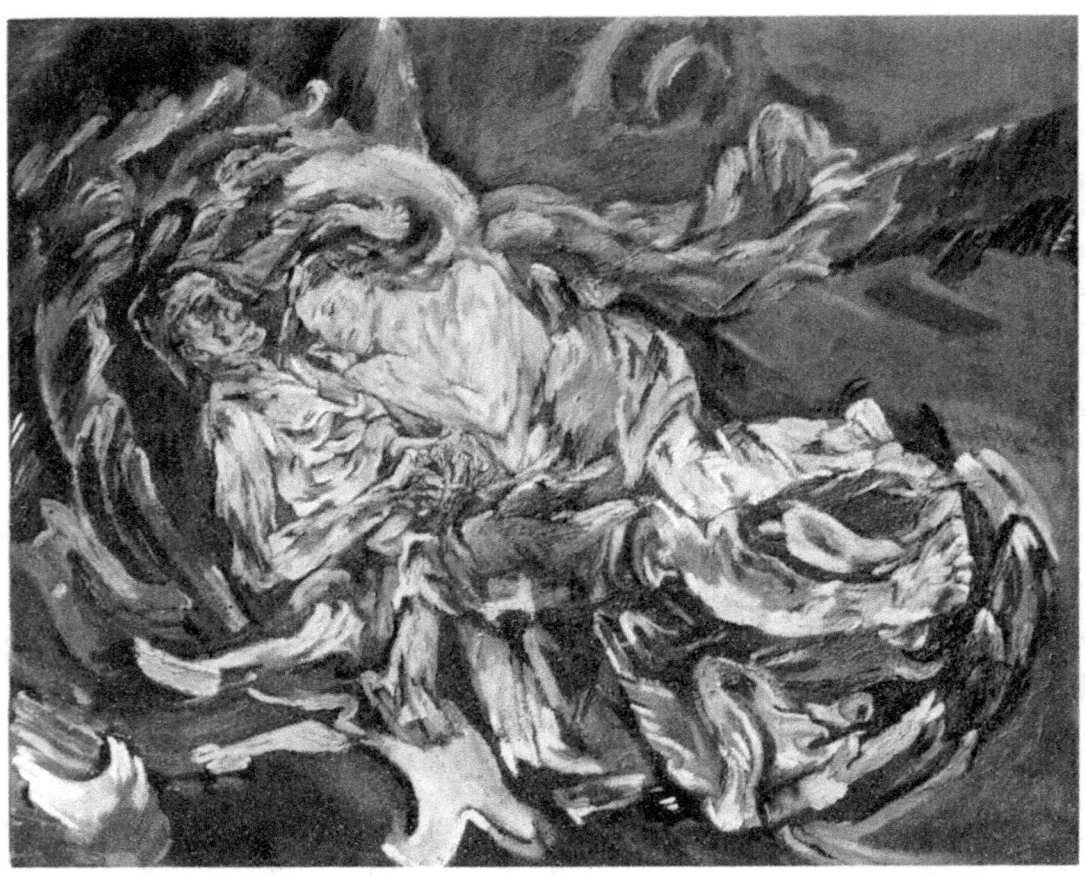

PL. 127. Kokoschka, *The Tempest*, 1914, oil.

PL. 128. Luca Signorelli, *The Damned* (detail), 1499–1503, fresco.

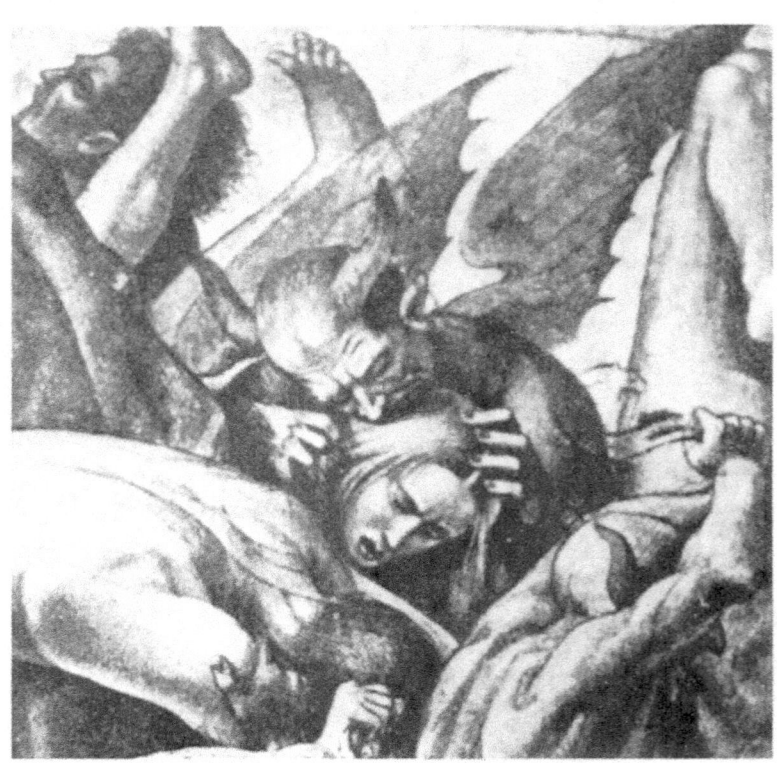

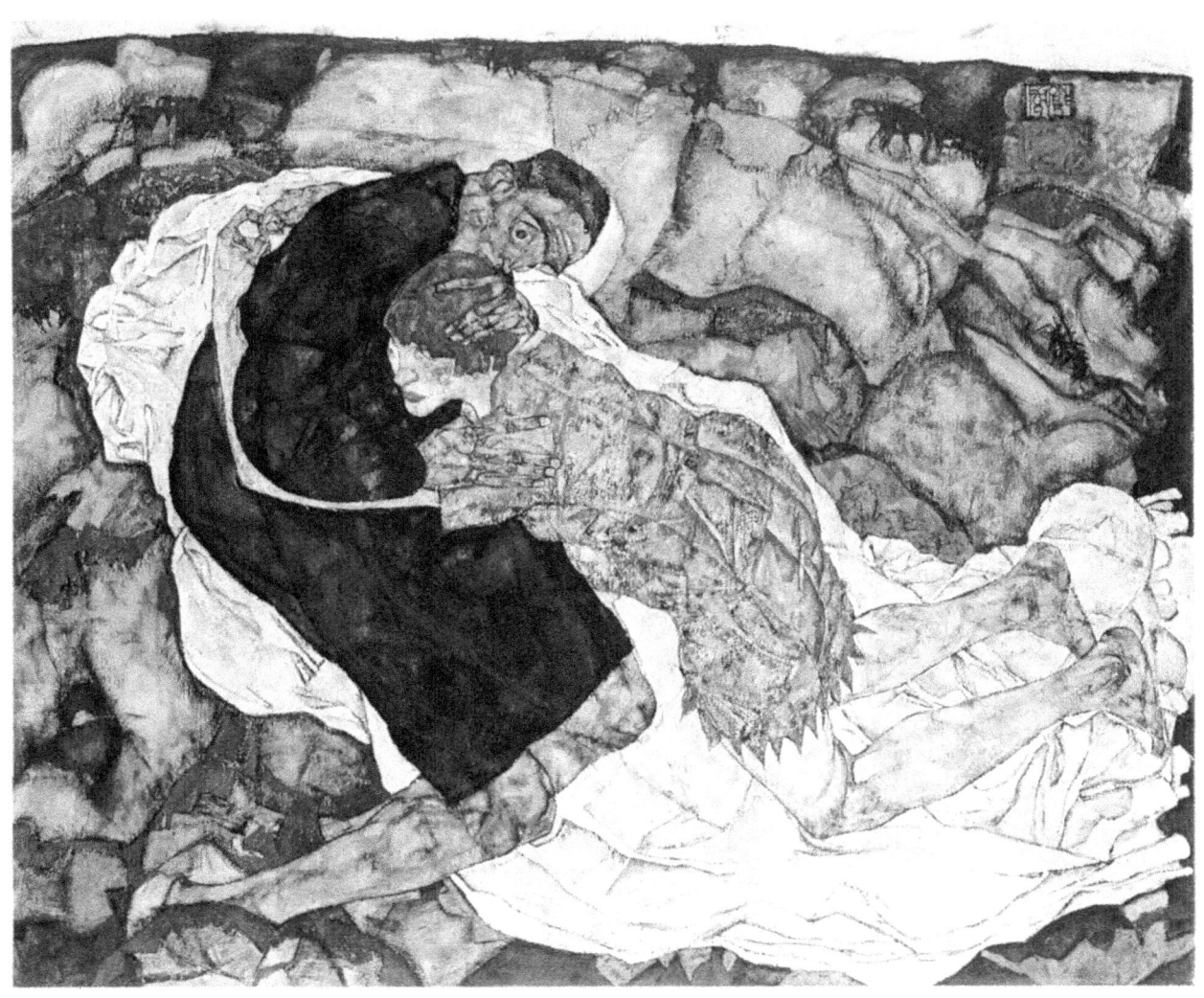

PL. 129. Schiele, *Death and Maiden ("Man and Girl")*, 1915, oil.

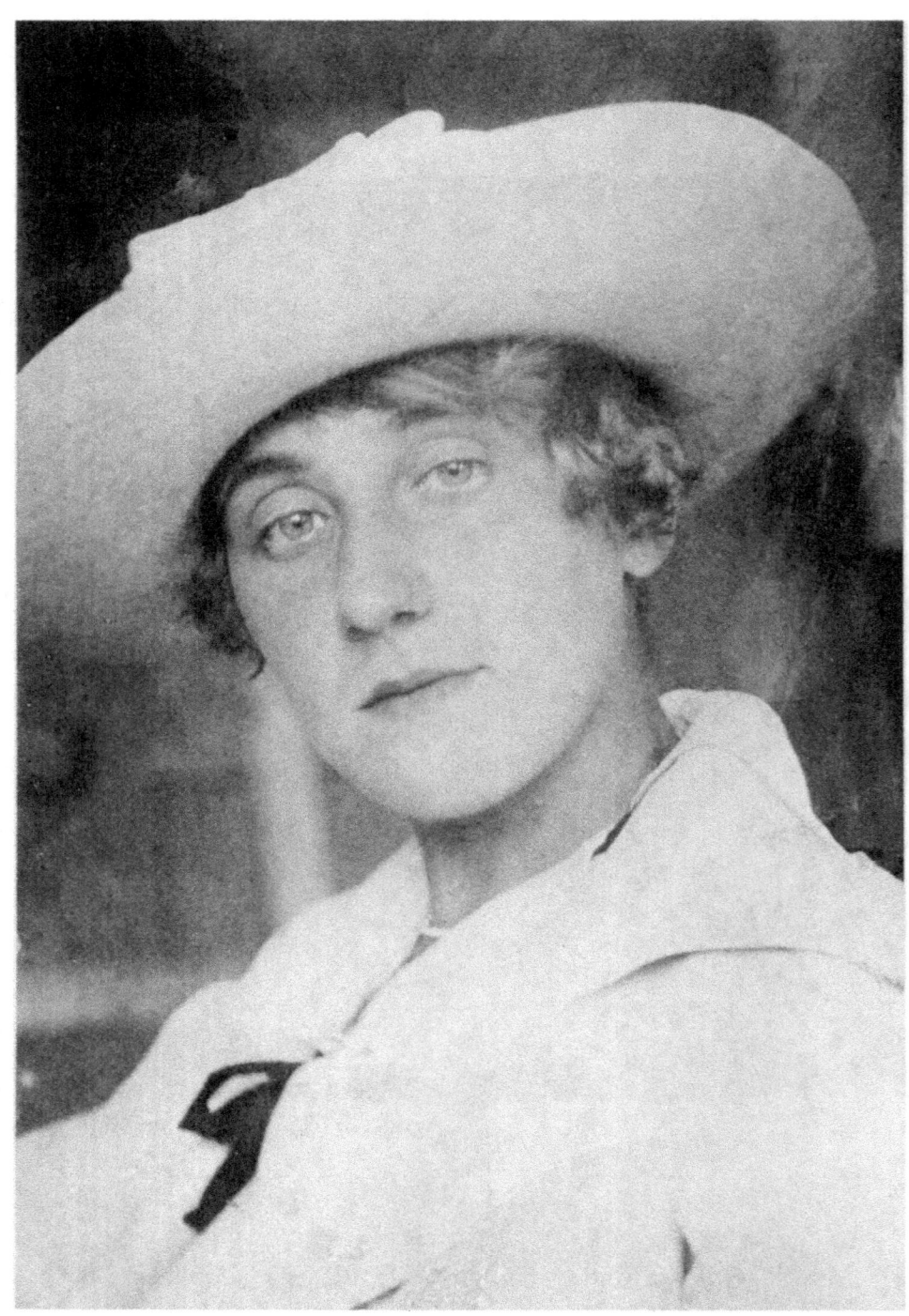

PL. 130. Edith Schiele, *ca.* 1917.

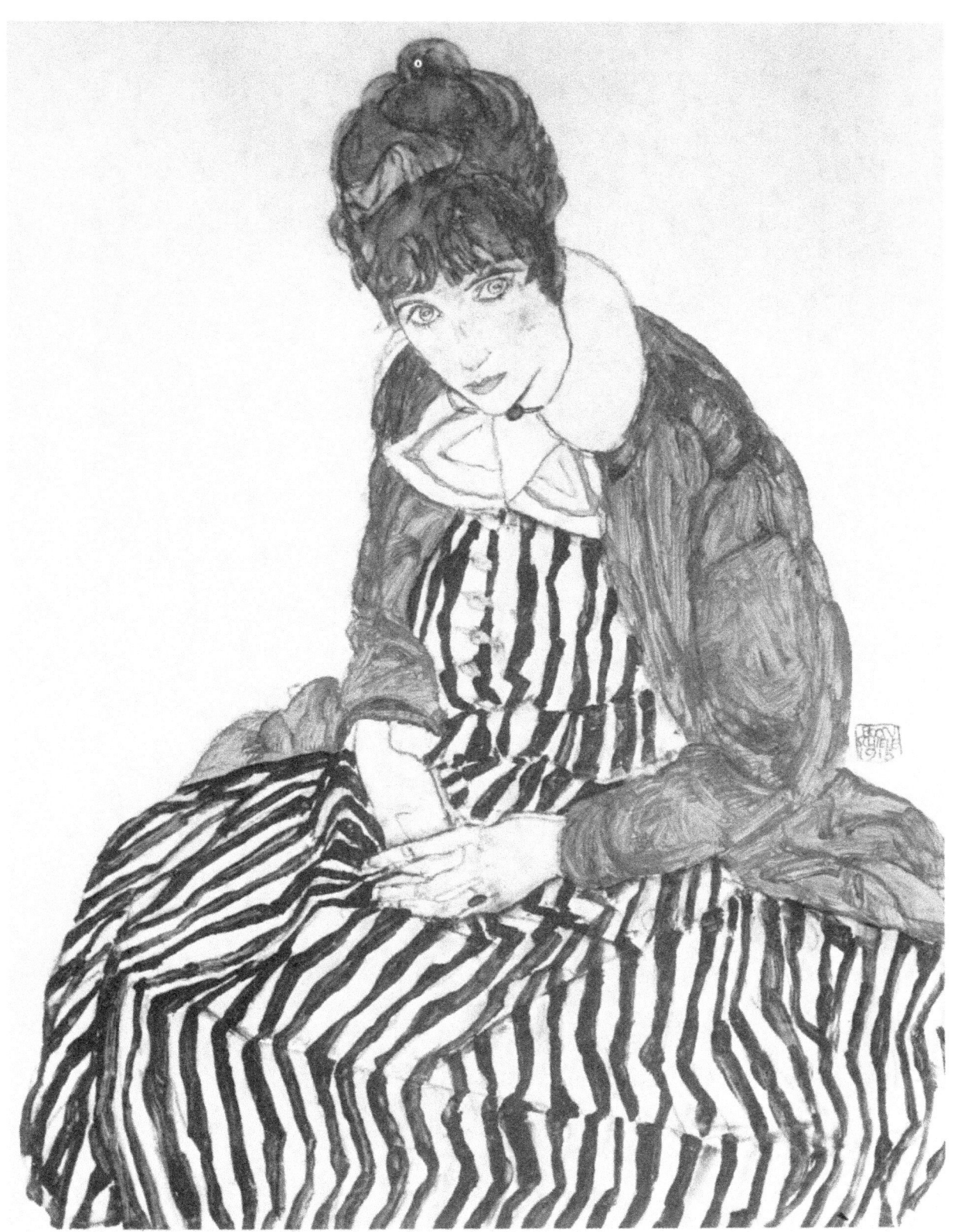

PL. 131. Schiele, *Study of Edith Schiele Seated*, 1915, pencil and watercolor.

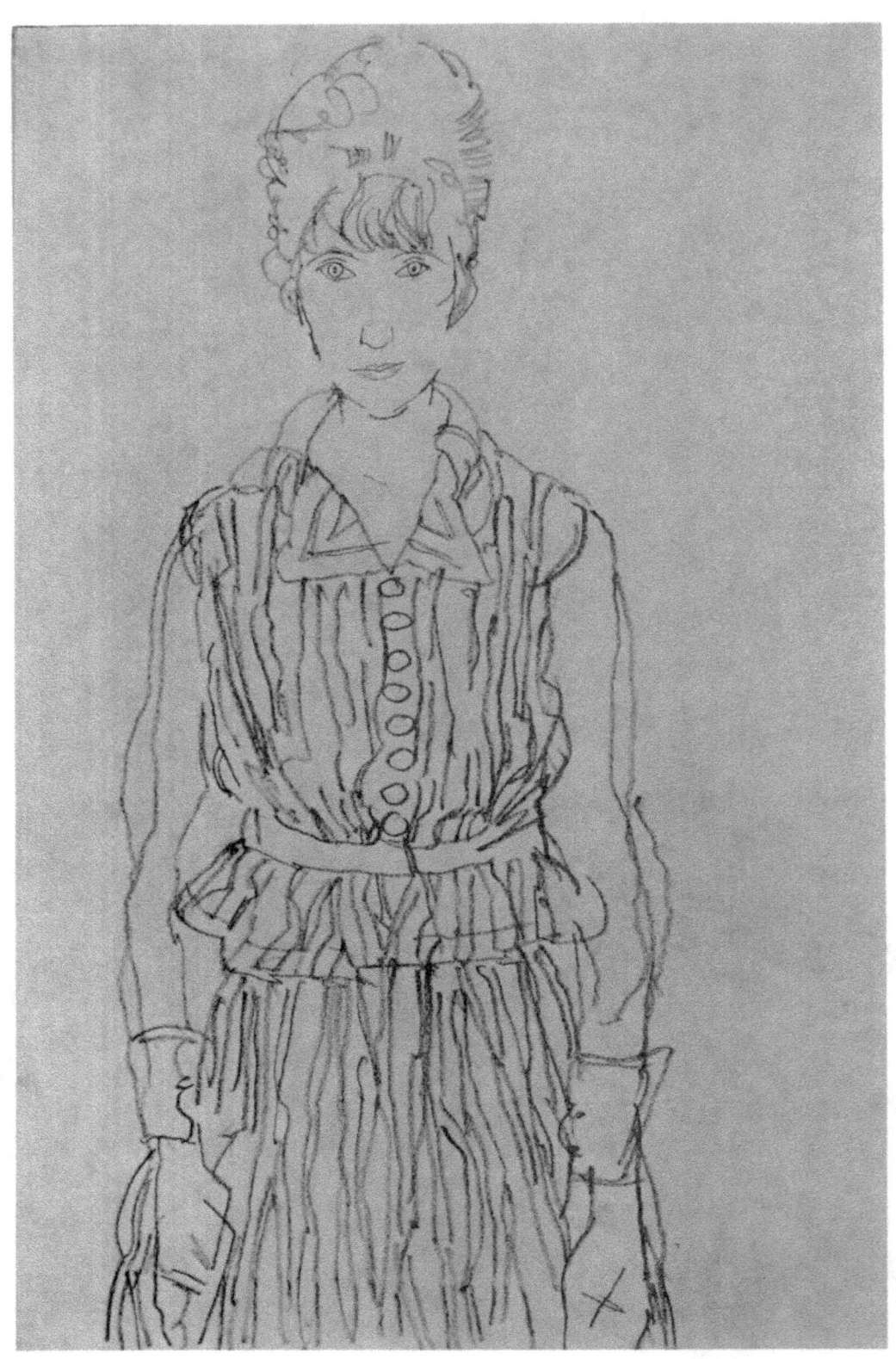

PL. 132. Schiele, *Study of Edith Schiele Standing with Arms at Sides*, 1915, pencil.

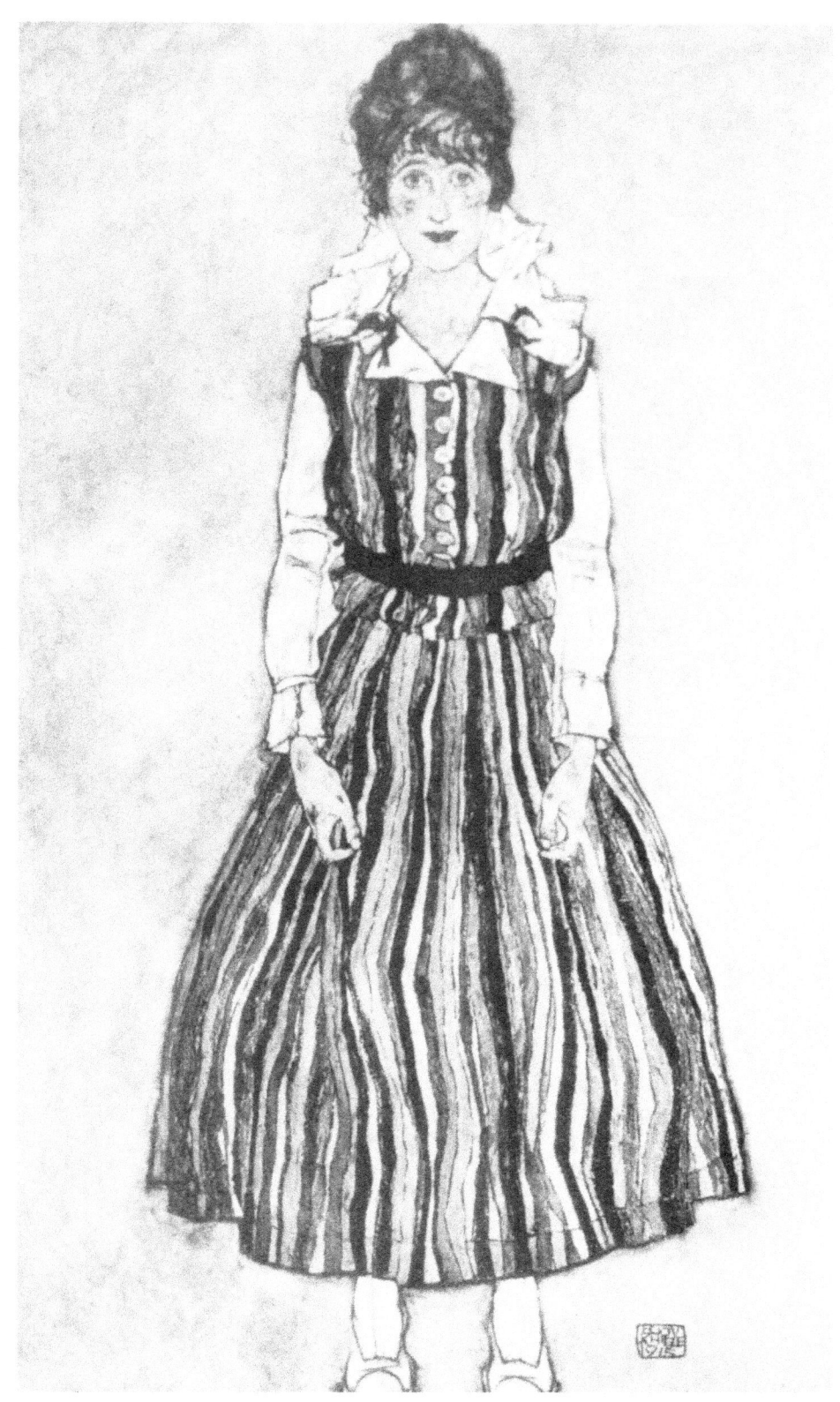

PL. 133. Schiele, *Portrait of Edith Schiele Standing*, 1915, oil.

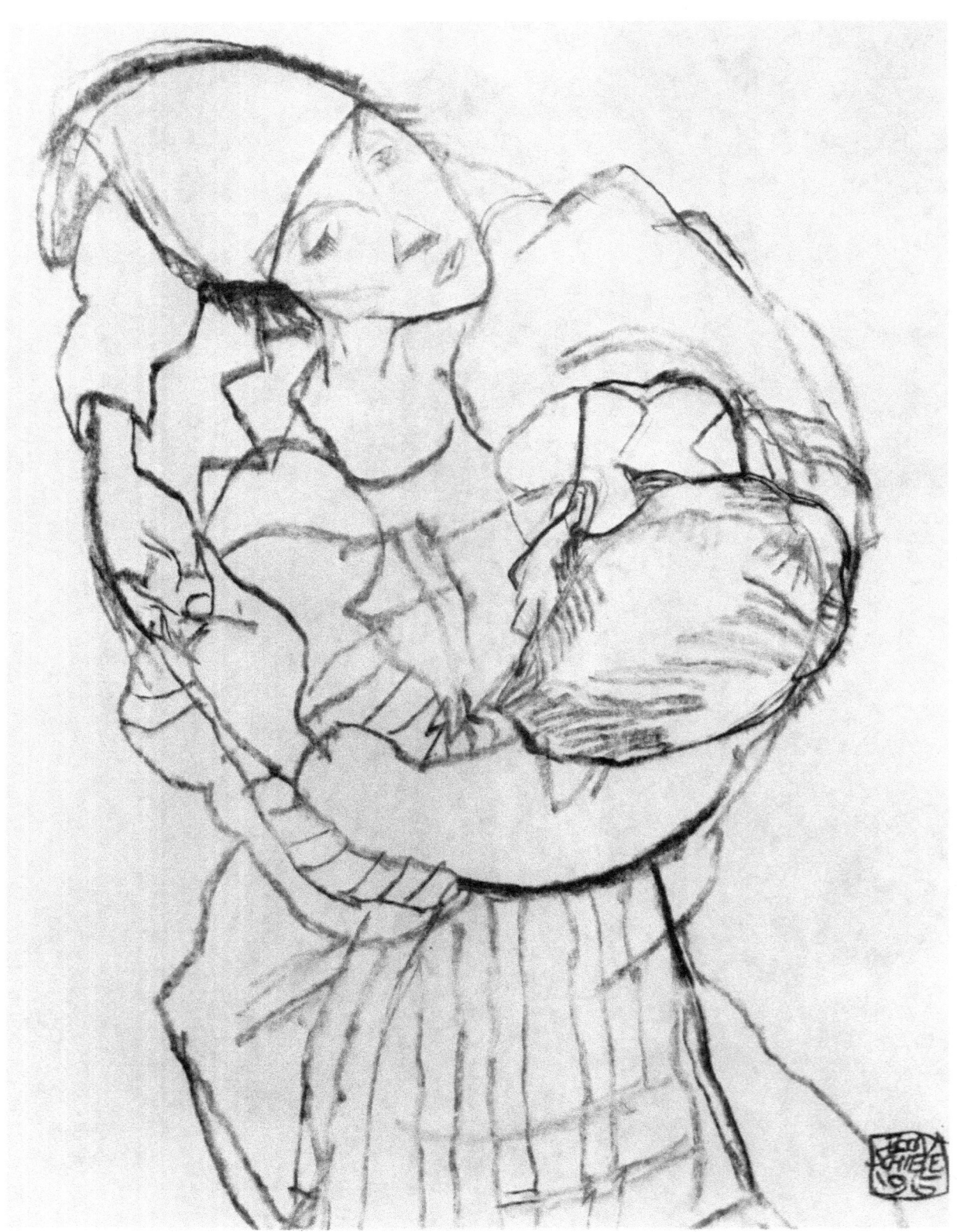

PL. 134. Schiele, *Embrace* [*I*], 1915, charcoal.

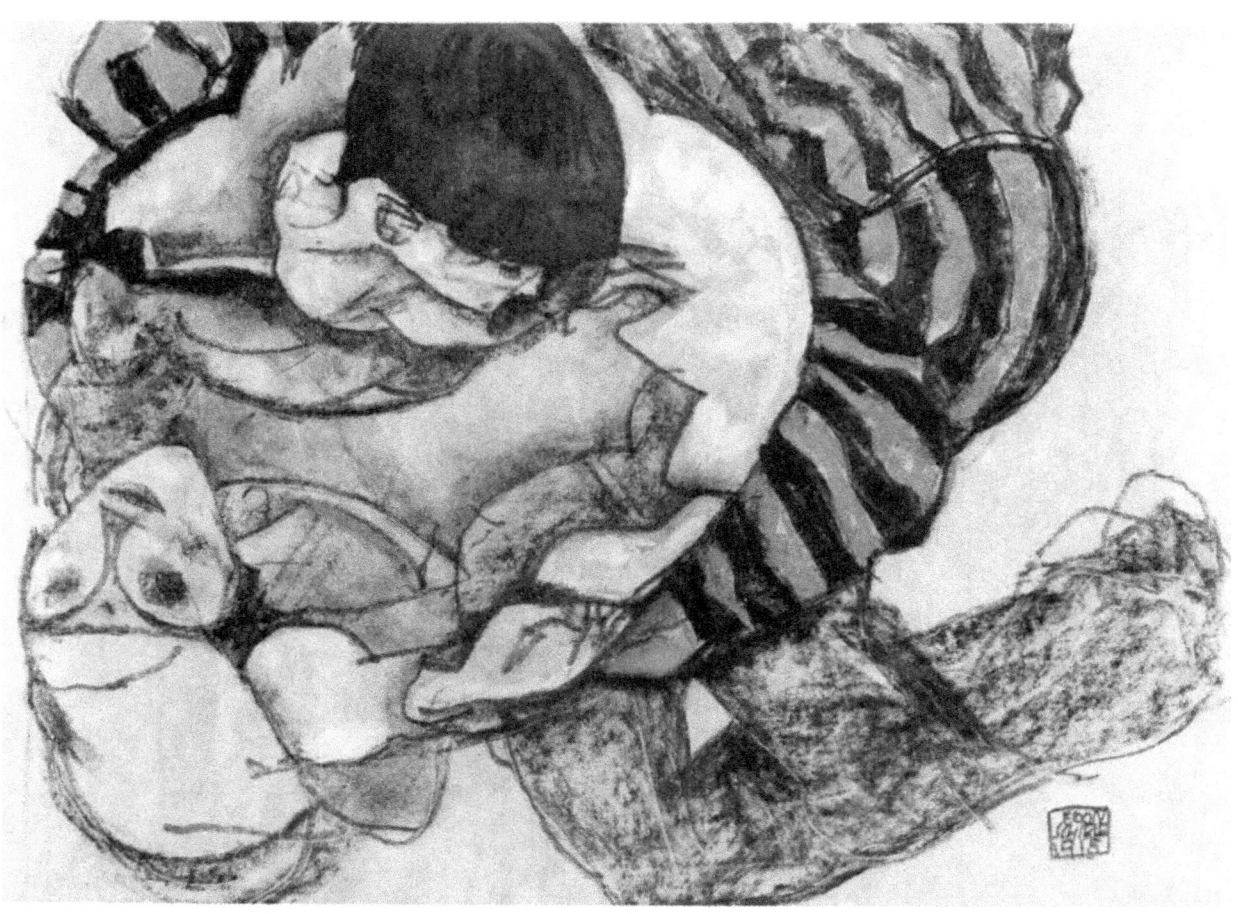

PL. 135. Schiele, *Embrace* [II], 1915, charcoal and tempera.

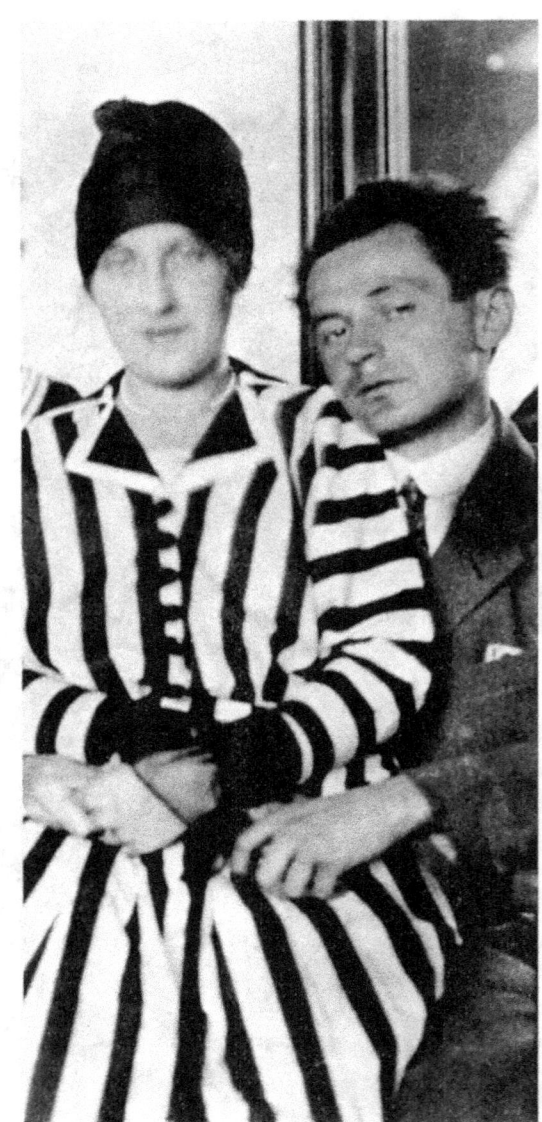

PL. 136. Egon and Edith Schiele, 1915.

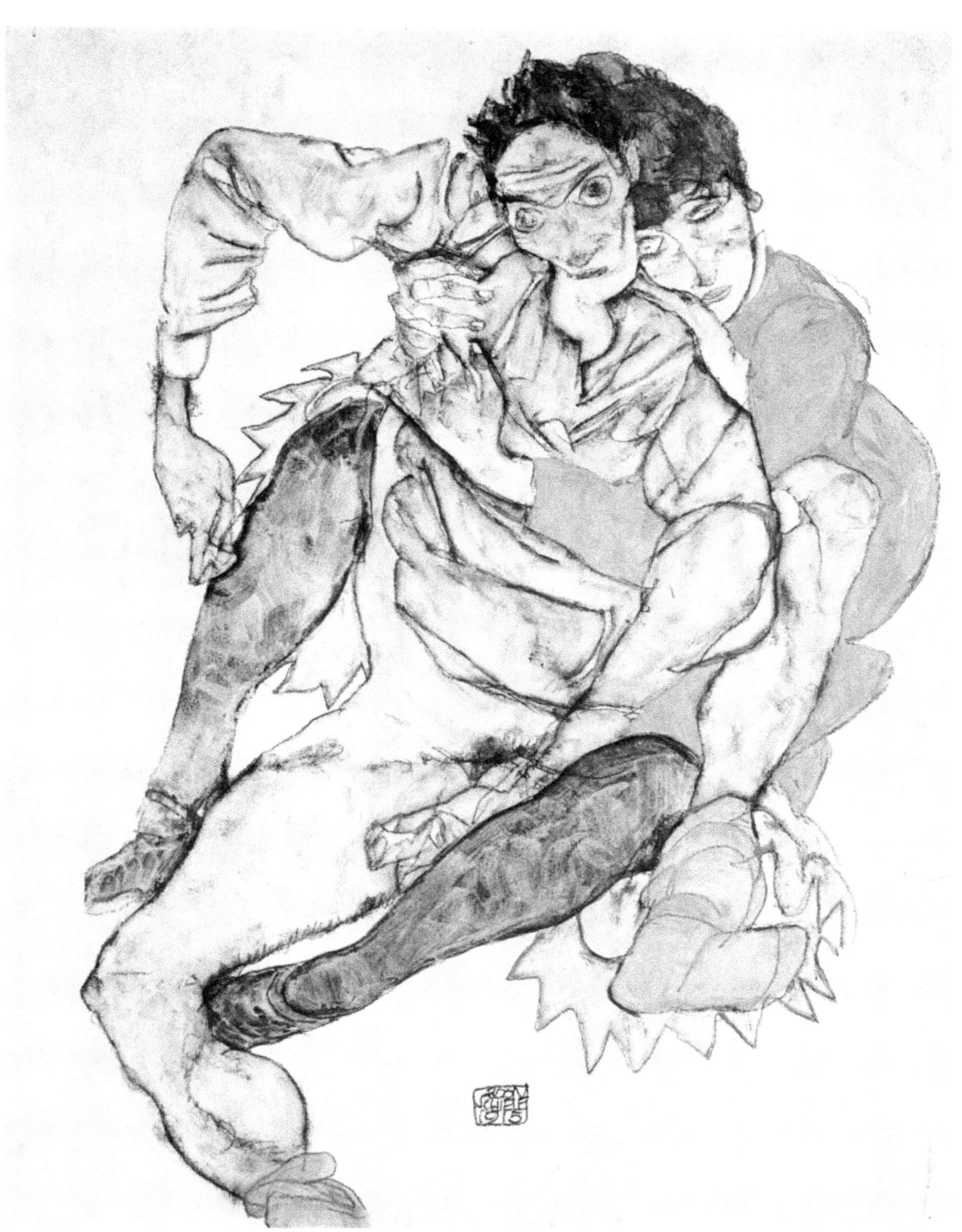

PL. 137. Schiele, *Embrace* [*III*], 1915, black chalk and watercolor.

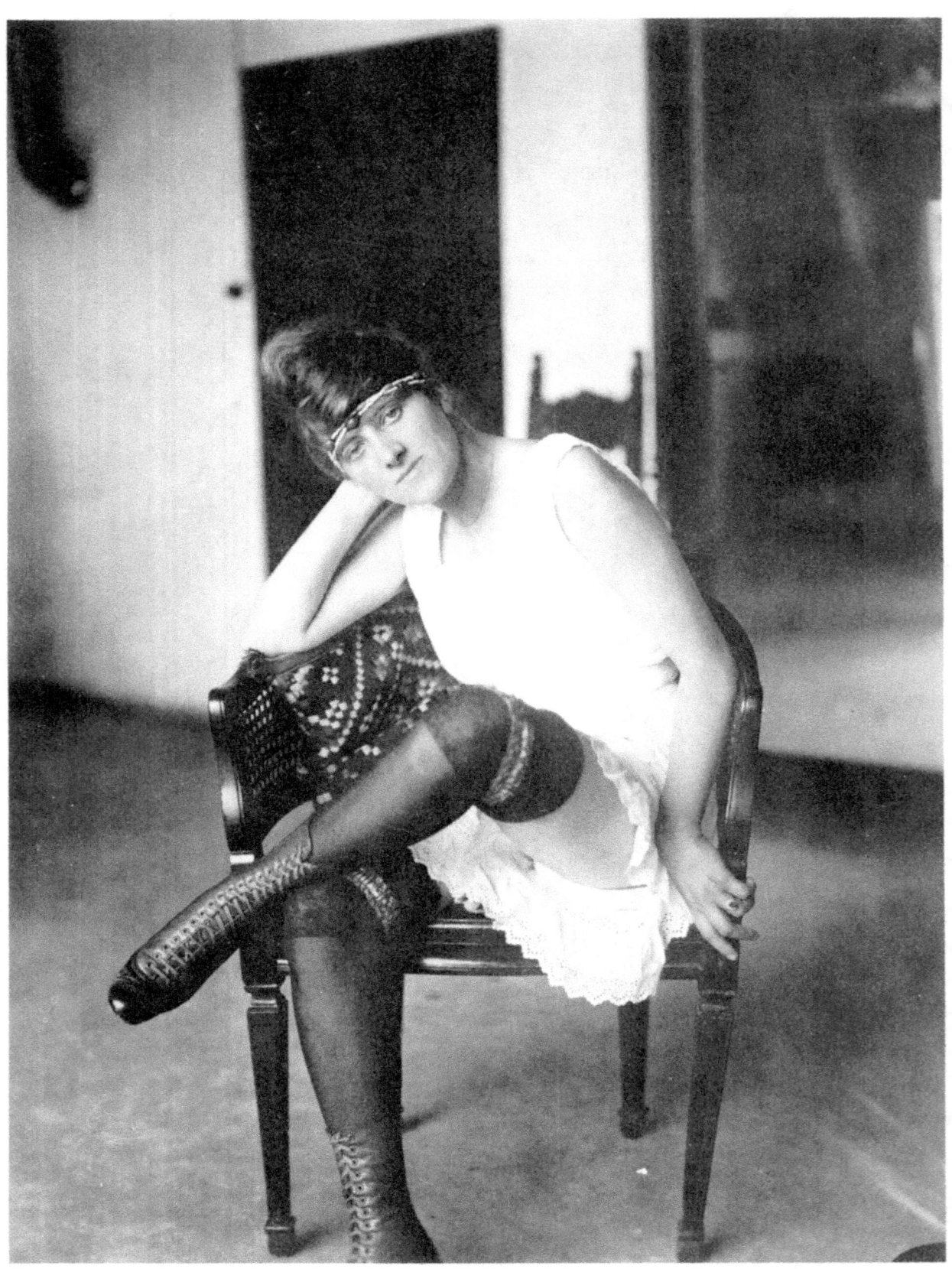

PL. 138. Adele Harms, 1917 (photograph by Egon Schiele).

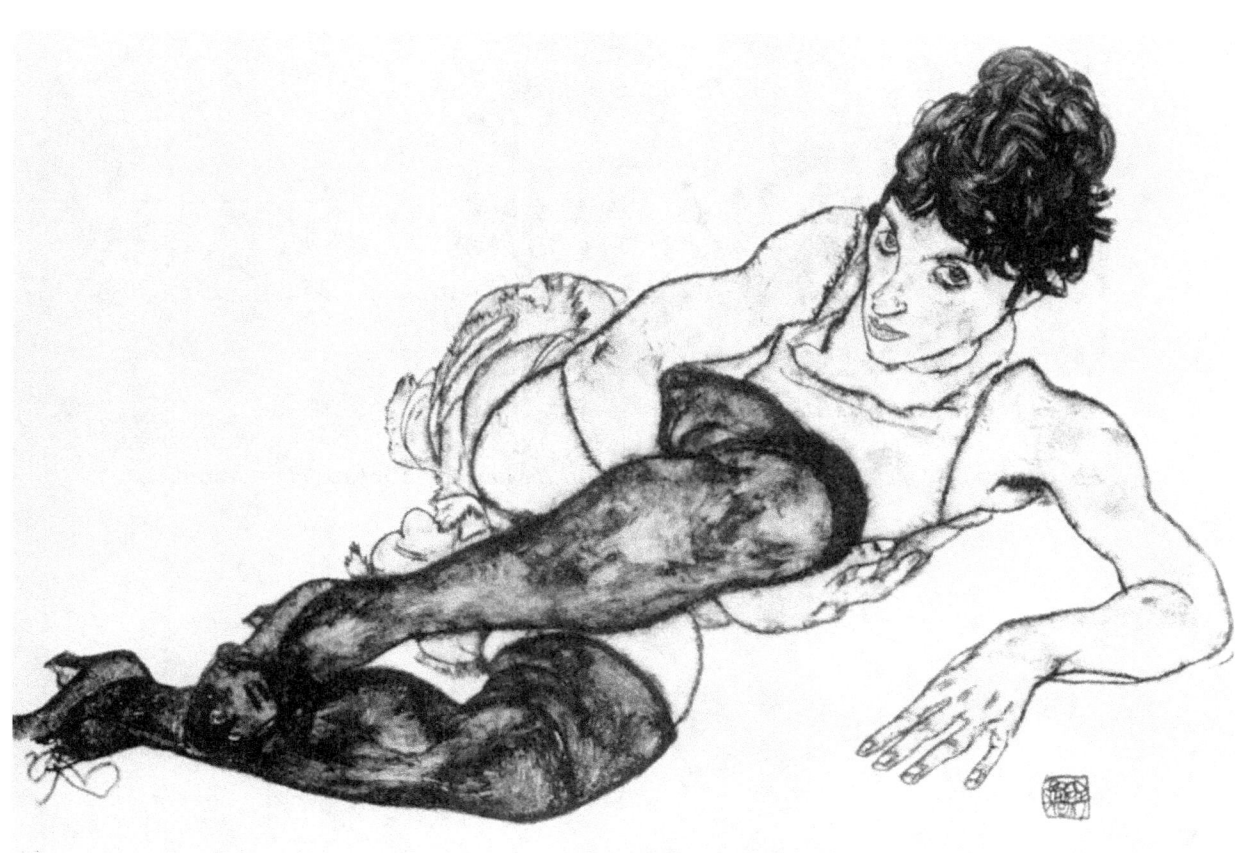

PL. 139. Schiele, *Portrait of Adele Harms Reclining*, 1917, black chalk and watercolor.

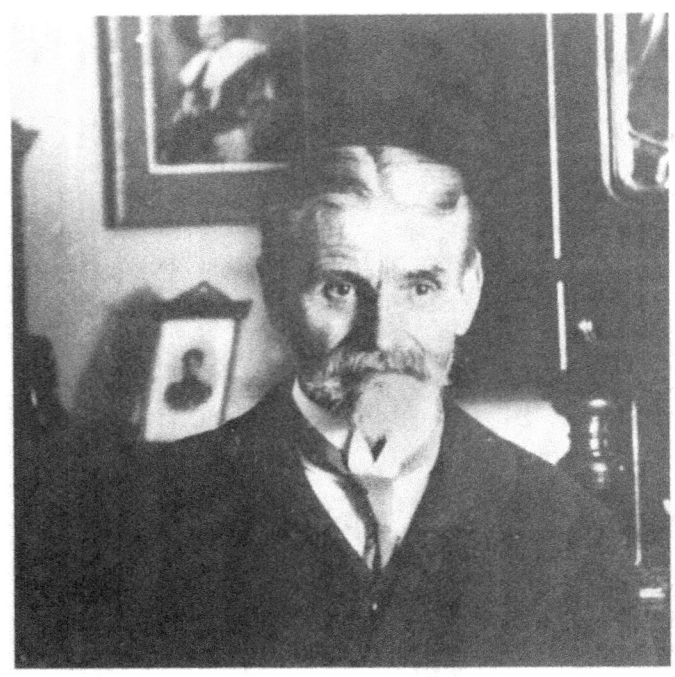

PL. 140. Johann Harms, *ca.* 1914.

PL. 141. Schiele, *Study for the Portrait of Johann Harms*, 1916, oil on paper.

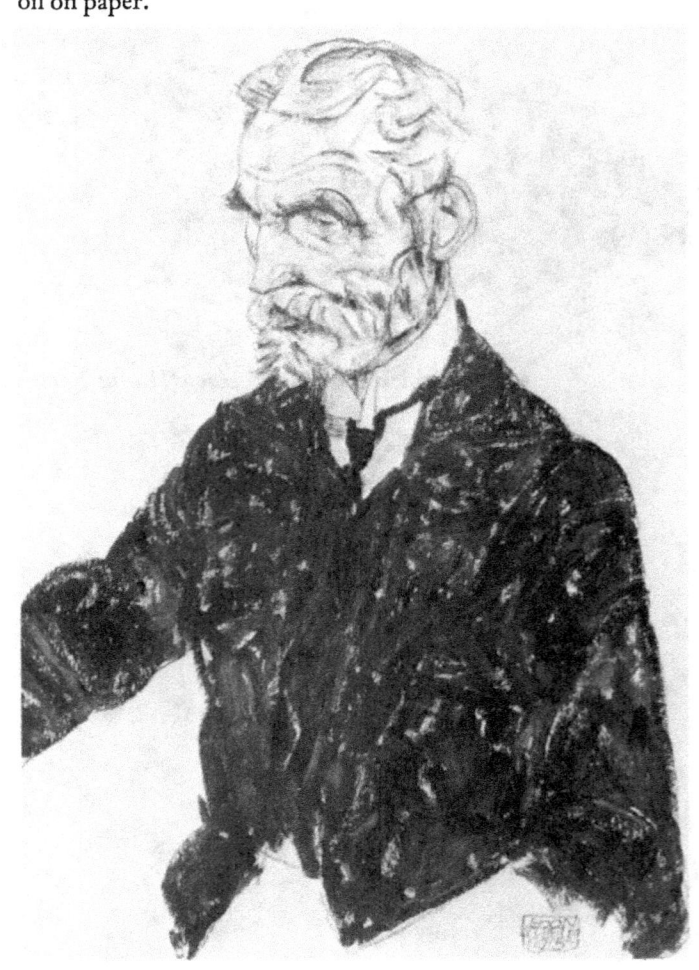

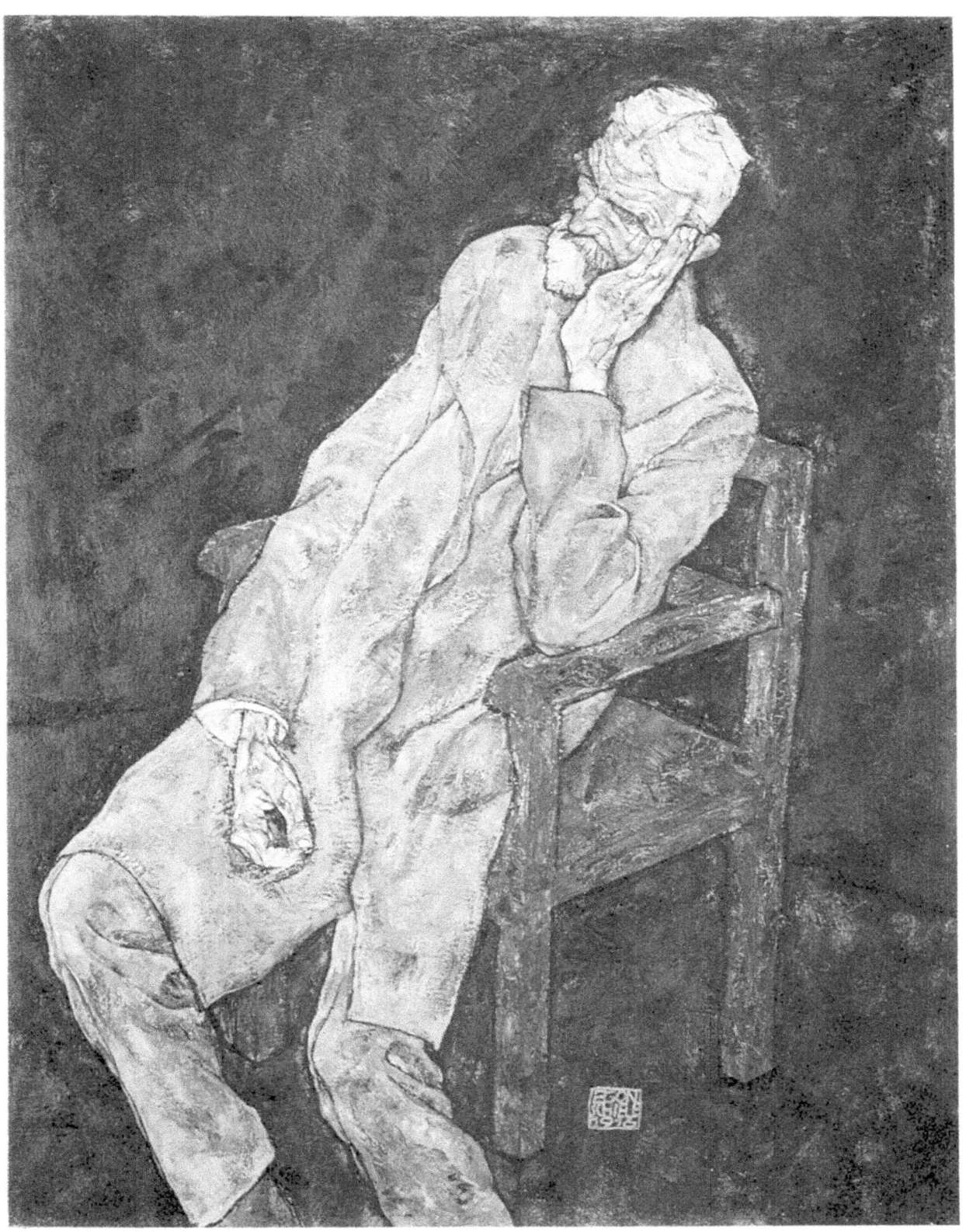

PL. 142. Schiele, *Portrait of Johann Harms*, 1916, oil.

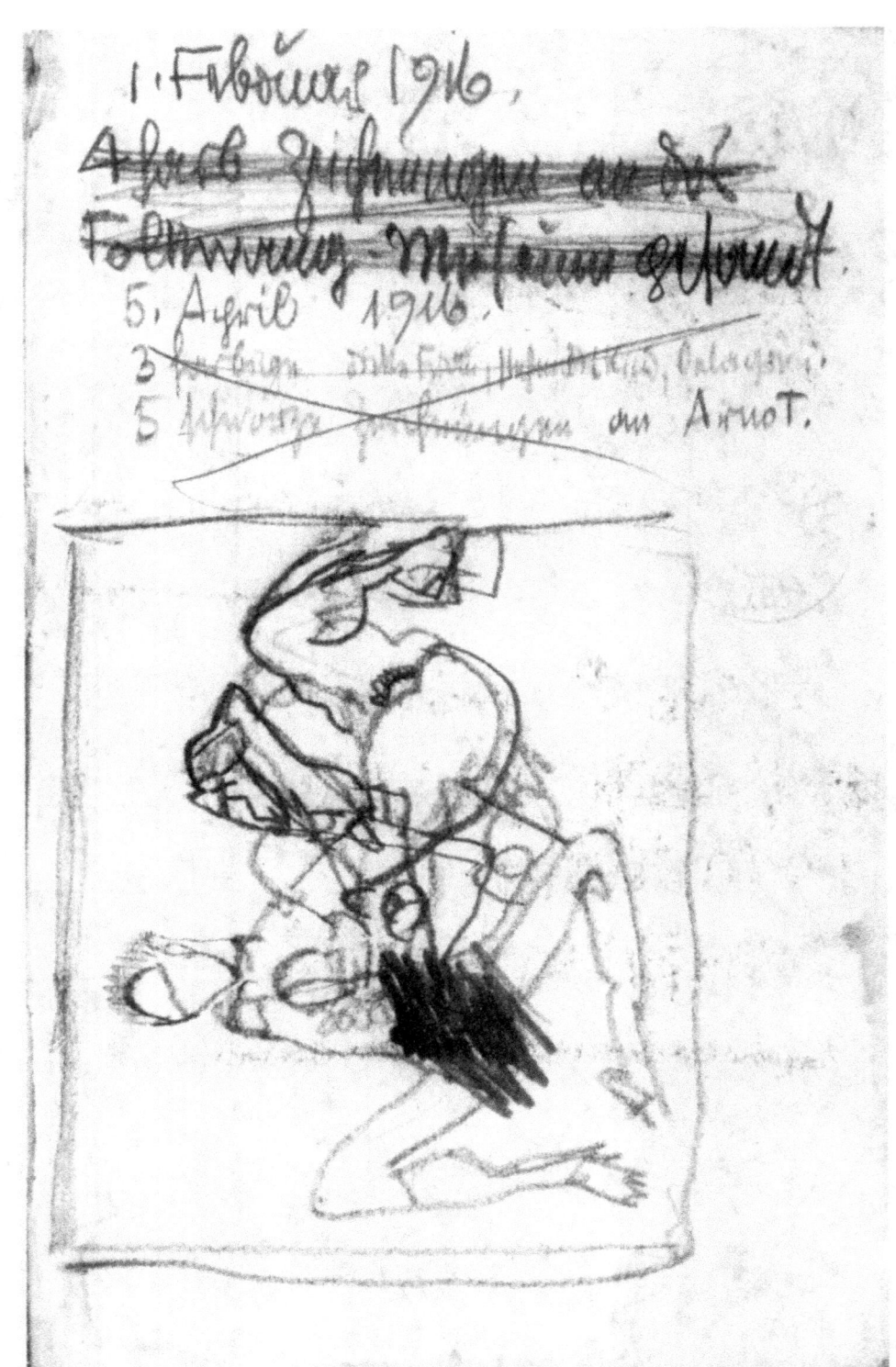

PL. 143. Schiele, A.E.S.A. Sketchbook IX, 1916, pencil, p. 1 *recto*.

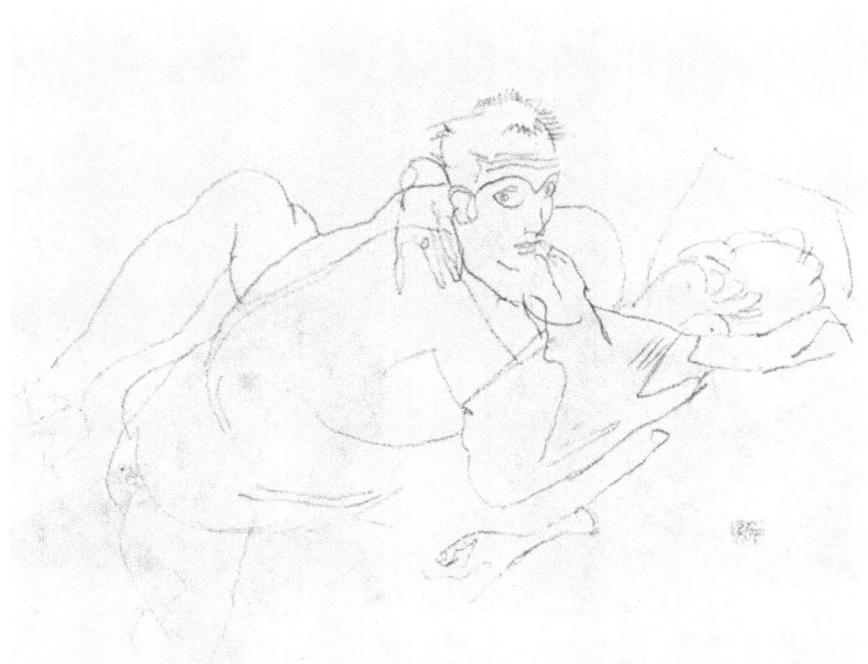

PL. 144. Schiele, *Lovers*, 1916, black chalk.

PL. 145. Schiele, Sketchbook, 1914–1917, pencil, p. 107.

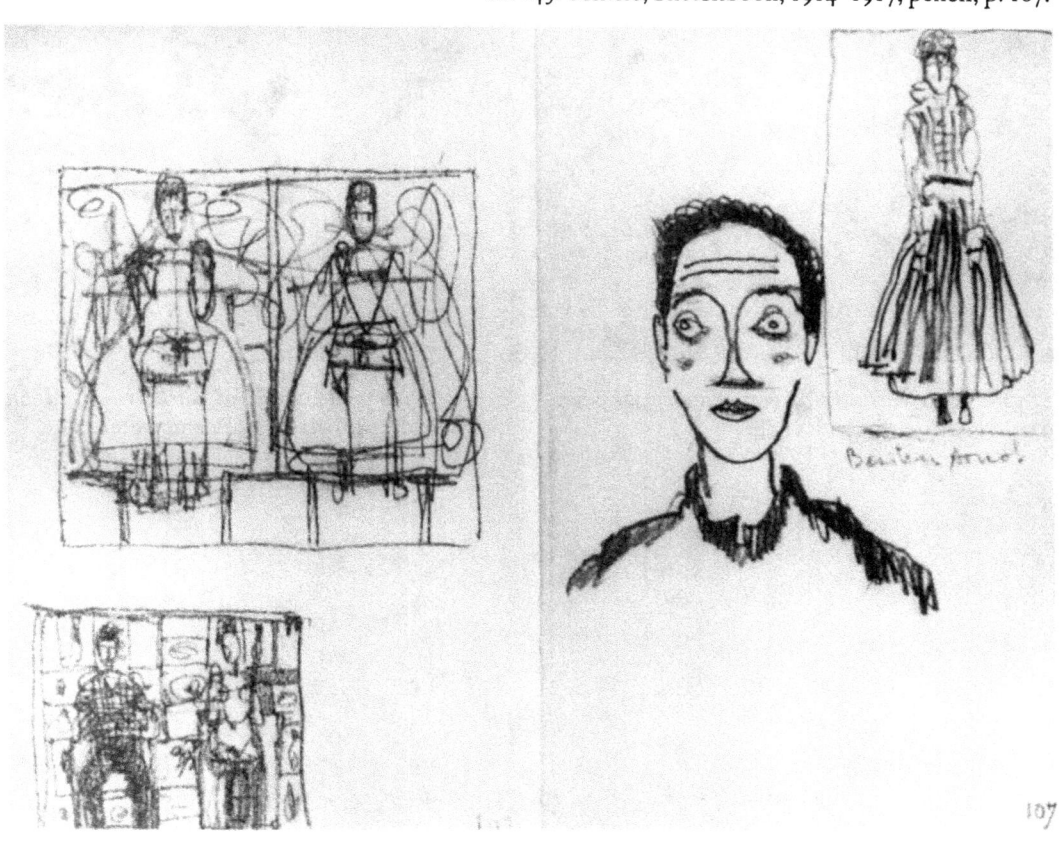

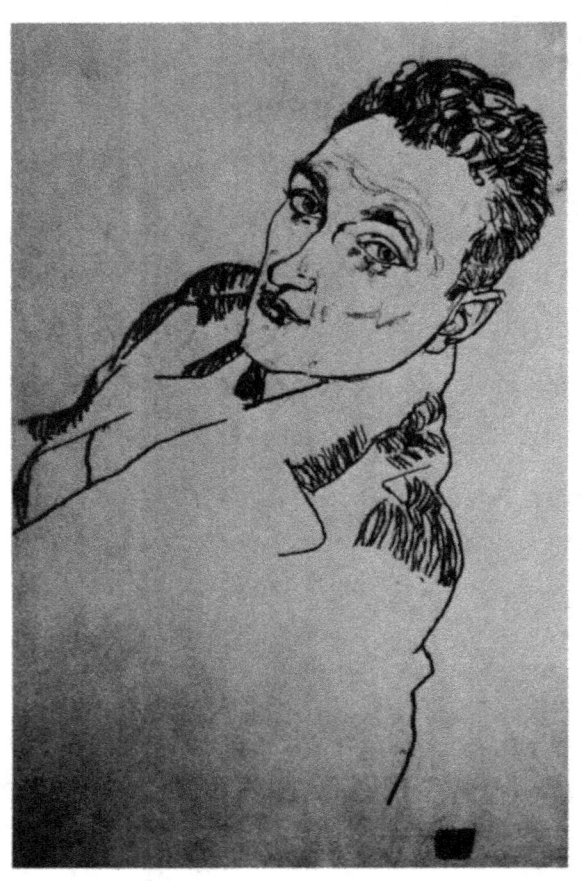

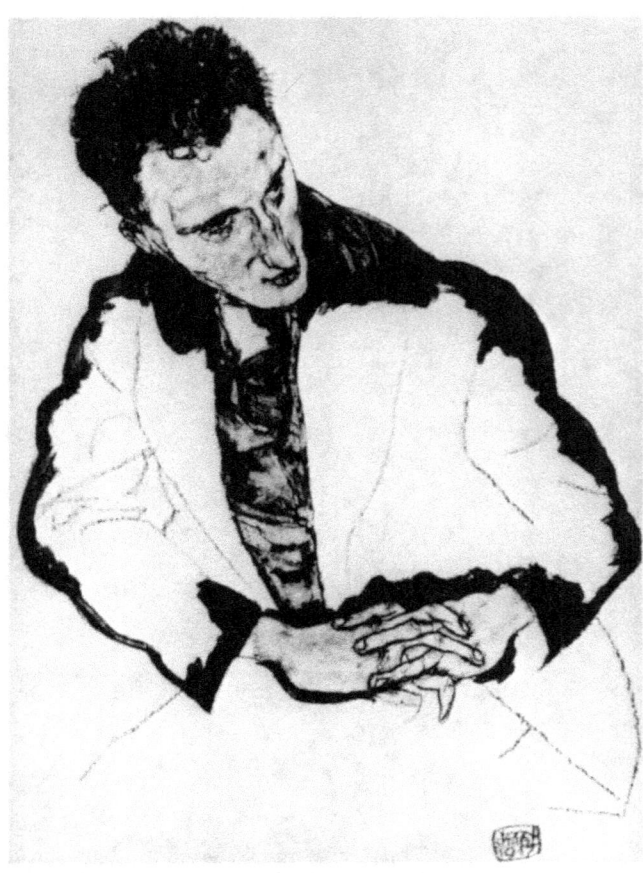

PL. 146. Schiele, *Study of Karl Grünwald Seen from Above*, 1917, black chalk.

PL. 147. Schiele, *Study of Karl Grünwald with Fingers Intertwined*, 1917, black chalk and watercolor.

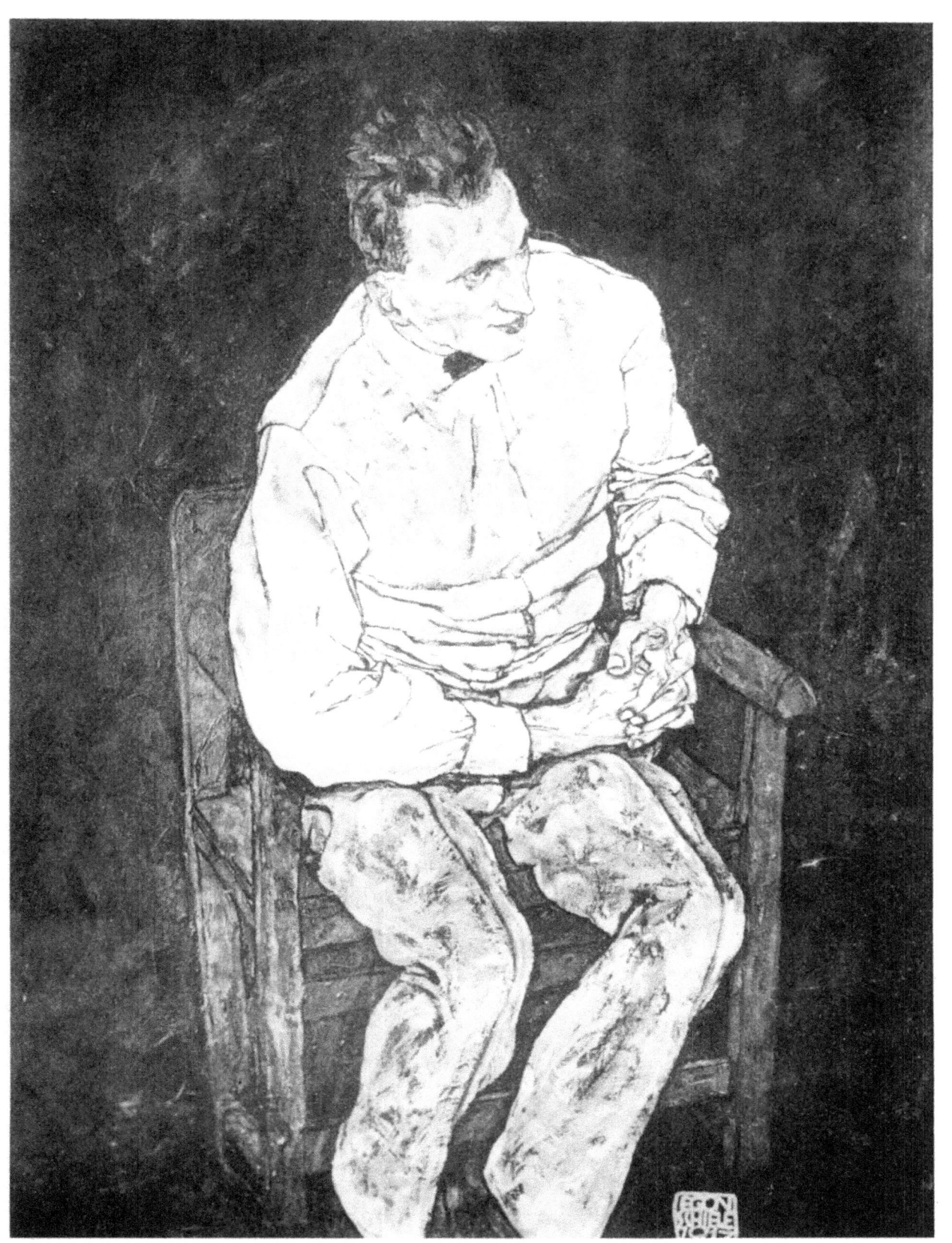

PL. 148. Schiele, *Portrait of Karl Grünwald*, 1917, oil.

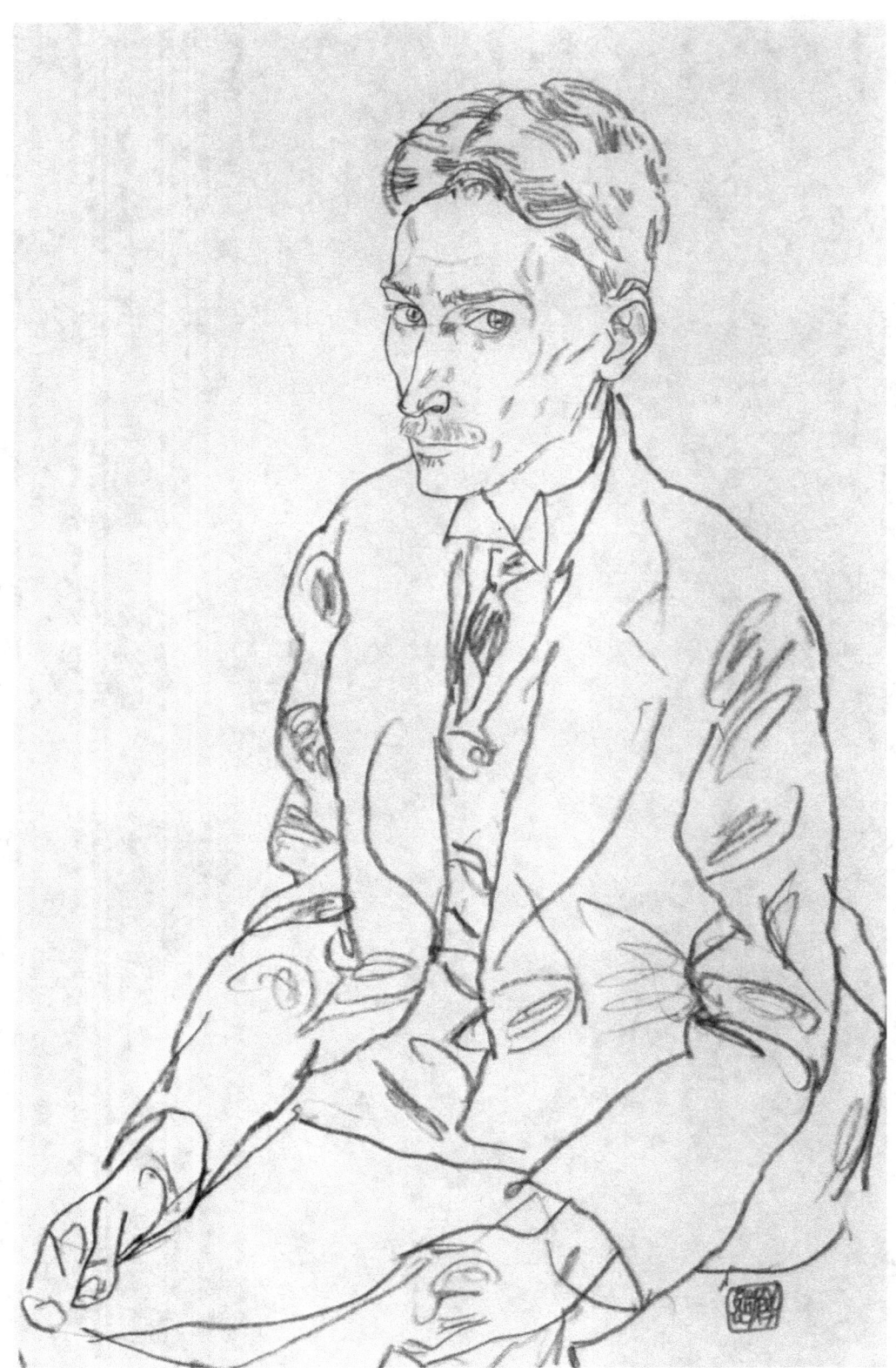

PL. 149. Schiele, *Study of Dr. Haberditzl Looking to the Right*, 1917, black chalk.

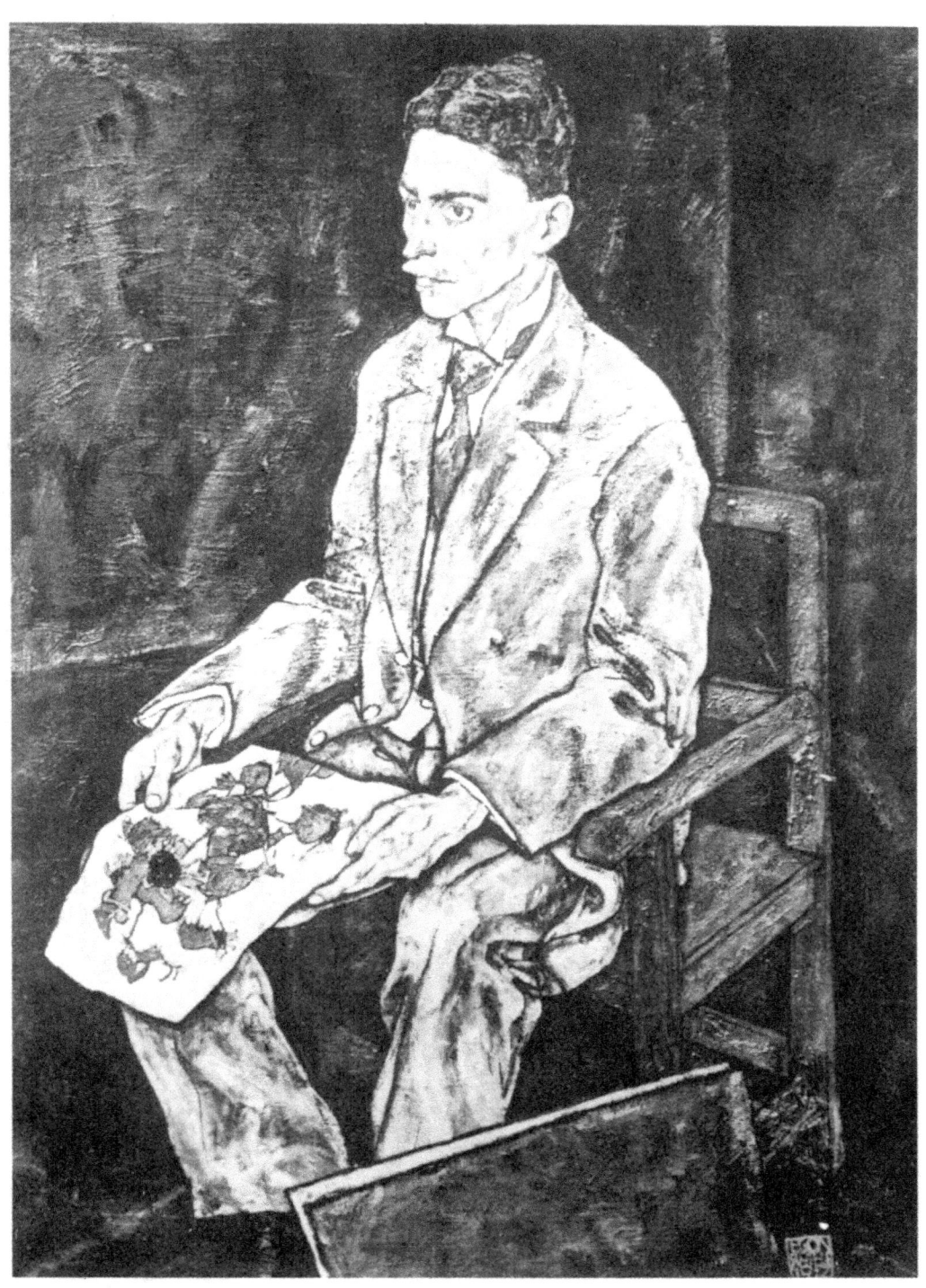

PL. 150. Schiele, *Portrait of Dr. Franz Martin Haberditzl*, 1917, oil.

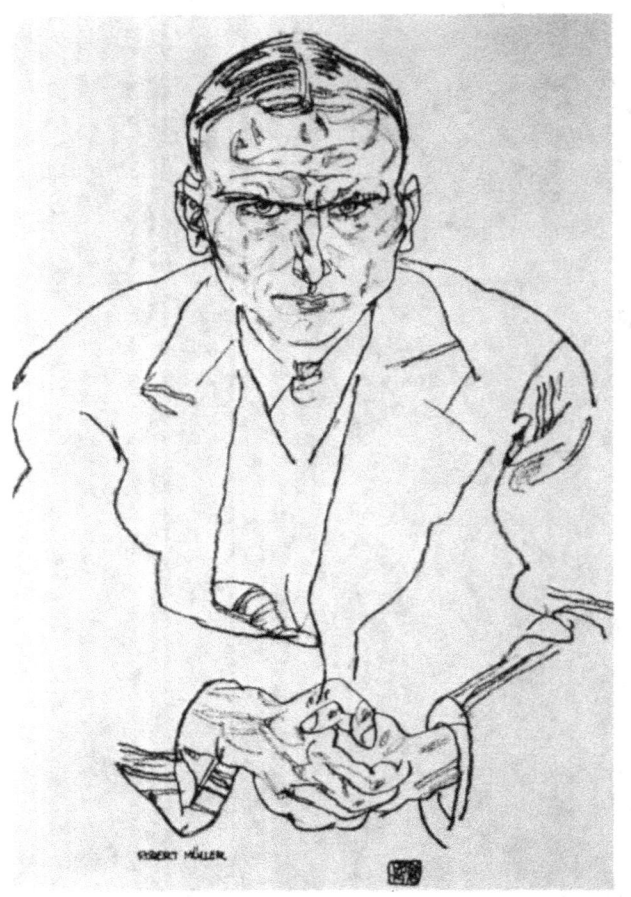

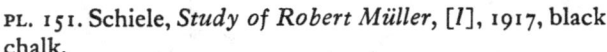

PL. 151. Schiele, *Study of Robert Müller*, [*I*], 1917, black chalk.

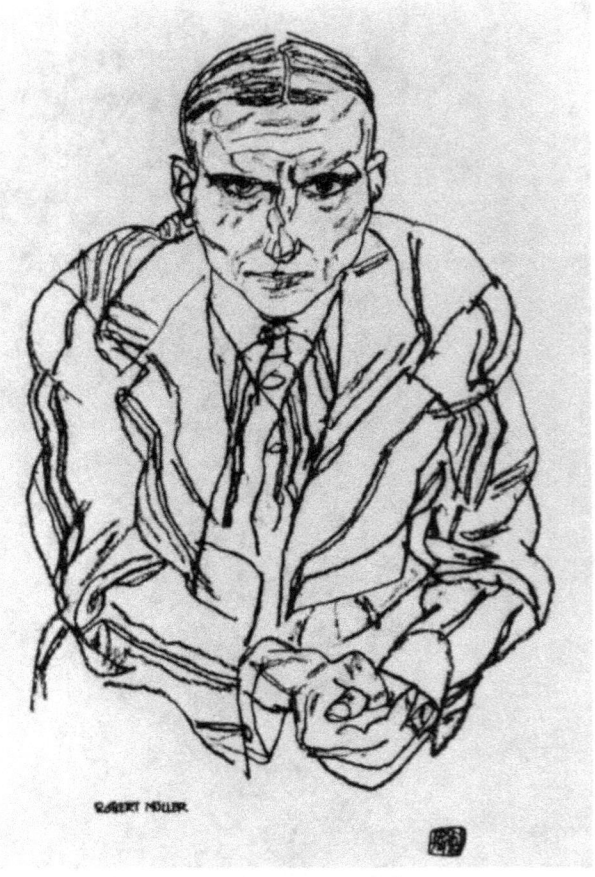

PL. 152. Schiele, *Study of Robert Müller*, [*II*], 1918, black chalk.

PL. 154. Robert Müller, *ca.* 1918.

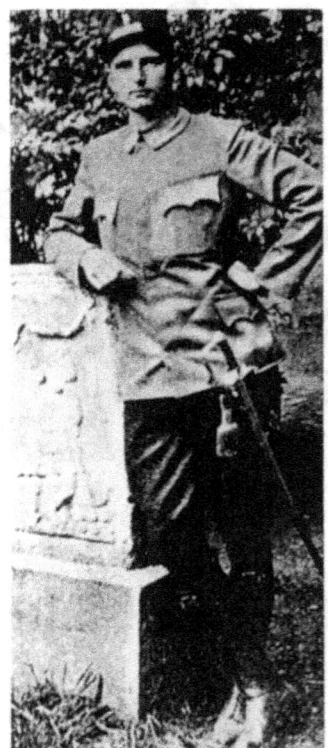

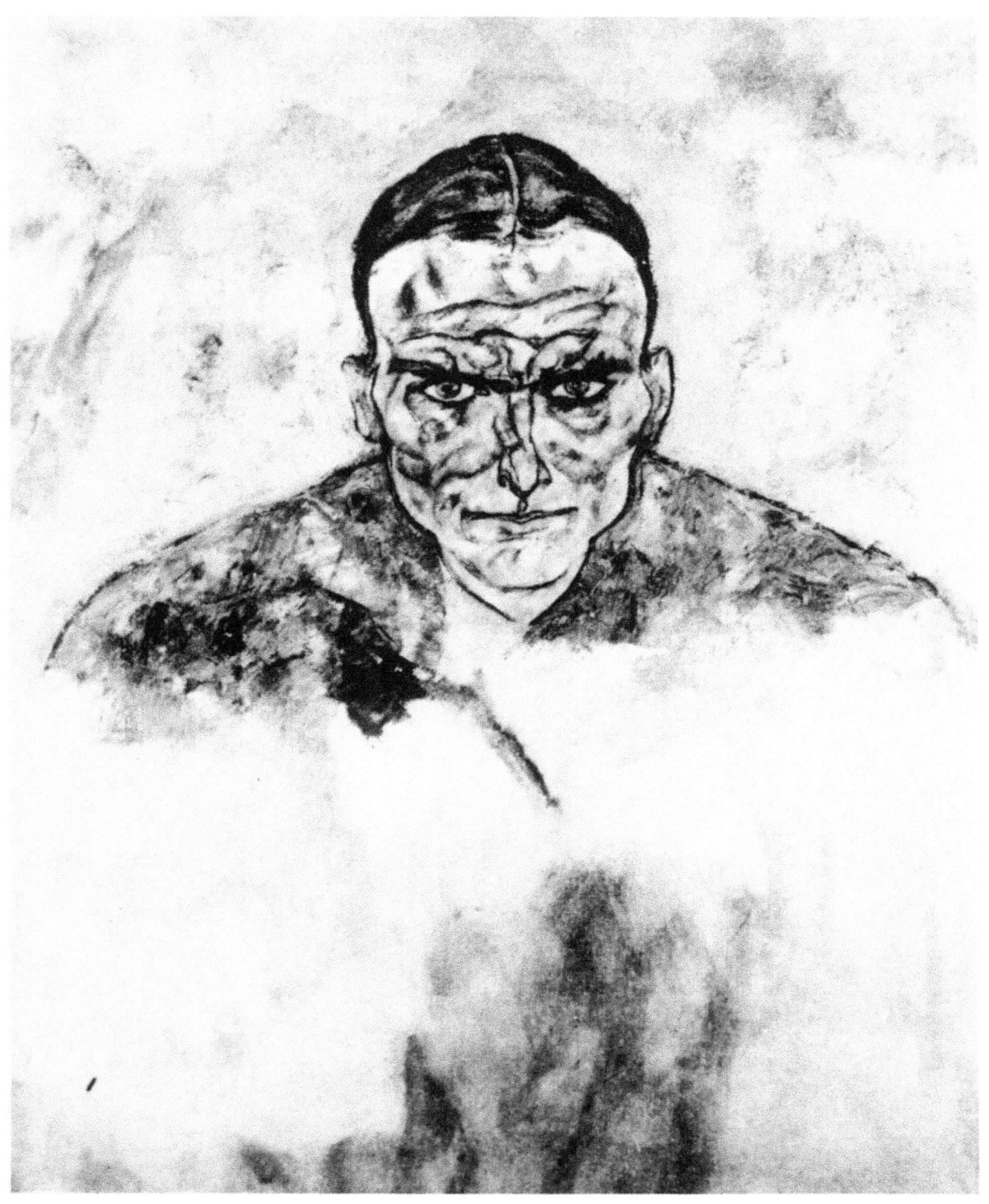

PL. 153. Schiele, *Portrait of Robert Müller* (uncompleted; fragment), 1918, oil.

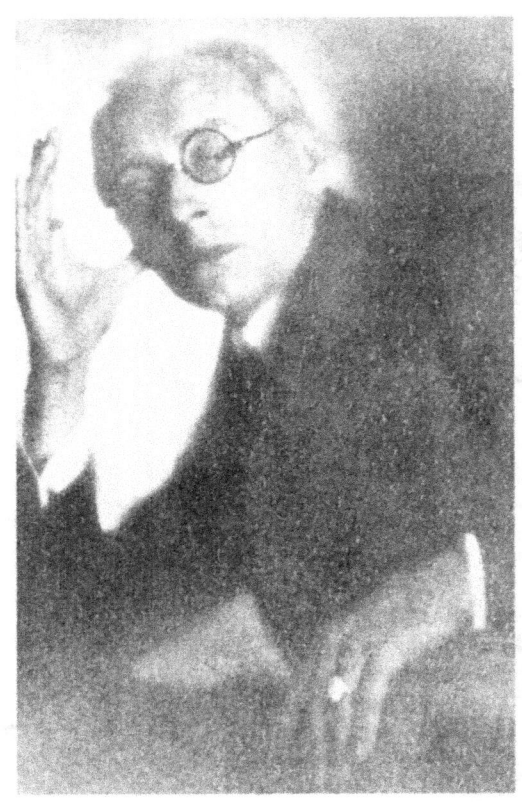

PL. 155. Franz Blei, 1918.

PL. 156. Schiele, *Portrait Sketch of Franz Blei with Arms Crossed*, 1918, black chalk.

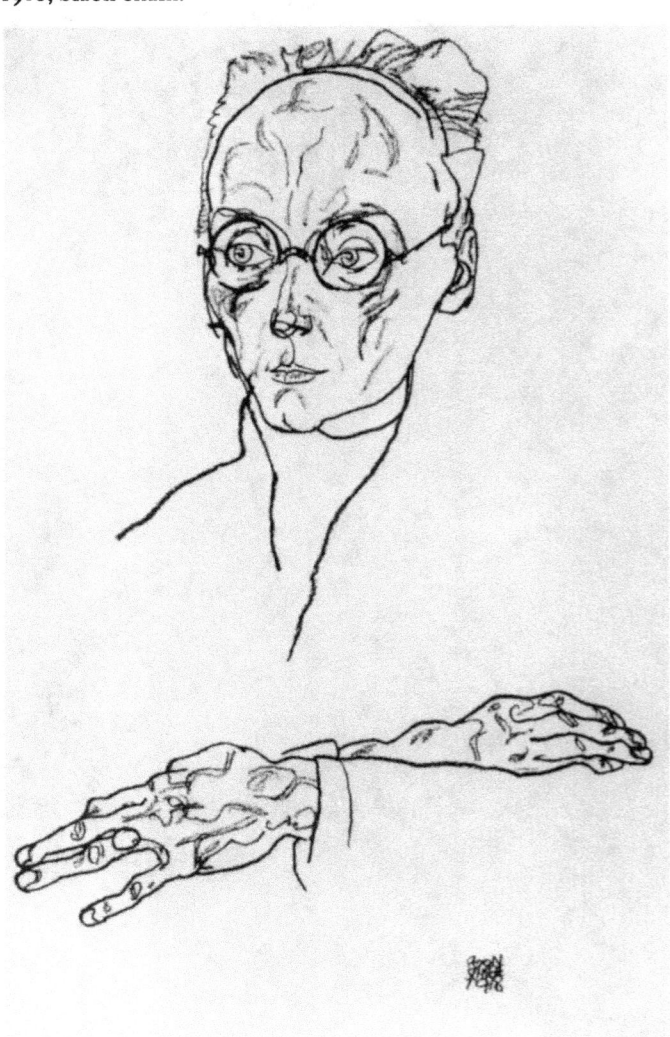

FRANZ BLEI

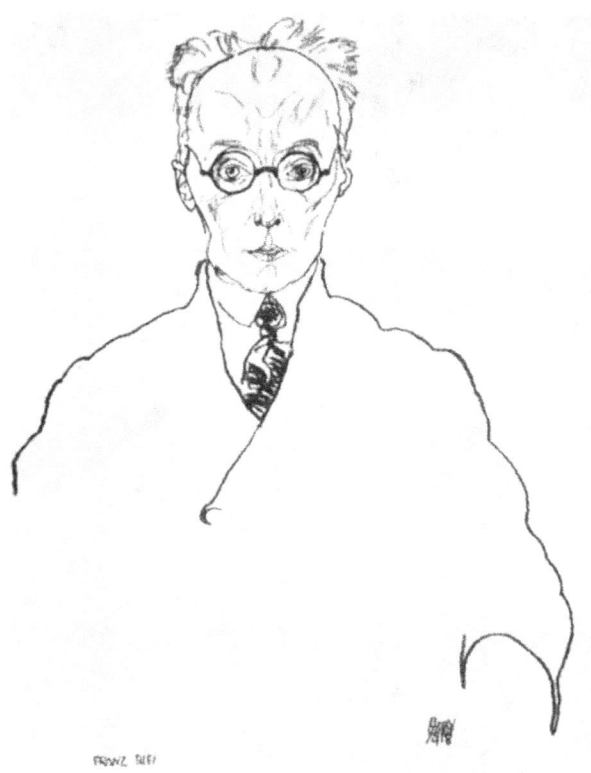

PL. 157. Schiele, *Portrait Sketch of Franz Blei, Frontal*, 1918, black chalk.

PL. 158. Schiele, *Portrait Sketch of Carl Otten*, 1914, pencil.

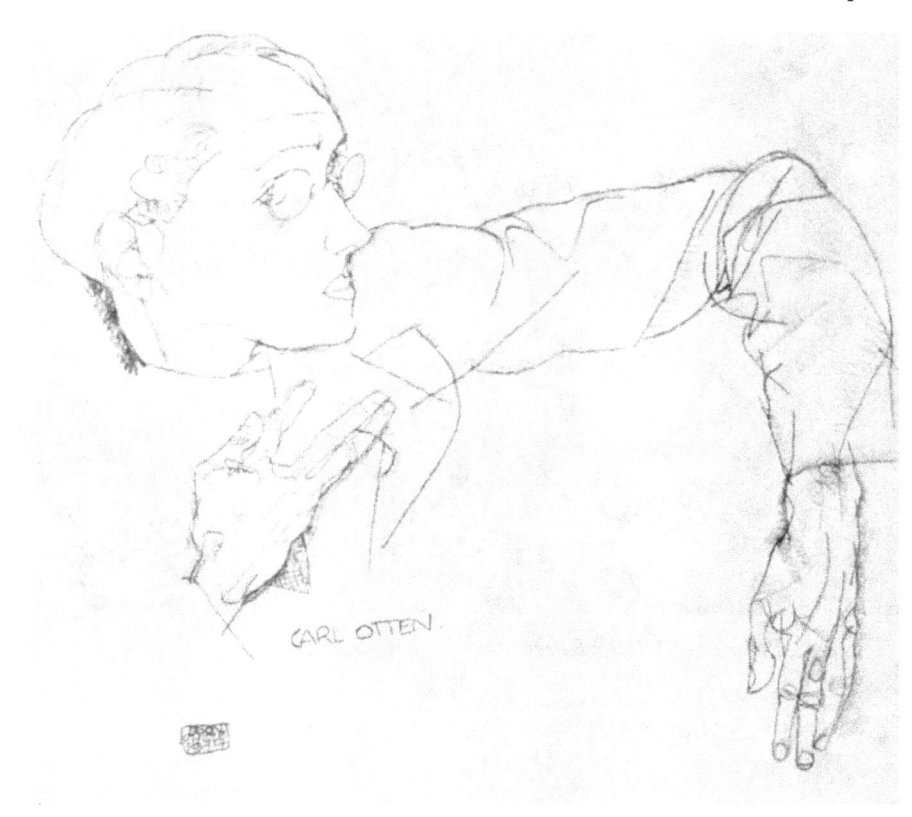

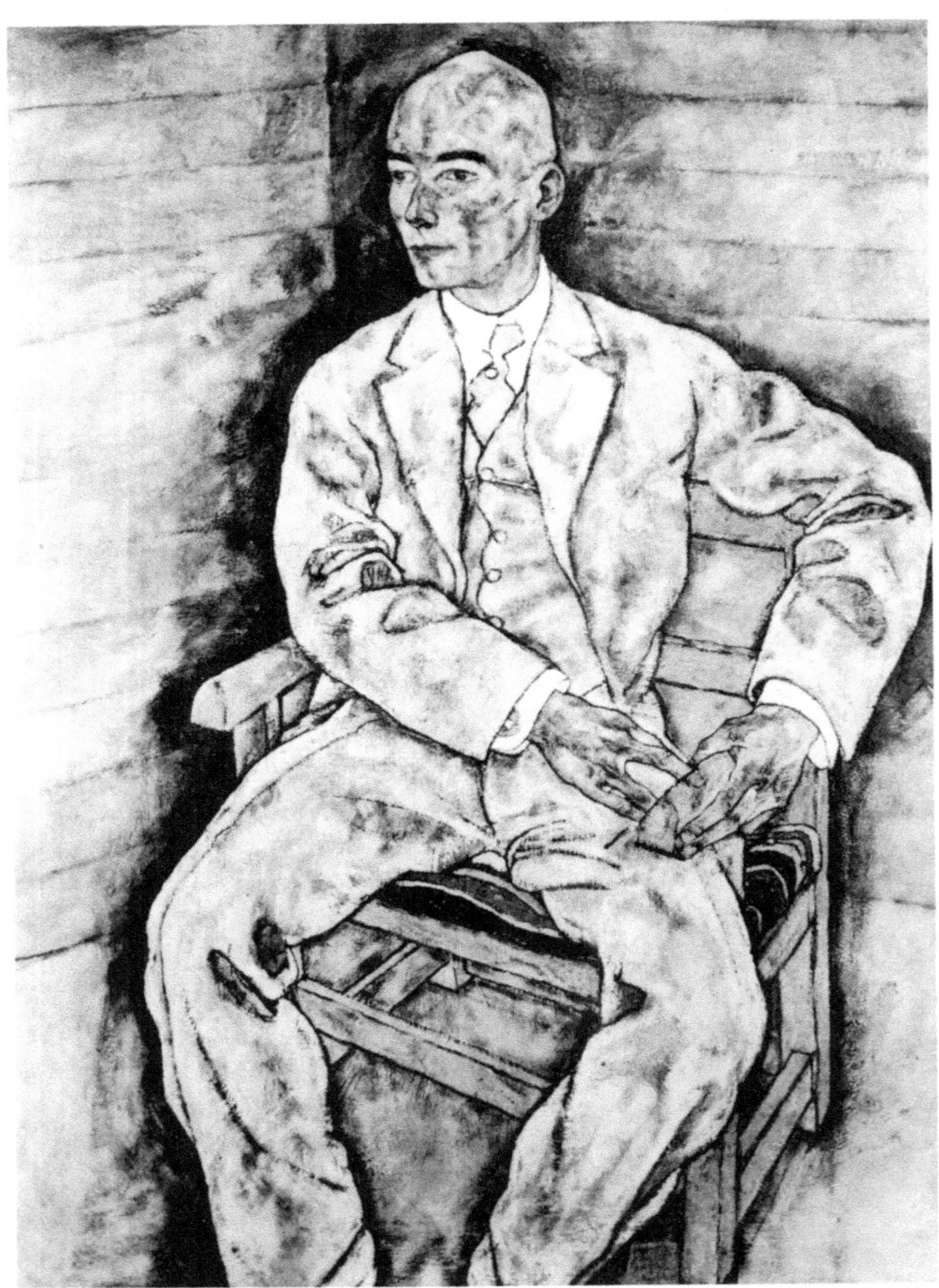

PL. 159. Schiele, *Portrait of Viktor Ritter von Bauer*, 1918, oil.

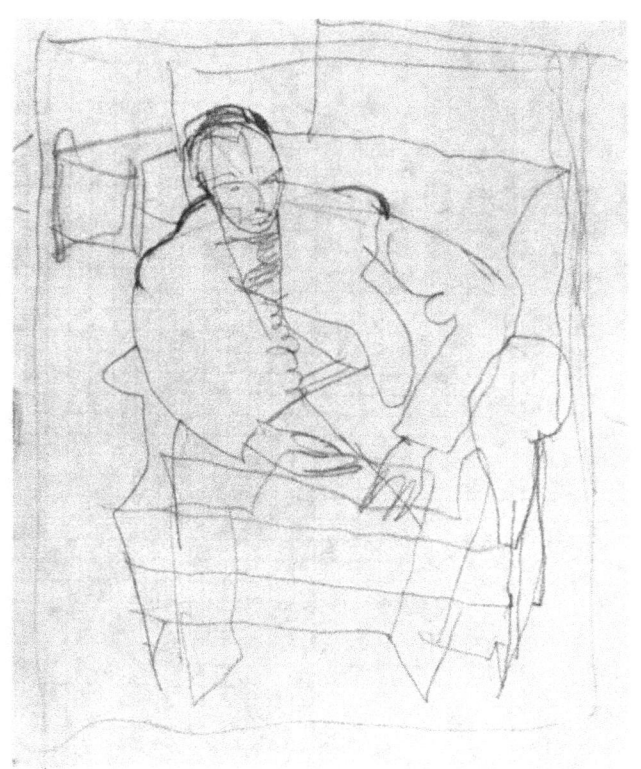

PL. 161a. Schiele, A.E.S.A. Sketchbook VII, 1917–1918, pencil, p. 16 *recto*.

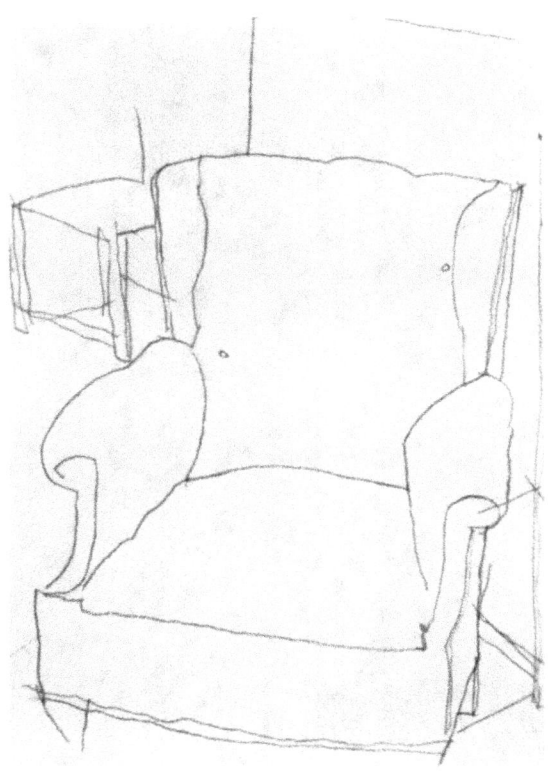

PL. 160. Schiele, *Armchair Study for the Portrait of Dr. Hugo Koller*, 1918, black chalk.

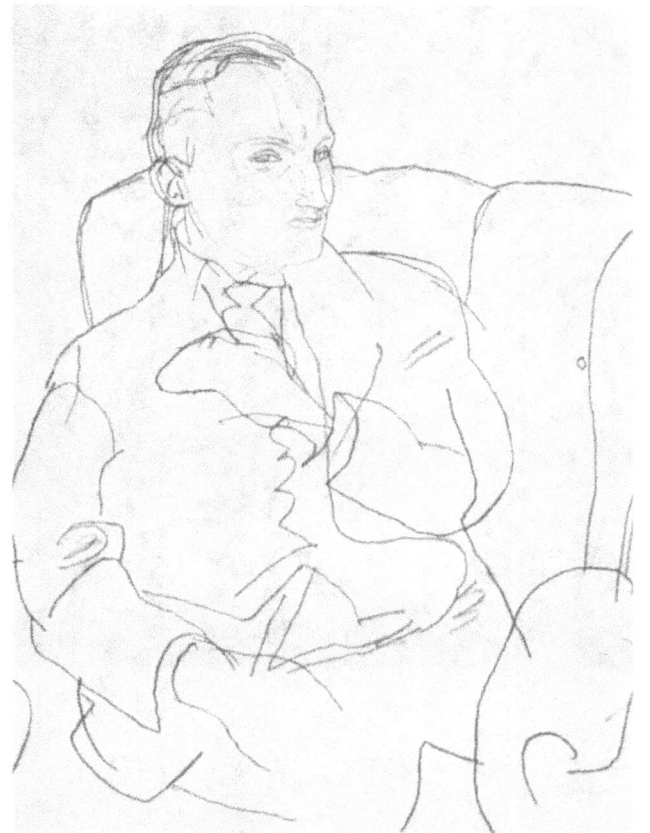

PL. 161b. Schiele, *Study of Dr. Koller with Left Arm Raised*, 1918, black chalk.

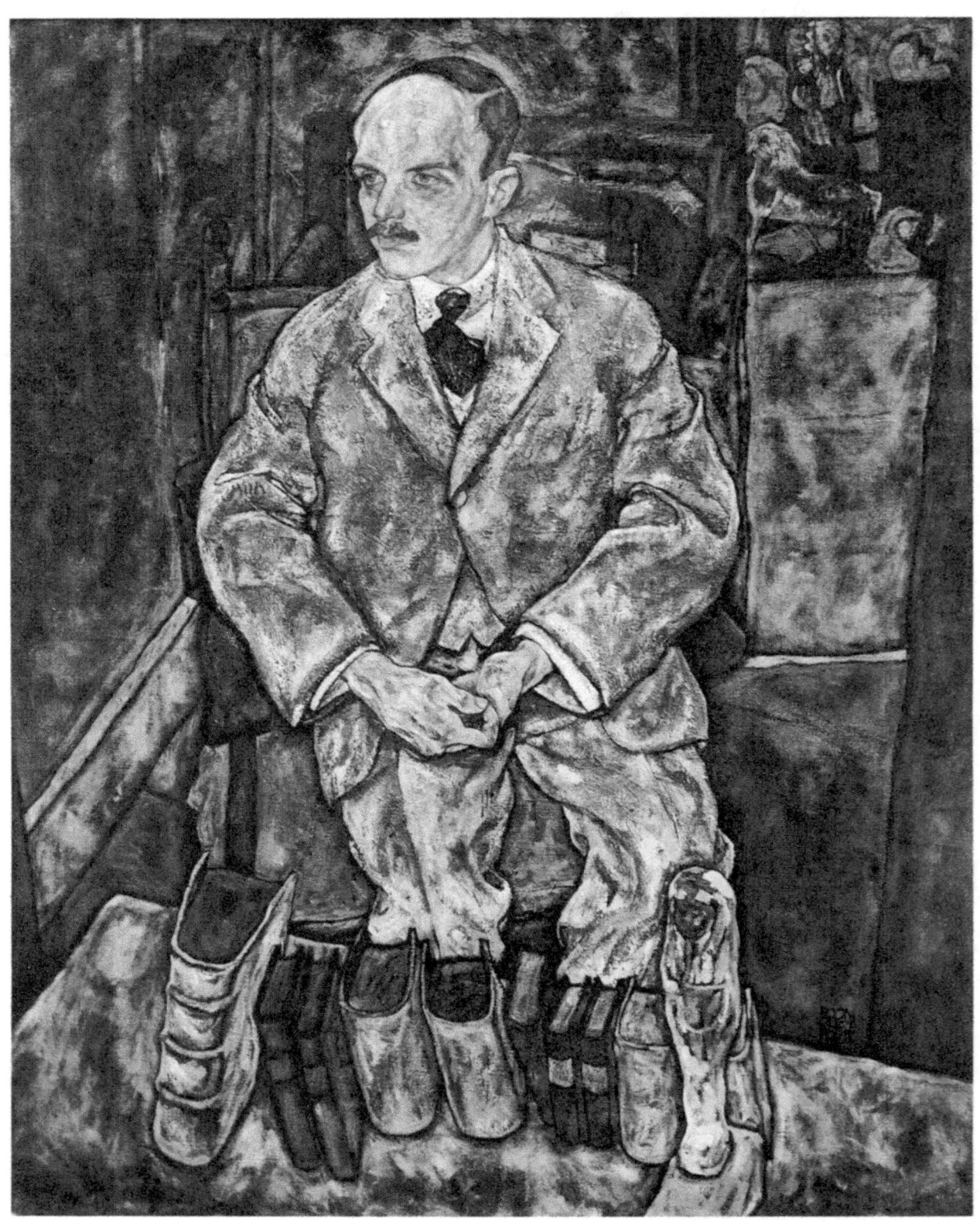

PL. 162. Schiele, *Portrait of Guido Arnot*, 1918, oil.

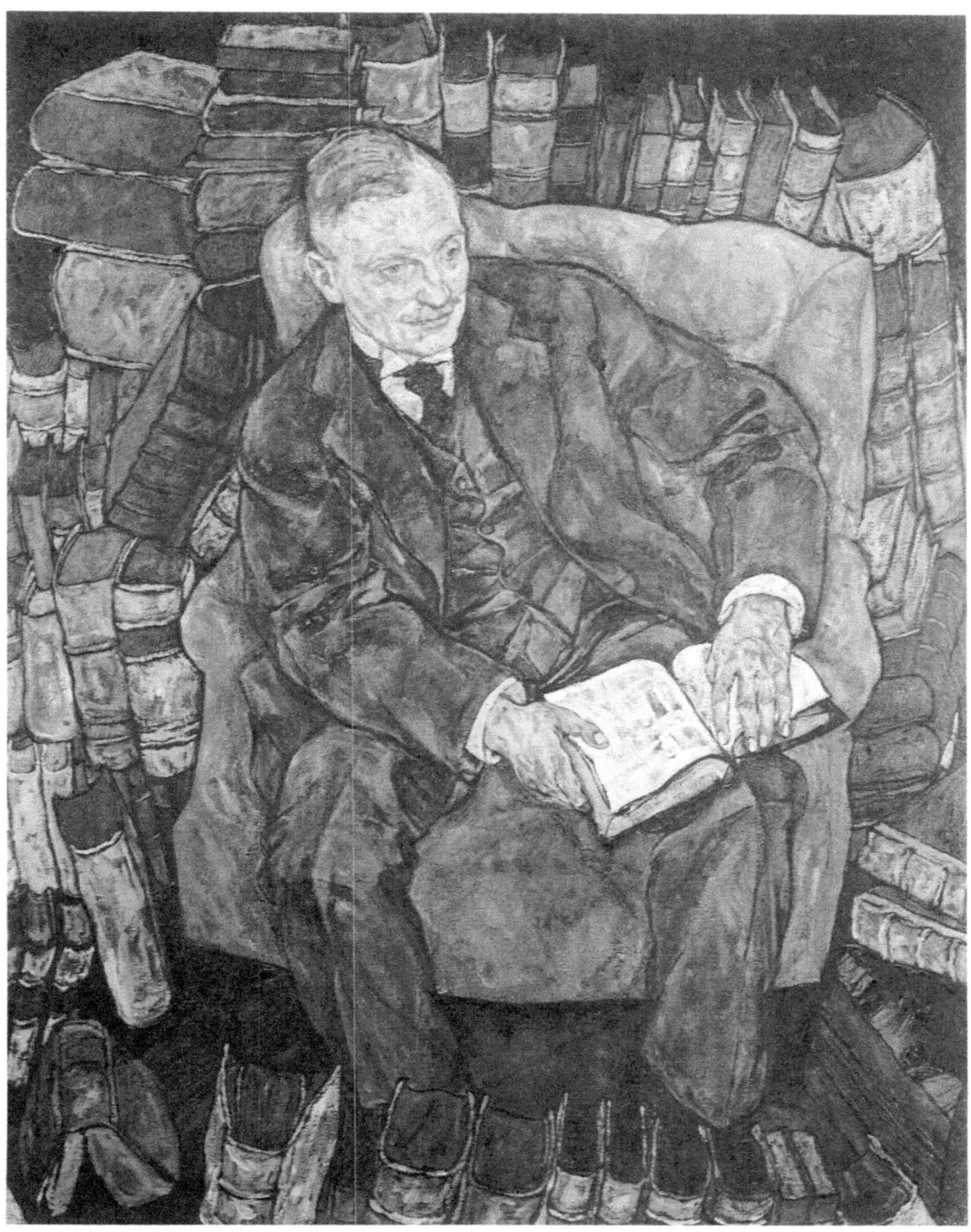

PL. 163. Schiele, *Portrait of Dr. Hugo Koller*, 1918, oil.

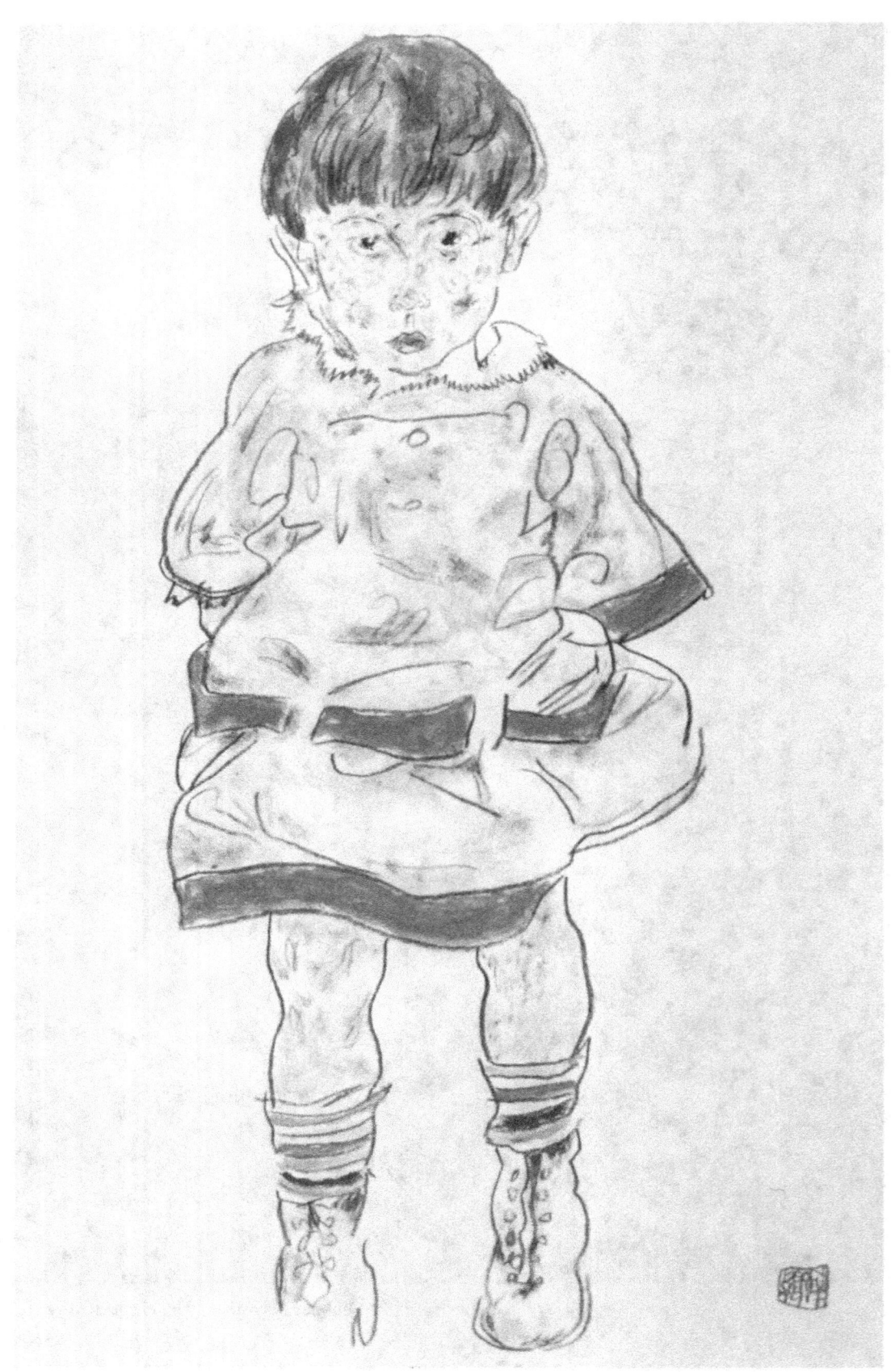

PL. 164. Schiele, *Study of Anton Peschka, Jr., Frontal*, 1917, black chalk and watercolor.

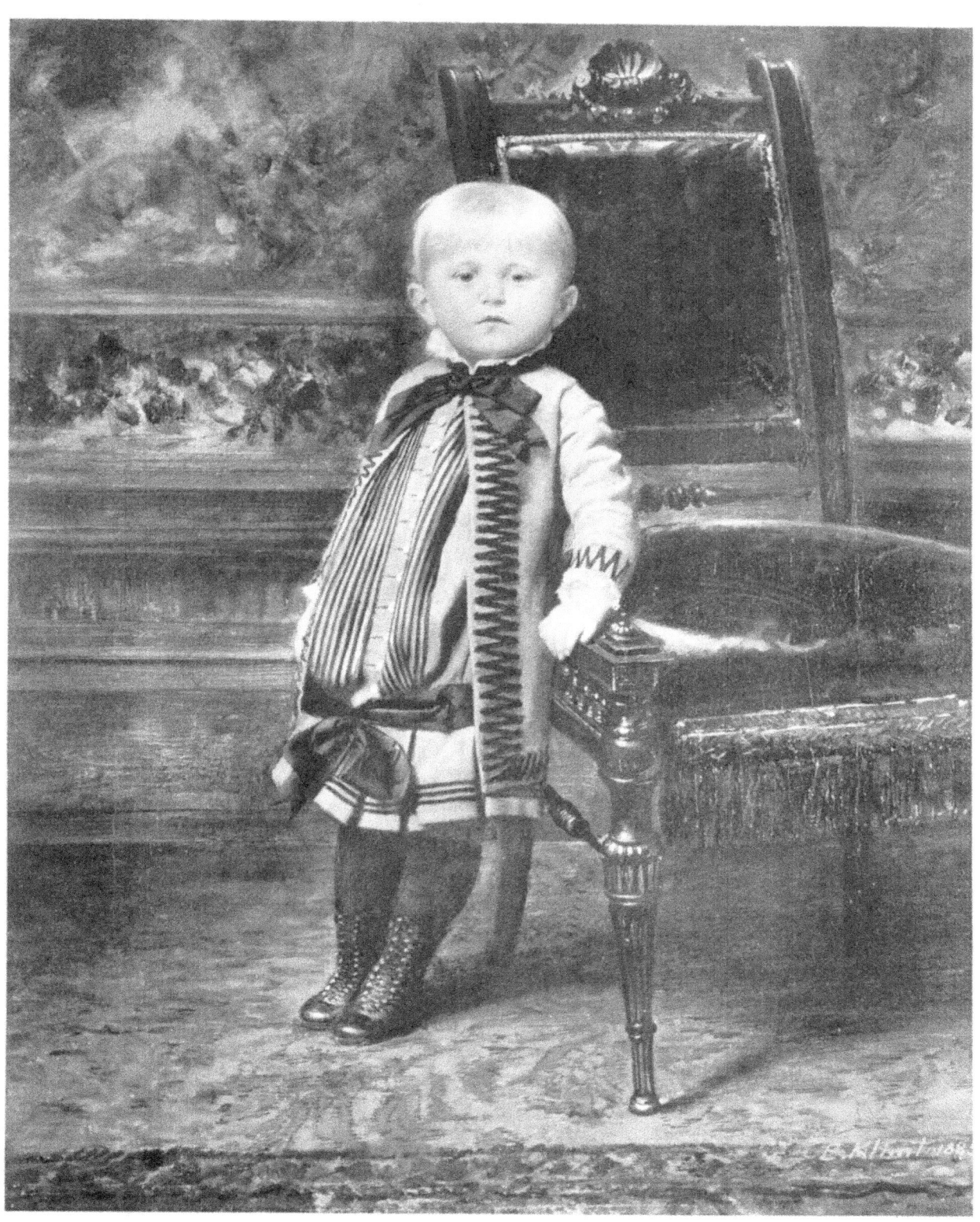

PL. 165. Ernst Klimt, *Portrait of a Boy*, 1885, oil.

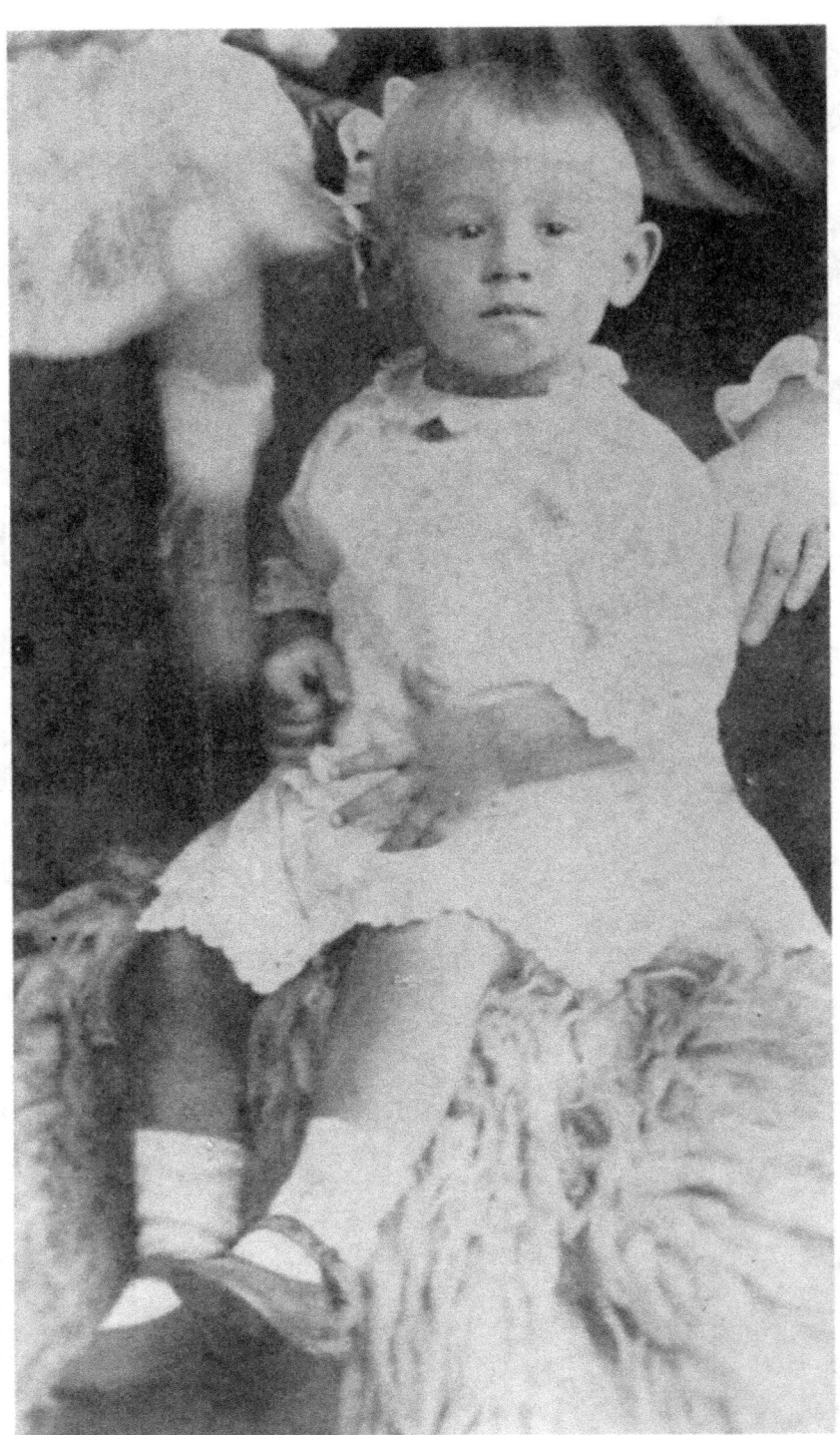

PL. 166. Anton Peschka, Jr., 1918.

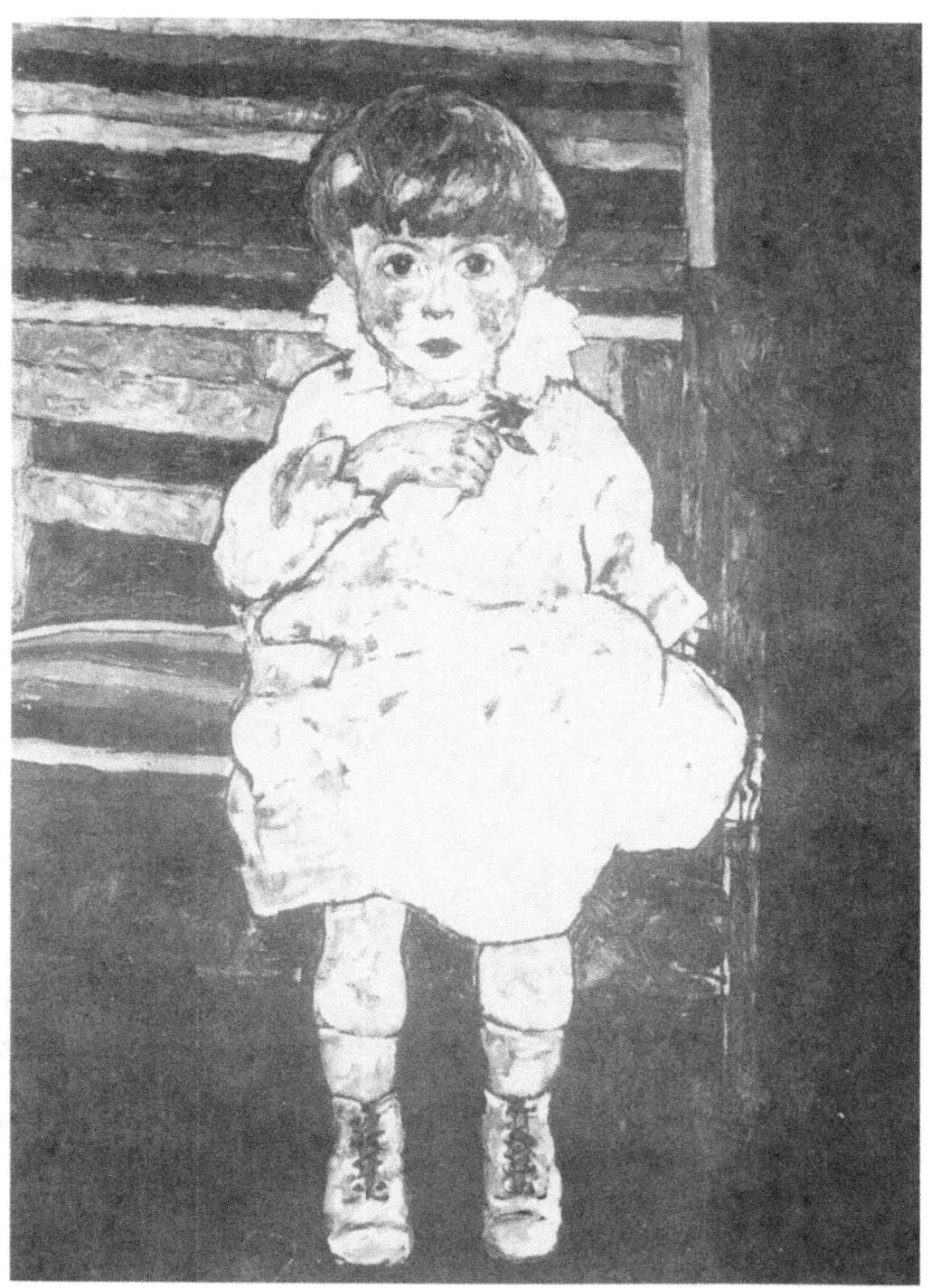

PL. 167. Schiele, *Portrait of Anton Peschka, Jr.*, 1918, oil.

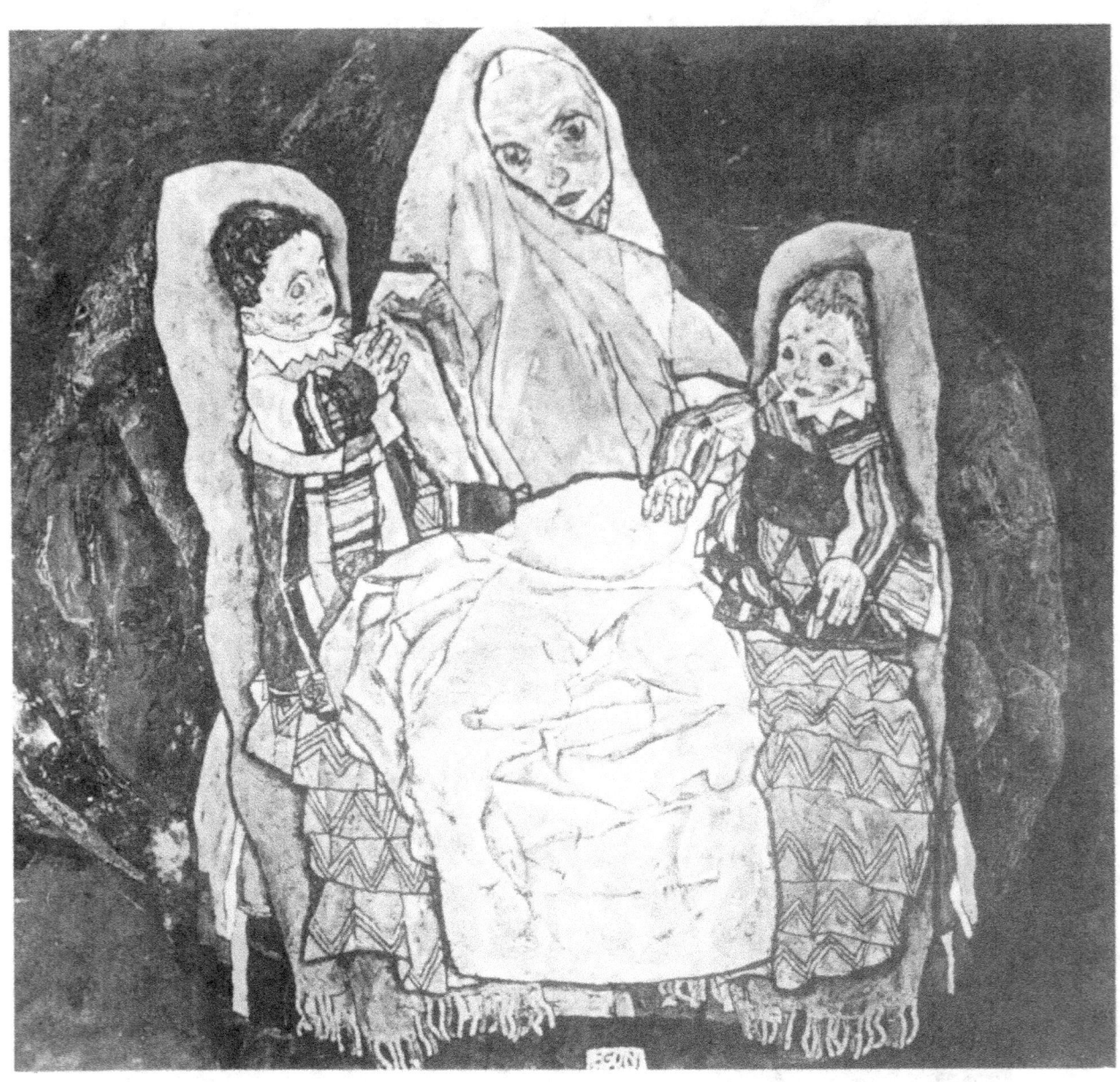

PL. 168. Schiele, *Mother with Two Children*, 1915–1917, oil.

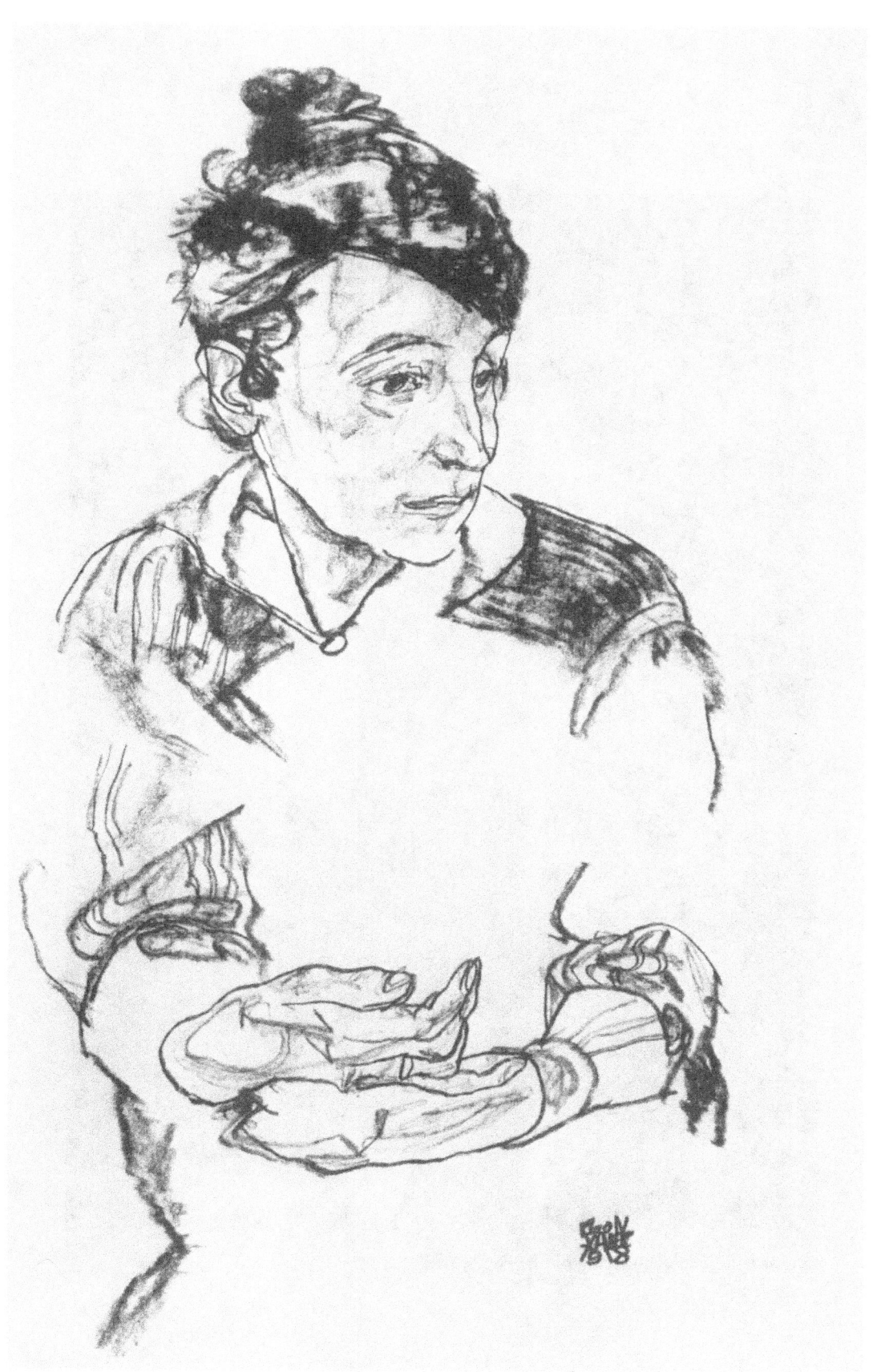

PL. 169. Schiele, *Portrait of Marie Schiele*, 1918, black chalk.

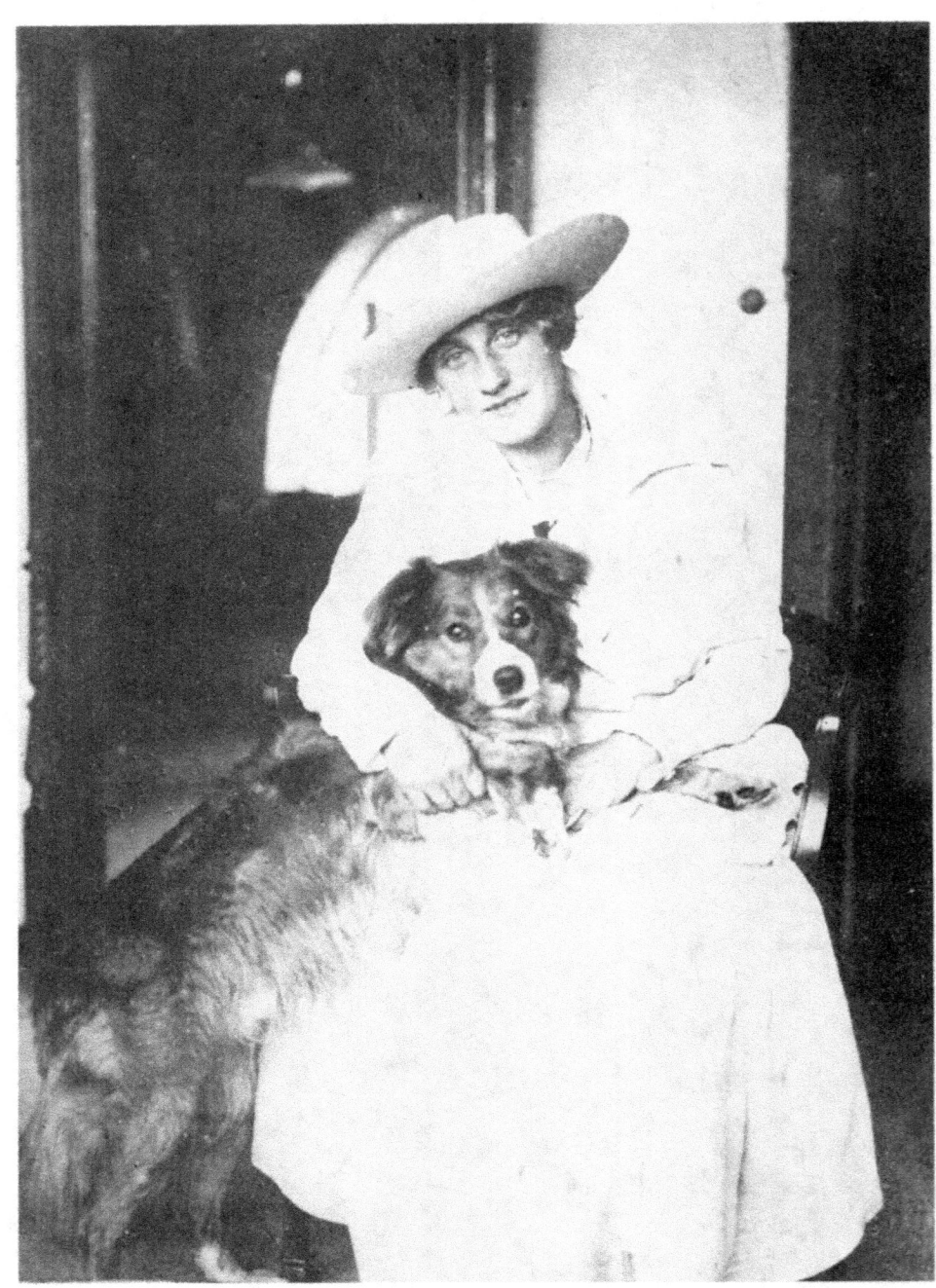

PL. 170. Edith Schiele seated with the dog "Lord," *ca.* 1917.

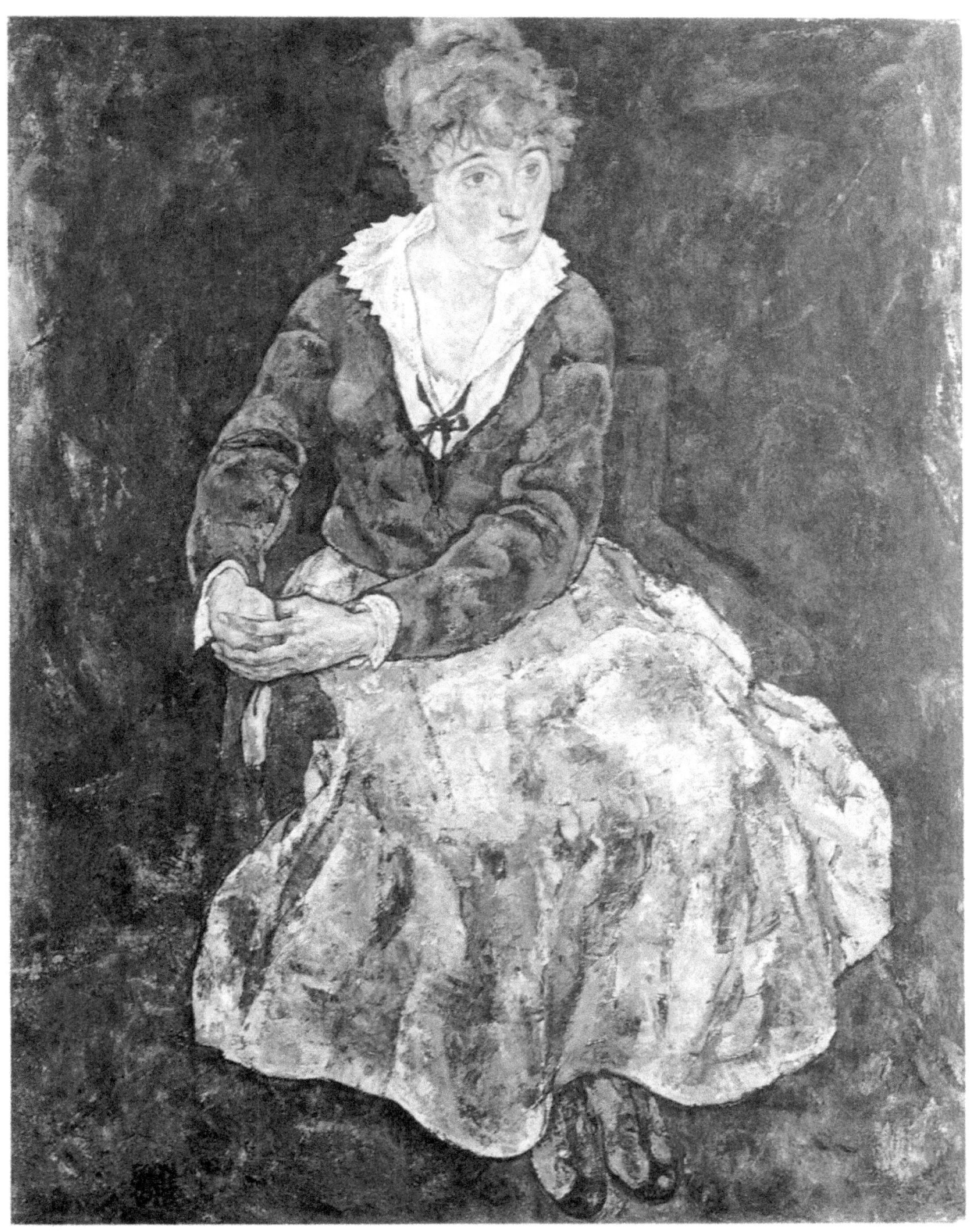

PL. 171. Schiele, *Portrait of Edith Schiele Seated*, 1917–1918, oil.

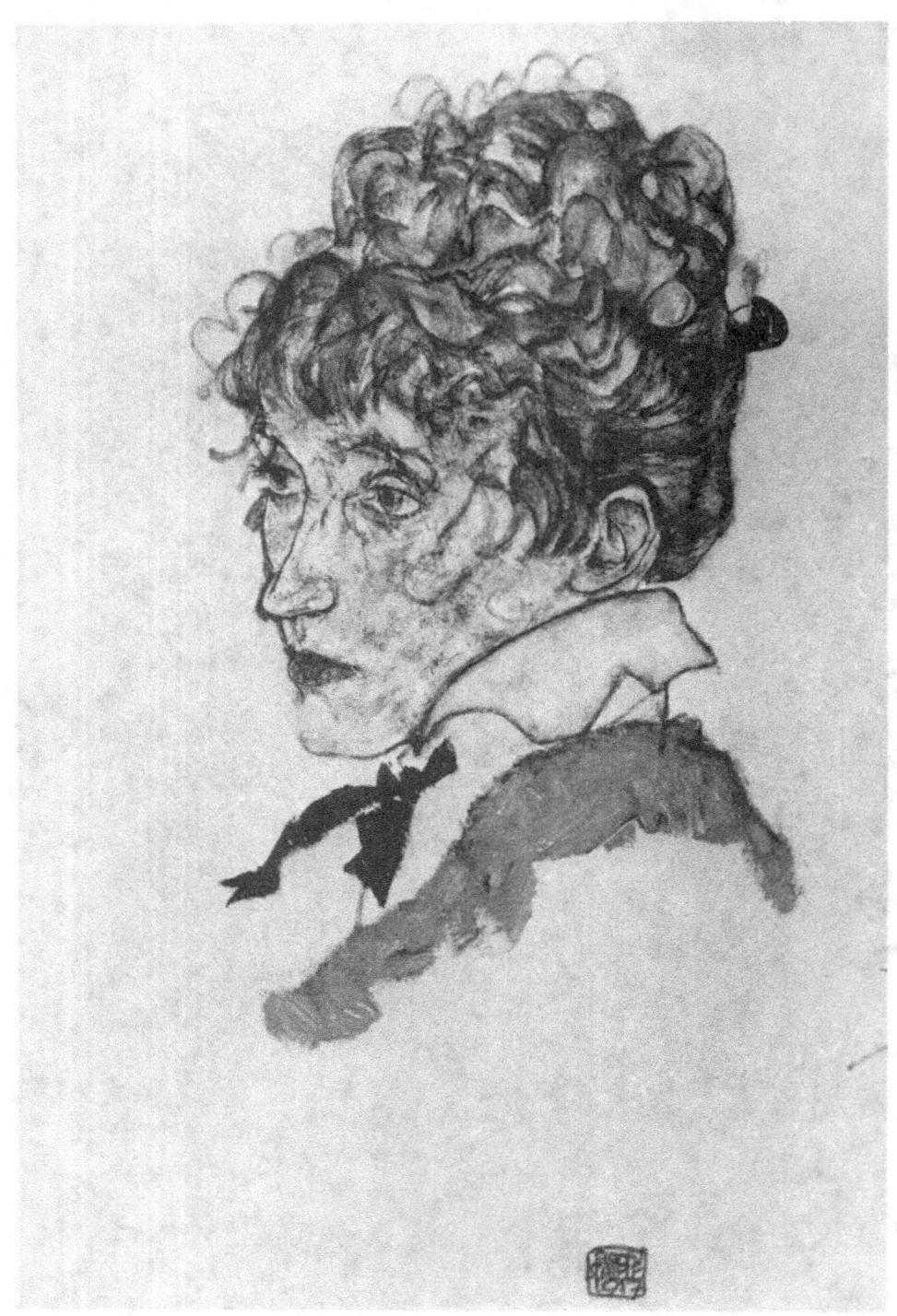

PL. 172. Schiele, *Edith in Three-Quarter View*, 1917, black chalk and watercolor.

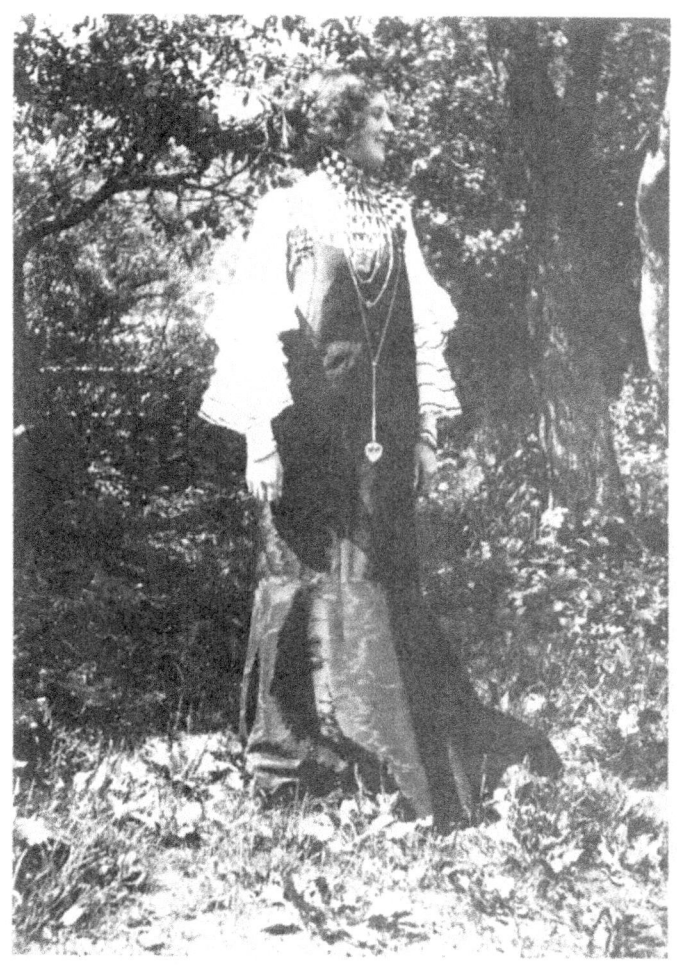

PL. 173. Emilie Flöge *ca.* 1905 (photograph by Gustav Klimt).

PL. 174. Klimt, *Portrait of Emilie Flöge*, 1902, oil.

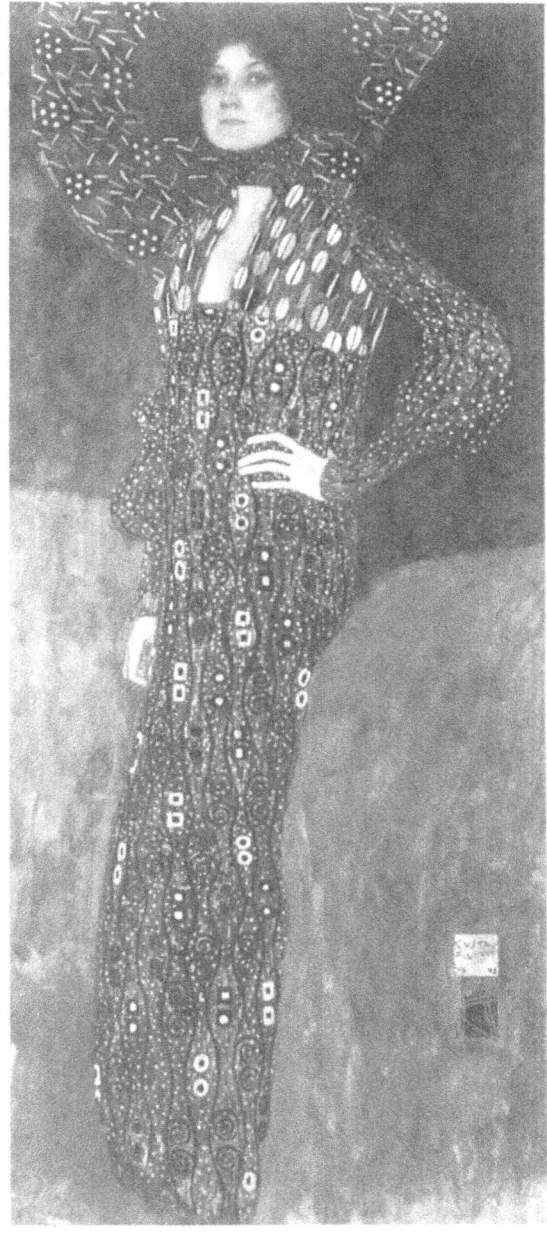

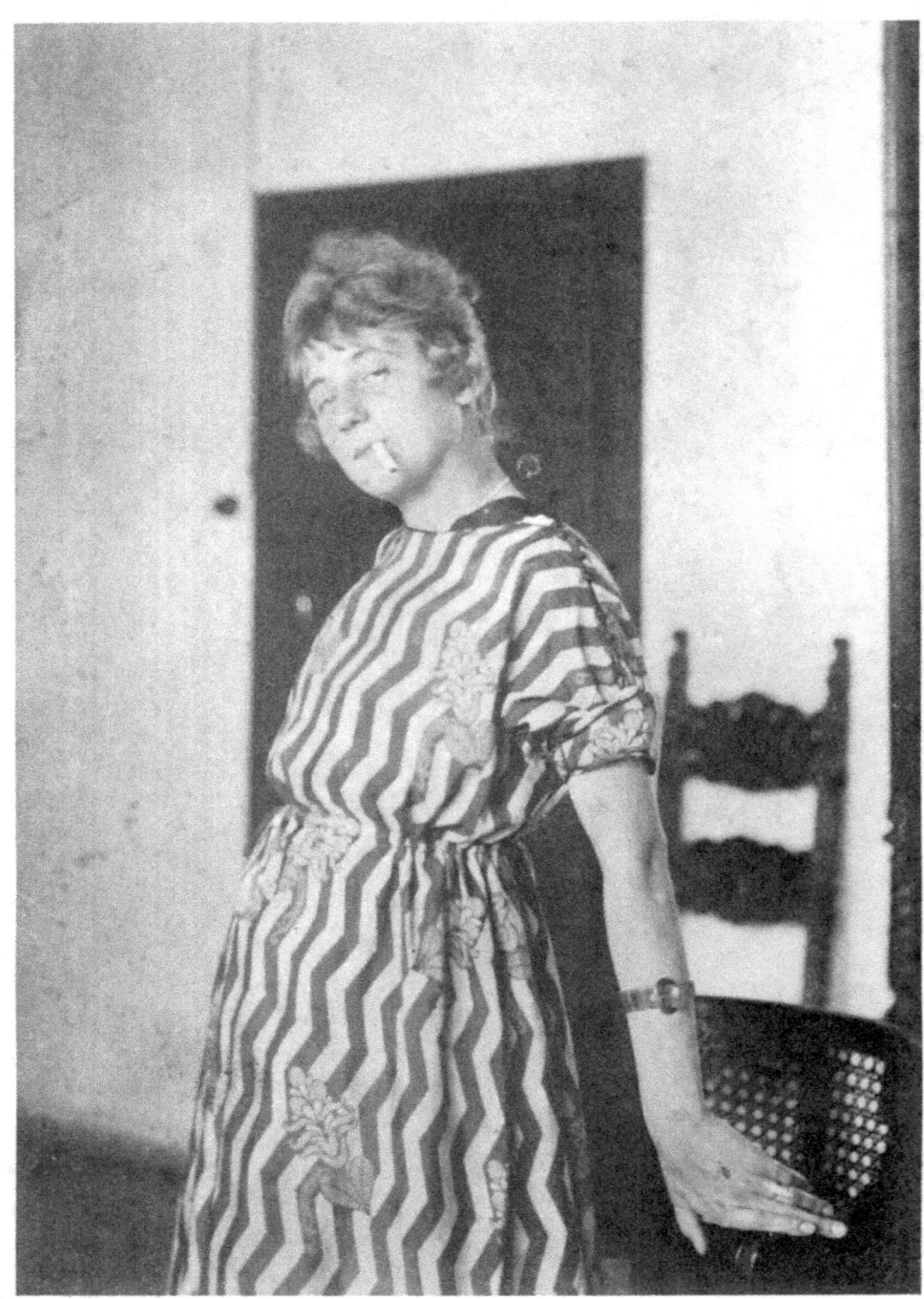

PL. 175. Edith Schiele, *ca.* 1916.

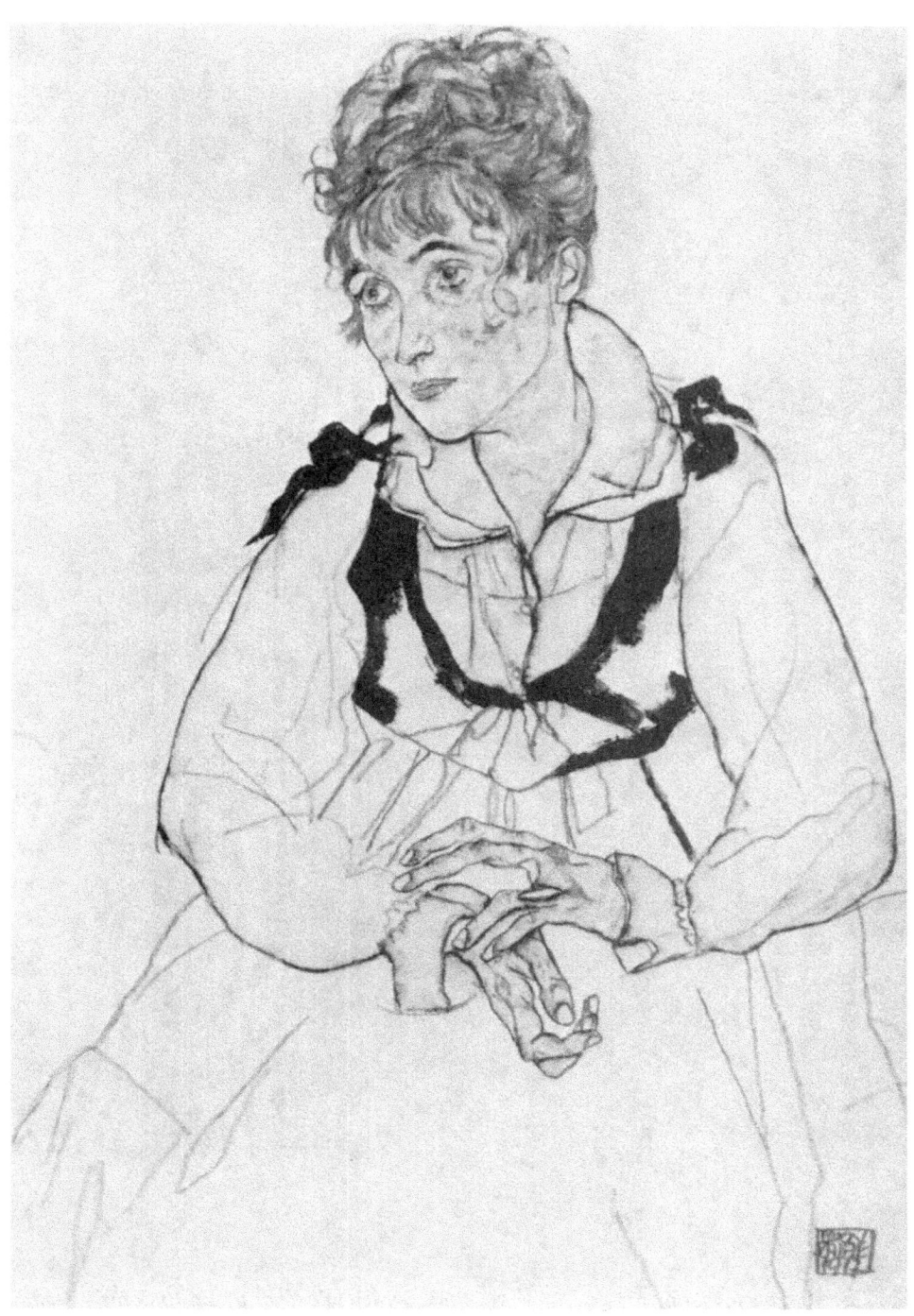

PL. 176. Schiele, *Study of Edith Schiele Seated with Hand to Cuff*, 1917, black chalk and watercolor.

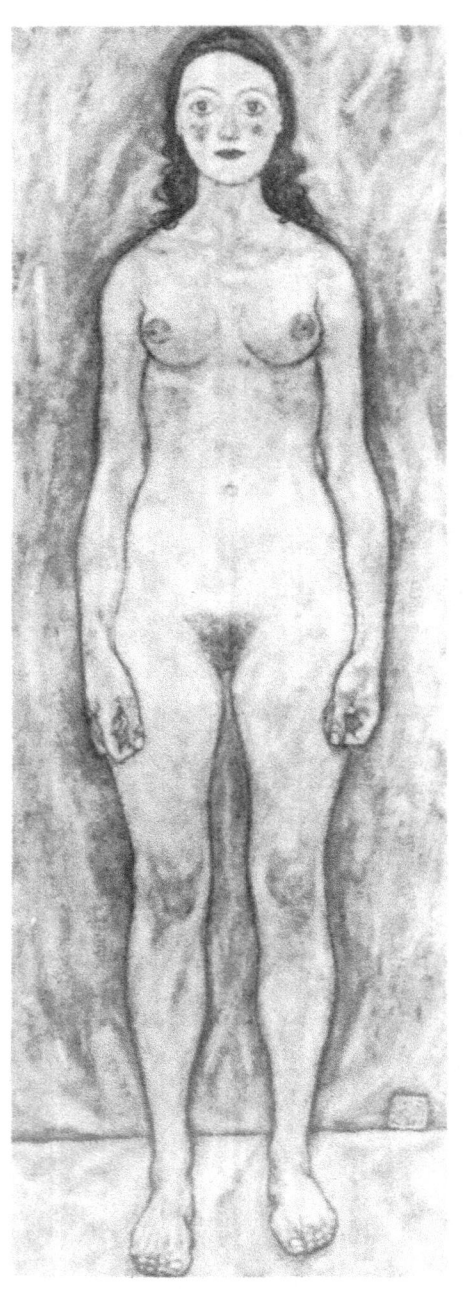

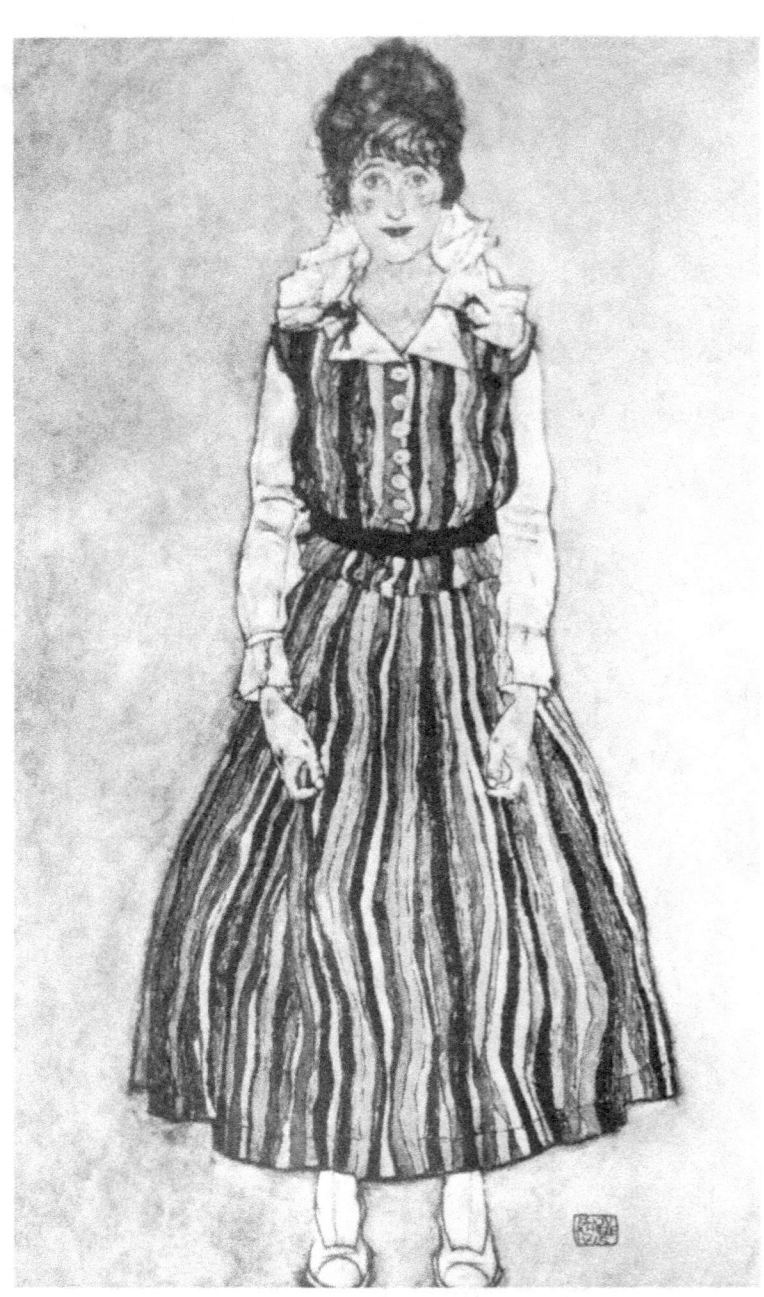

PL. 177. Schiele, *The Virgin*, 1917, oil.   PL. 178a. Schiele, *Portrait of Edith Schiele Standing*, 1915, oil.

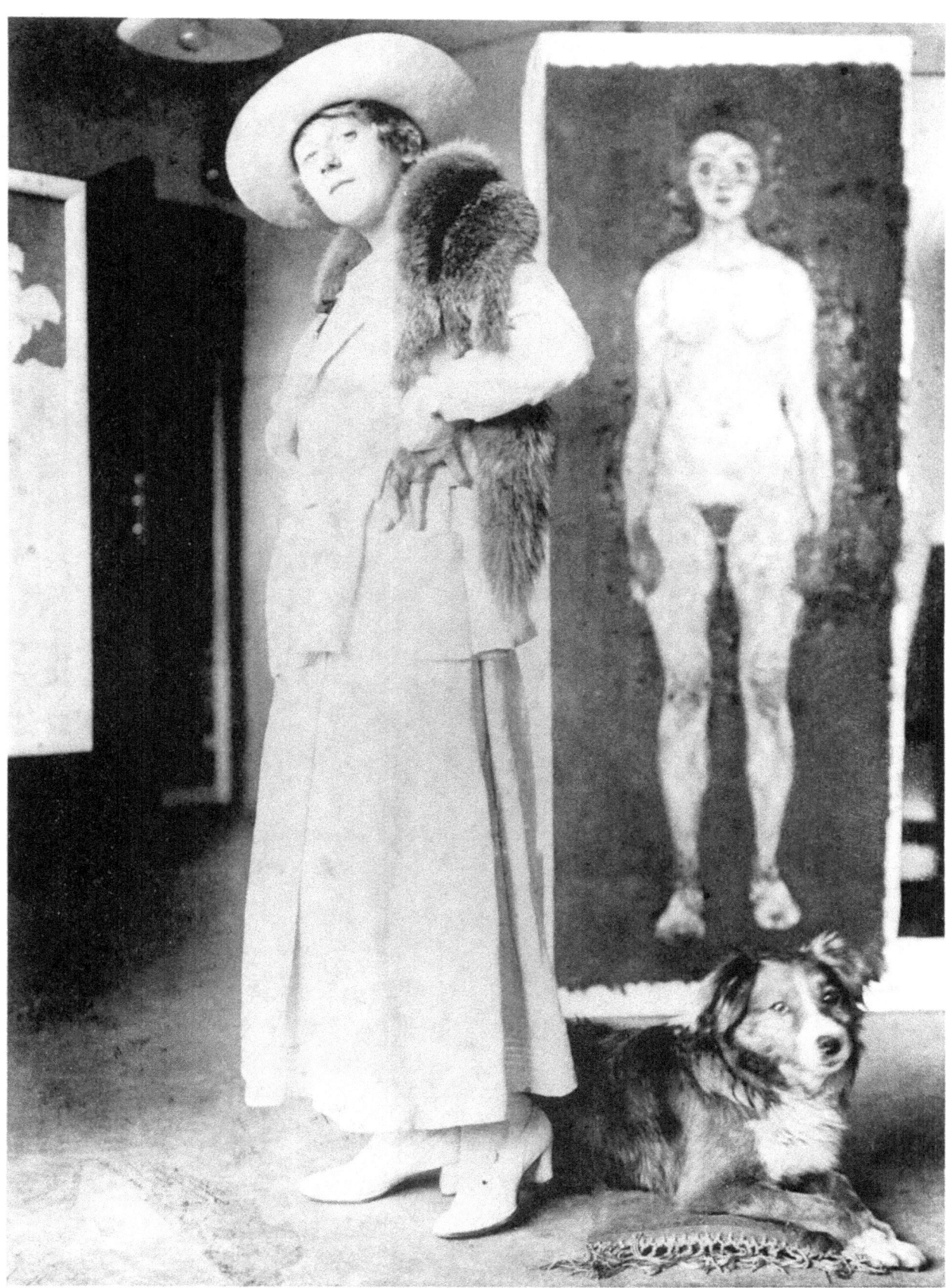

PL. 178b. Edith Schiele standing before Schiele's *The Virgin*, ca. 1917 (photograph by Egon Schiele).

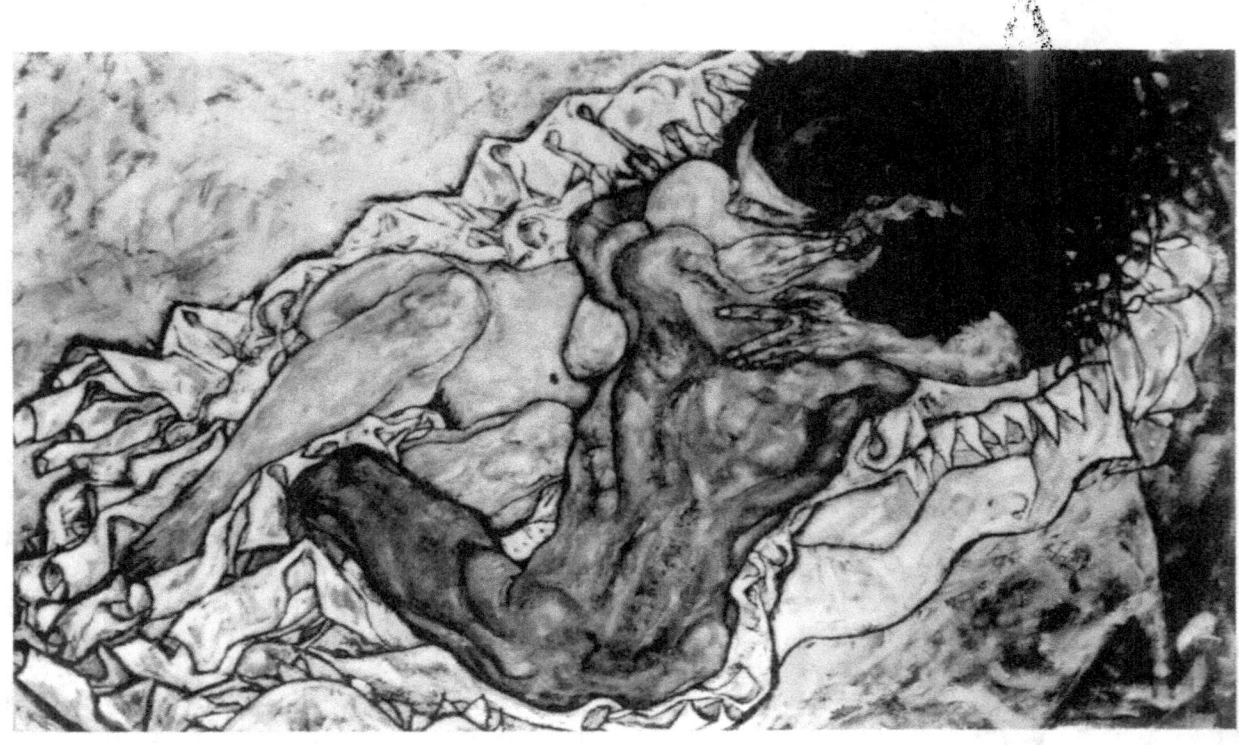

PL. 179. Schiele, *The Embrace ("Lovers")*, 1917, oil.

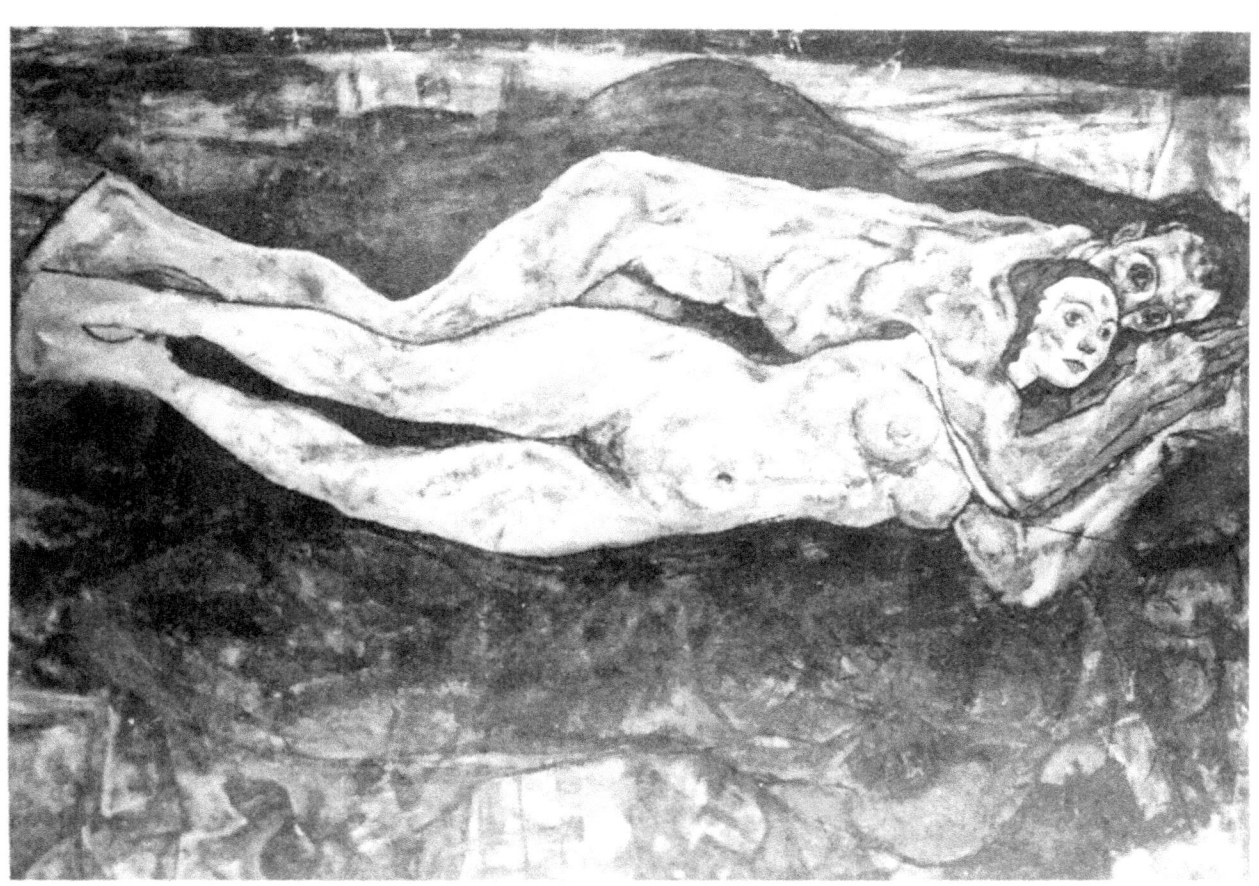

PL. 180. Schiele, *Man and Woman* (unfinished), 1917–1918, oil.

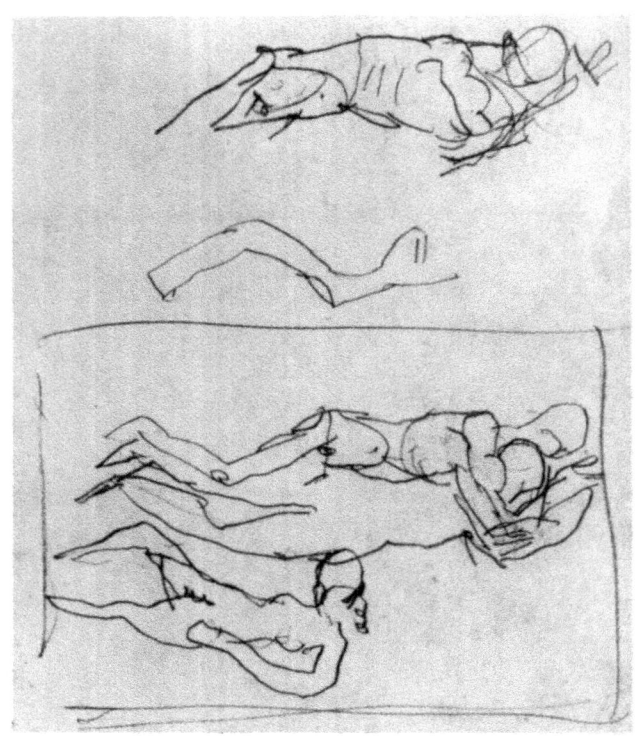

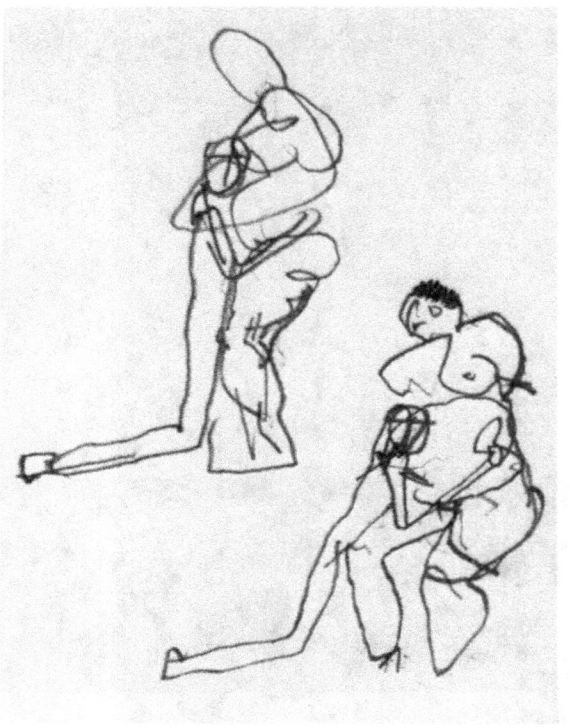

PL. 181. Schiele, A.E.S.A. Sketchbook VII, 1917–1918, pencil, p. 21 *recto*.

PL. 182. Schiele, A.E.S.A. Sketchbook V, 1915, pencil, p. 17 *recto*.

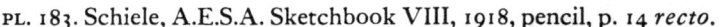

PL. 183. Schiele, A.E.S.A. Sketchbook VIII, 1918, pencil, p. 14 *recto*.

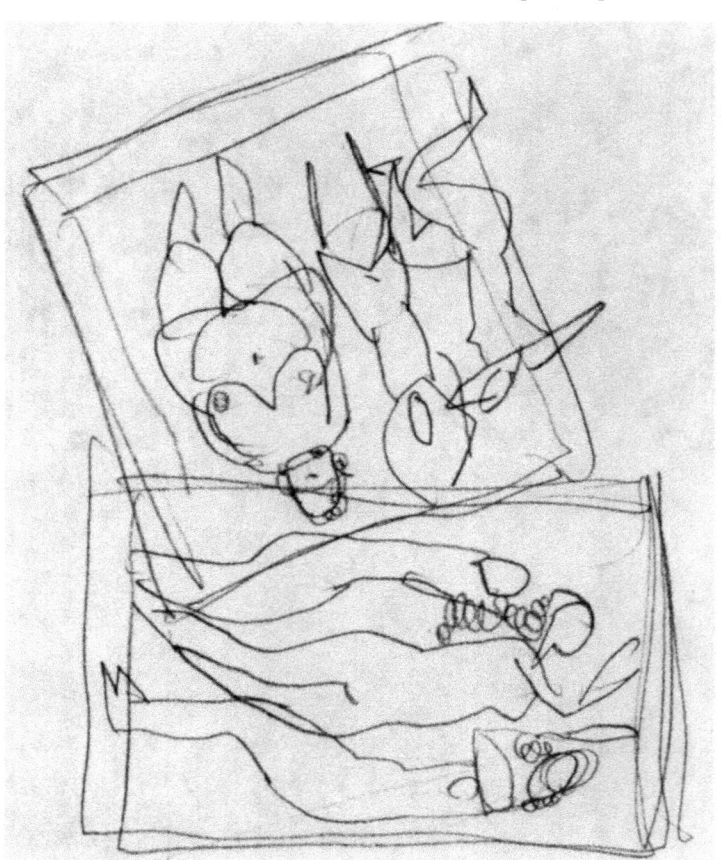

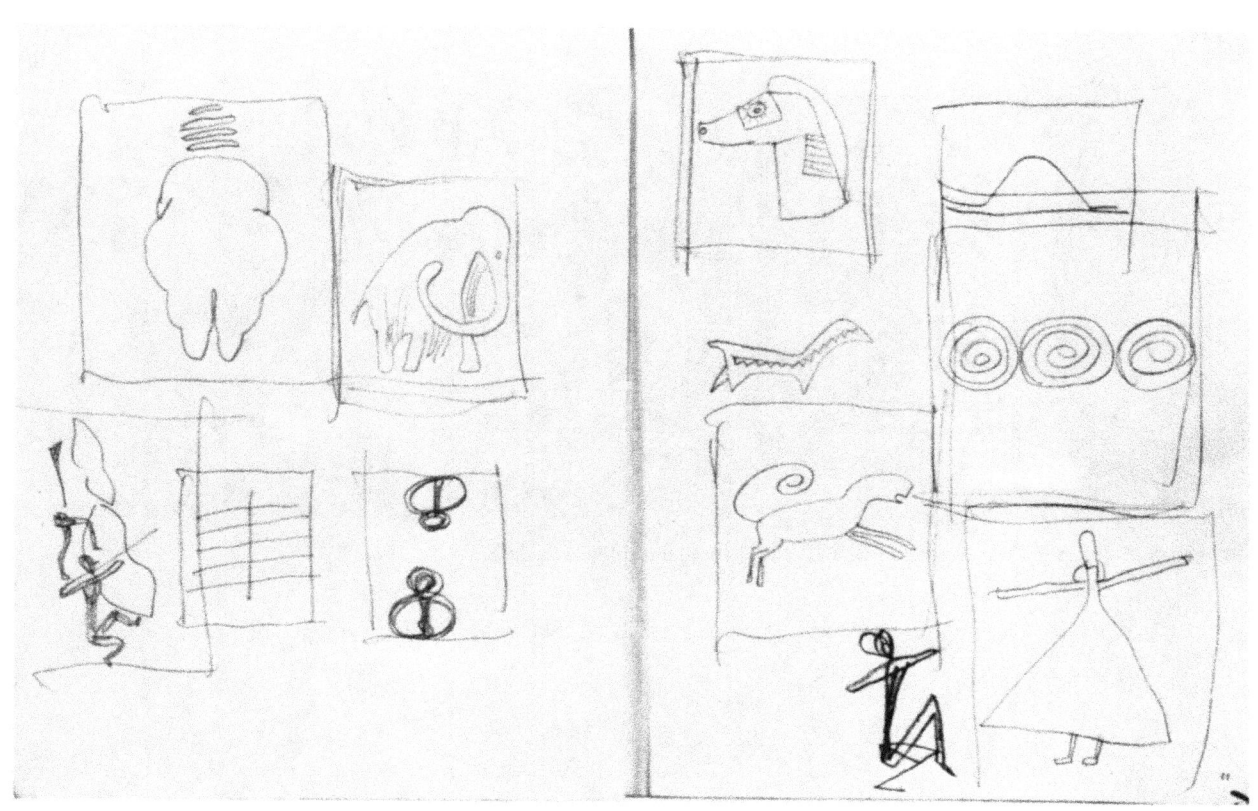

PL. 184. Schiele, A.E.S.A. Sketchbook VIII, 1918, pencil, pp. 10 *verso*, 11 *recto*.

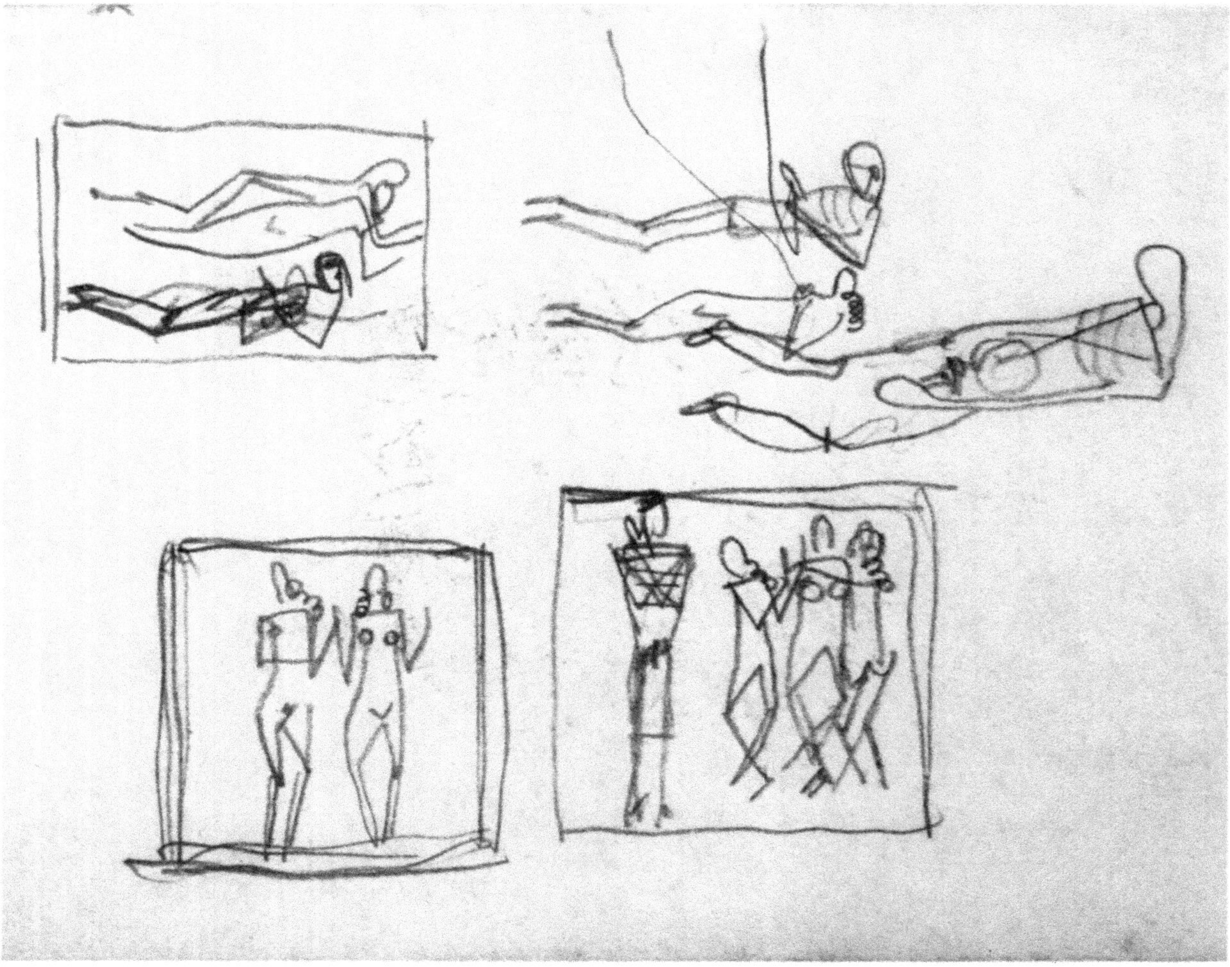

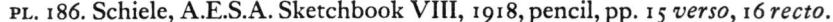

PL. 185. Schiele, A.E.S.A. Sketchbook VII, 1917–1918, pencil, p. 26 *verso*.

PL. 186. Schiele, A.E.S.A. Sketchbook VIII, 1918, pencil, pp. 15 *verso*, 16 *recto*.

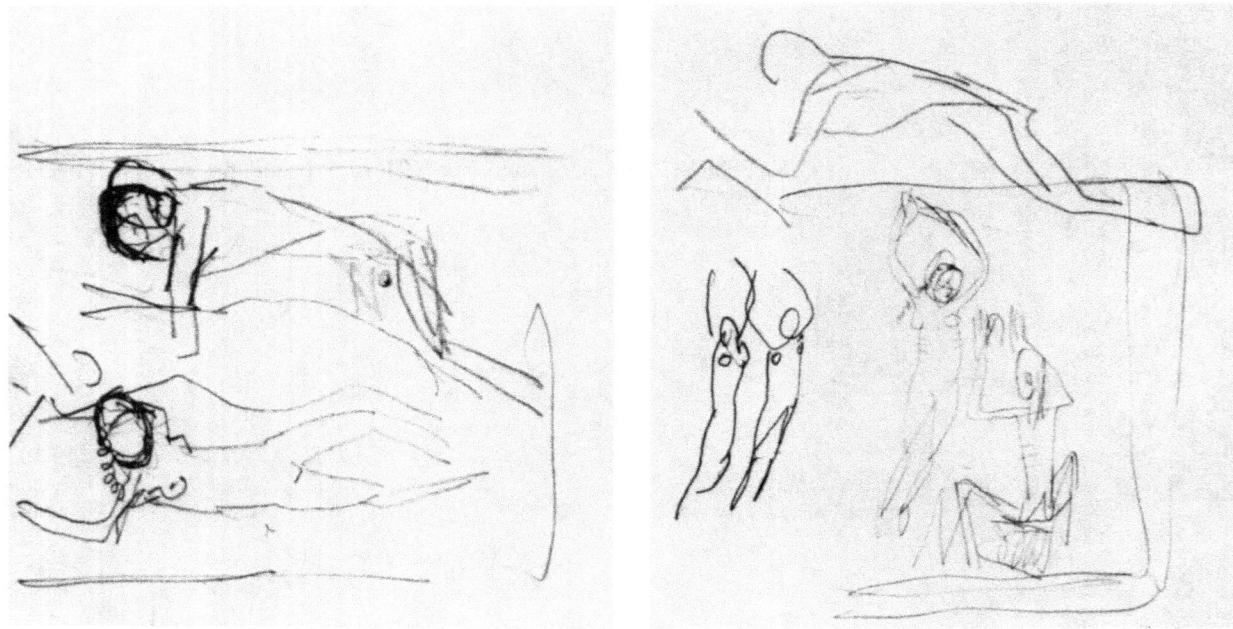

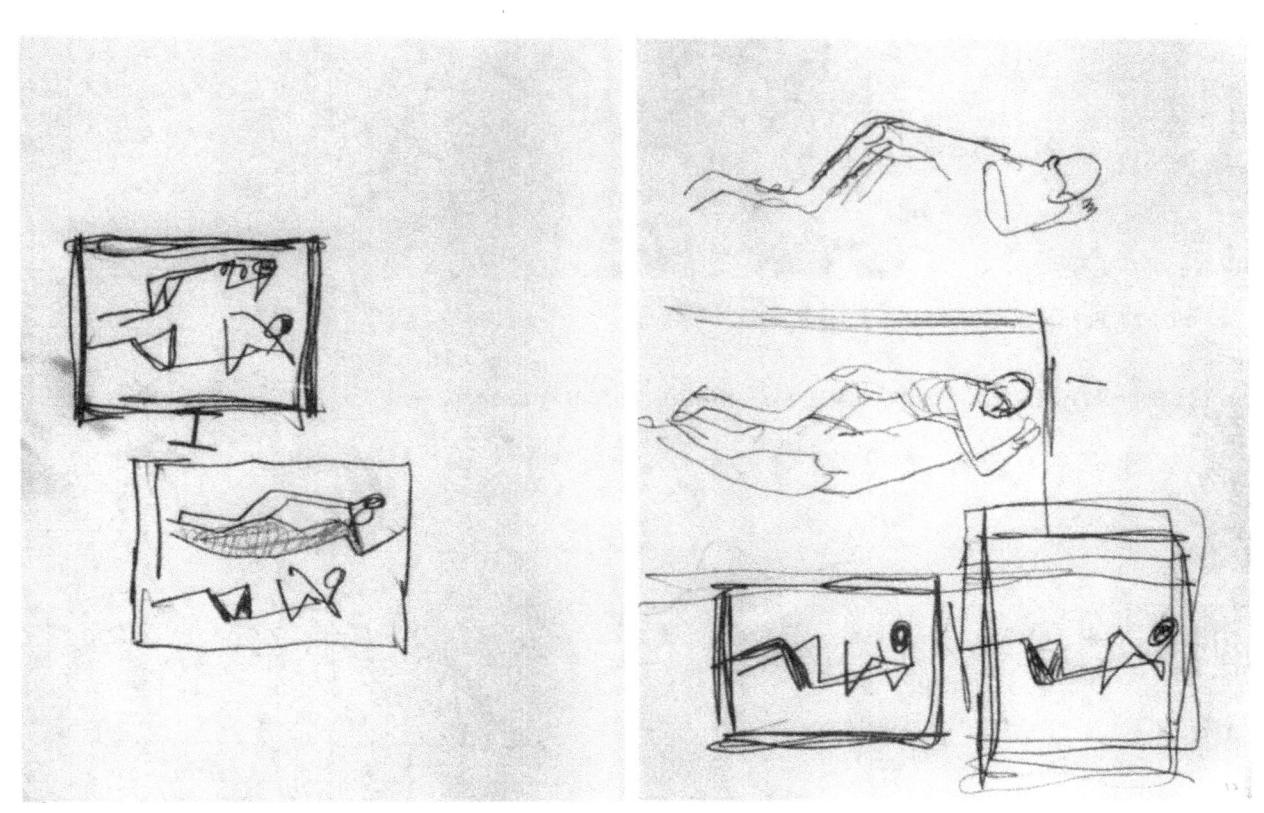

PL. 187. Schiele, A.E.S.A. Sketchbook VIII, 1918, pencil, pp. 22 *verso*, 23 *recto*.

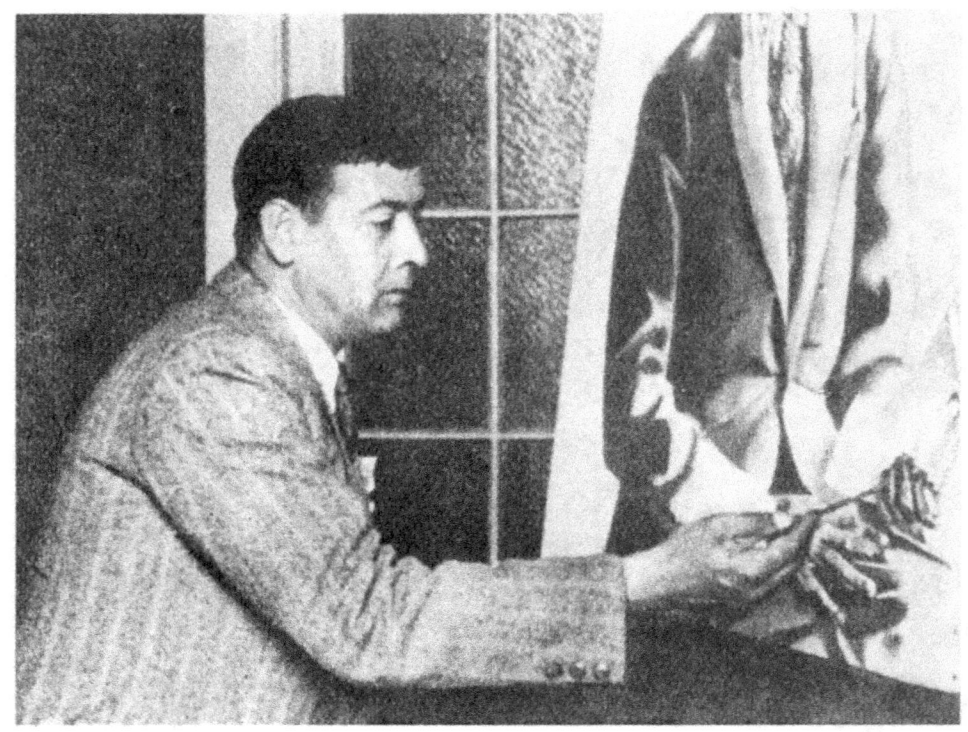

PL. 188. Paris von Gütersloh, *ca.* 1928.

PL. 189. Schiele, A.E.S.A. Sketchbook VII, 1917–1918, pencil, pp. *13 verso, 14 recto.*

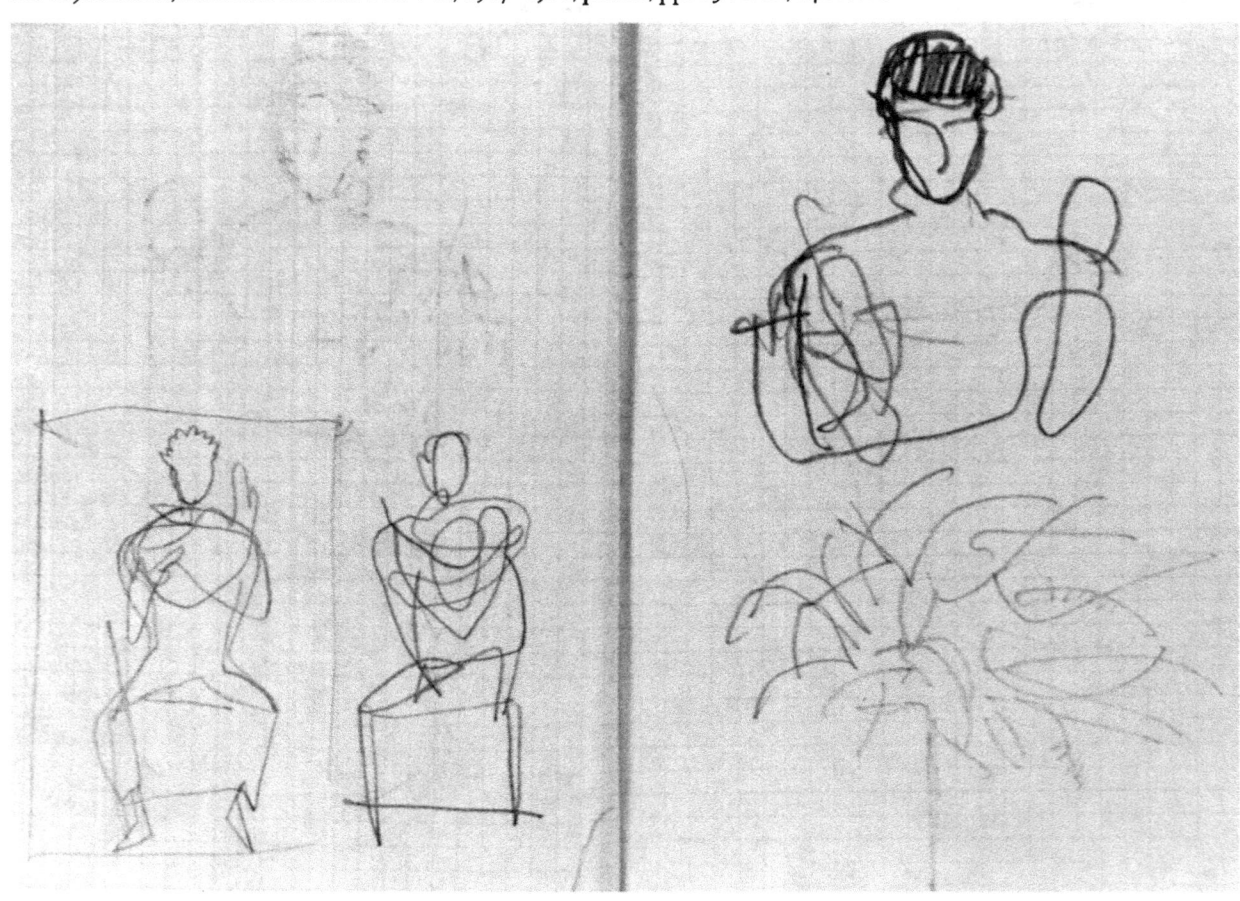

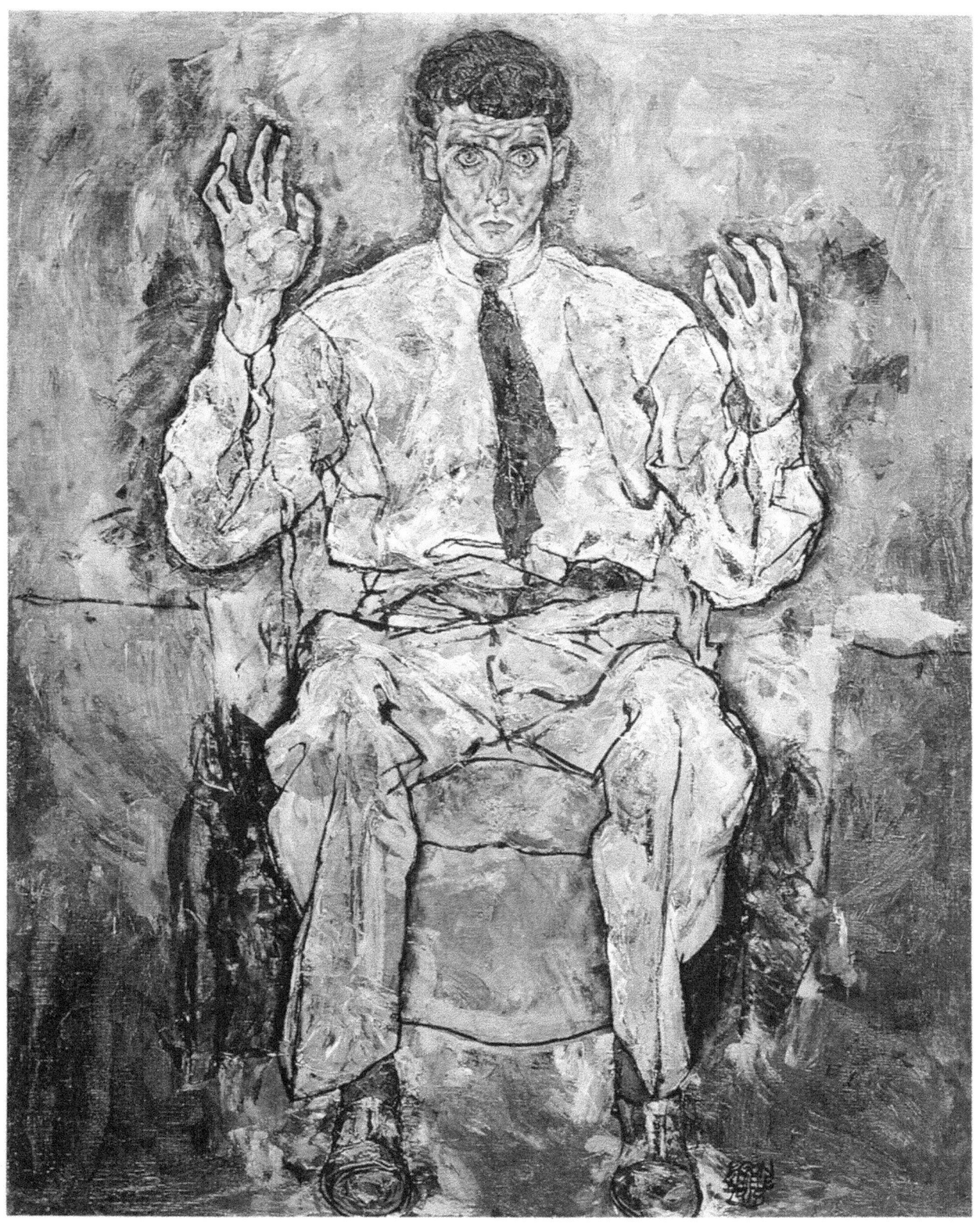

PL. 190. Schiele, *Portrait of Paris von Gütersloh* (unfinished), 1917–1918, oil.

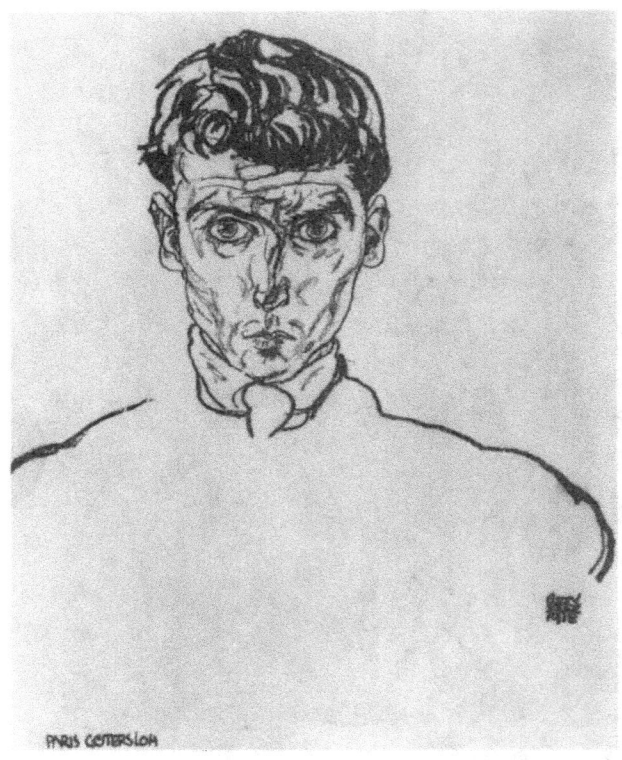

PL. 191. Schiele, *Study of Paris von Gütersloh*, 1918, black chalk.

PL. 192. Paris von Gütersloh, *Mirror Self-Portrait, ca.* 1920.

PL. 193. Paris von Gütersloh, *Portrait of Egon Schiele, ca.* 1918, pencil and watercolor.

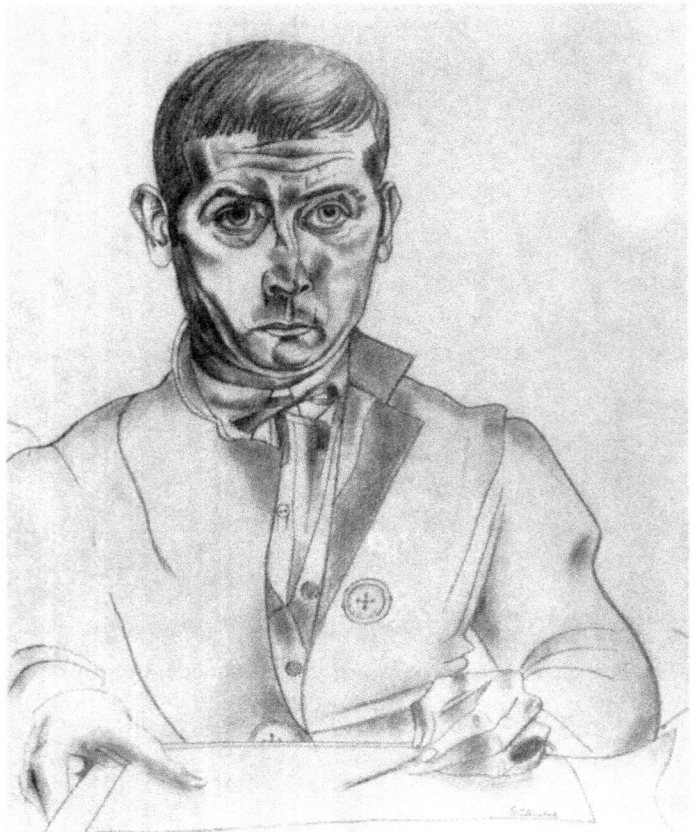

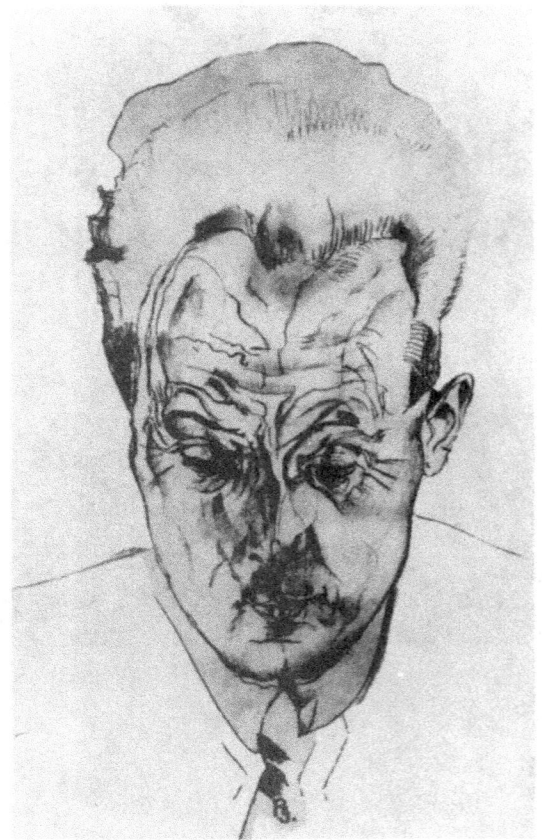

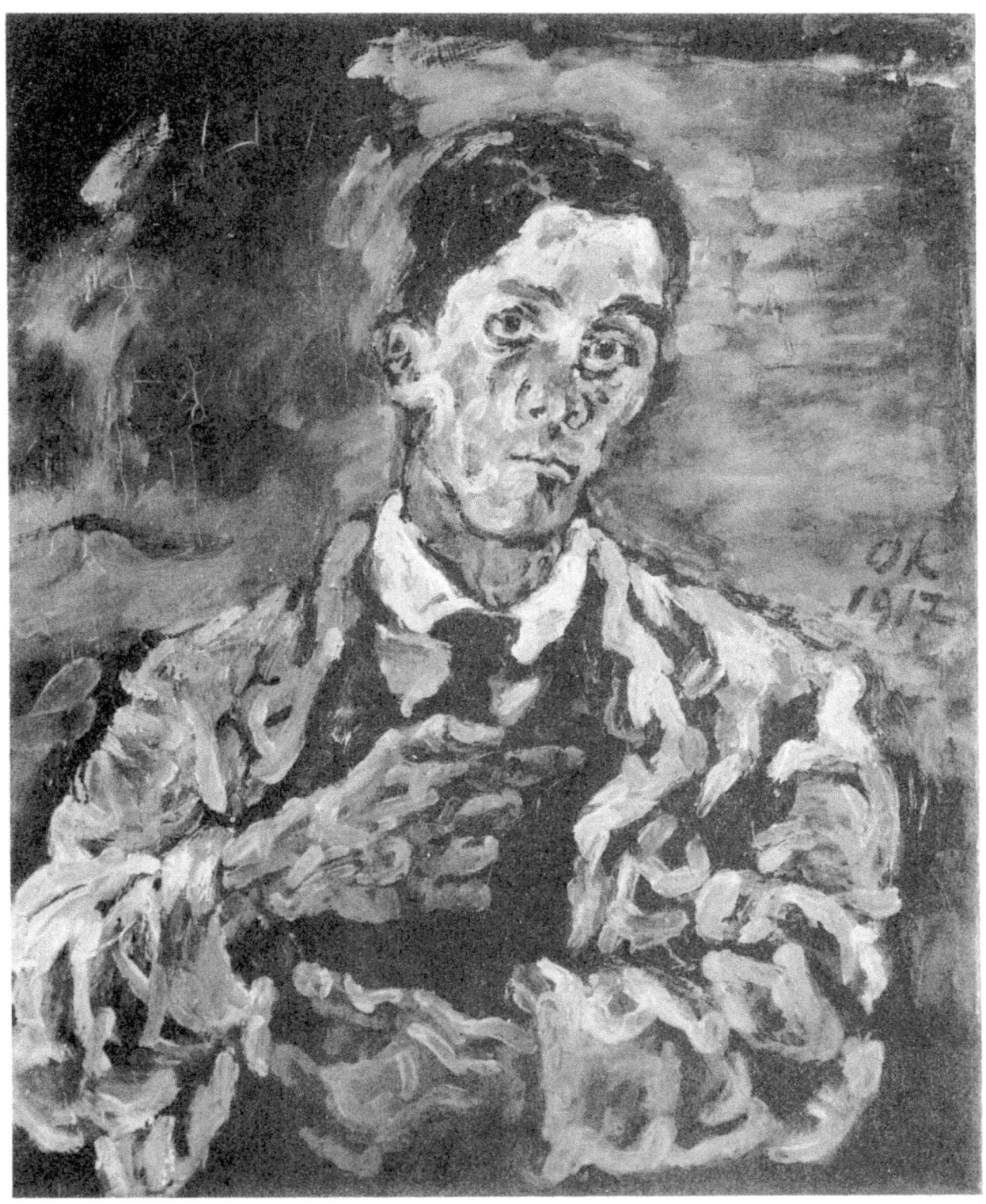

PL. 194. Kokoschka, *Self-Portrait*, 1917, oil.

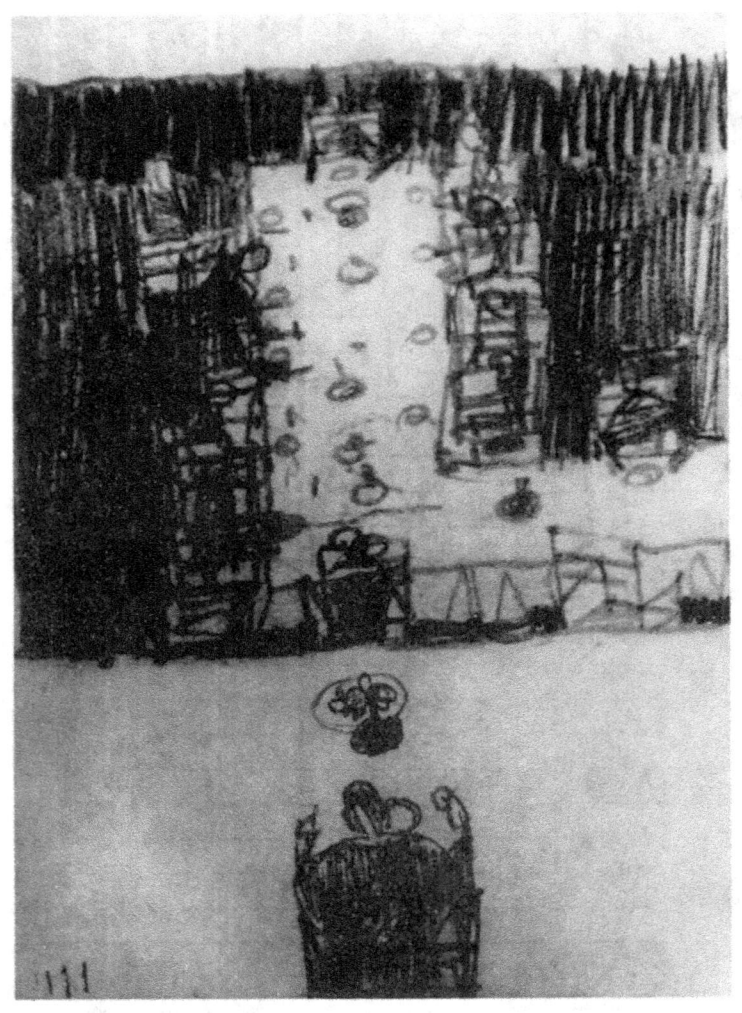

PL. 195. Schiele, Sketchbook, 1914–1917, pencil, p. 111.

PL. 196. Schiele, A.E.S.A. Sketchbook VIII, 1918, pencil, p. 1 *recto*.

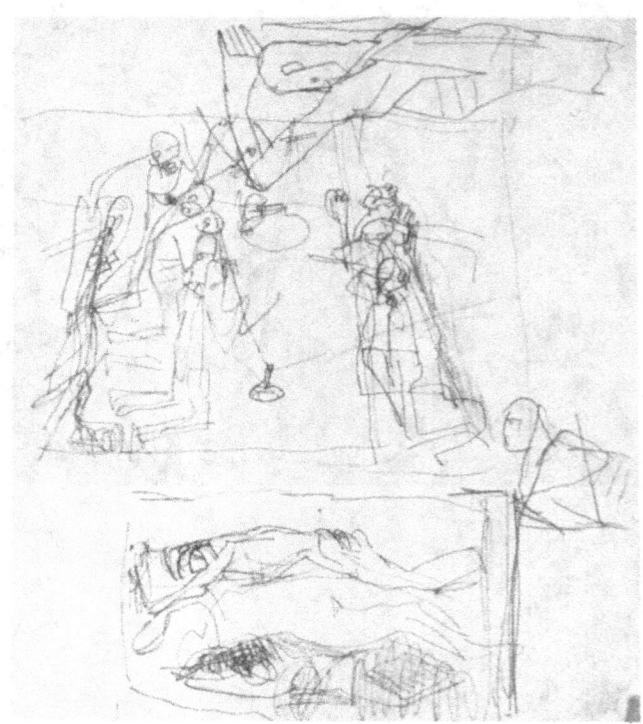

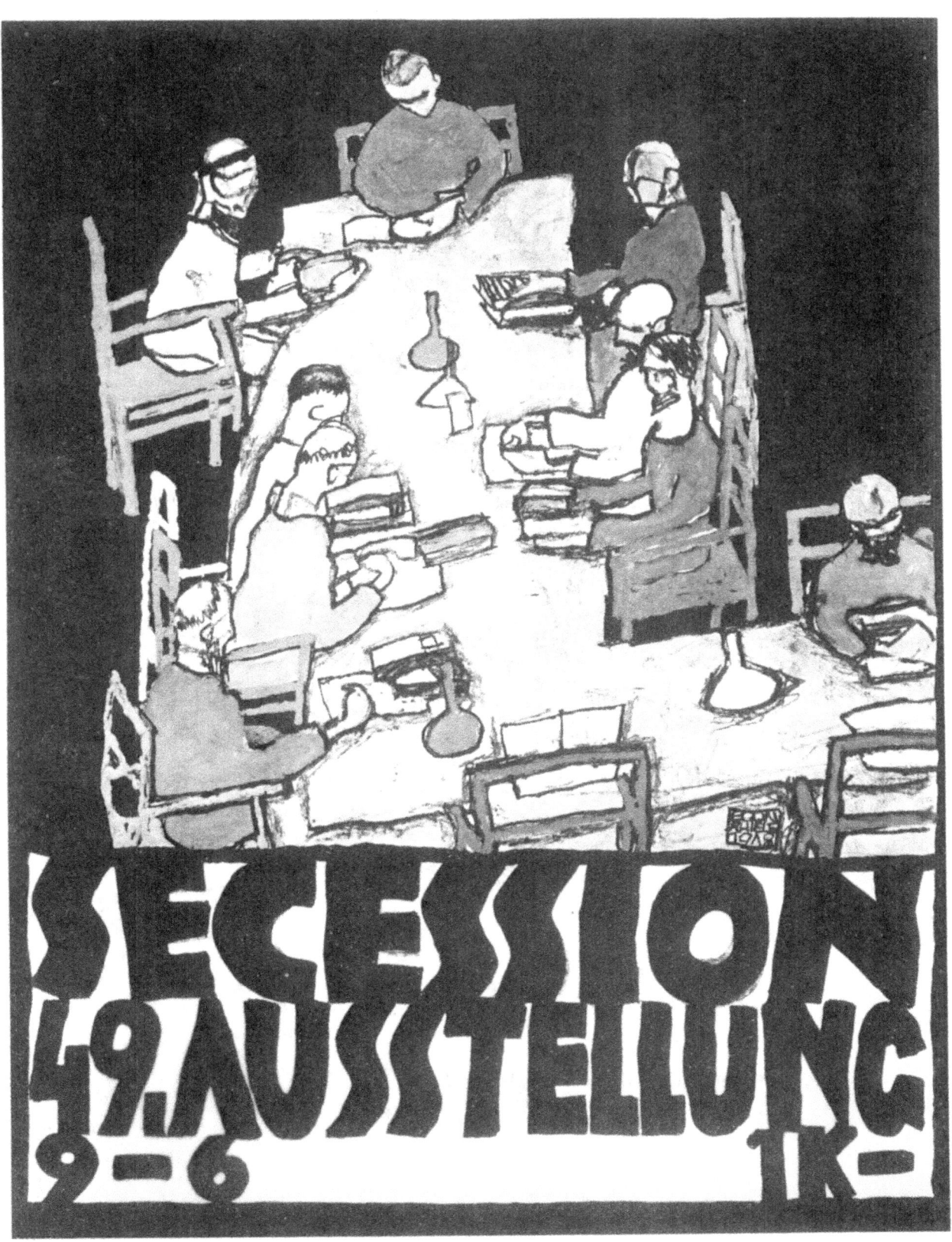

PL. 197. Schiele, *Round the Table (The Friends; "Secession 49. Ausstellung")*, 1918, color lithograph.

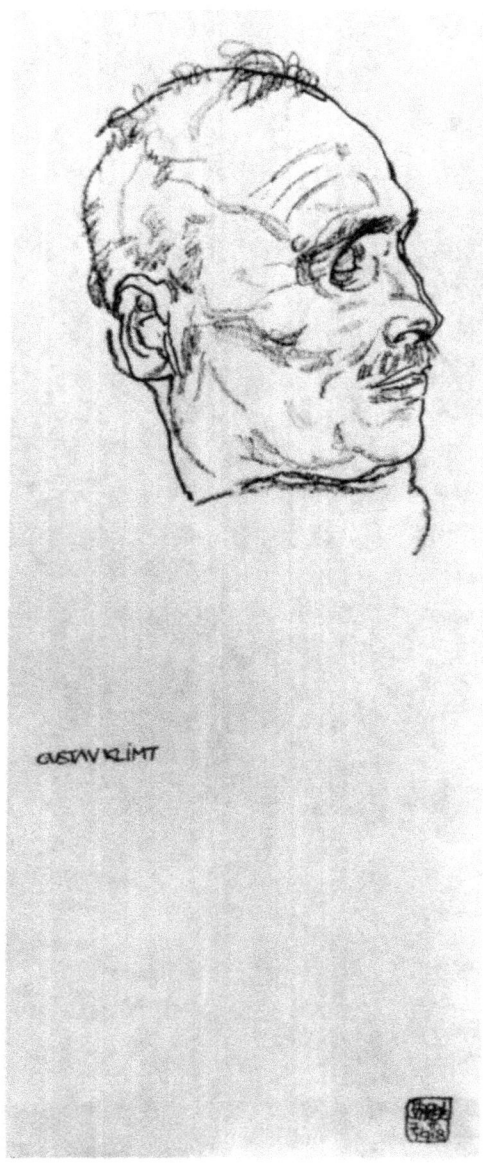

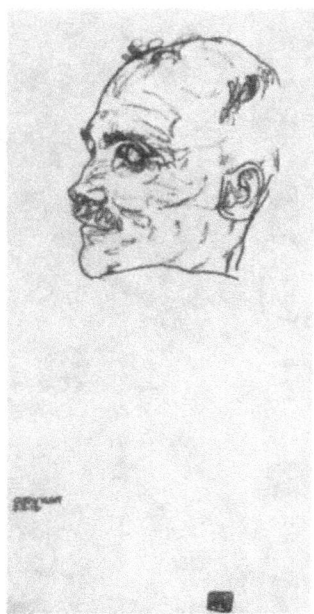

PL. 198b. Schiele, *Gustav Klimt on His Deathbed from the Right*, 7 Feb. 1918, black chalk.

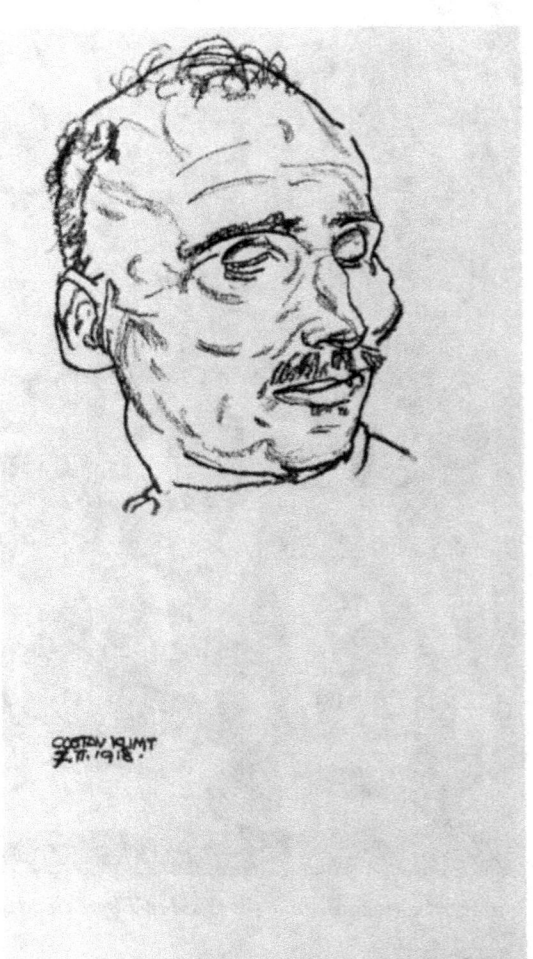

PL. 198a. Schiele, *Gustav Klimt on his Deathbed from the Left*, 7 Feb. 1918, black chalk.

PL. 198c. Schiele, *Gustav Klimt on his Deathbed*, 7 Feb. 1918, black chalk.

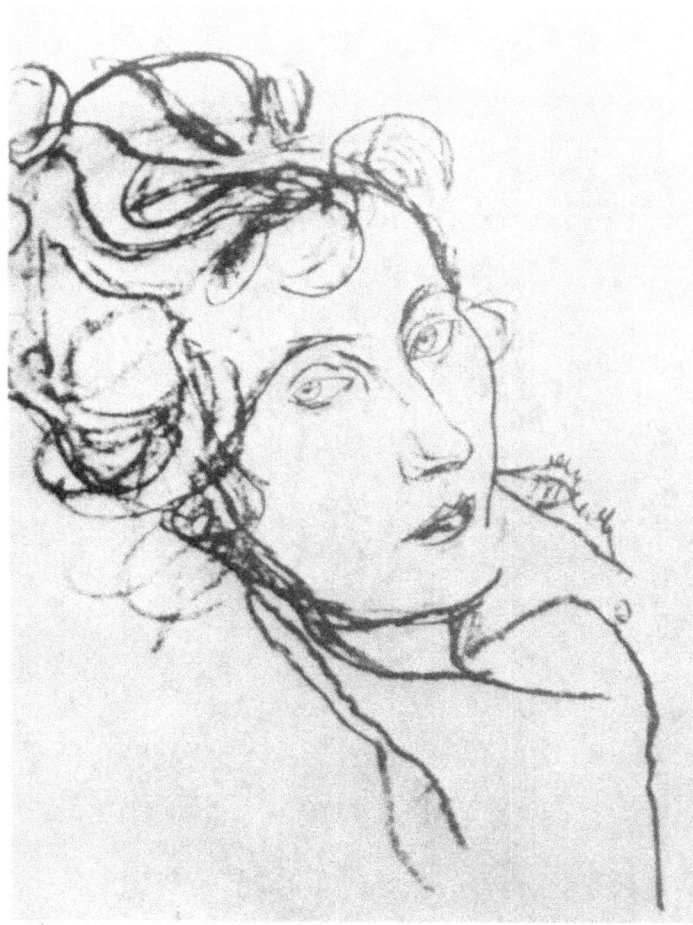

PL. 199a. Schiele, *Edith Schiele on Her Deathbed*, 27–28 Oct., 1918,
black chalk.

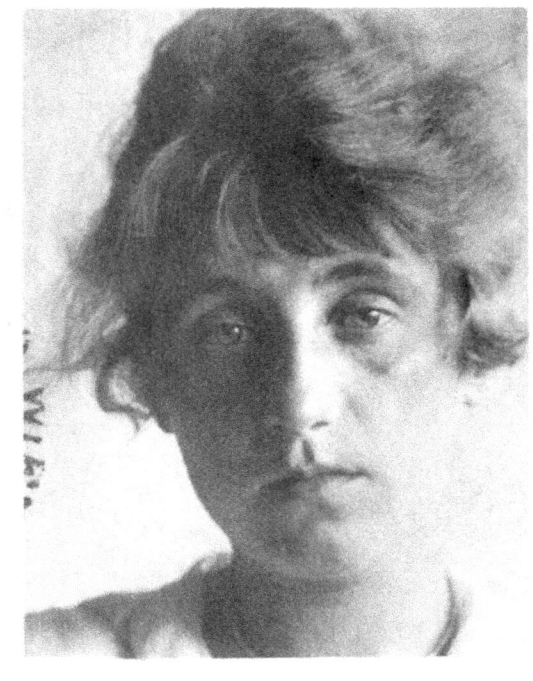

PL. 199b. Edith Schiele, *ca.* 1918.

PL. 199c. Edith Schiele's dying lines to her husband, 27 Oct. 1918.

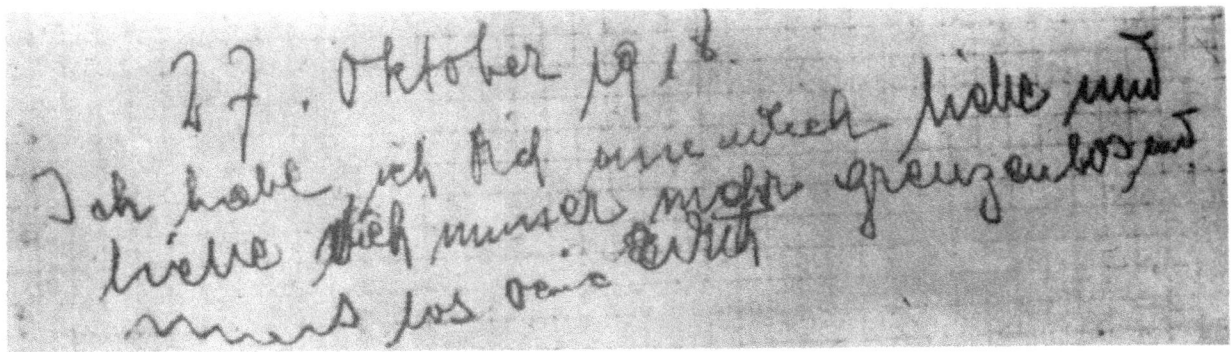

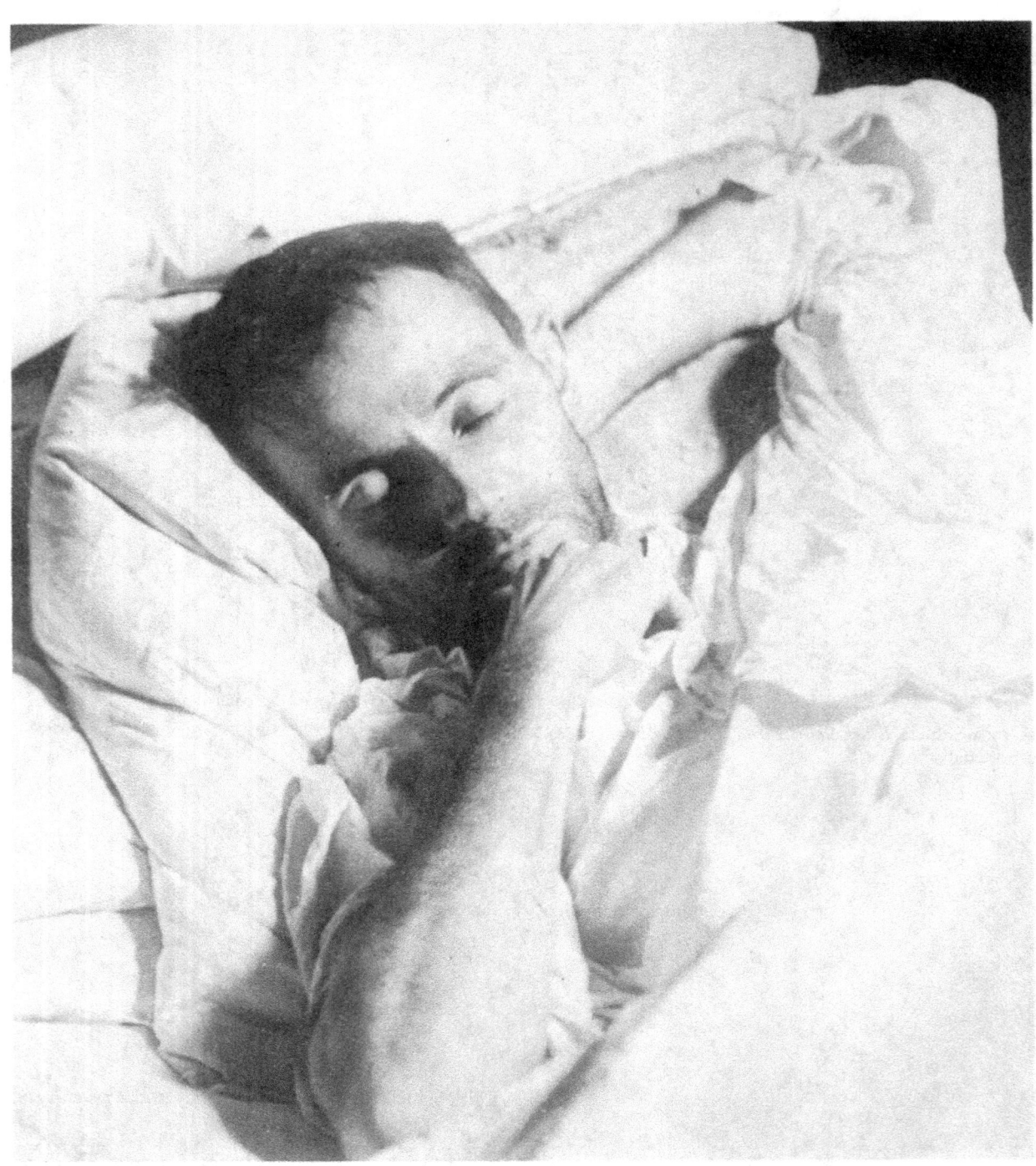

PL. 200. Egon Schiele on his deathbed, 1 Nov. 1918.

www.ingramcontent.com/pod-product-compliance
Lightning Source LLC
Chambersburg PA
CBHW081253170526
45165CB00011B/3302